Readings in

Information Retrieval

The Morgan Kaufmann Series in Multimedia Information and Systems

SERIES EDITOR, EDWARD FOX

Practical Digital Libraries: Books, Bytes, and Bucks
Michael Lesk

Readings in Information Retrieval
Edited by Karen Sparck Jones and Peter Willett

Introduction to Data Compression
Khalid Sayood

Forthcoming:

Digital Compression for Multimedia: Principles and Standards
Jerry D. Gibson, Toby Berger, Tom Lookabaugh, and David Lindbergh

Multimedia Servers: Design, Environments, and Applications
Asit Dan and Dinkar Sitaram

Readings in

Information Retrieval

EDITED BY

KAREN SPARCK JONES

UNIVERSITY OF CAMBRIDGE

PETER WILLETT

UNIVERSITY OF SHEFFIELD

MORGAN KAUFMANN PUBLISHERS, INC.

An Imprint of Elsevier

Amsterdam Boston Heidelberg London New York Oxford
Paris San Diego San Francisco Singapore Sydney Tokyo

Senior Editor	Jennifer Mann
Production Manager	Yonie Overton
Production Editor	Cheri Palmer
Editorial Coordinators	Marilyn Alan and Jane Elliott
Cover Art	Lauren Uram
Cover Production	Jamison Chandler/MacTemps
Text Design, Composition, and Pasteup	Susan M. Sheldrake
Copyeditor	Jennifer McClain
Proofreader	Pamela Sullivan
Indexer	Paul Kish
Printer	Edwards Brothers

Morgan Kaufmann Publishers
An Imprint of Elsevier
340 Pine Street, Sixth Floor
San Francisco, CA 94104-3205
www.mkp.com

Printed in the United States of America
06 5

Library of Congress Cataloging-in-Publication Data
Readings in information retrieval/edited by Karen Sparck Jones, Peter Willett.
p. cm.
Includes bibliographical references and indexes.
ISBN-13: 978-1-55860-454-4 ISBN-10: 1-55860-454-5
1. Information retrieval. 2. Information storage and retrieval systems. I. Sparck Jones, Karen, date. II. Willett, Peter, date.
Z695.9.R43 1997 97-18612
025.5'24—dc21 CIP

ISBN-13: 978-1-55860-454-4
ISBN-10: 1-55860-454-5

IN MEMORY OF

GERARD SALTON

Table of Contents

Preface .... **xi**

Acknowledgements .... **xiii**

Chapter 1 **Overall Introduction** **1**

Chapter 2 **History** **9**

The Thesaurus Approach to Information Retrieval 15
T. Joyce and R.M. Needham

The Automatic Derivation of Information Retrieval Encodements from Machine-Readable Texts 21
H.P. Luhn

Indexing and Abstracting by Association. Part I 25
L.B. Doyle

On Relevance, Probabilistic Indexing and Information Retrieval 39
M.E. Maron and J.L. Kuhns

The Cranfield Tests on Index Language Devices 47
C.W. Cleverdon

Computer Evaluation of Indexing and Text Processing 60
G. Salton and M.E. Lesk

Chapter 3 **Key Concepts** **85**

The Concept of "Aboutness" in Subject Indexing 93
W.J. Hutchins

The Testing of Index Language Devices 98
C.W. Cleverdon and J. Mills

Thesaurus 111
D.J. Foskett

Using Problem Structures for Driving Human-Computer Dialogues 135
P.J. Daniels, H.M. Brooks, and N.J. Belkin

Relevance: A Review of and a Framework for Thinking on the Notion in Information Science 143
T. Saracevic

Chapter 4 **Evaluation** **167**

A Study of Information Seeking and Retrieving.I. Background and Methodology 175
T. Saracevic, P. Kantor, A.Y. Chamis, and D. Trivison

On Selecting a Measure of Retrieval Effectiveness. Part I 191
W.S. Cooper

The Pragmatics of Information Retrieval Experimentation, Revisited 205
J. Tague-Sutcliffe

Presenting Results of Experimental Retrieval Comparisons 217

E.M. Keen

MEDLARS: Report on the Evaluation of Its Operating Efficiency 223
F.W. Lancaster

The TREC Conferences 247
D.K. Harman

Chapter 5 **Models** **257**

Getting Beyond Boole 265
W.S. Cooper

A Non-Classical Logic for Information Retrieval 268
C.J. van Rijsbergen

A Vector Space Model for Automatic Indexing 273
G. Salton, A. Wong, and C.S. Yang

The Probability Ranking Principle in IR 281
S.E. Robertson

Inference Networks for Document Retrieval 287
H. Turtle and W.B. Croft

ASK for Information Retrieval. Part I. Background and Theory 299
N.J. Belkin, R.N. Oddy, and H.M. Brooks

Chapter 6 **Techniques** **305**

An Algorithm for Suffix Stripping 313
M.F. Porter

Robust Text Processing in Automated Information Retrieval 317
T. Strzalkowski

Term-Weighting Approaches in Automatic Text Retrieval 323
G. Salton and C. Buckley

Search Term Relevance Weighting Given Little Relevance Information 329
K. Sparck Jones

Using Probabilistic Models of Document Retrieval
without Relevance Information 339
W.B. Croft and D.J. Harper

Some Simple Effective Approximations to the 2-Poisson Model
for Probabilistic Weighted Retrieval 345
S.E. Robertson and S. Walker

Improving Retrieval Performance by Relevance Feedback 355
G. Salton and C. Buckley

Using Interdocument Similarity Information
in Document Retrieval Systems 365
A. Griffiths, H.C. Luckhurst, and P. Willett

Chapter 7 **Systems** **375**

The SMART and SIRE Experimental Retrieval Systems 381
G. Salton and M.J. McGill

Architecture of an Expert System for Composite Document Analysis,
Representation, and Retrieval 400
E.A. Fox and R.K. France

User-Friendly Systems Instead of User-Friendly Front-Ends 413
D.K. Harman

The Okapi Online Catalogue Research Projects 424
S. Walker

TREC and TIPSTER Experiments with INQUERY 436

J.P. Callan, W.B. Croft, and J.S. Broglio

RUBRIC: A System for Rule-Based Information Retrieval 440
B.P. McCune, R.M. Tong, and J. Dean

TARGET and FREESTYLE: DIALOG and Mead Join the Relevance Ranks 446
C. Tenopir and P. Cahn

Chapter 8 Extensions 457

A Hypertext Environment for Interacting with Large Databases 469
M. Agosti, G. Gradenigo, and P.G. Marchetti

Automatic Analysis, Theme Generation, and Summarization of Machine-Readable Texts 478
G. Salton, J. Allan, C. Buckley, and A. Singhal

Querying Across Languages: A Dictionary-Based Approach to Multilingual Information Retrieval 484
D.A. Hull and G. Grefenstette

Experiments in Spoken Document Retrieval 493
K. Sparck Jones, G.J.F. Jones, J.T. Foote, and S.J. Young

Video Parsing, Retrieval and Browsing: An Integrated and Content-Based Solution 503
H.J. Zhang, C.Y. Low, S.W. Smoliar, and J.H. Wu

The Automatic Indexing System AIR/PHYS —From Research to Application 513
P. Biebricher, N. Fuhr, G. Lustig, M. Schwantner, and G. Knorz

A News Story Categorization System 518
P.J. Hayes, L.E. Knecht, and M.J. Cellio

Conceptual Information Extraction and Retrieval from Natural Language Input 527
L.F. Rau

A Production Rule System for Message Summarization 534
E. Marsh, H. Hamburger, and R. Grishman

The Application of Linguistic Processing to Automatic Abstract Generation 538
F.C. Johnson, C.D. Paice, W.J. Black, and A.P. Neal

Chapter 9 Envoi 553

Historical Note: Information Retrieval and the Future of an Illusion 555
D.R. Swanson

Author Index 563

Subject Index 567

Preface

Following their genesis in library-based systems for searching bibliographic records, information retrieval, or IR, systems are now used for searching a vast range of text databases. This Reader provides a comprehensive introduction to the research that has been carried out to develop and to test the models and the techniques that can be exploited for these systems, and that offer a basis for the design of retrieval methods for future systems not restricted to written documents.

The Reader commences with a general introduction to IR; there then follow seven chapters, each of which comprises a number of carefully selected papers, a brief introduction to the topic of that section, and sufficient references to enable the reader to explore the subject in more detail. The sequence of chapters proceeds from more general, fundamental concepts to more particular ones, focusing on the written document retrieval task; but because some key concepts are of wide applicability, we also show how this task relates to other document types and some other important information management tasks.

With the current interest in IR, the Reader has been designed to serve several audiences, both academic and professional. Academic interest in IR is concentrated in, but by no means restricted to, departments in computer science, library science, and information science, where IR is typically included as a one-semester module in a final-year undergraduate programme or in a postgraduate programme. The professional audience includes not just workers in the huge range of organisations that may need to utilise IR (such as libraries and information services, database hosts and database vendors, the legal and medical professions, news organisations, software houses, and multimedia companies, inter alia) but also, most importantly, the designers and implementers of IR systems. As we describe in Chapter 1, it has taken a very long time for the results that have been obtained by IR researchers to be embodied in the operational systems that are in use today. With the explosive growth in content-based retrieval occasioned by the World Wide Web, we hope that future IR systems will exploit to a much greater extent than heretofore the research results that are summarised in this Reader. We are thus addressing not only those who already recognise their engagement with IR but those in neighbouring areas of computing research and development, such as database systems, speech and language processing, and human-computer interaction, for whom the changing shape of computing technology is posing new challenges that are, in fact, retrieval challenges.

Many people have helped in the preparation of this Reader, and we are most grateful to them: first, Marilyn Alan, Jane Elliott, Jennifer Mann, and Cheri Palmer at Morgan Kaufmann for their editorial and contractual support; next, Ijsbrand Jan Aalbersberg, Maristella Agosti, Nick Belkin, Christine Borgman, Bruce Croft, Ed Fox, Jim French, Norbert Fuhr, Donna Harman, Bill Hersh, Peter Ingwersen, David Lewis, Tefko Saracevic, Alan Smeaton, Howard Turtle, Keith van Rijsbergen, and Ellen Voorhees for their comments on the organisation and constitution of the first draft of the Reader; then, Nick Belkin, Ed Fox, David Lewis, Howard Turtle, and Keith van Rijsbergen for also providing detailed critiques of the introductory texts accompanying each chapter; and finally, Ray Larson for his help in establishing the basic framework of the Reader.

We would also, here, like to make not merely a personal but a community acknowledgement to the late Gerard Salton, by dedicating this volume of readings to his memory. Gerard Salton led the field for more than thirty years in innovative, significant, and influential research. He worked on IR, regardless of fashion, because it is interesting and important. This collection naturally includes several major papers that he wrote. But his role in the development of effective approaches to IR was much wider, through the stimulus his ideas and experiments gave to others—whether to push his work further or to develop their own alternative ideas more properly. Thus both the confirmed general findings and the wide range of individual theories and practices that this volume presents owe much to Gerry.

Acknowledgments

The editors are pleased to thank the following authors and publishers for permission to include copyrighted material in the present volume:

Joyce, T., and Needham, R.M. (1958) The thesaurus approach to information retrieval. *American Documentation,* **9**, 192–197. Reprinted by permission of John Wiley & Sons, Inc.

Luhn, H.P. (1961) The automatic derivation of information retrieval encodements from machine-readable texts. In A. Kent (Ed.), *Information Retrieval and Machine Translation.* Vol. 3, Pt. 2, pp. 1021–1028. New York: Interscience Publication. Reprinted by permission of John Wiley & Sons, Inc.

Doyle, L.B. (1962) *Indexing and Abstracting by Association. Part 1.* SP-718/001/00. Santa Monica, CA: System Development Corporation. © Unisys Corporation.

Maron, M.E., and Kuhns, J.L. (1960) On relevance, probabilistic indexing and information retrieval. *Journal of the Association for Computing Machinery,* **7**, 216–244. © Association of Computing Machinery, Inc. Reprinted by permission.

Cleverdon, C.W. (1967) The Cranfield tests on index language devices. *Aslib Proceedings,* **19**, 173–192. Reprinted by permission of Aslib.

Salton, G., and Lesk, M.E. (1968) Computer evaluation of indexing and text processing. *Journal of the Association for Computing Machinery,* **15**, 8–36. © Association of Computing Machinery, Inc. Reprinted by permission.

Hutchins, W.J. (1978) The concept of "aboutness" in subject indexing. *Aslib Proceedings,* **30**, 172–181. Reprinted by permission of Aslib.

Cleverdon, C.W., and Mills, J. (1963) The testing of index language devices. *Aslib Proceedings,* **15**(4), 106–130. Reprinted by permission of Aslib.

Foskett, D.J. (1980) Thesaurus. In A. Kent, H. Lancour, and J.E. Daily (Eds.), *Encyclopaedia of Library and Information Science, Volume 30,* pp. 416–462. New York: Marcel Dekker. Reprinted with permission.

Daniels, P.J., Brooks, H.M., and Belkin, N.J. (1985) Using problem structures for driving human-computer dialogues. In *RIAO-85. Actes: Recherche d'Informations Assistee par Ordinateur,* pp. 645–660. Grenoble, France: IMAG.

Saracevic, T. (1975) Relevance: A review of and a framework for thinking on the notion in information science. *Journal of the American Society for Information Science,* **26**, 321–343. Reprinted by permission of John Wiley & Sons, Inc.

Saracevic, T., Kantor, P., Chamis, A.Y., and Trivison, D. (1988) A study of information seeking and retrieving. I. Background and methodology. *Journal of the American Society for Information Science,* **39**, 161–176. Reprinted by permission of John Wiley & Sons, Inc.

Cooper, W.S. (1973) On selecting a measure of retrieval effectiveness. Part 1. *Journal of the American Society for Information Science,* **24**, 87–100. Reprinted by permission of John Wiley & Sons, Inc.

Tague-Sutcliffe, J. (1992) The pragmatics of information retrieval experimentation, revisited. *Information Processing and Management,* **28**, 467–490. Reprinted with permission from Elsevier Science Ltd., Oxford, England.

Keen, E.M. (1992) Presenting results of experimental retrieval comparisons. *Information Processing and Management,* **28**, 491–502. Reprinted with permission from Elsevier Science Ltd., Oxford, England.

Lancaster, F.W. (1969) MEDLARS: Report on the evaluation of its operating efficiency. *American Documentation,* **20**, 119–142. Reprinted by permission of John Wiley & Sons, Inc.

Harman, D.K. (1995) The TREC Conferences. In R. Kuhlen and M. Rittberger (Eds.), *Hypertext - Information Retrieval - Multimedia: Synergieeffekte Elektronischer Informationssysteme, Proceedings of HIM '95,* pp. 9–28. Konstanz, Germany: Universitaetsforlag Konstanz.

Cooper, W.S. (1988) Getting beyond Boole. *Information Processing and Management,* **24**, 243–248. Reprinted with permission from Elsevier Science Ltd., Oxford, England.

van Rijsbergen, C.J. (1986) A non-classical logic for information retrieval. *Computer Journal,* **29**, 481–485. Reprinted by permission of the British Computer Society.

Salton, G., Wong, A., and Yang, C.S. (1975) A vector space model for automatic indexing. *Communications of the ACM,* **18**, 613–620. © Association of Computing Machinery, Inc. Reprinted by permission.

Robertson, S.E. (1977) The probability ranking principle in IR. *Journal of Documentation,* **33**, 294–304. Reprinted by permission of Aslib.

Turtle, H., and Croft, W.B. (1990). Inference networks for document retrieval. In J.L. Vidick (Ed.), *Proceedings of the Thirteenth International Conference on Research and Development in Information Retrieval,* pp. 1–24. New York: Association for Computing Machinery. © Association of Computing Machinery, Inc. Reprinted by permission.

Belkin, N.J., Oddy, R.N., and Brooks, H.M. (1982) ASK for information retrieval. Part I. Background and theory. *Journal of Documentation,* **38**, 61–71. Reprinted by permission of Aslib.

Porter, M.F. (1980) An algorithm for suffix stripping. *Program,* **14**, 130–137. Reprinted by permission of Aslib.

Strzalkowski, T. (1994) Robust text processing in automated information retrieval. In *Proceedings of the 4th Conference on Applied Natural Language Processing,* pp. 168–173. Stuttgart, Germany: Association for Computational Linguistics. Used by permission of the Association for Computational Linguistics. Copies of the publication from which this material is derived can be obtained through Priscilla Rasmussen (ACL), P.O. Box 6090, Somerset, NJ 08875, U.S.A.; +1-908-873-3898 (phone); +1-908-873-0014 (fax); acl@bellcore.com.

Salton, G., and Buckley, C. (1988) Term-weighting approaches in automatic text retrieval. *Information Processing and Management,* **24**, 513–523. Reprinted by permission of John Wiley & Sons, Inc.

Sparck Jones, K. (1979) Search term relevance weighting given little relevance information. *Journal of Documentation,* **35**, 30–48. Reprinted by permission of Aslib.

Croft, W.B., and Harper, D.J. (1979) Using probabilistic models of document retrieval without relevance information. *Journal of Documentation,* **35**, 285–295. Reprinted by permission of Aslib.

Robertson, S.E., and Walker, S. (1994) Some simple effective approximations to the 2-Poisson model for probabilistic weighted retrieval. In W.B. Croft and C.J. van Rijsbergen (Eds.), *Proceedings of the 17th International Conference on Research and Development in Information Retrieval,* pp. 232–241. London: Springer-Verlag. © Association of Computing Machinery, Inc. Reprinted by permission.

Salton, G., and Buckley, C. (1990) Improving retrieval performance by relevance feedback. *Journal of the American Society for Information Science,* **41**, 288–297. Reprinted with permission from Elsevier Science Ltd., Oxford, England.

Griffiths, A., Luckhurst, H.C., and Willett, P. (1986) Using interdocument similarity information in document retrieval systems. *Journal of the American Society for Information Science,* **37**, 3–11. Reprinted by permission of John Wiley & Sons, Inc.

Salton, G., and McGill, M.J. (1983). The SMART and SIRE Experimental Retrieval Systems, pp. 118–155. New York: McGraw-Hill. Reprinted with the permission of The McGraw-Hill Companies.

Fox, E.A., and France, R.K. (1987) Architecture of an expert system for composite document analysis, representation, and retrieval. *Journal of Approximate Reasoning,* **1**, 151–175. Reprinted by permission of the publisher from Fox, E.A., and France, R.K. © 1987 by Elsevier Science Inc.

Harman, D.K. (1992) User-friendly systems instead of user-friendly front-ends. *Journal of the American Society for Information Science,* **43**, 164–174. Reprinted by permission of John Wiley & Sons, Inc.

Walker, S. (1989) The Okapi online catalogue research projects. In C. Hildreth (Ed.), *The Online Catalogue. Developments and Directions,* pp. 84–106. London: Library Association. Reprinted by permission of Library Association Publishing.

Callan, J., Croft, W.B., and Broglio, J. (1995) TREC and TIPSTER experiments with INQUERY. *Information Processing and Management,* **31**, 327–332, 343. Reprinted with permission from Elsevier Science Ltd., Oxford, England.

McCune, B.P., Tong, R., and Dean, J. (1985) RUBRIC, a system for rule-based information retrieval. *IEEE Transactions on Software Engineering,* **SE-11**, 939–944. © 1985 IEEE. Reprinted, with permission, from IEEE Transactions on Software Engineering.

Tenopir, C., and Cahn, P. (1994) TARGET and FREESTYLE: DIALOG and Mead join the relevance ranks. *Online,* **18**(3), 31–47. Reprinted by permission of Online, Inc.

Agosti, M., Gradenigo, G., and Marchetti, P.G. (1992) A hypertext environment for interacting with large databases. *Information Processing and Management,* **28**, 371–387. Reprinted with permission from Elsevier Science Ltd., Oxford, England.

Salton, G., Allan, J., Buckley, C., and Singhal, A. (1994) Automatic analysis, theme generation, and summarization of machine-readable texts. *Science,* **264**, 1421–1426. Reprinted with permission. © 1994 American Association for the Advancement of Science.

Hull, D.A., and Grefenstette, G. (1996) Querying across languages: A dictionary-based approach to multilingual information retrieval. In H.-P. Frei, D.K. Harman, P. Schaeuble, and R. Wilkinson (Eds.), *Proceedings of the 19th Annual International Conference on Research and Development in Information Retrieval,* pp. 49–57. New York: Association for Computing Machinery. © Association of Computing Machinery, Inc. Reprinted by permission.

Sparck Jones, K., Jones, G.J.F., Foote, J.T., and Young, S.J. (1996) Experiments in spoken document retrieval. *Information Processing and Management,* **32**, 399–419. Reprinted with permission from Elsevier Science Ltd., Oxford, England.

Zhang, H.J., Low, C.Y., Smoliar, S.W., and Wu, J.H. (1995) Video parsing, retrieval and browsing: An integrated and content-based solution. In *Proceedings of ACM Multimedia '95,* pp. 15–24. New York: ACM Press. © Association of Computing Machinery, Inc. Reprinted by permission.

Biebricher, B., Fuhr, N., Lustig, G., Schwanter, M., and Knorz, G. (1988) The automatic indexing system AIR/PHYS—from research to application. In Y. Chiaramella (Ed.), *Proceedings of the 11th Annual International Conference on Research and Development in Information Retrieval,* pp. 333–342. New York: Association for Computing Machinery. © Association of Computing Machinery, Inc. Reprinted by permission.

Hayes, P.J., Knecht, L., and Cellio, M. (1988) A news story categorisation system. In *Proceedings of the Second Conference on Applied Natural Language Processing, Association for Computational Linguistics,* pp. 9–17. San Francisco: Morgan Kaufmann. Used by permission of the Association for Computational Linguistics. Copies of the publication from which this material is derived can be obtained through Priscilla Rasmussen (ACL), P.O. Box 6090, Somerset, NJ 08875, U.S.A.; +1-908-873-3898 (phone); +1-908-873-0014 (fax); acl@bellcore.com.

Rau, L.F. (1988) Conceptual information extraction and retrieval from natural language input. In *RIAO 88,* pp. 424–437. Paris: Centre des Hautes Etudes Internationales d'Informatique Documentaire. © 1997, General Electric Company, U.S.A.

Marsh, E., Hamburger, H., and Grishman, R. (1984) A production rule system for message summarisation. In *AAAI-84, Proceedings of the American Association for Artificial Intelligence,* pp. 243–246. Cambridge, MA: AAAI Press/MIT Press. Reprinted by permission of William Kaufmann Inc.

Johnson, F.C., Paice, C.D., Black, W.J., and Neal, A.P. (1993) The application of linguistic processing to automatic abstract generation. *Journal of Document and Text Management,* **1**, 215–241. Reprinted with permission.

Swanson, D.R. (1988) Historical note: information retrieval and the future of an illusion. *Journal of the American Society for Information Science,* **39**, 92–98. Reprinted by permission of John Wiley & Sons, Inc.

Chapter 1

Overall Introduction

INTRODUCTION

Computers had only been in existence for a few years before it was realised that they could be used for the implementation of what we would now refer to as a *database,* i.e., a set of linked files and associated software for the maintenance and the searching of the information contained within those files. The precise functionality of a database system depends crucially upon the characteristics of the information that it stores and processes, and this has led to the development of many different types of system. By far the best established are database management systems (DBMS), which support the storage and processing of numeric or tightly restricted language information and which are operated by nearly all types of modern organisation, from the local community group to the multinational company (Stonebraker, 1994). Though the idea of automating document retrieval dates back to the immediate postwar period, solid operational systems using computers for storing and retrieving textual information were established somewhat later than those for handling data. Initially, information retrieval (IR) systems were used mainly by librarians, who had long been obliged to carry out bibliographic searches using manual tools such as the card catalogue and universal classification schemes (e.g., the Library of Congress and Dewey Decimal Classifications) for books or, increasingly, journal articles, held offline. The advent of word processing software and then of the CD-ROM provided effective mechanisms for the creation and dissemination of machine-readable text, with these technological developments soon leading to a rapid, widespread growth in the usage of IR systems. This growth will increase still further with the current intense interest in Web-based distributed information processing, and in the application of IR techniques to nontextual media.

The focus upon textual information means that the requirements for, and the principal characteristics of, an IR system are very different from those for a DBMS system. The next section hence outlines the basic concepts of IR, emphasising their generality for a range of computational tasks; there follows a brief historical overview of the development of the subject. We then outline the organisation of the Reader, and complete this introduction by listing sources to which the reader can turn for further information on the topics discussed here.

BASIC CONCEPTS

Information retrieval is often regarded as being synonymous with *document retrieval* and, nowadays, with *text retrieval,* implying that the task of an IR system is to retrieve documents or texts with information *content* that is *relevant* to a user's information *need.* This task does, indeed, form the principal focus of the Reader, but (as discussed below) the approaches that have been developed for this purpose are also applicable to a whole family of related information processing tasks that lie between, on the one hand, *data retrieval* and, on the other, *fact* or *knowledge retrieval.*

Document retrieval subsumes two related, but different, activities: *indexing* and *searching.* Indexing refers to the way *documents,* i.e., the items in the file, and *requests,* i.e., expressions of the user's information need, are represented for retrieval purposes. Searching refers to the way the file is examined and the items in it are taken as related to a search *query.* This is a logical characterisation. How work is distributed between the time when items enter the file and when searching is done, and how the indexing and searching processes are carried out, can vary enormously.

The two activities of indexing and searching have formed the focus of most of the research that has been carried out by the IR community to date (see, e.g., Sparck Jones, 1981; van Rijsbergen, 1979), and this orientation is reflected in our choice of papers for this Reader. However, there is now increasing interest in complementary studies of the ways that people use IR systems and of how user-system interactions should be organised to facilitate effective retrieval (see, e.g., Fidel, 1984; Ingwersen, 1992). These activities will become of increasing importance with the explosion of interest in IR occasioned by the introduction of the World Wide Web. Indeed, with progress in technology, while indexing and searching are necessarily central to automated retrieval, they can support different forms of retrieval, like *browsing,* which can also be enhanced by sophisticated visual presentation.

The great majority of early IR systems were designed for use with bibliographic databases; i.e., they provided access to *references* to the end documents rather than to the documents themselves, and indexing and searching were thus applied to document surrogates, such as titles or abstracts. However, the plummeting costs of online storage over the years have meant that it is now normal to search the full texts of documents (as has always been the case in legal information systems that are used to gain access to statutes and case reports); moreover, the range of document types has widened from library catalogues and files of journal articles to encompass all types of textual entity. Thus, if from the abstract, machine point of view the main change has been that the *records* in the file have become longer, from a retrieval point of view there has been a truly fundamental change. For while searching could initially be done only on representations of documents that were certainly highly reductive of the end document's information content and might well be inaccurate, later searching could be on the whole end document. Even so, the basic requirement—to interpret a sequence of words as purveyors of information so as to retrieve documents relevant to the user's information need—is still the key retrieval challenge.

The inherent richness of language means that the indexing and searching operations described above can never result in the "perfect" retrieval of DBMS, where searches are for exact values, or ranges thereof. Much effort has hence been given to the establishment of quantitative methods for evaluating retrieval *effectiveness* in terms of the relevant items that are retrieved. The two most common measures of performance are *recall* (the percentage of the relevant items that are retrieved in a search) and *precision* (the percentage of the items retrieved in a search that are relevant). When averaged over large numbers of queries and with large files, IR systems have been found to operate at no more than 30% recall and 30% precision, with an increase in the one normally being accompanied by a decrease in the other (Cleverdon, 1972). These figures are in stark contrast with the 100% recall and 100% precision that characterise DBMS searches.

Information retrieval, even when confined to written documents and texts, is a broad task subsuming many varieties of file item and many kinds of user need, within many different types of retrieval system environment. But it is also important from an abstract perspective to recognise that retrieval, for all its variation, is essentially a *classificatory* activity. Documents are indexed to classify them with an eye to matching future requests, and searching classifies a file into matching and nonmatching parts (absolutely or to different degrees). In general, any of the primitive entities of a retrieval system—file documents, index terms, user requests—may be assigned to classes aimed at optimising retrieval effectiveness. Further, while in some cases classifications when once established are treated as effectively static (as in many conventional library cases), classification is more properly seen as a *dynamic* process, involving learning in response to training examples or feedback. From this point of view, document retrieval from a given file in response to a one-off user need, which may involve iterative cycles of searching and query revision, is just one of a family of selective retrieval tasks, including: *categorisation*, i.e., assigning incoming file items to some set of file headings, and *filtering* or *routing*, i.e., sending items from an incoming stream to particular individuals with standing statements of interest. In just the same way, the index descriptions of documents on which retrieval is based have relatives fulfilling similar purposes such as *extraction*, i.e., the identification within a text of prespecified types of information, and *summarising*, i.e., the abstraction of the most important parts of text content.

When stated in this way, it should be evident that IR is not restricted to the processing of written documents or texts, since the basic operations outlined above are applicable to searching other types of document, such as images, even if the details are necessarily different. Indeed, it is increasingly the case that file records, such as museum catalogue entries or journal articles, are multimedia ones calling both for a coherent philosophy of retrieval for records as wholes and for the integration of specific techniques individually suited to different information *types* like those exemplified by image and language. The same, of course, applies to exclusively text entities, where records of all sorts, such as library catalogue entries with different fields for author and title or e-mail messages with headers and bodies, embody different language types. It is also the case that systems must increasingly handle databases and records that not only contain different types of information but also different languages, and while there is a general expectation that models and techniques that are appropriate for one language are broadly applicable to another, much development may be required before this can be accomplished in practice.

It is nevertheless important to see that, even with *hybrid* searches such as those where different fields are distinguished, the same generic strategies may be helpful and that relations between types may be deliberately exploited. The same point applies to whole files, which may now be far more heterogeneous than old-fashioned document files and include entities at different levels, like *directories*, which may themselves be indexed and searched in the same style as the ultimate end documents. Indeed the notion of "end document" disappears in a sea of information entities.

This extension, on the one hand, of the notion of document in document retrieval is matched on the other by the extension of the task area beyond the different forms of retrieval, like routing, mentioned earlier. Accordingly, there are tasks, like information extraction and summarising, that share the requirement to identify important document content and that can thus share with retrieval both some general notions and some specific processing techniques. In the limit, a brief phrasal index description of a document is also a summary, though the contrasting emphases on the individual document and on the document file in the cases of summarising and retrieval, respectively, also indicate that these are members of a family of tasks rather than just the same task.

Most of the papers in this volume focus on IR in the sense of the document retrieval task. However, the Reader is more general in scope in two major ways. First, we introduce concepts and, more importantly, modern automatic techniques, that are in fact applicable to other classification tasks; second, in Chapter 8, we explicitly consider other, related tasks and their individual forms of the indexing and searching requirements that are generic to information transformation and recovery. It is thus important, throughout these readings, to see our presentation of IR through document retrieval as inclusive rather than exclusive, and as covering a wide area between data and knowledge.

DEVELOPMENT OF IR

The term "Information Retrieval" was coined in a paper by Mooers (1952) and later popularised in the nascent IR research community by the writings of Faithhorne (1961).

Sparck Jones (1981) suggests that the International Conference on Scientific Information, which was held in Washington in 1958 (Proceedings, 1959), marked the start of IR as we now recognise it. The following years saw seminal work by researchers such as Doyle (1961) and Salton (1968) who, in considering the automation of existing manual retrieval tasks and in comparing manual and automatic approaches to indexing, were led to develop new methods of retrieval. Further, as the growth of the specialised scientific literature in the fifties had stimulated the development of new forms of indexing language, this period also saw several tests of manual indexing languages, culminating in Cleverdon's second set of Cranfield experiments (1967), which established the basic evaluation procedures that are still in use today for testing the performance of IR systems and techniques. Examples of several of these groundbreaking studies are included in both Chapters 2 and 3 of this Reader. The large collection of papers in Saracevic (1970) includes not only many important items but clearly illustrates both the intellectual ferment and the research findings of this period when automated retrieval first really took off. It captures, in particular, the feeling that wholly new theories about information and its communication were needed to match the new technological world. More extended reviews of the early development of IR are presented by Stevens et al. (1965) and by Salton (1968), the latter being the first of five books by this author (Salton, 1968, 1971, 1975, 1989; Salton and McGill, 1983) that provide a fascinating personal view of the historical development of the field.

The concerns of researchers in IR have, historically, been very different from those of the producers of operational IR systems. Batch *current awareness* services, the precursors of the modern-day routing systems that were mentioned previously, started in both the USA and the UK in the mid-sixties, and the development of time-sharing operating systems and wide-area data communication networks soon led to the introduction of the first interactive retrieval systems such as DIALOG and MEDLINE, the descendants of which remain in operational use around the world to the present day. The characteristics of these early online systems are well displayed in Lancaster and Fayen (1973). The seventies saw the introduction of software packages for in-house information retrieval and this was followed by the introduction of *online public-access catalogues* (OPACs), both of these types of system enabling end users to carry out computer-based searches for themselves, without requiring the assistance of a search intermediary.

An important characteristic of operational systems is that, almost without exception until recently, they adopted the *Boolean* model of searching, in which a user's search terms are linked by the Boolean logical operators of AND, OR, and NOT: the OR operator is used to link together synonyms or alternatives; the AND operator is used to link together different facets of a multifaceted subject; and the NOT operator is used to eliminate documents indexed by terms that are known to be irrelevant to the query. The Boolean model (which is discussed in more detail in Chapters 5 and 7) is entirely appropriate for use in a DBMS context, where the well-defined nature of the stored data invites the use of *partial-match* (i.e., inclusive search) retrieval algorithms that result in a partition of a database into those records (typically few) that do satisfy the logical constraints of the query statement and the remainder that do not. However, it is far less obviously appropriate for use in an IR context, where users generally have only a vague picture of the sorts of document that might satisfy their information need, i.e., they exist in an "anomalous state of knowledge" (Belkin et al., 1982). The early and rapid adoption of the Boolean model as the general search strategy for retrieval systems is thus rather surprising; but is explained, on the one hand, by the constraints of the existing file-handling technology and, on the other, by the presumption that professional staff would be doing the actual searching and would have put considerable preparatory effort into analysing the user's situation and developing a sufficiently careful search expression to allow for the user's uncertain knowledge. Boolean searching also has the advantage that it is obvious to a user why a particular document has been retrieved by a particular query, which is often not the case with alternative approaches.

The Boolean model is, however, intrinsically restrictive, even if a search exploits a sequence of query versions, and researchers have thus generally eschewed Boolean searching in favour of retrieval algorithms that result in a ranking of a database, with the top-ranked documents being those that most closely match the query, using some quantitative definition of similarity, nearness, or goodness of fit. These matching documents are those most likely to be relevant to the user's information need, and their retrieval will hence maximise the effectiveness of retrieval; a quantitative rationale for this *probability ranking principle* is provided by Robertson (1977). That said, several different criteria can be used to define "most closely match," and ranked-output searching thus encompasses several different approaches to retrieval, as discussed in detail in later chapters. The emphasis on searching and matching strategies that deliver a ranked output (sometimes called *coordination level*, or *quorum*, for simpler cases or, more generally, *best match*) reflects the intensive and wide-ranging work on retrieval system theory that began in the sixties in response to the new challenges and opportunities of automated retrieval.

IR also differs from DBMS in that the imprecise character of natural language and the subjective nature of concepts such as "information need" and "relevance" have led to substantial research interest in studies of user behaviour. This has resulted in the application of techniques from the behavioural and cognitive sciences to complement, and to provide a context for, the computer science techniques that have predominated in IR research over the years (Ellis, 1992; Ingwersen, 1996).

Operational IR systems are now starting to make use of the results of IR research, in that best-match searching is becomingly increasingly available as a complement, or even as an alternative, to the long-established Boolean mechanisms. In-house systems, such as STATUS/IQ (Pearsall, 1989), were the first to adopt such research ideas, shortly followed by public online systems, such as ESA-IRS (Muhlhauser, 1985) and West Publishing Company (Pritchard-Schoch, 1993), and now by the new generation of search engines that has been developed for searching the World Wide Web (Berners-Lee et al., 1994). While the facilities offered by many of these engines are currently much inferior to those available from existing IR research systems, it can only be a matter of time before the huge resources now being ploughed into Web-based IR leads to the widespread adoption of leading-edge retrieval techniques. The distinctive properties of the Web have also presented distinctive new problems for those engaged in IR research, for example those stemming from its sheer scale and the extreme variety of material and those stemming from end document ownership. A further important recent development has been the annual Defence Advanced Research Projects Agency/National Institute of Standards and Technology (DARPA/NIST) Text Retrieval Conferences (TRECs), which began in 1992 (Harman, 1993). These are major evaluation exercises with many participants, using not just full text but also very much larger test databases than any previous systematic evaluations, and exploring not only "plain" retrieval but also an increasing range of specific issues. We can expect the consolidated findings from the succession of tests to enter operational practice in the future. Finally, while IR techniques were developed specifically for searching textual documents, they are also applicable to content-based retrieval from other sorts of database medium, and there is thus much current interest in the development of systems for multimedia retrieval.

The time is thus clearly ripe for this Reader, which is designed to provide an overview, covering both general theory and specific methods, of the development and current status of IR systems.

ORGANISATION OF THE READER

The remainder of the Reader is divided into seven chapters as follows:

- *History*, which covers some of the classical ideas and implementations bearing on or in automatic retrieval.
- *Key Concepts*, which covers the nature of documents, aboutness, indexing and index languages, requests, relevance, users, and searching.
- *Evaluation*, which covers notions of performance issues, factors and criteria, and IR test design and methodology.
- *Models*, which covers qualitative and quantitative models of various important aspects of the retrieval process.
- *Techniques*, which covers the detailed working out of the models and associated technologies, and also includes examples of systematic retrieval tests using these approaches.
- *Systems*, which exemplifies systems (both research and operational) that embody the various research ideas detailed elsewhere in the Reader.
- *Extensions*, which demonstrates the generality of the techniques described previously by illustrating their application to multimedia and multilingual environments, and by relating them to other information-processing tasks including categorising, extracting, and summarising.

Each chapter contains about half-a-dozen papers that have been carefully chosen to represent substantive research work that has been carried out in that area, preceded by an introductory overview of the area in question with leads into the individual selected papers and with further supporting references to enable the reader to explore the subject in more detail.

The seven-part categorisation we have chosen, like any categorisation, is somewhat artificial since there are very strong links between the various chapters. For example, some of the systems that are described exemplify specific models of retrieval; e.g., the SMART system and its successors have provided a vehicle for the implementation and testing of the many components of the vector processing model (Salton and McGill, 1983), while OKAPI has provided a similar vehicle for the probabilistic model (Robertson et al., 1993). We conclude with a single-paper *Envoi*.

SELECTION OF THE PAPERS

Many criteria can be used to select papers for inclusion in a collection such as this, and the editors have devoted much time to considering the following questions:

- Should one choose original research articles that provide a detailed account of some specific area but that may miss the broader picture provided by a good review article? We have chosen to select original articles, rather than reviews, since the inclusion of the former will enable readers to obtain a detailed insight into the models, techniques, and methodologies necessary for successful IR research. This should make them well prepared if, as we hope, they are encouraged to consider the use of these approaches in their own research work.
- Should one choose papers that are "citation classics" that have contributed to the growth of the subject, or papers that may be more appropriate for teaching newcomers to the field? We have chosen the former approach for much the same reasons as above, aiming to provide the necessary pedagogic basis by the chapter introductions and the extensive lists of supporting references.
- Should one choose the best papers within an area regardless of the extent to which these are distributed over the area, or seek area coverage even if this does not reflect the relative amount of work or solidity of ideas in different subareas? As we have been guided by the wish to cover as much as possible of the entire IR field in our collection, we have also sought balance within each chapter, though our concern with quality papers has meant that there are a few topics, noted where they occur, for which we could not find suitable papers.
- To what extent should one include recent material that, while appearing to be substantive in content, may not pass the test of time in the future? Or, in the converse case, hold only to confirmed work and thus exclude interesting older papers that have not had any significant following? The former question is a very difficult one since, as we have noted above, IR methods are starting to

be widely adopted, and there is thus a vast amount of new work appearing in the literature, the long-term merits at which we can only guess. In general, we have avoided recent material, with the specific exception of Chapter 8 (on Extensions), where we have sought to identify emerging applications of the basic IR technologies. We have equally eschewed papers which, however interesting in themselves, have neither had impact on nor have relations with other work in the field, though some of these appear in the secondary reference lists.

We emphasise that the considerations above have formed the basis for the selection of those papers that are included in the Reader in toto. Each chapter also has a carefully selected set of supporting references that includes papers that are valuable even if they do not meet all of the criteria above, that are excellent in content but too long for inclusion in a volume such as this, or that require substantial technical background for their appreciation.

IR is affected, as are many other computer-based subjects, by the headlong development of computing technology. This can cause some types of publication to become obsolescent, or even obsolete, extremely rapidly. This tendency is exemplified by the very extensive studies that have been carried out on novel algorithms for nearest-neighbour searching (see, e.g., Perry and Willett, 1983; Turtle and Flood, 1995) and for text compression (see, e.g., Bell et al., 1989; Cooper and Lynch, 1982), which were intended to reduce retrieval time and storage requirements, respectively, and on the use of novel types of parallel computer hardware (see, e.g., Cringean et al., 1991; Stanfill and Thau, 1991). Such work is of great importance but can be short-lived in its effect, and we have thus chosen to exclude work that relates specifically to the *efficiency* (as against the effectiveness) of IR systems, although this topic is covered in passing by some of the system-description papers in Chapter 7. Similar comments apply to the development of user interfaces for IR systems (Shaw, 1991), where the effects of technological improvements within just a short time period are well exemplified by comparing the papers by Kahle et al. (1993) and by Rao et al. (1995) and where activities such as the US Digital Libraries Initiative (*Communications of the ACM*, 1995; *Computer*, 1996; Lesk, 1997) are likely to bring about further substantial changes in the near future. More generally, indeed, this initiative can be expected to have far-reaching effects on the whole area of IR, and to establish new relations between retrieval and other areas of information processing.

More generally, we have excluded papers dealing with the strictly computational underpinnings of IR systems, in particular the whole area of file structure and organisation. Beyond noting, again in Chapter 7, that IR systems are conventionally implemented with *inverted files*, which can accommodate the changing sets and occurrences of access keys and the very variable lengths of internal objects, and that this type of file structure may have influenced some views of search logic, the essentials of IR with which we are concerned are independent of specific database implementations. Detailed discussion of such issues are provided by Frakes and Baeza-Yates (1992) and by Witten et al. (1994).

IR clearly has links with other areas as well as that of database management. These include human-computer interaction (HCI), natural language processing (NLP), and artificial intelligence (AI). We touch on these only from a strictly retrieval point of view, and take other Readings volumes for these areas as useful references for further reading (see, e.g., Baecker et al., 1995). There is, however, one further major area, normally labelled "library and information science," that is very close to ours. Seeking to satisfy a user's information need is clearly a common concern, so some fundamental concepts are the same. Calling our collection *Readings in Information Retrieval* nevertheless reflects key differences. One is that librarians have very many legitimate concerns outside the core indexing and retrieval task, such as the degree of subject coverage in a library's holdings. A second, much more significant one is that, while computers are extensively used in libraries for purposes such as circulation control, as a straightforward practical matter, the revolution embodied in the expression *information retrieval* refers to changes in indexing and searching stemming from automation. But as there are shared aims and notions, and as automation is also affecting conventional library indexing and searching as illustrated by the growth of OPACs, we draw attention, as a convenient entry to library and information science, to Kent et al. (1968ff.).

INFORMATION SOURCES

We have designed this collection of papers and supporting material as a comprehensive introduction to IR. But as an active and, by now, established field, IR has an extensive and detailed literature. The major sources of further information, covering all the aspects of the field as a whole, are as follows.

The most important books are the monographs by Frakes and Baeza-Yates (1992), Griffith (1980), Salton (1989), Saracevic (1970), Sparck Jones (1981), van Rijsbergen (1979), and Witten, Moffat, and Bell (1994) and the conference proceedings of the *Annual International Conference on Research and Development in Information Retrieval*, which is organised by the Special Interest Group on Information Retrieval of the Association for Computing Machinery (ACM SIGIR). The conference has been held annually since 1978, and the proceedings provide an unrivalled view of the development of IR over the last 18 years.

The principal journals in the field are the *ACM Transactions on Information Systems*, *Information Processing and Management* (formerly *Information Storage and Retrieval*), the *Journal of the American Society for Information Science* (formerly *American Documentation*), and the *Journal of Documentation*, but relevant material may be found (as is evidenced by the reference lists in this Reader) in a very wide range of computing, library, and information journals. The interested reader will also find much of interest in the *Annual Review of Information Science and Technology*, which contains extended review articles on a very wide range of topics and which has covered the field since 1966.

REFERENCES

Baecker, R.M., Grudin, J., Buxton, W., and Greenberg, S. (Eds.) (1995) *Readings in Human-Computer Interaction: Toward the Year 2000.* Second edition. San Francisco: Morgan Kaufmann.

Belkin, N.J., Oddy, R.N., and Brooks, H.M. (1982) ASK for information retrieval: Part 1. Background and theory. *Journal of Documentation*, **38**, 61–71.

Bell, T., Witten, I.H., and Cleary, J.G. (1989) Modelling for text compression. *ACM Computing Surveys*, **21**, 557–591.

Berners-Lee, T., Cailliau, R., Luotonen, A., Nielsen, H.F., and Secret, A. (1994) The World-Wide Web. *Communications of the ACM*, **37**(8), 76–82.

Cleverdon, C.W. (1967) The Cranfield tests on index language devices. *Aslib Proceedings*, **19**, 173–192.

Cleverdon, C.W. (1972) On the inverse relationship of recall and precision. *Journal of Documentation*, **23**, 195–201.

Communications of the ACM (1995) Special Issue: Digital libraries. *Communications of the ACM*, **38**(4), 22–96.

Computer (1996) Special Issue: Digital library initiative. *Computer*, **29**(5), 22–76.

Cooper, D., and Lynch, M.F. (1982) Text compression using variable-length to fixed-length encoding. *Journal of the American Society for Information Science*, **33**, 18–31.

Cringean, J.K., England, R., Manson, G.A., and Willett, P. (1991) Network design for the implementation of text searching using a multicomputer. *Information Processing and Management*, **27**, 265–283.

Doyle, L.B. (1961) Semantic road maps for literature searchers. *Journal of the Association for Computing Machinery*, **8**, 553–578.

Ellis, D. (1992) The physical and cognitive paradigms in information retrieval research. *Journal of Documentation*, **48**, 45–64.

Fairthorne, R.A. (1961) *Towards Information Retrieval.* London: Butterworths.

Fidel, R. (1984) Online searching styles: A case-study-based model of searching behaviour. *Journal of the American Society for Information Science*, **35**, 211–221.

Frakes, W.B., and Baeza-Yates, R. (Eds.) (1992) *Information Retrieval: Data Structures and Algorithms.* Englewood Cliffs, NJ: Prentice Hall.

Griffith, B.C. (Ed.) (1980) *Key Papers in Information Science.* White Plains, NY: Knowledge Industry Publications.

Harman, D.K. (Ed.) (1993) *The First Text REtrieval Conference* (TREC-1). Special Publication 500–207. Gaithersburg, MD: National Institute of Standards and Technology.

Ingwersen, P. (1992) *Information Retrieval Interaction.* London: Taylor Graham.

Ingwersen, P. (1996) Cognitive perspectives of information retrieval interaction: Elements of a cognitive IR theory. *Journal of Documentation*, **52**, 3–50.

Kahle, B., Morris, H., Goldman, J., Erickson, T., and Curran, J. (1993) Interfaces for distributed systems of information servers. *Journal of the American Society for Information Science*, **44**, 453–467.

Kent, A., and others (Eds.) (1968ff.) *Encyclopedia of Library and Information Science.* New York: Dekker.

Lancaster, F.W., and Fayen, E.G. (1973) *Information Retrieval On-Line.* Los Angeles: Melville Publishing.

Lesk, M.E. (1997) *Practical Digital Libraries: Books, Bytes and Bucks.* San Francisco: Morgan Kaufmann.

Mooers, C.N. (1952) Information retrieval viewed as temporal signalling. *Proceeding of the International Conference of Mathematicians, Cambridge, Massachusetts August 30–September 6, 1950.* pp. 572–573. Providence, R.I.: American Mathematical Society.

Muhlhauser, G. (1985) Dawn of next generation information retrieval. In D. Raitt (Ed.), *Proceedings of the 9th International Online Information Meeting*, pp. 365–371. Oxford: Learned Information.

Pearsall, J. (1989) STATUS/IQ: A semi-intelligent information retrieval system. *Information Services and Use*, **9**, 295–309.

Perry, S.A., and Willett, P. (1983) A review of the use of inverted files for best match searching in information retrieval systems. *Journal of Information Science*, **6**, 59–66.

Pritchard-Schoch, T. (1993) Natural language comes of age. *Online*, **17**(3), 33–43.

Proceedings of the International Conference on Scientific Information (2 volumes) (1959). Washington, DC: National Academy of Sciences—National Research Council.

Rao, R., Pedersen, J.O., Hearst, M.A., Mackinlay, J.D., Card, S.K., Masinter, L., Halvorsen, P.-K., and Robertson, G.G. (1995) Rich interaction in the digital library. *Communications of the ACM*, **38**(4), 29–39.

Robertson, S.E. (1977) The probability ranking principle in IR. *Journal of Documentation*, **33**, 294–304.

Robertson, S.E., Walker, S., Hancock-Beaulieu, M.M., Gull, A., and Lau, M. (1993) Okapi at TREC. In D.K. Harman (Ed.), *The First Text REtrieval Conference* (TREC-1). NIST Special Publication 500–207, pp. 21–30. Gaithersburg, MD: National Institute of Standards and Technology.

Salton, G. (1968) *Automatic Information Organisation and Retrieval.* New York: McGraw-Hill.

Salton, G. (Ed.) (1971) *The SMART Retrieval System.* Englewood Cliffs, NJ: Prentice Hall.

Salton, G. (1975) *Dynamic Information and Library Processing.* Englewood Cliffs, NJ: Prentice Hall.

Salton, G. (1989) *Automatic Text Processing. The Transformation, Analysis and Retrieval of Information by Computer.* Reading, MA: Addison-Wesley.

Salton, G., and McGill, M.J. (1983) *Introduction to Modern Information Retrieval.* New York: McGraw-Hill.

Saracevic, T. (1970) *Introduction to Information Science.* New York: Bowker.

Shaw, D. (1991) The human-computer interface for information retrieval. *Annual Review of Information Science and Technology*, **26**, 155–195.

Sparck Jones, K. (Ed.) (1981) *Information Retrieval Experiment.* London: Butterworths.

Stanfill, C., and Thau, R. (1991) Information retrieval on the Connection Machine: 1 to 8192 gigabytes. *Information Processing and Management*, **27**, 285–310.

Stevens, M.E., Heilprin, L., and Giuliano, V.E. (Eds.) (1965) *Statistical Association Methods for Mechanised Documentation. Symposium Proceedings.* Miscellaneous publication 269. Washington, DC: National Bureau of Standards.

Stonebraker, M. (Ed.) (1994) *Readings in Database Systems.* Second edition. San Francisco: Morgan Kaufmann.

Tague-Sutcliffe, J. (1995) *Measuring Information: An Information Services Perspective.* New York: Academic Press.

Turtle, H., and Flood, J. (1995) Query evaluation: Strategies and optimizations. *Information Processing and Management,* **31**, 831–850.

van Rijsbergen, C.J. (1979) *Information Retrieval.* Second edition. London: Butterworths.

Witten, I.H., Moffat, A., and Bell, T.C. (1994) *Managing Gigabytes: Compressing and Indexing Documents and Images.* New York: Van Nostrand Reinhold.

Chapter 2
History

The Thesaurus Approach to Information Retrieval 15
T. Joyce and R.M. Needham

The Automatic Derivation of Information Retrieval Encodements from Machine-Readable Texts 21
H.P. Luhn

Indexing and Abstracting by Association. Part I 25
L.B. Doyle

On Relevance, Probabilistic Indexing and Information Retrieval 39
M.E. Maron and J.L. Kuhns

The Cranfield Tests on Index Language Devices 47
C.W. Cleverdon

Computer Evaluation of Indexing and Text Processing 60
G. Salton and M.E. Lesk

GENERAL REMARKS

We have already noted, in the previous chapter, some major features of the development of IR as a whole. This chapter is intended to illustrate the early development of some key IR ideas. It thus focuses on the impact of automation in stimulating and shaping models and techniques for retrieval, but also shows how far back concepts that are now being applied operationally reach. It is easy to assume that, because computing technology changes so fast, any ideas underpinning its application are equally rapidly outdated. This is not the case. It is also extremely important for those now newly approaching IR not only to be aware that (as further discussed in Chapter 3) some ideas of *traditional*, manual systems remain valid but also to distinguish, within automated systems, between the *conventional* style represented by systems using Boolean logic and *modern* research-style systems offering ranked output. For those who see the faults of the conventional systems that were operationally dominant until the advent of the World Wide Web and are still, with their enormous literature indexes, extremely important, research in fact already offers an alternative approach that has only comparatively recently entered operational practice, for example in WIN (Pritchard-Schoch, 1993).

As this is both only a brief introduction and one concentrating on the history of the field from the perspective of the way the main currents evolved and were consolidated, there are aspects of and approaches to IR, as well as many detailed topics, that are not covered. Since the late forties, when Bush's groundbreaking paper, "As We May Think" (Bush, 1945; Smith, 1981), was published, there has been energetic and varied work, both theoretical and practical, in the field as a whole. In the earlier period in particular, the appearance and development of computing, along with the growth of the scientific literature, stimulated attempts to provide wide-ranging theories of information and communication suited to the modern world as well as, within the library world, novel approaches to document characterisation. This phase, up to about 1975, is very well illustrated in Fairthorne (1961), Kochen (1967), Saracevic (1970), and Griffith (1980). Thus Saracevic's collection includes a paper by Goffman on communication as an epidemic process. The great interest taken in new approaches to the design of languages for document indexing and classification is illustrated by Chan *et al.* (1985) and Gilchrist (1994).

This perception of the new information frontier also meant that work on IR was seen as part of a larger field including, in particular, what is now called natural language processing (NLP). This was symbolised by Masterman, Needham, and Sparck Jones's title "The Analogy between Mechanical Translation and Library Retrieval" at the 1958 International Conference on Scientific Information (*Proceedings of the International Conference on Scientific Information*, 1959), noted in Chapter 1 as a major event and one reflecting an optimism well conveyed by the fact that Luhn provided "auto-abstracts" for one section's papers (Schultz, 1968); and books and conferences throughout the sixties regarded IR and computational linguistics/NLP as falling within a larger language-oriented area of research (see, e.g., Garvin, 1963). Salton (1968, Chapter 5) and Bely et al. (1970) clearly show this close relationship. The collapse of machine translation work in the later sixties, putting computational linguistics as a whole under a cloud, and the largely independent growth of artificial intelligence (AI) promoted a separation during the seventies, which was increased by the lead taken within IR by purely statistical methods independent of NLP. It is only recently that relations between IR and NLP have been noticeably reestablished, as we see later in Chapter 6 and, especially, in Chapter 8.

This reflects the steady improvement of NLP technology, encouraging on the one hand the belief that it may be both viable and valuable in retrieval for the full-text case and on the other the growth of effort on closely related information tasks, like data extraction from retrieved texts, as illustrated by the multitask US TIPSTER Programme (Defence Advanced Research Projects Agency, 1996). Sparck Jones (1994) provides a history of NLP. For longer historical perspectives on the field as a whole, not confined to automated IR and setting it in a larger context, see Vickery (1994) and *Information Processing and Management* (1996).

AUTOMATED RETRIEVAL METHODS

Modern IR systems, with their characteristic ranking and weighting, became established in two stages: the first, from about 1955 to 1975, when key ideas and techniques were advanced in research; the second, from 1975 onward, when these slowly spread into the operational world. As noted in Chapter 1, we are now facing new challenges presented by the growth of machine-readable material and of networked communications, which has stimulated new research. Thus within IR research specifically, an initial phase up to the late sixties, when new ideas were introduced, was followed by a deepening and consolidating of these ideas during the seventies, with some new beginnings in the eighties, and a quicker pace in the present decade.

Automated retrieval began in the fifties with the use of punched cards, which established the *postcoordinate* revolution, i.e., the realisation that indexing *terms* can be arbitrarily combined at search time to satisfy absolute or relative Boolean conditions: card sorting made finding documents sharing any set of terms easy. Postcoordination was more flexible than the normal term *precoordination* used to form fixed whole descriptions that were assigned to documents and through which they were reached (cf. Lancaster, 1972). Postcoordination implied that it was the user, rather than the librarian, who defined document topics. It was associated with the idea of *descriptors* forming an indexing vocabulary, perhaps consisting of simple rather than complex terms and perhaps also not having any classificatory structure. However, following the almost universal use of classifications for traditional library purposes, descriptor sets were often organised hierarchically to allow upward (more general) matching at search time. In this early work, the notion of vocabulary control associated with traditional approaches to indexing, i.e., with the use of a specially-designed *indexing language* (as exemplified by the Universal Decimal Classification, or UDC), was strong; and such sets of descriptors were therefore normally labelled *thesauri*, to reflect the idea that each descriptor captured a generic concept (for instance, that underlying a set of synonyms in ordinary language).

The postcoordinate approach was a response to the growth of literature, especially journal articles rather than books, and to its greater content specialisation. Thus a domain-oriented thesaurus was assumed to be more effective for retrieval than a universal classification scheme, through both a finer category grain and a freer possibility of term combination to define topics.

Early automation focused on searching, not on the primary indexing of the documents themselves. However, it was not long before the idea of automating the indexing itself was put forward, both to reduce the considerable effort involved in indexing and to reflect more closely the actual content of documents. It was argued, in particular, that thesauri could be built automatically from the actual words used in documents, by exploiting the statistics of term *associations*, so derived thesaurus labels could then be automatically assigned to documents. Paradoxically, this suggestion emphasised the document *words* themselves as true content indicators, so simple indexing using the *natural language* to be found in the documents could be seen as the default if neither manual nor automatic thesauri were available; minimal vocabulary normalisation (to promote recall) could be achieved just by (automatic) stemming, to reduce variant word forms like singulars and plurals to their common root. More importantly, it was recognised that the *redundancy* of natural language in its initial text form, i.e., repetition of concepts and words, could be profitably exploited when "all in" queries, with many terms, were encouraged in order to support both precision through conjoint matches on several terms and recall through matches on alternative terms. These ideas are particularly associated with such workers as Luhn, Doyle, and Needham, as illustrated in the papers selected for inclusion in this chapter.

This development was further supported by the findings of early comparative evaluations, which showed postcoordination and natural language performing very competitively for very little effort when compared with existing approaches based on precoordinate indexing and controlled vocabularies (Cleverdon, 1967), but also by the difficulty of obtaining significant performance improvements through the use of collectionwide statistical associations. However, though the work on automatic thesauri was not directly productive, it had an important consequence in the context set by using natural language words taken from documents. It drew attention to the significance of variable word frequencies and so led to the development of statistically based *weighting* schemes, something completely outside the framework of conventional indexing, which at most allowed for one or two importance levels for terms. Testing showed statistical weighting was advantageous (and it was natural for automatic systems since the necessary facts could be easily gathered), as shown here in the paper by Salton and Lesk. The further development of statistical approaches to weighting are detailed in Chapters 5 and 6.

The final piece of the modern jigsaw was supplied by the notion of *relevance feedback*, using responses from the user that marked retrieved documents as relevant or nonrelevant: both term associations and term weighting could be profitably specialised for the individual user query by exploiting the extra information about good (or bad) terms that could be obtained from the relevance assessment of initial search output. This was information that could be provided without much user effort and was ideally suited to automatic application.

All of these ideas were vigorously investigated during the sixties. This early work was, moreover, distinguished as much by work on appropriate theory (e.g., Maron and Kuhns, 1960), to motivate the statistical techniques being applied, as by retrieval experiment. At the same time, other experiments had been conducted with, for example, automatic parsing to derive complex natural language index terms, though these were not shown to give superior retrieval performance with the small test collections then used. Further, while most work focused on the treatment of index terms, there was also work exploiting incidence data to group documents by their term co-occurrences, aimed at directly structuring the document space in a manner promoting effective retrieval. Such *document clustering* research was begun by Salton's group in the sixties (Salton, 1971) but was more evident in research during the seventies (see, e.g., van Rijsbergen and Croft, 1975), though, overall, it has not proven itself for retrieval effectiveness, regardless of whether it can be an aid to efficiency, and its possible roles in modern large-scale systems are unclear.

Thus, by the beginning of the seventies, some key statistical and probabilistic notions had been established, as had some general methodologies for retrieval system evaluation: these offered some useful performance measures, like *precision* and *recall*, both of which emphasised the need for *factor* decomposition in test design and identified some important performance factors, like indexing exhaustivity. The idea of relevance feedback, developed by Rocchio (1965) and intensively studied by Salton's group in the late sixties (Salton, 1971), can be taken as beginning the second phase of IR research as such, building on the first phase that introduced and indicated the value of statistically based approaches. In the seventies, the ideas and techniques of the sixties were refined and consolidated to give substantive models, like the vector and probabilistic ones, and particular techniques for weighting and feedback, that were justified by an increasing range of well-conducted tests, as described in more detail in later chapters.

However, beyond the general idea of postcoordination, the research ideas of the sixties were not adopted for operational implementation. The technological development of automated retrieval systems during the sixties was manifest in the growth of search services, like DIALOG or MEDLARS, which continued to rely on manual indexing using manually constructed indexing languages. These services concentrated their efforts on search support and paid very necessary attention to rapid and reliable operation on a large scale, while also addressing user interests in database coverage or document delivery. The notion of natural language indexing slowly filtered into these systems as an extra or fallback. But they were still used through professional intermediaries, aware of the many problems of formulating effective searches for large files. Moreover, the belief that carefully constructed indexing languages (manual thesauri, classifications) *must* be superior to simple natural language remained strongly held and was difficult to overcome from research evidence based only on very small document files.

The wind of change began to be felt in the operational world in the later seventies and to blow more strongly in the eighties, for a combination of reasons. Ever-increasing volumes of material made the maintenance of manual indexing vocabularies, and indexing itself, more costly and less cost-effective. The spread of full text, rather than just document titles or abstracts, suggested that approaches exploiting redundancy in indexing would be more appropriate than those relying on content distillation. The continuing signals from research, both confirming earlier findings in new studies and extending indexing and searching technologies (as shown in Chapters 6 and 7), added to this pressure for the adoption of the new methods and styles. The general spread of computing encouraged a relaxation of traditional paradigms. More computer power, and more computing facilities for end users, encouraged direct searching that bypassed the professional intermediary. Finally, the self-confidence of those working in mainstream computing encouraged them to march in and provide retrieval facilities, indifferent to the professional claims (and also real skills) of librarians and information officers, but more open in principle and sometimes in practice to the lessons of retrieval research.

All of this is crystallised in the explosion of new services for the Internet that has characterised the nineties. The application of modern, statistically motivated approaches has also been encouraged by the sharp rise in experimental scale, as well as general visibility, of retrieval system development and evaluation through the (D)ARPA/NIST Text Retrieval (TREC) Programme, which is discussed in detail in Chapter 4. The TREC experiments have demonstrated the continuing viability, for large-file full-text retrieval, of the statistical approach, while also encouraging new work, within this framework, to meet the new conditions. Importantly, these experiments have involved not only researchers but also an increasing number of system vendors. Conventional services are having to change under these new pressures, while many of the user needs to which they sought to respond via intermediaries may now be mediated through modern workstation interfaces. But the current environment also calls for new research, notably to deal with vast files (with corresponding high term frequencies), and heterogeneous file content (with wildly variable term co-occurrences and document lengths): both of these present challenges to the received research wisdom, while the extension to nontextual media presents a wealth of new research opportunities, as summarised in Chapter 8. There is especially a need for research on user interface design, exploiting new presentational and interactive devices to suit new data and search conditions—for example, to address competing demands for window real estate.

Even so, it is important to recognise that in the new services the essential problems of retrieval have not been overcome, merely shifted to new places, and in particular that it remains essential, for modern approaches to work properly, to ensure that the user supplies "good" requests, i.e., ones with redundancy. At the same time, even if the current retrieval environment is new, it is important to understand the message of past research and not to invent old wheels, especially square ones.

The papers in this chapter illustrate the earlier history of IR, and specifically the key period up to about 1968. They are chosen, from a rich and stimulating literature, both to introduce the innovations of automatic indexing and searching and to show what respectable antiquity they in fact have. They have also been deliberately chosen as presenting the ideas and findings of the period without excessively heavy technical baggage. For more historical detail on the specific automatic indexing and searching themes of this introduction, see Salton (1987), Sparck Jones (1981, Chapter 12; 1991), Stevens (1965), and Stevens et al. (1965).

SELECTED READINGS

The paper by Joyce and Needham (1958) reflects the arrival of the thesaurus, previously advocated by Luhn (Schultz, 1968) and noted by Vickery (1960) as a "new word in documentation". More specifically, it is a response to the limitations of earlier coordinate indexing systems using descriptors, proposing a thesaurus to overcome the various problems of missing matches or false matches that can arise with large/tolerant or small/rigorous descriptor vocabularies and with more or less coverage of document content in indexing descriptions. The paper then develops the suggestion that a thesaurus of index terms can be organised as a lattice (not a hierarchy), where the inclusion relation defining the lattice models a scale of relevance for the terms. Thus, while the basic search operations were very simply implemented using "peekaboo" cards, the paper notes the flexibility offered by the structure. It also suggests the use of frequency information, with vector matching, to control crude incidence matching.

Luhn's paper (1961) addresses the question of fully automatic indexing, focusing on the use of keywords taken from documents. This has the advantage that an author's own words are used to represent document content, without any constraint from an artificial classification or subject-labelling scheme, and without any prior restriction on how a future inquirer might be obliged to approach the document. Luhn also notes the value of a large number of keywords *per* document description, rather than the conventional few class or subject labels, and indeed envisages indexing using full texts: this allows matching on many words conjointly, which is discriminating, and Luhn further illustrates the use of numerical similarity measures for description matching. As indicated in this comparatively brief paper, Luhn combined a far-ranging view of the future with an engineer's practicality, and his research was a major influence on the early development of IR. The collection in Schultz (1968) demonstrates this more fully, and Luhn (1959), in particular, shows how comprehensive a view he took of the value of statistics about words for information retrieval and related tasks. This overview paper—unfortunately not well suited for reproduction here—covers the use of frequency data for term vocabularies, for individual document representation, for establishing term relations, and for both retrieval and related tasks like abstracting (which is discussed in Chapter 8).

The papers by Joyce and Needham (1958) and Luhn (1961) introduce some of the new ideas about how to do automatic indexing. Doyle (1962) illustrates the further exploration and extension of these ideas intended to exploit the indexing value of statistically derived vocabularies. He considers first the question of how (pairwise) term relationships should be defined and then the way they should be used, whether autonomously within the system or interactively by the user in search formation. He advocates the latter, showing how association maps (which he had memorably labelled "semantic road maps" (Doyle, 1961)) displaying term linkages and also individual document data, could be offered to and exploited by the user, online, in browsing and searching. Doyle's paper emphasises the role of clusters of associated terms and thus reflects work in the field generally where, in a natural progress, researchers had moved from relations between pairs of terms to those between sets. However, while Doyle sees an important role for statistically based clusters within the overall retrieval system, he also sees the user exploiting his own cognitive clusters in roaming the map and picking out sets of terms of interest.

Statistical term associations carry implications about probable term utility. Thus, while one major area of early research was in exploiting the value of term occurrences and co-occurrences for retrieval, another was in the development of a proper probabilistic theory of retrieval.

Maron and Kuhns (1960) was important as the first solid development of the probabilistic view of retrieval., centred on the notion of relevance: it thus offers a comprehensive formal model, but one intended to respond to the human user's key status as well as to objective properties of the system data. Like others at the time, Maron and Kuhns start from the limitations of traditional and conventional library systems and the possibilities opened up by automation. Thus existing systems, using strict Boolean methods, fail to deal adequately with semantic noise. Automation makes a more sophisticated approach based on term weighting possible, so that in searching documents are ranked by their "relevance number", indicating their probability of relevance to the user's information need. The paper assumes that the initial weight for terms, as well as the terms themselves, will be assigned by human indexers. However given this initial data, the authors propose search strategies that exploit statistical properties of the document file in order to modify requests or candidate output sets so as to emerge with a better final output. Their strategies for "groping in the index space" include, in particular, the use of term and document associations, and of term significance based on collection frequency. These ideas were more fully developed by later workers, as illustrated in, e.g., several of the papers in the Techniques chapter of this Reader. Section 5 of the paper, not reproduced here, reports on modest but promising experiments. This work and Kuhn's complement one another in relation to what is needed for fully automatic indexing.

Much of the early work on automatic IR was long on ideas but short on experiment, particularly for proper evaluation as opposed to feasibility testing. However, the interest within conventional library and documentation circles in novel indexing languages as a way of coping with the increasingly specialised technical literature, and the heated arguments between the advocates of different languages, prompted the first serious tests of comparative performance. These were tests that assumed manual document indexing, though within an overall framework increasingly seen as using at least punched cards, or even full-blown computing, for searching. Following the pioneering Cranfield-1 evaluation (Cleverdon, 1962), Cleverdon's Cranfield-2 experiments were a milestone in the design and conduct of retrieval tests (cf. Sparck Jones, 1981, Chapter 13). They also, to Cleverdon's, his colleagues', and the community's surprise, demonstrated the value of simple natural language indexing as opposed to highly controlled "artificial" languages. These studies, which are represented here by Cleverdon (1967), established a protocol for testing that has lasted to this day, through the careful attention to separate performance factors (including but not confined to the languages being tested), to the choice of performance measures (preeminently recall and precision), and to test methodology overall. One of the major aspects of performance characterisation was the recall-precision graph, showing the inverse relation between the two variables as a searching strategy was relaxed.

As just noted, Cleverdon's tests were of manual indexing, with mechanistic searching. Salton's work, from the beginning of the sixties, was focused on automatic systems and specifically on automatic indexing, even if he was willing to allow that manual thesauri might be helpful. Within the framework of the SMART Project, Salton developed the vector model of retrieval and the SMART software system both as an experimental vehicle and as a prototype for operational systems; he carried out extensive experiments on many indexing and searching techniques (notably on stemming, simple versus complex terms, complex terms defined only by word proximity or by syntactic relations, and conventional and statistical thesauri), using a range of performance measures and addressing such issues as significance testing on results. The work was also important because testing was done with several (albeit small) document and request collections. At an early stage, Salton recognised that term weighting, in response to term incidence data, could be easily implemented in an automatic system. His findings overall lent powerful support to the claim that basically simple approaches using natural language words could give competitive system performance. Thus the results brought together in the paper selected here (Salton and Lesk, 1968) showed the value of stemming and weighting when applied to the words in document abstracts, with some further (though not large) performance improvement from the use of thesaurus relations between terms. This paper did much to establish an automatic indexing and system baseline, familiar up to today. It was followed by the important detailed studies reported in Salton (1971), which introduced the major idea of search feedback and which thus completed the set of basic techniques that are discussed in Chapter 6.

REFERENCES

*Note: *** after a reference indicates a selected reading.*

Bely, N., Borillo, A., Virbel, J., and Siot-Decauville, N. (1970) *Procédures d'Analyse Sémantique Appliqués a la Documentation Scientifique.* Paris: Gauthier-Villars.

Bush, V. (1945) As we may think. *Atlantic Monthly,* July, 101–108.

Chan, L.M., Richmond, P.A., and Svenonius, E. (Eds.) (1985) *Theory of Subject Analysis: A Sourcebook.* Littleton, CO: Libraries Unlimited.

Cleverdon, C.W. (1962) *Report on the Testing and Analysis of an Investigation into the Comparative Efficiency of Indexing Systems.* Cranfield, England: College of Aeronautics.

Cleverdon, C.W. (1967) The Cranfield tests on index language devices. *Aslib Proceedings,* **19**, 173–192.***

Defence Advanced Research Projects Agency (1996) *TIPSTER Text Program Phase II. Proceedings of a Workshop Held at Vienna, Virginia, May 6–8, 1996.* San Francisco: Morgan Kaufmann.

Doyle, L.B. (1961) Semantic road maps for literature searchers. *Journal of the Association for Computing Machinery,* **8**, 553–578.

Doyle, L.B. (1962) *Indexing and Abstracting by Association. Part 1.* SP-718/001/00. Santa Monica, CA: System Development Corporation.***

Fairthorne, R.A. (1961) *Towards Information Retrieval.* London: Butterworths.

Fairthorne, R.A. (1964) Basic parameters of retrieval tests. *Proceedings of the American Documentation Institute,* **1**, 343–345.

Garvin, P.L. (Ed.) (1963) *Natural Language and the Computer.* New York: McGraw-Hill.

Gilchrist, A. (1994) Classification and thesauri. In B.C. Vickery (Ed.), *Fifty Years of Information Progress: A Journal of Documentation Review,* pp. 85–118. London: Aslib.

Griffith, B.C. (Ed.) (1980) *Key Papers in Information Science.* White Plains, NY: Knowledge Industry Publications.

Information Processing and Management (1996). Special issue: History of information science. *Information Processing and Management,* **32**, 1–88.

Joyce, T,. and Needham, R.M. (1958) The thesaurus approach to information retrieval. *American Documentation,* **9**, 192–197.***

Kochen, M. (Ed.) (1967) *The Growth of Knowledge.* New York: John Wiley.

Lancaster, F.W. (1972) *Vocabulary Control for Information Retrieval.* Washington, DC: Information Resources Press.

Luhn, H.P. (1959) *Potentialities of Auto-Encoding of Scientific Literature.* Technical Report RC-101. Yorktown Heights, NY: IBM Research Centre.

Luhn, H.P. (1961) The automatic derivation of information retrieval encodements from machine-readable texts. In A. Kent (Ed.), *Information Retrieval and Machine Translation*. Vol. 3, Pt 2., pp. 1021–1028. New York: Interscience Publication.***

Maron, M.E. (1961) Automatic indexing: an experimental inquiry. *Journal of the Association for Computing Machinery*, **8**, 404–417.

Maron, M.E. (1965) Mechanised documentation: The logic behind a probabilistic interpretation. Statistical methods for mechanised documentation. In M.E. Stevens, V.E. Giuliano, and L.B. Heilprin (Eds.), *Statistical Association Methods for Mechanised Documentation. Symposium Proceedings*. Miscellaneous publication 269, pp. 9–13. Washington, DC: National Bureau of Standards.

Maron, M.E. and Kuhns, J.L. (1960) On relevance, probabilistic indexing and information retrieval. *Journal of the Association for Computing Machinery*, **7**, 216–244.***

Pritchard-Schoch, T. (1993) Natural language comes of age. *Online*, **17**(3), 33–43.

Proceedings of the International Conference on Scientific Information (1959). 2 volumes. Washington, DC: National Academy of Sciences—National Research Council.

Rocchio, J.J. (1965) Relevance feedback in information retrieval. In G. Salton (Ed.), *Scientific Report ISR-9 (Information Storage and Retrieval) to the National Science Foundation*, pp. XXIII-1–XXIII-11. Cambridge, MA: Computation Laboratory, Harvard University.

Salton, G. (1968) *Automatic Information Organisation and Retrieval*. New York: McGraw-Hill.

Salton, G. (Ed.) (1971) *The SMART Retrieval System*. Englewood Cliffs, NJ: Prentice Hall.

Salton, G. (1987) Historical note—the past thirty years in information retrieval. *Journal of the American Society for Information Science*, **38**, 375–380.

Salton, G., and Lesk, M.E. (1968) Computer evaluation of indexing and text processing. *Journal of the Association for Computing Machinery*, **15**, 8–36.***

Saracevic, T. (Ed.) (1970) *Introduction to Information Science*. New York: Bowker.

Schultz, C.K. (Ed.) (1968) *H.P. Luhn: Pioneer of Information Science*. New York: Spartan Books.

Smith, L.C. (1981) 'Memex' as an image of potentiality in information retrieval research and development. In R.N. Oddy, S.E. Robertson, C.J. van Rijsbergen, and P.W. Williams (Eds.), *Information Retrieval Research*, pp. 345–369. London: Butterworths.

Sparck Jones, K. (Ed.) (1981) *Information Retrieval Experiment*. London: Butterworths.

Sparck Jones, K. (1991) Notes and references on early classification work. *ACM SIGIR Forum*, **25**(1), 10–17.

Sparck Jones, K. (1994) Natural language processing: A historical review. In A. Zampolli, N. Calzolari, and M. Palmer (Eds.), *Current Issues in Computational Linguistics: In Honour of Don Walker*, pp. 3–16. Dordrecht, Netherlands: Kluwer.

Stevens, M.E. (1965) *Automatic Indexing: A State of the Art Report*. Monograph 91. Washington, DC: National Bureau of Standards (2nd edition 1970).

Stevens, M.E., Heilprin, L., and Giuliano, V.E. (Eds.) (1965) *Statistical Association Methods for Mechanised Documentation. Symposium Proceedings*. Miscellaneous publication 269. Washington, DC: National Bureau of Standards.

van Rijsbergen, C.J., and Croft, W.B. (1975) Document clustering: An evaluation of some experiments with the Cranfield 1400 collection. *Information Processing and Management*, **11**, 171–182.

Vickery, B.C. (1960) Thesaurus—a new word in documentation. *Journal of Documentation*, **10**, 181–189.

Vickery, B.C. (Ed.) (1994) *Fifty Years of Information Progress: A Journal of Documentation Review*. London: Aslib.

THE THESAURUS APPROACH TO INFORMATION RETRIEVAL

*T. JOYCE and R. M. NEEDHAM**

An article by Dr. Vannevar Bush[1] which appeared in 1945 may be considered the beginning of the literature on mechanised information retrieval. In this article Dr. Bush described an imaginary machine, the "Memex", in which a research worker could store his personal library (principally on microfilm) together with other reports, papers, and records; and from which he would be able to select instantly all references relevant to the information he desired.

Dr. Bush's article is chiefly of interest today for its account of the inadequacies of conventional systems of library classification and the resulting tendency to neglect existing information in research work. "Even the modern great library is not generally consulted: it is nibbled at by a few... our ineptitude at getting at the record is largely caused by the artificiality of systems of indexing."

Since the importance of this problem became widely understood, a number of retrieval systems have been either designed or proposed. These systems normally involve the following, which may be wholly or partly mechanised:

1) The documents or other records which are to be added to the system are processed by recording information about them which will assist in their retrieval.
2) The requests for information are processed in a similar, though not necessarily identical, manner.
3) The documents and the requests are then compared or matched in such a way as to segregate those which are relevant to the information requested. Subsequently, several lists, or an ordering of documents, may be prepared according to the degree of relevance.
4) Thus is made possible access to the documents, or copies of them may be provided.

Broadly speaking, there have been two basic approaches to the first stage of information retrieval, namely the scanning or processing of the documents:

1) *Classifying* or grouping in a particular order — possibly physically on bookshelves — according to a predetermined scheme. This is the principle upon which almost every library operates, and upon which the conventional library classifications (Dewey, Bliss, etc.) are based.

However, conventional classifications possess inherent weaknesses which do not appear to have been overcome by constant revision. It is not always clear to which class, or subclass, a document should be assigned, and rules must be devised to make possible the selection of one class from the two or more which may be appropriate. Unless there are duplicate copies or an adequate system of cross-references, this may mean that not all the documents which are relevant to a given class are to be found in that class, and hence may not be retrieved when they are wanted.

2) *Indexing* the documents by selecting terms (also known as descriptors, concepts, aspects) which provide a sufficient indication of the subject-matter of the document to ensure that it will be retrieved according to the specifications of the request.[2,3]

Retrieval is often carried out by superimposing punched cards or metal plates representing the terms or descriptors, in which the holes represent the documents to which the terms apply. In Zatocoding,[4] a set of random numbers is assigned to each descriptor to be encoded, and each number corresponds to a hole to be punched in a given field on cards representing the documents.

The principal difference among the various systems is in the nature of the terms used to index the documents. These vary from several thousand in the Uniterm system (with little or no attempt to remove synonyms), to a few

*Cambridge Language Research Unit, Cambridge, England.

hundred, or even less than a hundred, descriptors in the Zatocoding system. Uniterms have an advantage in that they can be selected easily. Terms which actually appear in the documents are employed and can be 'posted' on the Uniterm cards without reference to a standard list. Descriptors (in Zatocoding) have the advantage of consistency in use — the same concept will always be represented by the same descriptor or set of descriptors.

There are two main difficulties encountered in the application of any system of 'multiple aspect indexing':

1) It may not be clear whether or not a particular term should be associated with a document. To some extent, any decision respecting the subject content of a document may be said to be subjective and may be biased by expectations of future information requests. Admittedly, it may be possible to index a research paper completely and satisfactorily by means of certain terms. In the case of a more discursive document, the decision as to which terms to employ must necessarily be more difficult. If one errs on the side of generosity in the allocation of terms, the possibility of 'false drops' is increased. If, on the other hand, subject analysis is incomplete, there is danger that some documents may not be retrieved even though they are definitely relevant to the information requested.

It is also clear that the phrasing of the request will, in certain important respects, affect the nature of the search. A loosely worded request may produce no documents at all, or it may produce an impossibly large number. One may say that the enquirer is getting no more than he deserves: he should learn from his experience. On the other hand, it may be said that one of the functions of a retrieval system is to produce material from a field of which the enquirer has no knowledge but which is nevertheless relevant to his enquiry. One may compare the situation with that of a well-organised index, from which it is often possible to get new relevant information. The enquirer should employ a tightly worded request, but if he does not get what he wants on the first attempt the system should be capable of producing a secondary list of references perhaps less directly relevant, but still useful.

The random superimposed coding of Zatocoding does do this to some extent but not in an organised way. Briefly, if the mechanical selector is set to work for a number of descriptors — say A, B and C — it will produce all the cards bearing the three descriptors, together with a small random number bearing only two. Mooers claims that these 'false drops' have a certain value.[5]

"These samplings are very useful because they lead to information the existence of which in the file might not otherwise have been discovered. They also permit reformulations of better search prescriptions. Because the random samplings are usefully biased to the desired subjects, they have been called 'subject induced extra selections'."

2) Multiple aspect indexing will tend to produce false drops which could have been avoided had the structural content of the documents been in some way taken into account. Thus, there will be no distinction made between a paper on exports from Britain to the U. S. A., and another on exports from the U. S. A. to Britain. Also, a document giving information upon the 'economic comparison of steam railway locomotives and diesel highway truck tractors' may be retrieved through a request for material on the cost of operation of railway diesel locomotives (example from Mooers). This problem is considered further below.

The Thesaurus Approach

As mentioned above, where a large number of terms are employed for the indexing process, synonyms or near-synonyms are bound to occur. These may lead to the non-retrieval of relevant documents unless, in some way, allowance is made for them. This is also true for general terms. For example, if it is desirable that a paper dealing with 'personal income tax and social security payments' should be retrieved when there is a request for material on 'the financing of social security', it will not be found unless it is also indexed under 'taxation', or there is a procedure for indexing all documents on income tax under 'taxation.'

The problems arising from synonymity with a large number of terms do not arise where only a few terms are employed, provided care has been taken to make them mutually exclusive. This is so with Zatocoding. On the other hand, selecting the Zatocoding descriptors, when indexing each individual document, requires more intelligence than selecting Uniterms from a considerably longer list, when the Uniterms selected are, for the most part, words which actually occur in the document.

In order to combine the advantage of the systems which employ a large number of terms with that of the systems employing a small number, the suggestion has been made that a thesaurus should be employed. For example, Bernier[6] writes: "A limited thesaurus would seem to be another effective way of bringing the relevant terms to the attention of the searcher if the vocabulary proves too large to be read completely each time for selection."

A pilot scheme for a retrieval system at the library of the Radar Research Establishment at Malvern* employs about 75 terms comprising a list which is effectively a thesaurus. The following entries, selected more or less at random, will illustrate this:

2. Add (gain, superimpose, sum, application, join, towards)
10. Calculate (compute, analog, digital, count, enumerate)
28. Generate (excitation, construct, make, produce, prepare, design)
41. Micro (miniature, small, narrow)
60. Square (area, surface, mean, square, field, plane)
73. Star (solar flares, prominences, eclipse, meteors, sun)

An alphabetic dictionary of terms which occur in R.R.E. reports and requests has been prepared, giving references to one or more of the listed head-words. For each report that is indexed, the relevant terms are selected (these can often be derived from the title or from the abstract), and the corresponding head-numbers looked up and noted. The reports are represented by holes punched in plates representing the heads. Requests are dealt with in the same way, the plates corresponding to the relevant heads being held in register so that reports are indicated by spots of light.

In a paper by H. P. Luhn[7] the thesaurus approach is carried still further. Luhn believes that it can be applied as follows:

1) Words of similar or related meaning are grouped into 'notional families', similar to the heads in *Roget's Thesaurus*.

2) The encoding of documents in terms of notional elements is effected by means of the dictionary of notations, the result being a mechanically prepared notional abstract.

3) For retrieval, the enquirer is asked to prepare an essay giving as many details as he can concerning his problem. This is encoded in the same manner, and the question notional pattern is compared with the notional patterns of the documents. "Since an identical match is highly improbable, this process would be carried out on a statistical basis by asking for a given degree of similarity."

The Thesaurus Approach of the Cambridge Language Rsearch Unit

As we have seen, the employment of a large number of terms, when indexing a collection of documents, must somehow take account of the existence of synonyms. On the other hand, the employment of a comparatively small number, particularly if the notions represented by the terms are not supposed to overlap, makes the indexing process considerably more difficult. These disadvantages can be avoided if a thesaurus is employed together with an alphabetic index which includes all the terms by which one might wish to index a document.

The thesaurus approach of the Cambridge Language Research Unit originated in three papers by M. Masterman, M. A. K. Halliday, and A. F. Parker-Rhodes presented to the M.I.T. Conference on Machine Translation in October 1956. They regarded language as consisting of words which necessarily derive much of their significance from their context. This is in opposition to the view that words have precise meanings, some words unfortunately having several.

The developments of these ideas, which were the first use of the thesaurus in a mathematical way, may be seen in the papers referred to above,[8,9,10] and in a number of other papers and notes by members of the Unit.[11] It is not easy to test these ideas as applied to machine translation without a large vocabulary based on a complete and successful treatment of syntax. Various tests of the procedures described in the papers mentioned above, contain several kinds of intuitive simplification, and are therefore not entirely satisfactory. Nevertheless, the approach obviously contains immense possibilities.

It has been widely observed that there is a

*Information supplied by Mr. S. Whelan of the R.R.E.

close analogy between machine translation and information retrieval (R. A. Fairthorne, G. King, A. Uttley), and after conversations with Dr. Uttley investigations were started into an application of this approach to retrieval work.

We first decided that it was essential to preserve, as units of the system, the key terms used in any document, thus to retain the advantages of such a system as Uniterm.

It was therefore necessary to make *term abstracts* of all the documents — since the choice of terms is not limited this presents no great difficulty — and to start from the term vocabulary found in them.

This term vocabulary was then arranged so that the property of accommodating near-synonyms held at all levels. It appeared that this could be done by arranging the words in a partial-ordering relation, expressed informally thus: If you ask for A you mustn't complain if you get $B' = A \geqslant B$. If you ask for something about Russian grammar you can reasonably be given something about Russian nouns. Also, if you ask either for something about mechanical processes, *or* about translation, you can hope and expect to be given something about machine translation. The difference between this arrangement of terms and that described by R. H. Richens,[12] who arranged the terms according to the hierarchic classification of the U.D.C., is that terms representing the meets of classes represented by other terms are freely employed, as well as are the joins. This eliminates the difficulty referred to above, which is inevitably encountered in a hierarchic classification, in that it may be difficult to decide into which sub-class a document should go, while at the same time making it possible to allow for structure.

To make use of the convenient algebraic properties of lattices, the figure our procedure yields can be readily turned into a lattice by including latent elements where needed to satisfy the lattice axioms. (We find that the idea of a terms vocabulary as a lattice of this kind occurs both in Fairthorne[3] and Mooers.[5])

Terms are to be treated only as synonymous if it appears that, for any conceivable extension of the library, there will never be any need to distinguish between them. For example, in a machine translation vocabulary, 'multiple meaning problem', 'plurivalence of meaning', and 'ambiguity' (in one sense) would be regarded as synonymous. Since, in all other cases the actual terms in the vocabulary are treated as distinct, although of course they may be close to one another in the lattice, it is possible to answer a very precise information request. But, at the same time some procedure for providing a scale of relevance is necessary. As considerable accuracy in specifying both documents and requests in the terms of the system is possible, the system cannot be a 'one-shot' one (that is: no initial output, no retrieval) in case the request is stated too exclusively.

As in other systems, the documents are represented by holes in punched cards which represent the various terms, and in addition, *when a hole is punched in any term card, all the cards representing terms at higher levels of the lattice such that the inclusion relation holds between them and the original term are also punched.* This can be easily accomplished if there is a suitable system of cross-references among the term cards themselves. A term abstract is then made of each information request received, the corresponding term cards are removed from the card file and held in register, and the first output (if any) is recorded.

The original course used to produce a scale of relevance[8] would, in the present context, work as follows: from the terms of the request select all appropriate term cards, including those to which there are cross-references (i.e. those representing all terms above the original terms in the lattice). Thus, for a request for material on mechanical translation of Russian prepositions, the cards for *machine translation*, *Russian*, *preposition*, and also for *machines*, *translation*, *languages*, *parts of speech*, *word classes*, *grammar*, *linguistics*, and *language* would be withdrawn from the card file. These would then be superimposed in all possible pairs, and all the documents revealed would be noted. The documents would then be consulted in order of frequency of appearance in the list of outputs. Clearly this process would be very laborious for requests involving any number of terms. Fortunately various simplifications can be made for practical use.

First, it can be shown that it is not necessary to compare the cards in pairs. The same scale will result from simply counting the occurrences of the document holes in the same set of cards. This might be useful for a mechanical method, but for hand use another equivalent method is more convenient. Under certain conditions* the first two stages of the scale are given by the following procedure. Choose as most relevant the set given by superimposing the actual cards representing the terms of the request. Then substituting for each card in turn a card covering it in the lattice, and note the set of outputs. This second set of outputs, having substituted all the covering elements, will constitute the second relevance class. This proves in practice to be far enough along the scale of relevance to give the documents needed. For the request given above it yields the desired result in five 'peek-a-boo' operations as against 11 counts and an addition.

Structure of Information

It has been noted that, particularly in large libraries, a high proportion of false drops could be caused by failure of the system to take account of the structure of the documents. There will come a time when there will be, for example, so many documents with the notional abstract a,b,c,d,e,f, that it is necessary to distinguish among them when this cannot be done effectively by including more terms.

One possible solution would be to take account of the frequency of occurrence of the different terms. The matching operation would then be between vectors, the elements of which are frequencies, and the matching relation would be the vector distance relation. The fault here would be that distance between long and short books on the same subject would be large. This could perhaps be overcome if the frequency vectors were normalised, or logarithms of frequencies were used. This method of giving both a scale of relevance and a reference to structure has not been tested because it is physically difficult. It does however appear to be a most complete treatment and will be tried if the more tractable methods prove insufficient.

Also one might treat a set of terms as a single term the place of which in the lattice is the lattice meet of the terms of the set. An example is provided by the terms 'machine' and 'translation'. These have a meet 'MT'. Thus a document about MT will be coded as MT, and a document which has references both to M & T but not to MT will be coded under M & T separately. A request involving MT will then not yield the latter at the first stage of relevance. This process may be elaborated to any extent that is found necessary. It is structurally similar to that proposed by Mooers,[5] involving interlocking descriptor sets, and the coding of n-tuples taken from these as if they were themselves descriptors, and may be illustrated by the same kind of example. The use of groups of terms or descriptors in this way, which may be made a fairly elegant process, although there is an essential arbitrariness in deciding when to apply it, seems to be the best that can be done without coding the documents in a way that will be to some extent message-preserving. The difficulties of message-preserving abstracting and coding are well known. The one that is most important in this context is that operations may no longer be carried out independently of the order of the cards and terms, and some asymmetrical operations will be necessary. All this detracts very much from the manipulative simplicity of the system.

Conclusion

The system given above has been, and is being, tested on the offprint library of the Cambridge Language Research Unit. Investigations of the use of compressed coding to lessen the physical work are continuing. A description of the technique and apparatus will appear in another communication.

The tests in progress, together with comparison with the published details of other systems, lead us to claim the following advantages for our system:

1) It has the advantages of descriptor or head systems in its treatment of related terms without
   a) the difficulty of abstracting for them,
   b) leaving the advantages of their hierarchies unrecognised,
   c) their inflexibility in an expanding library.

2) It uses a scale of relevance and does not, therefore, fail if there is no initial output.

3) It retains the advantage of Uniterms in that it cannot be caught by an unforeseen change in the structure of the library.

4) It can deal with a request in general terms without producing at once all the detailed

*The condition is that if Σ is the set of terms of the request and $J(\Sigma)$ is the set of elements of the lattice which are a, some $a \in \Sigma$, and $J'(\Sigma)$ the set obtained by removing from $J(\Sigma)$ the elements substituted for, then $J(J'(\Sigma)) = J(\Sigma)$. (See (13)).

work on the subject. This is illustrated by the classification we have established, which will be discussed in detail in a following paper.

REFERENCES

1. V. Bush, "As we may think", *Atlantic Monthly*, v. *176* (1945), p. 101-108.
2. J. W. Perry, A. Kent, & M. Berry, *Machine Literature Searching*, New York, Interscience, 1956.
3. R. A. Fairthorne, "The patterns of retrieval", *American Documentation*, v. *7*, (1956), p. 65-70.
4. C. N. Mooers, "Zatocoding and developments in Information Retrieval", *Aslib Proceedings*, v. *8*, (1956), p. 1-20.
5. C. N. Mooers, "Information Retrieval on Structured Content", *3rd London Symposium on Information Theory*, '55, p. 121-134.
6. C. L. Bernier, "Correlative Indexes II: Correlative trope indexes", *American Documentation*, v. *8*, (1957), p. 103-122.
7. H. P. Luhn, *A Statistical Approach to Mechanised Literature Searching"*, New York, I.B.M. Research Center, 1957.
8. M. Masterman, "Potentialities of a Mechanical Thesaurus", *M.I.T. Conference on MT*, 1956.
9. M. A. K. Halliday, "The thesaurus type mechanical dictionary and application to English Preposition Classification", *M.I.T. Conference on MT*, 1956.
10. A. F. Parker-Rhodes, "An Algebraic Thesaurus", *M.I.T. Conference on MT*, 1956.
11. *C.L.R.U. Series on Mechanical Study of Context*, privately circulated, 1957.
12. R. H. Richens, "An Abstracting and Information Service for Plant Breeding and Genetics", in Casey & Perry, *Punched Cards and Their Application in Science and Industry"*, New York, Reinhold, 1951.
13. R. M. Needham, "A property of finite lattices", *C.L.R.U. Research Note*, 1957.

CHAPTER 45

The Automatic Derivation of Information Retrieval Encodements from Machine-Readable Texts

H. P. LUHN

International Business Machines Corporation, Advanced Systems Development Division, Yorktown Heights, New York

I. INTRODUCTION

The ever increasing production of scientific and technical literature has, in recent years, accentuated the difficulty of extending conventional methods of organizing such literature for retrieval. A great deal of attention is presently given to the development of mechanical information retrieval systems which have for their objective the reduction of manual effort for locating information pertinent to a given topic that might be contained in large collections of documents. While the feasibility of such systems has in part been established by full scale operations, they remain dependent upon human effort. The documents of a collection must still largely be analyzed and encoded "by hand." Thus, a key problem of coping with the ever growing supply of new literature is still begging for a solution.

There is at present a great deal of duplication of effort in that the encoding of identical documents for retrieval is carried on in several places. The elimination of this duplication in some orderly fashion might go far in relieving the pressure, at least temporarily. The pooling of effort necessary to accomplish this, can, however, be effective only if the encoding would be performed in a uniform manner. It has been proposed that a "common language for machine searching and translation" (1) would bring about the desired standardization.

If it is reasonable to assume, however, that there will not be sufficient qualified manpower available to satisfy encoding and translation requirements regardless of the economies effected by standardization, then methods still have to be found by which machines can substantially assist the human encoder. There is a question then of whether the quest for a common artificial language is justifiable, in view of the impending automation, or the language itself is practical.

In the following, some approaches to a solution to this problem will be explored and examples given. These approaches are based on the general availability of the text of documents in machine-readable form, as may be assumed to be the case in the near future. The discussion is relevant primarily to the retrieval of ideas, experiences, comments, etc.; that is, to the expressions of intellect rather than factual details.

I. THE PRACTICABILITY OF A COMMON LANGUAGE

The concept of a common language for facilitating the processing of texts by machines for purposes of information retrieval implies the necessity of translation. Even if an author were to write in terms of such a language, the need for translation is not removed since an artificial common language would be too restrictive for use as a natural language.

One of the objectives of a common language is the standardization or normalization of notions by means of definitions. The assignment of a suitable standard definition to an author's expression of a certain notion is subject to the translator's interpretation and therefore a variable factor. Furthermore, both the formulation of definitions and the translator's interpretations are strictly based on past knowledge and experience. Aspects of documents which might prove important in the light of future inquiry are therefore liable to be made inaccessible. Under these circumstances there is a serious doubt as to the effectiveness of storing information in translated form, i.e., coded in terms of a "common language for machine searching and translation."

If on the other hand it should be possible for machines to store information in terms of the author's own language, the act of interpretation may be shifted to the instant of inquiry. This would make it possible to have the inquirer formulate his own definitions and interpret information in the light of the latest developments and with respect to his particular problem. It would permit complete freedom as to the aspect from which an inquirer needs to view past information. The lack of this freedom is typical of present classification systems which invariably restrict the avenues of approach. This restrictiveness would tend to persist if a common language were used.

The argument for storing uninterpreted textual material also accords best with the statistical fact that only a fraction of stored information is ever referred to again. The intellectual effort invested initially in the interpretation of information for translating it into a common language can be only partly recovered. This wastefulness will become intolerable in the face of the anticipated growth of the literature output. Therefore the method of storing uninterpreted information can check this problem by limiting effort to the productive phase of the information retrieval process.

The foregoing arguments point up the limitations of an artificial common language. The question arises: what are natural languages lacking that gives rise to the demand for a substitute language? Since we are here concerned with the communication of ideas, it is difficult to see how the interposition of an artificial language can in practice overcome a problem which is inherent in language itself, including the artificial language. The result can only be a compounding of the problem.

It must be realized that in the area of information retrieval here discussed it is not possible to retrieve specific information per se but only clues to the chance existence in storage of information having various degrees of relationship to a given topic. It is only by interpretation of the original text that the actual presence of pertinent information can be discovered and established.

III. MACHINE TALENTS

If the reduction of intellectual effort in the encoding phase of information retrieval systems is desirable and automatic processes must be reverted to, there is the question as to the extent to which machines can assist. Based on the availability of text in machine-readable form, can a machine produce clues which can serve in a manner similar to those derived manually? Since this question cannot be answered at this time for lack of experience, it might be useful to review some of the approaches that might be taken toward the solution of this problem. Obviously it cannot be expected that machine products in this area will be similar to man made products, particularly since the faculty of interpretation is beyond the talent of machines. It will therefore be necessary to settle for the best a machine can do in its own right. Ways need to be found for man to interpret the clues a machine is capable of producing. It is believed that this is feasible, once the machine talents are understood and that man can learn to properly interpret machine manifestations as he has learned to interpret many other non-human manifestations in the past.

IV. AUTOMATIC DERIVATION OF CLUES

Broadly speaking, the formulation of clues based on human interpretation of texts take the form of abstracts, extracts or assignments of subject headings or categories. These processes have in essence the effect of reducing the wordage of a text to a few statements or words, chosen with deliberation for their significance and value as clues. A machine substitute for such processes of compacting and contracting would consist of a systematic reduction of the text on the basis of its statistical properties. Methods for performing such encodements on certain types of text have been described elsewhere (2, 3, 4) and will therefore not be gone into here. The end products may consist of a frequency ranking of certain words occurring in the text, or of an extraction of certain sentences or portions of sentences in accordance with a statistical evaluation of the words contained therein.

The encodements here referred to consist of a far greater range of identifying elements than is customary in manually encoded systems. This is necessary to compensate for the machine's lack of discriminatory power and to minimize the effects of "noise" created by this lack.

V. WORD LISTS

A clue to similarity of subject matter may be derived from the choice of words a document exhibits. If the document contains many of the words required to phrase the topic of a given inquiry, the probability of their subject matters being similar should be high. The comparison of word lists may be carried out on a one-to-one basis, and the degree of similarity may be measured by the fraction of matching words.

If frequency of occurrence is an indication of the significance of certain words used by an author, the machine can readily rank such words by frequency or can weigh each word by its relative frequency with respect to all the words of a given text.

One such method is illustrated in Fig. 1 as applied to the determination of similarity between documents. A coefficient of similarity is computed based on relative frequency of words common to pairs of documents. The coefficient equals the sum of the lesser relative frequency values of matching word pairs. When this method is used for retrieval, an inquiry may be posed in terms of a vocabulary typical of the topic in question, and the words of this vocabulary may be weighted arbitrarily to reflect relative emphasis.

The vocabulary method of detecting similarity of texts may be refined and modified in many ways to meet specific requirements. For instance the coefficients of similarity may be made to reflect a measure of both the relative frequency and ranking of words (5). An up-to-date consolidation of all individual vocabularies may be provided as a guide for formulating inquiries. This may further be combined with a listing of synonyms and near-synonyms for inclusion as alternatives in the inquirer's vocabulary.

VI. KEYWORDS IN CONTEXT

A rather comprehensive automatic method for providing clues to pertinent literature involves the extraction of significant words (keywords) together with significant modifying words adjoining them. Listing such keywords in context in alphabetic order provides an index in which all identical keywords are grouped and an account is given of the various associations and meanings that each keyword has throughout the document collection.

The method of generating Keyword in Context indexes has been described in an earlier paper (6). A sample page of such an index is shown in Fig. 2. The number to the right of each entry refers to the related document as listed in the bibliography associated with the index.

COEFFICIENTS OF SIMILARITY (s) BETWEEN DOCUMENTS

An Example Involving the Following 3 Documents:

A. Mechanism Discovered in the Brain Which Unlocks Stream of Consciousness Record. (N. Y. Times, Nov. 24, 1957)*

B. The Brain as a Tape Recorder. (Time, Dec. 23, 1957)*

C. The Reticular Formation. (Scientific American, May, 1957)*

NOTE: Documents A and B deal with precisely the same subject, while C deals with some other aspect of the human brain.

Absolute and Relative Frequencies of Top-frequency Words Shares by at Least 2 Documents.

Word	Document A		Document B		Document C	
	abs.	rel.	abs.	rel.	abs.	rel.
Brain	12	.082	12	.109	29	.080
Experience	10	.069	7	.064	11	.030
Record	10	.069	3	.027	-	-
Area	9	.062	-	-	12	.033
Conscious	8	.055	3	.027	-	-
Patient	7	.048	8	.078	-	-
Dr. Penfield	6	.041	6	.055	-	-
Electric	6	.041	6	.055	-	-
Time	6	.041	5	.046	-	-
Hear	5	.034	9	.082	-	-
Stimulated	5	.034	4	.086	27	.074
Cortex	4	.027	-	-	26	.072
Detail	4	.027	4	.086	-	-
Function	4	.027	-	-	11	.030
Temporal	4	.027	5	.046	-	-
Respond	4	.027	-	-	11	.030

Coefficients

s (A, B) = .495
s (A, C) = .260
s (B, C) = .147

Method:

$s(X, Y) = \sum_i \min(f_i, g_i)$, where the sum is taken over all words shared by the documents X and Y. f_i is relative frequency of word number i in X and g_i is the same for Y.

*By permission of publisher.

Fig. 1.

KEYWORD-IN-CONTEXT INDEX

COULOMB	EXCHANGE ENERGY FROM SHELL-MODEL WAV	1719
	EXCITATION OF PROTONS IN HELIUM II B	0011
OF ATOMIC AND MOLECULAR	EXCITATION BY A TRAPPED-ELECTRON ME	0150
THERMAL	EXCITATIONS IN LIQUID HE3.	1465
ENERGIES OF GROUND AND	EXCITED NUCLEAR CONFIGURATIONS IN TH	0452
	EXCITED STATES OF V51 AND CR53.	1691
4-PLUS	EXCITED STATE IN OSMIUM-188.	1717
NTERNAL PHOTOEFFECT AND	EXCITON DIFFUSION IN CADMIUM AND ZIN	0123
OF THE CONTRIBUTION OF	EXCITONS TO THE COMPLEX DIELECTRIC	1555
THERMAL	EXPANSION OF SOME CRYSTALS WITH THE	0136
ENERGY LEVELS IN	F18 FROM THE N14/ALPHA,ALPHA/N14 AND	0547
ON FROM AL27-PLUS-P AND	F19-PLUS-P.	0239
TIC MEASUREMENTS OF THE	FE-CR SPINELS.	1603
BARIUM	FERRATE III.	0326
MAGNETOSTATIC MODES IN	FERRIMAGNETIC SPHERES.	0059
NICKEL-IRON	FERRITE.	0397
TRANSITION TO THE	FERROELECTRIC STATE IN BARIUM TITANA	0413
SUPERCONDUCTIVITY AND	FERROMAGNETISM IN ISOMORPHOUS COMPOU	0089
INTERPLANETARY MAGNETIC	FIELD AND ITS CONTROL OF COSMIC-RAY	0589
MAGNETIC	FIELD DEPENDENCE OF ULTRASONIC ATTEN	0080
RELATIVISTIC	FIELD THEORY OF UNSTABLE PARTICLES.	0283
QUANTUM	FIELD THEORIES WITH COMPOSITE PARTIC	0669
A GENERALLY CONVARIANT	FIELD THEORY.	1826
AND SURFACE STATES FROM	FIELD-INDUCED CHANGES IN SURFACE REC	0369
NGULAR DISTRIBUTIONS IN	FISSION INDUCED BY ALPHA PARTICLES,	0536
UTRON CROSS SECTIONS OF	FISSIONABLE NUCLEI.	0203
AL COSMIC-RAY INTENSITY	FLUCTUATIONS OBSERVED AT SOUTHERN ST	1798
	FLUX OF COSMIC-RAY PARTICLES WITH Z-	0597
NEUTRINO CORRELATION IN	FORBIDDEN BETA DECAY.	0244
	FOURIER COEFFICIENTS OF CRYSTAL POTE	0073
RVATION IN THE DECAY OF	FREE AND BOUND LAMBDA PARTICLES.	0605
STEADY-STATE	FREE PRECESSION IN NUCLEAR MAGNETIC	1693
	FREQUENCY SHIFT OF THE ZERO-FIELD HY	0449
DECAY OF	GADOLINIUM-159.	0262
	GAMMA RADIATION FROM AL27-PLUS-P AND	0239
ECTIONAL CORRELATION OF	GAMMA RAYS IN GE72.	0229
CISION DETERMINATION OF	GAMMA RAYS FOLLOWING P,P-PRIME-GAMMA	0532
	GAMMA-RAY THRESHOLD METHOD AND THE O	0461
P/S32 AND S32/P,P-PRIME	GAMMA/S32.	1702
ONSTANT OF YTTRIUM IRON	GARNET AT O DEG K.	0395
LORENTZIAN	GAS AND HOT ELECTRONS.	1567
TIBILITY OF AN ELECTRON	GAS AT HIGH DENSITY.	0328
UCTIVITY OF AN ELECTRON	GAS IN A GASEOUS PLASMA.	0001
OF AN ELECTRON GAS IN A	GASEOUS PLASMA.	0001
DUCED BY VARIOUS BUFFER	GASES.	0449
BUFFER	GASES.	0450
IONIZED	GAS.	1441
EZORESISTANCE IN N-TYPE	GA,AS.	1533
IN ELECTRON-IRRADIATED	GE AT 80 DEG K.	0362
LATION OF GAMMA RAYS IN	GE72.	0229
NERAL RELATIVITY AS THE	GENERATORS OF COORDINATE TRANSFORMAT	0287
ETORESISTANCE IN N-TYPE	GERMANIUM AT LOW TEMPERATURES.	0317
CONDUCTION ELECTRONS IN	GERMANIUM.	0298
IATIVE RECOMBINATION IN	GERMANIUM.	0330
PARTICLES IN LINEARIZED	GRAVITATIONAL THEORY.	0674
ENERGIES OF	GROUND AND EXCITED NUCLEAR CONFIGURA	0452
	GROUND STATE OF TWO-ELECTRON ATOMS.	1649
KINEMATICS OF	GROWING WAVES.	1488
RIC CONSTANTS OF ALKALI	HALIDE CRYSTALS.	0090
	HALL EFFECT, MAGNETORESISTANCE, AND	0381
TWO	HALL EFFECTS OF IRON-COBALT ALLOYS.	1516
	HALL MOBILITY OF CARRIERS IN IMPURE	0044
A DILUTE BOSE SYSTEM OF	HARD SPHERES. I. EQUILIBRIUM PROPERT	1419
OLUME ANOMALY OF LIQUID	HE3 ARISING FROM ITS NUCLEAR SPIN SY	1483
L EXCITATIONS IN LIQUID	HE3.	1465
OF 95-MEV PROTONS WITH	HE4.	1658
SPECIFIC	HEAT OF LI,F AND KI AT LOW TEMPERATU	0049
TION OF DONOR STATES IN	HEAT-TREATED SILICON.	1546
UCLEAR ENERGY LEVELS IN	HEAVY ELEMENTS.	0518
XCITATION OF PROTONS IN	HELIUM II BY COLD NEUTRONS.	0011
MAGNETIC MOMENT OF	HELIUM IN ITS 3S1 METASTABLE STATE.	1627
LITY OF LI-PLUS IONS IN	HELIUM.	0445
OF SN, IN, TA, TL, AND	HG.	0031
ISOMERS IN TB158 AND	HO163.	0489
LORENTZIAN GAS AND	HOT ELECTRONS.	1567
ICROWAVE PROPAGATION IN	HOT MAGNETO-PLASMAS.	1460
OF THE ELECTRON ON THE	HYDROGEN ENERGY LEVELS.	1637
DISSOCIATION OF THE	HYDROGEN MOLECULE ION BY ELECTRON IM	0155
SS OF SLOW ELECTRONS IN	HYDROGEN.	0159
	HYDROMAGNETIC EQUATIONS FOR TWO ISOT	1441
SHIFT OF THE ZERO-FIELD	HYPERFINE SPLITTING OF CS133 PRODUCE	0449
NARROW	HYPERFINE ABSORPTION LINES OF CS133	0450
	HYPERFINE-STRUCTURE SEPARATIONS AND	0186
MASSES OF CHARGED SIGMA	HYPERONS AND THE NEGATIVE K MESON.	0622

Fig. 2.

Applied to titles and possibly abstracts of documents, the keyword in context method provides many points of access for conducting a search. In printed form the indexes can be searched rapidly by eye, so that the need for machines at the retrieval phase of the system is largely obviated. Since they can be prepared automatically, the indexes also serve as an effective means for disseminating information about new literature at the instant it becomes available.

Wherever a rather extensive analysis of texts is essential, the keyword in context method may be broadened to include entire texts. In this case the determination of what is to be considered a keyword has to be refined in order to prevent the index from assuming unwieldy proportions. This is accomplished by having the machine first compile a wordlist from a representative sample of the texts of a collection. The list is then edited by removing from it those words which are desired to serve as keywords. The remainder represents the words to be disregarded by the machine. Through this arrangement any new word will be treated as a keyword although it may subsequently be demoted by adding it to the list of insignificant words.

VIII. CONCLUSION

The desirability of a standard encoding language must be considered in the light of machine potentialities. Where it is possible to handle natural languages automatically, the advantages of interposing an artificial encoding language, however well standardized, are doubtful.

If machines are utilized in a manner which exploits their inherent capabilities to the fullest, there should be little doubt that they can assist significantly in meeting the information retrieval demands of the future. The mechanical derivation of encodements directly from original texts should materially simplify the problem of furnishing clues which will lead an inquirer to potential sources of useful information. The concept of shifting interpretive processes essentially to the instant of retrieval should result in a substantial saving of overall intellectual effort.

REFERENCES

1. International Conference for Standards on a Common Language for Machine Searching and Translation, Cleveland, Ohio, September 6-12, 1959, sponsored by Western Reserve University and Rand Development Corporation, Cleveland, Ohio.
2. Luhn, H. P., A Statistical Approach to Mechanized Encoding and Searching of Literary Information, "IBM Journal of Research and Development," October 1957.
3. Luhn, H. P., Potentialities of Auto-Encoding of Scientific Literature, RC 101 IBM Research Center Yorktown Heights, N. Y., 1959.
4. Luhn, H. P., The Automatic Creation of Literature Abstracts, "IBM Journal of Research and Development," April 1958.
5. Stiassny, S., Coefficients of Similarity Between Documents, IBM Advanced Systems Development Division, Yorktown Heights, N. Y., 1959.
6. Luhn, H. P., Keyword-In-Context Index for Technical Literature (KWIC Index), RC 127, IBM Advanced Systems Development Division, Yorktown Heights, N. Y., 1959.

Indexing and Abstracting by Association

Part I

Lauren B. Doyle

System Development Corporation

Santa Monica, California

I. Representing Knowledge

A traditional task of librarians has been to give the library user a condensed representation of the contents of the library. Such a representation must be made up of small elements, to permit rapid perusal by the user; and it must be well-organized, to permit the user to find his way among these elements. Examples, of course, are card catalogues, alphabetized lists of subject headings, and classification schemes.

Organization of the library itself or of its condensed representations is a difficult problem. Mortimer Taube (1) expressed the problem succinctly in regard to classification systems when he said, "...Classification fails... in the arbitrary disassociations which are imposed on related ideas by the requirements of the system...." Unfortunately, Taube's solution of this problem was to do away with all organization except that of alphabetical order of lists of document tags used in coordinate searching.

Actually, the desired impetus might well be in the opposite direction: to seek a form of organization which preserves the relationships that Taube says are broken in a classification system. There should be nothing incompatible between organization and complete portrayal of relationships; indeed, the very purpose of organization in a library is the indication of relatedness.

We have to inquire how and why relationships are broken in some forms of organization.

Some reference media use alternative forms to emphasize this or that class of relationships. The information seeker chooses the form which is structured according to relationships of interest. As an example, one would not use a gazetteer if he were interested in geographical relationships between cities; he would go directly to the map. Analogously, for a sense of relatedness between topics, one doesn't consult a card catalogue, he looks up the classification scheme.

It is to be noted that in going from one organizational scheme to another something is given up as well as gained. For example, if all cities were classified according to major industry, most geographical relationships could not be represented in the organization. Magnitogorsk and Pittsburgh would be side by side, but a town with no steel industry 5 miles from Pittsburgh would necessarily be a considerable "topical distance" from Pittsburgh in our chosen scheme. As Claridge (2) said, "Any form of generic relationship can be taken as the basis of classification, but once this is chosen, generic searches on other bases have become impossible."

There are some interesting solutions to the broken-relationship problem aside from that adopted by Taube. The most obvious one is to simply present to the library user several alternative organizational forms, each using a different basis for generic grouping. Though this has not been economical in the past, it may prove to be so in the future.

A less obvious solution is to present an organization in which genera are blended together in proportion to their probability of being used in searching. In current library practice, such a procedure would spell chaos; however, it is not to be forgotten that the human brain must operate on just such a basis, as anyone who has ever played the game "20 questions" would realize. We habitually group concert musicians by type of instrument and nationality, and then nimbly shift over to grouping by usage and physical properties when we think of various kinds of material. Even more to the point, such a mental scheme would not preclude the grouping of musicians by physical property, e.g., Joseph Szigeti is bald, Nathan Milstein is not bald, Jack Benny is variable. Such a grouping, less likely to be used in mental look-up of musicians, would probably atrophy and therefore be relatively unavailable. Nevertheless it is not completely excluded from the system.

Both these solutions, if economically achievable, would probably be superior to coordinate indexing. Like coordinate indexing, they both increase the number and variety of relationships which can be used in searching; but unlike it, they retain elements of organization and hence guidance for the searcher. Of these two solutions, the latter has the advantage of convenience over the former, since it may be representable in one coherent scheme; any switching of attention back and forth between separate alternative organizational forms would tend to be cumbersome and inhibiting.

We would prefer, then, to have a representational scheme which is coherent, organized, and made up of a greater and more varied assemblage of relationships than any traditional library organization could offer. Such a scheme would almost certainly have to be represented in two dimensions rather than one. Probably many students of library science have wistfully contemplated the possibility of representing knowledge in two (or more) dimensions, and have been discouraged by soberer heads who dismissed the undertaking involved as not being worth the effort.

But such sobriety is destined for rapidly declining prevalence as a result of a revolution in information processing technology which will bring radically new capabilities to librarians. The new technology will be based on two electronic machines, the high-speed digital computer and the photoelectric print reader. Page-scanning devices will feed the contents of books directly into computer storage, wherein words and sentences will be manipulated at speeds 5 to 10 million times as great as those possible manually.

In the computer the librarian has at his disposal a powerful organizing instrument. Demonstrations of this potential have been made on a small scale by several workers. Maron (3) has shown that documents can be automatically assigned to categories. Borko (4) went a step farther, showing that the categories themselves can be automatically generated by means of factor analysis of the distribution of words in text. Neither of these efforts has dealt with the arrangement of categories, though the possibility of automatically generating a structure is latent in Borko's work.

For several years the author has been investigating the possibility of using a computer to analyze text on a library-sized scale and to derive interpretable and usable condensed representations of libraries. This article will present some of the most recent conceptual advances which have sprung from the investigation. As in a previous article (5), the author will treat word association maps derived through statistical analysis of text, and will try to show how stores of printed information might eventually be organized, represented, and retrieved in terms of such maps.

II. Associations Derived from Text

The frequencies of words in the text of an article are greatly dependent on the topic an author chooses to write about and the aspects of it he wishes to stress. This assumed relationship lies behind much of the work in automatic abstracting and automatic indexing (6).

If authors writing on special topics use certain words with unusual frequency, a consequence of this should be unusual co-occurrence of certain pairs of words within the text of the same documents. For example, one would expect the words "discovery" and "elliptical" to co-occur in articles about comets, and one would therefore expect that in any library containing appreciable material on comets the words "discovery" and "elliptical" should co-occur to an extent greater than predictable on the basis of chance assignment of words to documents.

When pairs of words co-occur strongly in text it should not be surprising to find the members of the pairs associated in the minds of the authors of books in which they co-occur. While it is true that in the sense of "free association" any word can be associated with any other word in the mind of a particular person, one may reasonably surmise that:

A. An author writing a document is not free-associating, but is making an effort to communicate and is therefore constrained to use verbal tags which have a high probability of making sense to the reader. In most professional fields one avoids the standard vocabulary only when the risk of not communicating is overbalanced by the necessity to convey a special meaning.

B. This being so, the statistical effects of whatever degrees of freedom are left to authors in self-expression within the topical framework are apt to be cancelled out by different behavior of other authors writing on the same topic. On the other hand, since authors are "obliged" to use the professional vocabulary in labelling the mental model of what is being talked about, a statistically reinforcing effect should come as a result of similar choices by a variety of authors writing on the same topic, leading to a consensus of co-occurrence which should be measurable.

Thus, the kinds of associations leading to co-occurrences wherein many authors will reinforce each other are the kinds that interest us most when we analyze text for retrieval purposes; these are the associations which have something to do with the topic to which these authors address themselves. Accordingly, we might as well refer to the corresponding co-occurrences as "associations of words in text." Next we will try to define an association in text so that it can be measured, and so that the strongest and most significant associations can be identified and possibly made use of in retrieval. The hope is that ultimately associations in text can be selected and arranged in patterns by completely automatic means.

Measuring associations

In the light of the foregoing considerations we say: "Words in text are associated to the extent that they co-occur in sentences, in paragraphs, in books, or in whatever unit of text is adopted for purposes of analysis." To simplify the picture somewhat for this discussion, we restrict ourselves to books and articles as units of text, hoping that many of the emergent conclusions will also apply when the units happen to be sentences or paragraphs.

In defining co-occurrence one has a choice of attitudes:

A. Regard two words as co-occurring if they are both present at least once in the book.

B. Do not consider two words as co-occurring unless both have frequencies in the book which are greater than some established or computed value.

C. Rather than say a given pair of words does or does not co-occur, speak in terms of "amount of co-occurrence" which varies as some function of the frequency of both words in the book.

Though the latter attitude is more sophisticated and will probably be the one to prevail in the long run, the former two attitudes lead to definitions of co-occurrence which are easier to apply in initial studies of text associations. Our preference at this stage is attitude B, and specifically to use a cutoff rank such that in any book the N most frequent content words can be said to co-occur with each other, thus giving N (N-1)/2 co-occurring pairs. Refinements in such a definition can be introduced in later studies when and if they are found to be needed.

At this point it is desirable to make a distinction between the frequency and the prevalence of a word in a given library. Frequency is the total number of times a word appears in a library corpus of text. Prevalence is the total number of books in which a word appears (or exceeds the cutoff frequency, or some other criterion for occurrence). The two quantities, of course, are not necessarily proportional, because clustering of words can be made to affect prevalence without affecting frequency.

In prevalence we find a quantitative measure in terms of which we can compute the "consensus of co-occurrence" throughout a given library. (As pointed out earlier in this section, for pairs of words which are "associated" we expect to find a consensus of co-occurrence wherein many authors writing about the same topic have somewhat similar sets of word pairs co-occurring in their books and articles.)

It is this "consensus of co-occurrence" that we would like to measure, and the question now arises as to what the measurement function should be. We could start by assuming that such a function would involve the following variables, given word A and word B: prevalence of word A (=A), prevalence of word B (=B), prevalence of the co-occurrence of word A and word B, i.e., the intersection of sets of books containing word A and word B (=f), and the total number of books in the library (=N). Stiles (7), makes this assumption in a similar situation and uses a form of the chi-square formula,

$$\log_{10} \frac{(|fN - AB| - N/2)^2 N}{AB(N - A)\ (N - B)}$$

which he calls the "association factor."

Borko (4), in his study of distribution of words in text, uses another statistic, the Pearson correlation coefficient,

$$\frac{fN - AB}{\sqrt{AB\ (N - A)\ (N - B)}}$$

in which f, N, A, and B have the same meanings as in the Stiles formula in the limiting case we are considering (i.e., Borko addresses himself to "frequency" rather than "prevalence," but his statistic can be used in dealing with the latter).

These two functions have in common, among other things, the term "fN - AB," which reflects the departure of f from statistical expectation under conditions of random assignment of words to documents. The value of the term is zero when f turns out to be the expected number of documents in which words A and B should co-occur. One using Borko's statistic would speak, in this case, of having "zero correlation."

The use of such sampling statistics as these, however, is subject to scrutiny under some conditions. The critical question is: "If we have a large number of different cases (i.e., word pairs) where the values of f, A, and B are the same, but where N varies, do we also want the function to vary, in step with N?" If we are sampling a population, the answer is yes, because the varying ratio of N to the other parameters represents varying characteristics of the population. On the other hand, if we are not sampling a population but only describing the characteristics of the document collection itself (i.e., calling the document collection a population instead of a sample), then it is conceivable that N could be an irrelevant variable.

Indeed, some library situations can be imagined in which the presence of N in an association measurement function leads to undesirable results. Consider two somewhat esoteric topical words, such as "neural" and "synapse." We would not expect to find these words occurring outside a narrow band of literature in physiology and another narrow band in the field of artifical intelligence. Assume we have 100 books in neurophysiology in which (given some criterion for occurrence) "neural" occurs in 80 of the books and "synapse" occurs in 75; assume "neural" and "synapse" co-occur in only 58 books. In other words, in the formulae given above we'd have A = 80, B = 75, f = 58, and N = 100. The value of fN - AB works out to be minus 200, which in the Borko formula would constitute a low order negative correlation.

Now we place these books in a technical library of 9,900 books, none of which concern neurophysiology or contain the words "neural" or "synapse." In analyzing the resultant 10,000 book library we find that A, B, and f are the same as they were in the 100 book accession. But N now equals 10,000, leading to an overwhelmingly positive correlation for occurrence of words A and B. Accordingly, the words are strongly associated in the library, whereas they were not associated in the 100 books, according to either of the above measurement functions.

Is it justifiable in a case of accession such as this to have the association strength between two words undergo such a radical change? It is if we want the association to be an attribute of the whole library. It is not if we want the association to be an attribute of the 100 books on neurophysiology, whose intrinsic nature did not change as a result of their being added to the 9,900 book library.

The latter attitude is preferable if we want associations in text to have some relationship, in their quantitative aspects, to the cause-and-effect processes by which documents are generated. Neurophysiological authors, who presumably intercommunicate, might be said to be the "aggregate cause" of the co-occurrence pattern of words like "neural" and "synapse." However, and this is the cogent point, they can't be said to be responsible in any causal sense for the size and composition of the libraries into which their books eventually gravitate. From this viewpoint, then, the variable N introduces an unwanted effect on the value of the association strength between two words.

Such considerations have persuaded the author to adopt a simple "descriptive statistic" which is a function only of A, B, and f,

$$\frac{f}{A + B - f}$$

which measures the ratio of the logical product to the logical sum to two sets of books: those in which word A occurs and those in which word B occurs.

Experimentation with the function has indicated that it tends to favor word pairs having approximately equal prevalence (the maximum value of 1.00 is possible only when two words are equally prevalent). Whether or not this is a drawback remains to be seen. It is noted also that the Pearson correlation coefficient, above, has this property, although to a lesser extent. Less equal prevalence implies weaker co-variance and would naturally lead to smaller maximum values for the correlation coefficient.

association maps

We have talked about what associations in text represent, and about how to define and measure them. The next question is what to do with them to aid the cause of information retrieval.

Stiles (7) and Maron (8) both advocate direct use of associations in machine literature searching. With non-associative methods, as have been plentifully discussed in the literature of information retrieval, searchers compose requests or prescriptions consisting of combinations of subject tags--combinations which the searcher expects documents he is looking for to bear; then machines search for references to documents having tags corresponding to those in the request.

However, with associative methods, machines yield not only references which match the prescribed combination of tags, but also references with tags that are strongly associated (statistically) to the prescribed tags. Maron predicted and Stiles has reported increases in accuracy of retrieval through the use of associations. Though both these researchers were applying associative methods to collections of subject tags assigned to documents by librarians, the same principles should apply when one is dealing with subject words selected from text by machine.

The author (5) has expressed the view that humans should be capable of doing a better job of searching than machines, if confronted with well-organized material. This suggests that computers be used to analyze text and produce exotic indexes of a type never before feasible. If this view is sound, then permuted title indexes and KWIC indexes (9, 10) should be merely a sample of things to come.

If human associative processes are responsible for the associations found in text, then the reverse relationship should hold: that a human searcher, presented with a representation of text-derived associations, will be able to recognize as cognitive units many of the associated word pairs. This opens up the possibility of an index which is organized associatively rather than alphabetically. Thus, instead of a machine using only statistical associations in searching, we would have a man-machine combination having the benefits of both statistical associations and the highly individual cognitive associations which enable the human searcher to be selective in following statistically associative pathways.

When the author began to investigate this possibility in 1959, he arbitrarily adopted a diagrammatic or map-like representation of text associations, in the hope that reasons for adopting a different form might eventually suggest themselves. However, though there have been important modifications of the original map idea, the map still remains the basic form.

An association map is shown in Figure 1. It was derived from a 90 x 90 correlation matrix*, where every one of 90 key words in a corpus of 618 Psychological Abstracts was correlated to every other one of the 90 words, by means of the Pearson correlation coefficient, for co-occurrence in individual abstracts. On the map, word pairs are connected by links which show the strength of association; dashed linkages are weaker than solid linkages. Where two-word term usage has been responsible for the co-occurrence, arrows point toward the second word of the term. Numbers beside the links are the values of the correlation coefficient.

*The 90-by-90 matrix involved the same words and abstracts as those in Borko's experiment (4).

The map in Figure 1 was hand-drawn from correlation data computed by an IBM 7090 program. There is no intrinsic reason, however, why such a map could not be generated entirely automatically and the output presented, say, on a display scope. In Section III, where the use of maps in retrieval will be discussed, the possibility of doing exactly this becomes very attractive.

A major determining parameter of the map's final form is the cutoff value chosen for the association measurement function. For Figure 1, +.15 was chosen as the minimum correlation to be shown on the map. (Three or four somewhat smaller correlations are also shown in order to make the map a complete network; such exceptions could also be made in a completely automatic map-generating process.) The value +.15 is nearly optimal as a cutoff value in Figure 1. If a larger value had been chosen, such as +.17, the map disintegrates through lack of associative links. If a smaller value had been chosen, such as +.13, the number of links becomes so large that topological difficulties arise in two-dimensional representation: links frequently have to cross each other and follow circuitous paths.

One can follow a different policy, having a variable cutoff point rather than a constant one. In the Figure 1 map more than a dozen words out of the 90 did not correlate as high as +.15 with any other word. One can bring all of these words into the network by lowering the threshhold for those words which do not associate strongly. Another way of accomplishing the same result is to adopt a rule that the number of associative links for any given word must fall within a certain range, say, one through four, regardless of the strengths of associative links. Of course, the choice of rules for determining which links will be shown on the map would depend on the use to which the map will be put.

Another question involved in determining the map's form is that of overall organization. If, in generating the map, the only set of rules used are those having to do with formation of links between word pairs, a somewhat arbitrary organization will usually result. Even on a small map some obvious dislocations of related groups will occur. For example, the Figure 1 map has two clusters of words separated which one would intuitively expect should be closely connected: The group "clinical, psychiatric, treatment, patient (s)" and the group "case (s), group, therapy, psychotherapy." Indeed, in Borko's factor analysis (4) seven of these eight words have high loadings of factor number 6, clinical psychology and psychotherapy.

As discussed in a previous article (5) the associative chips should not be permitted to fall where they may, and improvement of the map's raw form is both desirable and feasible. Such improvement can be accomplished by automatic methods such as factor analysis or by human decisions of a type a librarian might make. In the latter case, it is rather interesting to note that any human patch-up work done on automatically generated association maps would be one of the most economical uses of human editing in all language

Figure 1
An Association Map Based on
Pearson Correlation Coefficients

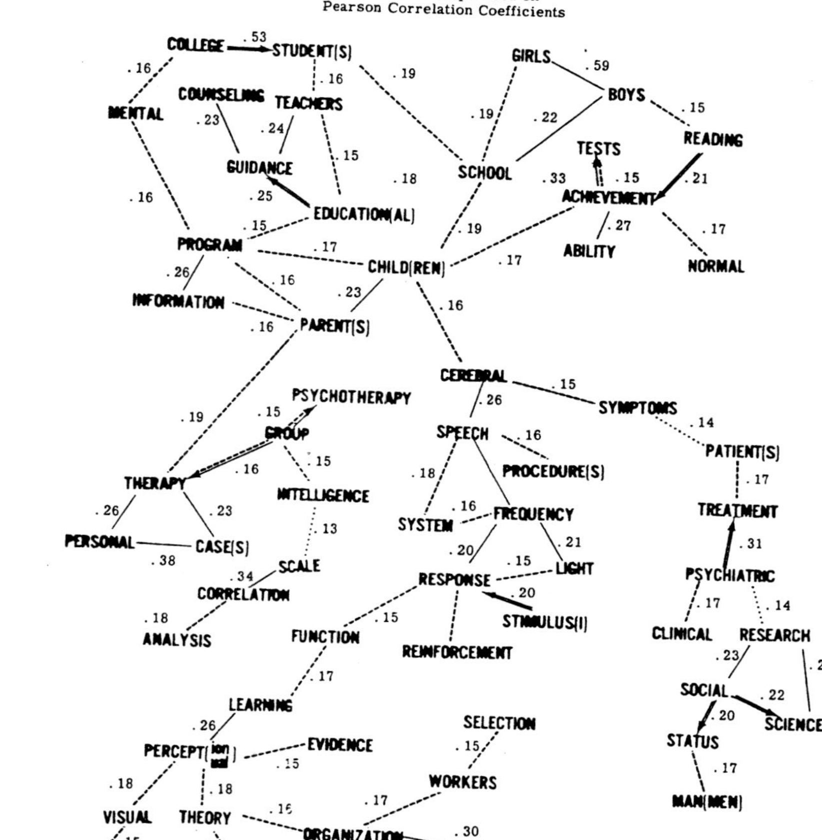

data processing, because of the large degree of condensation which accompanies the formation of an association map. To put it another way, in the current state of the art, the amount of human labor required in post-editing a million-word corpus of mechanically translated text would be huge, but the corresponding association map would contain only several hundred words, and the reduction of editing labor could conceivably be as large as a thousand-fold. This reasoning assumes that the human would know how and why to edit the map and would not have to refer to the uncondensed corpus.

This section has discussed the basic ideas of associations in text and their representations as maps. We are now in a position to consider, in Section III, the use of association maps in information retrieval. In Part II of this paper, to be subsequently issued, we can return to the topic of the map itself and how to make it a more effective instrument.

III. Association Maps As Components of Retrieval Systems

An association map brings a literature searcher face-to-face with a library. The map is capable of filling the specification of Section I for a highly condensed and highly organized representation of a library. We now have to inquire how far we are from realizing this capability and what we have to do to integrate association maps into operating retrieval systems.

First of all, the point has to be restated that association methods of interrogating information stores offer certain advantages over usual machine searching methods, especially when the association linkage patterns are shown directly to the searcher. In ordinary machine searching one composes a request to the machine consisting of combinations of key words or subject tags which one, in effect, recalls from his own (mental) association network. These words or tags may not correspond well to the array of words or tags in the library. In particular, there are certain to be some tags which one does not think up, but which belong to documents relevant to one's need.

Swanson (11) and others have offered thesauri of synonyms and related terms as a solution to this problem. An association map is in a sense an extension of this solution; it is a gigantic, automatically derived thesaurus. Confronted by such a map, the searcher has a much better "association network" than the one existing in his mind, because it corresponds to words actually found in the library and, therefore, words which are best suited to retrieve information from that library.

In a retrieval system, the part played by an association map would be as a point of departure for more detailed searching. As a searcher scans such a map, his eye should soon come to rest in a cluster of words which equate semantically to the topic in which he is searching. There is a reasonable guarantee that this will happen because, as discussed in Section II, the very cognitive processes which lead to the generation of pairs and clusters of co-occurring words should lead to the recognition of the pairs and clusters as represented on a map. When this recognition occurs, the next step in the operation of the system is to give the searcher more information about those documents which have "caused" a particular cluster of words.

This further information can be given in several ways, depending on the number of documents represented by the cluster which the searcher picked out. If the number is large, say between 100 and several thousand, we can give the searcher a "sub-association map" based only on this subset of the library. As will be made evident in the forthcoming Part II of this paper, this map will be a highly detailed elaboration of the searcher's cluster. If the number is moderate, about several dozen documents, we can give the searcher a series of diagrammatic proxies, each of which stands for an individual document and shows the relationships between the document's major key words. If the number is less than one or two dozen, we can present the searcher with automatic abstracts. The general principle intended here is the same one alluded to by Bar-Hillel (12) on page 11 of his Technical Report No. 3, namely, the smaller the number of documents which have yet to be screened by a searcher, the greater the amount of information per document it is practical to give the searcher as a basis for further screening. This principle, which Bar-Hillel stated in somewhat particulate form, has been generalized in an interesting note by Wyllys (13).

We now have an over-all picture of the association map in an information retrieval setting. The primary map is a view of the entire library at a distance. Subsequent operations can be visualized as focusing on smaller and smaller portions of the library, with "microscopes" of successively higher power, bringing out more and more detail about each remaining potentially relevant document.

modes of operation

Many ways of making an association map part of a retrieval system are conceivable; some ways would require a great deal of research and development, but others would require simply a short computer program. As an example of the latter, computer-based Uniterm systems could be augmented with a program which measures associations among the uniterms and prints them out in order of association strength. A map could be drawn from this in a few hours, reproduced, and distributed among the users of the system.

In the long run we hope for more organic, highly automated systems which can carry out smoothly the process of focusing on successively smaller portions of the library, as described above. At this point two modes of operation of such systems are distinguishable: an off-line and an on-line mode. The off-line mode would make use of a book or file of association map printouts and the on-line mode, which would be both more flexible and more costly, would represent association maps on display scopes. In the off-line mode, the searching pathways used in going from large to small portions of the library would have to be standard or fixed for all searchers. In the on-line mode, the various stages of the search process would be under individual control of the searcher at the display console, and therefore more adaptable to his momentary needs.

Figure 2 presents a flow chart of the process for both the off-line and on-line modes. The initial elements common to both modes would be a map index, which operates like the index to a street map, and a primary map based on the complete contents of the library. The primary map would be in printout form in the off-line mode, but it might also be desirable to have it as a printout in the on-line mode as well, in order to cut down the time a searcher would spend operating a display console.

From this point on there is a divergence in the mechanics of the search process, beginning in the second box of Figure 2, where the searcher has much more freedom in designating clusters in the on-line mode. Things are "cramped" in the off-line mode: because a printout index must be limited in size, clusters which are involved in subsequent stages of the search process must be very limited in number; therefore, to gain maximum probably utility per cluster, purely statistical criteria should be used in determining cluster membership for the off-line mode. Here, a factor analysis methodology (4) would be appropriate.

However, in the on-line mode there is no necessity to confine one's operations to purely statisticaly clusters. If a searcher believes that two words which are not statistically associated are nevertheless cognitively related, he should be given the means of following up his hunch. A casual inspection of an association map makes convincing the speculation that such incidents will be numerous.

Thus, the searcher departs from the primary map to any of a small number of sub-maps based on statistical clusters in the off-line mode (Box 3a in Figure 2) or to any of a practically unlimited number of "cognitive clusters" sub-maps in the on-line mode (Box 3). The sub-maps in the on-line mode are, of course, generated on the spot at the command of the searcher at the display console; he will designate a certain group of words (we'll discuss later in the section how the designation might be made), and thereupon the computer will pick out the subset of documents which is a function of the group (the author recommends the logical sum as the safest and simplest function, and eschews complicated Boolean statements) and will generate a map for display.

Continuing the description of the off-line mode, as shown in Figure 2, the association maps for the statistical clusters should be similar in appearance to the primary map, with one possible exception: whenever the population of

Figure 2

Flow Chart of Search Stages in the use of an Association Map

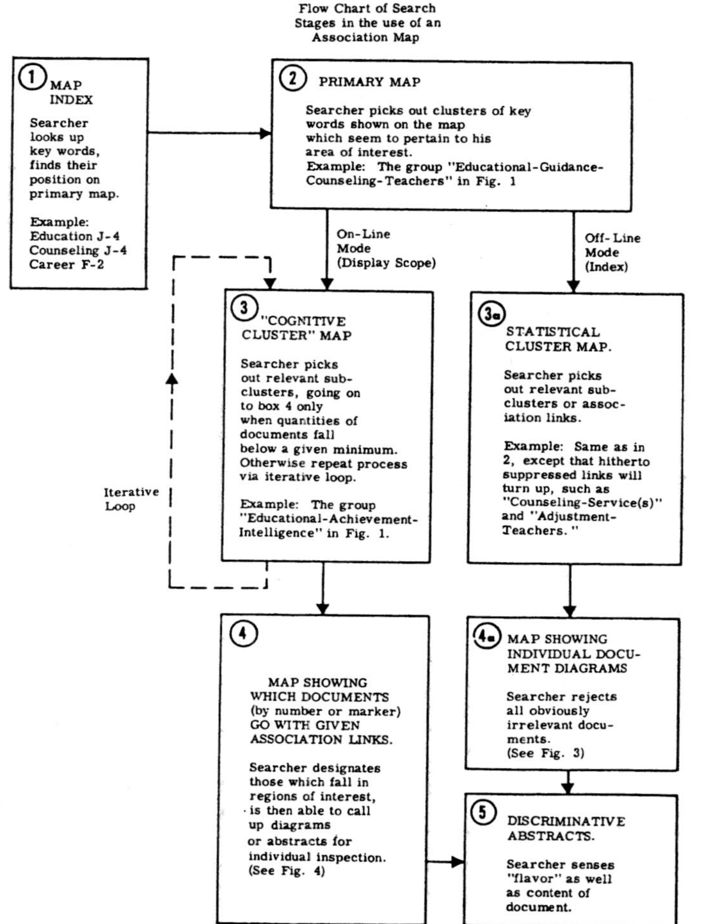

documents corresponding to the cluster is small enough, we can probably make references to the individual documents alongside the appropriate words or word-pair links. This would bring us to Box 4a in Figure 2.

An example of how this might be done is shown in Figure 3. Recalling the discussion in Section II of the definition of co-occurrence, we know that the computer would have as raw material for the maps a great many lists of key words; each list of key words will have been derived from some corresponding document, probably via statistical analysis of the entire text of the document. With little extra strain on storage, some simple indications of relationships between the key words can also be added to each list, primarily relationships based on adjacency or close proximity of the words in text. These indications can subsequently be used to generate diagrammatic representations of individual documents such as are shown in Figure 3.

The representations of Figure 3 were derived by the author from real documents, as was the association framework to which they are attached. The associated words are shown in capital letters, and each document is represented by a group of lower-case-lettered words within a dotted-line envelope. Arrows connecting pairs of words show which word is second whenever the words occur adjacently or in close proximity (separated by one or two other words). Words not cleanly satisfying adjacency or proximity criteria are connected by a simple line, indicating unusual co-occurrence in the same sentences. Some arrows have a bar at the base; the bar indicates that the term or phrase begins at that point. Where it is not present three and four-word terms can often be discerned, such as "cognitive language processing system."

A variety of rules can be used in the positioning of these document diagrams on the map. For example, they can be attached to the most frequent word of the document which is also represented on the map. This rule tends to give poor results, because topically close documents have a tendency for a large number of them to have the same key word as "most frequent." In Figure 3 more than half of the documents had "word" as the most frequent word. Another rule is to position the document diagram near the most frequent two words which are also linked together on the map. This gives more satisfactory results.

The next question is which key words to show in the diagram. The author used the 11 most frequent key words of each document as starting material for generating the map (the association function given at the end of the first half of Section II was used in the generation process, which was done by hand). But showing all 11 of the words would make an unnecessarily complicated diagram. A better policy is to let the number of words in the diagram be a function of how "different" a given document is from its closest neighbors, or more specifically, how few of its key words are widely prevalent on the key word lists of the other documents. For example, document D-32 (upper left, Figure 3) had very few words in common with the other documents, so a mere

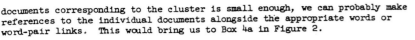

Figure 3
Final Stage of Off-Line Search:
Expanded Links and Diagrammatic
Representations of Individual Documents.

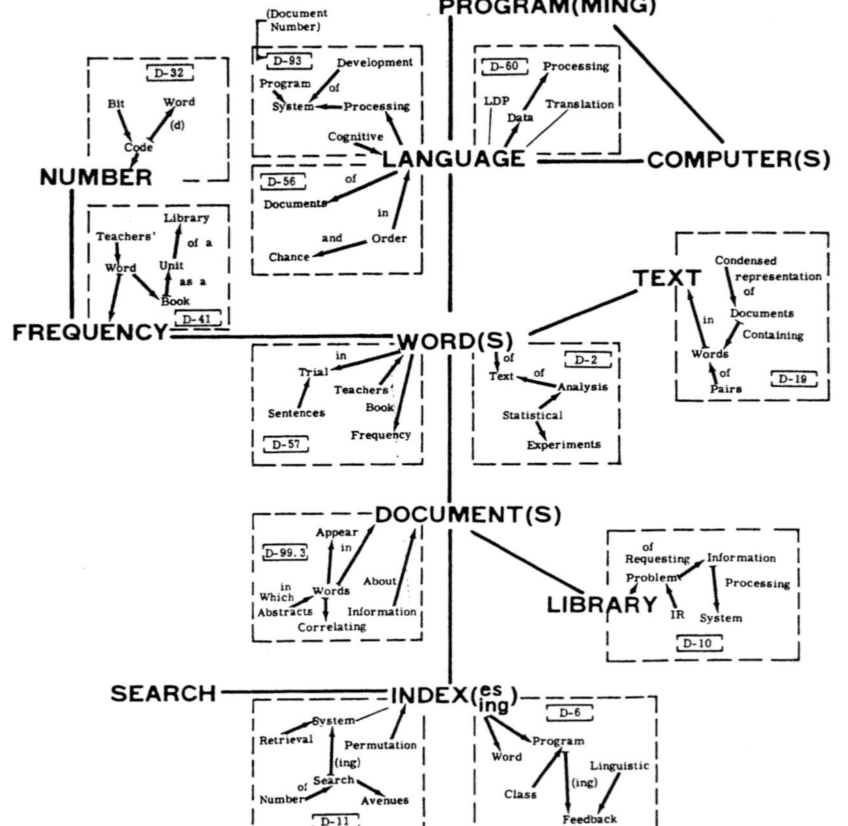

four words give a picture of what the document is about. On the other hand, document D-11 (bottom) is less unusual, and therefore more words are needed to convey to the searcher its distinct topical slant. The principle behind this will be discussed later in this section, under the heading "abstracting for discrimination."

The Figure 3 diagrammatic representations are so terse and unusual in form that a person might at first be inclined not to have confidence in them. A certain amount of experience in using such diagrams would probably be necessary before the user would "have faith" that the diagrams do indeed give a remarkably good indication of what the documents are about. For example, document D-32 talks about n-bit code numbers and coded words literally from stem to stern; its title is "Language Condensation for Digital Storage." The reader, breathing a sigh of comprehension in reading this title, may think "Why not include the title instead of the diagram on the map?" Hereupon the point is reinforced that the reader is used to titles and is not used to the diagrams. Time and evaluations from a human factors standpoint will tell at what point in the search process titles should be introduced.

It is important to realize that wherever a searcher is puzzled by a diagram, further information (such as titles, abstracts) will be available in Box 5 of Figure 2 to alleviate his uncertainty. Such moments of uncertainty should become less frequent as the searcher gains experience with the correspondence between documents and representations of their most frequent words.

As stated earlier, the on-line process is more flexible than the off-line, because the computer (in response to the searcher's signals at the display console) is capable of generating condensed representations for any one of an unlimited number of subsets of the library. In the off-line mode the allowable size of the printout limits the number of subsets which can be represented.

There is, however, a price to be paid for the flexibility, and in Figure 2 this price manifests itself in the iterative loop attached to Box 3. The loop means that the searcher has to keep repeating the process of picking out "cognitive clusters" until the document subset is small enough to allow individual document diagrams or representations to be shown on the scope. Each repetition of the loop prunes down the size of the subset. Two factors combine to increase the number of repetitions required in a given search:

(a) Because the searcher is able to deal with clusters which are not strictly statistical in nature, the reduction in the size of the subset will not be as great, in going from a cluster to a sub-cluster, as would be the case with a statistical cluster, all other things being equal. The manifold co-occurrences of the words in a statistical cluster causes such great overlap in the subsets tagged by each word in the cluster that the logical sum of all these subsets is at minimum; this is, by definition, the thing about a cluster that makes it "statistical."

(b) A searcher will find, through experience or through training, that he will get greater percentage recovery of relevant documents if he is generous in designating the words in his cluster, and thus inevitably he winds up with larger subsets. The option of being lavish doesn't exist in the off-line mode, with its fixed subsets and clusters.

The searcher eventually prunes down the subset of potentially relevant documents to the point that individual documents can be represented on the display. With the intrinsic flexibility of the computer-display-console combination, there are uncountably many sub-modes that we can offer a searcher at this point--in contrast to the off-line mode, where standard search paths are required.

Figure 4 illustrates one interesting possibility. With the briefest possible representation of documents on a map, we can introduce them individually at a much earlier stage of the search process, i.e., when the potentially relevant subset is still fairly large. The Figure 4 map, derived from Scientific American articles on physics, shows how a circle-arrow-number combination can be made to provide a fairly information-rich representation of individual documents.

As an example, document number 43 (shown near the top, center, of Figure 4) is given as a circle positioned near the word "measure," with a short arrow pointing toward the word "G-factor" and a long arrow pointing between the words "moment" and "precise." The "most frequent word list" for document 43 reads: "G-factor, moment, predict, experiment, measure, magnetic, electron, anomalous, muon, and precision." When these words are located on the map (all but "anomalous," which was excluded by a map-generation rule which required key words to be on more than one "most frequent word list" to qualify for position on the map), the function of the arrows becomes understandable. The length and direction of the arrows simply directs the "sweep of the eye" to words which might describe the document.

It doesn't matter at this point that the searcher isn't given more precise information about each document. The capability we want the searcher to have at this stage is easy rejection of obviously irrelevant documents; in this rejection process we want to keep the "information processed per document" by the searcher's brain at a minimum. For example, a searcher interested in bubble chamber literature would instantly exclude document number 38 (by the word "meson") from further consideration because the arrow is pointing toward the wrong set of words. (Note: If any of the words in the cluster in the lower left of Figure 4 were on document 38's word list, a second and shorter arrow would be added to the circle, informing the searcher that further investigation of this document is desirable.)

One skeptical about the ease of this process of rejecting documents as irrelevant would be somewhat naturally inclined to visualize for comparison the same

Figure 4

FINAL STAGE OF ON-LINE SEARCH: DISPLAY OF INDIVIDUAL DOCUMENT MARKERS AT THEIR POINTS OF GREATEST CONTRIBUTION TO THE MAP STRUCTURE.

(Note: Letters vary in size in proportion to the prevalence of the word. All capital-lettered words exceed all lower-case-lettered words in prevalence.)

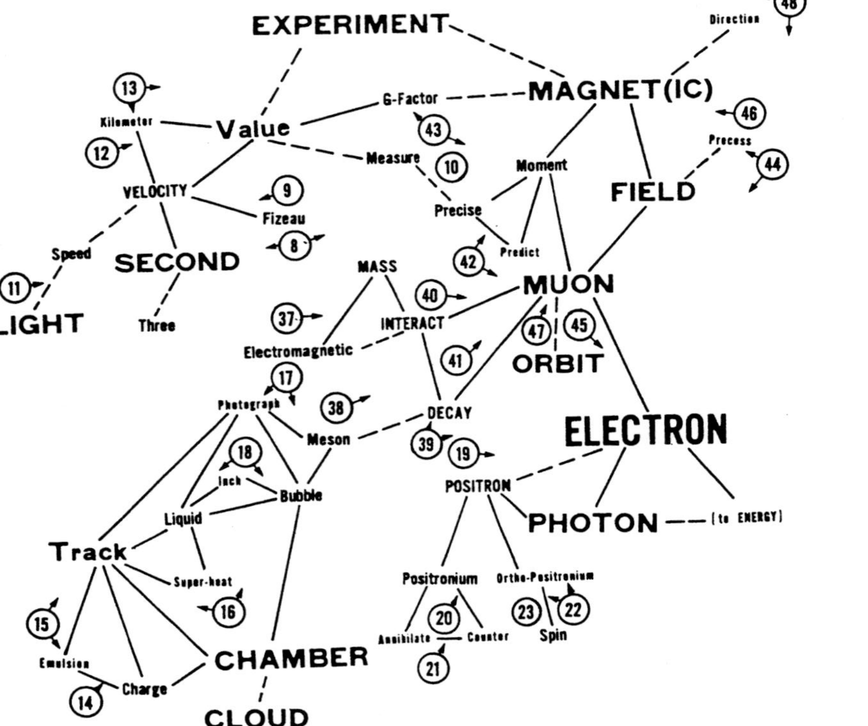

rejecting process taking place as a searcher thumbs through abstracts. But this comparison would not tell the full story, because it leaves out the benefits of organization and grouping which the map provides. Documents can be rejected not just individually, but in groups of 5 or 6 at a time, as fast as the meaning of a given small cluster of words can be comprehended. Truly there is more here than "meets the eye."

Documents not rejected can be "designated" for further investigation. One way of doing this is to punch the number into computer storage, using typewriter keys at the console. A far more elegant and simple way is through the use of a device known in the SAGE air defense system as a "light gun." A light gun is a small photoelectric cell which can be manually aimed at a point on a display scope. A computer program can activate (i.e., strike with a burst of electrons from the cathode) each document number every few hundred milliseconds or so; then when the searcher aims his "light gun" at, say, document 38, the photocell catches the flash when the electron burst strikes the phosphor on the screen. The computer is able to sense that the time of activation of the photocell coincides with the time at which the particular burst was fired at number 38. Thus, the searcher "designates" a document of interest. This same device can be used to designate words in clusters at earlier stages of the process.

Figure 2 shows presentation of abstracts as the final stage for both the on-line and off-line modes. Here again the off-line mode gives greater flexibility.

In an off-line situation the abstracts (automatic or otherwise) are in rigid one-to-one correspondence to the documents. In an on-line mode, however, each document can have any number of abstracts; indeed, abstracts can be generated on demand to emphasize or de-emphasize aspects of a document, as befits the requirements of the searcher.

It is admitted that Figures 2 through 4 and the previous discussion do not constitute a particularly precise picture of the two modes of using association maps. Indeed, if he imagines the gyrations a computer would have to go through, especially in the on-line mode, the reader may feel that the abilities of computers (and of programmers) are being wildly overestimated. If such a feeling has been provoked, it is time to stress that the principles given herein can be applied in a large number of ways, and they are sufficiently adaptable that any upper limits on library size or complexity of procedure should be tolerable. This being the case, it does not hurt to think in terms of what is nominally possible, even if the equipment to carry it out doesn't happen to exist at the moment.

abstracting for discrimination

In the early days of automatic abstracting, the word-frequency information which determined the selection of the output sentences came entirely from within the document. Edmundson and Wyllys (6) were probably the first to publicly advocate contrasting word frequencies within a document to word frequencies in a given field, and of using these relative frequencies as criteria for scoring and selecting sentences. The author (5) suggested that the principle be broadened to include word frequency data from any and all document subsets of interest in a given library. The chief reason for such broadening would be to provide searchers with a capability to discriminate between topically close documents.

Automatic abstracts, as currently conceived, are not likely to bring out the discriminative aspects of a document, i.e., those aspects which make it "different" from documents on similar topics. Yet it is these different aspects which are the essence of what the author of a document is trying to convey; these aspects may well be the closest links to his reason for writing the document. Any professional man who does not have the time to read the literature of his field exhaustively, or any information searcher who does not wish to read unnecessarily many documents, is interested not only in getting a terse picture of what each potentially interesting document is about, but in what each such document is about that all other documents are not about.

The same statistical data which go into the making of association maps can be used in the terminal stages of the searching process, particularly in the off-line mode, to give discriminatory abstracts. Such brief representations as are shown in Figure 3 can give some of this discriminatory information; but for many documents the searcher will need an abstract, either because he can't interpret the diagram or because he needs more information to decide on relevance. At the Figure 3 stage of the process we might think of two classes of words, generic words and discriminating words. Generic words are those common to many of the documents in the cluster, and therefore the words whose co-occurrences "cause" the map structure. Discriminating words are those which other authors of topically close documents do not use, and which therefore have a chance of indicating some special purpose or motive of a particular document.

It might seem that if a searcher is familiar with the cognitive significance of the cluster he is probing, it would suffice to give him abstracts consisting entirely of discriminating words. However, even if we're sure of this familiarity, there are two reasons why we might also want to include some generic words in the abstract: (a) there is no guarantee that the document's author didn't use the generic words in a different sense than that implied by the cluster, and (b) it is important to show how the discriminating words relate to the generic words.

To give a picture of how different abstracts based on discriminating words and those based on generic words can be, the author simulated automatic abstracting procedures using 24 documents on information retrieval* as working material. The generic words in these documents turned out to be, for example, "document," "information," "library," "computer," etc. Two of the 24 documents were gone through sentence by sentence, each sentence being scored for (a) the density of words which were most prevalent in the 24 documents as a whole, and (b) the density of words which were frequent in the individual document but not prevalent in the 24 documents. The highest scoring sentences were then picked out to form, respectively, "generic abstracts" and "specific abstracts."

The results are given, with generic words and discriminating words underlined in the corresponding abstracts:

Document A

Generic Abstract:

"In other words, when a man walks up to the library, he may be presumed to be out of adjustment with respect to the library on two counts.

We look for machine searching eventually, yes, but in the meantime indexing may be a better way of exploring the feasibility of machine searching than machine searching itself would be.

Also, such a language is a potential machine language, more so than a mnemonic language would be."

Specific Abstract:

"This is a formidable group of people, and many of them are eyeing the IR problem with great relish.

As the experimental system evolves, so the problem will evolve, and so the people must evolve in their thinking.

They could be linguistic problems, programming problems, or problems in system organization, semantics, psychology, or even sociology."

*System Development Corporation internal documents and working papers.

Document B

Generic Abstract:

"Typical language processing operations will be translation, analysis, and retrieval of text.

In terms of word frequencies, other statistical measures can be derived, such as coefficients of joint occurrence of different words, clustering tendencies of words, rank-frequency curves, etc.

A word token is an occurrence of a word type in text."

Specific Abstract:

"Only then, in terms of an artificial language which is synonym-free and homonym-free, would he conduct his statistical analysis.

Do the experiments reflect a wide variety of possible statistical analyses?

Synonym removal has no effect on the outcome of this statistical experiment."

The reader should permit himself to disregard the admittedly low quality of the above abstracts, and take note of his response to what the abstracts appear to say. To one of the above generic abstracts, one might have the response: "This sounds like a document on retrieval of language data." On the other hand, the specific abstracts make one aware of the distinctive "flavor" of the document, its quality of being different from closely related documents.

The specific abstracts, however, do not have the desirable property of relating the discriminating words and the generic words. It might seem that a regular Luhn-type automatic abstract would do this, because the most frequent words in a given document are likely to consist of both discriminating and generic words. However, unless heuristics are placed in an automatic abstracting program to insure the presence of both types of words, there is no guarantee that occasional abstracts will not be lacking in either discriminating or generic words; the balance between the two types of words should be under programmed control.

What happens if a rule is used that both types of words should be present in a sentence before it can be accepted as part of an abstract? The author applied such a rule to Documents A and B (the same ones as above), together with the same word-density scoring as was used in the above abstracts. The results are given with generic words underlined and discriminating words capitalized.

Document A

"When these limits are exceeded, the PROBLEM of requesting information will compare in magnitude to the PROBLEM of requesting information from a library.

One hears talk about intermediate languages, standardized languages, and even meta-languages as containing the seeds of a solution to the IR PROBLEM.

We would no more want documents read and categorized by PEOPLE than would the mechanical translation PEOPLE want PEOPLE to translate any part of their input text."

Document B

"One will measure some STATISTICAL PROPERTY of a word type, another will determine some PROPERTY of sets of items retrieved by two-term logical-product search, and still another will determine some PROPERTY of word frequency.

Only then, in terms of an artificial language which is SYNONYM-FREE and homonym-FREE, would he conduct his STATISTICAL ANALYSES.

The word-pair list, especially, will be required in the construction of a SYNONYM-FREE language.

Here again ignoring the low quality of these abstracts, we note that they do indeed give a picture of the relationship between generic and discriminating words. These "composite abstracts" combine the generic character of the document and its specific "flavor" to an extent not found in either the generic abstracts or the specific abstracts. For example, the specific abstract of document A would have given no indication that the document was on information retrieval were it not for the accidental frequent use of the abbreviated form "IR." And the generic abstract for document A gives only a slight hint that the document is broad-scale discussion of the nature of the information retrieval problem; this comes out in the composite abstract, however, because the words "people" and "problem" do in fact give a good picture of the overview character of the document, especially when one keeps in mind that those words recur throughout the document. The composite abstract of document B, moreover, gives a remarkably accurate statement of what that document is really about--although this is probably a stroke of luck.

Word frequencies, of course, are not the only characteristics of a document which distinguish it from its closest topical neighbors; frequencies just happen to be easiest thing for us to get our hands on in programmed analysis of text. At later stages of development in natural language processing research, more elusive distinctive qualities of a document can hopefully be ferreted out. For example, we have not yet talked about frequencies of terms or phrase-length constructions, which a combination of statistical and structural linguistic technique should enable us eventually to deal with.

summarizing, retrieval by association

Section III has presented a sketch of a retrieval system which takes advantage of the statistics of the distribution of key words in libraries. The author realizes acutely that to many readers the retrieval formulation given here must seem outrageously complicated.

Two counterarguments come to mind. First, a distinction must be made between the difficulty of describing and designing a system and the difficulty of using it. We are quite familiar with the former, but woefully unfamiliar with the latter--to the extent, perhaps, of not appreciating the countless variables which we can control to bring about desirable effects. For example, in Figure 4 the variation in letter size as a function of prevalence is such a simple idea, and yet extremely powerful: it gives one that all-important feeling of proceeding from the general to the specific.

The second counterargument is that, thanks to the experiments of Swanson (11) and others, we are just beginning to get a feeling for the great difficulty of machine searching of text and of the inadequacy of current retrieval methods to put the human brain truly in contact with the library. One aspect of the common, everyday, operating human brain has been studiously overlooked among retrieval thinkers--its capacity to be reminded of things it didn't realize it wanted. This capacity makes every literature searcher more of a browser than he thinks; in effect, he unwittingly conducts many literature searchers simultaneously, and not just one. In the light of this, is it not then evident that our method of "retrieval by association" can bring the typical human searcher greater satisfaction than anything advocated so far?

REFERENCES:

(1) Taube, Mortimer, Machines and Classification in the Organization of Information, Documentation, Inc., Technical Report No. 2, ASTIA AD No. 22426, Washington, D. C., 1953.

(2) Claridge, P. R. P., Information Handling in a Large Information System, Preprints of Papers for the International Conference on Scientific Information, Area 5, Washington, D. C., Nov. 1958, pp. 377-394.

(3) Maron, M. E., Automatic Indexing: An Experimental Inquiry. Journal of the Association for Computing Machinery, Vol. 8, No. 3, July 1961, pp. 404-417.

(4) Borko, H., The Construction of an Empirically Based Mathematically Derived Classification System, Proceedings of the Western Joint Computer Conference, May 1962 (in press). (Also available as SP-585, System Development Corporation research paper.)

(5) Doyle, L. B., Semantic Road Maps for Literature Searchers, Journal of the Association for Computing Machinery, Vol. 8, No. 4, Oct. 1961, pp. 553-578. (Also available as SP-199, System Development Corporation research paper.)

(6) Edmundson, H. P., and Wyllys, R. E., Automatic Abstracting and Indexing--Survey and Recommendations, Communications of the ACM, Vol. 4, No. 5, May 1961.

(7) Stiles, H. E., The Association Factor in Information Retrieval, Journal of the Association for Computing Machinery, Vol. 8, No. 2, April 1961, pp. 271-279.

(8) Maron, M. E., and Kuhns, J. L., On Relevance, Probabilistic Indexing, and Information Retrieval, Journal of the Association for Computing Machinery, Vol. 7, No. 3, July 1960, pp. 216-244.

(9) Ohlman, H. M., Hart, L. D., and Citron, Joan, A Permutation Index to the Preprints of the International Conference on Scientific Information, SP-44, System Development Corporation, 1958.

(10) Luhn, H. P., Keyword-in-Context Index for Technical Literature (KWIC Index), IBM Research Center document RC 127, Yorktown Heights, New York, 1959

(11) Swanson, D. R., Searching Natural Language Text by Computer, Science, Vol. 132, No. 3434, Oct. 1960, pp. 1099-1104.

(12) Bar-Hillel, Y., Some Theoretical Aspects of the Mechanization of Literature Searching, Technical Report No. 3., U. S. Office of Naval Research, April 1960.

(13) Wyllys, R. E., Automatic Analysis of the Contents of Documents, Part II: Document Searches and Condensed Representations. FN-6170, System Development Corporation, Jan. 1962.

On Relevance, Probabilistic Indexing and Information Retrieval*

M. E. Maron

The RAND Corporation, Santa Monica, California

AND

J. L. Kuhns

Ramo-Wooldridge, Canoga Park, California

Abstract. This paper reports on a novel technique for literature indexing and searching in a mechanized library system. The notion of *relevance* is taken as the key concept in the theory of information retrieval and a comparative concept of relevance is explicated in terms of the theory of probability. The resulting technique called "Probabilistic Indexing," allows a computing machine, given a request for information, to make a statistical inference and derive a number (called the "relevance number") for each document, which is a measure of the probability that the document will satisfy the given request. The result of a search is an ordered list of those documents which satisfy the request ranked according to their probable relevance.

The paper goes on to show that whereas in a conventional library system the cross-referencing ("see" and "see also") is based solely on the "semantical closeness" between index terms, statistical measures of closeness between index terms can be defined and computed. Thus, given an arbitrary request consisting of one (or many) index term(s), a machine can elaborate on it to increase the probability of selecting relevant documents that would not otherwise have been selected.

Finally, the paper suggests an interpretation of the whole library problem as one where the request is considered as a clue on the basis of which the library system makes a concatenated statistical inference in order to provide as an output an ordered list of those documents which most probably satisfy the information needs of the user.

1. *Introduction*

One of the really remarkable characteristics of human beings is their ability to communicate with and operate on information formulated in ordinary language. We somehow are able to determine the meanings of words and sentences so as to make judgments about sameness of meaning, redundancy, inconsistency, relevance, etc., in spite of the fact that ordinary language is extremely complex and fraught with vagueness and ambiguity. Since there are no strict rules which prescribe how words are to be put together to convey various kinds and shades of meanings, it is difficult indeed to think of using machines to perform the following kinds of operations on ordinary language: automatic analysis to detect and remove redundant information, automatic abstracting of relevant information, automatic verification of information (i.e., given some items of data, deciding whether or not they are inconsistent with any other data already in storage), automatic deduction (i.e., logical derivation), automatic correlation of data so as to establish trends and deviations from trends, and so on. Yet, if the capabilities of digital computers are to be exploited to the fullest extent, we would hope that someday they can be programmed to operate on ordinary language on the basis of its meaning (content). It appears that as a first step in the direction of the automatic processing of ordinary language, as typified by the above examples, the problems of information identification and retrieval must be met and dealt with successfully. We therefore turn our attention to the problems of mechanizing a library.

There are a number of obvious difficulties associated with the so-called "library problem" (i.e., the problem of information search and retrieval). The one usually cited relates to the fact that documentary data are being generated at an alarming rate (the growth rate is exponential—doubling every 12 years for some libraries), and consequently considerations of volume alone make the problem appear frightening. However, the heart of the problem does not concern size, but rather it concerns meaning. That is to say, there have been a number of "hardware" solutions to the problem of library size (e.g., use of microfilm, microcards, minicards, magnacards, etc.), but the major difficulties associated with the library problem remain, namely, the identification of content, the problem of determining which of two items of data is "closer" in meaning to a third item, the problem of determining whether or not (or to what degree) some document is *relevant* to a given request, etc.

The jumping-off point for our approach to automatic information retrieval is the recognition that the core of the problem is that of adequately identifying the information content of documentary data. In the discussion that follows we introduce arithmetic (as opposed to logic alone) into the problem of indexing and thereby pave the way for the use of mathematical operations so as to compute a number, called the relevance number, which is a measure of the probable relevance of a document for a requestor. Thus, the fundamental notion which acts as a wedge to drive an opening into the basic problem of information retrieval is that of the relevance number, which provides a means of ranking documents according to their probable relevance. However, the solution to the problem of information retrieval involves more than ranking by relevance—it involves the proper selection of those documents which are to be ranked. In order to get at this "selection" problem, it is necessary to establish various measures of closeness of meaning, and an approach to this semantical problem is via statistics. We define various measures of closeness between documents and between requests for information so that given an arbitrary request a machine can automatically elaborate upon a search in order to retrieve relevant documents which would not otherwise have been selected.

We divide the paper into three parts: (a) a discussion of the conventional approach to the library problem, (b) an exposition of the solution given by Probabilistic Indexing, (c) a discussion of some preliminary experiments to test these new techniques and procedures.

* Received October, 1959. This research was carried out while both authors were at Ramo-Wooldridge and was supported by the United States Air Force with funds from Contract No. AF30(602)-1814, monitored by the Rome Air Development Center, New York.

2. *Conventional Approach to an Automatic Retrieval System*

2.1. *The Role of Indexes.* Because, at least for the immediate future, no machine can actually read a document and decide whether or not its subject matter relates to some given request subject, it is necessary to use some intermediate identifying tags, namely, an indexing system. An index to a document acts as a tag by means of which the information content of the document in question may be identified. The index may be a single term or a set of terms which together tag or identify the content of each document. The terms which constitute the allowable vocabulary for indexing documents in a library form the common language which bridges the gap between the information in the documents and the information requirements of the library users.

In principle, an indexer reads an incoming document, selects one or several of the index terms from the "library vocabulary," and then coordinates the selected terms with the given document (or its accession number). Thus, the assignment of terms to each document is a go or no-go affair—for each term either it applies to the document in question or it does not. Furthermore, the processes of indexing information and that of formulating a request for information are symmetrical in the sense that, just as the subject content of a document is identified by coordinating to it a set of index terms, so also the subject content of a request must be identified by coordinating to it a set of index terms. Thus, the user who has a particular information need identifies this need in terms of a library request consisting of one or several index terms or logical combinations thereof.

2.2. *The Mechanization.* Given a set of tags (index terms) which identify the content of each document and a set of tags which describe a request for information, the problem of automatic searching resolves itself to that of searching for and matching tags or combinations thereof. Once a set of index terms has been assigned to each document in the library, this information can be encoded in digital form, put on a suitable machine medium, and searched automatically. In the past, literature searching has been done automatically on punched cards using the IBM sorter, on magnetic tape using an electronic computer such as the IBM 709, on photographic film as a continuous strip such as in the case of the Rapid Selector, or in discrete records on photographic film as, for example, in the Minicard system. In each case a machine searches and retrieves (either copies of the document, abstracts, or a list of accession numbers) by matching document index terms with the terms and logic of the given request.

2.3. *The Notion of Semantic Noise.* The correspondence between the information content of a document and its set of indexes is not exact because it is extremely difficult to specify precisely the subject content of a document by means of one or several index words. If we consider the set of all index terms on the one hand and the class of subjects that they denote on the other hand, then we see that there is no strict one-to-one correspondence between the two. It turns out that given any term there are many possible subjects that it could denote (to a greater or lesser extent), and, conversely, any particular subject of knowledge (whether broad or narrow) usually can be denoted by a number of different terms. This situation may be characterized by saying that there is "semantic noise" in the index terms. Just as the correspondence between the information content of a document and its set of indexes is not exact, so also the correspondence between a user's request, as formulated in terms of one or many index words, and his real need (intention) is not exact. Thus there is semantic noise in both the document indexes and in the requests for information.

One of the reasons that the index terms are noisy is due to the fact that the meanings of these terms are a function of their setting. That is to say, the meaning of a term in isolation is often quite different when it appears in an environment (sentence, paragraph, etc.) of other words. The grammatical type, position and frequency of other words help to clarify and specify the meanings of a given term. Furthermore, individual word meanings vary from person to person because, to a large degree, the meanings of the words are a matter of individual experience. This is all to say that when words are isolated and used as tags to index documents it is difficult to pin down their meanings, and consequently it is difficult to use them as such to accurately index documents or to accurately specify a request.

2.4. *Conventional Stopgaps.* Many workers in the field of library science have attempted to reduce the semantic noise in indexing by developing specialized indexing systems for different kinds of libraries. An indexing system tailored to a particular library would be less noisy than would be the case otherwise. (In a sense, to tailor an index system to a specific library is to apply the principle of an ideoglossary, as it is used in machine language translation, to remove semantic ambiguity.) In spite of careful work in the developing of a "best" set of tags for a particular library, the problem of semantic noise and its consequences remain, albeit, to a lesser extent.

Another attempt to remove the semantic noise in request formulations has to do with the use of logical combinations of index terms. That is to say, if two or more index terms are joined conjunctively, it helps to narrow or more nearly specify a subject. On the other hand, the same set of terms connected disjunctively broadens the scope of a request.[1] Thus, using logical combinations of index terms, one would hope to either avoid the retrieval of irrelevant material or avoid missing relevant material. However, although a request using a set of index terms joined conjunctively does decrease the probability of obtaining irrelevant material, it also increases the probability of missing relevant material. The converse holds for a request consisting of a disjunction of index terms. This difficulty in the conventional approach is inherent in its go or no-go nature.

The fact that conventional searching consists in matching noisy tags implies that the result of a search provides documents which are irrelevant to the real needs of the requestor, and, even worse, some of the really relevant documents are not retrieved. Thus, in spite of specialized indexing systems and in spite of the

[1] We use the words "conjunction" and "disjunction" to denote the logical connectives "and" and "or." This usage is continued when classes, instead of propositions, are under discussion (as is the case for a possible interpretation of the index terms mentioned above), although in this case "intersection" and "union" are more appropriate.

use of logical combinations of index terms, the major problem is still that of properly identifying the subject content of both documents and requests. The problem of accurately representing the information content of a document by means of some kind of tags in such a way that a machine can operate on these tags in order to search for documents with the same meaning, related meanings, relevant meanings, etc., is still unsolved.

In the following section we shall present the basic notions of the technique of Probabilistic Indexing and show that this approach to the library problem improves retrieval effectiveness both by reducing the probability of obtaining irrelevant documents and by increasing the probability of selecting relevant documents. Furthermore, the technique of Probabilistic Indexing provides as the result of a search an ordered list of those documents which satisfy the request, ranked according to relevance.

3. *Derivation of the Relevance Number*

3.1. *Initial Remarks.* To say that index tags are noisy is to say that there is an uncertainty about the relationship between the terms and the subjects denoted by the terms. That is to say, given a document indexed with its assigned term (or terms), there is only a probability that if a user is interested in the subject (or subjects) designated by the tag he will find that the document in question is relevant. Conventional indexing consists in having an indexer decide on a yes-no basis whether or not a given term applies for a particular document. Either a tag is applicable or it is not—there is no middle ground. However, since there is an uncertainty associated with the tags, it is much more reasonable and realistic to make this judgment on a probabilistic basis, i.e., to assert that a given tag may hold with a certain degree or weight. Given the ability to weight index terms, one can characterize more precisely the information content of a document. The indexer may wish to assign a low weight such as 0.1 or 0.2 to a term, rather than to say that the term does not hold for the document. Conversely, the indexer may wish to assign a weight of 0.8 or 0.9 to a term, rather than to say that it definitely holds for a document. Thus, given weighted indexing, it is possible to more accurately characterize the information content of a document. The notion of weighting the index terms that are assigned to documents and using these weights to compute relevance numbers is basic to the technique which we call *Probabilistic Indexing.*

3.2. *Notions of Relevance and Amount of Information.* One of our basic aims is to rank documents according to their relevance, given a library request for information. The problem then is to take relevance, which is a primitive notion, and explicate it—in the sense of making the concept precise—hopefully, to give a quantitative explication. If we cannot have a quantitative measure for relevance, at least we would like a comparative measure so that ranking of documents by relevance will be possible. In some sense the problem of explicating the notion of relevance (which is the basic concept in a theory of information retrieval) is similar to that of explicating the notion of amount of information (which is the basic concept of communication theory). In Shannon's work on information theory we find that one notion of amount of information has been explicated in terms of probabilities so that one can establish a quantitative measure of the amount of information in a message.[2] We approach the notion of relevance also in a probabilistic sense.

3.3. *First Step.* By "$P(A,B)$" we mean the probability of an event of class B occurring with reference to an event of class A. We shall be interested in the following classes of events:

(a) D_i : obtaining the ith document and finding it relevant.
(b) I_j : requesting information on the field of interest (subject, area of knowledge) designated by the jth index term I_j.
(c) A: requesting information from the library.

Thus

$P(A.I_j,D_i)$ = the probability that if a library user requests information on I_j, he will be satisfied with document D_i.

As the first step in the explication of relevance we assert:
If $P(A.I_j,D_1) > P(A.I_j,D_2)$, *then* D_1 *is more relevant than* D_2.

3.4 *Next Step.* In the elementary calculus of probability, one can immediately derive by the inverse inference schema (closely associated with Bayes' Theorem):

$$P(A.I_j,D_i) = \frac{P(A,D_i)\cdot P(A.D_i,I_j)}{P(A,I_j)}\,. \tag{1}$$

For any given request I_j, $P(A,I_j)$ is a constant, and consequently we may rewrite (1) as follows:

$$P(A.I_j,D_i) \sim P(A,D_i)\cdot P(A.D_i,I_j) \tag{2}$$

where $P(A,D_i)$ is the a priori probability of document D_i, and $P(A.D_i,I_j)$ is the probability that if a user wants information of the kind contained in document D_i he will formulate a request by using I_j. Thus, if we can obtain the values called for in the right-hand side of (2), then we can compute a quantity proportional to the value $P(A.I_j,D_i)$. We call this quantity the *relevance number* of the ith document with respect to the given request.

Immediately the problem of estimating these values confronts us. Consider first the estimate of $P(A.D_i,I_j)$. In principle, one could obtain an estimate of this probability via a statistical sampling process, but such a procedure would of course be extremely impractical, and it turns out that it is unnecessary. When an individual indexes a document (i.e., when he decides which terms to use to tag a document) he intuitively estimates this probability—in the conventional case automatically converting the probabilities to either 0 or 1. We now assert that

[2] C. E. Shannon and W. Weaver, *The Mathematical Theory of Communication*, The University of Illinois Press, Urbana, Illinois (1949).

the weight of a tag for a document, i.e., the degree with which the tag holds for a document, when properly scaled, can be interpreted as an estimate of $P(A.D_i,I_j)$. Thus we have from (1) and (2)

$$P(A.I_j,D_i) = \alpha_j \cdot P(A,D_i) \cdot \omega_{ij}, \tag{3}$$

where "ω_{ij}" denotes *the degree to which the j-th index term applies to the i-th document*, $P(A,D_i)$ is the a priori probability of document D_i, and α_j is the scaling factor times the reciprocal of $P(A,I_j)$. If we interpret the a priori probability so that it corresponds to statistics on document usage, i.e., so that $P(A,D_i)$ is the quotient of the number of uses of document D_i by the total number of document uses, then it is easy to show on the basis of (1) and (3) that ω_{ij} and $P(A.D_i,I_j)$ are related by

$$\omega_{ij} = \beta_j \cdot P(A.D_i,I_j), \tag{4}$$

where

$$\beta_j = \frac{\sum_i P(A,\ D_i) \cdot \omega_{ij}}{P(A,\ I_j)}. \tag{5}$$

In other words, in (4), β_j plays the role of an error factor in the estimation of $P(A.D_i,I_j)$ by the value ω_{ij}; (5) tells us how to estimate, in turn, the value of this error factor by using all the weights for a given tag as well as the statistical data $P(A,I_j)$. An improved estimate, therefore, is given by redefining the weight of a tag as follows:

$$w_{ij} = \omega_{ij}/\beta_j = \text{improved estimate of } P(A.D_i,I_j). \tag{6}$$

We call this value "the modified weight." The reader is referred to the Appendix for the details on the extension of the weight of a single index term to the weight of any Boolean function of index terms.

To summarize, library statistics provide us with $P(A,D_i)$, the weights coordinated with the index terms, when properly scaled, give us estimates of $P(A.D_i,I_j)$, and consequently we can compute the value of the relevance number $P(A.I_j,D_i)$ by means of which documents can be ranked according to their probable relevance to the requestor.

3.5. *Question Concerning Estimation.* At this point one might raise the following question. If the indexer is required to estimate $P(A.D_i,I_j)$, why not have him estimate $P(A.I_j,D_i)$ directly, since this is the goal of the computations? Actually this is not quite correct since the general goal of the computations is the determination of $P(A.R,D_i)$, where R is any Boolean function of the index terms. Clearly the indexer cannot make a single estimate of $P(A.R,D_i)$ since the value depends on the particular request R and hence there would have to be as many estimates of $P(A.R,D_i)$ as there would be R's. In order to avoid this situation, it would be necessary to transform $P(A.R,D_i)$ so that R goes from the reference class to the attribute class. Once we do this the problem is to compute $P(A.D_i,R)$ given all of the values of $P(A.D_i,I_j)$ as j varies over the range of tags that are contained in R. Thus, it turns out that $P(A.R,D_i)$ cannot be estimated directly—we must obtain it from $P(A.D_i,R)$, which in turn must be computed from $P(A.D_i,I_j)$.[3] That is to say, we need the value of $P(A.D_i,I_j)$ anyway, and any other estimates are superfluous.[4]

4. *Automatic Elaboration of the Selection Process*

4.1. *Initial Remarks.* The technique of Probabilistic Indexing, as we have seen, allows a computing machine, given a request for information, to derive a relevance number for each document. This relevance number is a measure of the document's relevance. The result of a search is an ordered list of those documents which satisfy the request, ranked according to their relevance numbers. We would prefer to have a technique which not only decides which of a given class of documents is most probably relevant, next most probably relevant, etc., but which also decides whether the class itself of retrieved documents is adequate (at least in the sense of determining whether or not it excludes some documents which are relevant to the user's *information needs* but are not computed as probably relevant due to inadequacies in the user's description of his information need). That is to say, if we consider the request as a *clue* which the user gives to the library to indicate the nature of his information needs, then we should raise the following question: Given a clue, how may it be used by the library system to generate a best *class* of documents (to be ranked subsequently by their relevance numbers)? Thus given the clue, how can we elaborate upon it automatically in order to produce a best class of retrieved documents? Let us turn our attention to this problem.

4.2. *Search Strategies and the Notion of Closeness.* A library request (a clue) is a Boolean function whose variables are index terms, each of which, in turn, selects a class of documents via a logical match. That is to say, all of those documents whose index terms are logically compatible with the logic and the tags of a request R constitute the class of retrieved documents C. Our goal is to extend the class C in the most probable "direction," and this can be done in two ways. One method involves the transforming of R into R', where R' in turn will select a class of documents C' which is larger than C and contains more relevant documents. A second method does not modify R but rather uses the class C to define a new class C''. A set of rules which prescribe how to go from a given request R to a class of retrieved documents is called a strategy. A strategy, in turn, involves the use of several different techniques for measuring the "closeness" between index terms and between documents. Before proceeding, let us introduce some further notations to make more precise what we have been saying.

[3] See Appendix.

[4] Even if every request were of the elementary form $P(A.I_j,\ D_i)$, it would be better to estimate $P(A.D_i,I_j)$ and compute $P(A.I_j,D_i)$ rather than to estimate the latter directly. This second argument in favor of the estimation of $P(A.D_i,I_j)$ over $P(A.I_j,D_i)$ appears when we consider the consistency of the comparative values. The indexer looks at each document, then runs through the various possible index terms which apply. In general $P(A.D_i,I_j)$ will vary over a much larger range than $P(A.I_j,D_i)$ as j varies, and therefore it is easier psychologically for the indexer to rank correctly the values over the larger range.

We understand by "basic selection process" the rule which uses the request to select the class of documents whose tags are logically compatible with the logic and tags of the request, and we denote this basic selection process by the functional notation "f". Thus f is the transfer function from inputs (requests) to output (class of retrieved documents) and we write

$$f(R) = C \tag{7}$$

where, again, R is the request and C is the class of retrieved documents. The problem is to enlarge C so as to increase the probability that it will contain relevant documents and to decrease the probability that it will contain irrelevant documents. We approach this problem in the following way: Suppose R' is a request similar in meaning to R; then we can take as a possible modification of f, say f',

$$f'(R) = f(R) \vee f(R') = C \vee C' \tag{8}$$

(where "$\vee$" designates class union). This modification can be made precise if we are able to invent a closeness measure on the request space to measure similarity in meaning. Since we are not sure what "meaning" is and much less able to assign a numerical quantity to it, this is rather difficult; but we shall show later that statistics can provide such measures. For the present, suppose we actually do have such a measure; then we can generate a modified selection function f' by defining $f'(R)$ to be the union of all classes $f(R')$ where the "closeness" between R and R' exceeds some specified number, say ϵ. Symbolically, this is written

$$f'(R) = \bigcup_{[Q(R,\,R') > \epsilon]} f(R'). \tag{9}$$

Analogously, if we have a "distance" function in the document space[5] which gives "distance" as a numerical measure of dissimilarity of information content, then a completely different modification f'' of f arises via

$$f''(R) = C'' \tag{10}$$

where C'' consists of all documents whose distance from $C = f(R)$ is less than ϵ.

Thus, we see that a machine strategy can elaborate upon the basic selection process in order to improve the search in one of two different ways. The first is to establish a measure for "closeness" in request space so as to formulate R', given R. The other way is to use the class of documents C, obtained by the initial request R, to define a new class C''. Both of these methods are discussed below.

4.3. *Notion of Index Space.* Geometrically speaking, one may think of the set of n index terms which constitute the library catalog "vocabulary" as points in an n-dimensional space. The points in this space are not located at random, but rather, they have definite relationships with respect to one another, depending on the meanings of the terms. For example, the term "logic" would be much closer to "mathematics" than to "music." One always finds, when looking up index terms in the catalog of a conventional library, other terms listed under "see" and "see also." This cross-indexing ("see/see also") aspect of a library indicates some of the relationships that index terms have for one another; i.e., it indicates some of the relationships between points in index space.

The numerical evaluation of relationships between index terms can be made explicit by formulating probabilistic weighting factors between them. Once numerical weighting factors are coordinated with the distances, the cross-indexing aspect of a library can be mechanized so that, given a request involving one (or many) index terms, a machine could compute other terms for which searches should be made. That is to say, a request places one at a point, or several points, in index space, and, once the "closeness" measures between points are arithmetized, a machine could determine which other points to go to in order to improve the request. Thus, the elaboration of a request on the basis of a probabilistic "association of ideas" could be executed automatically.

4.4. *Automatic Groping in Index Space.* There are at least two different kinds of relationships that can exist between the points in index space, viz., semantical relationships and statistical relationships. The most elementary semantical relationship is that of synonymity, but in addition to synonymity there are other semantical relationships such as "partially implied by" and "partially implies." Such relationships between terms are based strictly on the meanings of the terms in question—hence the word "semantical." Another class of relationships is statistical, i.e., those based on the relative frequency of occurrence of terms used as indexes. The distinction between semantical and statistical relationships may be clarified as follows: Whereas the semantical relationships are based solely on the meanings of the terms and hence independent of the "facts" described by those words, the statistical relationships between terms are based solely on the relative frequency with which they appear and hence *are* based on the nature of the facts described by the documents. Thus, although there is nothing about the meaning of the term "logic" which implies "switching theory," the nature of the facts (viz., that truth-functional logic is widely used for the analysis and synthesis of switching circuits) "causes" a statistical relationship. (Another example might concern the terms "information theory" and "Shannon"—assuming, of course, that proper names are used as index terms.)

Once the various "connections" between the points of index space have been established, rules must be formulated which describe how one should move in the maze of connected points. We call such rules "heuristics." They are general guides for groping in the "maze" in the attempt to create an optimal output list of documents for any arbitrary request. The heuristics would enable a machine to decide, for a given set of request terms, which index terms to "see" and "see also," and how deep this search should be and when to stop, etc. Generally speaking, the heuristics would decide which index terms to look at next, on the basis of the semantical and statistical connections between terms, and the heuristics would decide when to stop looking, on the basis of the number of

[5] We use "distance" in document space, "closeness" in request space. The reason is that our measures in request space have the nature of "coefficients of association" rather than the properties of mathematical distance functions.

documents that would be retrieved and the relevance numbers of those documents. (Remember that each point in index space defines a class of documents, viz., all of those documents which have been assigned the index terms in question with a nonzero weight.) Given this understanding of heuristics, we see that an over-all search strategy is made up of components, some of which are heuristics; i.e., the sequence of devices, rules, heuristics, etc., which lead from inputs (requests) to outputs (classes of retrieved documents) is the strategy.

4.5. *Three Measures of Closeness in Index Space.* In order to clarify the notion of developing heuristics which would determine how a computer should "grope" in index space, consider the following example. Assume that we compute the frequency, $N(I_j)$, with which each term is used to tag a document, and also that we compute the frequency, $N(I_j.I_k)$, with which pairs of terms are assigned to documents. We can then compute the conditional probability $P(I_j,I_k)$ that if a term I_j is assigned to a document then I_k also will be assigned:

$$P(I_j\,,I_k) = \frac{N(I_j\,.\,I_k)}{N(I_j)} \tag{11}$$

We do this for all pairs I_j, I_k.

Assume now that I_j' is the index term which has the highest conditional probability given I_j; i.e., I_j' is the index term for which $P(I_j,I_k)$ is a maximum. Then given a request, $R = I_j$, for all documents tagged with I_j, we form a new request, $R' = I_j \vee I_j'$, which searches for all documents tagged with either I_j or I_j'. Thus, the rule is now to consider R' instead of R.

This procedure tells us which tags are closest (in one sense) to given ones, but we still have no *measure* of the "closeness" (hereafter written without quotes) and such a measure is needed as a part of the associated computation rule. That is to say, we elaborate upon R and obtain R' by searching for documents indexed under tags closely related to those in the original request, but clearly the relevance numbers that we derive for these additional documents should be weighted down somewhat in order to indicate that they were obtained only from tags which are close to those in the original request. We measure the closeness as follows: Let $p_j = P(I_j,I_j')$ and normalize p_j over the set of tags used in the request so that

$$\bar{p}_j = \frac{p_j}{\sum p_j}\,.$$

Now, instead of using $w_i(I_j')$ (the weight assigned to I_j' for the ith document) in the search computation, we replace it by $\bar{p}_j \cdot w_i(I_j')$. The extended search that we have just described is an elementary form of only one of a class of possible heuristics based on the statistical relationships between tags.

A second elementary heuristic which looks even more promising is called the "inverse conditional" search, and it involves measuring closeness of tags to I_j in terms of the conditional probability from I_k to I_j (instead of conversely as described above). That is to say, we compute the $P(I_k,I_j)$ which is maximum as I_k varies, and this provides the tag which most strongly implies the given tag I_j. Thus, instead of asking for that tag which is most strongly implied (statistically) by an arbitrary tag in the request, we ask for the tag which most strongly *implies* (statistically) the given tag. Using this method to determine the closeness of tags we establish a measure for the closeness by normalizing the probability as before. That is, define

$$p_j = P('I_j\,, I_j),$$

$$\bar{p}_j = \frac{p_j}{\sum p_j}$$

and, again, the corresponding computation rule is now $\bar{p}_j \cdot w_i('I_j)$, where $'I_j$ is the I_k which makes $P(I_k,I_j)$ a maximum for a given I_j.

Having discussed two possible measures of closeness, viz., the conditional probability $P(I_j,I_k)$ and the inverse condition probability $P(I_k,I_j)$, we now consider a third statistical measure which appears to be the most promising of the three. This is one of several possible *coefficients of association* between predicates.[6]

The particular coefficient we have chosen arises in the following way. Consider the tags I_j and I_k, and partition the library by four classifications, viz., documents indexed under both I_j and I_k, those indexed under I_j but not I_k, those indexed under I_k but not I_j, and those not indexed under either. Letting "$\bar{I}_j$" denote the complement of the class I_j, etc., these four classes are given by $I_j.I_k$, $I_j.\bar{I}_k$, $\bar{I}_j.I_k$, $\bar{I}_j.\bar{I}_k$, respectively. The classification and the number of documents is shown most conveniently in a table:

	I_k	$\bar{I}_k$	
I_j	$x = N(I_j.I_k)$	$u = N(I_j.\bar{I}_k)$	$N(I_j)$
$\bar{I}_j$	$v = N(\bar{I}_j.I_k)$	$y = N(\bar{I}_j.\bar{I}_k)$	$N(\bar{I}_j)$
	$N(I_k)$	$N(\bar{I}_k)$	n

We have adjoined to the table the row and column sums and n (the total number of documents).

Now, using the notation of formula (11), we say that I_j is *statistically independent* of I_k if

$$P(I_j,I_k) = P(I_k). \tag{15}$$

This can be shown to be equivalent to

$$P(I_j.I_k) = P(I_j)\cdot P(I_k); \tag{16}$$

so that rewriting in terms of frequencies we have an additional equivalence:

$$N(I_j.I_k) = N(I_j)\cdot N(I_k)/n. \tag{17}$$

[6] G. U. Yule, On measuring association between attributes, *J. Royal Stat. Soc.*, *75* (1912), 579–642.

For any pair I_j, I_k, (17) suggests that we look at the excess of $N(I_j.I_k)$ over its independence value; i.e., the quantity

$$\delta(I_j,I_k) = N(I_j.I_k) - N(I_j)\cdot N(I_k)/n. \quad (18)$$

It can be shown that this function δ has the property

$$\delta(I_j,I_k) = \delta(\bar{I}_j,\bar{I}_k) = -\delta(\bar{I}_j,I_k) = -\delta(I_j,\bar{I}_k), \quad (19)$$

and thus δ is associated with the difference over independence values in all four classifications. Yule[7] lists some basic properties that a coefficient of association between I_j and I_k should have. We call this coefficient "$Q(I_j,I_k)$". (1) $Q(I_j,I_k)$ should be zero when $\delta(I_j,I_k) = 0$ and, moreover, $Q(I_j,I_k)$ should vary as $\delta(I_j,I_k)$ for fixed n and fixed row and column totals; (2) the maximum of $Q(I_j,I_k)$ should occur when I_j is contained in I_k ($u = 0$), or I_k is contained in I_j ($v = 0$), or I_j and I_k give the same class ($u = v = 0$); (3) the minimum of $Q(I_j,I_k)$ should occur when I_k is contained in $\bar{I}_j$ ($x = 0$), or $\bar{I}_j$ is contained in I_k ($y = 0$), or I_j is the complement of I_k ($x = y = 0$); (4) it should have a simple range of values, say from -1, to 1. A coefficient[8] that has all of these properties is:

$$Q(I_j,I_k) = (xy - uv)/(xy + uv), \quad (20)$$

where the intimate connection with δ is indicated by the fact that the numerator of Q is, in fact, $n\delta$.

The generation of a heuristic now proceeds by the rules for the previous measures. Given $R = I_j$, we select the term I_k (different from I_j) with the maximum coefficient $Q(I_j,I_k)$. This value will be between 0 and 1, or no term will be selected. Then R is extended to

$$R' = I_j \vee I_k,$$

and in the search computation we multiply the weight $w_i(I_k)$ by $Q(I_j,I_k)$.

We now have the possibility of generating more elaborate heuristics. The heuristics just described can be called "one-deep." Applying the procedure again, we arrive at "two-deep" heuristics. At this second level, however, several possibilities arise. Having gone from I_j to $I_j \vee I_k$, we can now find the term most closely associated to I_k, say I_l, thus obtaining (two-deep chain search):

$$R'' = I_j \vee I_k \vee I_l.$$

Alternately, we can choose the term of second highest association with I_j, say I_m, thus obtaining (two-deep hub search)

$$R'' = I_j \vee I_k \vee I_m.$$

We also have the possibility of changing the measure of closeness for the second search, thus building as complex a search strategy as we wish.

[7] Loc. Cit.

[8] The coefficient recommended by Yule, *loc. cit.*, is not Q, but $Z = (\sqrt{xy} - \sqrt{uv})/(\sqrt{xy} + \sqrt{uv})$. The range of variation of both Q and Z is the same and since both lead to equivalent heuristics we have chosen Q for its computational simplicity. For refined work we might adopt Z.

4.6. *Heuristics in the Document Space.* Having shown how to generate heuristics by elaborating on the original requests, let us now look at the problem of implementing formula (10). We call such heuristics "extension heuristics"; i.e., we extend an initially retrieved class of documents by considerations concerning this class itself—holding that this class gives clues as to the meaning of the original request. Now we would prefer not only to extend this class by measures of distance between documents but also introduce such measures into a "generalized" relevance number computation. That is to say, we would like to combine heuristics in such a way that documents with associated ranking numbers are retrieved, not just classes of documents. We would also like to use the values $w_i(R)$ in the computation.

First, we note that the Pythagorean distance between two rows of the probabilistic matrix gives a measure of dissimilarity of information content (as well as dissimilarity of distribution of information) between documents corresponding to these rows. Call this distance, $\Delta(D_i,D_j)$. We can use this distance function to compute the distance of any document from the class C of documents retrieved by the basic selection process. This is all the theory required to implement formula (10).[9]

Next is the problem of defining the generalized relevance number. There are infinitely many possibilities here, and which is the "best" is still an open problem. However, an extremely natural one arises as follows: We consider the values $w_i(R)$ as measures of closeness between R and the documents. To combine these values with $\Delta(D_i,D_j)$, we convert closeness to "distance" by some device such as considering the negative of the logarithm of $w_i(R)$. We define

$$d(R,D_i) = -\log w_i(R). \quad (21)$$

D_i will be retrieved by R if and only if $d(R,D_i)$ is finite; thus this characterizes the class of retrieved documents. Now take that document D_i in the class of retrieved documents such that $\Delta(D_i,D_j)$ is a minimum.[10] Then we take

$$g(R,D_j) = \sqrt{\Delta^2(D_i,D_j) + \log^2 w_i(R)} \quad (22)$$

as the measure of "distance" between R and D_j.[11] Note that if D_j is a retrieved document, then $\Delta(D_i,D_j)$ is zero and

$$g(R,D_j) = -\log w_j(R).$$

Furthermore, if D_j has not been retrieved (initially),

$$g(R,D_j) > -\log w_i(R),$$

where i is the accession number of the document nearest to D_j. Thus the ranking by the g-function will always put an adjoined document below its associated

[9] Another measure of dissimilarity is to take, not the Pythagorean distance, but the sum of the absolute values of the differences between rows; i.e., $\sum_k |w_{ik} - w_{jk}|$; in fact, several other measures of dissimilarity appear worthy of study. Our discussion is perfectly general, and the reader may take $\Delta(D_i,D_j)$ as any such measure.

[10] If D_i is not unique, choose the one in the minimal set with the largest $w_i(R)$.

[11] It may be preferable to "weight" each of the components $\Delta(D_i,D_j)$, $\log w_i(R)$ in (22). Suitable values of these weights are to be determined by experimentation.

document in the class C. We may now finish the computation by subtracting the logarithm of the *a priori* probability of a document from its g-value (analogous to multiplying $w_i(R)$ by $P(A,D_i)$ to obtain the relevance number). The final heuristic is then obtained by choosing a suitable cutoff point in the list of adjoined documents—taking only those with generalized relevance numbers less than some specified value.

4.7. *Extension of the Request Language*. It is obvious that the richer the request language the more precise is the user's description of his information need. However, as the language becomes descriptively richer, the processing of retrieval prescriptions becomes more complex because of the difficulties discussed in section 1. A rather simple extension of our request language does, however, present itself. This richer language also has the virtue of adaptability to the automatic procedure we envisage. That is, we permit the requestor to assign numerical weights to index terms according to how important a role he wishes them to play in the processing of his request. These request weights can be used to scale down the index term weights and/or to serve as control numbers in search strategies.

4.8. *Search Strategies*. We have presented some of the heuristics that appear to have the best possibility of being useful components of a search strategy. We also have formulated some principles for a general approach to the problem of automatic elaboration of the selection process. Let us now illustrate these ideas by constructing an over-all search strategy.

First we list the variables involved:

1. Input
   a. The request R
   b. The request weights
2. The Probabilistic Matrix $[w_{ij}]$
   a. Dissimilarity measures between documents (e.g., Δ-values)
   b. Significance measures for index terms (An index term applied to every document in the library will have no significance, while an index term applied to only one document will be highly significant. Thus significance measures are related to the "extension number" for each term, i.e., to the number of documents tagged with the term—the smaller this number, the greater the significance of the index term.)
   c. "Closeness" measures between index terms (e.g., Q-values, etc.)
3. The a priori Probability Distribution
4. Output (by means of the basic selection process, i.e., the logical match plus the inverse inference schema (1) with all of its ramifications and refinements)
   a. The class of retrieved documents, C
   b. n, the number of documents in C
   c. Relevance numbers
5. Control Numbers
   a. n_0, the maximum number of documents that we wish to retrieve
   b. Relevance number control; e.g., we may ignore documents with relevance number less than a specified value.
   c. Generalized relevance number control. Similar to the above, but this applies to the computation described in section 4.6.
   d. Request weight control; i.e., we elaborate on index terms in the request if their request weight is higher than some specified value.
   e. Significance number of index term control; i.e., we give index terms of certain significance (defined in terms of their extensions) special attention.
6. Operations
   a. Basic selection process; denote this by "f".
   b. Elaboration of the request by using "closeness" in the request space. Denote this by "H". Thus the operation H will transform the request R into a new request R'. More precisely H is the heuristic: elaborating the index terms in R with request weights greater than the request weight control number and/or index term significance greater than a specified value.
   c. Adjoining new documents to the class of retrieved documents by using "distance" in the document space. Denote this by "h". Thus the operation h will transform the class C of retrieved documents into a new class, say D. More precisely, h is the heuristic: trim C to documents having relevance number greater than the control number and then annex to C all of the documents with generalized relevance number in a certain range.
   d. Merge: any merging operation between two classes; e.g., forming their intersection, their union, trimming by using relevance number and then forming union, etc.

Next we combine these to obtain the strategy shown in figure 1. This strategy is to be regarded as a particularly simple example, its goal to obtain a specified number of documents (say n_0) having the best chance of satisfying the request. Thus, the decision to elaborate, centers on answering the question: Is the number of documents selected greater than or equal to n_0? In figure 1 we refer to the heuristic H as simply "elaborate the request." The actual transfer function H involves using control numbers to limit the elaboration. Furthermore, these control numbers can be varied from one application of H to the next. Similarly we refer to the heuristic H as simply "extend the class," but we point out that this too involves control numbers. Finally, a word about the classes C, C', D, etc. These are actually lists of documents ranked by relevance numbers. Thus the instruction "trim C to n_0" means "cut off the list to the n_0 documents with highest relevance numbers." The output of the system will be an ordered list of document accession numbers.

• • •

THE CRANFIELD TESTS ON INDEX LANGUAGE DEVICES

CYRIL CLEVERDON

Librarian, College of Aeronautics, Cranfield

Evening meeting, London, Thursday 27th April 1967

The investigation dealt with the effect which different devices have on the performance of index languages. It appeared that the most important consideration was the specificity of the index terms; within the context of the conditions existing in this test, single-word terms were more effective than concept terms or a controlled vocabulary.

THE first Aslib-Cranfield project attempted to investigate the operational performance of four different indexing systems, namely the Universal Decimal Classification, a facet classification, an alphabetical subject catalogue and the Uniterm system of co-ordinate indexing.[1,2] In terms of performance, it was found that all systems operated at very much the same level of efficiency.

In the course of this first project, an evaluation was made of a test collection of some 1,100 documents in the index of metallurgical literature of Western Reserve University, and comparison was made with a faceted index, covering the same set of documents, that was compiled at Cranfield.[3] The results from these tests were to establish the measures that can be used in evaluating the operational performance of information retrieval systems. The two measures, namely *recall ratio* and *precision ratio*, were not only important in themselves, but provided a clue to the composition of index languages, for detailed analysis of the results of the two tests showed that each indexing system was made up of a basic vocabulary together with a number of devices. These devices fall into two main categories; there are *recall devices*, which are intended to increase the probability of retrieving more relevant documents. Examples of such recall devices are the grouping of synonyms, the confounding of word forms, or the formation of classes of related terms. On the other hand *precision devices* are intended to ensure that non-relevant documents are not retrieved, and examples of such precision devices are co-ordination (whether pre-co-ordination or post-co-ordination), links and roles.

The analysis of the test results in Cranfield I showed that all indexing systems were an amalgam of recall and precision devices, and that these interacted with each other in such a complex manner that it was impossible to measure their effect on the overall performance of any indexing system. The Universal Decimal Classification, for instance, is a very complex system, and includes every possible device. It incorporates recall devices, such as the control of synonyms, by means of the alphabetical index:

e.g. Air Cushion Vehicles 629.137
Ground-effect machines 629.137
Hovercraft 629.137

Word forms are also brought together by the alphabetical index:

e.g. Weld 621.791
Welded 621.791
Welding 621.791

Generic relations are shown in the schedules:

e.g. 662 Beverages
662.3 Wines

Pre-co-ordination of terms frequently occurs in the schedules:

e.g. 533.6.071 Wind tunnels
533.6.071.4 Wind tunnel instruments

Alternatively, co-ordination can be obtained by the use of the colon sign or brackets:

e.g. 338:633.1 Cereal production
942(42) English history

Links are also shown by the colon sign:

e.g. 669.71 : 621.791 Welding of aluminium

Roles are indicated by the context of the schedules:

e.g. *Input* Wood (fuel) 662.63
Output Wood (forestry) 634.08

The second Cranfield project was therefore designed to investigate such index language devices in isolation and in all practical combinations, and attempt to measure the effect which each device had on performance. For this purpose a test collection was established consisting of 1,400 research papers, mainly in the field of aerodynamics. Each document was 'indexed' in three different ways (Fig. 1); first, the most important concepts were selected and were recorded in the natural language of the document. The single words in each of the concepts were then listed, and finally the concepts were combined in different ways to form the main themes of the documents. At the time of indexing, each concept was given a 'weighting' (1, 2 or 3) to indicate its relative importance. The concepts in the main theme of the document would be weighted '1', the less important concepts '2' and the minor concepts '3'.

For the testing, 221 questions were used, these being questions which had been provided by the authors of a number of research papers. The first task was to determine the relevance of every document in the collection to each of the questions. The relevance decisions, which were finally decided by the originators of the questions, were in a scale of from 1 to 4, which had the following requirements.

1. References which are a complete answer to the question.
2. References of a high degree of relevance, the lack of which either would have made the research impracticable or would have resulted in a considerable amount of extra work.

B1590 Base Document A137	AUTHOR STONE, A. TITLE Effect of stage characteristics and matching on axial flow compressor performance REFERENCE *Trans. American Soc. of Mechanical Engineers*, c–, 1958, p. 1273	Indexer J.M.	Date 17-6-63

	THEMES (*partitioning*)		*CONCEPTS* (*Interfixing*)		*CONCEPTS* (*Interfixing*)	*TERMS & WEIGHTS*		*TERMS & WEIGHTS*	
A	cd *effect of* a *use of* ef	a	Stage characteristics	t	Range of operations	Stage	1	Blade	3
B	——— b ———	b	Stage matching	u	Stage flow co-efficient	Characteristic	1	Range	2
C	cdh	c	Axial flow compressor	v	Mass flow	Matching	1	Operations	2
D	cdi *effect of* j *with* k	d	Stage performance	w	Choking flow	Axial	1	Mass	2
E	cdl *effect of* g	e	Test data		co-efficient	Flow	1	Choking	2
F	cmp *effect of* n	f	Analysis	x	Surge line	Compressor	1	Line	2
G	———vo	g	Mach number	y	Change in slope	Performance	1	Slope	3
H	cmdq	h	Velocity distribution	z	Knee double valued	Test	1	Knee	3
I	cmdr	i	Temperature		performance curve	Data	1	Double	3
J	cmdt *effect of* sg		co-efficient	aa	Unstalling hysteresis	Analysis	1	Curve	3
K	cmu *effect of* g	j	Flow co-efficient		Inlet guide vane stagger	Mach	2	Unstalling	3
L	———v	k	Constant flow angle	bb	Uprating stage one	Velocity	2	Hysterisis	3
M	cbv *effect of* w	l	Cascade losses		Uprating stage two	Distribution	2	Inlet	3
N	cbx *effect of* o	m	Idealized compressor		Blade stagger	Temperature	3	Guide	3
O	cbxy *effect of* o	n	Total pressure ratio	cc	Stage loading	Co-efficient	3	Vane	3
P	cbz *effect of* aa	o	Percentage of design	dd	Annular area	Constant	3	Stagger	3
Q	cu *effect of* bb		speed	ee		Angle	3	Uprating	3
R	———cc	p	Performance	ff		Cascade	3	One	3
S	———dd	q	Stalling point	gg		Loss	3	Loading	3
T	cx *effect of* ee	r	Compression surges			Idealized	2	Annulus	3
U	———ff	s	Pitch line blade speed			Total	3	Area	3
V	———gg					Ratio	3	Number	2
W	———vq					Percentage	2	Line	3
						Design	2	Valued	3
						Speed	2	Two	3
						Stalling	2	Pressure	2
						Point	2		
						Surge	2		
						Pitch	3		

FIGURE 1 INDEXING SHEET FOR DOCUMENT 1590

3. References which were useful, either as general background to the work or as suggesting methods of tackling certain aspects of the work.
4. References of minimum interest, for example, those that have been included from an historical viewpoint.

In a normal search, the document collection is divided into two groups, consisting of the documents that are retrieved and the documents that are left in the system. Each of these groups can be subdivided into those documents that are relevant and those documents that are not relevant. This is usually presented as in Fig. 2.

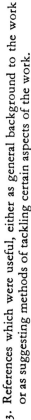

	RELEVANT	NON-RELEVANT	
RETRIEVED	a	b	a + b
NOT RETRIEVED	c	d	c + d
	a + c	b + d	a + b + c + d = N (Total Collection)

FIGURE 2 2 x 2 CONTINGENCY TABLE

For the purpose of evaluating an information retrieval system, performance is presented by plotting the recall ratio $\left(\frac{100a}{a+c}\right)$ against either the precision ratio $\left(\frac{100a}{a+b}\right)$ or the fallout ratio $\left(\frac{100b}{b+d}\right)$. The fallout ratio is particularly useful when comparing performances of document collections of different sizes, but the precision ratio is more satisfactory for most of the results obtained in the Cranfield work.

Three main types of index language were investigated. For the first, single terms only were used; examples of these are given in the final columns of Fig. 1 and all such terms are in the natural language of the documents. It was these natural language terms which were used for the basic index language of this type; for the second Single Term index language, synonyms were grouped; for the third, word forms were confounded. Further Single Term index languages had groups of terms based on different hierarchical classes (Fig. 3).

The second main type of index language used the concepts as given in Fig. 1, with some slight simplifications; again the basic Simple Concept index language used these terms as they occurred in the documents, and fourteen other index languages were formed on the basis of various groupings of these terms (Fig. 4). The third main type consisted of six different index languages which were based on various groupings of a set of controlled terms (Fig. 5).

In addition, there were four further index languages where the index terms represented all the key words in the titles or in the abstracts. In each case these were tested in the natural language and with word forms confounded.

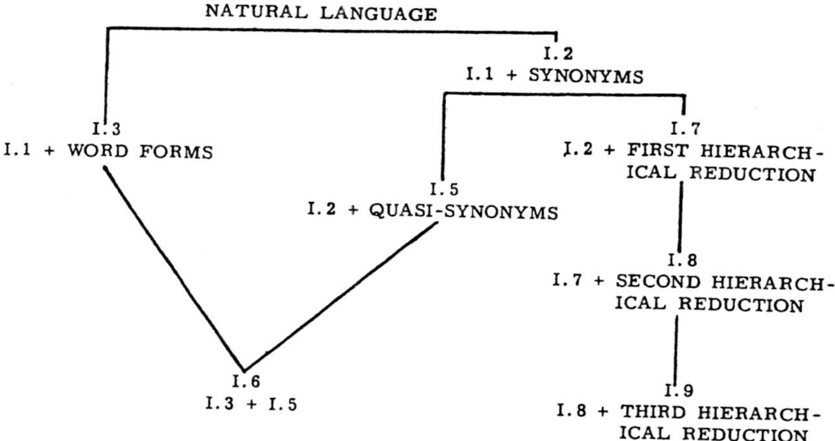

FIGURE 3 SINGLE TERM INDEX LANGUAGES

The searches were carried out in such a way that there was absolute consistency, except for a single variable, such as the index language or the search rule or the relevance decision. Consider, for instance, the question '*Small deflection theory* of *simple supported cylinders*'. This is the question exactly as stated by its originator, and it contains six key terms. With the basic single term index language, the first search was made for a match in all six terms, and this retrieved three documents. For a match of any five terms, ten documents were retrieved; for a match of any four terms fourteen documents were retrieved; forty-three documents were retrieved at a match of three terms, 177 documents at a match of two terms and 722 documents when any single term was accepted on its own.

For comparison we consider the results obtained with Index Language 1.6; in this case the change is that the single terms are grouped into classes formed by synonyms, word forms and quasi-synonyms. It is now found that at a match of all six terms, four documents have been retrieved; at a match of five terms, fourteen documents were retrieved; for a match of four terms, thirty-eight documents were retrieved; 125 documents were retrieved at a match of three terms, this being nearly three times as many as were retrieved at this level with Index Language I.1. However, in this particular case, whereas only two of the six relevant documents were retrieved at a match of three with Index Language I.1, five relevant documents are retrieved with Index Language I.6.

When the results of a number of searches are aggregated, test results are obtained which can be presented in the manner shown in Figs. 6 and 7. The single variable in these two sets of results is the index language; Fig. 6 shows the results for Index Language I.1, which used single terms in the natural language. Figure 7 presents the results for Index Language I.6 where the single terms are grouped into classes formed by synonyms, word forms and quasi-synonyms.

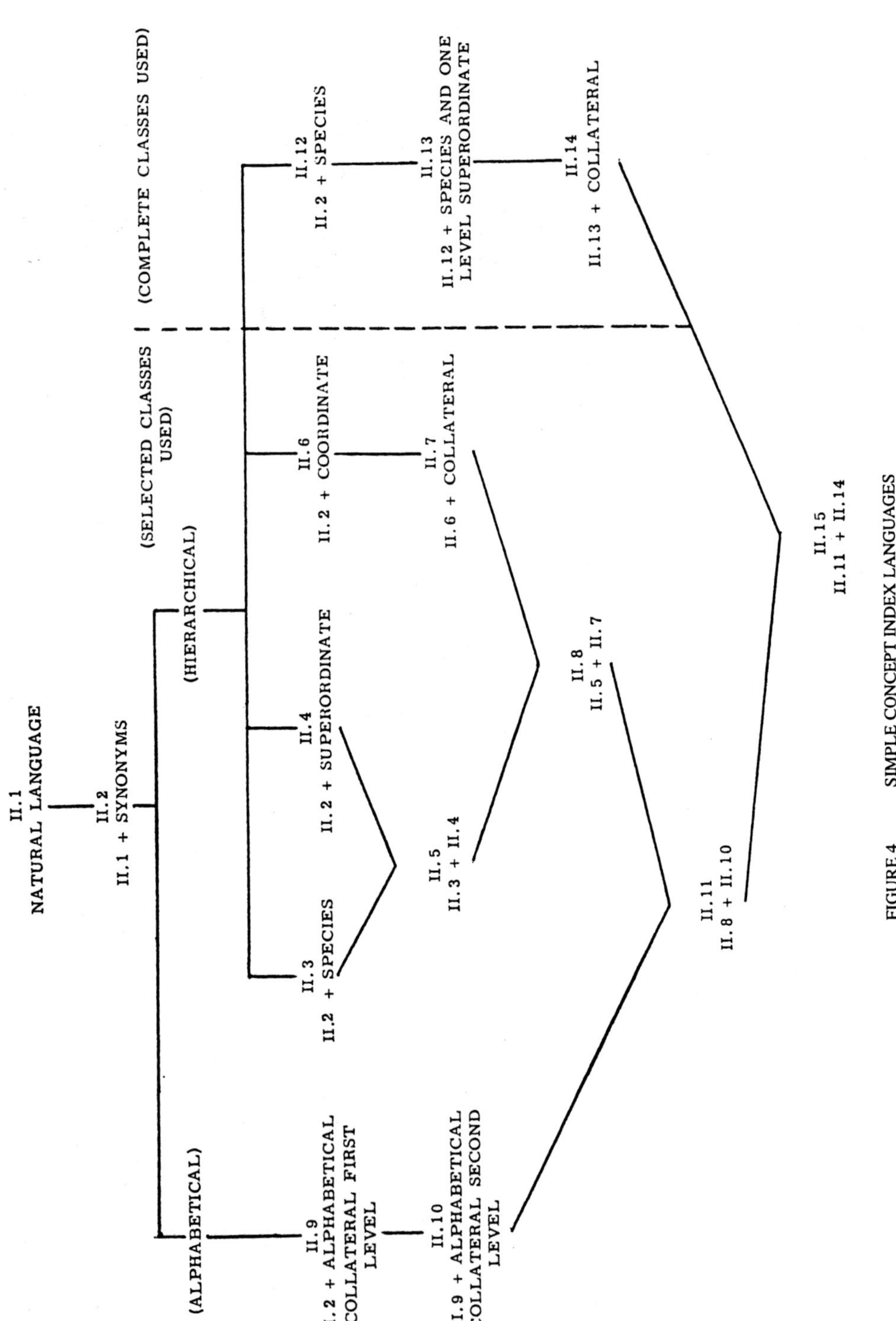

FIGURE 4 SIMPLE CONCEPT INDEX LANGUAGES

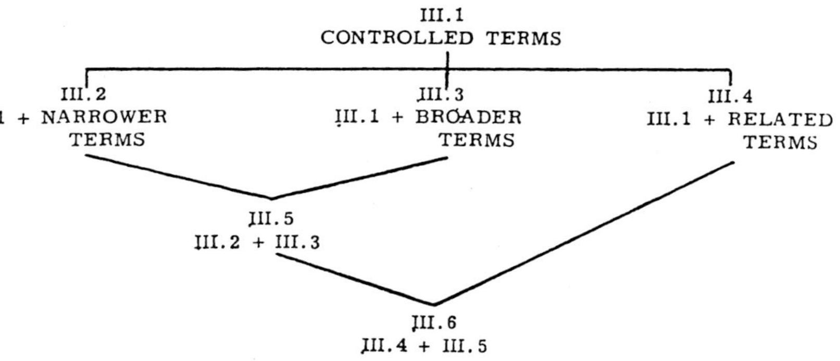

FIGURE 5 CONTROLLED TERM INDEX LANGUAGES

The tables show the number of relevant and non-relevant documents retrieved at various coordination levels and from these figures are calculated the recall ratio, the precision ratio and the fall-out ratio.

These two sets of results can be presented on a recall-precision plot as in Fig. 8; from this it can be seen that at any given recall ratio up to 95 per cent, Index Language I.1 has a higher precision ratio than Index Language I.6.

In addition to the results of the type already shown, many further tests were made to determine the effect of different variables. Figure 9, for instance, shows the effect of introducing certain rules concerning the search strategy, and Figure 10 is a plot showing the effect of the four different levels of relevance. In this latter case a plot showing recall and fall-out ratios is presented. This is done because the effect of changing the relevance levels is to alter the number of relevant documents and thereby change the generality number. Due to this change in generality number, a recall/precision plot would have shown the best performance with documents relevance 1–4 and the worst performance with documents relevance 1. While it is practical to make the necessary adjustments in precision ratio, the fallout ratio automatically compensates for the change in the generality number and correctly shows that the best performance is obtained with relevance 1 documents.

The plots and the test results illustrate the inverse relationship, first postulated in the earlier Cranfield work,[2] which exists between recall and precision. Whereas the maximum possible recall ratio of 100 per cent can be obtained by, if necessary, looking at every document in the collection, the inevitable effect of bringing about any improvement in the precision ratio is a drop in the recall ratio. In reverse, if one wishes to increase the number of relevant documents which are being retrieved, this can only be done by increasing to a greater extent the number of non-relevant documents also retrieved. This is always the case when operating within any given system, although it does not, of course, apply for comparisons between different systems.

It is estimated that some 300,000 test results were obtained in the project, and while the results appeared consistently to show the same trends, it was difficult

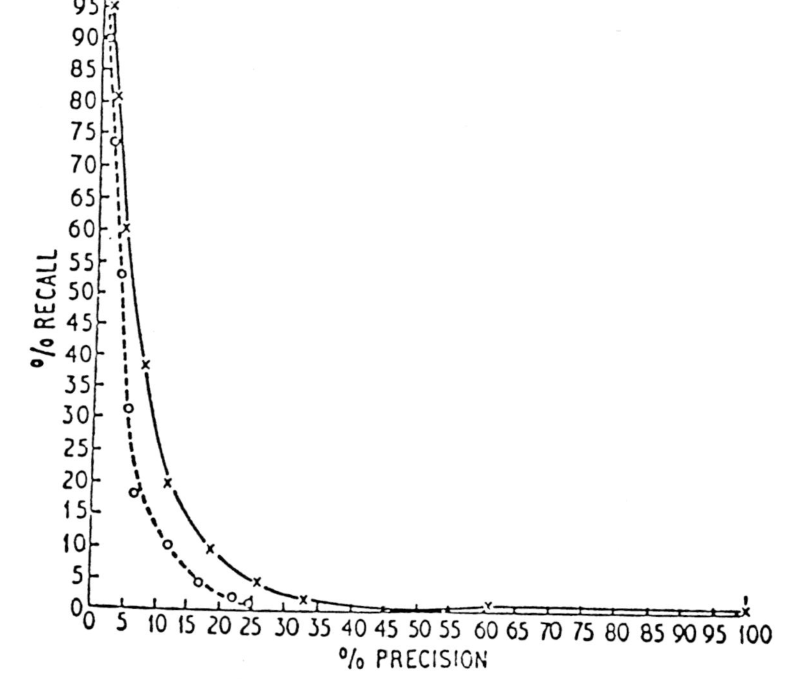

FIGURE 8 RECALL/PRECISION PLOT FOR INDEX LANGUAGES I.1 AND I.6 AS GIVEN IN FIGURES 6 AND 7

to present them in a manner which gave a direct comparison between the different systems. Many proposals have been made for a single performance measure, and a large number of these were considered in detail in the project report.[4] All these measures had a similar weakness in that they could only represent a single recall/precision point. This meant that a 'score' of, say, 85 might imply a recall ratio of 80 per cent and a precision of 5 per cent, or a recall ratio of 20 per cent and a precision ratio of 65 per cent or any other of a whole series of single points. The emphasis in the Cranfield work has been on the overall performance of a system which is obtained by changing a single variable, such as the co-ordination level; this produces a series of points giving a performance curve as already shown in Figure 8, and it was this overall performance which we wished to compare. The answer lay in a form of the normalized recall ratio as first used by Professor Salton.

The investigations undertaken by Salton with the SMART system[5] were basically similar to those which were being done at Cranfield. In both cases the intention was to compare the effect of using different devices or options, but there were, of course, important differences, apart from the fact that Salton used a large computer while Cranfield used simple but laborious clerical techniques

Index Language I.1.a. (S.T. Natural language. Coordination)

Exhaustivity of Indexing 3
Search Rule A
Document Relevance 1-4

Number of Documents in Collection 1,400
Number of Questions 221 (Subset 3)
Number of Relevant Documents 1,590
Generality Number 5.1

Coord-ination Level	Documents Retrieved Rel.	Documents Retrieved Non-rel.	Recall Ratio a/a+c	Precision Ratio a/a+b	Fallout Ratio b/b+d	x	y	z
1	1,510	159,122	95.0%	0.9%	51.696%	221	221	221
2	1,283	58,122	80.7%	2.2%	18.883%	221	221	221
3	946	21,933	59.5%	4.1%	7.125%	215	220	220
4	606	7,359	38.1%	7.6%	2.390%	187	212	212
5	314	2,380	19.7%	11.6%	0.773%	131	197	197
6	154	699	9.7%	18.0%	0.227%	86	164	164
7	74	216	4.7%	25.5%	0.070%	50	140	140
8	22	43	1.4%	33.8%	0.014%	18	105	105
9	8	5	0.5%	61.5%	0.002%	8	78	78
10	1	0	0.1%	100.0%	0.000%	1	52	52
11	0	0				0	32	32
12	0	0				0	15	15
13	0	0				0	8	8
14	0	0				0	4	4
15	0	0				0	3	3

FIGURE 6 RESULTS OF SEARCHES USING INDEX LANGUAGE I.1

Index Language I 6.a (S. T. Synonyms, Quasi-synonyms, Word forms. Coordination)

Exhaustivity of Indexing 3
Search Rule A
Document Relevance 1 - 4

Number of Documents in Collection 1,400
Number of Questions 221 (Subset 3)
Number of Relevant Documents 1,590
Generality Number 5.1

Coord-ination Level.	Documents Retrieved Rel.	Non-rel.	Recall Ratio a/a+c	Precision Ratio a/a+b	Fallout Ratio b/b+d	x	y	z
1	1,557	(-)	97.9%	(-)	(-)	221	0	221
2	1,430	116,374*	89.9%	1.2%*	37.783%*	221	44*	221
3	1,165	45,101*	73.3%	2.5%*	14.643%*	218	109*	220
4	848	18,373*	53.3%	4.4%*	5.965%*	206	142*	212
5	503	8,895*	31.6%	5.4%*	2.888%*	169	177*	197
6	295	3,874*	18.6%	7.1%*	1.257%*	119	161*	164
7	161	1,136	10.1%	12.4%	0.369%	83	140	140
8	72	344	4.5%	17.3%	0.112%	54	105	105
9	24	82	1.5%	22.6%	0.027%	25	78	78
10	6	18	0.4%	25.0%	0.006%	12	52	52
11	0	1	0.0%	0.0%	0.0003%	1	32	32
12	0	0				0	15	15
13	0	0				0	8	8
14	0	0				0	4	4
15	0	0				0	3	3

FIGURE 7 RESULTS OF SEARCHES USING INDEX LANGUAGE 1.6

FIGURE 9 EFFECT ON PERFORMANCE OF CHANGES IN SEARCH RULES

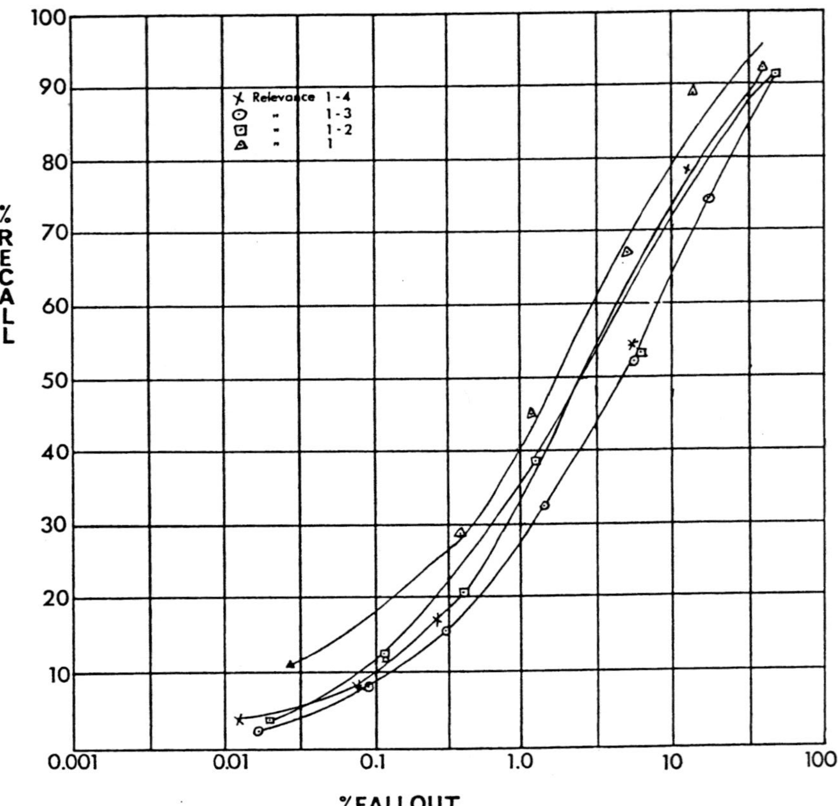

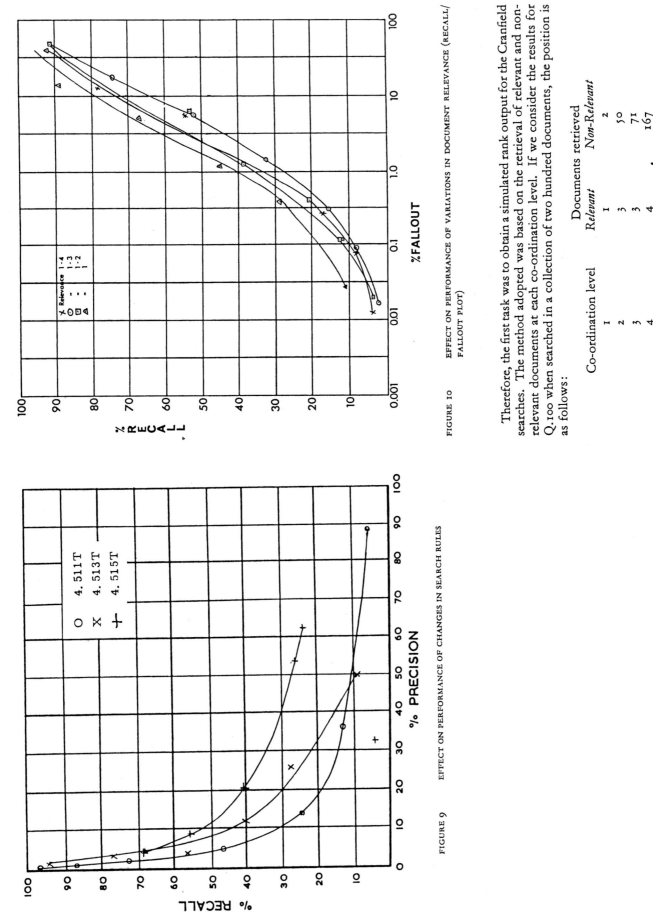

FIGURE 10 EFFECT ON PERFORMANCE OF VARIATIONS IN DOCUMENT RELEVANCE (RECALL/FALLOUT PLOT)

Therefore, the first task was to obtain a simulated rank output for the Cranfield searches. The method adopted was based on the retrieval of relevant and non-relevant documents at each co-ordination level. If we consider the results for Q.100 when searched in a collection of two hundred documents, the position is as follows:

	Documents retrieved	
Co-ordination level	*Relevant*	*Non-Relevant*
1	1	2
2	3	50
3	3	71
4	4	167

By using such figures, a rank order number could be assigned to each relevant document by means of the equation

$$c_{R_n} = X_c + (n - Y_c)\left(\frac{x_c + 1}{y_c + 1}\right)$$

where c_{R_n} is the rank order number of the nth relevant document to be retrieved

c is the co-ordination level at which the *nth relevant document* is retrieved

x_c is the additional number of *documents* retrieved at coordination level c. (i.e. those not retrieved at a higher co-ordination level)

y_c is the additional number of *relevant documents* retrieved at co-ordination level c. (i.e. those not retrieved at a higher co-ordination level)

X_c is the total number of documents retrieved before searching at co-ordination level c. (i.e. at higher coordination levels)

Y_c is the total number of *relevant documents* retrieved before searching at co-ordination level c. (i.e. higher co-ordination levels)

c_{R_n} is taken to the nearest whole number but if its value falls exactly between two whole numbers, it is taken to the lower whole number for odd numbered questions and to the higher whole number for even numbered questions.

ABSTR NEW QS
TOP 15 RELEVANT

1	792	7	712
2	797	19	711
3	799	97	713
4	324	101	708
5	683	149	709
6	992		
7	712		
8	707		
9	416		
10	321		
11	655		
12	33H		
13	874		
14	316		
15	919		

RNK REC = 0·0402
LOG PRE = 0·2509
NOR REC = 0·6328
NOR PRE = 0·3390
OVERALL = 0·2911
NOR OVR = 0·3390

INDEX NEW QS
TOP 15 RELEVANT

1	792	3	712
2	683	69	708
3	712	80	711
4	797	139	713
5	988	153	709
6	572		
7	437		
8	799		
9	682		
10	675		
11	670		
12	316		
13	681		
14	701		
15	707		

RNK REC = 0·0338
LOG PRE = 0·2433
NOR REC = 0·5600
NOR PRE = 0·3115
OVERALL = 0·2771
NOR OVR = 0·3115

CRAN CONCON
INDEX F NULL
TOP 15 RELEVANT

1	597	6	708
2	792	25	712
3	717	46	711
4	799	102	709
5	748	136	713
6	708		
7	316		
8	451		
9	11A		
10	37I		
11	683		
12	10A		
13	670		
14	916		
15	08D		

RNK REC = 0·0476
LOG PRE = 0·2605
NOR REC = 0·6923
NOR PRE = 0·3717
OVERALL = 0·3081
NOR OVR = 0·3717

FIGURE 11 EXAMPLES OF RANKED OUTPUT OBTAINED WITH SMART FOR QUESTION 147

Q	REL	1	2	3	4	5	6 -7	8 -10	11 -15	16 -20	21 -30	31 -50	51 -75	76 -100	101 -125	126 -150	151 -175	176 -200
79	3	x									x					x		
100	4		x							x	x					x		
116	6							x		x	x	x	x		x			
118	5	x					x	x			xx							
119	6			x		x	x				x		xx					
121	3	x	x	x														
122	5	x				x		x			x	x						
123	4	x		x		x											x	
126	2	x	x															
130	4	x						x	x		x							
132	4				x							x			x		x	
136	6		x	x		x	x	xx										
137	6		x			x		xx	xx									
141	1	x																
145	12	x	x	x	x			x	x	x		xxx	x	x				
146	9		x	x	x	x			x		x	x		x		x		
147	5							x			x		x			x	x	
148	4	x	x		x		x											
167	4	x				x		x						x				
170	2		x											x				
181	2				x						x							
182	4				x									x	x			x
189	2										x	x						
190	7	x	x	x			x		x			x			x			
223	2	x	x															
224	5								x		x	x	x	x				
225	6							x	x		x	x			x	x		
226	7	x	x	x		x						xx	x					
227	2	x		x														
230	7	x	x					x		x	x	xx						
250	8	x	x	x		x	x	x	xx									
261	4	x	x	x	x													
264	2	x	x															
266	5								x	x	x	x		x				
268	5	x	x	x	x		x											
269	4	x	x		x		x											
272	4	x	x		x					x								
273	7	x	x	x	x		x		x		x							
274	5				x		x			x			x			x		
317	2					x		x										
323	5					x			x	x	x	x						
360	8		x		x	x	x	x	x	xx								
Totals		23	21	13	13	12	11	16	14	10	18	17	8	7	5	6	3	1
Recall		12	22	29	35	41	47	56	62	67	76	85	89	92	95	98	99	100
Precision		55	51	45	42	39	32	26	20	16	12	8	6	4	4	3	3	2

FIGURE 12 DOCUMENT OUTPUT CUT-OFF SCORE SHEET FOR INDEX LANGUAGE I.1

With Question 100, no documents are retrieved at a co-ordination level higher than four, so for this question, the various values are as follows:

Question 100

At level c = 4, then $x_4 = 3$, $y_4 = 1$, $X_4 = 0$, $Y_4 = 0$
At level c = 3, then $x_3 = 50$, $y_3 = 2$, $X_3 = 3$, $Y_3 = 1$
At level c = 2, then $x_2 = 21$, $y_2 = 0$, $X_2 = 53$, $Y_2 = 3$
At level c = 1, then $x_1 = 97$, $y_1 = 1$, $X_1 = 74$, $Y_1 = 3$

∴ For Relevant Document 1, retrieved at level 4:

$$4R_1 = 0 + (1 - 0)\left(\frac{3 + 1}{1 + 1}\right) = 0 + 2 = 2$$

For Relevant Document 2, retrieved at level 3:

$$3R_2 = 3 + (2 - 1)\left(\frac{50 + 1}{2 + 1}\right) = 3 + 17 = 20$$

For Relevant Document 3, retrieved at level 3:

$$3R_3 = 3 + (3 - 1)\left(\frac{50 + 1}{2 + 1}\right) = 3 + 34 = 37$$

For Relevant Document 4, retrieved at level 1:

$$1R_4 = 74 + (4 - 3)\left(\frac{97 + 1}{1 + 1}\right) + 74 = 49 = 126$$

The normalized recall ratio was obtained by taking the sum of the recall ratios of seventeen standardized cut-off groups, and dividing by seventeen. Figure 12 shows a typical score sheet based on simulated ranking for forty-two questions with a single language while Fig. 13 presents the results for eight single term index languages.

As Salton had used the Cranfield test collection with the SMART system, it was possible to check the proposed method, and this showed that the Cranfield normalized recall ratios produced a performance ranking which closely matched that obtained with the original SMART measure. This being the case, the results of the tests on thirty-three index languages were recalculated to give the normalized recall ratios.

It must be emphasized that, for reasons which are considered at length in Chapter 5 reference 4, the use of a document output cut-off method means that recall ratios and precision ratios are interdependent. For a single system, the inverse relationship of recall and precision will always hold; however, if in a second system there is, as compared to the first, an increase in the recall ratio, then there must always be a corresponding increase in the precision ratio. Because of this, it is immaterial whether one obtains the normalized recall ratio or the normalized precision ratio.

Figure 14 shows the thirty-three index languages tested at Cranfield in a ranked order based on the normalized recall ratios. The relationship of the index languages to each other is shown in detail in figures 3, 4, and 5. Generally speaking, the Single Term index languages are found at the head of the list, the Simple Concept index languages at the bottom and the Controlled Term index languages are in the middle position.

There are a number of points of special interest in this table. The only difference between index language I.1 (rank order 3) and II.1 (rank order 33) is that the latter interfixes the single terms of the former, e.g. the single terms 'axial', 'flow', 'compressor' are combined to form the simple concept term 'axial flow compressor' (Fig. 1). However, the effect of this is to change the ranking from 3 to 33.

The only improvement on the Single Term natural language (I.1) is by the control of synonyms or the confounding of word endings. Any further extension of the classes of terms results in a drop in performance. The reverse, however, is true of the group of Simple Concept index languages, where the performance with the natural language terms is so poor that grouping of terms brings about a significant improvement. Intermediary is a third group of index languages, based upon a controlled term vocabulary. Here the broadening of the basic terms by forming groups with related terms brings about a small loss in performance.

Numerous additional tests were made (and are reported in reference 4) to investigate various factors, such as the level of relevance of the documents, the effect of varying the search procedure, or the effect of various precision devices such as interfixing or partitioning. None of these appear in any way to affect the general results as presented in Fig. 14.

When considering the somewhat unexpected results of this project, one must, of course, bear in mind the environment in which the tests were made, but there appears to be nothing in the test design which could have so consistently influenced the results. Certainly it would be absurd to say that in all situations the most effective form of index language is one that combines simple post-co-ordination with natural language single terms which are uncontrolled except for the grouping of synonyms and terms having the same root. Yet that is what happened in this particular environment, and one can only say that it would be an unusual coincidence if a situation had been selected which was unique in the whole field of science and technology.

ORDER	NORMALISED RECALL		INDEXING LANGUAGE
1	65.82	I-3	Single terms. Word forms
2	65.23	I-2	Single terms. Synonyms
3	65.00	I-1	Single terms. Natural Language
4	64.47	I-6	Single terms. Synonyms, word forms, quasi-synonyms
5	64.41	I-8	Single terms Hierarchy second stage
6	64.05	I-7	Single terms. Hierarchy first stage
7=	63.05	I-5	Single terms. Synonyms. Quasi-synonyms
7=	63.05	II-11	Simple concepts. Hierarchical and alphabetical selection
9	62.88	II-10	Simple concepts. Alphabetical second stage selection
10=	61.76	III-1	Controlled terms. Basic terms
10=	61.76	III-2	Controlled terms. Narrower terms
12	61.17	I-9	Single terms. Hierarchy third stage
13	60.94	IV-3	Abstracts. Natural language
14	60.82	IV-4	Abstracts. Word forms
15	60.11	III-3	Controlled terms. Broader terms
16	59.76	IV-2	Titles. Word forms
17	59.70	III-4	Controlled terms. Related terms
18	59.58	III-5	Controlled terms. Narrower and broader terms
19	59.17	III-6	Controlled terms. Narrower, broader and related terms
20	58.94	IV-1	Titles. Natural language
21	57.41	II-15	Simple concepts. Complete combination
22	57.11	II-9	Simple concepts. Alphabetical first stage selection
23	55.88	II-13	Simple concepts. Complete species and superordinate
24	55.76	II-8	Simple concepts. Hierarchical selection
25	55.41	II-12	Simple concepts. Complete species
26	55.05	II-5	Simple concepts. Selected species and superordinate
27	53.88	II-7	Simple concepts. Selected coordinate and collateral
28	53.52	II-3	Simple concepts. Selected species
29	52.47	II-14	Simple concepts. Complete collateral
30	52.05	II-4	Simple concepts. Superordinate
31	51.82	II-6	Simple concepts. Selected coordinate
32	47.41	II-2	Simple concepts. Synonyms
33	44.64	II-1	Simple concepts. Natural language

FIGURE 14 ORDER OF EFFECTIVENESS BASED ON NORMALISED RECALL FOR 33 CRANFIELD INDEX LANGUAGES

DOCUMENT OUTPUT CUT-OFF	I-1 R	I-1 P	I-2 R	I-2 P	I-3 R	I-3 P	I-5 R	I-5 P	I-6 R	I-6 P	I-7 R	I-7 P	I-8 R	I-8 P	I-9 R	I-9 P
1	12	55	12	57	12	57	13	60	11	52	10	48	9	43	8	36
2	22	51	23	54	23	54	19	45	21	49	21	49	19	44	16	37
3	29	45	30	47	30	48	28	44	29	46	29	46	28	44	22	34
4	35	42	36	42	37	43	32	38	35	42	33	39	32	38	27	32
5	41	39	41	39	43	40	36	34	40	38	40	38	38	36	33	31
6-7	47	32	48	32	48	32	45	30	47	32	46	31	46	31	40	27
8-10	56	26	55	26	56	26	53	25	55	26	53	25	55	26	47	22
11-15	62	20	63	20	64	20	59	19	62	19	63	20	62	20	58	18
16-20	67	16	67	16	70	17	65	15	66	16	67	16	68	16	63	15
21-30	76	12	76	12	76	12	73	12	73	12	76	12	76	12	72	11
31-50	85	8	85	8	86	8	82	8	83	8	86	8	85	8	82	8
51-75	89	6	89	6	89	6	88	6	89	6	91	6	91	6	89	6
76-100	92	4	92	4	93	4	91	4	92	4	93	4	93	4	93	4
101-125	95	4	95	4	95	4	94	4	95	4	95	4	96	4	95	4
126-150	98	3	98	3	98	3	96	3	97	3	97	3	98	3	97	3
151-175	99	3	99	3	99	3	98	3	99	3	99	3	99	3	98	3
176-200	100	2	100	2	100	2	100	2	100	2	100	2	100	2	100	2
NORMALISED RECALL	65.00		65.23		65.82		63.05		64.47		64.05		64.41		61.17	

SINGLE TERM LANGUAGES

I-1	Natural language
I-2	Synonyms
I-3	Word endings
I-5	Synonyms and quasi-synonyms
I-6	Synonyms, word endings, and quasi-synonyms
I-7	Hierarchical reduction first stage
I-8	Hierarchical reduction second stage
I-9	Hierarchical reduction third stage

FIGURE 13 RECALL AND PRECISION RATIOS AND NORMALISED RECALL FOR SINGLE TERM INDEX LANGUAGES
(R = Recall Ratio, P = Precision Ratio)

It is necessary to try to explain what has been happening in these tests so as to bring about the results as given. It must be emphasized that with the exception of Languages IV.1, IV.2, IV.3, and IV.4, in all the systems shown in Fig. 14 everything has been held constant except the index language. This is to say that we are dealing with the same documents which have all been indexed in the same way; a set of questions which have been searched in exactly the same way for each index language; a set of relevance decisions which are always the same. The only variation is the relationship of the index terms to the natural language terms of the documents.

This can be considered as a matter of specificity of the index terms. In Index Language I.1 the specificity is exactly the same as that of the single terms of the natural language. Synonyms and word endings provide, overall, a slight reduction in specificity, and also give a small improvement in performance. However, beyond this stage, the further reductions in specificity, provided by the formation of classes based on quasi-synonyms or hierarchical grouping, results in a loss in performance.

In Index Language II.1 the specificity is exactly the same as the concepts of the natural language, and these represent a higher level of specificity that the single terms. 'Constant wall temperature' is a far more specific index term than the separate single terms 'Constant', 'Wall' and 'Temperature', and, as previously noted, the result of this higher level of specificity brings about a large fall in performance. Because the Simple Concept index terms are over-specific, it is found that the broadening of the classes by any means brings about an improvement in performance. However, this improvement does not result in any Simple Concept index language reaching the level of performance of that obtained by the single terms.

The Controlled Term index languages, with ranks of 10, 11, 14, 16, 17 and 18, occupy an intermediary position. One can suggest that two conflicting factors are present. Some of the index terms were compound terms (e.g. 'Pressure welding' or 'Hydraulic equipment') and were therefore more specific than the single terms. On the other hand, a number of natural language terms were grouped to form a single term, and thereby maintain Rule T–1 of the E.J.C. Thesaurus of Engineering Terms, which warns against being too specific. It is difficult to say which of these factors was responsible for the loss in performance as compared to single terms; the only clue is that any broadening of the classes from the basic terms give a slight loss in performance, and it would therefore seem that, overall, the terms were not sufficiently specific.

This matter of specificity is related to the number of index terms (but *not* code terms) in the index language and if we plot the normalized recall ratio against the number of terms in the index language the result is shown in Fig. 15. This indicates that in the environment of this test, an index language having 2,541 terms was the most efficient.

The second factor which appears to have an important effect on performance is the level of exhaustivity of indexing. Index Languages I.1, IV.1 and IV.3 represent three levels of exhaustivity of indexing; figures are also available for Index Language I.1 when the exhaustivity is reduced by omitting terms weighted 3 and then omitting terms weighted 2 and 3. Figure 16 shows the average number of terms of these five levels of exhaustivity and the normalized recall ratios, and the plot of figure 17 shows that the performance is optimised at a level of 33 terms; below this figure the results indicate that insufficient terms are being used, but the sixty terms of the abstracts would appear to be at too high a level of exhaustivity, since there is a large drop in performance.

Index Language	Number of terms	Normalized recall Ratio
I.9	306	61·17%
I.7	1,217	64·05%
I.3	2,541	65·82%
I.2	2,988	65·23%
I.1	3,094	65·00%
II.13	6,000*	55·88%
II.4	8,000*	52·05%
II.1	10,000*	44·64%

* *Estimated*

FIGURE 15 NORMALIZED RECALL RATIOS FOR INDEX LANGUAGES WITH VARYING NUMBERS OF INDEX TERMS

Index Language		Average No. of Terms	Normalized Recall Ratio
Titles		7	59·76%
Level 1	Single Term Natural Language	14	62·88%
Level 2	Single Term Natural Language	22	63·57%
Level 3	Single Term Natural Language	33	65·00%
Abstracts		Approx. 60	60·94%

FIGURE 16 NORMALIZED RECALL RATIOS FOR FIVE LEVELS OF EXHAUSTIVITY OF INDEXING

A clue as to how the exhaustivity of indexing and the specificity of the index language work together is provided by the comparison of Index Languages IV.1 with IV.2, and IV.3 with IV.4. With Index Language IV.1 where only the terms in the titles were used, the exhaustivity is too low. By moving to Index Language IV.2, where word forms have been confounded, the lower specificity results in an improvement of the normalized recall ratio from 58.94 per cent to 59.76 per cent. With Index Language IV.3, it has been shown that the use of all the terms in the abstracts is at too high a level of exhaustivity of indexing; when in Index Language IV4 word forms are confounded, the lower specificity now results in a loss in performance from 60.94 per cent to 60.82 per cent.

As with Cranfield I, the outcome of this test is to raise more new questions than questions it answers. It would be absurd for any organization to abandon conventional indexing and controlled index languages, whether thesauri or classification, on the basis of these test results. It would, to the author, seem equally absurd to aver that any system is operating at maximum efficiency

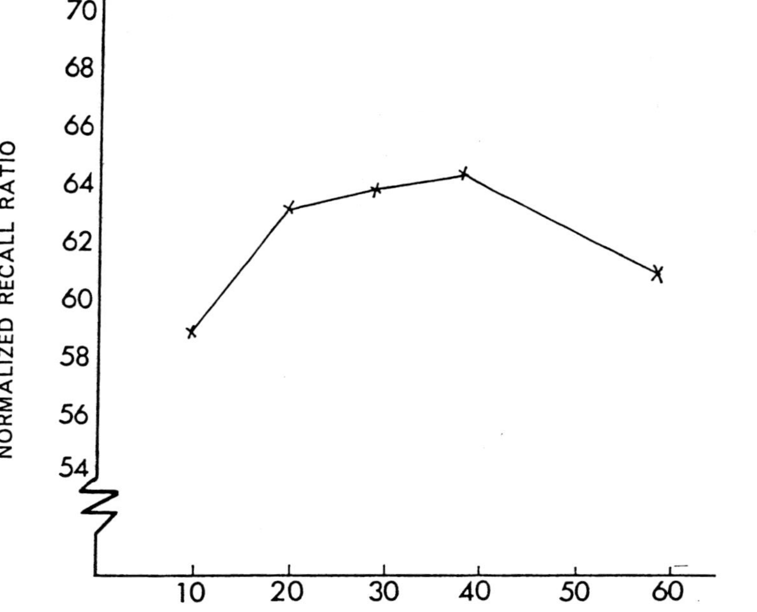

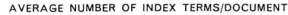

FIGURE 17 PLOT OF NORMALIZED RECALL RATIOS FOR FIVE LEVELS OF EXHAUSTIVITY OF INDEXING

unless a careful evaluation of the operational and economic characteristics of the system has been made. For this purpose, this test has shown that the use of single terms in the natural language, with true synonyms and word endings confounded, is a perfectly reasonable—and relatively simple—index language to use for comparison purposes. In practically all circumstances it would seem that such an index language is more economical than any other; it will be interesting to see whether in some cases it also turns out to be more efficient.

REFERENCES

1 CLEVERDON, C. W. Report on the first stage of an investigation into the comparative efficiency of indexing systems. Cranfield, 1960.

2 CLEVERDON, C. W. Report on the testing and analysis of an investigation into the comparative efficiency of indexing systems. Cranfield, 1962.

3 AITCHISON, J., *and* CLEVERDON, C. W. Report of a test on the Index of Metallurgical Literature of Western Reserve University. Cranfield, 1963.

4 CLEVERDON, C. W., MILLS, J., *and* KEEN, M. Factors determining the performance of indexing systems (Aslib-Cranfield Research Project). 2 vols. Cranfield, 1966.

5 SALTON, G. The evaluation of computer-based information retrieval systems. In Proceedings of the 1965 Congress of the International Federation for Documentation, pp. 125–33. Washington: Spartan Books, and London: Macmillan, 1965.

This study provides a summary of the SMART *system organization with emphasis on the evaluation procedures incorporated into the system. Experimental retrieval results are then given using document collections in the areas of computer science, documentation, and aerodynamics. In particular, the retrieval effectiveness of the following system parameters is covered: demand length, query-document matching functions, term weights, word stem generation methods, synonym recognition use, phrase recognition procedures, and hierarchical expansion methods. The evaluation results are used to derive design criteria for modern information systems.*

7

COMPUTER EVALUATION OF INDEXING AND TEXT PROCESSING†

G. SALTON and M. E. LESK

7-1 INTRODUCTION

Throughout the technical world, a growing interest is evident in the design and implementation of mechanized information systems. Over the last few years, the general feeling that something should be done to help organize and store some of the available information resources has given way to the widespread impression that modern computing equipment may in fact be capable of alleviating and solving to some extent the so-called information problem. Specifically, it is believed that the required capacity to store many data or document collections of interest does exist, that procedures are available for analyzing and organizing the information in storage, and that real-time software and hardware can be used to ensure the retrieval of stored information in response to requests from a given user population in a convenient form and at little cost in time and effort [1], [2], [3].

Before investing the necessary resources required for the implementation of sophisticated information services, it is necessary to generate the detailed systems specifications and to determine which of many possible alternative design features should in fact be implemented. This, in turn, must be made to depend on experimentation in a controlled environment to test and evaluate the effectiveness of various possible search and analysis procedures. The SMART document retrieval system, which has been operating on an IBM 7094 for over two years, has been used extensively to test a large variety of automatic retrieval procedures, including fully automatic information analysis methods, automatic procedures for dictionary construction, and iterative search techniques based on user interaction with the system [4], [5], [6], [7].

The present study summarizes the results obtained with the SMART system over a two-year period starting in 1964 and presents evaluation output based on the processing of three document collections in three different subject fields. Conclusions are drawn concerning the most likely analysis methods to be implemented in an operational environment. The emphasis throughout is on text analysis procedures because they form an important part of a document-handling system. Several operational problems, including the actual network implementation of a retrieval system are not covered; cost and timing estimates are also excluded because these are tied directly to the specific environment within which a given system actually operates.

First, the basic features of the SMART system are described, and then the design of the main experiments is outlined; this includes the statistical procedures used to test the significance of the evaluation output obtained. Then the principal evaluation results are presented, and tentative conclusions are reached concerning the effectiveness of automatic text analysis procedures as part of future information systems. The results derived from the present experiments are also compared briefly with the output obtained with several other testing systems.

7-2 THE SMART SYSTEM

7-2-A Basic Organization

The SMART system is a fully automatic document retrieval system operating on the IBM 7094. The system does not rely on manually assigned keywords or index terms for the identification of documents and search requests, nor does it use primarily the frequency of occurrence of certain words or phrases included in the document texts. Instead, the system goes beyond simple word-matching procedures by using a variety of intellectual aids in the form of synonym dictionaries, hierarchical arrangements of subject identifiers, phrase-generating methods, and the like, in order to obtain the content identifications useful for the retrieval process.

The following facilities incorporated into the SMART system for purposes of document analysis are of principal interest:

(a) A system for separating English words into stems and affixes which can be used to reduce incoming texts into *word stem* form.

†This study was published as Section III in *Scientific Report ISR-12*, June 1967. It also appeared in *Journal of the ACM*, Vol. 15, No. 1, January 1968, pp. 8–36.

(b) A synonym dictionary, or thesaurus, which replaces significant word stems by *concept numbers*, each concept representing a class of related word stems.

(c) A *hierarchical arrangement* of the concepts included in the thesaurus which makes it possible, given any concept number, to find its "parent" in the hierarchy, its "sons," its "brothers," and any of a set of possible cross references.

(d) *Statistical association* methods which compute similarity coefficients between words, word stems, or concepts, based on co-occurrence patterns between these entities in the sentences of a document or in the documents of a collection; associated items can then serve as content identifiers in addition to the original ones.

(e) *Syntactic analysis* methods which permit the recognition and use, as indicators of document content, of phrases consisting of several words or concepts where each element of a phrase must hold a specified syntactic relation to each other element.

(f) *Statistical phrase* recognition methods which operate like the preceding syntactic procedures by using a preconstructed phrase dictionary, except that no test is made to ensure that the syntactic relationships between phrase components are satisfied.

(g) *Request-document matching* procedures which make it possible to use a variety of different correlation methods to compare analyzed documents with analyzed requests, including concept weight adjustments and variations in the length of the document texts being analyzed.

Stored documents and search requests are processed by the system without any prior manual analysis using one of several hundred automatic content analysis methods; those documents which most nearly match a given search request are identified. Specifically, a correlation coefficient is computed to indicate the degree of similarity between each document and each search request, and documents are then ranked in decreasing order of the correlation coefficient [4], [5], [6]. Then a cutoff can be selected, and documents above the chosen cutoff can be withdrawn from the file and turned over to the user as answers to the search request.

The search process may be controlled by the user in that a request can be processed first in a standard mode. After analysis of the output which is produced, feedback information can then be returned to the system where it is used to reprocess the request under altered conditions. The new output can be examined again, and the search can be iterated until the right kind and amount of information are obtained [7], [8].

The SMART systems organization makes it possible to evaluate the effectiveness of the various processing methods by comparing the output obtained from a variety of different runs. This is achieved by processing the *same* search requests against the *same* document collections several times, while making selected changes in the analysis procedures between runs. By comparing the performance of the search requests under different processing conditions, it is then possible to determine the relative effectiveness of the various analysis methods. The evaluation procedures actually used are described in the next section.

7-2-B Evaluation Process

The evaluation of an information search and retrieval system can be carried out in many different ways depending on the type of system considered—operational, experimental with user populations, or laboratory—on the viewpoint taken—the user, the manager, or the operator—and on other factors—such as the special aims of the evaluation study. A large number of different variables may affect the results of any evaluation process. These include the kind of user population, the type and coverage of the document collection, the indexing tools, the analysis and search methods incorporated into the system, the input–output equipment, the operating efficiency, cost and time lag, and many others.

In the present context, the user's viewpoint is taken, and the overriding criterion of systems effectiveness is taken to be the ability of the system to satisfy the user's information need. Management criteria such as cost are not considered, even though in the final analysis the problem is of primary importance; the most effective system will not be of use if the operations are too costly to be performed. However, costs are difficult to measure in an experimental situation where unusual fluctuations may occur because of many extraneous factors. Furthermore, the immediate need is for a measurement of the effectiveness of the intellectual tools used to analyze and search the stored information, since these are responsible in large part for the retrieval results. Costs can be taken into account later, for example, by providing several classes of service at varying cost.

The evaluation measures actually used are based on the standard *recall* and *precision* measures. In an operational situation, where information needs may vary from user to user, some customers may require high recall—the retrieval of almost everything that is likely to be of interest—while others may prefer high precision—the rejection of everything likely to be useless. Everything else being equal, a perfect system is one which exhibits both a high recall and a high precision.

If a cut is made through the document collection to distinguish retrieved items from nonretrieved on the one hand, and if procedures are available for separating relevant items from nonrelevant ones on the other hand, the standard recall R and standard precision P may be defined as follows:

$$R = \frac{\text{Number of items retrieved and relevant}}{\text{Total relevant in collection}},$$

and

$$P = \frac{\text{Number of items retrieved and relevant}}{\text{Total retrieved in collection}}.$$

The computation of these measures is straightforward only if exhaustive relevance judgments are available for each document with respect to each search request, and if the cutoff value which distinguishes retrieved from nonretrieved material can be determined unambiguously [8], [9], [10].

In the evaluation work carried out with the SMART system, manually derived, exhaustive relevance judgments are used because all the document collections processed are relatively small. Moreover, the choice of a unique cutoff is avoided by computing the precision for various recall values and exhibiting a plot showing recall against precision. An example of such a graph is shown in Fig. 7-1 for query Q145, processed against a collection of 200 documents in aerodynamics. A total of 12 documents in the collection were judged relevant to the request, the relevance judgments being performed by a subject expert independently of the retrieval system. The ranks of the relevant documents produced by the search system after ordering of the documents in decreasing correlation order are shown in Fig. 7-1(a). For the retrieval process illustrated in Fig. 7-1, these ranks range from 1 for the relevant document with the highest request-document correlation to 78 for the relevant item with the lowest correlation. By choosing successive cutoff values after the retrieval of 1, 2, 3, . . . , n documents, and computing recall and precision values at each point, a recall-precision table can be constructed, as shown in Fig. 7-1(b). The recall-precision graph obtained from this table is represented in Fig. 7-1(c).

RELEVANT DOCUMENTS		
Rank	*Number*	*Correlation*
1	80	.5084
2	102	.4418
3	81	.4212
10	82	.2843
11	193	.2731
14	83	.2631
15	87	.2594
20	88	.2315
40	86	.1856
50	109	.1631
69	84	.1305
78	85	.1193

(a)

RECALL-PRECISION AFTER RETRIEVAL OF X DOCUMENTS		
X	*Recall*	*Precision*
1	0.0833	1.0000
2	0.1667	1.0000
3	0.2500	1.0000
9	0.2500	0.3333
10	0.3333	0.4000
11	0.4167	0.4545
13	0.4167	0.3846
14	0.5000	0.4286
15	0.5833	0.4667
19	0.5833	0.3684
20	0.6667	0.4000
39	0.6667	0.2051
40	0.7500	0.2250
49	0.7500	0.1837
50	0.8333	0.2000
68	0.8333	0.1470
69	0.9167	0.1594
77	0.9167	0.1428
78	1.0000	0.1538

(b)

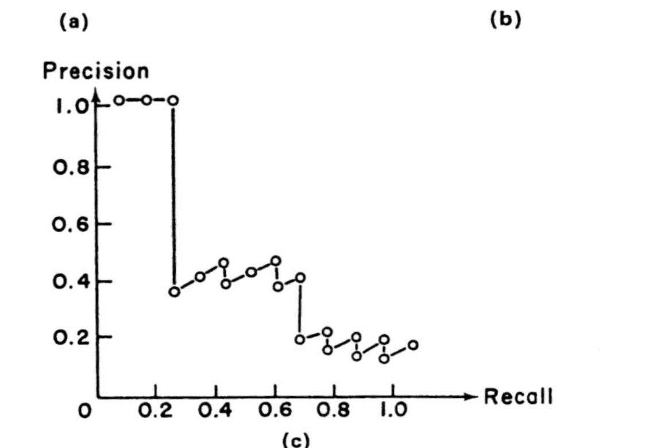

(c)

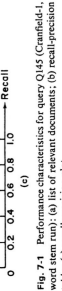

Fig. 7-1 Performance characteristics for query Q145 (Cranfield-1, word stem run): (a) list of relevant documents; (b) recall-precision table; (c) recall-precision plot.

Recall-precision graphs, such as that of Fig. 7-1(c), have been criticized because a number of parameters are obscured when plotting recall against precision—for example, the size of the retrieved document set and the size of the collection [11]. Such plots are, however, effective in summarizing the performance of retrieval methods averaged over many search requests, and they can be used advantageously to select analysis methods which fit certain specific operating ranges. Thus, if it is desired to select a procedure which favors the retrieval of *all* relevant material, then one must concentrate on the high recall region; similarly, if *only* relevant material is desired, the high precision region is of importance. In general, it is possible to obtain high recall only at a substantial cost in precision and vice versa [8], [9], [10].

In addition to the standard recall and standard precision measures, whose values depend on the size of the retrieved document set, it is also possible to use indicators which are independent of the retrieved set. In particular, since the SMART system produces ranked document output in decreasing order of correlation between documents and search requests, evaluation measures can be generated based on the ranks of the set of relevant documents, as determined by the automatic retrieval process, compared with the ranks of the relevant documents for an ideal system where all relevant items are retrieved before any nonrelevant ones are retrieved.

Two particularly attractive measures with this property are normalized recall and normalized precision, which are defined as follows [7], [9]:

$$R_{\text{norm}} = 1 - \frac{\sum_{i=1}^{n} r_i - \sum_{i=1}^{n} i}{n(N-n)},$$

and

$$P_{\text{norm}} = 1 - \frac{\sum_{i=1}^{n} \log r_i - \sum_{i=1}^{n} \log i}{\log N!/(N-n)!\,n!}$$

where n is the size of the relevant document set, N is the size of the total document collection, and r_i is the rank of the ith relevant document when the documents are arranged in decreasing order of their correlation with the search request.

These measures range from 1 for a perfect system, in which all relevant items are placed at the top of the retrieved list, to 0 for the worst case where all nonrelevant

(c) Using the cutoff value calculated in this manner for the number of retrieved documents, the precision value is generated corresponding to the specified recall.

(d) The precision values obtained for a given recall value are averaged over a number of search requests, and the resulting point is added to the recall-precision plot.

(e) The ten individual points on the plot are joined to produce an average recall-precision curve.

Averaged evaluation results are presented for three different document collections in Sec. 7-3.

7-2-C Significance Computations

For each search request and each processing method, the evaluation procedure incorporated into the SMART system produces 14 different statistics, including 4 global statistics (rank recall, log precision, normalized recall, and normalized precision), and 10 local statistics (standard precision for 10 recall levels). A problem then arises concerning the use of these 14 statistics for the assessment of systems performance. In theory, comparisons between different processing methods are easy to make by contrasting, for example, the recall-precision plots obtained in each case. In practice, it is difficult to draw "hard" conclusions because the variation in performance between individual requests is large, because the 14 measures have different ranges, and because it is unclear a priori whether the magnitude of a given recall or precision value is significant or not. In particular, given a specified recall or precision value, it is of interest to determine whether values as large, or larger, as the given one could be expected under random circumstances, or whether on the contrary the probability of obtaining a given specified value for an average system is very small.

Because of the large request variance and the differences in the range of the various parameters, the significance computations incorporated into the SMART system are based on *paired comparisons* between the request performance using processing method A, and the performance using method B. In particular, the difference in magnitude is computed for each of the 14 pairs of statistics obtained for each request for each pair of processing methods. These differences are then averaged over many requests, and statistical computations are used to transform the averaged differences into probability measurements. Each of the 14 values obtained in this manner represents the probability that if the performance level of the two methods A and B were in fact equally high for the given statistic (except for random variations in the test results), then a test value as large as the one actually observed would occur for a system. A probability value of 0.05 is usually taken as an upper bound in judging whether a deviation in test values is significant or not. Using this probability value as a limit, the corresponding test difference would in fact be significant 19 times out of 20; only 1 time out of 20 would two equally effective systems be expected to produce as large a test difference.

Because it is difficult to judge systems performance by using 14 different probability values corresponding to the 14 evaluation measures, an *aggregate probability*

items are retrieved before any relevant ones. Furthermore under certain circumstances, the normalized measures can be shown to be closely related to the standard measures as follows [12]:

$$R_{\text{norm}} \approx \frac{1}{N} \sum_{i=1}^{n} R(i),$$

when the number of relevant documents n is small compared to the collection size N, and

$$P_{\text{norm}} \approx \frac{1}{N} \sum_{i=1}^{n} P(i)$$

for large N and not too small n. $R(i)$ and $P(i)$ correspond, respectively, to the standard recall and precision values after the retrieval of i documents.

Two further overall measures of retrieval effectiveness, analogous to the normalized measures but somewhat simpler to compute, are the "rank recall" and "log precision" measures, defined as

$$\text{Rank recall} = \frac{\sum_{i=1}^{n} i}{\sum_{i=1}^{n} r_i},$$

and

$$\text{Log precision} = \frac{\sum_{i=1}^{n} \log i}{\sum_{i=1}^{n} \log r_i},$$

where again n is equal to the number of relevant documents, and r_i is the rank (in decreasing correlation order) of the ith relevant document. Like the normalized measures, rank recall and log precision are functions of the rank of the relevant documents, but contrary to the earlier situation, these measures do not take into account the collection size N.

Under normal circumstances, the results of a systems evaluation must reflect overall system performance, rather than the performance for individual requests only. In these circumstances, it is convenient to process many search requests and to use an average performance value as a measure of retrieval effectiveness [12]. For the overall evaluation measures (normalized recall, normalized precision, rank recall, and log precision), the averaging process presents no problem because only a single set of values is obtained in each case for each request. The averaging method is more complex for the standard recall-precision graph, since a continuous set of values is involved, and the number of relevant documents differs from request to request. In the SMART system, the averaging process for the recall-precision graph corresponding to many search requests is performed as follows:

(a) Ten specified standard recall values are selected ranging from 0.1 to 1.0.

(b) For each recall level, the number of documents which must be retrieved in order to obtain the specified level is determined.

value is computed from 14 individual probabilities. The significance of this aggregate depends on the independence of the various individual tests.

Two separate testing procedures are incorporated into the SMART system. The first one uses the well-known *t test* based on Student's t distribution [13]. This test requires an underlying normal distribution of the data used in the test process, as well as the independence among the search requests processed against the document collections. The t test process takes into account the actual magnitude of the differences for the statistics being calculated, and the resulting probabilities are considered to be reliable indicators of system differences.

A less demanding testing procedure is furnished by the *sign test*, where the magnitude of the differences in the statistics is not taken into account, but the sign of the differences is (that is, an indication of whether method A provides a larger test result than B or vice versa) [14]. An attractive feature of the sign test is that normality of the input data is not required, and since this normality is generally hard to prove for statistics derived from a request-document correlation process, the sign test probabilities may provide a better indicator of system performance than the t test.

The t test computations are performed as follows: let m_{ijA} be the value of statistic i for request j, using method A (for example, the value of the rank recall or the normalized recall). Then, given two processing methods A and B, and a set of k requests, the average of the differences for statistic i are computed. Specifically,

$$d_{ij} = m_{ijA} - m_{ijB},$$

and

$$D_i = \frac{1}{k} \sum_{j=1}^{k} d_{ij}.$$

The difference computations for two statistics (rank recall and log precision) are shown in Table 7-1. The average differences are then used to obtain the standard deviation of the differences $(SD)_i$ and the t test values T_i, where

$$T_i = \frac{D_i}{(SD)_i} k.$$

The t-test values T_i are now converted to probabilities P_{ti} using Student's t distribution with k degrees of freedom.

The probabilities derived from the 14 statistics are then used to compute an aggregate probability by first converting the two-tailed t test to a one-tailed test, changing each probability to chi-square, adding the chi-square values, and finally reconverting to a probability P_t, using a chi-square distribution with 28 degrees of freedom [13]. Specifically, let s be the sign of the sum of the differences D_i, or

$$s = \text{sign}\left(\sum_i D_i\right).$$

Then

$$\text{if sign } D_i = s \Rightarrow P'_{ti} = \tfrac{1}{2} P_{ti},$$

Table 7-1

COMPUTATION OF RECALL AND PRECISION DIFFERENCES FOR INDIVIDUAL REQUESTS

(Method A: Stem Concon; Method B: Thesaurus)

REQUEST NAME	RANK RECALL		DIFFERENCE	LOG PRECISION		DIFFERENCE
	Method A	*Method B*		*Method A*	*Method B*	
AUTOMATA PHR	0.5238	0.9649	−0.4411	0.7126	0.9881	−0.2755
COMP SYSTEMS	0.0725	0.1228	−0.0503	0.3783	0.4806	−0.1023
COMPS-ASSEMB	0.3714	0.7428	−0.3714	0.8542	0.9453	−0.0911
CORE MEMORY	0.0691	0.1064	−0.0373	0.3157	0.3695	−0.0538
DIFFERNTL EQ	0.5298	0.7574	−0.2276	0.8620	0.9219	−0.0599
ERROR CONTRL	0.1460	0.1875	−0.0415	0.5342	0.5972	−0.0630
M10-COUNTERS	0.8182	0.7347	0.0835	0.8682	0.8599	0.0083
M2-TRANSMIT	0.0522	0.0963	−0.0441	0.2819	0.4698	−0.1879
M3-INFORM	0.1968	0.3134	−0.1166	0.6300	0.7666	−0.1366
M8-STORAGE	0.0375	0.2763	−0.2388	0.2670	0.4666	−0.1996
MISSILE TRAK	1.0000	0.7500	0.2500	1.0000	0.6309	0.3691
MORSE CODE	1.0000	1.0000	0.0000	1.0000	1.0000	0.0000
PATTERN RECG	1.0000	1.0000	0.0000	1.0000	1.0000	0.0000
RANDOM NUMBS	0.0517	0.2000	−0.1483	0.1750	0.3408	−0.1658
SOLSTAT CIRC	0.2766	0.3402	−0.0636	0.6921	0.7912	−0.0991
SWITCH FUNCS	0.3529	0.4444	−0.0915	0.7416	0.8005	−0.0589
THIN FILMS	0.2157	0.8462	−0.6305	0.6294	0.9242	−0.2948
Total	6.7142	8.8833	−2.1691	10.9422	12.3531	−1.4109
Average value over 17 requests	0.3950	0.5225	−0.1276	0.6437	0.7267	−0.0830

alternatively

$$\text{if sign } D_i \neq s \Rightarrow P'_{ti} = 1 - \tfrac{1}{2} P_{ti}.$$

The chi square of the sum is now obtained such that

$$\chi^2 = -\sum_{i=1}^{14} - 2 \log P'_{ti}.$$

Finally, this value is converted to the desired probability P_t.

The t-test computations are shown for two sample analysis methods A and B in Table 7-2. The values in the first two columns of Table 7-2 represent averages over 17 search requests for each of the 14 evaluation measures. The final probabilities P_{ti} range from a high of 0.107 for the standard precision at recall value 1, to a low of 0.0007 for the normalized precision. The final probability value P_t is smaller than 1.10^{-4}, thus indicating that the combination algorithm concentrates on the significant tests, while ignoring the less significant ones. The validity of the process depends on

Table 7-2

t-TEST COMPUTATIONS FOR 14 DIFFERENT RECALL AND PRECISION MEASURES

(Averages over 17 requests, Method *A*: Stem Concon; Method *B*: Thesaurus)

	EVALUATION MEASURE		AVERAGE VALUE		DIFFERENCE OF AVERAGE	STANDARD DEVIATION	*t*-TEST VALUE	PROBABILITY
			Method A	*Method B*				
1.	Rank recall		0.3950	0.5225	−0.1276	2.07E–01	2.54E 00	0.0219
2.	Log precision		0.6437	0.7267	−0.0830	1.47E–01	2.33E 00	0.0334
3.	Normed recall		0.9233	0.9675	−0.0442	5.35E–02	3.41E 00	0.0036
4.	Normed precision		0.7419	0.8639	−0.1219	1.20E–01	4.19E 00	0.0007
5.	Precision Graph (Precision for ten recall levels)	0.1	0.7385	0.9735	−0.2351	2.88E–01	3.37E 00	0.0039
6.		0.2	0.6544	0.8973	−0.2428	2.82E–01	3.55E 00	0.0026
7.		0.3	0.5844	0.8245	−0.2401	2.51E–01	3.95E 00	0.0011
8.		0.4	0.5326	0.7551	−0.2226	2.39E–01	3.84E 00	0.0014
9.		0.5	0.5187	0.7146	−0.1959	2.00E–01	4.04E 00	0.0009
10.		0.6	0.5035	0.6499	−0.1464	1.59E–01	3.79E 00	0.0016
11.		0.7	0.4452	0.6012	−0.1561	1.79E–01	3.59E 00	0.0024
12.		0.8	0.4091	0.5514	−0.1423	2.24E–01	2.62E 00	0.0184
13.		0.9	0.3794	0.4973	−0.1179	2.29E–01	2.12E 00	0.0499
14.		1.0	0.3106	0.4118	−0.1012	2.44E–01	1.71E 00	0.1070

Combined Significance: Total Chi Square: 1.67E–02
Total probability of *B* over *A*: 0.0000

an assumption of independence among the 14 measures, which is true to a limited extent for the measures used.

The sign test uses the binomial instead of the t distribution to produce a probability value. Specifically, given two processing methods for which the null hypothesis applies (that is, two equivalent methods), each d_{ij} has an equal chance of being positive or negative; moreover, since the search requests are assumed unrelated (independent) and randomly distributed, the signs of the differences are unrelated. The number, let us say M, of positive signs is accordingly distributed binomially with P equal to one-half and k equal to the number of requests.

M can then serve as a statistic to test the null hypothesis by taking large values of M as significant evidence against the equivalence of the two methods tested. Obviously, a test based on rejecting the equivalence hypothesis for large values of M is equivalent to a test based on rejection for small values of M', the number of negative signs. As before, a probability of 0.05 may be taken as an upper limit for rejecting the equivalence assumption.

Since the sign test does not depend on the magnitudes of the differences, the number of positive or negative signs can be cumulated directly. In particular, the number of requests preferring method A is summed over all measures, as well as the number of requests preferring method B. These totals are then subjected to the same testing process, as follows. Let t be a tolerance value, taken as 0.001 for the present test; further, for each statistic i, let

$$k_{ai} = \text{number of } d_{ij}\ (j = 1, \ldots, k) \text{ exceeding } +t,$$
$$k_{bi} = \text{number of } d_{ij} \text{ smaller than } -t,$$

and

$$k_{ci} = \text{number of } d_{ij} \text{ such that } |d_{ij}| \leq t,$$

where the number of requests $k = k_{ai} + k_{bi} + k_{ci}$.

The sign test probability for statistic i is now computed as follows:

Let

$$k_{vi} = k_{ai} + k_{bi},$$

and

$$k_{wi} = \min(k_{ai}, k_{bi}).$$

Then

$$P_{si} = \sum_{j=1}^{k_{wi}} \frac{k_{vi}!}{j!\,(k_{vi} - j)!}\, 2^{-k_{vi}+1}.$$

The overall probability P_s can be cumulated directly for the 14 evaluation measures. Specifically, if

$$k_a = \sum_i k_{ai},$$
$$k_b = \sum_i k_{bi},$$
$$k_v = k_a + k_b,$$

and

$$k_w = \min(k_a, k_b),$$

then

$$P_s = \sum_{j=1}^{k_w} \frac{(k_v)!}{j!\,(k_v - j)!}\, 2^{-k_v+1}.$$

The sign test computations are shown in Table 7-3 for the same processing methods and search requests used previously as examples in Tables 7-1, 7-2, and 7-3. The individual probabilities P_{si} range in values from 0.0010 to 0.1185. Again the overall probability is smaller than 1.10^{-4}; this is also reflected by the fact that method B is preferred 165 times, while A is superior only 26 times, with 47 ties.

Since the 14 statistics used may not be fully independent, a question arises concerning the interpretation of the cumulated t-test probability P_t, and the cumulated sign test probability P_s. As a general rule, the equality hypothesis between two given methods A and B can be rejected safely when both probabilities P_s and P_t do not exceed 0.001 in magnitude, implying that most of the individual probabilities P_{si} and P_{ti} are smaller than 0.05, and when the same test results are obtained for all document collections being tested. If, on the other hand, the values of the final prob-

Table 7-3

Sign Test Computations for 14 Different Recall and Precision Measures

(Averages over 17 Requests, Method A: Stem Concon; Method B: Thesaurus)

Evaluation Measure		Number of Requests Superior (Method A)	Number of Requests Superior (Method B)	Number of Requests Equal (A and B)	Probability (B over A)
Rank recall		2	13	2	0.0074
Log precision		2	13	2	0.0074
Normed recall		2	13	2	0.0074
Normed precision		2	13	2	0.0074
Recall-precision graph	0.1	0	9	8	0.0039
	0.2	0	11	6	0.0010
	0.3	1	12	4	0.0034
	0.4	1	11	5	0.0036
	0.5	0	13	4	0.0002
	0.6	3	11	3	0.0574
	0.7	2	12	3	0.0129
	0.8	3	12	2	0.0352
	0.9	4	11	2	0.1185
	1.0	4	11	2	0.1185
Combined significance for 14 measures		26	165	47	0.0000

abilities are larger, or if the test results differ from one collection to the next, additional tests would seem to be required before a decision can be made.

7-3 EXPERIMENTAL RESULTS

7-3-A Test Environment

The principal parameters controlling the test procedure are listed in Tables 7-4, 7-5, and 7-6, respectively. The main properties of the document collections and search requests are shown in Table 7-4. Specifically, results are given for three document collections in the following subject fields:

(a) Computer Science (IRE-3): a set of 780 abstracts of documents in the computer literature, published in 1959–1961 and used with 34 search requests.

Table 7-4

DOCUMENT COLLECTION AND REQUEST CHARACTERISTICS

	Characteristics		IRE-3	CRAN-1	ADI
Document collection	Number of documents in collection		780	200	82
	Average number of words (all words) per document	full text	–	–	1380
		abstract	88	165	59
		title	9	14	10
	Average number of words (common words deleted) per document	full text	–	–	710
		abstract	49	91	35
		title	5	11	7
	Average number of concepts per analyzed document	full text	–	–	369
		abstract	40	65	25
		title	5	9	6
Search requests	Number of search requests		34	42	35
	Average number of words per request (all words)		22	17	14
	Request preparation				
	(a) short paragraphs prepared by staff members for test purposes		√		√
	(b) short paragraphs prepared by subject experts previously submitted to operational system			√	

Table 7-5

RELEVANCE DISTRIBUTION AND ASSESSMENT

Characteristics	IRE-3	CRAN-1	ADI
Preparation of relevance judgments			
(a) dichotomous prepared by staff experts based on abstracts using full relevance assessment	√		
(b) dichotomous prepared by subject experts based on abstracts and full text (full relevance assessment)		√	
(c) dichotomous prepared by staff experts based on full text using full relevance assessment			√
Number of relevant documents per request (all requests)			
(a) range	2–65	1–12	1–33
(b) mean	17.4	4.7	4.9
(c) generality (mean divided by collection size)	22.2	23.6	59.2
Number of relevant documents per specific request			
(a) number of specific requests	17	21	17
(b) mean number of relevant	7.5	3.0	2.1
Number of relevant documents per general request			
(a) number of general requests	18	21	18
(b) mean number of relevant	25.8	6.4	7.4

Table 7-6

GENERAL TEST ENVIRONMENT

Characteristics	IRE-3	CRAN-1	ADI
User population			
(a) 10 students and staff experts	√		√
(b) 42 subject experts		√	
Number of retrieved documents per request	all	all	all
Number of indexing and search programs used			
(a) matching algorithms	2	2	2
(b) term weight adjustment	2	2	2
(c) document length variation	3	4	3
(d) basic dictionaries (suffix "s", stem, thesaurus, stat. phrases, hierarchy, syntax)	6	5	5
(e) concept-concept association dictionaries	2	3	1
(f) total basic options	144	240	60

(b) Documentation (ADI): a set of 82 short papers, each an average of 1380 words in length, presented at the 1963 Annual Meeting of the American Documentation Institute and used with 35 search requests.

(c) Aerodynamics (CRAN-1): a set of 200 abstracts of documents used by the second Aslib–Cranfield Project [15] and used with 42 search requests.

Each of these collections belongs to a distinct subject area, thus permitting the comparison of the various analysis and search procedures in several contexts. The ADI collection in documentation is of particular interest because full papers are available rather than only document abstracts. The Cranfield collection, on the other hand, is the only one which is also manually indexed by trained indexers, thus making it possible to perform a comparison of the standard keyword search procedures with the automatic text-processing methods.

The procedure used to collect relevance assessments and the related statistical information concerning the average number of relevant documents per request are summarized in Table 7-5. Exhaustive procedures were used to assess the relevance of each document with respect to each search request. Only one person (the requestor) was asked to collect the judgments for each request, and dichotomous assessments were made to declare each document as either relevant or not. In the words of a recent study on evaluation methodology, the process used consists of "multiple events of private relevance" [17].

Additional data concerning the user population and the number of search programs employed are given in Table 7-6. In each case, the user population consisted of volunteers who were asked to help in the test process. Several hundred analysis and search methods incorporated into the SMART system were used with the three document collections. Results based on about 60 of these processing methods are exhibited in the present study.

The methods chosen are generally useful in answering a number of basic questions affecting the design of automatic information systems. For example, can automatic text-processing methods be used effectively to replace a manual content analysis? If so, what part or parts of a document should be incorporated in the automatic procedure? Is it necessary to provide vocabulary normalization methods to eliminate ambiguities caused by homographs and synonymous word groups? Should such a normalization be handled by means of a specially constructed dictionary, or is it possible to replace thesauri completely by statistical word association methods? Which dictionaries can be used most effectively for vocabulary normalization? What should the role of the user be in formulating and controlling the search procedure? These and other questions are considered in the evaluation process described in the remainder of this chapter.

7-3-B Document Length

A primary variable of interest is the *length* of each document to be used for content analysis purposes. This fundamental question enters into many of the arguments between advocates of automatic systems and others who hold that manual content analysis methods are essential, because in an automatic environment, it is not normally possible to process the full text of all documents.

In Fig. 7-2, three analysis systems based only on document titles are compared with systems based on the manipulation of complete document abstracts. In each case, weighted word stems, extracted either from the titles or from the abstracts of the documents, are matched with equivalent indicators from the search requests. Figure 7-2 exhibits recall-precision graphs, averaged respectively over 34, 42, and 35 search requests for the computer science, aerodynamics, and documentation collections. In every case, the abstract process is found to be superior to the "title only" option, particularly at the high recall end of the curve, since the abstract curve comes closest to the upper right-hand corner of the graph where both recall and precision are equal to 1. [For an ideal system which retrieves all relevant items before any irrelevant ones, the recall-precision curve shrinks to a single point with coordinates (1, 1)].

The significance output for the graphs shown in Figs. 7-2 through 7-9 is collected in Table 7-7. In each case, reference is made to the graphs being compared, and the combined probability values P_s and P_t are listed with an indicator specifying the preferred method. The superiority of the abstract-stem process of Fig. 7-2 is reflected in the significance output of Table 7-7. The probability of a correct null hypothesis is smaller than 1.10^{-4} for both the sign and the t tests, thus showing that document titles are definitely inferior to doument abstracts as a source of content indicators.

The ADI documentation collection was used to extend the analysis to longer document segments. The results of a comparison between document abstract processing (60 words) and full text processing (1400 words) show that the full text process is superior to the abstract process. The improvement in performance appears smaller than that shown in Fig. 7-2 for the title-abstract comparison. In particular, the t-text probabilities for the abstract—full text comparisons are too large to permit an unequivocal rejection of the null hypothesis in this case.

In summary, document abstracts are more effective for content analysis purposes than are document titles alone; further improvements appear possible when abstracts are replaced by large text portions; however, the increase in effectiveness is not large enough to reach the unequivocal conclusion that full text processing is always superior to abstract processing.

7-3-C Matching Functions and Term Weights

It is easy in an automatic text-processing environment to differentiate among individual content indicators by assigning weights to the indicators in proportion to their presumed importance. Such weights can be derived in part by using the frequency of occurrence of the original text words which give rise to the various indicators, and in part as a function of the various dictionary-mapping procedures. Thus, ambiguous terms which in a synonym dictionary would normally correspond to many different thesaurus classes, can be weighted less than unambiguous terms. The SMART system includes procedures for testing the effectiveness of such weighted (numeric)

Table 7-7

COMBINED SIGNIFICANCE OUTPUT

RETRIEVAL METHODS BEING COMPARED	CORRESPONDING GRAPH NUMBER	DOCUMENT COLLECTION					
		IRE-3		*CRAN-1*		*ADI*	
		P_s	P_t	P_s	P_t	P_s	P_t
Title stem (*A*) Abstract stem (*B*)	Fig. 7-2	0.0000 (*B* > *A*)	0.0000 (*B* > *A*)	0.0000 (*B* > *A*)	0.0000 (*B* > *A*)	0.0000 (*B* > *A*)	0.0000 (*B* > *A*)
Abstract stem (*A*) Full text stem (*B*)		–	–	–	–	0.1420 (*B* > *A*)	0.0892 (*B* > *A*)
Abstract thesaurus (*A*) Full text thesaurus (*B*)		–	–	–	–	0.0064 (*B* > *A*)	0.0987 (*B* > *A*)
Numeric stem (*A*) Logical stem (*B*)	Fig. 7-3	0.0000 (*A* > *B*)	0.0000 (*A* > *B*)	0.0000 (*A* > *B*)	0.0000 (*A* > *B*)	0.3736 (*A* > *B*)	0.0040 (*A* > *B*)
Cosine logical stem (*A*) Overlap logical stems (*B*)	Fig. 7-4	0.0000 (*A* > *B*)	0.0000 (*A* > *B*)	0.0000 (*A* > *B*)	0.0000 (*A* > *B*)	0.0891 (*A* > *B*)	0.0148 (*A* > *B*)
Overlap numeric stem (*A*) Overlap logical stem (*B*)		–	–	0.3497 (*B* > *A*)	0.1427 (*B* > *A*)	–	–
Overlap numeric stem (*A*) Cosine numeric stem (*B*)		–	–	0.0000 (*B* > *A*)	0.0000 (*B* > *A*)	–	–
Word stem (*A*) Suffix "s" (*B*)		0.0000 (*A* > *B*)	0.0000 (*A* > *B*)	0.0000 (*B* > *A*)	0.0000 (*B* > *A*)	0.0000 (*A* > *B*)	0.0000 (*A* > *B*)
Thesaurus (*A*) Word stem (*B*)	Fig. 7-5	0.0000 (*A* > *B*)	0.0000 (*A* > *B*)	0.0020 (*A* > *B*)	0.1483 (*A* > *B*)	0.0000 (*A* > *B*)	0.0000 (*A* > *B*)
Old thesaurus (*A*) New thesaurus (*B*)	Fig. 7-6	0.0000 (*B* > *A*)	0.0000 (*B* > *A*)	0.0000 (*B* > *A*)	0.0000 (*B* > *A*)	–	–

Table 7-7—Cont.

RETRIEVAL METHODS BEING COMPARED	CORRESPONDING GRAPH NUMBER	DOCUMENT COLLECTION					
		IRE-3		*CRAN-1*		*ADI*	
		P_s	P_t	P_s	P_t	P_s	P_t
Thesaurus (*A*) Phrases, weight 1.0 (*B*)		1.0000 (*A* > *B*)	0.8645 (*B* > *A*)	0.0001 (*A* > *B*)	0.1120 (*A* > *B*)	0.0391 (*B* > *A*)	0.1171 (*B* > *A*)
Word stem (*A*) Stem concon (*B*)	Fig. 7-7	0.1948 (*A* > *B*)	0.0566 (*A* > *B*)	0.0086 (*B* > *A*)	0.0856 (*B* > *A*)	0.4420 (*B* > *A*)	0.6521 (*B* > *A*)
Concon all, 0.60 (*A*) Concon 3–50, 0.60 (*B*)		–	–	0.0000 (*B* > *A*)	0.0525 (*B* > *A*)	–	–
Concon 3–50, 0.60 (*A*) Concon 6–100, 0.45 (*B*)		–	–	0.0001 (*B* > *A*)	0.0991 (*B* > *A*)	–	–
Thesaurus (*A*) Hierarchy parents (*B*)	Fig. 7-8	0.1047 (*A* > *B*)	0.1676 (*A* > *B*)	–	–	–	–
Thesaurus (*A*) Hierarchy brothers (*B*)	Fig. 7-8	0.0000 (*A* > *B*)	0.0000 (*A* > *B*)	–	–	–	–
Thesaurus (*A*) Hierarchy sons (*B*)		0.0000 (*A* > *B*)	0.0000 (*A* > *B*)	–	–	–	–
Thesaurus (*A*) Hierarchy cross ref. (*B*)		0.0000 (*A* > *B*)	0.0000 (*A* > *B*)	–	–	–	–
Index stem (*A*) Abstract stem (*B*)	Fig. 7-9	–	–	0.0465 (*A* > *B*)	0.0415 (*A* > *B*)	–	–
Index stem (*A*) Stem concon (*B*)	Fig. 7-9	–	–	0.0020 (*A* > *B*)	0.0176 (*A* > *B*)	–	–
Index new thesaurus (*A*) Abstract, new thesaurus (*B*)	Fig. 7-9	–	–	0.0019 (*A* > *B*)	0.0001 (*A* > *B*)	–	–

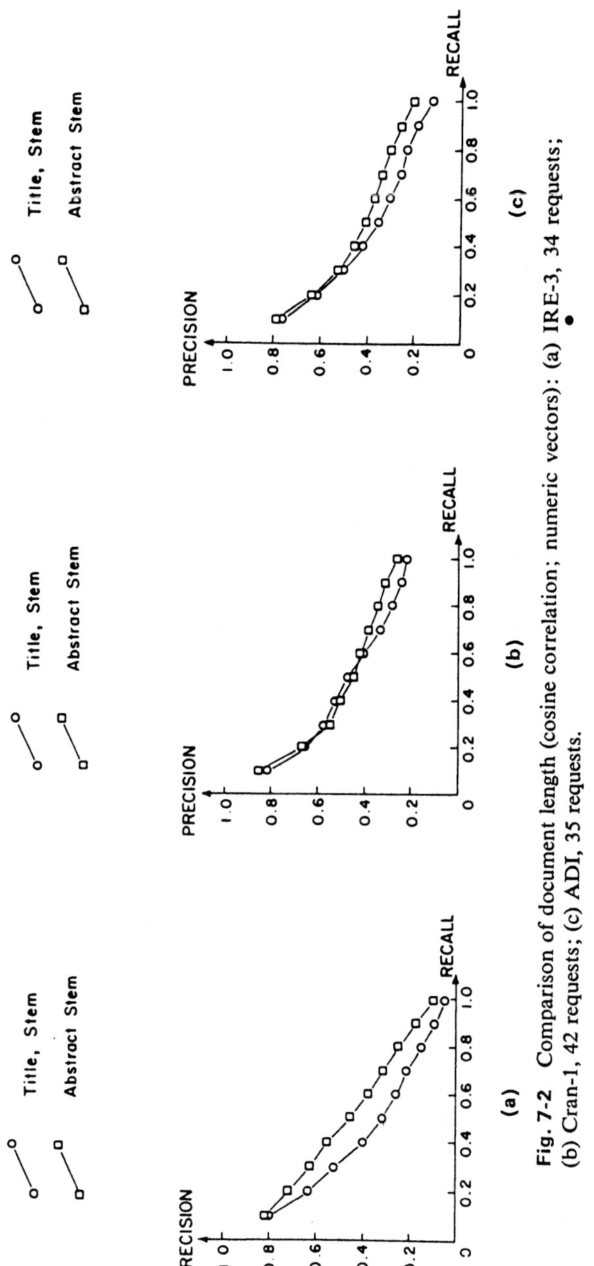

Fig. 7-2 Comparison of document length (cosine correlation; numeric vectors): (a) IRE-3, 34 requests; (b) Cran-1, 42 requests; (c) ADI, 35 requests.

content indicators compared with nonweighted (logical) indicators, where all term weights are either 1 or 0 (1 if a given term is assigned to a given document, and 0 if it is not).

The recall-precision graphs for the three collections used previously are shown in Fig. 7-3, and the corresponding significance output is reproduced in Table 7-7. In each case, weighted word stems extracted from document abstracts or full text are compared with nonweighted (logical) stems. The results are clearly in favor of the weighted process for all three collections, the largest performance differences being registered for the IRE collection in computer science. The recall-precision graph for the ADI collection also appears to show a considerable advantage for the weighted process, and this is reflected in the t-test probability of 0.0040. However, when the magnitudes of the results are disregarded, it is found that nearly as many evaluation parameters favor the nonweighted process as the weighted one for the documentation collection. Therefore the test results are not wholly significant for that collection. On the whole, it appears that weighted content indicators produce better retrieval results than nonweighted ones, and that binary term vectors should therefore be used only if no weighting system appears readily available.

Another variable affecting retrieval performance which can be incorporated easily into an automatic information system is the correlation coefficient used to determine the similarity between an analyzed search request and the analyzed documents. Two of the correlation measures which have been included in the SMART system are the cosine and overlap correlations which are defined as follows:

$$\text{Cos}(\mathbf{q}, \mathbf{d}) = \frac{\sum_{i=1}^{n} \mathbf{d}_i \mathbf{q}_i}{\sqrt{\sum_{i=1}^{n} (\mathbf{d}_i)^2 \times \sum_{i=1}^{n} (\mathbf{q}_i)^2}},$$

and

$$\text{Ovlap}(\mathbf{q}, \mathbf{d}) = \frac{\sum_{i=1}^{n} \min(\mathbf{q}_i, \mathbf{d}_i)}{\min\left(\sum_{i=1}^{n} \mathbf{q}_i, \sum_{i=1}^{n} \mathbf{d}_i\right)},$$

where $\mathbf{q}$ and $\mathbf{d}$ are considered to be n-dimensional vectors of terms representing an analyzed query $\mathbf{q}$ and an analyzed document $\mathbf{d}$, respectively, in a space of n terms assignable as information identifiers.

Both the cosine and the overlap functions range from 0 for no match to 1 for perfect identity between the respective vectors. The cosine correlation is more sensitive to document length, that is, to the number of assigned terms because of the factor in the denominator and tends to produce greater variations in the correlations than the overlap measure.

A comparison of cosine and overlap-matching functions is shown in the output of Fig. 7-4. In each case, logical (nonweighted) vectors are used with either of the two correlation methods. The results are clearly in favor of the cosine-matching function, although the sign test result for the ADI collection is not sufficiently one-sided to reach a hard conclusion in that case.

The combined effect of parameter adjustment in both the weighting and the correlation method can be studied by combining the output of Figs. 7-3 and 7-4. The significance data of Table 7-7 indicate that the weakest method appears to be the combination of logical vectors with the overlap correlation, and the most satisfactory results are obtained with the numeric (weighted) term vectors and the cosine correlation.

It should be noted that the overlap-logical process corresponds to the standard keyword-matching method used in almost all operational, semimechanized retrieval situations. In such cases, nonweighted keywords assigned to each document are compared with keywords attached to the search requests, and a count is taken of the number of overlapping keywords. The resulting coefficient is then equivalent to a non-normalized overlap function. It would appear from the results of Figs. 7-3 and 7-4, that standard keyword-matching systems can be improved by the simple device of using a better matching function and assigning weights to the keywords.

To summarize: weighted content identifiers are more effective for content description than nonweighted ones, and the cosine correlation function is more useful as a measure of document-request similarity than the overlap function; therefore advantage can be taken of the computational facilities incorporated into many mechanized information systems, and service can be improved by using more sophisticated request-document matching methods.

7-3-D Language Normalization—The Suffix Process

If natural language texts are to form the basis for an automatic assignment of information identifiers to documents, then the question of language normalization is of primary concern. Indeed, no human intermediaries exist who could resolve some of the ambiguities inherent in the natural language itself, or some of the inconsistencies introduced into written texts by the authors or writers responsible for the preparation of the documents.

A large number of experiments have been conducted therefore with the SMART system, using a variety of dictionaries for purposes of language normalization in each of the three subject fields under study. The performance of the following dictionaries is studied in particular:

(a) *Suffix "s"* process, where words differing by the addition of a terminal "s" are recognized as equivalent (for example, the words "apple" and "apples" are assigned a common identifier, but not words "analyzer" and "analyzing".

(b) The *word stem dictionary*, where all words which exhibit a common word stem are treated as equivalent; for example, "analysis", "analyzer", "analyst", and so on.

(c) The *synonym dictionary*, or thesaurus, where a set of synonymous, or closely

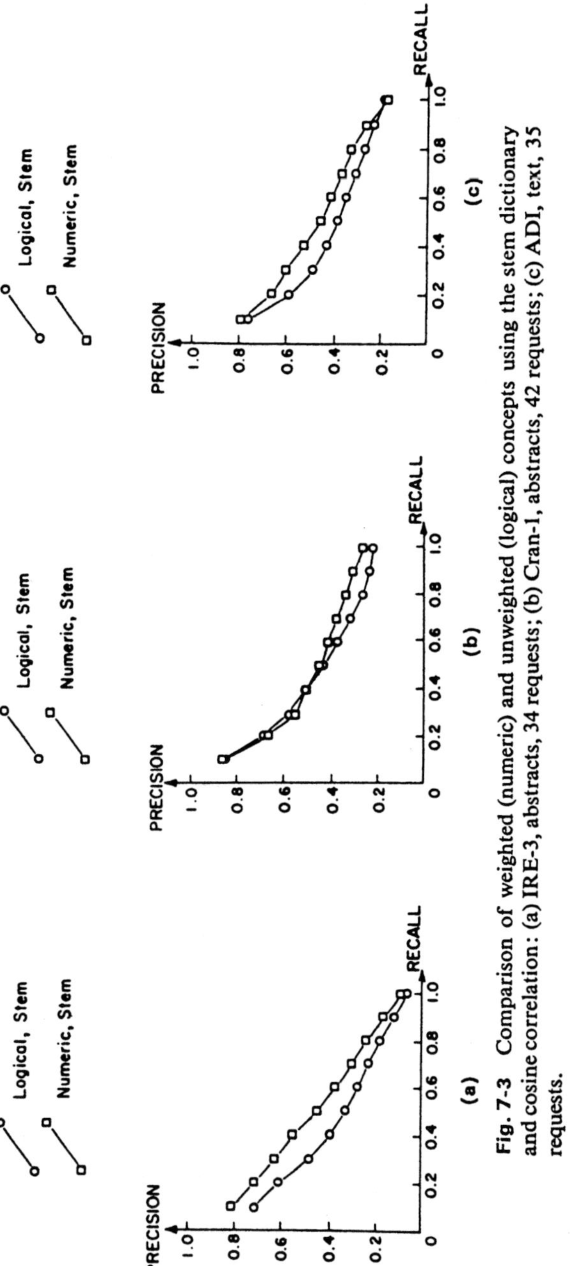

Fig. 7-3 Comparison of weighted (numeric) and unweighted (logical) concepts using the stem dictionary and cosine correlation: (a) IRE-3, abstracts, 34 requests; (b) Cran-1, abstracts, 42 requests; (c) ADI, text, 35 requests.

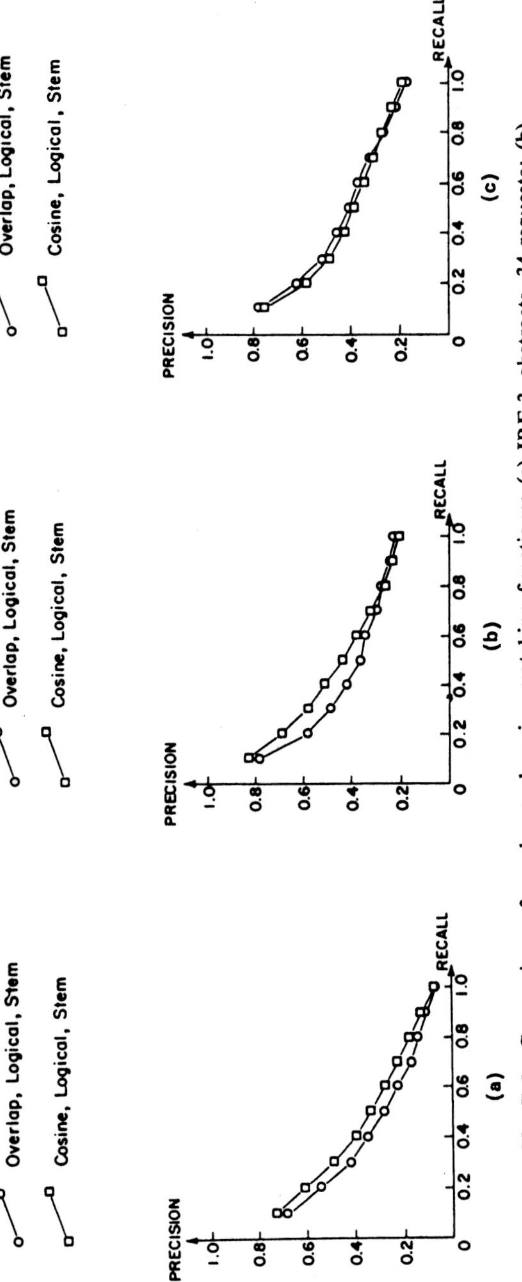

Fig. 7-4 Comparison of overlap and cosine matching functions: (a) IRE-3, abstracts, 34 requests; (b) Cran-1, abstracts, 42 requests; (c) ADI, text, 35 requests.

related terms are all placed into a common thesaurus class, thus ensuring that common identifiers are derived from all such terms.

(d) The *statistical phrase dictionary* which makes it possible to recognize "phrases" consisting of the juxtaposition of several distinct concepts; thus if a given document contains the notion of "program", as well as the notion of "language", it could be tagged with the phrase "programming language"; the statistical phrase dictionary incorporated into the SMART system is manually constructed and contains a large variety of common noun phrases for each of the subject areas covered.

(e) The *concept association method* where concepts are grouped not by reference to a preconstructed dictionary but by using statistical co-occurrence characteristics of the vocabulary under investigation.

A comparison of the suffix "s" dictionary with a complete word stem dictionary is illustrated in the output of Table 7-7. In the former case, the texts of documents and search requests are looked up in a table of common words so as to delete function words and other text items not of immediate interest for content analysis purposes; the final "s" endings are then deleted so as to confound words which differ only by a final "s." In the latter case, a complete suffix dictionary is also consulted, and the original words are reduced to word stem form before request identifiers are matched with document identifiers.

The results obtained from the experiments are contradictory, in the sense that for two of the collections used (IRE-3 and ADI) the more thorough normalization inherent in the word stem process, compared with suffix "s" recognition alone, improves the search effectiveness; for the third collection (Cranfield), the reverse result appears to hold. For none of the collections is the improvement of one method over the other really dramatic, so that in practice either procedure might be used reasonably.

The discrepancy between the IRE and ADI results, on the one hand, and the Cranfield results, on the other, may be caused by differences in the respective vocabularies. Specifically, the Cranfield texts are substantially more technical in nature, and the collection is more homogeneous than is the case for the other collections. In order to differentiate between the various document abstracts, it is then important to maintain finer distinctions for the Cranfield case than for ADI and IRE, and these finer differences are lost when several different words are combined into a unique class through the suffix cutoff process. The argument can be summarized by stating that dictionaries and word normalization procedures are most effective if the vocabulary is redundant and relatively nontechnical; in the reverse case, such procedures may not in fact result in processing advantages.

7-3-E Synonym Recognition

One of the perennial problems in automatic language analysis is the question of language variability among authors and the linguistic ambiguities which result. Therefore several experiments have been performed using a variety of synonym dictionaries for each of the three subject fields under study (*Harris-2* and *Harris-3* dictionaries for the computer literature, *quasi-synonym* or *QS* lists for aeronautical engineering, and a regular thesaurus for documentation). Use of such a synonym dictionary permits the replacement of a variety of related terms by similar concept identifiers, thereby ensuring the retrieval of documents dealing with the "manufacture of transistor diodes" when the query deals with the "production of solid state rectifiers".

The output of Fig. 7-5 which represents a comparison of the word stem matching procedure with a process including a thesaurus lookup operation for the recognition of synonyms shows that considerable improvements in performance are obtainable by means of suitably constructed synonym dictionaries. The improvement is again smallest for the Cranfield collection in part for the reasons stated already in Sec. 7-3-D, and in part because the dictionary available for this collection was not constructed originally to mesh in with the SMART retrieval programs. However in the present case, the synonym recognition seems to benefit the Cranfield material also. The significance output for Fig. 7-5 shows that all thesaurus improvements are fully significant, with the exception of the t test for the Cranfield collection. The null hypothesis can therefore be rejected unequivocally for all collections except Cranfield.

The differences observed in the performance of the various synonym dictionaries suggest that not all dictionaries are equally useful for the improvement of retrieval effectivenes. The experiments conducted with the SMART system in fact led to the principles of dictionary construction outlined previously in Chapter 6 and reference [17].

The differences in search effectiveness for two sets of two synonym dictionaries are shown in Fig. 7-6. The less effective dictionaries (Harris-2 for the IRE collection, and "old " quasi-synonym for the Cranfield) were in each case constructed manually by specialists using ad hoc procedures set up for the occasion. The other two dictionaries are improved versions obtained manually by using some of the dictionary construction principles listed previously. The significance output shows that fully significant improvements are obtained from one dictionary version to the next. It may be noted in this connection that the synonym recognition results of the main Cranfield experiments [18] were obtained with the "old", less effective synonym dictionary, rather than with the new one.

In summary, it appears that dictionaries providing synonym recognition produce statistically significant improvements in retrieval effectiveness compared with the word stem matching process; the improvement is largest for dictionaries obeying certain principles with regard to the word groupings which are incorporated.

7-3-F Phrase Recognition

The SMART system makes provision for the recognition of "phrases" to identify documents and search requests, rather than only individual concepts alone. Phrases can be generated using a variety of strategies. For example, a phrase can be assigned

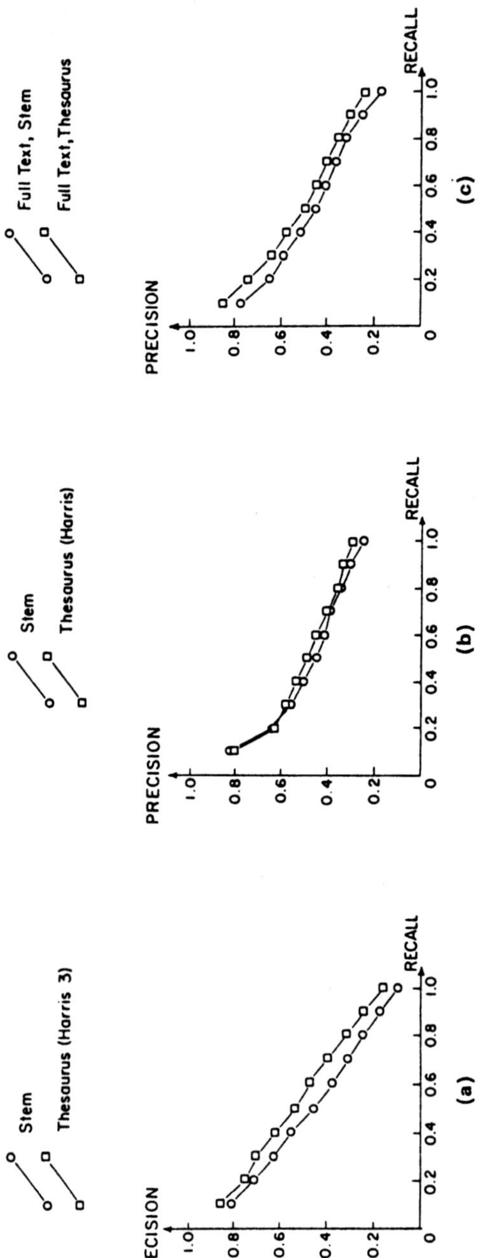

Fig. 7-5 Comparison of synonym recognition (thesaurus) with word stem matching process: (a) IRE-3, 34 requests; (b) Cran-1, abstracts, 42 requests; (c) ADI, full text, 35 requests.

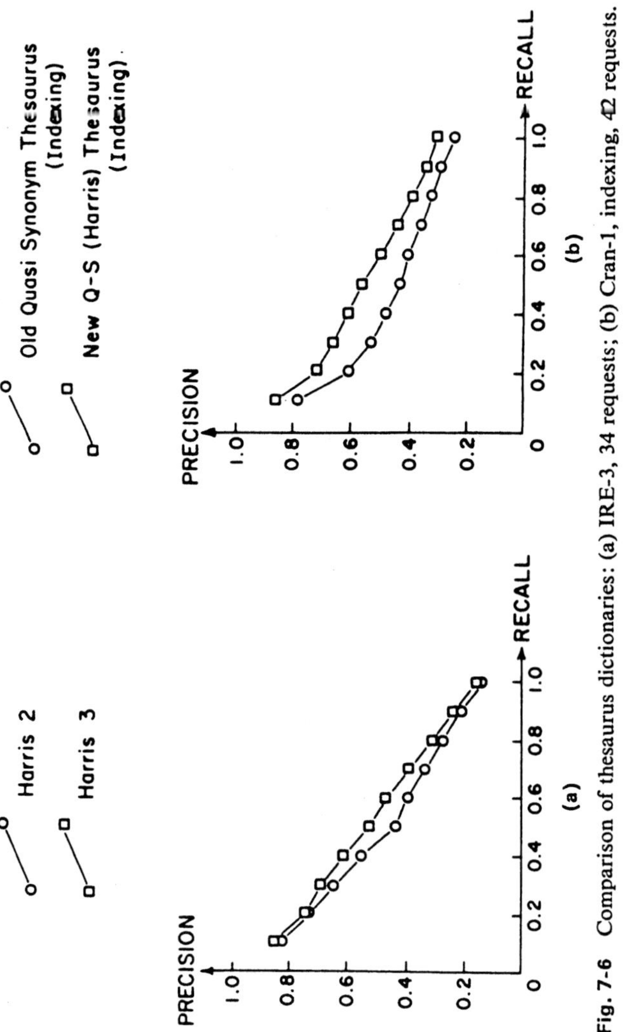

Fig. 7-6 Comparison of thesaurus dictionaries: (a) IRE-3, 34 requests; (b) Cran-1, indexing, 42 requests.

any time the specified components co-occur in a given document or in a given sentence of a document; alternatively, more restrictive phrase generation methods can be used by incorporating a syntactic recognition routine into the phrase generation process to check the syntactic compatibility between the phrase components before a phrase is actually accepted [19].

In the SMART system, the normal phrase process uses a preconstructed dictionary of important phrases, and simple co-occurrence of phrase components, rather than syntactic criteria, is used to assign phrases to documents. Phrases seem to be particularly useful as a means of incorporating into a document representation those terms whose individual components are not always meaningful by themselves. For example, "computer" and "control" are reasonably nonspecific, while "computer control" has a much more definite meaning in a computer science collection.

The results of the phrase lookup procedure compared with the equivalent process using only a synonym dictionary indicate that for two of the collections the phrase dictionary offers improvements in certain ranges of the recall and precision curve. The output of Table 7-7 shows, however, that the improvements are not significant, and on the whole the phrase dictionary does not appear to offer any real help in the middle recall range. Whether this result is due to the recognition of false phrases where phrase components are all present in the text but do not really belong together (such as in the phrase "solid state" in the sentence "people whose knowledge is solid state that computer processing is efficient") remains to be seen. The available evidence would seem to indicate that the presence of such false phrases is quite rare and that a more serious deficiency is the small size of the statistical phrase dictionary from which many potentially useful phrases may be absent.

Phrases can also be recognized by using the statistical properties of the words in a text, rather than a preconstructed dictionary of phrase components. Specifically, if two given terms co-occur in many of the documents of a collection, or in many sentences within a given document, a nonzero correlation coefficient can be computed as a function of the number of co-occurrences. If this coefficient is sufficiently high, the two terms can be grouped and can be assigned jointly to documents and search requests. Associative methods are therefore comparable to thesaurus procedures except that the word associations reflect strictly the vocabulary statistics of a given collection, whereas a thesaurus grouping may have more general validity [20, 21].

Many possible methods exist for the generation of statistical word associations. Specifically, by varying several parameters suitably, a number of different types of term associations can be recognized; furthermore, once an association between term pairs is introduced, it is possible to assign to it a smaller or a greater weight. Two main parameters that can be used in this connection are the cutoff value K in the association coefficient below which an association between terms is not recognized and the frequency of occurrence of the terms being correlated. When all terms are correlated, no matter how low their frequency in the document collection, a great many spurious associations may be found; on the other hand, some correct associations may not be observable under any stricter conditions. Increasingly more restrictive association procedures, applied first only to words in the frequency range 3 to 50 and then in the frequency range 6 to 100, eliminate many spurious associations but also some correct ones.

Figure 7-7 shows a comparison of the word-stem matching process with the statistical term-term association method (labeled "stem concon" in Fig. 7-7 to indicate a concept-concept association in which word stems are manipulated). The applicable frequency restrictions for the concept pairs and the cutoff values K are also included in Fig. 7-7. The output of Fig. 7-7 and the corresponding significance computations indicate that for the Cranfield collections, in particular, the term associations provide some improvement over the word stem process; local improvements for certain recall ranges are also noticeable for the ADI and IRE collections. Only for Cranfield does the sign test appear to be of some statistical significance, so that based on the present tests, no strong claims of overall effectiveness can be made for the association process.

The conclusion is reinforced by performing a comparison between the thesaurus lookup process and the word stem association method. Table 7-7 shows that the advantage is clearly and significantly with the more powerful thesaurus method for both the ADI and IRE collections. For Cranfield, the advantage is still slightly with the word stem association process particularly at the high recall end, where the more exhaustive indexing procedures represented by the stem associations supplies additional useful information identifiers and serves therefore to maintain the finer distinctions among the Cranfield documents. However, the superiority of the association method is not statistically significant for Cranfield, so that the conclusion reached previously must stand.

Table 7-7 also includes a comparison of various word stem association strategies performed for the Cranfield collection. The output suggests that the more restrictive association processes are more effective as a retrieval aid than the more general ones. Specifically, as the number of generated association pairs grows, too many of them appear to become spurious, thus depressing the retrieval performance. In practice, limitations should be imposed on the number and types of associated terms actually used.

To summarize, the phrase generation methods, whether implemented by dictionary lookup or by statistical association processes, appear to offer improvements in retrieval effectiveness for some recall levels by introducing new associated information identifiers not originally available; the improvement is not, however, sufficiently general or substantial, when averages over many search requests are considered, to warrant incorporation into automatic information systems, except under special circumstances where suitable control procedures can be maintained.

7-3-G Hierarchical Expansion

Hierarchical arrangements of subject identifiers are used in many standard library classification systems and are also incorporated into many nonconventional information systems. Subject hierarchies are useful for the representation of generic inclusion relations between terms, and they also serve to broaden, narrow, or otherwise "expand" a given content description by adding hierarchically related terms to

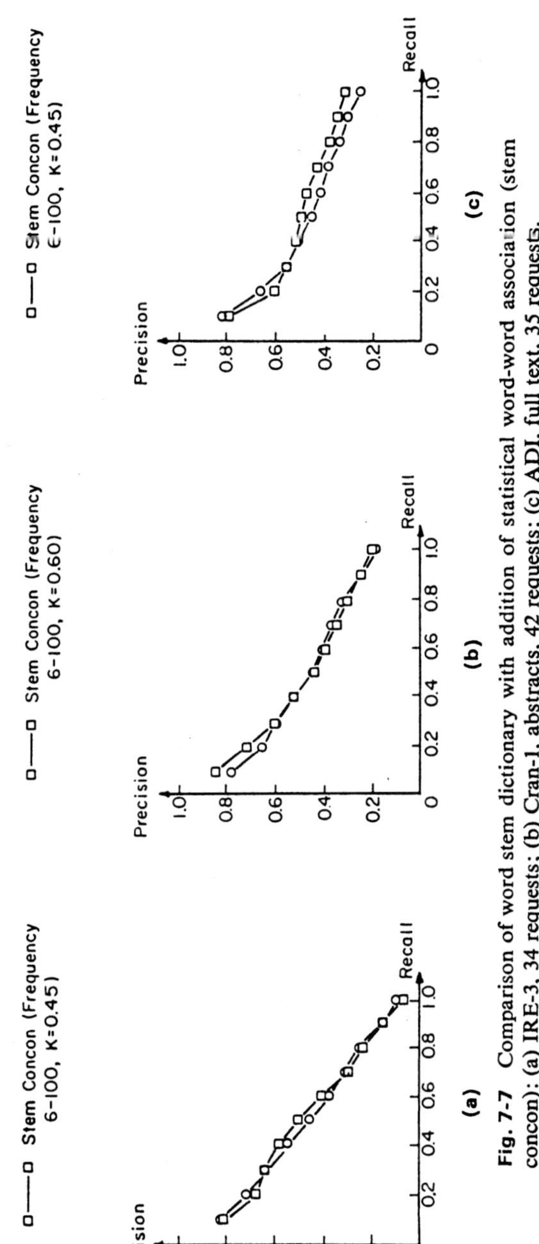

Fig. 7-7 Comparison of word stem dictionary with addition of statistical word-word association (stem concon): (a) IRE-3, 34 requests; (b) Cran-1, abstracts, 42 requests; (c) ADI, full text, 35 requests.

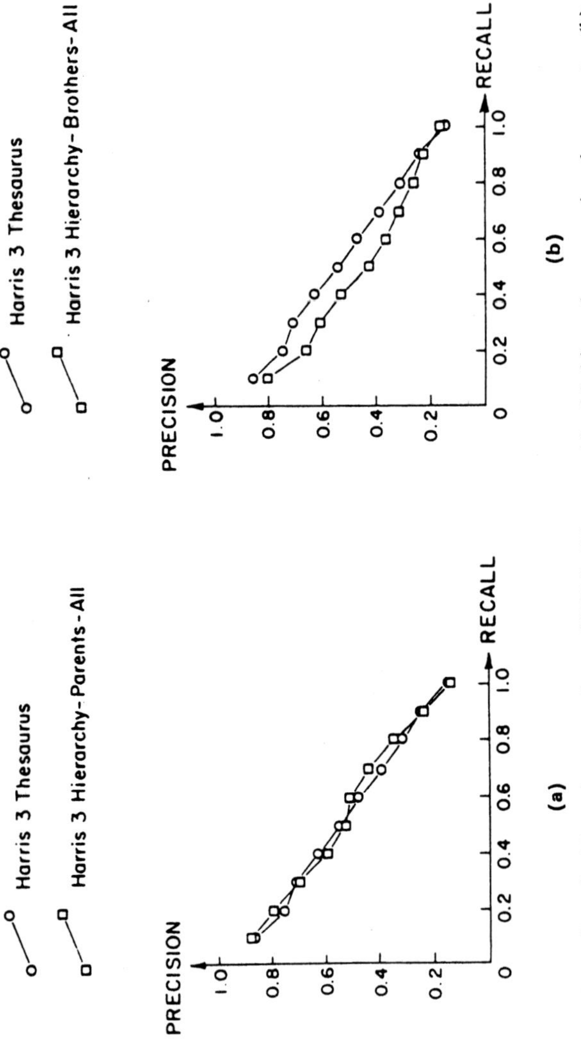

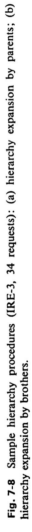

Fig. 7-8 Sample hierarchy procedures (IRE-3, 34 requests): (a) hierarchy expansion by parents; (b) hierarchy expansion by brothers.

those originally available. Specifically, given an entry point in the hierarchy, it is possible to find more general terms by going "up" in the hierarchy (expansion by parents), and more specific ones by going "down" (expansion by sons); related terms which have the same parent can also be obtained (expansion by brothers); finally any available cross references between individual entries can be identified (expansion by cross references).

A hierarchical arrangement of thesaurus entries was used with the IRE collection to evaluate the effectiveness of the hierarchical expansion procedures. In the test process carried out with the SMART system, the concepts present in both the document and request vectors were looked up in the hierarchy, and appropriately related hierarchy entries were added to the original content identifiers. The expanded document vectors which resulted were then matched with the requests, and documents were arranged in decreasing correlation order as usual. A comparison of the standard thesaurus process with two of the four hierarchical expansions described previously is shown in Fig. 7-8, and the corresponding significance output is included in Table 7-7.

In each case it is seen that the standard thesaurus process alone is superior; moreover, the equality hypothesis can be rejected unequivocally for the expansions by brothers, sons, and cross references. A question exists only for the expansion by parents, where more general terms are added to the original identifiers. Figure 7-8(a) shows, in particular, that this expansion process does in fact improve retrieval performance for certain recall levels.

Of course many alternative methods exist for using a hierarchy. It is possible, for example, to expand requests without expanding the documents or vice versa; terms obtained from the hierarchy can also *replace* the original content identifiers instead of being added to them. In general, the expansions tend to produce large-scale disturbances in the information identifiers attached to documents and search requests. Occasionally, such a disturbance can serve to crystallize the meaning of a poorly stated request, particularly if the request is far removed from the principal subjects covered by the document collection. More often, the change in direction specified by the hierarchy option is too violent, and the average performance of most hierarchy procedures does not appear to be sufficiently promising to advocate their immediate incorporation in an analysis system for automatic document retrieval.

7-3-H Manual Indexing

The Cranfield collection was available for purposes of experimentation both in the form of abstracts and in the form of manually assigned index terms. The indexing performed by trained indexers is extremely detailed, consisting of an average of over 30 terms per document. As such, the indexing performance may be expected to be superior to the subject indexing normally used for large document collections. Therefore a meaningful comparison with standard manual keyword indexing systems may not be possible. A comparison of index term performance with certain automatic procedures using document abstracts is represented in Fig. 7-9, together with the corresponding significance output in Table 7-7. Figures 7-9(a) and 7-9(b) show that the overall performance of a straight index term match is only slightly superior to a match of word stems abstracted from the document abstracts; for certain recall ranges, the automatic word-word association method in fact proves to be more effective than a manual index term match. In any case, Table 7-7 shows that the null hypothesis which postulates equivalence cannot be rejected in that instance.

When the index terms are looked up in the thesaurus and a comparison is made with the thesaurus process for the document abstracts, a clearer advantage is apparent for the indexing; that is, the identification of synonyms and related terms inherent in the thesaurus process seems of greater benefit to the indexing than to the automatic abstract process. Even there, however, the advantage for the index term process is not fully significant.

Based on those results, it is not possible therefore to say that the automatic text processing is substantially inferior to the manual-indexing method; indeed, one is tempted to say that the efforts of the trained indexers may well have been superfluous for the collection at hand, since equally effective results could be obtained by simple word-matching techniques. Such a result appears even more probably in the case of larger or less homogeneous collections, where the manual indexing tends to be less effective because of the variabilities among indexers and the difficulties of ensuring a uniform application of a given set of indexing rules to all documents. The computer process in such cases does not necessarily decay as the collections grow larger, and the evaluation output may then be more favorable for the automatic procedures.

7-4 CONCLUDING COMMENTS

A summary of the main evaluation output is contained in Table 7-8, where eight processing methods are presented in order for the three document collections used. The measure used to rank the output is a combined coefficient consisting of the sum of the normalized recall and the normalized precision. The following principal conclusions can be drawn from the data of Table 7-8:

(a) The order of merit for the eight methods is generally the same for all three collections, with the possible exception of the suffix "s" method which performs better than average for CRAN-1 and worse than average for ADI.

(b) The performance range of the methods used is smaller for the Cranfield collection than for the other two collections.

(c) The use of logical vectors (disregarding term weight), overlap correlation, and titles only is always less effective than the use of weighted terms, cosine correlation, and full document abstracts.

(d) The thesaurus process involving synonym recognition always performs more effectively than the word stem or suffix "s" methods when synonyms are not recognized.

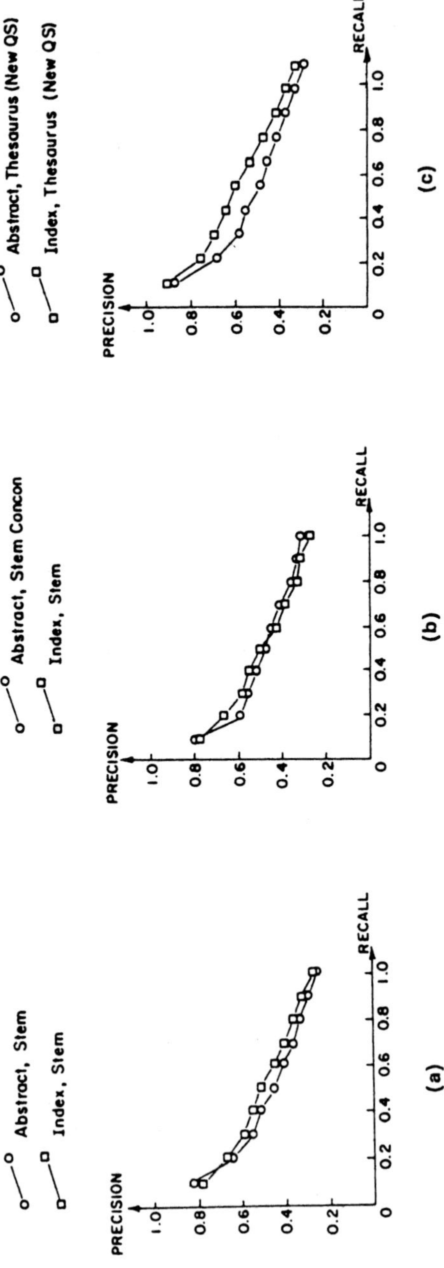

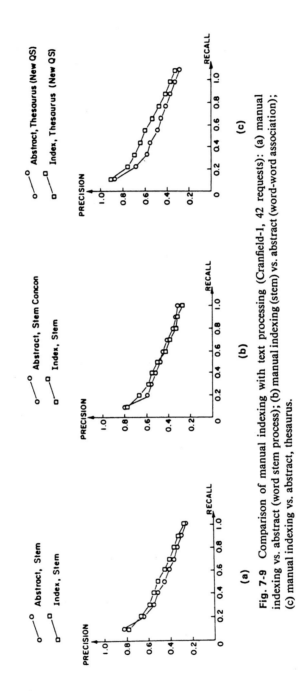

Fig. 7-9 Comparison of manual indexing with text processing (Cranfield-1, 42 requests): (a) manual indexing vs. abstract (word stem process); (b) manual indexing (stem) vs. abstract (word-word association); (c) manual indexing vs. abstract, thesaurus.

Table 7-8

OVERALL MERIT FOR EIGHT PROCESSING METHODS USED WITH THREE DOCUMENT COLLECTIONS

	IRE-3			CRAN-1			ADI		
ORDER	D*	*Method*	M†	D	*Method*	M	D	*Method*	M
1	*D4*	stat. phrase	1.686	*D3*	thesaurus	1.579	*D4*	stat. phrase	1.456
2	*D3*	thesaurus	1.665	*D1*	suffix "s"	1.574	*D3*	thesaurus	1.448
3	*D2*	stems	1.570	*D4*	stat. phrase	1.566	*D5*	concon	1.367
4	*D5*	concon	1.559	*D5*	concon	1.556	*D2*	stems	1.335
5	*D1*	suffix "s"	1.530	*D2*	stems	1.535	*D2*	no weights	1.294
6	*D2*	no weights	1.494	*D2*	no weights	1.477	*D2*	title only	1.293
7	*D2*	overlap	1.455	*D2*	title only	1.430	*D1*	suffix "s"	1.283
8	*D2*	title only	1.369	*D2*	overlap	1.407	*D2*	overlap	1.241
Range		0.317			0.172			0.215	

**D*: Dictionary used—*D1*: Suffix "s"; *D2*: Word Stem; *D3*: Thesaurus; *D4*: Stat. Phrase; *D5*: Word-Word Association.

†*M*: Merit measure (normalized recall plus normalized precision).

(e) The thesaurus and statistical phrase methods are substantially equivalent; other dictionaries perform less well (with the exception of suffix "s" for Cranfield).

These results indicate that, in automatic systems, weighted terms should be used, derived from document excerpts whose length is at least equivalent to that of an abstract; furthermore, synonym dictionaries should be incorporated wherever available. Other local improvements may be obtained by incorporating phrases, hierarchies, and word-word association techniques. The Cranfield output shows that the better automatic text-processing methods (abstracts—thesaurus) may not be substantially inferior to the performance obtained with manually assigned index terms.

A comparison of the test results obtained here with other related studies is difficult to perform. For the most part, only fragmentary results exist which do not lend themselves to a full analysis [16], [22]. The Cranfield project studies contain the only available extensive test results, including the performance of manually assigned index terms, phrases, and dictionary concepts together with a wide variety of "recall devices" (procedures that broaden or generalize the meaning of the terms) and "precision devices" (procedures that add discrimination and narrow the coverage of the terms) [18]. The principal conclusions reached by the Cranfield project are also borne out by the SMART studies: that phrase languages are not substantially superior to single terms as indexing devices, that synonym dictionaries improve performance, but that other dictionary types, such as hierarchies, are not as effective as expected.

Further experiments leading to the design of automatic information systems should be performed in different subject areas with larger document collections. Furthermore, it becomes increasingly important to evaluate also the search procedures likely to be used in an automatic systems environment, particularly those real-time search methods where the user can control the search strategy to some exent, by providing suitable feedback information. Work in this direction is continuing [7], [23], [24].

Acknowledgement: The assistance of Mr. Cyril Cleverdon and Mr. Michael Keen in making available the documents and dictionaries used by the Aslib–Cranfield Research Project is gratefully acknowledge. Mr. Keen was also instrumental in preparing many of the output graphs included in this study.

REFERENCES

[1] Committee on Scientific and Technical Information (COSATI), Recommendations for National Document Handling Systems, *Report PB 168267*, distributed by the Clearinghouse for Federal, Scientific and Technical Information, Springfield, Va., November 1965.

[2] M. Rubinoff, ed. *Toward a National Information System*, Spartan Books, New York, 1965.

[3] G. S. Simpson and C. Flanagan, Information Centers and Services, in *Annual Review of Information Science and Technology*, C. Cuadra, ed. Chap. XII, John Wiley & Sons, Inc., New York, 1966.

[4] G. Salton, A Document Retrieval System for Man-machine Interaction, *Proceedings of the ACM 19th National Conference*, Philadelphia, 1964.

[5] G. Salton and M. E. Lesk, The SMART Automatic Document Retrieval System—An Illustration, *Communications of the ACM*, Vol. 8, No. 6, June 1965.

[6] G. Salton, Progress in Automatic Information Retrieval, *IEEE Spectrum*, Vol. 2, No. 8, August 1965.

[7] J. J. Rocchio, Jr. and G. Salton, Information Search Optimization and Iterative Retrieval Techniques, *Proceedings of the AFIPS Fall Joint Computer Conference*, Las Vegas, Nev., November 1965, Spartan Books, New York, 1965.

[8] J. J. Rocchio, Jr., Document Retrieval Systems—Optimization and Evaluation, Doctoral thesis, *Report ISR-10* to the National Science Foundation, Harvard Computation Laboratory, Cambridge, Mass., March 1966.

[9] C. W. Cleverdon, The Testing of Index Language Devices, *Aslib Proceedings*, Vol. 5, No. 4, April 1965.

[10] G. Salton, The Evaluation of Automatic Retrieval Procedures—Selected Test Results Using the SMART System, *American Documentation*, Vol. 16, No. 3, July 1965.

[11] R. A. Fairthorne, Basic Parameters of Retrieval Tests, *1964 ADI Annual Meeting*, Philadelphia, October 1964.

[12] G. Salton, Evaluation of Computer-Based Retrieval Systems, *Proceedings 1965 International FID Congress*, Spartan Books, New York, 1966.

[13] R. A. Fisher, *Statistical Methods for Research Workers*, Hafner Publishing Company, New York, 1954.

[14] J. L. Hodges and E. L. Lehmann, *Basic Concepts of Probability and Statistics*, Holden-Day, Inc., San Francisco, 1964.

[15] C. W. Cleverdon, J. Mills, and M. Keen, Factors Determining the Performance of Indexing Systems, *Design*, Vol. 1, Aslib–Cranfield Research Project, Cranfield, England, 1966.

[16] V. E. Giuliano and P. E. Jones, Study and Test of a Methodology for Laboratory Evaluation of Message Retrieval Systems, *Report ESD-TR-66-405* Little, Brown & Company, Boston, August 1966.

[17] G. Salton, Information Dissemination and Automatic Information Systems, *Proc. IEEE*, Vol. 54, No. 12, December 1966.

[18] C. W. Cleverdon and M. Keen, Factors Determining the Performance of Indexing Systems, *Test Results*, Vol. 2, Aslib–Cranfield Research Project, Cranfield, England, 1966.

[19] G. Salton, Automatic Phrase Matching, in *Readings in Automatic Language Processing*, D. Hays, ed., American Elsevier Publishing Company, Inc., New York, 1966.

[20] L. B. Doyle, Indexing and Abstracting by Association, *American Documentation*, Vol. 13, No. 4, October 1962.

[21] V. E. Giuliano and P. E. Jones, Linear Associative Information Retrieval, in *Vistas in Information Handling*, P. Howerton, ed., Spartan Books, New York, 1963.

[22] B. Altman, A Multiple Testing of the Natural Language Storage and Retrieval ABC Method: Preliminary Analysis and Test Results, *American Documentation*, Vol. 18, No. 1, January 1967.

[23] E. M. Keen, Semi-Automatic User Controlled Search Strategies, *Proceedings of the Fourth Annual National Colloquium on Information Retrieval*, A. B. Tonik, ed., Int. Information Inc., Philadelphia, 1967, pp. 141–154.

[24] G. Salton, Search Strategy and the Optimization of Retrieval Effectiveness, *Report ISR-12* to the National Science Foundation, Department of Computer Science, Cornell University, Ithaca, N.Y., 1967; also in *Mechanized Information Storage, Retrieval, and Dissemination*, K. Samuelson, ed., North Holland Publishing Co., Amsterdam, 1968, pp. 73–107.

Chapter 3
Key Concepts

The Concept of "Aboutness" in Subject Indexing 93
W.J. Hutchins

The Testing of Index Language Devices 98
C.W. Cleverdon and J. Mills

Thesaurus 111
D.J. Foskett

Using Problem Structures for Driving Human-Computer Dialogues 135
P.J. Daniels, H.M. Brooks, and N.J. Belkin

Relevance: A Review of and a Framework for Thinking on the Notion in Information Science 143
T. Saracevic

This section presents the key concepts that characterise IR. As indicated in the general introduction in Chapter 1, retrieval systems are designed to find documents relevant to users' needs for information about some topic. Decomposing this statement lays bare the essentials of retrieval and, hence, the issues that have to be addressed in designing useful systems. The way these issues are approached may then be motivated by one of the types of retrieval model considered in Chapter 5, from which particular techniques in turn follow, as discussed in Chapter 6.

We consider first the nature of information needs and documents, then indexing languages and descriptions, searching and matching, and the impact of the context within which an automated system operates.

INFORMATION NEEDS AND DOCUMENTS

Documents can in principle be any information-conveying items. However, though there is increasing interest in multimedia systems and hence in, e.g., image retrieval (as discussed in Chapter 8), documents in which information is conveyed in *natural language* have a special importance because it is our ordinary human means of communication. Retrieval systems are thus primarily concerned with documents in natural language, albeit documents of a wide range of types and with many variations in language. Retrieval systems have also, till recently, been confined to written documents. In general, we will assume retrieval is of written documents and, indeed, for printed rather than handwritten ones; but the basic notions and issues of retrieval apply to other types of material.

Documents convey information *about* something—a topic, subject, or whatever. IR in the broadest sense subsumes on the one hand user calls for specific documents ("known item" searches), and on the other explicit requests for specific data or facts. But the normal presumption in document retrieval is that the user wishes to find out about a *topic* or *subject* and is thus, while interested in data or facts, not yet in a position to specify precisely what data or facts are required. Indeed, requests for facts are also often requests for information about facts with their context. There is clearly no definite distinction between document and data retrieval, but document retrieval concentrates on the important, very common, situation where the user seeks a body of information about some necessarily (for them at the time) inadequately defined topic. Again, while users may have questions for which they want answers (cf. O'Connor, 1981), document retrieval in general cannot be taken just as question answering, since the user may not be in a position to formulate any very useful questions (Sparck Jones, 1990). Thus, if the aim is to provide for question answering, this should be seen as one function within the compass of a multifunction inquiry system.

Information, as the "substance" sought, while clearly the crucial ultimate deliverable, is also manifestly a vague and subtle substance. More to the point, it is a situation-specific product of the interaction between a user and a document (Wilson, 1973) and, as such, is only an indirect deliverable. Attempts to define it as a base for systems have generally been at a very high level of abstraction (cf. Hayes, 1993) that is often difficult to interpret and apply. *Aboutness* as a property of documents is in principle more accessible, but while it is a critical property of documents, it has its own intractability (see Hutchins's paper in this section), which thus constrains system design and performance. In particular, while aboutness clearly has something to do with document meaning (since documents are natural language objects), document meaning, i.e., the meaning of a text or discourse, is itself complex and intractable (cf. Blair, 1992), and the relation between meaning and aboutness is also a tricky one. While meaning is the province of such disciplines as linguistics, appropriate theories of discourse meaning are lacking, and it is thus not surprising (as Chapter 5 shows) that there are no solid, meaning-based retrieval models.

In order to obtain documents *relevant* to their *needs,* users have to express these needs, and they do this in natural language, as *requests.* But language is generally indeterminate and is the major contributor to the essential indeterminacy of retrieval (Blair, 1986). Thus, given that any request is only one possible way of expressing some topic need, and indeed (through the user's lack of information) may also be an inadequate characterisation of the topic, the root issue in retrieval is ensuring that a document a system matches with a request is actually about the topic of user interest.

Further, user information need is a complex notion, as Hewins (1990) clearly shows. Quite apart from document topic, it can cover a range of requirements like presentation level (e.g., elementary or advanced) and document style (e.g., popular or specialised), which may themselves not be easily specified. At the same time, need in terms of topic is not simple because, as the user is seeking information they do not already have, the topic may itself not be well understood, and the level of (mis)understanding may change during the course of the search. The study of users' information-seeking dialogues as illustrated in Belkin et al. (1987) shows, through the process of elicitation and reformulation of need, how uncertain and complicated needs can be. Moreover, what is *relevant* to a user's need is not strictly a document but the *content* of a document. The root challenge in retrieval is that user need and document content are both *unobservables,* and so is the relevance relation between them: relevance is the central concept in IR. The complexities of relevance and the difficulties of operationalising it, both as a basis for system design and as the means of system evaluation (see Chapter 4), are clear from Saracevic's paper in this section (Saracevic, 1975), which is as pertinent now as when it was originally written. A retrieval system nevertheless seeks to capture the relevance relation by establishing a *matching* relation between the two expressions of information in the document and the request, respectively.

In order to optimise this matching, a retrieval system works with characterisations of documents and requests in an *indexing language.* These characterisations are designed to meet two requirements. One is ensuring that if the *representations* of documents and requests match, the corresponding relevance relations hold; and the other is that the means of achieving this do not also allow or encourage matches where the relevance relation does not hold. The normal retrieval situation is where only a very small subset of the entire document file is relevant to a user need. A retrieval system has, in *indexing,* both to overcome surface differences of topic expression in document and request, in order to ensure that documents with relevant content (*relevant documents* for short) do match, and to avoid surface similarities of topic expression that permit matches on documents that are not relevant.

INDEXING, DESCRIPTIONS, AND LANGUAGES

Indexing—the provision of document and request *representations,* or *descriptions,* in an indexing language—is therefore the primary and distinctive action in operating a retrieval system: a retrieval system presupposes indexing, and system performance depends on the quality of the indexing. This is true, however unobvious at first sight, for modern full-text retrieval systems just as much as for old-fashioned libraries full of books, since indexing is an abstract notion that can be realised in very many ways. In particular, even if an entire user request is simply adopted as a search query and matched entire against the whole body of each document, seeking an occurrence of the complete request text, this implies, as a logical matter, that requests and documents are indexed by their respective complete texts.

A traditional library classification (like the Library of Congress one) is clearly an indexing language, since class labels are assigned as document descriptions to items in the file, and also to requests to form the *queries* for the actual searching. A thesaurus, like MeSH (Medical Subject Headings), is similarly an index language. A set of words extracted from a document and used as keywords provides a description for matching against words similarly extracted from a request: in this case, the only difference from the previous ones is that the indexing language vocabulary is defined a posteriori as the complete set of keywords for the whole file.

These different examples also show that it may or may not be the case that there is a presumption that matching is required on entire descriptions. When broad subject classes are used, as in the traditional library case, documents (explicitly) and requests (implicitly) are described by a single label that must match for retrieval. However, if entire texts, or full-content word lists, are used as descriptions, matching cannot be expected to be complete.

As the examples further suggest, individual index *terms* for an indexing language may be more or less close in meaning to the same word symbols in their normal natural language uses (which holds even when numerical class marks are used since these are interpreted via the natural language labels or definitions associated with them). There may or may not also be a classificatory structure over the indexing vocabulary, e.g., with hierarchic links. Document descriptions, and the queries representing requests, may have structures that range from simple unordered term sets to one with more complex groupings or relations between terms, as defined by the index language grammar, which may allow, e.g., Boolean formulae or semantic case relations. What *paradigmatic* and *syntagmatic,* i.e., permanent classificatory or temporary combinatory, relations are provided for a vocabulary and allowed in document and request representations are naturally important for retrieval effectiveness.

The nature of indexing languages is, as noted in the introduction to Chapter 2, one of the major traditional concerns for library and information service and system providers, and the range of possibilities is large (Chan et al., 1985; Dym,

1985; Foskett, 1980; Hutchins, 1975; Lancaster, 1972). The question of what, if any, fundamental difference automation makes is therefore important, especially as a difference of principle because automation offers new approaches to indexing, rather than as one of practice in relation to whether traditional manual indexing with its languages can be automated. As noted in Chapter 2, the fact that conventional automated IR systems may offer only natural language keyword indexing is not sufficient justification for advocating "new" automated approaches, using fancy indexing languages or descriptions, that are actually revivals of manual indexing styles (cf. Sparck Jones, 1992).

The various properties or features that indexing languages have can be seen as *devices* serving specific retrieval functions and, as discussed in Chapter 4, one of the important contributions of early retrieval evaluations was to make the notion of index language device explicit, with a view to assessing whether and how specific devices worked (Cleverdon and Mills, 1963; Keen, 1973).

The fact that document descriptions are not provided at *file time*, when documents enter a collection, but at *search time* through the retrieval process, does not imply that there are no document index descriptions. Thus, if a user searches a file of full document texts for matches against one or more query terms, those terms in the document that match constitute, for that particular search, the actual or *final* document index description. In such a situation, there is still an indexing language and indexing. The difference between this case and the more traditional one is that the system is more flexible, and responsive to users, because no decisions have been taken at file time as to how documents should be described to meet future, unknown needs. The document, in its raw form, is left open to the variety of index descriptions that the user's request, and the system's mediating indexing and searching apparatus working from the request, together impose on it. Thus, referring to Chapter 2, at the general level, systems with search time indexing are ones with *post-coordinate* indexing.

In modern systems where full text constitutes an *initial* document description, the potential for different actual matching descriptions is in principle largest, since indexing methods can be applied that check for complex expressions with an internal syntactic and semantic structure. However, the use of full text is normally far from implying that either initial or final descriptions involve any significant interpretative understanding of document meaning or content. Thus the matching operations allowed in typical operational situations actually have only the document word set as initial descriptions, or perhaps also word pairs defined by adjacency. More complexity may, however, be introduced into the final document descriptions constructed at search time, through the use of word proximity operators in the query.

But it should be noted that while it is one major advantage of search time indexing that complete descriptions are not required to match, and indeed in the full text case can hardly be expected to, it is also the case that where a short description has been assigned to a document at file time, for instance as a set of keywords, this need not imply that the complete description has to match for retrieval. It is also possible to choose, whether at file or search time, to confine indexing only to some parts of the whole document, e.g., main articles in a legal document, or to *surrogates* for the ultimate full text, e.g., titles or abstracts: these parts or surrogates are taken as the indexing *sources* for the entire document. Documents may alternatively be divided into portions, or *passages*, taken as independent indexing sources for the document or even as separate documents to be retrieved.

Indexing at search rather than file time has the advantage, as a matter of retrieval principle, that it does not preempt the future; it also has the practical advantage that indexing effort is not devoted to documents that are outside the scope of the requests that actually occur. It does, however, place pressure on the user to start the retrieval process sensibly since nothing has been done to "draw out" document content in a potentially helpful way; and it places more pressure on the system designer to supply an appropriate mediating apparatus to connect requests with relevant documents. This has to be powerful enough to generate or modify document and request representations that overcome the surface limitations of the given forms of documents and requests that "say the same thing in different words". There are further challenges for modern system designers in whether the required processes can actually be automated or are economically viable. Of course, indexing at search time does not imply that the actual documents are sequentially scanned then. It relies on organisational preprocessing through inverted files (see Chapter 7) and may be constrained by the form that these take: for example, whether specific locations for each word occurrence within a document have been recorded, or just presence and frequency.

At the same time, the assumption so far in this introduction has been that indexing is primarily grounded in the straightforwardly linguistic parts of documents, e.g., title and text, and that indexing languages refer to document content as thus *directly* expressed. However, as in traditional libraries, non-language index *keys* like author names are also used, as they are extremely useful means of document access. Other *indirect* content indicators, including citations (Garfield, 1955; Kessler, 1963; Small, 1973), are very valuable, and retrieval systems may now exploit a range of *header* and similar keys as found with e-mail and the increasing use of URLs (universal resource locators). The latter in particular can function both as unique labels for end documents and as starting points for focused, hypertext-based browsing.

Thus there are important questions about the appropriate response to the fact that documents typically have a complex administrative structure reflected in the familiar different fields of library catalogues and now amplified by the ballooning of the full-text field. These include the type of index language suited to each field, which may be quite different, and how information from the different indexing sources represented by different fields may be combined. Thus, if the language used for different fields is the same, as with title and text, this may reinforce topic specification. But if the languages are of fundamentally different types, as with author and text, they may provide complementary means of topic characterisation. One feature of modern systems has been the greater flexibility allowed to cross field boundaries, as with searching on personal names in either author or text fields. The complicated interactions between sources and languages, with their implications not only for the content of index descriptions but for other properties like their level of detail, are illustrated by Katzer et al. (1982) and Tenopir (1985).

The use of full text also raises the issue of what role the structure of the text body has in retrieval. Documents, as discourse, have an organisational structure which groups, relates, and emphasises topics. Hutchins (1978) considers the way document discourse structure may bear on retrieval, and Liddy (1991) examines the structure of abstract texts. But beyond some use of structurally significant text areas (e.g., opening paragraphs) and elements (e.g., section headings), and of paragraphs as natural indicators of discourse units and topic divisions, there has been little work on the retrieval use of the rich structure that indubitably exists in discourse. This may be because IR is a relatively coarse-grained task, and the discourse structure of documents is more relevant to extracting or summarising and to hypertext (see Chapter 8) than to retrieval proper. However, it may also be attributed on the one hand to the fact that evaluation of the ways structure contributes to performance is very hard, and on the other to the fact that identifying within-text discourse structure automatically is an open research problem.

All of these points serve to emphasise the key part played by *redundancy* in retrieval. As all the elements of natural language (and of specialised sublanguages in fact) are ambiguous, because multifaceted, what topics or concepts are actually expressed in a document emerges (as in a pointillist painting) by repetition and convergence. Index descriptions, of documents and requests, should therefore seek to compensate for the uncertainties of topic expression by their own redundancy. The techniques discussed in Chapter 6 show ways in which this is done.

SEARCHING AND MATCHING

Indexing and searching, intimately related as the twin faces of retrieval, subsume several lower-level operations that may or may not be independent of one another according to the particular model of retrieval on which a system is based. From the point of view of *searching,* these are *inspection, matching, scoring,* and *output*. Thus, in systems where documents are clustered, so whole groups of documents are given a common representation for initial inspection and may be rejected en bloc if this representation does not sufficiently match a query, individual documents within a cluster that in fact share terms with a query may never be inspected. Matching establishes what is in common between document and query representations, normally what terms are shared, while scoring assigns a particular value, according to the chosen system function, to the match. As suggested by the earlier remarks on indexing, matching may on the one hand be all or nothing, so documents are either retrieved or not retrieved, or may grade documents according to the degree to which they match a query. Finally, what and how output is delivered may depend on other criteria, e.g., limiting volume. In practical operation, the way data about search results and documents themselves are presented to the user is very important.

Matching and scoring are the core retrieval operations; but the complex possibilities for system design are evident in many modern approaches using weighting, where one document may be ranked more highly in the output than another through sharing fewer, but more highly weighted, terms with the query. The rank position of a document is thus a function not just of its own match with the query, as in a conventional Boolean system, but of that of other documents as well (though Boolean systems may order output by, date, for example). Again the value of a term may depend not only on properties of the individual document and request but also of the document file as a whole. From this it follows that the value of a term for a document, and indeed its actual or effective assignment to the document, depends not only on the nature of a request but on the time that the request is submitted.

In general in modern systems, when compared with traditional or conventional ones, not just document retrieval but also document indexing depends on the user's request, while the values of terms are determined by the properties of the document set as well as by those of individual documents and requests. As a natural corollary, matching is relative rather than absolute, subsuming (but without requiring explicit prespecification) a search strategy allowing for those combinations of search terms that deliver first the best (highest scoring) match, then the next best, in rank order. What is sometimes called a document's *retrieval status value* is therefore properly seen as determined not only by its own individual relationship with a query but by its relationships with other documents, as more or less strongly related to the query than they are.

INDEXING-SEARCHING DEPENDENCIES AND ISSUES

Indexing and searching thus interact to define IR system capabilities. But index languages are the foundation for everything else, so there are important questions to be asked about indexing languages and the way they may be used to provide or modify document and request representations. These are:

- What are the minimal indexing *elements*, e.g., stems or full words?
- What are the index *terms* like; e.g., are they elements alone or do they have more complex forms like multiword *compound terms*?
- What are the means of *marking* terms as more or less important, e.g., by flagging as obligatory or by weighting?
- What are the *relations* between elements forming terms and between terms forming descriptions; e.g., are these *syntagmatic* relations limited to simple coordination or are they drawn from a richer stock of grouping or labelling *operators*?

- What are the available permanent, or *paradigmatic,* links between elements or terms, that can be exploited to form representations or to revise them in searching?
- What are the *decomposition* or *modulation* operations allowed on descriptions to derive alternative matching possibilities; e.g., substitution of generically related terms, suppression of terms in subordinate relations?

As noticed earlier, virtually every possible view of what makes the best indexing language, index representation, and permitted modulation operation has been advocated in the manual case, and many have been actually implemented in practice. However (as mentioned in the introduction to Chapter 2), systematic tests from the sixties onward suggested that many of the more elaborate schemes offer no special advantage. It was found sufficient to use simple word stems as elements and also as terms, and coordinated representations that were completely unconstrained in allowing any terms to be dropped from the initial query in order to secure matches. This approach was effective, especially when document or request representations were enhanced with the weighting that automation made possible. It also became apparent that some indexing resources, e.g., association or classification relations among vocabulary terms, were only or most helpful when applied under the constraints of relevance information. Thus a term should not be added to a query just through its association with a given query term in the file as a whole, but only if associated in relevant documents.

It is nevertheless not clear how well the *benchmark,* statistics-enhanced simple term approach stands up to really large-scale conditions. This is one issue the TREC Programme is examining, but current file sizes are outstripping the TREC data scale. There is currently little interest, largely because of cost, in comparisons between modern natural-language-based techniques and conventional indexing e.g., using a controlled vocabulary. The issue now is rather whether modern versions of conventional ideas, e.g., linguistically motivated compound terms, are of value, and whether, if they are, they can be implemented automatically. It is, however, important for those advocating "obvious" improvements over the benchmark type of approach to be aware that they may be claiming potential gains from mere automated implementations of earlier manual approaches not found to be effective or, at any rate, cost-effective. Further, it is necessary to show that linguistically motivated compounds are not only better than single terms but also than compounds defined by statistical associations or user-specified proximity.

Thus it is especially necessary to state whether proposed elaborate automatic indexing techniques are intended to replicate former manual ones (perhaps with improvements, e.g., through greater consistency of implementation), to emulate their performance, or to offer some wholly novel retrieval resource. In the context of large systems in particular, it is also necessary to consider indexing devices according to whether they presuppose document processing or may be confined to query development from requests. This is important too because evidence from past investigations suggests that concentrating on query development is much more valuable than devoting effort to a priori document indexing. From this point of view, as the TREC Programme illustrates, while all the filing and searching operations in modern systems are automated and file time document processing may be minimised for economy reasons, it is natural not only to encourage careful manual query development but also to exploit, for this, indexing resources that have been manually constructed (e.g., word classifications). But the precise payoffs from different forms and amounts of human and machine effort are a key issue in current retrieval research.

Thus the critical questions modern systems have to address are, first, a general one:

- What determines good indexing terms and good index descriptions, given both the necessity and the opportunities of automation?

and second, a specific one:

- How, given the available benchmark provided by coordination and weighted terms, can performance be further improved? For example, are compound terms useful and, if so, how should they be handled in operations like weighting and query modulation?

It is essential to emphasise here that while the expression *index description* applies to both documents and requests, interpreting the user's need as stated in a request (or as manifested by marking approved documents) presents its own particular challenges, regardless of the fact that with search time indexing this interpretation is necessarily important. Thus, precisely what elements of a request should be extracted and organised to drive the search, through one or more queries, depends on a view of what a good search query is, irrespective of the fact that it is formally an index description.

Before either question above can be answered, moreover, further points have to be taken into account. In discussing indexing and searching so far, the presumption has been that *indexing policy* and *searching strategy* are primarily narrow, technical matters. But, in fact, both are broader notions. Thus traditional indexing languages, like subject classification schemes, imply decisions about the degree of language *specificity* with which it is desirable to treat topics: for instance, if there is only the class "Mathematics", it is impossible to distinguish documents about algebra from ones about geometry. The degree of description *exhaustivity* refers to the extent to which all, or only some, of the topics in a document figure in its description. When natural language and full text are used, these points no longer straightforwardly apply. However, there is a closely related issue to be addressed in automatic indexing; namely that (for a given vocabulary), the more document terms are available for matching, the less any one of them will be a useful one for distinguishing this document from others. This is the relation between description exhaustivity and description specificity, reflecting van Rijsbergen's conflict between "representation without discrimination" and "discrimination without representation" (van Rijsbergen, 1979, p. 29). As Chapters 5 and 6 make clear, devices like weighting are forms of response to these issues in the modern system context.

Equally, while we have just treated searching as a purely technical matter of internal machine operation, in accord with our emphasis on automatic processes, this is just one part of the much larger notion of information seeking that necessarily depends on and involves the user, and may thus take forms beyond that represented by the "find documents on X" paradigm: for example, *browsing* and (half-remembered) *item location*.

These and other types of retrieval requirement imply a need for a system to offer a range of strategies to meet the different kinds of problem such types of retrieval present.

SYSTEM CONTEXT

Thus the particular devices chosen for a system must be responses to its wider *environment*, which subsumes such important factors as the nature of the documents in the file, the kinds of users the system has, the sorts of relevance need to be met, and so forth. For instance, in a given case it may be perfectly reasonable to institute an indexing policy that limits indexing to titles and abstracts, not only because these are seen as handy full-document distillations but because the more detailed content coverage that full text offers is not required for the actual system users. Similarly, it may be appropriate to implement a searching strategy with default backup to broader terms if matching fails, because users typically have rather unfocused subject needs. Again, if the users of a particular system, when left to themselves, tend to follow certain kinds of retrieval strategy, like "berrypicking" (Bates, 1989), the system indexing and matching should be designed to support this effectively.

The presumption so far in this introduction has been that the design aim for automated retrieval systems is to shift as much of the work as possible from the user to the machine, and that the system's indexing and searching resources are autonomously applied. In fact, the human as information seeker is not merely the original initiator of the whole process but a necessarily active and interactive participant in it, however much (as evidenced further in Chapters 6–8) the system attempts to function not just as a dumb data basher but as an intelligent assistant. The user's involvement applies from the beginning to the end of the entire information seeking effort, not just to online interaction with an automated system; but it is especially important during the search session itself. There is thus the general issue to consider: "Where should the person stop and the information search start?" (Bates, 1990), as well as the characteristics of users apart from their actual subject need; for example, their background or skills. Altogether, as the discussions in Bates (1986, 1989), Borgman (1985, 1989), and Fidel (1984, 1991) show, there are many important and complex properties both of users and of their modus operandi that have to be taken into account in overall system design. From a broad perspective, interface facilities for browsing, scanning, and so forth also play a part in retrieval functionality and thus help to determine the shape of the central indexing and retrieval processes.

At the same time, while methods of indexing and searching have been applied, or may be intended to be applicable, to different types of document or literature, the nature of the document material in the file is important. In the past, books were regarded as somewhat different from, e.g., scientific articles, and it was recognised that humanities papers, say, might not behave in the same way as chemistry ones. In the many evaluation tests done in the past decades, retrieval techniques have been compared across test collections with different properties, with the aim of showing that superiority of one over another is preserved. But while absolute performance naturally differs a good deal, there has been little serious investigation of the impact of document characteristics like different genres on performance. Properties of documents and literatures are an important area where useful papers are surprisingly lacking.

Finally, as will be evident from the point made about the role of indexing, there are properties of files as a whole that affect retrieval. These refer first to the statistical characteristics of large document sets, where the same distributional patterns appear in many different guises (Brookes, 1977) and may be exploited as in term weighting schemes. There is also *makeup*, as where a file covers many different subject areas, or kinds of document, a point that is becoming increasingly important with the explosion of heterogeneous online resources within what may be labelled the universal file. These include both end documents in the ordinary sense and many types and levels of metadocument, to which it is both desirable, and may be feasible, to apply the same IR techniques. Searchers may not be aware of such file properties, but it may be difficult for systems to respond to them automatically, at least fully rather than partially or incidentally. Indeed, there is what may be called the hidden information content of a file, where concepts only become apparent when several documents are considered together and not in isolation. From this point of view, offering the user many, rather than few, documents might be deemed valuable, though getting the information synergy from disparate documents described by Swanson (1986) may be too hard to achieve.

In fact, the nature of document files and of individual documents, of subject areas, of users, and of their information needs, all vary enormously and are environment factors that have to be taken into account in system design. The challenge for system builders is therefore either to be able to apply a range of methods, well founded on tests for the effects of different environment conditions, or to have a single, good, general-purpose way of doing retrieval.

The papers in this chapter are chosen first as considering the situation properties of retrieval (aboutness, relevance, etc.) and second as examining the essential questions of indexing and searching. Types of retrieval model that can be drawn from these analyses appear in Chapter 5. But as retrieval is an empirical matter, it is necessary to evaluate models, however plausible they may seem, by performance testing; and testing is also needed to assess the detailed alternative interpretations of general arguments. The next chapter therefore examines evaluation issues and notions in information retrieval.

SELECTED READINGS

Hutchins (1978) addresses a foundation issue for indexing, in a thought-provoking way. He examines the assumption that the business of indexing is to state what a document is about in the sense of providing a summary of the document content. His claim is that an alternative view of aboutness, grounded in the thematic organisation of texts, may be more appropriate. Thus he illustrates a text-linguistic structure with a complex thematic progression embodying the author's argument, and suggests that this organisation, in which given and new with respect to document content are clearly indicated, is pertinent to indexing to meet ignorant users' needs. Thus indexing should mark the presupposed knowledge of the text, so that users can identify those documents where the entry point to new material is right for them, in terms of what they already know.

The paper by Cleverdon and Mills (1963) reflects the authors' experience of conducting a serious comparative study of indexing systems, and marks the important contribution the Cranfield work made to the decompositional analysis of IR systems, in terms of performance factors, that is required to ensure well-motivated comparative evaluation. The important point here is the way in which the notion that indexing languages are characterised by functional devices (which was an important topic in the animated discussions of the period) is treated. Thus the paper lays out the range of generic devices and illustrates how, in the indexing of the test documents, basic descriptions in a theory-neutral natural language style were supplied that provided support for these devices in a clear and plain way. This meant that it was then possible to derive further descriptions using a set of specially designed indexing languages with various devices and device combinations, so that the effect on retrieval performance of each device was made clear (Cleverdon, 1967). As the authors note, many existing languages offered varied device sets, so that simply comparing the performance of these languages as wholes could not show which devices were responsible for their respective performances.

The paper by Foskett (1980) is one of the few overview papers we have included in the Reader. The historical and continuing importance of its topic, the thesaurus, makes it difficult to select a single primary paper from the mass of literature on thesauri, but equally makes a discussion of the ways the notion of thesaurus has been interpreted essential. Manually constructed thesauri have been and are widely used in bibliographic services, both as primary indexing tools and also as search aids: there are many that have survived through decades under continuous adaptation to the specialised subject areas for which this type of indexing language was originally designed. Thesauri have at the same time proved difficult to construct automatically. They rest on two foundations: the definition of individual (complex) concepts and their linking by simple relations, especially but not exclusively hierarchical; and the importance for information characterisation and discovery of the concepts and associations between concepts that thesauri provide, means that thesauri continue to be seen as desiderata, if not for primary indexing at any rate for search formulation. Foskett's account illustrates the wide range of forms that thesauri can take and the retrieval functions they are intended to serve.

We have noted that the properties and activities of the user are complex matters for system design, and that it is essential to see the entire retrieval process from end to end as intrinsically interactive even if, as with earlier bibliographic services, the end user was not interacting online with the system. Daniels et al. (1985) report work done before end user interaction was commonplace, analysing the interaction between an end user and a librarian to prepare the honed search specification submitted to the machine. The authors view their analysis as the basis for developing a model of what an automated intelligent intermediary would have to do (Brooks et al., 1985). However, we have chosen the paper here because the authors lay out the various subtasks that characterise information seeking, and show how information interaction dialogues are cooperative efforts that address the different subtasks that have to be carried out for the complete information access task, doing this in a locally flexible and adaptive but globally useful way. Thus the authors' decomposition identifies such subgoals as establishing the user's background knowledge of a field, and the context of the current need, the type of output required, and so on, as well as the definition of the search topic and the formulation of the actual search specification. The problem structure the paper presents is seen in other publications by the authors as of very wide applicability to information seeking of any kind, while it also offers a useful framework for thinking about document retrieval in general.

Finally, Saracevic (1975) provides both a discussion of the nature of relevance and a review of the different ways in which it has been treated, analysed from the perspective of communication of knowledge. Thus relevance is seen as an extremely broad, and also controversial, notion that has developed a particular flavour within the narrower compass of information science as concerned with the effective transmission of scientific knowledge. Different definitions of relevance essentially reflect different views of what is required for effective communication within this framework. For example, relevance may be interpreted from the system point of view, or from the destination one, or from the subject knowledge or from a pragmatic, problem-solving point of view. These views in turn then lead to various specific procedures or measures as the basis for establishing the effectiveness of an information provision system. However, as Saracevic argues, it is more valuable to see relevance as necessarily implying relationships between its various specific manifestations.

REFERENCES

*Note: *** after a reference indicates a selected reading.*

Bates, M.J. (1986) Subject access in online catalogs: A design model. *Journal of the American Society for Information Science*, **37**, 357–376.

Bates, M.J. (1989) The design of browsing and berrypicking techniques for the online search interface. *Online Review*, **13**, 407–424.

Bates, M.J. (1990) Where should the person stop and the information search start? *Information Processing and Management*, **26**, 575–591.

Belkin, N.J., Brooks, H.M., and Daniels, P.J. (1987) Knowledge elicitation using discourse analysis. *International Journal of Man-Machine Studies*, **27**, 127–144.

Blair, D.C. (1986) Indeterminacy in subject access to documents. *Information Processing and Management*, **22**, 229–242.

Blair, D.C. (1992) Information retrieval and the philosophy of language. *Computer Journal*, **35**, 200–207.

Borgman, C.L. (1985) Why are online catalogues hard to use? Lessons learned from information retrieval studies. *Journal of the American Society for Information Science*, **36**, 387–400.

Borgman, C.L. (1989) All users of information retrieval systems are not created equal: An exploration into individual differences. *Information Processing and Management*, **25**, 237–251.

Brookes, B.C. (1977) Theory of the Bradford Law. *Journal of Documentation*, **33**, 180–209.

Brooks, H.M., Daniels, P.J., and Belkin, N.J. (1985) Problem descriptions and user models: Developing an intelligent interface for document retrieval systems. In *Informatics 8: Advances in Intelligent Retrieval*, pp. 191–214. London: Aslib.

Chan, L.M., Richmond, P.A., and Svenonius, E. (Eds.) (1985) *Theory of Subject Analysis: A Sourcebook*. Littleton, CO: Libraries Unlimited.

Cleverdon, C.W. (1967) The Cranfield tests on index language devices. *Aslib Proceedings*, **19**, 173–192.

Cleverdon, C.W., and Mills, J. (1963) The testing of index language devices. *Aslib Proceedings*, **15**(4), 106–130.***

Daniels, P.J. (1986) Cognitive models in information retrieval—an evaluative review. *Journal of Documentation*, **42**, 272–304.

Daniels, P.J., Brooks, H.M., and Belkin, N.J. (1985) Using problem structures for driving human-computer dialogues. In *RIAO-85. Actes: Recherche d'Informations Assistee par Ordinateur*, pp. 645–660. Grenoble, France: IMAG.***

Dym, E.D. (Ed.) (1985) *Subject and Information Analysis*. New York: Marcel Dekker.

Fidel, R. (1984) Online searching styles: A case-study-based model of searching behaviour. *Journal of the American Society for Information Science*, **35**, 211–221.

Fidel, R. (1991) Searchers' selections of search keys. *Journal of the American Society for Information Science*, **42**, 490–527.

Foskett, D.J. (1980) Thesaurus. In A. Kent, H. Lancour, and J.E. Daily (Eds.), *Encyclopaedia of Library and Information Science, Volume 30*, pp. 416–462. New York: Marcel Dekker.***

Garfield, E. (1955) Citation indexes for science. *Science*, **122**, 108–111.

Hayes, R.M. (1993) Measurement of information. *Information Processing and Management*, **29**, 1–11.

Hewins, E.T. (1990) Information need and use studies. *Annual Review of Information Science and Technology*, **25**, 145–172.

Hutchins, W.J. (1975) *Languages of Indexing and Classification*. Stevenage, Herts.: Peter Peregrinus.

Hutchins, W.J. (1978) The concept of "aboutness" in subject indexing. *Aslib Proceedings*, **30**, 172–181.***

Ingwersen, P. (1992) *Information Retrieval Interaction*. London: Taylor Graham.

Katzer, J., McGill, M.J., Tessier, J.A., Frakes, W., and DasGupta, P. (1982) A study of the overlap among document representations. *Information Technology: Research and Development*, **1**, 261–274.

Keen, E.M. (1973) The Aberystwyth index languages test. *Journal of Documentation*, **19**, 1–35.

Kessler, M.M. (1963) Bibliographic coupling between scientific papers. *American Documentation*, **14**(4), 10–25.

Lancaster, F.W. (1972) *Vocabulary Control for Information Retrieval*. Washington, DC: Information Resources Press.

Liddy, E.D. (1991) The discourse-level structure of empirical abstracts: An exploratory study. *Information Processing and Management*, **27**, 55–81.

O'Connor, J. (1981) Answer-passage retrieval by text searching. *Journal of the American Society for Information Science*, **31**, 227–239.

Saracevic, T. (1975) Relevance: a review of and a framework for thinking on the notion in information science. *Journal of the American Society for Information Science*, **26**, 321–343.***

Small, H. (1973) Co-citation in the scientific literature: A new measure of the relationship between scientific documents. *Journal of the American Society for Information Science*, **24**, 265–269.

Sparck Jones, K. (1990) *Retrieving Information or Answering Questions. British Library Annual Research Lecture, 1989*. London: British Library.

Sparck Jones, K. (1992) Assumptions and issues in text-based retrieval. In P.S. Jacobs (Ed.), *Text-Based Intelligent Systems*, pp. 157–177. Hillsdale, N.J.: Lawrence Erlbaum.

Stiles, H.E. (1961) The association factor in information retrieval. *Journal of the Association for Computing Machinery*, **8**, 271–279.

Swanson, D.R. (1986) Undiscovered public knowledge. *Library Quarterly*, **56**, 103–118.

Swanson, D.R. (1988) Historical note: Information retrieval and the future of an illusion. *Journal of the American Society for Information Science*, **39**, 92–98.

Tenopir, C. (1985) Full text database retrieval performance. *Online Review*, **9**, 149–164.

van Rijsbergen, C.J. (1979) *Information Retrieval*. Second edition. London: Butterworths.

Wilson, P. (1973) Situational relevance. *Information Storage and Retrieval*, **9**, 457–471.

The concept of 'aboutness' in subject indexing

W. J. Hutchins

The Library, University of East Anglia, Norwich

Paper presented at a Colloquium on Aboutness held by the Co-ordinate Indexing Group, 18 April 1977

The common view of the 'aboutness' of documents is that the index entries (or classifications) assigned to documents represent or indicate in some way the total contents of documents; indexing and classifying are seen as processes involving the 'summarization' of the texts of documents. In this paper an alternative concept of 'aboutness' is proposed based on an analysis of the linguistic organization of texts, which is felt to be more appropriate in many indexing environments (particularly in non-specialized libraries and information services) and which has implications for the evaluation of the effectiveness of indexing systems.

Introduction

THE LITERATURE OF INDEXING AND CLASSIFICATION contains remarkably little discussion of the processes of indexing and classifying. We find a great deal about the construction of index languages and classification systems, about the principles of classification, about the correct formulation of index entries (*e.g.* the uses of standard citation orders and of chain indexing) and about the evaluation of indexes and information systems. But we find very little about how indexers and classifiers decide what the subject of a document is, how they decide what it is 'about'. The great majority of works on indexing and on information retrieval (however broadly defined) contain a statement somewhat similar to the following quotation from the PRECIS manual:[1]

> It has been found most convenient to start an explanation of PRECIS by assuming that the indexer, having examined a document, has established in his mind some meaningful sequence of words which summarizes its subject content. The manual goes on from that point to explain how such a phrase should . . . be analysed into its separate components and then organized into a string . . . (p. 4).

The basic assumption is that indexers are able to state what a document is 'about' by formulating an expression which 'summarizes' the content of the document. Indexing is traditionally seen as a process of 'summarization'. It is assumed that the relationship between a document and its index entry (or entries) is one of some kind of semantic condensation: the index entry represents a 'summary' of the content of the whole text.

The process is generally seen to involve the selection of 'key' words or phrases from the text, expressions which are 'significant' indicators of content and which together sum up the message of the document (e.g. Vickery[2]). This view underlies most experiments in automatic indexing and abstracting. In many it is assumed that 'key' words can be identified as those which occur most frequently in the text, disregarding the 'function words' (articles, prepositions, conjunctions, etc.) and other common words of high frequency in similar texts. Such statistical methods of extracting 'key' words have now achieved considerable subtlety and some degree of success (Salton's work[3]), but they have inadequacies which other researchers have tried to reduce by the development of other means of identifying 'significant' expressions. Indexers know from experience the value of reading prefaces, scanning chapter headings and indexes, looking at conclusions, etc. as 'short cuts' in deciding what a document is about. Edmundson[4] has experimented with refined versions of such 'hints for indexers' (following the earlier work of Baxendale[5]), selecting 'key' words from the beginnings of paragraphs, chapter headings and concluding sections, and on the basis of 'cue words' such as *result, therefore, since*, etc.

However different in approach, the basic assumption is the same. The objective of indexing (whether automated or not) is seen as the provision of an expression or of a set of 'key' words which as a whole represents a 'summary' of the document's content. This basic assumption has rarely been questioned—indeed it is rare to find any awareness that such an assumption has been made. The traditional view finds universal acceptance, namely that for the purposes of document indexing and information retrieval the 'aboutness' of a document is to be equated with some kind of 'summary' of its contents.

Why should the assumption be questioned? First, we are all aware of the inadequacies of present indexing practice and, despite impressive achievements, there is not much sign that automatic systems can or will do much better than human ones. We should be prepared to consider alternative approaches. Secondly, it is surely right to ask ourselves whether a concept of 'aboutness' which may well be appropriate in the context of literary criticism, in the anlysis of political speeches, or indeed for the purposes of abstracting—to which I shall be returning later—is necessarily equally valid in the context of subject indexing. We should consider whether a different concept of 'aboutness' might not be more appropriate in many indexing environments. Lastly, we should ask ourselves to what extent true 'summarization' is in fact attempted in everyday indexing practice.

I shall be putting forward an alternative concept of 'aboutness' based largely on a linguistic analysis of text structure, which could form a sounder foundation of indexing procedure in many contexts and which reflects more realistically the information needs of many users of libraries and information services.

Thematic structure of texts

I begin by sketching in broad outline the basic features of text structure, concentrating particularly upon the thematic organization of texts.[6]

In any sentence or utterance, whatever the context in which it may occur, there are some elements which the speaker or writer assumes his hearer or reader knows of already and which he takes as 'given', and there are other elements which he introduces as 'new' elements conveying information not previously known. The 'given' elements may be related either to items which have been mentioned earlier in the discourse or they may be related to objects or events which, in the context of the discourse, are taken to be common knowledge for both speaker and hearer (or writer and reader). Those 'given' elements relating to previous discourse are generally signalled linguistically by such devices as the use of anaphoric pronouns (*he*, *she*, *it*, *they*, etc.), definite articles, demonstratives (*this*, *that*), relative clauses (*the man I told you about*), or by simple repetition of the earlier expression. The particular means employed depends very much on the relative distance of the previous mention, the need to distinguish among similar phenomena, the demands of stylistic variety and emphasis, etc. Similar formal means are used to refer to anything taken as 'given' from the environment of the discourse: pronouns, relative clauses, deictic articles, etc. Whatever their origin we may regard the 'given' elements of a sentence as constituting its 'theme'; and those elements expressing anything 'new' or otherwise unpredictable (from the text or environment) as constituting its 'rheme'. (In this account of 'given' and 'new' and of 'theme' and 'rheme' I have had to simplify considerably a very complex area of linguistic usage—for more detail see the book edited by Daneš,[7] and the monograph by Halliday and Hasan[8].)

In the normal case, the 'theme' precedes the 'rheme'. It is natural for speakers and writers to start from what is known or can be presumed to be known before going on to impart 'new' information. It is natural to begin by saying which 'given' elements are going to be talked 'about', *i.e.* to express in the 'theme' what the sentence (as a whole) is 'about'. It is equally natural for the thematic elements, where they relate to previous discourse, to refer back to some elements of the immediately preceding sentence. In this way the speaker or writer can convey his message by a natural progressive accumulation of 'new' information. In crude terms there are basically two ways a theme may be related to a preceding sentence or clause: either it refers to elements of the foregoing 'rheme' or it repeats some or all of the preceding 'theme' (Daneš[9]). We have thus two basic types of thematic progression: linear progression (figure 1) and parallel progression (figure 2).

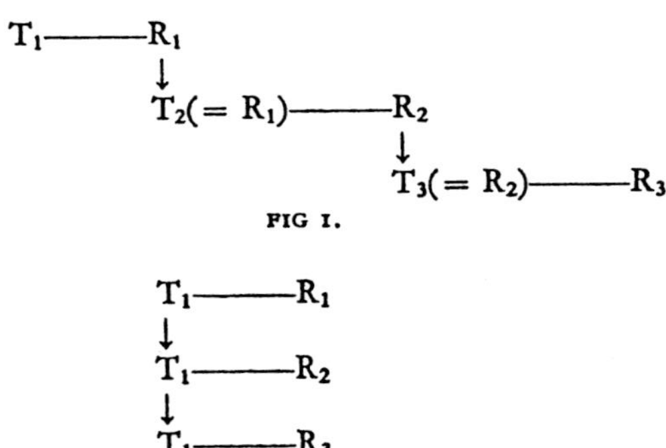

FIG 1.

FIG 2.

Linear progression may be illustrated by the sentence sequence:

The boy (T_1) was reading a book (R_1). It (T_2) was about elephants (R_2). These animals (T_3) are found in Africa and India (R_3).

Parallel progression may be illustrated by:

The boy (T_1) came home from school (R_1). First he (T_1) had something to eat (R_2). Then he (T_1) went off to play football in the park (R_3).

These two types of progression provide the foundations for the thematic organization of texts. Typically a paragraph or larger segment of text consists of a mixture of linear and parallel progressions starting from an initial sentence. A common example is the exposition of a 'split rheme' (figure 3).

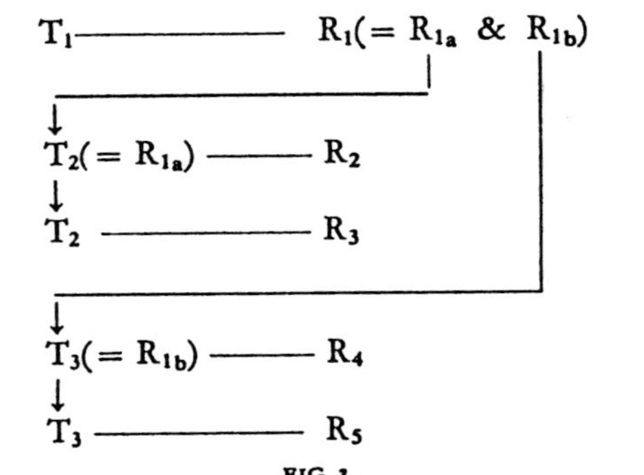

FIG 3.

This mixed thematic progression may be illustrated by the short paragraph:

> All substances are divided into two classes: elementary substances and compounds. An elementary substance is a substance which consists of atoms of only one kind. . . . A compound is a substance which consists of atoms of two or more different kinds . . .

The initial sentence ($T_1 - R_1$) may be regarded as the 'theme sentence' for the whole paragraph, as the foundation upon which the speaker or writer builds his message. The analogy can be pursued further: the 'theme sentence' of a paragraph may be related either to elements introduced as 'new' in an earlier paragraph or to elements of the 'theme sentence' of a preceding paragraph. Clearly, we may have similar types of thematic progression among text segments much larger than individual sentences. In the normal case, we should expect the initial sentences of a text to represent the foundations upon which the writer organizes what he wants to say. The first paragraphs of a text establish, therefore, the 'theme' for the text as a whole; they express in essence what the text is going to be 'about'.

This is, of course, still only a crude picture of the mechanisms of text structure. Many other organizational principles play a role in the structuring of text;

in narratives, for example, the demands of plot and characterization, the need to depict the topographical, social and psychological settings of actions and events all play a large part in determining text structures. One structural feature common to all texts is that of semantic progression, the requirement that components of the text should be related to each other by some 'logical' connections—where the 'logic' may vary between the extremes of strict philosophical logic and of weaker common-sense plausibility. At the sentence level, the 'logic' of semantic progression requires, for example, that the statement of a condition (*if X*) should be followed by its consequent (*i.e. If X, then Y*); otherwise the progression is incomplete. At the paragraph level, the operation of semantic progression may be seen in the expectation that after a sentence stating, *e.g.* that *X has three components* there should follow sentences describing each component in turn; a failure to do so would be a violation of semantic progression. Finally at the level of the whole text, there are similar expectations of 'logical' development; one of them, for example, is that if a writer has begun by describing a particular 'problem' he will, at some later stage in the text, offer an appropriate 'solution'; another is that if some 'hypothesis' about a state of affairs has been put forward there will be described some 'tests' or arguments supporting or rejecting the hypothesis. (Such kinds of semantic progression seem to underlie a large proportion of scientific and scholarly texts.)[10]

Writers and readers: assumptions and expectations

Every speaker and writer has to make some assumptions about the knowledge and interests of his hearers and readers, whatever the context in which he may be speaking or writing. These assumptions are usually undefined and are very often purely intuitive. Nobody can ever begin speaking or writing without assuming something; nobody can ever begin from absolute scratch—even with very young children we all make numerous assumptions about what they know already. How are the writer's assumptions about readers reflected in his text? From what we have been saying the answer should be clear. The most explicit expressions of assumed or presupposed 'knowledge' are to be found whenever an author treats some elements as 'given' which he has not previously introduced as 'new' information or which he has not chosen to describe or explain in any detail. These elements he takes for granted; he assumes that anyone reading his text (or rather, anyone he expects to read his text) will already have some knowledge of the objects or events he is referring to; in other words, he presupposes a certain level of knowledge of what he is going to talk about.

The same process is at work in a less explicit way when the author establishes the thematic foundation of his text. In the initial passages of a document an author makes numerous presuppositions about the knowledge, interests and attitudes of his potential readers. He will assume a certain linguistic competence, a certain level of general knowledge, a certain cultural and educational background, and normally also some kind of general interest or inquisitiveness in the topic he is going to write about. In some cases his assumptions take on more specific and definable forms (many documents, for example, require an above average knowledge of highly specialized disciplines); these he will normally be well aware of and will take care to make explicit. But there will always be some presuppositions* that remain hidden and which become evident only when a reader does not share them.

It is not, of course, only in the initial passages of a text that an author refers to elements taken as 'given'; at any point in his text he may mention some phenomenon or event which he presumes that his readers know something about already. Nevertheless, it is in these early sections where the thematic base is being established that the author's presuppositions are most in evidence and where they have greatest effect, for it is in the opening paragraphs that the author must succeed in making contact with his readers. It is here that the reader learns the intentions of the author and how much he is expected to know of the topic already.

This brings us to the question of what readers normally expect from documents. Readers approach documents from such a variety of objectives, motives, temperaments, ideologies, predispositions and states of knowledge that any attempt to give a meaningful answer would seem to be doomed from the outset. Nevertheless, we can make certain generalizations. Leaving aside novels, poetry and other creative writings it is generally true to say that the reader of a document hopes to learn something 'new' as a result of reading it. He comes to the document with an interest, a desire or a need to 'improve' in some way his present state of knowledge. What he wants is a document which contains information that is 'new' to him and which assumes no more knowledge than he has already. These, then, may be regarded as the basic conditions which must be satisfied: (i) the information conveyed as 'new' (*i.e.* not presupposed) in the document must include some that the reader did not know before; and (ii) the knowledge taken as 'given' (*i.e.* presupposed) must be at a level lower than, or roughly equal to, that of the reader. Failure to satisfy both conditions leads to frustration or, at best, annoyance for the reader: to read something which tells him nothing 'new' is just a waste of his time, to try to read something beyond his present capabilities may produce very little from a great deal of effort. Of course, the fulfilment of the basic conditions does not guarantee that the reader will in fact 'improve' his knowledge. Many other factors may lead to a failure: the reader may not understand the author's line of reasoning, he may misinterpret some crucial point, or he may disagree with the author's argument in some area where he holds strong beliefs or prejudices. Although such failures of communication are by no means irrelevant to the activities of libraries and information services, it will be generally agreed that they lie outside the responsibility of the indexer: his concern is with the 'subjects' of documents and not with the success or failure of authors to communicate or of readers to understand what they read.

By contrast, the basic conditions for the initial contact of reader and document are at the heart of the indexing process. How do we provide the documents that readers need at a level which is appropriate to their present knowledge? We may, I think, identify two basic types of document need, although perhaps rarely encountered in their 'pure' states: one is the need felt by the reader who

* In this paper the term 'presupposition' is used not in the tightly defined sense employed by many philosophers, logicians and (now) many linguists as the necessary antecedent or condition of a statement, but in the looser everyday sense of whatever is taken as granted.

wants to find out more on some particular subject which he has come across—he knows very little about it and wants to learn more; the other is the need of the reader who knows quite a lot about a subject—who may even be an expert in it—who wants to know what 'new' things have been written on it. The first need will generally be satisfied by a book which starts from a foundation of knowledge roughly comparable to the reader's and in which most of what the author conveys as 'new' information will in fact be previously unknown to the reader. The second need will be satisfied by a document which, though its presupposed level of knowledge may well be considerably below the actual state of knowledge of the reader, does in fact say something that he did not know before.

Indexing and the needs of readers

The 'summarization' approach to indexing is clearly able to cater for the second type of document need, since the objective is to provide index entries which together represent the whole content of documents. Index entries cover not only the 'given' elements of texts but also the 'new' elements. In theory, an index user may be referred to documents from any one of the 'topics' which have been dealt with, whether these have been assumed by the authors to be known already to potential readers or whether they have been introduced as 'new' subjects. This is precisely what the reader interested in the latest developments of a particular subject wants; he wants to know which (recent) documents have treated the subject, since any one of them may potentially report something of importance for his particular needs.

But if the 'summarization' approach appears to satisfy the second type of need, it would seem inherently incapable of dealing with the first type of need. Since all elements of texts are treated as being equally significant, the entries for a particular topic in an index may refer in some cases to knowledge presupposed in documents and in other cases to 'new' information—and no distinction is made between the two kinds of reference. But what the reader with our first type of need wants is not all the documents treating in some way a particular topic, but just one document (or a small selection of documents) which can extend his own knowledge, which starts from a level of knowledge in the relevant area which is roughly comparable to his own.

What I am suggesting, therefore, is that for this type of document need an index system should work with a definition of the 'aboutness' of documents which is formulated in terms of the knowledge presupposed by the authors of the texts. If index entries express this kind of document 'aboutness' then the basic conditions mentioned above for reader–document contact should be met: the user of the index is referred to documents on a topic about which he knows roughly what the authors of those documents presuppose of their readers, and he can seek out the documents (or just one of them) with some confidence that he will in fact learn something 'new' about the topic. (He will not be referred to documents where the topic is not one of the basic 'themes' of the text.) He is thus brought into contact with documents which have the potential to enlarge his present state of knowledge—even if for other reasons which we have mentioned they do not in fact succeed in doing so. In essence, an index system based on such a concept of 'aboutness' would lead the reader (index user) from what he knows already to what he does not yet know; it satisfies his need for information whose nature he cannot define (because he does not know what it is) by referring him to texts which progress from already familiar territory.

Objectives of indexing

This concept of 'aboutness' would clearly be most appropriate in those information services where indexers are unable to specify precisely the kind of readers they are serving, *i.e.* in general public and academic libraries and in national bibliographical services. In these contexts it is not possible to make any general assumptions about the cultural and educational backgrounds of readers. The 'summarization' approach, however, requires indexers to formulate some notion, however vague, of the typical or 'ideal' user of the index system. Summarization cannot be completely neutral: the indexer must make some assumptions about what aspects of a text will be of interest to users, he must take into account the general or average knowledge of users. This is because in producing a 'summary' the indexer is in effect producing a kind of 'text', and like the author of any text he must 'write' for a particular audience; he must have some image of his recipient and 'compose' with him in mind.* By contrast, the 'presupposition' approach to 'aboutness' (as we might call the concept I have been describing) does not compel indexers to make any assumptions about the general knowledge or cultural background of a 'common' or 'ideal' reader. The indexers' task is to establish and record the topic or topics which the authors of documents themselves assume their readers should be starting from; they are required only to take account of the authors' own assumptions about their ('ideal') readers; they do not have to formulate their own image of readers. In this way, in theory at least, any 'interference' by the indexer between reader and documents should be minimized.

In the context of the special library and similarly specialized information services, the 'summarization' approach to subject indexing is most appropriate. Indexers are generally able to define clearly the interests and levels of knowledge of the readers they are serving; they are thus able to produce 'summaries' biased in the most helpful directions for their readers. More importantly, indexers can normally assume that most users are already very knowledgeable on most of the topics they look for in the indexes provided. They can assume that the usual search is for references to all documents treating a particular topic, since any one may have something 'new' to say about it that the reader did not know before. The fact that some references will lead users to texts which tell them nothing they did not previously know should not normally worry them unduly—it is the penalty they expect to pay for the assurance that the search has been as exhaustive as feasible.

It might well be objected that if the 'presupposition' approach to document 'aboutness' were followed, indexes would be no longer capable of satisfying the exhaustive search, the need for references to all documents on a topic. This would indeed be so, but one may legitimately ask whether present indexes based

* I have given elsewhere a fuller description of the linguistic processes of 'summarization' in indexing.[11]

on a 'summarization' concept of 'aboutness' succeed in this aim. The evidence of most tests of the effectiveness of indexes in information retrieval[12] would seem to demonstrate that exhaustiveness can be achieved only at the cost of the retrieval of an unacceptably large amount of irrelevant material and that any attempts to reduce the volume of 'dross' usually result in the failure to retrieve some material which is relevant to the topic sought.

In any case, should indexes be attempting to provide for such a need? Is it not better covered by the abstracting services? Abstracts are specifically intended as 'summarizations' of the contents of documents; they are designed to inform users what the authors have to say on a particular topic. From an abstract the user seeking 'new' information about a subject can usually decide whether the document referred to will in fact satisfy his particular need. Where good abstracts exist there would seem to be little justification for an index to attempt to cater for the exhaustive search. Only where an information service operates in a specialized field not covered satisfactorily by abstracts can there be a sound case for indexing in depth based on the 'summarization' approach.

Conclusions and implications

My general conclusion is that in most contexts indexers might do better to work with a concept of 'aboutness' which associates the subject of a document not with some 'summary' of its total content but with the 'presupposed knowledge' of its text. The 'summarization' of document contents is best left to the abstracting services and to those specialized libraries and information services where depth indexing is feasible and justified by the document needs of the readers they serve.

What would be the practical effects of a change of attitude to document 'aboutness'? It can be objected that it is surely no easier to establish the knowledge an author presupposes of his readers than it is to make a summary of a document's content. This is probably true; the indexer has an equally difficult task with either approach. The difference is then only one of the purpose and objectives of indexing: how do we bring together readers and the documents they need? What kinds of need are we trying to satisfy? If it is agreed that most readers (in a particular indexing environment) want just one or two documents on a topic at a level which is appropriate to their present knowledge of the subject, then indexers should take the 'presupposition' approach to 'aboutness'. How would indexers discover what knowledge authors presuppose? From the description above it should be clear that they would look most closely at the early passages of a text where the author lays the foundations of what he is going to say. They would look, in other words, at prefaces and introductory sections of texts. But this is what the great majority of indexers do at present; in deciding what a text is 'about' they rarely feel the need to look beyond the introductory passages of a document. Even though they intend (consciously or not) to 'summarize' the content, what they do in fact may be very similar to what I have been describing. If (to give a crude example) an author says that 'this book is about industrial archaeology', the indexer will generally assume that this probably represents a reasonable summary of its contents. But the phrase 'industrial archaeology' is also an expression which the author assumes his readers have some knowledge of already; he presumes that they have some concept of what 'industrial archaeology' might refer to, and that (more importantly) they have an interest in learning more about it. Thus both approaches to indexing would result in the same index entry *Industrial archaeology*.

The difference then is less one of practical procedures and more of general attitude to the objectives of indexing. A change to a 'presupposition' concept could for instance affect the way we evaluate the effectiveness of an indexing system. The now traditional parameters of 'recall', 'precision' and 'fallout' are clearly valid for systems in which success is measured in terms of the ability to retrieve all documents which have something to say on a particular topic—that is to say, in systems based on the 'summarization' approach.* But where this is not the case we need perhaps different parameters. Other measures of effectiveness must be identified for systems in which success is achieved if the reader obtains one document which is genuinely capable of enlarging and enriching his present state of knowledge and where readers do not want to have documents that tell them nothing they do not know already or that start from a level of knowledge they do not possess.

The emphasis in most writings on information retrieval has been on the specialized services catering for the exhaustive search, where the 'summarization' concept of 'aboutness' is quite appropriate. Perhaps we should now examine more closely the general information services where the needs of users are different and where the concept of 'aboutness' I have been describing may well be more relevant.

REFERENCES

1 AUSTIN, D. J. *PRECIS: a manual of concept analysis and subject indexing.* London, Council of the British National Bibliography, 1974.

2 VICKERY, B. C. *On retrieval system theory.* 2nd ed. London, Butterworths, 1965.

3 SALTON, G. *The SMART retrieval system: experiments in automatic document processing.* Englewood Cliffs, N.J., Prentice-Hall, 1971.

4 EDMUNDSON, H. P. New methods in automatic extracting. *Journal of the Association for Computing Machinery,* 16 (2), 1969, p. 264–85.

5 BAXENDALE, P. B. Machine-made index for technical literature—an experiment. *IBM Journal of Research and Development,* 2 (4), 1958, p. 354–61.

6 HUTCHINS, W. J. On the problem of 'aboutness' in document analysis. *Journal of Informatics,* 1, 1977, p. 17–35.

7 DANEŠ, F. *ed. Papers on functional sentence perspective.* The Hague, Mouton, 1974 (Janua Linguarum, Series Minor, 147).

8 HALLIDAY, M. A. K. *and* HASAN, R. *Cohesion in English.* London, Longman, 1976.

9 DANES, F. Functional sentence perspective and the organization of text, in Daneš, F. (*ed.*) *Op. cit.*, p. 106–28.

10 HUTCHINS, W. J. On the structure of scientific texts, *UEA Papers in Linguistics,* 5, 1977, p. 18–39.

11 HUTCHINS, W. J. *Languages of indexing and classification: a linguistic study of structures and functions.* Stevenage, Peregrinus, 1975.

12 CLEVERDON, C. W. Evaluation tests of information retrieval systems, *Journal of Documentation* 26, 1970, p. 55–67. CLEVERDON, C. W. On the inverse relationship of recall and precision, *Journal of Documentation,* 28, 1972, p. 195–201. LANCASTER, F. W. *Information retrieval systems: characteristics, testing and evaluation.* New York, Wiley, 1968. ROBERTSON, S. E. The parametric description of retrieval tests. *Journal of Documentation,* 25, 1969, p. 1–27 and p. 93–107.

* This includes most experimental systems of automatic indexing; in the contexts in which they are designed to operate the 'summarization' approach is clearly most appropriate.

THE TESTING OF INDEX LANGUAGE DEVICES

CYRIL W. CLEVERDON

Director, Aslib Cranfield Research Project

and

J. MILLS

Deputy Director, Aslib Cranfield Research Project

One-day conference, London, 5th February 1963

INTRODUCTION

THE evaluation of information retrieval systems has recently become an important matter. In the past, however, most reports or proposals on this type of work appear largely to have ignored the efficiency of operation of the central core of an IR system, namely those operations concerned in the compilation and use of the index. The only aspects to receive consideration are the physical form of the index and the design of thesauri or classifications. The former activity has been slanted towards the use of computers and has tended to assume that this type of equipment will, *ipso facto,* give an improved performance but has made no attempt to justify cost factors which may be one hundred times that of conventional techniques. Work on thesauri and classifications, where it has been practical in nature, appears to consist of compiling lists of terms which go out of favour as quickly as any list of subject headings in the past; the more popular theoretical approach is the setting up of models or the use of increasingly abstruse and complex algebras. From the results and conclusions of the experimental work at Cranfield; it would seem that many of these investigations are comparatively trivial.

In this paper we set out the fundamental operations involved in compiling and using an index, show how the various factors can influence the operating efficiency, and consider the methods to be used in the present Aslib Cranfield investigation.

DEFINITIONS

As the analysis of indexing has become more detailed, there has been an increasing requirement for the more precise definition of the various operations. We have endeavoured to use terms in their conventional meanings wherever possible, but it has frequently been necessary to modify, or to find new terms.

An *information retrieval system* is the complete organization for obtaining, storing and making available information. This could be a definition of a conventional library, but an IR system would be expected to exploit the information in a positive manner and to have extra facilities such as people on the staff capable of evaluating information before it is passed to the inquirer. It would also be expected to have a *subject index* to the items in the store, the index being the physical equipment which permits of the retrieval of references in the searches. The index may be in the form of a card catalogue, a printed list, a set of peek-a-boo cards, a computer, or any other convenient equipment. The arrangement within the index will depend upon the *index language** and this may be a straightforward alphabetical arrangement of terms, or a classified arrangement of terms, or any variation of these methods. The index language may be used in a *pre-co-ordinate* or *post-co-ordinate* manner. The former implies that the co-ordination of separate concepts is done at the time of indexing and the entries in the subject index will show this co-ordination. The latter implies that the co-ordination of concepts is done at the time of searching, so the entries in the subject index will refer only to single elements.

The *vocabulary* of the index language is the complete collection of sought terms in the natural language, including all necessary synonyms, that are used in the set of documents and are therefore required for entry points to the index language. An *index term,* on the other hand, is an actual term or heading used in the index language, and may be a word or words, as with alphabetical subject indexes, uniterm indexes or zatocoding, or may be notational elements, such as a group of numbers in the Universal Decimal Classification, or may be non-meaningful groups of letters, as in the Western Reserve University Metallurgical Index.

Concept indexing is the intellectual process of deciding which are the concepts in a particular document that are of sufficient importance to be included in the subject index. Conventionally, this involves a 'Yes' or 'No' assessment, for a concept either is, or is not, considered worthy of inclusion in the subject index. It is possible for the indexer to indicate the relative importance of different concepts in a document by *weighted indexing,* which involves the assignment to each concept of a weighting number.

The *exhaustivity* of the concept indexing is a comparative term; at a high level it implies that an entry is made for every possible concept in a document. At a low level it implies that a selection has been made and a smaller number of concepts have been used. *Specificity* is also a comparative term. A concept can be translated into an indexing language in such a way that the index term is co-extensive with a concept. This is a high level of specificity and implies that the index term covers the concept but nothing else besides the concept. Alternatively, the translation can be to a less specific (often called 'broader') index term which includes the concept being indexed as well as other concepts.

Syntactic indexing implies the use of headings which display the relationship between the various elements, as distinct from those which merely show the existence of several attributes relevant to the subject indexed.

* In recent papers we have been using the term 'descriptor language' following on the usage of Mr B. C. Vickery. However, Mr Calvin Mooers has pointed out that the word 'descriptor', although now somewhat debased in common usage, originally had a precise meaning. We have agreed to restrict our use of the word to this precise meaning and have therefore decided upon the term 'index language'.

A *search programme* is the formalization of the search request and it can show the same characteristics as outlined above for indexing, i.e. it entails a statement of the concepts, which can be at varying levels of exhaustivity, and can be translated into indexing terms of varying specificity.

The *operating efficiency* of an index language will depend upon its performance as regards recall and relevance. *Recall ratio* equals $\frac{100R}{C}$, where C equals the total number of documents in the collection which have an agreed standard of relevance to a given question, while R equals the number of those relevant documents retrieved in a single search. On the other hand, *relevance ratio* equals $\frac{100R}{L}$, where L equals the total number of documents retrieved in a single search. Operating efficiency is affected by the exhaustivity and specificity of the indexing, as well as the search programme, and by varying any of these factors, one will obtain a performance curve which plots recall ratio against relevance ratio. *Economic efficiency* deals with the performance of the complete index.

A *set of documents* is any collection of documents which are, or will be, used as the basis of a single subject index. The set can be large or small, restricted to an organization's research papers, or be a heterogeneous collection of journal articles, research reports, patents, etc., in many different languages, but homogeneous in that they will be used as the raw material of a single index. A *set of questions* is a collection of questions to be put to a single subject index, either at present, or at any time in the future when the index is still intended to be operating.

THE PREPARATION OF AN INDEX

Assuming there is agreement concerning the set of documents to be indexed, the following operations have to be carried out in compiling and using an index:

1. Assess the subject matter of each document in relation to the requirements of the users, and decide which subjects should be included in the index. This is concept indexing, and is at present, and for the foreseeable future, an intellectual operation. With a pre-co-ordinate index, it is also necessary to decide on the appropriate combinations of concepts and, if the index language is to show relationships, the syntax.
2. Translate the subject concepts into the index language. This is a clerical task, except in those cases where a new term has to be added to the vocabulary of the index language.
3. Place the indexing decisions into the index, which may involve preparing and filing catalogue cards, punching holes in a card or cards, or making marks on tape. This again is a clerical process.
4. Make a concept analysis of the question and decide on the priority of alternative search programmes. As with concept indexing, this is an intellectual process.
5. Translate the search concepts into the index language, a purely clerical task.
6. Operate the physical retrieval mechanism of the index.

The Aslib Cranfield Project has been primarily concerned with operations 1, 2, 4 and 5, and it has only been due to the necessity of having the index in the physical form that we have been involved with 3 and 6. It is certain that these two latter points play no part in deciding on the operating efficiency, except in so far as that one technique might be more, or less, prone to clerical errors than another. They can, however, significantly affect the economic efficiency of an index.

Involved in these operations is the variable of the index language. Whichever type of index language is used, it is certain that all the stages 1 to 6 have to be carried out. More important is it to note that the only two operations which have a true intellectual content are completely divorced from any consideration of the index language.* The basic concept analysis of the document and the basic concept analysis of the question, with the auxiliary decision of which concepts should be included in the index or the search programme, will be the same irrespective of which index language is used. It is probably the case that many indexers tend to think in the terms of the index language and their concept indexing decisions may be thereby influenced, but fundamentally it is true that concept indexing is a separate process which should not be affected by the index language.

INDEX LANGUAGES

The common basic requirement of all index languages is a complete vocabulary of all the sought terms, including all necessary synonyms, that are used in the indexing of a set of documents. This may be likened to an uncontrolled set of uniterms, and must be the basic structure for all index languages; and, whatever ultimate form an index language may take, it can only operate at maximum efficiency by having such a vocabulary. To this basic structure can be added a number of devices which are intended to improve the recall ratio or the relevance ratio. These devices (see Vickery[1]) can be listed as follows:

A. *Devices which, when introduced into an uncontrolled vocabulary of simple terms, tend to broaden the class definition and so increase recall*

1. Confounding of true synonyms.
2. Confounding of near synonyms; usually terms in the same hierarchy.
3. Confounding of different word forms; usually terms from different categories.
4. Fixed vocabulary; usually takes the form of generic terms, but may use 'metonymy' for example, representing a number of attributes by the thing possessing them.
5. Generic terms.
6. Drawing terms from categories and, within these, facets; this controls the generic level of terms, and to a certain degree controls synonyms.

* It is, of course, true that the compilation and maintenance of the index language can fairly be said to be an intellectual task. Its use, however, within the context of an indexing operation is a separate matter which requires only clerical operations.

7. Representing terms by analytical definitions (semantic factors), in which inter-relations are conveyed by relational affixes or modulants; the generic level will usually be more specific than when control is by categories.
8. Hierarchical linkage of generic and specific terms, and, possibly, of co-ordinate terms.
9. Multiple hierarchical linkage, i.e. linking each term to a number of different generic heads.
   It should be noted that devices 8 and 9 are not usually (as the others are) methods of class definition determining the structure or constituents of individual subject descriptions; they are ancillary devices (manifested as systematic sequence, or classified arrangement, as a thesaurus, as a network of *see also* references, etc.) indicating the existence of classes wider than these individual descriptions.
10. Bibliographical coupling, and citation indexes; these, also, are ancillary devices which indicate the existence of wider classes, the latter reflecting the use made of the documents and a probability of relevance arising from this.

B. *Devices which tend to narrow the class definition and so increase relevance*

11. Correlation of terms: although implicit in some form in all practical indexing, this device is not inevitable; i.e. the use of a single term to define a class may retrieve quickly and economically, if the term is sufficiently rare in the context of the system.
12. Weighting, i.e. attempts to express the particular relevance of each concept used in indexing a document to the whole document. It may take two forms:
    i. An attempt to assess subjectively the relative 'information content' of each term within the context of the system;
    ii. An objective measure, based on statistical counting of the word frequencies, etc.
13. Indicating connections between terms (interlocking):
    a. Without explicit expression of particular relations (interfixing); this may take at least three forms:
       i. Partitioning of the document; e.g. if the same document deals with the Conductivity of titanium and the Hardness of copper at a particular temperature, partitioning makes it clear that the document has at least two separate 'themes'.
       ii. Interfixing within a theme (or 'information item'); e.g. Lead (1) Coating (1) Copper (2) Pipes (2) makes it clear that the subject is the Lead coating of copper pipes and not the Copper coating of lead pipes.
       iii. If terms are recorded physically in a linear sequence, a citation order (a regulated sequence in which terms from different categories are cited), will convey relations.
    b. With explicit expression of particular relations; this is necessary in cases where simple interfixing cannot cope with the possible ambiguities; e.g. to distinguish which particle is the projectile, which the target, and which the product, in a report in nuclear physics. Two forms are usually recognized:
       i. Role indicators: these are usually limited in number and express the basic or most common relations found in the subject field concerned; e.g. Product, Starting material.
       ii. Relational terms: these are more freely developed, the name of a relation being used in the same way as any other term. It may, however, be cited only in the framework of a limited number of fundamental relations, as in Farradane's system.

    A third form sometimes to be found in conjunction with *a*, *iii* above is that of distinctive facet indicators which convey clearly the exact category to which the next term belongs.

Any operating index language is an amalgam of some of these devices; for example a modern faceted classification uses hierarchical linkage within its facets, combines (correlates) terms from different categories (according to a strict citation order so as to maximize the mutual exclusiveness of its classes), provides a degree of multiple hierarchical linkage through its relative alphabetical index, controls synonyms, may control near synonyms, and may confound word forms to a mild degree.

A machine-orientated retrieval system may use correlation as its basic device, but supplement this with confounding of synonyms, confounding of near synonyms, of word forms, show hierarchical and multiple hierarchical linkage to some degree (often via a thesaurus), and use links and roles.

A simple, manual Uniterm system will use correlation as its basic device, but may add to this the confounding of true synonyms, of near synonyms and (possibly) of word forms, a modest degree of hierarchical linkage, and roles.

PERFORMANCE MEASUREMENT

The technique evolved in the Aslib Cranfield tests for the measurement of operating efficiency depends on two factors—the percentage of relevant documents retrieved as against the total of relevant documents in the collection (recall ratio), and the percentage of relevant documents among those actually retrieved (relevance ratio). The original Aslib Cranfield project established the former by conducting searches for questions which had been based on documents known to be in the collection, and the result of this showed that, on an average, about 80 per cent of the source documents were being retrieved. It could be said that this figure did not have particular significance, since it is obviously possible to obtain 100 per cent recall by looking at every document in the collection. Quite apart from going to this extreme, it would have been possible to improve the figure of 80 per cent by 'broadening' the search programme or, as we should say, by making the search programme less specific and/or less exhaustive. The only control on this figure of 80 per cent was that a limit was put on the level of exhaustivity of the search programme. (See Cleverdon,[2] page 14), but this was rather crude, and (as discussed in chapter 6 of the same reference), an attempt was made to assess the relevance ratio. This proved to be exceedingly difficult, but it was obvious that it was an essential part of performance measurement, and, in the test of the WRU metallurgical literature[3] the work was done more thoroughly, as is discussed later in this report. The result of a complete analysis of recall and relevance means that it is possible to plot a series of points, depending, for instance, on the search programme, and produce a performance curve as shown in Fig. 1a.

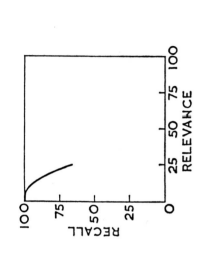

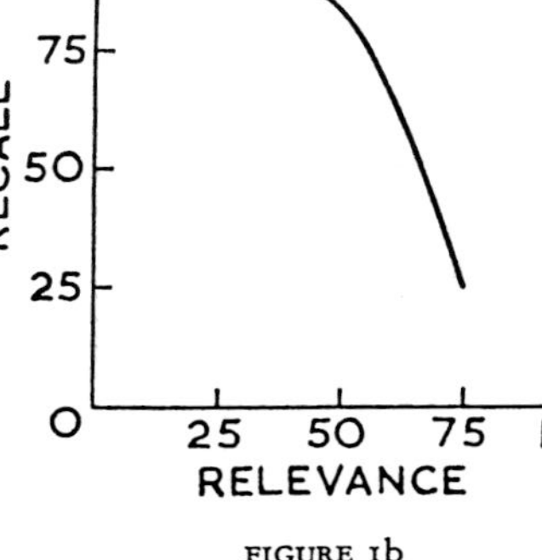

FIGURE 1c

ASSUMPTION FOR FUTURE WORK

A basic premise of the following arguments is that, for a given set of documents and a given set of questions, there will be a maximum retrieval performance; whatever type of index language is used, the performance curves will not be materially altered, and, in fact, the only reason for any major variation from this curve will be inadequacies of the intellectual performance in decisions concerning subject concepts, either in indexing or in searching. For sets of documents in different subject fields, the resulting performance curves would probably differ, and if the same set of documents were used in two separate situations, since there could be two different sets of questions, this in turn could result in different performance figures. Tests at Cranfield have been concerned mainly with the subject fields of science, engineering, and metallurgy, and with these types of document sets and question sets, it appears that the maximum retrieval performance would be as in Fig. 1a. If the subject matter of the collection were organic chemistry, the resulting performance curve might be as Fig. 1b; for sociology it might be as Fig. 1c.

It has to be assumed in this discussion that we are considering idealized conditions, and do not have to take into account losses due to human error. This has been investigated in the first project, and the general allowance to be made for this is known or, alternatively, can easily be ascertained in any given situation, by using the Cranfield test procedure. We have postulated that there is a fixed maximum performance curve for any given set of documents and questions, and have suggested that, with the type of document and question sets tested at Cranfield, this might range from 100 per cent recall at less than 1 per cent relevance to 50 per cent recall at 30 per cent relevance. The important problem to investigate is how an index can be operated most efficiently at any particular point or within any particular range. As an example, it might be a requirement of an index that it should have a recall level of not less than 95 per cent. Alternatively, the requirement may be that the index should normally operate at a level of 25 per cent relevance ratio, but that it should, when required, be capable of giving a recall figure of 90 per cent.

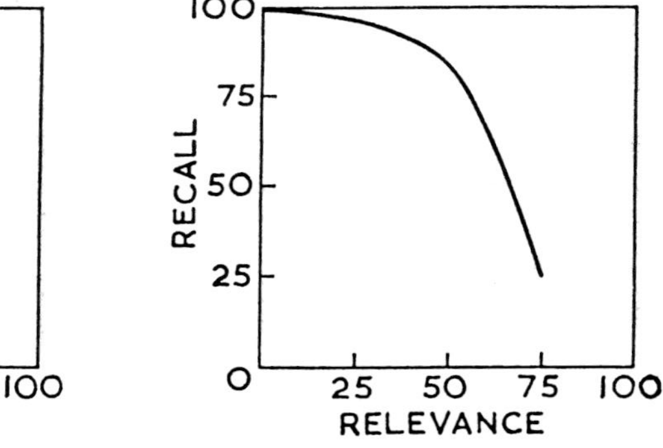

FIGURE 1a

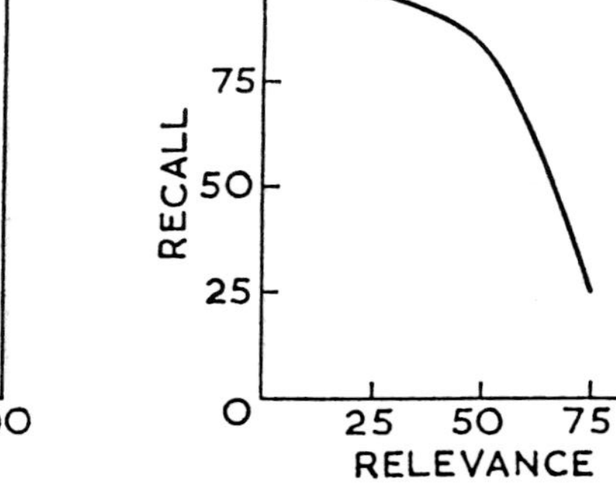

FIGURE 1b

In such an investigation, there are a number of factors to be considered, and of major importance is the concept indexing. Some groups working in this area seem to place more emphasis on search analysis, in finding how variations in search programmes will affect the efficiency, but this seems to be rather a cart-before-the-horse approach. It is at the stage of concept indexing that the future potential performance of the resulting indexes is determined; if a concept is not included, it will not be possible to recall the particular document by that concept, and vice versa. Concept indexing is, it must be emphasized, an intellectual process that cannot be avoided. Current literature sometimes implies that keyword-in-context title indexing, for instance, is automatic indexing. It is automatic in its preparation of the physical index, but the intellectual stage of concept indexing is still there; the only difference is that in this case the concept indexer is the person who wrote the title.

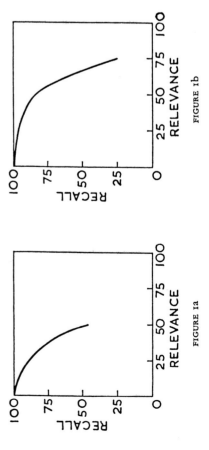

It is the decisions of concept indexing which result in the level of exhaustivity achieved. The extremes of exhaustivity range from where the whole text is included to where only a single concept is indexed for each document. The effect of high or low exhaustivity on the basic performance curve can be readily shown. 100 per cent recall can always be obtained by doing no indexing but by having available for searching the text of every document in the collection. On the other hand, if only a single concept from each document is included in an index, then it is apparent that there will be a considerable drop in recall. We can, therefore, say that, if all other factors are held constant, the effect of lowering the level of exhaustivity will be to drop the recall figure. This will in turn result in an improved relevance figure, and briefly it can be said that

a high level of exhaustivity of indexing results in high recall and low relevance;

a low level of exhaustivity of indexing results in low recall and high relevance.

Little work has been done on the effect of exhaustivity of indexing, and practice varies widely (see chapter 7 of reference 4) without the appearance of any positive reasoning behind the decisions. Inevitably a high level of exhaustive indexing results in higher input costs, and this could be a determining factor with certain physical forms of index. In the Western Reserve University test an attempt was made to ascertain the effect of varying the exhaustivity with the facet index that was prepared at Cranfield. In this index the average number of entries originally included for each document was 12½, and the effect of reducing this by stages to an average of three entries per document was investigated. Table 1 shows the effect that this had on recall and relevance of the documents.

TABLE 1

RECALL AND RELEVANCE RATIO IN FACET CATALOGUE OF WRU TEST AT VARYING INDEX ENTRIES

		Relevance 2		*Relevance 2 and 3*	
No. of entries	*No. of documents retrieved*	*Recall ratio*	*Relevance ratio*	*Recall ratio*	*Relevance ratio*
		%	%	%	%
12½	891	83	16.3	64.1	34.6
8	824	80.6	17.1	60.6	35.5
5	643	73.1	19.9	50.7	38
3	491	64.6	23	42.1	41.3

This effect will operate irrespective of which index language is used, and, in passing, it should be noted that the same situation prevails in reverse with the decisions concerning concepts to be used in the search programme. However, before going into the matter of search programmes, we will consider the translation of the concept indexing into the index language.

The aspect of the input stage which is concerned with index languages is specificity, and we suggest that, in so far as their operating performance is concerned, a fundamental difference—and probably the most important difference—between index languages is their hospitality for specificity; this we now consider in its simpler form and show its direct relationship to the index language. It is assumed that an index language includes, as a minimum, all the categories of the subject field, whether given in detail or not, of the documents being indexed.

The first stage, i.e. concept indexing, with its decision concerning the level of exhaustivity of indexing, is assumed to have been completed for a given document and we have concepts A_1, B_1, C_1, D_1, E_1 and F_1. The next stage is translating these into the index language. Assume three hypothetical index languages, I, II, and III containing respectively, 10,000, 1,000 and 100 index terms. In index language I, there is a straight translation of the concepts into A_1(I), B_1(I), C_1(I), D_1(I), E_1(I), F_1(I). Index language II translates into A(II), B(II), C(II), D(II), E(II), F(II) (where A is the containing head for A_1, A_2, A_3 and B the containing head for B_1, B_2, etc.). Descriptor language III translates into ABC(III) and DEF(III) (where ABC is the containing head for A, B, C, A_1, A_2, etc.).

The level of specificity which can be given to the indexing is obviously very different in each of these three index languages; the result is that in a search where the requirements are for A_1, B_1, C_1, although index language III will retrieve all the relevant documents that are retrieved by index language I, it will also bring out, for example, documents coded A_2, B_2, C_2, resulting in a larger number of irrelevant documents and therefore a lower relevance ratio. In reverse, though the relevance ratio of a search in index language I will be relatively high, it is likely to miss some of the relevant references which would be found by the same search programme by index language III. It might, therefore, be the case that the normal operating level of index languages I, II and III, with all other conditions fixed, would be as shown by points 1, 2 and 3 in Fig. 2. Again, one notes that a lowering of relevance results in higher recall, and of specificity it can be said that

a high level of specificity in the index language results in high relevance and low recall;

a low level of specificity in the index language results in low relevance and high recall.

Considering again the basic performance curve (Fig. 3), we have shown that the maximum recall figure which can be obtained is limited by the level of exhaustive indexing; the maximum relevance figure is limited by the specificity possible in the index language. Therefore, a system which combines a high level of exhaustive indexing with the use of a highly specific index language would have the potentiality, dependent upon the search programme, of operating over the wide range of the curve between points A and B. However, a system which combines a low level of exhaustivity and a less specific index language might not be able to operate beyond the narrower limits shown by points C and D, whatever type of search programme was used. However, if this limited range gives a satisfactory performance figure, then it will be obviously more economical to operate.

It is now possible to consider the effects of exhaustivity and specificity in the search programme. Assume that the concept programme of a question requires that a search should be made for A_1, B_1, C_1 and D_1. If it is decided to 'broaden' the search, then this can be done in two ways. On the one hand, it is possible to drop one of the concepts, so that the search is now for A_1, B_1 and C_1. This we would describe as making the search less exhaustive. Alternatively, it is possible to make the search less specific, by substituting A for A_1 or B for B_1 (where A is taken to be an inclusive term covering A_1, A_2, A_3, etc.). It is obvious that by broadening the search in either of these ways, the recall ratio will be improved. In particular, however, we should consider the matter of specificity in indexing and specificity in the search programme. To return to the index languages considered earlier, if one has coded according to index language III, then it is useless to attempt a programme that has a high level of specificity. In fact, it is impossible to do this, since the index language does not include

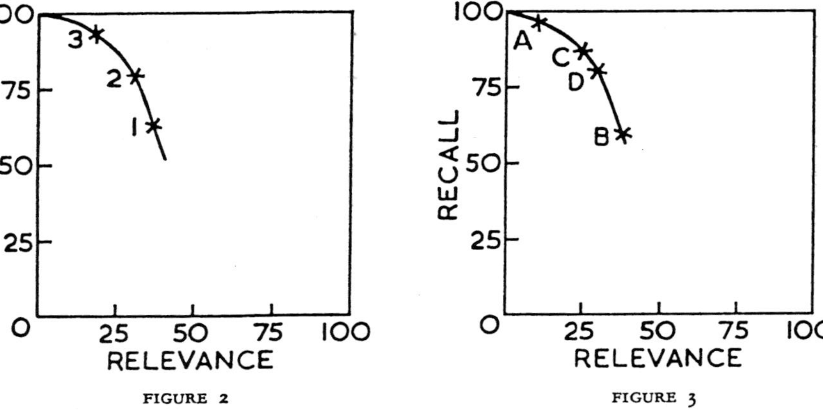

FIGURE 2

FIGURE 3

index terms of the required specificity. However, with index language I, it is possible to have a highly specific search programme, which would give a high relevance ratio but a low recall ratio (i.e. point 1 in Fig. 2). If it is desired to improve the recall ratio, then the search programme can be made less specific, until it reaches a level of specificity of the term codes of index language III. By this time it can be assumed that the recall ratio will have risen to the same level as with index language III (i.e. point 3 in Fig. 2). It is, therefore, shown that, as far as operating efficiency is concerned, there will be for every index language—depending upon its hospitality for specific indexing—a maximum relevance ratio which cannot be exceeded. It will, however, always be possible (by varying the search programme) to improve the recall ratio along the fixed performance curve up to its maximum level, this being dependent on the exhaustivity of the indexing.

AIDS TO EFFICIENCY

If, as is not wholly unreasonable, we consider as a median in the range of indexing languages, one which consists of nothing except an uncontrolled vocabulary of sought terms, then many of the indexing devices mentioned in an earlier section of this paper can be seen to be working in opposing directions. Any device which reduces the number of index terms is working towards improved recall, with the inevitable result that there will be a fall in relevance. Other devices, such as role indicators, are, in effect, increasing the number of index terms and are thereby improving relevance but decreasing recall. These devices have been discussed in an earlier section and the part they will play in the further work will be considered later, but we would now consider the effect of one type of device which is found in many operating index languages.

In the introduction, we said that much of the present theoretical work being done on index languages was trivial. This comment is based on what appear to be logical deductions from the experimental work undertaken at Cranfield. The theoretical work which we have in mind is all concerned with what might be described as the grouping of the terms in the index language. This work is proceeding in many directions; facet classification, clumps, logical associations, word pairs, etc. To describe all this work as trivial shows that we have moved away from a main stream of development in information retrieval, and it may appear difficult to justify the statement. We would first make the point that we say that this work is trivial and do not say that it is useless. This could be translated into more precise figures by suggesting the following. Assume an imperfect index language, covering the field of engineering and metallurgy, which consisted only of an alphabetical list of index terms, and with a normal operating efficiency of 75 per cent recall and 20 per cent relevance. If one gave to this index language the additional device of a grouping of the terms, then we suggest that the recall ratio of 75 per cent might be achieved with a relevance of 21 per cent or, alternatively, that with a relevance of 20 per cent one might have a recall ratio of 78 per cent.

The purpose of any grouping of terms is to lead the searcher to related terms which might have been used by the indexer for relevant information. It is logical to assume that this is a worthy objective and it has been a common assumption that it is also a vitally important objective. Why is it, in fact, of such little importance? The reason is because it is incorrect to assume that the comparison is between an index language without a grouping of terms and an index language with a grouping of terms. The comparison is, in actual fact, between an index language with a pre-arranged grouping of terms and an index language with a grouping of terms that is special and personal each time it is used. In other words, a searcher, whether a librarian or a subject specialist, is capable, to a greater extent than has been generally appreciated, of making a grouping of related terms at the time of the search and in relation to the particular subject of the search. The problem is that a single classification schedule, a single set of cross-references, a single set of thesauri-type headings, or a single set of any other form of grouping, however logically or abstrusely derived, is most unlikely to be of equal value to all the different types of user of an information retrieval system. With a metallurgist, a chemist, a mineralogist, a mining engineer or a design engineer, a single term might well have five different sets of associations, and the individual concerned will be able to decide for himself, at the time of the search, the set of related terms that would be an improvement on a set of pre-arranged groupings. It would, therefore, appear logical that the best method would be to devise a separate set of groupings for each type of user, so as to maximize the chances of improving recall with a minimum drop in relevance. It should be noted that such groupings can be devised independently of the index language, and can therefore be used with any index language.

It is, however, necessary to qualify the above comments, and also to return to the point, raised earlier, concerning the presumed difference in the shape of the performance curve for subject indexes in different subject fields. If we consider pure data retrieval, of the type where it is required to know, for instance, the names of all persons in an organization who joined more than ten years ago, who are graduates and whose salary is less than £1,800 a year, it might be expected that all the relevant information and only relevant information would be retrieved. As one passes from the field of data retrieval to the field of information retrieval, the terminology becomes less precise in its meaning, there is an increasing number of errors due to confusion and the performance of the subject index becomes progressively worse. We have suggested that chemistry, being more precise in its terminology, would permit the compilation of a subject index having an improved performance curve in comparison with an index in the field of engineering and metallurgy of the type tested at Cranfield. On the other hand, many areas in the social sciences have a vague terminology. For example, in the opening pages of this paper, it was considered necessary to give the definitions of many terms that have been used, and it would take little effort to find examples of the same term being used with other meanings, or other terms being used for the same meaning. In such circumstances, it is hardly surprising that retrieval performance is hampered, and it is reasonable to suggest that there would be an increased requirement for a grouping of the index terms. Workers in the field of engineering and metallurgy appear to be sufficiently well acquainted with the terminology of the subject field to make their own grouping of terms, with the result that an index language which lacks a pre-arranged grouping of terms is only marginally inferior to an index language which has such a grouping of terms. We can, therefore, assume that any subject field that has a more precise terminology than engineering will have even less need for a grouping of the index terms.

THE FUTURE WORK OF THE CRANFIELD PROJECT

It might be said of Cranfield I that its main endeavour was that it tried to measure the operating efficiency of complete indexing languages in a simulated real life situation, and also that it used, as its major measure of performance, a relatively crude gauge of relevance based on the retrieval or non-retrieval of a single source document. Cranfield II will differ in both major respects; firstly, it will try to measure the impact on recall and relevance of particular indexing devices—the elements which go to make up a complete index language; and secondly, it will try to use decidedly more precise measures of relevance.

The devices that have been identified are listed earlier, but some further observations on them seem to be called for:

i. Their significance is that they provide different ways of defining classes, i.e. different ways of indicating relations between the concepts which are the subject of a document. Consequently, they differ in the degree to which they produce broader or narrower classes, and thereby assist or hinder specificity and exhaustivity.

ii. The function of class definition in indexing is that the assignment of a document to a particular class or classes (x, say) may allow us to ignore other classes (not-x), on the assumption that the kind of document we seek, if it is not in class x, cannot be in class not-x. Classes are established which will predictably include certain documents, and as predictably exclude others. This assumption can never be realized fully in practice, for classes in documentary classification can never be quite mutually exclusive. A documentary subject description ABCDE is never more than a statement of what the document is *mainly* about. ABCDE does not necessarily exclude FG; these may feature in it in some minor way. A report on 'Laminar boundary layer flow' will reveal, in a single casual aside, half-way through the text, that 'Three-dimensional boundary layer' is assumed. If this concept (three-dimensional) is not indexed, it does not mean that the concept really is banished from the subject content of the article. It is this awkward indeterminancy of the literature to be indexed which we seek to circumvent by exhaustive indexing.

iii. Different class definitions have different focusing or resolving power. If we take the simple correlation of keywords in the title and abstract of a document as a relatively crude device for establishing classes, then other devices, if added to these, either enlarge the scope of the classes or constrain them further. For example, to confound verbal forms, so that the class designations 'Heat', 'Heated', 'Heating', 'Hot', are extended to designate a single class covering all these different concepts, would clearly broaden the description. This would inevitably increase recall and reduce relevance—but by how much? Or, if we now introduce role indicators into our index language, so that a class designation 'Zinc' becomes several different classes according to the role played by Zinc in the particular subject description, e.g. Zinc (starting material), or Zinc (product), or Zinc (agent), then these classes are clearly narrower, and recall will now decrease and relevance increase. But again, by how much?

iv. Certain of the devices, such as generic and specific terms linked hierarchically, might appear to perform a function different from that of mere class definition. The difference between the operation of *arrangement* in an index, which is designed to display relations between ostensibly separate classes (the chief function normally associated with classification), and the operation of class definition, is often overlooked. In traditional classification, different principles of division might be applied to produce different classes, and then these classes are arranged, usually in some systematic order. But the two operations, of division to produce classes, and the arrangement of those classes, are quite distinct.

The functions of arrangement are well known. It may show clearly various connections between classes (and this function is itself a looser form of class definition); it may help the programming of searches, by suggesting other approaches; it may be economically efficient in the performance of these functions by reason of physical juxtaposition of entries or documents. Cranfield I appeared to indicate that the differences in the arrangement of classes (full classification, A/Z direct, A/Z indirect—i.e. alphabetico-classed) are only of marginal importance in retrieval. But we need to remember context here; the context for which the findings seemed to be valid was that of indexing, not the physical arrangement of documents (which rules out the entire field of shelf display); of a special field, rather than a general collection, where interconnections between classes are more difficult to display thoroughly and far more difficult for a librarian to carry around in his head; of indexing by experienced and skilled indexers, with equally intelligent searchers.

Is arrangement, then, a device to be tested here? Hierarchical linking is certainly to be tested, but how it is implemented—whether by a classified arrangement in the index itself, or by a thesaurus, or by systematic connectives in an alphabetical catalogue—is probably outside the field of our inquiry just now. But independently of the convenience of different methods of performing the function of hierarchical linkage, the extension of the field of likely search which this device implies may be regarded as a form of class definition, whereby membership of a given class carries with it an explicit or implicit indication of the existence of a wider class containing it. Much the same may be said of semantic factoring; for example, to index 'Tempering' as a kind of process, acting on a metal, making use of heat . . . is another device for extending the field of likely search, of broadening the effective class definition.

v. It might be argued that an index language is more than the sum of its parts, and that evaluation of the contribution to recall and relevance of isolated devices will not help to evaluate the complete index languages which are the practical concern of workers in information retrieval. But the evaluation of complete languages is clearly incomplete so long as we do not know which features of these languages are making them work as they do. For example, it could be argued that the good performance of the Universal Decimal Classification in Cranfield I owed much to the unusually thorough A/Z index made for it. It has already been observed that a complete language will invariably contain an assortment of different indexing devices, and the investigation should give some definite measure of the separate contributions these devices make to recall and to relevance.

METHOD OF INVESTIGATION

To obtain reliable measurements of the impact on recall and relevance of the different devices requires careful precautions for their isolation. This will be done by operating in the laboratory conditions which are provided by a set of questions and a strictly limited number of documents providing the answers to be retrieved, so that there can be a 'closed' collection, in which the relevance to each question of each document in the collection is known. The questions and documents are being assembled as follows.

The assumption is that a research paper is written as the result of an investigation which has been undertaken to provide the answer to a question or questions in the mind of its author; also, that if an author cites references these must have something to do with the subject of the paper. In the field of high speed aerodynamics there are generally from five to ten references attached to each research paper. We are writing to four hundred or more authors of research papers (both theoretical and experimental) in this field. Each author is asked to state, as nearly as possible in the form of a search question, the basic problem which was the reason for the investigation. Also, if there were any subsidiary questions which arose in the course of the work, he is requested to enter up to three of these (see Fig. 4, sheet 1). He is then asked to indicate the relevance of the references to each question in the following scale of 1 to 5:

1. References which are a complete answer to the question. Presumably this would only apply for supplementary questions, i.e. (B), (C) or (D) since if they applied to the main question there would have been no necessity for the research to be done.
2. References of a high degree of relevance, the lack of which either would have made the research impracticable or would have resulted in a considerable amount of extra work.

ASLIB CRANFIELD INVESTIGATION INTO
PERFORMANCE OF INDEX LANGUAGES

Please complete and return to:
C. W. Cleverdon,
The College of Aeronautics,
Cranfield, Bletchley,
Bucks., England.

AUTHOR J. F. Clarke
TITLE Reaction-resisted Shock Fronts.
REFERENCE College of Aeronautics Report No. 150, May 1961.

BASIC QUESTION

(A) Has anyone investigated the role of chemical reactions in determining shock wave structure?

(B) Papers on acoustic wave propagation in reacting gases.

(C) Have other types of 'non-viscous' compression waves been investigated analytically or observed experimentally

(D) Is there any simple, but realistic, "model" gas which can be used to expedite analysis?

FIGURE 4 (SHEET 1)

LIST OF REFERENCES

Ref. No.		ASSESSMENT Question A	B	C	D
1.	Clarke, J.F. Flow of chemically reacting gas mixtures. College of Aeronautics Report 117.	5	1	5	3
2.	Clarke, J.F. Linearized flow of a dissociating gas. Jnl. Fluid Mech., 7, 1960, pp 577-595.	5	1	5	5
3.	Griffith, W.C. and Kenny, A. Jnl. Fluid Mech. 3, 1957, p.268.	5	5	1	5
4.	Lighthill, M.J. Survey in Mechanics, Ed. by G.K. Batchelor and R.M. Davies, Cambridge University Press, 1956.	2-3	3	1	5
5.	Lighthill, M.J. Dynamics of a dissociating gas. Jnl. Fluid Mech., 2, 1957, pp 1-32.	5	5	5	1

FIGURE 4 (SHEET 2)

3. References which were useful, either as general background to the work or as suggesting methods of tackling certain aspects of the work.
4. References of minimum interest, for example those that have been included from a historical viewpoint.
5. References of no interest.

The references will now constitute the basic indexing collection. The original papers which cited the references will be discarded, since the correlation between them and the questions they were designed to answer might be undesirably high. Ultimately, it is intended to obtain a collection of some 1,500 documents and some 400 questions, and for each question there will be some documents with a certain stated degree of relevance to them.

However, it is possible, even probable, that for each question some of the other documents in the collection (i.e. those not quoted as references by the author of the original paper) are also relevant in some degree. The only way to establish this reliably is to examine the whole collection in respect of each single question. This will be done by a number of post-graduate students working in the subject field. Any further documents which they think might be relevant to the question will be sent to the author of the original paper, who will assign relevance values to them as he did to the references in his paper.

What will emerge will be a closed system in which we have a set of documents (about 1,500) and a set of questions (about 400), and in which every document has been checked against every question. Therefore we know, for every question, exactly which documents in the collection are relevant, and to what degree. It might work out, say, that for a given question there will be two documents that are really important, four of which are useful, three which are marginal in relevance, with all the rest irrelevant.

Perhaps the most difficult problem in the above procedure is that of giving a measure of the relevance to a question of a particular document. It is probable that a serious element of subjectivity is likely to remain in any measure attempted. Certainly, to attempt too much refinement here is to risk deceiving ourselves; so we are attempting only the few broad distinctions listed above.

Promise of a more objective measurement of relevance may lie in the degree to which a question description matches a document description, and this is being explored. The distinction between 'relevance' and 'pertinence' drawn in some recent papers is certainly a real one. A document may match a question exactly in the matter of conceptual content (which is what we describe in indexing) and yet be of no use (not pertinent) to the requester because it is in a foreign tongue, is too mathematical in treatment, or has been superseded by another paper. Some of these factors can be handled in the index by means of further description, such as the well-known 'form' divisions of book classification and cataloguing. Others are not measurable in any laboratory investigation (e.g. 'I've read this already').

INDEXING

All index languages consist in the first place of a substantial reduction of the language of the original collection of documents themselves to a relatively small and limited index language. This is true even of automatic retrieval systems in which the whole file is scanned, for the machine has built into it a programme which has already rejected much of the language of the text being scanned, for example its articles, conjunctions, etc.

The indexing devices to be measured may be regarded as refinements, of one sort or another, to be imposed on the crude index language (not just vocabulary, but essential relations also) which is obtained by selecting the significant words in the title, summary and text of the document indexed. So our first task is to establish this crude language for each document, and thus for the whole collection. This must provide the raw material, the basic information regarding the document's subject content, to allow us to index the document subsequently with maximum exhaustivity and specificity.

These terms, exhaustivity and specificity, have already been defined, but further explanation of their practical implications seems desirable. Both for indexing and for searching programmes, we regard the limits of broadness and narrowness to be contained within a framework determined by the specificity and exhaustivity of the descriptions used. In indexing, the specificity of a term refers to the degree to which it reflects the precise generic level of the concept it stands for; for instance, to index a 'slender delta wing' specifically is to index it as just this, and nothing less. To index it as a 'delta wing' is to describe a genus to which it belongs, not the particular species itself—and such indexing is not specific. It might be called less specific or more generic—the terms are purely relative.

This is, of course, nothing more than the traditional genus/species relation, which is sometimes thought to be the only acceptable relation in strict classification. Its significance in indexing is that it refers to an inclusion relation which is permanent in character; slender delta wing, for example, is always a kind of delta wing, being included in it, and a document on the one will always be of some relevance to a document on the other.

Exhaustivity in indexing refers to the degree to which we recognize (i.e. include in our subject descriptions) the different concepts in a subject which are *not* in a genus/species relation—which, in other words, come from different categories or facets. For example, a paper on the 'calculation of the laminar boundary layer on a slender delta wing' is exhaustively indexed only if all three categories present are recognized, i.e. the kind of aircraft structure, the kind of aerodynamic flow, and the kind of activity directed at the subject (calculation as distinct from experimentation, say). It might be said that exhaustivity covers also the recognition of the different elements in a hierarchy—e.g. of 'slender' as well as of 'delta'. But the idea of specificity takes care of this; a specific indexing description automatically recognizes those links in a chain which constitute sought terms in the indexing sense, as this example demonstrates.

Exhaustivity does cover, however, recognition of different co-ordinate terms from one hierarchy; e.g. exhaustive indexing of a document on the conductivity of metals *a, b, c, d* and *e* would require the separate indexing of each metal.

Except for the Whole/Part relation, these non-hierarchical relations are not inclusion relations, and the connections between members of different categories are not so permanent or so predictable as the connections between members of the same hierarchy, e.g. whereas a search for information on 'Slender, delta wings' would automatically find relevant a document on 'Delta wings', it would not necessarily find a document on 'Boundary layer' to be so.

Earlier on, we have stated that greater exhaustivity in indexing makes for higher recall and lower relevance, whilst greater specificity makes for lower recall and greater relevance. This may puzzle some readers when they consider the effect on a single subject description of these factors. For example, to index a report as being about '*slender* delta wings' rather than just 'delta wings' narrows the class definition and so reduces the number of documents in the class—i.e. it improves relevance, but reduces recall. If we index a report as being about '*experiments* on the boundary layer of a delta wing', rather than just 'boundary layer of a delta wing', we again narrow the class definition (this time by correlation), and so reduce the number of documents in the class; again, we improve relevance, but reduce recall.

It is clear from this that we must distinguish between exhaustive indexing in the sense of making a single subject description truly exhaustive of the subject of the document, and exhaustive indexing in the sense of providing the maximum number of retrieval handles or access points necessary to full retrieval. An indexing system could recognize all the three categories in the above subject by means of separate entries, one for the kind of wing, one for the kind of flow, and one for the kind of intellectual operation. At no point would any one subject description be completely precise, i.e. exhaustive of the categories in the complete subject. But they will collectively exhaust it and provide all the required access points. It is this second sense of the term 'exhaustivity' which we use here. Indeed, it is open to argument whether the first meaning is a practical possibility in indexing. A single subject description of a complete report, to be truly exhaustive, would need to be, at the very least, of the dimensions of a full WRU type abstract. If, however, we recognize that in practice, thorough indexing partitions a document into its 'information items' (or 'themes' as we tend to call them), then exhaustive indexing, in the sense of a single subject description of a theme being a precise and exhaustive description of that theme, may well be an objective.

SPECIFICITY AND EXHAUSTIVITY IN INDEXING AND SEARCHING

Below are two grids, showing the degrees of exhaustivity and specificity possible in the indexing of a document and in the framing or programming of a search question (which is really a form of indexing of the subject implied by the question) to which that document is relevant. The document and question are taken, with slight simplifications, from reference 2, page 223.

Document

'An approximate method of calculating the laminar boundary layer on a delta wing.'

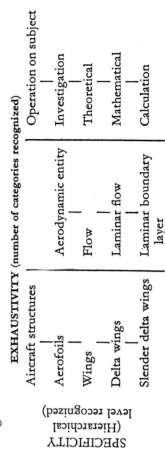

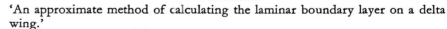

EXHAUSTIVITY (number of categories recognized)

SPECIFICITY (Hierarchical level recognized)			
	Aircraft structures		Operation on subject
	Aerofoils	Aerodynamic entity	Investigation
	Wings	Flow	Theoretical
	Delta wings	Laminar flow	Mathematical
	Slender delta wings	Laminar boundary layer	Calculation

A linear statement of the precise subject omitting implicit terms would be

Slender delta wings—Laminar boundary layer—Calculation

Varying the specificity of indexing—this implies indexing the terms within one or more categories at levels above that constituting 'specific' indexing, e.g. varying the level in the structures category (by omitting the specification 'Slender') would give

Delta wings—Laminar boundary layer—Calculation

or varying the level in the Aerodynamic Entities category would give

Slender delta wings—Laminar flow—Calculation

It should be noted that part of the hierarchy of both 'Structures' and of 'Flow' could be varied in their order of subordination; i.e. they could be altered to: Wings—Slender—Delta, and to Flow—Boundary layer—Laminar. This possibility might add a complication to a pre-co-ordinate system.

Varying the exhaustivity of indexing—this implies the non-recognition of one or more of the categories, e.g. omission in the indexing of the Operations category would give

Slender delta wings—laminar boundary layer

Omission of the Structures category would give

Laminar boundary layer—Calculation

Question

Three-dimensional boundary layer on slender wings

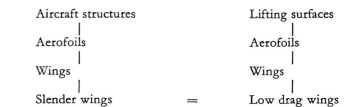

Aircraft structures	Aerodynamic entity
Aerofoils	Flow
Wings	Boundary layer
Slender wings	3-dimensional boundary layer

A linear statement would be

Slender wings—3-dimensional boundary layer

Varying the specificity in searching is exactly analogous to varying the specificity of indexing, e.g. varying the specificity in the Aerodynamic Entity category would mean a search for the broader subject

Slender wings—Boundary layer

Varying the exhaustivity in searching is exactly analogous to varying the exhaustivity of indexing, e.g. the omission of the Structures category would mean a search for the broader subject

Three-dimensional boundary layer

The hierarchical relations shown above are incomplete in two ways.

1. *Multiple generic links* are not shown. For example, a slender wing, from another viewpoint, could be characterized as a low drag wing factor. Theoretically any one term may be considered as a species in a number of different hierarchies, and the grid above could be enlarged within each category to show this:

Aircraft structures		Lifting surfaces
Aerofoils		Aerofoils
Wings		Wings
Slender wings	=	Low drag wings

2. *Co-ordinate relations* are not shown, although theoretically these may include potentially useful connections, as *Turbulent* boundary layer on slender delta wing.

In the first place, both the indexing and searching will be exhaustive and specific within the capabilities of a given index language; for instance, our first test might be of a language consisting simply of the correlation of uncontrolled 'uniterms'. In the example above, this would mean a search for the description 'Three-dimensional boundary layer on a slender wing' in a file in which the document is indexed as 'Calculation of laminar boundary layer on a slender delta wing'. We will then vary one element at a time, e.g. we will assume a degree of indexing which is less specific, first within one category, then within two categories, and so on, whilst holding the question exhaustive and specific. At each stage, figures for recall and relevance will be noted. Next, the exhaustivity of indexing is varied, then the specificity of the question, and so on.

After completing this stage, a particular indexing device is introduced which has been absent so far; for example, to the simple correlation of uncontrolled 'uniterms' we may introduce the confounding of verbal forms and note its impact on recall and relevance, again testing within a range of variables of specificity and exhaustivity of indexing and searching.

The number of different permutations of variables implied in the above programme is obviously vast and will constitute one of the major problems. We anticipate, however, that many of the theoretically possible combinations of factors will rule themselves out as having no retrieval or search significance; reducing the specificity of the Structure category to 'Wing', say, and reducing exhaustivity by omitting the Flow category would give us a description 'Wings—Calculation', which is obviously worthless.

PROBLEMS OF BASIC INDEXING

To provide the raw indexing material for subsequent processing we begin by recording the product of the 'concept indexing'. This means that we enter on a master sheet (see Fig. 5) a statement of what we consider to be all the significant terms, indicating as far as is necessary the relations between them. This is being entered at four levels of description, namely:

i. Abstract

ii. Themes

B 1069	AUTHOR G. E. Kaattari TITLE Predicted shock envelopes about two types of vehicles at large angles of attack.	*Indexer*	*Date*	
Base Document A32	REFERENCE NASA Tech. Note D–860	FWL	4/2/63	

ABSTRACT Presents methods for predicting detached shock envelopes of two atmosphere entry vehicles, one a high-drag capsule shape, the other a slender triangular wing (conical vehicle). Predicted and measured shock envelopes were compared for Mach range of 3 to 15 for vehicles at high angle of attack.

THEMES	CONCEPTS & WEIGHTS		TERMS & WEIGHTS		TERMS & WEIGHTS	
Atmosphere entry vehicle—at high angle of attack—in hypersonic flow (Mach 3 to 15)—detached shock envelope of—theory.	Atmosphere entry vehicle	8	Atmosphere	3	Slender	8
	High angle of attack	9	Entry	3	Triangular	8
High-drag capsule entry vehicle—at high angle of attack—in hypersonic flow (Mach 3 to 15)—detached shock envelope of—prediction.	Hypersonic flow	7	Vehicle	[illegible]	Wing	8
	Mach 3 to 15	6	High	9	Conical	8
	Detached shock envelope	10	Angle of attack	9	Standoff	6
Slender triangular wing (conical) entry vehicle—at high angle of attack—in hypersonic flow (Mach 3 to 15)—detached shock envelope of—prediction.	Theory	10	Hypersonic	7	Angle	6
	High-drag capsule	8	Flow	7	Continuity	7
	Slender triangular wings	8	Mach 3 to 15	6	Mass	7
Conical entry vehicles—at high angle of attack—in hypersonic flow (Mach 3 to 15)—shock standoff angles—prediction of.	Conical vehicle	8	Detached	10	Wave	10
	Shock standoff angle	6	Shock	10	Surface	5
Continuity of mass flow between shock wave and entry vehicle surface.	Mass flow continuity	7	Envelope	10	High	8
	Entry vehicle surface	5	Theory	10	Shock	6
			Drag	8	Entry	5
			Capsule	8	Vehicle	5

FIGURE 5

iii. Concepts
iv. Terms

The abstract provides a brief but general statement of the subject content of the complete document. The themes are required to show the relationship of the concepts, and will be used in connection with such indexing devices as partitioning, interlocking and interfixing. With the concepts, it will be noted that the same concept may occur in different themes, and similarly the same term may appear in two or more concepts. It should be emphasized that we have no particular system in mind when doing this initial indexing; it is completely neutral.

An additional type of statement that we provide is the weighting of the different concepts, and thus the terms. This is a relatively untried device that appears to have the possibility of being a particularly powerful tool in improving the relevance ratio. If one is doing intellectual indexing, it seems reasonable to suggest that the weighted indexing should also be a subjective assessment. If the indexing is to be done by using statistical techniques, then obviously the assignment of weights is a ready by-product.

If the impact on recall and relevance of the various devices is to be isolated, we cannot afford to have variations in other factors introducing uncontrolled influences. We cannot afford a situation, for example, where the figures for the effect of a particular device are criticized as unreliable because the indexer had omitted some vital term or relation. In particular, we want to be sure that all the relevant documents can be retrieved when indexing is exhaustive and specific, i.e. all the facilities indexwise must be available for complete retrieval from the index language (remembering that complete retrieval is always available to any librarian if he is prepared to abandon his index language and search the whole collection). This will be ensured by checking the indexing of a document against the questions to which it is known to be relevant and making quite sure that the raw indexing material does have this necessary data.

It is an implicit assumption of the provisions we intend to make for indexing that the ability of any index language to describe a subject closely or precisely is crucial if a high relevance ratio is required. If the index language (its vocabulary and its syntax) does not allow precise description, then the most exhaustive and specific searching will not improve matters in this respect. It is interesting to note that the age-old arguments about whether a classification should be detailed or not now has the basic issue determined with reasonable precision. While a detailed classification will provide precision for those who need it, but can be used broadly by those who do not, a broad classification provides facilities only for the second eventuality. At the same time, it is possible that the surprising degree of correspondence in the recall performance of the four different systems in Cranfield I can be attributed largely to the care with which the vocabulary was established in each case, even though the syntax of the schemes varied considerably. It should be noted, however, that the presence or absence of provision for the display of relations will, in certain circumstances, have the same effect on recall and relevance as the presence or absence of provision for vocabulary terms, e.g. a search for *x as an agent* will not be retrieved independently of *x as a patient* unless the index language allows the difference in role to be indicated.

Earlier in this paper, we suggested that the subject area covered by an indexing system might prove to be the most potent factor of all in determining a performance curve. We hope to be able to shed some light on this by testing an index in the field of the social sciences, where we may find that the potency of particular devices will vary significantly from their potency in a relatively unambiguous area like high speed aerodynamics.

REFERENCES

1. VICKERY, B. C. On retrieval system theory. London, Butterworths, 1961.
2. CLEVERDON, C. W. Report on the testing and analysis of an investigation into the comparative efficiency of indexing systems. Cranfield, [College of Aeronautics], October 1962. (Aslib Cranfield Research Project.)
3. AITCHISON, JEAN, *and* CLEVERDON, CYRIL. Report of a test on the index of metallurgical literature of Western Reserve University. [To be published.]
4. CLEVERDON, C. W. Report on the first stage of an investigation into the comparative efficiency of indexing systems. Cranfield, College of Aeronautics, September 1960. (Aslib Cranfield Research Project.)

Theory of Clumps

See *Clumps, Theory of*

D.J. Foskett

THESAURUS

The word *thesaurus* derives from Greek and Latin words which mean "a treasury," and it has been used for several centuries to mean a lexicon or treasury of words. An interesting and entertaining historical account has been given by Karen Sparck Jones, who traces the origins of "synonymy" in dictionaries and identifies the main difference from natural language: the thesaurus involves "vocabulary normalisation" (*1*). Modern usage may be said to date from 1852, when the first edition of the *Thesaurus of English Words and Phrases* was published by Peter Mark Roget. His subtitle reads: "classified and arranged so as to facilitate the expression of ideas and to assist in literary composition." The value and importance of *Roget* may be judged from the fact that new editions have appeared regularly right up to the present day. The addition of "and phrases" in the title has great significance, as anyone knows who has used *Roget* for literary composition; and it is also significant in a discussion of the role of the thesaurus in information storage and retrieval.

This role began in earnest in the early 1950s, particularly through the work of Hans Peter Luhn. Luhn himself was clear about the relation of his own use of the word to that of Roget, but the confused way in which the idea was applied by several others was pointed out in 1960 by B. C. Vickery, who showed that at least four different meanings were used in the literature of information science at that time. The most common interpretation was as an alphabetical list of single words, with related words listed under each, in various ways. Since then, attempts have been made to tidy up this situation, and the definition used here is that of the World Science Information System of UNESCO, known as UNISIST:

> A thesaurus may be defined either in terms of its function or its structure.
>
> In terms of function, a thesaurus is a terminological control device used in translating from the natural language of documents, indexers or users into a more constrained "system language" (documentation language, information language).
>
> In terms of structure, a thesaurus is a controlled and dynamic vocabulary of semantically and generically related terms which covers a specific domain of knowledge.

Roget's own thesaurus is very far from being a simple alphabetical list of words; the main structure is in fact the list of words and phrases set out in a series of categories defined in very general terms such as Existence, Quantity, Time, Space, Matter, Intellect, and Sentient and Moral Powers. Each of these categories has a number of subdivisions, each containing several words. Each word is identified by an arabic numeral, and below it are listed all the synonyms and other related words and phrases which concern the same concept. Under Space, for example, we find the subdivision "relative space," which includes the following entry:

> 183. **Situation** — *N.* situation, position, locality, locale, status, latitude and longitude; standpoint, post; aspect, attitude, posture, pose.
>
> place, site, base, station, seat, venue, whereabout, environment, neighbourhood; bearings, &c. 278; spot &c. 182.
>
> top- ge-ography; map &c. 554.
>
> *V.* be-situated, -situate; lie; have its seat in.
>
> *Adj.* situ-ate, -ated; local, topical, topographical &c. *n.*
>
> *Adv.* in situ; here and there; here-, there-, where-abouts; in place, here, there.

As can be seen, each of the words and phrases listed under each term heading is assigned to a grammatical category: noun, verb, adjective, and adverb. Following the section that lists all the terms in categories there is a second list of all these terms in alphabetical order; under each term in this section there appears a list of related terms with different category numbers. The heading term also appears in those categories, according to its various shades of meaning:

position
circumstances 8
term 71
situation 183
proposition 514
assertion 535
situation
circumstances 8
place 183
location 184
business 625
out of a — 185

Thus *Roget's Thesaurus* is a classification scheme for terms with a relative alphabetical index. It can be seen at once that its value consists in being a structure for relating concepts to one another through their various meanings; this is what makes *Roget* familiar to all concerned with the quality of style in writing. As Roget put it in his own original introduction, he did not set out to provide a dictionary but a structure of concepts in which:

> . . . the idea being given, to find the word or words by which that idea may be most fitly and aptly expressed. For this purpose, the words and phrases of the language are here classed, not according to their sound or their orthography, but strictly according to their signification.

The use of a thesaurus in modern information storage and retrieval systems has not been so much for the purpose of finding fit and apt means of expression as for controlling a vocabulary in the process of analysis of information. According to Mary Elizabeth Stevens, in her biographical note on Luhn, he was thinking about "families of notions" as early as 1951 (*2*). He certainly advanced this idea in his work at the Research Center of the I.B.M. Corporation, where he was looking for a simple way of using a computer to record a system of authorized words for use in subject indexing, with a regular structure of cross-references. His paper of 1957, "A Statistical Approach to Mechanised Literature Searching," is usually held to be the first published expression of this opinion, and in it he specifically states:

> The procedure to be described is similar to the one used by P M Roget for compiling his Thesaurus for English Words. . . . the third step is a preparation of a card index for all transcribed sentences. A concordance that can then be worked out with the aid of these cards will result in the grouping of words of similar or related meaning into "notional families." This is so similar to the work required for the creation of Roget's thesaurus that basic organization of his book may well serve as the skeleton for this process (*3*, p. 89a).

Most of the modern thesauri, on the other hand, began by making the alphabetical list the major element; in the early days, some had no listing in categories at all. But it was soon found that even in a computerized system some kind of classificatory structure was an advantage for both indexer and searcher, and consequently there have been introduced arrangements of terms in categories for most of the more recent thesauri. There is now an enormous literature on the subject, including several books; in English, there are works of an introductory nature by Jean Aitchison and Alan Gilchrist (*4, 5*), and a vast, encyclopedic survey by Dagobert Soergel (*6*). All of these can be strongly recommended. The journal *International Classification* has as its subtitle "Journal on Theory and Practice of Universal and Special Classification Systems and Thesauri," and a review of recent work has been made by F. W. Lancaster (*7*).

Even if the modern thesaurus does on occasion help an author to find an appropriate or felicitous word and therefore enhance his style, its primary object is to act as an indexing language for use in information storage and retrieval. Any such language must be based on the literature of the subject field which it sets out to cover; it must be able to accommodate all the terms found in that literature, and this will certainly include many words that are not germane to that field but belong to marginal fields. Although this causes trouble for indexers and searchers, it is nonetheless a reflection of the nature of knowledge itself, which is of course not neatly divided into self-contained and mutually exclusive compartments but is an intricate mesh of ideas which react with other ideas; each individual person has such an intricate network stored in his brain, derived from his unique set of experiences. It is for this reason that any index language must contain as many guides to related concepts as are necessary to cope with the many different "patterns of knowledge" that already exist in the heads of the indexers and searchers who use that index language. Such a scheme of words must be a growing organism, always subject to revision, and thus there must be some means for introducing new words and concepts at appropriate places. This particular need has always been advanced as the strongest argument in favor of the simple alphabetical list, on the grounds that any such new word can easily be inserted in its correct place in the alphabetical order. Against this must be set the fact that this applies only to a single-language system, whereas the growing need today is for multilingual thesauri which can be used in several different countries. In addition, unless an index has some form of structure, a user will have no means of knowing whether he has selected the correct term when making or consulting the index. Even with a structure, it is still somewhat cumbersome to pursue a train of references in alphabetical indexes. For example, the article "Nine Years' Toxicity Control in Insecticide Plants," from *Index Medicus* though not indexed under either "toxicity" or "toxicology," may still be traced from the cross-reference from "toxicology" to "poisons," despite the fact that the article is not indexed under "poisons" either; the explanation is that in this index "poisons" stands next to "poisoning" and it is here that the article is actually indexed. This is a cumbersome and chancy process, but there is a path to be found if the searcher thinks to look for it and takes the trouble to follow up the trail of cross-references.

Purpose of a Thesaurus

The major purposes of a thesaurus include the following:

1. To provide a map of a given field of knowledge, indicating how concepts or ideas about concepts are related to one another, which helps an indexer or a searcher to understand the structure of the field.
2. To provide a standard vocabulary for a given subject field which will ensure that indexers are consistent when they are making index entries to an information storage and retrieval system.
3. To provide a system of references between terms which will ensure that only one term from a set of synonyms is used for indexing one concept, and that indexers and searchers are told which of the set is the one chosen; and to provide guides to terms which are related to any index term in other ways, either by classification structure or otherwise in the literature.
4. To provide a guide for users of the system so that they choose the correct term for a subject search; this stresses the importance of cross-references. If an indexer uses more than one synonym in the same index—for example, "abroad," "foreign," and "overseas"—then documents are liable to be indexed haphazardly under all of these; a searcher who chooses one and finds documents indexed there will assume that he has found the correct term and will stop his search without knowing that there are other useful documents indexed under the other synonyms.
5. To locate new concepts in a scheme of relationships with existing concepts in a way which makes sense to users of the system.
6. To provide classified hierarchies so that a search can be broadened or narrowed systematically, if the first choice of search terms produces either too few or too many references to the material in the store.
7. A desirable purpose, but one which it would be premature to say is being achieved, is to provide a means by which the use of terms in a given subject field may be standardized.

In practice, the use of a controlled vocabulary to make subject indexes in libraries is by no means new. Lists of "subject headings," such as those of Minnie E. Sears and the Library of Congress, have been in popular use since the 19th century. E. J. Coates has made an analysis of some of them in his book *Subject Catalogues: Headings and Structure* (*8*), showing how imperfect is the relationship between the Library of Congress list and its own classification scheme. On the whole, such lists were designed as aids to indexing only—that is, with the compiler of an index in mind, rather than a searcher. Naturally, an indexer would take on the role of a searcher when consulting the subject catalog to ensure that a new book would be entered under the same headings as previous books on the same subject. It is surprising, therefore, that the modern development of the thesaurus, with much the same objectives, should originate from users rather than from librarians. Significant features were that it happened in the area of scientific and technical literature and in institutions having easy access to computers, with their ability to process large amounts of data in a very short time. Searches carried out in such circumstances demanded ready access to highly specific subjects with many facets. If we take the relatively simple article mentioned earlier, "Nine Years' Toxicity Control in Insecticide Plants," it will be clear that this might be approached from at least four different directions: toxicity (poisons, poisoning, health, hygiene), control (measurement, restriction), insecticide (insects, pests, infestation), and plants (factories, industry, production). Approaches beginning with any one of these words should lead the searcher to this particular article.

It will also be clear that using only one facet will bring the searcher a large number of documents from the collection, and that many of them will not be helpful. The search must be narrowed down by coordinate indexing. The order in which the words are arranged has considerable significance too, because a searcher will not be looking for documents which deal with, for example, the control of toxicity of insecticides in plants, a subject in the same general area of knowledge but not the same specific subject.

A thesaurus which acts efficiently as a controlled language for indexing and retrieval therefore has to provide specific terms, general terms to which the specific terms are related, and a secondary network of other terms which may from time to time be related in the subject literature. It is, in fact, an improved version of the "list of subject headings," and in at least one case, the Medical Subject Headings (MESH) used in the MEDLARS scheme of the National Library of Medicine, the present thesaurus has grown out of the original list and continues to use the same title.

It should be noted that not everyone agrees on the need for a controlled vocabulary in information storage and retrieval. At a symposium on "A Comprehensive On-line Computer System for Special Libraries" held at the Building Research Station in England in December 1974, H. H. Neville and his colleagues announced their intention of moving over to a "natural language system" (*9*)—mainly on the grounds that controlled-language systems are becoming ever more elaborate, need increasing amounts of staff time at input, and perform no better in retrieval. A middle road has some advocates: "free language entry," that is, a system with no restriction on the number of terms in use and with a minimal structure of references to cope with synonyms and similar close relationships. There seems to be little difference between this and the "list of subject headings" used in most libraries.

Yet the fact remains that more and more organizations are compiling thesauri and continue to find them useful, to the extent that several "guidelines" for construction have been published: Guidelines for monolingual and for multilingual thesauri have been produced by UNISIST (*10*), and the British Standards Institution has completed a draft specification. Most of the organizations which have published a thesaurus have included information on its structure and use, and two international centers for collecting thesauri have been set up, at Case Western Reserve University in the United States and at the Central Institute for Scientific, Technical, and Economic Information in Warsaw. Each of these centers now holds several hundred examples, and new ones are reported in every issue of the *FID/CR Newsletter* published by the Documentation Research and Training Center of the Indian Statistical Institute in Bangalore.

In this article, therefore, no attempt is made to give a complete list or even to cite all the major thesauri; a selection is provided, and anyone wanting to use a thesaurus for their own field will be well advised to consult one of the centers to find out whether any example already exists.

Format

A thesaurus usually has at least two major parts: (*a*) a list of words grouped systematically into sets or categories, now often called "facets," in each of which all the words have some intrinsic relation to each other (such as chemical elements, mammals, industrial occupations, and member states of the United Nations); and (*b*) an alphabetical list, which may take more than one form, of all the terms from all the categories, with a notation which refers each term to the category of which it is a member. C. van der Merwe, in his *Thesaurus of Sociological Research Terminology*, published by Rotterdam University, expresses this relation thus:

> This combination of a systematic classification scheme and a controlled index language determines the structure of the thesaurus. Although an alphabetical index of terms has been added as an extra aid, the thesaurus in a more narrow sense consists of terms that have been arranged in a logical order by subject rather than in an alphabetical order (*11*, p. 7).

The relative importance of these two parts varies greatly from one thesaurus to another, and in some cases the principles on which the categories are based are far from clear.

The *Thesaurus of Engineering and Scientific Terms* (TEST), one of the largest and best known, covers a very wide range of subjects, as its name implies (*12*). It was produced as a cooperative effort between the Engineers Joint Council and the Department of Defense of the United States, and its object is "to produce a comprehensive thesaurus of scientific and technical terms for use as a basic reference in information storage and retrieval systems and to provide a vocabulary groundwork by means of which the interchange of information might be enhanced" (*12*, p. 1). In addition to compiling a data bank of some 150,000 terms, an important early step was the formulation of rules and conventions; these were first published as the *Manual for Building a Technical Thesaurus* (ONR-55) by the Office of Naval Research and were later included as an appendix to the printed TEST. These are commonsense rules and have been followed to a greater or lesser degree by several other compilers; they are, however, somewhat less detailed than later examples such as the *UNISIST Guidelines*. The major part of TEST is the alphabetical list, which is actually called "Thesaurus of Terms," as distinct from the other sections:

"Permuted Index," "Subject Category Index," and "Hierarchical Index." There is much duplication between these groups, especially the Thesaurus of Terms and the Permuted Index. Since the Thesaurus of Terms includes entries for "vocational guidance" and "vocational interests," for example, it is hard to see the necessity for entries of "vocational guidance" and "vocational interests" under "vocational" in the Permuted Index. The Subject Category Fields and Groups include those shown in Figure 1, and although these categories are identified by subject, they are in fact arranged in alphabetical order (with the exception of No. 10); the subgroups are likewise alphabetical, without regard for closely related subjects. Some subgroups appear more than once, but not consistently; for example:

05 09 Personnel selection, training, and evaluation
06 14 Personnel selection and maintenance (medical)

Such a subgroup could better be treated only once, in 05 09, or alternatively, in every category where personnel are involved. It could also be given the same subgroup number in each category.

A similar type of arrangement can be found in the thesaurus of the American Psychological Association (APA), which has three sections: "Relationship Section," "Rotated Alphabetical Terms Section," and "Postable Terms and Term Codes Section." Extracts from the three sections of the APA thesaurus are given in Figures 2, 3, and 4 (*13*). Duplication between the Relationship Section and the Rotated Alphabetical Terms Section is reduced by not including in the latter those terms which are not to be used for indexing documents—like "concept (self)," "conditioned reflex," and "conditioning (classical)," from all of which there are references to the term which is to be used. As in TEST, the normal sequence of terms is alphabetical. In the second edition of the APA thesaurus, some 180 terms have been deleted because an analysis showed that they had never been used as access points to the psychological literature in the cumulated machine-readable data base of *Psychological Abstracts* (PA). The new Rotated Alphabetical Terms Section includes terms having several words, listed in alphabetical sequence under each word in turn. The Postable Terms and Term Codes Section replaces the former alphabetical section and includes the numeric codes for each term from the PA data base.

If the compiler follows the principles of facet analysis, the place of each term should be easy to see, since the facets will be based on a logical approach to the subject field. Probably the best-known example of this is the *Thesaurofacet*, compiled by Jean Aitchison and her colleagues for the English Electric Company (*14*). This is certainly one of the most thoroughgoing and successful attempts to construct for a thesaurus a detailed and systematic analysis or classification of a very large subject area, engineering—using the technique of facet analysis and deriving the whole of the alphabetical listing from the classification schedules. Figure 5 shows how the two parts of the *Thesaurofacet* complement each other and contrasts the amount of information given by this relationship with that provided by the type of entry found in more conventional systems.

Subject Category Fields and Groups

01 Aeronautics
- •01 01
- 01 02 Aeronautics
- 01 03 Aircraft
- 01 04 Aircraft flight instrumentation
- 01 05 Air facilities

02 Agriculture
- 02 01 Agricultural chemistry
- 02 02 Agricultural economics
- 02 03 Agricultural engineering
- 02 04 Agronomy and horticulture
- 02 05 Animal husbandry
- 02 06 Forestry

03 Astronomy and astrophysics
- 03 01 Astronomy
- 03 02 Astrophysics
- 03 03 Celestial mechanics

04 Atmospheric sciences
- 04 01 Atmospheric physics
- 04 02 Meteorology

05 Behavioral and social sciences
- 05 01 Administration and management
- •05 02 Information sciences
- 05 03 Economics
- 05 04 History, law, and political science
- 05 05 Human factors engineering
- 05 06 Humanities
- 05 07 Linguistics
- •05 08
- 05 09 Personnel selection, training, and evaluation
- •05 10 Psychology
- 05 11 Sociology

06 Biological and medical sciences
- 06 01 Biochemistry
- 06 02 Bioengineering
- 06 03 Biology
- 06 04 Bionics
- 06 05 Clinical medicine
- 06 06 Environmental biology
- 06 07 Escape, rescue, and survival
- 06 08 Food
- 06 09 Hygiene and sanitation
- •06 10
- 06 11 Life support
- •06 12 Medical equipment and supplies
- 06 13 Microbiology
- 06 14 Personnel selection and maintenance (medical)
- 06 15 Pharmacology
- 06 16 Physiology
- 06 17 Protective equipment
- 06 18 Radiobiology
- 06 19 Stress physiology
- 06 20 Toxicology
- 06 21 Weapon effects

07 Chemistry
- 07 01 Chemical engineering
- 07 02 Inorganic chemistry
- 07 03 Organic chemistry
- •07 04 Physical and general chemistry
- 07 05 Radio and radiation chemistry

08 Earth sciences and oceanography
- 08 01 Biological oceanography
- 08 02 Cartography
- 08 03 Dynamic oceanography
- 08 04 Geochemistry
- 08 05 Geodesy
- 08 06 Geography
- 08 07 Geology and mineralogy
- 08 08 Hydrology and limnology
- 08 09 Mining engineering
- 08 10 Physical oceanography
- 08 11 Seismology
- 08 12 Snow, ice and permafrost
- 08 13 Soil mechanics
- •08 14 Geomagnetism

09 Electronics and electrical engineering
- 09 01 Components
- 09 02 Computers
- 09 03 Electronic and electrical engineering
- 09 04 Information theory
- 09 05 Subsystems
- 09 06 Telemetry

•10 Nonpropulsive energy conversion
- 10 01 Conversion techniques
- 10 02 Power sources
- 10 03 Energy storage

11 Materials
- 11 01 Adhesives and seals
- 11 02 Ceramics, refractories, and glasses
- 11 03 Coatings, colorants, and finishes
- 11 04 Composite materials
- 11 05 Fibers and textiles
- •11 06 Metals
- 11 07 Miscellaneous materials
- 11 08 Oils, lubricants, and hydraulic fluids
- 11 09 Plastics

FIGURE 1. *Extract from TEST.*
Reproduced by permission of the Engineers Joint Council.

ROTATED ALPHABETICAL TERMS SECTION

Community

Obstetrical **Complications**
Postsurgical **Complications** (Physica
Comprehension
Comprehension Tests
Listening **Comprehension**
Number **Comprehension**
Reading **Comprehension**
Sentence **Comprehension**
Compressed Speech
Compulsions
Compulsive Repetition
Obsessive **Compulsive** Neurosis
Obsessive **Compulsive** Personality
Computer Applications
Computer Assisted Diagnosis
Computer Assisted Instruction
Computer Programing Languages
Computer Simulation
Computer Software
Computers
Analog **Computers**
Digital **Computers**
Concentration Camps
Concept Formation
Concept Learning
Conservation **(Concept)**
Self **Concept**
Temporal Spatial **Concept** Scale
Tennessee Self **Concept** Scale
Concepts
God **Concepts**
Mathematics **(Concepts)**
Conceptual Imagery
Brain **Concussion**
Conditioned Emotional Responses
Conditioned Responses
Conditioned Stimulus
Conditioned Suppression
Conditioning
Avoidance **Conditioning**
Classical **Conditioning**
Escape **Conditioning**
Eyelid **Conditioning**
Operant **Conditioning**

Atmospheric **Conditions**
Working **Conditions**
Bone **Conduction** Audiometry
Cones (Eye)
Confabulation
Conference Proceedings
Confession (Religion)
Confidence Limits (Statistics)
Conflict
Marital **Conflict**
Role **Conflicts**
Conformity (Personality)
Mental **Confusion**
Congenital Disorders
Drug Induced **Congenital** Disorders
Congenitally Handicapped
Self **Congruence**
Conjoint Therapy
Connective Tissue Cells
Connective Tissues
Connotations
Consanguineous Marriage
Conscience
Conscious (Personality Factors)
Consciousness Disturbances
Consciousness Raising Groups
Consciousness States
Conservation (Concept)
Conservation (Ecological Behavior)
Conservatism
Political **Conservatism**
Wilson Patterson **Conservatism** Scale
Consistency (Measurement)
Consonants
Constipation
Test **Construction**
Mental Health **Consultation**
Professional **Consultation**
Consumer Attitudes
Consumer Behavior
Consumer Protection
Consumer Psychology
Consumer Research
Consumer Surveys

Conditioned

FIGURE 3. *Extract from the Rotated Alphabetical Terms Section of the* Thesaurus of Psychological Index Terms. *Reproduced by permission of the American Psychological Association.*

Experience has proved, therefore, that in order to provide maximum efficiency and ease of use, a thesaurus should have at least two major parts, the systematic and the alphabetical, and in fact there are many thesauri which have more than two parts. The extra ones usually turn out to be variations on the two basic forms.

Terms

The basic elements in a thesaurus are the individual words, terms, or phrases, and these are often called "descriptors" or "keywords." Some writers use these two as synonyms; others make distinctions of various types. The *UNISIST Guidelines* chooses "descriptor," which is a general term used in documentation systems. But there is an important psychological factor to be borne in mind,

RELATIONSHIP SECTION

Community

Community Welfare Services — (Continued)
Related: Welfare Services (Government)
Companies
Use: Business Organizations
Comparative Psychology
Broader: Psychology; Sciences; Social Sciences
Compatibility (Interpersonal)
Use: Interpersonal Compatibility
Compensation (Defense Mechanism)
Broader: Defense Mechanisms
Compensatory Education
Broader: Curriculum
Related: Education/; Educational Programs
Competition
Broader: Social Behavior
Complex (Electra)
Use: Electra Complex
Complex (Oedipal)
Use: Oedipal Complex
Complexity (Cognitive)
Use: Cognitive Complexity
Complexity (Stimulus)
Use: Stimulus Complexity
Complexity (Task)
Use: Task Complexity
Compliance
Broader: Social Behavior
Comprehension
Used for: Understanding
Narrower: Listening Comprehension; Number Comprehension; Reading Comprehension; Sentence Comprehension
Related: Meaning; Meaningfulness
Comprehension Tests
Related: Measurement/
Compressed Speech
Broader: Speech Processing (Mechanical); Verbal Communication
Compulsions
Narrower: Compulsive Repetition
Related: Mental Disorders/

Compulsions — (Continued)
Related: Obsessions; Obsessive Compulsive Neurosis; Obsessive Compulsive Personality
Compulsive Neurosis
Use: Obsessive Compulsive Neurosis
Compulsive Repetition
Used for: Repetition (Compulsive)
Broader: Compulsions
Computer Applications
Narrower: Computer Assisted Diagnosis; Computer Assisted Instruction; Computer Simulation
Related: Computers
Computer Assisted Diagnosis
Broader: Computer Applications; Diagnosis
Related: Medical Diagnosis; Psychodiagnosis
Computer Assisted Instruction
Used for: Instruction (Computer Assisted)
Broader: Computer Applications; Teaching; Teaching Methods
Related: Individualized Instruction; Programed Instruction; Teaching Machines
Computer Programing Languages
Used for: FORTRAN; Programing Languages (Computer)
Related: Computers; Data Processing
Computer Programs
Use: Computer Software
Computer Simulation
Broader: Computer Applications; Simulation
Related: Simulation Games
Computer Software
Used for: Computer Programs; Programing (Computer)
Related: Computers; Data Processing; Systems/
Computers
Broader: Apparatus
Narrower: Analog Computers; Digital Computers
Related: Automation

Computers — (Continued)
Related: Computer Applications; Computer Programing Languages; Computer Software; Cybernetics; Data Processing; Systems/
Concentration Camps
Used for: Camps (Concentration)
Related: Correctional Institutions
Concept (Self)
Use: Self Concept
Concept Formation
Used for: Conceptualization
Broader: Cognitive Processes
Related: Concepts; Conservation (Concept); Egocentrism
Concept Learning
Narrower: Nonreversal Shift Learning; Reversal Shift Learning
Related: Concepts; Learning/
Concepts
Used for: Information (Concepts)
Related: Concept Formation; Concept Learning; Information/
Conceptual Imagery
Used for: Imagery (Conceptual)
Broader: Imagery
Related: Imagination
Conceptualization
Use: Concept Formation
Concussion (Brain)
Use: Brain Concussion
Conditioned Emotional Responses
Used for: CER (Conditioning)
Broader: Classical Conditioning; Conditioned Responses; Conditioning; Emotional Responses; Operant Conditioning; Responses
Conditioned Inhibition
Use: Conditioned Suppression
Conditioned Reflex
Use: Conditioned Responses

FIGURE 2. *Extract from the Relationship Section of the* Thesaurus of Psychological Index Terms. *Reproduced by permission of the American Psychological Association.*

Cobalt **POSTABLE TERMS AND TERM CODES SECTION** Delirium

09920 Cobalt
09930 Cocaine
09940 Cochlea
09950 Cochran Q Test
09960 Cockroaches
09970 Codeine
10000 Coeducation
10040 Cognition
10050 Cognitive Ability
10060 Cognitive Complexity
10070 Cognitive Contiguity
10080 Cognitive Development
10090 Cognitive Discrimination
10100 Cognitive Dissonance
10110 Cognitive Generalization
10120 Cognitive Mediation
10130 Cognitive Processes
10140 Cognitive Style
10150 Cohabitation
10200 Cold Effects
10220 Colitis
10230 Coll Ent Exam Bd Scholastic Apt Test
10250 Collective Behavior
10260 College Academic Achievement
10290 College Dropouts
10300 College Environment
10320 College Students
10330 College Teachers
10350 Colleges
10370 Colon Disorders
10380 Color
10390 Color Blindness
10400 Color Perception
10410 Color Pyramid Test
10430 Colostomy
10440 Columbia Mental Maturity Scale
10450 Coma
10470 Commissioned Officers
10480 Commitment (Psychiatric)
10510 Communes
10540 Communication Skills
10550 Communication Systems
10560 Communication Theory
10570 Communication/
10580 Communications Media
10590 Communism
10600 Communities
10620 Community Attitudes
10627 Community College Students
10630 † Community Colleges
10640 Community Facilities
10647 Community Mental Health
10650 Community Mental Health Centers
10654 † Community Mental Health Services
10660 Community Mental Health Training
10670 Community Psychiatry
10680 Community Psychology
10690 Community Services
10700 Community Welfare Services
10720 Comparative Psychology
10740 Compensation (Defense Mechanism)
10745 Compensatory Education
10750 Competition
10810 Compliance
10820 Comprehension
10830 Comprehension Tests
10840 Compressed Speech
10850 Compulsions
10890 Compulsive Repetition
10900 Computer Applications
10910 Computer Assisted Diagnosis
10920 Computer Assisted Instruction
10930 Computer Programing Languages
10950 Computer Simulation
10960 Computer Software
10970 Computers
10980 Concentration Camps
11000 Concept Formation
11010 Concept Learning
11030 Concepts
11040 Conceptual Imagery
11070 Conditioned Emotional Responses
11090 Conditioned Responses
11100 Conditioned Stimulus
11110 Conditioned Suppression
11120 Conditioning
11190 Cones (Eye)
11200 Confabulation
11210 Conference Proceedings
11220 Confession (Religion)
11230 Confidence Limits (Statistics)
11250 Conflict
11270 Conformity (Personality)
11290 Congenital Disorders
11300 Congenitally Handicapped
11310 Conjoint Therapy
11320 Connective Tissue Cells
11330 Connective Tissues
11340 Connotations
11350 Consanguineous Marriage
11360 Conscience
11370 Conscious (Personality Factors)
11380 Consciousness Disturbances
11387 † Consciousness Raising Groups
11390 Consciousness States
11400 Conservation (Concept)
11403 † Conservation (Ecological Behavior)
11405 Conservatism
11420 Consistency (Measurement)
11430 Consonants
11440 Constipation
11470 Consumer Attitudes
11480 Consumer Behavior
11490 Consumer Protection
11500 Consumer Psychology
11510 Consumer Research
11520 Consumer Surveys
11540 Contact Lenses
11548 † Content Analysis
11550 Content Analysis (Test)
11560 Contextual Associations
11580 Contingency Management
11630 Contraceptive Devices
11710 Conversation
11730 Conversion Neurosis
11750 Convulsions
11756 † Cooperating Teachers
11760 Cooperation
11790 Coping Behavior
11800 Copper
11830 Cornea
11860 Coronary Thromboses
11900 Corpus Callosum
11910 Correctional Institutions
11980 Cortical Evoked Potentials
12000 Corticosteroids
12010 Corticosterone
12020 Corticotropin
12040 Cortisone
12045 Costs and Cost Analysis
12070 Counseling Psychology
12080 Counseling/
12090 Counselor Attitudes
12100 Counselor Characteristics
12120 Counselor Education
12150 Counselor Role
12160 Counselor Trainees
12170 Counselors
12180 Counterconditioning
12190 Countertransference
12195 Countries
12210 Courage
12215 † Course Evaluation
12260 Cousins
12300 Crabs
12310 Crafts
12330 Cranial Nerves
12340 Cranial Spinal Cord
12360 Crayfish
12380 Creativity
12390 Creativity Measurement
12400 Credibility
12430 Crime
12440 Criminal Conviction
12450 Criminal Law
12460 Criminals
12470 Criminology
12490 Crises
12510 Crisis Intervention
12520 Crisis Intervention Services
12530 Critical Flicker Fusion Threshold
12540 Criticism
12570 Crocodilians
12590 Cross Cultural Differences
12610 † Crowding
12620 Cruelty
12630 Crustacea
12640 Crying
12650 Crying Cat Syndrome
12670 Cuba
12680 Cues
12690 Cultism
12700 Cultural Assimilation
12710 Cultural Deprivation
12730 Cultural Test Bias
12750 Culture (Anthropological)
12760 Culture Change
12770 Culture Fair Intelligence Test
12780 Culture Shock
12790 Curare
12800 Curiosity
12810 Curriculum
12820 Curriculum Development
12830 Cursive Writing
12840 Cushings Syndrome
12850 Cutaneous Sense
12860 Cybernetics
12875 † Cyclic Adenosine Monophosphate
12880 Cycloheximide
12890 Cyclothymic Personality
12900 Cynicism
12910 Cysteine
12920 Cytochrome Oxidase
12930 Cytology
12940 Cytoplasm
12950 Czechoslovakia

12970 Dance
12980 Dance Therapy
12990 Dark Adaptation
13000 Darwinism
13020 Data Processing
13040 Daughters
13070 Day Care Centers
13080 Daydreaming
13090 DDT (Insecticide)
13100 Deaf
13110 Death and Dying
13115 † Death Anxiety
13120 Death Attitudes
13150 Death Rites
13160 Decarboxylases
13166 † Decentralization
13170 Deception
13180 Decerebration
13190 Decision Making
13200 Decompression Effects
13210 Decortication (Brain)
13230 Deer
13240 Defecation
13250 Defense Mechanisms
13260 Defensiveness
13290 Dehydrogenases
13297 † Delay of Gratification
13300 Delayed Auditory Feedback
13310 Delayed Development
13320 Delayed Feedback
13340 Deletion (Chromosome)
13360 Delirium

† New term added in 1978

FIGURE 4. *Extract from the Postable Terms and Term Codes Section of the* Thesaurus of Psychological Index Terms. *Reproduced by permission of the American Psychological Association.*

namely, standard usage, which clearly favors the use of the word "term." This will be evident when (before dealing with the form of the descriptors themselves) we consider two other pieces of thesaurus apparatus: (*a*) definitions and explanations and (*b*) the symbols of relationships. Both of these are usually found only in the alphabetical part, though they can also have value in the systematic part, and some compilers use them there as well.

Definitions and explanations have to be given wherever there is a need to state the precise meaning of a particular term in the particular context of any thesaurus. The term "elevation" has several different meanings in technology, and the terms "pavement" and "public school" have more or less opposite meanings in the United Kingdom and the United States. To ensure consistency in use, and in order not to mislead searchers, it is necessary to add a "scope note" (SN) immediately under the term, thus:

Public School
SN In the United Kingdom, an independent foundation which does not receive funds from the state, and which is a member of the Headmasters Conference or the Girls' Public Day School Trust.
In the United States, a school established and supported by the state system of education.

Dagobert Soergel gives good examples of such homographs (*6*):

Seal 1 (*marine animal*)
Seal 2 (*documents*)
Drill 1 (*instruction*)
Drill 2 (*agriculture*)
Drill 3 (*fabric*)

Not every term needs a scope note, but their presence is of considerable help in using a thesaurus correctly and, indeed, in reaching a correct understanding of the field of knowledge concerned.

THE COMPLIMENTARY PARTS OF THE THESAUROFACET

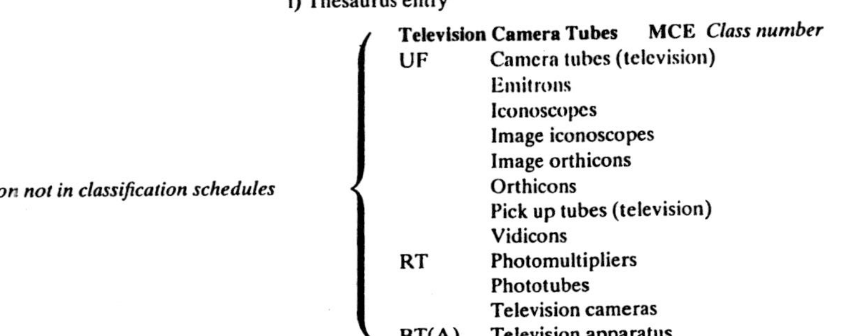

(Continued)

ii) Classification schedules

Information not in Thesaurus
Related terms (RT):
(i) Image converter tubes
(ii) Image intensifiers
(iii) Storage tubes
(iv) Television picture tubes
(v) Television colour picture tubes

Narrower terms (NT):
Television colour camera tubes
Broader terms (BT):
(i) Cathode ray tubes
(ii) Electron beam deflection tubes
(iii) Electron tubes

M	*ELECTRONIC ENGINEERING*
MA	**ELECTRON TUBES** (Cont'd) *BT*
MBT	Electron beam deflection tubes *BT*
MBV	Indicator tubes (tuning)
MBW	Trochotrons
MC	Cathode ray tubes *BT*
MC2	*RT* { Image converter tubes
MC4	Image intensifiers
MC6	Storage tubes
MCE	**Television camera tubes**
MCI	Television colour camera tubes *NT*
MCL	*RT* { Television picture tubes
MCO	Television colour picture tubes
MCQ	X ray tubes

CONVENTIONAL THESAURUS ENTRY

In the Thesaurofacet underlined items are shown in the classification schedules and not in the thesaurus

Television Camera Tubes

UF	Camera tubes (television)
	Emitrons
	Iconoscopes
	Image iconoscopes
	Image orthicons
	Orthicons
	Pick up tubes (television)
	Vidicons
RT	Image converter tubes
	Image intensifiers
	Photomultipliers
	Phototubes
	Storage tubes
	Television cameras
	Television colour picture tubes
	Television picture tubes
NT	Television colour camera tubes
BT	Cathode ray tubes
	Electron beam deflection tubes
	Electron tubes
	Television apparatus

FIGURE 5. *Extract from* Thesaurofacet.
Reproduced by permission of the English Electric Company.

Relationships and the symbols used to express them have always been an integral part of lists of subject headings. They have been of two simple forms, nearly always called "see" and "see also" references. Their significance is plain from their names: a "see" reference is added to a term not used in the system, pointing to the term used instead, a synonym or near-synonym, a "see also" reference is added to a term which can be used, pointing to other terms at which additional useful information may also be indexed. The well-known *Sears List of Subject Headings*, now edited by Barbara Westby (*15*), has an additional refinement, using *x* and *xx* to show the reciprocal references from the "see" and "see also" references themselves:

Classical dictionaries
x Dictionaries, Classical
xx History, Ancient
History, Ancient
See also **Archeology; Bible; Civilization, Ancient; Classical dictionaries; Geography, Ancient; Inscriptions; Numismatics;** also names of ancient races and peoples (e.g. **Hittites**; etc.); and names of countries of antiquity
x Ancient history
xx **World history**
History—Atlases. *See* **Atlases, Historical**
History, Biblical. *See* **Bible—History of Biblical events**
History—Chronology. *See* **Chronology, Historical**
History, Church. *See* **Church history**
History, Constitutional. *See* **Constitutional history**
History—Criticism. *See* **Historiography**
History—Dictionaries
x Historical dictionaries

This simple solution has also been used by MESH, with X for "see" and XU for "see under"; it also has XR for "related" and XS for "specific" terms:

Armed Forces Personnel
X Military Personnel
Kefir
XU Milk

The symbols to express these relationships in thesauri have now become more or less standardized, as follows:

SN	Scope note
USE	Equivalent to "see" reference
UF	Use for, the reciprocal of USE
BT	Broader term, in a hierarchical array
NT	Narrower term, in a hierarchical array; the reciprocal of BT
RT	Related term, expressing any useful relationship other than BT/NT

There are many, usually minor, variations of these. The *Information Retrieval System Subject Authority List* of the American Petroleum Institute, which has gone through a number of revisions, now has "see" and "see also" references in addition to "use" and "used for." The *Thesaurofacet* has extra symbols to mean that a term may appear in more than one hierarchy according to context, and that the term may form part of a multiword term which is in common use and so must appear in the system as such:

BT	Broader term
BT(A)	Additional broader term
NT	Narrower term
NT(A)	Additional narrower term

RT	Related term
Synth	Synthesized
S	Constituent term in synthesized index term
UF	Use for
*	Cross-reference in classification schedules

As will now be clear, the word "term" is the one most commonly used to name a "descriptor" and to point to other "descriptors" in the system. None of the thesauri published so far use symbols based on "descriptor"; for example, BD, ND, RD. It would therefore seem sensible to standardize use of the word "term" for these individual basic elements of a thesaurus, and this word is henceforward used with this meaning in this article.

Forms of Terms

The *UNISIST Guidelines* identify two major types of term: (*a*) terms denoting concepts or concept combinations and (*b*) terms denoting individual entities. The latter terms are also called proper names (or identifiers). Proper names may be:

Project names
Nomenclatures
Identification numbers or symbols
Geographical or geopolitical names
Trademarks
Names of persons and organizations
Abbreviations and acronyms
Other proper names (e.g., programming systems)

Identifiers differ from concept terms in that they are specific to one, named entity and cannot usually be attached to another as an alternative. When they appear in the literature, they have to be used in the index, since they are more or less unique to their own entity (in much the same way that an author's name uniquely identifies his work). It is true that a search for information about, say, the State of Illinois may be helped by documents about the United States or the Middle West, but such part-whole relations are not a common feature among identifiers. One such example is the Geographical List in the *Thesaurus of Terms for Indexing the Literature of Mineral Processing and Metals Extraction*, published by Warren Springs Laboratory of the U.S. Department of Industry in 1974. Where it is necessary to include identifiers of such a common type, a compiler might better turn to an existing list rather than begin to invent his own, which is not likely to end up very different. An identifier naming a new form of entity, such as Hovercraft, must always be included, because this is the term which searchers will naturally expect to find in the index. This applies even where, as in the case of Hovercraft, it would be possible to synthesize a description from terms already in the thesaurus.

Most of the identifiers listed here have already been published in lists which are in fact easily available, and there should be little difficulty in attaching them to a thesaurus. It would be desirable for more use to be made of them, again in the interests of standardization and of its concomitant, compatibility between different systems.

In most thesauri, terms are single-word, plural nouns. Exceptions always have to be made where this use results in ambiguity, unfamiliarity, or nonsense. Nouns are chosen because they are the most concrete part of speech; a single-word adjective or adverb would not usually convey much specific meaning, while a verb concept, though it can be specific, is usually converted into the gerund form used as a noun: "cleaning," "reading," etc.

The choice between singular and plural forms is much more complex. Some words have two different connotations in the two forms: in law, "damage" is not the singular of "damages." The plural form is the more favored choice, on the grounds that most thesaurus terms represent classes of things and it therefore seems more like natural usage to prefer the plural: "automobiles," "children." On the other hand, the singular form often makes more sense when used to synthesize a compound; in the *London Education Classification/Thesaurus*, the singular is preferred for this reason. "Child" is used instead of "children" in order to be able to synthesize "child development," "child psychology," and similar commonly found compounds. Some guidelines are necessary, and the rules given for TEST, one of the largest thesauri, show the complexity of the issue (see Figure 6).

But many concepts cannot be adequately represented by single words, and compounds are of necessity included in most thesauri. Since a major objective of a thesaurus is to facilitate coordinate indexing, it seems logical to avoid compounds as entry terms, though it will be desirable to put in a "use" reference from any compound not used. This often occurs when a form of adjective-plus-noun is in common use as an inquiry term, but the inclusion of such forms would result in unhelpful bulking under the adjective, with hosts of such compounds enumerated. In the field of education, for example, the adjective "educational" is commonly found in compounds: "educational philosophy," "educational psychology," etc. In that context, the adjective is actually nonsignificant as an identifying term, yet the *ERIC Thesaurus* has nearly 100 such compounds listed at "educational," covering several pages. It is better to invert, using "philosophy of education" and "psychology of education," which are equally readily understood and used as inquiry terms. "Educational technology," on the other hand, has now become a term of art and cannot be replaced by "technology of education," which has a somewhat different meaning. TEST has very many compound terms: In addition to "boundaries" and "boundary layer," for example, it includes "boundary layer control," "boundary layer flow," "boundary layer separation," "boundary layer stability," and "boundary layer transition"—in spite of the fact that terms like "flow" and "stability" also have substantive entries of their own. The Introduction to the *ERIC Thesaurus*, commenting on the "multiword term problem," points out that this is one of the most difficult tasks facing anyone constructing an indexing scheme, and states that ERIC prefers to draw far more heavily on multiword terms on the grounds that these are more often used by educators than is necessary in the physical sciences. The author of this Introduction, Frederick Goodman, warns that this approach must be used with care:

> . . . it might be dangerous to have the following four descriptors: GROUP TESTS, GROUP INTELLIGENCE TESTS, GROUP TESTING, and GROUP INTELLIGENCE TESTING. A searcher might search on one or two of those terms and assume that he had found all the relevant documents (*16*).

Some commonly used compound terms may be avoided by the expedient of coordinating two (or more) single-word terms which will be required in the thesaurus

TYPE OF TERM	*USE SINGULAR FORM*	*USE PLURAL FORM*
Material terms, such as: chemical compounds mixtures materials	When term is specific, as: urea cellophane beeswax	When term is generic, as: amines solvents plastics
Terms representing properties, conditions, characteristics	When term is specific, as: viscosity temperature purity opacity	When term is generic, as: physical properties process conditions
Terms representing equipment, devices, physical objects, and elementary particles	Do not use singular	Use plural, as: pulverizers regulators mesons teeth stars
Class of use terms	Do not use singular	Use plural, as: adhesives catalysts
Process terms	Use singular, as: constructing installing modulating	Do not use plural
Proper names (A proper name is defined as the name for a *single unique* item)	Use singular, as: Hookes Law Pluto	Do not use plural
Disciplines, fields, subject areas	Use singular according to common usage, as: chemistry hydraulics engineering	Do not use plural (Words such as "hydraulics" are actually singular)
Events or occurrences	Do not use singular	Use plural, as: ambushes explosions discharges

FIGURE 6. *Extract from TEST (Table 1. Guidelines to Singular-Plural Usage). Reproduced by permission of the Engineers Joint Council.*

anyway. This gives greater flexibility and escapes the problem mentioned by Goodman. E. J. Coates points out another interesting factor here (*8*): the terms "child psychology" and "animal psychology" are well known and used, and their inclusion would be justifiable. But no one would ever think of using "boy psychology" or "chimpanzee psychology," though both are logical subsets of the others and there is plenty of literature on each. Coates makes the point that in these cases, inversion or coordination will produce the perfectly acceptable compounds "psychology-plus-animals," and "psychology-plus-children." The *UNISIST Guidelines* go even further, giving as an example the single word "shipbuilding," which is to be separated into "ships" plus "building." The advantage of such a procedure is that it releases both terms for use in other combinations. Where this is done, the *UNISIST Guidelines* also suggest the addition of another symbol, UFC (use for combination), to the symbols of relationship in order to draw attention to the fact that a compound is involved; the TEST practice is to place a dagger (†) in front of a term to show that two or more terms have to be used in combination to identify the term not used:

Bombs (Ordnance)   1902
UF   † Smoke bombs

Smoke bombs
USE   Bombs (Ordnance)
and   Smoke ammunition

Thesaurofacet recognizes the problem by providing a pair of symbols: *Synth* at a term which should be made by synthesis, with *S* as its reciprocal:

Cold rolling   TH/TD 2
Synth
    RT Cold mills
S   BT Rolling
S   BT(A) Cold working

There are many terms with "cold" which are syntheses, but there are also exceptions, such as "cold cathode tubes."

To deal with the question of which form to use, some authors have advocated the device of truncation, in which only the root part of a word is used, with several alternative endings. In many cases, this will cover noun, adjective, verb, and adverb forms—even, in some instances, more than one of each. Thus the root "machin-" would cover all the words beginning with those letters: "machine," "machined," "machining," "machinable," etc. The device can achieve particularly good results in a computerized system containing many compound or precoordinated terms, but it needs to be used with care; its apparent simplicity can easily result in the unlucky searcher receiving a pile of references which are irrelevant because the different suffixes add meanings from different contexts, such as "machination" and the "damage"/"damages" example in law.

Relationships

In addition to synonyms/near-synonyms, the other two types of relationship are those of hierarchy and association, or co-occurrence. These are usually symbolized by BT/NT and RT. Broader/narrower terms are reciprocals because they cannot exist without each other: To be a broader term necessarily implies at least one other term which is narrower. Related terms are also reciprocal in a different sense; one would expect that if Term *A* is RT to Term *B*, then Term *B* must be RT to Term *A*, but in practice this is not always expressed in the schedules, being catered for by other means such as classification.

The hierarchical BT/NT relationship is a classificatory one. A BT must be a class term with (usually) an array of NT listed beneath it. On the other hand, each NT will normally have only one BT listed beneath it, though exceptions to this can arise, partly because some terms can actually exist as members of more than one class, but also because the NT itself may be a compound, in which each element of the compound has an upward reference to its own BT:

AC generators
BT AC machines
Electric generators

Where the thesaurus includes a detailed systematic part based on a scheme of classification, the selection of BT/NT is simple, because these terms will already be set out there in a series of classified arrays; they will usually have indentations in the schedule to show which terms are subordinate to which. The more general the term, the more terms will be subordinate to it, but the division of a generic term into its various species will be shown in a series of steps:

Mammals
Primates
Apes
Gorillas

Criminology
Delinquents
Juvenile Delinquents
Hooligans

In such hierarchies, all the indented terms are subordinate, or NT, to the main heading, or class term, which is likewise BT to all of them. In practice, it expands the size of the thesaurus considerably to list all such NT under the main heading, and it is almost equally effective for search purposes to list only one step of any multistep hierarchy. Thus, from the example given, we could derive the following:

Criminology
NT Delinquents

Delinquents
BT Criminology
NT Juvenile Delinquents

Hooligans
BT Juvenile Delinquents

Juvenile Delinquents
BT Delinquents
NT Hooligans

Some thesauri, however, do refer to more than one level of a hierarchy. In the *SPINES Thesaurus* produced by UNESCO for the UNISIST Project, it was decided to do this, and the thesaurus refers to several levels of NT (*17*). Under R&D (an abbreviation for research and experimental development) we find:

5757 R&D
NT 1 EXPERIMENTAL DEVELOPMENT
NT 1 RESEARCH
NT 2 APPLIED RESEARCH
NT 3 PROCESS RESEARCH
NT 3 PRODUCT RESEARCH
NT 2 FUNDAMENTAL RESEARCH

The reciprocal entries include:

435 APPLIED RESEARCH
BT 1 RESEARCH
BT 2 R&D
NT 1 PROCESS RESEARCH
NT 1 PRODUCT RESEARCH

An intermediate step is taken by the *INSPEC Thesaurus* produced by the Institution of Electrical Engineers in London, in the areas of physics, electronics, electrotechnology, and control (*18*). This specifies that BT means one level up and NT means one level down, but it introduces the relationship of TT (top term[s]) in a hierarchy to show the main class term of any specific term:

a.c. generators
UF alternators
NT asynchronous generators
synchronous generators
BT a.c. machines
electric generators
TT electric machines

TEST offers an economy of a slightly different kind. By prefixing a dash (—) symbol before a term, it indicates that the term has other NT shown only under the main entry:

Bomb fuzes
RT Acoustic fuzes
— Impact fuzes
Nose fuzes
— Time fuzes

Impact fuzes

RT Base fuzes
— Bomb fuzes
Grenade fuzes

Another very effective means of economy in the alphabetical part may be gained where the systematic part consists of a correctly laid out scheme of classification, as in *Thesaurofacet* and in the *Thesaurus of Education Terms* by G. C. Barhydt and C. T. Schmidt (*19*). Both use a reference to the classified schedules instead of those BT/NT entries which are derived from the same hierarchy in the classification. In the Barhydt-Schmidt thesaurus, Facet 1 is "people," and Subfacet 1003 is "teaching staff," which includes the following:

FACET 1
SUB-FACET 1003
ASSISTANT PROFESSOR
ATHLETIC COACH
LECTURER
PROFESSOR
SCHOOL TEACHER
TEACHER

The related alphabetical array entries include the following (where * means a very general term which should only exceptionally be used):

PROFESSOR
RT 1003
SCHOOL TEACHER
USE TEACHER
TEACHER
SN *
UF INSTRUCTOR
SCHOOL TEACHER
RT 1003

The notation 1003 thus refers the user to the faceted section, where that entry contains a number of other related terms: "exchange teacher," "relief teacher," "visiting teacher," and so on. Only occasionally does this particular thesaurus use BT and NT; the explanation lies in the fact that the terms in each subfacet are set out in alphabetical order, as shown in 1003, with no visible distinction between coordinate and subordinate terms (as would be shown in a regular classification schedule).

Most thesauri, however, do make a clear distinction. But whereas BT and NT are reasonably simple to identify, related terms present a much more complex issue, and no system has yet succeeded in defining precisely which terms should be enumerated as RT to any other term. One reason is that the RT relation may be designed to suit specific user groups, and so no actual generalized rule is possible. Using a properly designed classification schedule as a basis, one could say that, for a beginning, coordinate terms with the same generic term have a prima facie claim to be shown as RT to each other; they are related in at least one aspect, because they are members of the same class and are neither BT nor NT to each other:

TRANSPORT INDUSTRY
Water Transport
Inland Water Transport
Sea Transport
Dock Work

Here, the last three terms can be listed as RT to each other, since a searcher looking at one term will be glad to be reminded of the other two. But compare this sequence:

TRANSPORT INDUSTRY
Air Transport
Rail Transport
Road Transport
Water Transport

Here, the last four terms are coordinates in relation to the generic term "transport industry," but the case for making them RT in the alphabetical part of a thesaurus is much less obvious.

The *UNISIST Guidelines* state that "the associative relation is usually employed to cover the other relations between concepts that are related but are neither consistently hierarchical nor equivalent (e.g. similarity, antonymity)" (*10*). The *Guidelines* then go on to list a number of types of relation that may be symbolized by the use of RT in the thesaurus:

— antonymity, i.e. a concept is the opposite of another concept: HARDNESS RT SOFTNESS
— co-ordination, i.e. concepts are derived from a superordinate concept by the same step of division: GENERIC RELATION RT PART-WHOLE RELATION
— generic relation, i.e. something is the predecessor of another thing: FATHER RT SON
— concurrent use of two concepts: EDUCATION RT TEACHING
— cause and effect: TEACHING RT LEARNING
— instrumental relation: WRITING RT PENCILS
— material relation, i.e. something is the material of which another thing is made: PAPER RT BOOKS
— similarity of different kinds (physical similarity, similarity of material, similarity of processes etc.): TEACHING RT TRAINING

These *Guidelines* admit, however, that even this list covers only some of the possible examples, and they add the necessary warning that any additional relations should be clearly defined and coded. Aitchison and Gilchrist suggest that "the part-whole relationship is the strongest non-hierarchical relationship, the other relationships being more tenuous and difficult to categorize" (*4*, p. 29). The types they offer are derived from the work of the British Classification Research Group, expounded by B. C. Vickery (*20*):

Species of same genus — B Scope displays
RT C Scope displays (both being types of two-dimensional radar displays)

Thing	
Thing/part	Doors RT Knobs
Thing/property	Lasers RT Coherence
Thing/process	Roads RT Road engineering
Thing/thing as attribute	Arcs RT Arc furnaces
Thing/application	Adaptive filters RT Signal processing
Property	
Property/process	Charge (electric) RT Charge measurement
Property/property as attribute	Skew RT Skew girders
Process	
Process/thing (agent)	Temperature measurement RT Thermometers
Process/property	Detonation RT Detonation waves
Near synonym	Fretting RT Spalling

Where a strictly faceted classification scheme is used as the basis, it will often be found that certain terms in one facet have a very close relationship in practice with particular terms in another facet. This may well occur in fields like product engineering, where certain materials will be treated by specific tools and processes, such as "aluminum—extrusion—presses." This can be a valuable source of RT, and is in fact a combination of two of the relations itemized by Aitchison and Gilchrist. It is also one of the serious arguments in favor of using a faceted structure in the systematic part of a thesaurus, since it is a sure technique for itemizing such terms precisely in conceptual relations with each other, according to the logic and practice of the subject field in question.

The most extensive research in this area is probably that carried out at the Documentation Research and Training Center in Bangalore under the direction of A. Neelameghan; his paper, presented with several others at the 1975 DRTC Seminar, contains a detailed analysis of nonhierarchical associative relations and the computer generation of RT links. He identifies these links as "facet relation (FR), speciator relation (SpR), co-ordinate relation (CR), and phase relation (PR), according to Ranganathan's model for structuring of subject" (*21*).

Another method of reaching a similar result by means of computer processing has been examined by Karen Sparck Jones in her *Automatic Keyword Classification* (*22*). She has expounded the concept of "substitutible terms," that is, terms which are able to substitute for one another in a document or request: "A request containing *b* could be satisfied by a document containing *b* or *e* or *f* indifferently, on the assumption that documents which contained any of these words would be about the same thing" (*22*, p. 8). From this starting point, she went on to carry out computer analyses of texts, noting those words which appear concurrently with one another, and identified four distinct types of term associations. These she called strings, stars, cliques, and clumps, which are best illustrated graphically:

Type 1 Strings

Type 2 Stars

Type 3 Cliques

Type 4 Clumps

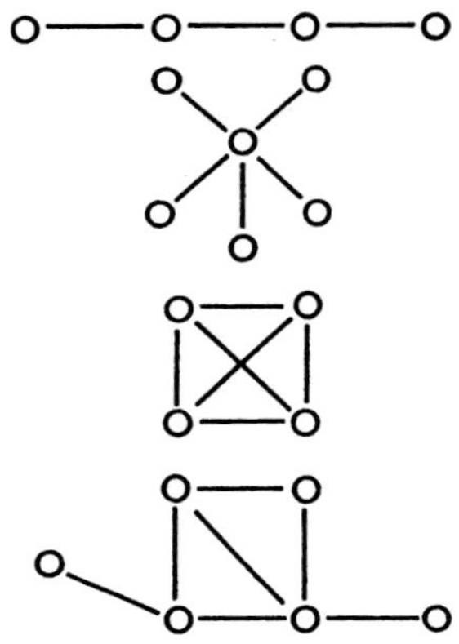

As she admits, this is a simplified view of these types, and other relationships could also develop in the strings and stars; but from the point of view of a thesaurus, such patterns could well be helpful in deciding which terms ought to be specified as RT in dealing with a particular subject literature, on the basis of co-occurrence in that literature. Furthermore, since this work was based on an actual set of documents, and tested on them, it has also served to underline the important fact that information retrieval systems have to cope with real literature, and that the literature in any subject directly reflects the way in which those working in that subject think about it.

Many research workers, particularly in the fields of language and comprehension, have shown that this type of associative relationship performs a most important function in the communication process. In brief, by ordering terms into more or less mutually exclusive categories, we come to understand the structure of subjects and are more easily able to learn about them. One of the clearest statements on this point was made by the eminent psychologist J. S. Bruner, reporting on a conference on education in science held at Woods Hole, Cape Cod, in September 1959: "Perhaps the most basic thing that can be said about human memory, after a century of intensive research, is that unless detail is placed into a structured pattern, it is rapidly forgotten" (*23*, p. 24).

The logical relation of genus/species has been of fundamental importance to our understanding of the world around us at least since the time of Aristotle, and all of the major schemes of bibliographical classification are based on it. But it is clearly not the only relationship that can exist, and furthermore, any entity may be a species of more than one class. Many psychologists have carried out tests on the role this relation plays in the development of the child's thinking powers, and they have shown that other relations come into the picture very early in life. For example, an orange is a species of citrus fruit and also of the class of round objects, and a child will demonstrate an understanding of the latter by bowling it along the floor. In the classic work *The Early Growth of Logic in the Child: Classification and Seriation*, J. Piaget and B. Inhelder show that multiplicative classifications develop in the child's mind as early as simple linear arrangements: that is, the ability to put things in groups as well as in straight lines (*24*).

In the simple generic hierarchy, each step of division is made by separating out those entities in a group which display one particular property, giving in principle two groups symbolized as *A* and *not-A*. This is not sufficient to express the multiple relationships between phenomena which exist in the real world and are described in the literature, and therefore any index language system which aims to reflect the literature has to be able to deal with more than the genus/species, or BT/NT, relation. R. A. Fairthorne once put it very succinctly when he wrote that "bibliographic classifications have no unique complement, and are therefore lattice systems, not Boolean Algebras" (*25*). In any subject field, a lattice of terms can easily enough be formed by dividing the terms, not into single hierarchies as in the Decimal Classification but into several categories of facets which are mutually exclusive. If we look at the literature of a subject, the topics written about soon reveal the appropriate facets. This approach is used in many thesauri; in the *Construction Industry Thesaurus* of the U.K. Department of the Environment, for example, the facets are Time, Place, Properties and Measures, Agents of Construction, Operations and Processes, Materials, Parts, and Construction Works (the end products, what Ranganathan would call the "Personality facet" of the subject) (*26*). In the alphabetical index, terms are referred by notation symbols to their place in the faceted schedules, as in *Thesaurofacet*.

To give a brief practical example—if we take the field of occupational safety and health, we find topics like these in the literature:

Chromate dermatitis from chrome glue
Dust sampling methods in the pottery industry
Safety precautions for use with blind workers
Statistics of accidents in the iron and steel industry
Provision of spectacles for oxy-acetylene welding

From examination of these and other documents, we can easily deduce several facets, as shown in the *CIS Thesaurus* of the International Occupational Safety and Health Information Center at the International Labor Organization in Geneva (*27*):

1. Occupational hazards (chromates, dust)
2. Consequences of these hazards (dermatitis, accidents)
3. Techniques of investigation of hazards and consequences (sampling)
4. Protective and remedial measures (safety precautions, spectacles)
5. Places of occurrence (pottery industry, welding)
6. Groups of persons affected (blind workers)

It will be obvious that, with rare exceptions where a term has more than one significance, terms selected on this basis can logically belong to only one category.

This technique has several important values. It enables a thesaurus to be constructed in a highly systematic way, using only elementary terms in the vast majority of places; it gives a clear guideline for the enumeration of many RT; it can be used as a check on the completeness and consistency of the listings. A negative example will serve to underline these advantages. The *ERIC Thesaurus* has some 50 "Descriptor Groups" added to later editions, which are set out in alphabetical, not systematic, sequence with no apparent logical structure or connections. Many compound terms are listed, often even when their component single terms are also listed. Thus in "Group 010 Abilities," we find the term "readiness," and in "Group 440 Reading," we find the term "reading"; but in addition, in "Group 180 Education," we find the compound precoordinated as "reading readiness."

In "Group 010 Abilities," in fact, some 80% of the terms are actually compounds. Of these, 29 out of 60 are compounded with the term "skills"; these include "agricultural skills," "alphabetizing skills," and "locational skills (social studies)." The term "skill obsolescence" is also included in 010, but "skill development" accurs in "130 Development," and "skill analysis," in "150 Employment."

Separation of related terms occurs with and without cross-references. "Group 060 Behavior" has a reference "*see also* Psychology," but in "Group 420 Psychology" there are no "see also" references at all. Many inconsistencies occur between "Group 040 Attitudes and "Group 420 Psychology":

040	Attitudes	420	Psychology
	Parent Attitudes		Affection
	Persistence		Curiosity
	Resentment		Insecurity
	Self-esteem		Parent Influence
	Teacher Motivation		

"Group 040 Attitudes" also includes "family attitudes" and "mother attitudes" but not "father attitudes," and "social attitudes" and "scientific attitudes" but not "artistic attitudes."

Other inconsistencies occur in the placing of curriculum subjects:

110	Curriculum	140	Education
	Science Courses		Art Education
	Science Curriculum		Music Education
	Science Programs		Science Education
	Sciences	260	Humanities
	[but not Humanities or Social Sciences]	480	Social Sciences

In Groups 260 and 480, the mixture of terms can only indicate a haphazard method of selection.

The introduction of Descriptor Groups constituted a great improvement for users of the *ERIC Thesaurus* compared with the first drafts, but once it had been decided to include a section for such groups, more attention might have been given to their nature and their relations with each other.

The conclusion is inescapable: A thesaurus benefits greatly in use, both for indexing and for searching, if the choice of terms and relations can clearly be seen to reflect the logical structure of a subject, instead of appearing to be a haphazard collection of terms which happen to turn up in the literature. This applies most strongly in those fields of knowledge—in the social sciences especially—where the terminology used by the experts themselves is not very precise.

Layout of the Thesaurus

The simplest way to lay out a thesaurus is to have one single list of terms in alphabetical order, with a minimum of references; such a product would certainly also be the least effective in practice. This reflects one of the great contradictions in the production of any bibliographical tool, and one that is very hard to resolve. It is this: How far can one reasonably go in refining the tool so that great effort may be required at the input stage, in the hope and expectation that many small individual efforts will be saved at the output stage? Clearly, the more complex the structure of a thesaurus, the more closely it will approach the complexity of the real world and the literature that describes the real world. It will give the indexer a refined and powerful technique, but one which will require a great deal of subtle thinking and skill if it is to be used to maximum advantage. For the searcher, on the other hand, it should present no difficulties because it will have foreseen and catered for all possible approaches, so that whatever search term may be chosen, it will lead unerringly to the relevant documents. In principle, one should always choose the best tool, because that will be the one to do the best job with the least effort. But economic considerations may make it necessary to choose a cheaper model, which will put more effort on the shoulders of the searcher.

One finds, in fact, a very wide variety of forms of presentation. The *London Education Classification (28)* has a highly structured faceted scheme as the basis, from which the alphabetical listing and its references have been made (see Fig. 7). The *EUDISED Multilingual Thesaurus* (29), which took the London scheme as its starting point, also has a strongly faceted structure but arranges its terms in a somewhat different way, bringing the references into each facet and making much more use of alphabetical order of terms in facets. This is probably easier to produce by computer, but it does, of course, result in some nonlogical sequences, and it is different in different languages, as shown by comparing the English edition with the Spanish (see Figs. 8 and 9). The sequence of the subfacets themselves is unchanged, since this depends on the numerals (10100, etc.) and not on the alphabet, and thus much of the original classificatory relationship is preserved. Like many thesauri which are computer generated, the *EUDISED Thesaurus* also has an alphabetical index which resembles a keyword-in-context (KWIC) type and brings together all the compound terms that include the same single-word terms (see Fig. 10).

A very different type of layout, though based on the same principle of displaying related terms in the classified section, is used by C. van der Merwe in the *Thesaurus of Sociological Research Terminology* (see Fig. 11). The classified array, shown in the left-hand column headed "Category," follows the sequence indicated by the notational symbols D.331.3, D.331.31, D.331.32, etc. Other classes where related terms will be found are also indicated by notational symbols, and these are shown in the right-hand column headed "Related Terms": "paired selection (D.21)," "factorial design (C.132.22)," etc. The alphabetical index, by inverting headings in the classified section, brings together all those terms which relate to "sampling," can be located from "sampling," or are accidental to "sampling" with two or more random starts.

Facet 1 Educands
- Educands, general
- Pre-school child, Infant, under 5 years
- Schoolchild, pupil
  - Child, pre-adolescent
  - Adolescent, "Teenager"
- Student
- Youth outside of school and college
- Adult
- Exceptional Educand
  - Genius, prodigy
  - Gifted, brilliant, able
  - Handicapped
    - Physically handicapped
    - Mentally handicapped
    - Maladjusted, Emotionally disturbed
    - Socially handicapped, Culturally deprived

Facet 2 Educational Institutions: Schools, Colleges, Universities
- Educational Institutions, and systems
- Home Education
- Nursery
- Primary, Elementary (5–11)
- Secondary (11–18)
  - Stages
    - Lower
    - Middle
    - Upper
  - English types of school (or favoured country)
    - Comprehensive
    - Grammar
    - "Public School"
- Post-Secondary Education
  - University
  - University of the Air
- Further Education
- Adult Education
- Continuing Education, Lifelong Education

FIGURE 7. *Extract from* London Education Classification.
Reproduced by permission of the University of London Institute of Education Library and the authors.

```
ADOLESCENT - ADOLESCENT - JUGENDLICHER
   UF:  TEENAGER
   NT:  BOY
        GIRL
   RT:  ADOLESCENCE
        PUBERTY
        YOUTH

ADULT - ADULTE - ERWACHSENER
   BT:  AGE GROUP
   NT:  ELDERLY PERSON
        PARENTS
   RT:  ADULT EDUCATION
        MATURITY

BOY - GARCON - JUNGE
   BT:  ADOLESCENT
        MAN
   RT:  BOYS' SCHOOL
        SEX

CHILD - ENFANT - KIND
   NT:  ADOPTED CHILD
        BACKWARD CHILD
        CHILD OF DIVORCED PARENTS
        ILLEGITIMATE
        INFANT
        NEGLECTED CHILD
        ONLY CHILD
        PRE-SCHOOL CHILD
        PROBLEM CHILD
        WAIFS AND STRAYS
   RT:  CHILD CARE
        CHILD DEVELOPMENT
        CHILD LABOUR
        CHILD PROTECTION
        CHILD PSYCHIATRY
        CHILD PSYCHOLOGY
        CHILD REARING
        CHILDHOOD
        CHILDREN'S BOOK
        FATHER-CHILD RELATION
        MOTHER-CHILD RELATION
        ORPHAN
        PAEDIATRICS
        PARENT-CHILD RELATION
        PRE-ADOLESCENCE
        PUPIL

ELDERLY PERSON - PERSONNE AGEE - ALTER MENSCH
   BT:  ADULT
   NT:  RETIRED PERSON
   RT:  OLD AGE

GIRL - JEUNE FILLE - MAEDCHEN
   BT:  ADOLESCENT
        WOMAN
   RT:  GIRLS' SCHOOL
        SEX

INFANT - ENFANT DU PREMIER AGE - KLEINKIND
   BT:  CHILD
   RT:  CHILD REARING
        DAY-NURSERY
        INFANCY
        INFANT MORTALITY
        NURSERY RHYME

PRE-SCHOOL CHILD - ENFANT D'AGE PRE-SCOLAIRE -
  VORSCHULKIND
   BT:  CHILD
   RT:  PRE-SCHOOL AGE

RETIRED PERSON - PERSONNE RETRAITEE - RUHESTAENDLER
   BT:  ELDERLY PERSON
   RT:  PENSION
        RETIREMENT

TEENAGER
  USE:  ADOLESCENT
```

FIGURE 8. *Extract from the* EUDISED Multilingual Thesaurus (*English version*). *Reproduced by permission of the Council of Europe and Jean Viet.*

```
ADOLESCENTE - ADOLESCENT - ADOLESCENT
   NT:  MUCHACHA
        MUCHACHO
   RT:  ADOLESCENCIA
        JUVENTUD
        PUBERTAD

ADULTO - ADULT - ADULTE
   BT:  GRUPO DE EDAD
   NT:  PADRES
        PERSONA DE EDAD
   RT:  EDUCACION DE ADULTOS
        MADUREZ

JUBILADO - RETIRED PERSON - PERSONNE RETRAITEE
   UF:  RETIRADO
   BT:  PERSONA DE EDAD
   RT:  JUBILACION
        PENSION DE JUBILACION

MUCHACHA - GIRL - JEUNE FILLE
   BT:  ADOLESCENTE
        MUJER
   RT:  ESCUELA FEMENINA
        SEXO

MUCHACHO - BOY - GARCON
   BT:  ADOLESCENTE
        HOMBRE
   RT:  ESCUELA MASCULINA
        SEXO

NINO - CHILD - ENFANT
   NT:  HIJO DE PADRES DIVORCIADOS
        HIJO NATURAL
        HIJO UNICO
        NINO ABANDONADO
        NINO ADOPTADO
        NINO DE PRIMERA INFANCIA
        NINO DESATENDIDO
        NINO PROBLEMA
        NINO RETRASADO
        PARVULO
   RT:  ALUMNO
        AYUDA A LA INFANCIA
        DESARROLLO DEL NINO
        HUERFANO
        INFANCIA
        LIBROS PARA NINOS
        PEDIATRIA
        PREADOLESCENCIA
        PROTECCION A LA INFANCIA
        PSICOLOGIA DEL NINO
        PSIQUIATRIA INFANTIL
        PUERICULTURA
        RELACION MADRE-NINO
        RELACION PADRE-NINO
        RELACION PADRES-NINO
        TRABAJO DEL NINO

NINO DE PRIMERA INFANCIA - INFANT - ENFANT DU PREMIER
  AGE
   BT:  NINO
   RT:  CANCION DE CUNA
        GUARDERIA
        MORTALIDAD INFANTIL
        PRIMERA INFANCIA
        PUERICULTURA

PARVULO - PRE-SCHOOL CHILD - ENFANT D'AGE PRE-SCOLAIRE
   BT:  NINO
   RT:  EDAD PREESCOLAR

PERSONA DE EDAD - ELDERLY PERSON - PERSONNE AGEE
   BT:  ADULTO
   NT:  JUBILADO
   RT:  VEJEZ

RETIRADO
  USE:  JUBILADO
```

FIGURE 9. *Extract from the* EUDISED Multilingual Thesaurus (*Spanish edition*).

```
CHILD
   ABNORMAL CHILD       10310
      USE:   EXCEPTIONAL
   ADOPTED CHILD      10350
   BACKWARD CHILD      10340
   CHILD      10100
   CHILD CARE      25720
   CHILD DEVELOPMENT       17200
   CHILD EMPLOYMENT       25550
      USE:   YOUTH EMPLOYMENT
   CHILD LABOUR      25550
   CHILD OF DIVORCED PARENTS       1035C
   CHILD PROTECTION      25720
   CHILD PSYCHIATRY      18651
   CHILD PSYCHOLOGY      17100
   CHILD REARING      11200
   CHILD-FATHER RELATION      17760
      USE:   FATHER-CHILD RELATION
   CHILD-MOTHER RELATION      17760
      USE:   MOTHER-CHILD RELATION
   CHILD-PARENT RELATION      17760
      USE:   PARENT-CHILD RELATION
   CHILD-SCHOOL RELATION      16320
      USE:   TEACHER-PUPIL RELATION
   FATHER-CHILD RELATION      17760
   MOTHER-CHILD RELATION      17760
   NEGLECTED CHILD      10350
   ONLY CHILD      18150
   PARENT-CHILD RELATION      17760
   PRE-SCHOOL CHILD      10100
   PROBLEM CHILD      10350
   RETARDED CHILD      10340
      USE:   BACKWARD CHILD
   SCHOOL CHILD      10210
      USE:   PUPIL
CHILDHOOD
   CHILDHOOD      18160
CHILDREN
   CHILDREN'S BOOK      14220
CHILE
   CHILE      30200
CHINA
   CHINA      30300
   CHINA MAINLAND      30300
      USE:   CHINA PR
   CHINA PR      30300
   CHINA R      30300
CHOICE
   CAREER CHOICE      16130
      USE:   OCCUPATIONAL CHOICE
   OCCUPATIONAL CHOICE      16130
   VOCATIONAL CHOICE      16130
      USE:   OCCUPATIONAL CHOICE
CHRISTIAN
   CHRISTIAN EDUCATION      12680
CHRISTIANITY
   CHRISTIANITY      26430
CHURCH
   CHURCH      26430
CINEMA
   CINEMA      14530
   CINEMA CLUB      14530
```

FIGURE 10. *Extract from the* EUDISED Multilingual Thesaurus *Index. Reproduced by permission of the Council of Europe and Jean Viet.*

Linking by classified notation also occurs in the bilingual *CIS Thesaurus*, where RT are listed in the "faceted thesaurus" while the "alphabetical index" lists all those places in the facets where a particular term occurs in compound combinations (see Fig. 12).

In his excellent manual, D. Soergel discusses the question of layout in considerable detail in his Chapter D, and he is in no doubt as to the proper example to follow: "Notwithstanding the deviation in the arrangement of most other thesauri,

Category	Descriptors	Unauthorized Terms	Related Terms
	Random start		
D.331.3 Stratified sampling	*Stratified sampling*	Stratified probability sampling Density sampling	Paired selection (D.21) Lattice sampling (D.22) Design effect (D.33) Stratified cluster sampling (D.331.4) Optimum stratification (H.216) Relational analysis (K.221)
	— Balanced sample		
	Poststratification	Stratification after selection	
D.331.31 Proportionate sampling	*Proportionate sampling*	Proportional stratified sampling Self-weighting sample Equal allocation	Representativeness (D.32) Systematic sampling (D.331.2)
D.331.32 Disproportionate sampling	*Disproportionate sampling*	Disproportional stratified random sampling Controlled sampling	Factorial design (C.132.22)
	— Oversampling		Sample size (D.321)

FIGURE 11. *Extract from* Thesaurus of Sociological Research Terminology. *Reproduced by permission of Rotterdam University Press.*

notably TEST, Roget has found the most meaningful form, the one most appropriate to the intended use of a thesaurus" (*6*, p. 183). Soergel has improved on the original, however, in the "Roget-Soergel Model," which has these sections: (0) introduction to the thesaurus, (1) classified index (schedule), (2) main part in classified arrangement, and (3) alphabetical index. He gives as an example (*6*, pp. 185–191) the subject "electron tubes," worked out in full according to this model, and he contrasts its obvious clarity and simplicity with an extract from the TEST Subject Category Index, which he rightly characterizes as a "coarse hierarchy."

Graphic Display

Graphic, or two-dimensional, displays of sets of terms and their interrelationships—like lists of subject headings—are not exactly new to librarians. The

Fewo	WOOD PRODUCTS - PRODUITS DU BOIS
	RT: WOODWORKING INDUSTRY
Fewob	BLOCKBOARD - PANNEAUX LATTES
Fewod	PLYWOOD - BOIS CROISE
Fewof	FIBREBOARD - PANNEAUX DE FIBRES
Fewol	WOOD WOOL - LAINE DE BOIS
Fewon	WOODPULP - PATE MECANIQUE
	RT: CELLULOSE
	PULP AND PAPER INDUSTRY
Fewop	PAPER - PAPIER
	RT: PACKAGING MATERIALS
	PAPER AND PAPER PRODUCTS INDUSTRY
	WASTEPAPER
Fewoq	CARDBOARD - CARTON
	RT: PACKAGING MATERIALS
Fewor	NATURAL RESINS - RESINES NATURELLES
Feworc	COLOPHONY - COLOPHANE
Fewos	TANNINS - TANINS
	RT: TANNING
	TANNING AGENTS
	TANNING INDUSTRY
Fewot	TURPENTINE - TEREBENTHINE
Fewou	CAMPHOR - CAMPHRE
Fewov	NATURAL RUBBER - CAOUTCHOUC NATUREL
	RT: RUBBER INDUSTRY
	SYNTHETIC RUBBER
Fewova	GUM ARABIC - GOMME ARABIQUE
Fewove	LATEX - LATEX
Fewovi	FOAMED RUBBER - CAOUTCHOUC-MOUSSE
Fewox	CHARCOAL - CHARBON DE BOIS
Fewoxa	ACTIVATED CARBON - CHARBON ACTIVE
	RT: ACTIVATED CARBON PNEUMOCONIOSIS
	ADSORBENTS
	CARBON PRODUCTS
Fewoy	WOOD TAR - GOUDRON DE BOIS

(a)

LOG	
LOG HANDLING	
— ROUND TIMBER HANDLING	Jdiko
LOG HAULAGE	Jso
LOG PONDS	
— SAWMILLING INDUSTRY	Xeha
LOGGING	
FORESTRY AND LOGGING	Xap
LOGGING	Xapo
LOGGING EQUIPMENT	Jsy
LOGGING OPERATIONS	Js
PAPER	
PAPER	Fewop
PAPER AND CARDBOARD CONVERTING INDUSTRY	Xejo
PAPER AND PAPER PRODUCTS INDUSTRY	Xej
PAPER CONVERTING MACHINES (WEB-FED)	Hns
PAPER GUILLOTINES AND TRIMMERS	Hrapa
PAPER HANGING	Jql
PAPER MAKING MACHINES	Hnr
PAPER REAM HANDLING	Jdise
PAPER ROLL HANDLING	
— REELED MATERIALS HANDLING	Jdir
PAPER SHREDDERS	Hryd
PULP AND PAPER INDUSTRY	Xeja
PAPERBOARD	
PAPERBOARD MILLS	
— PULP AND PAPER INDUSTRY	Xeja
PAPERS	
FILTER PAPERS	Hufmo
TEST PAPERS	Qicup

(b)

FIGURE 12. *Extracts from the* CIS Thesaurus: *(a) from the "faceted thesaurus" and (b) from the "alphabetical index." Reproduced by permission of the International Occupational Safety and Health Information Center, Geneva.*

idea, also like that of lists of subject headings, has been greatly developed and refined by some of the compilers and theoreticians of thesauri. The simplest and oldest form is the "family tree" type of structure, in which the various steps in the hierarchical subdivision of a class are shown; another familiar example is the management organization chart, which is also usually cast in this form. An example is:

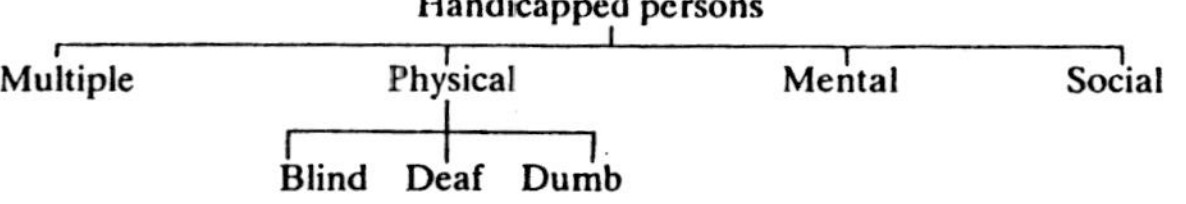

Such a list of connected terms is monohierarchical, in the sense that all the subdivisions stem from one main class, and from any one term there is only one chain of connections upward to that main class term. But a major use of graphic display in descriptions of thesauri has been precisely in order to illustrate the polyhierarchical nature of the relationships that the thesaurus can show—namely, that a concept represented by a term, whether single or compound, may often have a hierarchical relationship with more than one main class term. A simple example appears in the *UNISIST Guidelines:*

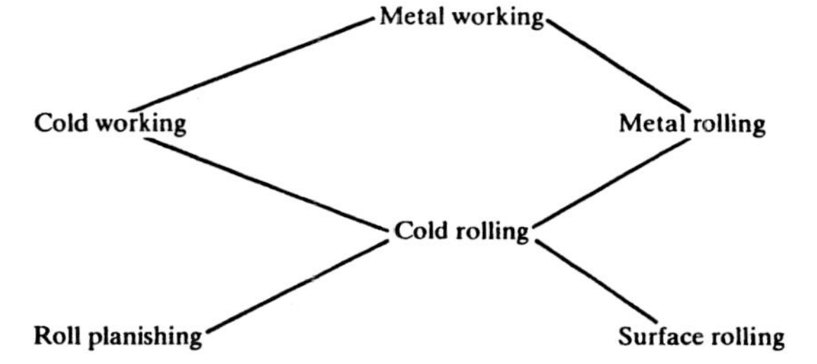

The extensive use of graphic display in this field, to the point that it has become an integral part of subsequent work on the thesaurus, probably began with that introduced into the Euratom Information and Documentation Center in Luxembourg. This was described in detail by its principal architect, L. N. Rolling, at the Second International Study Conference on Classification Research, organized at Elsinore, Denmark, in 1964 by the FID/CR Classification Research Committee of the International Federation for Documentation and the Danish Center for Documentation (*30*). Rolling gave a very complete account of the use of graphic displays, beginning with simple Venn or Euler Diagrams, and then enlarged on them in a number of different forms of graphic display, showing how they can demonstrate quite highly complicated networks. An arrowgraph is a stage more elaborate than the UNISIST example just given, and it is able to show reciprocal relations working in both directions between two terms (see Fig. 13). A more complex box-chart not only shows "neighbor" or contiguous relationships but can also include heirarchical relationships depending from the main term in each box (see Fig. 14).

Without going into the production of three-dimensional models, it is difficult to

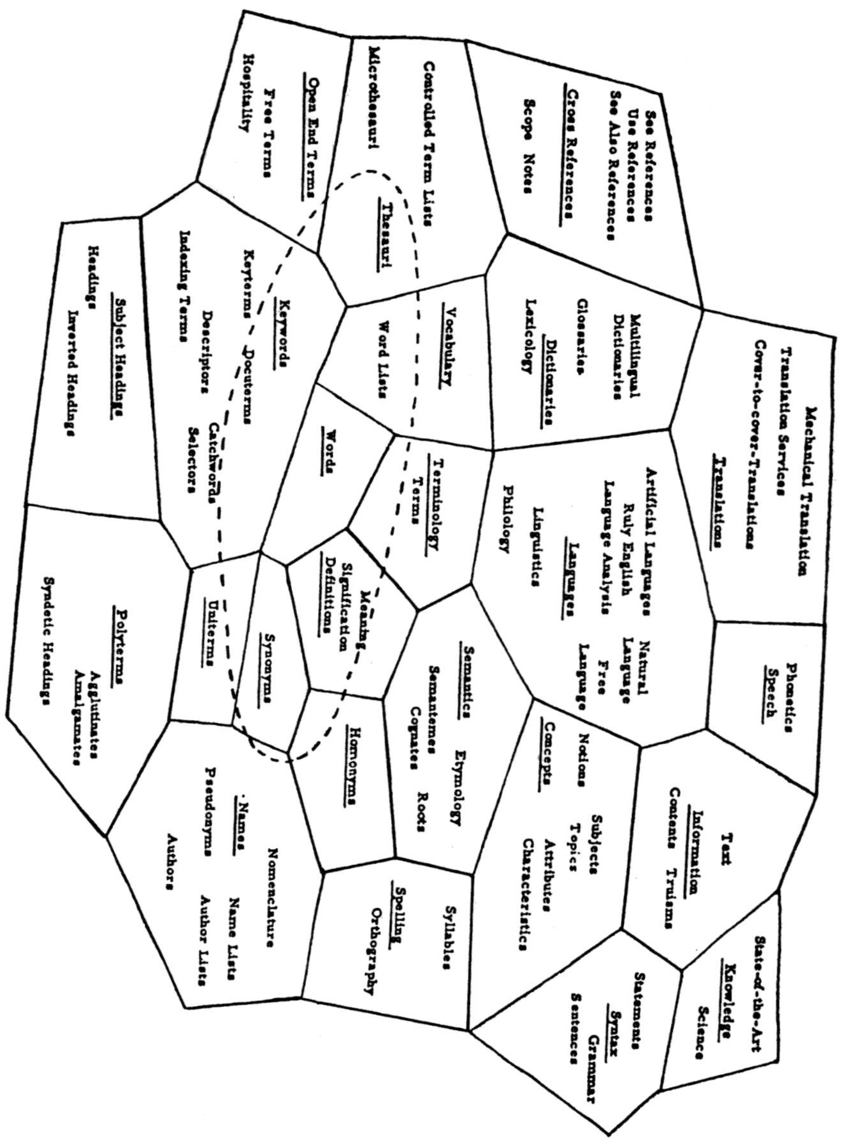

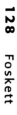

FIGURE 14. *Box-chart by L. N. Rolling. Reproduced by permission of Munksgaard, Copenhagen.*

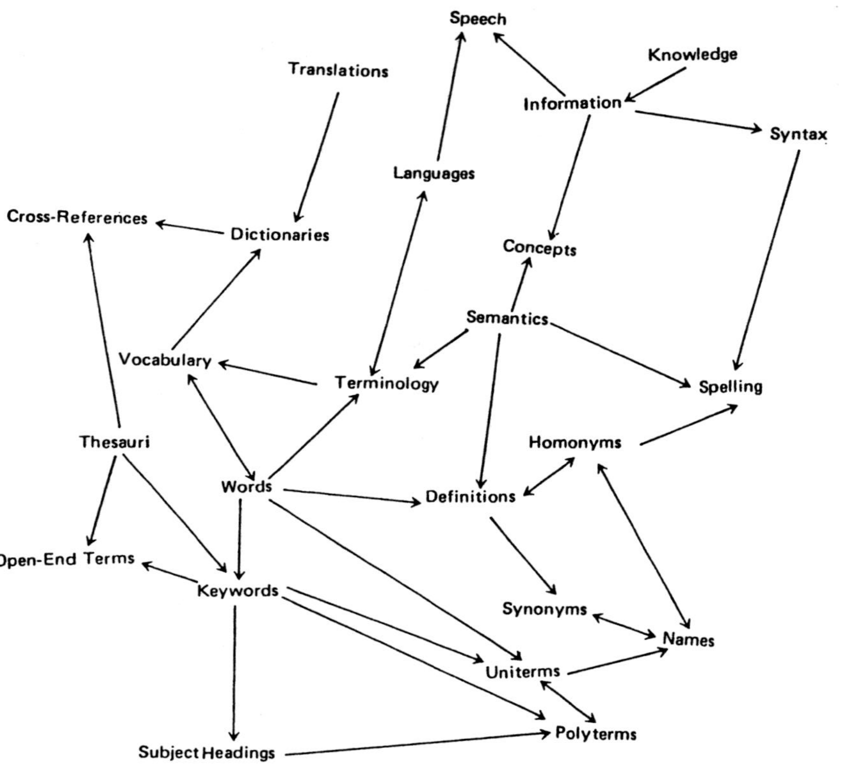

FIGURE 13. *Arrowgraph by L. N. Rolling. Reproduced by permission of Munksgaard, Copenhagen.*

envisage a more thoroughgoing use of graphic display than the three-volume *SPINES Thesaurus* produced by UNESCO for the UNISIST Project (*17*). The whole of Volume 3 is devoted to "Terminological Graphic Displays," though the enthusiasm of the designers appears to have somewhat got the better of their bibliographical judgment, and the volume is of a very large and unwieldy format, about the size of an elephant folio. There are 34 of these displays showing, in two dimensions, all the terms in the thesaurus in their various contexts of meanings and relationships. Each right-hand page shows a term in a central box, with lines joining it to its related terms in the other boxes, or "polygons"; these links are mainly those to terms in the same hierarchy as the central term, but they also indicate synonymous terms not used. On the back of each page there are an explantory note on how to use the displays, a list of all the RT which relate to the central term (or "Top Term") on the front of the page, and a complete display of all the relations between the complete set of the 34 graphic displays. Each display, of course, has a different term in its central box, so that any term may be looked at in the context of all its relations included in the thesaurus (see Figs. 15–17).

Revision

An argument often leveled against schemes of classification as instruments for arranging and indexing documents is that, once published, they at once become fossilized and unable to cope with the ever-advancing dynamic continuum of knowledge—which is, of course, precisely what they set out to do. The thesaurus, it is claimed, does not suffer from this disability and is thus to be preferred as a superior tool. Such comments seem to indicate an unawareness of two factors: (*a*) the well-constructed thesaurus itself depends on a classificatory structure, whether this is acknowledged or not; and (*b*) keeping up to date, for any indexing language, simply means adding new words to an existing list, according to the format of that list. It makes little difference whether the list is in alphabetical or classified sequence, the new words have to be inserted in their appropriate place. At first blush, it appears easier to add to a simple alphabetical list, provided that all are actually agreed on the form of the word (which often differs even between the United Kingdom and the United States). But once the question of BT, NT, and RT arises, we are at once in the realm of classification, like it or not. Those who protest that new terms cannot be "fitted" into a classification scheme have overlooked the 19 editions of the Decimal Classification, the P-Notes of the Universal Decimal Classification, the new editions of Library of Congress Classification classes, and so on. As a matter of fact, they are also confusing classification with notation, which is another matter entirely.

A thorough and well-conceived scheme for the process of revision is essential for any indexing language. All that has to be decided is how to do it. This boils down to two main choices, with some variations: (*a*) new editions of the whole scheme, published as often as possible; and (*b*) piecemeal revision, adding new terms as they arise.

The first method has been the most favored and is used by the Engineers Joint Council for TEST and by the National Center for Educational Communication for the *ERIC Thesaurus*. It is much tidier, much more satisfactory for the compiler, who sees the product in a new and up-to-date dress; and it is more convenient for the user, who does not have to keep making amendments to his probably already battered copy. But it has some disadvantages. New editions are more costly to produce, and inevitable delays are involved because it only becomes worth publishing a whole new edition when enough amendments have been accumulated to provide an edition that is significantly new. It is also more expensive for the user, who will be buying a lot of material which he already has, in the form of everything that has not been amended. Preparation of new editions encourages the compiler to tamper with the existing text, not always effecting an improvement. As an example of how alterations which are unsatisfactory and inconsistent come about, largely through lack of a proper structure, we may consider the treatment by ERIC of the terms "ability," "creative ability," "creativity," and "intelligence," which varies considerably between the first and the subsequent editions, with no apparent reason for the changes and no improvement in the relational structure. Where a complete new edition is published, especially if this is within a relatively short time after the

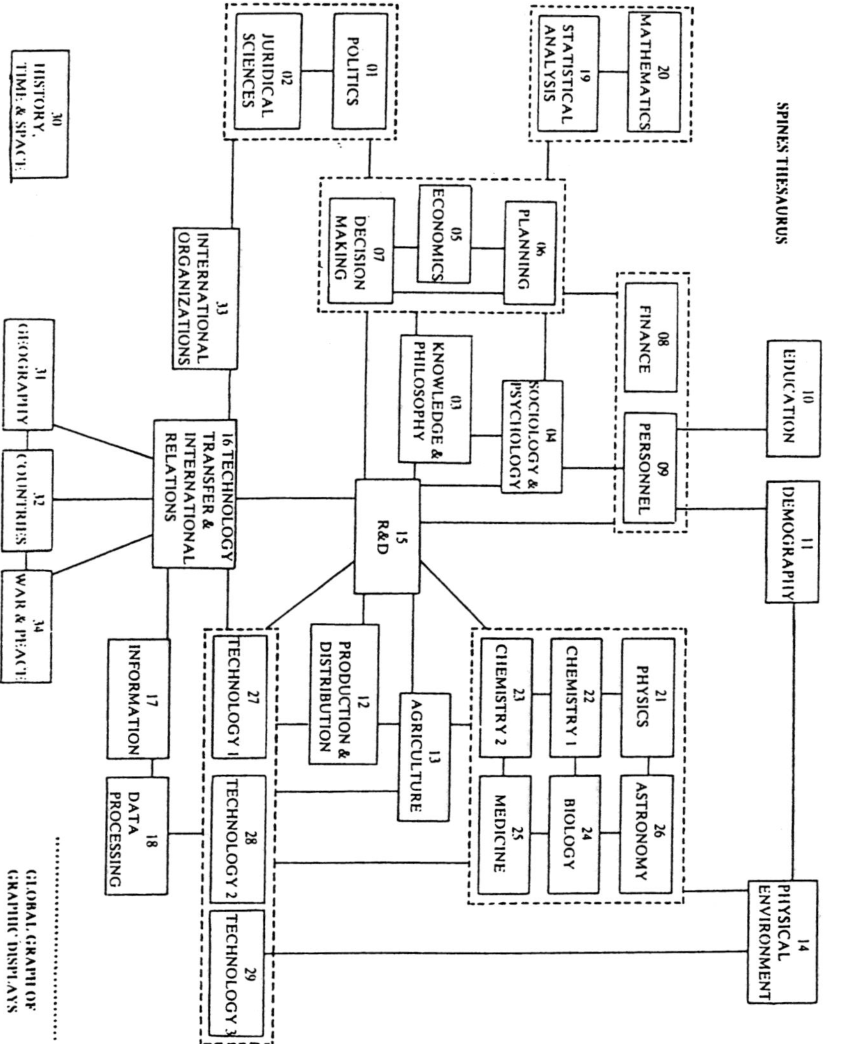

FIGURE 15. *Extract from the* SPINES Thesaurus.
Reproduced by permission of UNESCO, Paris.

ASSOCIATIVE RELATIONS BETWEEN TOP DESCRIPTORS OF GRAPHIC DISPLAY 18, AND EXTERNAL TOP DESCRIPTORS

18-01 DATA PROCESSING EQUIPMENT		**18-02 DATA PROCESSING**	**18-03 COMPUTER SOFTWARE**	
ELECTRONIC TECHNOLOGY	27-11	INFORMATION SCIENCES 17-07	SYSTEMS	07-03
OFFICE EQUIPMENT	29-17			

FIGURE 16. *Extract from the* SPINES Thesaurus. *Reproduced by permission of UNESCO.*

DATA PROCESSING EQUIPMENT

calculators
— accounting machines
— calculating machines
— desk calculators

COMPUTERS
— business computers
— industrial computers
— scientific computers

minicomputers
microcomputers
general purpose computers
special purpose computers
analog computers
hybrid computers
digital computers
synchronous computers
asynchronous computers
first generation computers
— vacuum tube computers
second generation computers
— solid state computers
third generation computers
— solid logic computers
virtual machines
— virtual computing machines

COMPUTER PERIPHERAL EQUIPMENT
— computer auxiliary equipment

computer consoles
— computer control panels

COMPUTER HARDWARE
— hardware (computers)
— computer systems

offline equipment
online equipment

CENTRAL PROCESSING UNITS
— central processors
— CPU

microprocessors

STORAGE DEVICES
— computer memories
— memory devices

storage capacity
random access
— direct access
serial access
computer registers
core storage
delays lines (computers)
magnetic cards
magnetic discs
magnetic drums
magnetic tapes
punched cards
— aperture cards
punched tapes
— paper tapes

(continued)

— console typewriters (computer)
computer display devices*

COMPUTER TERMINALS

remote terminals
— teleprocessing devices

curve followers
data processing collators
key punches
plotters
— graph plotters
storage devices converters*
summary punches

film readers
— microfilm viewers
printers (data processing)

thick film storage
thin film storage
input output devices*
— computer input devices
— computer output devices
computer circuits

character recognition devices
— magnetic ink character recog.
— mark detection
— mark sensing devices
— optical character recognition
punched card equipment*
— unit record equipment
punched tape equipment
— paper tape punches
— punched tape readers

FIGURE 17. *Extract from the* SPINES Thesaurus. *Reproduced by permission of UNESCO.*

previous, an explanation of changes should be given. This is not only desirable from the user's point of view, but it also forces the compiler to think deeply about any proposed changes and their justification. Where this cannot be done, and where the previous edition is out of print and still in demand, it would seem preferable simply to issue a reprint.

Piecemeal revision means publishing additions and corrections as often as the occasion arises. The obvious advantage of this is that users can keep their copies continuously up to date with a minimum of labor for both compiler and user. It does require a certain firmness of purpose on the part of the user, however, and amendment slips are fragile things which can easily get lost. The most necessary feature of this type of revision procedure, therefore, is a vehicle of regular communication between compiler and users. Experience with the UDC P-Notes, each of which arises from a separate operation and is issued separately, shows that it can become a very laborious, even haphazard process.

But since a complete edition must itself, in the nature of things, be compiled piecemeal, there seems to be no reason why both revision methods should not be used in combination, especially if there is a regular means of communication to hand. ERIC, for example, publishes "New Thesaurus Terms" in its *Research in Education* and *Current Index to Journals in Education;* both of these are organized by means of its own thesaurus, and so a subscriber will need to possess a copy of the thesaurus if he is to make the best use of the two indexes to current documents. This not only provides regular and continuous communication between compiler and user, it can also mean that a user in straightened circumstances may not have to buy every new complete edition, so long as he faithfully adds all new terms to his own copy.

For both compiler and user, this combination of methods provides the best system. A thesaurus compiler who hopes and expects that his scheme will be widely used would be well advised to set up a regular revision service if he cannot make use of an already existing vehicle. This has a further advantage: If the users recognize that they have such a regular channel of communication, they may be encouraged to use it in the other direction and offer helpful suggestions for improvements based on actual practice in retrieval systems.

Machine Compilation

The development of computer technology has greatly assisted in the compilation and revision of thesauri, and most major organizations now use this technique, so that several programs are available. Much of the research in this area—like that of Karen Sparck Jones (*22*) and Gerard Salton (*31*)—has been based on the analysis of texts in order to work out the relations that occur between the semantic contents of words and phrases as they appear in actual documents. Although this contribution has considerable theoretical interest, probably the most important advantage of the use of computers is that the whole of a thesaurus is held in machine-readable form, available for immediate consultation in an on-line dialogue with a user, who then knows that he is accessing the thesaurus in its most up-to-date form. In his article "Vocabulary Control in Information Retrieval Systems" (*7*), F. W. Lancaster discusses several important functions that may be performed by storing a thesaurus in machine-readable form:

1. Checking for consistency and acceptability of terms
2. Maintaining statistics on the use of terms
3. Maintaining the "tracings" necessary to ensure that, if a term is deleted from the vocabulary or modified in some way, all the terms that are connected with this term (through some form of reference) are also appropriately modified
4. Maintaining records of term "history"
5. Automatic optimization of a searching strategy
6. Facilitating the conduct of generic searches
7. Automatic generation of cross-references for printed indexes

To these may also be added the facility for editing at the terminal whenever the need arises, so that the machine-stored thesaurus is always kept up to date in a quick, efficient, and relatively inexpensive way. If it can thus be made available for on-line access to users, they too can easily check to bring their own copies up to date without having to wait for a printed amendment.

Relations Between Thesauri

With so many organizations finding the need for a thesaurus, and so many thesauri being compiled, it seems surprising that more attention has not been given to the question of compatibility between the various schemes. In particular, one might expect this to apply to publishers of thesauri which cover the same or similar ground. That it has not happened so far is due to a variety of circumstances. First, only in recent years has there been any attempt to set up standard methods of construction. Second, many organizations seem to set about their task in total unawareness of either traditional subject heading lists or existing thesauri in their own or in related fields. Making a virtue out of such accidents, it is often claimed that one of the major attractions of a thesaurus is precisely that it can be tailor-made to suit the particular requirements of a particular organization—an attraction, it is said, which more than compensates for the costs of constructing a thesaurus in intellectual isolation.

The situation is changing, and the trend toward cooperation will doubtless continue—because there is a greater need, and because of the greater facility which has arrived in the wake of developments in the computer industry; and also, of course, because of growing awareness of the value of international cooperation in intellectual matters, in a world becoming ever more conscious of the value of cooperation in science and industry. The United Nations and its many specialized agencies, other international organizations such as Euratom, and the transnational corporations have all played a role in this development, and they are now being followed by international governmental organizations such as the European Communities Commission and the Council for Mutual Economic Assistance.

Where the method of construction is the same, it is a simple matter for one scheme to borrow parts of another. The *London Education Classification* thesaurus and the *Thesaurofacet* are both constructed by means of facet analysis, and so is the *London Classification for Business Studies* (LCBS), from which a new thesaurus is now being compiled. The LCBS has a facet for education which is an abridged version of some sections of the *London Education Classification;* the *Thesaurofacet* has a facet for management which is in its turn extracted from the LCBS.

A determined effort at this sort of economy has been started by the United Nations family of organizations, mainly through work in the social sciences by G. K. Thompson at the International Labor Organization (ILO). The result is the *Macrothesaurus* (*32*), described in a background paper by Thompson in 1974 (*33*). An "Interim Caretaker Group for the Macrothesaurus" was established at the ILO by the International Committee on Social Sciences Documentation, which has for many years stressed the need for coordination in the social sciences, where fields of study have large areas of overlap and the terminology is not nearly as precise as it is in the physical sciences. The initiative was taken in the late 1960s by the Organization for Economic Cooperation and Development (OECD), whose Development Center was active in the field of information storage and retrieval. This brought together the ILO, the Food and Agriculture Organization (FAO), the International Committee on Social Sciences Documentation, and the Deutsche Stiftung für Entwicklungsländer [German Foundation for International Development]. The "Aligned List of Descriptors" was first published for discussion in 1969. Many other organizations in the international field expressed interest; some had already compiled their own lists, and contributed them, so that the original Aligned List came to be much larger and more wide ranging. It is now "an author-

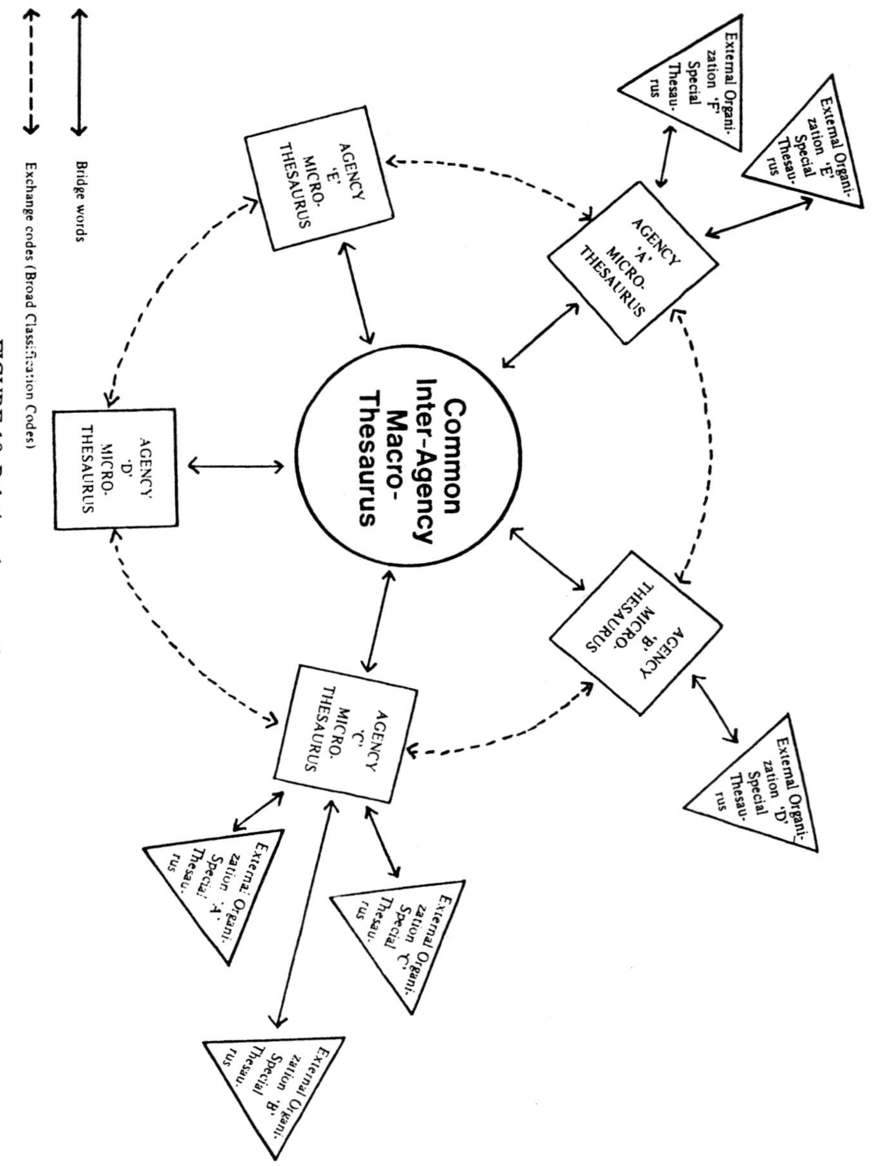

FIGURE 18: Relations between thesauri

ity list of terms on economic and social development, for use in the international context." It is titled *Macrothesaurus* because it was derived from several separate lists, and it endeavored to incorporate all of their terms in one single framework which would be acceptable to all of the original compilers. Each institution can take those parts of interest to itself, develop them more fully if necessary for its own purposes within the overall framework, and use the remainder to deal with the ever-present problem of "marginal fields."

The *Macrothesaurus* is divided into 19 facets, as follows:

01 International Cooperation. International Relations.
02 Economic Policy. Social Policy. Planning.
03 Economic Conditions. Economic Research. Economic System.
04 Institutional Framework.
05 Culture. Society.
06 Education. Training.
07 Agriculture.
08 Industry.
09 Commerce. Trade.
10 Transport.
11 Currency. Financing. International Monetary Relations.
12 Management. Productivity.
13 Labour.
14 Demography. Population.
15 Biology. Food. Health.
16 Environment. Natural Resources.
17 Atmospheric Science. Earth Sciences.
18 Science. Research. Methodology.
19 Information. Documentation.

It is published by the OECD in English, French, German, and Spanish, and responsibility for its upkeep has been assumed by the United Nations family. Headquarters for the *Macrothesaurus* are based at the ILO, where G. K. Thompson has acquired much valuable experience in the use of computers for compiling and printing thesauri, and for their use in all aspects of information storage and retrieval. Already a number of improvements have been incorporated based on the suggestions of the cooperating bodies. Considerable reference was made, for example, to Jean Viet's *Thesaurus for Information Processing in Sociology* (*34*) for several sections, and in turn, Viet drew on "Section 06 Education" when he later compiled the *EUDISED Thesaurus*.

The kinds of relationship that may exist between such a "macrothesaurus" and the several "microthesauri" in its family are shown schematically in Figure 18.

In 1977 UNESCO published its own *Unesco Thesaurus*, which is subtitled "A Structured List of Descriptors for Indexing and Retrieving Literature in the Fields of Education, Science, Social Science, Culture and Communication." This was compiled by Jean Aitchison, and it follows to some extent the pattern which she established with the *Thesaurofacet*. It has been designed to be the working tool of the Computerized Documentation System (CDS) of UNESCO and will be used in indexing and retrieval of all documents and publications processed through the CDS. The terms from the *Unesco Thesaurus* are already being used to retrieve information from the data base established by the CDS, both for retrospective searches and in selective dissemination of information. It is in two volumes: Volume 1 contains the Introduction, the Classified Thesaurus, the Permuted Index, and the Hierarchical Display of Terms; Volume 2 contains the alphabetical part of the thesaurus. The *Unesco Thesaurus* was compiled originally by preparing an unstructured list of terms based on the *Macrothesaurus*, which was drafted in 1973/74 and circulated to many institutions, particularly in the UN family. As a result of this process, a new version was prepared, and the final version contains nearly 8,500 terms in all. There is a very good introduction, as one would expect from Jean Aitchison, and all aspects of the subjects are catered for. The *Unesco Thesaurus* also sets a fine example in the way in which considerable effort has been made to ensure compatibility with other thesauri and classification schemes such as the second edition of the *Bliss Bibliographical Classification*, the *London Education Classification*, and the *London Classification of Business Studies*.

The Thesaurus in Use

As this survey shows, the thesaurus can take several different forms, from the deceptively "simple" alphabetical list of terms to an intricate network of relationships like the *SPINES Thesaurus* and the *Thesaurofacet*. In every case, it will require an introductory section which explains how it can best be used. If this is not provided, the unlucky users will have to produce one for themselves; and this, paradoxically, is particularly true for the "simpler" types, because experience shows that they are the most difficult to use with consistency, especially where more than one person is involved in indexing. The reason for this becomes clear when we consider the purposes for which the thesaurus may be used. First, the purpose may be to index into one system subject information derived from several different sources which cannot be subjected to the constraints of the index system itself. Most of those sources are documents produced by individual authors who all base their writings on the thought patterns in their own minds, which are not necessarily the same pattern as that of the index system, even though all may be aiming at the same target: the accurate reflection of the real world and real phenomena. Second, the thesaurus may be used as an entry means for searching the file created by the index system, in order to find information for yet a third category of individual, an inquirer who may well be neither an author nor an indexer. This "matching" of terms cannot be done consistently if the thesaurus in use carries no rules of operation to guide the user to a correct selection of terms which will act as the bridge or intermediary between author and reader.

If the director of an information storage and retrieval system chooses to make use of a published thesaurus, he will naturally follow the rules set out by the original compiler; sometimes, unfortunately, these are not as full or precise as they should be, and compilers would do well to note that this is a fault which will certainly detract from the use and value of their systems. If, on the other hand, one chooses to compile one's own thesaurus (and the intellectual attraction of this is not to be underestimated), then a lesson may be learned from examples like TEST and the *Thesaurofacet*, which have well-written and detailed introductions giving both full explanations of how the thesaurus is constructed and all the information a user will require in order to use it efficiently. An introduction should therefore aim to cover all the sections that make up this article: the limits of the field or fields covered, the choice and form of terms, the network of relations, the form of presentation, and the use of special features like the graphical displays of the *SPINES Thesaurus*.

Conclusion

The thesaurus as a tool for librarians and information scientists represents the latest stage in a long line of works whose aims are to codify the language of discourse for the purposes of information storage and retrieval, and as a result, to improve the effectiveness of communication between people. Since language itself is constantly developing as the human race progresses, we cannot expect to find one perfect and absolute form, nor even one absolute set of rules and principles that will endure forever without change. Indeed, it will be to our advantage to recognize the need for constant revision of old forms and invention of new. What is important is that we should follow the advice we often give to others: Make use of the literature and so of the efforts and achievements of our predecessors. In this way, and only in this way, can each generation build on the foundations already laid by its forbears; and in this way too, we will learn more readily from our contemporaries. If we have the will to do this, then the thesaurus, being an instrument for effecting communication, can play a small but significant part in the improvement of understanding and harmony among the peoples of the world.

REFERENCES

1. Karen Sparck Jones, "Some Thesauric History," *Aslib Proc.*, **24,** 408–411 (July 1972).
2. Mary Elizabeth Stevens, H. P. Luhn: Information Scientist," in *H. P. Luhn . . .* , Ref. 3, p. 26b.
3. Claire K. Schultz, ed., *H. P. Luhn: Pioneer in Information Science*, Spartan Books, New York, 1968, 320 pp.
4. Jean Aitchison and Alan Gilchrist, *Thesaurus Construction: A Practical Manual*, Aslib, London, 1972, 95 pp.
5. Alan Gilchrist, *The Thesaurus in Retrieval*, Aslib, London, 1971, 184 pp.
6. Dagobert Soergel, *Indexing Languages and Thesauri: Construction and Maintenance*, Melville Publishing Co., Los Angeles, Calif., 1974, 632 pp.
7. F. W. Lancaster, "Vocabulary Control in Information Retrieval Systems," in *Advances in Librarianship* (Melvin J. Voigt and Michael J. Harris, eds.), Academic Press, New York, 1977, Vol. 7, pp. 1–40.
8. E. J. Coates, *Subject Catalogues: Headings and Structure*, Library Association, London, 1960, 186 pp.
9. H. H. Neville, "Comprehensive On-line Computer System for Special Libraries, *Aslib Proc.*, **27**, 188–216 (May 1975).
10. UNESCO, *UNISIST Guidelines for the Establishment and Development of Monolingual Thesauri*, UNESCO, Paris, SC/WS/555, 1973, 37 pp.
11. C. van der Merwe, *Thesaurus of Sociological Research Terminology*, Rotterdam University Press, Netherlands, 1974, 471 pp.

12. Engineers Joint Council, *Thesaurus of Engineering and Scientific Terms*, EJC, New York, 1967, 890 pp.
13. American Psychological Association, *Thesaurus of Psychological Index Terms*, 2nd ed., APA, Washington, D.C., 1977, 282 pp.
14. Jean Aitchison et al., *Thesaurofacet: A Thesaurus and Faceted Classification for Engineering and Related Subjects*, English Electric Co., Whetstone, 1969, 491 pp.
15. Barbara Westby, ed., *Sears List of Subject Headings*, 9th ed., H. W. Wilson Co., New York, 1965, 641 pp.
16. Frederick Goodman, "Introduction," in *ERIC Thesaurus*, CCM Information Corp., New York, 1972, 330 pp.
17. UNESCO, *SPINES Thesaurus: A Controlled and Structured Vocabulary of Science and Technology for Policy-Making, Management and Development*, UNESCO, Paris, 1976, 3 vols.
18. B. J. Field, *INSPEC Thesaurus (a Thesaurus of Terms for Physics, Electrotechnology, Computers and Control)*, Institution of Electrical Engineers, London, 1973, 2 vols.
19. Gordon C. Barhydt and Charles T. Schmidt, *Information Retrieval Thesaurus of Education Terms*, Case Western Reserve University, Cleveland, 1968, 133 pp.
20. B. C. Vickery, *Classification and Indexing in Science*, 3rd ed., Butterworths, London, 1975, 228 pp.
21. A. Neelameghan, "Non-hierarchical Associative Relationships: Their Types and the Computer Generation of RT Links," in *Seminar on Thesaurus in Information Systems*, Bangalore, December 1–5, 1975, pp. A1–A8.
22. Karen Sparck Jones, *Automatic Keyword Classification for Information Retrieval*, Butterworths, London, 1971, 253 pp.
23. J. S. Bruner, *The Process of Education*, Vintage Books, New York, 1960, 97 pp.
24. Bärbel Inhelder and Jean Piaget, *The Early Growth of Logic in the Child: Classification and Seriation*, Routledge and Kegan Paul, London, 1964, 302 pp.
25. R. A. Fairthorne, "The Mathematics of Classification," *Proc. British Soc. International Bibliography*, **9**, 35–42 (October 1947).
26. M. J. Roberts et al., *Construction Industry Thesaurus*, Department of the Environment, London, 1972, 341 pp.
27. International Occupational Safety and Health Information Center, *CIS Thesaurus*, International Labor Organization, Geneva, 1976.
28. D. J. Foskett and Joy Foskett, *The London Education Classification: A Thesaurus/Classification of British Educational Terms*, 2nd ed., University of London Institute of Education Library, 1974, 165 pp.
29. Jean Viet, *EUDISED Multilingual Thesaurus*, Mouton, Paris, 1973, 391 pp.
30. Lol N. Rolling, "The Role of Graphic Display of Concept Relationships in Indexing and Retrieval Vocabularies," in *Classification Research: Proceedings of the Second International Study Conference* (Pauline Atherton, ed.), Munksgaard, Copenhagen, 1965, pp. 295–320.
31. Gerard Salton, *Experiments in Automatic Thesaurus Construction for Information Retrieval*, Cornell University, Ithaca, N.Y., 1971, 27 pp.
32. Organization for Economic Cooperation and Development, *Macrothesaurus: A Basic List of Economic and Social Development Terms*, OECD, Paris, 1972, 225 pp.
33. George K. Thompson, *Background Paper on the Macrothesaurus*, International Labor Organization, Geneva, 1974, 14 pp.
34. Jean Viet, *Thesaurus for Information Processing in Sociology*, Mouton, The Hague, 1971, 336 pp.

BIBLIOGRAPHY

No attempt has been made here to set out a complete bibliography on the thesaurus, which would run to many hundreds of items. The two centers, at Cleveland and Warsaw, have catalogs, and there are also several other selective bibliographies. New thesauri are reported in the *FID/CR Newsletter* from Bangalore. The items listed here are therefore confined to those which give further information about matters in the text of the article, or which are located in items which may be unusual, unexpected, or difficult to find.

Aitchison, Jean, "Thesaurofacet: A New Concept in Subject Retrieval Schemes," in *Subject Retrieval in the Seventies* (Hans Wellisch and Thomas D. Wilson, eds.), Greenwood Publishing Co., Westport, Conn., and School of Library and Information Services, University of Maryland, pp. 72–98.

Batten, W. E., ed., *EURIM II*, Aslib, London, 1977.

Documentation Research and Training Center, Bangalore, *Seminar on Thesaurus in Information Systems*, jointly organized by DRTC and INSDOC, December 1–5, 1975, DRTC, Bangalore, 1976.

Foskett, D. J., *A Study of the Role of Categories in a Thesaurus for Educational Documentation*, Council of Europe, Strasbourg, EUDISED Project DECS/Doc (73) 8, 1974, 38 pp.

Gilchrist, Alan, "Intermediate Languages for Switching and Control," *Aslib Proc.*, **24**, 387–399 (July 1972).

Gilchrist, Alan, "The Role of Thesauri in Mechanized Systems," *Indexer*, **9**, 146–154 (October 1975).

Horsnell, Verina, ed., *Informatics 2: Proceedings of a Conference Held by the Aslib Coordinate Indexing Group on 25–27 March, 1974*, Aslib, London, 1975, 100 pp.

Jones, Karen Sparck, "Some Thesauric History," *Aslib Proc.*, **24**, 408–411 (July 1972).

Kutten, Aaron, *Thesauri Bibliography*, Elyachar Library, Technion Israel Institute of Technology, Haifa, 1975.

Laureilhe, Marie-Thérèse, *Le Thésaurus: Son rôle, sa structure, son elaboration*, Presses de l'E.N.S.B., Lyon, 1977.

Richmond, Phyllis A., "A Thesaurus within a Thesaurus: A Study in Ambiguity," in *Towards a Theory of Librarianship: Papers in Honour of Jesse Hauk Shera* (Conrad H. Rawski, ed.), Scarecrow Press, Metuchen, N.J., 1973, pp. 268–301.

Rolling, Lol N., "Compilation of Thesauri for Use in Computer Systems," *Inform. Storage and Retrieval*, **6**, 341–350 (October 1970).

Shepherd, Michael, and Carolyn Watters, "Computer-generation of Thesaurus," *Library Science with a Slant to Documentation* (Thesaurus Ser. 1), **12**, 40–54 (June 1975).

Thorp, Alan L., and W. E. Robbins, "Using Computers in a Natural Language Mode for Elementary Education," *Int. J. Man-Machine Studies*, **7**, 703–725 (November 1975).

Unesco Thesaurus: A Structured List of Descriptors for Indexing and Retrieving Literature in the Fields of Education, Science, Social Science, Culture and Communication (Jean Aitchison, comp.), UNESCO, Paris, 1977, 2 vols.: Vol. 1: Introduction, Classified Thesaurus, Permuted Index, Hierarchical Display; Vol. 2: Alphabetical Thesaurus.

Walkley, Janet, and Barbara Hay, "An Annotated List of Thesauri Held in the Aslib Library," *Aslib Proc.*, **23**, 292–300 (June 1971).

Wall, Eugene, "Symbiotic Development of Thesauri and Information Systems: A Case History," *J. Amer. Soc. Information Science*, **26**, 71–79 (March–April 1975).

Willetts, Margaret, "Investigation of the Nature of the Relation between Terms in Thesauri," *J. Documentation*, **31**, 158–184 (September 1975).

DOUGLAS J. FOSKETT

USING PROBLEM STRUCTURES FOR DRIVING HUMAN-COMPUTER DIALOGUES

P.J. DANIELS, H.M. BROOKS*, N.J. BELKIN**
Department of Information Science
The City University
Northampton Square
London EC1V 0HB
England

*also with
Central Information Services
University of London

Abstract:

We discuss aspects of the design of an intelligent interface for direct end-user access to document retrieval systems, based on the idea that the computer half of such an interface must build up complex models of the user and the user's problem in a cooperative dialogue with the user. We suggest that a general problem structure for the document retrieval problem could provide a means for driving and guiding such a human-computer dialogue in this domain. On the basis of a detailed discourse analysis of six human-human information interactions, a candidate problem structure is proposed, with some suggestions as to how it might be used to understand information interaction, and to guide a human-computer dialogue.

**To whom communications about this paper should be sent.

1. Introduction

Within the next ten years, computer-mediated access to knowledge bases of all sorts will have spread throughout our society. Most such access will be in support of problem management for relatively naive end participants in information systems, who will typically have ill-formed problems and not easily specifiable information requirements. It is therefore vital that the access or query mechanisms to the knowledge bases which will be used be capable of dealing with non-specific enquiries in a natural manner. Since all information systems at present force users to specify precisely their information requirements, usually in a highly un-natural manner, it is clear that a new approach to this problem is needed, based on the related ideas of naturalness and non-specifiability. We believe that fundamental to any such approach is the recognition that the user is an integral part of the information system, the other components being a knowledge resource and some intermediary mechanism between them. The last two components can be considered together as the information provision mechanism.

The basic problem with which we are concerned is the design of information provision mechanisms (IPMs) which cooperate with human users, in the task of finding information which might help the users in managing the problem which prompted them to instigate the information system. There are many possible approaches to this problem. Here we concentrate upon one particular aspect - the intermediary component of the IPM, which interacts with the user. In particular, we suggest a possible model for design of human-computer information dialogues, in the document retrieval context, which is based explicitly on a notion of the problem which the two parties (user and IPM) are cooperating on.

This paper derives from earlier work concerned with the issues of non-specifiability of information requirements (Belkin, Oddy & Brooks, 1982), information provision for problem management (Belkin, Seeger & Wersig, 1983), and the functional analysis of human information dialogues (Brooks & Belkin, 1983; Belkin & Windel, 1984), which we will very briefly review here.

Belkin, Oddy and Brooks (1982) report on a design study for an interactive document retrieval system based on the hypothesis that users in such systems cannot, in principle, specify their information requirements. They suggest that in this case, the IPM should attempt to represent the anomalous state of knowledge (ASK) underlying the information behaviour, rather than trying to force the user to try to make some sort of specification of requirements. Especially important to us here is the idea of non-specifiability, and the means by which the ASK was evoked and represented.

Belkin, Seeger and Wersig (1983) stressed that the IPM should support the user in problem management. They suggested that this implies that the IPM has a number of <u>functions</u> which it must perform, in cooperation with the user, in order to produce an adequate response. These functions included such things as modelling the user, describing the user's problem, determining the state of the user in the problem solving process, and so on. The whole was labelled a Distributed Expert Problem Treatment (DEPT) model. This work has subsequently been evaluated and extended by simulations of such a system (Belkin, Hennings & Seeger, 1984). From our point of view here, the significance of this work is in its functional analysis of the IPM.

Brooks and Belkin (1983), concerned with the issue of building a document retrieval IPM which would allow direct end user access, suggested that such an IPM should simulate some of the functions that a human intermediary performs in the document retrieval situation. They therefore used the DEPT functions to analyze transcripts of the interactions between users and intermediaries in document retrieval systems. The work we report on here follows their lead in analysis of human-human dialogues, although we begin with a slightly different analytic schema, which arises from our somewhat different goals.

Belkin & Windel (1984) report briefly on the analysis of a dialogue between a student and an advisor in a student advisory service, in which they suggest that the moves in the dialogue can be interpreted as being dependent on a highly structured model that the advisor holds of the problem the two of them are working on. This <u>problem structure</u>, or mental model, in effect drives the dialogue, and might even predict the moves of the advisor. This interpretation of the user-advisor interaction seems to us promising in terms of leading to schemata which might organize a human-computer dialogue of the kind with which we are concerned.

Our specific aim, therefore, is to attempt to identify and define a problem structure associated with the information system, which might be capable of driving the computer half of a human-computer information dialogue, and of interpreting the human half correctly. Our method is to analyze human-human information dialogues. For the purposes of the research project reported on here, we consider one kind of information dialogue, that associated with the document retrieval situation.

<u>Figure 1. Goal Hierarchy for the Document Retrieval Problem.</u>

LEVEL	GOAL
1	User leaves the system
2	User is satisfied
3	Appropriate response to user
4	Appropriate search formulation
5	Subgoals to achieve Level 4 goal
6	Subgoals to achieve Level 5 goals

The general document retrieval problem can be broken down into several levels of goals that are to be achieved (figure 1). At the highest level, the goal is that the user leaves the system (level 1). One way to achieve this goal is to have the user satisfied with the interaction (goal level 2). One way to achieve this goal is for the IPM to provide the user with some appropriate response (goal level 3). And in order to produce an appropriate response, it is necessary, in the document retrieval situation, that an appropriate search formulation be constructed (level 4). At this point, of appropriate search formulation, we begin our detailed analysis. We consider level 4 as the problem on which the two participants are collaborating, and thus we look at it in order to see what specific activities take place, and what goals are set, in order to achieve the level 4 goal of an appropriate search formulation. These are the level 5 goals of document retrieval, with a sixth level of specific tasks associated with each of the level 5 goals.

2. Methods

Our data for analysis consist of natural language human-human interactions, assuming that the goals or functions which appear in successful or good information interactions should be simulated in human-computer interactions. The collection of data took place at several academic online information retrieval services at London University, where trained intermediaries carry out searches of bibliographic databases. The users are primarily post-graduate students, but also include academic staff, and other types of researchers. Audio recordings were made of six presearch interviews, carried out by four different intermediaries, from the point that the user entered the service until the beginning of the online search, when the intermediary logged on to the system. The interviews were then transcribed from the tapes according to a specific format which included means for representing breath pauses, silences and their duration, failed utterances and extralinguistic phenomena such as coughs, laughter, etc. The transcription of each dialogue was then checked by another of the team, the transcript was divided into utterances, which were the units used for analysis, and this division was again checked by another person.

An utterance can be defined as a speech sequence by one participant during the conversation. It may or may not comprise of complete grammatical entities, and may be terminated by a contribution made by the other participant. If the contribution of one participant takes the conversational turn, the previous speech sequence is regarded as a completed utterance (Brooks & Belkin, 1983; Price, 1983).

Our aim was to discover which goals may exist at level 5 of Figure 1; that is, the individual subgoals which must be achieved during the interaction between user and intermediary before the goal at level 4 can be fulfilled. The analysis was carried out according to these level 5 goals, rather than according to functions (Brooks & Belkin, 1983; Belkin & Windel, 1984) because the specific purpose of each utterance had to be identified and, at this level, the functional analysis seemed too gross.

One interview (interview no. 4) was subjected to four separate analyses by four different people, each of whom attempted to identify and categorize the goal or goals which were occurring in each utterance. The results of this analysis stabilized the inventory of goals, and also suggested that analysis according to focus, and focus shift was possible.

The focus of a dialogue (Grosz, 1978) can be said to highlight that part of the mutual knowledge of the participants relevant at any given point in a dialogue, by grouping together those concepts or themes that are in the focus of attention. The current focus is likely to dictate the structure of the discourse, and the topics to which reference can be made at that given moment. In the analysis of our six interviews, shifts of focus were generally indicated by the occurrence of 'frame' words (Sinclair & Coulthard, 1975), often accompanied by pauses of varying duration. Frame words can be characterized as words or phrases that indicate that some kind of boundary has been reached within the discourse, and that therefore a shift of focus is about to occur. Examples of such frame words include:

Yeah (.) OK (.) emm (...) (Interview 4)

Right OK (,) right (..) (Interview 190684hba)

now the next thing is to get (,) our strategy (Interview 190684hba)

Each of the remaining five interviews was analyzed by one person, assigning specific goals for each utterance, and partitioning into foci, and the results were cumulated for all six interactions. At this point we achieved the final inventory of level 6 goals and foci.

Figure 2. Level 6 goals for document retrieval interaction.

GOAL/ACRONYM	DESCRIPTION
1. CAPAB	Explain the capabilities of the system to user.
2. UGOAL	Determine the user's goals.
3. USER	Determine the status of the user.
4. KNOW	Determine the user's state of knowledge of the field.
5. IRS	Determine the user's familiarity with information retrieval systems.
6. PREV	Determine the user's previous reference activities.
7. PREVNON	Determine the user's previous non-reference activities.
8. PDIM	Determine the problem dimension; this refers to anything which is temporally coded within the state of research.
9. SUBJ	Define the subject area or background to the search.
10. SLIT	Determine formal characteristics of the subject literature.
11. RES	Specify the content of the user's research.
12. TOPIC	Specify the search topic.
13. DOCS	Determine the content or description of documents that the user would like to retrieve.
14. TERMS	Select the terms for searching.
15. QUERY	Formulate the query.
16. STRAT	Evolve the search strategy (how query will be implemented).
17. DB	Select the databases to be searched.
18. OUT	Determine the output requirements.
19. EXPL	Bring the user's knowledge of information retrieval up to the minimum level necessary for functioning.
20. DISP	Literal display of some aspect of the system.
21. INFORM	Explain the intermediary's intentions to the user.
22. PLAN	Specify the plan of the interview, the structure of activity.
23. MATCH	Compare models that participants hold of aspects of other.

Figure 3. Level 6 goals grouped by level 5 goals, and goals which were instantiated as foci of the dialogues.

LEVEL 5 GOALS / LEVEL 6 GOALS*	GOALS INSTANTIATED AS FOCI OF DIALOGUE
Problem Mode (PM)	
CAPAB	
User Model (UM)	User Model (includes all 4 UM level 6 goals)
UGOAL	
USER	
KNOW	
IRS	Experience of IRS
BACK	
Problem State (PS)	
PREV	Previous Reference Activities
PREVNON	
PDIM	
Problem Description (PD)	Problem Description (includes RES, DOCS, TOPIC, USER, KNOW)
SUBJ	Subject Area of Search
RES	User's Research Problem
TOPIC	Topic of Search
DOCS	Document Description
SLIT	
Retrieval Strategies (RS)	
TERMS	Term Selection
QUERY	Query Formulation
STRAT	Search Strategy
DB	Database Selection
Response Generator (RG)	
OUT	Output Requirements
Explain (EX)	
EXPL	Explanation
INFORM	
DISP	
Meta-Goals	
MATCH	
PLAN	Planning Interaction Goal 4

*Acronyms identified in figure 2.

3. Results

Utterance-by-utterance analysis of the data elicited a common set of 23 goals at level 6, listed in figure 2. Analysis of the interviews according to focus, and focus shift, produced a set of sixteen foci, listed as part of figure 3. Figure 4 is an excerpt of the transcript for interview 4, which we use as an example to show how the analysis was applied. The end of the second focus (characterized as 'search topic') in this interview is signalled by the frame words 'Uhmhmm' (utterance no. 30), and the beginning of the third focus therefore is at utterance no. 31. The level 6 goal for utterances 31 and 32 is DOCS (see figure 2 for identification of these goals), and 33 has goals TOPIC and DOCS. 35 has been characterized as RES and SUBJ, and it is the final utterance in this focus. The shift to the next focus is indicated by the occurrence of the frame word 'what?' at the beginning of utterance 37.

Figure 4. Sample transcript of interaction.

```
I  three countries/29        but, are, you prepared to read stuff
U                       Uhmhmm/30

I  about, I dunno, ya know, anywhere else in the world, i::f/31
U                                                            yeah,

I                                        if it's         Yeah, if it's
U  if it's related to the questions I'm asking/32

I  about community education, but primarily in Africa (.)
U

I  a::nd (.) and then those three countries/33
U    Uhmhmm/34                                     Then I'm looking at (.)

I
U  a history as well, because these three (..) the reason I chose them

I                                                            Uhmhm/36
U  is because they've got a history of community education (breath)

I                                                     What (.) they
U  which was introduced during colonial times (...)/35

I  actually called it community education (.) or/37
U
```

The results of our analyses indicate that the majority of level 6 goals tend to constitute foci in their own right, although subsidiary goals do appear within these foci. Detailed analysis of each focus is currently being undertaken in order to identify patterns of interaction and organization of goals within the foci.

In order to discover the logical and temporal ordering of the foci within each interview, a graph was drawn for each interaction, showing the proportion of time (as indicated by number of utterances) occupied by each particular focus during the interaction, and at which stages in the interaction focus shifts occurred.

Comparison of these six graphs reveals that not all of the sixteen foci appear in every interview, but that certain, temporally-ordered patterns of foci tend to occur. Some foci tend to cluster together at particular stages of the interview, and there are points where certain foci tend not to occur. Foci 1-5 (user model, user's experience of information retrieval systems, previous reference activities, problem description and subject area) with one exception, do not appear in the latter half of any interaction. Foci 9 (with one exception), 10 and 11 (select terms, formulate query and formulate search strategy) tend to appear at the later stages of the interaction. Focus 12 (select data-base) also appears more frequently at the later stages, whereas focus 13 (output requirements) tends to occur during the middle stages of the interview. Foci 3,4,5,6,7 and 8 (previous reference activity, topic description, subject area, research, search topic and document description) tend to cluster together mainly at the beginning of the interview, although foci 6 and 7 do also occur throughout the interview. Focus 15 (explain) occurs fairly consistently throughout the interaction. Foci 2,4,5 and 16 (user's experience of information retrieval systems, problem description, subject area and goal 4) appear very infrequently during the course of the interaction.

4. Discussion

The aim of this research has been to derive a candidate problem structure for the interview held between a human intermediary and the end user prior to an online search being carried out. We propose a single problem structure, which is multi-dimensional, and capable of representing individual aspects of interviews whilst retaining a commonality of form. Along one dimension stands the hierarchy of goals (figure 1).

We have shown that it is possible to classify the individual utterances of the interview transcripts on the basis of the level 6 goals these utterances are directed towards. Moreover, the analysis has revealed distinct groupings of adjacent utterances into larger units or foci, which appear to be involved with the attainment of higher goals at level 5.

We propose that the level 5 goals are goal equivalents of the functions of the MONSTRAT model (Belkin, Seeger & Wersig, 1983; Belkin, Hennings & Seeger, 1984). That is, the level 5 goals include the goals of deriving a model of the user; determining the state of the user in the problem solving process; eliciting a description of the user's problem, and so on. Taking the level 5 goals to be the goal equivalents of the MONSTRAT functions, we found that the foci could be grouped according to the level 5 goal toward which they were directed (Figure 3).

The goals are mostly self-explanatory, and concern the accomplishment of the MONSTRAT function they relate to. Explain has a slightly different character from the rest, because it was found to be used by the intermediary in order to bring the user to some minimum level of knowledge about the retrieval system, so that the user could participate usefully in the next task. In other words, it was involved with the facilitation of other level 5 goals, particularly that of Retrieval Strategies. The foci 'Plan' and 'Goal 4' are special cases. Plan is concerned with the accomplishment of level 4, and so operates at a higher level in the goal hierarchy than the other foci. Similarly, Goal 4 represents an attempt by the participant directly to accomplish goal 4, deriving an effective search formulation, without passing through the lower levels of the goal hierarchy.

We are not suggesting that the foci listed here represent a complete set of possible foci. There are no foci involved, for instance, with the goal of establishing the Problem Mode. This is largely because questions of problem mode had been dealt with prior to these interviews taking place. The exception is interview 190684hba, where the question of the system's capabilities arose repeatedly and was in fact the crucial factor in the user's problem. It never appeared as a focus, however, which is perhaps the reason for the ineffectiveness of this particular interview. Other MONSTRAT functions such as Input Analysis, Dialogue Mode, Output Generator have not been included as level 5 goals because they were not present, or occurred outside the interviews recorded and analyzed here.

It is also possible to group the level 6 goals according to the level 5 goal to which they appear primarily to relate (Figure 3). MATCH and PLAN are exceptions, the former because it is primarily a means of checking the validity of results of all of the other level 6 goals, the latter because it appears to be involved with higher level goals.

The foci often encompass more than one level 6 goal. In many cases this may be merely the associated level 6 goal plus PLAN and/or EXPL. The focus 'Select Database, for instance, was usually found to contain the level 6 goals DB, EXPL and PLAN. However, some foci involved much more complex patterns of level 6 goals, which seems to suggest that while level 6 goals may map onto particular level 5 goals, subsidiary level 6 goals may be called into play within the context of the focus. Some patterns of interaction were so complex, that no single level 6 goal could be identified as the major focus. Thus, we identified the foci 'User Model' and 'Problem Description', which correspond to level 5 goals rather than level 6.

The other crucial dimension in the problem structure is that of time. Initial data indicate that while the sequence of goals is non-linear and iterative, there seem to be particular patterns of sequencing,' perhaps related to other variables such as problem type, intermediary's model of user, and so on. We found, for example, that the Explain focus tended to have an initial level 6 goal sequence of IRS, followed by EXPL, indicating that the intermediaries tend to first assess the user's level of knowledge about the information retrieval system and then supply explanations as appropriate. The sequencing of the goals reflects, perhaps, the nature of the task and the need to conform to Grice's maxim of quantity (Grice, 1975), as much as anything else.

Emerging from the analysis, therefore, is a multidimensional candidate problem structure whose constituent parts are the level 5 goals, and the logical and temporal relations between them. This structure is shown in figure 5. The arrows indicate the direction of input potentially necessary for the accomplishment of the directed-to goal. Input elicited from the user has not been included, although it obviously represents a large proportion of the information input needed to accomplish goals such as user model and problem description.

The foci can be seen as concentrating the participants' attention on the accomplishment of a particular goal, with shifts of focus moving attention from goal to goal across the problem structure (cf. Grosz, 1978). Focussing on a particular level 5 goal may generate the need to acquire input derived from other goals, and thus results in the complex level 6 goal sequences found in the data. Instantiating particular level 6 goal sequences in turn results in the generation of particular sequences of utterances whose purpose is to accomplish the level 5 goals.

Questions still to be answered concern the temporal sequencing of goals, and in particular how the participants decide whether or not a particular goal has been fulfilled. The amount of iteration present in the sequencing of foci suggests that the measure of goal attainment is a dynamic one. New information elicited during a particular focus may propagate through the problem structure and alter the thresholds of other goals; perhaps causing a goal tagged as 'fulfilled' to be retagged 'unfulfilled', and resulting in an eventual focus shift back to the 'unfulfilled' goal. There may also be some weighting of goals according to their perceived importance. This perceived importance may be derived

Figure 5. A problem structure for the document retrieval problem.

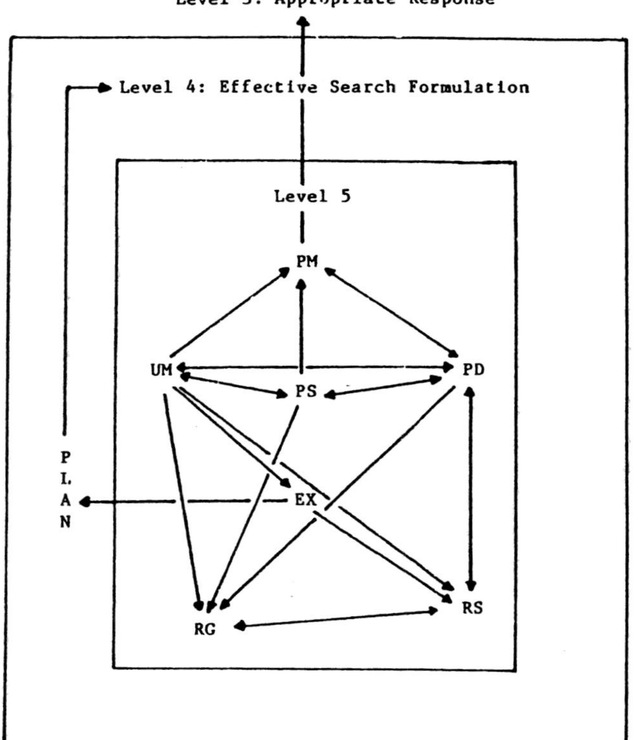

LEVEL 5 GOALS:
PM - Problem Mode; PD - Problem Description; UM - User Model
PS - Problem State; EX - Explain; RG - Response Generator
RS - Retrieval Strategies

Arrows indicate logical (empirically established) relations. Temporal sequence of Level 5 goals approximately from top to bottom, with iteration and recursion.

from variables such as user status, problem type, and so on.

We are as yet a long way from implementing an 'automated intermediary', but we are beginning to determine the essential components and the structure such a system must possess.

5. Conclusions

We have presented here a candidate problem structure for the document retrieval problem, derived from an analysis of online reference interviews. Although the nature of the analysis was different from that carried out to derive the MONSTRAT model, there are points of similarity and indeed, the level 5 goals appear to be the goal equivalents of the MONSTRAT functions. It is also interesting that similar patterns of temporal sequencing were found to those discovered in the MONSTRAT simulation (Belkin, Hennings & Seeger, 1984).

The present analysis has concentrated largely on the structural elements of the discourse, especially in defining the set of foci and goals. We intend now to examine in more detail the temporal aspects, in particular the shifting of foci across the structure, and to look for a set of rules for focus shifts. Another area of examination is the pattern of level 6 goals underlying the foci. We would like to establish which level 6 goals are essential to which foci, and what the temporal relations between level 6 goals might be. Some of these results will be ready by the time of the conference.

What we believe we have demonstrated is that it is possible to analyze some dialogues from the point of view of the problem with which they are concerned, and that by doing this it is possible to derive a problem structure which could be suitable for driving a human-computer dialogue concerned with this problem. We hope that the candidate problem structure which we have developed for the document retrieval problem will provide the basis for the user-computer interactive component of an automated system for end-user access to text data bases.

6. References

BELKIN, N.J., HENNINGS, R.-D. and SEEGER, T. Simulation of a distributed expert-based information provision mechanism. Information Technology: Research and Development, v. 3 (1984): in press.

BELKIN, N.J., ODDY, R.N. and BROOKS, H.M. ASK for information retrieval. Part I: Background and theory; Part II; Results of a design study. Journal of Documentation v.38 nos. 2&3 (1982): 61-71, 145-164.

BELKIN, N.J., SEEGER, T. and WERSIG, G. Distributed expert problem treatment as a model for information system analysis and design. Journal of Information Science v. 5 no. 5 (1983): 153-167.

BELKIN, N.J. and WINDEL, G. Using MONSTRAT for the analysis of information interaction. In: IRFIS 5. Proceedings of the Fifth International Research Forum in Information Science, Heidelberg, 1983. Amsterdam, North Holland, 1984: 359-382.

BROOKS, H.M. and BELKIN, N.J. Using discourse analysis for the design of information retrieval interaction mechanisms. In: Research and Development in Information Retrieval. Proceedings of the Sixth Annual International ACM SIGIR Conference, Washington, D.C. 1983. New York, ACM, 1983: 31-47.

GRICE, H.P Logic and conversation. In: Syntax and semantics, volume 3. Speech Acts. Ed. by P. Cole and J.L. Morgan. New York, Academic Press, 1975: 41-58.

GROSZ, B.J. Discourse knowledge. In: Understanding spoken language. Ed. D.E. Walker. New York, Elsevier-North Holland, 1978: 229-346.

PRICE, L.E.T. Functional and satisfaction analyses of information interaction dialogues. M.Sc. Thesis, Department of Information Science, The City University, London, 1983.

SINCLAIR, J. McH. & COULTHARD, R.M. Towards an analysis of discourse. The English used by teachers and pupils. Oxford, Oxford University Press, 1975.

RELEVANCE: A Review of and a Framework for the Thinking on the Notion in Information Science *

Information science emerged as the third subject, along with logic and philosophy, to deal with relevance—an elusive, human notion. The concern with relevance, as a key notion in information science, is traced to the problems of scientific communication. Relevance is considered as a measure of the effectiveness of a contact between a source and a destination in a communication process. The different views of relevance that emerged are interpreted and related within a framework of communication of knowledge. Different views arose because relevance was considered at a number of different points in the process of knowledge communication. It is suggested that there exists an interlocking, interplaying cycle of various systems of relevances.

Tefko Saracevic
School of Library Science
Case Western Reserve University
Cleveland, OH 44106

• Preface: Where Lies the Importance of Thinking on Relevance?

From the small world of our everyday lives to the large world of mankind, the complexity and interdependence between the spheres of our lives and worlds has increased tremendously and so has our awareness of the ensuing problems. The problems of our civilization and "mankind at the turning point," as documented by Mesarovic and Pestel (*1*), the problems of post-industrial society as envisioned by Bell (*2*), and the problems of modern living and quality of life, as experienced by all of us, have one thing in common: to work toward their rational resolution, we need the resolve and wisdom to act. Knowledge and information are not the only aspects that create a resolve and instill wisdom. But they are important aspects. And the complexity of our present problems has probably made them into the most important aspect.

The effective communication of knowledge—effective information systems—thus becomes a crucial requirement for the resolution of a variety of problems. For different problems, different information systems (libraries included) have been developed or envisioned. Today most, if not all, information systems have one common demand thrust upon them: to increase effectiveness of communication and of services. For instance, the emergence of new services, such as urban information and referral services, and of new concepts in systems, such as information utilities and on-line information retrieval networks, can be directly traced to such a demand and to attempts at resolving some of the above problems.

In the most fundamental sense, relevance has to do with effectiveness of communication. Underlying all information systems is some interpretation of the notion of relevance. In this paper, I intend to explore the meaning of relevance as it has evolved in information science and to provide a framework within which various interpretations of relevance can be related.

Hopefully, the future thinking on relevance may be advanced within the suggested framework. The better we understand the meaning of relevance from different points of view, the better we understand various "systems

*Work in part supported by NSF Grant GN-36085. A version of this article is planned to appear in: *Voigt, M.J.* and *M.H. Harris*, ed., *Advances in Librarianship*, Vol. 6, New York: Academic Press (Planned publication date: 1976).

of relevance" [a term borrowed from philosopher Schutz (*3*)]—the better information systems could be built. In addition, the better we understand relevance, the better chance we have of avoiding failures and of restricting the variety of aberations committed in the name of effective communication. In that lies the importance of advancing the thinking on relevance.

• Introduction: How Relevance in Information Science Is Involved in Controversy and How It Is Interpreted in Other Subjects.

If I were to follow the tradition of much of the writing on relevance in information science, I would start with the often found statement that the understanding of relevance is wrought with controversy, that much of the thinking is muddled philosophical rambling and that the talk about relevance uses a bewildering array of terminology. But if we were to look through the history of science, we would find that such controversy has been a part of the struggle to understand many phenomena and notions in all of scholarship. That is, the evolution of thinking on relevance is no different than the evolution of thinking on so many other notions throughout the history of science.

A "paradigm" of the evolution of thinking on a notion in science can be made: *recognition of a problem*—first simple definitions and statements; *challenge*—refinement and broadening; *restatement*—hypotheses, theories, observations and experiments; *synthesis; restatement; challenge* and so on until the thinking temporarily reaches a satisfactory consensus and resolution (fully understanding that eventually it will be supplanted), a dead end or abandonment. By 1975, the thinking on relevance in information science has reached one of the *challenge* stages (about the third). But, before examining how information science became involved with relevance, let us consider the interpretation of the notion of relevance in other subjects as a broader context that should be taken into account by information scientists and librarians concerned with relevance.

LOGIC

Information science is not the only subject concerned with the notion of relevance. For two thousand years, logicians and philosophers have been struggling with the notion. They have developed extensive theories and interpretations. In logic, the notion of relevance has been involved in specifying and explaining various relationships, especially those of deduction, implication, entailment and logical consequence and to a lesser extent, in induction and concept formation. Relevance is used to state that a necessary condition for the validity of an inference from A to B is that A be relevant to B. In modern times, Carnap [(*4*) and in other works] among others, has extensively discussed relevance and irrelevance, here in regard to probabilities and confirmation of conclusions from premises. Anderson and Belnap (*5*) have vividly pointed out the fallacies of relevance and have provided, within the structure for a pure calculus of entailment, an "axiomatic system that captures the notion of relevance": relevance exhibits the properties of identity, transitivity, permutation and self-distribution.

PHILOSOPHY

Philosophers have involved, in a general way, the notion of relevance in the explanations of "aboutness" and in the theory of meaning. And, in a very specific way, relevance has been involved in explication of relations between different realities. In modern times the most powerful philosophical discussion of relevance was provided by Schutz (*3*) in his posthumously published notes. Schutz was concerned with making it possible to understand "what makes the social world tick," that is what makes it at once social and world. He contended that the social world ("lifeworld") is not simply one homogeneous affair, rather it is articulated or stratified into different realities, with relevance being the principle at the root of the stratification of the "lifeworld." Schutz elucidated three basic interdependent systems of relevances: *topical relevances, motivational relevances* and *interpretational relevances.* The circular interrelationship between the three systems has been graphically represented as shown in Fig. 1.

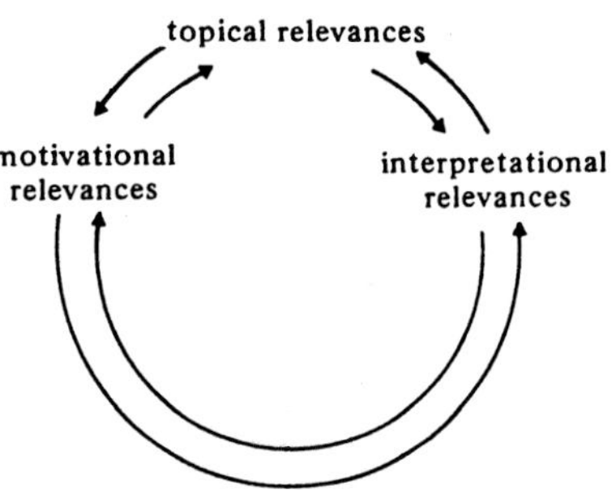

Fig. 1.

First are the topical relevances which involve perception of something being problematic "in the midst of the unstructuralized field of unproblematic familiarity." Interpretive relevances involve the stock of knowledge at hand in grasping the meaning of that which is perceived. Motivational relevances refer to the course of action to be adopted. The goals of such action motivates in turn the process of obtaining additional interpretative material; the perception may also be affected in this dynamic interaction.

INTERACTION

The thinking in logic has provided some information scientists [*e.g.*, Hillman (*6*), Cooper (*7*)] with a necessary framework for their theoretical work on relevance. However, the thinking in philosophy, unfortunately, has not been directly recognized by any information scientists to date, although such works as that by Schutz, may have provided a direct framework for some of the views on relevance in information science [*e.g.*, Foskett (*8*), Wilson (*9*), Kemp (*10*) and others]. Generally, some arguments that were already argued out may have been avoided.

Some other subjects have dealt with relevance, but none as directly and extensively as logic and philosophy. These subjects are sociology, in the sociology of knowledge; psychology, in the studies of perception, learning, and capacity of memory; and linguistics, in the studies of semantics and pragmatics. It has remained for information science to struggle with relevance in relation to communication and to emerge as the third subject that directly contributed to the thinking on that so elusive and so human a notion.

• How Information Science Became Involved with Relevance.

Relevance was the key notion in the emergence of information science and it has remained the basic notion in most of its theories and all of its practice. Thus, a review of relevance has to begin with a review of information science.

A field of activity and a subject of study are defined, fundamentally, by the problems attacked and operationally by the solutions offered and methods used, that is, by the work done. As problems and/or solutions change over time, specific definitions of a field or subject change as well.

Information science is a field and a subject that is concerned with problems arising in communication of knowledge in general and with records in such communication in particular, from both applied and basic points of view. It shares this concern with other fields, notably those of librarianship and of documentation; thus, this sharing of concerns specifies the fundamental relationship between information science and librarianship. It follows that the thinking on relevance in information science should be of direct interest to librarianship and vice versa.

We may further define information science by enumerating the areas of applied (*i.e.*, professional or practical) and of basic (scientific) concerns and work. Of major interest to practical applications of information science have been: 1) technical aspects of the communication of knowledge, which involve a variety of applications of information technology for information processing and transmission; 2) representational aspects, which involve the development of a variety of languages, vocabularies and classifications for representing information, various types of file organization and procedures and logic for retrieval; 3) systems aspects which involve the design, development and operations of a variety of information systems in general and information retrieval (IR) systems in particular, and also involve the development of complex information networks and of an information industry.

On the theoretical side, information science studies have dealt with the behavior and effects of information as a phenomenon and communication as a process; information users and uses; the processes in and evaluation of information systems; and finally, the various aspects of the ecological environment of information systems, such as the structure of scientific and other literatures and the structure and relations in scientific and other social communications. Quantitative studies involving characteristics and empirical laws in communication have created study areas of their own under the names of bibliometrics and scientometrics (a more appropriate universal term may be "informetrics, in line with sociometics, econometics, psychometrics, etc.). Studies in the ecology of communication have carved out for information science a scientific problem area, which is contributing to the coagulation of information science as a scientific subject.

But why has all this happened? Why has information science emerged on its own and not as part of librarianship or documentation, which would be most logical? It has to do with relevance.

Why, then, has relevance emerged as a central notion of information science? It has to do with interpretation of the problems in scientific communication.

SCIENTIFIC COMMUNICATION

Although it proliferated into other areas, information science has its roots in the problem encountered in scientific communication. So has documentation, one of its predecessors. To achieve an understanding of relevance and indeed of information science, as well as some understanding of relations between information science and documentation and between information science and librarianship, one has to achieve some understanding of the nature of scientific communication.

Modern science has developed a particular mechanism of communication which began with the appearance of the first scientific journals in the 17th Century and has remained the same to this date. This mechanism is based on the following: the systematic and selective publication of fragments of work–items of knowledge related to a broader problem rather than complete treatises; the selective derivation from and selective integration into a network of other works; and an evaluation before and after publication. All of this is ultimately aimed toward the creation of what Ziman (*11*) calls "public knowledge," that is "the aim of scientists is to create, criticize and contribute to a rational consensus of ideas and information."

It is this selective concern with fragments of knowledge that is enabling effective functioning of science and that has led to concern with relevance. That is, to be effective, scientific communication, and indeed science itself, has to deal not with any old kind of information but with relevant information. And the history of science is the history of that effectiveness.

Ziman (*12*), Price (*13*) and others have pointed out that the invention of the mechanism for the systematic publication of fragments of scientific work may well have been the key event in the history of modern science. This invention has enabled science to grow so much faster than the rest of scholarship.

There are many other aspects that play a role in scientific communication (*e.g.*, invisible colleges, conferences, professional societies, the system of recognition and challenge, and the whole governance of science). However, all follow from and end up in this particular selective mechanism.

BALANCING COMMUNICATION ECOLOGY

Over these last three centuries, communication in science has developed into an ecological system with elaborately organized and interdependent subsystems or strata [Warren and Goffman (*14*)]. Periodically, there have been upsets in that ecology caused by various factors. In this century such upsets have been caused by a combination of effects due to: 1) the large quantitative increases in the number of scientists and subsequently in the number of publications; 2) the qualitative difficulties in selection; 3) the breakdown of boundaries between subjects and 4) the increases in specializations. As a consequence of the ecological imbalances and the resultant problems in scientific communication, fields of activity have emerged that are directly and primarily concerned with a study of and a *fix* for these upsets.

At the turn of this century documentation emerged, which defined the problem at that time as one of the organization of knowledge; thus, it developed a concern with classification, indexing, etc. Indexing and abstracting services emerged as a *fix*. After the second World War information science emerged, which defined the problem at that time as one of providing the scientist with information; thus it developed a *concern with relevance* for it was perceived that the *amounts* of nonrelevance endanger communication. Information retrieval systems emerged applying a *technological fix* to the problem.

Shera and Egan (*15*) thought that the emergence of documentation was due to the "failure of librarianship" to address itself to the problem of scientific communication. In turn, one may think that the emergence of information science is due to the failure of documentation to address itself to the problems of the output of scientific communication. However, fields do not really develop because of the failure of other fields, but because they carve out a problem area for themselves and because they build a rational consensus of ideas and information about the problem that leads to solution. The success or failure lies in the adequacy of defining and then addressing the problem. The success of information science, whatever there is, is due to the fact that it did address itself to relevance, and the failure, whatever it may be, will be because it did not address relevance adequately.

INFORMATION AND RELEVANT INFORMATION

As far as I can determine, S.C. Bradford was the first one to use the term *relevant* in the context that it is used today in information science. In the 1930's and 40's, he talked about articles "relevant to a subject." In the 40's and 50's, development of information retrieval (IR) systems began. From the onset, the main objective of IR systems was a provision of relevant information to users. A worldwide consensus emerged on that.

The distinction between *information* and *relevant information* was made in recognition of the selective mechanism of scientific communication and in order to underline the user orientation of IR systems. However, that distinction, although intuitively quite clear, became and has remained a major point of discord due to a lack of a consensus on meaning. From the outset it was recognized that relevance indicates a relation. But what relations does it involve? Between what elements? What factors affect the relation? The thinking on relevance in information science evolved around these questions and so has the controversy. To understand the thinking and possibly unravel the controversy, we first have to build a framework within which this could be achieved, a framework within which the thinking on relevance can be advanced.

• How to Construct a Framework for Viewing Relevance from Intuitive Understanding and Then on to More Elaborate Communication Models.

INTUITIVE UNDERSTANDING

Intuitively, we understand quite well what relevance means. It is a primitive "y' know" concept, as is information for which we hardly need a definition. When in communication with no particular outcome in mind (small talk, for instance), relevance plays little or no role. However, if and when any productive contact is desired, consciously or not, we involve and use this intuitive notion of relevance. This affects the whole process of communication, overtly or subtly. Thus, our intuitive understanding of relevance has something to do with productive, effective communication—how well the process was conducted, how good were the results. Relevance is, then, a fundamental aspect of human communication.

We also understand intuitively that this effectiveness, this productivity, depends on a great many factors which could involve different criteria. And like so many other things in life, relevance is relative. Some things are more relevant than others, some things are not relevant any more, and some have a chance of becoming relevant. Relevance depends a great deal on what we already know and on what is generally known. We must admit that there are various aspects that at times predominate in determining relevance, such as: what we think we want and how we ask for it; how we understand what is asked and what we think is really asked; what is wanted in contrast to what is really needed; who is asked, who is asking; what the situation is; what will be done with what is provided; and so on. In other words, we know that we can look at relevance from different points of view. And that is the problem.

COMMUNICATION

To create a framework for reviewing and relating the different views of relevance in information science, first we have to consider the process of communication. Communication is a process where something called information is transmitted from one object to another [Goffman (*16*), via Shannon-Weaver (*17*), via Aristotle]. The first object can be called the source; the second, the destination. A dynamic, interactive feedback can occur between a source and a destination; they can exchange roles [Wiener (*18*)]. Communication can be considered as a process on its own, as Shannon did in information theory, or as a process effecting other processes, as Wiener did in founding Cybernetics. That is, the role of environment can be considered. We may not know what information is as a phenomenon, any more than we know what energy, matter, gravity or electricity is; but we can study its behavior and effects. As Shannon and Weaver pointed out, three levels of problems can occur in communication: 1) technical, 2) semantic, and 3) behavioral. Semantic problems obviously also involve the technical and behavioral problems involve the other two.

In this context of communication and communication problems, we can consider *relevance as a measure* of the effectiveness of a contact between a source and a destination in a communication process.* And, since a measure is a relation, relevance is also a relation.

COMMUNICATION OF KNOWLEDGE

Communication is used in many diverse contexts; *e.g.*, media, signal transmission, speech and hearing, rhetoric, propaganda, advertising, medicine, psychoanalysis, etc. Thus, communication has related but different connotations. *Information* is used in Roget in at least seven diverse senses; and, when considering synonyms, there are over 100 associated words. In Shannon's information theory, information is restricted to the context of signals; information is very specifically defined as a property of a collection of coded signals or messages which reduce the receiver's uncertainty about which message is sent. Information theory treats only the technical problems of communication.

In information science, the connotation of *communication* and *information* is extended to, and limited to, the context of *knowledge* as used in the theory of knowledge. Information science attempts to treat all three levels of communication problems. For information science to keep this context and connotation in mind, we use the term *communication of knowledge*, although strictly speaking it is not knowledge but data, information or information conveying objects that are being transmitted.† In simple terms, the distinction is as between "to know" and "to inform."

We may think of public knowledge as being organized into a structure of subjects, represented in a language and recorded into a literature, elements of which can be called documents. Broadly speaking then, subject knowledge is represented by subject literature; thus, documents may convey information. The structures of subject knowledge and of subject literature, although related, are not the same. And the structure of linguistics or other symbolic representations is still different.

Both a source and a destination involved in the communication of knowledge have, as one of the elements, a file (or files) where subject knowledge and/or its representations are stored in an organized manner. (Examples of files are memory, library collection, catalog, computer file, data bank, store of sentences, and the like.) *Communication of knowledge is effective when and if information that is transmitted from one file results in changes in another. Relevance is the measure of these changes.*

Changes consist of additions to, deletions from, or reorganization of the files of knowledge and/or the files of representations. One can take a much broader view and argue that communication of knowledge is effective when and if it has directly observable results, such as changes in actions or behavior. The argument is grossly

*There is a great distinction between a measure (*e.g.*, time), a measuring unit (hour), a measuring instrument (watch) and measuring (determining elapsed time between events). We can consider revelance as a measure without defining other aspects. In information science a persistent confusion between these aspects exists, especially in test and evaluation.

†For the explication of important distinctions and relations between data, information, knowledge, understanding and wisdom, as well as between fact-retrieval, document-retrieval and question-answering, which fall broadly within information-retrieval, see Kochen (*19*). For information science an applicable definition is given by Bell (*2*). "Knowledge is a set of organized statements of facts or ideas, presenting a reasoned judgment or an experimental result, which is transmitted to others through some communication medium in some systematic form." And public knowledge, as mentioned before, is applicably defined by Ziman (*11, 12*), as "a rational consensus of ideas and information."

deficient in that such results are effected by a great many other factors, in addition to and unrelated to, the communication of knowledge.

In any case, since so many elements are involved in the communication of knowledge and in its effectiveness, relevance can be considered from different points of view (*e.g.*, involving elements of subject knowledge, of subject literature, of any representation of the source's file, of the destination's file, or of the processes). One can consider them separately or together in various combinations or in various hierarchies. And there are still other aspects to consider.

INFORMATION SYSTEMS

Imbedded in the communication of knowledge may be information systems which are aimed at enabling, enhancing, preserving or extending the process. And associated with such systems are sources and files. An information system selects from existing subject knowledge, subject literature and/or any of its representations, organizes the selections in some manner in its files, and disseminates the selections in some manner to given destinations. Other communication systems, such as signal transmission systems, graphic reproduction systems and computing systems, can be associated with information systems.

A variety of information systems has been built for a variety of types of communication of knowledge, uses, conditions and environments; desires for effectiveness or efficiency; and understandings of what the information problems are. Underlying all of them, one can find explicitly stated or implicity assumed some interpretation of the notion of relevance. Therefore, when considering relevance, one may also have to involve aspects of information systems. And there are still other aspects to consider.

ENVIRONMENT; VALUES

Communication of knowledge and information systems can be considered by themselves, but they do not exist in a vacuum. They operate within, by means of, and under constraints imposed by their environment. They affect and are affected by the environment. The same knowledge communication process, the same information system, can be related to a number of realities of an environment, to a number of environments and can perform many functions.

Knowledge, information, communication, information systems—all are imbedded in, all reflect some system of human values—ethical, social, philosophical, political, religious and/or legal values. Therefore, when considering relevance, one may also involve aspects of the environments, realities and values.

SUMMARY

Given that, in the context of information science, relevance is considered as a measure of the effectiveness of the contact between a source and a destination in a communication process (with all the other considerations described) —then, in considering what factors and relations are involved in relevance, we can consider the various elements or aspects of the:

1. Subject knowledge,
2. Subject literature,
3. Any other linguistic or symbolic representation,
4. Source, especially the file or files,
5. Destination, especially the file or files,
6. Information systems,
7. Environments, realities, functions and
8. Values.

The majority of works on relevance in information science have concentrated on determining:

1. What factors or elements enter into the notion of relevance?
2. What relation does the notion of relevance specify?

The controversy stems either from insistence that *only* some of the enumerated factors or relations are *the* factors or relations, or from the failure to recognize the existence of some other factors. The confusion stems from a very low adherence to the basics of semantic hygiene.

I wish to suggest that all the works, views and ensuing conflicts on relevance that have emerged so far in information science can be interpreted within the above framework. Moreover, I suggest that when and if a complete theory of relevance emerges in the context of information science, it will have to emerge within this framework and incorporate at least the enumerated aspects.

• How the *System's View* of Relevance Developed and How *IT* Has Been Challenged.

LOGIC OF RETRIEVAL

The Second World War spurred unprecedented scientific and technological activity resulting in a mass of reports and literature. The end of the War brought suggestions (as by Vannevar Bush) to apply the emerging computer technology to control records of science and technology. As a result, information retrieval (IR) systems emerged in the late 40's and early 50's, developed by such pioneers as Taube, Perry, Mooers and Luhn. Principles of information retrieval that were laid down then have remained to this day.

It has been accepted explicitly or implicitly that the main objective of an IR system is to retrieve information relevant to user queries. The logic of search and retrieval is based on the algebra of sets, Boolean algebra, which is well formulated and thus easily applicable to computer manipulations. Inherent in the application of this logic is the fundamental assumption: those documents (answers, facts, data) retrieved are also those relevant to the query; those not retrieved are not relevant. In some systems documents can be ordered (evaluated, associated) as to their relevance and retrieved when some specified threshold is reached, and even presented in some ordered form; but, even here, the assumption that retrieved/not retrieved corresponds to *relevant/not relevant* still holds.

FALSE DROPS

The early pioneers quite correctly recognized that not all that will be retrieved will be relevant [Mooers (*20*), Perry (*21*) and Taube (*22*)]. Their concern was with non-relevance, with unwanted retrieval, rather than relevance. They diagnosed that the *false drops, noise, false coordinations* and *extra tallies* are due to internal malpractices—the ineffectiveness of whatever document representation was used and/or the inadequacy in the way these were applied. Thus, the *system's view* of relevance was a result of the thinking that relevance is mostly affected by the internal aspects and manipulations of the system. Relevance was conceived in terms of indexing, coding, classification, linguistic manipulations, file organization, and eventually question analysis and searching strategies. This thinking led to development of a myriad of schemes, and to attention to input processing and manipulation almost to the exclusion of other aspects. In theoretical works, linguistics has been the subject of a great deal of attention because it is believed that it will lead to better representation schemes.

COMPLETENESS OF VIEW

Clearly, internal aspects of any system affect its performance. How a source manipulates information certainly influences the effectiveness of the contact with a destination, but it is not the exclusive aspect that enters into considerations of relevance. Therefore, the system's view of relevance, although correct, is incomplete. However, the most glaring incompleteness of that view does not lie in the fact that it does not recognize other aspects, but in the fact that it does not recognize selection into the system per se as one of the system's aspects that enters into relevance. As a result, to this date, selection into IR systems remains an aspect to which little attention is paid—articles on the topic of selection are scarce, investigations are few.

However, there has been another school of thinking, though it has not gained wide acceptance, in which selection into the system is the most important aspect that enters into relevance (exposed mostly by information scientists from Battelle Memorial Institute). Information analysis centers have developed as a result of this view. Since this view has not received a broader support of the people in the field, relatively few information analysis centers are in existence.

FIRST CHALLENGE

The challenge to the simplicity of the *system's view* began with the 1958 International Conference for Scientific Information (*23*). Later more substantiated challenges were offered in serious attempts to construct a theoretical framework for relevance [Hillman (*6*) and Goffman (*24*)]. Among others, these suggestions were offered:

1. The notion of relevance should be considered independently and prior to any particular method of representation or IR system;
2. There is a relevance to a subject;
3. Relevance is multivalued, a matter of degree, and not a simple yes/no decision;
4. Relevance of given documents may change as a result of other documents, as stock of knowledge at hand changes.

As powerful as these arguments were; they really did not succeed in widely spreading a different view of relevance. It remained for the great debate that followed the first attempts to test and evaluate IR systems to swing the pendulum to an opposite view.

TEST AND EVALUATION

Pioneers of IR development were, by and large, engineers and scientists. It was logical for them to think of testing a system or a method as soon as it was conceived. The first quantitative measuring units proposed were the familiar recall and precision* by Kent, Perry and associates (*25*). Although often challenged as to their adequacy, these or similar measuring units have remained in use to this day, and their use has spread worldwide. (There is a whole literature and many theoretical works on measuring units for IR systems, but they are not of direct interest to considerations of the notion of relevance.) Underlying these measuring units is relevance as a measure, as a criterion that reflects the performance of IR systems. Relevance was selected as a result of the recognition that the prime objective of IR systems is to provide relevant information to user queries.

The testing of IR systems began in the 1950's as unverified claims and counterclaims mounted and as investments rose. During the late 50's and early 60's, large scale tests conducted by C. Cleverdon at Cranfield and later tests by others caught universal attention. The number of papers reporting results was small, but the number of papers discussing the tests was very large. The

**Recall* is the ratio of relevant answers retrieved over the total number of relevant answers in the file. *Precision* is the ratio of relevant answers retrieved over the total number of answers retrieved. Precision was originally called relevance, but the name was changed because of complaints of semantic confusion.

great testing debate of information science ensued with periodic ripples to this date. The debate did not concentrate at all on the results but on the methods, and the central issue was a measuring methodology. How was the relevance of the answers determined? How should it be determined? Who are to be the relevance judges? How is the relevance judgment to be passed?

The debate imperceptibly, but completely, shifted the problem of relevance from the source to the *destination*. At issue was relevance judgment. The thinking that the notion of relevance is most connected to user judgment, or the *destination's view* of relevance, was born.

- **How the *Destination's View* Emerged Equating Relevance with Relevance Judgment and How Experimentation Was Spurred.**

The great testing debate in the early and mid-60's in large part turned into a relevance debate. As a result, relevance definitions proliferated by the dozen and a few hypotheses emerged. Eventually, two schools of thought developed.

One school has suggested that relevance is such an elusive and subjective property that it cannot serve as a criterion for performance testing [*e.g.*, Doyle (*26*)]. The other school took the view that experimentation with revelance judgments should precede adoption or non-adoption of relevance as performance criterion [*e.g.*, Cuadra (*27*)]. Thus, psychology entered information science largely as a result of concern with relevance, or rather with relevance judgments.

In 1964, the National Science Foundation called an invitational conference of leaders in the field to assess the results of IR testing and to chart new paths. One of the conclusions stated that the "major obstacle to progress in evaluation of IR systems is the lack of sufficient knowledge regarding. . .human assessments of the relevance of retrieved documents" (*28*). This spurred experimentation with relevance judgments, which in turn solidified the *destination's view* of relevance. Experiments were clearly affected by the definitions and hypotheses that emerged.

DEFINITIONS

Numerous definitions of relevance were offered in the 60's, mainly as a result of the criticism that it is not clear what the term means. There was a rather naive belief that a *good* definition by itself would make it clear and that the controversy would then go away. A *good* definition, in this context, referred to a paraphrase. By themselves, paraphrases, of course, do no such thing. However, relevance definitions were a form of hypotheses enumerating factors that entered into the relations. Thus, the definitions played an important role in setting the boundaries of experiments. Definitions fell into a general pattern:

> Relevance is the *A* of a *B* existing between a *C* and a *D* as determined by an *E*.

In various definitions the slots were filled with fillers such as these:

A	*B*	*C*
measure degree dimension estimate appraisal relation	corresondence utility connection satisfaction fit bearing matching	document article textual form reference information provided fact

D	*E*
query request information used point of view information requirement statement	person judge user requester information specialist

As an aid to their experiments, Cuadra and Katter (*29*) established this definition:

> Relevance is the correspondence in context between an information requirement statement and an article; *i.e.*, the extent to which the article covers material that is appropriate to the requirement statement.

The most obvious criticism of these, as all other paraphrasing type definitions, is that they do not first establish primitive terms and then proceed to more complex definitions, using proofs or evidence where necessary; but they simply substitute terms that are as undefined as the term which they tried to define was at the outset. The most obvious advantage of paraphrasing definitions is that such definitions provide a preliminary context for further work.

HYPOTHESES

The hypotheses offered in relation to experimentation with relevance judgments by and large concentrated on enumerating and classifying the factors that affect relevance judgments. For instance, Rees and Saracevic (*30*) hypothesized on the variables and conditions under which the judgment would achieve a high degree of agreement. O'Connor (*31*) concentrated on the reasons for relevance judgments disagreements, on conditions under which agreement may or may not coincide, and related these conditions to unclearness. Cuadra and Katter (*29*) provided the handiest classification scheme and the largest enumeration of factors affecting relevance judgment. They suggested the following general classes of variables that affect relevance judgment:

1. Documents and document representation,
2. Queries (or as they said: "Information Requirement Statements"),
3. Judgmental situations and conditions,
4. Modes of expression, and
5. People (judges).

All the hypotheses have given no direct consideration to the *system's view* of relevance. However, by acknowledging that documents and document representations are some of the factors affecting relevance judgment, a relation between the *system's view* and the *destination's view* of relevance is established.

The most obvious criticism of all the offered hypotheses is that they are not like rigid scientific hypotheses that can be directly tested under controlled conditions. They are axiomatic in nature, somewhat extending previous definitions and classifications. Still they have been a step in the right direction for they have led toward experimentally observed evidence and away from anecdotal types of evidence.

EXPERIMENTS

The first experimental observation related to relevance was reported in 1961. Until 1970, about two dozen experiments were reported. No experiments directly dealing with relevance were reported after 1970, as far as I can determine. Synthesis of the experiments is presented in the *Appendix.* The relatively small number of experiments, and the evident moratorium on relevance experimentation after 1970, may look strange, but it should be put in the context of the activities in the field of information science. The field is highly pragmatic; funds are expended mostly for practical and technological achievements; research funding is not as forthcoming in the 70's as it was in the 60's; and research interests have shifted.

All of the experiments could be criticized easily for methodological deficiencies, with some praised for their achievements. [For a lengthy review see Saracevic (*32*).] However, the experiments do offer important clues as to the nature of some of the factors that affect human revelance judgments. For some factors the experimental results provide ballpark estimates of the comparative extent to which they affect relevance judgments. For practitioners and researchers, these experimental findings could be of interest by themselves.

COMPLETENESS OF VIEW

The *destination's view* of relevance has concentrated on factors that affect human relevance judgment. It has equated relevance with relevance judgment. Certainly these factors affect relevance, but they are still only one of the aspects that influences the measure of the effectiveness of the contact between a source and a destination in a communication process. The destination's view is not incorrect at all. As is the *system's view*, it is merely incomplete.

As mentioned, there were a few hypotheses suggested and a few experiments carried out. But we cannot assume that the hypotheses and experiments dealt with all, or even most, of the factors related to human relevance judgments. To the contrary, they just scratched the surface; the area is in dire need of further hypotheses and experiments.

One of the most obvious aspects not investigated is the effect of the limitations of human memory on relevance judgments. Miller (*33*) and others discussed "the magical number seven" as describing limits of human information processing. As the effect of selection from the subject has not been investigated from the *system's view*, the effect of another type of selection has also not been investigated from the *destination's view*, namely the selection due to the limitation of human memory in information processing. Such limitation is fully recognized in the practice of providing information. The effectiveness of communication and this process of selection are closely related. This has not been investigated, and it would be a most promising and important area of study.

• How Bibliometrics Evolved and How It Is Related to the *Subject Literature View* of Relevance.

Up to the 1970's, most of the works directly concerned with relevance in information science have concentrated either on *system's* or on *destination's* view of relevance. However, chronologically speaking, both of these views were preceded by the *subject literature view* of relevance. As mentioned, S.C. Bradford was concerned in the 1930's and 40's with articles "relevant to a subject." His work pioneered the area that later became known as bibliometrics, the "quantitative treatment of the properties of recorded discourse and behavior appertaining to it" [Fairthorne (*34*)]. Although some bibliometric work was continued in the 40's and 50's, it wasn't until the 60's that work in bibliometrics started attracting more people and more attention; and it wasn't until the 70's that it started to blossom.

In bibliometrics a number of empirical laws have been uncovered, theories have been suggested and quantitative observations have been made. But the strength of the work in bibliometrics lies in the direct connection between empirical laws and theories on one hand, and observation on the other. (Unfortunately, by the way, this is not usual in most areas of work in information science or librarianship, including relevance.) Excellent reviews of bibliometric works have appeared, such as that by Fairthorne (*34*), who concentrated on showing relationship between various bibliometric and other hyperbolic distributions; by Brookes (*35*), who summarized bibliometric applications of significance to information science and librarianship; by Line and Sandison (*36*), who synthesized approximately 180 studies that deal with obsolescence and changes in use of literature over time. Admittedly, bibliometric works have not been concerned with relevance, not directly; but even if not mentioned or realized, a concern with relevance is fundamental to most bibliometric works and also to bibliographic controls. Let me elaborate further on this point and suggest the nature of the *subject literature view* of relevance.

DISTRIBUTIONS: BRADFORD, LOTKA, ZIPF AND/OR MANDELBROT

Originally Bradford was interested in the rate that given sources, such as journals, contained items (articles) relevant to a given subject; he was interested in the pattern of a statistical distribution which will describe the relation between a quantity (journals) and a yield (articles). He observed that the scatter of articles on a subject across journals in which they appeared forms a regular pattern of diminishing returns, and he stated his law of literature scatter.*

For a century or so, a similar statistical relation between a quantity and a yield was observed in relation to many phenomena (*e.g.*, Pareto distribution of income). Explanations and interpretations were given according to the interests of the subject and the nature of the phenomena. In other words, a similar statistical distribution described patterns of many phenomena without assuming proximity of causes. The distributions afford a method of description (conformity or non-conformity) and prediction. They do not describe the underlying causes and mechanisms. In information science, the family of these distributions was given the names of Bradford, Lotka, Zipf and/or Mandelbrot (*see* Fairthorne's review).

Lotka (*38*) investigated the productivity of authors in scientific subjects: he found that a large proportion of literature is produced by a small number of authors distributed so that the number of people producing n papers is approximately proportional to $1/n^2$. Zipf (*39*) investigated distribution of words in a text. The finding is similar: a small number of words appear very often and the frequency of use of words falls off in a regular pattern—if the words are ranked by frequency of appearance in a text, then rank times frequency is approximately constant. Price (*40*) investigated the pattern of citation networks and found that the number of papers cited at frequencies above average is small, forming a "research front." Urquhart (*41*) investigated the patterns of use of periodicals from a large scientific library; the use was heavily oriented toward a small portion of the collection. Saracevic (*42*) studied the distribution of documents retrieved as answers from an experimental IR system; he found that the distribution follows Bradford's law—taking all queries together, a small number of documents were repeatedly retrieved as answers forming a nucleus, with the rest falling off in the expected Bradford pattern. Then the relevance judgments of users on the same retrieved answers was studied; many were judged not relevant, but the distribution of those documents that were judged relevant again conformed to Bradford's law. Numerous other studies could be cited on the same or similar aspects—studies related to the use of libraries and of literature, distribution of index terms in subject indexes, citation patterns, etc. The observed statistical distributions are similar.

*Bradford (*37*) formulated the law as follows:
"... .if scientific journals are arranged in order of decreasing productivity of articles on a given subject, they may be divided into a nucleus of periodicals more particularly devoted to the subject and several groups or zones containing the same number of articles as the nucleus, where the number of periodicals in the nucleus and succeeding zones will be as $1:n:n^2:n^3$ ...."

SUBJECT LITERATURE VIEW OF RELEVANCE

Attempts were made to associate some of the facts studied in bibliometrics and the notion of relevance. In the Soviet Union, Kozachkov (*43*) related the notion of relevance to the "process of scientific cognition" and described various aspects of scientific literature as growth, scatter and obsolescence in terms of their relation to relevance. Saracevic (*32, 42*) synthesized a number of the distributions and findings in bibliometrics and interpreted them in terms of relevance calling them "relevance related distributions." The appearance of articles in journals, the contribution of authors to literature, the networks of citations, the changes in the use and the obsolescence of literature, the use of literature from libraries or IR systems, etc., are all manifestations of communications of knowledge. Sometimes it is not realized that these and similar manifestations are not independent of each other, even though they may be viewed one at a time. They are manifestations of a larger whole; namely, they relate to the structure of subject literatures. I wish to suggest that underlying all the above manifestations of communication of knowledge is the notion of relevance. These manifestations form the *subject literature view* of relevance.

So far, the investigations in information science have concentrated mostly on the statistical distribution patterns of these various manifestations. Obviously distribution patterns are but one aspect to be investigated; so much more remains to be learned even with regard to distributions. Still, what is emerging is a picture of the structure of subject literatures, of the patterns of what went on and what is going on. Needless to say, a rational forecast of what may be expected to be going on in the subject literatures, and with what probability, is dependent on the degree and the depth of familiarity with their structure. Here lies the great practical importance of works on the structure of subject literatures.

Of critical importance would be to investigate the mechanism that operates to form the given structure of subject literatures over time. As suggested by many, the mechanism underlying the investigated distribution is one of selection, a "success-breeds-success" mechanism, a Darwinian mechanism. Previously I suggested that the notion of relevance underlies the described manifestations. In generalizing, I wish to suggest that notion of relevance underlies all of the *mechanisms* that form the structure of subject literatures. Therefore, the notion of relevance also underlies the *structure* of the subject literature itself. I suggest that the given mechanisms exist and the given structures are found because of the requirements of effective communications necessary for survival, procreation and use of the subject knowledge. Thus, an association between relevance and the structure of subject literature exists as well. We may better understand both the structure of subject literature and the notion of relevance if we explore their association.

COMPLETENESS OF THE VIEW

Effectiveness of communication depends on many factors. Various views on relevance result from considering the effectiveness at different points of the process. Thus emerged different classification of the factors with different priorities. None of the views is by itself incorrect, but taking only one view is incomplete. Along with the *system's* and the *destination's* view of relevance, we may add the *subject literature view* of relevance. This view can be built around considerations of the structure of subject literatures. The view has not been developed to any extent yet, but there is a start. It is premature to talk about the completeness of the view.

The importance of the *subject literature view* of relevance to other views and to the total knowledge communication process, especially where information systems are involved, is great. For information systems, the process starts with subject literatures. The aim of information systems is to enable and to enhance contact between subject literature and users—destinations. Therefore, subject literature affects all aspects. The *system's view* of relevance has to take into account that selection from the literature to the system influences effectiveness of the source. The *destination's view* of relevance has to take into account that answers can be provided only within the subject knowledge and subject literature. This provides for a relation between the three views.

• How Splitting of the Notion Began and the *Subject Knowledge View* of Relevance Resulted.

In the early 1960's, direct suggestions that relevance involved numerous relations and that a distinction should be made between various relations were forthcoming. Most often a distinction was made between relevance and pertinence, stemming originally from the distinction made between a question and an information need.

THE CONCEPT OF INFORMATION NEED

Experience has taught us that at times, often unintentionally, a question does not exactly coincide with what a questioner had on his/her mind, that it may be difficult to verbalize a question even if it is in one's mind, and that people may tend to answer what they think the questioner should have asked, rather than answer the question as formulated.

Operationally in IR systems and libraries, question analyses, reference interviews, and the like are aimed at clarifying the questions and reducing any differences between the question as asked and the question in one's mind. The questioner's stock of knowledge at hand and the intended use of answers are also often probed to help in the provision of the most related answer.

Out of these experiences and out of the sociological concepts of *need* and *need-event* came the concept of information need in information science. Information need is a psychological state associated with uncertainty, and with the desire to know an unknown. "It is not directly observable. . . but it has a definite existence in the mind of the user at least and so it is useful to have a term by which one may refer to it." [Cooper (*7*)]. But the concept of information need has had its fierce critics in information science, as the general concept of need has had in sociology: "Numerous explanations, all unclear. . . sacred expression. . .cover up for question negotiation. . ." [O'Connor (*44*)]. However, to this date the concept of information need remains chiefly to distinguish between a state of the mind and the subsequent representation in a question.

PERTINENCE

The concept of information need brought out the notion of pertinence. Numerous authors made this following or similar distinction [*e.g.*, Rees and Saracevic (*45*)]. The question-asking, question-answering process can be represented by the diagram in Fig. 2.

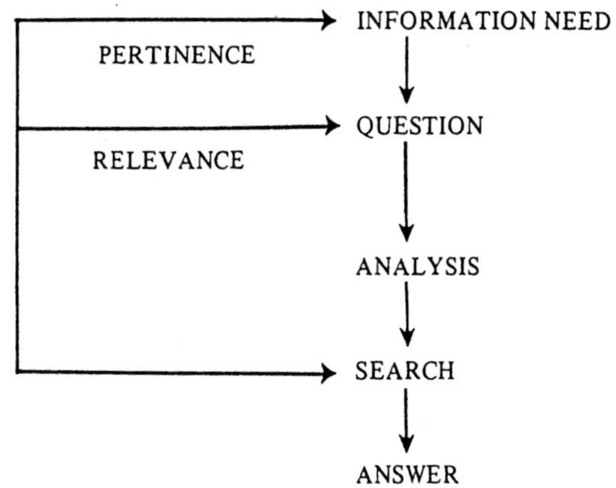

Fig. 2.

Relevance is the property which assigns certain members of a file (*e.g.*, documents) to the question; *pertinence* is the property which assigns them to the information need [Goffman and Newill (*46*)]. Subsequently, (as known from experience) some relevant answers are also pertinent; but there could be relevant answers that are not pertinent and pertinent answers that are not relevant. It has often been argued that, from the user's point of view, desirable answers are pertinent answers; but, in reality, an IR system can only provide relevant answers. That is, a system can only answer questions. It can only guess what the information need is. In practice, there is often a real tug of war in trying to satisfy information needs and not just answer questions.

FOSKETT'S PUBLIC KNOWLEDGE–PRIVATE KNOWLEDGE

Although information need is a satisfactory concept from a practical point of view, from a more theoretical point of view the whole concept of *need* in explaining states of mind, stocks of knowledge at hand, and ensuing changes is neither satisfactory nor comfortable. Given that a distinction between relevance and pertinence is to be made, many have felt that an explanation away from information need is required. Cooper (*7*) in defining logical relevance (discussed in a later section entitled, "How Theories of Relevance Have Covered Different Aspects and Why They Are Important") inspired a different explanation although he kept to the concept of an information need.

In a brief note, Foskett (*8*) suggested a different distinction between pertinence and relevance. Taking Ziman's "public knowledge" and augmenting it with Kuhn's paradigm on the pattern of thinking in a given field of science Foskett suggested that "relevance means being a part of a paradigm, or public knowledge, or consensus in a field; pertinence means related to the specific pattern of thought in a specific reader's mind."

KEMP'S PAIRS

Kemp (*10*) builds further from Foskett and discusses relevance and pertinence as related to public knowledge and private knowledge. He suggests that "relevance and pertinence each belong to a group of terms which have something in common—*public-ness* in one case and *private-ness* in the other," as shown in Table 1.

Table 1

Field	Public	Private
Information Science:	Relevance	Pertinence
Philosophy of Science:	Public Knowledge	Private Knowledge
Psychology:	Denotation	Connotation
Linguistics:	Semantics	Pragmatics
Sociology of Knowledge:	Formal Communication	Informal Communication

Furthermore, "relevance and pertinence are two different qualities, one capable of public objective assessment and the other being capable only of private subjective assessment." Pointing out similar distinctions from other fields, Kemp is providing an invitation to relate the knowledge on these other notions to the notion on relevance, an area certainly worth examining in great detail.

TWO *KNOWLEDGE VIEWS* OF RELEVANCE

Two *knowledge views* of relevance emerged from these delineations. In the suggested framework described previously in the section entitled "How to Construct a Framework for Viewing Relevance from Intuitive Understanding and Then on to More Elaborate Communication Models," we recognized that subject knowledge is at the outset of the knowledge communication process and that the destination (*e.g.*, a user) is at the end. We also recognized that the destination has a file—a mind in the case of a human being. There are a number of causes which can put the knowledge communication process into motion. One of them is the posing of a question by a destination. In this case there are two pairs of relations, two pairs of contact points that can be considered in determining what constitutes a measure of the effectiveness of the contact. The first pair of relations is between the *question* (or rather the subject content or topic of the question) and the existing *subject-knowledge*. This view corresponds, to some degree, to Schutz's "topical relevances" and to Kemp's concept of relevance as involving public knowledge. We may refer to it as *subject knowledge view of relevance*.

The second pair of relations is between *the file of the destination* (or rather, the subject content of the file, the user's stock of knowledge at hand) and the existing *subject knowledge*. This view corresponds, to some degree, to Schutz's "interpretational relevances" and to Kemp's concept of pertinence as involving private knowledge. We may refer to it as the *destination's knowledge view of relevance*, or simply as the *pertinence view of relevance*.

Both of these views involve subject knowledge on one end of the relation, but they distinguish what is on the other.

SUBJECT KNOWLEDGE VIEW OF RELEVANCE AND ITS COMPLETENESS

The *subject knowledge view* of relevance stresses the nature, structure and extent of the subject knowledge on a topic given by a question. Subject knowledge and subject literature are obviously related, but they are not the same. Each has a structure that is related but is also quite different. Each is dynamic but on differing parameters. Subject knowledge involves knowledge per se, including redundancy, association, organization, and sedimentation. Subject literature as a representation involves authors, documents, producers, scatter, etc., as well as redundancy, associations and organization, which may differ from those of knowledge. Basically, because of the redundancy of knowledge, we can have more than one set of answers to a question; because of the redundancy of literature, we can have more than one set of documents containing answers to a question. All this, and obviously much more including much that is not known on and about subject knowledge and subject literature, affects relevance. But one thing should be clear: relevance involving subject knowledge and relevance involving subject literature, although related, are not one and the same.

In the previous sections, it was established that every view of relevance, if considered by itself in isolation from other views, is incomplete by definition. Thus, let me consider only the completeness of further views within themselves.

In information science, there has been no work that has tried to directly relate the structure, properties and dynamics of subject knowledge to relevance. In philosophy this was attempted; *e.g.*, the work by Schutz. However, there have been numerous works in information science (and in other subjects) on or about subject knowledge that indirectly refer to and directly impinge upon relevance; *e.g.*, works by Price, Goffman, and Ziman. Conversely, relevance could be considered in the explanation of the mechanism underlying the various observations on the structure and dynamics of subject knowledge.

In discussing the completeness of the *destination's view* of relevance, it was suggested that the limits of human memory may play a significant role in explanations of relevance. Harmon (*47*) suggested the intriguing idea that the same limits of human memory affect the growth and formation of subjects and their break-up into specializations or related subjects. This may be a significant factor in explanations of the *subject knowledge view* of relevance.

The *subject knowledge view* has not been formed as yet in any detail, although considerable material from which it can be formed exists. I wish to suggest that the *subject knowledge view of relevance is fundamental to all other views of relevance,* because subject knowledge is fundamental to communication of knowledge. In that lies the importance and urgency of the work on that view.

PERTINENCE VIEW OF RELEVANCE AND ITS COMPLETENESS

The *destination's knowledge* or *pertinence view* of relevance stresses the content of the file of the destination. The interest in people as the ultimate destinations in knowledge communication is of overriding importance. Thus, in the *pertinence view* of relevance, determining factors are the nature, structure, and extent of one's stock of knowledge at hand, the process and sequence of its sedimentation, and the process of the mind's selectivity.

The *destination's view* of relevance (discussed previously in the section entitled "How the Destination's View Emerged Equating Relevance with Relevance Judgment and How Experimentation Was Spurred") attempts to incorporate all factors that enter into human relevance judgment. The stress is on judgment. One of these factors is the stock of knowledge at thand, which, in turn, is the base of the *pertinence view*. Therefore, the *destination's view* does incorporate the *pertinence view* of relevance, but the latter is much more to the point. The *pertinence view* has a firmer base than the broad *destination's view*, because of a considerable number of philosophical and psychological investigations that have been devoted to the understanding of how we know what we know. These could be directly related to the *pertinence view*. In comparison, there has been a much smaller number of investigations on human judgment; thus the broad *destination's view* has little to relate to.

No work on the *pertinence view* of relevance has gone beyond providing a general framework for the view, either in the concept of information need or in the contrast between public and private knowledge. There has been no enumeration of the specific elements and relations that are a part of either framework. Therefore, the view has only broad outlines—it is incomplete within these outlines. This incompleteness provides an invitation for research.

• How the Disenchantment with Relevance Led to Another Splitting and How the *Pragmatic View* of Relevance Evolved.

RELEVANCE IS "NO GOOD"

Not surprisingly, there has been some disenchantment and impatience with the notion of relevance. A lot of declarative criticism has been leveled: "not appropriate," "inadequate," "too confusing," "ambiguous," "overused," "nonmeasurable," "doesn't reflect X" (X being a myriad of factors enumerated by critics that, indeed, relevance does not reflect), "not a good criterion," etc. Such criticisms have been especially pointed by those concerned with practice and/or with testing. How, indeed, does one run a system if one declares that it is aimed toward relevance, which is such an ambiguous notion? How, indeed, does one test systems using measures or criteria as slippery and imprecise as relevance? The criticisms do have a point; but, they lose validity when put in a human context.

Relevance is a human notion. How does one do anything neatly and precisely and unambiguously with human notions? Twentieth century science in moving toward a study of human notions found that reductionism to the "preciseness" of natural science does not work. The meaning of effectiveness in systems dealing with human notions is not the same as in engineering or business, and treating them in the same way leads to social dissatisfaction. These aspects have not been taken into account by declarative critics of the use of the notion of relevance.

As a result of this disenchantment with the notion of relevance, substitutions have been suggested. *Usefulness, appropriateness, utility,* and other similar terms have been suggested and used as substitutions for relevance. Although the connotations of each of the substitutions is different, interestingly enough, the basic notion behind the use of the substitutions and of relevance is exactly the same. In these attempts the notion of relevance has not been abandoned, the word has been. As it was naive to think that a *good definition* (*i.e.*, a paraphrase) of relevance will resolve the problem, so it was equivalently naive to think that abandonment of the word will do it. However, although a mere substitution of words for notions does not resolve a problem, it can open new avenues of thinking.

CYBERNETICS; PRAGMATISM

In a number of fields, it has been realized that many of the processes can be looked at from the point of view of what happened to the results: what effect do processes have on other wholes and other processes? For instance, in cybernetics, Wiener looked at the governing effects of communication and, conversely, how the results of communication, through a feedback function, govern communication. He looked at how one process governs the other.

In logic and linguistics, the study of pragmatics emerged in addition to the traditional study of syntactics and semantics. Concern also developed over the interplay among the three. In the 19th century in philosophy, the school of thought called pragmatism developed, suggesting that the meaning of an idea consists of the pragmatic consequence of the idea. Radical pragmatism of the 20th century suggests that the activities of the consciousness, as actions in the outer world, have exclusively practical aims, in particular, aims designed to satisfy biological needs. In the fields of action—in manufacture, industry, production and governance—pragmatic concepts are quite prevalent.

It is not surprising then, that a *pragmatic view* of relevance has developed. However, it did not develop from cybernetics or the notion of pragmatics in logic, linguistics or philosophy, but rather strictly from the prevailing utilitarian, practical orientation of the fields of action. In addition, it developed from the demands and desire for justification in terms of cost-benefits that pervaded in the 60's and 70's, the social, behavioral and educational fields in general and information science in particular. The argument for the pragmatic view of relevance went as follows: it is fine for IR systems to provide relevant information, but the true role is to provide information that has utility—information that helps to directly resolve given problems, that directly bears on given actions, and/or that directly fits into given concerns and interests. Thus, it was argued that relevance is not a proper measure for a true evaluation of IR systems. A true measure should be utilitarian in nature.

COOPER'S UTILITY

In defining *logical relevance* (see the next section), Cooper (*7*) made a distinction between relevance and utility: ". . . *relevance* has to do with *aboutness* (or *pertinence* or *topic-relatedness*) and is ultimately defined in terms of logical implication, whereas *utility* is a catch-all concept involving not only topic-relatedness but also quality, novelty, importance, credibility and many other things." Building on this distinction, Cooper (*48*) provided the first in-depth treatment of utility instead of relevance as a measure of retrieval effectiveness. He has built his argument on the assumption that "the purpose of retrieval systems is (or at least should be) to retrieve documents that are useful, not merely relevant." With further elaboration: "The success of a retrieval system must ultimately be judged on the basis of a comparison of some kind involving costs and benefits." Cooper uses the suggested measure of *utility*: ". . . in a complete neutral sense. It is simply a cover term for whatever the user finds to be of value about the system output, whatever its usefulness, its entertainment, or aesthetic value, or anything else."

Since this review has *not* concentrated on the measures and measuring units for testing of information retrieval systems, it is really of little or no interest here, or to any explication of relevance, if relevance, utility or whatever specific measure should be applied to test and evaluate any specific information retrieval system. However, Cooper's ideas on utility are a beginning of the explication of still another view of relevance that evolved—the *pragmatic view*—thus they are included here. Moreover, Cooper astutely notes a relation between his utility and relevance.

As in the *pertinence view*, in the *pragmatic view* the approach was to split the notion of relevance in order to differentiate and to argue that relevance is one thing, but X (pertinence, utility) is another, even though they are related. Imperceptibly, the thinking on relevance was moving during the last decade toward the concept that there are a number of *kinds* of relevances involving different relations. Different names started to be employed to characterize different kinds of relevance.

WILSON'S SITUATIONAL RELEVANCE

Another and slightly different explication of the *pragmatic view* of relevance was provided by Wilson (*9*). Wilson's explanation starts from the assumption that "relevance is not a single notion but many." He makes a basic distinction between psychological and logical relevance. The former deals with actual uses and actual effects of information. The latter is a double concept "of a relation between an item of information and a particular individual's personal view of the world and his situation in it; and it is a concept in which relevance depends on logical bearing on some matter on which he has preferences."

To derive the notion of situational relevance, Wilson uses Cooper's definition of logical relevance derived from deductive logic and constructs a definition using probabilities of evidential relevance drawn from inductive logic. To specify the relations established by situational relevance, Wilson also uses the notions of an individual's: 1) concerns, 2) preferences over ranges of alternatives (similar to the use in economic theories), and 3) stock of knowledge. Situational relevance is defined as a relation between these three notions and an item of information, a relation which is established by inference either deductively (Cooper's logical relevance) or inductively (evidential relevance). "Situational relevance is relevance to a particular individual's situation—but to the situation as he sees it, not as others see it, nor as it *really* is." "Wilson suggests that situational relevance captures the "essentials of the vague popular notion of practical relevance. . .that must bear on our actions."

KOCHEN'S UTILITY FUNCTION

Kochen (*19*), in the first book ever that explicates rather than describes theoretical principles of information retrieval, made a distinction between "relevance as a relation between propositions and the recognition of relevance on its judgment by a user, which resembles a utility or significance judgment." This is the same distinction as Cooper's, but Kochen went further and formally defined the notion of utility.

Kochen adapted four well established axioms about preferences from utility theory to a strategy for searching document collections. Subsequently, he showed that, if a user is willing to abide by these axioms, then it is possible to provide for a given user with a given question a utility function that assigns a utility number to each document in the collection searched. [See Kochen (*19*) p. 138 for details.] Kochen recognizes that changes of preferences can take place over time, and thus, that the utility function can change as well. As with all utility functions, this one depends on the ability of users to assign preferences and associate probabilities, which is its fundamental weakness. In many ways one can argue that this expectation, although at times realistic, at other times certainly is not. Without preferences, there is no utility theory and subsequently no utility functions. But, bringing the notions of preferences and the whole armamentarium of the utility theory to considerations of relevance is an important contribution. It opens a new area of study which should be followed.

COMPLETENESS OF VIEW

Precise definition of logical relevance by Cooper inspired the development of the *pragmatic view* of relevance.

As with other views, the *pragmatic view* of relevance is incomplete, but less so. It does recognize some of the different aspects of relevance not recognized by other views. Explicitly, it allows for relevance to be measured at different points in the communication process. Significantly, there is a direct attempt (admittedly, barely a beginning attempt) to establish a relationship between different views of relevance. However, in the *pragmatic view* of relevance, immediate pragmatism of information in one form or another is the ultimate, definite, final criterion. What each individual does with information is superordinate to what the information is. A criticism of this view can be attempted from a platform of general criticism of pragmatism and cost-benefits.

Pragmatism has been a subject for serious criticism in philosophy. The chief criticism is that it applies to only one reality, that which is referred to as "paramount reality." It does not deal with the totality of human existence. And above all, it deals with that reality as if it were unquestionable.

In our times one of the operational reflections of pragmatism is the concept of cost-benefits, which is also subject to serious criticism. Clearly, the costs of a great many processes and actions can be, and must be, related to the accrued benefits. But, as many critics point out, a great many other processes and actions, especially those related to human notions, cannot and should not be judged on cost-benefit basis, especially not on that basis alone. Cost-benefits should not be an omni-criterion for all human actions and enterprises, whether or not they can be estimated. At any rate, in the case of knowledge, costs can be estimated; but true cost-benefits, hardly. Besides, decisions related to knowledge and knowledge systems are made primarily on ethical, political and sociological grounds, rather than on economic grounds.

There are limited situations where cost-benefits and relevance should be related. But, if the cost-benefits were to be universally applied to communication of knowledge, it would be the surest way to the destruction of its effectiveness. For instance: Would the Alexandrian library ever have been built if cost-benefit studies were a criterion for decision?

This should not be construed as a rejection of the *pragmatic view* of relevance. On the contrary, it is an important aspect to be explored, especially as to the factors involved in pragmatism of information and as to the relation to other views. What is rejected is the idea that pragmatism is the only, or even the basic, aspect to apply to relevance.

In the conclusion, let me relate three views centering around the destination. The *destination's view* concentrates on judgment, the *pertinence view* concentrates on the stock of knowledge at hand and the *pragmatic view* on immediate application or on the problem at hand. If the *pertinence view* is related to some degree to Schutz's "interpretational relevances," then the *pragmatic view* can be related to some degree to his "motivational relevances." The *pertinence view* is fundamental to both other views, for the stock of knowledge at hand is fundamental to a judgment and to a problem. The *pertinence view* can be considered without involving the other two views; the *destination's view* has to involve the *pertinence view*, and it can but does not have to, involve the *pragmatic view*; the *pragmatic view* has to involve the other two.

• How Theories of Relevance Have Covered Different Aspects and Why They Are Important.

I left for last the discussion of the most significant work on relevance in information science: the attempts to formulate theories of relevance. As few and as sketchy as they are, the theoretical works have resulted in: 1) drawing methods and results from other and more rigorous subjects to the study of relevance, 2) illuminating the nature of the notion more and better than all the discussions combined, and 3) specifying the various relations involved which now enables classification of relations and a deeper study of specific relations. As with other theoretical work in information science, theoretical works on relevance have had only an indirect effect on practice.

MARON–KUHNS' RELEVANCE NUMBER

Maron and Kuhns (*49*) presented one of the first large, formal theoretical treatises in information science. They were concerned with the derivation of a probabilistic measure that would enable the ranking of documents as to their relevance. Considering that the "problem of explicating the notion of relevance (which is the basic concept in a theory of information retrieval) is similar to that of explicating the notion of amount of information (which is the basic concept of Shannon's communication theory), . . . we approach the notion of relevance also in a probabilistic sense." Their conditional probability, which specifies the "relevance number," involves the relation between a user's *request*, the *subject area* of the request, designation by a given *representation*, and a given *document* provided by a *system*. Regardless of any applications, the significance of Maron-Kuhns' explication lies in: 1) enumeration of the above factors in italic affecting relevance, 2) envisioning that there is a relation between these various factors, and 3) introduction of the concept of probabilities in describing the relations.

The probabilistic approach has been successful in many subjects in relation to many complex phenomena. There exists a systematic, formal body of knowledge related to probabilities and to the treatment of measures as probabilities. However, formulating a measure in terms of probabilities is one thing; approximating probabilities (deriving numerical values) is another. Often this is a major problem in experimentation and practice; but, without formulation first, there is no approximation at all. Yet, even though Maron and Kuhns and many others have tried to approximate probabilities related to relevance, this experimental and practical problem remains unsatisfactorily resolved.

GOFFMAN'S RELEVANCE AS A MEASURE AND THE EPIDEMIC THEORY

In the mathematical theory of measures, four axioms describe the properties that a measure has to satisfy to be a measure: 1) it is real-valued and non-negative, 2) it is completely additive, 3) it has an order, and 4) it has an absolute zero. Goffman (*24*), used these properties to prove that, if relevance is determined solely on the basis of a query and each document in a file independently of other documents (the prevailing practice in IR systems), then relevance does not satisfy all of the axiomatic properties of a measure; *i.e.*, it is not completely additive. He also proved in another theorem that, if relevance is determined not only on the basis of query-document relation but also on the relations among documents, then relevance satisfies all the axiomatic properties of a measure. To be a measure, relevance also has to take into account association—the effects of the items of knowledge on each other. This, of course, supports efforts in associative indexing.

Goffman and Newill (*50*), elaborated on later by Goffman (*16*), developed an epidemic theory of communication equating the process of the spread of ideas to the spread of diseases. The notion of effective contact is central to the theory. A series of theorems proves the conditions under which the dynamics of the process changes over time in given populations. In the case of the information retrieval process (a sub-process in a communication process), relevance is considered the measure of the effectiveness of the contact. The information retrieval process is described as an interrogation procedure of a file of documents (objects which convey information). Assuming that a general measure of relevance is prababilistic, a series of mathematical definitions and theorems provides various conditions under which a set of documents exhibit various relations. Among others, Goffman proved mathematically that relevance is not associated with a unique subset of documents as answers from a file, and that more than one subset of answers is possible; that answers that were not initially relevant can become relevant in an appropriate sequence; and that relevance is an equivalence relation, which provides for a partitioning of a file in equivalence classes. It has been shown "that any measure of the effectiveness of information conveyed must depend upon what is already known. . . and (therefore, it is necessary to) introduce the notion of conditional probability of relevance."

The strength of the theory is that it provides for some of the dynamic aspects of communication and shows some of the complexity of relations of relevance as a measure using mathematical rigor. As a matter of fact, this is the only theory related to communication which has emerged in information science that attempts to show some of the dynamics of the process. It clearly shows the large role that the *interplay* among documents has on relevance.

One of the more interesting things that should be done is to relate the dynamics of this communication theory, where effectiveness of the contact is a central notion, to the so-called *relevance-related* distributions (as in Bradford), which are essentially static in nature but involve relevance as well.

HILLMAN'S SIMILARITY CLASSES

Hillman (*6*) introduced logic to the treatment of relevance in information science. In treating the basic problem of defining relevance, Hillman suggested the use of the constructs in formal logic, particularly Carnap's concept-formation theory. Assuming that the problem of mutual relevances of queries and documents involves conceptual relatedness, Hillman critically examined various aspects in the theory of concept formation showing their applicability or non-applicability to the definition of relevance. He suggested that to describe relevance-relations in terms of similarity classes would be most appropriate. The theory is not complete, but its strength lies in the critical examination of a number of constructs in logic as to their applicability to the study of relevance and, even more so, in drawing the attention of information scientists to logic.

COOPER'S LOGICAL RELEVANCE

It remained for Cooper (*7*), to fully employ the armamentarium of deductive logic in a carefully argued out definition of what he called logical relevance. He addressed the nature of inference involved in relevance. He assumed that relevance is a relationship "holding between pieces of stored information on the one hand and user's information needs formulated as information needs representation on the other. . .both are linguistic entities of some kind." As in logic, Cooper takes a sentence to be the basic information-conveying unit of language. He also assumes that an information need and the data in an information retrieval system can be represented by declarative sentences. And, as a fundamental construct, he takes the relationship of "logic consequences" (*entailment*, or *logical implication*) from deductive logic, where a sentence (called *conclusion*) is a logical consequence of a set of sentences (called *premises*) when a set of conditions is fulfilled.

Given these restrictions:

1. A search query is a yes-no type question; thus, it can be transformed in a pair of yes-no *component statements* (*e.g.*, Is hydrogen a halogen element?).
2. The data stored in a system is in well formed sentences so that a *premise set* for the component statement can be derived by logical consequence. *A minimal premise set* is a set as small as possible—if a member is deleted the component statement would no longer be a logical consequence of the premise set.
3. The retrieval is inferential; it deduces direct answers to input questions.

Then Cooper provides his "restricted definition":

"A stored sentence is *logically relevant* to (a representation of) an information need, if and only if it is a member of some minimal premise set of stored sentences for some component statements of that need."

In generalizing from that definition, Cooper shows that the *restricted definition* could also be applied to fact retrieval systems and even to document retrieval systems (but not precisely), taking the strategy of transforming whatever is stored into declarative sentences. The difficulties with this definition occur when dealing with induction (and inductive systems) rather than deduction, as fully acknowledged by Cooper; probabilities and degrees of relevance cannot be accommodated.

The strength of Cooper's approach is that it defines fully, and as precisely as deductive logic permits, one set of relations and one type of inference involved in relevance. As restricted as it is, Cooper's logical relevance has to be recognized as a first of its kind, inviting definitions of other possible types of inferences and providing grounds for differentiation. In his work on situational relevance, Wilson (*9*) (see the previous main section of this article), attempted briefly to incorporate inductive logic and probabilities into a definition of evidential relevance.

The *logical view* of relevance has concentrated on the *nature of relations* between elements, rather than on *enumeration of elements* that enter into relevance. The nature of these relations was treated as inferences. Two *logical views* emerged:

1. *Deductive inference view* drawing from deductive logic, and
2. *Probabilistic inference view* drawing from inductive logic and probabilities.

Since deductive logic is much more precise and complete than inductive logic, the first view is much more precise and complete than the second. The second view especially needs further elaboration.

COMPLETENESS OF THEORIES

None of the theories of relevance are complete in the sense that any of them incorporates all aspects of relevance. Each theory illuminates some aspect of relevance and provides a different method for describing the properties and relationships of the notion. No theory has, as yet, attempted to describe the mechanisms that account for the notion. In all probability, the forthcoming theories on relevance will be of a *step-by-step* nature, further illuminating some particular aspect of the notion.

Why so much stress on theories? The history of science provides numerous proofs that there is nothing more practical then a good theory. It can easily be demonstrated how different conceptions, views and pseudo-theories of relevance have led to the development of given systems and of given practices and standards in many types of information systems. Complete and valid theoretical thinking on relevance has a potential of having great impact on the practice of information retrieval and librarianship in particular and on the communication of knowledge in general. Lack of theory most often leads to guessing games with little probability of positive impact.

• Back to the Framework

This review is an inventory and a classification. On one hand, I have attempted to trace the evolution of thinking on relevance, a key notion in information science; on the other hand, I have also attempted to provide a framework within which the widely dissonant ideas on relevance that have emerged could be interpreted and related to each other. If the classification, the framework, is valid, it does provide a potential for uncovering gaps in knowledge and indicating possible directions of future work.

Since the notion of relevance is part and parcel of knowledge, information and communication, it also involves the complexities, puzzles and controversies of the larger phenomena. Intuitively, the notion of relevance has to do with the success of the communication process. Therefore, we have taken the notion of relevance fundamentally to be a notion of the measure of the effectiveness of the contact between a source and a destination in a communication process.

In a slightly different context, Weiler (*51*) remarked that "the arguments about relevance are arguments about the framework of our discussion." And this is exactly what arguments about relevance in information science have been all about. What aspect of communication, what relations, should be considered in specifying relevance? What factors are to be considered in determining relevance?

Some more *formal* answers to these questions have been attempted in information science. Differences in answers have formed different views of relevance. As yet, none of the views has achieved a stage of a broad consensus; rather the thinking on the notion of relevance in information science seems to have reached a stage of perpetuating challenge.

The process of the communication of knowledge was suggested as a framework for considerations of relevance and as a source of a scheme for classifying various views of relevance that have emerged in information science. Even while measuring the same thing, a process can be validly measured at a number of different points in the sequence of events which involves different elements and relations–creating different viewpoints. This was exactly what has happened with relevance. Relevance can be and has been considered at a number of different points in the process of communication of knowledge; thus different elements and relations were considered, and different viewpoints emerged. On a more specific level, relevance can be and has been considered in relation to specific types of knowledge communications.

Imbedded in the communication of knoweldge are information systems which aim at enabling and enhancing the process. Different systems aim at enhancing different aspects of the process or are directed toward different uses or environments. Relevance can also be and has been considered with or without involving any of the information systems or their elements.

SUMMARY OF DIFFERENT VIEWS

Taking into account different elements and/or the nature of different relations in the communication of knowledge, the following views of relevance, arranged approximately by the sequence of events in the process, have emerged.

The *subject knowledge view of relevance* has considered the relation between the knowledge on or about the subject *and* a topic (question) on or about the subject.

The *subject literature view of relevance*, closely related to the *subject knowledge view*, has considered: the relations between the subject *and* its representation, the literature, or the relation between the literature *and* a topic (question) on the subject.

The *logical view of relevance* has been concerned with the *nature of the inference* between premises on a topic and conclusions from a subject or subject literature. Two views have emerged: 1) the *deductive inference view*, which has considered the relation between premises *and* conclusions on the basis of logical consequence; and 2) the *probabilistic inference view*, which has considered the relation among premises, information as evidence *and* conclusions on the the basis of degree of confirmation or probabilities.

The *system's view of relevance* has considered the contents of the file and/or the processes of a given information system *and* the relation to a subject or a subject literature, a topic (question), or a user or users.

The *destination's view of relevance* has considered the human judgment on the relation between documents conveying information *and* a topic (question).

The *pertinence or destination's knowledge view of relevance* has considered the relation between the stock of knowledge at hand of a knower *and* subject knowledge, or subject literature.

The *pragmatic view of relevance* has considered the relation between the immediate problem at hand of a user *and* the provided information, involving utility and preference as the base for interference.

The following can be ascertained: Different views of relevance are not independent of each other. It seems that there exists an interlocking, interplaying cycle of the various systems of relevances (*i.e.*, various systems of measures). Some systems may be considered as special cases or subsystems of other more general systems. There is *no*, and there cannot be any *one specific*, view of relevance, for there does not exist any one system of relevance in communication. Different systems of relevances may involve some different factors, but they are coupled in such a way that they can hardly be considered without other systems of relevance. For instance, *pragmatic view* cannot be considered without involving the *pertinence view* or *destination's view* of relevance. None can be considered without *subject knowledge view*. Many practical problems in information systems and many cases of user dissatisfaction can now be explained as due to the existance of various systems of relevances.

Therefore, when considering relevance in a specific sense, one should be quite careful to indicate the elements and the nature of the relations between elements that are being considered. Different names can be given to the considerations of specific different sets of elements or different relations. This was started with names of *pertinence* and *logical relevance*. However, it should always be realized that any specific consideration of relevance is tied in with systems of relevances. A most significant advance in thinking on relevance will be achieved with the illumination of the interplay between these systems.

SPECULATION ON PROPERTIES AND FUTURE WORK

It has been explained that different views of relevance have arisen because in the communication of knowledge there are a number of dynamically interacting systems of relevances organized in some stratified or perhaps hierarchical fashion of complex systems. Each view has concentrated on one system. If this explanation is valid, then we may postulate that there should be some fundamental properties that are universal—common to all views or systems of relevance—and some unique properties that are specific to each system. At present we can only speculate that among the universal properties are:

> *Knowledge, knower*: all views assume a prior existence of a body of knowledge, or ideas or facts or their representations; or of a knower.
>
> *Selection*: implied by all views is a process of selection concentrating on elements or structure of above knowledge.
>
> *Inference*: selectivity is based on some form of inference.
>
> *Mapping:* the aim is some form of mapping of selected elements or structure of knowledge onto something—at a minimum onto some other elements or structure of knowledge.
>
> *Dynamics*: the dynamic interactions among properties are involved; changes in any property over time is possible.
>
> *Association:* the internal structure of elements of knowledge and other properties affect the dynamics and vice versa.
>
> *Redundancy:* more than one set of elements of knowledge, pattern of association or structure, form of inference, dynamics or mapping may satisfy the criteria of any and/or all properties.

If these, or some similar properties are indeed found to be universal to all views or systems of relevances, then an explication of each view will be incomplete if it does not in some way incorporate an explication of at least every one of the universal properties. Thinking on relevance can proceed in various directions, such as:

1. Taking a given view or system of relevance and proceeding to define fully all properties;
2. Taking a given property in one or a number of systems and defining and contrasting the nature of the property; for instance, this was started with the explications of the nature of inferences—deductive, inductive, probabilistic, preferential, etc.;
3. Taking a number of properties and explicating the interplay;
4. Taking a number of explicated systems of relevance and explicating the interplay between them. The ultimate thinking on relevance will be the one that explicates the interplay among all explicated systems of relevances.

In summarizing the framework for considering relevance, a number of elements or aspects have been enumerated. Information science has dealt with most of them, but not all. Most glaringly absent are considerations of environments and human values involved in communication of knowledge. Hopefully, future work on relevance will include these aspects as well.

Our understanding of relevance in communication is so much better, clearer, deeper, broader than it was when information science started after the Second World War. But, there is still a long, long way to go.

Appendix

Synthesis of the Experiments on Relevance in Information Science

The experiments are organized and synthesized according to the five general classes of variables that affect human relevance judgment, as suggested by Cuadra and Katter (reviewed in the section entitled "How the *Destination's View* Emerged Equating Relevance with Relevance Judgment and How Experimentation was Spurred" under the paragraphs on "Hypotheses"). To derive conclusions, I examined the data and results of the experiments rather than use the conclusions and claims of the authors. This synthesis is taken from Saracevic (*52*).

DOCUMENTS AND DOCUMENT REPRESENTATIONS

Documents and their representations were the first, and most frequently treated, variables in the study of relevance judgments. Documents evoked early interest since they are the items provided by IR systems to users, and thus observations concerning their effect upon the user and his judgment have direct practical implications for systems design and operations. The investigations covered:

1. The comparative effects on relevance judgments of titles, citations, abstracts and/or full texts (*53, 54, 55, 56, 57*);
2. The effects of stylistic characteristics of documents (*29*); and
3. The effects of degree of specificity and variations in document content in relation to queries (*29, 54*).

An analysis and correlation of experimental results suggest several conclusions:

1. It may be expected with a considerable degree of certainty that documents, or objects conveying information, are the major variables in relevance judgments.
2. Although a number of factors are aligned with documents as variables, the most important of these factors affecting relevance judgment appears to be the subject content of documents as compared to the subject content of the query. This finding relates to Schutz's "topical relevances."
3. Elements of style may also be expected to affect relevance judgments.
4. Highly specific subject content in a document appears to stimulate more relevance agreements.
5. Relevance judgments for the same article may be expected to differ from titles to full texts; titles should be utilized with considerable scepticism.
6. Relevance judgments for the same article may be expected to differ somewhat from abstracts to full texts, depending upon the abstract's type, length, detail, etc.

QUERIES

The query stimulates the generation of document as answers and documents are judged for relevance in relation to the query. Experimental observations were made on the query-document relationship:

1. The effects on relevance judgments of query specificity (*29*);
2. The effects on relevance judgments of judges' subject expertise at various stages of the research—the successive research stages were treated as enlargements of the queries (*54*);
3. The relation between the wording and phraseology of queries and documents judged relevant or non-relevant (*58*);
4. The relation between disagreements in relevance judgments and unclearness of query statements (*59*); and
5. The effect of judges' subject knowledge in relation to the subject content of queries (*29, 54*).

The following conclusions may be drawn:

1. The more judges know about a query, the higher is the agreement among judges on relevance judgments and the more stringent the judgments become.
2. The more judges discuss the inference from query to answer, the higher the agreement on relevance judgments.
3. A close similarity and correlation seems to exist between texts of queries and texts of relevant documents, which cannot be found between texts of queries and texts of non-relevant documents.
4. Document texts may be the most important factor in triggering relevance judgments in relation to stated queries; *i.e.*, if one finds a statement in a document resembling a query statement, one is assured of a high probability that the document will be considered relevant by the user stating the query.
5. The less one knows about a query, the greater the tendency to judge documents relevant. In specific terms, the less a system operator or user delegate knows about a query—its content, eventual use or the problem in relation to which the query is asked—the greater the temptation to judge documents relevant. These findings relate to Schutz's "innovational relevances."

JUDGMENTAL SITUATIONS AND CONDITIONS

This variable refers to the environment—real or constructed—within which relevance judgments are made. Two aspects are examined:

1. The effect of aspects and definitions of relevance upon relevance judgments (*29, 54*); and
2. The effect of time and stringency pressures on relevance judgments (*29*).

The results from these experiments are inconclusive and should be interpreted cautiously:

1. Not surprisingly, changes in experimental conditions may introduce changes in judgments;
2. Different definitions of relevance do not necessarily stimulate different relevance ratings; *i.e.*, people tend to treat relevance as a primitive notion; and
3. Greater pressure in the judgmental situations stimulates higher relevance ratings (*i.e.*, "more" relevant). This finding relates to Schutz's "motivational relevances."

MODES FOR EXPRESSION

This variable refers to the instruments (psychometric devices) by which judges express relevance judgments. Since instruments used for recording attitudes do affect the attitude, they become subjects of study. The experiments covered:

1. The comparative effects on relevance judgments of rating, ranking and ratio scales (*29, 54, 60*);
2. The effect of differing numbers of categories on rating scales (*29*);
3. The reliability of judgments as affected by different types of scales (*54*); and
4. The interaction of scale types with other variables tested (*29, 54*).

It may be concluded:

1. Different kinds of scales (rating, ranking and ratio scales) may produce slightly different judgments.
2. The more categories a rating scale has, the more comfortable the judges feel in their judgment; in any case, they may be more at ease with a scale having more than two and up to some ten categories.
3. It is not clear what type of scales are most reliable for use in recording relevance judgments. Some form of the ratio scale appears to have some advantage over other types of scales.
4. On the scales tested, judges with a high level of subject expertise tended to agree with themselves over a short period of time (*e.g.*, a month).
5. It was found that the end points of scales were used most heavily regardless of the number of categories in the scale; *i.e.*, documents tend to be rated very relevant or very non-relevant.
6. Relevance judgments of a group of judges on one document are not normally distributed but skewed in one direction.
7. It is most significant to note that the relative relevance score of documents in a group, expecially among the documents with high relevance, may be expected to be remarkably consistent even when judges with differing backgrounds make the relevance judgments. Thus, it may be more profitable to compare the relative position of documents in a set than to compare the relevance ratings assigned to individual documents.

PEOPLE

The fundamental factor studies in all experiments reviewed was the consistency of, or agreement in, relevance judgments as affected by certain human characteristics. These characteristics usually dealt with the degree of subject or professional education. It should be noted that the human element as a variable is present to some extent in all previous conclusions presented. The following were investigated:

1. The ability of people to judge consistently the relevance of documents to their general interest (*61*);
2. The comparison of users' and non-users' (delegated) and experts' and non-experts' relevance judgments (*62, 63*);
3. The effect on relevance judgments of the documents intended use (*29, 64*);
4. The effect of academic and professional training on relevance judgments (*29, 54*); and
5. The relation between relevance judgments assigned by judges and test results from IR systems (*65*).

On this most important variable, the conclusions are as follows:

1. It may be expected that the greater the judges' subject knowledge, the higher will be their agreement on relevance judgments. Subject knowledge seems to be the most important factor affecting the relevance judgment as far as human characteristics are concerned. This finding underlines the importance of considering the stock of knowledge at hand, when considering relevance and people.
2. It has also been demonstrated that the level of judges' subject knowledge varies inversely with the number of documents judged relevant; conversely, the less the subject knowledge, the more lenient are their judgments.
3. Non-subject-oriented groups (*e.g.*, subject information retrieval specialists and librarians) tend to assign relatively high relevance ratings. They will be inclined to provide a user with all or most of the relevant material that he himself would consider relevant and, in addition, some or considerably more material that he would not consider relevant. However, it may be expected that the ranking of documents as to degree of relevance will be similar for persons with extensive subject background (*i.e.*, users) and for suppliers of information (*i.e.*, delegates) with lesser subject backgrounds.
4. Familiarity with, and knowledge of, subject terminology has been shown to effect high relevance agreement.
5. It may be expected that a professional or occupational involvement with the problem giving rise to the query would increase agreement of relevance judgments among and between groups of subject specialists and suppliers of information. Increased professional involvement affects agreement among judgments, irrespective of the degree of subject knowledge.
6. The correlation in relevance agreements among people with high levels of subject expertise and the most professional involvement with the query has been found to be between .55 and .75; the correlation in relevance agreements among suppliers of information has been found to be between .45 and .60.
7. Differences in the intended use of documents may produce differences in relevance judgments,

suggesting that intended use becomes part of the query. This finding relates to Schutz's "interpretational relevances" and Wilson's "situational relevances."

8. Agreement as to what *is not* relevant may be expected to be greater than agreement as to what *is* relevant; judging relevance is not the same as judging non-relevance.
9. Tests of retrieval system performance, if of course they are well designed and controlled, may produce reliable comparative results within test experiments, regardless of relative instability of relevance judgments (instability within the range elaborated under previous conclusion 6.)

One of the major conclusions that can be drawn from experiments is that relevance judgments are not at all associated with a random distribution. Although it may appear that relevance judgment is a very subjective human process, it has associated with it some remarkable *regularity patterns.*

• Acknowledgments

The thoughtful suggestions of Professor Phyllis A. Richmond and the editing of Jane M. Wiggs are gratefully acknowledged. I am also indebted to my colleagues at the School of Library Science and at the Complex Systems Institute, Case Western Reserve University, for providing a conducive environment for this work and to my students for providing the challenge.

Reference Bibliography

1. **Mesarovic, M.** and **E. Pestel**, *Mankind at the Turning Point-The Second Report ot the Club of Rome*, New York: Dutton (1974).
2. **Bell, D.**, *The Coming of Post-Industrial Society—A Venture in Social Forecasting*, New York: Basic Books (1973).
3. **Schutz, A.**, *Reflections on the Problem of Relevance*, New Haven: Yale University Press (1970).
4. **Carnap, R.**, *Logical Foundations of Probability*, Chicago: University of Chicago Press (1950).
5. **Anderson, A.R.** and **N.D. Belnap, Jr.**, "The Pure Calculus of Entailment," *Journal of Symbolic Logic*, 27 (No. 1): 19-52 (1962).
6. **Hillman, D.J.**, "The Notion of Relevance (1), " *American Documentation*, 15 (No. 1): 26-34 (1964).
7. **Cooper, W.S.**, "A Definition of Relevance for Information Retrieval," *Information Storage and Retrieval*, 7 (No. 1): 19-37 (1971).
8. **Foskett, D.J.**, "A Note on the Concept of 'Relevance'," *Information Storage and Retrieval*, 8 (No. 2): 77-78 (1972).
9. **Wilson, P.**, "Situational Relevance," *Information Storage and Retrieval*, 9 (No. 8): 457-471 (1973).
10. **Kemp, D.A.**, "Relevance, Pertinence and Information System Development," *Information Storage and Retrieval*, 10 (No. 2): 37-47 (1974).
11. **Ziman, J.M.**, *Public Knowledge: An Essay Concerning The Social Dimension of Science*, London: Cambridge University Press (1968).
12. **Ziman, J.M.**, "Information, Communication, Knowledge," *Nature*, 224 (No. 5217): 318-324 (1969).
13. **Price, D.J. de S.**, *Little Science, Big Science*, New York: Columbia University Press (1963).
14. **Warren, K.G.** and **W. Goffman**, "The Ecology of the Medical Literatures," *American Journal of the Medical Sciences*, 263 (No. 4): 267-273 (1972).
15. **Shera, J.H.** and **M.E. Egan**, "A Review of the Present State of Librarianship and Documentation," in: **S.C. Bradford**, *Documentation*, 2nd ed. London: Lockwood, 11-45 (1953).
16. **Goffman, W.**, "A General Theory of Communication," in **T. Saracevic**, *Introduction to Information Science*, New York: Bowker, Chapter 13, 726-747 (1970).
17. **Shannon, C.E.** and **W. Weaver**, *Mathematical Theory of Communication*, Urbana: University of Illinois Press (1949).
18. **Wiener, N.**, *Cybernetics: Control and Communication in the Animal and the Machine*, 2nd ed. Cambridge, Massachusetts: MIT Press (1961).
19. **Kochen, M.**, *Principles of Information Retrieval*, Los Angeles: Melville (1974).
20. **Mooers, C.S.**, "Coding, Information Retrieval, and the Rapid Selector," *American Documentation*, 1 (No. 4): 225-229 (1950).
21. **Perry, J.W.**, "Superimposed Punching of Numerical Codes on Handsorted, Punch Cards," *American Documentation*, 2 (No. 4): 205-212 (1951).
22. **Taube, M.**, and Associates, "Storage and Retrieval of Information by Means of the Association of Ideas," *American Documentation*, 6 (No. 1): 1-17 (1955).
23. National Academy of Sciences, *Proceedings of the International Conference on Science Information*, 2 Vols., National Academy of Sciences, Washington, D.C. (1959). See: (a) **Vickery, B.C.**, 855-886; (b) **Vickery, B.C.**, 1275-1290; (c) Summary of the discussion of the Area 4: 803-811; and Area 6: 1395-1409.
24. **Goffman, W.**, "On Relevance as a Measure," *Information Storage and Retrieval*, 2 (No. 3): 201-203 (1964).
25. **Kent, A.**, **M. Berry**, **F.U. Leuhrs**, and **J.W. Perry**, "Machine Literature Searching VIII. Operational Criteria for Designing Information Retrieval Systems," *American Documentation*, 6 (No. 2): 93-101 (1955).
26. **Doyle, L.B.**, "Is Relevance an Adequate Criterion for Retrieval System Evaluation?" *Proceedings of the American Documentation Institute*, Part 2, Washington, D.C.: 199-200 (1963).
27. **Cuadra, C.A.**, *On the Utility of the Relevance Concept*, Technical Report SP-1595, Systems Development Corporation, Santa Monica, California (1964).
28. National Science Foundation, *Summary of Study Conference on Evaluation of Document Searching Systems and Procedures*, NSF, Washington, D.C. (1964).
29. **Cuadra, C.A.** and **R.V. Katter**, *Experimental Studies of Relevance Judgments*, TM-3520/001, 002, 003/ 00. 3 vols., Systems Development Corporation, Santa Monica, California (1967).
30. **Rees, A.M.**, and **T. Saracevic**, "The Measurability of Relevance," *Proceedings of the American Documentation Institute*, Washington, D.C., 3: 225-234 (1966).
31. **O'Connor, J.**, "Relevance Disagreements and Unclear Request Forms," *American Documentation*, 18 (No. 3): 165-177 (1967).

32. **Saracevic, T.**, *Introduction to Information Science*, New York: Bowker, Chapter 3, 110-151 (1970).
33. **Miller, C.A.**, "The Magical Number Seven, Plus or Minus Two: Some Limits on our Capacity for Processing Information," *Psychological Review*, 63 (No. 2): 81-97 (1956).
34. **Fairthorne, R.A.**, "Empirical Hyperbolic Distributions (Bradford-Zipf-Mandelbrot) for Bibliometric Description and Prediction," *Journal of Documentation*, 25 (No. 4): 391-343 (1969).
35. **Brookes, B.C.**, "Numerical Methods of Bibliographic Analysis," *Library Trends*, 22 (No. 1): 18-43 (1973).
36. **Line, M.B.** and **A. Sandison**, " 'Obsolescence' and Changes in the Use of Literature with Time," *Journal of Documentation*, 30 (No. 3): 283-350 (1974).
37. **Bradford, S.C.**, "The Documentary Chaos," in his *Documentation*, London: Lockwood, 106-121.
38. **Lotka, A.J.**, "The Frequency Distribution of Scientific Productivity," *Journal of the Washington Academy of Sciences*, 16 (No. 12): 317-323 (1926).
39. **Zipf, G.**, *Human Behavior and the Principle of Least Effort*, Cambridge: Addison-Wesley (1949).
40. **Price, D.J. de S.**, "Networks of Scientific Papers," *Science*, 149 (No. 3683): 510-515 (1965).
41. **Urquhart, D.J.**, "Use of Scientific Periodicals," *Proceedings of the International Conference on Scientific Information*, Washington, D.C., National Academy of Sciences, National Research Council, 277-290 (1959).
42. **Saracevic, T.**, *"On the Concept of Relevance in Information Science,"* Ph.D. Dissertation, Cleveland, Ohio: Case Western Reserve University (1970).
43. **Kozachkov, L.S.**, "Relevance in Informatics and Scientology," (In Russian) *Nauchno-Tekhnicheskaya Informatsiya*, Series 2, No. 8: 3-11 (1969).
44. **O'Connor, J.**, "Some Questions Concerning 'Information Need'," *American Documentation*, 19 (No. 2): 200-203 (1968).
45. **Rees, A.M.**, and **T. Saracevic**, "Conceptual Analysis of Questions in Information Retrieval Systems," *Proceedings of the American Documentation Institute*, Part 2, Washington, D.C., 175-177 (1963).
46. **Goffman, W.**, and **V.A. Newill**, "Methodology for Test and Evaluation of Information Retrieval Systems," *Information Storage and Retrieval*, 3 (No. 1): 19-25 (1966).
47. **Harmon, G.**, *Human Memory and Knowledge: A Systems Approach*, Westport, Connecticut: Greenwood (1973).
48. **Cooper, W.S.**, "On Selecting a Measure of Retrieval Effectiveness, Part 1," *Journal of the American Society for Information Science*, 24 (No. 2): 87-100 (1973).
49. **Maron, M.E.**, and **J.L. Kuhns**, "On Relevance, Probabilistic Indexing, and Information Retrieval," *Journal of the Association for Computing Machinery*, 7 (No. 3): 216-244 (1960).
50. **Goffman, W.**, and **V.A. Newill** "Communication and Epidemic Processes," *Proceedings of the Royal Society*, A., 298 (No. 1454): 316-334 (1967).
51. **Weiler, G.**, "On Relevance," *Mind*, 71: 487-493 (1962).
52. **Saracevic, T.**, "Ten Years of Relevance Experimentation: A Summary and Synthesis of Conclusions," *Proceedings of the American Society for Information Science*, 7: 33-36 (1970).
53. **Rath, G.J.**, **A. Resnick**, and **T.R. Savage**, "Comparisons of Four Types of Lexical Indicators of Content," *American Documentation*, 12 (No. 2): 126-130 (1961).
54. **Rees, A.M.**, **D.G. Schultz**, et al, *A Field Experimental Approach to the Study of Relevance Assessments in Relation to Document Searching*, 2 Vols. Cleveland, Ohio: Center for Documentation and Communication Research, School of Library Science, Case Western Reserve University (1967).
55. **Resnick, A.**, "Relative Effectiveness of Document Titles and Abstracts for Determining Relevance of Documents," *Science*, 134 (No. 3483): 1004-1006 (1961).
56. **Shirey, D.L.** and **H. Kurfeerst**, "Relevance Predictability. II: Data Reduction," in: **A. Kent et al.**, *Electronic Handling of Information: Testing and Evaluation*, Washington, D.C.: Thompson 187-198 (1967).
57. **Saracevic, T.**, "Comparative Effects of Titles, Abstracts and Full Texts on Relevance Judgments," *Proceedings of the American Society for Information Science*, Washington, D.C. 6: 293-299 (1969).
58. **Gifford, C.** and **G.J. Baumanis**, "On Understanding User Choices: Textual Correlates of Relevance Judgments," *American Documentation*, 20 (No. 1): 21-26 (1969).
59. **O'Connor, J.**, "Some Independent Agreements and Resolved Disagreements about Answer-Providing Documents," *American Documentation*, 20 (No. 4): 311-319 (1969).
60. **Katter, R.V.**, "The Influence of Scale Form on Relevance Judgment," *Information Storage and Retrieval*, 4 (No. 1): 1-11 (1968).
61. **Resnick, A.** and **T.R. Savage**, "The Consistence of Human Judgments of Relevance," *American Documentation*, 15 (No. 2): 93-95 (1964).
62. **Barhydt, G.C.**, "The Effectiveness of Non-User Relevance Assessments," *Journal of Documentation*, 23 (2): 146-149 and (3): 251 (1967).
63. **Hoffman, J.M.**, *Experimental Design for Measuring the Intra- and Inter-Group Consistence of Human Judgment for Relevance*, M.S. Thesis, Georgia Institute of Technology, Atlanta, Georgia (1965).
64. **Cuadra, C.A.** and **R.V. Katter**, "Opening the Black Box of 'Relevance'," *Journal of Documentation*, 23 (No. 4): 291-303 (1967).
65. **Lesk, M.E.**, and **G. Salton**, "Relevance Assessments and Retrieval System Evaluation," *Information Storage and Retrieval*, 4 (No. 3): 343-359 (1968).

Chapter 4
Evaluation

A Study of Information Seeking and Retrieving. I. Background and Methodology 175
T. Saracevic, P. Kantor, A.Y. Chamis, and D. Trivison

On Selecting a Measure of Retrieval Effectiveness. Part I 191
W.S. Cooper

The Pragmatics of Information Retrieval Experimentation, Revisited 205
J. Tague-Sutcliffe

Presenting Results of Experimental Retrieval Comparisons 217
E.M. Keen

MEDLARS: Report on the Evaluation of Its Operating Efficiency 223
F.W. Lancaster

The TREC Conferences 247
D.K. Harman

Just as with other services, those responsible for library and information services have addressed performance assessment and tried to evaluate service and, more narrowly, system performance. However, as information is essentially an invisible good, determining cost-benefit ratios is hard. Moreover, as with other such services, determining the precise contribution of the many components a system has is extremely difficult. For example, if a user has failed to retrieve anything helpful, is this to be attributed to collection coverage, document classification, or query formulation? For any individual information system with some specific character, there are several particular performance questions: how well does the system actually perform? how well could a system with the generic design in question perform? and how well, for the given document file and user population, could any system perform?

RELEVANCE JUDGEMENTS

It is evident that, given the fundamental intangibles of retrieval systems, it is difficult to get reliable and informative answers to the questions above, indeed increasingly so from the first to the last. The general problem that IR's "ineffable concepts" pose for retrieval evaluation is clearly shown in Belkin (1981). The special problem is not just that it is hard to reach the normal evaluation destination, being able to predict future from past performance: the problem is that it is normally impossible to obtain all the ground data that are in principle required for a full assessment of performance. This is because it is impossible, with any document file of nontrivial (and hence currently common) size, to determine whether each document in the file is relevant to any particular user need. It will therefore not be known what documents "ought" to be retrieved.

This is not merely a practical matter. It is indeed impossible for any individual to read, say, 100,000 documents, let alone millions. It is also, more significantly, impossible for any user to read a succession of documents as if each was wholly new, without being affected by what they have learnt through reading previous ones; yet such independent *relevance judgements* are required to provide the neutral, primary *evaluation data* for determining specific system performance.

It is further the case that as every information need is unique to a particular person at a particular time, performance evaluation depends on large populations of users and needs. In general, therefore, retrieval system evaluation implies compromises in relation to the authenticity, bias, and completeness of relevance judgements, with extensive sampling not only to offset these compromises but to cover the natural variation in user properties, needs, etc. Users with needs, document files, and relevance judgements are the necessary basis for evaluation. When frozen in the more limited form of user requests, files, and preserved judgement sets, these constitute the type of evaluation data commonly referred to as a *test collection*.

Of course, as Saracevic's paper in the previous chapter made clear, what makes a document relevant to a user need is not a straightforward matter, and relevance may be defined in many ways. Thus the crudely stated prime requirement for serious testing, namely that there be known relevant documents constituting the reference data against which system output is set, has to be carefully unpacked and interpreted to ensure that all the implications for the way performance is actually measured are clear. For example, if used to mean novelty, then output presentation order is critical and has to be recognised. The same applies if, as Cooper (1973) argues, the property sought of retrieved documents is subjective utility to the user rather than topic relevance, which Cooper sees as an objective property of documents in themselves. The important point is, nevertheless, that without given information about which documents are liked and which are not liked (by the user with the information need) there can be no performance assessment. This is true whether in reference to the system's ability to retrieve liked documents, to do this quickly, or to do it with little user effort.

However, while relevance judgements are required for overall performance evaluation, it may naturally be the case that local evaluations without them may be in order; for instance, evaluations of system interfaces for user convenience. On the other hand, in formal, and especially laboratory, evaluations, success in retrieving relevant documents is typically the only aspect of system performance considered.

SYSTEM EVALUATION

From a broader point of view, defining system performance solely in terms of success in retrieving relevant documents is clearly far too limited, and the evaluation of retrieval systems as wholes—indeed of information systems—has necessarily to examine a wide range of system characteristics and behaviour, and from many different points of view. *Information systems* are, moreover, abstract systems involving people as well as computational apparatus and serving many different information-processing and management activities. It has long been recognised, by librarians and economists alike, that evaluating the performance of information systems is extremely difficult, because of the problem of determining the value of information, the benefits and costs of having it, and hence the *utility* of some *information service* for its clients. It is in particular hard to make the distinction between service and clients or customers when, as is essentially the case not only in general but specifically in the interactive search case, the human customers are part of the abstract information management system.

We have not attempted in this volume to cover the evaluation of information systems in the broader sense or even of information services more narrowly conceived, as illustrated by a system's ability not only to locate wanted documents but to deliver them to the user in a convenient form and in a timely fashion. But it is essential to recognise that the evaluation even of a retrieval system, i.e., an indexing and searching system rather than an entire service, can encompass many different matters from the logical ("does it retrieve wanted documents?") via the financial ("does it do this cheaply?") to the human ("does it offer me handy tools for doing it?"). Thus, to use the evaluation terminology developed in Sparck Jones and Galliers (1996), the *setup* within which an automated retrieval system is embedded is as important as the system itself, and it is particularly important in evaluation to distinguish evaluation of a system, with respect to its external function in its setup, and evaluation with respect to its own internal objective.

METHODOLOGY

In general, proper evaluation calls for a careful methodology that treats the *subject* of the evaluation in a sufficiently comprehensive way and develops a detailed *scenario* for the actual evaluation. As with performance assessment in other contexts, information system evaluation can be categorised, broadly, in various ways. Thus evaluation may be from a manager's or a user's point of view; it may be internal in the sense of focusing on retrieval itself, or external, say, in addressing the cost of retrieval. Again, the output of a retrieval system evaluation may be a report showing what performance is, or an analysis showing why performance is what it is. The evaluation may be solitary, concerned only with a single system's modus vivendi, or comparative, to determine the effect of alternatives. Such dichotomies refer to characterising decisions that are all important for evaluation, in different combinations in individual evaluations. The choices just listed refer, however, only to a few broad headings, and much more refinement is needed to design and conduct any evaluation.

Thus, adopting Sparck Jones and Galliers's approach for illustrative purposes, it is necessary first to address the *remit* of the evaluation, subsuming its motivation, goal, and manner. For example, in relation to motivation, is the perspective financial, administrative, or scientific? Who are the interested parties promoting the evaluation (e.g., local managers, researchers) and who are the consumers for the findings? Then, given a clearly defined goal, choices have to be made of the manner of evaluation, including whether it focuses on the system's internal objective or its external function; whether it will only be an investigation or, more rigorously, an experiment; whether it will treat the system under study as a black box, defined only by its inputs and outputs, or as a glass box, examining its internal workings; whether it will use comparison with a benchmark or something else as a performance yardstick; whether it will be exhaustive or indicative in style; and whether qualitative or quantitative. The remit guides (and is in turn refined by) further choices in relation to the evaluation *design*. Thus, taking account of the test subject's constitution and context, it is necessary to identify the *performance factors* involved, both as *environment variables* and as *system parameters*; to determine the performance *gauges*, including broad *criteria*, specific *measures*, and detailed *methods* of applying these; to decide on evaluation data; and to establish the evaluation procedure for conducting the whole. It is evident that, when done thoroughly, a great deal of work is required even for a few tests, and certainly for an extensive evaluation programme. This is clearly illustrated by the detailed methodological guidance offered in Tague (1981, 1992, 1994). The care and attention needed in choosing and applying measures and methods is well shown in Keen (1971) and in Keen's subsequent paper reproduced here, while the paper in this chapter by Saracevic et al. illustrates careful methodology in action, especially in relation to the quantitative analysis of primary results, as required to determine the dependencies between performance factors. Studies like that of Saracevic et al. are not themselves primarily evaluations. But they are important as investigations of retrieval setups that help to define the many environment variables and values to be taken into account in more specific system evaluation.

Many evaluations have been conducted without comprehensive and rigorous specification. In practice, very many unexamined assumptions are made, and *default* models of retrieval testing have become entrenched with a life of their own which may not be well related to important retrieval realities. Thus many studies have applied the academic, laboratory approach well illustrated by the long-standing SMART work under Salton at Cornell without asking whether this approach, very valuable in itself, is always appropriate to the individual evaluation situation. This particular approach—abstracting IR systems from operational setups, considering only a limited set of environment variables, and using precision and recall computed from extensive evaluation data—defines what has become the default model of retrieval testing. This model has come to be entrenched in the current TREC Programme, and it is therefore important to recognise its limitations and the many other aspects of evaluation.

It is indeed necessary to understand that a methodology for evaluation ultimately invokes a *theory* of evaluation, grounded in an analysis of system objectives or functions and thus providing a sound justification for the choice of evaluation measures (see, e.g., Raghavan et al., 1989). This has to provide, for example, an appropriate way of relating basic measures like recall and precision that refer to simple classes of documents (relevant and retrieved, relevant but not retrieved, etc.) with ranked output.

EVOLUTION OF IR TESTING

The development of current evaluation concepts and methods of evaluation stems, as mentioned in Chapter 2, from the introduction of automation. It was thought necessary to discover whether automated retrieval systems were as good as manual ones, on the subsequently challenged assumptions that manual systems were good and that the goal of automated systems was to reach manual performance levels. However, there were two subsidiary themes. One was to assess the comparative performance of different indexing languages and search strategies offered as responses to the growth of the scientific literature, but still intended for manual application. The other was to evaluate different automated indexing and searching methods: these were initially seen as inferior substitutes for manual approaches that could not be automated (e.g., ones requiring full document text understanding), but were subsequently treated in their own right. In particular, as automation spread and new strategies were suggested that had never had manual analogues, e.g., ones involving statistical weighting, it was necessary to compare different specific ways of interpreting and implementing these notions.

The proposed, or actual, substitution of automatic for manual indexing and searching within a global framework of automated file management and first offline, then online, searching stimulated internal evaluation concentrating on the features of the system itself and then, naturally, on comparative system evaluation. Moreover, in the attempt to understand system behaviour and so be able to design better systems, evaluation was approached not just as *investigation* intended to determine and account, descriptively, for system performance but as *experiment* intended to explain performance analytically. This implied control of experimental variables, so the general idea of a performance test was given a tight, laboratory-oriented application.

Unfortunately, this has led to problems since control and realism conflict and it is difficult to balance them rationally. There are special challenges in designing and managing controlled experiments with real users engaged in online, interactive retrieval. But work on retrieval evaluation over the last four decades has helped to establish an appropriate framework and to gather experience in relation to the factors affecting performance and the gauges used to define it, as illustrated by, for example, Keen and Digger (1972) and Keen (1977). Retrieval performance factors cover, as environment variables, the properties of documents and of users, and, as system parameters, such matters as index language devices for description and search, methods of term choice for documents, type of interface resource for the user, etc. Thus the most important lessons of early retrieval system testing were those indicating the range of system factors to be considered and providing guidelines for feature decomposition for a given retrieval situation, especially in ensuring correct assignment of factors to environment or system.

The second major focus in retrieval evaluation has naturally been the performance gauges used, subsuming broad criteria, particular measures interpreting these general criteria, and detailed methods for operationalising the measures; for instance, in averaging over request sets, *micro-averaging* and *macro-averaging* (Tague, 1981) give different detailed views of the same output data. Even for internal system evaluation, it is useful to distinguish criteria referring to *effectiveness, efficiency,* and *acceptability*. Recall and precision are very widely used as measures for effectiveness, but they are by no means the only possible effectiveness measures and may, for instance, be given various specific forms where they may be viewed not just as pure effectiveness measures. Thus precision at a low output rank cutoff is intuitively a measure addressing acceptability as well as effectiveness in retrieving relevant documents. There is some conflict between formally appealing and intuitively open measures. For instance, one common measure, precision at recall levels, completely obscures realities about the numbers of documents involved, and single-number measures, convenient and attractive though they are as instant performance comparators, are far too summary to be genuinely informative. The considerations underlying definitions of effectiveness and specific measures are displayed in Cooper (1968), Swanson (1977), Swets (1967), and van Rijsbergen (1979).

There has been a gradual development of retrieval test methodology that is appropriate to the laboratory way of meeting important performance evaluation requirements, though in general more attention has been paid to the details of design than of remit, which has not always been fully enough examined. The definition of test data, an important element of evaluation design, has in particular been a subject of attention: what constitutes an adequate test collection?

TEST COLLECTIONS

Much early, and even comparatively recent, retrieval system testing has been on far too small a scale. This has been partly attributable to lack of clarity about what constitutes a statistically valid sample and, more importantly, one reflecting the raw numerical characteristics of large file retrieval. But it has been mainly the consequence of the effort and cost of providing relevance judgements, mentioned earlier. When many, very different approaches to retrieval are applied to the same collection, it is possible to *pool* their output and have the pooled data judged, which allows relative performance assessment for each approach. But for a long time test collections were used by only one or two projects, with a natural tendency to go on testing with the same material in order to maintain comparability with earlier work. During the seventies in particular, the need to check environment variables led to an increasing use of several collections for tests, but these were often arbitrarily different from each other and were typically still small. Even by 1990, while test collections had grown slowly since sixties data sets with only 35 requests against 82 documents, through 225 against 1400, to 93 against 11,429, experiments were still often conducted with collections of order 75 against 2000. The study described in Sparck Jones and van Rijsbergen (1976) had shown how complex and costly providing a coherent set of collections for the research community would be. At the same time, it became increasingly evident that large test collections were needed not only to capture user variation, mentioned earlier, and to support claims for statistical significance in findings, but also to demonstrate that performance levels and differences hold as document file sizes grow. This last was important not only for scientific reasons but also to achieve credibility with commercial system operators.

To a considerable extent, the requirement for varied and large collections has been met by the TREC Programme, summarised in Harman's paper selected here and covered in more detail in Harman (1993–1996), *Information Processing and Management* (1995), and Sparck Jones (1995). Both absolutely and by comparison with earlier test data, the files used are much larger than older ones and are for full text rather than just title or title/abstract. Thus, TREC-3 matched 50 requests against 742,611 documents averaging nearly 500 terms (i.e., stemmed content words) per document compared with older collections with 5 to 100 terms. However, the files are not natural accumulations, rather arbitrary aggregations, and the data has its limitations on the request side, well illustrating the practical difficulties of obtaining wholly satisfactory test data. This material will nevertheless be a very valuable community resource, particularly since it is complemented by the extensive results published for successive evaluation cycles. The TREC Programme as a whole, continuing over successive years from 1992, marks a new phase in retrieval evaluation in the form of laboratory experiment simply because of its many participants and continuity (Harman, 1993–96). Many quite different approaches to indexing and searching are covered, for the automated full-text retrieval that is an increasingly common situation, and at finer levels of granularity all the individual teams have made many specific comparisons. The overall range of system parameter variation is enormous, even if that for environment variables has been very much more limited. The programme illustrates the synergy that such collaborative competitions can achieve and has done much to consolidate earlier, more limited findings. It has confirmed in particular that similar performance can be achieved with very different approaches, and that ones applying relatively straightforward techniques with term weighting can do as well as much more elaborate ones.

However, while these techniques can be, and are being, exploited now in commercial systems (see Chapter 7), the nature of the TREC requests, which have mainly been highly honed, means that the TREC experience is not directly applicable to the many everyday contexts where brief and poorly considered requests are the normal search starting point.

SIGNIFICANCE TESTING

TREC also sharpens two major issues in IR evaluation. One is the nature and use of statistical significance testing. Since the form of the population distributions underlying the observed performance values is not known, only weak tests can be applied; for example, the sign test. Much earlier performance evaluation was reported without any reference to significance testing, though it is slowly becoming more common. The choice and application of statistical tests in IR within a general framework of proper quantitative analysis has been a particular concern for Tague-Sutcliffe (see Tague [1981], her paper in this chapter, and Tague-Sutcliffe [1994]) and is critical for test standards. For instance, when request differences including very large variations in relevance set sizes are taken into account, apparently substantial differences in performance are obliterated. It is certainly the case that it is too easily assumed that manifest performance differences are real. It is also the case that statistically significant differences may not be meaningful for the real user when translated into actual numbers of documents. From this point of view, many performance measures commonly used in retrieval testing, especially in the default manner, are unrealistic (for example, in computing recall and precision figures over far larger document sets than ordinary users would ever consider). It is thus important, as is indeed recognised in the official presentation of TREC results, to give figures for performance defined in different ways and, in particular, not to limit it to single-number measures like average precision.

EVALUATING INTERACTIVE SYSTEMS

The other major limitation of TREC so far, and the hole in mainstream IR research in its default mode, has been the failure to engage substantively with the evaluation of online interactive searching, especially by end users. Interactive searching, as illustrated by the growth of OPACs and the more recent explosion of Web browsing, is increasingly the dominant mode, but the presumed type of retrieval situation over decades of evaluation was primarily the one-off "offline" search. This allowed for careful formulation of the query before submission, as was the norm with information services staffed by specialists, but reflected the fact that with early automated systems the main file search was slow and expensive. The idea of incorporating *relevance feedback* in query reformulation dates back to the sixties, but has almost always figured in actual testing in a wholly impersonal and abstract form via the exploitation of the relevance judgements already available with test collections. This has been justified as simulating a desirable real situation where the end user is not required to think about query reformulation, but just to press a yes/no button and lie back and enjoy letting the system do all the real work. However, with modern direct search access, the assumption that preliminary work to prepare a query will have already been done (as in the old-fashioned, presearch interview) no longer holds, so much more direct participation in a genuinely interactive search with extensive query reformulation must be accepted.

There are manifestly system design problems for setups where "untutored" users submit (as they often do) very short queries, whether for searching against short or long documents. As importantly here, interactive end user searching presents serious challenges for evaluation, and it has proved extremely difficult to design and conduct proper investigations or, especially, experiments on interactive searching. There are several good reasons for this. The first is the well-known danger of observer interference with the subject user's natural search activity, for instance by asking questions about what they are doing. The second is that there is sufficient intrinsic variation in user needs and activities to make reliable comparisons with respect to the uses and values of different facilities very hard to obtain. These problems are well known to social scientists and make careful test design essential. However, there is a third problem with interactive retrieval, namely that of *nonreplicability*. Once a user has done a search seeking to satisfy some information need with some particular system or utility, they cannot, by definition, do another search for the same need with a different system. They will have learnt something bearing on their need from conducting the first search. This implies that, for far-reaching comparison studies, large samples of users are required, adding to the cost and effort of evaluation.

Evaluations of interactive searching, initially for professionals rather than ordinary end users, began in the eighties, but substantial well-conducted studies are uncommon, and both robust test methodologies and solid findings for the increasingly critical and central case of routine end user searching are still needed (Beaulieu et al., 1995; Robertson and Hancock-Beaulieu, 1992; Tague and Schultz, 1989). The difficulty of evaluation here is exacerbated by the rapid advance of interface technology, so there is the double requirement to determine what elements of performance are attributable to back-end system capabilities and what to front-end gizmos. For example, though windows are not themselves retrieval devices, they may affect the whole mode of interaction for the user and hence influence the demands the user indirectly puts on the back-end index and searching system. The arrival of the Web has indeed created a whole new evaluation environment not only through the opportunity for direct interaction but through other features of the setup, including data scale and heterogeneity, huge machine power, and the special type of information infrastructure embodied in URLs. These points apply whether the user is simply directly exploiting the whole structure or is searching via one of the IR engines now available, where matters are further complicated by a range of administrative constraints somewhat different from those that applied when automated retrieval began.

NOTABLE EVALUATIONS

While there have been a number of extended test programmes (the most notable being that carried out over several decades in Salton's SMART project work) that have had a cumulative impact of the kind also now expected of TREC, there have been individual evaluations that have been widely recognised as landmarks. One of these was that done at Cranfield, reported in Cleverdon's paper in Chapter 2, and another was Lancaster's MEDLARS evaluation (1969), which is included here. The STAIRS test conducted by Blair and Maron (1985) was also a landmark of a slightly different kind, in raising questions about natural language retrieval systems and focusing attention on precisely what can be legitimately claimed, especially in relation to large-scale operational systems. It also served to draw attention to what is meant by "natural language retrieval system", a notion somewhat differently interpreted in the conventional retrieval service context and in the research community. But quite apart from the actual results, the methodological aspects of the evaluation, for example, in determining recall for a large file, were especially important. (References for important response and successor papers are grouped under Blair and Maron (1985) in the list of references at the end of the chapter).

TEST FINDINGS

It is impossible to refer in any detail to the outcomes of forty years' consideration of how to test retrieval systems, or to the results of individual evaluations. Some particular tests appear in later chapters, showing performance for specific retrieval techniques and systems and making useful comparisons that serve to illustrate the levels of performance that are attained. Two major global points that can be made about the tests done over the four decades since modern testing began can nevertheless be appropriately made here. One is to confirm, if by now not surprisingly, the inverse relationship between recall and precision, and also that it is hard to raise joint performance, even in the favourable conditions represented by smaller test collections, beyond the 40%/40% level: with larger, realistic collections 30/30 is likely. The other is that despite the limitations of statistically based natural language indexing as a means of capturing information content, systems based on this approach provide very respectable performance that is hard to beat.

As indicated, IR evaluation, even in its narrow default case—represented by the application of recall and precision to the results of detached laboratory tests not directly involving real users—is not completely straightforward. Evaluation for the other information-processing tasks considered in Chapter 8 ranges from cases where such a narrow approach is appropriate, as illustrated by Lewis (1995), to tasks like summarising, where narrow default notions cannot be applied and evaluation is a major problem. The long testing tradition in IR has been exploited in these other areas, so measures labelled "recall" and "precision" may be applied, e.g., to information extraction. But their interpretation is then different, albeit sometimes in a way that is stimulating for IR evaluation.

Sparck Jones (1981) gives a comprehensive view of IR evaluation, covering both methodological issues and analyses of actual tests. The many aspects and issues of evaluation are also evident in the special issues on the subject in *Information Processing and Management* (1992) and *Journal of the American Society for Information Science* (1996).

SELECTED READINGS

The comprehensive study of Saracevic et al. (1988) was a major attack on the realities of retrieval as represented by the activities of users, without the abstraction typical of the default test mode. We reproduce the first part of this three-part paper here. (For reference details on all three parts, see the listing for Saracevic et al. at the end of the chapter.) As the paper notes, very little is actually known about these realities. The study therefore examined five major aspects of information seeking and retrieving (users, questions, searchers, searches, and outputs), doing this within the framework of an overall model of an information retrieval system in the abstract sense of "system", i.e., one that embodies the information seeker interacting with the machine system, not just the latter. Thus in this case, Sparck Jones and Galliers's setup was itself the test subject, and the study sought to capture as many as possible of its properties so that the environment variables for a machine system were fully analysed and understood. The quantitative and qualitative measures used to capture the embedded machine system's performance were consequently derived from the users' interests in both relevance and utility. One of the major features of the study was the very thorough application of statistical analysis, described in detail, which was used not only to establish the significance of the output performance figures for the machine searches themselves, but also, and more importantly, to establish their correlation with the different environment variables.

Saracevic et al.'s study as a whole shows a very careful methodology in which a wide range of factors and behaviours is considered, defined, observed, and analysed, exemplifying a detailed attention to the remit and design of an IR investigation. It illustrates in particular the issues to be addressed when, and the ways in which, characteristics of users are captured; for instance, their intentions, forms of knowledge, and so forth. As is evident, the work was not directly an evaluation of IR system performance in the ordinary sense, but a higher-level investigation of the nature of information-seeking behaviour with a view to identifying those factors that are important and with which, as environment variables, the designers of machine systems and interfaces should be especially concerned. At the same time, the detail of the study is suggestive in relation to the kinds of contextual characterisation that should be undertaken by those who wish to conduct comparative experiments to evaluate different interactive system facilities and devices.

Cooper (1973) seeks to capture the important idea, for information systems, of utility, and, specifically, of utility for the individual user. Cooper's proposal for doing this is presented via a detailed account of a naive evaluation methodology, which is also of interest as illustrating the kind of detail that needs to be covered in designing a specific evaluation procedure as the basis for performance measurement. The interpretation of utility that is embodied in the naive methodology is then justified, in dialectical argument against a series of objections, for instance, that utility is a subjective rather than objective criterion, to which Cooper replies that it is indeed subjective, and intentionally so. Both the actual hostile questions or comments and Cooper's responses provide a comprehensive view of what choosing a measure of system effectiveness involves. Cooper sees his naive methodology as establishing a utility-based reference standard against which proposed specific, and especially simpler, measures may be assessed for their ability to determine effectiveness in relation to what he regards as the prime requirement. Thus he objects to relevance, when defined as aboutness, for being an objective property of documents rather than a subjective property of system outputs. Cooper's paper is not actually concerned with the evaluation of interactive systems. But in presenting the operations of his naive methodology, he also displays many factors bearing on interactive evaluation.

We have already noted Tague's 1981 paper on the "how to do it" detail of retrieval experiment and the particular emphasis she places on the quantitative elements of evaluation. The paper selected for inclusion here (Tague-Sutcliffe, 1992), revisiting the theme and individual topics of the earlier one, provides an update motivated by the shift from offline to genuinely interactive searching and the need to rethink the pragmatic details of evaluation from this point of view. Thus the paper proceeds through a step-by-step discussion from the initial "whether to test" to "how to present the results". Tague-Sutcliffe concentrates, in particular, first on how to operationalise the variables, in fact covering both environment variables and system parameters, along with the choice of performance criteria and measures. She then focuses on the major issue, under data gathering, of obtaining requests and on the way that searching is organised so as to maintain proper control of the critical area of searching the same request with different systems/strategies. The presumption is that it is in practice necessary to "double up", i.e., not to restrict users or searchers to a single foray per request, and that undesirable learning biases can be avoided by careful experimental design. Tague-Sutcliffe also examines the question of collecting and analysing data about the search, both quantitative and qualitative, with the necessary attention to the statistical treatment of performance information and relationships among variables. As she notes, an IR test is not a project to be lightly undertaken, and this is especially the case when much human search effort is required. She therefore emphasises the need to ground any test in a thoroughly considered remit, to guide both the global and local decisions about the design and conduct of the test.

Keen (1992) focuses, assuming a sensibly intended and conducted investigation or experiment, on the fine-grained detail of how retrieval results should be treated and presented. Thus Keen shows that, even within a conventional framework focusing on recall-and precision-based measures, there are many tricky questions to be considered as to precisely how to treat results, first for a set of different request runs under aggregation and averaging, and second in comparison between strategies or systems that deliver intrinsically different kinds of output (for instance, Boolean searches providing sets and weighted searches producing a ranked output). Keen's figures illustrate very clearly the wide variation there is in raw retrieval performance across different requests, across different systems, and across different measures within the same general class. One of the lessons of this careful analysis of alternatives for the presentation of results is to emphasise how strongly the overall "shape" of performance, e.g., the changing relation between precision and recall over ranked output, depends on very detailed calculation and presentation decisions that might be thought of no major import, and how heavily averaging smoothes things out. The paper thus draws attention to the role of the methods level under performance gauges, as important in its way as the criteria and measures levels that are more often the subject of interest. Keen's points are important given the de facto standardisation in such major programmes as TREC on certain ways of measuring and presenting performance. This selectivity is already within a relatively clinical experimental context, and it is therefore necessary to bear in mind all the features of system behaviour that are not addressed at all within this performance-characterisation paradigm.

As noted, Lancaster's MEDLARS test (Lancaster, 1969) was a landmark one, especially in looking at the performance of an operational rather than experimental system. MEDLARS was an early, now conventional, information service, and Lancaster shows very clearly how the remit for his test followed from the fact that it was an operational system. Thus it addressed factors like file coverage that are typically neglected or irrelevant in laboratory situations. System performance was also coloured by the use of a particular controlled indexing language, MeSH, but this was a given, not a direct subject of assessment as an optional system parameter setting. Lancaster was obliged, by the very impressive scale of his test data, to address the question of obtaining a decent recall base independent of the searches, and he achieved a reasonable form of pool. Performance figures for recall and precision were computed. However, the major and most important part of the paper refers to the extensive failure analysis, designed to allocate system responsibility for relevant documents not retrieved or nonrelevant retrieved. This was done in terms of major performance factors, embodying indexing devices. Thus Lancaster examined failures of the indexing language, and of document and request indexing, with both of the latter considered in relation to indexing specificity and exhaustivity. The failure analysis was forced by the fact that Lancaster could not engage in comparative testing, but it is equally valuable as a means of interpreting comparative performance. Thus the TREC figures on requests above and below the median can draw attention to failures needing explanation. Lancaster's analysis showed failures primarily in the transition from user request, via the professional intermediary, to the query. These failure analyses were truly heroic given the scale of the test, but they are essential for performance understanding even though they are a challenge to carry out as systems grow. Lancaster's finding that the starting request is critical is also as pertinent now, though in a very different retrieval situation.

We have commented on the importance, both for evaluation and also retrieval research generally, of the ongoing TREC Programme. The Proceedings of the successive workshops provide enormous detail (Harman, 1993–96), while Harman's overview chapters in these Proceedings give the essentials and show how the programme has evolved. The paper included here (Harman, 1995) is a convenient introduction, covering the first three cycles of this very large evaluation enterprise, outlining the basic tasks, data (including provision of relevance judgements), and methods of evaluation, along with illustrative results from TRECs 1–3. One of the important features of TREC, a natural consequence of the many different participating teams, is that it allows both manual and automatic indexing for requests (though documents are not manually indexed), as well as a wide range of specific strategies, and thus offers an unrivalled series of direct performance comparisons. Harman summarises the different team approaches and illustrates performance from among the better sets of results. As she notes, the effect of the successive cycles was an improvement in performance, attributable partly to tuning to the type of data and task specifications, partly to the proper development of individual team approaches, and partly to a cheerful adoption by teams of one another's manifestly useful devices. The last two are clear benefits for the progress of IR research in general, while the first serves to emphasise the point that testing for tuning can be of real utility for operational systems.

Subsequent TRECs have developed a multitrack structure addressing a larger range of tasks, including grappling with the evaluation of interactive searching as more consonant with retrieval realities than the logically batched style of the initial cycles. At the same time, also in the direction of greater realism, it has worked with less well developed starting requests than those used up to TREC-3.

REFERENCES

*Note: *** after a reference indicates a selected reading.*

Beaulieu, M.M., Robertson, S.E., and Rasmussen, E.M. (1995) Evaluating interactive systems in TREC. *Journal of the American Society for Information Science,* **47**, 85–94.

Belkin, N.J. (1981) Ineffable concepts in information retrieval. In K. Sparck Jones (Ed.), *Information Retrieval Experiment,* pp. 44–58. London: Butterworths.

Blair, D.C., and Maron, M.E. (1985) An evaluation of retrieval effectiveness for a full-text document retrieval system. *Communications of the ACM,* **28**, 280–299. Also: Blair, D.C., and Maron, M.E. (1985) Technical correspondence. *Communications of the ACM,* **28**, 1238–1242; Salton, G. (1986) Another look at text-retrieval systems. *Communications of the ACM,* **29**, 648–656; Blair, D.C., and Maron, M.E. (1990) Full text information retrieval: further analysis and clarification. *Information Processing and Management,* **26**, 437–447; and Blair, D.C. (1996) STAIRS redux: Thoughts on the STAIRS evaluations, ten years after. *Journal of the American Society for Information Science,* **47**, 4–22.

Cooper, W.S. (1968) Expected search length: A single measure of retrieval effectiveness based on the weak-ordering action of retrieval systems. *American Documentation,* **19**, 30–41.

Cooper, W.S. (1973) On selecting a measure of retrieval effectiveness. Part 1. *Journal of the American Society for Information Science,* **24**, 87–100.***

Harman, D.K. (Ed.) (1993–1996) *Proceedings of the First/Second/Third/Fourth Text REtrieval Conference (TREC-1/2/3/4).* NIST Special Publications 500–207/215/225/236. Gaithersburg, MD: National Institute of Standards and Technology.

Harman, D.K. (1995) The TREC Conferences. In R. Kuhlen and M. Rittberger (Eds.), *Hypertext - Information Retrieval - Multimedia: Synergieeffekte Elektronischer Informationssysteme, Proceedings of HIM '95,* pp. 9–28. Konstanz, Germany: Universitaetsforlag Konstanz.***

Information Processing and Management (1992) Special Issue: Evaluation issues in information retrieval. *Information Processing and Management,* **28**, 439–528.

Information Processing and Management (1995) Special Issue: The second Text Retrieval Conference (TREC-2). *Information Processing and Management,* **31**, 269–448.

Journal of the American Society for Information Science (1996) Special Issue: Evaluation. *Journal of the American Society for Information Science,* **47**, 1–105.

Keen, E.M. (1971) Evaluation parameters. In G. Salton (Ed.), *The SMART Retrieval System,* pp. 74–111. Englewood Cliffs, NJ: Prentice Hall.

Keen, E.M. (1977) On the processing of printed subject index entries during searching. *Journal of Documentation,* **33**, 266–276.

Keen, E.M. (1992) Presenting results of experimental retrieval comparisons. *Information Processing and Management,* **28**, 491–502.***

Keen, E.M., and Digger, J.A. (1972) *Report of an Information Science Index Language Test. 2 Parts.* Aberystwyth: Wales, College of Librarianship. (See Chapter 16 especially.)

Lancaster, W.F. (1969) MEDLARS: Report on the evaluation of its operating efficiency. *American Documentation,* **20**, 119–142.***

Lewis, D.D. (1995) Evaluating and optimising autonomous text classification systems. In E.A. Fox, P. Ingwersen, and R. Fidel (Eds.), *Proceedings of the 18th Annual International Conference on Research and Development in Information Retrieval,* pp. 246–254. New York: Association for Computing Machinery.

Raghavan, V.V., Bollman, P., and Jung, C.S. (1989) Retrieval system evaluation using recall and precision: Problems and answers. In N.J. Belkin and C.J. van Rijsbergen (Eds.), *Proceedings of the 12th Annual International Conference on Research and Development in Information Retrieval,* pp. 59–68. New York: Association for Computing Machinery.

Robertson, S.E., and Hancock-Beaulieu, M.M. (1992) On the evaluation of IR systems. *Information Processing and Management,* **28**, 457–466.

Salton, G. (1992) The state of retrieval system evaluation. *Information Processing and Management,* **28**, 441–449.

Saracevic, T., Kantor, P., Chamis, A.Y., and Trivison, D. (1988) A study of information seeking and retrieving. I. Background and methodology. *Journal of the American Society for Information Science,* **39**, 161–176.*** Also: Saracevic, T., and Kantor, P. (1988) A study of information seeking and retrieving. II. Users, questions, and effectiveness, ibid., 177–196; and III. Searchers, searches, and overlap, ibid., 197–216.

Sparck Jones, K. (1975) A performance yardstick for test collections. *Journal of Documentation,* **31**, 266–272.

Sparck Jones, K. (Ed) (1981) *Information Retrieval Experiment.* London: Butterworths.

Sparck Jones, K. (1995) Reflections on TREC. *Information Processing and Management,* **31**, 291–314.

Sparck Jones, K., and Galliers, J.R. (1996) *Evaluating Natural Language Processing Systems.* Lecture Notes in Artificial Intelligence 1083. Berlin: Springer.

Sparck Jones, K., and van Rijsbergen, C.J. (1976) Information retrieval test collections. *Journal of Documentation,* **32**, 59–75.

Swanson, D.R. (1977) Information retrieval as a trial and error process. *Library Quarterly,* **47**, 128–148.

Swets, J.A. (1967) Effectiveness of information retrieval methods. *American Documentation,* **20**, 72–81.

Tague, J.M. (1981) The pragmatics of information retrieval experimentation. In K. Sparck Jones (Ed.), *Information Retrieval Experiment,* pp. 59–102. London: Butterworths.

Tague, J.M., and Schultz, R. (1989) Evaluation of the user interface in an information retrieval system. *Information Processing and Management,* **25**, 237–251.

Tague-Sutcliffe, J. (1992) The pragmatics of information retrieval experimentation, revisited. *Information Processing and Management,* **28**, 467–490.***

Tague-Sutcliffe, J.M. (1994) Quantitative methods in documentation. In B.C. Vickery (Ed.), *Fifty Years of Information Progress: A Journal of Documentation Review,* pp. 147–188. London: Aslib.

van Rijsbergen, C.J. (1979) Retrieval effectiveness. *Progress in Communication Sciences,* **1**, 91–118.

A Study of Information Seeking and Retrieving. I. Background and Methodology*

Tefko Saracevic
School of Communication, Information and Library Studies, Rutgers, The State University of New Jersey, 4 Huntington St., New Brunswick, N. J. 08903

Paul Kantor
Tantalus Inc. and Department of Operations Research, Weatherhead School of Management, Case Western Reserve University, Cleveland, Ohio 44106

Alice Y. Chamis† and Donna Trivison‡
Matthew A. Baxter School of Library and Information Science, Case Western Reserve University, Cleveland, Ohio 44106

The objectives of the study were to conduct a series of observations and experiments under as real-life a situation as possible related to: (i) user context of questions in information retrieval; (ii) the structure and classification of questions; (iii) cognitive traits and decision making of searchers; and (iv) different searches of the same question. The study is presented in three parts: Part I presents the background ot the study and describes the models, measures, methods, procedures, and statistical analyses used. Part II is devoted to results related to users, questions, and effectiveness measures, and Part III to results related to searchers, searches, and overlap studies. A concluding summary of all results is presented in Part III.

Introduction

Problem, Motivation, Significance

Users and their questions are fundamental to all kinds of information systems, and human decisions and human-system interactions are by far the most important variables in processes dealing with searching for and retrieval of information. These statements are true to the point of being trite. Nevertheless, it is nothing but short of amazing how relatively little knowledge and understanding in a scientific sense we have about these factors. Information retrieval systems, expert systems, management and decision information systems, reference services and so on, are instituted to answer questions by users — this is their reason for existence and their basic objective, and this is (or at least should be) the overriding feature in their design. Yet, by and large and with very few exceptions (see ref. 1) the basis for their design is little more than assumptions based on common sense and interpretation of anecdotal evidence. A similar situation exists with online searching of databases. While the activity is growing annually by millions of searches it is still a professional art based on a rather loosely stated set of principles (see ref. 2) and experience. While there is nothing inherently wrong with common sense, professional art, and principles derived from experience or by reasoning, our knowledge and understanding and with them our practice would be on much more solid ground if they were confirmed or refuted, elaborated, cumulated, and taught on the basis of scientific evidence.

Since 1980 a number of comprehensive critical literature reviews have appeared on various topics of information seeking and retrieving, among them reviews of research on

- interactions in information systems, by Belkin and Vickery [3]
- information needs and uses, by Dervin and Niles [4]
- psychological research in human computer interaction, by Borgman [5]
- design of menu selection systems, by Shneiderman [6]
- online searching of databases, by Fenichel [7] and Bellardo [8].

It is most indicative that an identical conclusion appears in every one of these reviews despite different orientation of

*Work done under the NSF grant IST85-05411 and a DIALOG grant for search time.

†Present address: Kent State University, Kent, Ohio
‡Present address: Dyke College, Cleveland, Ohio

Received February 5, 1987; accepted March 19, 1987.

the review and different backgrounds of the reviewers. They all conclude that research has been inadequate and that more research is needed. In the words of Belkin and Vickery: "... research has not yet provided a satisfactory solution to the problem of interfacing between end-user and large scale databases." Despite a relatively large amount of literature about the subject, the research in information seeking and retrieving is in its infancy. It is still in an exploratory stage.

Yet, the future success or failure of the evolving next generation of information systems (expert systems, intelligent front-ends, etc.) based on built-in intelligence in human-system interactions depends on greatly increasing our knowledge and understanding of what is really going on in human information seeking and retrieving. The key to the future of information systems and searching processes (and by extension, of information science and artificial intelligence from where the systems and processes are emerging) lies not in increased sophistication of technology, but in increased understanding of human involvement with information.

These conclusions form the motivation and rationale for the study reported here and describe our interpretation of the significance of research in this area in general.

Background

The work reported here is the second phase of a larger long-term effort whose collective aim is to contribute to the formal characterization of the elements involved in information seeking and retrieving, particularly in relation to the cognitive context and human decisions and interactions involved in these processes. The first phase, conducted from 1981 to 1983 (under NSF grant IST80-15335) was devoted to development of appropriate methodology; the study resulted in a number of articles discussing underlying concepts, describing models and measures, and reporting on pilot tests [9–18]. These articles explain the methodological background for the second phase.

The second phase is reported here. It was a study conducted from 1985 to 1987 (under grants listed under title) devoted to making quantified observations on a number of variables as described below. To our knowledge this is the largest and most comprehensive study in this area conducted to date. Still and by necessity (due to the meager state of knowledge and observations on the variables involved) this is an exploratory study with all the ensuing limitations. The results are really reflective of the circumstances of the experiments alone. While at the end generalizations are made, they should be actually treated as hypotheses ready for verification, refutation, and/or elaboration.

The third phase (planned for 1987 to 1989) will have as its objective to study in depth the nature, relations and patterns of some of the critical variables observed here. In this way we are trying to proceed (or inch) along the classic steps of scientific inquiry.

Organization of Reporting

A comprehensive final report to NSF deposited with ERIC and NTIS [19] provides a detailed description of models, methods, procedures, and results; a large appendix to the report contains the "raw" data and forms and flowcharts for procedures used. Thus, for those interested there is a detailed record of the study, particularly in respect to procedures and data.

In this journal, the study is reported in three articles or parts. This first part is devoted to description of models, measures, variables and procedures involved and relates the study to other works. The second part, subtitled "Users and Questions" presents the results of classes or variables that are more closely associated with information seeking; included in Part II are also results related to effectiveness measures. The third part, subtitled "Searchers and Searches" is devoted to the classes of variables that are more closely associated with information retrieving. A summary of conclusions from the study as a whole is also presented in Part III.

Objectives and Approach

As mentioned, the aim of the study was to contribute to the formal, scientific characterization of the elements involved in information seeking and retrieving, particularly in relation to the cognitive context and human decisions and interactions involved. The objectives were to conduct the observations under as real-life conditions as possible related to: (1) user *context* of questions in information retrieval; (2) the structure and classification of *questions;* (3) cognitive traits and decision-making of *searchers;* and (4) different *searches* of the same question.

The following aspects of information seeking and retrieving were studied as grouped in five general classes of the entities involved:

1. *User:* effects of the context of questions and constraints placed on questions.
2. *Question:* structure and classification as assigned by different judges and the effect of various classes on retrieval.
3. *Searcher:* effects of cognitive traits and frequency of online experience.
4. *Search:* effects of different types of searches; overlap between searches for the same question in selection of search terms and items retrieved; efficiehcy and effectiveness of searches.
5. *Items retrieved:* magnitude of retrieval of relevant and nonrelevant items; effects of other variables on the chances that retrieved items were relevant.

The approach was as real-life as possible (rather than laboratory) in the following sense:

- users posed questions related to their research or work and evaluated the answers accordingly; they were not paid for their time, but received a free search
- searchers were professionals, i.e. searching is part of their regular job; they were paid for their time
- searching was done on existing databases on DIALOG. There were no time restrictions
- items retrieved (i.e. answers) were full records as available from the given database.

The control was that all the searching was done under the same conditions. However, for control purposes there were two major restrictions departing from real-life situations: (i) only one and the same database was used for searching the same question by different searchers; in real-life more than one may be used; and (ii) searchers did not have access to users for interviews, they all received the same written question as elaborated by the user. These restrictions were posed because there was no way that we could control the observations otherwise. However, similar restrictions are not that uncommon in real-life searching.

Related Works

The enumerated reviews [3–8] provide an extensive coverage of works related to this study, particularly the review by Belkin and Vickery [3], thus only a brief overview is provided here.

Models of Information Seeking Context

An exhaustive list of variables by Fidel and Soergel [20] illustrates the complexity of the context and processes in online searching: they listed over 200 variables grouped into 8 broad categories. Other models in which some or other of these variables were highlighted greatly depended on a given view of the information seeking context. For a long time the predominant concept around which models revolved was the concept of information need; we shall mention Taylor's work [21] as representative of this school of thought. Slowly, modeling changed to that of problem orientation, viewing the problem behind the question, rather than information need as central to information seeking context. The work by Belkin and colleagues [1,22,23] is representative of the problem oriented school of thought, which has increasingly borrowed notions and approaches from cognitive science. The study reported here belongs in this problem oriented category, greatly affected by cognitive science.

Models of Questions

The nature of questions, as reviewed by Graesser and Black [24], has been a subject of study in a number of fields from philosophy and logic to computer science and artificial intelligence. Librarianship also has many works on classification of questions, some going back over 50 years [25]. More recently, the whole area of questions and questioning has become an intensive area of study in artificial intelligence because of its importance to natural language processing, question-answering systems, and expert systems. The book by Graesser and Black is representative of work in this area. So is the pioneering work by Lehnert [26]. Among other things, she provided a novel classification scheme for questions. The work on questions in artificial intelligence is innovative, but it also demonstrates that the progress in this area is slow and incremental. The study reported here in regard to structure and classification of questions is complementary to this work in artificial intelligence.

Models of Search Processes

A number of works in information science have been devoted to modeling and description of the search process. These range from simple flowcharts to complex analysis of the elements and steps involved. Here are some representative models that deal with

- elements and tactics in question analysis and search strategy, by Bates [27,28]
- types of search strategies, by Markey and Atherton [29]
- definition and principles of user interviews and search processes, by Soergel [30]
- identification of heuristics and tactics that are applicable to a wide range of search problems, by Harter and Peters [31]

Most of the descriptions in these studies have been inferred from observations of professional practice or describe desires to improve practice and make it more standardized. Remarkably few models have been put to a scientific test.

Empirical Studies

The factors affecting online searching and human-system interface have been studied in a number of experiments in which data were collected under (more or less) controlled conditions. Here is a list of representative topics in such studies (for others, see ref. 3)

- differences in searching and in search results as affected by various degrees of searching experience, by Fenichel [32]
- relationship between some given cognitive characteristics or educational level of searchers and type of searching and/or search results, by Bridle [33], Bellardo [34], and Woelfl [35]
- types of elements, sequences, and modifications in the search process, by Penniman [36,37], Fidel [38], and Oldroyd and Cetroen [39]

- effects of the type of training received by searchers, by Borgman [40]
- effects of various types of search questions and various user goals on searching, by Rouse and Rouse [41]
- observation of end user search behavior in an operational setting, by Sewell and Teitelbaum [42]
- conceptualization and test of the search process as an imperfect decision-making task, by Fischhoff and MacGregor [43]

The study reported here is closely related by type to the empirical studies reviewed above and as a result it builds on these studies.

General Model

Complex systems such as information retrieval systems (or information systems in general) can be modeled and studied in a number of ways. In the 1960s and 1970s the emphasis was on study and evaluation of input processes and components, such as various representations of documents (or texts) and subsequent retrieval effectiveness. In the 1980s a shift occurred toward study of output processes, users and interactions. In either case, a part of the larger system or a microsystem was isolated, modeled and studied.

Information seeking and retrieving is viewed here as such a microsystem of a larger information system. It is the microsystem that involves the user and interacts with the user and whose role it is to help the user in obtaining appropriate responses.

Figure 1 presents a general model of information seeking and retrieving describing the major events with the accompanying classes of variables. A similar model is found in Belkin and Vickery [3]. The interactive nature of this microsystem is its primary characteristic and one should envision arrows between all events and variables.

The model provides an overview of all events and variables involved in information seeking and retrieving. We follow this general model by presenting next, in greater detail, the model and measures for each class of variables selected for study in this project.

Event	Class of Variables
User (information seeker) has a problem which needs to be resolved	* User Characteristics * Problem statement
User seeks to resolve the problem by formulating a question and starting an interaction with an information system	* Question statement * Question characteristics
Presearch interaction with a searcher i.e. a human or computer intermediary	* Searcher characteristics * Question analysis
Formulation of a search	* Search strategy * Search characteristics
Searching activity and interactions	* Searching
(Possible: initial evaluation of results and reiterative searching)	(* Adjusted search)
Delivery of responses to user	* Items retrieved * Formats delivered
Evaluation of responses by user	* Relevance * Utility

FIG. 1. A general model of information seeking and retrieving.

Users and the Context of Information Seeking

There is more to a question than words expressing it. This is a well known truism examined from various viewpoints in psychology and cognitive science, philosophy, linguistics, artifical intelligence, librarianship, and information science [24]. We assume that the context of a question is a governing force describable by a set of variables affecting all events in information seeking and retrieving. The context can be considered as to its external or environmental aspects, or internal or cognitive aspects. Here we are concerned with the latter involving the following

1. *Problem* underlying the question (or more accurately, perception of the problem by the user).
2. *Intent* for use of the information by the user.
3. *Internal knowledge state* of the user in respect to the problem at hand.
4. *Public knowledge expectations* or estimate by the user.

Problem

Within the framework of information seeking, a problem is defined as an unknown in a work or situation of a potential user of an information system. A problem signifies that which causes difficulty in finding or working out a solution. We assume that information is necessary to solve problems, make decisions, or improve understanding. Such information can be obtained in many ways. One of them is to obtain or deduce it from the existing body of public knowledge, such as in organized retrieval systems, expert systems and the like.

In problem solving research in cognitive science a problem is said to exist when (a) it is at a given state, (b) it is desired to be at another state, and (c) there is no clear way to get from (a) to (b) [44,45]. Either of the two states could be well defined or poorly defined, leading to four obvious categories: both well defined, both poorly defined, first well defined and the other poorly defined, and vice versa.

Borrowing from these notions we have concentrated on observing the effects of the degree of how well the problem is defined, as perceived by the user. We also compared the user perception with that of a searcher.

Internal Knowledge State

People ask questions because they don't know something or they want to confirm something, or, in the words of

Belkin [1], because they have an anomalous state of knowledge in respect to a problem. Internal knowledge state refers to the degree of knowledge an information seeker has about the problem at hand and/or the question arising from the problem.

Internal knowledge state involves many aspects related to cognitive structures and processes: how knowledge is stored, organized, associated, retrieved, and changed in one's mind. A considerable amount of research in cognitive science is devoted to these questions (see ref. 46). Recognizing the great complexity of internal knowledge states, we have concentrated on a rather simple aspect in this study: the effects of the degree of internal knowledge about the problem or question at hand, as perceived by the user about his/her own knowledge. We have also compared the user indication of internal knowledge with that of the searcher.

Intent

An information seeker inevitably has some purpose in mind for the use of requested information. In the framework of information retrieval, the intent is defined as a planned or prospective use of information, including constraints, if any, on that information. In other words, the users have some preconceived ideas about

- the use of information in respect to the problem
- the amount of time and effort they are willing to spend in absorption of or deduction from the provided information
- the desirable characteristics of responses to the question, such as completeness, precision, reliability, timeliness, etc.
- the form characteristics of responses deemed most desirable, such as to the language, source, etc.
- the economic value they attach to responses.

The intent in information retrieval and the goal state in problem solving are related but not identical. They are treated separately because the information seeking intent can be a very specific aspect of problem solving, exclusively devoted to the use of supplied information within a broader context of a goal in problem solving.

Information seeking intent can be focused (where a type of use is more specified), and unfocused (where the use is less specified). We concentrated on the effects of the degree of how well the intent is defined, as perceived by the user. We also compared the user perception with that of the searcher.

Public Knowledge Estimate

Public Knowledge is the recorded knowledge on a subject in the public domain; in the context of information retrieval it refers to the records or literature on a subject. People ask questions within the framework of public knowledge. This involves a number of aspects such as their perception of what is (or what is not) there, how is it organized, what can they expect to get, etc. Thus, a user's estimate of public knowledge defines his/her expectations, which in turn affects the evaluation.

We concentrated on the effects of the estimate of public knowledge by the user. We also compared the user estimate with that of the searcher.

Measures of Information Seeking Context

Four Likert-type scales have been used to obtain an indication of the information seeking context first from users and then also as perceived by searchers.

1. PROBLEM DEFINITION SCALE
   "In your opinion, and on a scale from 1 to 5, would you describe your problem as weakly defined or clearly defined, with 1 being weakly defined and 5 being clearly defined?"

   : ____ : ____ : ____ : ____ : ____ :

   1 2 3 4 5

   weakly defined clearly defined

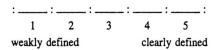

2. INTENT SCALE
   "On a scale from 1 to 5, would you say that your use of this information will be open to many avenues, or for a specifically defined purpose, with 1 representing open to many avenues and 5 representing a specifically defined purpose?"

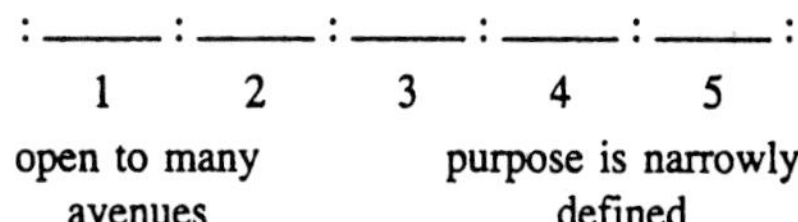

3. INTERNAL KNOWLEDGE SCALE
   "On a scale from 1 to 5, how would you rank the amount of knowledge you possess in relation to the problem which motivated this request?"

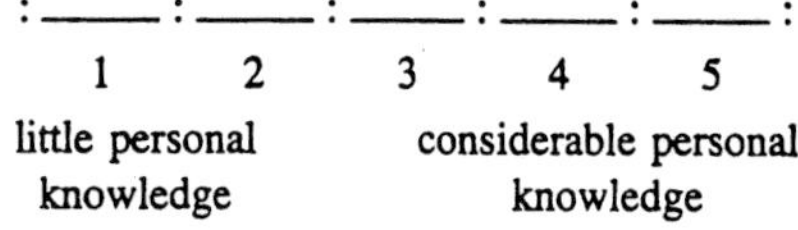

4. PROBLEM-PUBLIC KNOWLEDGE SCALE
   "On a scale from 1 to 5, how would you rank the probability that information about the problem which motivated this research question may be found in the literature?"

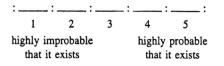

   : ____ : ____ : ____ : ____ : ____ :

   1 2 3 4 5

   highly improbable that it exists highly probable that it exists

Structure and Characteristics of Questions

Questions are a whole class of linguistic expressions, uttered with the intention of inducing a response. In addition to grammar, there is also a logic and pragmatic context of questions (e.g. refs. 47 and 48). Study of questions and questioning dates at least from Aristotle and encompasses a number of fields as reviewed by Kearsley [49]. As mentioned, this is a particular active area of research in artificial intelligence and cognitive science because of the significant implications for design of intelligent systems [24,26].

While questions can have a number of functions, of interest here are those that have a role in problem solving. Within the context of information seeking, questions are defined as statements that are verbalized (written or oral) representations of a problem at hand; their function is to elicit a response. We have concentrated on

1. Observing the effects of constraints on questions as indicated by users.
2. Describing and testing a structure of questions in information retrieval.
3. Developing and testing a classification scheme for questions in information retrieval oriented toward grouping of questions by several characteristics above and beyond their subject contents.
4. Observing the effects of different classes of questions.

Constraints on Questions

The user was asked to indicate for the question the following aspects considered as constraints

1. Do you want a broad or precise search?
2. What is the type of application of this research or work (undergraduate study; graduate study; faculty research; industrial; general; other)?
3. Do you want to place restrictions on the language of publication of the articles retrieved (English only; any language)?
4. Do you want to restrict the years of publication of the article retrieved (last 5 years; no limits; specify years: 19__ to 19__)?

Structure of Questions

As a rule, questions in information retrieval consist of three parts: a lead-in, a subject, and a query.

The lead-in is not directly searchable. It may consist of phrases such as: "I want information about . . . ." However, at times lead-in may have implication for searching; for instance "what is . . . " implies request for definition, "where is . . . " implies request for location, or "when was . . . " implies involvement of a time element. In such cases, lead-ins are important for recognizing presuppositions in a question, i.e. implications not directly expressed (see discussion below).

The subject of the question is the central concept of the question. It is a concept around which all other aspects of the question revolve and relate. A question can have more than one subject.

The query is the specific aspect asked about the question's subject. It is an attribute, characteristic, component, or part of the subject about which information is desired. There can be more than one query about a subject.

Example:

What are	the advertising expenditures	of the automobile industry?
LEAD-IN	QUERY	SUBJECT

In addition, questions may have constraints geared toward restricting or orienting the type of desired responses.

Classification of Questions

It is not uncommon to hear searchers describe given questions as: "complex," "specific," "very general," "difficult," "unsearchable," "unclear," and the like. In such cases searchers are (possibly even unwillingly) applying certain general attributes to classify questions. While no generally accepted classification of questions in information retrieval exists, it is of practical interest to specify certain attributes which could be used to classify or describe questions in information retrieval.

The scheme described here has been developed on the basis of criteria that might relate categorizations of questions to approaches to and outcomes of searching. Five categories are used: domain, clarity, specificity, complexity and presupposition.

1. **Domain:** classifies a question in the appropriate general subject or topic area in which it falls. This can be done on the basis of a general subject classification. In our case, we have chosen the list of DIALOG subject categories of their files as the subject classification scheme.
   Measure: for a question the classifier indicates the number or name associated with the given DIALOG category best fit for the question. More than one DIALOG category can be used, as necessary.
2. **Clarity:** classifies a question on the basis of degree of clarity in respect to (a) semantics (meaning of terms) and (b) syntax (relation and logic between terms).
   Measure: for a question the classifier indicates on a scale from 1 to 5 the degree of clarity, where 1 means "unclear" and 5 means "clear". Two scales are used:
   (a) For semantic clarity (meaning.of terms).
   (b) For syntactic clarity (relation and logic between terms).
3. **Specificity:** classifies a question on the basis of degree of specificity of (a) query terms and (b) subject terms. Specificity ranges from very general or broad (e.g. as found in a thesaurus under BT-Broader terms) to very specific or narrow (e.g. as found in a thesaurus under NT-Narrower terms).
   Measure: for a question the classifier indicates on a scale from 1 to 5 the degree of specificity, where 1

means "broad" and 5 means "narrow". Two scales are used
   (a) For terms associated with the query part of the question.
   (b) For terms associated with subject part.

4. **Complexity:** classifies a question on the basis of complexity for searching as related to number for search concepts involved. The search concepts are those that are used as search terms or will be translated into one or more search terms (i.e. a search concept can have more than one search term as its synonyms or near synonyms). The search concepts in both the query part and subject part of the question are added together.
   Measure: for a question the classifier indicates two aspects
   (a) On a scale from 1 to 5 the degree of complexity, where 1 means low complexity and 5 means high complexity.
   (b) The number of search concepts to be used as or translated into search terms.

5. **Presupposition:** classifies a question on the basis of presence or absence of implied (not explicitly stated) concepts derived from sharing of common linguistic and world knowledge. Of interest are those implied concepts that could be used as search terms or search constraints. Most commonly presuppositions are expressed by phrases such as "What is...", "Where is...", etc. implying existence or verification, identity or definition, quality, relation, number, location, or time.
   Measure: for a question the classifer indicates two aspects:
   (a) On a scale from 1 to 5 the degree of presence of presuppositions, where 1 means "no presupposition" and 5 means "many presuppositions".
   (b) The number of presuppositions that can be translated into search terms or search constraints.

Searchers

A large number of environmental (or external) and cognitive (or internal) factors, e.g. organizational setting, economic constraints, affect searcher's decisions and thus retrieval effectiveness and efficiency. While recognizing the external factors, we have concentrated on a limited number of cognitive traits of searchers:

1. Language ability or the ability to make inductive inferences through word association, as measured by a standard test called Remote Associates Test.
2. Logical ability or the ability to make deductive inferences as measured by a standard test called Symbolic Reasoning Test.
3. Preferred style or mode of learning as measured by a standard test called Learning Style Inventory.
4. Online experience as derived from a questionnaire given to searchers.

Remote Associates Test (RAT)

RAT is a test of semantic associations. It claims to test the ability to make inductive inferences. The test instrument was developed by Mednick and Mednick [50] and it has been widely applied and tested for fifteen years. The test presents the subjects with sets of three stimulus words and asks them to infer the fourth word that is related (or has something in common with) all three stimulus words, as in the following examples:

			Prescribed right answer
cookies	sixteen	heart ______	(sweet)
poke	go	molasses ______	(slow)
surprise	line	birthday ______	(party)
skunk	kings	boiled ______	(cabbage)

The test consists of thirty such matches to be made in twenty minutes. The score is a straight count of right (predetermined) answers out of thirty.

Symbolic Reasoning Test (SRT)

SRT is one of the tests in the Employee Aptitude Survey (EAS). The survey is a battery of 10 tests developed by Ruck and Ruck [51], widely used in business and industry for personnel selection. The Symbolic Reasoning Test, based as the name implies on symbols, claims to measure deductive inferences. This is a thirty item test done in five minutes. Each item specifies a relationship of A to B to C and requires a "true", "false", or "don't know" answer as in the following example:

$A > B > C$ therefore $A < C$: true, false, don't know

The test is scored on a straight count of correct answers.

Learning Style Inventory (LSI)

LSI is based on a theory describing learning as an integrated, four stage process that involves the use of four different cognitive modes as described by Kolb [52]: (i) Concrete Experience (CE); (ii) Reflective Observation (RO); (iii) Abstract Conceptualization (AC); (iv) Active Experimentation (AE). LSI claims to measure individual preferences for each of the above four basic modes for learning and places an individual in a composite category indicative of his/her learning style. The test has been widely applied and tested for over ten years. The respondent is asked to rank order from 1 to 4 a series of four statements in response to a question on how he/she learns. There are twelve sets to rank within twenty minutes; here are two examples

When I learn:

_ I like to deal with my feelings	_ I like to watch and listen	_ I like to think about ideas	_ I like to be doing things

I learn best from:

_ Personal relations	_ Obser- vation	_ Rational theories	_ A chance to try out and practice

Each column represents a separate learning mode arranged from left to right: CE, RO, AC, and AE. The raw scoring is done by adding all the rank numbers given by the respondent in a column. Two combination scores are obtained by subtracting Concrete Experience score from Abstract Conceptualization score (AC − CE), and the Reflective Observation score from Active Experimentation score (AE − RO). The combination scores are used to indicate an individual's learning style—the extent to which he/she emphasizes abstractness over concreteness (AC − CE) and action over reflection (AE − RO). These scores are also used to make a graph with AC − CE on the *Y* axis and AE-RO on the *X* axis. An individual is placed in one of the four quadrants characterizing a person as to style of learning as: (i) converger (lower left); (ii) diverger (upper right); (iii) assimilator (lower right); or (iv) accommodator (upper left). A person with a zero score on either AC − CE or AE − RO is considered indeterminate.

Searcher's Experience

The amount and type of experience a searcher had in online searching was obtained from a questionnaire. Since DIALOG was used for searching, the questions asked were specific to DIALOG system:

1. "How often do you search DIALOG?: daily, twice a week, once per week, twice per month, less."
2. "Indicate seven DIALOG databases you search most often in order of decreasing use."
3. "Indicate thesaurus most important to you when you search."

The answer to the first question has been used as a searcher's variable. The answers to the last two questions have been used to match the searchers with databases they are to search in the study, so that their background and the databases match as closely as possible.

Search

The elements and subprocesses in a search have been modeled and categorized in a number of ways [27 to 31]. While it is difficult to make a clear separation, a common way is to make a distinction between:

1. *Question Analysis:* procedures that deal with decisions on semantic and pragmatic (contextual) aspects of a question in preparation of a search statement, including determination of appropriate information sources, and a possible interview with a user.
2. *Formulation of Search Strategy:* procedures that deal with decisions on syntactic and logical aspects of the search statement, including incorporation of constraints, if any, and selection of tactics related to a desired level of effectiveness and efficiency.
3. *Searching:* procedures used in the conduct of a search, including the use of protocols and capabilities of given information systems and obtaining the responses.

In this study we have concentrated on several specific variables within Question Analysis and Search Strategy. We kept searching constant, meaning that the environment, hardware, software, procedures, and information system for all searches were the same.

Question Analysis

We have concentrated on two aspects:

1. Degree of overlap or agreement in selection of search terms by different searchers searching the same question based on the written question statement submitted by the user.
2. Differences in results among search statements derived from four different sources for search term selection, namely:

Type 1. From a statement about the problem at hand as tape recorded by the user, but without recourse to the written question.

Type 2. From the tape problem statement and the written question submitted by the user.

Type 3. From the written question using only the words in the question as search terms without any further elaboration.

Type 4. From the written question plus terms from an appropriate thesaurus for elaboration.

These four types of searches we labeled "project searches."

Search Strategy

We have concentrated on three aspects of the search statement as a whole:

1. Degree of overlap or agreement in retrieved items by search statements done by different searchers searching the same question based on the written question statement submitted by the user.
2. Differences in search effectiveness as expressed by measures based on relevance and utility judgements of users.
3. Differences in search tactics and efficiency as used by different searchers searching the same question; these characteristics are based on the level of effort used in a search as expressed by the tactics and efficiency measures described below.

Measure of Overlap in Search Terms

This measure indicates for each pair of searchers the degree of agreement or overlap in selection of search terms in searching of the same question. However, because there may be differences in how Searcher 1 agrees with Searcher 2, from how Searcher 2 agrees with Searcher 1 the measure is asymmetrical (e.g., in a search statement Searcher 1 uses two terms, and Searcher 2 uses six terms; the two terms of S1 are also used by S2, but S2 has four more terms, thus S1 is in 100% agreement with S2, but S2 is only in 33% agreement with S1). The overlap or agreement measures for search terms are:

$$S_{1,2} = \frac{|S_1 \cap S_2|}{|S_1|} = \frac{\text{no. of search terms in common}}{\text{total no. of terms used by Searcher 1}}$$

$$S_{2,1} = \frac{|S_1 \cap S_2|}{|S_2|} = \frac{\text{no. of search terms in common}}{\text{total no. of terms used by Searcher 2}}$$

Measure for Overlap in Output

This measure indicates for each pair of searchers the degree of overlap in retrieved items for the search of the same question. The overlap measure for output parallels the measure for the overlap or degree of agreement in search terms. It is calculated in the same way except that either the total number of retrieved items or else the number of relevant items retrieved is substituted for the number of search terms. Since the formula is the same as shown above, it is not repeated here. Both overlap measures are asymmetrical and both can be used for arranging data into a matrix and/or a histogram to study the distribution of overlap from a group as a whole.

Effectiveness Measures

Two sets of measures for evaluating the effectiveness of a search have been used, based on the two most often used criteria:

1. *Relevance:* the degree of fit between the question and the retrieved item. The criteria of *"aboutness"* is used.
2. *Utility:* the degree of actual usefulness of answers to an information seeker. The criteria used is the *value* to the information seeker.

In this study both relevance of items and the utility of the entire retrieved set have been established by users.

Definition of relevance. The following definitions have been provided to users for judging the answers (i.e. abstracts):

"Each abstract should be evaluated according to its degree of relevance to the question you submitted for searching. The degree of relevance should be determined using the following three point scale:

RELEVANT—Any document which on the basis of the information it conveys is considered to be related to your question, even if the information is outdated or already familiar to you.
PARTIALLY RELEVANT—Any document which on the basis of the information it conveys is considered only somewhat or in some part related to your question or to any part of your question.
NONRELEVANT—Any document which on the basis of the information it conveys is not at all related to your question."

Recall and Precision. These are measures based on the relevance judgement of users where:

Precision = probability that a retrieved item is relevant

Recall = probability that a relevant item in the file is retrieved

These probabilities were estimated as follows for a given search:

$$\text{Precision} = \frac{\text{No. of relevant items retrieved by the search}}{\text{Total no. of items retrieved by the search}}$$

$$\text{Recall} = \frac{\text{No. of relevant items retrieved by the search}}{\text{Total no. of relevant items in the union of items retrieved by all searchers for that question}}$$

Precision is easy to establish directly from the output of evaluated items for a search. Recall is not easy to establish, because it is never apparent how many items in a file are relevant to the question. Each question was searched by a number of searches and types of searches. A union of retrieved items from all searches for the question was established (i.e., by merging all the outputs and eliminating duplicates) and sent to the user for evaluation. In this way the evaluated items from the union served as the benchmark of individual search recall. This presents a *comparative* rather than absolute measure of recall performance for any given search.

Utility Measures. These are measures based on users' expression of degree of satisfaction and value of the retrieved items as a whole. Recall and precision are universally used measures. Unfortunately, there are no such universally used utility measures, thus we had to establish our own. The following questions were posed to the users which reflect utility based measures:

1. How much time did you spend reviewing these abstracts? ____
2. In an overall sense, if you were asked to assign a dollar value to the usefulness of this entire set of abstracts to you, what would that dollar value be?
   $______ ______ I cannot assign a dollar value
3. Could you rate your participation in this project and the information which resulted as:

   5 Worth much more than the time it has taken
   4 Worth somewhat more than the time it has taken
   3 Worth about as much as the time it has taken
   2 Worth less than the time it has taken
   1 Practically worthless

4. Problem Resolution Scale—On a scale of 1 to 5, what contribution has this information made to the resolution of the problem which motivated your question?

: ___ : ___ : ___ : ___ : ___ :

1 2 3 4 5

nothing contributed — substantial contribution

5. Satisfaction Scale—On a scale of 1 to 5, how satisfied were you with the results of the search?

: ___ : ___ : ___ : ___ : ___ :

1 2 3 4 5

dissatisfied — satisfied

Tactics and Efficiency Measures

The following measures have been used for online searches describing search characteristics as to:

1. Number of *commands* used by a search.
2. Number of command *cycles* used by a searcher. A cycle is a set of commands in sequence from those used to select, combine, and/or expand terms to a command used to type (or view) the results. A cycle ends with display (type, print) of intermediate or final items retrieved for a set of preceding commands.
3. Number of *search terms* used by a searcher searching a question.
4. *Preparation time* used by a searcher in preparing a search for a question.
5. Online *connect time* used by a searcher in searching a question.
6. *Total time* used by a searcher (connect time plus preparation time).

The first three measures reflect the search tactics and the last three the efficiency or costs associated with the search and searching.

Items Retrieved

Output from a search may be called by a number of names: references, answers, documents, abstracts, displays, etc. We have selected a neutral label, "items retrieved," to designate the output for a search, that is, the individual records retrieved from a database in response to a question. While databases provide different format options for each item retrieved, we have chosen to use the full database record of each and every item retrieved. Thus, "items retrieved" were *full records*. In all databases searched for the project, full records included bibliographic information, index terms and/or classification codes and an abstract.

We have concentrated on two aspects.

1. Observing the distributions of items retrieved.
2. Analyzing the chances or odds that an item retrieved will be relevant as affected by other variables.

The second aspect is actually a major point of the study.

Measures for Items Retrieved

The following measures of quantity were used:

1. Total number of items retrieved for a question calculated in two ways: (i) as a sum for all searches for the question *including* duplicates retrieved by different searches, and (ii) as a union of all searches for the question counting the distinct numbers only by *excluding* or eliminating the duplicates.
2. Total number of items evaluated by a user for a question again calculated in two ways. (The items evaluated for a number of question were smaller than items retrieved as described below under Procedures.)
3. Total number of items judged by users as relevant, partially relevant and not relevant for a question, again calculated two ways.

The quantities from the last measure have been used to calculate the chances of retrieval of a relevant item as a function of some other variable by a statistical method called Logarithmic Cross Ratio Analysis (described under Analysis Methods). These measures of performance when correlated with variables associated with users, questions, searchers and searches revealed effects which cannot be seen using the traditional measures of recall and precision.

Procedures

Users

On the basis of advertising about the project forty users volunteered to participate. The forty users that started with the project completed all their tasks from start to finish, thus, user response was 100%. Each of the forty users:

- filled out a short questionnaire about his/her background
- submitted one question for searching together with information on desired question constraints; thus, 40 questions were used in the study
- participated in a taped interview describing the problem underlying the question and the intent in use of information and indicated the context measures
- evaluated items retrieved in response to his/her question as to relevance and indicated the utility of the search as a whole.

The forms, instructions, and procedures used in these and all other tasks in the study, as well as the full statement of questions are assembled in the appendix to the Final Report for the project [19].

Searchers

On the basis of advertising and presentations at professional meetings we received an indication of interest from about forty information professionals, thirty-six of these eventually participated from beginning to end. These became known as "outside searchers." The outside searchers were paid $100 for their time. Each of the searchers:

- was tested on three cognitive tests described above and filled out a questionnaire on their search experience
- received instructions on procedures for searching in a presentation and in writing
- received five or six questions for searching (each question was searched by 5 different searchers, but since there were forty questions and thirty-six searchers some searched six questions); the questions they received were copies of written statements by the users, together with users' indication of constraints
- prepared a preliminary search strategy
- conducted the search and recorded the results. (The whole search was recorded on a disc and a printout).

No restrictions, such as time limits, were placed on searchers in preparation for and conduct of the search.

In addition, three searchers from the full time staff of the project were engaged in searching so called project searches, as described below. These became known as "project searchers". Thus, a total of thirty-nine searchers participated in the study.

Searching

Searching was done on DIALOG, the largest vendor in the world as to the number of databases and frequency of use. More searchers have more professional experience with DIALOG than with any other system, which was the reason for selecting it.

Each question was searched on one database only. The database was selected by the project team on the basis of closeness of fit between the question and the subject of the database. The searchers were assigned questions which matched as closely as possible their own database experience. Searching was done on microcomputers with preprogrammed log-on and downloading protocols. Appropriate thesauri and manuals were assembled and made available to all searchers. All searching was done in the same room and environment, and under the same conditions.

Project Searches

As mentioned, each question was searched by five outside searchers. In addition, there were four searches done in-house by the project staff. These additional searches were labeled "project searches", and the staff searchers as "project searchers." Thus, nine searches were done for each question: five by outside searchers and four by project searchers.

As mentioned, the objective of four project searches was to study various types of searches resulting from different sources for the search strategy. The sources for each type are enumerated above under "Question Analysis."

The project searches were done by three project searchers. They also conducted the taped interview with the users. However, the project searches were arranged so that they were done by the project searcher who did *not* do the interview. Thus, each project searcher heard the taped interview for the first time when the first project search was done. The project searchers took all the same cognitive tests as the outside searchers.

Question Structure and Classification

This part of the study had two separate objectives:

1. To test the suggested model of question structure and the scheme for question classification.
2. To observe the effects of different question classes.

For the first objective a separate experiment was conducted. It consisted of testing the consistency or degree of agreement in assigning question structure and classification classes by a number of judges. On the basis of advertising a group of twenty-one information professionals was assembled to assign the question structure and classification. These were a different group from the searchers and had nothing to do with searching. They are called "classification judges." The experiment consisted of each judge:

- receiving twenty questions for judging; these were selected at random from the forty questions submitted by users
- assessing the question structure on an appropriate form
- classifying each question as to domain, clarity, specificity, complexity, and presuppositions.

The results of classification were calculated for agreement. The classes (and questions in these classes), with significant agreement, were then used to analyze chances of retrieval of relevant answers, i.e. to address the second objective of this part of the study.

Prior to conducting the experiment with twenty-one judges, a pilot experiment was carried out with two other judges to observe if the procedures worked. They did. In the Final Report [19] we report results only on the two judges in the pilot study and not on the twenty-one judges in the experiment proper (the report was written before this part of the study was completed). Here we are reporting the results on twenty-one judges only, i.e., we are disregarding the pilot study.

Evaluation by Users

Here is a summary of steps involved in evaluation:

- the end result of each search was a list of accession numbers of items retrieved

- the accession numbers for retrieved items from nine searches for each question were merged and a union set created, i.e., the duplicates were eliminated, thus this union set consisted of all and only distinct items retrieved for the question
- if the union of retrieved items exceeded 150, only the first 150 items were designated to be sent to the user for evaluation. This was done to make evaluation manageable for the user, who, if presented with an overwhelming output might have considered the task unreasonable, and rightly so, and may not have finished. (However, for three questions that slightly exceeded the 150 limit we sent all retrieved items). Since all searchers had an equal chance to contribute to the retrieved set, including the first 150 items, there was no bias toward any searcher. DIALOG databases are organized on a last in/first out principle, thus the first 150 items represent the most recent additions to the databases and the literature
- the full record of each item retrieved in the union set to be sent to user was downloaded from DIALOG onto floppy disk and then printed
- to each item retrieved a line for evaluation was added:
  ___ Relevant ___ Partially Relevant ___ Nonrelevant
- the printout and a carbon copy were sent to the user for evaluation. The user also indicated the utility of the search as a whole. Finally, the user returned the original with his/her evaluation.

The relevance evaluations were recorded with accession numbers of each item retrieved to create a benchmark file against which the output of all searches was compared. In turn, a large master file was created containing values for all variables involved, including user evaluations. The master file served as a basis for statistical analysis.

Summary

The study involved the following:

- forty users, each providing one question and a taped interview on the problem at hand
- thirty-six outside searchers and three project searchers for a total of thirty-nine searchers
- for each of the questions five different outside searches and four project searches, for a total of nine searches per question
- all together for the forty questions 360 searches, consisting of 200 outside and 160 project searches.

In addition, a separate question structure and classification experiment involved twenty-one judges.

Methods of Statistical Analysis

Approach

The basis for statistical analysis was user evaluation of retrieved items. Every evaluation involved five distinct entities: (i) user, (ii) question, (iii) searcher, (iv) search, and (v) retrieved item. The analysis proceeded by examining these entities first one by one and then at several different levels of aggregation.

Any measured variable (using measures described above) describes one or more of the five entities. For instance, the cognitive characteristics of the searcher describe only a single entity, the searcher; the number of commands or the number of search terms used describe only another single entity, the search. On the other hand, user evaluation is a description of the relevance of a retrieved item by the user; and it relates two entities: user and retrieved item. The overall retrieval or precision scores for a given question combines several searches by several searchers and so are descriptive of three entities: the question, the searches, and the searchers together. And so on.

The data has been examined at each of such different levels of aggregation. Some of the levels of aggregation are more familiar in everyday practice, while others are more powerful in the search for possible explanatory relations. A data file was formed for each level of aggregation by retaining those variables that are meaningful at that level and ignoring the others. These files were used to investigate various statistical relationships.

The relationships (as well as other statistics) were analyzed and displayed by using BMDP and SPSSX statistical packages. BMDP is widely used in biomedical research and SPSSX in social science research. The BMDP Manual [53] provides a detailed description of statistical techniques used.

We distinguished between findings that are statistically significant and those that are also important, i.e. those findings that provided a substantial explanation of the relevance of retrieved items. When a statistically significant relationship is found it can be assigned some measure of association. This is a measure of the extent to which one of the variables in question (X—the one presumed independent) determines the other (Y—the one taken to be dependent). The fact that a relationship is significant does not mean that it is important.

We regarded a relationship as important if the independent variable explains a substantial amount of the observed variation in the dependent variable. The measures of importance that have been used in this study are the R-squared measure for regression analysis and the t-value for analysis of the log cross ratio. Below we review the two. The R-squared measure is reviewed only briefly because it is used widely in information science research, but the log cross ratio is reviewed in some detail, because to our knowledge this is its first application in research in this area. It is a powerful technique widely used in biomedicine and, as we found, a powerful tool for explanation of factors that affect chances of retrieved items being relevant.

Macro (Search-wise) and Micro (Item-wise) Analysis

Two levels of statistical analysis were used in this study: macro, or search-wise, and micro, or item-wise. On the search-wise level explanations were sought for the impact of given variables on precision and recall and on the odds of either being above average; that is, the macro analysis focused on the effectiveness of the searches as a whole. On the item-wise level, explanations were sought for the impact of given variables on the odds that retrieved items were relevant as opposed to not relevant. As the names imply, the search-wise analysis concentrates on traditional measures of precision and recall of the whole search, while the item-wise analysis ignores these measures and concentrates on the relevance of each item retrieved by a search. Regression and logarithmic cross ratio analyses were used for the former and logarithmic cross ratio analysis only for the latter.

Regression Analysis

In regression analysis, exploring the dependence of Y on X, we try to find the best straight line describing Y as a function of X. We may imagine all the values of Y and X plotted in a single graph.

When such a graph is made the values of Y will show some substantial variation. This degree of variation is conveniently summarized by a statistical quantity called the variance. The variance is the average value of the square of the difference between any particular value of Y and the average of all the values of Y. When a line is fit to the data, to explain Y, a certain amount of the value of Y remains unexplained. The average square of the unexplained part is called the residual mean square variation. The difference between the two is the part of the variance that is explained by the model. This may be expressed as a percentage of the original variance, which is called R-squared. Thus, if R-squared is 80%, the model explains 80% of the original observed variation in the values of Y. If R-squared is 10%, 90% of the original variation remains unexplained.

Logarithmic Cross Ratio Analysis

In analysis of what affects (i) retrieval of items judged by users as relevant or partially relevant, and (ii) precision and recall of searches we have used a powerful technique called cross product ratio analysis. The technique is described in chapter 11 of BMDP Manual [53] and a detailed discussion of the meaning of cross product odds ratio is given by Fleiss [54].

To apply the cross ratio analysis, each variable (for which such a distinction is meaningful) is broken into a class of high values and a class of low values. For convenience the mean is generally taken as the cut point or dividing line, thus "high" means above the mean and "low" below the mean. Since in micro analysis the dependent variable of greatest interest is the relevance of retrieved items we take for high value of the relevance, items judged "relevant" or "partially relevant". In macro analysis we take for high value searches having precision or recall above mean. Every case may then be classified into exactly one of four cells in a 2 × 2 table. The number of cases for which the variable is low and the item is not relevant (or below mean) is designated by "A" and so forth. The cross ratio for this table is defined as the ratio of two products: xpr = AB/CD.

For micro or item-wise analysis the values are displayed in the table as follows:

Dependent Variable	Independent Variable: Low (Below Mean)	Independent Variable: High (Above Mean)
Not Relevant	A	C
Relevant or Part. Rel.	D	B

Number in A indicates the number of items that were retrieved in association with low (below mean) value of the independent variable (e.g., by searches having below mean number of cycles) and at the same time were judged not relevant by users. When it is written in this form its meaning is rather obscure. But, it is easy to see that if A and B are large while C and D are small the cross product ratio will be large. The meaning becomes clearer if we consider the odds that a high value of the independent variable leads to relevant items. For high values of the independent variable the odds that a retrieved item will be relevant or partially relevant are given by B/C. For low values these odds are given by D/A. The ratio of these two odds ratios reflects the increase in odds due to moving from a low value of the variable to a high value of the variable. This ratio (B/C)/(D/A) is precisely equal to the cross product ratio i.e. AB/CD. For this reason the cross ratio is also referred to as the odds ratio.

For macro or search wise analysis the values are displayed in the table as follows:

Dependent Variable		Independent Variable: Low (Below Mean)	Independent Variable: High (Above Mean)
Precision (Recall)	Below mean	A	C
	Above mean	D	B

Number in A indicates the number of searches that were below the mean value of the independent variable (e.g., searches by searchers with below mean score on Remote Associates Test) and at the same time had a below mean precision (recall). As in the case of item-wise analysis described above, the ratio of the two odds ratios ((B/C)/(D/A) = AB/CD) reflects the increase in odds due to moving from a low value of the variable to a high value of the variable.

Since the cross product ratio is always positive and may become infinite, it is replaced by its logarithm which has a more symmetrical distribution and which, for samples as large as the ones we are using, is essentially normally distributed. Thus, in our discussion of the impact of independent variables we have consistently used the log odds ratio as a statistical indicator. Since the log odds ratio is distributed essentially normally, the t statistic (that is, the measured value of the log odds ratio divided by its standard deviation) is a measure of the statistical significance of the observed effect. At the same time, the value of the odds ratio itself gives us a simple way of describing the importance or odds of a particular variable.

The log odds ratio has been used because it is resistant to two types of sample selection bias, which may be present in this study. One type of selection bias is in the distribution of relevance. Although the average precision found in this project (about 50%) is similar to that found in other studies, the end users were self-selected, and this may introduce some unknown bias in judgements of relevance. Similarly, the searchers were self-selected and, particularly with regard to cognitive characteristics, may not be typical of searchers in general. The virtue of the log odds ratio, or of the cross product ratio, is that as long as the selection biases of two variables are independent of each other, the log odds ratio is unaffected by the bias. This feature makes the log odds ratio important in so called retrospective clinical studies, where it is not possible to form a random sample. It is appropriate, for the same reasons, in this study.

Example calculation of item-wise analysis. The variable in this example of log odds ratio calculation is the number of cycles used in searches. The cut point for cycles is 3.40—this is the mean number of cycles per search. Calculations involve 8956 cases representing the total number of items retrieved by 360 searches done by all searchers (9 searches per question, for 40 questions). Of these 5287 (59%) were judged by users as relevant or partially relevant and 3669 (41%) as not relevant. There were 3486 (38.9%) cases with cycles above the mean or cut point of 3.40 and 5470 (61.1%) below the mean. In other words, 3486 items were retrieved by searches that had more than 3.40 cycles per search.

Note that the number of cycles is a property of the search as a whole, and is inherited by each of the items retrieved in that search. Thus, we expect that the items retrieved in searches with high values of cycles have a better chance to be relevant, although each particular item may be either relevant or not relevant. In fact, in searches with cycles above the cut point 2145 were relevant or partially relevant and 1341 were not relevant.

The contingency table looks like this:

		Number of Cycles		
		Below Mean	Above Mean	Total
	Not Relevant	2328	1341	3669 41%
Users Judgement	Rel. or Part Rel.	3142	2145	5287 59%
	Total	5470 61.1%	3486 38.9%	8956 100%

We can calculate the odds of REL PREL in each column:

Above mean odds	2145/1341 = 1.5995:1
Below mean odds	3142/2328 = 1.3496:1
Ratio:	1.5995/1.3496 = 1.1851
LN	(1.1851) = 0.17
STD ERROR	(from BMPD) = 0.04
	t value = 3.84

Note: 0.04 is the standard error assuming the given value of logarithm of the odds ratio. The t value is calculated on the null assumption that the cross product ratio is 1.

This is an example of a statistically significant (t larger than 2) result at 95% significance. It says that items retrieved in cases with a high (above mean) number of command cycles are by a factor 1.1851, or 18% more likely to be relevant. In other words, the odds for an item to be relevant are 18% higher when a high number of cycles is in a search. To generalize, more cycles bring higher chances for relevance.

Example of Calculation of search-wise analysis. The variable in this example is the Concrete Experience (CE) score on the Learning Style Inventory (LSI) as taken by the 36 outside searchers. The cut point for CE is 24.70—this is the mean score on the CE for the searchers (the possible score had a range from 12 to 48). Calculations involve precision for 200 searches; the mean precision was 0.54. One hundred searches had above mean values of precision and 100 below mean. Ninety-nine (49.5%) searches came from searchers with below mean CE score and 101 (50.5%) with above mean CE score. Forty-one searches came from below mean CE scores and had below mean precision.

The contingency table looks like this:

		Learning Style Inventory		
		Concrete Experience		
		Below Mean	Above Mean	Total
	Below Mean	42	59	100 50%
Precision	Above Mean	58	42	100 50%
	Total	99 49.5%	101 50.5%	200 100%

We calculate the odds of precision in each column:

Above mean	42/59 = 0.7119:1
Below mean	58/41 = 1.4146:1
Ratio	0.7119/1.4146 = 0.5032
LN	(0.5032) = −0.69
Standard error	= 0.29
t-value	= −2.39

Since the t-value even if negative is above 2, this is a statistically significant result at 95%, but in a negative sense. It indicates that searches from searchers with above mean values of CE are by a factor of 0.4968 or 49.68% (1-0.5032) less likely to have high (above mean) values of precision. In other words, searches from searchers with high CE scores are about two times (1/0.503) more likely to have low (below mean) precision. To generalize: higher CE scores bring higher chances or odds for low precision or lower chances for high precision.

Such calculations and conclusions are applied to all meaningful variables with significant results, as presented in parts II and III in the series of articles on this study of information seeking and retrieving.

Acknowledgement

We gratefully acknowledge the splendid cooperation from our users, searchers, and classification judges. Although remaining anonymous, as is the custom, they made this study possible. Our thanks to Elizabeth Logan and Nancy Woelfl for participating in set-up of various experiments and for technical advice, and to Jun-Min Jeong, J. J. Lee, Moula Cherikh, and Altay Guvenir for programming.

This was the last research project conducted at the now defunct Mathew A. Baxter School of Information and Library Science, Case Western Reserve University (1904–1986). From its inception until the very end the School encouraged research and provided an atmosphere conducive to scholarship. In recognition, the project is dedicated to the alumni and faculty of the School.

References

1. Belkin N. J.; Oddy, H. M.; Brooks, H. M. "ASK for Information Retrieval: Parts I and II," *Journal of Documentation*. 38: 61–71, 145–164; 1982.
2. Harter, S. P. *Online Information Retrieval. Concepts, Principles, and Techniques*. New York: Academic Press; 1986.
3. Belkin, N.: Vickery, A. *Interaction in Information Systems: A Review of Research From Document Retrieval to Knowledge-Based Systems*. London: The British Library; 1985. (Library and Information Research Report 35).
4. Dervin, B; Nilan, M. "Information Needs and Uses." In: Williams, M., Ed. *Annual Review of Information Science and Technology*, Vol. 21. White Plains, NY: Knowledge Industry; 1986.
5. Borgman, C. "Psychological Research in Human-Computer Interaction." In: Williams, M., Ed., *Annual Review of Information Science and Technology*, Vol. 19. White Plains N. Y.: Knowledge Industry; 1984.
6. Schneiderman, B. "Designing Menu Selection Systems," *Journal of the American Society for Information Science*. 37(2): 57–70; 1986.
7. Fenichel, C. "The Process of Searching Online Bibliographic Databases: A Review of Research," *Library Research*. 2: 107–127; 1980.
8. Bellardo, T. "Scientific Research in Online Retrieval: A Critical Review." *Library Research*. 2: 231–237; 1981.
9. Derr, R. L. "A Classification of Questions in Information Retrieval by Conceptual Presupposition." In: *Proceedings of the 45th American Society for Information Science Annual Meeting*, 19: 69–71; 1982.
10. Derr, R. L. "A Conceptual Analysis of Information Need," *Information Processing and Management*, 19(5): 273–278; 1983.
11. Derr, R. L. "Information Seeking Expressions of Users," *Journal of the American Society for Information Science*, 35(2): 124–128; March 1984.
12. Derr, R. L. "Questions: Definitions, Structure, and Classification," *RQ*. 24: 186–190; 1985.
13. Derr, R. L. "The Concept of Information in Ordinary Discourse," *Information Processing & Management*. 21(6): 489–500; 1985.
14. Pao, M. L. "Specificity of Terms in Questions." In: *Proceedings of the 46th American Society for Information Science Annual Meeting*. 20: 26–27; 1983.
15. Saracevic, T. "On a Method for Studying the Structure and Nature of Requests in Information Retrieval," In: *Proceedings of the 46th American Society for Information Science Annual Meeting*. 20: 22–25; 1983.
16. Saracevic, T. "A Research Project on Classification of Questions in Information Retrieval—Preliminary Work," In: *Proceedings of the 43rd American Society for Information Science Annual Meeting*. 17: 146–148; 1980.
17. Saracevic, T. "Measuring the Degree of Agreement Between Searchers," In: *Proceedings of the 47th American Society for Information Science Annual Meeting*. 21: 227–230; 1984.
18. Saracevic, T. "Information Retrieval," In: E. H. Brenner and T. Saracevic, ed. *Indexing and Searching in Perspective*. Philadelphia, Pa: National Federation of Abstracting and Indexing Services; 1985. Ch. 4, pp. 4-1 to 4-29.
19. Saracevic, T.; Kantor, P.; Chamis, A. Y.; Trivison, D.; *Experiments on the Cognitive Aspects of Information Seeking and Retrieving. Final Report for National Science Foundation Grant IST-8505411*. Washington, D.C.: National Technical Information Service; Educational Research Information Center; (ED 281530). 1987.
20. Fidel, R.; Soergel, D. "Factors Affecting Online Bibliographic Retrieval: A Conceptual Framework for Research," *Journal of the American Society for Information Science*. 34(3): 163–180; 1983.
21. Taylor, R. "Question Negotiation and Information Seeking in Libraries," *College and Research Libraries*. 29(3): 178–194; 1968.
22. Belkin, N. "Anomalous States of Knowledge as a Basis for Information Retrieval," *The Canadian Journal of Information Science*. 5: 133–143; 1980.
23. Belkin, N. "Cognitive Models and Information Transfer," *Social Science Information Studies*. 4: 111–129; 1984.
24. Graesser, A. C.; Black, J. B. *The Psychology of Questions*. Hillsdale, N.J.: Lawrence Erlbaum; 1985.
25. Swift, I. I. "Classifying Readers' Questions," *Wilson Bulletin for Libraries*. 8(5): 274–275; 1934.
26. Lehnert, W. G. *The Process of Question Answering*. Hillsdale, N.J.: Lawrence Erlbaum; 1978.
27. Bates, M. J. "Information Search Tactics," *Journal of the American Society for Information Science*. 30(4): 205–214; 1979.
28. Bates, M. J. "Idea Tactics," *Journal of the American Society for Information Science*. 30(5): 280–289; 1979.
29. Markey, K.: Atherton, P. *ONTAP: Online Training and Practice Manual for ERIC Data Base Searchers*. Syracuse University, ERIC Clearinghouse on Information Research, Syracuse, N.Y.; 1978. (ED 106 109).
30. Soergel, D. *Organizing Information: Principles of Database and Retrieval Systems*. New York: Academic Press, 1985.
31. Harter, S.; Peters, A. "Hueristics for Online Information Retrieval: A Typology and Preliminary Listing," *Online Review*, 9: 407–424; 1985.
32. Fenichel, C. "Online Searching: Measures That Discriminate Among Users With Different Types of Experience," *Journal of the American Society for Information Science*. 23(2): 23–32; 1981.
33. Brindle, E. A. *The Relationship Between Characteristics of Searchers and Their Behavior While Using an Online Interactive Retrieval System*. Ph.D. dissertation. Syracuse, N.Y.: Syracuse University; 1981.
34. Bellardo, T. "An Investigation of Online Searcher Traits and Their Relationship to Search Outcome," *Journal of the American Society for Information Science*. 36(4): 241–250; 1985.

35. Woelfl, N. N. *Individual Differences in Online Bibliographic Searching: The Effect of Learning Styles and Cognitive Abilities on Process and Outcome*. Ph.D. dissertation. Cleveland, Ohio: Case Western Reserve University; 1984.
36. Penniman, W. D. "A Stochastic Process Analysis of Online User Behavior," *Proceedings of the American Society for Information Science*. 12: 147–148; 1975.
37. Penniman, W. D. *Modeling and Evaluation of Online User Behavior*. Final Report to the National Library of Medicine. Columbus, Oh: OCLC, 1981.
38. Fidel, R. "Online Searching Styles: A Case-Study-Based Model of Searching Behavior," *Journal of the American Society for Information Science*. 35(4): 211–221; July 1984.
39. Oldroyd, B. K.; Citroen, C. L. "Study of the Strategies Used in Online Searching," *Online Review*. 1: 295–310; 1977.
40. Borgman, C. *User's Mental Model of an Information Retrieval System: Effects of Performance*. Ph.D. dissertation. Palo Alto, CA: Stanford University; 1984.
41. Rouse, W.; Rouse, S. "Human Information Seeking and Design of Information Systems," *Information Processing and Management*. 20(3): 92–138; 1984.
42. Sewell, W.; Teitelbaum, S. "Observations of End-User Online Searching Behavior over Eleven Years." *Journal of the American Society for Information Science*. 37(4): 234–245; 1986.
43. Fischhoff, B.; MacGregor, D. "Calibrating Databases." *Journal of the American Society for Information Science*. 37(4): 222–233; 1986.
44. Newell, A. C.; Simon, H. A. *Human Problem Solving*. Englewood Cliffs, N.J.: Prentice-Hall; 1972.
45. Meyer, R. E. *Thinking and Problem Solving: An Introduction to Human Cognition and Learning*. Glenview, IL: Scott Foresman; 1977.
46. Simon, H. A. "Information-Processing Models of Cognition," *Journal of the American Society for Information Science*. 32(5): 364–377; 1981.
47. Belnap, N. D.; Steel, T. B. *The Logic of Questions and Answers*. New Haven, CT: Yale University Press; 1976.
48. Harrah, D. "A Logic of Questions and Answers." *Philosophy of Science*. 28: 40–46; 1961.
49. Kearsley, G. P. "Questions and Question-Asking in Verbal Discourse: A Crossdisciplinary Review." *Journal of Psychological Research*. 5(4): 355–375; 1976.
50. Mednick, S. A.; Mednick, M. T. *Examiner's Manual: Remote Associates Test, College and Adult Forms 1 and 2*. Boston: Houghton Miffin; 1967.
51. Ruck, F. L.; Ruck, W. L. *Employee Aptitude Survey Technical Report*. Los Angeles: Psychological Services; 1980.
52. Kolb, D. A. *Experiential Learning: Experience as the Source of Learning and Development*. Englewood Cliffs, N.J.: Prentice-Hall; 1984.
53. *BMDP Statistical Software, 1985 Printing*. Berkeley, CA: University of California Press; 1985.
54. Fleiss, J. L. *Statistical Methods for Rates and Proportions*. New York: Wiley; 1981 (see especially chapter 5).

On Selecting a Measure of Retrieval Effectiveness

It is argued that a user's subjective evaluation of the personal utility of a retrieval system's output to him, if it could be properly quantified, would be a near-ideal measure of retrieval effectiveness. A hypothetical methodology is presented for measuring this utility by means of an elicitation procedure. Because the hypothetical methodology is impractical, compromise methods are outlined and their underlying simplifying assumptions are discussed. The more plausible the simplifying assumptions on which a performance measure is based, the better the measure. This, along with evidence gleaned from 'validation experiments' of a certain kind, is suggsted as a criterion for selecting or deriving the best measure of effectiveness to use under given test conditions.

WILLIAM S. COOPER

School of Librarianship
University of California
Berkeley, California

• Part I. The 'Subjective' Philosophy of Evaluation

According to a recent survey by Robertson (*1*), the first system-analytic retrieval tests took place in the mid-1950's. Since that time, an astonishing amount of attention has been devoted to the problem of retrieval system evaluation. The number of full-scale system tests that had been attempted at the time of Robertson's survey was thirty-four, a figure which gives some idea of the considerable amount of practical effort expended on evaluation to date. And on the theoretical side literally dozens of measures of retrieval effectiveness have been proposed in the literature. This is readily confirmed by consulting in addition to (*1*) the earlier surveys in (*2*) and (*3*) and the pertinent chapters of the *Annual Review of Information Science and Technology*. Sessions on retrieval evaluation continue to attract increasing numbers of participants at professional society meetings, and a full-fledged textbook on the subject has now appeared (*4*). Yet, in spite of all this concerted attention to the problem on the part of highly qualified researchers, there is still no substantial agreement in the field as to what good retrieval performance is or how to measure it.

There does seem to be general agreement on the importance of the problem. In the present state of the art of retrieval system design—which is to say, in the absence of any extensive body of guiding theory—there seems to be little alternative, in deciding between two or more design possibilities, to actually trying out the different possibilities experimentally in some way to see which works best. 'Seeing which works best' requires, of course, a performance measure. It is possible that at some time in the future theoretical foundations for information retrieval may be developed, and that in particular, design equations may be derived which will allow a more analytic approach to design decisions (c.f. (*5*)). However, the derivation of design equations also presupposes an acceptable evaluation measure; and so whatever happens it seems inescapable that measures of retrieval effectiveness will continue to play a crucial role in the progress of the information retrieval field.

Although the need for an evaluation capability is universally conceded, some commentators have come to feel that the search for a *single* measure of effectiveness is misguided—that there is not now and never can be any one 'correct' way of measuring retrieval success. Others regard this attitude as a mere counsel of despair, and continue to look for the 'right' way to evaluate system output, in its most essential features at least, and relative to whatever the motive of the system evaluation happens to be. Now if there is any one 'right' way of measuring retrieval effectiveness, it remains to be discovered, or in any case it remains to be widely accepted. On the other hand if there is no single correct measure, it remains to specify how to select the combination of measures most appropriate to a given test and how to weight their relative importance in the comparison of two or more systems. In either case the task facing a would-be evaluator of a retrieval system today is to decide upon the basic criteria he will apply in selecting a measure: to evaluate the possible evaluations, in other words. His task is *not* merely to discover one more new and ingenious measure, for too many ingenious and superficially plausible measures have been invented already. The *embarras de richesses* is the problem, and the solution will have to be some compelling criterion for deciding which measure is best under given conditions.

What form might such a criterion take? One approach involves finding an 'ideal' way of measuring effectiveness which is correct in principle, even though it might be difficult or impossible to apply in practice. The general criterion for selecting a practical measure of effectiveness under given conditions would then be: choose the measure which approximates the ideal measure as closely as possible, under the limitations of the available resources. For this kind of approach to be successful, it would be necessary for the 'ideal' measure to be straight-forward and obvious, involving no confusing mathematical or theoretical complexities, and having an ultimate validity apparent on the basis of common sense alone. It would not necessarily make much use of the customary conceptual or experimental trappings of retrieval evaluations, and for this reason it might appear at first to be curiously naive, especially to the sophisticated researcher; but after some impartial reflection, its validity-in-principle should be discernable to anyone. It would not matter if this ideal measure were outrageously costly to apply, or if it presented any other practical difficulties however insuperable, so long as its desirability in principle were clear. Selecting an existing performance measure, or tailoring a new one to fit a given test situation, would then reduce to a matter of deciding on the most helpful and least harmful practical compromises to make with the ideal measure.

It is too much to hope that a measure of this ideal nature could ever be described in such a way as to appear totally convincing to everyone, one obvious difficulty being the problem of describing an idealized evaluation procedure in acceptable operational terms when this procedure may in fact be operationally impracticable. Nevertheless, by hypothesizing unlimited test resources and talents, it may be possible to specify, as a gedanken experiment at least, something approaching an ideal evaluation. What follows is an exploratory attempt in that direction. It is based on the assumption (truism?) that an ideal evaluation methodology must somehow measure the ultimate worth of a retrieval system to its users in terms of an appropriate unit of utility.

The present paper, the first of a two-part series, attempts to spell out what such a near-ideal evaluation procedure might be like. Since the procedure may at first appear curiously strange and naive, a number of potential objections to it are also discussed at some length. From the discussion, a basic philosophy of retrieval system evaluation emerges which, if accepted, provides a criterion for choosing a sound and workable measure of effectiveness under given test conditions. The second paper in the series will deal with the implementation of this criterion. Part I may be read independently of Part II, but not *vice versa.*

1. A Naive Evaluation Methodology

An ideal measure of retrieval effectiveness must measure somehow the retrieval system's 'ultimate worth' to its users. Unfortunately there is no practical procedure which is guaranteed to determine this worth with absolute precision and finality. Nevertheless, if considerations of time and expense and other practical difficulties are ignored, it is possible to conceive of ways in which this worth could be determined to at least a first approximation. Since there is probably no better way of getting at the value of a system than by questioning its users (and possibly other people) directly, the meaning of the phrase 'ultimate worth' is most readily clarified in terms of some kind of questioning or elicitation procedure. The following hypothetical investigation is illustrative of a comparative evaluation conducted without regard to time and expense, with the goal of estimating the ultimate system worth as well as is possible with an elicitation procedure carried out at the time the system is used.

Let us imagine that an investigator is asked to evaluate a reference or document retrieval system by its managers. The system is not just a paper tiger on a drawing-board, but is already a going concern. It is set up and working; real users are coming to it in large numbers in the hope of satisfying real-life information needs; and this has been going on long enough so that the character of the user population has stabilized. It is convenient to assume that the character of the document collection within which the system operates has also stabilized. The internal details of the retrieval system need not concern us—it is just a black box as far as the evaluation is concerned. However, it will simplify things a little to assume that the document collection and the system itself are all together in one place and that the users do all their reading of retrieved documents on location, making the system comparable to a noncirculating library. In such circumstances it is feasible for an investigator to observe the actions of a patron throughout his entire experience with the system, including all his experience with the fruits of his search as he reads or examines the documents retrieved by the system.

The need for an evaluation has arisen, we may imagine, because some clever design modification has been proposed which might substantially improve the system's retrieval performance. If we call the system as it stands System A, and the system which would result from the proposed modification System B, the investigator's task is to compare the retrieval effectivenes of A and B. To make things simple, let us suppose that the document collection itself would not be affected by the change from A to B, but only the indexing of the documents or the rules by which the system retrieves documents. We may assume also that the difference between systems A and B is of a kind that is not immediately apparent to the user from the input language used or the form or timing of the output; this is the most favorable case from the evaluator's point of view because it allows a 'blind' experimental design in which the user does not know which system is serving him. It is also helpful to assume that the switch from design A to design B and from B back to A can be made quickly and conveniently. In the case of a computerized system this would be so if the only difference between A and B were, say, the setting of some critical program parameter, or the use or non-use of some auxiliary subroutine. Finally, we assume that there is no reason to expect that the character of the user population would change significantly if system B were substituted for system A; that is to say, it would not be unfair to test out system B on the present user population of system A.

The investigator's first task is to decide upon a unit in terms of which the worth of systems A and B can be measured and compared. To obtain the background information he needs to make this decision, he interviews the managers of the system at some length. He determines, let us suppose, that their basic motive is a profit motive; they plan eventually to charge a fee for each use of the system and their reason for wanting a comparative evaluation of A and B at this time is to find out which mode of operation could ultimately be the most profitable. With this motive in mind, the investigator decides that the fundamental unit of worth for the evaluation should be a monetary one, say the dollar. This is to be his basis for comparing the relative effectiveness of the two systems as perceived by their users—it is for this test at any rate to be the unit of utility, or the *utile*. (The term 'utility' will be used here in a completely neutral sense. It is simply a cover term for whatever the user finds to be of value about the system output, whether its usefulness, its entertainment or aesthetic value, or anything else.)

The investigator's basic plan is to observe and question a large random sample of patrons as they use the system. The system users in the sample are chosen at random from among the patrons as they enter the library and are about to make use of the retrieval system. Thus it is, strictly speaking, system uses rather than system users that are sampled, as it is possible for the same user to be included in the sample more than once if he makes more than one use of the system during the period of the evaluation. Each patron so selected as a subject for the evaluation is clearly a legitimate user with a genuine information need, a real motive that has actually caused him to come to the system for help. The investigator asks him for permission to follow him around and ask him questions as he uses the system. The investigator does not suggest any hypothetical 'search question' to the user, but rather instructs him to try to fulfill his own needs using the system as he ordinarily would if the investigator were not there. (It is assumed that the investigator is skilled in the psychological techniques for eliciting information without disturbing a subject unduly while the subject is about his task.) The investigator offers to compensate the user for whatever extra time the questioning adds to the time he would otherwise have spent in the library. By making the compensation high enough, the investigator is able to ensure that virtually any patron so approached will agree to cooperate, thus eliminating any worries about a biased sample.

Half of the users in the random sample are to use the system in mode A, the other half in mode B, so that in effect there are really two random samples, one for each of the two systems. The assignment of users to systems is performed in such a way that each user has an equal chance of being assigned to either of the two systems. The investigator might well delegate the random assignment of users to systems to an assistant whose duty it is to set the retrieval apparatus secretly into the randomly assigned mode of operation as each patron of interest starts to use it. The virtue of having an assistant perform the switching between systems A and B is that it makes possible a double-blind experiment in which neither the user nor the investigator questioning him knows which system is currently in operation.

Now let us introduce a temporary simplifying assumption about the search pattern which the users of the system follow. We assume that, with the help of the system, a user's attention is directed first to one document, then another, then another, and so on, without his ever having to think about two documents simultaneously, or having to return his attention to a document once examined. His search pattern can be described as a simple sequence of documents, in other words. This is not to say that every document will be 'relevant' to his need, whatever that may mean, nor even that the user looks at each document in its entirety. Many of the documents in the sequence he will presumably judge unsatisfactory for his needs and discard, perhaps without reading more than the title and abstract, or perhaps even without looking at more than its indexing, which some systems might present to him in a preliminary stage of the retrieval. Other documents may interest him, in which case he reads them in their entirety then and there. The assumption is simply that there is some sequence of documents which represents his natural search order: that he devotes some detectable interval of time to each document in that sequence, and in the order indicated by the sequence. The sequence ends, of course, at the point where he either decides his need is satisfied, or gives up and goes home. This sequentiality assumption is not essential, but it simplifies the description of the elicitation procedure somewhat.

The questioning procedure is the same for all users in both samples. Basically, the investigator waits until his user-subject is through with the first document in his search sequence, and then, before he has had time to turn his attention to the second, questions him about his encounter with the first. The subject is asked, in effect, how many dollars his contact with that first document was worth to him, where any positive, zero, or negative amount is permissible as an answer. The elicitation of this figure is the most delicate part of the evaluation and must be done with great care, using the most refined elicitation techniques that are available. The investigator might for example start out by reminding the patron that his time spent with the document presumably had both penalties and rewards for him. The penalties included the time spent, the effort expended, possibly boredom, any unpleasantness occasioned by the content of the document (if it was read), and so on. The rewards were any useful information gleaned from the document, plus any entertainment or other nonutilitarian value it may have had for the user, and in general anything that might have tended to offset the penalties, in his opinion. The subject is then asked a question or series of questions whose import is: 'Did the rewards of your time spent on the document outweigh the penalties?' or more simply, 'Was your contact with the document worthwhile to you?' or 'Everything considered, are you better off now than if you had not spent that time doing whatever it was that you did with that document?' If the subject answers affirmatively to such questions, the investigator then asks, in effect, 'How many dollars would you have been (barely) willing to pay for the experience you just went through with that document, if you had had some way of knowing beforehand what the experience would be like?' The subject must then make an estimate, such as 'I think I would have been willing to pay as much as two dollars, but no more.' If on the other hand the subject answers negatively to the questions about overall worthwhileness, the investigator follows up with "How much would you have been willing to pay to *avoid* that experience?" Again he gets a dollar amount as an answer, though in this latter case it would be recorded as a negative amount. If, as the third possibility, the subject says he received just enough rewards from his contact with the document to offset the penalties incurred, the investigator records a zero. Hopefully the investigator would be far more skilled in elicitation techniques than these crude question-forms might suggest, but this is the general direction the questioning takes.

The investigator now has a figure, either positive, negative, or zero, which represents the user's best estimate of the personal worth to him, in dollars, of his encounter with document number one in his search sequence. This figure we shall call a *document-utility;* specifically, it is the document utility of the first document of this user's search. The investigator next lets the user go on to document number two, questioning him in exactly the same way when he is through with it, and obtaining a second document-utility figure for document number two of this search. If the user asks the investigator whether this figure should take into account the prior experience with document number one, the investigator replies that it should. Thus, if for example document two merely restates information already gleaned from document one and hence is of no actual benefit to this user, he may wish to assign it a negative document utility, no matter how 'relevant' its content might have been to the original information need. By the same token, if the second document is found to have valuable content it does not matter that this value can be seen only in the light of something learned from document one; document two still gets a positive rating. Thus the personal worth assigned to the second document is in general conditional on what was learned from the first. The investigator continues in this fashion for the third document, the fourth, and so on, getting a document-utility figure for each, the figure being dependent on the subject's entire past experience at the time including his experience with all previous documents in the search sequence.

When the user finally gets to the end of his search sequence, i.e. when he has either satisfied his information need or given up the search, the investigator totals the document-utility figures obtained for each document in the sequence. The sum he calls a *search-utility*: it is the utility of the system experienced by that user during his search to satisfy that information need. If the search utility is a positive number, it indicates the amount the subject would have been willing to pay for that particular use of the system. If negative, it tells how much he would have to be paid to go through the same experience again.

This entire procedure is repeated for every system user (or more precisely every system use or search) in both samples. The result is a large set of search utilities, one for each search conducted under system A, and one for each search under system B. The investigator averages the search utilities for system A; the resulting mean is his estimate of the 'system-utility', or more simply the *utility,* of system A, expressed as an average search-utility. He computes the utility of system B in a like manner. Finally, he subtracts the utility of system A from the utility of system B and computes a confidence interval around the difference in accordance with accepted statistical practice. The result of his investigation as he submits it to his sponsors has therefore the form of a single number with accompanying confidence limits; e.g. a final result of $3.5 \pm .2$ at the 99% confidence level would be interpreted to mean that the managers of the system could have that degree of statistical confidence that system B was worth, on the average, between \$3.30 and \$3.70 more per search than system A, in the judgement of the users.

The system managers want ultimately to be able to make a comparison between benefits and costs. The 'benefits' of an information system have been traditionally construed rather broadly to include anything from convenience of location to friendliness of personnel. However, in the present experiment all benefits were held constant between systems A and B except for one very critical benefit, a benefit having to do with that elusive quality of the search output which we have been calling 'retrieval effectiveness.' The only difference in benefits between the two systems is therefore this crucial difference in retrieval effectiveness, measurable as a difference in the utility experienced by the users. How the managers use the figure obtained for this difference by the investigator will depend on whether or not there is a corresponding difference in cost. If there is no difference in the respective costs of systems A and B (as might well be the case if e.g. B differed from A only in the setting of a program parameter which had no effect on running time), then the managers will simply choose the system for which the higher system utility is indicated, provided only that the difference in utility estimates is statistically significant. If on the other hand there is a difference in programming, installation, operating, or any other cost, this difference must be estimated on a per-search basis and compared with the difference in system utility. Thus for example if the investigator reports an advantage in utility of $3.50 ± .20 per search for system B, while it is estimated that a switch to B would cause only a $1.50 average increase in per-search cost, it would probably be rational for the managers make the change from A to B. This is because the switch could be expected to increase the benefits experienced by the users by an amount greater than the increase in the fees they would have to pay, enhancing the system's attractiveness to them, and hopefully increasing thereby the system's potential for profit, which was assumed for the sake of the illustration to be the underlying motive.

2. Potential Objections to the Naive Methodology

A common first reaction of thoughtful people to this naive approach to retrieval system evaluation seems to be one of scorn, or at least of the raising of a flock of objections. However, most of the objections either fail to bear close scrutiny, or else can be met by specifying minor improvements in the methodology. The predicated test conditions have to be remembered, however, including the assumptions that the system is a going concern, that the investigator is skilled at elicitation without disruption, and so on. Also, it has to be borne in mind that the procedure just described is not claimed to measure the exact 'true' utility of a system, since the true worth is probably not precisely determinable at all. The procedure gives only a crude gage of actual worth—an approximate reading which, though it could probably never reach the point of perfection, can doubtless be improved upon by various procedural refinements. Some possible refinements will be mentioned presently.

Here are a few of the potential objections to the "naive" methodology:

Objection 1. *The method of evaluation is entirely subjective.*

Reply. This is correct. The naive method is in the last analysis merely an orderly way of collecting and quantifying the users' personal, wholly subjective, evaluations of a system's worth. But is subjectivity necessarily bad? And if it is, is there any real alternative? Surely a service system of any kind exists for the satisfaction of its users, and the users themselves are generally the ones who know best whether their wants have been satisfied or not. Any so-called 'objective' method claiming to measure user satisfaction according to rigid and preconceived criteria is likely to diverge, to whatever extent it is 'objective,' from the user's actual criteria of satisfaction.

Traditional measures of retrieval effectiveness which rely on statistics about 'relevance judgements' may succeed in giving a superficial impression of objectivity. This is particularly true of the more sophisticated ones that are expressible as mathematical formulae with theoretically interesting derivations. However, no measure of this kind is really any more objective than the relevance judgements on which it is based. It is widely recognized by now that judgements of relevance are highly subjective indeed, and are influenced by a host of personal factors. Moreover, in traditional evaluation methodology, it is often not the system users themselves who make the relevance judgements, but outside judges who are in the position of having to second-guess the users' real information needs as best they can. Thus if the naive methodology is to be accused of subjectivity, traditional methodology is doubly accused, relying as it does on a judge's subjective guesses about a hypothetical user's subjective evaluations.

Objection 2. *Often a system user will, in his haste, discard a retrieved document after a cursory glance, when actually the document could have proved highly valuable had the user only taken the time to examine it more carefully. This shows that the subjective or perceived utility of a document is not necessarily its real utility.*

Reply. The perceived utility is the only utility that does the patron any good. The performance of the system ought therefore to be judged on the basis of how well it delivers this kind of actually experienced utility. The significant question is not what utility a document *could* have had or *should* have had for the user, but what utility it actually *did* have.

Objection 3. *The naive methodology measures utility, whereas the purpose of a retrieval system is to retrieve material that is relevant. Utility and relevance are not the same thing.*

Reply. The naive methodology is indeed based on utility rather than relevance, but this is a virtue, not a defect. According to one recent explication of 'relevance'

(*6*), the term has to do with 'aboutness' (or 'pertinence,' or 'topic-relatedness') and is ultimately definable in terms of logical implication, whereas 'utility' is a catch-all concept involving not only topic-relatedness but also quality, novelty, importance, credibility, and many other things. If one accepts this usage, one perceives that it is really documents with high utility, and not merely relevant documents, that the user wants to see. Thus the underlying premise of the objection is misguided; the purpose of a retrieval system is (or at least should be) to retrieve documents that are useful, not merely relevant.

OBJECTION 4. *But the naive methodology does not even measure utility, at least not in the usual sense of usefulness. A user might put a high price on a retrieved document for a purely frivolous reason, e.g. the fact that it happened to be written in a witty and engaging style.*

REPLY. As explained, the term 'utility' is used here as a cover term for anything about a document that the user values. If a user values a witty style as much as an informative content, who are we to say that he is wrong? Systems should be designed so as to optimize the satisfaction of their users, not the information scientists.

OBJECTION 5. *It may be desirable in theory for a system to retrieve on the basis of utility, but in practice it can retrieve only on the basis of relevance. For example, a computerized retrieval system could never judge the 'quality' of a document, let alone something like its 'wittiness'. Therefore, successful retrieval of relevant material is the only criterion on which system performance should be judged.*

REPLY. There are two answers to this. The first is that retrieval systems *can* take into account factors of utility other than relevance. There is no reason why our deliberations here should have to be limited to computer systems, and as soon as a human-powered system is contemplated, it becomes obvious that the system can make judgements of quality, importance, even wittiness. And even if we were to restrict attention to fully automated searching, it would still not be clear that relevance is the only mechanically useful utility trait. One could, after all, store encoded human estimates of quality, etc., to be searched mechanically in a computer. And if this is possible today, who knows what tomorrow may bring? Thus even quality and style, which are perhaps the most elusive factors in the utility of a document, cannot be excluded as a possible criterion upon which future retrieval rules may be partly based.

The second answer is that the 'therefore' in the objection is a *non sequitur*. Even if it were difficult to imagine retrieval system designs based on utility instead of relevance, it would still fail to follow that relevance should be the only basis for judging performance. If utility is what is ultimately wanted from a retrieval system, then its performance must in the last analysis be judged in terms of utility. A wheel-alignment specialist would not judge how well a car runs solely on the basis of how well its wheels were aligned, even if wheel alignment were the only repair operation he knew how to perform.

Why, it might be asked, does the reasoning behind this objection seem to influence intelligent researchers if it is so patently fallacious? (My own experience is that it does; I have encountered the argument more than once in discussions with colleagues.) The explanation is probably that: (1) All mechanizable retrieval strategies that have been formulated to date attempt to retrieve exclusively on the basis of relevance; and (2) those traditional evaluation methodologies which make use of relevance judges naturally stress judgements about relevance alone, since it would be difficult or impossible for judges to second-guess hypothetical users' feelings on any of the other more elusive aspects of utility. Because of these historical circumstances it is tempting, or so it would seem, to fall into the trap of thinking that relevance is what information retrieval is all about, whereas the more correct statement is that relevance is the only factor in utility that has been seriously exploited to date.

OBJECTION 6. *Suppose a patron were to submit a request for documents on solid-state circuitry, and the first document retrieved happened to be a book on chinchilla-raising which had nothing whatever to do with solid-state circuitry. The patron nevertheless reads it, finds it highly interesting and valuable, and becomes an immediate chinchilla-breeding enthusiast. Under the naive methodology the system would be given a high rating for the retrieval of this irrelevant document, which is absurd.*

REPLY. The naive methodology would indeed assign a high worth to the system for its performance, but to do so is not absurd. There are two possible explanations of this hypothetical system's curious behaviour in retrieving such a seemingly irrelevant document. The first is that it was merely a blunder, a poor retrieval prediction, and its high utility to the user merely a lucky fluke. If this was the case, one would expect the effect of such flukes to wash out in the statistics of a sufficiently large sample of users, and comparisons between two designs would not be invalidated. The second possibility is that the system was actually able somehow to predict, on some subtle but reasonable grounds, that the document in question would probably be valuable to the user in spite of its apparent irrelevance. In this case the system will tend to come up with such 'flukes' consistently, and should and will be rewarded for this capability by the naive evaluation measure. (This objection is not really a new one, but only another example of the common confusion about the purpose of a retrieval system being to retrieve relevant material rather than useful.)

OBJECTION 7. *The naive methodology is based on a monetary utile, but this choice is rather arbitrary in view of the existence of many other possible bases for utility comparisons.*

REPLY. This objection is directed at the dollar specifically, whereas the intended import of the naive methodology was only that *some* suitable unit of utility be chosen. The particular unit selected will depend on the circumstances at hand, including the motives for wanting to evaluate the system in the first place. One can reasonably maintain that the dollar is indeed a suitable unit under at least some circumstances—specifically, when there is a profit motive and the users pay for the system in monetary fees. However, it is easy to think of other situations in which some different unit of utility would be preferable to the dollar. Consider for instance the case of a free but cooperatively maintained retrieval system in which the users themselves donate all the spare-time labor needed to operate the system. Here there is no profit motive, and the users pay their 'fees' in their own labor. Under these circumstances it might be appropriate to take a man-hour of operating labor as the unit of utility instead of the dollar. The line of questioning adopted by the investigator would then be: 'How much time would you have been willing to spend performing typical system operation and maintenance tasks in exchange for your experience with this document?'

A rough guideline for choosing a unit of utility might be stated somewhat as follows: *Select a utile whose character matches as closely as possible the form in which the system is supported,* whether it be payment in dollars, hours of labor, or some other form of personal penalty or sacrifice. When this guideline is followed, the utility figures obtained will automatically be in a form which facilitates comparison with system costs, whether these costs have a monetary character or not. Hence they will be in a maximally useful form for decisions about the allocation of resources—specifically, decisions about which system design to implement with existing resources.

OBJECTION 8. *Knowledge is priceless. You can't put a dollar price-tag on knowledge; or at least, not on all kinds of knowledge. Hence a subject in the naive evaluation would be justified in refusing to give any definite dollar figure for the worth of what he had learned.*

REPLY. It is not knowledge but documents that the users are asked to put a dollar value on. People are obviously able to do this, because they do it every time they decide whether or not to buy a book in a bookstore. Their decision in the bookstore is, if anything, even more delicate than the decisions asked of them in the naive methodology, for in the bookstore they have usually not yet read the book in question, and so are forced to put a price on an unexpected utility rather than an actually experienced utility.

OBJECTION 9. *It may be correct in principle to say that each document considered must have a definite dollar value for the patron, but the patron will never be able to state this amount with any degree of precision.*

REPLY. This is probably true; if the investigator forces his subjects to give exact dollar figures, he must count on the presence of a certain 'random error' component in each answer. It works to the investigator's advantage, however, that in a sufficiently large random sample even very sizable random errors of estimate will tend to cancel each other out. Thus it is only systematic bias that is dangerous, as for example if all patrons were to tend to give utility estimates that were too high. And even a systematic bias of this sort may be tolerable for purposes of comparing two systems, provided the bias is the same for both systems.

OBJECTION 10. *The dollar is not an adequate unit of utility because it is not additive. A thousand dollars is not necessarily worth exactly a thousand times as much to a user as one dollar would be.*

REPLY. True. This difficulty has been overcome in the theory of business decisions by defining utiles in terms of dollars in a sophisticated manner which does not postulate a simple one-to-one relationship (see e.g. (7)). A similar development for the retrieval context would be a welcome further refinement of the naive methodology.

OBJECTION 11. *When the dollar is taken as the unit of utility, it is not clear whether the system user is supposed to think of the dollars as his own or his organization's. He is likely to be freer with expense account money than his own.*

REPLY. It would of course be necessary to clear up this kind of confusion in the user's mind before the questioning began. Under the assumptions of the illustration, the profit-conscious sponsors of the evaluation would be interested in comparing retrieval rules A and B on the basis of which of the two kinds of service the patrons would be willing to pay the most for, regardless of whether they happened to be paying out of an expense account or not. Under these circumstances the problem would be resolved by asking the user who would be footing the retrieval bill ultimately, he or his employer. If the former, the user would be instructed to think of the dollars as his own during the questioning; if the latter, he would be told to translate all questions into terms of expense-account dollars.

A related issue is the problem of what to do if neither the system user nor his employer has to pay anything at all for the use of the system. Many retrieval systems are financed by governmental or professional organizations or philanthropic foundations, and are made available free of charge to the public or some segment of it. In this situation, the users must be instructed to imagine during the questioning that they would be paying their dollars out of an expense account provided by the true sponsors of the retrieval system. For example, if the retrieval system is provided as a free service by the American Metallurgical Society, the users would be asked 'How much would you have been willing to pay out, in money provided by the American Metallurgical Society, for your experience with that document?' It might be necessary or at least advisable to fill the user in beforehand on what the American Metallurgical Society is, its aims and purposes, and possibly its financial condition and the possible alternative uses to which it could put the money; but there is in principle no reason why this could not be done.

(A good argument can be made that in the case of a sponsored system, the user should be asked not how much of the sponsor's money he *would* have been willing to pay, but rather how much he *should* have been willing to pay, i.e. how much the sponsor ought rationally to have been willing to spend to provide the user with the experienced retrieval results. This way of framing the question might help to prevent unscrupulous users from naming excessively large sums simply because the money they are hypothetically spending is not their own. However, this is a controversial point, because the 'should' wording introduces a suspiciously 'normative' flavor into the proceedings.)

OBJECTION 12. *A dollar is worth more to some people than to others. Its subjective usefulness to a given person depends on his wealth as well as his philosophy of life and other imponderables. Hence the dollar does not provide a constant standard of utility equally applicable for all system users.*

REPLY. The dollar doubtless has a very different subjective worth to different people, but that does not impair its appropriateness for the purposes of retrieval system testing. To see this, it is helpful to consider separately the two cases of systems run for a profit on their users' fees, and systems run for the public good by some agency. Under a pure profit motive, all that really matters in the end is how much a patron would be willing to pay. The personal, financial, or philosophical reasons for *why* he would be willing to pay just that much are of no importance. For making purely mercenary business decisions, then, the dollar is an appropriate unit of utility in spite of the fact that it is of unequal subjective worth to different users. In the case of an agency-supported system, on the other hand, the users are asked only how they would spend the agency's dollars, not their own. In this latter case there is just one payer involved, namely the agency, so the problem of differences in the dollar's worth to different parties does not arise.

OBJECTION 13. *The naive methodology fails to take into account output characteristics which the user himself is not in a position to perceive. For example, the truth, or accuracy, of what the retrieved documents assert is surely of importance in telling how well the system has served the user. But under the naive methodology, one could have an anomalous situation in which system A retrieved only accurate information and system B only mistaken information, yet users having no way of knowing whether what they had read was correct or not would evaluate the systems as having equal utility.*

REPLY. The operational question here in terms of elicitation methodology seems to be this. If the investigator knows whether the document the user has just read is accurate or not, should he share this knowledge with the user before asking him for his evaluation of the document, or should he keep it to himself? Imagine for example, that the document just read was full of lies and inaccuracies. This fact constitutes a special sort of auxiliary information about the document which, if supplied to the user, would surely lower his estimate of the worth of the document to him. Should the user be given this piece of auxiliary information or not?

"It all depends" is a tiresome answer, but the only correct one for this question. For one can conceive of some situations in which it would not be desirable to give the user the auxiliary information, and others in which it would. Here are two different illustrative situations which would call for opposite treatment in this respect:

Situation I (Auxiliary Information Undesirable): Suppose that a retrieval system is privately operated on a usage fee basis and that the only ultimate aim of the evaluation is to maximize profits by providing the kind of system the users would be willing to pay the most to use. Suppose also that the users will never have any way of finding out for themselves whether the documents supplied to them by the system are truthful or not. (Alternatively, one could imagine that if they do find out, the discovery will for some reason fail to influence future usage of the system.) In such circumstances, it is of no importance whether the users have really been well-served by the system or not, since all that will affect their rate of future usage is whether they *think* they have been well-served. Hence it would be most rational (though possibly unethical) to withhold the auxiliary information from the users, and so optimize system performance as perceived by users in a realistic state of ignorance.

Situation II (Auxiliary Information Desirable): But consider now a different set of circumstances in which the users pay no fees, the costs of the system being borne by an agency or foundation for some broad, benevolent purpose such as 'furthering scientific progress'. The system's users, we may imagine, are captive users, or for some other reason are unlikely to change their rates of future usage significantly in accordance with how well they think the system has served them in the past. The agency's purpose in having the evaluation performed is so that a rational choice can be made about what system design to implement in order to 'further the progress of science' the most. Now everyone would agree, one would hope, that a system that delivers accurate data to its users is likely to advance science faster than one that delivers lies. Hence it would be rational for the investigator to tell the user whether the retrieved data is accurate or not. Giving the user the auxiliary information to assist him in his judgement is desirable in this case because of the ultimate use to which the judgements will be put.

Evidently, then, there can be no blanket rule for whether to extend the naive methodology by introducing briefing sessions on accuracy into the elicitation process; it all depends on the special circumstances surrounding the retrieval test.

Only rarely will a given set of test circumstances be

neatly classifiable as either Type I or Type II. For even a profit-hungry entrepreneur normally has to take the ultimate worth (as opposed to the immediately perceived worth) of his product into account to some extent, since usually at least some of his potential customers will sooner or later be influenced by it to some degree. And similarly even the most altruistic sponsor, if he wants the services he is offering to be well-used, must concern himself to some extent with the ignorant forces that determine demand. Thus Situations I and II are at the endpoints of a spectrum. For mixed situations near the middle of the spectrum, it may make little difference whether auxiliary information is supplied or not.

The issue involved here is of course not confined to matters of accuracy alone. There are many other kinds of auxiliary information which, if made known to a user, could affect his subjective utility judgements: among them are information about a document's popularity or importance, its reception by critics, the status of its authors, etc. In fact, there is no end to the auxiliary information with potential for improving utility estimates. The upshot is that in Type II situations the naive methodology is open-ended, for it would always be possible to improve its results by rounding up still further auxiliary information to give to the users when they are making their utility estimates.

Objection 14. *The naive methodology elicits utility judgments only from the system users themselves. It may happen that someone else is actually in a better position to judge the usefulness of the retrieved information. For example, a senior scientist might have a wider perspective on the value of a piece of research than his assistant who applies to the system for data essential to it. As another instance a professor's colleagues might be able collectively to judge the effect of his information sources on his work more objectively than the professor could himself.*

Reply. In circumstances of Type I it would not matter whether others were in a better position to judge the ultimate social usefulness of the retrieved information since by assumption only the user's own evaluation will affect future usage behavior. In circumstances of Type II, however, one might indeed be able to improve on the naive methodology by interviewing other people in addition to the immediate users. A case in point would be one in which some party or parties other than the user possesses vastly more background information than the user himself—so much so that it is better to interview the other parties directly than to try to get them to impart all their background to the user as auxiliary information. The examples of the senior scientist and the professor's colleagues would fall into this category. Finally, in both Type I and Type II situations it is conceivable that the users may simply be intellectually incapable of understanding the investigator's questions, or of making the utility judgements necessary to answer them, so that better judgements could be obtained from others by proxy. A retrieval system for school children might fall into this category.

Objection 15. *The naive methodology elicits the users' judgement of utility immediately after he is through with a document, whereas its true utility might not become apparent to him until much later.*

Reply. This is a valid objection. One can readily conceive of a patron changing his utility estimate for a document quite radically a few hours, months, or even years after he has read it, either because it takes him that long to digest the document's content or because he learns new information in the meantime which alters his perceived usefulness of it.

A refinement in the naive methodology which would help to overcome this objection would be to reinterview each user periodically for a protracted period of time after his use of the system, thereby providing him with an opportunity to change any of his utility assignments in the light of new experience. This refinement would be a little like allowing him time to collect some of his own auxiliary information. As with other kinds of auxiliary information, however, supplying this background information would improve the evaluation only in circumstances of Type II; not Type I.

Objection 16. *A fair measure ought to take account of the amount of useful material not brought to the user's attention. It is for this reason that conventional evaluation procedures usually penalize a system if a large proportion of the relevant documents are not retrieved.*

Reply. The involvement of unexamined documents in a performance formula has long been taken for granted as a perfectly natural thing, but if one stops to ponder the situation, it begins to appear most peculiar. Why should the status of documents which the user has not examined have any influence on a user-oriented performance rating? Surely a document which the system user has not been shown in any form, to which he has devoted not the slightest particle of time or attention during his use of the system output, and of whose very existence he may be unaware, does that user neither harm nor good in his search. It is puzzling, to say the least, that the characteristics of such documents have conventionally been accorded great significance in evaluating what the system has done for the user. How could the properties of such documents possibly matter? Nor does it make it any less puzzling to add that the property these documents should be tested for is their potential 'relevance.' The burden of proof should therefore be on those who make this bizarre claim, to show why properties of documents that have not been brought to the user's attention should be taken into account in measuring the benefits received from the system.

The early history of the notion that the relevance or irrelevance of unretrieved documents is important seems to be somewhat as follows. The first attempts at evaluating retrieval output dealt with systems which simply retrieved an unordered set of documents. The most obvious thing to examine first about such output was the density of relevant (useful?) documents in the retrieved set. This proportion came to be called the *precision* (also "relevance ratio," "accuracy," "distillation," "acceptance rate," etc.) of the system. It was realized shortly thereafter that precision was not everything. For instance a retrieved set of only two documents with a precision of 50% was not necessarily as satisfactory as a retrieved set of twenty documents with the same precision—at least, it would not seem as satisfactory to a user wanting ten relevant documents. The percentage of the relevant documents that were retrieved was therefore proposed as a supplementary figure; it came to be known as *recall* ("sensitivity," "relevancy score," "completeness," "hit rate" "discrimination"). The recall measure was conceptually simple; it seemed plausible that high recall was somehow good and low recall bad; and recall and precision have remained the most commonly applied measures of effectiveness to this day.

Those who have applied precision and recall in actual evaluation experiments remark that a system's recall is vastly more difficult to estimate in practice than its precision. The reason is that in order to measure recall, one must obtain relevance judgements not only for the relatively small amount of material actually retrieved and examined by the user, but also for all the unretrieved documents, which normally constitute the vast bulk of the collection. The historic response to this difficulty has been to accept the challenge and to use the recall measure anyway, in spite of the difficulties and tremendous expenditure of labor involved in doing so. The irony of this situation from the present point of view is that the vast labor involved in estimating recall is largely wasted, since the relevance or irrelevance of unexamined documents has little bearing on system utility anyway. Instead of attempting to estimate recall in spite of all difficulties, what should have been done was to find a way to overcome the deficiencies of the precision measure without bringing a second measure into the picture.

Note that the historical objection to the use of the precision measure alone does not apply to the naive measure. If ten positive utility documents are badly needed, and one is not nearly enough, the naive measure will indeed give a higher score to a retrieved set of twenty documents than to a retrieved set of two, even though the precision of both outputs is 50% in the sense that half the retrieved documents in each have positive utility. Thus it is possible in principle to remove the obvious difficulties of the precision measure without the help of recall or any other secondary measure based on extraneous considerations about unexamined documents. In other words, a possible means of overcoming the historical difficulties of the precision ratio without importing a secondary measure might be to bring the precision measure closer in some way to the naive measure. This idea will be pursued in Part II.

Objection 17. *Sometimes a user is not interested so much in learning from what the retrieved documents say as he is in finding out whether or not certain kinds of documents exist in the collection. The classic example of an 'existence search' of this kind is the patent search, in which the inventor is interested only in whether or not there already exist patents covering his invention. A related situation is the one in which a scientist with a new idea searches the literature not for edification, but instead to find out whether anyone else has thought of the idea first. In both cases it would seem important to take into account whether or not the system located for the user whatever relevant information there may be. This is a case in which relevance properties of unexamined documents are clearly germane to retrieval evaluation.*

Reply. The existence search is indeed the one important case in which the relevance properties of unexamined documents may matter. For this case the (perhaps overly polemical) remarks given in reply to the previous objection must be modified, since the number of relevant documents missed in the unexamined bulk of the collection may be germane to the evaluation after all. This number (the number or percentage of relevant documents left unexamined or unretrieved) is best regarded as auxiliary information which in the case of an existence search could influence the user's subjective estimate of how well the system had served him. Note, however, that it is *only* this special case that calls for checking unexamined documents, and even then only in circumstances of Type II, not Type I. Thus the standard 'recall' figure is germane only under rather restricted conditions, and in any case should ideally never be used as a competing measure of effectiveness, but only as auxiliary information to be given to the user to aid him in forming his own utility estimate.

Objection 18. *The naive methodology pays no attention even to retrieved documents unless they are actively considered by the user at some point in his search sequence. Suppose the system operates as many do by retrieving an unordered set of documents which the user must search through in essentially random order. The user might well abandon his search in disgust before looking at everything that has been retrieved, whereas what had actually happened was that by bad luck alone all the useful retrieved documents happened to be among those not yet examined. Under these circumstances the measure would downgrade the system unjustly.*

Reply. It might downgrade the system 'unjustly' for some searches, but the downgrading would be offset in the final average, since in a sufficiently large random sample other searches would tend to get upgraded in a compensating manner.

Objection 19. *At some information centers, certain kinds of requests are deemed more important than others (e.g. 'emergency information needs') or certain classes of users are given preferred treatment (e.g. faculty over students). One would like a measure of effectiveness to take any such order of preference into account, stressing the worth of preferred searches over the others. Adopting the same unit of utility for all users would defeat this purpose.*

Reply. This problem takes care of itself. Under a profit motive, the users with the more urgent needs would presumably be willing to pay more, and any differences among their needs not reflected in how much they would be willing to pay are of no concern. Under a philanthropic motive, the reasons for giving certain users preferred treatment are presumably already inherent in the statement of the philanthropic agency's purpose in providing the system, so the judgements given by the users as to how to distribute the agency's dollars should automatically take them into account. Thus for example the agency would presumably be willing to spend more to meet a genuine emergency need, or to serve a user with a legitimate preferential status.

Objection 20. *The simplifying assumption that the user's search pattern is sequential is unrealistic. A user often turns his attention back to a document already examined. For example, a user might read just the title and abstract of each retrieved document first, taking note of those that looked probably useful, and only after that return his attention to the hopeful candidates in order to read their full text.*

Reply. The naive methodology is readily generalized to apply to more complicated search patterns. The only change needed is that instead of just one subjective utility being associated with each document, more than one figure per document must in general be elicited, a separate one for each encounter with that document during the course of the user's search. The search pattern is still conceived as a simple sequence through time, but the members of the sequence are now more appropriately referred to as 'document-encounters', and the figures of worth elicited for them 'document-encounter utilities', the possibility now being recognized that the same document may be encountered more than once during a search. When the search terminates, the investigator first adds up the separate utility estimates for each given document, obtaining a single document-utility figure for each document examined. He then totals the document utilities as before, and averages.

Objection 21. *Why is it necessary to obtain a separate utility figure for each document-encounter? It would be simpler for the investigator to elicit just a single composite estimate of the search utility from the user after the entire search had ended.*

Reply. It would indeed be a lot simpler and less trouble for all concerned. It is a shortcut method that might well yield just as good an estimate of the search utility as would the totalling of separate document-encounter utilities. However, the single figure would not provide much of a basis for a later analysis of *why* the system performed as well or as poorly as it did. Moreover, we will see in Part II that the notion of a separate utility for each examined document or document-encounter is useful when considering compromise versions of the naive methodology.

Objection 22. *The figures for system utility yielded by the naive methodology are not independent of the document collection in which the retrieval system operates. Hence it does not really measure the effectiveness of just the retrieval systems per se, since the effects of the system are confounded with those of the collection.*

Reply. The utility score assigned to a system by the naive measure is indeed dependent partly upon the collection in which the system is operating, and this is as it should be. In some situations it may be difficult even to make the distinction between the 'system' and the 'collection.' In cases where such a distinction can profitably be made, and it is systems (which in this context it might be preferable to call by some different name, say 'retrieval rules') rather than collections that are to be compared, care must be taken to hold the collection constant, and then to interpret the comparison as valid for that collection only. Similarly, if it is collections as distinct from retrieval rules that are to be compared, the retrieval rule must be held constant. In the third case, if the naive methodology is used to compare rule A operating in collection C with rule B operating in collection D, then nothing can be said either about A versus B or about C versus D. The most that can be determined is e.g. that A with C outperforms B with D.

Some authors have suggested that a system evaluation is worth while only to the extent that its results are generalizable beyond the immediate circumstances of the test. To this end it has been proposed, for example, that a retrieval rule's performance score in a collection be divided by the proportion of relevant documents in the collection. This normalization is supposed to make the scores of retrieval rules evaluated in different collections more comparable. Such devices may succeed in their purpose to some extent, and if a comparison of retrieval rules evaluated in different collections has to be made, these normalizations may be better than nothing. However, the safest and most scientific course is to avoid comparing retrieval rule performances at all unless they have been evaluated with respect to a common collection. For this reason we shall forego here any attempt to provide a way of 'normalizing' utility scores to make them less sensitive to collection characteristics. The naive methodology is to be regarded as evaluating not just retrieval rules but whole systems inclusive of the document collections the systems are operating in.

Objection 23. *A common set of users (more precisely, search requests) is not used for both systems. This invalidates the comparison of the systems. System A could appear to have a higher utility than system B simply because the two samples of users happened to be different in some important respect.*

Reply. The naive methodology is a completely randomized experimental design in which treatments A and

B are allotted to the subjects entirely by chance (*8*). This is a standard experimental design and is perfectly valid: the statistical analysis administered at the end of the experiment gives assurance that the observed difference in the effects of the two treatments is not due just to chance. The design of the experiment is not necessarily the most efficient one possible—stratified sampling and other techniques could conceivably be used to reduce the sample sizes needed—but it is safe enough from adverse effects of chance differences in the two user samples.

OBJECTION 24. *The construction of a confidence interval as described for the naive methodology is not necessarily the most appropriate statistical analysis to apply.*

REPLY. There are probably several other statistical analyses which would provide acceptable variants of the naive methodology, and there could be no objection to these. For example, in the absence of any cost differences between systems A and B, a common T-test would be sufficient, and the confidence interval could be dispensed with. In other circumstances, the confidence interval could be omitted in favor of a simple computation of the standard error of the difference between the means.

The confidence interval approach, though not the only acceptable one, has the special virtue of emphasizing that the result of a naive system comparison is a definite number, not just a decision as to which of two systems is preferable. Unlike many measures of effectiveness that have been used, the naive measure not only answers the question 'Which system is better?', but also the followup question 'How much better?', which is often of much greater practical importance in decision-making. In statistical terminology, the naive measure is valid on the 'ratio' level, not just the 'interval' or 'ordinal' levels. A measure which has this level of validity has a meaningful zero, a meaningful unit, and allows of meaningful manipulation under all standard arithmetic operations (*9, 10*).

OBJECTION 25. *The request language for system A might differ from that of system B. If this is the case, there is the relative difficulty and inconvenience of request formulation in the two input languages to consider, as well as the relative virtues of the retrieval results that ensue. The naive methodology considers only the latter.*

REPLY. This is correct. Like most other analytic measures of effectiveness that have been proposed, the naive measure is concerned only with how good the output of the system is, and has nothing to say about how much trouble it takes to formulate the input. It also says nothing about such matters as whether the information center is conveniently located, adequately staffed, open at convenient hours, etc. Such a measure is, however, sufficient for many practical and theoretical design purposes, as for example a decision about which of two retrieval rules to program when all other variables are held constant. And for those design decisions for which it is not sufficient by itself, the naive measure is at least expressed in units of utility which could provide a basis for evaluating other benefits of the system also, as well as for comparison with costs. For instance, the difficulty of the request formulation could be evaluated by the users in terms of whatever unit of utility had been adopted by asking them how many such units they would have been willing to pay to get out of the chore. In short, the naive measure is no more limited than other analytic performance measures in what it is able to evaluate, and less limited to the extent that evaluations of aspects of a system other than its output performance are easily compared with it.

OBJECTION 26. *In the naive methodology the user is questioned immediately after each encounter with each document. The interviews themselves might so disrupt his usual search habits that his patterns of usage of the system output could no longer be considered natural or typical after the first interview. As an illustration of this difficulty, consider the problems which would arise when a user scans quickly down a list of titles in search of interesting ones. The investigator would have trouble even in telling precisely when the user's attention had shifted from one document to another, let alone in breaking into the process at just that instant for an interview without disrupting the future course of the scan. Consider also the point at which the user terminates his search. It is likely in the naive methodology to be quite different from what it would have been under undisturbed conditions, since any extensive questioning that has gone on will fatigue or otherwise affect the subject and make him unable to tell where he would normally have given up.*

REPLY. This is a serious objection which suggests another possible refinement in the methodology. Instead of questioning the user after each encounter with a document, the investigator might do better to wait until the search was over, and then question the user retrospectively. What was lost in forgotten detail would probably be more than offset by the guarantee of a totally natural and undisturbed search pattern.

OBJECTION 27. *The naive measure is essentially an average utility per search. The 'search' is not the best entity to which to assign so fundamental a role. One objection to it is that it is sometimes difficult to specify just when a given search begins and when it terminates, especially in interactive systems. A more attractive alternative would be to compute, instead of a per-search utility, the total utility experienced by all users during a prescribed test period. This alternative obviates the need to say just when a user has ended one search and started another.*

REPLY. If there is any problem in making the defining rules for what constitutes a search comparable for the two systems, the suggestion is well taken and leads to another refinement in the methodology. Otherwise, a little thought reveals that the two ways of presenting the results would always lead to the same practical decisions about what system to implement, so that it does not really matter which of the two formulations the test data are given.

3. The Real Objections to the Naive Methodology

The discussion to this point suggests the following as a working hypothesis: *The naive methodology, especially when modified by refinements of the sort indicated in the last section, begins to at least approach a method of retrieval evaluation which is the 'best possible' in principle.* That is to say, there is nothing terribly seriously or fundamentally wrong with it *as a conceptual scheme.* No doubt there is room in it for further improvements and refinements; the assumption is merely that it is based on a sound general philosophy, and is at least somewhere in the neighborhood of a sound measure. If one had unlimited test resources, it would be hard to do very much better.

Unfortunately, time and resources are never unlimited in the real world, and this raises the issue of whether the naive methodology is at all practical. On the practical level, the difficulties are severe indeed, suggesting that the real objections to the measure are not objections of principle at all but of practice. Specifically, the practical difficulties are the following:

1. *The elicitation technique is delicate and time-consuming.* To judge from the literature on business decision-making, the elicitation of careful subjective utility estimates from a layman is a laborious task, often requiring round-about methods of questioning which translate the entire issue into lay terms. The possible additional tasks of having to question the user at later times for retrospective judgements, to supply the user with auxiliary information, and to question people other than the user, would multiply this labor. The convenient assumption of a non-circulating library does not always obtain, and this raises practical difficulties: if the naive methodology were carried out to the letter the investigator would have to follow the user home and spy on him until he has at last read the books he took out. And so on.

2. *The two samples of users have to be relatively large.* Other considerations aside, one would of course wish to use just one sample of users for the testing of both systems A and B, if only this could somehow be done. Holding the user sample constant in this way would allow the use of the much more efficient paired-comparison method. This experimental design would yield a valid comparison between A and B with a far smaller sample than is otherwise required for either A or B alone, since there would be no random variation between the two different samples to worry about (see e.g. (8, pp. 105 ff)). Unfortunately, however, the naive methodology definitely requires separate samples for separate systems. A patron with an information need cannot realistically be 're-used' with the same need once he has completed a search intended to satisfy that need. The requirement of two separate and large user samples greatly aggravates the laboriousness of the elicitation procedure.

3. *In practice it is likely that many samples of users, not just two, would be required.* So far, we have confined attention to comparisons involving only two retrieval systems. The more usual design problem is that there are many systems, or variants of systems, which one would like to test out simultaneously. Even a design decision about how to set the value of a single numeric parameter requires that as many values of the parameter be tested out as resources allow for. When more than one parameter has to be decided upon, there is of course a combinatorial effect. There is usually no shortage of hypotheses among system designers as to what the best retrieval design might be, and though it is trivial to generalize the naive methodology to more than two treatments in principle, the resulting multiplication of the required labor further compounds the disadvantages of the naive method in practice.

To illustrate a typical need to test out more than two systems, consider again the comparative evaluation of a retrieval rule A operating in a collection C as against a rule B operating in D. If one wants to know not only *which* system is better, but also *why* it is better, one must also evaluate A operating in D and B operating in C, in order to deduce whether it is the retrieval rule or the collection to which the success is to be attributed. This is an application of the statistical technique of 'partitioning' an experiment to allow for later analysis of the factors responsible for a difference in outcomes. The partitioning of an evaluation experiment, though necessary if any 'why' questions are to be asked, can clearly increase the total number of systems to be tested by a large factor.

4. *The methodology is applicable only to systems already in use.* What a system designer often wants is, by contrast, a method for comparing different possible designs while they are still on the drawing board.

Summarizing the real objections, then, the naive methodology tests working systems in a slow and tortuous manner in which the labor increases with the number of systems tested out, whereas for practical purposes one would like a test applicable to system designs as well as working systems, in which many designs may be evaluated with not much more work than one.

4. Summary of Part I

The success of a retrieval system must ultimately be judged on the basis of a comparison of some kind involving costs and benefits. In arriving at design decisions this usually involves making a comparison of the costs and/or benefits of one possible system vis-a-vis others. Some writers argue that the way a retrieval system is evaluated should depend on the 'point of view' that is taken—whether that of the system user, the manager, the owner, the designer, or whoever. This is surely true, but the fact remains that all these points of view are concerned with costs or benefits in one way or another.

On the benefits side of the ledger, there are many factors to consider, but the particular benefit which is unique to retrieval systems (as opposed to other kinds of service systems and organizations) is guidance in searching a document collection. Our contention has been that there can be in principle no better evaluation of this most essential aspect of a retrieval system's benefits than a subjective evaluation by its users, provided that such an evaluation is made with all due care, and is measured judiciously in terms of an appropriate utile. If there is a difference in cost as well as benefits among the different systems under comparison, this utile must among other things fulfill the requirement that it allow a meaningful comparison of benefits with costs.

The 'naive' test procedure of Section 1, as amended by the various qualifications in Section 2, provides a concrete illustration of how subjective evaluations could in principle be collected in such a way as to meet these requirements. It is based on a simple conceptual scheme for retrieval evaluation that is philosophically sound, or is at least close enough to being sound so that its general character seems unlikely to be totally devastated by future criticisms not yet thought of. But the naive methodology is far from sound from a practical point of view, since it would normally be infeasible to carry it out with limited resources. Hence it is not recommended that it actually be applied as it stands.

What is the use of the naive methodology, then? Its most important function is that of a conceptual standard against which other more practical measures of effectiveness may be compared. That is, when a practical measure of effectiveness must be selected, it can and should be chosen on the basis of how likely it is to lead to the same design decisions as the naive methodology would. For if the essential correctness of the naive method is accepted, it follows that the guiding rule for selecting a practical measure of retrieval effectiveness has to be: *Choose the measure that promises to yield results that are as similar as is possible under the practical limitations of the test resources to what would be obtained with the naive measure.* An inescapable if somewhat disheartening corollary is that if the available resources are insufficient to allow a method of testing having a reasonably high probability of leading to the same design decisions as the naive methodology would, then there is no use conducting the test.

It remains to go into the practical matter of how to select or invent efficient measures of effectiveness that are as similar in expected outcome to the naive measure as available resources allow. This matter will be the topic of Part II.

References

1. Robertson, S. E., The Parametric Description of Retrieval Tests, *Journal of Documentation,* 25 (No. 1): 1–27 and 25 (No. 2): 93–107 (1969).
2. Swets, J. A., Information Retrieval Systems, *Science,* 141: 245–250 (1963).
3. Giuliano, V., and P. Jones, *Study and Test of a Methodology for Laboratory Evaluation of Message Retrieval Systems,* Report ESD–TR–66–405, Arthur D. Little, Inc., Cambridge, Mass. (1966).
4. King, D. W., and E. C. Bryant, *The Evaluation of Information Services and Products,* Information Resources Press, Washington, D. C. (1971).
5. Cooper, W. S., On Deriving Design Equations for Information Retrieval Systems, *Journal of the American Society for Information Science* 21: 385–395 (1970).
6. Cooper, W. S., A Definition of Relevance for Information Retrieval, *Information Storage and Retrieval,* 7: 19–37 (1971).
7. Schlaifer, R., *Introduction to Statistics for Business Decisions,* McGraw-Hill, New York, (1961).
8. Winer, B. J., *Statistical Principles in Experimental Design,* McGraw-Hill, New York (1962).
9. Stevens, S. S., On the theory of Scales of Measurement, *Science,* 103: 677–680 (1946).
10. Stevens, S. S., Measurement, Statistics, and the Schemapiric View, *Science,* 125: 849–856 (1968).

THE PRAGMATICS OF INFORMATION RETRIEVAL EXPERIMENTATION, REVISITED

JEAN TAGUE-SUTCLIFFE
School of Library and Information Science, University of Western Ontario, London, Ontario, N6G 1H1, Canada

Abstract—The decisions that must be made by an investigator in carrying out an information retrieval experiment are described. Guidance is provided on a number of issues, specifically determining the need for testing, choosing the type of test (laboratory or operational), defining the variables, developing or using databases, finding queries, processing queries, assigning treatments to experimental units, collecting the data, analyzing the data, and presenting the results.

In 1981, I contributed a paper (Tague, 1981) with the title "The pragmatics of information retrieval experimentation" to a collection of papers in honor of Cyril Cleverdon, the pioneer of the information retrieval testing. The paper was an attempt to guide a novice information scientist in the actual conduct of an information retrieval experiment, so that it would really accomplish what the investigator had set out to do.

In the ensuing decade, a great deal of information retrieval experimentation has taken place and, in fact, it would not be incorrect to say that the field has blossomed beyond all expectation. New problems and foci have arisen. Technologies such as CD-ROM and improved communication networks have widened the availability of computer-based retrieval systems. Others, such as full-text databases and hypertext and hypermedia systems, have enlarged our notion of what constitutes an information record in an information retrieval system. A paradigmatic shift has occurred in the research front, to user-centered from system-centered models. Thus, the time seems ripe for an updating of the original paper.

The format of the original paper will be followed (i.e., to step through an information retrieval test procedure, indicating, at each step, the choices that will face the experimenter). As before, the emphasis will be on guiding decisions that will affect the validity, reliability, and efficiency of the experimental procedure, where these concepts are defined as follows:

Validity is the extent to which the experiment actually determines what the experimenter wishes to determine. Do the observed variables really represent the concepts under investigation? For example, does a five-point rating scale really measure user satisfaction? Does the number of search terms really measure search complexity? Does evaluation by a judge other than the user really represent document relevance? Can results obtained with student subjects be replicated in a corporate information center?

Reliability is the extent to which the experimental results can be replicated. Will another experimenter get consistent results? For example, will a test of the retrieval effectiveness of free vs. controlled indexing using 10 articles from a single journal, indexed by a single indexer, provide results that can be replicated elsewhere?

A bias is any feature of the experiment that contributes to a lack of reliability or validity. Aspects that contribute to a lack of reliability are small samples, unequal samples, nonrandom samples, and improper methods of statistical analysis. Aspects that contribute to a lack of validity are order effects, learning effects, models based on inappropriate axioms, improper operational definitions, observer inaccuracies, and extraneous subject-treatment interaction.

Efficiency is the extent to which an experiment is effective (i.e., valid and reliable, relative to the resources consumed). Results can usually be made more valid by employing a larger number of variables and more discriminating variables. Results can usually be made more reliable by increasing the size and representativeness of the database and user and query set. However, these choices usually cost more in terms of time and money. How much better are the results relative to this increased expenditure?

Performing a valid, reliable, and efficient information retrieval test involves a great deal of knowledge, skill, and perceptiveness on the part of the investigator, as the ensuing pages will make clear. Ideally, the investigator should have a background not only in the substantive areas of information retrieval and the subject matter of the documents, but also in the methodological areas of research design, statistical analysis, human factors in research, database design, and project management. For major formal retrieval tests, where large databases and retrieval systems will be developed, experimental factors controlled, and large numbers of queries processed, a team approach is desirable, to provide all of this expertise.

However, a great deal can be learned from informal tests, carried out by less highly trained investigators, perhaps system professionals, because these tests are often closer to the reality of an information service environment. Such tests will not usually lead to publications, but are undertaken to provide clues as to how improvements in a system can be made. This paper is addressed both to those undertaking formal tests which may lead to an enlargement of our general knowledge of retrieval systems and to those undertaking informal tests which may lead to a betterment of the system provided to a particular user group.

In updating the earlier presentation, I have relied on my own experience, the experience of doctoral students whom I have advised, and, of course, the literature published since 1981. Much valuable advice has been obtained, both formally and informally, from others. However, the final responsibility for these counsels, based on the personal view of the field I have acquired over the years, is my own. In information retrieval testing, as in many other aspects of life, final choices are as much an art as a science.

DECISION 1. TO TEST OR NOT TO TEST?

An experiment should have a purpose; it is a means to an end, not an end in itself. It is therefore essential that the investigator delineate clearly the purpose of the test, the addition to knowledge that will result from its execution, and ensure that this addition has not already been made.

To guarantee novelty, as well as to get some useful ideas about how others have attacked similar problems, it is essential to check the information retrieval literature. Review chapters in the *Annual review of information science and technology* are a good starting point, as are the proceedings of the annual International Conference on Research and Development in Information Retrieval, sponsored by the Association for Computing Machinery Special Interest Group on Information Retrieval (SIGIR). A number of online systems, or their print counterparts, are particular useful: ERIC, INSPEC, NTIS, LISA, INFORMATION SCIENCE ABSTRACTS, ONLINE CHRONICLE, COMPENDEX, MICROCOMPUTER INDEX, and MATHSCI.

The literature of the past 10 years has included some major information retrieval experiments, among others those described by Blair and Maron (1985), Croft *et al.* (1989), Harman and Candela (1990), Salton (1989), Saracevic *et al.* (1988), and Shaw (1990). It is highly recommended that these and other earlier experiments be studied before beginning a new one.

In the earlier paper, it was pointed out that there is a need for cumulative studies in information retrieval. Happily, this need appears closer to fulfilment now than 10 years ago. Tague (1987) found that research in information science is becoming more cumulative in terms of the impact factors of journals in the field (i.e., in terms of the average number of citations per article).

DECISION 2. WHAT KIND OF TEST?

Much research in information retrieval is concerned with determining the effect of one or more factors or treatments (the independent variables) on one or more performance outcomes (the dependent variables). In an experiment, as opposed to other kinds of research, there is some control of the independent variables and assessment of the resulting change in the dependent variable.

Sometimes the word "experiment" is reserved for situations in which not only the independent variables, but also the environmental or concomitant variables—other sources of variation in the dependent variables—are controlled. This is the situation, at least in theory, with a laboratory experiment. In information retrieval, a laboratory test is one in which the sources of variability stemming from users, databases, searchers, and search constraints are under the control of the experimenter. By contrast, an operational test is one in which one or more existing systems—with their own users, databases, searchers, and search constraints—are evaluated or compared.

In fact, there is a range from laboratory tests, with all four components (users, databases, searchers, search constraints) controlled, to tests in which three will be controlled (e.g., users, searchers, search constraints), to tests in which two will be controlled (e.g., users and searchers, but operational databases), to tests in which one only is controlled (e.g., searchers), to operational tests in which none is controlled.

What are the advantages and disadvantages of these various levels of variable control? If the test is of operational systems, one cannot generalize to other systems with any degree of confidence. Operational tests usually tell us something about the systems as a whole, but not their individual aspects. Thus, the purpose of the research is important in determining the level of control to be imposed. Laboratory tests, where the database and retrieval algorithms must be specially created, tend to be more expensive than operational tests with the same size database and numbers of queries. The experimenter must be sure of having the time, funding, and cooperation of users to bring the experiment to a conclusion. However, operational tests also require the acquiescence of others, usually the personnel and managers of the operational system. Generally speaking, operational tests are closer to "real life," but provide less specific information. Because fewer variables are controlled in an operational test, it is difficult to attribute observed results to particular causes.

DECISION 3. HOW TO OPERATIONALIZE THE VARIABLES

Whatever the degree of control chosen, for any experiment the investigator must, initially, clearly define the independent and dependent variables.

A variable is some attribute or feature—qualitative or quantitative—of a retrieval system. Many variables are involved in information retrieval experiments, and any given variable may play a number of roles—independent variable, dependent variable, environmental variable—depending on the purpose of the experiment. The variables studied in a sense define a discipline and serve as a shorthand for its important concepts. A major problem in designing any experimental study is deciding how actually to observe or measure these concepts—how to operationalize them.

What follows are simply some suggestions for operationalizing a number of the variables encountered in information retrieval, grouped under the components of an information retrieval process: database, information representation, users, queries, search intermediaries, retrieval process, retrieval evaluation.

Document collection or database

Variables in this category relate to the size, concentration, form, medium, subject coverage, and warrant or expected use of the database. Database here refers to a collection of documents, where a document, following Nelson's (1990) definition, is a package of information created by someone. Each document will consist of one or more information records (i.e., components of the package that can be individually accessed).

The size of a database may be measured in a number of ways: the number of documents, the number of records, or the storage requirements, in bytes or blocks. The concentration or homogeneity of the collection with respect to qualitative and quantitative variables can be described by functions of the class frequencies called concentration measures. These have been evaluated by Egghe and Rousseau (1989) on the basis of some desirable mathematical properties, with the result that the authors proposed, as the most satisfactory measures, the following: the coefficient of variation and its square, the Yule characteristic, the CON-index, Pratt's measure, the Gini index, the generalized Pratt index, Theil's measure, and Atkinson's index.

Other than size and concentration, the variables describing databases are all qualitative and the major problem, for operationalization, is defining appropriate categories. Form may relate to the completeness of the representation (e.g., citation, abstract, full-text) or the publication vehicle (e.g., monograph, journal article, technical report). Records that consist of citations, possibly with index terms and abstracts, and so refer to other full-text documents, are called document surrogates. With full-text databases, defining appropriate documents and records is important; for example, is a document a book or a chapter? Is a record a chapter, a paragraph, or a sentence. Communication medium (text, sound, table, picture, graph) and recording medium (paper, electronic) need to be distinguished. With multimedia databases, communicating medium becomes less a characteristic of the database as a whole than of individual documents or records.

Information representation

Information representation refers to the logical and physical structure of the stored information. The effect of this structure on retrieval has been one of the major foci of information retrieval experimentation. It can be represented, at a general level, by a model. Tague *et al.* (1991) discuss a number of models that have been used to describe the logical structure of the information base, including the boolean model, the vector space model, the relational model, the semantic model, the cluster model, the hypergraph model, and the production grammar model. Models used to describe the physical structure include b-trees and other multiway trees, hashing, signatures, and multilists.

Where indexing of the information records occurs, a number of operationalizations have been suggested for important aspects of the indexing process. These include the following:

1. Exhaustivity of indexing (i.e., the number of topics covered by the indexing). Operational definition: number of index terms/document.
2. Specificity of indexing (i.e., the precision of the subject descriptions). Operational definition: number of postings per term, or posting rate. This number may, however, depend on fashions in the literature as well.
3. Degree of control in indexing. Operational definition: proportion of free keywords vs controlled vocabulary terms assigned to documents.
4. Degree of linkage in a vocabulary. Operational definition: number of *see also* references in the dictionary.
5. Accommodation of vocabulary (i.e., extent to which user need not know exact terms). Operational definition: number of *see* references in the dictionary.
6. Term discrimination value (i.e., extent to which a term decreases the average similarity of the document set). For an operational definition, see Salton (1975).
7. Degree of pre-coordination of terms. Operational definition: number of index terms per index phrase. Averaging may take place over either all entries (types) in the dictionary of the language or over all tokens in the database.
8. Degree of syntactic control (i.e., grammatical operators, role operators, relational operators). Operational definition: number of operators per record.
9. Accuracy of indexing. Operational definition: number of indexing errors, as determined by a judge or by reference to a standard set of term assignments. Two types of errors may be distinguished: of omission and of commission. Validity is a problem here—why is the judge or standard "correct"?
10. Inter-indexer consistency. Operational definition: ratio of number of terms assigned by both indexers to number of terms assigned by either. There is a problem, however, in determining what constitutes a common term: exact match or same word root, possibly with different endings.

Where documents are clustered or classified, various types of clustering structures may be defined, including distinct vs overlapping clusters, hierarchical vs flat clusters, and clustering criterion (e.g., nearest neighbour, complete-link, centroid-based). Shaw (1990) suggests that any document clustering or partition is not meaningful unless it differs from random grouping.

Users

One of the major thrusts of the past decade has been the information user. Individual differences among users, in terms both of their personal characteristics and their reasons for seeking information, are now seen as important elements of the information retrieval process.

Many variables relating to the user are categorical. Some examples are:

1. type of user – student, scientist, businessperson, child;
2. context of use – occupational, educational, recreational;
3. kinds of information needed – aid in understanding, define a problem, place a problem in context, design a strategy, complete a solution;
4. immediacy of information need – immediate, current, future.

Many of these variables are a part of the approach to information seeking proposed by Dervin (1980), Belkin (1980), and others, and known as the sense-making approach. In this approach, users are seen as involved in a decision-making or problem-solving process. They are stopped in this process by a gap or anomaly and seek information in order to overcome it. In the time line method proposed by Dervin, the investigator tries to identify and categorize critical events in this process from interviews, observation, journal keeping, etc.

Following initiatives by Borgman (1987) and Saracevic and Kantor (1988), it has become common to measure personal characteristics, such as mathematical ability, language ability, logical ability, learning mode, educational level, and searching experience, of users and searchers. Experience is usually measured in terms of time (e.g., years of experience) or number of previous searches or use of a system. Psychometric scales can be used to measure many of the other personal characteristics and attitudinal variables. Typically, these scales are based on responses that consist of ratings – for example, poor, fair, satisfactory, good, excellent. Specific tests that have been used are the Learning Style Inventory, Remote Associates Test, and Symbolic Reasoning Test. Many of the tests are Likert scales, in which a subject's ratings for a set of items are summed. A useful text on psychometric measurement is Ghiselli *et al.* (1981). Rorvig (1988) reviews the use of psychometric measurement in information retrieval.

Queries and search statements

Query will be used here to mean the verbalized statement of a user's need. A *search statement* is a single string, expressed in the language of the system, which triggers a search of the database (i.e., causes a search algorithm to scan the database and identify a set or sequence of hits). A *search process* is a sequence of search statements, all relating to the same query. Search processes, rather than single search statements, are increasingly studied, as a result of the greater interactivity of present-day information retrieval systems.

Queries may be real-life (i.e., representing real information needs of a user) or artificial. One way of generating artificial queries is to derive them from titles and other parts of documents. For example, in an experiment, the title of a paper may be used as the query and the set of references in the paper as the set of relevant documents. However, many investigators believe that real queries and users are to be preferred. Real queries may be measured with respect to such variables as clarity and complexity using user- and searcher-rating scales.

Search statements consist of a structure of search elements (terms, truncated terms, classification codes, etc.) The structure depends on the model upon which the information retrieval system is based and could be a boolean expression (using connectives 'and', 'or', and 'not'), vector (set of weights indicating the importance of each of a set of terms in the query), an expression employing some other kind of syntax (role indicators, facets, word adjacency requirements), or natural language. In the latter case, there will need to be a computer-based natural language understanding system to process the search statements. Although a number of these are available, it must be remembered that they are not true understanding systems, but more or less successful algorithms for analyzing a natural language statement into component parts.

Search statements can be measured as to size: the number of search elements in a boolean search or the number of non-zero vector elements in a vector search. With boolean statements, we may also define exhaustivity and specificity. A boolean search statement must first be put into a standard form – disjunctive normal form, a disjunction of conjuncts. The exhaustivity of the search statement can then be defined as the number of conjuncts and the specificity as the average number of terms per conjunct.

The search process

The past decade has also seen an explosion of investigations of the search process. Searches may vary in many ways, at both the macro and the micro level. Variation can relate to interactions of people (user and searcher) and interactions of people with systems. Three macro-level variables attempt to capture these sources of variation.

1. *Delegated vs end-user searching.* Searches may be carried out by an intermediary or by the end user. Within delegated searches, there may be degrees of interaction between user and searcher. A variable that measures this degree of interaction is the amount of time the user and searcher are in direct contact. However, this variable may also reflect the complexity of the search.

2. *Search logic or technique used.* Belkin and Croft (1987) distinguish techniques based on individual documents (boolean, vector, extended boolean, natural language processing, relevance feedback) with those based on networks of documents (clustering, browsing, spreading activation). Vector-based searches will also differ on the document-query similarity measure used, for example, cosine, jaccard, or maximum entropy functions, and on the weighting function used for the query terms.

3. *Access modes for searcher:* commands, hypertext links, menus.

At the micro or individual search level, the search process can be described by the kinds of interaction between user and searcher when the search is delegated, or by the kinds of preliminary activities when it is not delegated, and by the kinds of commands and strategies employed during the search process. In the first two categories are such activities as question negotiation, explanation of system, selection of search elements, selection of search logic, selection of databases, and relevance feedback from an initial search. Time spent in each activity and commonly occurring sequences of activities can be determined.

Commands may also be classified (scanning dictionary, exploding term, selecting, displaying, printing documents, etc.) and the number of each type tabulated. Larger units may also be analyzed. Bates (1979) has defined an information search tactic as a move to further a search and has described 29 human information search tactics in four categories: monitoring (keeping the search on track), files structure (threading through the structure), search formulation (designing the formulation), and term (selecting and revising terms). Fidel (1985) has defined a move as a modification of a query formulation and has described 18 operational and 12 conceptual moves.

The length of a search can be described by the elapsed or connect time, by the number of commands entered, or by the number and length of the search cycles, where a cycle represents a sequence of commands from a search statement to a print statement.

Retrieval performance

The traditional measures of retrieval performance are recall and precision, defined as follows: Recall is the proportion of relevant documents retrieved and precision is the proportion of retrieved documents that are relevant. An alternative measure of performance is fallout, the proportion of nonrelevant items retrieved. Thus, if we make a four-way partition of the database as follows:

a is the number of relevant and retrieved references,
b is the number of nonrelevant and retrieved references,
c is the number of relevant and nonretrieved references,
d is the number of nonrelevant and nonretrieved references,

then we have:

$$\text{recall} = a/(a + c),$$
$$\text{precision} = a/(a + b),$$
$$\text{fallout} = b/(b + d).$$

The definitions of recall and precision presume that the relevant set and the retrieved set are well defined. In an age of interactive databases and, particularly, full-text interactive databases, these definitions present some problems. An investigator must clearly indicate how the states of being retrieved and being relevant are determined. In a full-text database, what units are retrieved and evaluated as to relevance—full papers, sections, paragraphs, sentences? In an interactive online or ondisk system, is a document retrieved when it is in the answer set to a search command, when its title is displayed, when its citation is printed, or when the full text is recovered?

If output is ranked, then recall and precision will depend on the stopping point, the point at which the user ceases to examine the ranked output. In this case, recall and precision can be calculated at each rank (i.e., using rank as a retrieval threshold). In general, as the number of documents retrieved increases, recall will increase. With a well structured search process one would also expect that as the number of documents retrieved increases, precision will decrease. However, this result will not necessarily occur. For example, if all the nonrelevant documents are retrieved first and then the relevant ones, recall and precision will increase together at the end of the search.

With ranked output, the overall recall and precision of the search may be described by normalized recall (R_{norm}) and precision (P_{norm}), defined by Salton (1975) as follows:

$$R_{\text{norm}} = 1 - \frac{\Sigma r_i - \Sigma i}{n(N - n)}$$

$$P_{\text{norm}} = 1 - \frac{\Sigma \log(r_i) - \Sigma \log(i)}{\log[n!/((N - n)!n!)]}$$

where n is the size of the relevant document set, N is the size of the total document set, and r_i is the retrieval rank of the ith relevant document.

A number of measures combine recall and precision into an overall retrieval performance measure. Van Rijsbergen (1979) suggested the E measure, defined as follows:

$$E = 1 - 1/[\alpha P^{-1} + (1 - \alpha)R^{-1}],$$

where P and R are precision and recall, respectively, and α is a parameter reflecting the relative importance of recall and precision for the user.

Shaw (1986) has suggested that the E measure leads to some inconsistencies and recommends, instead, the MZ metric, defined as follows:

$$D = 1 - 1/(P^{-1} + R^{-1} - 1).$$

Determination of recall is dependent on a determination of the full set of relevant documents. This has been a problem since the early days of retrieval testing. Some suggested solutions are the following:

1. The relevant set is predetermined by some means, for example, taking the title of a paper as the query and the cited documents as the relevant set. This approach operationalizes relevance in a very arbitrary fashion. For example, there may be other documents in the database that are also relevant.

2. A small document set is used for the test, and the relevance of all documents for all queries is assessed by users or system personnel. A problem is that small files may not be very reliable guides to results with large files.

3. A random sample of the nonretrieved set is taken and all documents in the set assessed as to relevance. The problem with this approach is that in most operational systems, the size of the relevant set is small compared to the size of the database, and hence a very large sample will be needed to assess the proportion of relevant documents accurately. For example, with large databases, for a 95% confidence level, an error in the estimated percentage of relevant documents of less than 1%, and the indicated actual percentage of relevant documents, one would need the following sample sizes.

Actual % relevant documents	Sample size for .1% accuracy
0.1%	3838
1.0	38032
10.0	345744

4. In comparative tests, relative rather than absolute recall is calculated. If a_i is the set of documents retrieved by the ith treatment and $N(a)$ the number of documents in a set a, the relative recall of the ith treatment is defined by $N(a_i)/U_jN(a_j)$, where the denominator represents the number of documents in the union of the sets retrieved for all treatments. Relative recall is useful in comparing a number of different retrieval strategies using the same database and query set. However, it should not be used to compare results from one experiment or database with another. McKinin *et al.* (1991) use this method for calculating recall in an operational system test under the name comprehensiveness.

5. With a large database, carry out a very broad search or examine subsets known to be rich in relevant items and then use the total number of relevant items found as the denominator for the recall ratio. This technique was used by Blair and Maron (1985), for example.

Recent investigators have broadened the scope of retrieval evaluation from a concentration on recall and precision to other dimensions of the retrieval process and to a deeper understanding of what is actually meant by relevance. Tague and Schultz (1989) suggest that there are actually four dimensions to the effectiveness of the retrieval process:

- How informative was the retrieved set? (precision)
- How complete was the retrieved set? (recall)
- How much time did the user spend with the system? (contact time)
- Was the experience with the system a satisfying one? (user friendliness)

Informativeness depends not only on what documents were retrieved, but also on the order in which they were retrieved. User friendliness can be measured by a number of variables such as number of keyboarding errors, number of commands entered per unit time, proportion of user vocabulary and syntax the system can recognize, proportion of system vocabulary and syntax the user utilizes, length of training time, and number of exasperation responses or terminations by the user.

A problem with relevance-based measures is that the concept of relevance has many different connotations, as Saracevic (1975) and Schamber *et al.* have pointed out. Pragmatically, the problem lies in determining the scale of relevance (binary, ranked, weighted) and in instructing the relevance judges (be they users or others) so that they will carry out relevance assessments in a consistent manner.

Historically, a distinction has been made between subject relevance (aboutness) and usefulness (pertinence). Usefulness or utility could be determined subjectively by the user or objectively by looking at whether or not the user used the document, the contact time with the document, or the results of contact with the document, such as improved productivity, development of a new product, or publication. However, more recently, Regazzi (1988) has provided experimental evidence of no difference in subjective judgments of subject relevance and usefulness. Regazzi also suggests that, in addition to relevance, documents should be rated for more specific attributes, including accuracy, completeness, content, or subject, suggestiveness of new ideas, timeliness, and treatment (clarity).

The new user-oriented approach to information retrieval suggests that rather than evaluating individual items as to relevance, we should evaluate the result of the overall retrieval service. Dervin and Nilan (1986) suggest that this needs to be done in categorical rather than quantitative terms. They present the following categories for the results of information providing:

- got picture
- had idea
- advanced understanding
- gained skill
- got started
- kept going
- got connected to others
- got support
- got rest/relaxation
- achieved happiness
- reached goal.

Cost studies also form a part of evaluation. These are not trivial undertakings and require meticulous record keeping and awareness of all factors that contribute to costs: personnel time, both professional and clerical, computer connect time, network use, database storage and update, amortized equipment costs, supplies, photocopying, and overhead.

Cost effectiveness and cost benefit are really two distinct concepts. The former relates the cost of a retrieval system to its effectiveness in serving its users. Thus, it can be measured by the ratio of cost to some performance measure such as recall or precision. The latter relates the cost of a retrieval system to its benefit to a society or community or institution. This might be measured by the extent to which potential users use the system, see barriers to use, or report satisfaction with use.

DECISION 4. WHAT DATABASE TO USE?

In this section we shall discuss the choice of experimental vs operational database, and in section 6 the choice of in-house vs externally-obtained database management and retrieval software. A number of combinations are possible. For example, both database and software might be developed in house, an externally developed database might be used with in-house software, commercial software might be used to develop and access an in-house database, or an operational online database and its software used.

In-house experimental databases are expensive to build and, hence, for most investigators, small. However, in some cases they are necessary—for example, when an experimental document representation approach is used. However, it is important to remember that results with a small collection cannot always be extrapolated to a large collection. The major reason for this caution is that, with a large collection, there may be a greater proportion of nonrelevant material than with a small collection. The sampling error in estimating system recall and precision from samples is inversely proportional to the square root of the collection size.

The planning and design stage is particularly important in developing an operational system, as this is when the major decisions are made. Specifically, decisions must be made relating to:

- coverage of the database—subject, time period, language;
- source of documents;
- source of vocabulary, use of authority files;
- form of documents—full-text, abstracts, citations;
- fields of the record or records for each document;
- display formats, ordering of records in displays; and
- windowing capabilities.

Most information retrieval systems are based on inverted files. Design of an inverted file system requires choices about the attributes to be indexed, whether the indexing will be of the complete string or individual words within the field, whether there will be a stop list, and whether words will be stemmed or truncated.

In cases where the focus of the experiment is on retrieval strategies, rather than information representation, test collections may be used in experiments. Some popular test collections are the *Cranfield*, *Medlars*, *Communications of the ACM*, and the *Ontap ERIC*, all of which contain queries and user evaluations as well as abstracts. There is a potential problem with overuse of a few test collections, however, as seemingly general results may stem from the peculiarities of the collections.

Operational systems may be used in two ways. Either tapes may be purchased and used in conjunction with software developed or purchased for the local computer, or the commercial online systems may be used directly. The latter approach makes sense when the focus of the investigation is on retrieval strategies used with existing systems, but will be found too restrictive if experimental retrieval approaches are being tested.

Usually investigators will opt for building experimental databases if they envisage a continuing, in-depth series of investigations of the basic variables of the retrieval process. If the investigation has more immediately practical ends, operational databases will be preferred. If the objectives of the experiment can be achieved by using a commercial online system, there seems to be good economic reasons for choosing this alternative.

DECISION 5. WHERE TO GET QUERIES?

A query is a verbalized information need. Queries provide the starting point for a database search, control the search process, and determine the value of the output. Because of their importance, it is unfortunate that getting good queries is one of the major problems of retrieval testing.

The user, the person with a real information need, is an obvious source of queries. Real users may be recruited through personal contacts with information service personnel or through advertising. However, many investigators find real users difficult to control and difficult to involve in the search process and evaluation in a predetermined fashion. Users do not willingly participate in tests, they will drop out before completing all requirements, particularly the evaluation of output, and will not obey instructions for maintaining the integrity of the experiment. These problems can often be minimized, however, by providing a monetary or other incentive to users to remain in the test. Typically, users are given all results from the searches of their queries and sometimes an honorarium as well. These days, users do not come cheap!

For the reasons given in the last paragraph, some retrieval testing is done with artificial queries or with people other than the user controlling the search process or evaluating the search output. How can such artificial queries be obtained? A popular technique, as we have already indicated, is to use the title of a paper as the query and the references cited as the set of relevant answers. Another is to use the records of past queries which are frequently kept by libraries and information services. The problem with artificial queries is that they do not represent the information need of a person involved in the test. It is therefore not possible to obtain additional information about the query (i.e., the need) or to obtain a definitive set of relevance evaluations. The end user is really the only judge of the relevance of documents to his or her information need. Where relevance is judged by others, inconsistencies may result (i.e., two judges may have differing opinions).

In comparative testing situations, where two or more treatments are being compared, it is important that the investigator not be too deeply involved in the searching and evaluation of output phases. To reduce the possibility of bias or favouring desired outcomes, the investigator should function primarily as a planner. Other system personnel or research assistants should carry out the searching and evaluation of output.

Most investigators agree that experiments with real users are to be preferred when the necessary control is possible. However, because of the many differences among users, both in personal characteristics and information requirements, it will be necessary to work with large numbers of queries in order, in most cases, to arrive at a reasonable degree of reliability in the estimation of the effects of different treatments or approaches to retrieval. It is important, also, that results for users of one type not be generalized to all users. For example, results from retrieval experiments carried out with student users should not be generalized to the information needs of experienced professionals.

DECISION 6. HOW TO PROCESS QUERIES

Processing queries involves decisions about the software to be used to access the database and about the procedures to be laid down for the searchers.

As mentioned earlier, the investigator must decide whether to develop his or her own database management and retrieval software or to use an existing system, whether commercial or experimentally developed. The decision will depend, in part, on the purposes of the test.

If novel approaches to retrieval are being tested, tailor-made software will be a necessity. Another advantage is that, with a tailor-made system, one can collect more detailed information about system use, for example, numbers of accesses of specific entries in the inverted file, and hence conduct a more discriminating study. For present-day retrieval testing, a user-logging capability is usually essential. This capability can be built into the tailor-made system; however, commercial and public-domain packages are also available.

As with in-house database development, detailed specification and planning is necessary with in-house retrieval software development. Experienced programmers should be employed and professional standards required. The investigator should work closely with the programmer in designing the system. The software should be well documented, structured, and completely debugged. Use of the software by non-experts and modification by other programmers should not present any problems.

Although tailor-made systems are expensive and take a long time to build (typically at least a year), they can provide a base for a continuing series of investigations if they are well designed. Time given to the design phase is therefore well repaid by the extended lifetime of the experimental system. In this regard, it is often useful to allow one or two extra fields in the database record, in case additional information is needed in later studies.

On the other hand, if ways of using existing systems are being investigated, there appears to be little reason not to use the software of the system. As well, many commercial database products such as DBASE, or automated library systems such as INMAGIC, can be used for retrieval experiments where the focus is on such aspects as user-searcher interaction or searcher behaviour. Even when the focus is on the retrieval algorithms themselves, they can often be adapted, with suitable pre- or post-processing software, to meet the needs of the study.

It is extremely important that procedures be standardized during the search process. Extraneous sources of variation must not be allowed to bias the results. Such control is obviously easier in an experimental rather than an operational setting, but even in the latter case much can be achieved by appropriate documentation, instructions, and training for those involved in the test searching.

The aim of these controls is to make those aspects of the search that are not being manipulated experimentally as much alike as possible. Thus, searchers need to be instructed about amount and kind of interaction with the user, mechanisms for searching, what search aids, such as thesauri, can be used, and the form of output required. System personnel should understand exactly what information the investigator hopes to obtain and should be given the necessary tools to collect this information.

Training and practice sessions for all searchers should be held prior to the test, and during the test the investigator or a research assistant should be available to handle unforeseen problems. During the practice sessions, the investigator should try to observe the point at which fatigue sets in and, during the actual experiment, schedule appropriate breaks so that this does not become a biasing factor. Many extraneous sources of variation arise from computer system breakdowns, and these can be eliminated by careful prechecking of the search environment, to be sure supplies are available and all equipment is in working order.

DECISION 7. HOW WILL TREATMENTS BE ASSIGNED TO EXPERIMENTAL UNITS?

This decision relates to the design of the test. Sparck-Jones (1988) has said:

> The most important problem we have to face in test, and especially experimental, design is that as we increase the emphasis on interaction with the individual user, we get less repeatability. This is not a new problem, but it is exacerbated by the complexity of the system, the power of the interface, and the need for tests on a large scale. Interactive searching for a given requirement with one strategy implies learning, which interferes with the user's operation with another strategy.

Although there is no perfect solution to this problem, use of standard experimental designs can alleviate this problem to some extent. Haas and Kraft (1984) provide an excellent introduction to the use of experimental designs as a method of eliminating bias. They distinguish an experiment, in which there is a random assignment of cases to treatments or independent variable levels, and quasi experiments, in which there is a nonrandom assignment. More detailed information can be found in Cochran and Cox (1957) and Winer (1971).

A complete information retrieval experiment is concerned with assessing the effects of one or more classes of treatments or factors on one or more performance measures determined for each of a sample of experimental units. For example, the treatments might be different forms of document representation or different approaches to query negotiation with the user or different kinds of search strategies. In multifactor experiments there will be more than one set of treatments or factors. For example, both the form of document representation and the type of search strategy might be varied.

To eliminate bias, proper assignment of experimental units to factor levels or combinations of factor levels in multifactor experiments is essential. This means units must be assigned randomly and, if factor level interactions are possible, there must be replication (i.e., more than one unit must be assigned to each combination of levels).

In information retrieval experiments, the sources of variation are the treatments or factors under investigation, the queries, the users, the searchers, the searching order, the documents, and random effects. What constitutes an experimental unit will depend upon the purpose and design of the experiment and is defined by the points in the experimental process at which performance is measured. Thus, an experimental units might be:

1. a query, where the performance measure was user satisfaction with the system's response,
2. a search of query, where different strategies for the same query were being assessed on the basis of recall and precision,
3. a search of a query by a particular searcher, where more than one searcher searched a query and different strategies were being assessed on the basis of recall and precision,
4. a document retrieved by a search, where different kinds of document representations were being assessed on the basis of whether or not they resulted in retrieval of a relevant document,
5. a step in a search strategy, where each step was assessed on the basis of the number of relevant documents it produced.

Table 1. Completed crossed design

	t_1	t_2	t_3
s_1	q_1, q_2	q_3, q_4	q_5, q_6
s_2	q_7, q_8	q_9, q_{10}	q_{11}, q_{12}
s_3	q_{13}, q_{14}	q_{15}, q_{16}	q_{17}, q_{18}
s_4	q_{19}, q_{20}	q_{21}, q_{22}	q_{23}, q_{24}

Some commonly used experimental designs are: completely crossed designs, randomized block designs, repeated measures designs, Latin squares, and Greco-Latin squares. In these designs, bias is reduced by random assignment of experimental units to treatments and by replication of treatments. The designs will be described using typical retrieval test examples.

Suppose that three different approaches to retrieval strategy are being compared using four searchers and queries from users of an operational system. Relative recall and precision will be used as the two performance measures. In Tables 1–5, the following definitions apply.

Experimental strategies (treatments): t_1, t_2, t_3

Searchers: s_1, s_2, s_3, s_4

Queries: $q_1, q_2 \cdots q_{24}$

Blocks of similar queries: Q_1, Q_2, Q_3, Q_4, where $Q_i = \{q_{i,1}, q_{i,2}, q_{i,3}, q_{i,4}, q_{i,5}, q_{i,6}\}$

Time periods: p_1, p_2, p_3.

In a completely crossed design (see Table 1), each searcher uses each strategy and so would be randomly assigned a different set of one or more queries for each strategy. Thus, at least 12 queries would be needed. If interactions between searcher and strategy were to be assessed, there would need to be more than one query for each combination of strategy and searcher. Table 1 shows an example of how queries would be distributed over strategies and searchers. The problem with this approach is that there is such a large variation among queries with respect to recall and precision that these variations may mask variations caused by the search strategies that the experiment is investigating.

In a repeated-measures design, each searcher has a query set and would search this query set using each strategy (see Table 2). This approach eliminates the problem of a large inter-query variation masking treatment effects, but presents another one, that of sequence effects. Sequence can operate in either a positive (learning) or negative (fatigue) fashion. In the example, as searchers proceed through the different strategies with a query, they gain an understanding of what is available in the database relative to the query, and hence may perform better on later than on earlier searches. On the other hand, they may become tired, and perform worse on later than on earlier searches. Or a searcher may learn something with one strategy that makes another strategy more difficult to learn. The bias resulting from this learning effect can be reduced if the order of searching using different strategies is varied over the query set.

Table 2. Repeated measures design

	t_1	t_2	t_3
s_1	q_1, q_2	q_2, q_1	q_1, q_2
s_2	q_3, q_4	q_4, q_3	q_3, q_4
s_3	q_5, q_6	q_6, q_5	q_5, q_6
s_4	q_7, q_8	q_8, q_7	q_7, q_8

Table 3. Randomized incomplete block design

	t_1	t_2	t_3
s_1	$q_{1,1}, q_{2,1}$	$q_{1,2}, q_{2,2}$	$q_{1,3}, q_{2,3}$
s_2	$q_{1,4}, q_{3,1}$	$q_{1,5}, q_{3,2}$	$q_{1,6}, q_{3,3}$
s_3	$q_{2,4}, q_{4,1}$	$q_{2,5}, q_{4,2}$	$q_{2,6}, q_{4,3}$
s_4	$q_{3,4}, q_{4,4}$	$q_{3,5}, q_{4,5}$	$q_{3,6}, q_{4,6}$

If it is possible to separate the set of queries into subsets of similar queries or queries from similar users (blocks), then a randomized block design can be used. The assumption here is that the within block variation is small. In a completely randomized block design, at least one query from each block is assigned to each combination of searcher and strategy. In an incomplete randomized block design, each combination does not occur within each block, but each combination occurs within the same number of blocks, and each block is used for the same number of levels of each factor. It is assumed there is no interaction between the blocks and the other factors (strategies and searchers). See Table 3 for an example of an incomplete randomized block design. An advantage of this design is that learning effects are eliminated, since searchers search different queries for each strategy. However, this solution does require some control of the query set (i.e., there must be equal-sized blocks of similar queries).

Another way to control sequence effects is by using a Latin square design. A Latin square is an *n* by *n* table or array in which the entries in the table are *n* distinct symbols, assigned so that each appears once in each row and in each column. In an experimental design, the rows and columns represent levels of two factors (for example, strategy and searcher). The entries in the body of the table represent experimental units or sets of randomly assembled experimental units (for example, sets of queries). For a Latin square to be used as an experimental design, the number of levels of each factor must be equal to *n* and the number of experimental units a multiple of *n*. Table 4 provides an example of a Latin square design. Latin square designs assume that there is no interaction between the factors represented by the rows and the columns.

A Greco-Latin square is obtained by combining two Latin squares in such a way (called orthogonally) that each factor level combination occurs the same number of times. This is often useful if there are two factors as well as sequence effects, since the sequence of administering the treatment can be treated as an additional factor. Table 5 shows the Greco-Latin design for a test of three strategies, three search time periods, three searchers, and three sets of queries.

Latin squares and Greco-Latin squares can be repeated as many times as needed for the experiment. Regazzi (1988) presents a good example of a repeated Greco-Latin square. The main effects are context (relevance or utility), type of subject (researcher or student), and level of subject (senior or junior) (i.e., a 2 × 2 × 2 design). Each of the eight main effect combinations in the design are assigned four subjects, four topics, and 16 documents. A Greco-Latin square (shown in Table 6) is used which equalizes the effects of topic and document orders of presentation to the subjects.

The size of the sample is another aspect of experimental design. The more factors and factor levels, the larger must be the set of experimental units, since there must be at least

Table 4. Latin square design

	t_1	t_2	t_3
s_1	q_1, q_2	q_3, q_4	q_5, q_6
s_2	q_3, q_4	q_5, q_6	q_1, q_2
s_3	q_5, q_6	q_1, q_2	q_3, q_4

Table 5. Greco-Latin square design

	p_1	p_2	p_3
s_1	t_1, Q_1	t_2, Q_2	t_3, Q_3
s_2	t_2, Q_3	t_3, Q_1	t_1, Q_2
s_3	t_3, Q_2	t_1, Q_3	t_2, Q_1

one unit within each cell of the design, and preferably more than one, if interactions are to be studied. The sample size determines the reliability and discrimination of the test (i.e., for a specified confidence level, what minimum difference between treatment effect can be determined). To double the discrimination of a test one needs to quadruple the sample size, and, in general, to increase the discrimination n-fold, one needs n^2 times the sample size.

DECISION 8. HOW TO COLLECT THE DATA?

Data becomes available at each stage of an information retrieval test. If investigators were to collect all available data, they would be inundated. It is essential to plan data collection carefully, so that, normally, only that data relevant to the purposes of the test will be collected. I say "normally" because often something will catch the experimenter's attention and she or he may wish to gather information about it, as a pilot study, to be followed by a later, full-scale investigation.

Data collected in an information retrieval test can be categorized by the component it describes: the information store or database, the people (users, searchers), the processes (searching, indexing, evaluating), and the results (effectiveness, cost, value).

Data about the information store can be obtained from its originator or by appropriate statistical processing, if it is in electronic format. It is important, if a database is purchased, that the vendor be asked for information such as size, period covered, language restrictions, record structure, etc. It is surprising how many operational systems keep virtually no statistics on such important characteristics. The cost of doing your own analysis of the database is considerable.

With tailor-made retrieval systems, it is usually possible to incorporate a statistical reporting system into the system design. In this way, information about the database (size and growth rate of collection, size and growth rate of index) and its use (number of times various index entries or retrieval features are accessed) can be automatically and continuously generated.

Data on the people involved in a study can be obtained through observation, interviews, questionnaires, protocols, and computer logs. In all cases, the variables that will be recorded and their scales should be determined in advance and standardized for all who will participate in the test by means of well structured data collection instruments and instructions.

Table 6. Greco-Latin square subplot design (Regazzi, 1988)

Subject	Period 1	2	3	4
1	Topic A Docs: 1,2,3,4	Topic D 13,14,15,16	Topic C 9,10,11,12	Topic B 5,6,7,8
2	Topic B Docs: 7,8,5,6	Topic A 3,4,1,2	Topic D 15,16,13,14	Topic C 11,12,9,10
3	Topic C Docs: 10,9,12,11	Topic B 6,5,8,7	Topic A 2,1,4,3	Topic D 14,13,16,15
4	Topic D Docs: 16,15,14,13	Topic C 12,11,10,9	Topic B 8,7,6,5	Topic A 4,3,2,1

Observation may be obtrusive (obvious to the person observed) or unobtrusive. Many kinds of observations might be either; for example, observing time spent by users at an online catalog or at the shelves in a library collection. Though such observation is useful, one must have confidence in the observers, that they have not missed anything through fatigue, inattention, or bias. Another problem with obtrusive observation is that those observed may act differently than they would under normal circumstances (the so-called Hawthorne effect, named after the Hawthorne plant of the Western Electric Company, where the effect was first noticed in industrial productivity research in the 1920s).

The widespread use of online searching has made it possible, through user transaction logs, to collect detailed information on searching to a degree not previously possible. It is even possible to track user paths in hypertext systems. However, it is important that the confidentiality of the user be respected in this process. Users should be informed that their searches are being logged and no personal identification should be attached to a search without the user's permission. A good source on ethical procedures in using human subjects is the American Psychological Association's *Ethical principles in the conduct of research with human participants* (1982).

With user search protocols, users describe their thought processes during a search verbally, and this verbal record is taped for later analysis. Data collected in this fashion can often supplement and explain computer transaction logs. Users should practice the verbalization process before the actual testing begins.

Questionnaires and interviews may be used to collect information on the people involved in a test and on the test results. A problem with questionnaires is the low response rate and the self-selection of the responders. However, in some situations (for example, a classroom) it may be possible to reach high response levels. It is important that the questions in both questionnaires and structured interviews be pretested, so that problems with them will be caught early.

Collecting information about the results of a search is particularly difficult because it usually involves feedback from the user. If users are presented with search results in the form of lists of references and asked to return the list with evaluative information (e.g., relevance judgments), a duplicate list should be provided, so that users can retain one for their own use. If users examine search hits online they may be able to provide evaluative information online as well. This approach is becoming more feasible with full-text systems, where the user need not go offline to examine a separate document. Investigators should take advantage of this capability of full-text systems, by incorporating suitable evaluation data collection devices, perhaps via pop-up windows, in the design of any tailor-made system.

How the data will be analyzed should be considered in designing data collection procedures, so that the data can be efficiently input to the data analysis programs. Even with observation, questionnaires, and interviews, the data can be recorded in machine-readable form through mark sense forms or notebook-type computers. Most statistical analysis programs expect the data about a 'case' or experimental unit to be entered together in a standard way. If it is collected in this way, the entire process becomes simplified.

Data collected in coded form is always easier to analyze than data collected in natural language form. By coded form we mean that each observation has been assigned to a one of a predefined set of categories. However, sometimes natural language input is necessary to understand all the dimensions of a situation. In this case, some automated kind of automated data entry—tape recording or direct computer entry—is essential to safeguard the integrity of the data.

DECISION 9. HOW TO ANALYZE THE DATA?

The approach to data analysis will depend on the form of the data. If it has been collected in a coded form, whether quantitative or qualitative, some kind of statistical analysis can be used. If it is in natural language form, for example tapes of interviews, then some kind of categorization and coding must be carried out before the standard statistical methods are applied. However, statistical analysis can be applied to coded qualitative data using a number of nonparametric approaches.

Methods of statistical analysis are usually characterized as descriptive or inferential. Descriptive methods describe the data set itself, but do not attempt to go beyond it. Inferential methods, on the other hand, draw conclusions about populations or random processes on the basis of random samples or realizations of the process. Thus, to use inferential techniques, one must be able to assume that either the sample or the process is random. For example, the accesses of an online library catalog might be regarded as accesses by a random sample of users from the set of all potential users at that time, or a realization in a particular time period of a process, accessing the catalog by a group of users, which occurs randomly over time.

Descriptive methods

Descriptive methods should be used to summarize all data, whether qualitative or quantitative in nature, and whether or not inferential methods will also be applied. Even with such qualitative data as types of users or questions or search tactics, tables and histograms showing frequencies and cross-tabulations are very useful.

With quantitative data, such as recall and precision scores, graphs are often more effective than tables, though the tables are needed as well, for exact values. The recall-precision graph has become a standard way of describing the outcome of retrieval experiments in which the documents are output as a ranked list.

Statistical measures of central tendency, variation, and association should be used to supplement the information provided by tables and graphs. The appropriate measure depends on the scale of measurement. For nominal variables, such as subject area of question, the appropriate measure of central tendency is the mode, the appropriate measure of variation is a measure of concentration, and the appropriate measure of association is the contingency coefficient. For ordinal or ranked variables, such as user satisfaction ratings, the appropriate measure of central tendency is the median, the appropriate measure of variation is the range or interquartile range, and the appropriate measure of association is the rank correlation coefficient. For truly quantitative data, such as counts or ratios or measurements, the mean is the appropriate measure of central tendency, the variance or standard deviation the measure of variation, and the product-moment correlation coefficient the measure of association.

When there are several independent variables or treatments in a test, statistics of the performance measures should be provided at various levels of aggregation. For example, if a test looks at the effect of both search strategy and searcher experience on recall and precision, the two performance measures should be averaged for each strategy level, each experience level, and each combination of strategy and experience level.

Two kinds of averaging have been suggested for summarizing recall and precision values for a set of queries: micro-averaging and macro-averaging. These are defined as follows:

$$m_{p1} = \Sigma r_i / \Sigma n_i \qquad m_{p2} = [\Sigma(r_i/n_i)]/q$$

$$m_{r1} = \Sigma r_i / \Sigma t_i \qquad m_{r2} = [\Sigma(r_i/t_i)]/q$$

where r_i is the number of relevant and retrieved documents, n_i the number of retrieved documents, and t_i the number of relevant documents for the ith query, q the number of queries, and m_{p1} and m_{r1} are the micro-averages and m_{p2} and m_{r2} the macro-averages for precision and recall, respectively. The choice of averaging method depends upon whether one wishes to give documents or queries equal weight in the averaging process.

In order to construct a recall-precision graph for a set of queries, the points at which recall and precision values will be averaged over queries and displayed on the graph must be determined. There are four possibilities:

1. Average recall and precision across queries at fixed document-query similarity scores. This method works well with coordination level scores (number of terms matching between query and document) when queries have similar numbers of terms (and hence possible coordination levels). It is problematic if queries have varying numbers of terms or if similarity scores assume a large number of value (as, for example, with the cosine similarity measure).

2. Average recall and precision across queries at fixed document ranks. This method is useful when the document-query scores assume a large number of values, but is problematic when the retrieved set size differs greatly from one query to another.

3. Average recall and precision values at either fixed scores or fixed ranks and then interpolate precision at standard recall values, for example, at intervals of 0.1 from 0 to 1. This method gives a smoother curve than the first two methods, but is not as close to the actual data points. Two interpolation methods have been suggested: linear interpolation and interpolation to the left between averaged recall values (pessimistic interpolation).

This method has the advantage that it is independent of the properties of the queries, the documents, and the similarity function, and so can be used to compare different tests. Further details on this method will be found in Spark-Jones (1978) and the earlier version of the present paper. Figure 1 provides an example, from a recent paper (Fagan, 1989), of a recall-precision graph at standard recall values.

Statistical inference

There are many techniques of statistical inference. The ones to be used depend on the purposes of the test, the scale of the variables, and the distribution of the test statistics. From the point of view of statistical analysis, the purposes of research can be characterized as follows: estimation, comparison of treatments or effects, exploration of relationships, forecasting, and determination of the structure of multivariate data. Scales of measurement are traditionally categorized as nominal, ordinal or ranked, equal interval, and ratio (i.e., with a natural zero point). However, in determining appropriate methods of statistical inference, a distinction is often made between discrete and continuous variables. Statistical techniques based on statistics having normal (gaussian) or related distribution (chi-square, t, F) are called parametric; others are called nonparametric. Frequently, whether or not a statistic has a normal or related distribution is dependent on the sample

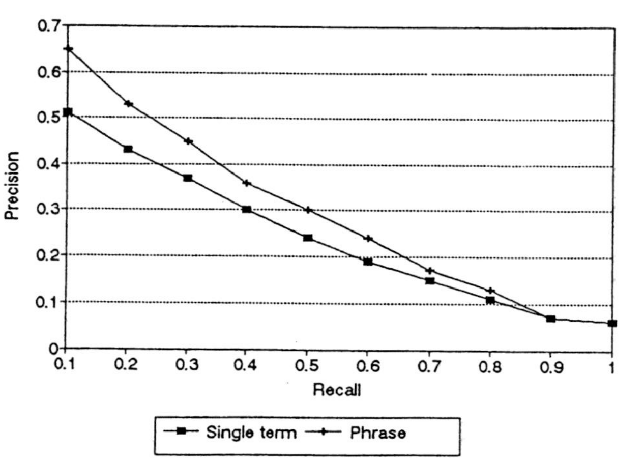

Fig. 1. Precision at standard recall values (Fagan, 1989).

size, with statistics from small samples being less likely to be normally distributed. Thus, nonparametric methods are most often used with small samples.

Estimation means estimating population or process parameters from the data. Some examples are estimation of the average recall and precision for a type of retrieval strategy, estimating average cost of a search on a database, and estimating the percentage of users who prefer a particular interface. In estimation, some indication should be given of error probabilities, either through confidence intervals or through standard errors.

Comparison of treatments or effects is frequently the major objective of a retrieval test, whether it is of the controlled, laboratory type, or based on the analysis of data from an operational setting. For example, the effect of different approaches to searching or of different databases might be compared, based on recall and precision, with the effect of searcher experience also assessed.

The analysis of variance is the primary technique used for assessing differences for all but the simplest experimental designs. To use this technique, it must be reasonable to assume that the dependent variable or performance measure is approximately normal, variances for different treatment groups are approximately equal, and the effects and interactions of the independent variables (treatments) are additive. When ratios such as precision and recall are used as the performance measures, an arcsine transformation of the square root of the original values will frequently result in a dependent variable that satisfies the requirements of the analysis of variance.

With small samples for each treatment combination, or with dependent variables such as user satisfaction ratings which are ordinal in scale, nonparametric analogues of the analysis of variance are to be preferred. When only two groups are being compared, a *t* test may be used if the same assumptions can be made as with the analysis of variance. Otherwise a nonparametric test such as the Mann-Whitney should be used.

When both dependent and independent variables are nominal, as would be the case, for example, if one were investigating the effect of the source of query vocabulary (user, intermediary, thesaurus) and type of search strategy (boolean, vector) on whether a retrieved document was relevant or nonrelevant, the preferred methodology now is a loglinear or a logistic analysis. This approach can be used to investigate the effect and interactions of the vocabulary and strategy on relevance/nonrelevance. It can also be used to test the order of a markov chain, for example, the chain of commands a user enters in an online search.

Saracevic *et al.* (1988) suggest using the crossproduct odds ratio. Each variable (dependent and independent) must be recoded as a binary variable if it is not already in this form. One way is dividing cases according to whether the case is above or below the mean. For large samples the logarithm of the cross product odds ratio has a *t* distribution and can be used to test for a significant relationship.

Exploring relationships between a search performance measure and one or more quantitative variables (e.g., size of the database or time spent searching) is usually carried out through regression techniques (i.e., expressing the performance measure as a function of the other variables). This function permits one to predict performance level for combinations of the other variables. Confidence intervals may be set up for the predicted values; however, the validity of this procedure depends on the approximate normality of the variables.

Although superficially like regression, *forecasting* future values of a variable on the basis of past values (e.g., use of a database on the basis of past use) is not really amenable to simple regression techniques. The reason is that regression is based on the assumption of independent observations, whereas observations that form a time series are frequently correlated. Time series analysis consists of analyzing a series in terms of trends (like regression), periodic components, and random fluctuations.

Multivariate techniques are increasingly used in the analysis of information retrieval tests. These techniques are appropriate when a large number of variables are determined for each experimental unit (i.e., when each experimental unit has a 'profile'). Some examples are: personal characteristics of each user or searcher, weights of index terms in each document, and the various measures of performance (informativeness, stopping point, user friendliness, time, etc.) for each search.

The most frequently used multivariate techniques in information retrieval testing are clustering, multidimensional scaling and factor analysis, and discriminant analysis. In clustering, units are grouped into clusters on the basis of their profile similarities. For example, documents are clustered on the basis of their index-term weight similarities. In multidimensional scaling and factor analysis, an attempt is made to reduce a larger set of variables to a small number that are mathematical combinations of the original variables and that, in some sense, represent underlying factors or dimensions of the set. For example, the many personal characteristics of searchers might be reduced to three, one representing experience, one representing mathematical ability, and the other representing linguistic ability. In discriminant analysis, units can be identified as belonging to one of several populations, and an attempt is made to predict population membership based on mathematical functions of the measured variables. For example, users indicate whether they prefer to do their own searches or use an intermediary. An attempt is then made to predict this preference on the basis of a variety of personal characteristics.

Some good intermediate level explanations of the statistical approaches described above will be found in Berenson *et al.* (1983) and in Miller and Wichern (1977). Conover (1980) provides an extended coverage of nonparametric tests, Fineberg (1980) of the loglinear model, Winer (1971) of the analysis of sophisticated experimental designs, Box and Jenkins (1976) of time series analysis, and Morrison (1976) of multivariate techniques.

Implementation of the analysis is usually done through such statistical software as SPSS (Statistical Package for the Social Sciences), SAS (Statistical Analysis System), and BMDP (Biomedical Data Program). The actual tests available vary from one package to another, to some extent, and from one installation to another. Micro and mainframe versions are both available. The microcomputer versions, though more interactive, may not be able to handle very large data sets. It is wise to check the documentation of the package you intend to use at the research design stage. Requirements of the package may, for example, determine the optimal order of recording and the coding of the data. Also, the great variety of statistical techniques now available in statistical packages make it tempting to use ones that are not appropriate to the data or the purpose of the experiment. Never use results from a computer analysis unless you understand the assumptions of the analysis and the meaning of the output.

DECISION 10. HOW TO PRESENT RESULTS

The question of how to present results resolves into two: how to describe the test and where to publish.

In the past decade, there has been a great improvement in editorial practices in information science journals, and it is really no longer necessary to encourage investigators, as I did in the original version of this paper, to write up information retrieval experiments as experiments, not narratives. This standard has won general acceptance.

In other words, the normal order of presentation will be as follows:

1. Purpose of the test: an explanation of why it was undertaken and what the investigators hoped to discover.
2. Background of the test: references to previous work relating *specifically* to the test (*not* a history of information retrieval).
3. Methodology: a description of the test environment and test procedures in sufficient detail that another investigator can replicate it; acknowledgment of problems that arose with the methodology during the actual testing.
4. Presentation of results: verbal, tabular, and graphical presentations, clearly identified and labelled.
5. Conclusions: a review and summary of what has gone before; an explanation of the major contribution made by the research and its implications for future research.

The past decade has not, however, reduced the vested interest most investigators feel in the theories or hypotheses they are testing. Therefore it is probably worthwhile to reiterate the warning against exaggerated claims made in the first version of this paper. Nothing should be claimed, in presenting a test, that cannot be verified by an independent investigator.

The widespread use of word processing systems has made the actual production of reports on information retrieval tests much more efficient that a decade ago. However, the problem still remains—where to present the report. If research is contracted or internal to a commercial organization, there may be no choice; the report simply goes to the sponsoring body. However, most research in information retrieval can be presented to the larger scientific community. Conferences such as the International Conference on Research and Development in Information Retrieval, sponsored jointly by the Association for Computing Machinery Special Interest Group on Information Retrieval (SIGIR), are a good starting point and provide an opportunity to get feedback from colleagues.

More formal publication is usually in journals. Of the information science journals, the *Journal of the American Society for Information Science, Information Processing & Management*, and the *Journal of Documentation* appear the popular choices of investigators in information retrieval. Computer-based information retrieval studies, particularly at the theoretical level, will also be found in a number of computer science journals, including the *Communications of the ACM, Information Systems*, and the *ACM Transactions on Information Systems*.

CONCLUSION

An information retrieval test is not a project to be lightly undertaken. The decisions we have described should not be made on an *ad hoc* basis as the research proceeds. The investigator should think through the entire project, from statement of objectives to presentation of conclusions, before commencing even such initial activities as obtaining a retrieval system or building a database.

To summarize the preceding pages, and to provide an example, let us help a novice information retrieval investigator, who wants to compare the effectiveness of three forms of online catalog (OPAC) to the monographs in a corporate library, develop a test for this purpose. The three forms under consideration are: (a) the traditional catalog record, including author, title, and imprint information; (b) the traditional record plus the book's table of contents; (c) the traditional record plus the back of the book index. The pragmatic approach we have presented suggests the following decisions should be made in the planning stage of the test.

1. *Need for testing.* The investigator must decide whether there is, in fact any need to do a test. She (we will suppose the investigator female) articulates the ultimate purpose of the test, namely, to reach a decision about whether or not to change the nature of the present OPAC (the traditional record) to one or both of the other forms. She does a literature search, finds reviews such as an ARIST chapter (Hildreth, 1985), and reads some earlier studies, such as that by Cochrane (1985), to see what other tests of this question have discovered. She suspects that the other results may not apply to her specialized group of users, and so decides to embark upon the test.

2. *Type of test.* The investigator now formulates the specific objectives of the test: to determine the relative effectiveness of the traditional catalog, the table of contents enhanced catalog, and the index enhanced catalog in serving the information needs of the users of the corporate library. Because of the immediately practical, as opposed to the theoretical aim of the test, she decides that it will be predominantly an operational one, with real users and items in the existing library. However, since in her environment it would not be feasible to involve and control all users and all library items in the test, subsets will have to be selected.

3. *Definition of variables.* The investigator must now define the independent, dependent, and environmental variables. The primary independent variable is defined by the objective of the test: type of OPAC, with three levels: traditional, table of contents, and index. The investigator needs to decide, as well, if there are other variables that may affect the outcome of the test and so need to be identified as independent variables, for example, type of user (managerial, technical, clerical, library professional, etc.) or type of query (factual, methodological, professional upgrading, research project backgrounding, etc.). The dependent variable—effectiveness in satisfying information needs—must be operationalized in terms of one or more specific variables, for example, recall, precision, informativeness, type or degree of user satisfaction, etc.

4. *Database development.* The investigator must now decide how to develop the database for the test, since it incorporates new approaches and so will have to be created for the test. She needs to determine how a subset of items from the existing catalog will be selected, whether randomly, by topic, by date, or by other approach, for the first module. She needs to design the record descriptions for the two experimental modules: those incorporating table of contents and index information. She needs to determine the size of the experimental database, based on test reliability requirements and time and resources available. She needs to consult with database experts concerning the overall design of the database.

5. *Finding queries.* The investigator has decided to get queries from the existing users of the library. However, in order to collect data on their use of the catalogs and obtain effectiveness scores, willing users will have to be recruited for the test. In a corporate library, where many users may be personally known to the investigator, this recruitment may not present a problem. However, the investigator should be confident that, with whatever recruitment procedures she elects, the users in the test represent a random selection from the set of all users, even if this means offering special inducements for participation.

6. *Retrieval software.* Since two experimental databases must be constructed for the test, it will also be necessary to acquire or develop retrieval software and interfaces for these. The approach here will probably depend on the software used for the existing OPAC, since one would want the interfaces for the three levels of the primary independent variable—type of OPAC—to be as alike as possible. The investigator, in consultation with computer information system experts, should estimate the time and resources that will be required to develop or adapt software for this purpose.

7. *Experimental design.* The investigator must now decide how she will assign queries to the three types of catalogs. Will she use a completely crossed design, in which different queries are searched on the three catalog types? Or will she use a repeated measures design, in which each query is searched on all three catalogs? If the latter design is chosen, how will order effects be controlled? Can the secondary independent variables, such as type of user or type of query, be considered as blocks in a randomized or incomplete block design? Or will they interact with the primary independent variables? In making these choices, the investigator must also consider how many queries one can realistically expect to obtain.

8. *Data collection.* All of the data that will be needed to carry out the analysis should be identified and forms developed for collecting this data. The investigator must plan how values of the independent variables will be recorded for each catalog search. Will it be necessary to incorporate a transaction logging module into the retrieval system? What kinds of information are needed from the users in order to determine the values of the dependent variables?

9. *Data analysis.* The scale of the independent and dependent variables and the experimental design selected will, for the most part, determine the appropriate statistical methods for the investigator to employ in the analysis. These methods should be identified, with expert assistance if necessary. However, the investigator should ensure that the methods developed for collecting data are the most efficient ones for input to whatever statistical package has been selected for the analysis.

10. *Presenting results.* Even though, in our example, the test was undertaken to facilitate an internal decision, it would be advisable for the investigator to plan on writing it up, if only as an internal report. Thus, whatever decision is made can be justified to others.

In this paper, I have tried to update the advice I gave in the earlier version and, at the same time, restate, in summary form, concerns that have continued to be major issues in information retrieval testing. Much of what I have presented I have learned from my own attempts at information retrieval testing, and those of my students. I do not claim that our solutions are the only ones. I simply hope that they will prove helpful to other investigators.

REFERENCES

American Psychological Association (1982). *Ethical principles in the conduct of research with human participants.* Washington, DC: American Psychological Association.

Bates, M. (1979). Information search tactics. *Journal of the American Society for Information Science, 30*(4), 205–214.

Belkin, N. (1980). Anomalous states of knowledge as a basis for information retrieval. *Canadian Journal of Information Science, 5*, 133–143.

Belkin, N., & Croft, B. (1987). Retrieval techniques. *Annual Review of Information Science and Technology, 22*, 109–146.

Berenson, M., Levine, D., & Goldstein, M. (1983). *Intermediate Statistical Methods and Applications: A Computer Package Approach.* Englewood Cliffs, NJ: Prentice-Hall.

Blair, D., & Maron, M. (1985). An evaluation of retrieval effectiveness for a full-text document-retrieval system. *Communications of the ACM, 28*(3), 289–299.

Box, G., & Jenkins, G. (1976). *Time series analysis: Forecasting and control.* San Francisco: Holden-Day.

Cochran, W. & Cox, G. (1957). *Experimental design.* New York: Wiley.

Cochrane, P. (1985). *Redesign of catalogs and indexes for improved online subject access.* Phoenix, AZ: Oryx.

Conover, W. (1980). *Practical nonparametric statistics*, 2nd edition. New York: Wiley.

Croft, B., Lucia, T., Cringean, J., & Willett, P. (1989). Retrieving documents by plausible inference: an experimental study. *Information Processing & Management, 25*(6), 599–614.

Dervin, B. (1980). Communication gaps and inequities: Moving toward a reconceptualization. In B. Dervin & M. Voigt (Eds.), *Progress in Communication Sciences*, (Vol. 2, pp. 73–112). Norwood, NJ: Ablex.

Dervin, B., & Nilan, M. (1986). Information needs and uses. *Annual Review of Information Science and Technology, 21*, 3–34.

Egghe, L., & Rousseau, R. (1989). Elements of concentration theory. In L. Egghe & R. Rousseau (eds.), *Informetrics 89/90* (pp. 97–138). Amsterdam: Elsevier.

Fagan, J. (1989). The effectiveness of a nonsyntactic approach to automatic phrase indexing for document retrieval. *Journal of the American Society for Information Science, 40*(2), 115–132.

Fidel, R. (1985). Moves in online searching. *Online Review, 9*(1), 61–74.

Fineberg, S. (1980). *Analysis of cross-classified categorical data.* Cambridge, MA: MIT Press.

Ghiselli, E., Campbell, J., & Zedeck, S. (1981). *Measurement theory for the behavioral sciences.* San Francisco: Freeman.

Haas, D., & Kraft, D. (1984). Experimental and quasi-experimental designs for research in information science. *Information Processing & Management, 20*(1–2), 229–237.

Harman, D., & Candela, G. (1990). Retrieving records from a gigabyte of text on a minicomputer using statistical ranking. *Journal of the American Society for Information Science, 41*(8), 581–589.

Hildreth, C. (1985). Online public access catalogs. *Annual Review of Information Science and Technology, 20*, 233–285.

McKinin, E., Sievert, M., Johnson, E., & Mitchell, J. (1991). The Medline/full-text research project. *Journal of the American Society for Information Science, 42*(4), 297–307.

Miller, R., & Wichern, D. (1977). *Intermediate business statistics.* New York: Holt, Rinehart & Winston.

Morrison, D. (1976). *Multivariate statistical methods*, 2nd edition. New York: McGraw-Hill.

Nelson, T. (1990). The once and future literature. *Journal of Information Science, 16*, 339–343.

Regazzi, J. (1988). Performance measures for information retrieval systems—An experimental approach. *Journal of the American Society for Information Science, 39*(4), 235–251.

Rorvig, M. (1988). Psychometric measurement and information retrieval. *Annual Review of Information Science and Technology, 23*, 157–190.

Salton, G. (1975). *Dynamic information and library processing.* Englewood Cliffs, NJ: Prentice-Hall.

Salton, G. (1989). *Automatic text processing: The transformation, analysis and retrieval of information by computer.* Reading, MA: Addison-Wesley.

Saracevic, T. (1975). Relevance: a review of and a frameword for the thinking on the notion in information science. *Journal of the American Society for Information Science, 26*, 321–343.

Saracevic, T., Kantor, P., Chamis, A., & Travison, D. (1988). A study of information seeking and retrieving, I. Background and methodology. *Journal of the American Society for Information Science, 39*(3), 161–176.

Saracevic, T., & Kantor, P. (1988). A study of information seeking and retrieving. II. Users, questions, and effectiveness. *Journal of the American Society for Information Science, 39*(3), 177–196.

Saracevic, T., & Kantor, P. (1988). A study of information seeking and retrieving. III. Searchers, searches, and overlap. *Journal of the American Society for Information Science, 39*(3), 197–216.

Schamber, L., Eisenberg, M., & Nilan, M. (1990). A re-examination of relevance: Toward a dynamic, situational definition. *Information Processing & Management, 26*(6), 755–790.

Shaw, W. (1986). On the foundation of evaluation. *Journal of the American Society for Information Science, 37*(5), 346–348.

Shaw, W. (1990). Subject indexing and citation indexing—Part II: An evaluation and comparison. *Information Processing & Management, 26*(6), 705–718.

Sparck-Jones, K. (1978). Performance averaging for recall and precision. *Journal of Informatics, 2*, 95–105.

Sparck-Jones, K. (1988). A look back and a look forward. In Y. Chiaramella (Ed.), *11th International Conference on Research & Development in Information Retrieval, Grenoble, France, June 13–15, 1988* (pp. 13–30). Grenoble: Presses Universitaires de Grenoble.

Tague, J. (1981). The pragmatics of information retrieval experimentation. In K. Sparck-Jones (Ed.), *Information Retrieval Experiment* (pp. 59–102). London: Butterworths.

Tague, J., & Schultz, R. (1989). Evaluation of the user interface in an information retrieval system: A model. *Information Processing & Management, 24*(4), 377–389.

Tague, J. (1987). The role of research in information and library education. In R. Gardner (Ed.), *The education of library and information science professionals* (pp. 121–134). Littleton, CO: Libraries Unlimited.

Tague, J., Salminen, A., & McClellan, C. (1991). A complete model for information retrieval systems. In *Proceedings of the ACM SIGIR International Conference on Research and Development in Information Retrieval, Chicago, October, 1991* (pp. 14–20). New York: ACM Press.

Van Rijsbergen, C. (1979). *Information retrieval*, 2nd edition. London: Butterworths.

Winer, B. (1971). *Statistical principles in experimental design*, 2nd edition. New York: McGraw-Hill.

PRESENTING RESULTS OF EXPERIMENTAL RETRIEVAL COMPARISONS

E. MICHAEL KEEN
Department of Information & Library Studies, University College of Wales,
Aberystwyth, SY23 3AS, U.K.

Abstract—Methods of calculating and presenting results from experimental retrieval comparisons are considered and illustrated by some new laboratory results. The measures used center on Recall and Precision. Topics of data calculation, single value measures, benchmark results, data aggregation, statistical significance, and the presentation of performance differences are discussed. User-oriented presentations can be used to simulate different needs such as high or low levels of Recall. Several methods of retrieval cutoff can be used as the control variable, but the document cutoff is the most useful. Two difficult performance comparisons are illustrated: Boolean versus Ranked output retrieval and non-iterative versus relevance feedback.

1. INTRODUCTION

New ideas and theories about information retrieval continue to receive their first experimental evaluation in the controlled conditions of the laboratory experiment before being taken to real-user environments for further testing. There is no perfect paradigm for the laboratory test, and though the 13 contributors to Sparck-Jones (1981) clearly acknowledged the crucial role of the Cranfield research projects, they did not withhold criticisms nor did they fail to identify some of the continuing problem areas in methodology. Things have not changed since 1981. The same standard test collections with queries and relevance judgments continue to be used, especially in the exploration of automatic non-Boolean retrieval techniques. If a technique can be shown to be beneficial in the artificiality and reduced scale of an experiment then it seems worth exploring further. However, we must be cautious about the converse of this approach: It may well be that some techniques not performing well in the laboratory may be due to the small scale or strong controls inevitable in that environment.

This writer believes that controlled experiments still have a continuing role in exploring new ideas. So, the clear and accurate presentation of test results is a very important matter, since further developments depend on this. The problems of performance presentation and comparison were considered first in the mid 1960s, and though no single best method emerged, researchers now present data in generally similar ways. A selection of these will be discussed in this paper and particular ones advocated. Two themes will recur: The first is that since searchers of all kinds of systems inspect documents output one at a time, whether they are retrieved in groups or strongly ranked in relation to the query, the use of a "document cutoff" as the control variable is one of the most satisfactory methods of presenting comparisons. This is true not only when a single component is being varied, such as a term weighting method, but also when a dissimilar system is to be compared, such as Boolean match versus Ranked retrieval. It is also argued here to be essential for assessing the merit of interactive strategies, such as relevance feedback, from a user viewpoint.

The second theme is that even tightly controlled tests can incorporate procedures and measures that reflect the actual or simulated activities and preferences of users. For example, the measures of Recall and Precision can be applied to differing user needs, such as cases desiring high Recall or those being satisfied by low Recall or a few relevant items for which high Precision is the goal.

Some of the main methods and stages used in calculating performance will be discussed first, illustrated by some new test results from a project in progress. Methods of assessing performance differences will then be discussed, followed by two difficult test comparison cases to illustrate the themes of document cutoff and user simulation.

2. CALCULATION OF EXPERIMENTAL DATA

After test searches have been conducted and given the availability of relevance judgments, data analysis is then undertaken to obtain results of at least a descriptive kind, and hopefully predictive as well, so that conclusions can be drawn. The substantial trustworthiness of relevance judgments for comparative test purposes will be assumed and not defended here. Summarizing test data requires decisions of many kinds. For example, at what points in the searches shall performance measures be applied; what control variable will be employed for this; what measures of performance merit will be used; what performance benchmark results will be provided; how will search data be aggregated; what descriptive statistics will be used; what performance relationships will be displayed; how will performance differences be judged; what methods of statistical inference are appropriate; and so on.

The illustrative descriptive statistical results to be used are taken from an on-going research project into term matching methods for Ranked output retrieval. The systems under test are listed in Table 1 and include recent unpublished test runs central to the research which has been described in Keen (1991a, in press a,b). The standard test collection in use is the records from Library and Information Science Abstracts in 1982 containing titles, abstracts, and index terms, totalling 6004 records, and a set of 35 queries and relevance judgments obtained from Sheffield University.

2.1 *Measures and control variables*

This paper will concentrate on retrieval results that reflect success in retrieving relevant documents and in suppressing irrelevant ones; equally important criteria also needing measurement include time, storage capacity needed, and so on. Retrieval results need to incorporate three performance metrics: Recall ability (relevant retrieved as a proportion of total relevant or total relevant required), Precision performance (relevant retrieved as a proportion of total retrieved), and a control variable at which Recall and Precision measures are made (such as the number of query terms matching or specified output rank position as a cutoff point). These results can reflect the final performance at the end of the search, or can be averaged over many points during the search, or can reflect the progress of a search at many standardized points.

For example, in the test results presented in Table 1 here, following the method used in Keen (1991a), Recall is fixed at three levels and the control variable is the document cutoff for each search of a query that achieves the Recall threshold (or exceeds it). At these

Table 1. Results of tests on the Library and Information Science Abstracts collection showing the use of the Recall cutoff control variable at three thresholds

	Low Recall Threshold 25% (mean 40%)			Medium Recall Threshold 50% (mean 57%)			High Recall Threshold 75% (mean 86%)		
	Precision ratio	Output position		Precision ratio	Output position		Precision ratio	Output position	
System	mean	median	mean	mean	median	mean	mean	median	mean
1. Best possible	100%	2	3.2	100%	4	5.7	100%	6	8.0
2. Random match	4.2%	144	171.4	4.2%	206	297.2	4.2%	341	448.5
3. Quorum	45.4%	9	21.5	31.1%	28	44.3	22.0%	79	111.1
4. Direct Collection Frequency	41.8%	12	38.1	29.4%	30	72.8	17.8%	87	176.7
5. Inverse Collection Frequency	56.8%	5	19.4	42.5%	25	38.3	29.8%	53	91.3
6. Collection & Record Frequency	60.0%	6	14.1	53.6%	14	30.2	39.8%	38	65.4
7. Collection F. & Pairs Distance	70.6%	4	8.9	54.0%	12	22.9	38.2%	44	60.5

levels two different measures of Precision are presented, the conventional Precision Ratio and the Output position, which is really the number of documents retrieved. This last measure is averaged two different ways here, thus giving three results to consider for each of the three Recall levels.

Precision is the researcher's ratio measure almost universally used, but output position seems an intuitively useful user-oriented measure; one could ask a user, for example, whether retrieving half the relevant documents at rank position 12 (system 7) rather than 28 (system 3) would be worth a given penalty in, say, search time or storage capacity.

The idea of Recall targets has been used before in testing index languages (Keen 1973), and as here its importance is that the discovery of a system performing well at low Recall but poorly at high Recall, or vice versa, would be an important finding which would have been obscured had only one target been used or the results averaged over the targets. Of course, if it is found that systems do not exhibit such a "crossover" in performance, then an average over the targets is justified. Harman (1991) and Salton and Buckley (1988) both present Precision averaged over performance at Recall 25%, 50%, and 75%, but do not say whether their original data exhibit any cases of performance crossover. One such case is seen in Table 1, since system 7 is better than 6 at low Recall, very slightly so at medium Recall, and slightly worse than 6 at high Recall in two of the three measures. The Recall targets used in Keen (1973) not only specified the amount of relevant documents but demanded their degree or relevance, with one target accepting only items judged highly relevant.

In case the use of the Recall target as the control variable is affecting the test comparisons, Fig. 1 shows a quite different performance calculation. Here the control variable is the document cutoff, taken at 10 points between positions 1 and 50. At each point a Recall/Precision pair is computed for the individual queries, then averaged by the arithmetic mean. The graph in Fig. 1 shows the seven systems as Table 1. Restricting the Recall to the 50th cutoff is again done for user simulation reasons—it seems unlikely that with a collection of 6000 items a user will want to examine more than 50 documents, even though Recall in absolute terms fails to reach 60% for systems 3 or 5.

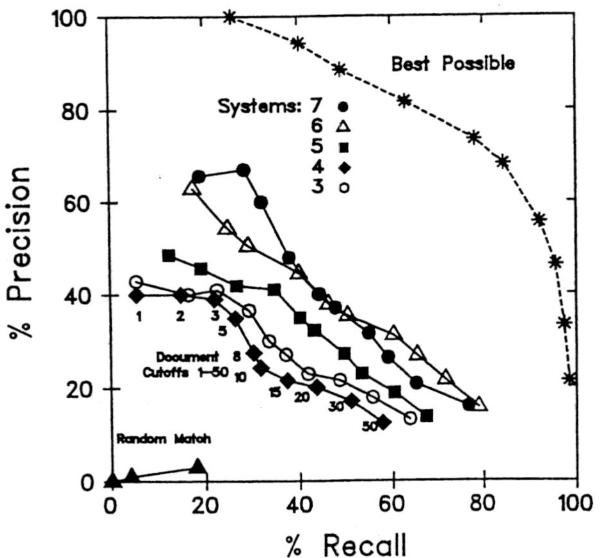

Fig. 1. Graph of the test systems identified in Table 1 showing the use of the document cutoff control variable.

But the strong similarity of the performance picture of the graph and the Recall cutoff is seen both in the relative positions of the systems and in the clear performance crossover of systems 6 and 7. The graph does show a big drop in absolute performance, for example, at 57% Recall (the actual mean of the 50% Recall target), system 7 shows 54% Precision in Table 1, about 28% Precision in the graph. The graph presents meaningful information from the user viewpoint: performance can be read off the plot at any specified value of document cutoff, Recall, or Precision, to get the remaining two values, assuming the validity of the straight line interpolation used.

The Table 1 Recall cutoff and Fig. 1 document cutoff alternatives follow closely the two methods of presentation called by Van Rijsbergen the predictive and descriptive approaches, respectively (Van Rijsbergen, 1981). In the predictive approach, the effectiveness of the queries is established with no account taken of what control variables are utilised, then the averaging is done at Recall effectiveness points. This, Van Rijsbergen says, answers the question "What is the probability of a retrieved document being relevant for a query at a particular Recall value?" In the descriptive approach, a correspondence between different queries is set up at fixed control variable values, even though these values may not represent the same measuring point for all queries, then averaging is done at these points. This answers the question "What is the probability that a retrieved document is relevant for the system operating at that level of Recall?" Of course, it is impossible to devise one measuring point for heterogeneous queries that represents the same for all; for example, if the control variable is document cutoff then the 10th document is a good leveller from a searcher viewpoint, but if one query matches 14 documents and another 2758 (as in the current tests), then another leveller could be a cutoff representing the same proportion of matches giving an alignment of point 10 for the query matching 14 and point 1970 for that matching 2758, a match of about 71%.

Drawing Recall/Precision graphs by document cutoff has the great merit that it avoids problems of interpolation and extrapolation, as discussed by a number of researchers from Cranfield-2 onwards. Graphs are in fact often drawn using the Recall cutoff at 10 levels extending to 100% Recall—a rather misleading result, as almost no retrieval algorithm matches every relevant document; so to get complete data the unmatched relevant are given random rank positions in the unmatched portion of the collection. This inflates the absolute results and makes the gap between user and results more distant than it need be.

Counts of queries that do or do not retrieve any relevant documents at a given cutoff are sometimes given, and seem a helpful addition as a secondary indication of performance. Query counts favouring one system as opposed to another, usually a pair of systems, are a natural additional result as well, because they lead straight to statistical significance testing. Table 2 presents such counts for six pairs of the four systems, and will be commented upon later.

Table 2. Various calculations of performance differences using Precision at Low Recall for six pairs of four of the systems identified in Table 1

System pairs	Precision at Low Recall				Queries favoring			Significance tests	
	arith.	means	Difference	Improvment					
a b	a	b	a-b	a-b/b	a	b	=	Sign	Wilcoxon
7 > 3	70.6%	45.4%	25.2%	55.5%	25	2	8	.0000	.0001
7 > 5	70.6%	56.8%	13.3%	24.3%	17	5	13	.0169	.0042
5 > 3	56.8%	45.4%	11.4%	25.1%	18	6	11	.0227	.0078
7 > 6	70.6%	60.0%	10.6%	17.7%	18	7	10	.0433	.0133
6 > 3	60.0%	45.4%	14.6%	32.2%	20	11	4	.1496	.0187
6 > 5	60.0%	56.8%	3.2%	5.6%	15	11	9	.5572	.6961

2.2 *Single value measures*

One quite popular single value measure is the effectiveness equation of Van Rijsbergen (1979), which simply combines a pair of Recall/Precision values. It always seems to be used with six values, one set of three using an early document cutoff (usually 10), and the other set of three at cutoffs 20 or 30; these choices both fall too close to medium Recall, and do not properly simulate the low and high Recall user, for which 5 and 50 would, respectively, be better choices. Croft *et al.* (1989) do use cutoff 5. The three variants adjust the weight given to the Recall value in the equation and usually cover equal weight, half the weight, and twice the weight. So, presenting six results for a given option naturally results in a lot of data to be presented, as is seen in experiments reported by Griffiths *et al.* (1986), Al-Hawamdeh & Willett (1989a,b) and Harman (1991), for example.

In fact an inspection of the effectiveness measures results in these three papers shows that the options under test give very substantially the same merit in each set of six results, with occasional changes of 1% and rarely 2% in the differences. There are no cases of even a hint of crossing performance, so this shows that weighting Recall by half or by two is not strong enough, nor are the cutoffs sufficiently extreme. In none of the examples examined do the researchers make any real comment on, or justification for, this practice of redundant presentation. It is interesting to observe that Van Rijsbergen (1981) himself suggests a rather different use of his own effectiveness measure, namely, that of comparing the results of a single Recall/Precision pair at one point (e.g., the end of a Boolean search) with points chosen from a system producing a Recall/Precision curve. No example of this is known.

The presentation of just one result for each system such as Precision averaged over a number of Recall points has already been mentioned, and is one good way of reducing multiple performance results to a single measure. This is not the same thing as a single value measure. It is especially useful if many results are to be compared or if performance is to be related to another measured variable, such as time. But any single measure presentation, or use of single value measures, involves a loss of information and removes the ability to confirm results by complementary techniques and by contrasting performance at different points of interest to users.

2.3 *Benchmark results*

Table 1 and Fig. 1 include four performance benchmark test results, one high and three low, to help judge the merit of the three systems primarily under test. Systems 1 and 2 are the two ultimate benchmarks. The Best Possible reflects the fact that the 35 queries have differing numbers of relevant items in the collection. In Table 1, for example, the Output Position measures for the test systems are to be judged again the Best Possible values, either median or mean, obviously because they represent perfection. In Fig. 1 the Best Possible performance starts with 100% Precision at low Recall, but as Recall rises, Precision departs from perfection, because at cutoffs of more than one document, some irrelevant items have to be counted in calculating the best possible curve. A truly perfect result would mean knowing exactly when to stop each individual search, and only that would produce a curve of rising Recall at perfect Precision. Even Recall does not reach 100% in Best Possible in the graph because the plot stops at cutoff 50 and one query has 53 relevant. But the curve provides a proper visual picture of perfection against which the systems tested may be judged.

The other ultimate result is random match. A random result could be computed by placing all the relevant items in random positions in the whole collection, but that is clearly such a low benchmark and so radically influenced by collection size that something different was done here. All matching relevant items were placed in random positions just among the matching items to generate a kind of random search match result. On an individual query basis, therefore, it is quite possible for the actual result to be worse than this random one. But as the overall average shows with both Recall and document cutoff, random match is many times worse than the results of the systems under test.

Systems 3 and 4 are tested options which could be used as retrieval strategies, but are included as baseline benchmarks due to their nature. System 3, quorum, is often called simple matching or coordination levels, as it is just the sum of the query/document term matches and produces a very weakly ranked output. If the sophisticated algorithms under test cannot significantly improve on this basic result, then such systems do not offer performance improvements worth considering.

System 4 is a test of the converse of a theory in order to see how strongly system 5 (the system reflecting the theory) improves performance. The equations used are given in Keen (in press b). The well established theory is that query terms should be weighted inversely according to their use in the collection, so the converse is weighting directly in relation to their use in the collection. The theory is often misleadingly called "inverse document frequency." Thus the converse might well be described as "perverse document frequency," as these results do show the expected merit, with the converse result a little worse than quorum.

2.4 *Data aggregation*

Although processing the raw data comes earlier in time than the average results that have been discussed, it is always necessary to have a clear view of the desired end before the detail of computation is embarked upon. Just a selection of issues will be mentioned on the subject of aggregation, since it is an area that, surprisingly, is still riddled with possibilities and pitfalls, and often does not meet the statistical *desiderata* for a good experiment. Tague (1981) provides a description of the 10 decision areas in experimentation; see also her paper in this issue.

The present project had to make decisions on how to deal with tied ranks, how to score the Precision ratio before any relevant documents are retrieved, and what Recall/Precision scores to use for document ranks 15 and onwards in two queries where matching documents did not reach this number. Relevant documents were placed in random positions; Precision was counted as zero before relevant documents were retrieved; and the Recall/Precision score for the last matching rank was frozen for later ranks. All these were reasonable but arbitrary choices.

Creating the averages of Recall and Precision ratios was done query-by-query before the ratios were themselves averaged, as this method seems correct both because queries should exert equal weight in the final average and the use of any statistical significance tests on ratio results requires it. But because documents and queries are not really drawn from large sample populations by approved sampling methods, these decisions can only be regarded as sensible but not mandatory.

The non-normal statistical distribution of most retrieval data is well known, and the output position measure in Table 1 shows how extreme this problem is by the large difference seen in every case in the two measures of central tendency, the median and the arithmetic mean. Even the conventionally calculated median is not the most accurate indicator of central tendency, and in previous tests the cumulative frequency distribution of the data was subject to a best fit line and then the middle position read off that plot to get a slightly better median (Keen, 1973).

2.5 *Statistical significance*

The most obviously useful technique of statistical inference in performance tests that compare systems is the testing for significance of that difference. Many tests, but not all, result in matched pairs data derived from the same queries being processed against two systems. But the demands of conventional parametric statistical tests are not met in the non-normal distribution of the data, and non-parametric tests have been employed even though they lose slightly in power efficiency.

For example, Table 2 takes the Precision Ratio results at low Recall from Table 1 for the six pairs of the four main systems under test and gives query counts, the Sign test results, and the Wilcoxon matched-pairs signed-ranks test results. The latter takes into account the magnitude of the differences in each query pair, but the precise suitability of the data for the Wilcoxon test has a measure of doubt about it. As can be seen from the table, the Sign and Wilcoxon tests do give a similar picture except for system pair 6 versus 3, where the Wilcoxon finding may reflect its more efficient use of data.

Non-matched pair tests using independent samples pose great difficulties in sample sizes and statistics (see Robertson, 1990, for example) but this area is extremely important for user evaluation of interactive systems where the learning effect prohibits the matched pairs approach. Robertson and Thompson (1987) used a non-parametric test for significance here also, the Mann-Whitney U test.

3. ASSESSING PERFORMANCE DIFFERENCES

Having briefly outlined some of the tools needed to process test data, attention will now turn to methods of assessing the validity, significance, and importance of performance differences.

3.1 *General approach*

In comparison tests, results are usually sought to provide either just an order of merit of the options or, in addition, an assessment of the magnitude of the difference between the options under test. This has to be done for each posited or simulated circumstance so that the results can be related to user needs or some other variable. For example, using the greater-than sign to mean "better than," the four main systems in Table 1 can be said to show the order 7 > 6 > 5 > 3 in Precision and mean Output Position at low Recall, all three measures at medium Recall, and mean Output position at high Recall. The order is 6 > 7 > 5 > 3 for the remaining measures, namely median Output Position at low and high Recall and Precision at high Recall.

The amount of difference can be displayed for given pairs of systems under test both by displaying the value achieved by each system and by computing a difference score between the means. Table 2 does this for just one of the nine results in Table 1 (Precision at Low Recall) using the four main systems under test (3, 5, 6, and 7). Thus System 7 scores 70.6% and System 3 scores 45.4% Precision, so the difference is 25.2%; or is it 55.5%, a calculation of percentage improvement that uses a different base figure? Confusion in terminology reigns here; Salton and Buckley (1990) call this latter calculation the "improvement," but Fagan (1989) calls it a "change," and other terms used include "advantage," "increase," and the + symbol. It is often not clear which calculation is in use, but the terms "difference" and "improvement" are used here to distinguish the two methods.

Improvement values can, of course, exceed 100%, so to process ratio results that are already interpretable as percentages (whether recorded as decimals or percentages) by the percentage improvement – a sort of double percentage – seems liable to mislead. Though the difference and improvement computations in Table 2 do correlate generally, there is one reversal, and where performance results from different test collections are involved, a difference on a poorly performing collection shows much greater improvement values than the same difference on a better performing collection. In fact, the latter result may well be a more important result. So use of improvement percentages is called into question by the present writer as being liable to mislead, an unhelpful metric, and at odds with statistical significance testing in which it is the difference that is being examined.

3.2 *Practical and consistent differences*

Table 2 has shown that system 7 is better than all others at least at the 5% level of statistical significance on both tests, and that only the difference between systems 6 and 5 is never significant. But is this significance of practical importance?

Sparck-Jones (1974) proposed that practical significance, or importance, should be based on the differences in the mean results (not the improvements!), and that differences would be regarded as "material" if >10%, "noticeable" if 5%–10%, and "not noticeable" if <5%. This pragmatic approach has been followed occasionally, for example, by Fagan (1989), and does seem a useful approach. Five of the comparisons in Table 2 are materially different by this criterion, with the sixth not noticeable. A combination of practical and statistical significance is clearly the best approach.

In tests of many options or systems and in tests where several collections are used, the number of results can be very large, running into hundreds sometimes (e.g., Salton & Buckley, 1988). In some cases researchers present just an order of merit and do so by assigning ranks to the systems on the basis of the results. Unless actual results values or differences from some benchmark are also presented, it is very difficult to interpret these results in a practical way. However, consistency in order of merit may well be very important – a result neither statistically significant nor judged practically important does seem worth noting if it occurs repeatedly in different tests or in different performance measures. For example, Harman's (1991) tests of suffixing algorithms showed no clear performance differences, but Keen's (in press a) view is that since in the 198 measures presented 131 show suffixing better than (and 47 equivalent to) no suffixing, then a consistency indication is something worth recognising.

Statistical testing of ranking consistency can easily be done, as Al-Hawamdeh and Willett (1989a,b) show, where nine index term weighting schemes are tested against 20 documents, so Kendall's Coefficient of Concordance (W) was used. But a test result of this kind needs judging together with the magnitude of difference observed in order to assess its practical importance.

4. SOME DIFFICULT PERFORMANCE COMPARISONS

4.1 *Boolean versus Ranked output retrieval*

Comparisons between Boolean and non-Boolean are not commonly attempted, and encounter difficulties with finding a control variable fair to both systems. The strict laboratory approach is typified by Al-Hawamdeh and Willett (1989a), where an equivalent document cutoff for the two systems was imposed at the data analysis stage. A more natural and unconstrained searcher cutoff was used by Robertson and Thompson (1987). Just for the record, in both these tests the performance differences would be categorised as not noticeable.

The present project has included some Boolean and Ranked output system searches to obtain realistic results using the same test collection and queries, and to explore the potential of the two systems for the low Recall user. The Boolean searches were carried out by an experienced searcher in an interactive system, so the stopping rules that give rise to a natural final searcher cutoff for each query will no doubt have been a subjective mixture of factors, such as what has been retrieved, time spent, availability of further search terms, likelihood of finding more relevant, and so on. This data gave averages of 66% Recall at 35% Precision and involved retrieving 16.8 (median 14) documents per query. This Recall/Precision point could reasonably be plotted against the laboratory results in Fig. 1, where it would be seen to lie in a slightly better position than system 7 at a document cutoff between 15 and 20. System 7 was, of course, denied the effects of interactive searching.

To get a more realistic comparison between Boolean and Ranked output, a search tool was devised to give the opportunity for searches of a Ranked system to use a pragmatic natural searcher cutoff. The tool available for this has so far been restricted to providing ranking according to the quorum algorithm, with no changes in search terms or iterative searching possible. But the searcher was free to inspect the document output in decreasing match order, or to jump around the ranked output at will, inspecting records at different levels of quorum match and looking at records in two display formats. The final searcher cutoff was slightly later than the Boolean results, 24.1 documents (mean), 21 (median), and the performance 54% Recall at 19% Precision. This result can be used to obtain a comparison of document cutoff versus searcher cutoff in exactly the same system by visualising this result on Fig. 1 again. The searcher cutoff seems to give a very similar result to document cutoff, as at 24 documents the quorum system 3 scored 52% Recall at 20% Precision.

Turning to a direct comparison of the two searcher cutoff results, Boolean interactive is materially superior to Quorum non-interactive in both Recall and Precision. However, this data is analysed further in Figs. 2 and 3 to explore ways of looking further at the lower Recall performance potential of these two systems. Figure 2 uses one possible control vari-

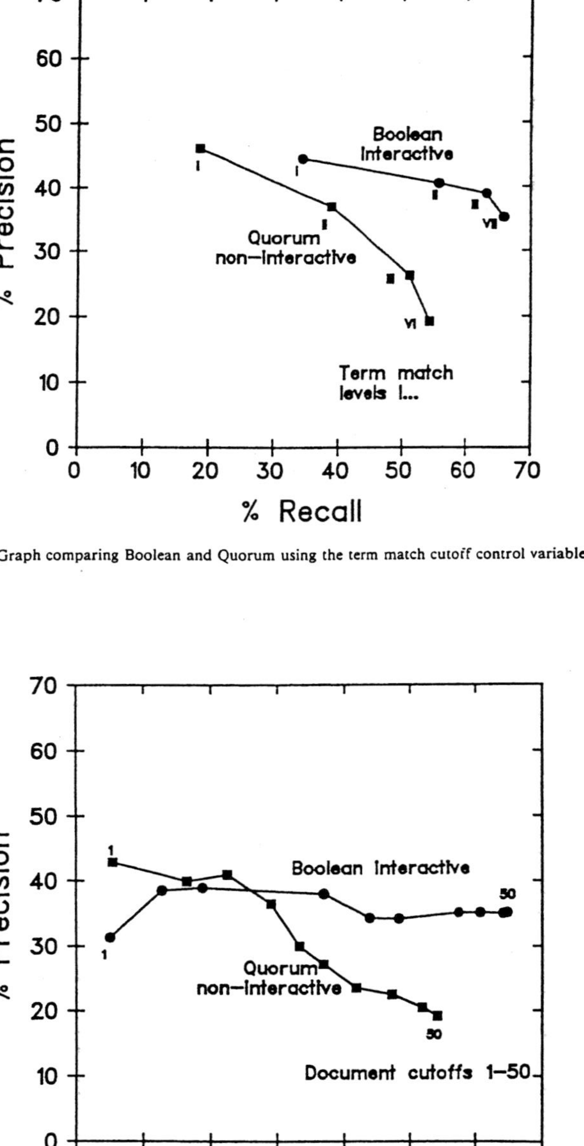

Fig. 2. Graph comparing Boolean and Quorum using the term match cutoff control variable.

Fig. 3. Graph comparing Boolean and Quorum using the document cutoff control variable.

able to do this, namely, the term match cutoff. Boolean searches employed around three term match statements, with a maximum of six. Quorum searches were very similar; about three term levels were inspected with a maximum of seven. So, four of these sets of term match levels are used in Fig. 2 as points for the low Recall plots. Quorum starts off with a slightly better Precision than Boolean, but does so at half the Recall, and then the divergence between Recall lessens and between Precision increases.

Figure 3 uses the document cutoff as the control variable. This is applied to both Boolean and Quorum output by placing documents judged relevant in random rank positions within each term match level. Below about 30% Recall the merit of the systems is reversed from term cutoff, with Quorum doing a little better.

In both plots the Boolean curve rises more steeply as Recall increases than Quorum, almost defying the inverse relationship between Recall and Precision; this would seem to be due to early search statements retrieving items irrelevant to the query, then the searcher finding the right term combination which gives, at a single query level, a sudden increase in both Recall and Precision. Visually superimposing the plots would reveal that the term cutoff gives a much better Recall/Precision tradeoff at all levels except at the common final point – the term matched sets of documents as aligned by that cutoff are logically a better point at which to stop the searches than choosing an arbitrary number of documents, such as 5 or 10.

A further possible visualisable comparison is the Boolean result from Fig. 2 with its term match cutoff, and the quorum result from Fig. 3 with its document cutoff a natural choice for ranked output. This in fact separates the two systems by the largest gap in the four sets of data. It is quite a valid comparison, provided that the twin differences of system and of curve-generating cutoff are appreciated to be entering into the comparison.

Although both plots give valuable insights into performance, it must be concluded that for general use the document cutoff is most suitable, because even Boolean searchers inspect documents output one at a time, and can stop searching in the middle of a term matched set, and also because ranked output systems that are both more advanced than Quorum and interactively used do not provide discrete term match levels, since query/document correlation values provide strong ranking. Whichever method is used, and the use of both brings fresh insights, it is argued to be important to devise methods that are clearly user-oriented so that laboratory simulation results will be understood by the world of practitioners.

4.2 *Non-iterative versus relevance feedback*

A similar user-oriented approach to the evaluation of relevance feedback is also advocated. Interactive results are obviously difficult to evaluate, and more than one method is needed to isolate different factors. For example, Salton and Buckley (1990) isolate the value of the feedback effect itself by a residual collection evaluation scheme; they compute both initial and feedback results as full Recall/Precision data before applying a single value measure. But this result needs complementing by a user-oriented method, because the real option a user faces is not an initial search versus a feedback search, but it is:

1. a search confined to the "initial" or single search attempt, with the user proceeding to examine as much of the ranked output as desired, or
2. a search that starts by an initial search (for perhaps 10 of the documents), followed by one or more feedback runs which, to the user, constitute documents 11-and-following new ones not appearing in the first 10.

The evaluation scheme for this is called frozen ranks (Salton, 1970), and this approach can be represented as a Recall/Precision graph as Keen (1968, Fig. 7) showed. Figure 4 is a new plot of this kind to show how it can be done using some recent frozen ranks evaluation results from Harman (1988, Table 1). (It involves some interpolation of published data and is used just as a presentation illustration, not a set of definitive results). Figure 4 shows how the single search option gives a result for document cutoffs 5 to 50 from about 30% to 70% Recall, and the feedback option for comparison is the initial search at ranks

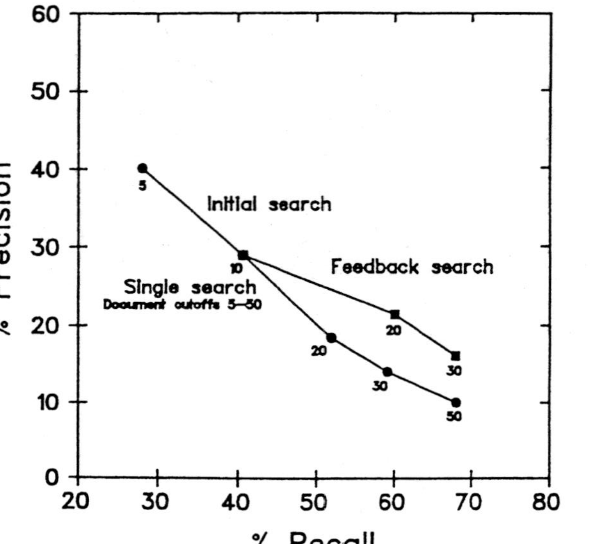

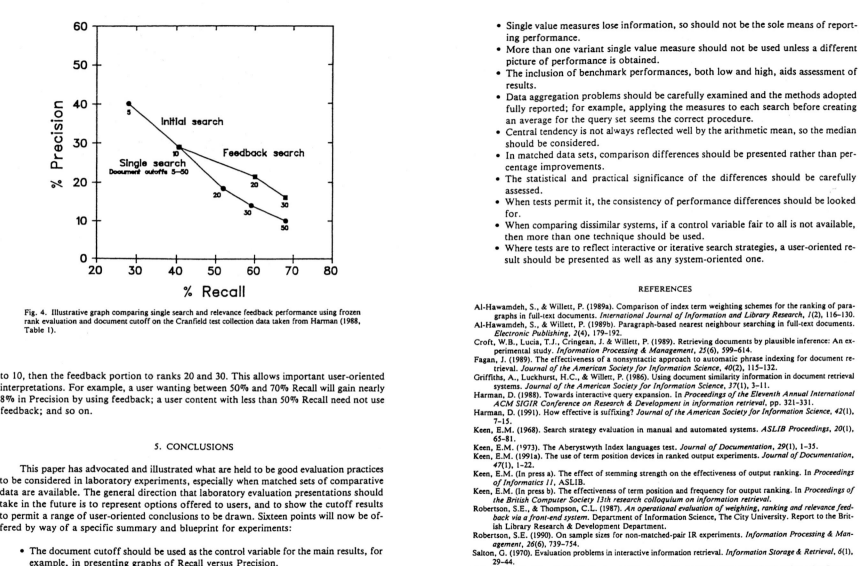

Fig. 4. Illustrative graph comparing single search and relevance feedback performance using frozen rank evaluation and document cutoff on the Cranfield test collection data taken from Harman (1988, Table 1).

to 10, then the feedback portion to ranks 20 and 30. This allows important user-oriented interpretations. For example, a user wanting between 50% and 70% Recall will gain nearly 8% in Precision by using feedback; a user content with less than 50% Recall need not use feedback; and so on.

5. CONCLUSIONS

This paper has advocated and illustrated what are held to be good evaluation practices to be considered in laboratory experiments, especially when matched sets of comparative data are available. The general direction that laboratory evaluation presentations should take in the future is to represent options offered to users, and to show the cutoff results to permit a range of user-oriented conclusions to be drawn. Sixteen points will now be offered by way of a specific summary and blueprint for experiments:

- The document cutoff should be used as the control variable for the main results, for example, in presenting graphs of Recall versus Precision.
- The document cutoff can be used for non-ranking systems, such as Boolean.
- Some of the performance graphs should include realistic levels of Recall ceiling.
- Results at different recall targets should be presented both to represent varieties of need and to check that system merit is not affected by these varieties.
- Employing the document cutoff at which given Recall targets are achieved is a good comparative strategy for laboratory results, although it will inflate the absolute values of the measures.
- For systems producing ranked output, a simple measure such as the output position for a given Recall is useful.
- Single value measures lose information, so should not be the sole means of reporting performance.
- More than one variant single value measure should not be used unless a different picture of performance is obtained.
- The inclusion of benchmark performances, both low and high, aids assessment of results.
- Data aggregation problems should be carefully examined and the methods adopted fully reported; for example, applying the measures to each search before creating an average for the query set seems the correct procedure.
- Central tendency is not always reflected well by the arithmetic mean, so the median should be considered.
- In matched data sets, comparison differences should be presented rather than percentage improvements.
- The statistical and practical significance of the differences should be carefully assessed.
- When tests permit it, the consistency of performance differences should be looked for.
- When comparing dissimilar systems, if a control variable fair to all is not available, then more than one technique should be used.
- Where tests are to reflect interactive or iterative search strategies, a user-oriented result should be presented as well as any system-oriented one.

REFERENCES

Al-Hawamdeh, S., & Willett, P. (1989a). Comparison of index term weighting schemes for the ranking of paragraphs in full-text documents. *International Journal of Information and Library Research, 1*(2), 116–130.

Al-Hawamdeh, S., & Willett, P. (1989b). Paragraph-based nearest neighbour searching in full-text documents. *Electronic Publishing, 2*(4), 179–192.

Croft, W.B., Lucia, T.J., Cringean, J. & Willett, P. (1989). Retrieving documents by plausible inference: An experimental study. *Information Processing & Management, 25*(6), 599–614.

Fagan, J. (1989). The effectiveness of a nonsyntactic approach to automatic phrase indexing for document retrieval. *Journal of the American Society for Information Science, 40*(2), 115–132.

Griffiths, A., Luckhurst, H.C., & Willett, P. (1986). Using document similarity information in document retrieval systems. *Journal of the American Society for Information Science, 37*(1), 3–11.

Harman, D. (1988). Towards interactive query expansion. In *Proceedings of the Eleventh Annual International ACM SIGIR Conference on Research & Development in information retrieval*, pp. 321–331.

Harman, D. (1991). How effective is suffixing? *Journal of the American Society for Information Science, 42*(1), 7–15.

Keen, E.M. (1968). Search strategy evaluation in manual and automated systems. *ASLIB Proceedings, 20*(1), 65–81.

Keen, E.M. (1973). The Aberystwyth Index languages test. *Journal of Documentation, 29*(1), 1–35.

Keen, E.M. (1991a). The use of term position devices in ranked output experiments. *Journal of Documentation, 47*(1), 1–22.

Keen, E.M. (In press a). The effect of stemming strength on the effectiveness of output ranking. In *Proceedings of Informatics 11*, ASLIB.

Keen, E.M. (In press b). The effectiveness of term position and frequency for output ranking. In *Proceedings of the British Computer Society 13th research colloquium on information retrieval.*

Robertson, S.E., & Thompson, C.L. (1987). *An operational evaluation of weighting, ranking and relevance feedback via a front-end system.* Department of Information Science, The City University. Report to the British Library Research & Development Department.

Robertson, S.E. (1990). On sample sizes for non-matched-pair IR experiments. *Information Processing & Management, 26*(6), 739–754.

Salton, G. (1970). Evaluation problems in interactive information retrieval. *Information Storage & Retrieval, 6*(1), 29–44.

Salton, G., & Buckley, C. (1988). Term-weighting approaches in automatic text retrieval. *Information Processing & Management, 24*(5), 513–523.

Salton, G., & Buckley, C. (1990). Improving retrieval performance by relevance feedback. *Journal of the American Society for Information Science, 41*(4), 288–297.

Sparck-Jones, K. (1974). Automatic indexing. *Journal of Documentation, 30*(4), 393–432.

Sparck-Jones, K. (Ed.) (1981). *Information retrieval experiment.* London: Butterworths.

Tague, J.M. (1981). The pragmatics of information retrieval experimentation. In K. Sparck-Jones (Ed.), *Information retrieval experiment* (pp. 59–102). London: Butterworths.

Van Rijsbergen, C.J. (1979). *Information retrieval.* London: Butterworths.

Van Rijsbergen, C.J. (1981). Retrieval effectiveness. In K. Sparck-Jones (Ed.), *Information retrieval experiment* (pp. 32–43). London: Butterworths.

MEDLARS: Report on the Evaluation of Its Operating Efficiency

A comprehensive program to evaluate the performance of MEDLARS was conducted by the National Library of Medicine in 1966 and 1967. This report describes the methodology used and presents a summary of the principal results, conclusions, and recommendations.

F. W. LANCASTER †

Special Assistant to the Associate Director for Library Operations
National Library of Medicine
Bethesda, Maryland

• MEDLARS: General Background

The Medical Literature Analysis and Retrieval System (MEDLARS) has been discussed in detail elsewhere (*1*). Only the most salient characteristics will be described here.

MEDLARS is a multipurpose system, a prime purpose being the production of *Index Medicus* and other recurring bibliographies. However, the present study concentrated on the evaluation of the *demand search* function (i.e., the conduct of retrospective literature searches in response to specific demands). The base of the retrospective search module consists of more than 800,000 citations to journal articles in the biomedical field input to the January 1964 and subsequent issues of the monthly *Index Medicus*. This data base is presently growing at the approximate rate of 200,000 citations annually. Journal articles, of which roughly 45% are in languages other than English, are indexed at an average level of 6.7 terms per item, using a controlled vocabulary of *Medical Subject Headings* (MeSH). About 10,000 searches are now formulated annually in the United States; additional searches are handled at MEDLARS centers in the United Kingdom and in Sweden.

Approximately 2400 scientific journals are indexed regularly. About one-third of these are indexed *exhaustively* ("depth journals") at an average of 10 terms per article, and the remainder are indexed less exhaustively ("non-depth journals") at an average of slightly under four terms per article.

MeSH consists of about 7000 fairly conventional precoordinate type subject headings. A hierarchical classification ("tree structure") of these terms is available to the indexers and the search analysts. In January 1966, subheadings were introduced into the system. Subheadings, of which 53 were in use in 1966, are general concept terms (e.g., BIOSYNTHESIS, COMPLICATIONS) which can be affixed to main subject headings, thus effecting greater specificity through additional precoordination. Each subheading can only be used with main subject headings from specified MeSH categories. For example, the subheading ABNORMALITIES can only be used with Category A (anatomical) terms, while CONGENITAL is only applicable to Category C (disease) terms. These and other indexing conventions are spelled out in detail in a *MEDLARS Indexing Manual* revised annually.

A demand search is presently conducted, on a Honeywell 800 computer, by serial search of the index term profiles of the 800,000 citations on magnetic tape. This search is essentially a matching process: the index term profiles of journal articles are matched against a *search formulation*, which is a translation of a subject request into the controlled vocabulary of the system. Requests for demand searches are mostly received by mail at NLM, either embodied in a letter or on a "demand search request form"; a higher proportion of the requests processed by regional *MEDLARS* centers are made by personal visit to the center. The search formulations are prepared, by search analysts, in the form of Boolean combinations of main subject headings and subheadings. A generic search (known at NLM as an "explosion") can be conducted by means of the tree structure. An "explosion on A9.44.44" means that a search is conducted on the generic term RETINA (identified as A9.44.44 in the

† Present affiliation: WESTAT Surveys, Inc., Bethesda, Maryland.

tree structure) and all the terms subordinate to it in the hierarchy, namely FUNDUS OCULI, MACULA LUTEA, and RODS AND CONES.

The final product of a MEDLARS search is a computer-printed *demand search bibliography,* in up to three sections of varying specificity, the citations usually appearing in alphabetical order by author within each section. Accompanying each bibliographic citation is a complete set of tracings (i.e., a record of all the index terms assigned to the article).

• The MEDLARS Evaluation

Purpose

Planning of the MEDLARS evaluation began in December 1965, the principal objectives being:

1. To study the demand search requirements of MEDLARS users.
2. To determine how effectively and efficiently the present MEDLARS service is meeting these requirements.
3. To recognize factors adversely affecting performance.
4. To disclose ways in which the requirements of MEDLARS users may be satisfied more efficiently and/or economically. In particular, to suggest means whereby new generations of equipment and programs may be used most effectively.

The prime requirements of demand search users were presumed to relate to the following factors:

1. The *coverage* of MEDLARS (i.e., the proportion of the useful literature on a particular topic, within the time limits imposed, that is indexed into the system).
2. Its *recall* power (i.e., its ability to retrieve "relevant" documents, which, within the context of this evaluation, means documents of value in relation to an information need that prompted a request to MEDLARS).
3. Its *precision* power (i.e., its ability to hold back "non-relevant" documents).
4. The *response time* of the system (i.e., the time elapsing between receipt of a request at a MEDLARS center and delivery to the user of a printed bibliography).
5. The *format* in which search results are presented.
6. The amount of *effort* the user must personally expend in order to achieve a satisfactory response from the system (*2*).

The evaluation program was designed to establish user requirements and tolerances in relation to these various factors, and to determine the MEDLARS performance with regard to these requirements. In particular, we wanted to identify the principal causes of search failures, thus allowing corrective action to be taken to upgrade system performance.

The two most critical problems faced in the design of the evaluation were:

1. Ensuring that the body of test requests was, as far as possible, representative of the complete spectrum of "kinds" of requests processed.
2. Establishing methods for determining recall and precision performance figures.

The Test User Population

Through the detailed analysis of demand searches conducted at NLM in 1965, we established a list of twenty organizations that would form a suitable "test user group" for the purposes of the evaluation. The composition of this group was based upon the following considerations:

1. *Volume of requests.* Based on past performance these organizations were expected collectively to submit a minimum of 400 requests in the 12-month period allocated to the data gathering phase of the project. Based on a "pretest" conducted early in 1966, a return rate (of relevance assessments) of about 75% was anticipated. It was felt that the approximately 300 test searches that would thus be fully completed would be adequate to allow a meaningful study of major causes of system failure.

2. *Type of request.* Using as a guide the categories into which *Medical Subject Headings* are divided, we arrived at eight broad subject areas into which any MEDLARS request will tend to fall: *preclinical sciences, disease* (pathology), *technics* (surgical, diagnostic, analytical), *behavioral sciences, public health, drug/biology* (pharmacology), *drug/disease* (drug therapy), and *physics/biology* (effect of physical phenomena on the body). Judging from their 1965 requests, we expected that the test group would submit requests that would be representative of all these subject areas.

3. *Type of organization.* The group was selected to include representatives of the principal types of organization (clinical, research, academic, pharmaceutical, federal regulatory) making use of MEDLARS.

4. *Mode of user/system interaction.* The group was selected to include organizations whose members would, collectively, be likely to submit requests in all of the three possible modes: *personal* (the requester makes a visit to a MEDLARS center and negotiates his requirements directly with a search analyst), *no interaction* (the request comes directly by mail from the requester), and *local interaction* (the request comes by mail but is submitted by a librarian or information specialist on behalf of the requester).

The 20 major medical organizations thus selected to form the test user group were formally invited to participate in the evaluation program, and all agreed to do so. In addition, we decided to include in the evaluation a number of requests made, within the test period, by private practitioners.

Establishing the Performance Figures

The operating efficiency of MEDLARS was evaluated on the basis of its performance in relation to the demand search requests made, in a 12-month period, by individual physicians and other scientists affiliated with the 20 major medical organizations agreeing to cooperate in the study. While the organizations comprising the test user group had agreed to cooperate in the evaluation program (e.g., the dean of a medical school or the director of a research institute), the individual requesters knew nothing of the evaluation program until they submitted their requests. At that time they were asked to cooperate by allowing us to use their requests as "test requests." There is, then, no artificiality about the body of test requests. Each quite definitely represents an actual information need. For each of the test requests, a search was conducted and a computer printout of citations (*demand search bibliography*), which is the normal product of a MEDLARS search, was delivered to the requester. A duplicate copy of this printout was used in the extraction of a random sample of 25 to 30 of the retrieved citations. Photocopies of these sample articles were submitted to the requester for assessment, a second copy of each being retained for analysis purposes. This figure of 25 to 30 represents an upper bound on the number of articles for which we felt we could reasonably expect to obtain careful assessments. If the search retrieved a total of 30 articles or less, we normally submitted all for assessment.

We believe categorically that, within the environment of an operating retrieval system, where the performance of the entire system is being evaluated, a "relevant" document is nothing more nor less than a document of some value to the user in relation to the information need that prompted his request. In other words, in a real operating situation, a "relevance assessment" is a value judgement made on a retrieved document. We also believe that, to obtain valid precision figures and other data for analysis purposes, value judgments carefully made on a sample of a complete search output are of much greater value than less careful assessments made grossly on the complete output.

A *Form for Document Evaluation* was attached to each article submitted for assessment. This form ascertained whether or not the requester was previously aware of the retrieved item, and asked him to assess the article as of major, minor or no value *in relation to the information need that prompted his request to MEDLARS*. Most importantly, the requester was required to substantiate these judgments by indicating why particular items are of major value, others minor, and yet others of no value. These substantiations are of great utility in the analysis of search results. To get some idea of the serendipity value of searches, the requester was asked to indicate whether or not an article judged of no value in relation to the need that prompted his request was in fact of interest in relation to some other need or project. Finally, if the user was unable to assess the article because of inability to read the language (approximately 45% of the data base is not in English), the form determined whether or not he intended to obtain a complete or partial translation of its contents.

While precision figures for a MEDLARS search present no particular problem, it is extremely difficult to estimate the recall ratio for a "real-life" search in a file of over half a million citations. The only way to obtain a true recall figure is to have the requester examine and make assessments on each and every document in the file. While this is feasible in certain experimental situations, it is obviously out of the question for a collection of the MEDLARS size. The size of the base also rules out any hope of obtaining recall figures by conventional random sampling among the documents not retrieved by a particular search.

We therefore estimated the MEDLARS recall figure on the basis of retrieval performance in relation to a number of documents, judged relevant by the requester, *but found by means outside MEDLARS*. These documents could be, for example, (1) known to the requester at the time of his request, (2) found by his local librarian in non-NLM generated tools, (3) found by NLM in non-NLM-generated tools, (4) found by some other information center, or (5) known by authors of papers referred to by the requester.

For every test request we attempted to obtain a record of any articles within the time span of MEDLARS that the requester already knew to be relevant to the subject of his request. A form *Record of Known Relevant Documents* was completed by the requester after he had submitted his request but before he received the results of a MEDLARS search.

If the requester was able to supply a substantial quantity of citations not found by him in *Index Medicus* (citations found through direct search of *Index Medicus* should theoretically introduce a substantial bias into the recall estimate, since MEDLARS indexing is *Index Medicus* indexing plus), this was accepted as the recall base without further expansion. However, if the requester knew of no articles, or only one or two, an attempt was made to find additional potentially relevant items *by means outside the system*. These might be articles found by the librarian of the organization submitting the request, searching in tools not generated by the National Library of Medicine. Alternatively, they could be found by conventional manual literature searches conducted by members of the Evaluation Group in non-NLM generated tools held at the Library. In some cases, the one or two citations supplied by the requester would yield additional possibly relevant items, by means of a search in the *Science Citation Index*, or through direct contact with the authors of these known relevant papers. Occasionally it was possible to obtain additional items from a specialized information center such as the Parkinson's Disease Information and Research Center at Columbia University.

Although all these methods were tried, experience showed that conventional manual searching at NLM was the method most likely to expand the recall base with the minimum of effort. The documents found by

TABLE 1. Estimating recall ratio

Document Sources	Documents found outside of MEDLARS	Documents judged relevant
Requester	2	2
Local librarian	7	4
NLM staff		
Other center		
Authors of papers referred to by requester		
Totals	9	6

MEDLARS Retrieves 4/6.

Recall ratio for single request: 4/6 × 100 = 66%

these various methods extraneous to MEDLARS were considered no more than "possibly relevant." They were not incorporated into the *recall base* until the requester had examined them and judged them as of some value in relation to his information need. To achieve this, these additional items were interspersed with the *precision set* (i.e., the articles selected by random sampling from the MEDLARS search printout). The requester then assessed the enlarged set at one time.

Table 1 illustrates the way in which this method of obtaining a recall estimate works. In this instance, the requester is able to name two relevant documents, and his local librarian finds an additional seven which she believes to be relevant to the physician's request. The user, asked to make assessments of these seven documents, judges four to be relevant. We now have six known relevant documents upon which to base our recall figure. If all are in the MEDLARS data base, but only four are retrieved, we can say that the recall ratio for this search is 66%. This method works equally well, of course, whether the "possibly relevant" documents are discovered by the local librarian, NLM staff (in non-NLM tools), or by some other specialized information center, or are named by the author of a relevant paper referred to by the original requester.

Another way of considering this method of obtaining a recall estimate is illustrated by Figure 1.

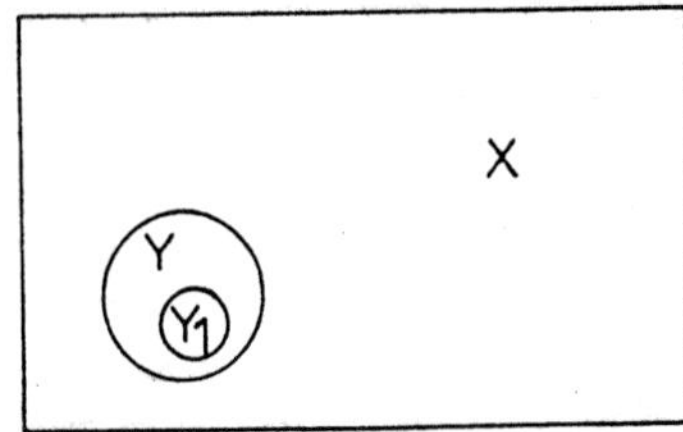

FIG. 1. Method used to compute recall estimate

TABLE 2.

	Major	Minor	No value	Not assessed
Known in advance	3	1		
Not known	1	5	8	5

The area X represents the entire MEDLARS collection. For any particular request made to the system, if the requester examined each and every item in the collection, he would be able to identify a subset, Y, of items which he considered of value in relation to his information need. All other items in the collection (X−Y) are of no value (i.e., "not relevant"). Unfortunately, except by complete examination of the collection, there is no foolproof method of establishing for any one request the exact subset Y of relevant items. However, we can establish a subset of the subset. That is, by methods outlined above, we can find some group, Y_1, of articles which the requester agrees to be relevant. We now establish the recall estimate on the basis of the performance of the system in relation to this particular group of relevant items. Thus, if we know 10 relevant articles within the data base, and MEDLARS retrieves seven of these, but misses three, we say that the MEDLARS recall ratio for this search is 70%, the assumption being that the "hit rate" for the group of documents Y_1 will approximate to the hit rate for the larger group Y.

Recall and precision figures are merely yardsticks by which we measure the effect of making certain changes in our system or in ways of operating the system. Although the recall estimate obtained by the present methodology may be slightly inflated or slightly deflated in relation to "true recall," since the method used to obtain the estimate was held constant throughout the evaluation program, the figures are still valid indicators of performance differences in various situations.

When the completed relevance assessment forms were returned, they were attached to the duplicate copies of the articles to which they related, and the recall and precision figures of the search were derived as illustrated in Table 1 and Table 2. In this case the requester was presented with a random sample of 25 articles, of which he assessed 20 (he could not assess the other five because they are in languages with which he is unfamiliar), judging 10 to be of value ("relevant") and 10 of no value. The *precision ratio* for this search is therefore 10/20× 100, or 50%. The *novelty ratio* (proportion of the articles judged of value that were brought to the requester's attention for the first time by the MEDLARS search) is 6/10.

ANALYSIS OF SEARCH FAILURES

Having derived the performance figures for a test search, the next step involved the detailed intellectual analysis of reasons why recall and precision failures occurred. The sample test results presented in Table 1 and Table 2 show that, in this particular search, we are faced with the analysis of (1) two *recall failures* (two of the six "known relevant" articles were not retrieved), and (2) ten *precision failures* (10 of the 20 articles assessed by the requester were judged of no value). The two recall failures and the 10 precision failures are not the only failures occurring in the search. They are the only ones that we know of, and as such they are accepted as exemplifying the complete recall and precision failures (i.e., they are symptomatic of problems occurring in this search).

The "hindsight" analysis of a search failure is the most challenging aspect of the evaluation process. It involves, for each "failure," an examination of the full text of the document; the indexing record for this document (i.e., the index terms assigned, which are obtained by printout from the magnetic tape record); the request statement; the search formulation upon which the search was conducted; the requester's completed assessment forms, particularly the reasons for articles being judged "of no value"; and any other information supplied by the requester. On the basis of all these records, a decision is made as to the prime cause or causes of the particular failure under review.

The MEDLARS Test Results

In the period from August 1966 to July 1967, 410 test requests were processed to the point of submitting photocopies of sample articles to requesters. From these, 317 sets of relevance assessments were returned (i.e., a 77% return rate), and 302 of these searches were completely analyzed.

For three of the 302 searches we were unable to obtain a recall base, but for the remaining 299 searches we have both a precision ratio and a recall ratio. When we take the individual performance ratios for the 299 test searches and average them, we arrive at the results displayed in Table 3. Over a substantial representative sample of MEDLARS requests, the system was found to be operating, on the average, at 57.7% recall and 50.4% precision. That is, on the average, over the 299 test searches, MEDLARS retrieved a little less than 60% of the total of relevant literature within its base. At the same time, on the average, approximately 50% of the articles retrieved were of some value to requesters in relation to the information needs prompting their requests. Approximately 26% of the articles retrieved were judged of major value by the requesters. Alternatively, we can say that MEDLARS is retrieving about 65% of the major value articles, accompanied by around 50% irrelevancy.

Table 3. Summary of average recall and precision ratios for 299 searches *

Overall precision ratio	50.4%
Precision ratio based on major value articles only	25.7%
Overall recall ratio (complete recall base)	57.7%
Recall ratio based on major value articles only (274 searches)	65.2%

* Omitting 3 that have no recall base. All figures in this table are calculated by averaging the individual ratios.

In the 302 searches analyzed, there were 238 in which recall failures were known to have occurred, and we know of 797 cases of recall failure (i.e., 797 articles that should have been retrieved, because they were judged "of value" but were not retrieved) over these 238 searches. There were 278 searches in which precision faiures were known to have occurred, and we know of 3038 cases of precision failure (i.e., 3038 articles that were retrieved but judged "of no value"). All these failures were analyzed in detail. The results appear in Tables 4 and 5.

The figures quoted are not absolute figures for the total number of failures occurring. For example, in Table 5, the figure of 534 precision failures due to "lack of appropriate specific terms" is quoted. This does not mean that in 278 searches only 534 unwanted articles were retrieved because of lack of specificity in the vocabulary. We know of 534 and these exemplify a much larger number of failures of this type.[1] The meaningful figures are the percentages in this case; lack of specificity in the vocabulary contributed to 17.6% of all the precision failures, and affected the precision performance of 20.9% of all the 278 searches in which precision failures occurred.

• Analyses of Failures: Explanatory Notes

We will now consider in detail the various factors contributing to recall and precision failures under the principal system components responsible: indexing, searching, index language, and the user-system interface. In these analyses, three terms appear that are given special meaning, and therefore require precise definition, namely *exhaustivity*, *specificity*, and *entry vocabulary*.

Exhaustivity and Specificity of Indexing

Exhaustivity and *specificity* are terms that apply both to the indexing of a document and to the preparation of a search formulation for a request. By *exhaustivity of indexing* we mean the extent to which the potentially indexable items of subject matter contained in a document are in fact recognized in the "conceptual analysis" stage of indexing and translated into the language of the system. For example, consider an article that discusses the use of radioisotope brain scanning in the localization of five

[1] In actual fact, over 4,000 precision failures in the 278 searches.

TABLE 4. Reasons for 797 recall failures in 238 of 302 searches examined

Source of failure	Number of missed articles	Percentage of total recall failures	Number of searches	Percentage of the 238 searches
Index Language				
Lack of appropriate specific terms	81	10.2	29	12.2
Searching				
Searcher did not cover all reasonable approaches to retrieval	171	21.5	80	33.6
Search formulation too exhaustive	67	8.4	31	13.0
Search formulation too specific	20	2.5	9	3.8
"Selective printout"	13	1.6	7	2.9
Use of "weighted" terms	2	0.2	1	0.4
Other searching failures due to sorting, screening, clerical error	6	0.8	5	2.1
Searching totals	279	35.0	133	55.9
Indexing				
Insufficiently specific	46	5.8	31	13.0
Insufficiently exhaustive	162	20.3	100	42.0
Exhaustive indexing (searches involving negations)	5	0.6	4	1.7
Indexer omitted important concept	78	9.8	61	25.6
Indexer used inappropriate term	7	0.9	7	2.9
Indexing totals	298	37.4	203	85.3
Computer Processing	11	1.4	7	2.9
Inadequate User-System Interaction	199	25.0	70	29.4
Total factors identified as contributing to 797 recall failures	868			

different types of lesions. If we completely omit to use an index term that would encompass one of these lesions, we are not indexing the subject matter of this document exhaustively. On the other hand, consider an article that presents case histories on, say, 20 patients. If the indexer includes terms to cover all diseases and abnormalities mentioned, all diagnostic techniques used, and all therapeutic procedures, including specific drugs employed, the subject matter of the document has been covered highly exhaustively.

A high level of exhaustivity of indexing will tend to result in a high recall performance for a retrieval system, but also in a low precision performance. Conversely, a low level of exhaustivity of indexing (i.e., inclusion of "most important" concepts only) will tend to produce a high precision, low recall performance. Exhaustivity of indexing is largely controlled by a policy decision of system management. At NLM, guidelines are given to indexers on the number of subject headings that may be applied to an article. This establishes a general exhaustivity level. Within this established level, the indexers choose terms to express what they consider to be the most important concepts discussed in an article. In the analyses, failure to retrieve a relevant document due to the fact that a particular concept was not indexed was called a recall failure due to lack of exhaustivity of indexing. Similarly, the retrieval of an unwanted document because of inclusion of minor importance concepts in indexing was called a precision failure due to exhaustivity of indexing. It is obvious that there is no "correct level" of exhaustivity in any absolute sense. There should, however, be an optimum level in relation to the types of request made of a particular retrieval system.

Specificity of indexing refers to the generic level at which a particular item of subject matter is recognized in indexing. For example, consider indexing the topic "tetrodotoxin." This could be expressed specifically by a single term TETRODOTOXIN, or we could deliberately

TABLE 5. Reasons for 3038 precision failures in 278 of 302 searches examined

Source of failure	Number of unwanted articles	Percentage of total precision failures	Number of searches	Percentage of the 278 searches
Index Language				
Lack of appropriate specific terms	534	17.6	58	20.9
False coordinations	344	11.3	108	38.8
Incorrect term relationships	207	6.8	84	30.2
Defect in hierarchical structure	9	0.3	5	1.8
Index Language totals	1094	36.0	255	91.7
Searching				
Search formulation not specific	462	15.2	87	31.3
Search formulation not exhaustive	356	11.7	62	22.3
Searcher used inappropriate terms or term combinations	132	4.3	31	11.2
Defect in search logic	33	1.1	6	2.2
Searching totals	983	32.4	186	67.0
Indexing				
Exhaustive indexing	350	11.5	137	49.3
Insufficiently exhaustive (searches involving negations)	5	0.2	2	0.7
Indexer omitted important concept (search involving negations)	1	0.0	1	0.4
Insufficiently specific	1	0.0	1	0.4
Indexer used inappropriate term	36	1.2	26	9.4
Indexing totals	393	12.9	167	60.1
Inadequate User-System Interaction				
Explicable	464	15.3	85	30.5
Inexplicable	39	1.3	26	9.4
Inadequate Interaction totals	503	16.6	111	39.9
Computer Processing	3	0.1	3	1.1
Value Judgment	71	2.3	40	14.4
"Inevitable" retrieval	4	0.1	4	1.4
Total factors identified as contributing to 3038 precision failures	3051			

choose to express this subject precisely by the joint use of two terms, TOXINS and PUFFER FISH (recording this decision in our *entry vocabulary* as: Tetrodotoxin *index under* TOXINS and PUFFER FISH). Alternatively, we could index this topic at a higher generic level (i.e., at the level of "toxins produced by fish") by the joint use of a term FISH and a term TOXINS. Climbing one level higher in the generic tree, we could index the topic under a term ANIMAL TOXINS, or ZOOTOXINS, or by the joint use of the term TOXINS and the term ANIMALS. We could, of course, choose to be even more general and index this specific toxin under the very broad term TOXINS.

Obviously, a high level of specificity in indexing will tend to produce a high precision capability in a retrieval system, whereas a low level of specificity will result in a low precision capability. This can be demonstrated by Figure 2. Unless we uniquely define that class of documents dealing with tetrodotoxin, we will never be able to retrieve documents on this subject except as part of a larger class of documents—in this case, as part of the class "fish toxins," the class "animal toxins," or the class "toxins." The greater the specificity of the indexing (i.e., the smaller the size of the document classes uniquely defined), the greater will be our precision capabilities.

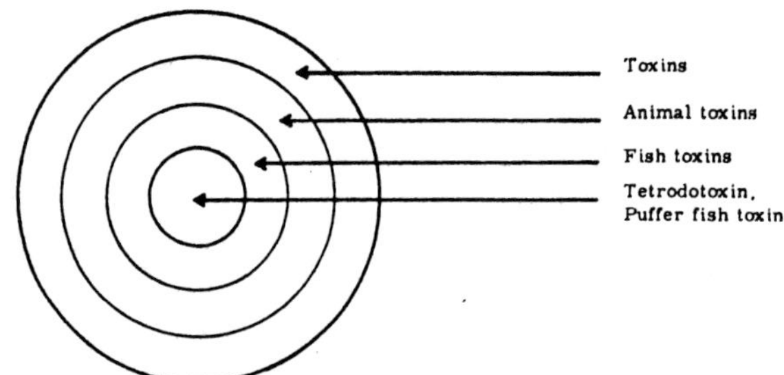

Fig. 2. Diagram of specificity in document classes

On the other hand, a high level of specificity in indexing will also tend to reduce recall. Reconsidering Figure 2, if we search only the class "tetrodotoxin" for a request on this subject, while those documents retrieved will tend to be highly relevant, we may well be missing some potentially useful items that have been assigned to the more general class "fish toxins" (for example, articles on tetrodotoxin not recognized by the indexer as being on this precise subject, or articles on fish toxins in general which contain substantial information relevant to the subject of puffer fish toxin).

To improve our recall, we can compensate for a high level of specificity in indexing by means of our searching strategies. That is, we can broaden the class of acceptable documents by searching at a higher generic level—in this case by accepting the entire class "fish toxins." However, no variations in searching strategy will ever be able to compensate for lack of specificity in indexing. If we subsume the class "tetrodotoxin" under the general class "animal toxins," there is no searching strategy that will allow us a very high-precision search on the subject of tetrodotoxin, since this class of documents is no longer uniquely defined.

Unlike exhaustivity (which is controlled in general by a policy decision of system management, and in particular by decisions made by individual indexers), specificity is governed by the index language. Although the degree of specificity in indexing is governed by properties of the index language, the indexer can in fact index a particular topic at a higher level of specificity than that allowed by the index language. This can either be a deliberate decision made by the indexer (e.g., he chooses to index an article on a number of pulmonary conditions under the term LUNG DISEASES rather than under terms for the specific diseases concerned) or it can be an indexing error (i.e., the indexer chooses a more general term because he is unaware of the existence of the specific term). In the analyses, failures due to lack of specificity in indexing (i.e., due to an indexer using a term of a higher generic level than that allowed by the index language) are distinguished from failures due to inherent lack of specificity in the index language.

Exhaustivity and Specificity in Searching

At the searching stage, the notions of exhaustivity and specificity are much less precise than they are in indexing; in fact, they tend to merge into one another. To take a very simple example, imagine a request for literature on oximetry applied to patients with pulmonary emphysema. This request involves only two facets or categories: the measurement technique facet and the disease facet. If we recognize both facets or categories, and demand their co-occurrence in our search formulation, we are being *exhaustive* in our formulation.

However, we can recognize each of these facets at any of several levels, as illustrated below:

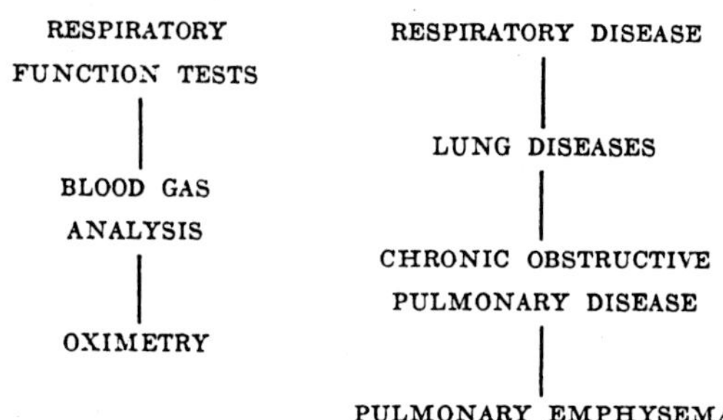

If we specify that both facets occur at exactly the level of specificity demanded in the request, i.e., we use terms defining the classes "oximetry" and "pulmonary emphysema," we are being fully exhaustive and fully specific in our search formulation for this request. We can, therefore, expect that the group of retrieved documents will, in the main, be highly relevant to the request (i.e., we will achieve a high precision search).

To improve our recall for this request, by pulling in a larger class of potentially relevant documents, we can move in one of two directions. Either we can reduce the exhaustivity of the formulation or we can reduce its specificity. We reduce specificity by moving up in one of the hierarchies, without omitting it entirely. For example, we could move to the more generic class "blood gas analysis" and demand that this co-occur with a term indicating "pulmonary emphysema." Or we could reduce specificity in the disease category and ask, as an example, for the co-occurrence of the class "lung diseases" and the class "oximetry." Of course, we can reduce specificity in more than one category simultaneously. For instance, we could demand co-occurrence of the class "blood gas analysis" and the class "lung diseases." Alternatively, we can broaden our search, with the object of improving recall, by reducing exhaustivity in the formulation (i.e., by omitting a category entirely). If we asked only for the class "oximetry," we would be searching at a low exhaustivity level for the stated request.

Both high level of exhaustivity and high level of specificity in searching, since they reduce the class of acceptable documents, make for high precision and low recall. Broadening the class of acceptable documents, by reducing specificity and/or exhaustivity in the formulation, will tend to improve recall and reduce precision.

In the analysis, failures to retrieve wanted documents because of a stringent search formulation were characterized as failures due to "formulation too exhaustive" or "formulation too specific." Conversely, failures to hold back unwanted documents due to a relaxed search requirement were characterized as failures due to "formulation not specific" or "formulation not exhaustive."

Obviously, there can be no such thing as a "correct level of exhaustivity" or a "correct level of specificity" in searching. Varying these levels, to widen or narrow the class of documents accepted in the search, is an essential part of searching strategy. The larger the class of documents retrieved, the greater we can expect to be our recall; the smaller the class of documents retrieved, the greater we can expect to be our precision (providing, obviously, that we are enlarging or reducing the class of acceptable documents in a sensible fashion).

Entry Vocabulary

The importance of an adequate entry vocabulary can be demonstrated by a reconsideration of Figure 2. We said earlier that the class of documents dealing with "tetrodotoxin" can be uniquely defined in the language of the system, or that the class can be subsumed under some larger class, thereby losing its separate identity. We also said that the precision performance of a system is directly controlled by the size of the document classes uniquely defined by the index language (i.e., by the level of specificity in indexing). However, from the point of view of recall, it matters little whether we uniquely define a class or subsume it under some larger class, *as long as we record the decision taken.* Thus, to return to our toxin example, we can uniquely define the class "tetrodotoxin," we can subsume it under "fish toxins," we can subsume it under "animal toxins," or we can subsume it under "toxins." Whichever decision we make, the class of documents relating to "tetrodotoxin" can be retrieved in subsequent searches, *providing we have an entry in our entry vocabulary* to tell us where this particular document class has been put, as:

Tetrodotoxin index under FISH TOXINS
or
Tetrodotoxin index under ANIMAL TOXINS
or
Tetrodotoxin index under TOXINS

Obviously, the precision will deteriorate with the size of the document class retrieved. However, our entry vocabulary leads us to the group of wanted documents and allows us to retrieve it, however it has been subsumed.

An adequate entry vocabulary is essential to ensure that indexers and searchers consistently use the same terms, or term combinations, to describe identical items of subject matter. A rich entry vocabulary will include all words and phrases used in documents to describe notions that have been recognized in the conceptual analysis stage of indexing and translated into the language of the system. It will also include words and phrases used in requests to describe notions about which literature exists in the system. The quality of an entry vocabulary can substantially affect the recall performance of an information retrieval system.

• The Indexing Subsystem

From Tables 4 and 5, it can be seen that the indexing subsystem contributed to 37% of the recall failures and was in fact the largest contributor to this group of failures, but to only 13% of the precision failures. There are two distinct types of failure: (1) those due to indexer errors; and (2) those due to a policy decision governing the number of terms assigned to an article (i.e., the policy regarding *exhaustivity* of indexing).

Indexer errors are themselves of two types: (1) omission of a term or terms necessary to describe an important topic discussed in an article, and (2) use of a term that appears inappropriate to the subject matter of the article. Omissions will normally lead to recall failures, while use of an inappropriate term can cause either a precision failure (the searcher uses this term in a strategy and retrieves an irrelevant item) or a recall failure (the searcher uses the correct terms and a wanted document is missed because labeled with an incorrect term). Use of inappropriate terms (i.e., sheer misindexing) is negligible in MEDLARS, contributing to about 1% of the precision failures and 1% of the recall failures. The misindexings that do occur appear not to be errors of carelessness. Rather they appear due to the general misuse of a particular term at some point in time. For example RADIOISOTOPE SCANNING was used indiscriminately for any radioisotope monitoring operation, whether or not scanning was involved.

Indexer omissions, on the other hand, contribute significantly to almost 10% of all the recall failures, and were wholly or partly responsible for at least one missed article in 25% of all the searches in which recall failures occurred. These omissions are fairly gross errors and cannot be attributed primarily to a policy decision governing indexing exhaustivity. We have distinguished recall failures due to indexer omissions from recall failures due to lack of exhaustivity of indexing, as follows:

1. *Indexer omission.* A topic that appears central to the subject under discussion in the article is not covered at all in the indexing. It is felt that the omitted topic is so important that it should be covered even in "non-depth" indexing.
2. *Lack of exhaustivity.* An item of subject matter treated peripherally in the article is not covered in the indexing. The topic is not crucial to the article, and was presumably excluded in favor of other topics due to general policy regarding the average number of terms to be assigned, and perhaps also to the short time period allowed for indexing (an experienced indexer at NLM will index 40 to 50 articles per day).

The following are two examples of indexer omissions discovered in test searches:

Search 20. An article on the effect of visual deprivation on growth of the visual cortex in mice was indexed under CEREBRAL CORTEX and VISION and DARKNESS, but should also have been indexed under GROWTH and SENSORY DEPRIVATION. It is from a depth-indexed journal and was not retrieved in a search relating to growth in the nervous system, although it was regarded as of major value.

Search 39. A major value article on reversible sterility following discontinuance of medroxyprogesterone was not retrieved because the crucial term STERILITY, FEMALE was not applied. The search was on prolonged amenorrhea and infertility following discontinuance of oral contraceptives.

Although a certain number of indexing omissions are to be expected under the pressures of a tight production schedule, some of those occurring are difficult to excuse, particularly when a term appearing in the title of an article is omitted. For example, search #45 relates to electrical brain stimulation in elicitation of species-specific behavior. One of the missed articles, from a 1966 issue of *Behavior,* was not indexed under ELECTRIC STIMULATION even though entitled "Behavioral effects of electrical stimulation in the forebrain of the pigeon."

Some of these cases of indexer omission can be attributed to the fact that no MeSH term exists for the missed notion, and there is nothing in the entry vocabulary to say how the topic is to be indexed. As a result, the indexer either omits the topic entirely or indexes it much too generally. This type of failure was found, for example, in search #190, which relates to deiodination of thyroxine. A major value article, unretrieved, deals with flavin photodeiodination of thyroxine. There is no MeSH term for "photodeiodination," or indeed for "deiodination," and there is nothing in the entry vocabulary to say how this concept is to be indexed. Consequently, the notion was completely ignored in indexing, although it might reasonably have been translated into IODINE. Similar, but much more drastic, failures occurred in other searches. Search #102 sought articles on hemodynamic analysis using Fourier series. Many major value articles (for example, on the Fourier analysis of vascular impedance) were missed. Despite the fact that "Fourier analysis" or "Fourier series" appeared prominently in these articles, this aspect was ignored by the indexers. Presumably these failures are due partly to lack of an adequate entry vocabulary. There is no specific term for Fourier series. Despite this, relevant articles could have been retrieved were there an entry in the entry vocabulary to tell indexers and searchers that "Fourier analysis" is to be subsumed under the broader term MATHEMATICS or whatever other term is chosen to express the topic. On the surface, it may appear strange that there should be so few instances of misindexing (that is, use of inappropriate terms) but so many cases of indexer omissions. The explanation may be simple. The work of the inexperienced indexers is scanned ("revised") by senior indexers. Usually the inappropriate terms will stand out quite clearly and are easily corrected in this revision process. However, omissions are not so readily detected by the reviser because this would involve a careful examination of the article. Consequently, errors of omission are more likely to creep through than examples of sheer misindexing.

Failures Due to Exhaustive Indexing or Lack of Exhaustivity

As previously mentioned, the more exhaustively we describe (by means of index terms) the subject matter of documents, the greater will be the recall potential of the system. Conversely, because of the inverse relationship between recall and precision, the more exhaustive the indexing, the more precision failures are likely to occur. This is partly attributable to the greater potential for false term coordinations, and partly to the fact that exhaustive indexing will cause retrieval of articles in response to requests to which they relate very weakly. In the operation of any retrieval system we are likely to find recall failures caused by indexing that is not sufficiently exhaustive. At the same time, we will discover precision failures due primarily to the fact that exhaustive indexing has brought out articles on topics for which they contain very little information.

This is exactly what happens in MEDLARS. Twenty percent of the recall failures are attributed to lack of exhaustivity of indexing, while 11.5% of the precision failures are caused largely by exhaustive indexing. Articles from "depth" journals (about one-third of all the 2400 journals regularly indexed) are presently indexed at an average of about 10 index terms per article, while the non-depth articles are indexed at an average of slightly less than four terms per article. The overall average for depth and non-depth is about 6.7 terms per item. In addition, some of the terms assigned to both depth and non-depth articles are chosen to be the headings under which entries for the articles will appear in *Index Medicus*. Only the terms representing the most important topics discussed in an article are chosen as *print* or *IM* terms. Thus, the *print* terms can function as *weighted index terms*. At present, there are approximately 2.6 print terms per article.

Recall Failures due to Indexing of Insufficient Exhaustivity

One example is adequate to illustrate a typical recall failure due to indexing of insufficient exhaustivity. Search #535 relates to the transmission of viral hepatitis by parenteral inoculations of materials other than blood or blood products or during venipuncture. One major value article that was not retrieved deals with hepatic inflammation in narcotic addicts. The fact that viral hepatitis is transmitted by contaminated injection equipment was mentioned in the text but was not covered by the indexing.

Precision Failures due to Exhaustive Indexing

Exhaustive indexing will contribute to a small proportion of the precision failures in certain searches and will be largely responsible for all the precision failures in others. For example, one of the irrelevant items retrieved in a search on the crystalline lens in vertebrates deals with the correlation between mast cells and the histamine content of the eye in cattle. It was indexed under LENS, CRYSTALLINE even though only one item of data on the lens is presented. Search #13, on blood or urinary steroids in human breast or prostatic neoplasms, retrieved two types of irrelevant article due to exhaustive indexing:

1. Articles in which the required neoplasm aspect is barely mentioned (for example, an article indexed under BREAST NEOPLASMS deals with plasma androgens in women and discusses a number of patients, only one of whom had breast cancer).
2. Articles in which the urinary aspect is very slight (PROSTATIC NEOPLASMS *and* URINE retrieved, for example, a single case report on prostatic cancer in which a urinary hormone assay value is presented in a table).

In other searches, exhaustive indexing had quite a drastic effect on precision. A search on the action of chloramphenicol retrieved 339 citations. In about 50% of the articles cited, the reference to chloramphenicol is very slender (e.g., it is used as an incubation medium in a bacterial study). The precision ratio for this search was only 20%.

Effect of Exhaustivity Levels

Seventy-three searches were selected for additional analysis to determine the effect of indexing exhaustivity on performance. This group of searches included 39 recall failures due to lack of exhaustivity and 69 precision failures due to exhaustive indexing. It was noted that the average number of index terms assigned to the 39 missed articles was 7.6, while the average number assigned to the 69 retrieved but unwanted items was 11.8.

It was also possible to derive figures indicative of performance variations caused by differences between depth and non-depth indexing. The combined random sample forming the overall precision base for the test searches consisted of 6491 articles, 4884 from depth journals and 1607 from non-depth. The overall precision ratios for these components, calculated by the *average of numbers,* was 2386/4672 (51.1%) for the depth articles and 533/1266 (43.7%) for non-depth.

The recall difference between depth and non-depth indexing was calculated on a sampling basis. Twenty searches having large requester-supplied recall bases were selected. The combined recall base consisted of 225 articles, 201 from depth journals and 24 from non-depth. The overall recall ratio for the depth journals, calculated by the *average of numbers* was 141/201 (70.1%). The overall recall ratio for non-depth was 13/24 (54.2%).

A further analysis was performed to determine what type of performance could be expected if the much lower level of exhaustivity adopted for *Index Medicus* (about 2.6 terms per article) was also the only level available in the retrospective search system. Because *print* terms are asterisked in the computer printout of index records (tracings), it was possible to determine the recall and precision results for a number of the test searches based only on these terms. The analysis simply involved the matching of tracings, for both recall and precision base documents, against the search formulation prepared for the request, and the counting of all articles that would have been retrieved had the indexing consisted only of the *print* terms. A total of 111 searches were analyzed. However, in the case of 23 of these searches the comparison was unreasonable because the search formulation used as a coordinate a term (a check tag such as HUMAN, or a technic term such as MICROSCOPY, ELECTRON) that would either never be used as a *print* term or would be used very rarely. Consequently, in nine of these searches no documents would have been retrieved on *print* terms only, while only a handful would have been retrieved in the other 14 searches. These 23 searches were therefore eliminated, all further analysis being conducted on the remaining 88.

The total combined recall base for these 88 searches comprised 633 articles. In the searches on the full MEDLARS indexing, 382 were retrieved, giving an overall recall ratio (by the *average of numbers*) of 60%. Only 280 of the articles would have been retrieved on the *print* terms however (i.e., a recall ratio of 44%). In other words, the much reduced exhaustivity of *Index Medicus* indexing led to the loss of one relevant document in every four.

The total combined precision base for the 88 searches consisted of 1716 documents, of which 890 were judged relevant (i.e., a precision ratio of 52%). Only 783 of these articles, of which 466 (60%) were relevant, would have been retrieved on the basis of the *print* terms only. In other words, searching on *Index Medicus* terms alone would have lost 344 of the 890 relevant documents (49%) with a compensatory gain in precision, because 509 of the 826 irrelevant items (61%) would also have been filtered out.

Summarized, the figures are as follows:

	Recall ratio %	*Precision ratio* %
Complete indexing	60	52
Index Medicus indexing only	44	60

These figures, of course, demonstrate the customary effect of variations in indexing exhaustivity: the more terms used, the greater will tend to be the recall but the lower the precision; the fewer, more selective the terms used, the lower will tend to be the recall and the higher the precision.

We can now look at this combined evidence relating to recall and precision performance as related to exhaustiv-

TABLE 6. Effect of indexing exhaustivity on retrieval performance in MEDLARS

Exhaustivity level	Recall ratio %	Precision ratio %
Depth indexing (10 terms approximately)	70	51
Non-depth indexing (4 terms approximately)	54	44
Index Medicus terms (2.6 terms approximately)	44	60

ity of indexing in MEDLARS. The data are presented in Table 6.

All other things being equal, we would expect that these results would show a strict inverse relationship between recall and precision. This is apparent in the relationship between the *Index Medicus* terms and the depth indexing. However, the results for the non-depth indexing do not correspond to the expected pattern: both recall and precision for the non-depth articles are lower than for depth articles. This is due to the fact that the non-depth articles are indexed not only with fewer terms, but also with more general terms. We will return to this matter, and discuss its implications, later.

Two small experiments were conducted to determine (1) whether re-indexing "in depth" of unretrieved non-depth articles would appreciably improve recall; and (2) whether re-indexing of nonretrieved depth articles, again in depth, would allow their retrieval. Eighteen non-depth articles that were unretrieved in a number of test searches (although the failure was not necessarily attributed primarily to non-exhaustive indexing) were re-indexed according to "depth" standards. Sixteen of the articles were indexed by three separate indexer-reviser pairs, and the other two articles were indexed by two separate indexer-reviser pairs. The average number of terms assigned in the original non-depth indexing was 5, while the average term assignment for the re-indexing was 11.2.

Seven of the 18 articles (38.9%) would have been retrieved on the basis of at least one out of three versions of the re-indexing, while 6 of the 18 (33.3%) would have been retrieved on the basis of at least two of the three versions.

The failure to retrieve 5 of the 18 articles was originally attributed to non-exhaustive indexing, and all 5 of these would have been retrieved by at least one of the three versions of the re-indexing, while 4/5 (80%) would have been retrieved on the basis of at least two of the three versions.

Thirteen of the failures were not originally attributed to nonexhaustive indexing, but two of these articles could in any case have been retrieved by the additional index terms assigned in the depth indexing. In other words, exhaustive indexing has a certain "fail-safe" property which, under certain conditions, will compensate for other system failures, such as inadequate searching strategies.

The above experiment suggests that depth indexing of non-depth articles might allow retrieval of between 30% and 40% of the relevant non-depth articles that are presently unretrieved in MEDLARS searches.

The second small experiment involved the re-indexing of 13 articles from depth journals that were not retrieved because of indexing of insufficient exhaustivity. These articles were selected at random from all the recall failures of this type. It was not to be expected that this reindexing would have much effect on recall. The articles were originally indexed in depth at an average of 7.2 terms per item. The omitted topics are comparatively minor aspects of the articles, and only indexing at a substantially higher level of exhaustivity would be likely to affect recall significantly. The test confirmed this. The re-indexing was done by one experienced indexer at a slightly higher level of 9.1 terms per item, but the topic originally omitted from the indexing was added to only two of the 13 articles.

Failures due to Lack of Specificity in Indexing

Only one precision failure was attributed to the failure of an indexer to use the most specific MeSH term available. However, 5.8% of all the recall failures were due to lack of specificity in indexing. In MEDLARS, lack of specificity and lack of exhaustivity of indexing are both closely related to policy regarding indexing depth (i.e., the average number of terms assigned). Articles from non-depth journals tend to be indexed in general terms. For example, search #64, on spina bifida and anencephalus, failed to retrieve a number of non-depth articles because they were indexed more generally under ABNORMALITIES. In depth indexing, the specific malformations would have been indexed.

General Observations on Exhaustivity and Specificity of Indexing in MEDLARS

1. Indexing exhaustivity is, of course, a relative matter. We have already mentioned the article on mast cells and histamine content of the eye in cattle, which was retrieved on the term LENS, CRYSTALLINE although only one item of data was given on this topic. The requester regarded it as of no value in relation to his research on the crystalline lens in vertebrates. Therefore, we must say that exhaustive indexing was largely responsible for this precision failure and, judged in relation to this request, assignment of the term LENS, CRYSTALLINE was unjustified. Visualize, however, a second, much more specific request for articles presenting data on the histamine content of the crystalline lens. In response to this request, the above article is highly relevant and may in fact be one of the few articles in which measured values are quoted. Judged in relation to this request, the term LENS, CRYSTALLINE is completely justified.

2. On the whole it is better to err on the side of exhaustive indexing. It is difficult to retrieve an article on X if X has not been covered in the indexing of the item. On the other hand, within MEDLARS the searcher has a limited capability for reducing the exhaustivity by searching only on *Index Medicus* terms, and thus improving precision for any one search (although inevitably losing some recall). Alternatively, the searcher may use what is in effect a weighting device by demanding that the key term of a request (LENS, CRYSTALLINE in the above example) must be a *print* term, but not putting any such restriction on the coordinate terms. This procedure is likely to improve precision with rather less drastic effects on recall.

3. The artificial separation of all MEDLARS journals into depth and non-depth appears, from the detailed search analyses, to lead to indexing anomalies that can cause both recall and precision failures. Although many of the articles from non-depth journals seem somewhat superficial and repetitive, others are very substantial papers which, because of a general policy decision, are indexed completely inadequately. On the other hand, half-column letters in *Lancet* are sometimes assigned 15–20 terms and are thus retrieved in searches to which they contribute little or nothing. A policy of treating each article on its own merit, whatever journal it comes from, would reduce such seeming anomalies.

4. From the point of view of machine retrieval, the policy of indexing non-depth articles in general terms is indefensible. To quote but one example, in the analysis of search #531 an article from a non-depth journal (*Poultry Science*), entitled "Role of *streptococcus faecalis* in the antibiotic growth effect in chickens" was examined. Found by manual search, but missed by MEDLARS, it was indexed only under EXPERIMENTAL LAB STUDY, INTESTINAL MICROORGANISMS and POULTRY. Use of the general term INTESTINAL MICROORGANISMS for the specific organism implicated is inexcusable. On the basis of this indexing, one could not reasonably expect the article to be retrieved in response to a request on "streptococcus faecalis in poultry" or one on "effect of penicillin on steptococcus faecalis" or even one on "antibiotic growth effect in poultry," to all of which specific topics it is highly relevant. In fact, on the basis of the indexing one could only reasonably expect to retrieve it in a search on intestinal microorganisms of poultry, to which general subject it is indeed a slight contribution.

It is always a mistake to index specific topics under general terms. In the above example, use of the term STREPTOCOCCUS FAECALIS would allow retrieval of this item in response to a request involving this precise organism. On the other hand, the article could still be retrieved in a more general search relating to intestinal microorganisms, because the searcher is able to "explode" on all bacteria terms. The article could have been indexed very adequately under five terms: POULTRY, PENICILLIN, STREPTOCOCCUS FAECALIS, GROWTH, and EXPERIMENTAL LAB STUDY. *As the article is presently indexed, it is difficult to visualize a single retrospective search in which it would be retrieved and judged of major value.* In other words, this citation and others indexed in such general terms are merely occupying space on the citation file.

• The Searching Subsystem

Considering recall and precision failures together, the searching subsystem is the greatest contributor to all the MEDLARS failures, being at least partly responsible for 35% of the recall failures and 32% of the precision failures. We can distinguish three types of searching failure:

1. Recall failures due to the fact that the searcher did not cover all reasonable approaches to the retrieval of relevant articles.
2. Pure errors involving the use of inappropriate terms or the use of defective search logic.
3. Failures due to the levels of specificity and/or exhaustivity adopted in searching strategies.

Recall Losses due to Failure to Cover All Reasonable Approaches to Retrieval

In the recall analysis, 21.5% of all the failures were attributed to the fact that the searcher did not cover all reasonable approaches to the retrieval of literature relevant to the request. In other words, 21.5% of the missed relevant articles could have been retrieved on terms or term combinations which, the author feels, the searcher might reasonably have been expected to use in the search formulation. This "failure to cover all reasonable approaches" in searching was a major contributor to recall losses in the 302 searches analyzed, being second only to failures of user-system interaction, which were responsible for 25% of the recall losses. There are really two categories of failures of this type:

1. Failure to use one particular relevant term, or term combination, in a formulation which otherwise reflects the complete interests stated in a request.
2. Failure to cover a complete aspect of the request as stated by the requester.

The first type has less drastic results than the second but neverthless can substantially reduce the recall ratio for a search, as the following illustrate:

Search #19. In a search on nervous-tissue culture as affected by electrical stimulation, and certain other variables, the searcher did not explode on NERVOUS SYSTEM in coordination with TISSUE CULTURE and terms for the specific factors of interest. A directly related article could have been retrieved on CEREBRAL CORTEX *and* TISSUE CULTURE *and* ELECTRIC STIMULATION

Search #34. In a search on potassium shifts in isolated cell preparations, no use was made of the term CELL MEMBRANE PERMEABILITY. Used in conjunction with POTASSIUM CHLORIDE, it would have brought out several major value articles.

More drastic failures occur when the searcher omits a complete aspect of a topic that is explicitly stated in the request. This type of failure is particularly prone to occur with fairly long, multifaceted request statements. Whether the searcher overlooks the aspect through careless reading or deliberately ignores it is difficult to establish. An example of this type of failure occurred in search #174, which relates to testicular biopsy in cases of infertility. One aspect of interest (the effect of surgical and hormonal therapy on sperm count, testicular morphology, and fertility) was completely omitted from the formulation, contributing to the low recall ratio of 3/11 (27.3%).

PRECISION FAILURES DUE TO SEARCHING ON INAPPROPRIATE TERMS OR TERM COMBINATIONS

Whereas omission of appropriate terms from a search formulation will lead to recall failures, use of inappropriate terms or term combinations will cause precision failures. The author attributes 4.3% of the precision failures to this cause. For example:

Search #47. In a search on computer recognition of cells, one strategy involved the coordination of CYBERNETICS with all cell terms. CYBERNETICS is inappropriate to a request on cell recognition, which is essentially a pattern recognition problem. It caused retrieval of articles on cells as cybernetic systems and was responsible for about one-third of the irrelevancy in this search.

Inappropriate *term combinations* tend to occur with fairly complex search formulations in which a list of terms in a logical sum (*or*) relation is *anded* with a second list of summed terms. While the overall strategy may appear sensible, some of the combinations resulting may be irrational in relation to the request.

RECALL AND PRECISION FAILURES DUE TO VARIATIONS IN EXHAUSTIVITY OF THE FORMULATION

As previously mentioned, varying the exhaustivity and/or specificity of the formulation is an essential part of searching strategy. In fact, the central problem of searching is the decision as to the most appropriate level of specificity and exhaustivity to adopt for a particular request. The less specific and exhaustive the formulation, the more documents will be retrieved; recall will tend to increase and precision to decrease. The more specific and exhaustive the formulation, the fewer documents will be retrieved; recall will tend to deteriorate and precision to improve. For each particular request, we must decide in which direction to go. In other words, how near to 100% recall does the requester really want to approach, bearing in mind that the closer we get to this figure the more documents we are likely to retrieve and the lower is likely to be the precision of the search?

An *exhaustive* search formulation is one that demands the co-occurrence of all the notions asked for, in some relationship, by the requester (although not necessarily at the level of specificity stated in the request). Consider search #115, which concerns various specific intestinal microorganisms causing diarrhea or dysentery in cases of protein deficiency or kwashiorkor. This request involves a relationship between three separate notions: (1) certain specific intestinal microorganisms, (2) the disorder of diarrhea or dysentery, and (3) the disorder of protein deficiency or kwashiorkor.

The searcher was fully exhaustive in the formulation, allowing an article to be retrieved only if (1) it has been indexed under the term PROTEIN DEFICIENCY *or* the term KWASHIORKOR, and (2) it had been indexed under a term indicating the involvement of some microorganism, *and* (3) it had been indexed under a term indicating diarrhea or dysentery.

With an exhaustive formulation such as this, we can expect high precision. That is, most of the articles retrieved are likely to be relevant. On the other hand, our strategy may be too exhaustive; it may be asking too much to expect a relevant article to have been indexed under *all* of the notions demanded by the requester. This was exactly the case in search #115, which retrieved nothing, although relevant literature exists and some could have been retrieved with the less exhaustive strategy:

PROTEIN DEFICIENCY
or *and* diarrhea terms
KWASHIORKOR

Exhaustivity of the search formulation is obviously related to the *coordination level* (i.e., the number of index terms required to co-occur before an article can be retrieved), but there is no strict one-to-one relationship between exhaustivity and coordination level. For example, PROTEIN DEFICIENCY *and* DYSENTERY *and* INTESTINAL MICROORGANISMS is a three-term coordination that is exhaustive in that it covers all the related notions demanded by the requester, but so also does PROTEIN DEFICIENCY *and* DYSENTERY, BACILLARY, which is a two-term coordination. Moreover, by varying the coordination level, we may be varying the *specificity* rather than the *exhaustivity* of the search.

For example, consider a request for "metastatic fat necrosis as a complication of pancreatitis." The formulation PANCREATITIS *and* NECROSIS is exhaustive in that it asks for the co-occurrence of the two notions specified. The three-term coordination PANCREATITIS *and* NECROSIS *and* ADIPOSE TISSUE is merely more specific in relation to the request.

Exhaustive search formulations were responsible for 8.4% of the recall failures, and nonexhaustive search formulations were responsible for 11.7% of the precision failures. Some further examples follow:

Exhaustive Formulations

Search #217. The request is for "influence of the styloid process on facial and head pains." The searcher required that some term indicating "face" or "head" be present, as well as a term indicating "pain" and the term for site of the "styloid process" (TEMPORAL BONE). This seems unnecessarily exhaustive because it is reasonable to assume that pain relating to the temporal bone would involve face or head. The simple, less exhaustive formulation TEMPORAL BONE *and* PAIN would materially have improved recall.

Search #460. This search concerned optical or spectral properties of malignant cells which would permit their detection with sufficient efficiency for counting. This request really boils down to "optical and spectral properties of malignant cells." However, in addition to requiring that a neoplasm term should co-occur with an optical property term, the searcher demanded that a "diagnosis" term should also be present. Recall was 76.5% but could have been 100% with a less exhaustive formulation.

Nonexhaustive Formulations

Search #9. The request relates to various aspects of induced hypothermia. This was searched on the single term HYPOTHERMIA, INDUCED. This retrieved 860 citations and predictably obtained 100% recall (25/25). However, the precision ratio was only 30%.

Search #18. In a search on "renal amyloidosis as a complication of tuberculosis," the strategy: amyloid term *and* tuberculosis term, omitting the requirement for kidney involvement, was responsible for most of the irrelevancy.

RECALL AND PRECISION FAILURES DUE TO VARIATIONS IN SPECIFICITY OF THE FORMULATION

Only 2.5% of all the recall failures were attributed to the use of a specific search formulation. *This does not mean that reduction of searching specificity could not substantially have improved recall in many searches*—obviously it could. It merely means that only in the case of 20 missed documents, out of the total of 797 examined, could the blame be put primarily on a search formulation unnecessarily specific in relation to the stated request. On the other hand, 15.2% of all the precision failures could be attributed to lack of specificity in the search formulation. In the same way that reduction of exhaustivity in a formulation will tend to improve recall but reduce precision, so reduction in search specificity (if it involves logical generalization) will tend to improve recall but reduce precision. Some examples are given below:

Search #3. A request on "electron microscopy of lung or bronchi" was broadened to LUNG/CYTOLOGY, thus improving recall but inevitably losing precision.

Search #19. In a search on nervous tissue culture, the "tissue culture" was generalized to IN VITRO. This led to about 80% irrelevancy in the search.

Search #101. The ease with which an explosion can be conducted appears to have led the searcher into a very poor search. The request refers to various aspects of personality in relation to choice of medical specialty. The searcher exploded on SPECIALISM and coordinated this set of terms with a group of behavioral terms. Unfortunately SPECIALISM brings out all the terms covering individual medical specialties (e.g., PATHOLOGY, PEDIATRICS, PSYCHIATRY, GERIATRICS). Coordinated with the behavioral terms, this retrieved 459 citations (e.g., on personality changes in aging, on doctor-patient relations in pediatrics) of which less than 20 are of any possible relevance.

Although it is terribly dangerous to generalize on the matter of searching strategy and the correct level of generality to adopt, a detailed study was undertaken to determine if any useful pointers could be derived to assist the searcher in deciding (a) when to broaden a search, (b) the best way to broaden, and (c) what type of search generalization is unwarranted. This study is presented in the full report of the project (*3*).

• Joint Causes of System Failures

Now that both indexing failures and searching failures have been discussed, it is appropriate to re-emphasize the fact that not all failures are attributed to a single cause. Sometimes they are attributed jointly to two parts of the system. This is particularly true in the case of the relationship between indexing and searching. Occasionally we must say "if the indexer had included *X*, the document would have been retrieved, but it would also have been retrieved had the searcher used *Y*." This occurred, for example, in search #276, on keratinization of the gingiva. The search was conducted on

		GINGIVA
KERATIN	*and*	GINGIVAL DISEASES
		GINGIVAL HYPERPLASIA
		GINGIVAL HYPERTROPHY

One of the recall base articles, missed by the above strategy, could have been retrieved had the searcher also used KERATIN *and* GINGIVITIS. On the other hand, the indexer might well have applied the term GINGIVA to this article, as well as GINGIVITIS, because it deals with the effect of powered toothbrushing on gingival inflammation and keratinization. This is the type of failure which, in the analysis, was jointly attributed to both indexing and searching.

• Recall and Precision Failures due to the Index Language

The quality of the index language is probably the most important single factor governing the performance of a retrieval system. Poor searching strategies and inadequate or inconsistent indexing can mar the performance of a system, but indexing and searching, however good, cannot compensate for an inadequate index language. In other words, indexers and searchers can perform only as well as the index language allows.

The index language contributed to 10.2% of the MEDLARS recall failures and to 36% of the precision failures. These failures are of two principal types: failures due to lack of specificity in the terms and failures due to ambiguous or spurious relationships between terms.

Lack of specificity in the index language can cause either recall failures or precision failures. In the present evaluation, it was responsible for 10.2% of all the recall failures and 17.6% of all the precision failures. Although an oversimplification, it is convenient to consider the index language of MEDLARS, or any other retrieval system, as comprising two vocabularies: (1) the controlled vocabulary of terms that indexers must use in describing the content of a document (i.e., the 7000 MeSH terms), and (2) the vocabulary of natural language words and phrases, occurring in documents and requests, that map onto the controlled vocabulary terms. This latter vocabulary we have described as an *entry vocabulary*. Within MEDLARS, the entry vocabulary is partly built into *Medical Subject Headings* through the use of references. For example, under CHARCOT-MARIE DISEASE in MeSH we find the instruction *see under* MUSCULAR ATROPHY. The former term is an *entry vocabulary* term: it does not uniquely define a class of documents in the system, because the class of "documents on Charcot-Marie Disease" is subsumed under the broader class of "documents on muscular atrophy," and thus has no separate identity. Within the Index Section at NLM is a further entry vocabulary, on 5″×3″ cards, of additional natural language terms that map onto MeSH terms. This entry vocabulary, known as the *authority file* consists of about 18,000 entries, of which approximately two-thirds relate to drugs and chemicals.

It is worthwhile returning to the earlier discussion on the matter of the entry vocabulary, and to the illustration given in Fig. 2. Consider articles on the subject of tetrodotoxin. We decide not to uniquely define this class of documents, but to subsume it under the more generic class "fish toxins," this topic being defined by the joint use of, say, a term ANIMAL TOXINS and a term FISH. Even though we do not uniquely define the class "tetrodotoxin," we must include it in our entry vocabulary, as a reference:

Tetrodotoxin *use* ANIMAL TOXINS *and* FISH

We must do this to:

1. Indicate that documents on this specific topic have been input to the system, and
2. Ensure that all indexers use the same term combination to enter articles on this precise topic into the system, and
3. Ensure that searchers use the right term combination to retrieve relevant literature.

Thus, although we do not uniquely define the class "tetrodotoxin," we should still be able to retrieve literature on this precise topic because our entry vocabulary tells us precisely where to look. That is, lack of specificity in the vocabulary will not cause recall failures in this case. However, we cannot retrieve articles on tetrodotoxin *alone;* we must retrieve the entire class of articles on fish toxins. Thus, lack of specificity will cause precision failures in a search on tetrodotoxin. In other words, if we do not uniquely define a particular class of documents, but still use our entry vocabulary to indicate how this class has been subsumed, we will get precision failures due to lack of specificity in the vocabulary, but not recall failures attributable to this cause. If we omit the notion even from our entry vocabulary, we will get both recall failures and precision failures. Some examples will help to illustrate this point:

Search #6. A search relating to aortic regurgitation had low precision because the 1963 and 1964 material was indexed under the more general term AORTIC VALVE DISEASES.

Search #70. A search on bacterial identification by computer achieved only 33.3% recall and 47.8% precision. There is no specific term for *bacterial identification* (speciation). The combination of bacteria terms *and* analysis or automation terms retrieved many articles on bacterial analysis (e.g., chromatographic purification) having nothing to do with species *identification.* Recall failures in this search can also be attributed to lack of specificity in the index language. "Bacterial identification by computer" is really "numerical taxonomy." There is no term for this, or for "numerical analysis," and nothing in the entry vocabulary to say how it is to be treated. This led to the complete omission of the topic in the indexing of several relevant articles.

Search #102. A search on the use of Fourier series in hemodynamic analysis achieved only 54.5% recall and 8% precision; 99 citations were retrieved. There is no specific term for "Fourier analysis" and nothing in the entry vocabulary to say how this notion is to be subsumed. Consequently, the concept was omitted in the indexing of several pertinent articles. Moreover, the searcher was forced into very general combinations (e.g., hemodynamics terms *and* MATHEMATICS or MODELS) which caused considerable irrelevancy.

Search #160. This search, on nephrogenic diabetes insipidus, clearly illustrates the importance of an adequate entry vocabulary. In an attempt to restrict the search to *nephrogenic* diabetes insipidus, the searcher coordinated DIABETES INSIPIDUS with kidney or kidney disease terms. This resulted in the low recall ratio of 1/9 (11.1%) because the topic is generally indexed only under DIABETES INSIPIDUS, with no co-occurring kidney term. However, the searcher had no way of knowing this because there is nothing in the entry vocabulary to say how this notion is to be indexed.

These examples illustrate overall index language deficiencies in MEDLARS and suggest areas (e.g., the behavioral sciences) in which the system is particularly weak. To pinpoint more precisely the subject areas in which the vocabulary is suspect, a breakdown by subject field was made for all the searches in which were found recall and/or precision failures due to lack of specificity in the index language.

Over one third of the searches falling in the general area of the behavioral sciences are marred because of lack of specificity in the vocabulary, while one-third (2/6) of the searches relating to public health are similarly affected. In the area of "technics," 27.6% of all the searches are affected by lack of specificity. On the whole, the language in this area is reasonably unambiguous. However, performance will depend upon the availability of specific terms. As already noted, there is no term covering high frequency radio therapy (diapulse) so that search #467 could operate at only 10.5% precision.

A quarter of the PHYSICS/BIOLOGY searches are affected by lack of specificity in the vocabulary (it is difficult to distinguish various types of radiation; e.g., ionizing from non-ionizing). About 23.6% of the searches falling into the DISEASE category are affected by lack of specificity, whereas only 17.6% of the PRECLINICAL SCIENCES searches are similarly affected. In other words, for the types of requests put to MEDLARS in the preclinical area, the vocabulary is shown to be reasonably adequate. The performance in the disease area will depend entirely upon whether or not terms for specific disease entities are available in either MeSH or the entry vocabulary. If we have no term for "colitis cystica profunda" we can hardly expect to achieve a satisfactory result in a search on this topic. On the whole, the search analyses have shown the MEDLARS vocabulary to be unexpectedly weak in the clinical area. Not only does it fail to express precisely a significant proportion of the pathological conditions occurring in requests, some of which are not particularly obscure (e.g., perforation of the gallbladder), but it is also deficient in its ability to express various *characteristics* of a disease. For example, we cannot indicate *extent* of pathological involvement (*diffuse* lesions of the lung, *solitary* pulmonary nodule). Nor can we readily distinguish *symptomatic* from *asymptomatic;* co-existent, unrelated conditions from true sequelae; or the situation of one disease simulating (masquerading as) another.

Again from the search analyses, the vocabulary appears weak in areas that impinge upon medicine. For example, in search #102, the terms MATHEMATICS, MODELS and COMPUTERS are as close as the searcher was able to get to the topic of "Fourier analysis." Similarly, in search #242, MICROWAVES was the only term available to express "masers."

Before leaving the matter of specificity in the vocabulary, it is worthwhile mentioning, or re-emphasising, the following:

1. There is a difference between failures due to lack of specificity in the vocabulary and failures due to lack of specificity in searching. In the former case, there is no specific term available so the searcher is obliged to use more general terms. In the second case, the searcher broadens the search even though more specific terms, of varying degrees of appropriateness to the request, exist in the vocabulary. As an example, we can consider a search on medicine in Somalia. Lack of a specific term before 1966 made it necessary for the searcher to include AFRICA, EASTERN in the formulation (*lack of specificity in the index language*), but the searcher went beyond the deficiency in the vocabulary by exploding on AFRICA, EASTERN, and thus bringing in articles indexed under ETHIOPIA and SUDAN (*lack of specificity in searching*). In some searches, although there was no specific MeSH term to cover a request topic (e.g., searches relating to ultrastructure), the author felt that the searcher generalized more than was necessary. In such cases, some of the failures were attributed to lack of specificity in the vocabulary, others to lack of specificity in searching.

2. To correct *precision failures* due to lack of specificity, requires that terms or term combinations *that uniquely define* the notion not presently covered specifically, be introduced into the vocabulary. To correct *recall failures,* we do not need a unique designation, but we must include the notion in our entry vocabulary.

3. The evaluation has shown the MEDLARS entry vocabulary to be very inadequate. Recall failures in the test searches could have been reduced by 10% if a satisfactory entry vocabulary had been available. Lack of an adequate entry vocabulary can lead to (1) indexer omissions, or lack of exhaustivity of indexing (the indexer does not know how to index a particular notion so leaves it out); (2) indexing inconsistencies; (3) recall failures; (4) precision failures (the searcher does not know how a particular notion has been treated, and is thus forced to use every possible term combination). Moreover, the fact that a term appears in an entry vocabulary indicates that literature on the topic exists in the system. Without such an entry, we have no assurance that MEDLARS even contains any articles on, say, some obscure syndrome. Consequently, we may willingly accept a negative result from the system when such a result is incorrect.

The value of the entry vocabulary is well illustrated by a search on "irradiation of mammalian oocytes." The searcher relied on OVUM *and* irradiation terms. The authority file contains an entry, dated July 31, 1966, which instructs "Oocytes *use* OVUM." But articles indexed before this date were indexed with no consistency (some were indexed under GERM CELLS), while this precise notion was omitted in various other articles (indexed only under CELL DIVISION).

5. Searching difficulties are caused by the fact that the vocabulary has been developed without consistency as to levels of specificity (degree of pre-coordination). Thus we have a specific term VAGOTOMY, for example, but we cannot express "pyloroplasty" except by PYLORIC STENOSIS *and* SURGERY, OPERATIVE, or by PYLORUS/SURGERY. Consequently, although we can say VAGOTOMY/ADVERSE EFFECTS, we have no precise way of expressing "adverse effects of pyloroplasty."

6. The MEDLARS index language is gradually becoming more specific. Not all of the failures attributed to lack of specificity indicate current inadequacies. That is, in some cases terminological changes have been made, but the searcher is still required to use nonspecific terms to retrieve material indexed before the specific terms were introduced. To discover what proportion of the failures, attributed to lack of specificity, represent terminological changes since rectified, and what proportion represent terminological deficiencies still existing, a special analysis of a sample of 100 searches was conducted. In this group of 100 searches, 24 contained recall and/or precision failures due to lack of specificity in the vocabulary. There were 25 separate terms involved, and 13 (52%) of these deficiencies no longer exist in MEDLARS (i.e., appropriate specific terms are now available. Note that the introduction of subheadings, in 1966, markedly increased the specificity of the vocabulary. It is now possible to express various notions (e.g., "epidemiology" and "etiology") which were not adequately covered in the vocabulary before the subheadings were introduced.

Failures due to False Coordinations and Incorrect Term Relationships

Ambiguous and spurious relationships between terms accounted for approximately 18% of all the precision failures. In one sense, all terms assigned in the indexing of a particular article must be considered related in some way, even if it is only a proximity relationship (i.e., the terms are common to a particular index term profile). However, consider a search involving a simple two-term logical product relation, A *in relation to* B. Although all the articles retrieved by this coordination should be indexed under the term A and also under the term B, some of these articles may be irrelevant because the term A and the term B are not directly related in the article (a *false coordination*), while others may be irrelevant because, while A is related to B, the terms are not related in the way that the requester wants them (an *incorrect term relationship*).

To clarify the distinction between false coordinations and incorrect term relationships, consider a search relating to phosphate excretion. A term combination used in this search was PHOSPHATES *and* URINE. One of the articles retrieved by this combination discusses urinary excretion of Toxogonin, which is mentioned as being an antidote to alkyl-phosphate poisoning. Hence, the term URINE is not directly related to the term PHOSPHATE (i.e., it is a false coordination). The same terms retrieved a second article, not on excretion of phosphates, but on a phosphate precipitation method of determining magnesium in urine. This is an *incorrect term relationship:* URINE is related to PHOSPHATE, but not in the way that the requester wants these terms related.

False coordinations were responsible for 11.3% of the precision failures, *incorrect term relationships* for 6.8%. Some further examples follow.

False Coordinations

Search #71. In a search on mongolism occurring with leukemia, the combination LEUKEMIA *and* MONGOLISM retrieved a number of articles in which the two terms refer to different patients (e.g., general articles on sex-chromatic abnormalities). This type of failure is always likely to occur in MEDLARS when two disease terms are coordinated. In a search on the neuropathy of multiple myeloma, the coordination of MULTIPLE MYELOMA *and* neurological disease terms caused about 40% irrelevancy, while a search on ventricular septal defect in association with mitral stenosis or mitral insufficiency, achieved only 26% precision because in most of the retrieved articles the two terms are not related.

Search #96. LUNG *and* NYMPH NODES retrieved articles that do not deal with pulmonary lymphatics (the two are discussed separately).

Incorrect Term Relationships

Search #39. The search relates to cases of prolonged amenorrhea or infertility following discontinuance of oral contraceptives. But about a third of the articles retrieved deal with therapeutic use of contraceptive agents in the treatment of menstruation disorders, and not with side effects. This search illustrates the principal type of relational indicator needed by MEDLARS, namely an indicator of *sequence* or *cause-effect* relationship. The same type of failure is likely to occur in searches on radiation and drug effects, because it is sometimes difficult to distinguish therapy from adverse effects. For example, in search #95, on the effect of radiation on hair growth, HAIR REMOVAL *and* RADIOTHERAPY retrieved articles on therapeutic use of irradiation (e.g., in alopecia mucinosa) as well as articles on radiation *damage* to hair.

Search #67. In a search on lipids in annelids, the combinations CEPHALINS *and* LEECHES and CHOLESTEROL *and* NEMATODA retrieved a number of articles not on lipids of worms, but on the effect of lipids *on* worms (e.g., effect on leech muscle preparation).

Search #73. In a search on bovine leukosis, CATTLE *and* LEUKEMIA retrieved articles not on cattle leukosis but on the reaction of sera from human leukemia patients, or the reaction of mouse leukemia viruses, with bovine cell cultures.

Value of Subheadings

In the literature of documentation, the solution generally offered to the problem of false coordination is the *link,* while the solution generally offered to the problem of incorrect relationships is the *role indicator.* However, in the search analyses it was repeatedly discovered that both types of problem could now frequently be avoided by the use of subheadings. Moreover, failures of this type were found to be virtually nonexistent when indexer and searcher had both made correct use of subheadings.

This led the writer to undertake an investigation to determine just what proportion of all the failures of this type could be corrected by the use of subheadings (either existing subheadings or subheadings that could readily be devised.)

In 45 searches examined 20 examples of false coordinations and 22 examples of incorrect term relationships were encountered. A total of 16 (80%) of the false coordinations could have been prevented by subheadings, 12 of these by existing subheadings and 4 by suggested new subheadings. A total of 20 (90%) of the incorrect term relationships could be prevented by subheadings, 14 by existing subheadings and 6 by suggested new subheadings.

Full details of this analysis are given in the full report (*3*). It is sufficient to say that subheadings, properly used, are capable of solving 80–90% of the precision failures attributable to false coordinations and incorrect term relationships. The subheadings ADVERSE EFFECTS and THERAPEUTIC USE serve to distinguish articles on therapy from articles on side effects. ETIOLOGY is another subheading useful in obviating the sequential or cause-effect type of problem. The subheading COMPLICATIONS tends to tie two disease terms together and thus avoid some of the false coordinations that occur when we *and* these terms. That is, in an article indexed *disease A*/COMPLICATIONS and also *disease B*/COMPLICATIONS there is a high probability that both conditions co-exist in the same patient. However, the subheading COMPLICATIONS does not solve the sequential problem. Does condition A lead to condition B, or does B lead to A? It would be necessary to introduce a new subheading SEQUELAE to cope with this type of situation.

More freely available subheadings would tend to reduce problems stemming from variations in the specificity (by pre-coordination) of the vocabulary. We can now say BLOOD PRESERVATION, but we can only express "plasma preservation" by the coordination of BLOOD PRESERVATION and PLASMA, which leads to false coordinations. A generally applicable subheading PRESERVATION, in place of the pre-coordinations that exist in parts of the vocabulary, would solve this type of problem.

Of particular value within MEDLARS are *paired subheadings*. That is, subheadings that tend to tie two terms together and at the same time indicate the relationship between these terms. Such subheading pairs act simultaneously as links and as roles. They function in much the same way as the paired role indicators introduced by Western Reserve University (*property given* and *property given for*) and the Engineers Joint Council (causative agent, thing affected). For example the coordination of TOLBUTAMIDE *and* DIABETES MELLITUS, in a search on therapeutic use of oral hypoglycemic agents in diabetes, will retrieve irrelevant articles on the "tolbutamide tolerance test." But the coordination TOLBUTAMIDE/THERAPEUTIC USE *and* DIABETES MELLITUS/DRUG THERAPY not only tends to tie the two terms together, but also shows their relationship.

• Recall and Precision Failures due to User-System Interaction

Defective user-system interaction contributed to 25% of the recall failures and 16.6% of the precision failures in the present evaluation.

A recall failure due to defective interaction implies that the stated request is more specific than the actual area of information need. Articles of value to the requester in relation to his need are not retrieved because the searcher adheres to the stated request.

A precision failure due to defective interaction implies that the stated request is more general than the actual information need. Articles of no value to the requester are retrieved. These match his stated request but are of no value because of some additional limitation or requirement that was not given in the request statement.

In some searches there is a partial overlap between stated request and information need and in these cases it is likely that both recall and precision failures will result from inadequate interaction.

There appear to be basically two types of interaction failure (*4*).

1. The situation, long known to librarians, of the user who puts an imperfect request (i.e., a request that does not precisely match his information requirement), or the situation in which the information need is captured imperfectly by a librarian or search analyst.

2. The situation in which the user puts a request that is a fair reflection of his information need, but recall failures result from the fact that he is not fully aware of the types of article that exist and could be of use to him. This type of failure can only be solved by a browsing or *iterative* search. About 20% of the MEDLARS test searches involving inadequate interaction were judged to be of this type (i.e., the situation in which the requester could never precisely define his need except through some browsing in the literature).

In this evaluation program, a discrepancy between a stated request and an information need has been determined on the basis of:

1. The requester's relevance assessments, particularly the reasons given for judging certain articles of value and others of no value.
2. Revised request statements supplied by the requester in a covering letter to the Evaluator or on the test form *Revised Statement of MEDLARS Request*.
3. The requester's *Record of Known Relevant Documents*.
4. In a few cases, by telephone contact between the Evaluator and the requester.

Some examples of search failures attributed to defective interaction (i.e., failures due to request statements that imperfectly represent the area of information need) follow.

Search #5. The request is for "crossing of fatty acids through the placental barrier; normal fatty acid levels in placenta and fetus." Recall was only 25% because the requester is interested in the broader area of *lipid* transfer and also in lipid levels in the *newborn infant.*

Search #11. This search was a complete failure, retrieving 1167 articles of which only one was relevant. The request statement was "cancer in the fetus or newborn infant," but the area of need appears to the relationship between teratogenesis and oncogenesis at the cellular level.

Search #24. The request relates to the metabolism of steroids in liver or liver disease, but the requester did not indicate that animal studies were of no interest.

Search #32. This is an example of a request too specific in one aspect, insufficiently specific in another. The request is for "homonymous hemianopsia in visual aphasia," but the actual area of interest encompasses homonymous hemianopsia *and other visual field defects* in patients having aphasia *as a result of a tumor or cerebrovascular accident.*

Search #52. The request reads "skin grafts in monkeys." Only *homografts* are of interest.

In the design of the evaluation, we hypothesized that, of the modes of interaction presently used within MEDLARS, the most desirable would be the *personal interaction* mode (i.e., the situation in which the requester visits a MEDLARS center and discusses his needs personally with a search analyst). The other modes (mailed request direct to the system, and the request transmitted through a local librarian) would be likely to be less successful on the whole. This hypothesis was not supported by the test results. Table 7 presents the performance figures for 299 searches broken down by mode of interaction, from which it can be seen that the performance for the "no local interaction" group (i.e., request mailed directly to the system) is noticeably better than the performance for the other groups. Of course there are other variables that could be affecting the results in this table, including the variable of the MEDLARS center performing the search, the subject field, and the type of organization submitting the request. However, when each of these variables is held constant, and the results are tabulated by mode of interaction, the trend displayed in Table 7 is consistently maintained. Moreover, when we take the group of 134 searches in which, from the requester's relevance assessments, we know that interaction failures have occurred (i.e., failures due to request statements that do not closely correspond to the actual area of interest), we find that 37.8% of all the "no local interaction" searches contain failures attributed to inadequate interaction, whereas 46.8% of the "local interaction" searches and 50% of the personal interaction searches contain failures of this type.

TABLE 7. Breakdown of MEDLARS performance figures by mode of interaction

Mode of interaction	Precision ratio %	Recall ratio %
Personal interaction (109 searches)	49.3	56.4
Local interaction (79 searches)	46.9	55.0
No local interaction (111 searches)	53.9	60.8

From these results, and from the detailed search analyses, it appears that the best request statements (i.e., those that most closely reflect the actual area of information need) are those written down by the requester in his own natural-language narrative terms. When he comes to a librarian or search analyst, and discusses his need orally, a transformation takes place and, unfortunately, the request statement captured by the librarian or searcher is frequently a less perfect mirror of the information need then the one prepared by the requester himself in his own natural language terms. When the user writes down his request, he is forced to think of what exactly he is looking for. In this, he is not particularly influenced by the logical and linguistic constraints of the system. When making a personal visit to a MEDLARS center, if he has not gone through the discipline of recording his request, he has a less well formed idea of what he is seeking. When this somewhat imprecise need is discussed with a search analyst, in terms of *Medical Subject Headings,* it tends to become forced into the language and logic of the system.

IMPROVING REQUEST STATEMENTS

The large number of failures attributed to the area of user-system interaction prompted the conduct of a detailed analysis of the searches involved. This analysis was intended to determine what data, if it could have been collected from the requester, would have helped to define more exactly the area of his actual information requirement. Put differently, can we design a search request form that, without being too complex, will assist the requester in defining the exact scope of his need, and at the same time will give the searcher data adequate for a proper understanding of the requester's need?

The following observations resulted from this analysis:

1. Obviously, the prime requirement is a complete statement of what the requester is looking for. This should be a statement in the requester's own natural-language, narrative form. It must *not* be deliberately phrased in the language of the system. It must *not* be artificially structured in a form that the requester believes will approximate to a MEDLARS search strategy.

2. Knowing the *purpose* of a search would clearly

have helped, in a number of cases, to precisely define its scope. We only know of these cases because the requester has told us the reason for his search after it was completed. It is not unlikely that those data would have helped to define the scope of many of the other searches. For example, the request for search #11 came out as "cancer in the fetus or newborn infant," while the actual area of interest covers "the relationship between teratogenesis and oncogenesis at the cellular level." The search might have been successful had the requester informed us, as he did post facto, that he had been asked to write an article, for *Advances in Teratology*, on "some aspect of cell differentiation or malformations and how they are related to the cancer problem."

Knowing the purpose of a search may help to establish the recall and precision requirements and tolerances of users. A physician writing a book on "connective tissue in ocular disease," and asking for a search on this subject, will demand high recall and tolerate low precision. That is, he will be prepared to examine a comparatively large number of nonrelevant citations to assure himself that he is not missing any articles of prime importance. On the other hand, we have a requester who is preparing a seminar, for nurses, on kidney transplantation. He does not necessarily want everything, but would like to see a number of recent major surveys of the entire subject. The requirement is for high precision, and a low recall will be tolerable.

3. The titles of articles that the requester knows to be relevant at the time he makes his request (collected in the present evaluation program on the form *Record of Known Relevant Documents*) can be of great potential value in helping to define the scope of a search. For example, search #5 relates to "crossing of fatty acids through the placental barrier; normal fatty acid levels in placenta and fetus." The fact that the requester is really concerned with a broader topic (crossing of *lipids* through the placental barrier; normal *lipid* levels of placenta, fetus, or *newborn infant*) is well illustrated by the titles supplied in advance by him:

"Release of free fatty acids from adipose tissue obtained from newborn infants"

"Changes in the nucleic acid and phospholipid levels of the liver in the course of fetal and postnatal development"

"The amount of lipids and proteins in the foetus of rats and rabbits and in newborn infants"

Note that titles of "known relevant" articles will be most useful in indicating a request more specific than the actual information need. If the titles quoted are obviously outside the scope of the stated request, this is an indication of a request statement that is too precise.

On the other hand, if the titles supplied are more specific than the stated request, this does not really tell us very much—since they are included within the scope of the search as defined by the request statement. Sometimes, however, the cited titles will relate to a topic *much more precise* than the general area covered by the request statement, and this will tend to identify a request that is probably too general in relation to the precise information need For example, the requester of search #11, on "cancer in fetus or newborn infant," could name only one known relevant paper before the search, namely: "Association of Wilm's tumor with aniridia, hemihypertrophy and other congenital malformations." The fact that the requester could name only one relevant article, and that so much more specific than the statement of his need, surely suggests that the request statement is much broader than it should be.

We are not, of course, advocating that search formulations be based on titles of known relevant papers rather than request statements. The two complement each other. The "known relevant" titles are most useful in signalling the fact that the request statement is probably imperfect and needs further clarification.

4. Occasionally, the requester's estimate of the volume of the relevant literature published on the subject of his request, within the time span of MEDLARS, will also signal a request statement that may either be too broad or too narrow. The danger here is that the requester may base his estimate on the request statement rather than on the volume of literature he expects on the *precise* topic of interest.

5. One of the problems is to get the requester to be sufficiently precise when he makes a narrative statement. We do not want him to omit any aspect of interest, but we would like to be able to eliminate certain categories of articles that will be of no possible use to the requester. In other words, we want to know what we can definitely exclude from a search. It is difficult usually for the requester to think in terms of exclusions when he prepares his narrative statement of need. Therefore we must help him to usefully delimit the scope of the search.

This could be done, for example, by incorporating into the request form a brief, carefully designed questionnaire relating to the previously recorded narrative statement. Certain types of exclusions, or limitations of scope, are applicable to many MEDLARS searches. For example, some requesters are interested only in humans, others are interested in both human and animal studies. Some requesters are interested only in particular sexes or age groups (e.g., "young, healthy, adult males"). Experimental studies are the sole concern of some requesters, while clinical case histories are all that is wanted by others. Some will accept all clinical studies, including single case reports, while others are only interested in "large series" of cases Again, one requester will be interested in a particular organ under normal physiological conditions, while another will be concerned with pathological conditions of the same organ, or in certain pathological conditions only (e.g., *not* neoplasms).

Such generally applicable limitations on a search could easily be incorporated into the demand search request form, either in the form of direct questions or by the use of check-off boxes (these would resemble the "check-tags" appearing on the MEDLARS indexing *Data Form* for generally applicable descriptors; e.g., age groups, sex, experimental animals, type of study). Very many request statements could have been made much more exact if the requester had been given this assistance in defining the scope of the search.

Having gone through this questionnaire approach, we should end up with a very precise statement of the requester's information need, including limitations that he would not think to include in his original request statement. We are now able, in our searching strategy, to eliminate a large segment of the data base (within the limitations of the vocabulary) that is of no interest to the requester, allowing us to undertake a broader search in the pertinent segment, while still obtaining a tolerable precision ratio.

6. The request form should also be designed to determine the recall and precision requirements and tolerances of the requester. At its simplest, the form could merely ascertain whether the requester would like all papers making some reference to the subject matter of interest, or whether he wants only papers in which the subject matter is treated centrally Alternatively, it could be made more complex by allowing the requester to choose from a number of alternatives. For example:

"Which would you prefer:

1. A search retrieving about 60% of the relevant articles within MEDLARS, but with about 50% irrelevancy in the search?
2. A search retrieving about 90% of the relevant articles within MEDLARS, but with about 80% irrelevancy in the search?"

• Additional Analyses

The full report of the study contains additional analyses that can merely be mentioned here:

1. *Indexing coverage.* Collectively, the participating requesters knew 1054 relevant articles at the time they make their MEDLARS request, and 89.2% of these were found to be in the system at the time the various searches were conducted. An additional 6.1% of the articles were "not yet indexed." Assuming that these items in the indexing backlog would eventually get into the system, we can say that the ultimate MEDLARS coverage of the relevant journal literature, as known by requesters, was 95%.

2. *Use of foreign language literature.* Although 40-45% of the entire data base consists of foreign articles, the useful foreign language component in the 302 test searches was found to be no more than 16%. In 55 searches (18.2%) only English articles were requested. In an additional 35, some additional language restrictions (e.g., "English, French and German") was imposed. In the 212 searches without language restriction, MEDLARS retrieves roughly in the proportion of 70% English to 30% foreign (English articles are indexed with more terms, on the average). Only 60% of the foreign articles retrieved in these searches could be assessed by the requesters and of these only 40% were judged of value.

3. *Journal usage factors.* It was possible to produce lists of both "depth" and "non-depth" journals ordered on the basis of the number of times each title appeared in the combined random sample of 6491 articles drawn from the 302 searches. From these tabulations it was possible to plot percentage of total retrievals against percentage of total journals cited. As expected, a comparatively small percentage of the journals contributed to a large percentage of the retrievals: the top 10 journals (0.7% of the 1387 separate journals represented in the 6491 retrievals) accounted for approximately 10% of the retrievals; 157 journals (11.3%) accounted for 50% of the retrievals.

4. *Effect of system response time.* Only 21 of the 302 searches (7.0%) were significantly reduced in value by processing delays.

5. *Serendipity value of MEDLARS searches.* Averaged over the 302 searches, it was discovered that requesters were glad to learn of the existence (because of other needs or projects) of 18% of the articles judged "of no value" in relation to the information needs prompting the MEDLARS requests. This, however, is undoubtedly an inflated estimate of the serendipity value of the machine search, because it is based on the requester's evaluation of actual articles spoonfed to him in photocopy form.

6. *Output screening.* Working from search printouts (titles and index terms), neither an M.D. on the staff of the Library (over 10 searches), nor an experienced search analyst (over 19 searches), were able to make "relevance predictions" that closely replicated the actual assessments made by requesters when seeing the articles themselves. On the basis of this performance, they would have screened out about 7% of the irrelevant material over the 29 searches, but at the same time they would have discarded about 8% of the articles subsequently judged relevant.

• Conclusions

The test results have shown that the system is operating, on the average, at about 58% recall and 50% precision. On the average, it retrieves about 65% of the *major value* literature in its base at 50% precision. Averages, however, are somewhat misleading. A scatter diagram shows that few of the individual search results fall in the area bounded by the average ratios ± 5%. Some of the searches appear to have performed very well, with high recall accompanied by high precision. Others achieved completely unsatisfactory recall results. By a careful examination of a sample of searches at each end of the distribution, it has been possible to identify the most important factors governing the success or failure of a MEDLARS search.

We can take the average figures achieved in the test searches by each of the five MEDLARS processing centers and plot them as recall/precision points. By extrapolation from these points, we can hypothesize a generalized MEDLARS performance curve looking something like that of Fig. 3. The fact that, on the average, MEDLARS is operating at 58% recall and 50% precision indicates that, consciously or unconsciously the MEDLARS searchers choose to operate in this general area. It would be possible for MEDLARS to operate at a different performance point on the recall/precision curve of Fig. 3. By broadening of search strategies, the system could obtain a much higher average recall ratio, but this could only be achieved at a much lower average precision. From Fig. 3 it can be seen that there are differences in searching policies between the various centers, center E choosing to operate in a high precision mode, while center A appears to favor higher recall. The other centers use strategies that compromise more between recall and precision.

In operating at 58% recall and 50% precision, MEDLARS is retrieving an average of 175 citations per search. To operate at an average recall of 85–90% and an average precision ratio in the region of 20–25% implies that the system would need to retrieve an average of perhaps 500–600 citations per search. Are requesters willing to scan this many citations (75% of which will be completely irrelevant) in order to obtain a much higher level of recall? Clearly each individual has his own requirements in relation to the tradeoff between recall and precision. It is obviously important that we establish *for each request* the recall requirements and precision tolerances of the requester, thus allowing the search analyst to prepare a strategy geared as required to high recall, high precision, or some compromise point in between.

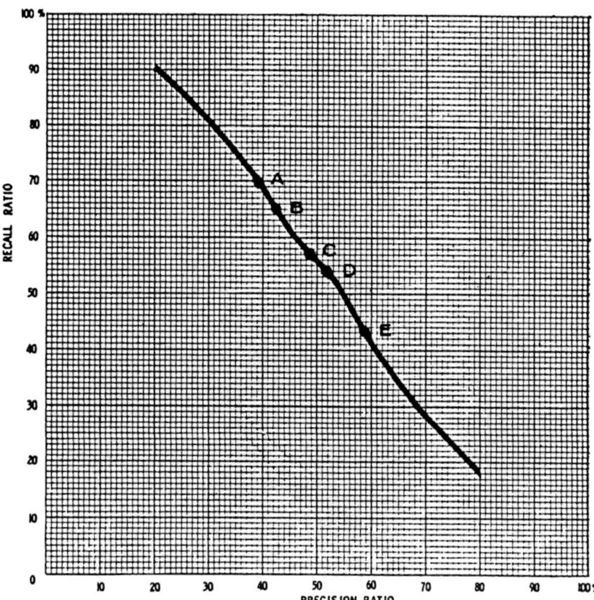

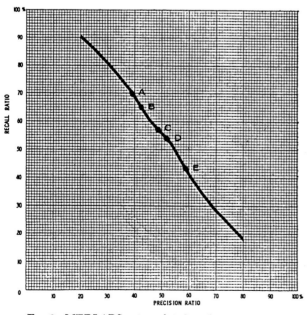

Fig. 3. MEDLARS extrapolated performance curve

The purpose of a comprehensive system evaluation, such as the one reported, is not simply to determine the present performance level but also to discover what needs to be done to upgrade the performance of the present system, i.e., what can be done to move the generalized performance curve of Figure 3 up and over to the right. On the basis of the diagnostic search analyses, it has been possible to make recommendations on actions designed to improve the overall operating efficiency of the system. Some of the more important of these are enumerated below:

1. Direct attention should be devoted to the improvement of user request statements because it is in this area that most immediate benefits in performance appear possible. The present search request form should be re-designed to demand greater participation from the user in making his precise requirements known to the system. All requesters should be required to complete this form personally, even in situations in which the requester makes a personal visit to a MEDLARS center or to his local library.

2. The search request form should record the recall and precision requirements and tolerances of the individual user, and search analysts should make use of this data in the formulation of appropriate strategies.

3. Consideration should be given to the possibility of establishing, and recording in machinable form, standard strategies for search elements likely to recur in a number of different searches.

4. The present distinction between "depth" and "non-depth" journals should be abandoned; each article should be treated on its own merit and sufficient terms assigned to index the extension and intension of its content. According to our best estimates, the present overall level of exhaustivity appears adequate to meet the type of demand currently being made of the system.

5. The further development of the MEDLARS vocabulary should be based primarily on continuous inputs from the indexing and searching operations. The entry vocabulary should be expanded and made readily available to every indexer and searcher.

6. The use of subheadings should be extended but additional precision devices, including links and role indicators, should not be incorporated into the system at the present time.

7. Steps should be taken to effect greater integration between the activities of indexing, searching and vocabulary control.

A large-scale study of the type that has been undertaken exposes the greatest weaknesses of a system, but, no matter how comphehensive, it cannot discover more than a small fraction of its specific (e.g., terminological) inadequacies. The Library is now investigating the feasibility of applying the procedures used in the present evaluation to the continuous monitoring of MEDLARS performance. By these quality control procedures we will: (1) attempt to ensure that each search meets the performance needs of the individual MEDLARS user; and (2) collect necessary data to allow the continued improvement of indexing policies, searching strategies, vocabulary development, and modes of interaction with the user. Only by continuous self-appraisal can a large information system make itself responsive to the needs of the scientific community.

• Acknowledgments

The author wishes to acknowledge the assistance and encouragement given to him by members of the MEDLARS Evaluation Advisory Committee: Charles J. Austin, University of Colorado Medical Center; Julian Bigelow, Institute for Advanced Study, Princeton; Cyril Cleverdon, College of Aeronautics, Cranfield, England; W. D. Climenson, Central Intelligence Agency; Eugene Harris, National Institutes of Health; and Calvin Mooers, Rockford Research Institute. For their advice and criticism he is deeply indebted.

References

1. Austin, C. J., *MEDLARS 1963–1967,* National Library of Medicine, Bethesda, Md., 1968.
2. Cleverdon, C. W., J. Mills, and M. Keen, *Factors Determining the Performance of Indexing Systems, Vol. 1, Design,* ASLIB Cranfield Project, London, 1966.
3. Lancaster, F. W., *Evaluation of the MEDLARS Demand Search Service,* National Library of Medicine, Bethesda, Md., 1968.
4. Lancaster, F. W., *Information Retrieval Systems: Characteristics, Testing, and Evaluation,* Wiley, New York, 1968.

The TREC Conferences

Donna Harman
National Institute of Standards and Technology

Abstract

There have been three TREC conferences to date, with the goal of these conferences being to bring research groups together to discuss their work on a verly large test collection. There has been a wide variation of retrieval techniques reported on, including methods using automatic thesaurii, sophisticated term weighting, natural language techniques, relevance feedback, and advanced pattern matching. As results have been run through a common evaluation package, groups have been able to compare the effectiveness of different techniques, and discuss how differences between the systems affected performance.

1. Introduction

In November of 1992 the first Text REtrieval Conference (TREC-1) was held at NIST. The conference, co-sponsored by ARPA and NIST, brought together information retrieval researchers to discuss their system results on a new large test collection (the TIPSTER collection). This conference became the first in a series of ongoing conferences dedicated to encouraging increased interaction between research groups in industry and academia. From the beginning there has been an almost equal number of universities and companies participating, with an emphasis on exploring many different types of approaches to the text retrieval problem.

The research done by the various groups in the three TRECs has been highly varied, but has followed a general pattern. TREC-1 required significant system rebuilding by most participating groups to the huge increase in the size of the document collection (from a traditional test collection of several megabytes in size to the 2 gigabyte TIPSTER collection). The TREC-1 results should be viewed therefore as only very preliminary due to severe time constraints. The second TREC conference (TREC-2) occured in August of 1993, less than 10 months after the first conference. In addition to 22 of the TREC-1 groups, nine new groups took part, bringing in the total number of participating groups to 31. Many of the original TREC-1 groups were able to "complete" their system rebuilding and tuning, and in general the TREC-2 results show significant improvements over the TREC-1 results. In some senses, however, the TREC-2 results should best be viewed as an excellent baseline for more complex experimentation.

The TREC-3 results reflect some of that more complex experimentation. For some groups that meant more extensive experiments based on their basic system techniques. For other groups it involved trying techniques from other groups and exploring more hybrid approaches. Some groups tried approaches that were radically different from their original approaches. As should be expected, those groups new to TREC had the same scaling problems as seen in TREC-1.

This paper provides an overview of the three TREC conferences, with an extended description of the task and the data. Then results from the three conferences are discussed, with an emphasis on the most recent TREC-3 results. For more details on any of the conferences, including information about specific system techniques and analysis, see the conference proceedings [Harman 1993, 1994, 1995]. (Additionally a special issue of *Information Processing and Management* based on TREC-2 is in press.)

2. The Task and the Participants

The three TREC conferences have all centered around the same task, with a schematic of that task shown in Figure 1. The task is based on traditional information retrieval models, and TREC evaluation has used traditional recall and precision measures. Two types of retrieval are being evaluated in TREC -- retrieval using an "adhoc" query such as a researcher might use in a library environment, and retrieval using a "routing" query such as a profile to filter some incoming document stream.

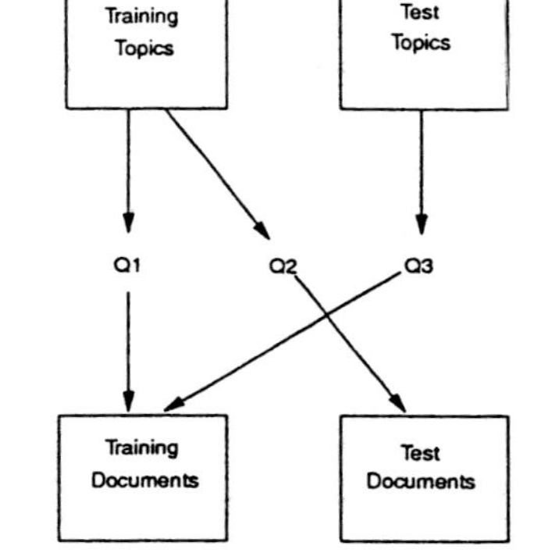

Figure 1. The TREC Task.

Figure 1 shows the various components of TREC and reflects the four data sets (2 sets of topics and 2 sets of documents) that are provided to participants. These data sets (along with a set of relevance judgments for the training topics) are used to construct three sets of queries. Q1 is the set of queries (probably multiple sets) created to help in adjusting a system to this task, to create better weighting algorithms, and in general to train the system for testing. The results of this research are used to create Q2, the routing queries to be used against the test documents. Q3 is the set of queries created from the test topics as adhoc queries for searching against the training documents. The results from searches using Q2 and Q3 are the official test results sent to NIST.

Each of the three TREC conferences used different combinations of topics and documents from the collection for training and test material. The training material has generally consisted of 2 gigabytes of documents, with an additional gigabyte of test material. Each set of test topics has contained 50 topics. For example, TREC-3 used topics 1-150 as training topics, with disks 1 and 2 as the training documents. Topics 101-150 were used as the routing topics for the (disk 3) test documents. Fifty new topics (150-200) were used as the test topics against disks 1 and 2.

Because TREC participants use a wide variety of indexing/knowledge base building techniques and a wide variety of approaches to generate search queries, it is important to establish clear guidelines for the evaluation task. The guidelines deal with the methods of indexing/knowledge base construction and with the methods of generating the queries from the supplied topics. In general, they are constructed to reflect an actual operational environment, and to allow as fair as possible a separation among the diverse query construction approaches. Three generic categories of query construction were defined in TREC-3, based on the amount and kind of manual intervention used.

AUTOMATIC (completely automatic initial query construction)
MANUAL (manual initial query construction)
INTERACTIVE (use of interactive techniques to construct the queries)

The TREC-1 and 2 conferences did not use interactive query construction, but made some preliminary attempts at this with a "feedback" category.

The participants are able to choose from three levels of participation: Category A, full participation, Category B, full participation using a reduced dataset (1/4 of the full document set), and Category C for evaluation only (to allow commercial systems to protect proprietary algorithms). Groups can submit up to two runs for the routing task, the adhoc task, or both, and are requested to send in the top 1000 documents retrieved for each topic for evaluation.

There were 25 groups participating in TREC-1 (see Table 1), plus three contractors from the ARPA TIPSTER project. Twenty-two of these groups returned for TREC-2 plus 9 new groups joined (see Table 2). For TREC-3 there were 33 groups (see Table 3).

Table 1. TREC-1 Participants (12 companies, 13 universities)

Advanced Decision Systems	Bellcore
Carnegie Mellon University	CITRI, Australia
City University, London	Conquest, Inc.
Cornell University	GE Research and Development Center
GTE Laboratories Incorporated	New York University
OCLC Online Computer Library Center, Inc.	PARA Group
PRC, Inc.	Queens College
Siemens Corporate Research Inc.	Systems Environment Corporation
TRW Systems Development Division	Universitaet Dortmund, Germany
University of California - Berkeley	University of Central Florida
University of Illinois at Chicago	University of Pittsburgh
VPI&SU (Virginia Tech)	
TIPSTER Contractors	
HNC Inc.	Syracuse University
University of Massachusetts at Amherst	

Table 2. TREC-2 Participants (14 companies, 17 universities)

Advanced Decision Systems	Bellcore
Carnegie Mellon University	CITRI, Australia
City University, London	Conquest, Inc.
Cornell University	Dalhousie University
Environment Research Institute of Michigan	
GE Research and Development Center	HNC Inc.
Institute for Decision Systems Research	Mead Data Central
New York University	PRC, Inc.
Queens College Rutgers University	Siemens Corporate Research Inc.
Swiss Federal Institute of Technology (ETH)	Syracuse University
Systems Environment Corporation	Thinking Machines Corporation
TRW Systems Development Division	Universitaet Dortmund, Germany
University of California - Berkeley	University of California - UCLA
University of Central Florida	University of Illinois at Chicago
University of Massachusetts at Amherst	VPI&SU (Virginia Tech)
Verity Inc.	

Table 3: TREC-3 Participants (14 companies, 19 universities)

Australian National University	Bellcore
Carnegie Mellon University/CLARITECH	CITRI, Australia
City University, London	Cornell University
Dublin City University	Environment Research Institute of Michigan
Fulcrum	George Mason University
Logicon Operating Systems	Mayo Clinic/Foundation
Mead Data Central	National Security Agency
New York University	NEC Corporation
Queens College	Rutgers University (two groups)
Siemens Corporate Research Inc.	Swiss Federal Institute of Technology (ETH)
TRW/Paracel	Universitaet Dortmund, Germany
University of California - Berkeley	University of Central Florida
University of Massachusetts at Amherst	VPI&SU (Virginia Tech)
University of Minnesota	University of Toronto
Universite de Neuchatel, Switzerland	Verity Inc.
West Publishing Co.	Xerox Palo Alto Research Center

3. The Test Collection

Like most traditional retrieval collections, there are three distinct parts to this collection -- the documents, the queries or topics, and the relevance judgments or "right answers". These test collection components are discussed briefly in the rest of this section.

3.1 The Documents

The documents are distributed as CD-ROMs with about 1 gigabyte of data each, compressed to fit. The following shows the actual contents of each disk.

Disk 1

- WSJ -- *Wall Street Journal* (1987, 1988, 1989)
- AP -- *AP Newswire* (1989)
- ZIFF -- Articles from *Computer Select* disks (Ziff-Davis Publishing)
- FR -- *Federal Register* (1989)
- DOE -- Short abstracts from DOE publications

Disk 2

- WSJ -- *Wall Street Journal* (1990, 1991, 1992)
- AP -- *AP Newswire* (1988)
- ZIFF -- Articles from *Computer Select* disks
- FR -- *Federal Register* (1988)

Disk 3

- SJMN -- *San Jose Mercury News* (1991)
- AP -- *AP Newswire* (1990)
- ZIFF -- Articles from *Computer Select* disks
- PAT -- U.S. Patents (1993)

Table 4 shows some basic document collection statistics. Note that although the collection sizes are roughly equivalent in megabytes, there is a range of document lengths from very short documents (DOE) to very long (FR). Also the range of document lengths within a collection varies. For example, the documents from AP are similar in length (the median and the average length are very close), but the WSJ and ZIFF documents have a wider range of lengths. The documents from the *Federal Register* (FR) have a very wide range of lengths.

Table 4: Document Statistics

Subset of collection	WSJ (disks 1 and 2) SJMN (disk 3)	AP	ZIFF	FR (disks 1 and 2) PAT (disk 3)	DOE
Size of collection (megabytes)					
(disk 1)	270	259	245	262	186
(disk 2)	247	241	178	211	
(disk 3)	290	242	349	245	
Number of records					
(disk 1)	98,732	84,678	75,180	25,960	226,087
(disk 2)	74,520	79,919	56,920	19,860	
(disk 3)	90,257	78,321	161,021	6,711	
Median number of terms per record					
(disk 1)	182	353	181	313	82
(disk 2)	218	346	167	315	
(disk 3)	279	358	119	2896	
Average number of terms per record					
(disk 1)	329	375	412	1017	89
(disk 2)	377	370	394	1073	
(disk 3)	337	379	263	3543	

The documents are uniformly formatted into SGML, with a DTD included for each collection to allow easy parsing.

<DOC>
<DOCNO> WSJ880406-0090 </DOCNO>
<HL> AT&T Unveils Services to Upgrade Phone Networks Under Global Plan </HL>
<AUTHOR> Janet Guyon (WSJ Staff) </AUTHOR>
<DATELINE> NEW YORK </DATELINE>
<TEXT>
American Telephone & Telegraph Co. introduced the first of a new generation of phone services with broad implications for computer and communications
.
.
</TEXT>
</DOC>

3.2 The Topics

In designing the TREC task, there was a conscious decision made to provide "user need" statements rather than more traditional queries. Two major issues were involved in this decision. First there was a desire to allow a wide range of query construction methods by keeping the topic (the need statement) distinct from the query (the actual text submitted to the system). The second issue was the ability to increase the amount of information available about each topic, in particular to include with each topic a clear statement of what criteria make a document relevant.

The topics were designed to mimic a real user's need, and were written by people who are actual users of a retrieval system. Although the subject domain of the topics was diverse, some consideration was given to the documents to be searched. The topics were constructed by doing trial retrievals against a sample of the document set, and then those topics that had roughly 25 to 100 hits in that sample were used. This created a range of broader and narrower topics.

The following is one of the topics used in TREC-1 and TREC-2.

<top>
<head> Tipster Topic Description
<num> Number: 066
<dom> Domain: Science and Technology
<title> Topic: Natural Language Processing

<desc> Description:
Document will identify a type of natural language processing technology which is being developed or marketed in the U.S.

<narr> Narrative:
A relevant document will identify a company or institution developing or marketing a natural language processing technology, identify the technology, and identify one or more features of the company's product.

<con> Concept(s):
1. natural language processing
2. translation, language, dictionary, font
3. software applications

<fac> Factor(s):
<nat> Nationality: U.S.
</fac>
<def> Definition(s):
</top>

Each topic is formatted in the same standard method to allow easier automatic construction of queries. Besides a beginning and an end marker, each topic has a number, a short title, and a one-sentence description. There is a narrative section which is aimed at providing a complete description of document relevance for the assessors. Each topic also has a concepts section with a list of assorted concepts related to the topic. This section is designed to provide a mini-knowledge base about a topic such as a real searcher might possess. Additionally each topic can have a definitions section and/or a factors section. The definition section has one or two of the definitions critical to a human understanding of the topic. The factors section is included to allow easier automatic query building by listing specific items from the narrative that constrain the documents that are relevant. Two particular factors were used in the TREC-2 topics: a time factor (current, before a given date, etc.) and a nationality factor (either involving only certain countries or excluding certain countries).

The new topics used in TREC-3 reflect a slight change. The topics in TREC-1 and 2 (topics 1-150) were not only very long, but contained complex structures. They were intended to represent the long-standing information needs for which a user might be willing to create elaborate topics and therefore are more suited to the routing task than to the adhoc task, where users are likely to ask much shorter questions.

The new topics used in TREC-3 (topics 151-200) are not only much shorter, but missing the complex structure of the earlier topics. In particular the concepts field has been removed because it was felt that real adhoc questions would not contain this field and because inclusion of the field discouraged research into techniques for expansion of "too short" user need expressions.

In addition to being shorter, the new topics were written by the same group of users that did the assessments. In specific, each of the new topics were developed from a genuine need for information brought in by the assessors. Each assessor constructed their own topics from some initial statements of interest, and performed all the relevance assessments on these topics (with a few exceptions).

The following is one of the new topics used in TREC-3.

<num> Number: 168
<title> Topic: Financing AMTRAK

<desc> Description:
A document will address the role of the Federal Government in financing the operation of the National Railroad Transportation Corporation (AMTRAK).

<narr> Narrative: A relevant document must provide information on the government's responsibility to make AMTRAK an economically viable entity. It could also discuss the privatization of AMTRAK as an alternative to continuing government subsidies. Documents comparing government subsidies given to air and bus transportation with those provided to AMTRAK would also be relevant.

</top>

3.3 The Relevance Judgments

The relevance judgments are of critical importance to a test collection. For each topic it is necessary to compile a list of relevant documents; hopefully as comprehensive a list as possible. For the TREC task, three possible methods for finding the relevant documents could have been used. In the first method, full relevance judgments could have been made on over one million documents, for each topic, resulting in over 100 million judgments. This was clearly impossible. As a second approach, a random sample of the documents could have been taken, with relevance judgments done on that sample only. The problem with this approach is that a random sample that is large enough to find on the order of 200 relevant documents per topic is a very large random sample, and is likely to result in insufficient relevance judgments. The third method, the one used in TREC, was to make relevance judgments on the sample of documents selected by the various participating systems. This method is known as the pooling method, and has been used successfully in creating other collections [Sparck Jones & van Rijsbergen 1975]. The sample was constructed by taking the top 100 documents retrieved by each system for a given topic and merging them into a pool for relevance assessment. This is a valid sampling method since all the systems used ranked retrieval methods, with those documents most likely to be relevant returned first. The sample is then given to human assessors for relevance judgments.

Evaluation of retrieval results using the assessments from this sampling method is based on the assumption that the vast majority of relevant documents have been found and that documents that have not been judged can be assumed to be not relevant. A test of this assumption was made between TREC-2 and TREC-3, using TREC-2 results. Thirty-six (18 adhoc and 18 routing) topics were selected for additional relevance assessments, using a pseudo-random selection based only on the number of original relevant documents and on selecting equal numbers of topics from each assessor. For each selected topic, a new pool of documents was created by taking the top 200 documents from 7 different runs known to achieve good results and to have little overlap in their document selection. New judgments were made on this pool, using the same judges that made the original decisions for each topic.

Table 5 gives the results of this test. On average, 30 new relevant documents (16%) were found for each of the topics, with a median of only 21 (11%) new relevant documents per topic. The median is much lower than the average because of the relatively large number of new documents found for those 5 topics with over 30% additional relevant documents found.

Table 5: Analysis of Completeness of Relevance Judgments (TREC-2)

Percent New Rel.	No. of Topics	Average New Rel.	Average Total Rel.	Average No. Jud.	Average "Hardness"
0%	5	0	46	381	0.3477
1-9%	11	10	173	257	0.4190
10-19%	9	36	277	343	0.2610
20-29%	6	47	185	190	0.3660
30-33%	5	73	242	233	0.5212
Average (over all 36 topics)		30	193	282	
Median		21	190	220	
Average (over the 18 routing topics)		18	188	373	
Median		8	160	376	
Average (over the 18 adhoc topics)		42	197	190	
Median		28	209	150	

There is some correlation between the number of new relevant documents found and the original number of relevant documents, particularly in that topics with few relevant documents initially tended to have few new ones found. In contrast, there is no correlation between the number of new relevant documents found and the number of new judgments made, or between the number of new relevant found for a topic and the "hardness" of that topic (a measure of average system performance for that topic). More new relevant documents were found for the adhoc task than for the routing task. This may reflect more "available" relevant documents for the adhoc task (twice the amount of searchable text) or may be caused by the more complete and accurate queries used in routing task due to the training data.

A different measure of the effect of pooling can be seen by examining the overlap of retrieved documents. Table 6 shows the statistics from the merging operations in the three TREC conferences. For TREC-1 and TREC-2 the top 100 documents from each run (33 runs in TREC-1 and 40 runs in TREC-2) could have produced a total of 3300 and 4000 documents to be judged (for the adhoc task). The average number of documents actually judged per topic (those that were unique) was 1279 (39%) for TREC-1 and 1106 (28%) for TREC-2. Note that even though the number of runs has increased by more than 20% (adhoc), the number of unique documents found has almost halved. The percentage of relevant documents found, however, has not changed much. The more accurate results going from TREC-1 to TREC-2 mean that fewer "noisy" non-relevant documents are being found by the systems. This trend was continued in TREC-3, even though the pooling method was changed.

Table 6: Overlap of Submitted Results

	Adhoc			Routing		
	Possible	Actual	Relevant	Possible	Actual	Relevant
TREC-1	3300	1279 (39%)	277 (22%)	2200	1067 (49%)	371 (35%)
TREC-2	4000	1106 (28%)	210 (19%)	4000	1466 (37%)	210 (14%)
TREC-3						
at 100	4800	1005 (21%)	146 (15%)	4900	703 (14%)	146 (21%)
at 200	9600	1946 (20%)	196 (10%)	9800	1333 (14%)	187 (14%)

Because of expected constraints in assessor time, only one run from each TREC-3 group was judged, with the groups specifying which run. However, due to the increase in overlap (as shown in Table 6), and more efficient judging, extra time became available and the decision was made to judge the top 200 documents for those runs. Table 6 gives the results of the TREC-3 mergings at both 100 documents and 200 documents. The percentage of unique documents found continues to drop compared with TREC-2, with a major drop for the routing. The total number of relevant documents found in TREC-1, TREC-2, and TREC-3 has dropped only somewhat, however, and that drop has been caused by a deliberate tightening of the topics between TREC-1 and TREC-2. Table 6 also shows the drop in relevant documents found beyond the 100 document cutoff. This not only reflects the ranking done by the systems, but shows the diminishing numbers of relevant documents to be found even as the judged pool continues to grow.

After pooling, each topic was judged by a single assessor to insure the best consistency of judgment. Some testing of this consistency was done after TREC-2, and showed an average agreement between two judges of about 80%. More consistency testing will be done in the future.

4. Evaluation

An important element of TREC was to provide a common evaluation forum. Standard recall/precision figures were calculated for each TREC system the results. Figure 2 shows typical recall/precision curves. The x axis plots the recall values at fixed levels of recall, where

$$Recall = \frac{\textit{number of relevant items retrieved}}{\textit{total number of relevant items in collection}}$$

The y axis plots the average precision values at those given recall values, where precision is calculated by

$$Precision = \frac{number\ of\ relevant\ items\ retrieved}{total\ number\ of\ items\ retrieved}$$

These curves represent averages over the 50 topics. The averaging method was developed many years ago [Salton & McGill 1983] and is well accepted by the information retrieval community. The curves show system performance across the full range of retrieval, i.e., at the early stage of retrieval where the highly-ranked documents give high accuracy or precision, and at the final stage of retrieval where there is usually a low accuracy, but more complete retrieval. Note that the use of these curves assumes a ranked output from a system. Systems that provide an unranked set of documents are known to be less effective and therefore were not tested in the TREC program.

The curves in figure 2 show that system A has a much higher precision at the low recall end of the graph and therefore is more accurate. System B however has higher precision at the high recall end of the curve and therefore will give a more complete set of relevant documents, assuming that the user is willing to look further in the ranked list.

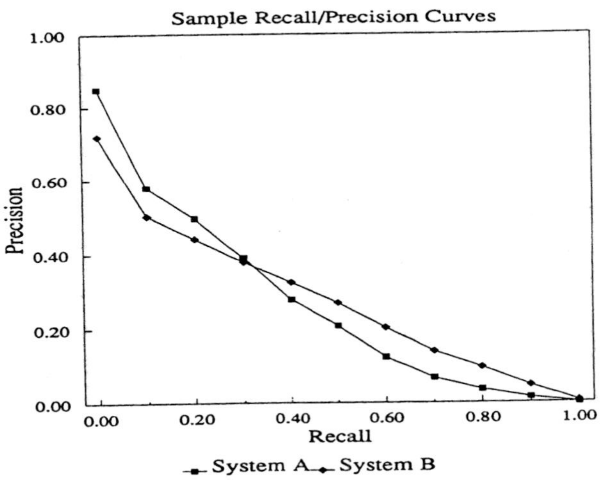

Figure 2. A Sample Recall/Precision Curve.

5. Results

The following is a brief summary of the TREC results. For more details, readers are referred to the proceedings. All the systems mentioned in the discussions have individual papers in the specific conference proceedings, but the references have been omitted due to space limitations.

5.1 TREC-1 Results

The major outcome of TREC-1 was that the TREC task could be done at all. The deadlines for submitting results were very tight, data generally arrived later than expected, and the fact that 27 groups turned in results required heroic efforts by many participants. The huge scale-up in the size of the document collection required major work from all groups in rebuilding their systems. Much of this work was simply a system engineering task: finding reasonable data structures to use, getting indexing routines to be efficient enough to finish indexing the data, finding enough storage to handle the large inverted files and other structures, etc.

The results of the TREC-1 conference should therefore be viewed only as a preliminary baseline for what could be expected from systems working with large test collections. Groups had no time for the system "tuning" of algorithms to handle the large numbers of documents. The longer documents also required major adjustments to the algorithms themselves (or loss of performance). This is particularly true for the very long documents in the *Federal Register*. Since a relevant document might contain only one or two relevant sentences, many algorithms needed adjustment from working with the abstract length documents found in the old collections. Additionally many documents were composite stories, with different topics, and this caused problems for most algorithms.

The second reason these results are preliminary is that groups were working blindly as to what constitutes a relevant document. There were no reliable relevance judgments for training, and the use of the long topics was completely new. This means that results were heavily influenced by an almost random selection of what parts of the topic to use. Groups also had to make often primitive adjustments to basic algorithms in order to get results, with little evidence of how well these adjustments were working. The large scale of the whole evaluation precluded any tuning without some relevance judgments, and the relevance judgments that were provided were generally sparse and sometimes inaccurate. These problems particularly affected those systems that needed training for routing.

Because of the preliminary nature of the results, very little can be said about which techniques seemed to perform the best. It was clear that the simple systems did the task well, much better than could have been expected. The automatic construction of queries from the topics did as well as, or better than, manual construction of queries, and this was encouraging for groups supporting the use of simple natural language interfaces for retrieval systems.

5.2 TREC-2 Results

In general the TREC-2 results showed significant improvements over the TREC-1 results. Many of the original TREC-1 groups were able to "complete" their system rebuilding and tuning tasks. The results for TREC-2 therefore can be viewed as the "best first-pass" that most groups can accomplish on this large amount of data. The adhoc results in particular represent baseline results from the scaling-up of current algorithms to large test collections. The better systems produced similar results, results that are comparable to those seen using these algorithms on smaller test collections.

Figure 3 shows the recall/precision curves for the six TREC-2 groups with the highest non-interpolated average precision using automatic construction of queries. The results marked "INQ001" are the INQUERY system from the University of Massachusetts (Callan, Croft & Broglio paper). This system uses probabilistic term weighting and a probabilistic inference net to combine various topic and document features. The "dortQ2" results from the University of Dortmund come from using polynomial regression on the training data to find weights for various pre-set term features (Fuhr, Pfeifer, Bremkamp, Pollmann & Buckley paper). The "Brkly3" results from the University of California at Berkeley come from performing logistic regression analysis to learn optimal weighting for various term frequency measures (Cooper, Chen & Gey paper). The "CLARTA" system from the CLARIT Corporation expands each topic with noun phrases found in a thesaurus that is automatically generated for each topic (Evans & Lefferts paper). The "crnlL2" run is the SMART system from Cornell University (Buckley, Allan & Salton paper), but using less than optimal term weightings (by mistake). The "lsiasm" results are from Bellcore (Dumais paper). This group uses latent semantic indexing to create a reduced dimension vector represention for the documents. The run marked "lsiasm" represents only the base SMART pre-processing results, however. Due to processing errors the "improved" LSI run produced unexpectedly poor results.

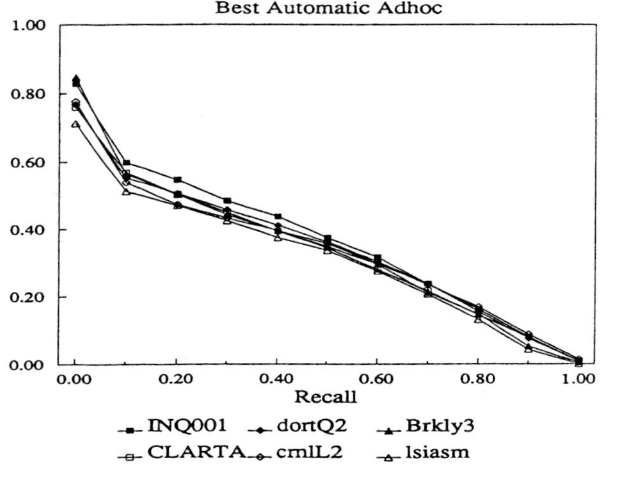

Figure 3 -- Best Automatic Adhoc Results

Several comments can be made with respect to these adhoc results. First, the better results (most of the automatic results and the three top manual results) are very similar and it is unlikely that there is any statistical differences between them. There is clearly no "best" method. Whereas the averages for the systems may be similar, however, the systems do better on different topics and retrieve different subsets of the relevant documents.

A second point that should be made is that the automatic query construction methods continue to perform as well as the manual construction methods. Two groups (the INQUERY system and the CLARIT system) did explicit comparision of manually-modified queries versus those that were not modified and concluded that manual modification provided no benefits. The three sets of results based on completely manually-generated queries had even poorer performance than the manually-modified queries. Note that this result was specific to the very rich TREC-2 topics; it was not clear that this would hold for the short topics normally seen in other retrieval environments.

The routing results showed the most improvement over TREC-1. Some of this improvement was due to the availability of large numbers of accurate relevance judgments for training (unlike TREC-1), but most of the improvements came from new research by participating groups into the best ways of using the training data.

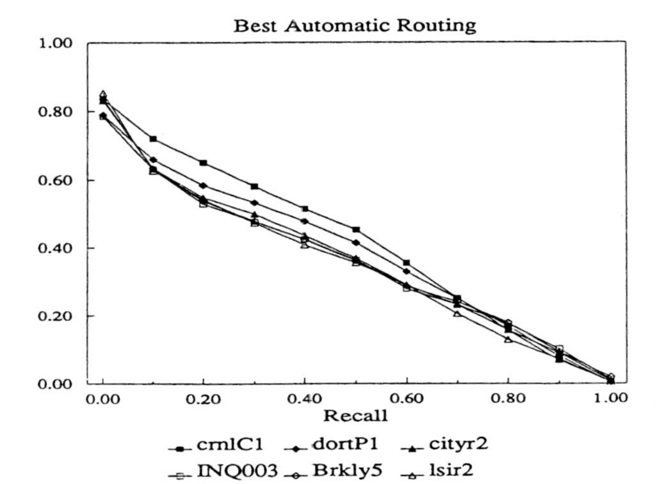

Figure 4 -- Best Automatic Routing Results

Figure 4 shows the recall/precision curves for the six TREC-2 groups with the highest non-interpolated average precision using automatic construction of the routing queries. The plot marked "crnlC1" is the SMART system, using the basic Rocchio relevance feedback algorithms, and adding many terms (up to 500) from the relevant training documents to the terms in the topic. The "dortP1" results come from using a probabilistically-based relevance feedback instead of the vector-space algorithm, and adding only 20 terms from the relevant documents to each query. These two systems have the best routing results. The "Brkly5" system uses logistic regression on both the general frequency variables used in their adhoc approach and on the query-specific relevance data available for training with the routing topics. The results marked "cityr2" are from City University, London (Robertson, Walker & Hancock-Beaulieu paper). This group automatically selected variable numbers of terms (10-25) from the training documents for each topic (the topics themselves were not used as term sources), and then used traditional probabilistic reweighting to weight these terms. The "INQ003" results also use probabilistic reweighting, but use the topic terms, expanded by 30 new terms per topic from the training documents. The results marked "lsir2" are more latent semantic indexing results from Bellcore. This run was made by creating a filter of the singular-value decomposition vector sum or centroid of all relevant documents for a topic (and ignoring the topic itself).

As was the case with the adhoc topics, the automatic query construction methods continue to perform as well as, or in this case, better than the manual construction methods. All six results with manually-generated queries perform worse than the six runs with automatically-generated queries. The availability of the training data allows an automatic tuning of the queries that would be difficult to duplicate manually without extensive analysis.

Unlike the adhoc results, there are two runs ("crnlC1" and "dortP1") that are clearly better than the others, with a likely significant difference between the "crnlC1" results and the "dortP1" results and also likely significant differences between these results and the rest of the automatically-generated query results. In particular the use of so many terms (up to 500) for query expansion by the Cornell group was one of the most interesting findings in TREC-2 and represents a departure from past results (see Buckley, Allan, & Salton paper for more on this).

5.3 TREC-3 Results

The TREC-3 results show improvements over the TREC-2 results, but more importantly feature some very complex retrieval techniques. A dominant issue in the adhoc task was the removal of the concepts field in the topics and many of the participating groups designed their experiments around techniques to expand the shorter and less "rich" topics.

Figure 5 shows the recall/precision curves for the 6 TREC-3 groups with the highest non-interpolated average precision using automatic construction of the adhoc queries.

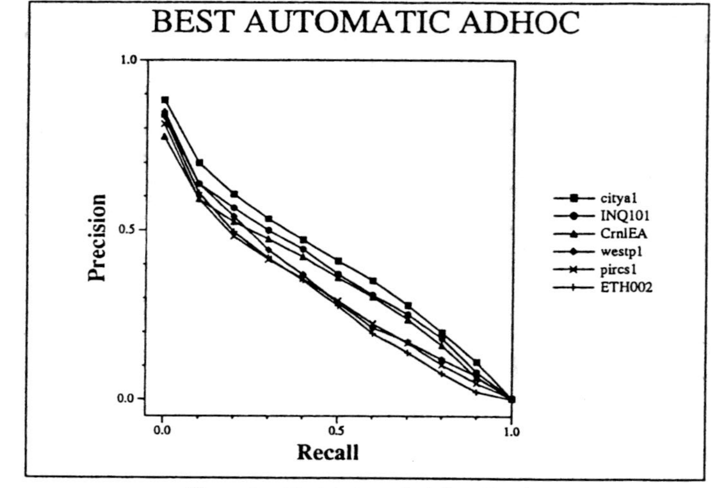

Figure 5 -- Best Automatic Adhoc Results

cityal -- City University, London (Robertson, Walker, Jones, Hancock-Beaulieu & Gatford paper), used the same term weighting as in TREC-2, but expanded the topics by up to 40 terms (average around 20) automatically selected from the top 30 documents retrieved (on a trial retrieval run).

INQ101 -- University of Massachusetts at Amherst (Broglio, Callan, Croft & Nachbar paper) used their probabilistic inference net technique and expanded the topics by 30 phrases that were automatically selected from a phrase "thesaurus" that had been previously built (automatically) from the entire corpus of documents.

CrnlEA -- Cornell University (Buckley, Salton, Allan & Singhal paper) used the vector-space SMART system, and a massive Rocchio topic expansion (500 terms + 10 phrases) based on the top 30 documents.

westpl -- West Publishing Company (Thompson, Turtle, Yang & Flood paper) used their commercial product (based on the same inference method used in INQ101), but did only minimal topic expansion.

pircsl -- Queens College, CUNY (Kwok, Grunfeld & Lewis paper) used a spreading activation model, with topic expansion by allowing activation from the top 6 documents in addition to the terms in the original topic.

ETH002 -- Swiss Federal Institute of Technology (ETH) (Knaus, Mittendorf & Schauble paper) used a completely new method in TREC-3 based on combining information from three very different retrieval techniques (a vector-space system, a Hidden Markov passage retrieval method and a topic expansion method based on document links generated automatically using on common phrases).

All of the systems except the Cornell system also used some form of passage retrieval or subdocuments to add precision to their results. Both main types of term expansion, term expansion based on a pre-constructed thesaurus and term expansion based on selected terms from the top X documents, worked well. The top 3 runs (cityal, INQ101, and crnlEA) have excellent performance (see Figure 5) in the "middle" recall range (30 to 80%), with this performance likely coming from the query expansion.

Figure 6 shows the recall/precision curves for the 6 TREC-3 groups with the highest non-interpolated average precision using manual construction of adhoc queries.

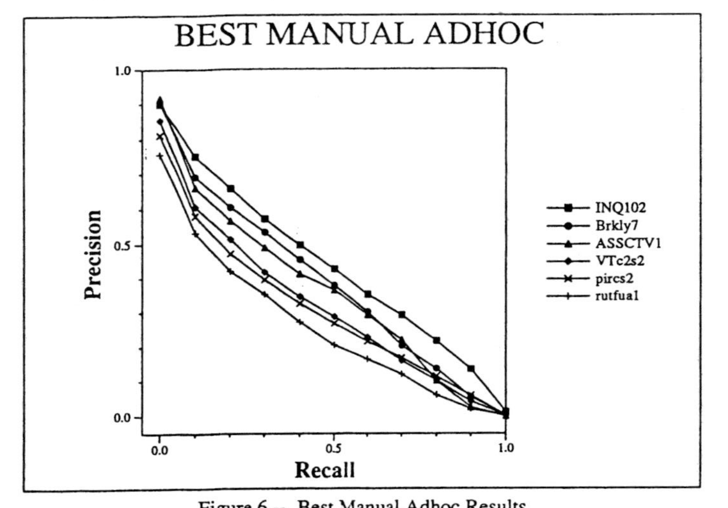

Figure 6 -- Best Manual Adhoc Results

INQ102 -- a manual modification of the INQ101 run, with strict rules for the modifications to only allow removal of words and phrases, modification of weights, and addition of proximity restrictions.

Brkly7 -- University of California, Berkeley (Cooper, Chen & Gey paper) used a manual expansion of the queries by adding synonyms found from other sources, with the retrieval system being the logistic regression model used in TREC-2, but with different term distribution factors.

ASSCTV1 -- Mead Data Central, Inc (Lu & Keefer paper) did a manual expansion of queries using an associative thesaurus built from the TREC data and used the SMART system as the retrieval tool.

VTc2s2 -- Virginia Tech (Shaw & Fox paper) used a combination of multiple types of queries, with 2 types of natural language vector-space queries and 3 types of manually constructed P-Norm ("soft Boolean") queries.

pircs2 -- a modification of the PIRCS system to use manually constructed soft Boolean queries.

rutfual -- Rutgers University (Kantor paper) used data fusion methods to combine the retrieval ranks from three different retrieval schemes (2 Boolean and one natural language) all using the INQUERY system.

In TREC-3, as opposed to TRECs 1 and 2, the manual query construction methods performed better than their automatic counterparts. The removal of some of the topic structure (the concepts) has allowed differences to appear that could not be seen in earlier TRECs. Topic expansion was necessary to produce top scores, and the superiority of the manual expansion over no expansion in the Berkeley runs should not be surprising. Less clear is why the manual modifications in the INQ102 run showed superior performance to their automatic run with no modifications. The likely explanation is that the automatic term expansion methods are relatively uncontrolled in TREC-3 and manual intervention plays an important role.

For the TREC-3 routing, many groups made only minor modifications to their TREC-2 techniques (and concentrated on the adhoc task). Other groups used the opportunity to try massive query expansion, while still others tried techniques for selecting specific terms for expansion.

Figure 7 shows the recall/precision curves for the six TREC-3 groups with the highest non-interpolated average precision using automatic construction of the routing queries.

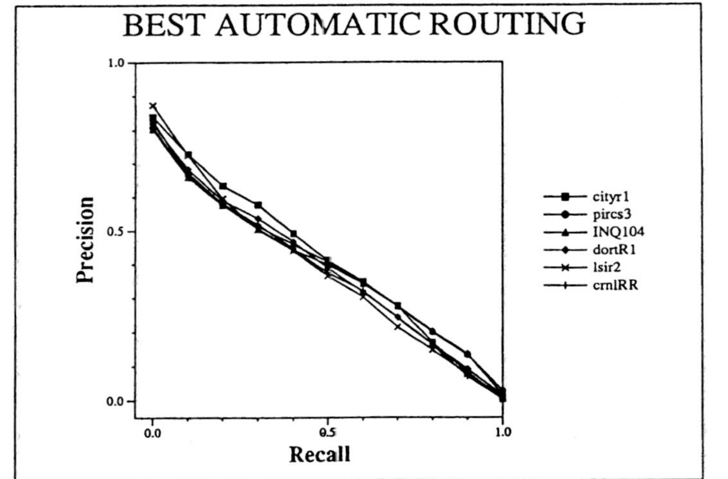

Figure 7 -- Best Automatic Routing Results

cityr1 -- City University, London used the relevant documents to learn the optimal terms to use for query expansion, selecting only about 11 terms on average.

pircs3 -- Queens College, CUNY used spreading activation based on a selection of only about 12-35% of the relevant material (subdocuments) available.

INQ104 -- University of Massachusetts at Amherst used an adaptation of the Rocchio algorithm, picking the top 32 terms plus 30 terms "in proximity" to those terms.

dortR1 -- University of Dortmund, Germany (Walczuch, Fuhr, Pollman & Sievers paper) used the SMART system with Rocchio expansion and different term weighting.

lsir2 -- Bellcore, used latent semantic indexing to construct a centroid of the relevant documents, similar to their TREC-2 routing run.

CrnlRR -- Cornell University used Rocchio feedback with over 500 terms, similar to the TREC-2 work.

The routing results showed some improvement over the TREC-2 results, but also showed some very interesting extensions of the research started in TREC-2. The term optimization done by City University and the massive query expansion done by several of the other groups illustrate the broad spectrum of machine learning techniques that seem to work well in the routing task. As in TREC-2, the manually-constructed queries had much poorer results; the use of extensive training data allows automatic query construction that is impossible to duplicate manually.

In addition to the main tasks done in TREC-3, four issues were further explored by some of the groups.

- there was increased attention to the efficiency issues, an area that TREC has not addressed sufficiently.
- Several groups tried experiments using the different document "subcollections" to simulate distributed server operations.
- TREC-3 introduced a second language (Spanish) to the task, with four groups working with a small Spanish collection in addition to their work in English.
- There was a heightened interest in the interactive query construction method, with several groups banding together to construct a trial set of rules for evaluation of interactive systems.

6. Summary

The TREC conferences have demonstrated a wide range of different approaches to the retrieval of text from large document collections. There has been significant improvement in retrieval performance -- the Cornell group calculated about a 20% improvement in their results for the adhoc task between EACH TREC. The conference itself has provided the opportunity for an open exchange between the research groups in universities and in commercial organizations.

There will be a fourth TREC conference in 1995, and most of the systems that participated in TREC-3 will be back, along with additional groups. Besides the main tasks, additional "tracks" or special interest groups will be tried, including the areas of retrieval in other languages, interactive retrieval, and retrieval from multiple subcollections.

7. References

Harman D. (Ed.). (1993). *The First Text REtrieval Conference (TREC-1).* National Institute of Standards and Technology Special Publication 500-207, Gaithersburg, Md. 20899.

Harman D. (Ed.). (1994). *The Second Text REtrieval Conference (TREC-2).* National Institute of Standards and Technology Special Publication 500-215, Gaithersburg, Md. 20899.

Harman D. (Ed.). (1995). *The Third Text REtrieval Conference (TREC-3).* National Institute of Standards and Technology Special Publication 500-225, Gaithersburg, Md. 20899.

Salton, G. and McGill, M. (1983). *Introduction to Modern Information Retrieval.* New York, NY.: McGraw-Hill.

Sparck Jones K. and Van Rijsbergen C. (1975). *Report on the Need for and Provision of an "Ideal" Information Retrieval Test Collection*, British Library Research and Development Report 5266, Computer Laboratory, University of Cambridge.

Chapter 5
Models

Getting Beyond Boole 265
W.S. Cooper

A Non-Classical Logic for Information Retrieval 268
C.J. van Rijsbergen

A Vector Space Model for Automatic Indexing 273
G. Salton, A. Wong, and C.S. Yang

The Probability Ranking Principle in IR 281
S.E. Robertson

Inference Networks for Document Retrieval 287
H. Turtle and W.B. Croft

ASK for Information Retrieval. Part I. Background and Theory 299
N.J. Belkin, R.N. Oddy, and H.M. Brooks

INTRODUCTION

As we have described in Chapter 2, the first researchers in IR soon realised that the computer could provide a huge range of possible alternatives to the catalogues, classification codes, and so forth that had provided the basis for manual IR systems. This realisation, coupled with the striking results of the Cranfield experiments, engendered a strongly empirical approach to research in IR that has continued to the present day. Since the mid-seventies, this *practice-based* approach has increasingly been augmented by more formal, *theory-based* approaches that try to *model* various aspects of an information retrieval system. Given an appropriate model, it is now possible not just to state that retrieval strategy A is better than retrieval strategy B (using one of the evaluation mechanisms discussed in Chapter 4) but also to provide a rationale (either a posteriori or, preferably, a priori) for why this should be so.

An important advantage of adopting a model-based approach to IR is that any model will be based on some set of underlying *assumptions*. The need to spell these out in detail when the model is being developed facilitates the analysis and rationalisation that may be necessary if limitations become apparent when the model is implemented with real sets of documents, queries, and relevance judgements. In this way, theory drives experiment by suggesting new tests that should be carried out, and experiment drives theory by providing results that can be used to modify, and hopefully improve, the original model. The linking of theory and practice means that model-based approaches play an increasingly justified role in IR research, with the improvements in effectiveness resulting from their use (as exemplified by the techniques discussed in Chapter 6) now starting to be translated into operational systems (as discussed in Chapter 7). At the same time, as the TREC experience shows, in a wholly new study and test situation, the relationship between underlying general model and specific implementation techniques may be uncertain or complicated, particularly when many individual devices and strategies are combined and a cheerful pragmatism reigns. However, the fact that some explicitly model-based approaches have consistently performed well in TREC reinforces the case for seeking explanatory models for IR.

CHARACTERISTICS OF IR MODELS

There are many levels at which IR procedures can be modelled, as is easily illustrated by considering the *cognitive* models that are currently attracting much interest (Ellis, 1989; Ingwersen, 1992). These are discussed in more detail below, but for the present we need to note merely that they seek to provide a *holistic* view of IR. The models thus include not only the retrieval mechanism that is used to match a query with a set of documents but also: the ways in which the user's information need can be formulated as a query that can be searched by that mechanism; the human-computer interaction that needs to take place to ensure the most appropriate processing of that query; and the social and cognitive environments in which that interaction takes place. The models that are appropriate in a context such as this are clearly very different in generality, and equally different in their disciplinary bases, to the models (such as the *vector processing* and *probabilistic* models described below) that provide an explicit statement of the precise workings of the searching mechanism, i.e., of the means by which the set of terms describing a query is matched against corresponding sets of terms representing each of the documents in a database (with the various classes of model, and specific models within a class, differing only in the precise way in which these matching operations are carried out). Intermediate between these two extremes are models, such as those based on *hypertext* (see, e.g., Agosti et al., 1992) or on *distributed expert systems* (see, e.g., Belkin et al., 1987), that define an approach to searching but that do not necessarily specify in detail how this approach should be implemented.

The models that are used in IR are increasingly quantitative in nature, drawing upon disciplines such as logical inference, statistics, and set theory, and while this orientation is markedly at variance with the purely empirical bases of much early experimentation in IR, there are very good reasons for such an orientation. In an early review of models in IR, Robertson (1977a) noted that he had focused on mathematical models "not because mathematics *per se* is necessarily a good thing but because the setting up of a mathematical model generally presupposes a careful formal analysis of the problem and specification of the assumptions and explicit formulation of the way in which the model depends on the assumptions." Such a quantitative approach is, of course, both less applicable and less appropriate to approaches that draw their inspiration from the behavioural and cognitive sciences.

We have noted, in Chapter 1, that the Reader excludes material under the general heading of library and information science. More specifically, in the present context, we have excluded material relating to what is commonly referred to as *infometrics* or *bibliometrics.* This covers a range of quantitative topics based upon the *bibliographical distributions* that underlie many library and information phenomena, such as the analysis of library circulation data, and the publication and citation behaviour of academic researchers (see, e.g., Fairthorne, 1969; Garfield, 1979; Tague-Sutcliffe, 1994). While there is a strong modelling component in much of this work, it generally has little direct relevance to the indexing and searching tasks that lie at the heart of IR, that on the distribution of word occurrence frequencies in natural language texts being the obvious exception. Finally, we note that the need to choose a small, discrete set of papers for inclusion in the Reader necessarily means that the discussion focuses on the distinct characteristics of a small number of types of model. It must, however, be emphasised that there are strong relationships between the various models that we describe (Ellis, 1992; Robertson et al., 1982; Turtle and Croft, 1992).

LOGICAL MODELS

Boolean logic has long formed the basis for the overwhelming majority of both numeric database systems and conventional IR systems. In a Boolean retrieval system, the query terms are linked by the logical operators AND, OR, and NOT, and the search engine then returns those documents that have combinations of terms satisfying the logical constraints of the query, with supplementary facilities being provided to allow proximity and truncation searching. The inclusion of both types of search facility in online database-host systems, as well as the ability to restrict searches to particular fields or date ranges, etc., permits quite sophisticated types of query to be searched online (see, e.g., Hartley et al., 1990).

The Boolean model is well understood, but has inherent limitations that lessen its attractiveness for text searching (Cooper, 1988; Salton et al., 1983). The first major problem is that, without a fair degree of training, it is difficult to formulate any but the simplest of queries using the Boolean operators; accordingly, trained intermediaries often have to carry out a search on behalf of the user who has the actual information need. Secondly, there is very little control over the size of the output produced by a particular query. Without a detailed knowledge of the contents of the file, the searcher will be unable to predict a priori how many records will satisfy the logical constraints of a given query, with the result that several reformulations of a query may be required before an acceptable volume of output is produced. A third problem is that Boolean retrieval results in a simple *partition* of the database into two discrete subsets, namely, those records that match the query and those that do not. All of the retrieved records are thus presumed to be of equal usefulness to the searcher, and there is no mechanism by which they can be ranked in order of decreasing probability of relevance. Finally, there are no obvious means by which one can reflect the relative importance of different components of the query, since Boolean searching implicitly assumes that all of the terms have weights of either unity or zero, depending upon whether they happen to be present or absent in the query.

These limitations have encouraged the development of *fuzzy set* models, which relax the strict class membership characteristics of Boolean logic and which attracted much attention in the early eighties (Bookstein, 1986). More recently, van Rijsbergen (1986) has suggested that the principal responsibility of an IR system is the selection of those documents d from a database in response to a query q that satisfy the logical implication $d \rightarrow q$, where "$\rightarrow$" denotes the type of implication that is defined by the particular logic that is adopted and where d and q are formal representations of the semantics of the document and the query. This is clearly far removed from the way that most people view the act of retrieval; however, it is possible to interpret other retrieval models, including the Boolean and probabilistic models, as forms of logical implication, and the approach has already been substantially developed, most notably in the *inference networks* that are discussed below in the section on probabilistic models.

VECTOR PROCESSING MODELS

Apart from Boolean logic, the model that has had most influence on the development of IR and, subsequently, on the development of operational IR systems, is the vector processing model, which provided the basis for the extended series of experiments carried out by Salton and his associates (Salton, 1971, 1981) and which was implemented as the SMART system that is described in Chapter 7. The essential idea is that indexing terms are regarded as the coordinates of a *multidimensional information space.* Documents and queries are represented by vectors in which the i-th element denotes the value of the i-th term, with the precise value of each such element being determined by the particular term weighting scheme that is being employed. The complete set of values in a vector hence describes the *position* of the parent document or query in the space, and the similarity between a document and a query (i.e., their separation in the space) is then calculated by comparing their vectors using a similarity measure such as the cosine coefficient.

This simple, *geometric* interpretation of retrieval is intuitively appealing and is also readily comprehensible to the nonspecialist; more importantly, it provides a unifying basis for a very wide range of retrieval operations, including indexing, relevance feedback, and document classification. Indexing involves the assignment of content descriptors to documents in such a way that the latter can readily be distinguished from each other by a query. Indexing in this model can thus be visualised as separating documents from each other in the multidimensional term space described previously: indeed, it is possible to evaluate the effectiveness of a potential indexing term by its *discrimination value,* which quantifies the extent to which the use of that term leads to the documents in a database being separated from each other. Another important component of IR, relevance feedback, applies user judgements of the relevance of previously assessed output to reformulate a query and is naturally implemented in the vector processing model by modifying the vector describing the query. The intuitive account of relevance feedback as either *reweighting* existing query terms or *altering* query composition by adding or deleting terms can be given a uniform, model-driven treatment via weighting alone. For example, *query expansion* is done by assigning nonzero values to those elements of the vector corresponding to terms that are to be added to the original set of query terms.

The vector processing model (like all of the others discussed here) focuses on the matching of a query against each of the documents in turn, so that the decision as to which documents should be retrieved depends upon the query-document relationship and takes no explicit account of the relationships that exist between documents. However, it is easy to show that documents that are similar to each other, i.e., that lie in the same part of the multidimensional term space, are likely to be jointly co-relevant to the same requests and should thus be stored and retrieved together. This observation, which forms the basis for the *Cluster Hypothesis* of van Rijsbergen and Sparck Jones (1973), suggests that matching a query against clusters of documents will result in higher levels of retrieval effectiveness than a matching operation that takes no account of the similarity relationships existing between the documents in a database (Willett, 1988). Unfortunately, as described in Chapter 6, it has not been possible thus far to develop operational implementations that achieve the expected results.

The vector processing model is one of many that seeks to overcome the limitations of the Boolean model, but it does have inherent limitations of its own. Most obviously, the use of indexing terms to define the dimensions of the space in which retrieval takes place involves the assumption that the terms are *orthogonal,* an assumption that is not correct (Raghavan and Wong, 1986). Practical limitations include: the need for several query terms if a discriminating ranking is to be achieved, whereas only two or three ANDed terms may suffice in a Boolean environment to obtain a high-quality output; and the difficulty of explicitly specifying synonymic and phrasal relationships, tasks that are easily handled in a Boolean environment by means of the OR and AND operators, respectively. These limitations suggest the need for models that use concepts from both approaches, emphasising the positive characteristics of each while, at the same time, minimising their negative characteristics (see, e.g., Bookstein, 1981; Paice, 1984; Salton et al., 1983). More generally, the vector processing model does not of itself impose very strong constraints on the numerical entities in description vectors, which have to be independently motivated.

PROBABILISTIC MODELS

The success of the SMART project rapidly established vector processing as the principal model of IR, and much of the published literature, right up to the present day, is based, explicitly or implicitly, on this model. However, the mid-seventies saw the development of an alternative model, which took as its starting point the assumption that the principal function of an IR system is to rank the documents in a collection in order of decreasing probability of relevance to a user's information need, an assumption that is commonly referred to as the *probability ranking principle*. The importance of this model in the recent development of IR warrants an explicit statement of the principle (due to Cooper as quoted by Robertson [1977b]): "If a reference retrieval system's response to each request is a ranking of the documents in the collection in order of decreasing probability of usefulness to the user who submitted the request, where the probabilities are estimated as accurately as possible on the basis of whatever data has been made available to the system for this purpose, then the overall effectiveness of the system to its users will be the best that is obtainable on the basis of that data."

The rationale for introducing probabilistic concepts is obvious: information retrieval systems deal with natural language, and this is far too imprecise to enable a system to state with certainty which documents will be relevant to a particular query (a situation that is in marked contrast to the unambiguous retrieval operations that are required for searching in numeric database management systems). It is thus hardly surprising that probabilistic notions were introduced in the earliest days of IR (Maron and Kuhns, 1960), but many years were to pass before Robertson and Sparck Jones (1976) provided a practical demonstration of the power of this approach in a study of schemes for the weighting of query terms using relevance information. The basic idea here is to use data about the distribution of the query terms in documents that have been assessed for relevance, this information permitting the calculation of query term weights that define the probabilities of relevance and non-relevance of previously unjudged documents. The precise form of the resulting weighting scheme depends upon assumptions regarding the nature of the *statistical independence* of terms and the contributions of query terms that are, or are not, present in a document. Robertson and Sparck Jones showed that the best performance was obtained using the most reasonable set of assumptions, and subsequent experiments demonstrated the value of the resulting weights in relevance feedback experiments with several document test collections (see, e.g., Sparck Jones, 1980).

Robertson and Sparck Jones's work adopted a probabilistic approach to searching; but probabilistic considerations are also applicable to the indexing component of an IR system (Bookstein and Swanson, 1974; Robertson et al., 1981), as had been noted earlier in the paper by Maron that is included in Chapter 2, and probabilistic models thus became rapidly established (van Rijsbergen, 1979). The OKAPI system described in Chapter 7 illustrates the practical implementation of such ideas. There are, however, many ways in which probabilistic concepts can be brought to bear on IR. One approach that has occasioned much recent interest is the use of inference networks to rank documents in order of decreasing probability that they satisfy the user's information need (rather than the probability that they are relevant, as in the basic probabilistic model discussed previously) (Turtle and Croft, 1990). An important characteristic of the inference net model is that it explicitly allows for the inclusion of, and the interactions between, different types of information (such as the document or query representations resulting from the use of several different indexing methods) in deciding the extent to which the need is satisfied by a particular document.

Methods for combining evidence have been extensively studied in the AI community, and one such method, the *Bayesian inference network*, is used to encode the available information in a network structure that contains various types of node. Each leaf document node is associated with a set of child nodes that characterise its contents, and there is a similar set of nodes describing the query concepts. Probabilities are associated with each network node, and data structures associated with these nodes are used to specify how to combine evidence from different sources of information about a document and how to relate the resulting evidence to the query concepts representing the user's need. The final outcome is an overall estimate of the probability that a particular document satisfies that particular need. Extensions of the model have been described to include relevance feedback and indexing, and an implementation, the INQUERY system (discussed in Chapter 7), has found wide acceptance as a tool for members of the IR research community and as the basis for operational systems.

COGNITIVE MODELS

The models that have been discussed so far concern themselves with the form of document and request index representations and the operations that can be carried out on these representations. Within this area, they allow for a rich range of term types, including complex ones; of means of description development, as in relevance feedback; and of search strategies, whether single or combination ones. But these models are still significantly limited, in that little or no consideration is given to the social and cognitive contexts in which these indexing and searching tasks are carried out (Ingwersen, 1992). The rationale for a cognitive approach was first identified by De Mey (1980), who stated that "any processing of information, whether perceptual or symbolic, is mediated by a system of categories of concepts which, for the information-processing device, are a model of the world". This viewpoint has encouraged the development of several IR models that accord a much greater degree of prominence to the user than is the case with the models described previously. These new approaches are likely to be of great significance if one is to design effective retrieval systems for inexperienced users, for whom database searching may be of only minor importance.

Cognitive models focus on users' information-seeking behaviour (i.e., on the formation, nature, and properties of a user's information need) and on the ways in which IR systems are used in operational environments. The studies that have been carried out thus far in this area have demonstrated: the various sorts of information that a user may require for searching; the ways in which information needs may change during the course of an interaction with an IR system, this necessitating the design of flexible interfaces that can facilitate user-system interactions; and the extent to which the various representational and searching tools that are now available (as discussed in Chapter 6) need to be combined if retrieval is to be successful.

It is important to note that work in this area covers a much wider range of topics than do the other approaches discussed in this chapter, as is entirely appropriate given the holistic view that the cognitive models adopt of the retrieval process. For example, even if we restrict attention to the much cited work of Belkin and his collaborators, areas that have received significant attention include empirical studies of information-seeking behaviour (such as the paper in Chapter 3 on using problem structures for driving human-computer dialogues), the modelling of distributed expert systems (Belkin et al., 1987), and the design of user-friendly system interfaces (Ingwersen, 1992). A comparable diversity of focus is apparent in the many other behavioural and user-centred studies that have been reported in the IR literature (see, e.g., Bates, 1989; Borgman, 1989; Ellis, 1989; Ingwersen, 1992). We have chosen to group all such studies under the single heading of "Cognitive Models" since they share a common focus in the user, a view supported by Ellis (1992) when differentiating between what he refers to as "the physical and cognitive paradigms in information retrieval research" (where the former subsumes all of the work that has been carried out on the indexing and searching tasks that lie at the heart of the other models in this chapter). Ingwersen (1996) draws a similar distinction between these two approaches, while acknowledging the many relationships that exist between them; e.g., he highlights the strong links that exist between his cognitive theory of IR and the logical inference models discussed above. Ingwersen also notes that the effectiveness of the former will be maximised by the use of many different types of text representation and searching mechanism, a focus that provides a link to current work on the application of *data fusion* (Belkin et al., 1995), and other sorts of data combination approach, to IR. There is thus much evidence, both direct and indirect, to support the use of cognitive models, and it now remains to be seen whether they can yield robust implementations that are amenable to detailed testing and evaluation: some initial experiments are discussed by Logan et al. (1994).

SELECTED READINGS

Cooper (1988) notes that "the prevalence of conventional Boolean systems today does not reflect their inherent virtue so much as a historic head start" and provides a concise summary of the inherent limitations of the Boolean model, highlighting the problems of query formulation, of ranking, and of differentiating between terms that have been referred to previously. This opinion piece is complemented by suggestions as to the ways in which the various limitations can be overcome, or at least alleviated.

The idea of retrieving documents on the basis of the extent to which they logically imply a request was first suggested by van Rijsbergen (1986). The use of natural language in document retrieval, and of speech or images in multimedia retrieval, means that there is always a measure of uncertainty associated with such an implication, thus necessitating the use of probabilistic approaches that allow the specification of plausible, rather than strict, inferences. The selected paper presents the use of plausible inference in IR and then goes on to relate the approach to the Boolean, vector processing, and probabilistic models of retrieval.

The vector processing model has been extensively discussed in the many publications from the SMART group: that included here (Salton et al., 1975a) has been chosen since it covers several of the major contributions of this group to the development of IR. Specifically, the paper investigates the extent of the link between retrieval effectiveness and the distribution of document vectors in the multidimensional term space that lies at the heart of the vector processing model. The first part of the paper demonstrates that there is an inverse relationship, as the model would predict, between effectiveness and the density of the documents in the space, with high performance being obtained when the documents are as separated as possible and low performance being obtained when term weighting and clustering procedures are adopted to modify this separation. The paper then goes on to investigate the relationship between term frequency and term discrimination value and demonstrates that the most effective terms for indexing purposes are those of low to medium frequencies of occurrence, a finding that provides a basis for systematic procedures to maximise the effectiveness of indexing.

Robertson (1977b) provides a detailed account of the mathematical basis for the probability ranking principle and hence for the use of probabilistic methods in IR. Specifically, he proves that application of the principle (i.e., the ranking of the documents in a database in order of decreasing probability of relevance) will optimise performance parameters that are very closely related to traditional measures of retrieval effectiveness, such as recall and precision. The paper is of importance in two ways: firstly, and most obviously, for the proof itself; secondly, for the care with which Robertson spells out the limitations of the proof, which involves the assumption that the relevance of a particular document to a request does not depend on the other documents in the collection and which only holds for a single request.

The paper by Turtle and Croft (1990) provided the first detailed exposition of the inference network model. The authors begin by noting that the model is intended to support the use of multiple document representations, of different types of query, and of procedures that facilitate matching the vocabularies used to describe documents and queries. They then go on to justify the use of Bayesian inference networks, linking them to the existing probabilistic and logical models, before providing a detailed account of how such networks can be implemented in the context of an IR system.

Cognitive approaches to IR are illustrated by one of the first papers to focus upon the user of an IR system rather than the mechanics of the system itself. The difference in approach from the models described previously is made manifest in the opening paragraphs of the paper selected here, where Belkin et al. (1982a) state that "This new approach recognises that a fundamental element in the IR situation is the development of an information need out of an inadequate state of knowledge. From this realisation it goes on to say that for IR to be successful, that information need must be represented in terms appropriate for just that task, with the remaining elements of system (i.e., document representation, retrieval mechanism) being represented or constructed on the basis of that representation." The paper spells out some of the implications of this focus on need and representation and provides some initial thoughts on how they might be implemented; this implementation is discussed in more detail in a companion paper (Belkin et al., 1982b).

REFERENCES

*Note: *** after a reference indicates a selected reading.*

Agosti, M., Gradenigo, G., and Marchetti, P.G. (1992) A hypertext environment for interacting with large databases. *Information Processing and Management*, **28**, 371–387.

Bates, M.J. (1989) The design of browsing and berrypicking techniques for the online search interface. *Online Review*, 13, 407–424.

Belkin, N.J. (1990) The cognitive viewpoint in information science. *Journal of Information Science*, **16**, 11–15.

Belkin, N.J., Borgman, C.L., Brooks, H.M., Bylander, T., Croft, W.B., Daniels, P., Deerwester, S., Fox, E.A., Ingwersen, P., Rada, R., Sparck Jones, K., Thompson, R., and Walker, D. (1987) Distributed expert-based information systems: An interdisciplinary approach. *Information Processing and Management*, **23**, 395–409.

Belkin, N.J., Kantor, P., Fox, E.A., and Shaw, J.A. (1995) Combining the evidence of multiple query representations for information retrieval. *Information Processing and Management*, **31**, 431–448.

Belkin, N.J., Oddy, R.N., and Brooks, H.M. (1982a) ASK for information retrieval. Part I. Background and theory. *Journal of Documentation,* **38**, 61–71.***

Belkin, N.J., Oddy, R.N., and Brooks, H.M. (1982b) ASK for information retrieval. Part II. Results of a design study. *Journal of Documentation,* **38**, 145–164.

Bookstein, A. (1981) A comparison of two systems for weighted Boolean retrieval. *Journal of the American Society for Information Science,* **32**, 275–279.

Bookstein, A. (1986) Probability and fuzzy-set applications to information retrieval. *Annual Review of Information Science and Technology,* **29**, 117–151.

Bookstein, A. (1989) Set-oriented retrieval. *Information Processing and Management,* **25**, 465–475.

Bookstein, A., and Swanson, D.R. (1974) Probabilistic models for automatic indexing. *Journal of the American Society for Information Science,* **25**, 312–318.

Borgman, C.L. (1989) All users of information retrieval systems are not created equal: An exploration into individual differences. *Information Processing and Management,* **25**, 237–251.

Brooks, H.M., Daniels, P.J., and Belkin, N.J. (1985) Problem descriptions and user models: Developing an intelligent interface for document retrieval systems. In *Informatics 8: Advances in Intelligent Retrieval,* pp. 191–214. London: Aslib.

Burt, P.V., and Kinnucan, M.T. (1990) Information models and modelling techniques for information systems. *Annual Review of Information Science and Technology,* **25**, 175–208.

Chiaramella, Y., and Chevallet, J.P. (1992) About retrieval models and logic. *Computer Journal,* **35**, 233–242.

Cooper, W.S. (1988) Getting beyond Boole. *Information Processing and Management,* **24**, 243–248.***

Croft, W.B. (1980) A model of cluster searching based on classification. *Information Systems,* **5**, 189–195.

Daniels, P.J. (1986) Cognitive models in information retrieval—an evaluative review. *Journal of Documentation,* **42**, 272–304.

De May, M. (1980) The relevance of the cognitive paradigm for information science. In O. Harbo and L. Kajberg (Eds.), *Theory and Application of Information Research. Proceedings of the 2nd International Research Forum on Information Science,* pp. 49–61. London: Mansell.

Ellis, D. (1989) A behavioural model for information retrieval systems design. *Journal of Information Science,* **15**, 237–247.

Ellis, D. (1992) The physical and cognitive paradigms in information retrieval research. *Journal of Documentation,* **48**, 45–64.

Fairthorne, R.A. (1969) Empirical hyperbolic distributions (Bradford-Zipf-Mandelbrot) for bibliometric description and prediction. *Journal of Documentation,* **25**, 319–343.

Fuhr, N. (1989) Models for retrieval with probabilistic indexing. *Information Processing and Management,* **25**, 55–72.

Garfield, E. (1979) *Citation Indexing: Its Theory and Application in Science, Technology and Humanities.* New York: John Wiley.

Harter, S.P. (1975a) A probabilistic approach to automatic keyword indexing. Parts 1 and 2. *Journal of the American Society for Information Science,* **26**, 197–206 and 280–289.

Hartley R.J., Keen, E.M., Large, J.A., Tedd, L.A. (1990) *Online Searching: Principles and Practice.* London: Bowker Saur.

Ingwersen, P. (1992) *Information Retrieval Interaction.* London: Taylor Graham.

Ingwersen, P. (1996) Cognitive perspectives of information retrieval interaction: Elements of a cognitive IR theory. *Journal of Documentation,* **52**, 3–50.

Logan, B., Reece, S., and Sparck Jones, K. (1994) Modelling information retrieval agents with belief revision. In W.B. Croft and C.J. van Rijsbergen (Eds.), *Proceedings of the 17th Annual International Conference on Research and Development in Information Retrieval.* pp. 91–100. London: Springer-Verlag.

Maron, M.E., and Kuhns, J.L. (1960) On relevance, probabilistic indexing and information retrieval. *Journal of the Association for Computing Machinery,* **7**, 216–244.

Miller, W.L. (1971) A probabilistic strategy for MEDLARS. *Journal of Documentation,* **27**, 254–266.

Paice, C.P. (1984) Soft evaluation of Boolean search queries in information retrieval systems. *Information Technology: Research and Development,* **3**, 33–42.

Raghavan, V.V., and Wong, S.K.M. (1986) A critical analysis of the vector space model for information retrieval. *Journal of the American Society for Information Retrieval,* **37**, 279–287.

Robertson, S.E. (1977a) Theories and models in information retrieval. *Journal of Documentation,* **33**, 126–148.

Robertson, S.E. (1977b) The probability ranking principle in IR. *Journal of Documentation,* **33**, 294–304.***

Robertson, S.E., Maron, M.E., and Cooper, W.S. (1982) Probability of relevance: A unification of two competing models for document retrieval. *Information Technology: Research and Development,* **1**, 1–21.

Robertson, S.E., and Sparck Jones, K. (1976) Relevance weighting of search terms. *Journal of the American Society for Information Science,* **27**, 129–146.

Robertson, S.E., van Rijsbergen, C.J., and Porter, M.F. (1981) Probabilistic models of indexing and searching. In R.N. Oddy, S.E. Robertson, C.J. van Rijsbergen, and P.W. Williams (Eds.), *Information Retrieval Research,* pp. 35–56. London: Butterworths.

Salton, G. (Ed.) (1971) *The SMART System—Experiments in Automatic Document Processing.* Englewood Cliffs, NJ: Prentice Hall.

Salton, G. (1975) *A Theory of Indexing.* Philadelphia, PA: Society for Industrial and Applied Mathematics.

Salton, G. (1981) The SMART environment for retrieval system evaluation—advantages and problem areas. In K. Sparck Jones (Ed.), *Information Retrieval Experiment,* pp. 316–329. London: Butterworths.

Salton, G. (1988) A simple blueprint for automatic Boolean query processing. *Information Processing and Management,* **24**, 269–280.

Salton, G., Fox, E.A., and Wu, H. (1983) Extended Boolean information retrieval. *Communications of the ACM,* **26**, 1022–1036.

Salton, G., Wong, A., and Yang, C.S. (1975a) A vector space model for automatic indexing. *Communications of the ACM,* **18**, 613–620.***

Salton, G., Yang, C.S., and Yu, C.T. (1975b) A theory of term importance in automatic text analysis. *Journal of the American Society for Information Science,* **26**, 33–44.

Sebastiani, F. (1994). A probabilistic terminological logic for modelling information retrieval. In W.B. Croft and C.J. van Rijsbergen (Eds.), *Proceedings of the 17th Annual International Conference on Research and Development in Information Retrieval,* pp. 122–130. London: Springer-Verlag.

Sparck Jones, K. (1980) Search term relevance weighting—some recent results. *Journal of Information Science,* **1**, 325–332.

Tague-Sutcliffe, J.M. (1994) Quantitative methods in documentation. In B.C. Vickery (Ed.), *Fifty Years of Information Progress: A Journal of Documentation Review,* pp. 147–188. London: Aslib.

Turtle, H., and Croft, W.B. (1990). Inference networks for document retrieval. In J.L. Vidick (Ed.), *Proceedings of the 13th International Conference on Research and Development in Information Retrieval,* pp. 1–24. New York: Association for Computing Machinery.***

Turtle, H.R., and Croft, W.B. (1992) A comparison of text retrieval models. *Computer Journal,* **35**, 279–290.

van Rijsbergen, C.J. (1977) A theoretical basis for the use of co-occurrence data in information retrieval. *Journal of Documentation,* **33**, 106–119.

van Rijsbergen, C.J. (1979) *Information Retrieval.* Second edition. London: Butterworths.

van Rijsbergen, C.J. (1986) A non-classical logic for information retrieval. *Computer Journal,* **29**, 481–485.***

van Rijsbergen, C.J., and Lalmas, M. (1996) An information calculus for information retrieval. *Journal of the American Society for Information Science,* **47**, 385–398.

van Rijsbergen, C.J., and Sparck Jones, K. (1973) A test for the separation of relevant and non-relevant documents in experimental test collections. *Journal of Documentation,* **29**, 251–257.

Willett, P. (1988) Recent trends in hierarchic document clustering: A critical review. *Information Processing and Management,* **24**, 577–597.

GETTING BEYOND BOOLE

William S. Cooper
School of Library and Information Studies, University of California, Berkeley, CA 94720, U.S.A.

Abstract—Although most computer-based information search systems in current use employ a Boolean search strategy, there is by no means a clear consensus throughout the information retrieval research community that the conventional Boolean approach is best. The well-known drawbacks of the Boolean design include an inhospitable request formalism, frequent null output and output overload, and lack of provision for differing emphasis on different facets of the search. Nontraditional design principles that overcome these problems are already known and available in the research literature. In this article several such alternative approaches are sketched and their advantages over the Boolean design indicated.

In the 1950s, the era in which serious thought was first given to the possibility of computerized information searching, it was proposed that search requests might advantageously be formulated as Boolean combinations of document descriptors. This suggestion seemed to meet with the immediate approval of most mathematicians, computer scientists, and technically oriented information professionals. At that time only Bar-Hillel, a mathematical logician, objected strenuously [1].

A decade later, when the first large-scale bibliographic retrieval services were set up, the Boolean approach was adopted as the underlying retrieval strategy. Since then it has become the more-or-less standard search mode for almost all the commercial search services and in most automated library catalogs. It is also used in the command languages of many database management systems, office information systems, personnel search systems, and various other information access programs for scholarly, institutional, or personal use. In fact, insofar as search systems in actual operation today are concerned, the Boolean request form is quite ubiquitous. Thus it may come as a surprise to some readers to learn that specialists in information retrieval are by no means unanimous in their praise of the Boolean approach, that the research literature is full of alternative proposals, and that knowledgeable information scientists who think the standard Boolean design could be significantly improved on probably constitute an overwhelming majority.

Admittedly, there is as yet no clear consensus among researchers as to which of the many available non-Boolean designs is best, and this lack of a single clear alternative candidate has doubtless been a factor tending to perpetuate the current monopoly of Boolean systems in the marketplace. Nevertheless, it is not difficult to point to well-researched retrieval strategies that are clearly superior to the Boolean in at least some important respects. This article sketches briefly a few of these possibilities for the benefit of system designers who might not otherwise be aware of them. A commercial implementation of any of them would be a practical advance and might help the information community to break through the Boolean barrier toward some of the more sophisticated designs that are already familiar to information retrieval researchers and experimenters.

Several proposals will be sketched in order of increasing sophistication and decreasing conformity with the conventional Boolean design. Although some of them may be novel in detail, the general principles behind these designs are all to be found in the research literature. The design ideas will be presented in the form of certain problems inherent in the Boolean search logic, and the proposed post-Boolean solutions to these problems.

PROBLEM 1: THE UNFRIENDLINESS OF BOOLEAN FORMULAS

Those who were initially enthusiastic about Boolean retrieval in the 1950s and 1960s were presumably computer people and other mathematically minded folk who already knew some Boolean algebra or could easily learn it. It is doubtful that many of them were typical potential lay users of retrieval systems, or they would have had more doubts about the suitability of the Boolean request language.

As anyone who has had occasion to teach the Boolean request form knows, at first there is a marked tendency among learners to confuse the Boolean AND with the OR. This is an understandable mixup for English speakers because in ordinary conversation a noun phrase of the form "A AND B" usually refers to *more* entities than would "A" alone, whereas in the information retrieval usage it refers to *fewer* documents than would be retrieved by "A" alone. In training courses for future information professionals, the confusion usually subsides after some on-line search experience, but occasionally it resurfaces; and in any case one would ideally wish for a request language that could be used immediately by naïve users without long explanations or hours of practice.

The AND/OR difficulty is by no means the only tricky aspect of the Boolean language. Even after the learner has the correct meanings of the Boolean operators clearly in mind, he or she must still gain facility in combining them, and this takes practice. There are connective symbols to be memorized, parentheses to be matched up, scope problems to be dealt with, conventions about connective priorities to be grasped, and so forth. Computer professionals, librarians-in-training, and some others may willingly jump these minor hurdles in order to learn a retrieval language, but it is doubtful whether large numbers of less highly motivated individuals would spend the effort required to feel at home with the Boolean formalism if they were not forced to do so by a lack of available alternatives.

Solution: Symbol-free faceted requests

In training sessions on how to use Boolean retrieval systems, it is often suggested that the learner start out each search by writing down a separate list of search terms for each aspect or "facet" of his or her information need [2]. The student is then taught to combine these lists of quasi-synonymous words or phrases, or concept clusters, into the form of a Boolean request by ORing within the lists and ANDing between them. For instance, an information need describable by the three concept clusters (1) A, B, (2) C, and (3) D, E, F, G would get transformed into the faceted request (A OR B) AND C AND (D OR E OR F OR G). Negated facets can also be included if need be, as in the request form (A OR B OR C) AND NOT (D OR E). Whether consciously or unconsciously, most experienced searchers lean heavily on this approach, and in practice the vast majority of Boolean search requests turn out to be special cases of the faceted request form. One suspects that those who do eventually learn to cope comfortably with the Boolean formalism manage the trick by using faceted requests almost exclusively.

But if the faceted request form is the only Boolean form that is ordinarily used or needed, why should the average searcher be forced to confront Boolean algebra at all? The user need only be given the idea, perhaps with the help of a homely example or two, of how to describe his or her information need by constructing the lists of quasi-synonymous terms. There need be no mention of Boolean connectives or search logic. Once they are constructed and entered into the computer, the user's concept lists can be transformed automatically into the faceted Boolean form needed for the search in a process that is invisible to the user and with which he or she need never be concerned. Any programmer experienced in the design of "friendly" interfaces should be able to provide convenient facilities for entering, editing, modifying, and rearranging such lists of terms. Although still in essence a (restricted) Boolean input language, this nonthreatening protocol could probably be grasped by anyone in a matter of minutes.

PROBLEM 2: NULL OUTPUT AND OUTPUT OVERLOAD

A well-known problem with Boolean systems is that a Boolean search request often results in null retrieval as first formulated. In fact, in conventional bibliographic search systems an empty or too tiny output is typical for requests that AND together more than three or four facets. The user is then forced to reconstruct his or her request, and following the line of least resistance, he or she usually does so by removing one or more of the original facets. After sufficient amputation of this sort has been performed on the request a non-null output is generally obtained, but only at a certain cost in time and frustration. Worse, the original sense of the request has been degraded by this process of excision.

On the other side of the coin, there is sometimes far too much output, leaving the user at a loss as to where to start looking through it. In such cases one could wish for some hints from the system as to what parts of the retrieved material are likeliest to be relevant, but in a pure Boolean design no such hints are forthcoming.

Solution: Ranking by coordination level

If the Boolean request has been entered into the system in faceted form, as suggested, the output can be ordered by the number of facets (disjunctive expressions) that are satisfied. Any unit of stored information satisfying all of the request's facets will be in the top rank of the output, any which satisfies all but one will be in the second rank, and so forth until some arbitrary limit on the length of the output has been reached. Under normal circumstances such an output will never be null; and by scanning through it from the top down the user will be led to examine what is probably the most hopeful material first, stopping either when his or her information need is met or when the density of relevant material becomes too low to warrant continuing. This kind of ranking will be in agreement with what is intuitively desirable provided all the request's facets are of approximately equal importance in representing the user's needs.

This general solution to the null-output and output-overload problem has been variously referred to as "coordination-level matching," "overlap ranking," and "vector product" retrieval [2–4]. It represents a distinct departure from pure Boolean logic but is thought by many specialists to produce better results than the traditional Boolean approach.

PROBLEM 3: UNDIFFERENTIATED FACETS

It is often the case that a searcher will feel that some aspects of his or her information need are more important or essential to the search than others. But in conventional Boolean designs there is no way in which the user can communicate this to the system, nor any way for the system to exploit such information to improve the retrieval results.

Solution: Weighted request terms

If (as already recommended) each search request is entered into the system in the form of one or more term lists (facets), the opportunity can easily be provided to any user who wishes to do so to enter a numeric weight along with each list. Larger numeric weights would indicate aspects of the search that have greater subjective significance in the user's mind. Output is ranked by taking into account not only the number of facets satisfied but also their numeric weights. The most straightforward formula is a simple sum-of-weights ranking criterion. (Example: Suppose in the two-facet request (A OR B) AND C the user has given facet A OR B the weight 3 and facet C the weight 5. Then stored records bearing the descriptor C along with either A or B would stand at the top of the output ranking with weight 8; next would come those without A or B but with C with a weight of 5; and finally those with either A or B but not C with a weight of 3.) In some schemes negative facets—that is, facets that in traditional Boolean formulation of the request would have been prefaced by the NOT connective—may be given negative weights.

Many researchers regard weighted-request retrieval as highly promising and a number of such systems have been set up on an experimental basis. However, there has as yet been little experience with the use of weighted systems by large populations of typical users. Consequently, not much is known about how willing or able the average user might be to provide the subjective quantitative judgements demanded by such schemes. Until more experience has been gained, conservative user-interface designs should certainly make the assignment of facet weights optional. There is no problem in doing so, for when a user declines to assign any weights, the system need only assign equal weights to all facets as default values.

An interesting compromise possibility would avoid asking the searcher to assign actual numbers. Instead, the user would be instructed merely to order the facets (term lists) down or across the screen in approximate descending order of importance in the information need. In a system with good editing facilities, including a facility for quickly and conveniently rearranging the lists into any desired order (e.g., with a mouse), users who would otherwise be loath to give any judgments about relative importance of facets might be coaxed into doing so in effect by way of the ordering. The system would then assign weights by an arbitrary scheme that gives larger weights to facets ranked higher by the user.

Considerable research has been carried out on weighted-request systems, including the use of both user-supplied subjective weights as just described, and computer-derived weights of various sorts. Weighted indexing (as distinguished from weighted requesting) is also possible (e.g., an index term can be assigned to a document with a weight equal to the number of times it occurs as a word in that document). Various mathematical formulas have been proposed for exploiting request term weights and indexing weights for retrieval purposes, including some which have interesting vector-space interpretations (see e.g., [3,4]). Although these formulas do not always have as firm a theoretical basis as one could wish, it seems likely (and experiments would appear to verify) that any of them would tend to work better than a system design that does not allow the use of weights at all.

PROBLEM 4: INTERPRETING THE WEIGHTS

The thorniest problem connected with any weighted request scheme is the question of what the weights assigned to the request terms or facets are supposed to mean. For many users it will seem an inadequate explanation merely to say that the weights are supposed to express the relative "importance" of the facet to the information need. What does "importance" mean, after all, and how should one go about quantifying it in one's mind? Moreover, even for those users who are willing to hazard a quantitative estimate of importance, it is far from clear how the system should manipulate the resulting numbers to achieve optimal retrieval. Although the various formulas just alluded to for exploiting the weights are all fairly plausible, they are, in the last analysis, somewhat arbitrary.

Solution: The probabilistic interpretation

One of the things information retrieval researchers have accomplished in the past decade has been to put retrieval theory on a firmer statistical basis (for surveys see [5–7]). The starting point of information retrieval theory is the recognition that the items in the system output produced in response to a search query should in general be ranked in descending order of probability of usefulness to the searcher. This is the so-called Probability Ranking Principle [8–11]. From this principle it follows that clues supplied to a retrieval system should, whenever feasible, be provided in a form that will make it easy to estimate the required probabilities of usefulness. In particular, when term request facet weights are permitted they should if possible be given a probabilistic interpretation.

One such interpretation is the following: When a searcher includes in his request a term (or facet) T with weight W, the weight W is to be regarded as the searcher's subjective estimate of the probability that a stored record having the term T among its index terms would be relevant to his information need. For example, a surefire term whose presence on a document is almost a guarantee in the user's mind of the document's pertinence would be assigned a probability of close to one in the request, whereas terms that would have been negated in a traditional Boolean request would be assigned a probability close to zero. Equivalently, but less formally, the user might be instructed to try to imagine the set of all documents in the collection that bear the descriptor T and to guess at the proportion of those documents that might be useful. For instance, when documents are stored in full-text form and all content words contained in a document are regarded as descriptors of it, the weight assigned to a request term such as TRANSISTOR would be the searcher's guess as to the fraction of documents containing occurrences of the term TRANSISTOR that would be useful.

With the request term weights so interpreted, it is possible to program the computer to estimate a probability of usefulness for each document in the collection. The simplest known formula for doing this is one given by Robertson and Sparck Jones, whose paper may be consulted for the mathematics [12], cf. [13]. The system output given in response to the request then consists of all documents for which this estimated probability is greater than some threshold probability, arranged in descending order of the estimated probability. The scheme has been shown to be computationally feasible in experimental setups (e.g. [14]), and though the probability-of-usefulness estimates so obtained are very crude, they have at least some foundation in statistical theory and the output rankings they produce are probably superior to those of ad hoc schemes.

It is not yet known how many retrieval system users would be willing to make probabilistic guesses of the kind called for by this design. However, it is not implausible that some might find probability estimation no harder than trying to quantify an ill-defined concept such as "importance." It can be taken for granted that the users' probabilistic guesses would usually be very rough, but again this must be weighed against the alternative of an arbitrary weighting scheme under which the output ranking rule is theoretically unmotivated. In any case there would seem to be no harm in making the probabilistic interpretation available to those users who wish to learn it. Even for users who refuse to make the effort to think probabilistically, preferring to assign weights merely by subjective "importance," there is no evidence that the probabilistic retrieval algorithm would perform any worse than its ad hoc competitors.

For users willing to attempt the kind of scientific guesswork the probabilistic approach calls for, various aids might prove useful. Consider again the situation of a searcher who has decided to include TRANSISTOR among his or her request terms and is in the process of assigning a weight to it. At a minimum, the number of records in the collection containing occurrences of TRANSISTOR should be displayed as background information to aid his or her decision. In addition, it would be helpful to display beside it another number, derived from prior experimental data, representing the proportion of records typically found useful in a set of this size defined by a request term. If the user does nothing, this second number would be taken as the default-value probability weighting for the term. If on the other hand the user is willing to provide his own subjective probability estimate for the term, he or she could do so simply by modifying the displayed number.

There is experimental evidence that even in the absence of any user-supplied request term weightings, retrieval effectiveness can generally be improved by having the system arbitrarily assign somewhat larger weights to request terms that are more specific (in the sense of indexing fewer documents) and smaller weights to terms that are broader. The user interface just described would automatically confer this benefit as a byproduct.

Probabilistic ranking within the output obtained from a conventional Boolean query is also a possibility (see e.g. [15] and the article "Probabilistic Methods for Ranking Output Documents in Conventional Boolean Retrieval Systems" in this issue). Hybrid systems of this sort would seem an attractive option to offer to those users who happen to be accustomed already to the Boolean request format and for that reason prefer it.

PROBLEM 5: TERM DEPENDENCIES

The probabilistic retrieval formula proposed by Robertson and Sparck Jones was derived with the help of a strong simplifying assumption concerning the statistical independence of index terms in the document collection. It is an assumption that is only approximately true, at best. The performance of probabilistic retrieval systems could presumably be improved if this assumption could be removed or replaced by a weaker assumption that would allow data concerning term dependencies to be used as part of the procedure for estimating the usefulness probabilities of the output documents.

Solution: Advanced statistical techniques

Various ways of using term dependency data to improve probabilistic retrieval computations have been explored. One possibility, proposed by van Rijsbergen, is based on the notion of a "maximum spanning tree" [16,17]. A related approach makes use of the so-called Maximum Entropy Formalism [18–20]. The latter is especially flexible in that it eliminates the need for statistical independence assumptions while making use of whatever probabilistic data or constraints might happen to be available. However, we mention these schemes only as possible future solutions to the dependency problem, not as immediate practical proposals, because it is not yet clear which (if any) of them will prove to be computationally feasible. This is an area of ongoing research.

SUMMARY

We have tried to suggest, by describing a series of gentle steps away from the standard Boolean design, that it should be possible to improve considerably upon the fundamental design features of most present-day retrieval systems and that this can be done simply by exploiting ideas that are already available in the research literature. The prevalence of conventional Boolean systems today does not reflect their inherent virtue so much as a historic head start.

With the advent of the mini- and especially the microcomputer, new opportunities have been and will continue to present themselves for introducing superior designs, either as intelligent interfaces for making better use of established Boolean services, or as independent search systems of various kinds. It is to be hoped that these opportunities will not be lost simply through a lack of awareness of the available alternatives.

REFERENCES

1. Bar-Hillel, Y. A logician's reaction to theorizing on information search systems. American Documentation. 3:103–113; 1957. Reprinted in: Bar-Hillel, Y., Language and information. Reading, MA: Addison-Wesley; 1964.
2. Lancaster, F.W. Information retrieval systems: Characteristics, testing and evaluation (2nd ed.). New York: Wiley; 1979.
3. Salton, G. Automatic information organization and retrieval. New York: McGraw-Hill; 1968.
4. Salton, G.; McGill, M.J. Introduction to modern information retrieval. New York: McGraw-Hill; 1983.
5. Robertson, S.E. Theories and models in information retrieval. Journal of Documentation, 33(2): 126–148; 1977.
6. Maron, M.E. Probabilistic retrieval models. In: Dervin, B.; M. Voigt, editors. Progress in communication sciences vol. V. Norwood, NJ: ABLEX; 1984; 145–176.
7. Bookstein, A. Probability and fuzzy-set applications to information retrieval. In: Williams, M.E. editor. Annual review of information science and technology, vol. 20. Washington, DC: ASIS; 1985; 117–142.
8. Cooper, W.S. The suboptimality of retrieval rankings based on probability of usefulness. Technical Report, School of Library and Information Studies, University of California, Berkeley, CA 94720; 1976.
9. Robertson, S.E. The probability ranking principle in I.R. Journal of Documentation, 33(4): 292–304; 1977.
10. Cooper, W.S.; Maron, M.E. Foundations of probabilistic and utility-theoretic indexing. Journal of the Association for Computing Machinery, 25(1): 67–80; 1978.
11. Robertson, S.E.; Maron, M.E.; Cooper, W.S. Probability of relevance: A unification of two competing models for document retrieval. Information Technology: Research and Development, 1(1): 1–21; 1982.
12. Robertson, S.E.; Sparck Jones, K. Relevance weighting of search terms. Journal of the American Society for Information Science, 27: 129–146; 1976.
13. van Rijsbergen, C.J.; Robertson, S.E.; Porter, M.F. New models in probabilistic information retrieval. British Library R & D Report No. 5587, Computer Laboratory, University of Cambridge, Cambridge, England; 1980.
14. Robertson, S.E.; Bovey J.D. A front end for IR experiments: Final report to the British Library Research and Development Department on project Number SI/G/569. Report No. 5807, Department of Information Science, The City University, London, England; 1983.
15. Radecki, T. A probabilistic approach to information retrieval in systems with Boolean search request formulations. Journal of the American Society for Information Science, 33(6): 365–370; 1982.
16. van Rijsbergen, C.J. A theoretical basis for the use of co-occurrence data in information retrieval. Journal of Documentation, 33(2): 106–119; 1977.
17. van Rijsbergen, C.J. Information Retrieval (2nd ed.). London: Butterworths; 1979; chapt. 6.
18. Cooper, W.S.; Huizinga, P. The maximum entropy principle and its application to the design of probabilistic retrieval systems. Information Technology: Research and Development, 1(2): 99–112; 1982.
19. Cooper, W.S. Exploiting the maximum entropy principle to increase retrieval effectiveness. Journal of the American Society for Information Science, 34(1): 31–39; 1983.
20. Kantor, P. Maximum entropy and the optimal design of automated information retrieval systems. Information Technology: Research and Development, 3: 88–94; 1984.

A non-classical logic for information retrieval

C. J. VAN RIJSBERGEN*
Department of Computer Science, University College, Dublin 4

Implicit in many information retrieval models is a logic. These logics are hardly ever formalised. This paper formalises a non-classical logic underlying information retrieval. It shows how a particular conditional logic is the 'right' logic to do Information Retrieval. Its relationship to existing retrieval mechanisms is investigated. The semantics of the logic are expressed in probability theory, and evaluated through a possible-world analysis, thus establishing an intensional logic. In doing so, we motivate a new principle, the **logical uncertainty principle,** ***which gives a measure of the uncertainty associated with an inference.***

Received January 1986

1. INTRODUCTION

This paper is to be seen as describing a new theoretical framework for investigating information retrieval. For some years now, I have felt the need to describe such a framework. It is especially important if one wants to develop information retrieval beyond the mere keyword approach. In the closing pages of my earlier book on the subject I said the following: 'It has never been assumed that a retrieval system should attempt to 'understand' the content of a document. Most Information Retrieval systems at the moment merely aim at a bibliographic search. Documents are deemed to be relevant on the basis of a superficial description. I do not suggest that it is going to be a simple matter to program a computer to understand documents. What is suggested is that some attempt should be made to construct something like a naïve model, using more than just keywords, of the content of each document in the system. The more sophisticated question-answering systems do something very similar. They have a model of their universe of discourse and can answer questions about it, and can incorporate new facts and rules as they become available.'[1]

When I wrote the above passage, I had no idea that progress in that direction was going to be so slow. The main obstacles appeared to be an adequate computable model of meaning, and its use in information retrieval operations. It was argued that even if we had an appropriate semantics for text, and it could be computed efficiently, we still would not know how to use it to retrieve documents in response to requests.

I would now like to counter this objection by saying that *the use of semantics comes via an appropriate logic.* I am not alone in think..g this; Cooper, in his book on logico-linguistics, would probably make the same claim.[2] Such a logic would be based on a formal semantics for text. The semantics would provide a limited representation of the meaning of any text but it would not be the meaning. A logic would then be interpretable in that semantics. It leaves me to say how such a logic can help in the retrieval of relevant documents. To understand this, one must think of documents as sets of sentences which are interpreted in the semantics, and think of queries as sentences too, the latter usually a single sentence. The single primitive operation to aid retrieval is then one of uncertain implication. In the extreme case, it would be logical implication, which through its interpretation in the formal semantics is logical consequence. That is, a document is retrieved if it logically implies the request. However, as we all know, documents rarely imply requests, there is always a measure of uncertainty associated with such an implication. And so a notion of probable, or approximate, implication is needed where a plausible inference instead of a strict inference is made, and the plausibility quantified through some measure. Modelling the information retrieval process in this way goes beyond the keyword approach, and specifies, once and for all, what relationship between a document and a request is to hold to compute probable relevance. The importance of this new way of looking at Information Retrieval derives from the realisation that with such a framework, Information Retrieval can advance with new developments in formal semantics for text. Starting with a keyword analysis which is a primitive semantics, we can go on to use our logic no matter how sophisticated our semantics is. At all times, we are attempting to infer requests (treated as sentences) from statements in the documents. The inference is possible because we have an interpretation of sentences in a document, we define this interpretation and can increase its complexity at will.

It is important to realise that the above approach is similar to the one adopted in database querying and question-answering. It is similar in that in all cases the answer is obtained through a process of logical satisfaction, i.e. looking at a common interpretation for premises and consequent. It is different in that in the case of Information Retrieval a request is typically a *closed* sentence (i.e. contains no variable) and the relationship computed between a document (the premises) and the request (the consequent) is paramount; i.e. if the relationship is sufficiently strong, the document is retrieved. In the case of Data Base Management Systems, a request is typically an *open* sentence (contains variables), the semantics giving an instantiation of the request, which is an answer.

Editor's Note: It may be thought that the publication of this paper is premature, in that the presentation of the proposed logic is not supported by rigorous mathematical argument. The purpose of publishing now is, however, to provoke reaction to a completely new direction for research in Information Retrieval. Responses will be especially welcome.

* Address for correspondence: Computing Science Department, The University, Glasgow G12 8QQ.

2. CLASSICAL INFORMATION RETRIEVAL

To begin with, I would like to say what Information Retrieval is. Let us assume that there is a large store of documents on a variety of topics. A user of such a store will have a need to know certain things, things that he does not know at present. He therefore expresses his information need in the form of a request for information. Information Retrieval is concerned with retrieving those documents that are likely to be relevant to his information need as expressed by his request. It is likely that such a retrieval process will be iterated, since a request is only an imperfect expression of an information need, and the documents retrieved at one point may help in improving the request used in the next iteration. It is important to realise that certain words in the above description are used carefully to avoid misunderstanding the idea of information retrieval.

Let us spell out the way in which the description is to be interpreted. A request for information is translated into a request for documents. The documents are assumed to contain the information, therefore the information is only retrieved indirectly. A request is an imperfect expression of a user's information need; only a user will be able to tell whether a document contains the information he is seeking. If it does contain the information sought then the document is considered relevant to the user's information need. This implies that documents are *not* relevant to *a request*; that is, identical requests submitted by two different users can be satisfied in different ways, one document may be relevant to one user and not to the other. Relevance is here connected firmly to 'aboutness', a document is not relevant because of its colour or shape. It is relevant because it is about the information sought.

In specifying a model for information retrieval, a small number of entities and concepts need to be defined. Superficially, this would appear to be a simple matter. The entities and concepts are document, request, property of a document and relevance. Anyone can give commonsense definitions of these; unfortunately, what is required is a *formal definition* so that an Information Retrieval system can be formally specified and therefore implemented on a computer.

Let us take a document as a set of sentences. Therefore, when a document is considered for retrieval, the sentences in the document are considered individually or perhaps jointly. In considering them, one is looking for a *relationship* between them and the request. Such a relationship needs to be computable if the Information Retrieval system is a computer-based one. If we take a request to be a sentence then the relationship to be computed is one between a set of sentences and a single sentence. This relationship must be such that it enables one to use it to determine whether a document is likely to be relevant or not. I use 'likely' because we are assuming that relevance is user-dependent and a request is an imperfect expression of an information need.

From a system's point of view, the computation of the relationship between document and request is central. How is one to specify this relationship? There are several ways of doing this, and each one has implications for how one represents a document and a query. Ideally, one would like this representation to be separated from the relationship computation; of course, this has proved to be almost impossible. In what follows, I propose that the right representation is given by a formal semantics for text (perhaps a Montague-style semantics, see Ref. 3). The detailed specification of a semantics will be the subject of a later paper. The relationship between a document and a request will be formalised as a logical implication to which a measure of uncertainty is attached. To motivate this 'implication' I shall give three examples in which standard Information Retrieval models are re-expressed in terms of uncertain implication.

2.1. Boolean retrieval

It is assumed that documents are represented by index terms, or keywords, and that requests are logical combinations (using AND, OR, NOT) of these terms. A document is deemed likely to be relevant, and hence retrieved, if the index terms in the document satisfy the logical expression in the request. For example:

$D_1 = \{A, B\}$
$D_2 = \{B, C\}$ A, B, C: index terms
$D_3 = \{A, B, C\}$
$Q = A \wedge B \wedge \sim C$
D_1: retrieved because D_1 is true implies Q is true
D_2, D_3: not retrieved.

The index terms are, in fact, the semantics, and indexing is seen as mapping a piece of text into its formal semantics. Formally, an index term is true for a document if it occurs in the set representing the document.

Notice the use of the *closed world assumption* here, that the absence of an index term in a document is assumed to imply that it is false for that document. The example makes clear that the relation computed between D and Q is one of logical implication. This is a simple set-up and commonly used in practice. Unfortunately, it does not model the uncertainty of relevance.

2.2. Co-ordination Level Matching

Just as in the example of Boolean retrieval above, documents are assumed to consist of sets of index terms, but requests are now also sets of index terms. The relationship between a document and a request is now computed in terms of the index terms they have in common. The likelihood of relevance is taken to be directly proportional to the number of index terms shared. For example, D_1, D_2, D_3 as before,

$$Q = \{A, B, C\}:$$

$$n(D_1 \cap Q) = 2$$
$$n(D_2 \cap Q) = 2$$
$$n(D_3 \cap Q) = 3$$

where $n(\ ) =$ number in set.

This relationship can be described in terms of the probability of a logical implication, so that $n(D \cap Q)$ is proportional to the probability of $D \rightarrow Q$. What is a probability of $D \rightarrow Q$? This depends first on how one interprets '$\rightarrow$'. It is not to be interpreted as the material implication $D \supset Q$, which is the usual truth-functional connective, only false when D is true and Q is false.

Intuitively, whatever the precise meaning of '$\rightarrow$', it is easy to understand that $D \rightarrow Q$, or that $D \nrightarrow Q$.

The problem is that when $D \nrightarrow Q$ we might still want to retrieve D because of its likelihood of relevance. To model this uncertainty of relevance, we use uncertainty of implication. If we assume $P(D \rightarrow Q) = P(Q \mid D)$, then with D and Q as sets we have:

$$P(D \rightarrow Q) = \frac{P(Q \cap D)}{P(D)} = \frac{n(Q \cap D)}{n(D)}$$

Treating $n(D)$ as constant, we get the relationship that $P(D \rightarrow Q)$ is proportional to the level of co-ordination.

2.3. Probabilistic Retrieval

In this example, documents are also represented by sets of index terms, and so are queries. However, this time the relationship between them is calculated by including estimates of the likelihood that a shared term indicates relevance. The emphasis is on somehow finding out how index terms discriminate between relevant and non-relevant documents. For example, a user might indicate that an index term is a good discriminator, i.e. it occurs far more frequently in relevant than in non-relevant documents. Such information for a number of terms is then pooled to estimate the probability of relevance of a particular document.

Consider a document represented by D that has not been retrieved before, its probability of relevance being given by $P(\text{rel} \mid D)$. This probability is assumed to be well formed in the sense that 'rel' and 'D' are events or propositions for which the relationship of probability holds. Unfortunately, this is not so; 'rel' is neither a proposition nor an event. Relevance is only given after the event of retrieval, and is a function of the user. Therefore, relevance can be used to conditionalise probabilities, but it cannot be given equal status with documents and requests, which are known before a retrieval operation.

Now, although 'D' appears as a simple event in $P(\text{rel} \mid D)$ its interpretation is far from simple. In the standard probability model we assume D to be a vector-valued random variable,[1] where its distribution is given by a mixture of two distributions, namely

$$P(D) = P(D \mid \text{rel})\, P(\text{rel}) + P(D \mid \text{nrel})\, P(\text{nrel})$$

(nrel = not-relevant).

To compute $P(\text{rel} \mid D)$ we use Bayes' Theorem:

$$P(\text{rel} \mid D) = \frac{P(D \mid \text{rel})\, P(\text{rel})}{P(D)}$$

In this computation the relationship between a document description and a request is given only indirectly. The request is used to start the iterative process in evaluating $P(\text{rel} \mid D)$. On the first cycle, one needs an estimate of $P(D \mid \text{rel})$, which can be obtained by using the request to retrieve some documents and assessing them for relevance. Another way of putting this is that P is *revised* to a different probability function P_{rel} in the light of information about relevance, and that

$$P(D \mid \text{rel}) = P_{\text{rel}}(D).$$

Putting it this way makes it clear that two users with differing ideas of relevance but submitting the same request can expect to get different probabilities of relevance, i.e. user 1 would get $P^1_{\text{rel}}(D)$ and user 2 $P^2_{\text{rel}}(D)$. This simply means that the probability function P can be revised in two different ways. But what about the case of the same relevance judgements but different requests, e.g. q_1 and q_2? As it stands, the probabilistic model does not deal with it directly. A recent attempt to deal with it can be found in (Ref. 4).

I would like to propose the following way of dealing with both cases; different relevance judgements and different requests.

Instead of calculating $P(D)$ or $P_{\text{rel}}(D)$, I propose $P(s \rightarrow q)$ or $P_{\text{rel}}(s \rightarrow q)$. Here s is a description of a document (for example, a set of sentences) and q a description of a request. $s \rightarrow q$ is a logical implication and $P(s \rightarrow q)$ is a measure of its uncertainty. In doing this, we have done two things: (1) separated the process of revising probabilities from the logic; and (2) separated the treatment of relevance from the treatment of documents and requests.

The general picture we now have is that the probability of relevance is given by the probability that q follows from s. However, this latter probability is a function of what the user already knows. His knowledge is expressed through relevance judgements and quantified through revision of the P to P_{rel}.

3. A CONDITIONAL LOGIC FOR INFORMATION RETRIEVAL

In re-expressing the three well-known retrieval models, Boolean, Co-ordination and Probabilistic, as examples of computation of logical implication, I have made the case (in part) that the fundamental retrieval operation is one of logical implication. This logical implication is not one of material implication, the usual truth-functional connective $A \supset B$, which is true in all cases except when A is true and B is false. To illustrate the difference between our earlier implication $A \rightarrow B$ and $A \supset B$ let me give a simple example. First, let us assume that the probability of a conditional of the form 'If A is true then B' is a conditional probability. Now consider a die and two events, A the event 'a number less than 3 will be rolled' and B the event 'an even number will be rolled'.

Then for the two 'implications' we get:

$$P(A \rightarrow B) = \frac{P(A \cap B)}{P(A)} = \frac{1/6}{2/6} = \frac{1}{2}$$

$$P(A \supset B) = P(\bar{A} \vee B) = \frac{5}{6}$$

This shows that by interpreting the probability of a conditional as a conditional probability rather than the probability of a material implication we get widely differing results. Of course, I would maintain that the conditional probability interpretation in the context of Information Retrieval is the right one.

There is another major reason why a conditional must not be identified with the material implication in logic. When using probabilistic inference, we want to ensure that the following *soundness criterion* holds.[5] It is impossible for the premises of an inference to be probable while its conclusion is improbable. To illustrate a violation of this, we take the well-known inference given $\sim A$ we can infer $A \supset B$. [Remember that we can logically infer a consequent from an antecedent, whenever interpretations making the antecedent true also make the consequent true.] In our example, whenever $\sim A$ is true, A will be false and hence $A \supset B$ will be true, independent of B's truth value.

If we identified $A \rightarrow B$ with $A \supset B$, then such an inference could easily violate the soundness criterion. It is easy to show situations (see diagram below) where $P(\sim A)$ is large and $P(A \rightarrow B) = P(B \mid A)$ (probability of consequent) is small. In other words, although '$\sim A$ infer $A \supset B$' is valid '$\sim A$ infer $A \rightarrow B$' should not be, if we take the probabilistic soundness criterion seriously.

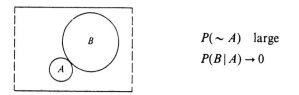

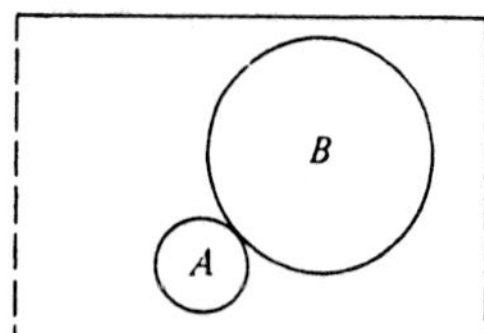

$P(\sim A)$ large

$P(B \mid A) \rightarrow 0$

A conditional logic will, therefore, in general, be different from a classical logic.[6] It is my contention that such a conditional logic (and there are several formulations) is the correct one for information retrieval.

4. HOW DO WE EVALUATE $P(s \rightarrow q)$?

First, let us consider the case without probabilities. To analyse this case, we will need to introduce *possible-world semantics*. An intuitive understanding of a possible world is that it is a complete specification of how things are, or might be, down to the finest semantically relevant details.[7] For our purposes, we will identify *documents* with *possible worlds*. This will raise problems of finiteness and structure which we will ignore for the moment.

Let s be a partial description of a document – this might be a set of sentences, or just a single index term – q being a request. In deciding whether to retrieve a document we would need to evaluate $s \rightarrow q$, that is, whether $s \rightarrow q$ is true or not. If s is true in a document d then $s \rightarrow q$ is true providing q is true. If s is not true in a document then we go to the *nearest* document d' to d in which it is true and consider whether q is true. If q is true in d' then $s \rightarrow q$ is true in d, otherwise it is false.

To give a simple example, s might be an index term, q the same or a different index term. If $s = q$, $s \rightarrow q$ is true follows trivially for those documents in which q occurs. The more interesting case is when $s \neq q$. In this case, to establish $s \rightarrow q$ in d find the nearest document d' in which s occurs and check for the occurrence of q. It is important to realise that because of the primitive nature of the semantics an example such as $s =$ FORTRAN, $q =$ PROGRAMMING LANGUAGE for which $s \rightarrow q$ is directly true in a more complex semantics, can only be handled indirectly.

The above process illustrates what is now widely known as the *Ramsey test*.[8] It might be summarised as follows:

> To evaluate a conditional, first hypothetically make the minimal revision of your stock of beliefs required to assume the antecedent. Then evaluate the acceptability of the consequent on the basis of this revised body of beliefs.

Note that the meaning of a conditional is not truth-functional under the above interpretation, i.e. its truth does not simply depend on the truth valuation of s and q in one world. It has become an *intensional* notion.

In document retrieval we are often faced with the situation where $s \rightarrow q$ is assumed false because s does not logically imply q. That is, assuming the truth of the sentences (index terms) in a document we cannot arrive at q. Boolean retrieval is an excellent example: given a truth valuation for the terms describing a document, we retrieve those documents which imply q (make q true for that valuation). What is suggested here is that a given document should be revised in a minimal way that makes s true. If, after that revision, q is true, then $s \rightarrow q$ is true and d should be retrieved. There are a number of ways of making this revision. One could restrict the revision to selecting a nearest document in which s is true, in which case no interaction from the user would be required. Or, one could involve the user in expanding the information contained in the document under consideration. Or, finally, one could do document expansion automatically using information already stored in the system. We will return to this notion of *minimal revision* when we attempt to formalise it.

Turning now to the *probabilistic* case, to evaluate $P(s \rightarrow q)$, we revise the probability function P to P' in a *minimal* way, so that $P'(s) = 1$. We then have that:

$$P(s \rightarrow q) = P'(q).$$

An example of such a revision is to make $P(s \rightarrow q) = P(q \mid s)$. In the case of Boolean semantics, where x, y are index terms and v a truth valuation:

$$v(x) = \begin{cases} 0 \\ 1 \end{cases}; \quad v(y) = \begin{cases} 0 \\ 1 \end{cases}$$

we get

$$P(x \rightarrow x) = 1$$

$$P(y \rightarrow x) = P(x \mid y).$$

In other words, a query consisting of the index term x is related to a document containing y by $P(x \mid y)$. If we restrict our worlds to documents already present, then we can interpret this as:

$$\frac{n(x \wedge y)}{n(y)}$$

the frequency of the co-occurrence of x and y divided by the frequency of y.

Of course, documents and queries are far more complex than is assumed above. It is not clear yet how one deals with arbitrary complex documents and queries. Generalising from the simple index-term approach we would need to specify a formal semantics in which documents and queries would be interpreted. To evaluate $s \rightarrow q$ would require a change in the interpretation function so that s would be true under the new interpretation, and $s \rightarrow q$ true, if q was true as well.

5. LOGIC OF UNCERTAINTY

In evaluating the truth of $y \rightarrow x$ or evaluating $P(y \rightarrow x)$, we are dependent on a notion of nearness (closeness) between worlds or documents. It is interesting to examine this in a little more detail. Remember our prime concern is to establish that '$y \rightarrow x$', or that $y \rightarrow x$, with sufficiently large probability. If for the current document $y \not\rightarrow x$, we look at the effect of changing/revising our current world and look at $y \rightarrow x$ in the revised world. These changes are to be made in a *minimal* way.

There is another way of looking at this revision process which may be more appropriate in the Information Retrieval context. I would like to generalise the Ramsey test and state a new, Logical Uncertainty Principle.

> Given any two sentences x and y: a measure of the uncertainty of $y \rightarrow x$ relative to a given data set is determined by the minimal extent to which we have to add information to the data set, to establish the truth of $y \rightarrow x$.

This is a slight generalisation of the foregoing. It denies that one can assess $y \rightarrow x$ with certainty if one has to revise the data set. It says nothing about how 'uncertainty' or 'minimal' might be quantified. It specifically relativises truth to a given data set. The semantics of the data have been left unspecified too. Nearness has been replaced by a measure of information.

Conventionally, uncertainty has been measured in information-theoretic terms. I will do the same. If we restrict ourselves to documents, and identify 'data set' with 'document', then we require an information measure to make the above principle precise. Formulating this, given any two documents w_1, w_2 we define conditional information measures $I(w_1 \mid w_2)$ and $I(w_2 \mid w_1)$, which give the information contained in w_2 about w_1 and vice versa. Notice that $I(.\mid.)$ is not symmetric, although one could define a symmetric *mutual* information:

$$I(w_1 : w_2) = I(w_1) - I(w_1 \mid w_2) = I(w_2) - I(w_2 \mid w_1).$$

The details are not important. What *is* important is that $I(.\mid.)$ can be used as a nearness measure, and that it can be defined *algorithmically* without recourse to random variables.[9] How is this done? Essentially, the conditional information measure $I(w_1 \mid w_2)$ is defined to be the smallest program needed to calculate w_1 from a minimal program for w_2. Now we have a nearness measure in terms of the information contained in one object about another. Given a document w, to find the nearest document in which a sentence is true we find that α for which $I(\alpha \mid w)$ is a minimum, subject to the sentence being true in α. In an intuitive sense this is the least revision of the given document, i.e. requires the smallest program to calculate α.

Of course, the principle does not specify that further information should come from the document collection. It may be that a thesaurus, or an expert assistant will be the source of the extra information. The revised document will then probably be different from any document already present. Let us consider an example of the second kind, an expert assistant.[10] Such an assistant might contain rules such as:

if a **then** b [0.9] i.e. $P(a \rightarrow b) = 0.9$.

If the query is y and the document contains x, then to derive the probability of $x \rightarrow y$, we would have to find intermediate steps. For example:

$$P(x \rightarrow a), \quad P(a \rightarrow b), \quad P(b \rightarrow y).$$

Each of these steps is either given by an expert assistant or can be evaluated from the document collection. How one combines these separate pieces of evidence to give a value for $P(x \rightarrow y)$ remains an open question. The reason it is an open question is related to the problematic status of $x \rightarrow y$ as a logical proposition and the consequent impossibility of simply embedding propositions of this kind. It is not clear that $a \rightarrow (b \rightarrow d)$ can be treated as $P(b \rightarrow d \mid a)$.[11] Clearly, one would like to do this, but simple approaches have led to the identification of $b \rightarrow d$ with $b \supset d$. At this stage I would *conjecture* that if one used a probability revision proposed by Lewis,[6] embedding would be allowed and would not lead to paradoxical results. However, this revision process may not be acceptable on other grounds. It would appear to me that a specification of a formal semantics for '$\rightarrow$' would be the way forward; it is the subject of a paper in preparation.

6. CONCLUSION

In this paper I have given a new framework for Information Retrieval based on non-standard logic. The fundamental primitive operation relating documents and queries is taken to be logical implication. This is not a truth-functional notion in the classical sense, but rather can only be evaluated by considering truth in other possible worlds. A new *logical uncertainty principle* is stated to characterise uncertainty associated with any logical implication, thereby quantifying the uncertainty of relevance.

REFERENCES

1. C. J. van Rijsbergen, *Information Retrieval*, 2nd edition. Butterworths, London (1979).
2. W. S. Cooper, *Foundations of Logico-Linguistics*. Reidel, Dordrecht (1978).
3. D. R. Dowty, R. E. Wall and S. Peters, *Introduction to Montague Semantics*. Reidel, Dordrecht (1981).
4. S. E. Robertson, M. E. Maron and W. S. Cooper, Probability of relevance: a unification of two competing models of document retrieval. *Information Technology: Research and Development* **1**, 1–21 (1982).
5. E. W. Adams, *The Logic of Conditionals*. Reidel, Dordrecht (1975).
6. W. L. Harper, R. Stalnaker and C. Pearce (eds), *Ifs*. Reidel, Dordrecht (1981).
7. R. Bradley and N. Schwartz, *Possible Worlds*. Basil Blackwell, Oxford (1979).
8. D. H. Mellor (Ed.) *Foundations: Essays in Philosophy, Logic, Mathematics and Economics: F. P. Ramsey*. Routledge & Keegan Paul, London (1976).
9. G. J. Chaitin, Algorithmic Information Theory. *IBM Journal of Research and Development* **21**, 350–359, 496 (1977).
10. W. B. Croft, *User-specified Domain Knowledge for Document Retrieval* 1986 (in press).
11. A. Appiah, Generalising the probabilistic semantics of conditionals. *Journal of Philosophical Logic* **13**, 351–372 (1984).

A Vector Space Model for Automatic Indexing

G. Salton, A. Wong
and C. S. Yang
Cornell University

In a document retrieval, or other pattern matching environment where stored entities (documents) are compared with each other or with incoming patterns (search requests), it appears that the best indexing (property) space is one where each entity lies as far away from the others as possible; in these circumstances the value of an indexing system may be expressible as a function of the density of the object space; in particular, retrieval performance may correlate inversely with space density. An approach based on space density computations is used to choose an optimum indexing vocabulary for a collection of documents. Typical evaluation results are shown, demonstating the usefulness of the model.

Key Words and Phrases: automatic information retrieval, automatic indexing, content analysis, document space

CR Categories: 3.71, 3.73, 3.74, 3.75

This study was supported in part by the National Science Foundation under grant GN 43505. Authors' addresses: G. Salton and A. Wong, Department of Computer Science, Cornell University, Ithaca, NY 14850; C. S. Yang, Department of Computer Science, The University of Iowa, Iowa City, IA, 52240.

[1] Although we speak of documents and index terms, the present development applies to any set of entities identified by weighted property vectors.

[2] Retrieval performance is often measured by parameters such as *recall* and *precision*, reflecting the ratio of relevant items actually retrieved and of retrieved items actually relevant. The question concerning optimum space configurations may then be more conventionally expressed in terms of the relationship between document indexing, on the one hand, and retrieval performance, on the other.

1. Document Space Configurations

Consider a document space consisting of documents D_i, each identified by one or more index terms T_j; the terms may be weighted according to their importance, or unweighted with weights restricted to 0 and 1.[1] A typical three-dimensional index space is shown in Figure 1, where each item is identified by up to three distinct terms. The three-dimensional example may be extended to t dimensions when t different index terms are present. In that case, each document D_i is represented by a t-dimensional vector

$$D_i = (d_{i1}, d_{i2}, \ldots, d_{it}),$$

d_{ij} representing the weight of the jth term.

Given the index vectors for two documents, it is possible to compute a similarity coefficient between them, $s(D_i, D_j)$, which reflects the degree of similarity in the corresponding terms and term weights. Such a similarity measure might be the inner product of the two vectors, or alternatively an inverse function of the angle between the corresponding vector pairs; when the term assignment for two vectors is identical, the angle will be zero, producing a maximum similarity measure.

Instead of identifying each document by a complete vector originating at the 0-point in the coordinate system, the relative distance between the vectors is preserved by normalizing all vector lengths to one, and considering the projection of the vectors onto the envelope of the space represented by the unit sphere. In that case, each document may be depicted by a single point whose position is specified by the area where the corresponding document vector touches the envelope of the space. Two documents with similar index terms are then represented by points that are very close together in the space, and, in general, the distance between two document points in the space is inversely correlated with the similarity between the corresponding vectors.

Since the configuration of the document space is a function of the manner in which terms and term weights are assigned to the various documents of a collection, one may ask whether an optimum document space configuration exists, that is, one which produces an optimum retrieval performance.[2]

If nothing special is known about the documents under consideration, one might conjecture that an ideal document space is one where documents that are jointly relevant to certain user queries are clustered together, thus insuring that they would be retrievable jointly in response to the corresponding queries. Contrariwise, documents that are never wanted simultaneously would appear well separated in the document space. Such a situation is depicted in Figure 2, where the distance between two x's representing two documents is inversely related to the similarity between the corresponding index vectors.

While the document configuration of Figure 2 may indeed represent the best possible situation, assuming that relevant and nonrelevant items with respect to the various queries are separable as shown, no practical way exists for actually producing such a space, because during the indexing process, it is difficult to anticipate what relevance assessments the user population will provide over the course of time. That is, the optimum configuration is difficult to generate in the absence of *a priori* knowledge of the complete retrieval history for the given collection.

In these circumstances, one might conjecture that the next best thing is to achieve a maximum possible separation between the individual documents in the space, as shown in the example of Figure 3. Specifically, for a collection of n documents, one would want to minimize the function

$$F = \sum_{i=1}^{n} \sum_{\substack{j=1 \\ i \neq j}}^{n} s(D_i, D_j), \tag{1}$$

where $s(D_i, D_j)$ is the similarity between documents i and j. Obviously when the function of eq. (1) is minimized, the average similarity between document pairs is smallest, thus guaranteeing that each given document may be retrieved when located sufficiently close to a user query *without also necessarily retrieving its neighbors*. This insures a high precision search output, since a given relevant item is then retrievable without also retrieving a number of nonrelevant items in its vicinity. In cases where several different relevant items for a given query are located in the same general area of the space, it may then also be possible to retrieve many of the relevant items while rejecting most of the nonrelevant. This produces both high recall and high precision.[3]

Two questions then arise: first, is it in fact the case that a separated document space leads to a good retrieval performance, and vice-versa that improved retrieval performance implies a wider separation of the documents in the space; second, is there a practical way of measuring the space separation. In practice, the expression of eq. (1) is difficult to compute, since the number of vector comparisons is proportional to n^2 for a collection of n documents.

For this reason, a clustered document space is best considered, where the documents are grouped into classes, each class being represented by a class centroid.

Fig. 1. Vector representation of document space.

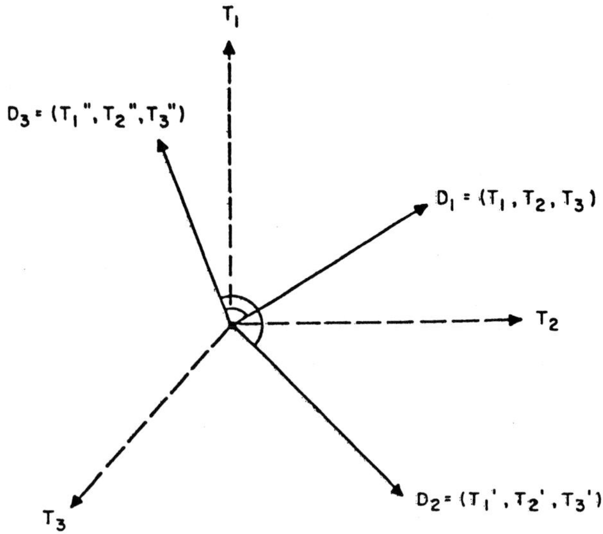

Fig. 2. Ideal document space.

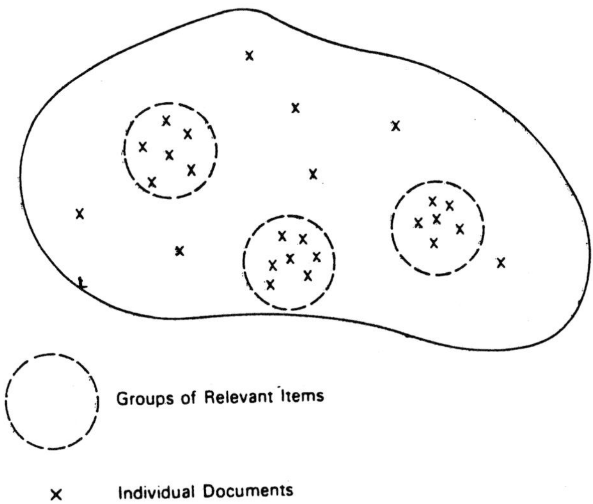

Fig. 3. Space with maximum separation between document pairs.

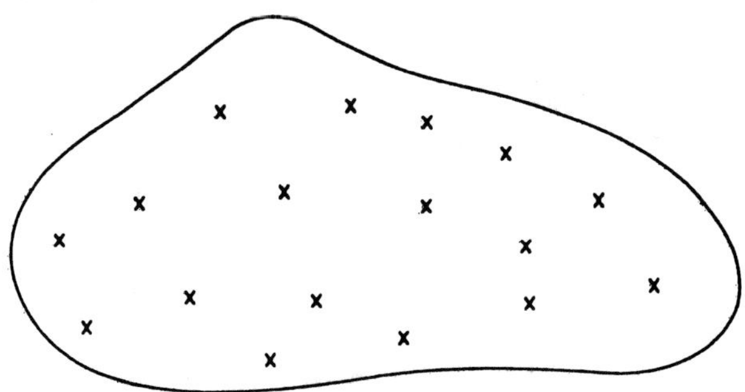

[3] In practice, the best performance is achieved by obtaining for each user a desired recall level (a specified proportion of the relevant items); at that recall level, one then wants to maximize precision by retrieving as few of the nonrelevant items as possible.

[4] A number of well-known clustering methods exist for automatically generating a clustered collection from the term vectors representing the individual documents [1].

Fig. 4. Clustered document space.

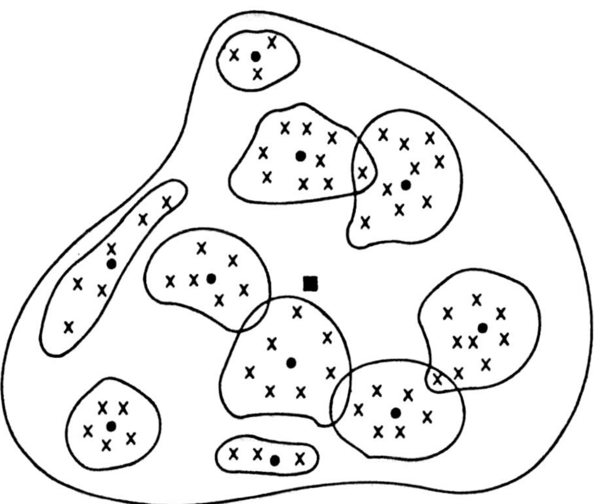

A typical clustered document space is shown in Figure 4, where the various document groups are represented by circles and the centroids by black dots located more or less at the center of the respective clusters.[4] For a given document class K comprising m documents, each element of the centroid C may then be defined as the average weight of the same elements in the corresponding document vectors, that is,

$$c_j = (1/m) \sum_{\substack{i=1 \\ D_i \in K}}^{m} d_{ij} . \tag{2}$$

Corresponding to the centroid of each individual document cluster, a centroid may be defined for the whole document space. This main centroid, represented by a small rectangle in the center of Figure 4, may then be obtained from the individual cluster centroids in the same manner as the cluster centroids are computed from the individual documents. That is, the main centroid of the complete space is simply the weighted average of the various cluster centroids.

In a clustered document space, the space density measure consisting of the sum of all pairwise document similarities, introduced earlier as eq. (1), may be replaced by the sum of all similarity coefficients between each document and the main centroid; that is

$$Q = \sum_{i=1}^{n} s(C^*, D_i), \tag{3}$$

where C^* denotes the main centroid. Whereas the computation of eq. (1) requires n^2 operations, an evaluation of eq. (3) is proportional to n whenever $s(D_i, D_j)$ is proportional to the inner product of the corresponding vectors.

Given a clustered document space such as the one shown in Figure 4, it is necessary to decide what type of clustering represents most closely the separated space shown for the unclustered case in Figure 3. If one assumes that documents that are closely related within a single cluster normally exhibit identical relevance characteristics with respect to most user queries, then the best retrieval performance should be obtainable with a clustered space exhibiting tight individual clusters, but large intercluster distances; that is, (a) the average similarity between pairs of documents within a single cluster should be maximized, while simultaneously (b) the average similarity between different cluster centroids is minimized. The reverse obtains for cluster organizations not conducive to good performance where the individual clusters should be loosely defined, whereas the distance between different cluster centroids should be small.

In the remainder of this study, actual performance figures are given relating document space density to retrieval performance, and conclusions are reached regarding good models for automatic indexing.

2. Correlation between Indexing Performance and Space Density

The main techniques useful for the evaluation of automatic indexing methods are now well understood. In general, a simple straightforward process can be used as a baseline criterion; for example, the use of certain word stems extracted from documents or document abstracts, weighted in accordance with the frequency of occurrence (f_i^k) of each term k in document i. This method is known as term-frequency weighting. Recall-precision graphs can be used to compare the performance of this standard process against the output produced by more refined indexing methods. Typically, a recall-precision graph is a plot giving precision figures, averaged over a number of user queries, at ten fixed recall levels, ranging from 0.1 to 1.0 in steps of 0.1. The better indexing method will of course produce higher precision figures at equivalent recall levels.

One of the best automatic term weighting procedures evaluated as part of a recent study consisted of multiplying the standard term frequency weight f_i^k by a factor inversely related to the document frequency d_k of the term (the number of documents in the collection to which the term is assigned). [2] Specifically, if d_k is the document frequency of term k, the inverse document frequency IDF_k of term k may be defined as [3]:

$$(IDF)_k = \lceil \log_2 n \rceil - \lceil \log_2 d_k \rceil + 1.$$

A term weighting system proportional to $(f_i^k \cdot IDF_k)$ will assign the largest weight to those terms which arise with high frequency in individual documents, but are at the same time relatively rare in the collection as a whole.

It was found in the earlier study that the average improvement in recall and precision (average precision improvement at the ten fixed recall points) was about 14 percent for the system using inverse document frequencies over the standard term frequency weighting. The corresponding space density measurements are shown in Table I(a) using two different cluster organizations for a collection of 424 documents in aerodynamics:

(i) Cluster organization A is based on a large number of relatively small clusters, and a considerable amount of overlap between the clusters (each document appears in about two clusters on the average); the clusters are defined from the document-query relevance assessments, by placing into a common class all documents jointly declared relevant to a given user query.

(ii) Cluster organization B exhibits fewer classes (83 versus 155) of somewhat larger size (6.6 documents per class on the average versus 5.8 for cluster organization A); there is also much less overlap among the clusters (1.3 clusters per document versus 2.1). The classes are constructed by using a fast automatic tree-search algorithm due to Williamson. [4]

A number of space density measures are shown in Table I(a) for the two cluster organizations, including the average similarity between the documents and the corresponding cluster centroids (factor x); the average similarity between the cluster centroids and the main centroid; and the average similarity between pairs of cluster centroids (factor y). Since a well-separated space corresponds to tight clusters (large x) and large differences between different clusters (small y), the ratio y/x can be used to measure the overall space density [5].

It may be seen from Table I(a) that all density measures are smaller for the indexing system based on inverse document frequencies; that is, the documents within individual clusters resemble each other less, and so do the complete clusters themselves. However, the "spreading out" of the clusters is greater than the spread of the documents inside each cluster. This accounts for the overall decrease in space density between the two indexing systems. The results of Table I(a) would seem to support the notion that improved recall-precision performance is associated with decreased density in the document space.

The reverse proposition, that is, whether decreased performance implies increased space density, may be tested by carrying out term weighting operations inverse to the ones previously used. Specifically, since a weighting system in *inverse* document frequency order produces a high recall-precision performance, a system which weights the terms directly in order of their document frequencies (terms occurring in a large number of documents receive the highest weights) should be correspondingly poor. In the output of Table I(b), a term weighting system proportional to $(f_i^k \cdot DF_k)$ is used, where f_i^k is again the term frequency of term k in document i, and DF_k is defined as $10/(IDF)_k$. The recall-precision figures of Table I(b) show that such a

Table I. Effect of Performance Change on Space Density

	(a) Effect of performance improvement on space density				(b) Effect of performance deterioration on space density			
	Cluster organization A (155 clusters; 2.1 overlap)		Cluster organization B (83 clusters; 1.3 overlap)		Cluster organization A (155 clusters; 2.1 overlap)		Cluster organization B (83 clusters; 1.3 overlap)	
Type of indexing	Standard term frequency weights (f_i^k)	Term frequency with inverse doc. freq. $(f_i^k \cdot IDF_k)$	Standard term frequency weights (f_i^k)	Term frequency with inverse doc. freq. $(f_i^k \cdot IDF_k)$	Standard term frequency weights (f_i^k)	Term frequency with document frequency $(f_i^k \cdot DF_k)$	Standard term frequency weights (f_i^k)	Term frequency with document frequency $(f_i^k \cdot DF_k)$
Recall-precision output*	—	+14%	—	+14%	—	−10.1%	—	−10.1%
Average similarity between documents and corresponding cluster centeroids (x)	.712	.668 (−.044)	.650	.589 (−.061)	.712	.741 (+.029)	.650	.696 (+.046)
Average similarity between cluster centroids and main centroid	.500	.454 (−.046)	.537	.492 (−.045)	.500	.555 (+.055)	.537	.574 (+.037)
Average similarity between pairs of cluster centroids (y)	.273	.209 (−.046)	.315	.252 (−.063)	.273	.329 (+.056)	.315	.362 (+.047)
Ratio y/x	.273/.712 = .383	.209/.668 = .318 (−19%)	.315/.650 = .485	.252/.589 = .428 (−12%)	.273/.712 = .383	.329/.741 = .444 (+16%)	.315/.650 = .485	.362/.696 = .520 (+7%)

* From [2].

weighting system produces a decreased performance of about ten percent, compared with the standard.

The space density measurements included in Table I(b) are the same as those in Table I(a). For the indexing system of Table I(b), a general "bunching up" of the space is noticeable, both inside the clusters and between clusters. However, the similarity of the various cluster centroids increases more than that between documents inside the clusters. This accounts for the higher y/x factor by 16 and 7 percent for the two cluster organizations, respectively.

3. Correlation Between Space Density and Indexing Performance

In the previous section certain indexing methods which operate effectively in a retrieval environment were seen to be associated with a decreased density of the vectors in the document space, and contrariwise, poor retrieval performance corresponded to a space that is more compressed.

The relation between space configuration and retrieval performance may, however, also be considered from the opposite viewpoint. Instead of picking document analysis and indexing systems with known performance characteristics and testing their effect on the density of the document space, it is possible to change the document space configurations artificially in order to ascertain whether the expected changes in recall and precision are in fact produced.

The space density criteria previously given stated that a collection of small tightly clustered documents with wide separation between individual clusters should produce the best performance. The reverse is true of large nonhomogeneous clusters that are not well separated. To achieve improvements in performance, it would then seem to be sufficient to increase the similarity between document vectors located in the same cluster, while decreasing the similarity between different clusters or cluster centroids. The first effect is achieved by emphasizing the terms that are unique to only a few clusters, or terms whose cluster occurrence frequencies are highly skewed (that is, they occur with large occurrence frequencies in some clusters, and with much lower frequencies in many others). The second result is produced by deemphasizing terms that occur in many different clusters.

Two parameters may be introduced to be used in carrying out the required transformations [5]:

$NC(k)$: the number of clusters in which term k occurs (a term occurs in a cluster if it is assigned to at least one document in that cluster); and

$CF(k, j)$: the cluster frequency of term k in cluster j that is, the number of documents in cluster j in which term k occurs.

For a collection arranged into p clusters, the average cluster frequency $\langle CF(k) \rangle$ may then be defined from $CF(k, j)$ as

$$\langle CF(k) \rangle = (1/p) \sum_{j=1}^{p} CF(k, j).$$

Given the above parameters, the skewness of the occurrence frequencies of the terms may now be measured by a factor such as

$$F_1 = |\langle CF(k) \rangle - CF(k, j)|.$$

On the other hand, a factor F_2 inverse to $NC(k)$ [for example, $1/NC(k)$] can be used to reflect the rarity with which term k is assigned to the various clusters. By multiplying the weight of each term k in each cluster j by a factor proportional to $F_1 \cdot F_2$ a suitable spreading out should be obtained in the document space. Contrariwise, the space will be compressed when a multiplicative factor proportional to $1/(F_1 \cdot F_2)$ is used.

The output of Table II(a) shows that a modification of term weights by the $F_1 \cdot F_2$ factor produces precisely the anticipated effect: the similarity between documents included in the same cluster (factor x) is now greater, whereas the similarity between different cluster centroids (factor y) has decreased. Overall, the space density measure (y/x) decreases by 18 and 11 percent respectively for the two cluster organizations. The average retrieval performance for the spread-out space shown at the bottom of Table II(a) is improved by a few percentage points.

The corresponding results for the compression of the space using a transformation factor of $1/(F_1 \cdot F_2)$ are shown in Table II(b). Here the similarity between documents inside a cluster decreases, whereas the similarity between cluster centroids increases. The overall space density measure (y/x) increases by 11 and 16 percent for the two cluster organizations compared with the space representing the standard term frequency weighting. This dense document space produces losses in recall and precision performance of 12 to 13 percent.

Taken together, the results of Tables I and II indicate that retrieval performance and document space density appear inversely related, in the sense that effective indexing methods in terms of recall and precision are associated with separated (compressed) document spaces; on the other hand, artificially generated alterations in the space densities appear to produce the anticipated changes in performance.

The foregoing evidence thus confirms the usefulness of the "term discrimination" model and of the automatic indexing theory based on it. These questions are examined briefly in the remainder of this study.

4. The Discrimination Value Model

For some years, a document indexing model known as the term discrimination model has been used experi-

Table II. Effect of Cluster Density on Performance

	(a) Effect of low cluster density on performance				(b) Effect of high cluster density on performance			
	Cluster organization A (155 clusters; 2.1 overlap)		Cluster organization B (83 clusters; 1.3 overlap)		Cluster organization A (155 clusters; 2.1 overlap)		Cluster organization B (83 clusters; 1.3 overlap)	
	Standard cluster density (term frequency weights)	Low cluster density (emphasis on low frequency and skewed terms)	Standard cluster density (term frequency weights)	Low cluster density (emphasis on low frequency and skewed terms)	Standard cluster density (term frequency weights)	High cluster density (emphasis on high frequency and even terms)	Standard cluster density (term frequency weights)	High cluster density (emphasis on high frequency and even terms)
Average similarity between documents and their centroids (x)	.712	.730 (+.018)	.650	.653 (+.003)	.712	.681 (−.031)	.650	.645 (−.005)
Average similarity between cluster centroids and main centroid	.500	.477 (−.023)	.537	.528 (−.009)	.500	.523 (+.023)	.537	.531 (−.006)
Average similarity between pairs of centroids (y)	.273	.229 (−.044)	.315	.281 (−.034)	.273	.290 (+.017)	.315	.364 (+.049)
Ratio y/x	.273/.712 =.383	.229/.730 =.314 (−18%)	.315/.650 =.485	.281/.653 =.430 (−11%)	.273/.712 =.383	.290/.681 =.426 (+11%)	.315/.650 =.485	.364/.645 =.561 (+16%)
Recall-precision comparison	—	+2.6%	—	+2.3%	—	−12.4%	—	−13.3%

mentally. [2, 6] This model bases the value of an index term on its "discrimination value" DV, that is, on an index which measures the extent to which a given term is able to increase the differences among document vectors when assigned as an index term to a given collection of documents. A "good" index term, that is, one with a high discrimination value, decreases the similarity between documents when assigned to the collection, as shown in the example of Figure 5. The reverse obtains for the "bad" index term with a low discrimination value.

To measure the discrimination value of a term, it is sufficient to take the difference in the space densities before and after assignment of the particular term. Specifically, let the density of the complete space be measured by a function Q such as that of eq. (3); that is, by the sum of the similarities between all documents and the space centroid. The contribution of a given term k to the space density may be ascertained by computing the function

$$DV_k = Q_k - Q, \tag{4}$$

where Q_k is the compactness of the document space with term k deleted from all document vectors. If term k is a good discriminator, valuable for content identification, then $Q_k > Q$, that is, the document space after removal of term k will be more compact (because upon assignment of that term to the documents of a collection the documents will resemble each other less and the space spreads out). Thus for good discriminators $Q_k - Q > 0$; the reverse obtains for poor discriminators, for which $Q_k - Q < 0$.

Fig. 5. Operation of good discriminating term.

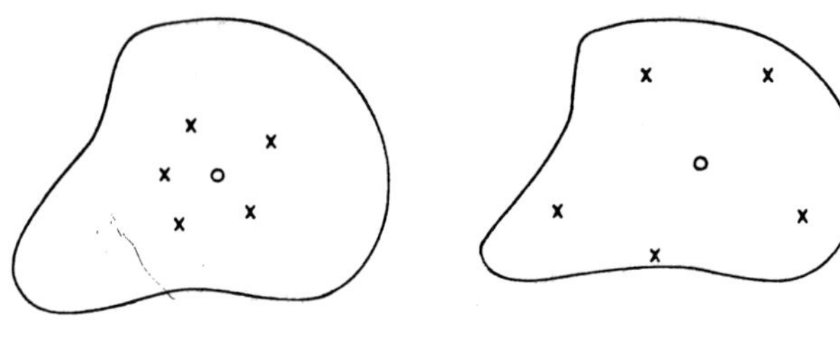

Before Assignment of Term — *After* Assignment of Term

x Document

O Main Centroid

Table III. Terms in Discrimination Value Order (1963 *Time* Magazine)

Good terms	Poor terms
1. Buddhist	7560. Work
2. Diem	7561. Lead
3. Lao	7562. Red
4. Arab	7563. Minister
5. Viet	7564. Nation
6. Kurd	7565. Party
7. Wilson	7566. Commune
8. Baath	7567. U.S.
9. Park	7568. Govern
10. Nenni	7569. New

Because of the manner in which the discrimination values are defined, it is clear that the good discriminators must be those with uneven occurrence frequency distributions which cause the space to spread out when assigned by decreasing the similarity between the individual documents. The reverse is true for the bad discriminators. A typical list including the ten best terms and the ten worst terms in discrimination value order (in order by the $Q_k - Q$ value) is shown in Table III for a collection of 425 articles in world affairs from *Time* magazine. A total of 7569 terms are used for this collection, exclusive of the common English function words that have been deleted.

In order to translate the discrimination value model into a possible theory of indexing, it is necessary to examine the properties of good and bad discriminators in greater detail. Figure 6 is a graph of the terms assigned to a sample collection of 450 documents in medicine, presented in order by their document frequencies. For each class of terms—those of document frequency 1, document frequency 2, etc.—the average rank of the corresponding terms is given in discrimination value order (rank 1 is assigned to the best discriminator and rank 4726 to the worst term for the 4726 terms of the medical collection).

Fig. 6. Average discrimination value rank of terms.

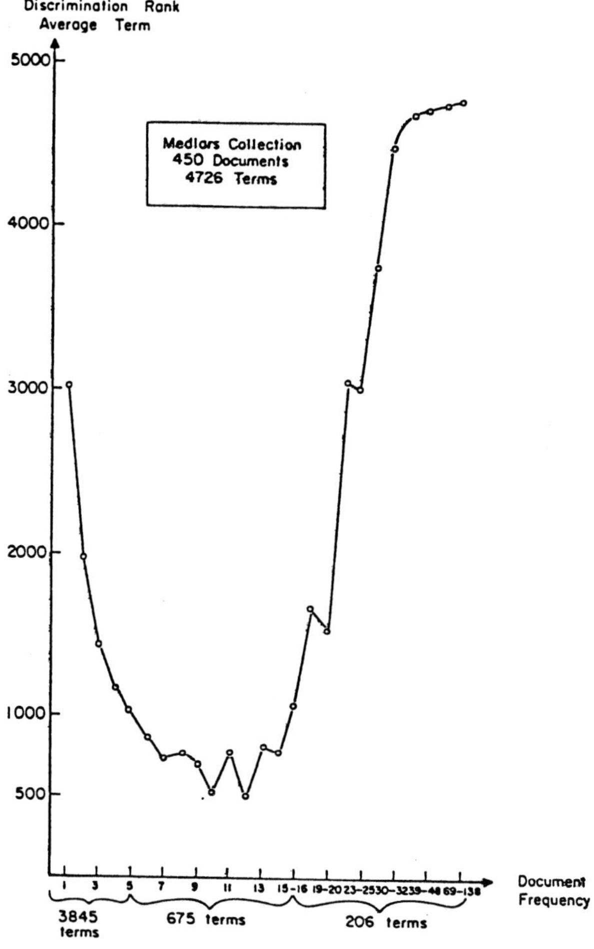

Fig. 6 shows that terms of low document frequency, i.e. those that occur in only one, or two, or three documents, have rather poor average discrimination ranks. The several thousand terms of document frequency 1 have an average rank exceeding 3000 out of 4726 in discrimination value order. The terms with very high document frequency, i.e. at least one term in the medical collection occurs in as many as 138 documents out of 450, are even worse discriminators; the terms with document frequency greater than 25 have average discrimination values in excess of 4000 in the medical collection. The best discriminators are those whose document frequency is neither too low nor too high.

The situation relating document frequency to term discrimination value is summarized in Figure 7. The 4 percent of the terms with the highest document frequency, representing about 50 percent of the total term assignments to the documents of a collection, are the worst discriminators. The 70 percent of the terms with the lowest document frequency are generally poor discriminators. The best discriminators are the 25 percent whose document frequency lies approximately between $n/100$ and $n/10$ for n documents.

If the model of Figure 7 is a correct representation of the situation relating to term importance, the following indexing strategy results [6, 7]:

(a) Terms with medium document frequency should be used for content identification directly, without further transformation.

(b) Terms with very high document frequency should be moved to the left on the document frequency spectrum by transforming them into entities of lower frequency; the best way of doing this is by taking high-frequency terms and using them as components of indexing *phrases*—a phrase such as "programming language" will necessarily exhibit lower document

Fig. 7. Summarization of discrimination value of terms in frequency ranges.

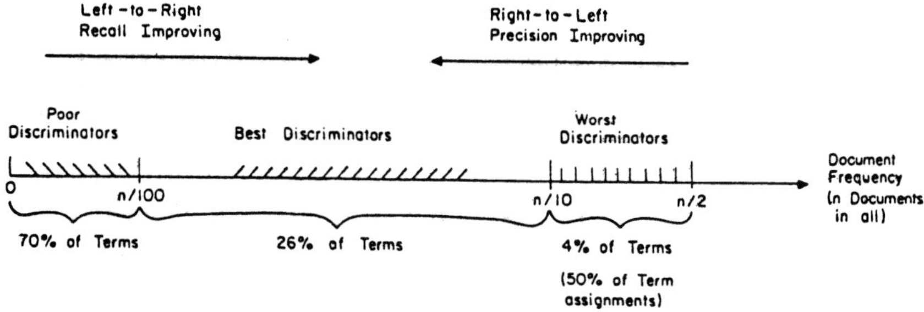

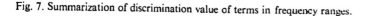

frequency than either "program", or "language" alone.

(c) Terms with very low document frequency should be moved to the right on the document frequency spectrum by being transformed into entities of higher frequency; one way of doing this is by collecting several low frequency terms that appear semantically similar and including them in a common term (thesaurus) class. Each thesaurus class necessarily exhibits a higher document frequency than any of the component members that it replaces.

The indexing theory which consists in using certain elements extracted from document texts directly as index terms, combined with phrases made up of high frequency components and thesaurus classes defined from low frequency elements has been tested using document collections in aerodynamics (CRAN), medicine (MED), and world affairs (TIME) [2, 6, 7]. A typical recall-precision plot showing the effect of the right-to-left phrase transformation is shown in Figure 8 for the Medlars collection of 450 medical documents.

Fig. 8. Average recall-precision comparison for phrases (Medlars: 450 documents, 24 queries).

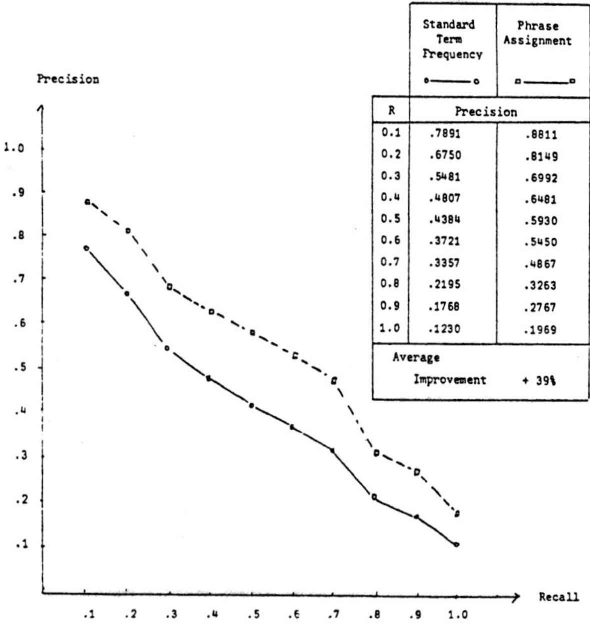

	Standard Term Frequency	Phrase Assignment
R	Precision	
0.1	.7891	.8811
0.2	.6750	.8149
0.3	.5481	.6992
0.4	.4807	.6481
0.5	.4384	.5930
0.6	.3721	.5450
0.7	.3357	.4867
0.8	.2195	.3263
0.9	.1768	.2767
1.0	.1230	.1969
Average Improvement		+ 39%

Table IV. Summary of Recall-Precision Evaluation (Three Collections)

	CRAN 424	MED 450	TIME 425
Automatic phrases vs. standard term frequency	+32%	+39%	+17%
Automatic phrases plus thesaurus vs. standard run	+33%	+50%	+18%
Best Precision			
low recall	0.89	0.88	0.85
medium recall	0.43	0.61	0.70
high recall	0.13	0.23	0.45

When recall is plotted against precision, the curve closest to the upper right-hand corner of the graph (where both recall and precision are close to 1) reflects the best performance. It may be seen from Figure 8 that the replacement of the high frequency nondiscriminators by lower frequency phrases improves the retrieval performance by an average of 39 percent (the precision values at the ten fixed recall points are greater by an average of 39 percent).

The performance of the right-to-left (phrase) transformation and left-to-right (thesaurus) transformation is summarized in Table IV for the three previously mentioned test collections. The precision values obtainable are near 90 percent for low recall, between 40 and 70 percent for medium recall, and between 15 and 45 percent at the high recall end of the performance spectrum. The overall improvement obtainable by phrase and thesaurus class assignments over the standard term frequency process using only the unmodified single terms ranges from 18 percent for the world affairs collection to 50 percent for the medical collection.

A conclusive proof relating the space density analysis and the resulting document frequency indexing model to optimality in the retrieval performance cannot be furnished. However, the model appears to perform well for collections in several different subject areas, and the performance results produced by applying the theory have not in the authors' experience been surpassed by any other manual or automatic indexing and analysis procedures tried in earlier experiments. The model may then lead to the best performance obtainable with ordinary document collections operating in actual user environments.

Received July 1974; revised March 1975

References

1. Salton, G. *Automatic Information Organization and Retrieval.* McGraw-Hill, New York, 1968, Ch. 4.
2. Salton, G., and Yang, C.S. On the specification of term values in automatic indexing. *J. Documen. 29,* 4 (Dec. 1973), 351–372.
3. Sparck Jones, K. A statistical interpretation of term specificity and its application to retrieval. *J. Documen. 28,* 1 (March 1972), 11–20.
4. Williamson, R.E. Real-time document retrieval. Ph.D. Th., Computer Sci. Dep., Cornell U., June 1974.
5. Wong, A. An investigation of the effects of different indexing methods on the document space configuration. Sci. Rep. ISR-22, Computer Sci. Dep., Cornell U., Section II, Nov. 1974.
6. Salton, G. A theory of indexing. Regional Conference Series in Applied Mathematics No. 18, SIAM, Philadelphia, Pa., 1975.
7. Salton, G., Yang, C.S., and Yu, C.T. Contribution to the theory of indexing. Proc. IFIP Congress 74, Stockholm, August 1974. American Elsevier, New York, 1974.

THE PROBABILITY RANKING PRINCIPLE IN IR

S. E. ROBERTSON

School of Library, Archive, and Information Studies, University College London

The principle that, for optimal retrieval, documents should be ranked in order of the probability of relevance or usefulness has been brought into question by Cooper. It is shown that the principle can be justified under certain assumptions, but that in cases where these assumptions do not hold, the principle is not valid. The major problem appears to lie in the way the principle considers each document independently of the rest. The nature of the information on the basis of which the system decides whether or not to retrieve the documents determines whether the document-by-document approach is valid.

A REFERENCE retrieval system should rank the references in the collection in order of their probability of relevance to the request, or of usefulness to the user, or of satisfying the user. This principle was first used explicitly by Maron and Kuhns.[1] Given that no system is capable of making a definitive assessment of relevance, it seems intuitively obvious that some such notion must be used; Maron and Kuhns accept the principle *a priori*. However, a closer analysis of the principle suggests that we need to examine carefully the assumptions on which it is based and the ways it might be interpreted. The object of this paper is to make a first attempt at such an analysis.

1. BACKGROUND

Maron and Kuhns's early paper introduced a very necessary new idea into discussion on the basic problems of retrieval. The idea was that since no retrieval system can be expected to predict *with certainty* which documents a requester might find useful, the system must necessarily be dealing with *probabilities*; we should therefore design our systems accordingly.

That said, the particular approach adopted by Maron and Kuhns in some ways confuses the issue (see Robertson).[2] They *define* the relevance of a document to an index term as the probability that a user using this term will be satisfied with this document: a definition which does not correspond to the usual use of the word 'relevance'.

In this paper, I will take relevance (or usefulness, or user satisfaction) to be a basic, dichotomous criterion variable, defined outside the system itself. The assumption of dichotomy is a strong one, and almost certainly not generally valid; discussions of a more complex model are given elsewhere.[2,3] Several more possible assumptions about the nature of this criterion variable are discussed below.

Given a dichotomous criterion variable, and a system which has some (essentially probabilistic) information about this variable, it seems obvious enough that the documents which are most likely to satisfy the user should be presented to him or her first. This idea has been used, in one form or another, by various people since Maron and Kuhns. Cooper[4] gives a formal statement of the principle:

> *The probability ranking principle* (*PRP*): If a reference retrieval system's response to each request is a ranking of the documents in the collections in order of decreasing probability of usefulness to the user who submitted the request, where the probabilities are estimated as accurately as possible on the basis of whatever data has been made available to the system for this purpose, then the overall effectiveness of the system to its users will be the best that is obtainable on the basis of that data.

However, Cooper goes on to show how counter-examples to the PRP can be constructed: situations in which a straightforward application of the principle leads to clearly less-than-optimal performance.*

Elsewhere,[3] before making use of the PRP, I have given a formal justification for it, on the basis of certain assumptions. In the present paper, after a discussion of the nature of the criterion variable, I give two such justifications. In the remainder of the paper, I begin to explore the areas not covered by these assumptions, from which Cooper's examples are taken.

2. THE CRITERION VARIABLE

The object of a reference retrieval system is to predict, in response to a request, which documents the requester will find relevant to his request, or useful to him in his attempt to find the answer. Relevance or usefulness must thus be defined outside the system itself, as a criterion for the system. What assumptions can we make about the nature and characteristics of this criterion variable?

I have already indicated that I will assume the variable to be dichotomous: that is, a document is either relevant or not, there are no in-between states. Indeed, the very statement of the PRP implicitly makes the same assumption. We might consider a more general principle which would get over this problem: Cooper, for example, considers ranking by 'expected utility', where the utility of a document is a continuous variable. In this paper, however, I deal only with the dichotomous case.

Does the relevance or usefulness of one document affect the relevance or usefulness of another? There are several aspects to this question. First, the fact that document A has been retrieved before document B (= is higher up the ordered list presented to the user, and has presumably been seen first) may affect the usefulness of B, if for example B simply repeats the same information as A. Second, the fact that document A has already been judged relevant by the user may provide some indication of the possible relevance of B. Third, even if the system does not know whether A has been judged relevant, it may know that there is a correlation between the acceptance of A and B for different users. Fourth, two documents taken together may be relevant where neither one is relevant on its own if they each tackle complementary aspects of the problem; and so on.

All these possibilities may affect the use of the PRP in different ways. For the purpose of defining a case in which the PRP holds unequivocally I make the following simplifying assumptions:

* As Cooper's paper has not been published, I present his main counter-example in the Appendix to this paper.

(*a*) The *relevance* of a document to a request is independent of the other documents in the collection;

(*b*) The *usefulness* of a relevant document to a requester may depend on the *number* of relevant documents the requester has already seen (the more he has seen, the less useful a subsequent one may be).

These assumptions raise some interesting questions about the nature of the information the system might use to predict relevance, and about the nature of the probability of relevance. Such questions are discussed below; in the meantime, the assumptions form a suitable basis for a justification of the PRP.

3. FIRST JUSTIFICATION: TRADITIONAL MEASURES OF EFFECTIVENESS

The object of this section is to prove that, under certain conditions, the PRP leads to optimum performance, where performance is measured by means of parameters which are very close to the traditional measures of retrieval effectiveness. An earlier version of this proof was first presented elsewhere.[3]

We first demonstrate a general result concerning the probabilities of any two events a, b ($\bar{a}$ denotes the event 'not a'). Two applications of Bayes's theorem give the following:

$$P(a|b)\,P(b) = P(a \cap b) = P(b|a)\,P(a)$$

Similarly:

$$P(\bar{a}|b)\,P(b) = P(b|\bar{a})\,P(\bar{a})$$

Hence:

$$\frac{P(a|b)}{P(\bar{a}|b)} = \frac{P(b|a)\,P(a)}{P(b|\bar{a})\,P(\bar{a})}$$

We now use the well-known logistic (or log-odds) transformation of a probability, which is defined by:

$$\text{logit } P(x) = \log \frac{P(x)}{1 - P(x)} = \log \frac{P(x)}{P(\bar{x})}$$

Hence:

$$\text{logit } P(a|b) = \log \frac{P(b|a)}{P(b|\bar{a})} + \log \frac{P(a)}{P(\bar{a})}$$

$$= \log \frac{P(b|a)}{P(b|\bar{a})} + \text{logit } P(a)$$

So we have demonstrated the following:

Lemma: For any two events a, b,

$$\text{logit } P(a|b) = \log \frac{P(b|a)}{P(b|\bar{a})} + \text{logit } P(a)$$

We now define the parameters of interest. The system is assumed to order (or partially order) the documents in response to a request, and a cut-off is applied to define the retrieved set. (Various possible algorithms which searchers might use to define the cut-off point are surveyed by Cooper;[5] a few specific ones are considered below.) Our parameters are:

$$\theta_1 = P(\text{document retrieved}|\text{document relevant})$$
$$\theta_2 = P(\text{document retrieved}|\text{document non-relevant})$$
$$\phi = P(\text{document relevant}|\text{document retrieved})$$
$$\gamma = P(\text{document relevant})$$

All these parameters relate to an individual request—indeed to an individual need. They correspond closely to the traditional proportion measures recall, fallout, precision and generality respectively (where these are calculated for individual requests); the exact relationship between the probabilities and the proportions can be expressed either as:

Recall is an *estimate* of θ_1

or as: θ_1 is *expected* recall

These matters are discussed further elsewhere.[3]

We also define some more parameters, relating to an individual document as well as to an individual request: for any given document d_i,

$$\theta_1(d_i) = P(\text{document is } d_i|\text{document relevant})$$
$$\theta_2(d_i) = P(\text{document is } d_i|\text{document not relevant})$$
$$\phi(d_i) = P(\text{document relevant}|\text{document is } d_i) = P(d_i \text{ is relevant})$$

Then we have:

$$\theta_1 = \sum_{d_i \in S} \theta_1(d_i)$$

$$\theta_2 = \sum_{d_i \in S} \theta_2(d_i)$$

(where S is the retrieved set)

Also $\phi(d_i)$ is the probability of relevance which the PRP says we should use to rank the documents.

From the lemma, we have:

$$\text{logit } \phi(d_i) = \log \frac{\theta_1(d_i)}{\theta_2(d_i)} + \text{logit } \gamma$$

or

$$\theta_1(d_i) = x_i\,\theta_2(d_i)$$

where x_i is monotonic with $\phi(d_i)$

(In particular, $x_i = \exp\,[\text{logit } \phi(d_i) - \text{logit } \gamma]$)

So if the cut-off is defined by a value of θ_2, we should clearly optimize retrieval (maximize θ_1) by including in the retrieved set those documents with the highest values of x_i—that is, those with the highest values of $\phi(d_i)$. In other words maximum expected recall for given expected fallout is obtained by ranking in order of $\phi(d_i)$ and applying a cut-off when the given fallout is reached.

Similarly, we can show that expected fallout is minimized for given expected recall, or that expected recall is maximized and expected fallout minimized if a given number of documents is retrieved, using the same document ordering. We can also apply the lemma again:

$$\text{logit } \phi = \log \frac{\theta_1}{\theta_2} + \text{logit } \gamma$$

to show that expected precision is maximized under any of the three cut-off criteria mentioned. Further, we could extend the analysis to a number of other effectiveness measures that have been proposed, including for example Cooper's[6] expected search length.

Thus we have proved that, under certain conditions, the PRP optimizes performance. With regard to the conditions, it should be noted that:

(*a*) the entire formalism makes the assumption suggested in §2, that the relevance of a document to a request does not depend on the other documents in the collection;

(*b*) the proof relates only to a single request; if a set of requests is being considered problems arise because the value of γ may differ from request to request, and because the measures of performance must in some way be averaged over the requests.

4. SECOND JUSTIFICATION: DECISION THEORY

The object of this section is to demonstrate that, under certain conditions, the PRP is the 'correct' decision procedure to use according to the dictates of Bayesian decision theory. An earlier version of this argument has been presented elsewhere.[7]

We define a 'loss function' associated with the decision as to whether or not to retrieve a document:

$$\text{Loss (retrieved}|\text{non-relevant)} = a_1$$

(that is, the loss associated with retrieving a non-relevant document is a_1), and

$$\text{Loss (not retrieved}|\text{relevant)} = a_2$$

Using the same notation as in the previous section, we suppose that we know the probability $\phi(d_i)$ of document d_i being relevant. If we retrieve it, the expected loss will be:

$$(1 - \phi(d_i))a_1$$

If we do not retrieve it, the expected loss will be:

$$\phi(d_i)a_2$$

So the optimum (loss-minimizing) decision is to retrieve d_i if:

$$\phi(d_i)a_2 > (1 - \phi(d_i))a_1$$

or:

$$\frac{\phi(d_i)}{1 - \phi(d_i)} > \frac{a_1}{a_2}$$

or:

$$\phi(d_i) > \frac{a_1}{a_2 + a_1}$$

Thus we can rank the documents in $\phi(d_i)$ order, and apply a cut-off where $\phi(d_i)$ falls below $a_1/(a_2 + a_1)$.

The assumption so far has been that a_1 and a_2 are constant for the situation under consideration. We can generalize the result somewhat, by supposing (as suggested in §2) that the usefulness of retrieving further relevant documents may diminish as some are retrieved. Then a_2 diminishes through the search; we have to recalculate after each document is presented to the user. But we can still apply the same rule, stopping where $\phi(d_i)$ falls below the current value of $a_1/(a_2 + a_1)$.

Thus the PRP is valid in decision-theoretic terms, under certain conditions. Again it should be noted that:

(*a*) the formalism again makes the assumptions about relevance and usefulness which were suggested in §2;

(*b*) again there will be problems associated with applying the result to a set of questions, because the values of a_1 and a_2 assigned by the users may be different.

5. A DIFFERENT RANKING PRINCIPLE

Why does PRP fail? In the examples given by Cooper,[4] the main problem seems to be in the calculation of the probabilities by cumulating over requests, where the requests vary in generality or total number of relevant documents. This clearly invalidates the argument of §3, which only works for a single request;* it also invalidates the decision theory approach of §4, since one cannot assume that the parameters a_1 and a_2 will be independent of the request.

In general, the PRP works document-by-document, whereas the results should be evaluated request-by-request. We can devise a form of ranking principle which works request-by-request which can be informally defined as follows:

> Documents should be ranked in such a way that the probability of the user being satisfied by any given rank position is a maximum.

This alternative principle deals successfully with some of the situations in which the PRP fails, but there are many problems with it. In this section, I attempt to define its uses and limitations.

We have first to define what is meant by 'satisfaction'. We must assume that the user searches down the ranked list until he is in some sense satisfied with the information obtained; we have to exclude, for example, the possibility of a 'frustration-point' cut-off criterion (in Cooper's[5] terms). We must also assume that this satisfaction is dichotomous. Examples of this kind of criterion are that the user is satisfied when he has retrieved a certain number or proportion of the relevant documents (such criteria are used by Keen and Digger[8] in their experiments).

The second problem with the request-based principle is exactly that it does not work document-by-document; it is difficult to imagine an algorithm which would find the correct order in any situation, other than the ridiculously clumsy method of looking at all possible rankings.† The third problem arises from the second: there may not exist an optimal ranking in the terms of the principle, because maximizing the probability of satisfaction at rank 1 may mean excluding

* One could generalize the argument of §3, by defining all the probabilities in terms of the set of requests rather than a single request. However, this would involve accepting as measures of effectiveness the 'micro-average' values of recall etc.—that is, the ratios of cumulative numbers of documents—for each document cut-off level. Such measures are in general of dubious value, and are clearly inadequate for the situation of Cooper's example, where different users will stop searching at different points.

† Stirling[10] has analysed the problem of devising such an algorithm. It is possible to do so. but the algorithm is still very time-consuming, and probably unusable for large collections, Stirling has demonstrated that it does, indeed, work better than the PRP.

the maximal probability of satisfaction by rank 10. We can demonstrate this fact with a simple example (a modification of one of Cooper's examples[4]), as follows.

We suppose that the system receives a request which indicates that the requester might fall into one of two groups: that is there are two distinct need-groups whose need is represented by the same formalized request. If he belongs to the first group (assume probability 2/3), there are three documents (d_1–d_3) which will interest him, and he wants to see all of them; if he belongs to the second, there is just one document (d_4) which he wants. The two obvious rankings in which the system could present the documents are:

Ranking *A*: d_1, d_2, d_3, d_4
Ranking *B*: d_4, d_1, d_2, d_3

If we plot the probability of satisfaction against rank for these two rankings, we obtain the graphs shown in Fig. 1.

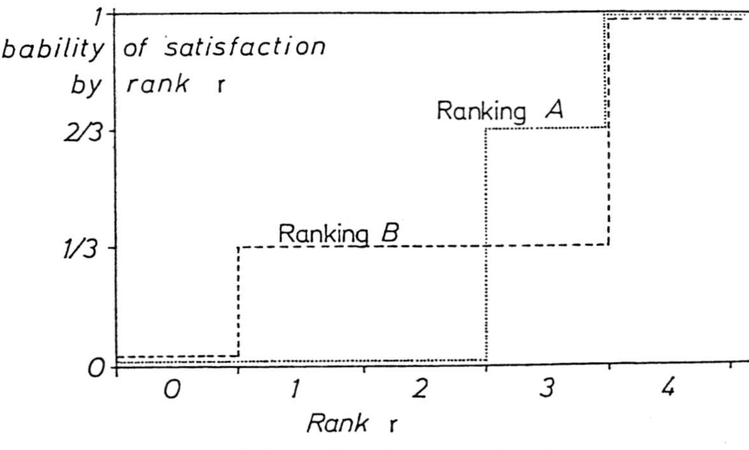

FIG. 1. *Probability of satisfaction at each rank*

Thus neither ranking maximizes the probability of satisfaction at *every* rank—indeed, it is not possible to do so.

We might therefore consider some modification of the principle to deal with this problem—say by maximizing the area under the curve of Fig. 1, or equivalently minimizing the area above it. In fact, the area above the curve and bounded by the lines shown is the expected search length or rather its arithmetic mean over the requests.

It can also be related to recall and fallout: we would be minimizing fallout (or rather, the micro-average of fallout over requests) for the given recall cut-off. Thus we end up with the following possible principle:

> Documents should be ranked in such a way as to maximize the area under the curve of probability of satisfaction against rank; or, equivalently, in such a way as to minimize expected search length (averaged over requests); or, equivalently, in such a way as to minimize fallout (micro-averaged over requests).

Such a principle, it should be noted, makes some assumptions about relative cost of (or losses due to) different events. For example, it is assumed equally valuable to reduce a comprehensive search from 100 to 99 documents, as it is to reduce a quick reference search from three to two documents. This assumption may be justified in cost-to-the-organization terms, but is unlikely to reflect the user-perceived value of the system. Unfortunately, the dilemma is not resolvable: in some circumstances an optimal ranking under one criterion *cannot be* optimal under another criterion.

The above principle is not likely to be of much practical use, for the two reasons given earlier:

(*a*) the fact that it relates only to satisfaction-point cut-off searches;
(*b*) the difficulty of devising an efficient algorithm for implementing it.

However, in the next section I show how the ideas behind it can shed some light on the original PRP.

6. DOCUMENT-BY-DOCUMENT APPROACHES

Ideally, one would like a ranking principle which, like the PRP, depends on the calculation of a single figure measure for each document, and the ranking of the documents in the order determined by this measure. However, in view of the discussion in the previous section, it seems unlikely that such a principle exists which could optimize performance under a range of conditions.

Is there any way in which we can modify the PRP in order to bring it closer to the request-based principle described in the last section, while maintaining its essentially document-by-document character? Two means suggest themselves.

We consider first the relationship between different need-groups represented by identical formalized requests, as in the example of the previous section. In that example, the PRP failed to give the ranking suggested by the request-based principle because it treated all relevant documents the same, even though one need-group required three documents for satisfaction, while the other group required only one. If we define the utility of a relevant document to be such that a total of one unit of utility is required for satisfaction, then we can rank the documents in order of expected utility. Thus in the example, documents d_1–d_3 are assumed to have utility 1/3 for the first need-group; document d_4 has utility 1 for the second need-group. Expected utility then yields the correct ranking according to the request-based ranking principle.

The second modification of the PRP relates to another example of Cooper's. We now assume the same situation as in the previous example, except that the first need-group is satisfied by any *one* of the documents d_1–d_3. The usual PRP suggests ranking the documents:

$$d_1, d_2, d_3, d_4$$

whereas the request-based principle suggests:

$$d_1, d_4, d_2, d_3$$

A modification of the PRP which gives the 'right' answer involves recalculating the probabilities of usefulness of the remaining documents after each document is retrieved. This modification, however, already destroys part of the document-by-document character of the PRP.

These two modifications do not by any means completely solve all the problems: one can make up more complex examples which show that the PRP, even with these two modifications, does not always produce the optimum ranking. They do, however, go some way towards bridging and interpreting the gap between the simply stated PRP and the general problem of finding a ranking which optimizes performance.

7. PROBABILITY AND INFORMATION

I now return to the basic idea behind the PRP. At the beginning of §2, I defined the object of a reference retrieval system as being to predict, in response to a request, which documents the requester will find relevant or useful. It is precisely this prediction process which the PRP was intended to formalize.

However, the discussions in Cooper's[4] paper and above suggest that the estimation of a 'probability of relevance' for each document may not be the most appropriate form of prediction. Going back to the definition, we can identify two main questions:

1. On the basis of what kinds of information can the system make the prediction?
2. How should the system utilize and combine these various kinds of information?

These questions represent, indeed, the central problem of retrieval theory. All theories or hypotheses about information retrieval (in the sense of reference or document retrieval) relate ultimately to these two questions, and all retrieval systems are based on some (explicit or implicit) theory or hypothesis.

As an example of a hypothesis which relates to the two questions, consider the idea of clustering documents. The justification for clustering documents has been expressed by van Rijsbergen and Sparck Jones[9] as the Cluster Hypothesis: that relevant documents are more like one another than they are like non-relevant documents. To express this hypothesis in prediction terms, the idea is that if document A matches the request and document B looks like document A, then this tells us something about the probable relevance of B, whether or not B itself matches the request.

What makes this example particularly interesting is that it is clear that the Cluster Hypothesis *cannot be* incorporated directly into a document-by-document calculation of probability of relevance, since the probability of relevance of document B in the example depends on the presence in the collection of document A. In practice, document cluster theory attempts to reduce the problem to the usual document-by-document form by first detecting the clusters, and then adding the information about cluster membership to the individual document records in some way. The subsequent retrieval operations can then be conducted in a document-by-document fashion.

No cluster theorist to my knowledge has attempted to approach the whole problem in terms of prediction. However, Goffman[11] suggested a method of retrieval based on the dependence between documents, and Croft and van Rijsbergen [12] have recently pointed out the similarities between Goffman's method and the clustering approach (and have given experimental evidence that the two methods give similar performance).

8. CONCLUSIONS

A retrieval system has to predict the relevance of documents to users on the basis of certain information. Whether the calculation of a probability of relevance, document-by-document, is an appropriate way to make the prediction depends on the nature of the relevance variable and of the information about it. In particular, the probability-ranking approach depends on the assumption that the relevance of one document to a request is independent of the other documents in the collection.

This assumption is as much about the nature of the information on the basis of which the system is trying to predict relevance, as it is about the nature of relevance itself. There are various kinds of dependency between documents, at various levels between the relevance itself and the information about it.

The probability ranking principle and its application can be regarded as a general theory of document-by-document information retrieval. But there exists no comparable theory for dealing with the more general problem of how to take account of dependency information. While dependency-oriented approaches to information retrieval, such as cluster-based retrieval, continue to be proposed, the development of such a general theory would seem to be of high priority.

REFERENCES

1. MARON, M. E. *and* KUHNS, J. L. On relevance, probabilistic indexing and information retrieval. *Journal of the Association for Computing Machinery*, *7*, 1960, 216–44.
2. ROBERTSON, S. E. The probabilistic character of relevance. *Information Processing and Management*, *13*, 1971, 247151.
3. ROBERTSON, S. E. *A theoretical model of the retrieval characteristics of information retrieval systems*. Ph.D. thesis, University of London, 1976.
4. COOPER, W. S. The suboptimality of retrieval rankings based on probability of usefulness. (Private communication.)
5. COOPER, W. S. On selecting a measure of retrieval effectiveness. *Journal of the American Society for Information Science*, *24*, 1973, 87–100 and 413–24.
6. COOPER, W. S. Expected search length: a single measure of retrieval effectiveness based on the weak ordering action of retrieval systems. *American Documentation*, *19*, 1968, 30–41.
7. ROBERTSON, S. E. *ans* SPARCK JONES, K. Relevance weighting of search terms. *Journal of the American Society for Information Science*, *27*, 1976, 129–46.
8. KEEN, E. M. *and* DIGGER, J. A. *Report of an information science index languages test*. College of Librarianship Wales, Aberystwyth, 1972.
9. VAN RIJSBERGEN, C. J. *and* SPARCK JONES, K. A test for the separation of relevant and non-relevant documents in experimental retrieval collections. *Journal of Documentation*, *29*, 1973, 251–7.
10. STIRLING, K. H. The effect of document ranking on retrieval system performance: A search for an optimal ranking rule. *Proceedings of the American Society for Information Science*, *12*, 1975, 105–6.
11. GOFFMAN, W. An indirect method of information retrieval. *Information Storage and Retrieval*, *4*, 1969, 361–73.
12. CROFT, W. B. *and* VAN RIJSBERGEN, C. J. An evaluation of Goffman's indirect retrieval method. *Information Processing and Management*, *12*, 1976, 327–31.

APPENDIX

The purpose of the appendix is to present in summary the counter-example to the probability ranking principle discovered by W. S. Cooper.[4]

Cooper considers the problem of ranking the output of a system in response to a *given* request. Thus he is concerned with the class of users who put the same request to the system, and with a ranking of the documents in response to this one request which will optimize performance for this class of users.

Consider, then, the following situation. The class of users (associated with this one request) consists of two sub-classes, U_1 and U_2; U_1 has twice as many members as U_2. Any user from U_1 would be satisfied with any one of the documents D_1–D_9, but with no others. Any user from U_2 would be satisfied with document D_{10}, but with no others.

Hence: any document from D_1–D_9, considered on its own, has a probability of $\frac{2}{3}$ of satisfying the next user who puts this request to the system. D_{10} has a probability of $\frac{1}{3}$ of satisfying him/her; all other documents have probability zero. The probability ranking principle therefore says that D_1–D_9 should be given joint rank 1, D_{10} rank 2, and all others rank 3.

But this means that while U_1 users are satisfied with the first document they receive, U_2 users have to reject nine documents before they reach the one they want. One could readily improve on the probability ranking, by giving D_1(say) rank 1, D_{10} rank 2, and D_2–D_9 and all others rank 3. Then U_1 users are still satisfied with the first document, but U_2 users are now satisfied with the second. Thus the ranking specified by the probability-ranking principle is not optimal. Such is Cooper's counter-example.

It might be argued that in this particular situation one could do something different anyway: for example, U_1 and U_2 users might distinguish between themselves, given a suitable prompting device such as a 'see also' heading. But the basic point remains: given some data about the possible relevance or usefulness of certain documents to certain people, a strict application of the probability ranking principle does not necessarily lead to optimum performance.

The above counter-example is the basis for the example used in §6 of the present paper. That of §5 is a second example presented by Cooper.

(Received 12 July 1977)

Inference Networks for Document Retrieval

Howard Turtle and W. Bruce Croft
Computer and Information Science Department
University of Massachusetts
Amherst, MA 01003

Abstract

The use of inference networks to support document retrieval is introduced. A network-based retrieval model is described and compared to conventional probabilistic and Boolean models.

1 Introduction

Network representations have been used in information retrieval since at least the early 1960's. Networks have been used to support diverse retrieval functions, including browsing [TC89], document clustering [Cro80], spreading activation search [CK87], support for multiple search strategies [CT87], and representation of user knowledge [OPC86] or document content [TS85].

Recent work suggests that significant improvements in retrieval performance will require techniques that, in some sense, "understand" the content of documents and queries [vR86, Cro87] and can be used to infer probable relationships between documents and queries. In this view, information retrieval is an inference or evidential reasoning process in which we estimate the probability that a user's information need, expressed as one or more queries, is met given a document as "evidence." Network representations show promise as mechanisms for inferring these kinds of relationships [CT89,CK87].

The idea that retrieval is an inference or evidential reasoning process is not new. Cooper's logical relevance [Coo71] is based on deductive relationships between representations of documents and information needs. Wilson's situational relevance [Wil73] extends this notion to incorporate inductive or uncertain inference based on the degree to which documents support information needs. The techniques required to support these kinds of inference are similar to those used in expert systems that must reason with uncertain information. A number of competing inference models have been developed for these kinds of expert systems [KL86,LK88] and several of these models can be adapted to the document retrieval task.

In the research described here we adapt an inference network model to the retrieval task. The use of the model is intended to:

- Support the use of multiple document representation schemes. Research has shown that a given query will retrieve different documents when applied to different representations, even when the average retrieval performance achieved with each representation is the same. Katzer, for example, found little overlap in documents retrieved using seven different representations, but found that documents retrieved by multiple representations were likely to be relevant [KMT+82]. Similar results have been obtained when comparing term- with cluster-based representations [CH79] and term- with citation-based representations [FNL88].

- Allow results from different queries and query types to be combined. Given a single natural language description of an information need, different searchers will formulate different queries to represent that need and will retrieve different documents, even when average performance is the same for each searcher [MKN79,KMT+82]. Again, documents retrieved by multiple searchers are more likely to be relevant. A description of an information need can be used to generate several query representations (e.g., probabilistic, Boolean), each using a different query strategy and each capturing different aspects of the information need. These different search strategies are known to retrieve different documents for the same underlying information need [Cro87].

- Facilitate flexible matching between the terms or concepts mentioned in queries and those assigned to documents. The poor match between the vocabulary used to express queries and the vocabulary used to represent documents appears to be a major cause of poor recall [FLGD87]. Recall can be improved using domain knowledge to match query and representation concepts without significantly degrading precision.

The resulting formal retrieval model integrates several previous models in a single theoretical framework; multiple document and query representations are treated as evidence which is combined to estimate the probability that a document satisfies a user's information need.

In what follows we briefly review candidate inference models, present an inference network-based retrieval model, and compare the network model to current retrieval models.

2 Inference networks

The development of automated inference techniques that accommodate uncertainty has been an area of active research in the artificial intelligence community, particularly in the context of expert systems [KL86,LK88]. Popular approaches include those based on purely symbolic reasoning [Coh85,Doy79], fuzzy sets [Zad83], and a variety of probability models [Nil86,Che88]. Two inference models based on probabilistic methods are of particular interest: Bayesian inference networks [Pea88,LS88] and the Dempster-Shafer theory of evidence [Dem68,Sha76].

A Bayesian inference network is a directed, acyclic dependency graph (DAG) in which nodes represent propositional variables or constants and edges represent dependence relations between propositions. If a proposition represented by a node p "causes" or implies the proposition represented by node q, we draw a directed edge from p to q. The node q contains a *link* matrix that specifies $P(q|p)$ for all possible values of the two variables. When a node has multiple parents, the link matrix specifies the dependence of that node on the set of parents (π_q) and characterizes the dependence relationship between that node and all nodes representing its potential causes.[1] Given a set of prior probabilities for the roots of the DAG, these networks can be used to compute the probability or degree of belief associated with all remaining nodes.

Different restrictions on the topology of the network and assumptions about the way in which the connected nodes interact lead to different schemes for combining probabilities. In general, these schemes have two components which operate independently: a *predictive* component in which parent nodes provide support for their children (the degree to which we believe a proposition depends on the degree to which we believe the propositions that might cause it), and a *diagnostic* component in which children provide support for their parents (if our belief in a proposition increases or decreases, so does our belief in its potential causes). The propagation of probabilities through the net can be done using information passed between adjacent nodes.

The Dempster-Shafer theory of evidence, although not originally cast as a network model, can be used as an alternative method for evaluating these kinds of probabilistic inference networks. Rather than computing the belief associated with a query given a set of evidence, we can view Dempster-Shafer as computing the probability that the evidence would allow us to prove the query. The degree of support parameters associated with the arcs joining nodes are not interpreted as conditional probabilities, but as assertions that the parent node provides support for the child (is *active*) for some proportion p of the time and does not support the child for the remainder of the time. For an *and*-combination we compute the proportion of the time that all incoming arcs are active. For an *or*-combination we compute the proportion of the time that at least one parent node is active. To compute the provability of the query given a document, we examine all paths leading from the document to the query and compute the proportion of time that all of the arcs on at least one proof path are active. Given the structure of these networks, this computation can be done using series-parallel reduction of the subgraph joining the document and query in time proportional to the number of arcs in the subgraph.

The Bayesian and Dempster-Shafer models are different and can lead to different results. However, under the assumption of disjunctive rule interaction (so called "noisy-OR") and the interpretation of an arc from a to b as $P(b|a) = p$ and $P(b|\neg a) = 0$, the Bayesian and Dempster-Shafer models will produce similar results [Pea88, page 446]. The document retrieval inference networks described here are based on the Bayesian inference network model.

The use of Bayesian inference networks for information retrieval represents an extension of probability-based retrieval research dating from the early 1960's [MK60]. It has long been recognized that some terms in a collection are more significant than others and that information about the distribution of terms in a collection can be used to improve retrieval performance. The use of these networks generalizes existing probabilistic models and allows integration of several sources of knowledge in a single framework.

[1] While this probability specification is generally referred to as a link matrix, it is actually a tensor.

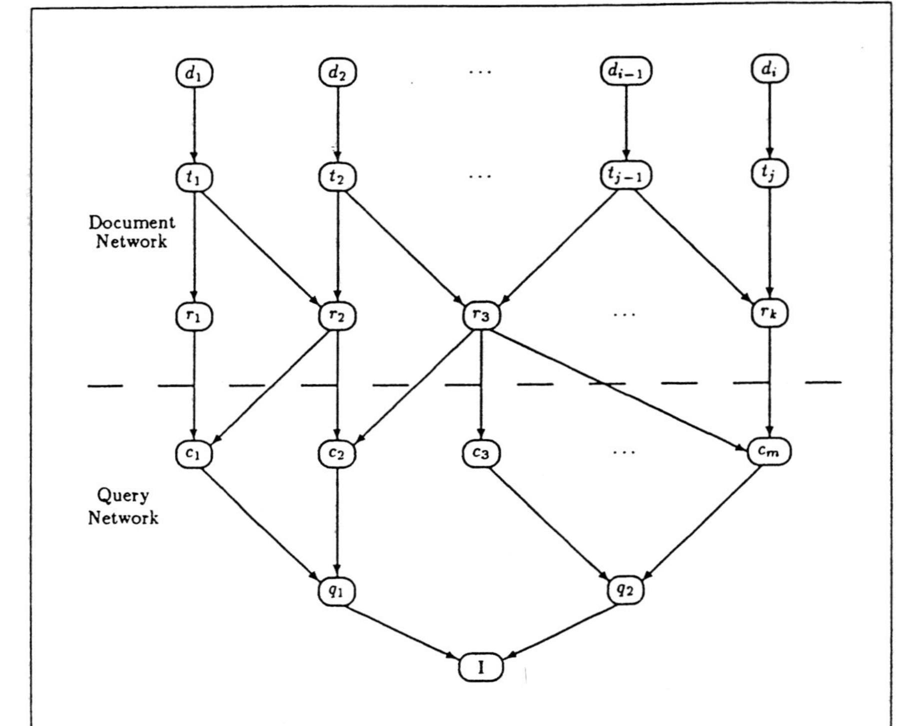

Figure 1: Basic document inference network

3 Basic Model

The basic document retrieval inference network, shown in Figure 1, consists of two component networks: a document network and a query network. The document network represents the document collection using a variety of document representation schemes. The document network is built once for a given collection and its structure does not change during query processing. The query network consists of a single node which represents the user's information need and one or more query representations which express that information need. A query network is built for each information need and is modified during query processing as existing queries are refined or new queries are added in an attempt to better characterize the information need. The document and query networks are joined by links between representation concepts and query concepts. All nodes in the inference network take on values from the set {*false*, *true*}.

3.1 Document network

The document network consists of document nodes (d_i's), text representation nodes (t_j's), and concept representation nodes (r_k's). Each document node represents a document in the collection. A document node corresponds to the event that a specific document has been observed. The form of the document represented depends on the collection and its intended use, but we will assume that a document is a well defined object and will focus on traditional document types (e.g., monographs, journal articles, office documents).

Document nodes correspond to abstract documents rather than their physical representations. A text representation node or text node corresponds to a specific text representation of a document. A text node corresponds to the event that a text representation has been observed. We focus here on the text content of documents, but the network model can support documents nodes with multiple children representing additional component types (e.g., figures, audio, or video). Similarly, a single text might be shared by more than one document. While shared components is rare in traditional collections (an example would be a journal article that appears in both a serial issue and in a reprint collection) and is not generally represented in current retrieval models, it is common in hypertext systems. For clarity, we will consider only text representations and will assume a one-to-one correspondence between documents and texts. The dependence of a text upon the document is represented in the network by an arc from the document node to the text node.

The content representation nodes or representation nodes can be divided into several subsets, each corresponding to a single representation technique that has been applied to the document texts. For example, if a collection has been indexed using automatic phrase extraction and manually assigned index terms, then the set of representation nodes will consist of two distinct subsets or content representation types with disjoint domains. Thus, if the phrase "information retrieval" has been extracted and "information retrieval" has been manually assigned as an index term, then two representation nodes with distinct meanings will be created. One corresponds to the event that "information retrieval" has been automatically extracted from a subset of the collection, the second corresponds to the event that "information retrieval" has been manually assigned to a (presumably distinct) subset of the collection. We represent the assignment of a specific representation concept to a document by a directed arc to the representation node from each text node corresponding to a document to which the concept has been assigned. For now we assume that the presence or absence of a link corresponds to a binary assigned/not assigned distinction, that is, there are no partial or weighted assignments.

In principle, the number of representation schemes is unlimited; in addition to phrase extraction and manually assigned terms we would expect representations based on natural language processing and automatic keyword extraction. For any real document collection, however, the number of representations used will be fixed and relatively small. The potential domain of each representation scheme may also be unlimited, but the actual number of primitive representation concepts defined for a given collection is fixed by the collection. The domain for most automated representation schemes is generally bounded by some function of the collection size (e.g., the number of keywords cannot exceed the number of words in a collection). For manual representation schemes the domain size is limited by the number of documents, the representation scheme itself (e.g., a controlled vocabulary), and the amount of time a human expert can spend analyzing each document.

The basic document network shown in Figure 1 is a simple three level DAG in which document nodes are roots, text nodes are interior nodes, and representation nodes are leaves. Document nodes have exactly one text node as a child and each text node has one or more representation nodes as children.

Each document node has a prior probability associated with it that describes the probability of observing that document; this prior probability will generally be set to 1/(collection size) and will be small for real collections. Each text node contains a specification of its dependence upon its parent; by assumption, this dependence is complete, a text node is observed ($t_i = true$) exactly when its parent document is observed ($d_i = true$).

Each representation node contains a specification of the conditional probability associated with the node given its set of parent text nodes. This specification incorporates the effect of any indexing weights (e.g., term frequency for each parent text) or term weights (e.g., inverse document frequency) associated with the representation concept. While, in principle, this would require $O(2^n)$ space for a node with n parents, in practice we use canonical representations that allow us to compute the required conditional probabilities when needed. These canonical schemes require $O(n)$ space if we weight the contribution of each parent or $O(1)$ space if parents are to be treated uniformly.

3.2 Query network

The query network is an "inverted" DAG with a single leaf that corresponds to the event that an information need is met and multiple roots that correspond to the concepts that express the information need. As shown in Figure 1, a set of intermediate query nodes may be used when multiple queries express the information need. These nodes are a representation convenience; it is always possible to eliminate them by increasing the complexity of the distribution specified at the node representing the information need.

In general, the user's information need is internal to the user and is not precisely understood. We attempt to make the meaning of an information need explicit by expressing it in the form of one or more queries that have formal interpretations. These queries may be generated from a single natural language description (e.g., keywords or phrases for a probabilistic search, a Boolean representation, sample documents, ...) or they may represent additional sources of information (e.g., an intermediary's description of the user or of the information need, or feedback provided by the user). It is unlikely that any of these queries will correspond precisely to the information need, but some will better characterize the information need than others and several query specifications taken together may be a better representation than any of the individual queries.

The roots of the query network are query concepts; they correspond to the primitive concepts used to express the information need. A single query concept node may have several representation concept nodes as parents. Each query concept node contains a specification of its dependence on the set of parent representation concepts. The query concept nodes define the mapping between the concepts used to represent the document collection and the concepts used in the queries. In the simplest case, the query concepts are the same as the representation concepts so each query concept has exactly one parent. In a slightly more complex example, the query concept "information retrieval" may have as parents both the node corresponding to "information retrieval" as a phrase and the node corresponding to "information retrieval" as a manually assigned term. As we add content representations to the document network and allow query concepts that do not explicitly appear in any document representation, the number of parents associated with a single query concept will increase.

A query concept is similar to a representation concept that is derived from other representation concepts (see section 5 for a discussion of derived representation concepts) and in some cases it will be useful to "promote" a query concept to a representation concept. For example, suppose that a researcher is looking for information on a recently developed process that is unlikely to be explicitly identified in any existing representation scheme. The researcher, if sufficiently motivated, could work with the retrieval system to describe how this new concept might be inferred from other representation concepts. If this new concept definition is of general interest, it can be added to the collection of representation concepts. This use of inference to define new concepts is similar to that used in RUBRIC [TS85].

The attachment of the query concept nodes to the document network has no effect on the basic structure of the document network. None of the existing links need change and none of the conditional probability specifications stored in the nodes are modified.

A query node represents a distinct query form and corresponds to the event that the query is satisfied. Each query node contains a specification of the dependence of the query on its parent query concepts. The link matrices that describe these conditional probabilities are discussed further in section 3.4, but we note that the form of the link matrix is determined by the query type; a link matrix simulating a Boolean operator is different than a matrix simulating a probabilistic or weighted query.

The single leaf representing the information need corresponds to the event that an information need is met. In general, we cannot predict with certainty whether a user's information need will be met by a document collection. The query network is intended to capture the way in which meeting the user's information need depends on documents and their representations. Moreover, the query network is intended to allow us to combine information from multiple document representations and to combine queries of different types to form a single, formally justified estimate of the probability that the user's information need is met. If the inference network correctly characterizes the dependence of the information need on the collection, the computed probability provides a good estimate.

3.3 Use of the inference network

The retrieval inference network is intended to capture all of the significant probabilistic dependencies among the variables represented by nodes in the document and query networks. Given the prior probabilities associated with the documents (roots) and the conditional probabilities associated with the interior nodes, we can compute the posterior probability or belief associated with each node in the network. Further, if the value of any variable represented in the network becomes known we can use the network to recompute the probabilities associated with all remaining nodes based on this "evidence."

The network, taken as a whole, represents the dependence of a user's information need on the documents in a collection where the dependence is mediated by document and query representations. When the query network is first built and attached to the document network we compute the belief associated with each node in the query network. The initial value at the node representing the information need is the probability that the information need is met given that no specific document in the collection has been observed and all documents are equally likely (or unlikely). If we now observe a single document d_i and attach evidence to the network asserting $d_i = true$ we can compute a new belief for every node in the network given $d_i = true$. In particular, we can compute the probability that the information need is met given that d_i has been observed in the collection. We can now remove this evidence and instead assert that some d_j, $i \neq j$ has been observed. By repeating this process we can compute the probability that the information need is met given each document in the collection and rank the documents accordingly.

In principle, we need not consider each document in isolation but could look for the subset of documents which produce the highest probability that the information need is met. While a general solution to this best-subset problem is intractable, in some cases good heuristic approximations are possible. Best-subset rankings have been considered in IR [Sti75], and similar problems arise in pattern recognition, medical diagnosis, and truth-maintenance systems. See [Pea88] for a discussion of the best-subset or belief revision problem in Bayesian networks. At present, we consider only documents in isolation because the approach is computationally simpler and because it allows comparison with earlier retrieval models that produce document rankings consistent with the Probability Ranking Principle [Rob77] in which documents are considered in isolation.

The document network is built once for a given collection. Given one or more queries representing an information need, we then build a query network that attempts to characterize the dependence of the information need on the collection. If the ranking produced by the initial query network is inadequate, we must add additional information to the query network or refine its structure to better characterize the meaning of the existing queries. This feedback process is quite similar to conventional relevance feedback.

3.4 Link matrix forms

For all non-root nodes in the inference network we must estimate the probability that a node takes on a value given any set of values for its parent nodes. If a node a has a set of parents $\pi_a = \{p_1, \ldots, p_n\}$, we must estimate $P(a|p_1, \ldots, p_n)$.

The most direct way to encode our estimate is as a link matrix. Since we are dealing with binary valued propositions, this matrix is of size 2×2^n for n parents and specifies the probability that a takes the value $a = true$ or $a = false$ for all combinations of parent values. The update procedures for Bayesian networks then use the probabilities provided by the set of parents to condition over the link matrix values to compute the predictive component of our belief in a or $P(a = true)$. Similarly, the link matrix is used to provide diagnostic information to the set of parents based on our belief in a. As mentioned earlier, encoding our estimates in link matrix form is practical only for nodes with a small set of parents, so our estimation task has two parts: how do we estimate the dependence of a node on its set of parents and how do we encode these estimates in a usable form?

We will describe four canonical link matrix forms, three for the Boolean operators and a fourth for simple probabilistic retrieval. For illustration, we will assume that a node Q has three parents A, B, and C and that

$$P(A = \text{true}) = a, \quad P(B = \text{true}) = b, \quad P(C = \text{true}) = c.$$

For *or*-combinations, Q will be true when any of A, B, or C is true and false only when A, B, and C are all false. This suggests a link matrix of the form

$$L_{\text{or}} = \begin{pmatrix} 1 & 0 & 0 & 0 & 0 & 0 & 0 & 0 \\ 0 & 1 & 1 & 1 & 1 & 1 & 1 & 1 \end{pmatrix}.$$

Using a closed form of the update procedures, we have

$$\begin{aligned} P(Q = \mathit{true}) &= (1-a)(1-b)c + (1-a)b(1-c) + (1-a)bc + a(1-b)(1-c) \\ &\quad + a(1-b)c + ab(1-c) + abc \\ &= 1 - (1-a)(1-b)(1-c) \end{aligned}$$

which is the familiar rule for disjunctive combination of events that are not known to be mutually exclusive. Similar matrix forms can be developed for *and* ($P(Q = \mathit{true}) = abc$) and *not* ($P(Q = \mathit{true}) = 1 - a$).

If we restrict the parent nodes for any of these logic operators to values 0 or 1 then Q must also have a value of 0 or 1. If we allow terms to take on weights in the range $[0,1]$ and interpret these weights as the probability that the term has been assigned to a document text, then these inference networks provide a natural interpretation for Boolean retrieval with weighted indexing. The use of these canonical forms to simulate Boolean retrieval is discussed in section 4.3

For probabilistic retrieval each parent has a weight associated with it, as does the child. In this weighted-sum matrix, our belief in Q depends on the specific parents that are true – parents with larger weights have more influence in our belief. If we let $w_a, w_b, w_c \geq 0$ be the parent weights, $0 \leq w_q \leq 1$ the child weight, and $t = w_a + w_b + w_c$, then we have a link matrix of the form

$$\begin{pmatrix} 1 & \frac{(w_a+w_b)w_q}{t} & \frac{(w_a+w_c)w_q}{t} & \frac{w_a w_q}{t} & \frac{(w_b+w_c)w_q}{t} & \frac{w_b w_q}{t} & \frac{w_c w_q}{t} & 1 - w_q \\ 0 & \frac{w_c w_q}{t} & \frac{w_b w_q}{t} & \frac{(w_b+w_c)w_q}{t} & \frac{w_a w_q}{t} & \frac{(w_a+w_c)w_q}{t} & \frac{(w_a+w_b)w_q}{t} & w_q \end{pmatrix}.$$

Evaluation of this link matrix form results in

$$P(Q = \mathit{true}) = \frac{(w_a a + w_b b + w_c c) w_q}{t}.$$

This link matrix can be used to implement a variety of weighting schemes, including the familiar term weighting schemes based on within-document term frequency (tf), inverse document frequency (idf) or both ($tf.idf$). To illustrate a $tf.idf$ weighting, let Q be a representation node and let A, B, and C be document nodes. Let w_a, w_b, and w_c be the normalized tf values for A, B, and C, let idf_q be the normalized idf weight for Q, and let

$$w_q = idf_q \cdot (w_a + w_b + w_c). \qquad (1)$$

Given our basic model, when A is instantiated, belief in Q is given by

$$\begin{aligned} \text{bel}(Q) &= \frac{w_a w_q}{w_a + w_b + w_c} \\ &= \frac{tf_a \cdot idf_q \cdot (w_a + w_b + w_c)}{w_a + w_b + w_c} \\ &= tf_a \cdot idf_q \end{aligned}$$

which is a form of $tf.idf$ weight. In general, when a document is instantiated all representation concept nodes to which it is attached take on the $tf.idf$ weight associated with the document/term pair.

The weight at Q has two distinct parts. The first part (idf_q in our example) acts to set the maximum belief achievable at a node. If, for some combination of parent values, our belief in Q is certain then this component disappears. Note that in this formulation, the idf component is dependent only upon the distribution of the term in the collection, not on the distribution of the term in relevant and non-relevant subsets. Relevance feedback is modeled as part of the query network and does not affect belief in representation concepts.

The second part ($w_a + w_b + w_c$ in our example) acts to normalize the parent weights. Equation 1 is appropriate for the basic model in which only one document is instantiated at a time. In the extended model of section 5 where multiple roots can be instantiated, this component is adjusted to normalize for the maximum achievable set of parent weights. In the general case, where all parents can take any value in the range $[0,1]$, this normalizing component disappears.

These canonical forms are sufficient for the retrieval inference networks described here, but many others are possible (see section 4.3 for other examples). Further, when the number of parents is small (say, less than 5 or 6) we can use the full link matrix if the dependence of a node on its parents does not fit a canonical form.

4 Comparison with other retrieval models

The inference network retrieval model generalizes both the probabilistic and Boolean models. Inference networks can be used to simulate both probabilistic and Boolean queries and can be used to combine results from multiple queries.

In this section we compare the inference network model with probabilistic (sections 4.1 and 4.2) and Boolean (section 4.3) models and show how inference networks can be used to simulate both forms of retrieval. We then consider how the probabilities required by the model can be estimated (section 4.4); the estimation problems are essentially equivalent to those encountered with probabilistic or vector-space retrieval.

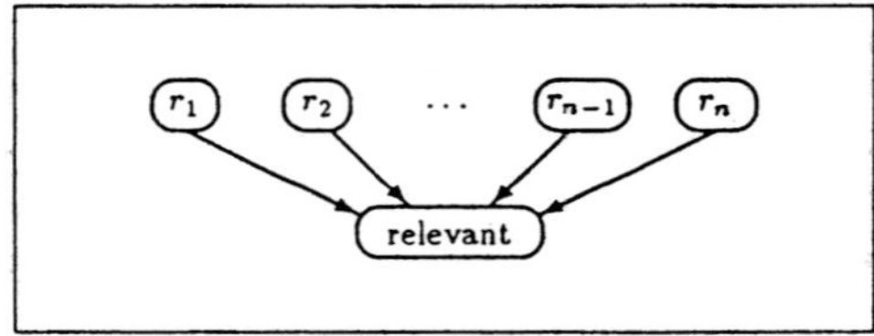

Figure 2: Inference network for binary independence model

4.1 Probabilistic retrieval models

Conventional probabilistic models [vR79,SM83] rank documents by the probability that each document would be judged relevant to a given query, $P(\text{relevant}|d_i)$.[2] This is, in many ways, similar to computing the probability that a user's information need is met given a specific document, $P(I|d_i)$. The principal differences between conventional probabilistic models and the model described here are: 1) most probabilistic models do not explicitly represent the query, 2) conventional probabilistic models do not distinguish between a document and its representations but treat a document as a single vector, and 3) the inference network model depends less upon Bayesian inversion than probabilistic models, Bayesian inversion is just one way to estimate $P(I|d_i)$ (or $P(Q|d_i)$ in the case of a single query).

In this section we summarize the major differences between the inference network and conventional probabilistic models by comparing the network model to the binary independence model. In the next section we provide a formal comparison of the inference network model with a recent probabilistic model that explicitly represents documents and queries.

An inference network that corresponds to the binary independence model [vR79] is shown in Figure 2. A document is represented by a vector whose components are indexing or representation concepts ($d_i = \{r_1, \ldots, r_n\}$). The set of concepts considered is generally restricted to the subset that actually occurs in the query. Comparing this network with that shown in Figure 1, we see that in the binary independence model, the document network is represented by a single level of representation nodes and the query network consists of a single relevance node. In order to implement this network we must somehow estimate the probability of relevance given the set of parent representation concepts and this estimate must incorporate all of our judgments about the probability that a representation concept should be assigned to a document, about the semantic and stochastic relationships between representation concepts, about the relationship between concepts named in the query and assigned to documents, and about the semantics of the query itself. This dependence is complex and its estimation is not a task we could expect users to perform willingly or reliably.

One approach to simplifying the estimation task is to invoke Bayes' rule so that we need only estimate the probability that each representation concept occurs in relevant or non-relevant documents. This approach does not help to provide initial estimates of the probability distributions since these "simpler" estimates must still incorporate all of the judgments required for the "hard" estimate. The advantage of this approach is that, given samples of relevant and non-relevant documents, it is easy to compute $P(r_i)$ for the relevant sample and to use the result as an estimate of $P(r_i|\text{relevant} = \textit{true})$. We can use a similar estimate for $P(r_i|\text{relevant} = \textit{false})$. Given a set of independence assumptions and estimates for $P(d_i)$ and $P(\text{relevant} = \textit{true})$ we can compute $P(\text{relevant}|d_i)$.[3] Estimating $P(\text{relevant}|d_i)$ without the use of Bayes' rule would be extremely difficult.

Essentially the same procedures can be used to estimate $P(Q|d_i)$. The main difference between the two estimates is that instead of using the representation concepts directly we must compute $P(c_j|\pi_{c_j})$ and compute an expected value for $P(c_j|d_i)$ in order to estimate $P(Q|d_i)$.

The question remains, however, whether estimates of $P(\text{relevant}|d_i)$ or $P(Q|d_i)$ obtained in this way match users' intuition about the dependence. The fact that relevance feedback does improve retrieval performance suggests that the estimates of $P(\text{relevant}|d_i)$ do capture at least some of the dependence, but these estimates are generally based on a small number of relevant documents and are necessarily rather coarse.

While it is clear that estimating $P(\text{relevant}|d_i)$ directly from a small number of documents is impractical, it may be possible to obtain estimates of $P(Q|\pi_Q)$. Users may, for example, be able to assign importance to the concepts in their query and may be able to identify significant interactions between concepts. These estimates could improve the initial estimate and might be used in conjunction with the estimates derived from training samples.

A second approach to simplifying the estimation task is to identify the different types of judgments that enter into the overall estimate and to develop estimates for each type of judgment separately. The model presented here represents one decomposition in which the task of estimating the probability that a given document satisfies an information need consists of judgments about the relationship of a document to its text, the assignment of representation concepts to the text, the relationships between query and representation concepts, and the relationship between queries, query concepts, and the information need. Other decompositions are certainly possible and can be accommodated within the same general framework. The set of relationships presented here incorporates those judgments most important for current generation document retrieval systems.

When viewed this way, the probabilistic and inference models use two similar approaches to the same estimation problem. The probabilistic model uses a single, general purpose rule and makes assumptions about term dependence in order to estimate $P(\text{relevant}|d_i)$. The model presented here views the problem of estimating $P(I|d_i)$ as consisting of a set of logically related estimates. Each estimate is made independently using procedures specific to

[2] Most probabilistic models do not actually compute $P(\text{relevant}|d_i)$, but simply rank documents using some function that is monotonic with $P(\text{relevant}|d_i)$. Like Fuhr ([Fuh89]), we believe that an estimate of the probability of relevance is more useful than the ranking by itself. A ranked list of documents in which the top ranked document has a probability of relevance of 0.5 should be viewed differently than a similar list in which the top ranked document has a probability of relevance of 0.95.

[3] $P(d_i)$ and $P(\text{relevant} = \textit{true})$ do not play a major role in probabilistic models that only produce a document ranking but are required to compute $P(\text{relevant}|d_i)$.

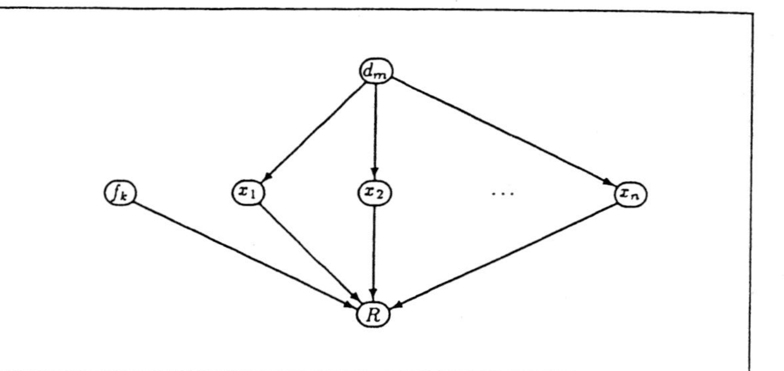

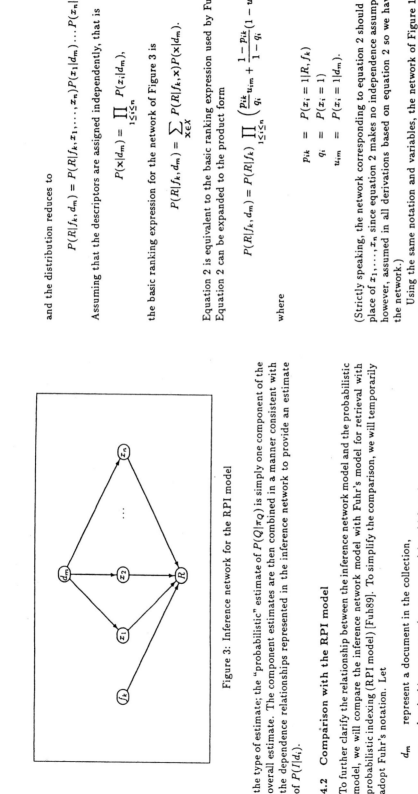

Figure 3: Inference network for the RPI model

the type of estimate; the "probabilistic" estimate of $P(Q|\pi_Q)$ is simply one component of the overall estimate. The component estimates are then combined in a manner consistent with the dependence relationships represented in the inference network to provide an estimate of $P(I|d_i)$.

4.2 Comparison with the RPI model

To further clarify the relationship between the inference network model and the probabilistic model, we will compare the inference network model with Fuhr's model for retrieval with probabilistic indexing (RPI model) [Fuh89]. To simplify the comparison, we will temporarily adopt Fuhr's notation. Let

d_m represent a document in the collection,

$\mathbf{x}$ be the binary vector $(x_1, x_2, \ldots, x_n)$ in which each x_i corresponds to a document descriptor (representation concept),

f_k represent the query, and

R represent the event that a document is judged relevant to a query.

All variables are binary valued. In this model, $P(x_i = 1|d_m)$ is interpreted as the probability that a descriptor r_i is a "correct" indexing of d_m. Let X be the set of possible values for $\mathbf{x}$, where $|X| \leq 2^n$.

The network shown in Figure 3 corresponds to the probability distribution

$$\begin{aligned} P(R, f_k, x_1, \ldots, x_n, d_m) &= P(R|f_k, d_m) \\ &= P(R|f_k, x_1, \ldots, x_n)P(x_1|d_m)\ldots P(x_n|d_m)P(f_k)P(d_m). \end{aligned}$$

We will evaluate this expression for a given document and query so f_k and d_m are known and the distribution reduces to

$$P(R|f_k, d_m) = P(R|f_k, x_1, \ldots, x_n)P(x_1|d_m)\ldots P(x_n|d_m).$$

Assuming that the descriptors are assigned independently, that is

$$P(\mathbf{x}|d_m) = \prod_{1 \leq i \leq n} P(x_i|d_m),$$

the basic ranking expression for the network of Figure 3 is

$$P(R|f_k, d_m) = \sum_{\mathbf{x} \in X} P(R|f_k, \mathbf{x})P(\mathbf{x}|d_m). \tag{2}$$

Equation 2 is equivalent to the basic ranking expression used by Fuhr [Fuh89, equation 9]. Equation 2 can be expanded to the product form

$$P(R|f_k, d_m) = P(R|f_k) \prod_{1 \leq i \leq n} \left(\frac{p_{ik}}{q_i} u_{im} + \frac{1 - p_{ik}}{1 - q_i}(1 - u_{im}) \right) \tag{3}$$

where

$$\begin{aligned} p_{ik} &= P(x_i = 1|R, f_k) \\ q_i &= P(x_i = 1) \\ u_{im} &= P(x_i = 1|d_m). \end{aligned}$$

(Strictly speaking, the network corresponding to equation 2 should have a single node $\mathbf{x}$ in place of $x_1, \ldots, x_n$ since equation 2 makes no independence assumptions. Independence is, however, assumed in all derivations based on equation 2 so we have chosen to show it in the network.)

Using the same notation and variables, the network of Figure 1 can be reduced to the network of Figure 4. This inference network is described by the probability distribution

$$\begin{aligned} P(R, f_k, x_1, \ldots, x_n, d_m) &= P(R|d_m) \\ &= P(R|f_k)P(f_k|x_1, \ldots, x_n)P(x_1|d_m)\ldots P(x_n|d_m)P(d_m). \end{aligned}$$

Comparing Figure 4 with Figure 3 we see that in the inference network model the query does not appear as a separate prior (root) but is explicitly conditioned on the representation concepts. Again, d_m is given, so we have

$$P(R|d_m) = P(R|f_k)P(f_k|x_1, \ldots, x_n)P(x_1|d_m)\ldots P(x_n|d_m).$$

Applying Bayes' rule we get

$$P(R|d_m) = P(R|f_k)\frac{P(x_1, \ldots, x_n|f_k)P(f_k)}{P(x_1, \ldots, x_n)}P(x_1|d_m)\ldots P(x_n|d_m).$$

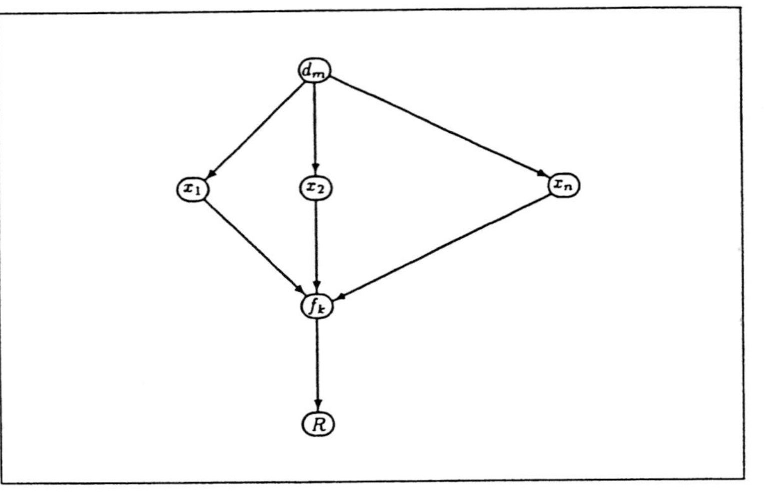

Figure 4: Example inference network

Assuming that the x_i are distributed independently in documents (4) and that the assignment of the x_i is independent of the query (5)

$$P(x_1,\ldots,x_n) = \prod_{1\le i\le n} P(x_i) \quad (4)$$

$$P(x_1,\ldots,x_n|f_k) = \prod_{1\le i\le n} P(x_i|f_k) \quad (5)$$

we have

$$P(R|d_m) = P(R|f_k)P(f_k)\sum_{\mathbf{x}\in X}\prod_{1\le i\le n}\frac{P(x_i|f_k)}{P(x_i)}P(x_i|d_m). \quad (6)$$

The application of Bayes' rule essentially inverts the network of Figure 4 to obtain the equivalent network shown in Figure 5[4]. Note that the use of Bayes' rule here is to allow us to derive a closed-form ranking expression that can be compared with the RPI model. In practice, we would use an estimate of $P(f_k|x_1,\ldots,x_n)$ and would not invert the network.

[4]While the networks in Figures 4 and 5 are equivalent in the sense that the computed probability distributions are the same, Figure 5 does not lend itself to normal belief network updating procedures. In order to produce the new $P(x_i|f_k, d_m)$ link matrix and the new prior $P(f_k)$ we must make use of the assumed value of $P(d_m)$. In essence, when we invert the network we fold the prior probability of d_m into the new link matrix and extract a new prior for the query. This means that to test the effect of a change in $P(d_m)$, we would have to recompute the link matrices at each x_i and compute a new $P(f_k)$. With the network in Figure 4, we can change our assumed value for $P(d_m)$ without changing the probability information stored at each node.

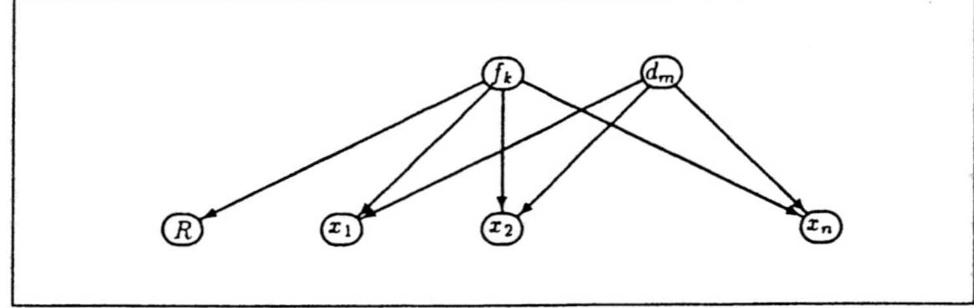

Figure 5: Effect of inversion

Equation 6 reduces to

$$P(R|d_m) = P(R|f_k)P(f_k)\prod_{1\le i\le n}\left(\frac{P(x_i=1|f_k)}{P(x_i=1)}P(x_i=1|d_m) + \frac{P(x_i=0|f_k)}{P(x_i=0)}P(x_i=0|d_m)\right).$$

If we let

$$\begin{aligned} p_{ik} &= P(x_i=1|f_k) \\ q_i &= P(x_i=1) \\ u_{im} &= P(x_i=1|d_m) \end{aligned}$$

we get the ranking expression

$$P(R|d_m) = P(R|f_k)P(f_k)\prod_{1\le i\le n}\left(\frac{p_{ik}}{q_i}u_{im} + \frac{1-p_{ik}}{1-q_i}(1-u_{im})\right) \quad (7)$$

Equation 7 differs from equation 3 in that p_{ik} is conditioned only on the query and not on R and the resulting probability is normalized by $P(f_k)$. The difference in conditioning for p_{ik} arises because the network of Figure 4 implicitly assumes that $\mathbf{x}$ and R are conditionally independent given the query, that is, $\mathbf{x}$ cannot influence our assessment of relevance except through its effect on the query. The network of Figure 3 assumes that $\mathbf{x}$ and f_k are independent, but not necessarily conditionally independent given R, that is, $\mathbf{x}$ and the query can influence our assessment of relevance independently. Under the assumption of conditional independence

$$P(\mathbf{x}|R, f_k) = P(\mathbf{x}|f_k)$$

and the p_{ik} terms are identical. $P(f_k)$ is constant for a given query and does not affect the ranking so, under the assumption of conditional independence, the rankings produced by the two models are identical.

The networks in Figures 3 and 4 help to clarify the differences between the probabilistic and inference network retrieval models. In the network of Figure 3, the query is modeled as a separate variable that is related to the possible document descriptions through the specification of $P(R|\mathbf{x}, f_k)$. The network of Figure 4 explicitly models the dependence of the query on the document representation and the dependence of relevance on the query. Again, the network of Figure 4 asserts the independence of the document representation and relevance given the query; the document representation cannot influence the probability of relevance except through its influence on the query.

The principal difference between the two models, then, lies in the dependencies assumed. While we have chosen Fuhr's model as the basis for comparison, network forms could be developed for the many other probabilistic formulations. The chief advantage of the inference network model is that it allows complex dependencies to be represented in an easily understood form and it allows networks containing these dependencies to be evaluated without development of a closed form expression that captures these dependencies.

4.3 Boolean retrieval

Using the canonical link matrix forms of section 3.4 we can implement Boolean retrieval as follows. For clarity, we assume that the query and representation vocabularies are identical so we can omit query concepts from the network. We also assume that when one document is instantiated all remaining documents are set to false.

1. Use a canonical *or* matrix at each representation node. When a document is instantiated, all representation concepts to which it has been attached will have $\text{bel}(r_i) = 1$. All remaining representation concepts have $\text{bel}(r_j) = 0$.

2. Build an expression tree for the query. The root of the tree is the query and all arcs in the tree are directed toward the root. The leaves of this tree will be representation concepts and the interior nodes will correspond to expression operators. At each operator node use the canonical link matrix form for that operator. Attach this tree to the document network.

3. Using the evaluation procedure described in section 3.3, instantiate each document in turn and record the belief in the query node. Any document for which $\text{bel}(Q) = 1$ satisfies the query, any node for which $\text{bel}(Q) < 1$ does not.

Under the assumptions above and using binary indexing, $\text{bel}(Q)$ can only have values 0 or 1 and the inference network simulates a conventional Boolean system exactly. If we relax the requirement that all uninstantiated documents be set to 0, then only documents for which $\text{bel}(Q) = 1$ satisfy the query and all remaining documents have a small but non-zero $\text{bel}(Q)$.

The same probabilistic interpretation of the Boolean operators applies equally well to weighted indexing. Using the approach described in section 3.4 we can incorporate indexing weights by replacing the *or* link matrix at the representation concept nodes with a weighted-sum matrix incorporating the appropriate *tf* and *idf* weights. In this case, when a document is instantiated, all representation nodes to which it is attached take on the *tf.idf* weight for that term/document pair and all remaining representation nodes take on bel = 0. These weights are then combined using the closed-form expressions of section 3.4. In short, the *tf.idf* weights are interpreted as probabilities and are combined using the normal rules for negation and for disjunctive or conjunctive combination of sets in an event space. As a result, the inference network model provides a natural interpretation of Boolean operations in probabilistic terms and of the meaning of indexing weights.

The binary nature of the retrieval decision in Boolean systems is frequently cited as a drawback [Cro86,SM83,Sal88]. We can relax our strict interpretation of the probabilistic semantics of the Boolean operators by allowing the number of parents=true to influence our belief. For example, we can choose a value $n \leq c \leq \infty$ and interpret the *and* operator to mean

$$\begin{aligned} P(Q_{and} = \text{true}|n \text{ parents} = \text{true}) &= 1 \\ P(Q_{and} = \text{true}|k \text{ parents} = \text{true}) &= 1 - \frac{n-k}{c}, \quad 0 < k < n \\ P(Q_{and} = \text{true}|\text{no parents} = \text{true}) &= 0 \end{aligned}$$

and the *or* operator to mean

$$\begin{aligned} P(Q_{or} = \text{true}|n \text{ parents} = \text{true}) &= 1 \\ P(Q_{or} = \text{true}|k \text{ parents} = \text{true}) &= \frac{k}{c}, \quad 0 < k < n \\ P(Q_{or} = \text{true}|\text{no parents} = \text{true}) &= 0 \end{aligned}$$

Since a node implementing the *not* operator has exactly one parent, its interpretation is unchanged. Under this interpretation, when $c = \infty$ the operators have their normal Boolean interpretation. As c decreases, our belief in Q depends increasingly on the number of parents that are true. When $c = n$ the distinction between *and* and *or* has disappeared and the link matrices for both operators are the same. The use of this parent weighting scheme is quite similar to the extended Boolean retrieval or p-norm model [Sal88,SM83]. The two approaches are equivalent when $c = n$ and $p = 1$ and when $c = p = \infty$; the resulting probability and similarity functions are monotonic for $n < c < \infty$ and $1 < p < \infty$.

4.4 Estimating the probabilities

Given the link matrix forms of section 3.4, we now consider the estimates required for the basic model of Figure 1. The only roots in Figure 1 are the document nodes; the prior probability associated with these nodes is set to 1/(collection size). Estimates are required for five different node types: text, representation and query concepts, query, and information need.

Text nodes. Since text nodes are completely dependent upon the parent document node, the estimate is straightforward. Since there is a single parent, a matrix form can be used; t_i is true exactly when d_i is true so

$$L_{text} = \begin{pmatrix} 1 & 0 \\ 0 & 1 \end{pmatrix}.$$

This matrix form is the inverse of that used for *not*.

Note that the distinction between document and text nodes is not required for the basic model and we often ignore text nodes for clarity. Text nodes are required if we support sharing of text by documents and to support the extended model of section 5 which includes citation links and document clustering. If we allow document nodes to share text nodes, then an *or* matrix is appropriate, t_i is true when any parent is instantiated.

Representation concept nodes. Link matrix forms for representation concepts were discussed in section 3.4. For binary indexing and unweighted terms an *or*-combination can be used. For *tf*, *idf*, or *tf.idf* weights a weighted-sum link matrix is used.

Query concept nodes. As we have seen, previous indexing research can be incorporated directly in the document network. The query network, particularly the links between representation and query concepts is less well understood. Here we are interested in estimating the probabilistic dependence of concepts mentioned in the user's query upon the representation concepts. Most current retrieval models view these two sets of concepts as identical under the assumption that the user knows the set of representation concepts and can formulate queries using the representation concepts directly. Under this assumption, the same link matrix as for text nodes should be used.

Research suggests, however, that the mismatch between query and indexing vocabularies may be a major cause of poor recall [FLGD87]. While our initial implementation is limited to linking query concepts to "nearly" equivalent representation concepts using a weighted-sum combination rule, it would appear that improved estimates of the dependence of query concepts on representation concepts could markedly improve performance. Two areas of research bear directly on improving the quality of these estimates: automatic thesaurus construction and natural language research aimed at extracting concept descriptions from query text, identifying synonymous or related descriptions, and resolving ambiguity.

Query nodes. The dependence of query nodes on the query concepts is more straightforward. For Boolean queries we use the procedure described in section 4.3. For probabilistic queries we use a weighted-sum matrix. In both cases we can adjust link matrix values if we have information about the relative importance of the query concepts.

Information need. The information need can generally be expressed as a small number of queries of different types (Boolean, *m*-of-*n*, probabilistic, natural language, ...). These can be combined using a weighted-sum link matrix with weights adjusted to reflect any user judgments about the importance or completeness of the individual queries.

5 Extensions to the basic model

The basic model described in section 3 is limited in at least two respects. First, we have assumed that evidence about a variable establishes its value with certainty. Second, we have represented only a limited number of dependencies between variables. In this section we will see that these limitations can be removed.

5.1 Uncertain evidence

The only use of evidence in the basic model is to assert that a document has been observed (d_i = *true*). During query processing we assert each document true and rank documents

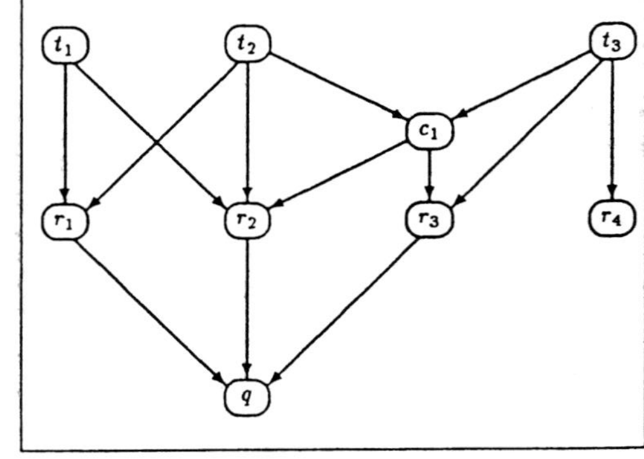

Figure 6: Document clustering model

based on the probability that the information need is met. Evidence is attached to a node a in a Bayesian network by creating a new *evidence* node b as a child of a. This new node b then passes a likelihood vector (both components of a likelihood ratio) to a. Since evidence is expressed in terms of likelihood we are not restricted to the values *true* and *false* but need only specify the likelihood of a = *true* and a = *false* given the evidence summarized at b. Thus we can "partially" instantiate nodes in the network when the evidence we have is not sufficient to establish the value of a proposition with certainty. This uncertain evidence can be used to model citation and document cluster information.

Document clustering. A variety of document clustering techniques have been developed for information retrieval [vR79]. Document clustering is generally used to find documents that are similar to a document that is believed relevant under the assumption that similar documents are related to the same queries. Our use of cluster information is somewhat different since we do not retrieve clusters, but we can incorporate cluster information by treating cluster membership as an additional source of evidence about document content. In the fragment shown in Figure 6, document texts t_1, t_2, and t_3 are indexed using representation concepts r_1, r_2, r_3, and r_4. Documents t_2 and t_3 have been identified as part of cluster c_1; both texts are linked to a cluster node and the cluster node is linked to the representation concepts that define the cluster. The cluster node is similar to a conventional cluster representative. Documents t_1 and t_2 are indexed by the same representation concepts (r_1 and r_2) and, if we assume equivalent conditional probabilities, would be ranked equivalently in the absence of the cluster node. With the addition of the cluster node, however, a new representation concept (r_3) is associated with t_2 by virtue of its cluster membership. Assuming that r_3 contributes positively to the belief in q, t_2 would be ranked higher than t_1. In practice, the links between documents and clusters are not represented in the network; evidence is attached to all clusters to which a document has been assigned when that document is instantiated.

Citation and nearest neighbor links. A variety of asymmetric relationships between pairs of documents can also be represented. These relationships are similar to clustering in that they use an assumed similarity between documents to expand the set of representation concepts that can be plausibly associated with a text. They differ in that they are ordered relations defined on pairs of documents rather than an unordered, set membership relationship between documents and clusters.

One example of this kind of relationship is the nearest neighbor link in which a document is linked to those documents judged to be most similar to the original. A second example is based on citations occurring in the text. Citation links may be useful if the type of reference can be determined to allow estimation of the probabilistic dependence between the nodes. Again, these links are not explicitly represented in the network; evidence is attached to a document's nearest neighbors and citation partners when the document is instantiated.

5.2 Additional dependencies

In the basic model, we assume that there are no dependencies between documents, between texts, between representation concepts, between query concepts, or between queries. While independence assumptions like these are common in retrieval models, it is widely recognized that the assumptions are unrealistic. In addition to the document cluster and citation information which is modeled as evidence, we would like to explicitly represent the term dependencies embodied in conventional term clusters and thesauri.

The basic mechanism for representing these dependencies is unchanged, we identify the set of nodes upon which a given node depends and characterize the probability associated with each node conditioned on its immediate parents. When adding these new links, however, we must be careful to preserve the acyclic nature of the inference network. Bayesian inference networks cannot represent cyclic dependencies, in effect evidence attached to any node in the cycle would continually propagate through the network and repeatedly reinforce the original node. In the basic model, no cycles are possible since nodes are only linked to node types that are lower in the DAG. The introduction of these new dependencies makes cycles possible.

Inference networks provide a natural mechanism for representing dependencies between representation concepts and between query concepts. Several automatic clustering techniques produce structures that can be used in an inference network. For example, dependence trees or Chow trees [vR79,Pea88] contain exactly the term dependence information required for an inference network in a form that is guaranteed to be cycle-free.

These networks can also be used to represent probabilistic thesaurus relationships. These relationships extend those of a conventional thesaurus by including conditional probability information. For example, a conventional thesaurus might list "house pet" as a broader term for "dog" and "cat"; the network representation will include a specification of the probability that "house pet" should be assigned given a document containing "dog" or "cat" in isolation, neither term, or both terms.

Synonyms, related terms, and broader terms can be represented by creating a new node to represent the synonym or related term class or the broader term and adding the new node as a child to the relevant representation concept nodes. We will generally prefer to add these nodes as part of the query network since their presence in the document network would represent a computational burden even when not used in a query. Although generally less useful, narrower term relationships can also be represented.

6 Conclusion

The retrieval model presented here provides a framework within which to integrate several document representations and search strategies. We are currently refining the model and conducting experiments to compare search performance based on this model with that of other models and to compare performance of potential representations and search strategies.

Acknowledgments

This work was supported in part by OCLC Online Computer Library Center, by the Air Force Office of Scientific Research under contract 90-0110, and by NSF Grant IRI-8814790.

References

[CH79] W. Bruce Croft and D. J. Harper. Using probabilistic models of document retrieval without relevance information. *Journal of Documentation*, 35:285–295, 1979.

[Che88] Peter Cheeseman. An inquiry into computer understanding. *Computational Intelligence*, 4:58–66, February 1988. Article is part of a debate between logic and probability schools in AI.

[CK87] Paul R. Cohen and Rick Kjeldsen. Information retrieval by constrained spreading activation in semantic networks. *Information Processing and Management*, 23(2):255–268, 1987.

[Coh85] Paul R. Cohen. *Heuristic Reasoning About Uncertainty: An Artificial Intelligence Approach.* Pitman, Boston, MA, 1985.

[Coo71] W. S. Cooper. A definition of relevance for information retrieval. *Information Storage and Retrieval*, 7:19–37, 1971.

[Cro80] W. Bruce Croft. A model of cluster searching based on classification. *Information Systems*, 5:189–195, 1980.

[Cro86] W. Bruce Croft. Boolean queries and term dependencies in probabilistic retrieval models. *Journal of the American Society for Information Science*, 37(2):71–77, 1986.

[Cro87] W. Bruce Croft. Approaches to intelligent information retrieval. *Information Processing and Management*, 23(4):249–254, 1987.

[CT87] W. Bruce Croft and Roger H. Thompson. I^3R: A new approach to the design of document retrieval systems. *Journal of the American Society for Information Science*, 38(6):389–404, November 1987.

[CT89] W. Bruce Croft and Howard Turtle. A retrieval model incorporating hypertext links. In *Hypertext '89 Proceedings*, pages 213–224, 1989.

[Dem68] A. P. Dempster. A generalization of Bayesian inference. *Journal of the Royal Statistical Society B*, 30:205–247, 1968.

[Doy79] John Doyle. A truth maintenance system. *Artificial Intelligence*, 12(3):231–272, 1979.

[FLGD87] G. W. Furnas, T. K. Landauer, L. M. Gomez, and S. T. Dumais. The vocabulary problem in human-system communication. *Communications of the ACM*, 30(11):964–971, November 1987.

[FNL88] Edward A. Fox, Gary L. Nunn, and Whay C. Lee. Coefficients for combining concept classes in a collection. In *Proceedings of the Eleventh Annual International ACM SIGIR Conference on Research and Development in Information Retrieval*, pages 291–308, New York, NY, 1988. ACM.

[Fuh89] Norbert Fuhr. Models for retrieval with probabilistic indexing. *Information Processing and Management*, 25(1):55–72, 1989.

[KL86] Laveen N. Kanal and John F. Lemmer, editors. *Uncertainty in Artificial Intelligence*. North-Holland, Amsterdam, 1986.

[KMT+82] J. Katzer, M. J. McGill, J. A. Tessier, W. Frakes, and P. DasGupta. A study of the overlap among document representations. *Information Technology: Research and Development*, 1:261–274, 1982.

[LK88] John F. Lemmer and Laveen N. Kanal, editors. *Uncertainty in Artificial Intelligence 2*. North-Holland, Amsterdam, 1988.

[LS88] S. L. Lauritzen and D. J. Spiegelhalter. Local computations with probabilities on graphical structures and their application to expert systems. *Journal of the Royal Statistical Society B*, 50(2):157–224, 1988.

[MK60] M. E. Maron and J. L. Kuhns. On relevance, probabilistic indexing and information retrieval. *Journal of the ACM*, 7:216–244, 1960.

[MKN79] Michael McGill, Mathew Koll, and Terry Noreault. An evaluation of factors affecting document ranking by information retrieval systems. Technical report, Syracuse University, School of Information Studies, 1979. Funded under NSF-IST-78-10454.

[Nil86] Nils J. Nilsson. Probabilistic logic. *Artificial Intelligence*, 28(1):71–87, 1986.

[OPC86] Robert N. Oddy, Ruth A. Palmquist, and Margaret A. Crawford. Representation of anomalous states of knowledge in information retrieval. In *Proceedings of the 1986 ASIS Annual Conference*, pages 248–254, 1986.

[Pea88] Judea Pearl. *Probabilistic Reasoning in Intelligent Systems: Networks of Plausible Inference*. Morgan Kaufmann Publishers, 1988.

[Rob77] S. E. Robertson. The probability ranking principle in IR. *Journal of Documentation*, 33(4):294–304, December 1977.

[Sal88] Gerard Salton. A simple blueprint for automatic boolean query processing. *Information Processing and Management*, 24(3):269–280, 1988.

[Sha76] Glen Shafer. *A Mathematical Theory of Evidence*. Princeton University Press, 1976.

[SM83] Gerard Salton and Michael J. McGill. *Introduction to Modern Information Retrieval*. McGraw-Hill, 1983.

[Sti75] K. H. Stirling. The effect of document ranking on retrieval system performance: A search for an optimal ranking rule. *Proceedings of the American Society for Information Science*, 12:105–106, 1975.

[TC89] Roger H. Thompson and W. Bruce Croft. Support for browsing in an intelligent text retrieval system. *International Journal of Man-Machine Studies*, 30:639–668, 1989.

[TS85] Richard M. Tong and Daniel Shapiro. Experimental investigations of uncertainty in a rule-based system for information retrieval. *International Journal of Man-Machine Studies*, 22:265–282, 1985.

[vR79] C. J. van Rijsbergen. *Information Retrieval*. Butterworths, 1979.

[vR86] C. J. van Rijsbergen. A non-classical logic for information retrieval. *Computer Journal*, 29(6):481–485, 1986.

[Wil73] Patrick Wilson. Situational relevance. *Information Storage and Retrieval*, 9:457–471, 1973.

[Zad83] Lotfi A. Zadeh. The role of fuzzy logic in the management of uncertainty in expert systems. *Fuzzy Sets and Systems*, 11:199–228, 1983.

THE

Journal of Documentation

VOLUME 38 NUMBER 2 JUNE 1982

ASK FOR INFORMATION RETRIEVAL: PART I. BACKGROUND AND THEORY

N. J. BELKIN
Centre for Information Science
The City University, London

R. N. ODDY
Computer Centre
The University of Aston, Birmingham

H. M. BROOKS
Centre for Information Science
The City University, London

We report the results of a British Library Research and Development Department-funded design study for an interactive information retrieval system which will determine structural representations of the anomalous states of knowledge (ASKs) underlying information needs, and attempt to resolve the anomalies through a variety of retrieval strategies performed on a database of documents represented in compatible structural formats. Part I discusses the background to the project and the theory underlying it, Part II (next issue) presents our methods, results and conclusions. Basic premises of the project were: that information needs are not in principle precisely specifiable; that it is possible to elicit problem statements from information system users from which representations of the ASK underlying the need can be derived; that there are classes of ASKs; and, that all elements of information retrieval systems ought to be based on the user's ASK. We have developed a relatively free-form interview technique for eliciting problem statements, and a statistical word co-occurrence analysis for deriving network representations of the problem statements and abstracts. Structural characteristics of the representations have been used to determine classes of ASKs, and both ASK and information structures have been evaluated by, respectively, users and authors. Some results are: that interviewing appears to be a satisfactory technique for eliciting problem statements from which ASKs can be determined; that the statistical analysis produces structures which are generally appropriate both for documents and problem statements; that ASKs thus represented can be usefully classified according to their structural characteristics; and, that of thirty-five subjects, only two had ASKs for which traditional 'best match' retrieval would be intuitively appropriate. The results of the design study indicate that at least some of our premises are reasonable, and that an ASK-based information retrieval system is at least feasible.

INTRODUCTION

IMPROVEMENTS IN THE performance of information retrieval (IR) systems as presently designed seem to be limited to only marginal gains in terms of complete recall and precision or complete user satisfaction (see, e.g. Robertson and Sparck Jones[1]). In these two papers *(Part II: Results of a design study,* to appear in *Journal of Documentation,* vol. 38 no. 3) we report on a design study[2] for an experimental IR system based on radically different hypotheses than those underlying present systems, which we think may allow the design of IR systems which produce significantly better performance than currently offered.

Recent work by Belkin[3-6] and others (see, e.g. Harbo and Kajberg[7] and Hollnagel[8]) has called into question some traditional assumptions of IR, in particular those concerning: the relationship of the request put to the IR system to the information need underlying the request; the basis for text and request representation in IR systems; and, the retrieval mechanisms suitable for IR. This new approach recognizes that a fundamental element in the IR situation is the development of an information need out of an inadequate state of knowledge. From this realization it goes on to say that for IR to be successful, that information need must be represented in terms appropriate for just that task, with the remaining elements of the system (i.e. document representation, retrieval mechanism) being represented or constructed on the basis of that representation. One means to an appropriate representation is consideration of the information need as an 'anomalous state of knowledge' (ASK).[6,9]

The ASK hypothesis is that an information need arises from a recognized anomaly in the user's state of knowledge concerning some topic or situation and that, in general, the user is unable to specify precisely what is needed to resolve that anomaly. Thus, for the purposes of IR, it is more suitable to attempt to describe that ASK, than to ask the user to specify her/his need as a request to the system.

Oddy's[10-12] experimental interactive IR system, THOMAS, was designed to allow information retrieval without query formulation, relying on the system to construct an 'image' of the user's need. The program operates upon a graph whose points represent documents, subjects and authors; the lines stand for associations. A structural image of the subject area of interest to the user is maintained during the online dialogue. Its main component is a subgraph of the program's document collection structure. Strictly speaking, this image is not asserted to be a representation of the user's need, but rather a formal context within which documents satisfying the need might be found. Thus it is the structural properties of the image, and not merely matching terms, which determine the program's choice of documents to show the user. The user may react to the documents, and their descriptions, and her/his response is used by the program to determine modifications to the image. This work has strong affinity to the ASK hypothesis, but is limited in its means for representation of document and user to traditional document descriptors, although in explicitly structural terms. In the design study, we investigated means of combining and extending these two developments to deal with complex IR situations in an entirely new way, which the ASK hypothesis predicts would produce better results than traditional IR systems. The design study attempted to resolve a number of problems raised by the hypotheses, and to provide a preliminary specification for a system which incorporates these new assumptions.

THEORETICAL BASIS OF THE ASK IR SYSTEM

The basis of the project we describe here is a combination of what we have rather loosely termed the 'ASK hypothesis' with the principles underlying Oddy's THOMAS system. In this section, we expand somewhat upon the theory underlying these two approaches to IR, and on how they can be combined into a framework suitable for what we think of as a 'second-generation' IR system. We begin by discussing what we see as the basic weakness of current IR systems.

The typical IR system now available, either operational or experimental, depends on what we call the 'best-match' principle. This principle, briefly stated, is that, given a representation of a request for information (e.g. a 'query' or set of index terms), the best possible system response will be the text whose representation most closely matches it. Leaving aside, for the moment, the problem of representation, one can identify two assumptions basic to the best-match principle: that it is possible for the user to specify precisely the information that she/he requires; and, that information needs (or at least expressions of them) are functionally equivalent to document texts.

Let us make clear how the best-match principle depends upon these two assumptions. It depends upon the first in that only those concepts and/or relations which are explicitly stated by the user as being significant are significant in the matching procedure. The user must be able to specify all of the relevant aspects of the problem, in order for the system to work optimally. If they are not stated, then documents treating these concepts (relations) cannot be retrieved (since they do not match what was specified), or will be ranked only very low in terms of probability or degree of relevance (since they match the specification only poorly). The best-match principle depends upon the assumption of equivalence between expression of need and document text in that it treats the representation of need as a representation of the document ideal for resolving that need.[13] The best-match principle looks first for a document which is just like the expression of need; that is, which is functionally equivalent to it.

Whether the best-match principle is a fundamental weakness in current IR systems is a function of the reasonableness of the two assumptions on which it is based. Simplifying assumptions, of course, are basic to the scientific enterprise. Later, we make some that may seem rather simple-minded, as well as merely simple. Nevertheless, such assumptions ought not stray too far away from what we conceive as the more complicated reality. Our contention, of course, is that the assumptions underlying the 'best-match' principle are sufficiently divorced from reality to make them quite untenable.

The specifiability assumption is by no means an obvious characteristic of the typical IR situation, which Wersig[14] has characterized as rooted in a 'problematic situation'. The problematic situation, and other related suggestions (e.g.[8,15]) emphasize that information need is in fact not a need in itself, but rather a means toward satisfying some more basic need, typically, in the situations with which information science is concerned, the resolution of a problem. The most general thing that one can say about such a circumstance is that the user, faced with a problem, recognizes that her/his state of knowledge is inadequate for resolving that problem, and decides that obtaining information about the problem area and its circumstances is an appropriate means towards its resolution. There are certainly occasions when one might be able to specify precisely what information is required to bring the state of knowledge to a structure adequate for resolution of the problem, but it seems obvious that the more usual situation will be that in which what is appropriate for the purpose is not known in advance. In such a situation, the best-match strategy does not seem a reasonable first choice for IR purposes.

The assumption that expression of information need and document text are functionally equivalent also seems unlikely, except in the special case in which the user is able to specify that which is needed as a coherent or defined information structure. A document, after all, is supposed to be a statement of what its author knows about a topic, and is thus assumed to be a coherent statement of a particular state of knowledge. The expression of an information need, on the other hand, is in general a statement of what the user does not know. Thus, the document is a representation of a coherent state of knowledge, while a query or other text related to an information need will be a representation of an anomalous, or somehow inadequate or incoherent state of knowledge. To assume that these two kinds of texts are alike in the characteristics useful for IR appears unwarranted, and at the very least ought to be investigated before being applied. Despite some work in philosophy, linguistics and artificial intelligence which seems to indicate that questions are different in kind from expository statements (e.g.[16-18]), IR based on the best-match principle uncritically accepts their equivalence.

The contradictions between 'reality' and the assumptions underlying best-match IR have indeed not gone unnoticed. Associative retrieval[19] and relevance feedback,[1] for instance, are significant attempts to resolve the problems inherent in the best-match principle. To some extent these techniques are undeniably successful. Relevance feedback, for instance, can be shown to improve retrieval performance in a variety of situations.[1] Nevertheless, one should note that neither of these approaches takes explicit account of the user's inability to express the information need in terms of the need itself. Both techniques attempt to deal with this problem on the basis of relationships among the documents in the collection, primarily those of word co-occurrence. Relevance feedback seems more responsive to the need issue, in that it uses information gathered from relevance judgements in modifying query formulations, and is therefore not solely dependent upon the characteristics of the document collection. It remains within the best-match paradigm, however, since it assumes that the eventual query formulation is equivalent to the ideal document. Associative retrieval extends the search without knowledge of the individual user's requirements on the basis of document collection characteristics alone. In a sense, this is a genuine recognition of the specification problem, but its distance from the user makes it somewhat unrealistic. Furthermore, it also assumes that the text and need representations are functionally equivalent.

These techniques have resulted in improvements in performance of IR systems, but improvements which, in terms of total recall and precision, or complete user satisfaction, are only marginal. In the end, the results of such modifications of the best-match principle should, we believe, encourage one either to look for theoretical limits on the performance of IR systems, or, to look for principles that take better account of the 'reality' of the IR situation. We opt for the second strategy as the more optimistic, although we recognize that the two are not mutually exclusive.

The assumptions underlying best-match IR mean that such systems cannot use information from the user about doubt, uncertainty or suspicion of inadequacy in the user's state of knowledge, since these factors will not be specified in the usual document, and are difficult for the user to specify. These, however, are the factors which prompt people to go to IR systems, and which ought therefore to be taken explicitly into account by any realistic IR procedure. One reason that best-match IR does not do this is because the problem is, in principle, extremely difficult. We suggest that one approach to taking account of these factors, which we call 'anomalies', is to try to represent them in terms of the user's larger-scale intentions and goals, without asking the user to specify the information needed to resolve the anomaly. Oddy's work on IR systems without query specification, combined with Belkin's speculations about the knowledge structures underlying information needs, seem to us appropriate means to this end.

Our basic orientation to the problem of combining these two approaches is the cognitive viewpoint,[20] which suggests that interactions of humans with one another, with the physical world and with themselves are always mediated by their states of knowledge about themselves and about that with which or whom they interact. Additionally, we look at the IR situation as a recipient-controlled communication system,[21] aimed at resolving the expressed information needs of humans, primarily via texts produced by other human beings. This communication system is outlined in Figure 1.

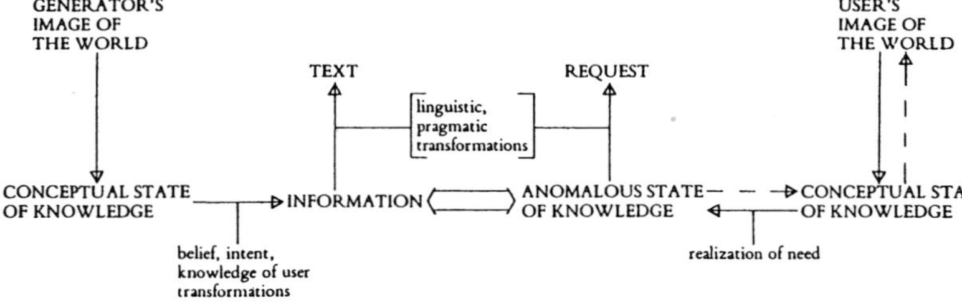

FIG. 1. *A cognitive communication system for information retrieval* (from Belkin,[9] p. 135)

Figure 1 suggests that the driving force of the IR situation is the user's problem, which leads to recognition of an inadequacy in her/his state of knowledge (an anomaly with respect to the problem). Whether an anomaly is resolved or not is evaluated in terms of the problem. It should be noticed that the problem determines not only the conceptual requirements of an appropriate response, but also the situational requirements such as, for instance, source of information, mode of information etc. (see Cooper[22] and Wilson[15] for more on such factors). It should also be noted that the anomaly, and the user's perception of the problem, will probably change with each instance of communication between user and mechanism. This dynamism implies that information systems ought to be highly iterative, and interactive.

Hollnagel has suggested a cognitive communication model[8] which is more active than that of Figure 1, and which perhaps takes better account of the interactive nature of this situation. His model suggest that the parties to the situation, the user and the mechanism, can be considered as partners in a dialogue, each, among other things, adapting its model of the other, and of the world, and therefore its response, according to what it has learned via communication with the other. Accurate models, and helpful dialogue then can in general be best arrived at through a series of interactions, rather than just an initial statement and subsequent response. This view of the IR situation leads to the conclusion that IR systems ought to be designed to be iterative and interactive. Relevance feedback is an example of a step in this direction.

Thus, the cognitive view of the IR situation leads us to some design principles for IR systems which we think incorporate the THOMAS and ASK approaches. These design principles require representation of the user's anomalies, evaluation in terms of the problem the user faces and iteration and interaction in retrieval.

Rather than to attempt to test the theoretical position underlying the ASK/THOMAS approach to IR by generating hypotheses from the theory which lead to falsifiable predictions, we decided to incorporate the theory in a general system design, and then to test the system against some well-specified goals. This general approach to understanding of a theory seems to us to be especially appropriate in our situation, where the theory itself is only partially developed in well-specified form, and where the problem area has a number of highly interactive components which may change significantly between experimental and 'real' settings. In such a situation, it seems reasonable to adopt an iterative methodology, in which the general principles lead to a specific system design, which is tested by reference to its feasibility in a real environment and its efficacy in solving the problem which it is set. At each stage of testing, the design can be modified according to results of the test, and thus the method is iterative, but in the end it is the system as a whole which is tested, rather than some particular aspect of it. This sort of program should begin with a general system based on theoretically motivated design principles, and with some study aimed at discovering whether the design is feasible. It is to these two points, in particular the latter, that the Design Study[2] was directed.

THE STRUCTURE OF THE ASK IR SYSTEM

Our first problem then was to design an IR system which would incorporate our theoretical ideas. Again, our basic premises arise from what we consider to be one of the central difficulties of IR: that people who use IR systems typically do so because they have recognized an anomaly in their state of knowledge of some topic, but they are unable to specify precisely what is necessary to resolve that anomaly. This can be seen as a restatement and perhaps extension of ideas proposed by Taylor.[23] Thus, we presume that it is unrealistic (in general) to ask the user of an IR system to say exactly what it is that she/he needs to know, since it is just the lack of that knowledge which has brought her/him to the system in the first place. This premise leads us to conclude that IR systems should be designed with the non-specifiability of information need as a major parameter. Furthermore, we assume that we can get closer to appropriate responses in an IR system via iteration and interaction. What sort of IR system could this be?

We consider that IR systems, in general, consist of: a mechanism for representing information need; a text store; a mechanism for representing and organizing texts; a mechanism for retrieving texts appropriate to particular information needs; and, usually, a mechanism for evaluating the effectiveness of the retrieval. Figure 2 indicates these components, and some other features, and the relationships among them.

From Figure 2, and experience, one can see that the starting points for IR system design are at either text or need representation, and that which of these one chooses, and the chosen method of representation, will strongly influence all the other elements of the IR system. Most previous systems have begun from the text representation end, with not very much influence from the need end. We have noted that need representation appears to be the fundamental problem of IR, and so we suggest that a good IR system should be one which begins with need representation and designs the rest of the system about a mechanism and formalism specifically designed for that purpose.

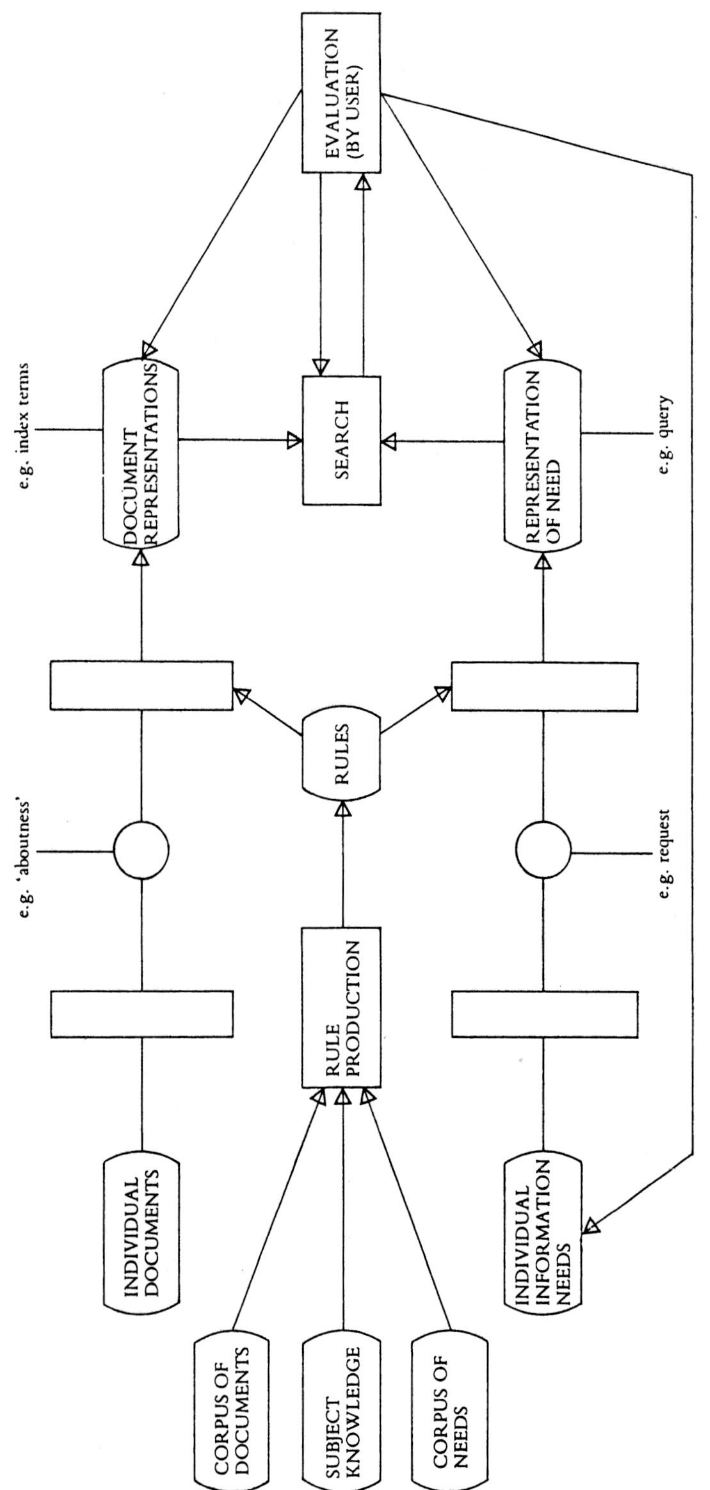

FIG. 2. *A model of information retrieval* (after Robertson[24])

Our mechanism is based on some experimental work by Belkin,[4] which indicated that networks constructed from constrained word associations yield reasonable representations of individuals' states of knowledge about the subject to which the associations are constrained. In the same experiment, a network generated from word co-occurrence analysis of a 3,000 word text (using the stimulus words of the word association test as major nodes) gave a reasonable representation of the 'information structure' of that text. The argument for using these techniques is based on the assumptions that concepts (represented by words) which are closely associated in an individual's state of knowledge will (a) be recalled close to one another in tasks such as word association; and, (b) occur in close proximity to one another in a text by that person on the specific topic.

The formalism used for representation, a network of concepts represented by words, depends upon our concept of a state of knowledge as a multi-dimensional structure. We have discussed this concept, as it applies to our work,[3-4,10] but the basic idea seems to us unexceptionable, except perhaps for the substitution of words for concepts. A network is certainly an effective way of representing this type of structure, and has the advantage, in our case, of being relatively easily derived from the sort of association data we use.

There is no question that this sort of representation of a state of knowledge (or of the information structure underlying a text) is simplistic and naïve, if one is attempting to obtain detailed representations for such purposes as natural language understanding, machine translation or retrieval from memory. On the other hand, it has the advantages of being fairly easily determined and reasonably machine-manipulable, important considerations in an IR context, where one needs to represent actual information needs and to manipulate large amounts of data. Our strategy for choice of formalism and mechanism for representation depends upon our assumption that there is no 'real' or 'true' representation of knowledge or information, but rather many possible representations, each appropriate to particular problems. We decided upon networks derived from association data as a potentially useful representation for the purposes of IR because of the advantages of this type of representation mentioned above, and because there has already been some experience with similar formalisms in IR. But we bear in mind that this is indeed a very simple model, and so treat it only as preliminary: if it works, we will be pleased, if not, then we will amend it in ways the evidence seems to indicate, or discard it for different models.

To this point, we have discussed means of representing information, or what people know about a topic. Yet our problem is to represent what someone does not know; that is, to represent an ASK. We obviously cannot use word association tests for obtaining the data for this purpose, since we would need to represent the ASK corresponding to a different topic for each user of the IR system, and thus would have no standard set of stimulus words. Our solution in this case derived, to some extent, from the suggestion by Wersig[14] that a 'problematic situation' underlies an information need. In terms of the ASK hypothesis, this means that the user, attempting to realize a goal or solve a problem, recognizes that her/his state of knowledge is inadequate (anomalous) in terms of the goal; resolution of the anomaly will help to solve the problem. Thus, if we are able to obtain a statement of the problem, this may give us the data from which we can construct a representation of the ASK. This, of course, is old hat to reference librarians. So the basic data for our representation of ASKs are narrative statements by the users of the IR system, of the problems which brought them to the system. We assume that some sort of associative analysis of those statements will yield representations of the ASKs inherent in the problematic situation, which will be useful within the context of an IR system aiming to resolve the ASKs.

We have now discussed representation of need and text. A second major mechanism is that of search, or retrieval. Here, our arguments against the best-match principle become important. We assume that one needs mechanisms which can recognize unspecified anomalies, and which can resolve, rather than match them. We recognize that there are ASKs which can be resolved by best-match type mechanisms, but we also recognize, on the basis of IR system experience, as well as theoretical speculation, that there must be ASKs for which this type of mechanism is not suitable. Therefore, our IR system design assumes that there exist different types of ASK which require different retrieval mechanisms.

The evaluative mechanism in an IR system is now recognized to have an importance equivalent to the representation and retrieval mechanisms, and this is the point at which we see the interactive component become most visible. There are many difficulties in establishing this mechanism, most of which we attempt to avoid here. But the basis of any evaluation must be the satisfaction of the user of the IR system with the system's performance in resolution of her/his ASK. Oddy[10] built his system THOMAS about this realization by making evaluation its driving force. THOMAS is truly interactive in that each retrieval depends upon the user's evaluation of the results of the previous retrieval. Thus, the evaluation mechanism feeds-back directly to the need-representation mechanism, modifying it according to the user's immediate, perceived judgement of the value of the mechanisms for resolving her/his information need. This sort of evaluation can thus cater for initial misrepresentation by the IR system and for changes in the anomaly and the problem which arise during the course of the search. In the IR system which we propose here, an additional factor for evaluation, multiple retrieval mechanisms, has been introduced. We assume, therefore, that an effective ASK-based system must be interactive in such a way as to incorporate direct evaluation by the user of retrieval output in terms suitable for modification of both need representation and choice of retrieval mechanism.

Thus, we propose that an IR system based on the representation of information need as an ASK look something like that outlined in Figure 3. We do not mean to suggest that this is the only possible such system, but rather only that this is a realization of these ideas, based on further assumptions about representation and on practicalities of IR.

1. USER'S PROBLEM STATEMENT
2. STRUCTURAL ANALYSIS OF PROBLEM STATEMENT
3. CHOICE OF RETRIEVAL STRATEGY ACCORDING TO TYPE OF ASK
4. ABSTRACT PRESENTED TO USER SIMULTANEOUSLY WITH EXPLANATION OF WHY TEXT WAS CHOSEN (STRATEGY AND SIGNIFICANT FEATURES)
5. STRUCTURED DIALOGUE BETWEEN SYSTEM AND USER FOR SYSTEM TO INFER USER'S EVALUATION OF:
   (A) METHOD OF CHOICE
   (B) SUITABILITY OF DOCUMENT TO PROBLEM
   AND/OR
   (C) WHETHER NEED HAS CHANGED
6. MODIFICATIONS ACCORDING TO EVALUATION OR FINISH
7. RETURN TO 2 OR 3 AS NECESSARY

FIG. 3. *An ASK-based information retrieval system design*

The system would work as follows:

1. The user discusses her/his information problem in an unstructured statement (say, 2–3 paragraphs long).
2. The problem statement is converted to a structural representation of the user's ASK by the text analysis program.
3. According to the type of problem structure (PS), one of several available retrieval mechanisms is chosen to interrogate the database (each member of which is represented by a structural representation of the information associated with the text). In this context, a retrieval mechanism is a strategy for resolving the anomalous aspects of a PS.
4. The abstract (i.e. the text) is printed out for the user to read. Simultaneously, the user is presented with a brief explanation of why that particular text was chosen (explanation of the retrieval mechanism), indicating aspects of the text structure which the system finds significant in that choice.
5. The system then initiates a structured dialogue with the user, based on the information presented to her/him, inferring from the response the user's attitude toward:
   (a) the method of choice;
   (b) the suitability of the text to the problem; and,
   (c) whether her/his information need has changed.
6. (a) the system changes retrieval mechanism if necessary, and/or
   (b) the system modifies the problem structure if necessary, or
   (c) the system stops if the user is satisfied.
7. The system returns to step 2 or 3.

Our design study intended to investigate the following aspects of the system, which we felt needed to be clarified before going on to actually implementing the system.

1. The text analysis program. This was based upon an existing algorithm[4] which determines statistically based structures. The suitability of the eventual algorithm must be tested on real problem statements (see 2 below) and on abstracts (see 3 below).
2. The feasibility of obtaining problem statements, the possible types of problem statement, and the analysis of problem statements. To these ends, a number of real problem statements were collected and analysed, and the analyses verified.
3. The feasibility of using abstracts as the basic documents in the system, and the analysis of abstracts. To these ends, real abstracts were collected and analysed, and the analyses verified.
4. Some specific retrieval mechanisms should be proposed, based in large part on the types of problem structures encountered, although the ASK hypothesis implies some strategies.
5. The interactive system (especially the dialogue with the user) should be specified (although not necessarily fixed).

In the event, we were unable to do much with points 4 and 5 in terms of empirical investigation, so that the Design Study aimed finally to consider the first three issues in detail, as necessary preliminaries to the design of an ASK-based IR system. In Part II, (*Journal of Documentation*, vol. 38, no. 3) we describe the methods and present the results and conclusions of the Design Study.

REFERENCES

1. ROBERTSON, S. E. *and* SPARCK JONES, K. Relevance weighting of search terms. *Journal of the American Society for Information Science, 27,* 1976, 129–46.
2. BELKIN, N. J. *and* ODDY, R. N. *Design study for an anomalous state of knowledge based information retrieval system.* British Library R & D Report No. 5547. Birmingham: Computer Centre, University of Aston in Birmingham, 1979.
3. BELKIN, N. J. *and* ROBERTSON, S. E. Information science and the phenomenon of information. *Journal of the American Society for Information Science, 27,* 1976, 197–204.
4. BELKIN, N. J. *A concept of information for information science.* Ph.D. Thesis, University of London, 1977.
5. BELKIN, N. J. Internal knowledge and external information. *In: CC77: The Cognitive Viewpoint.* Proceedings of an international workshop on the cognitive viewpoint, Ghent, 1977. Ghent: University of Ghent, 1977, 187–94.
6. BELKIN, N. J. The problem of 'matching' in information retrieval. *In:* O. Harbo and L. Kajberg, *eds. Theory and applications of information research.* Proceedings of the Second International Research Forum in Information Science. London: Mansell, 1980, 187–97.
7. HARBO, O. *and* KAJBERG, L., *eds. Theory and applications of information research.* Proceedings of the Second International Research Forum in Information Science. London: Mansell, 1980.
8. HOLLNAGEL, E. The relation between intention, meaning and action. *In:* M. MacCafferty and K. Gray, *eds. The analysis of meaning: Informatics 5.* London: Aslib, 1979, 135–47.
9. BELKIN, N. J. Anomalous states of knowledge as a basis for information retrieval. *Canadian Journal of Information Science, 5,* 1980, 133–43.
10. ODDY, R. N. *Reference retrieval based on user-induced dynamic clustering.* Ph.D. Thesis, University of Newcastle upon Tyne, 1975.
11. ODDY, R. N. Information retrieval through man–machine dialogue. *Journal of Documentation, 33,* 1977, 1–14.
12. ODDY, R. N. Retrieving references by dialogue rather than by query formulation. *Journal of Informatics, 1,* 1977, 37–53.
13. CLEMENT DAVIES, C. Reference retrieval by user-negotiated term frequency ordering within a dynamically adjusted notional 'document'. *Journal of Informatics, 2,* 1978, 62–76.
14. WERSIG, G. *Information—Kommunikation—Dokumentation.* Pullach bei München: Verlag Documentation, 1971.
15. WILSON, T. D. On user studies and information needs. *Journal of Documentation, 37,* 1981, 3–15.
16. BELKNAP, N. D. *and* STEEL, T. B. *The logic of questions and answers.* London: Yale University Press, 1976.
17. HUDSON, R. A. The meaning of questions. *Language, 51,* 1975, 1–31.
18. LEHNERT, W. G. *The process of question answering.* Hillsdale, N. J.: Lawrence Earlbaum Associates, 1978.
19. CROFT, W. B. *Organizing and searching large files of document descriptions.* Ph.D. Thesis, Computer Laboratory, University of Cambridge, 1978.
20. DE MEY, M. The cognitive viewpoint: its development and its scope. *In: CC77: The cognitive viewpoint.* Proceedings of an international workshop on the cognitive viewpoint, Ghent, 1977. Ghent: University of Ghent, 1977, xvi–xxxii.
21. PAISLEY, W. J. *and* PARKER, E. B. Information retrieval as a receiver-controlled communication system. *In: Education for information science.* Washington, D.C.: Spartan Books, 1965, 23–31.
22. COOPER, W. S. On selecting a measure of retrieval effectiveness. *Journal of the American Society for Information Science, 24,* 1973, 87–100.
23. TAYLOR, R. S. Question-negotiation and information seeking in libraries. *College and Research Libraries, 29,* 1968, 178–94.
24. ROBERTSON, S. E. Indexing theory and retrieval effectiveness. *Drexel Library Quarterly, 14,* 1979, 40–56.

Chapter 6

Techniques

An Algorithm for Suffix Stripping 313
M.F. Porter

Robust Text Processing in Automated Information Retrieval 317
T. Strzalkowski

Term-Weighting Approaches in Automatic Text Retrieval 323
G. Salton and C. Buckley

Search Term Relevance Weighting Given Little Relevance Information 329
K. Sparck Jones

Using Probabilistic Models of Document Retrieval without Relevance Information 339
W.B. Croft and D.J. Harper

Some Simple Effective Approximations to the 2-Poisson Model for Probabilistic Weighted Retrieval 345
S.E. Robertson and S. Walker

Improving Retrieval Performance by Relevance Feedback 355
G. Salton and C. Buckley

Using Interdocument Similarity Information in Document Retrieval Systems 365
A. Griffiths, H.C. Luckhurst, and P. Willett

INTRODUCTION

This chapter considers automated retrieval techniques, that is, the system techniques intended to exploit capabilities the user cannot be expected to possess (e.g., advanced algebra), to remove drudgery from the user, or to supplement and enhance the user's own efforts. We do not consider here the query development or searching techniques and strategies that users themselves, especially in interactive situations, may apply (cf. Chapter 3), though it is clearly essential to understand these in order that they may best be automatically assisted. We do not consider here, either, human-computer interface technology, particularly important though this is; some thoughts on this subject are, however, included in the following chapter on IR systems. Thus, this chapter considers the computational techniques that are required to carry out a best-match search of a text database. Given sets of terms that characterise a user's information need and the contents of each of the documents in a database, such a search involves calculating a score denoting a *similarity*, a *probability of relevance*, or a degree of *nearness* or *goodness of fit* between the sets of terms for the query and for each document (in what follows, we shall assume that this scoring function is a similarity, such as is calculated in the vector processing model, although the precise form of the function is determined by the particular retrieval model that is being used). The documents are then sorted into decreasing order of these scores, with the output of the search being a *ranked list*, in which the documents at the top of the list are those the system judges to be the best match with the query and that are thus displayed first to the user. User judgements of the relevance of these top-ranked documents can then be used as the basis for a subsequent, *relevance feedback* search, modifying the term status and composition of the initial query. We also summarise the use of *clustering* techniques in retrieval.

INDEXING TECHNIQUES

Over the years, the IR research community has devoted much attention to the development of methods for *automatic indexing*. *Manual indexing* is based on a detailed analysis and interpretation of the texts of documents or requests, and it was thus natural for early workers to apply linguistic techniques to the automatic selection of indexing terms. However, it was soon found (Salton, 1968) that stemmed keywords gave levels of retrieval performance that were comparable with, or superior to, those obtainable from manual application of controlled vocabularies or of phrase-based indexing, a result that was in accordance with the findings of the Cranfield-2 experiments (Cleverdon, 1967). Accordingly, interest then turned to the development of *statistical* methods for indexing, in which frequency criteria of various sorts were used to select words, or word stems, from the natural language of document texts (an approach that was first pioneered by Luhn, as detailed in his paper in Chapter 2). In fact, rather than applying sophisticated selection criteria, the tendency is increasingly to use nearly all of the words from a document or request text, with statistical information being used to differentiate the terms by means of an appropriate weighting scheme at search time, instead of selecting them when documents or queries are indexed. The only words that are generally not used for searching are those with very high frequencies; these are eliminated by means of a *stopword* list containing commonly occurring words that are unlikely to be of use for retrieval purposes. Different strategies may be adopted for documents and queries, with only a very few (if any) document words being stoplisted, but with a much larger set of stopwords being applied to queries, except in the context of phrases that may require the inclusion of frequent words that would be stoplisted if they were to appear on their own.

Once the set of words representing a request or document has been identified, some means must be found of overcoming the variation in word forms that is likely to be encountered in free-text databases. This is normally effected by means of a *conflation algorithm,* a computational procedure that reduces variants of a word to a single form. The rationale for such a procedure is that similar words generally have similar meanings and, thus, retrieval effectiveness may be increased if the query is expanded by including words that are similar in meaning to those originally contained within it. The most common conflation procedure is the use of a *stemming algorithm,* which reduces all words with the same root to a single form by stripping the root of its derivational and inflectional affixes; in many languages, only suffixes are stripped so that the algorithm performs a comparable role to that of manual, *right-hand truncation*. Most stemmers are based on a dictionary of common word endings that are searched for when a word is presented for stemming (Frakes, 1992). If a suffix is found to be present, it is removed, subject to a range of checks that, e.g., forbid the resulting stem have less than some minimal number of characters and that handle any changes in a word root that occur when a suffix is attached to it. Comparisons of the effectiveness of searches using stemmed and unstemmed texts in English have produced equivocal results (Harman, 1991; Hull, 1996), but the increasing number of tests that are now being carried out on languages having a greater degree of morphological complexity than English suggest that significant improvements in performance can be obtained by stemming (Kraaj and Pohlmann, 1996; Popovic and Willett, 1992).

Word stemming is easy to implement and provides a highly effective means of conflating morphological variants. However, many other types of word variant are likely to occur in free-text databases, and an alternative, and more general, approach involves the system calculating a measure of *string similarity* between a specified query term and each of the distinct terms in the database. Similar words can then be displayed at a terminal for inclusion in the query if the user so desires. The most common approach is based on *n-gram coding,* which involves fragmenting a word into a sequence of *n*-grams, i.e., strings of *n* adjacent characters, and then estimating the similarity between a pair of words by the similarity between the corresponding sets of *n*-grams (Frakes, 1992).

Stemming applies to individual words. Indexing also covers the treatment of multiword strings as conceptual units. As mentioned in Chapter 3, index descriptions can be *complex expressions* with a rich internal syntactic and semantic structure, or at least consist of a set of *compound terms,* nowadays often called *phrases.* These may be defined by NLP methods ranging from shallow syntactic parsing to full semantic analysis, to obtain what are generally labelled *syntactic phrases.* Or they may be defined by *proximity,* especially strict adjacency, relying only implicitly and not explicitly on linguistic structure. Such phrases may be further justified on statistical grounds by occurrence frequency, as *statistical phrases.* The range of phrase definitions and extraction methods is large (Fagan, 1989; Salton et al., 1990; Sparck Jones and Tait, 1984; Strzalkowski, 1994).

Term (including phrase) *weighting* is clearly also an indexing technique, since it defines the degree of importance of a term in a description. Thus, in general, weighting defines the significance of a term for an individual document or query as some function of its frequency in the document itself (taking the document's length into account) and its frequency in the document set.

When specific automated techniques are in question, the distinction between *file time* and *search time* application, discussed in Chapter 3, is critical. It is especially important to distinguish, for indexing, between time choices that are necessary and those that are contingent. The former make irrevocable commitments to terms or term status; the latter do not. As mentioned in Chapter 2, the historical shift has been from file time to search time operation both to avoid overcommitment on indexing decisions and because it is economically more sensible. Some indexing techniques, like stemming, may be treated as either file time or search time operations: with rule-based stemming as described above, the choice makes no formal difference, though the practical effects can be considerable; user truncation of query terms is obviously a search time action. The actual retrieval effects of the generic stemming idea can thus vary markedly according to timing policy. The creation of a phrase vocabulary for a whole file, as for example with the SMART statistical phrase list, is strictly a file time operation with the resulting advantage that phrases are available for query expansion in relevance feedback. When phrases, even of the same type, are defined only at search time, they are limited to the existing query and new ones cannot be added in expansion.

Search time operation is increasingly the norm, for good, practical reasons. Desired facts about the file properties of index descriptions, like the file frequencies of single terms or query phrases, can be found and exploited then. It is also possible, with current computing power, to carry out extensive operations on individual documents at search time; for example, to determine phrase presence. We therefore consider many IR devices and strategies under the "Searching Techniques" heading below. It is, however, necessary to bear in mind file time constraints on the formation and application of index keys, especially those associated with the use of an indexing vocabulary.

SEARCHING TECHNIQUES

We have noted above that best-match searching involves ranking the documents in a database in order of decreasing match with a query statement, this implying the calculation of some quantitative measure of similarity between the query and each of the documents. A similarity measure comprises two major components: the *term weighting* scheme, which allocates numerical values to each of the index terms in a query or document that reflect their relative importance; and the *similarity coefficient*, which uses these weights to calculate the overall degree of similarity between a query and a document. Of these, the former is by far the more important; indeed, one of the principal conclusions that can be drawn from all of the research that has been carried out over the years is that term weighting is the single most important factor in determining the effectiveness of an IR system (and it is for this reason that no less than five of the papers we have selected for discussion in this chapter are about term weighting).

Weights can be assigned to search terms using data about the frequency of occurrence in *individual documents*, in the *file as a whole*, or in the *query* (Salton and Buckley, 1988; Sparck Jones, 1973). Earlier experiments, which were typically with short documents (and also minimal requests), suggested that weighting based on file frequency and thus naturally applied to query terms at search time, is of great importance in determining the effectiveness of a search. There are two main types of query-term weights, these being the *initial weights* and the *relevance weights*. The former are used when a searcher first puts a query to a best-match system, while the latter are used once the searcher has had a chance to inspect the output from the initial search.

The most common type of initial weight is *collection frequency*, or *inverse document frequency* (IDF), weighting, which involves assigning weights to the terms in a query such that the weights are in inverse proportion to the frequency of occurrence of those terms in the database that is to be searched (Sparck Jones, 1972). The basis for IDF weighting is the observation that people tend to express their information needs using rather broadly defined, frequently occurring terms (see, e.g., Nelson, 1988), whereas it is the more specific, i.e., low-frequency, terms that are likely to be of particular importance in identifying relevant material. This is because the number of documents relevant to a query is generally small, and thus any frequently occurring terms must necessarily occur in many irrelevant documents; infrequently occurring query terms, conversely, have a greater probability of occurring in relevant documents and should thus be considered as being of greater potential importance when searching a database. These considerations lead to the use of a weight that is inversely proportional to a term's collection frequency, and this weighting scheme has been found to give results that are consistently superior to those resulting from unweighted query terms.

If the terms are to be weighted using document data, then the most common approach (and a very natural one for full text) involves *term frequency weighting*, where the term frequency of a term represents its frequency of occurrence within the text of an individual document, usually normalised by document length. Several types of term frequency weight have been discussed in the past (see, e.g., Fuhr, 1989; Salton and Buckley, 1988), though with the continuing TREC evaluation a general form for weighting is becoming established. It is common to carry out the initial search by means of the so-called *tf.idf* weight, which involves multiplying the term frequency weight by the collection frequency weight, suitably normalised, for each document-to-query match.

When someone carries out a search, it is natural for them to modify the query in the light of previously inspected search output. *Relevance feedback* is the name given to techniques that try to carry out such query modification by automatic, rather than by manual, means (Robertson and Sparck Jones, 1976; Rocchio, 1971; Salton and Buckley, 1990), and relevance feedback is thus a specific example of the more general subjects of machine learning and pattern recognition.

When relevance feedback is to be used, an initial search is carried out as described previously, e.g., using IDF weights, and the user inspects a few top-ranking documents (perhaps 5 or 10 of them) to ascertain their relevance to the query. In the basic approach to feedback searching, the user's relevance data enables the system to calculate a new set of weights that should more accurately reflect the importance of each of the query terms. However, rather than just modifying the weights of the original query terms, the system can modify the query by the addition or deletion of terms (which are, logically, also examples of reweighting operations).

The basic assumption is that a query term that occurs frequently in documents that are judged to be relevant to a particular query, and infrequently in documents that are judged to be nonrelevant, is a "good" term, in some sense, for that query: such good query terms should thus be allocated greater weights than the other query terms. This intuitively reasonable idea has formed the basis for relevance feedback methods that are based on several of the models described in Chapter 5. These methods use the searcher's relevance judgements on the initial output to calculate new weights that should more correctly represent the relative importance of the various query terms. The resulting relevance weights are used in the second, feedback search, which can be iterated at will until the user is satisfied with the output from the search.

The use of the available relevance data to reweight the original query terms is a limiting case of a more general approach to relevance feedback in which the system can change the *constitution* of the query by adding or deleting terms, this corresponding to the assignment of a nonzero weight to a previously zero-weighted term and vice versa. Thus, it is possible to calculate relevance weights for all of the terms in the documents that have been judged relevant and then to expand the query by the addition of some of the most highly weighted terms that had not previously been included. Again, if some of the original terms are found to occur primarily in nonrelevant documents, then it may be helpful to remove them from the query prior to the feedback search. There is considerable discussion as to precisely how relevance-based query modification should be carried out to maximise search effectiveness (Efthimiadis, 1995; Harper and van Rijsbergen, 1978; Salton and Buckley, 1990).

Clearly, the two specific issues arising in the practical application of relevance feedback are the amount of relevance data needed for useful performance improvement (and also likely to be obtainable from the user) and the degree of query expansion. There is evidence that, though the weight estimation is not very reliable, very small amounts of relevance data can be helpful (Sparck Jones, 1979b). The evidence on expansion is more equivocal (as shown specifically in successive TREC tests), since it appears to depend, in a rather complicated way, on the *exhaustivity* of request and document descriptions, particularly the former, as well as on the amount of relevance data to hand. That is to say, it is unlikely that large-scale expansion is generally valuable. However, some expansion certainly is valuable, so only the level has to be determined empirically in different retrieval situations. Indeed, it appears that expansion is a sufficiently useful technique to enable it to be applied successfully by *assuming* that the top-ranked documents are relevant, without explicit judgements. Such ideas have been around for many years (Attar and Fraenkel, 1977; Croft and Harper, 1979), but it is only now that the TREC Programme is providing substantive evidence of their effectiveness (Xu and Croft, 1996).

CLUSTERING TECHNIQUES

The stemming, indexing, weighting, and feedback techniques described above lie at the heart of modern approaches to IR (although the precise way that they are implemented will vary from model to model and from system to system, even if attention is restricted to the retrieval of textual documents). There are, however, many other techniques that have been—and continue to be—the subject of much interest. In particular, the description given thus far has taken no account of the extensive studies that have been made of *document clustering* and *term clustering*, which seek to utilise information about the similarity relationships existing between documents and between terms, respectively.

Automatic classification, clustering, or *cluster analysis,* is a multivariate statistical technique that groups together similar objects in a multidimensional space. Similarities can be calculated between pairs of documents on the basis of the numbers of index terms that they have in common (in just the same way as one calculates the similarity between a document and a query), and the application of a cluster analysis method to a document database will hence result in the grouping together of documents that have large numbers of terms in common. As discussed in Chapter 5, the *Cluster Hypothesis* states that similar documents tend to be relevant to the same requests, and a clustering method should hence provide a way of bringing together the relevant documents for a query, thus permitting very high-precision searches to be carried out when queries are subsequently applied to the clustered file. It is fairly easy to demonstrate that such groupings of relevant documents do result when a document database is clustered and that searches of such a clustered file can, in principle, be more effective than conventional, nonclustered searches (Jardine and van Rijsbergen, 1971). In practice, however, it has not been possible consistently to obtain such improvements in performance, despite the many different searching algorithms and clustering methods that have been tested for this purpose (Willett, 1988).

Similar comments apply to term clustering, which can be viewed as an inverse of document clustering in that the inter-term similarities here are calculated on the basis of the numbers of documents in which pairs of terms co-occur. The use of *term co-occurrence data* would appear to provide a simple and direct way of identifying semantic relationships between terms, and hence of constructing a thesaurus by automatic, rather than by manual, means. The resulting thesaurus can then be used to increase the recall of a search by identifying matches between documents and queries even if they are characterised by different indexing terms. Van Rijsbergen (1979) has postulated the *Association Hypothesis,* which states that "if an index term is good at discriminating relevant from non-relevant documents, then any closely associated index term is also likely to be good at this". Hence, if one assumes that the original terms in a query are good indicators of relevance, then the hypothesis provides a rationale for automatic query expansion, in just the same way as the Cluster Hypothesis provides a rationale for the use of document clustering. Unfortunately, while early experiments (Sparck Jones, 1971; Stiles, 1961) suggested that co-occurrence-based expansion could improve retrieval performance, later, more detailed studies were notably unsuccessful. In some cases, indeed, fully automated query expansion in the absence of relevance data was found to result in significant decreases in performance (Peat and Willett, 1991; Smeaton and van Rijsbergen, 1983); the main use of co-occurrence data may hence be to suggest terms that are related to those in a user's query, with expansion being carried out by the searcher.

Thus, while these two cluster-based approaches both seem to provide a simple, direct way of improving the effectiveness of retrieval, it has not been possible so far to obtain the expected benefits in practice. One reason for this, in relation to term clustering, is that in earlier work co-occurrences were defined with respect to whole document term lists; this was not too weak a co-occurrence frame when documents were represented by abstract-length texts or simple lists of extracted keywords. More recent research has taken the *sentence,* a short, fixed-length *text window,* or even *adjacency* as the frame, and emphasised the identification of "true" term pairs—statistical phrases—rather than the larger term classes that generally result from traditional co-occurrence studies. It is also the case that such term pairs are used as additional index units, alongside their constituent terms, rather than as devices allowing term substitution or as replacing term members. The retrieval effects are thus rather different from those sought earlier and seem (from SMART evidence, for example) to be more helpful. It is also possible that terms, or sets of terms, based on such tightly drawn frames may supply individual additional index terms of value, especially when used in conjunction with weighting. A comparable shift of focus is also observable in the case of document clustering, where the necessary inter-document similarities have traditionally been generated from complete files of documents but where there is now interest in the use of search time clustering of database subsets, e.g., as a way of summarising the outputs of nonclustered searches (Cutting et al., 1993).

In conclusion, then, the work that has been carried out to date has not provided unequivocal evidence for the effectiveness of cluster-based techniques; moreover, much of this work has been restricted to very small datasets because of the substantial computational requirements associated with these techniques. Studies are, however, continuing in the context of TREC (Caid et al., 1995), and if it does prove possible to identify effective approaches, then the computing power that is now available should permit their use on a scale that was quite inconceivable even a few years ago.

SELECTED READINGS

The first two papers discuss techniques for the indexing of documents and queries. As Frakes (1992) notes, many different stemming algorithms have been described in the literature: that chosen for inclusion here is the algorithm due to Porter (1980). This has become almost a de facto standard for use in experimental IR systems; indeed, although developed for use with English texts, versions of the algorithm have been reported recently for languages as diverse as Dutch and Latin. A word that is to be stemmed is characterised by its *measure,* which describes the number of constituent alternating vowel-consonant sequences. Suffixes are removed in a series of steps, each of which involves checking conditions relating to the remaining stem, the suffix to be removed, and the value of the measure. There are several reasons for the popularity of the Porter algorithm: it is conceptually very simple; it seems to work at least as well as other, more complex algorithms; and the original paper provides a sufficiently detailed description to enable it to be implemented very easily. A coding of the algorithm in the C programming language is included as an appendix to the paper by Frakes (1992).

With the noticeable exception of stemming, IR systems have traditionally made very little use of NLP techniques, whether as a means of locating terms to use for indexing or of defining compound terms. There has recently been a resurgence of interest in the use of NLP in IR, occasioned not just by the improved linguistic techniques that are now available (Lewis and Sparck Jones, 1996; Smeaton, 1992) but also by the need to search the full texts of documents, rather than the short, title-and-abstract surrogates that have traditionally been used to represent the document content. In particular, as discussed previously, there has been much interest in the use of both *syntactic* and *statistical* techniques for the identification and use of phrasal representations (Fagan, 1989; Salton et al., 1990; Sparck Jones and Tait, 1984). The current state of the art is exemplified by the work of Strzalkowski (1994), who has implemented a range of NLP routines as a database and query preprocessor for the PRISE system that is described by Harman in Chapter 7. A database text is first processed by a part-of-speech tagger, a morphological stemmer, and then a fast syntactic parser. The search tree resulting from the parser is analysed to identify certain classes of phrase, and these phrases are then analysed to identify semantic relationships (such as generalisation, specialisation, and synonymy) with the words in the user's natural language request. Strzalkowski also considers the need for weighting schemes that differentiate between matching words and matching phrases.

The next five papers discuss the use of statistical techniques for weighting indexing terms. Salton and Buckley (1988) review the use of statistical information for weighting document terms and query terms in the vector processing model, and discuss the implementation of weights that involve collection frequencies, term frequencies, and length normalisation. They go on to provide a detailed comparison of initial searches that involve no less than 287 different combinations of document and query weights. The best results were obtained with weighting schemes that involve length normalisation for documents and both collection frequency and term frequency information, appropriately parameterised, for document terms and query terms. Later TREC work under SMART and by others confirmed the value of these three sources of weighting information, though the detailed ways in which they are exploited differ.

Many of the weighting schemes considered by Salton and Buckley are empirical in origin; e.g., the term frequencies are typically obtained simply by counting the number of occurrences of a term in a document or query. The discussion of IR models in Chapter 5 would suggest that better results might be expected from the use of weighting schemes for which there is some theoretic rationale, and the next three papers to be considered here all focus upon the probabilistic model. This model assumes that relevance data are available that enable the calculation of the probabilities that a particular term does, or does not, occur in a relevant document, with these probabilities being used to calculate relevance weights for the feedback search. Initial studies with the model (Robertson and Sparck Jones, 1976; Sparck Jones, 1979a) demonstrated the very substantial increases in performance that could be achieved; however, these studies assumed that a very large amount of relevance data was available for the calculation of the weights for the feedback search—a situation that is only likely to occur in a *filtering* environment, where user assessments of search output can be built up over time (as discussed in Chapter 8). The paper included here (Sparck Jones, 1979b) investigates the value of relevance weighting when only a limited amount of relevance data is available, such as the one or two relevant documents that are the typical outputs of an initial search. Not only do the experiments demonstrate clearly the effectiveness of relevance weighting in such circumstances, but they also help to explain why these particular weights function so well in practice. Specifically, the paper shows that use of the weights results in a substantial reduction in the numbers of nonrelevant documents that are retrieved, so that even if (as occurs with one of the test collections that was studied) there is some slight loss in recall, this is more than compensated for by a substantial increase in precision.

Croft and Harper (1979) discuss the implementation of probabilistic retrieval strategies when no relevance data are available, i.e., when the initial search takes place. By making several inherently reasonable assumptions about the probabilities necessary for the model, their analysis leads to the interesting, and intellectually satisfying, conclusion that the widely used collection frequency (or IDF) weight is simply a limiting case of probabilistic relevance weights, thus providing a firm rationale for the use of IDF weighting in an initial search. In similar vein, Robertson and Walker (1994) discuss the incorporation of term frequency and document-length information in the probabilistic model, the basic version of which specifically assumes binary indexing for the document terms and takes no account at all of document length. Robertson and Walker start from an established, but highly complex, formal model that involves many different parameters, specifically the 2-Poisson model of indexing described by Harter (1975). They then introduce a series of approximations to simplify the various formulae and, hence, to enable the necessary computations to be carried out. The resulting encodings of term frequency and document-length information can then be used either for an initial search (in combination with IDF weights) or for a feedback search (in combination with relevance weights).

The probabilistic model provides a quantitative basis for the reweighting of the terms in a user's original query once some relevance assessments have been obtained, but the basic model needs modification if these assessments are to be used to suggest additional terms and their associated weights for query expansion (Robertson, 1986). This is in marked contrast to the vector processing model, where the terms and associated weights comprising the original query are modified by consideration of the terms that occur in the documents that have been judged previously to be relevant or nonrelevant (Rocchio, 1971). We illustrate these contrasting approaches with a further paper by Salton and Buckley (1990), who discuss the implementation of relevance feedback using the probabilistic and vector processing models, focusing upon the effects of different expansion strategies. This study (like that described in Salton and Buckley [1988]) involved six different document test collections, and the paper contains an interesting discussion of the effects of collection characteristics on performance. This is an important point since much IR research has considered just a single collection, typically the Cranfield collection in much of the early work, without any consideration being given as to the generality of the conclusions resulting from that research. The current TREC experiments are also important in throwing light on the effect of file size.

The final paper here has been chosen to exemplify the very extensive studies that have been carried out on the implementation of document clustering methods. Griffiths et al. (1986) present a detailed comparison of several different hierarchic clustering methods and find that the best results are obtained with methods that result in large numbers of small clusters. This finding motivates the second part of the paper, which demonstrates the effectiveness and the efficiency of a very simple form of cluster consisting of just a document and its nearest neighbour. The authors also consider the effect of combining clustered and nonclustered searches to give a single search output. The idea of combining different sorts of information is not new (Katzer et al., 1982) but is currently attracting much interest in the form of so-called *data fusion* techniques, which provide a quantitative means of merging the rankings resulting from several different retrieval strategies (Belkin et al., 1995).

In closing this chapter, we must emphasise that the body of techniques described here represents our view of the state of the art as of the mid-nineties. As the dates of publication of several of the selected papers demonstrate, much that has been discussed would have been little different if this Reader had appeared a decade ago. However, this should not be taken as implying a static research area; rather, it reflects the fact that the ongoing research activity represented by the TREC Programme has confirmed many of the findings of earlier experiments with far smaller test collections. It is not necessary in a volume such as this to provide a detailed coverage of the programme, but it is appropriate, as the frequent references to it imply, to emphasise that it provides a highly prominent playground for those working on IR techniques (see, e.g, Harman, 1996). For example, in addition to supporting earlier results, TREC has also encouraged interest in other topics, such as the use of noun phrases and the development of term weighting (as exemplified by the papers chosen for inclusion here by Strzalkowski and by Robertson and Walker, respectively), and we can only guess at the further advances that may be expected as this series of research conferences continues. In particular, most of the research that has been carried out so far, and especially the systematic experimental research both in TREC and elsewhere, has involved *batch*, or *pseudo-interactive*, retrieval systems: it may thus be that the techniques that we have described will prove to be less than optimal once it becomes possible to carry out detailed experiments with truly interactive systems, these including both conventional systems involving large bibliographic databases and the new retrieval environments provided by the Web.

REFERENCES

*Note: *** after a reference indicates a selected reading.*

Attar, R., and Fraenkel, A.S. (1977) Local feedback in full-text retrieval systems. *Journal of the Association for Computing Machinery*, **24**, 397–417.

Belkin N.J., Kantor, P., Fox, E.A., and Shaw, J.A. (1995) Combining the evidence of multiple query representations for information retrieval. *Information Processing and Management*, **31**, 431–448.

Buckley, C. (1993) The importance of proper weighting methods. In *Human Language Technology; Proceedings of an ARPA-Sponsored Workshop, March 1993*, pp. 349–352. San Francisco: Morgan Kaufmann.

Caid, W.R., Dumais, S.T., and Gallant, S.I. (1995) Learned vector-space models for document retrieval. *Information Processing and Management*, **31**, 419–429.

Callan, J.P. (1994) Passage-level evidence in document retrieval. In W.B. Croft and C.J. van Rijsbergen (Eds.), *Proceedings of the 17th Annual International Conference on Research and Development in Information Retrieval*, pp. 302–310. London: Springer-Verlag.

Cleverdon, C.W. (1967) The Cranfield tests on index language devices. *Aslib Proceedings*, **19**, 173–192.

Croft, W.B., and Harper, D.J. (1979) Using probabilistic models of document retrieval without relevance information. *Journal of Documentation*, **35**, 285–295.***

Cutting, D.R., Karger, D.R., and Pederson, J.O. (1993) Constant interaction-time scatter/gather browsing of very large document collections. In R. Korfhage, E.M. Rasmussen, and P. Willett (Eds.), *Proceedings of the 16th Annual International Conference on Research and Development in Information Retrieval*, pp. 126–134. Washington, DC: Association for Computing Machinery.

Deerwester, S., Dumais, S.T., and Furnas, G.W. (1990) Indexing by latent semantic analysis. *Journal of the American Society for Information Science*, **41**, 391–407.

Efthimiadis, E. (1995) User choices: A new yardstick for the evaluation of ranking algorithms for interactive query expansion. *Information Processing and Management*, **31**, 605–620.

Fagan, J.L. (1989) The effectiveness of a non-syntactic approach to automatic phrase indexing for document retrieval. *Journal of the American Society for Information Science*, **40**, 115–132.

Frakes, W.B. (1992) Stemming algorithms. In W.B. Frakes and R. Baeza-Yates (Eds.), *Information Retrieval. Data Structures and Algorithms*, pp. 131–160. Englewood Cliffs, NJ: Prentice Hall.

Fuhr, N. (1989) Models for retrieval with probabilistic indexing. *Information Processing and Management*, **25**, 55–72.

Fuhr, N., and Buckley, C. (1991) A probabilistic learning approach for document indexing. *ACM Transactions on Information Systems*, **9**, 223–248.

Griffiths, A., Luckhurst, H.C., and Willett, P. (1986) Using inter-document similarity information in document retrieval systems. *Journal of the American Society for Information Science*, **37**, 3–11.***

Harman, D.K. (1991) How effective is stemming? *Journal of the American Society for Information Science*, **42**, 321–331.

Harman, D.K. (Ed.) (1996) *The Fourth Text REtrieval Conference (TREC-4)*. Special Publication 500–236. Gaithersburg, MD: National Institute of Standards and Technology.

Harper, D.J., and van Rijsbergen, C.J. (1978) An evaluation of feedback in document retrieval using co-occurrence data. *Journal of Documentation*, **34**, 189–216.

Harter, S.P. (1975) A probabilistic approach to automatic keyword indexing. Parts 1 and 2. *Journal of the American Society for Information Science*, **26**, 197–206 and 280–289.

Hull, D.M. (1996) Stemming algorithms: A case study for detailed evaluation. *Journal of the American Society for Information Science*, **47**, 70–84.

Jacobs, P.S. (Ed.) (1992) *Text-Based Intelligent Systems*. Hillsdale, NJ: Lawrence Erlbaum.

Jardine, N., and van Rijsbergen, C.J. (1971) The use of hierarchic clustering in information retrieval. *Information Storage and Retrieval*, **7**, 217–240.

Katzer, J., McGill, M.J., Tessier, J.A., Frakes, W., and DasGupta, P. (1982) A study of the overlap among document representations. *Information Technology: Research and Development*, **1**, 261–274.

Kraaj, W., and Pohlmann, R. (1996) Viewing stemming as recall enhancement. In H.-P. Frei, D.K. Harman, P. Schäuble, and R. Wilkinson (Eds.), *Proceedings of the 19th Annual International Conference on Research and Development in Information Retrieval*, pp. 40–48. New York: Association for Computing Machinery.

Kwok, K.L. (1995) A network approach to probabilistic information retrieval. *ACM Transactions on Information Systems*, **13**, 325–353.

Lewis, D.D., and Sparck Jones, K. (1996) Natural language processing for information retrieval. *Communications of the ACM*, **39**(1), 92–101.

Logan, B., Reece, S., and Sparck Jones, K. (1994) Modelling information retrieval agents with belief revision. In W.B. Croft and C.J. van Rijsbergen (Eds.), *Proceedings of the 17th Annual International Conference on Research and Development in Information Retrieval*, pp. 91–100. London: Springer-Verlag.

Lovins, J.B. (1968) Development of a stemming algorithm. *Mechanical Translation*, **11**, 22–31.

Lovins, J.B. (1971) Error evaluation for stemming algorithms as clustering algorithms. *Journal of the American Society for Information Science*, **22**, 28–40.

Mittendorf, E., Schäuble, P., and Sheridan, P. (1995) Applying probabilistic term weighting to OCR in the case of a large alphabetic library catalogue. In E.A. Fox, P. Ingwersen, and R. Fidel (Eds.), *Proceedings of the 18th Annual International Conference on Research and Development in Information Retrieval*, pp. 328–335. New York: Association for Computing Machinery.

Nelson, M.J. (1988) Correlation of term usage and term indexing frequencies. *Information Processing and Management*, **24**, 541–547.

O'Connor, J. (1980) Answer-passage retrieval by text searching. *Journal of the American Society for Information Science*, **31**, 227–239.

Peat, H.J., and Willett, P. (1991) The limitations of term co-occurrence data for query expansion in document retrieval systems. *Journal of the American Society for Information Science*, **42**, 378–383.

Popovic, M., and Willett, P. (1992) The effectiveness of stemming for natural-language access to Slovene textual data. *Journal of the American Society for Information Science*, **43**, 384–390.

Porter, M.F. (1980) An algorithm for suffix stripping. *Program*, **14**, 130–137.***

Robertson, S.E. (1986) On relevance weight estimation and query expansion. *Journal of Documentation*, **42**, 182–188.

Robertson, S.E., and Sparck Jones, K. (1976) Relevance weighting of search terms. *Journal of the American Society for Information Science*, **27**, 129–146.

Robertson, S.E., and Walker, S. (1994) Some simple effective approximations to the 2-Poisson model for probabilistic weighted retrieval. In W.B. Croft and C.J. van Rijsbergen (Eds.), *Proceedings of the 17th International Conference on Research and Development in Information Retrieval*, pp. 232–241. London: Springer-Verlag.***

Rocchio, J.J. (1971) Relevance feedback in information retrieval. In G. Salton (Ed.), *The SMART System: Experiments in Automatic Document Processing*, pp. 313–323. Englewood Cliffs, NJ: Prentice Hall.

Salton, G. (1968) *Automatic Information Organisation and Retrieval*. New York: McGraw-Hill.

Salton, G. (1981) The SMART environment for retrieval system evaluation—advantages and disadvantages. In K. Sparck Jones (Ed.), *Information Retrieval Experiment*, pp. 316–329. London: Butterworths.

Salton, G., and Buckley, C. (1988) Term-weighting approaches in automatic text retrieval. *Information Processing and Management*, **24**, 513–523.***

Salton, G., and Buckley, C. (1990) Improving retrieval performance by relevance feedback. *Journal of the American Society for Information Science*, **41**, 288–297.***

Salton, G., Buckley, C., and Smith, M. (1990) The application of syntactic methodologies in automatic text analysis. *Information Processing and Management*, **26**, 73–92.

Smeaton, A.F. (1992) Progress in the application of natural language processing to information retrieval tasks. *Computer Journal*, **35**, 268–278.

Smeaton, A.F., and van Rijsbergen, C.J. (1983) The retrieval effects of query expansion on a feedback document retrieval system. *Computer Journal*, **26**, 239–246.

Sparck Jones, K. (1971) *Automatic Keyword Classification for Information Retrieval*. London: Butterworths.

Sparck Jones, K. (1972) A statistical interpretation of term specificity and its application in retrieval. *Journal of Documentation*, **28**, 11–21; see also Correspondence, ibid., 164–165.

Sparck Jones, K. (1973) Index term weighting. *Information Storage and Retrieval*, **9**, 619–633.

Sparck Jones, K. (1979a) Experiments in relevance weighting of search terms. *Information Processing and Management*, **15**, 133–144.

Sparck Jones, K. (1979b) Search term relevance weighting given little relevance information. *Journal of Documentation*, **35**, 30–48.***

Sparck Jones, K. (1980) Search term relevance weighting—some recent results. *Journal of Information Science*, **1**, 325–332.

Sparck Jones, K., and Tait, J.I. (1984) Automatic search term variant generation. *Journal of Documentation*, **40**, 50–66.

Stiles, H.E. (1961) The association factor in information retrieval. *Journal of the Association for Computing Machinery*, **8**, 271–279.

Strzalkowski, T. (1994) Robust text processing in automated information retrieval. In *Proceedings of the 4th Conference on Applied Natural Language Processing*, pp. 168–173. Stuttgart, Germany: Association for Computational Linguistics.***

van Rijsbergen, C.J. (1979) *Information Retrieval*. Second edition. London: Butterworths.

Willett, P. (1988) Recent trends in hierarchic document clustering: a critical review. *Information Processing and Management*, **24**, 577–597.

Xu, J., and Croft, W.B. (1996) Query expansion using local and global document analysis. In H.-P. Frei, D.K. Harman, P. Schäuble, and R. Wilkinson (Eds.), *Proceedings of the 19th Annual International Conference on Research and Development in Information Retrieval*, pp. 4–11. New York: Association for Computing Machinery.

An algorithm for suffix stripping

M.F. Porter

Computer Laboratory, Corn Exchange Street, Cambridge

ABSTRACT

The automatic removal of suffixes from words in English is of particular interest in the field of information retrieval. An algorithm for suffix stripping is described, which has been implemented as a short, fast program in BCPL. Although simple, it performs slightly better than a much more elaborate system with which it has been compared. It effectively works by treating complex suffixes as compounds made up of simple suffixes, and removing the simple suffixes in a number of steps. In each step the removal of the suffix is made to depend upon the form of the remaining stem, which usually involves a measure of its syllable length.

1. INTRODUCTION

Removing suffixes from words by automatic means is an operation which is especially useful in the field of information retrieval. In a typical IR environment, one has a collection of documents, each described by the words in the document title and possibly the words in the document abstract. Ignoring the issue of precisely where the words originate, we can say that a document is represented by a vector of words, or *terms*. Terms with a common stem will usually have similar meanings, for example:

CONNECT
CONNECTED
CONNECTING
CONNECTION
CONNECTIONS

Frequently, the performance of an IR system will be improved if term groups such as this are conflated into a single term. This may be done by removal of the various suffixes -ED, -ING, -ION, -IONS to leave the single stem CONNECT. In addition, the suffix stripping process will reduce the total number of terms in the IR system, and hence reduce the size and complexity of the data in the system, which is always advantageous.

Many strategies for suffix stripping have been reported in the literature.[e.g. 1–6] The nature of the task will vary considerably depending on whether a stem dictionary is being used, whether a suffix list is being used, and of course on the purpose for which the suffix stripping is being done. Assuming that one is not making use of a stem dictionary, and that the purpose of the task is to improve IR performance, the suffix stripping program will usually be given an explicit list of suffixes, and, with each suffix, the criterion under which it may be removed from a word to leave a valid stem. This is the approach adopted here. The main merits of the present program are that it is small (less than 400 lines of BCPL), fast (it will process a vocabulary of 10,000 different words in about 8.1 seconds on the IBM 370/165 at Cambridge University), and reasonably simple. At any rate, it is simple enough to be described in full as an algorithm in this paper. (The present version in BCPL is freely available from the author. BCPL itself is available on a wide range of different computers, but anyone wishing to use the program should have little difficulty in coding it up in other programming languages.) Given the speed of the program, it would be quite realistic to apply it to every word in a large file of continuous text, although for historical reasons we have found it convenient to apply it only to relatively small vocabulary lists derived from continuous text files.

In any suffix stripping program for IR work, two points must be borne in mind. Firstly, the suffixes are being removed simply to improve IR performance, and not as a linguistic exercise. This means that it would not be at all obvious under what circumstances a suffix should be removed, even if we could exactly determine the suffixes of the words by automatic means.

Perhaps the best criterion for removing suffixes from two words W_1 and W_2 to produce a single stem S, is to say that we do so if there appears to be no difference between the two statements 'a document is about W_1' and 'a document is about W_2'. So if W_1='CONNECTION' and W_2='CONNECTIONS' it seems very reasonable to conflate them to a single stem. But if W_1='RELATE' and W_2='RELATIVITY' it seems perhaps unreasonable, especially if the document collection is concerned with theoretical physics. (It should perhaps be added that RELATE and RELATIVITY *are* conflated together in the algorithm described here.) Between these two extremes there is a continuum of different cases, and given two terms W_1 and W_2, there will be some variation in opinion as to whether they should be conflated, just as there is with deciding the relevance of some document to a query. The evaluation of the worth of a suffix stripping system is correspondingly difficult.

The second point is that with the approach adopted here, i.e. the use of a suffix list with various rules, the success rate for the suffix stripping will be significantly less than 100%, irrespective of how the process is evaluated. For example, if SAND and SANDER get conflated, so most probably will WAND and WANDER. The error here is that the -ER of WANDER has been treated as a suffix when in fact it is part of the stem. Equally a suffix may completely alter the meaning of a word, in which case its removal is unhelpful. PROBE and PROBATE for example, have quite distinct meanings in modern English. (In fact these would not be conflated in our present algorithm.) There comes a stage in the development of a suffix stripping program where the addition of more rules to increase the performance in one area of the vocabulary causes an equal degradation of performance elsewhere. Unless this phenomenon is noticed in time, it is very easy for the program to become much more complex than is really necessary. It is also easy to give undue emphasis to cases which appear to be important, but which turn out in practice to be rather rare. For example, cases in which the spelling of the root of the word changes with the addition of a suffix, as in DECEIVE/DECEPTION, RESUME/RESUMPTION, INDEX/INDICES, occur much more rarely in real vocabularies than one might at first suppose. In view of the error rate that must in any case be expected, it did not seem worthwhile to try and cope with these cases.

It is not obvious that the simplicity of the present program is any demerit. In a test on the well known Cranfield 200 collection [7] it gave an improvement in retrieval performance when compared with a very much more elaborate program which has been in use in IR research at Cambridge since 1971 [2,6]. The test was done as follows: the words of the titles and abstracts in the documents were passed through the earlier suffix stripping system, and the resulting stems were used to index the documents. The words of the queries were reduced to stems in the same way, and the documents were ranked for each query using term coordination matching of query against document. From these rankings, recall and precision values were obtained using the standard recall cutoff method. The entire process was then repeated using the suffix stripping system described in this paper, and the results were as follows:

earlier system		present system	
precision	recall	precision	recall
0	57.24	0	58.60
10	56.85	10	58.13
20	52.85	20	53.92
30	42.61	30	43.51
40	42.20	40	39.39
50	39.06	50	38.85
60	32.86	60	33.18
70	31.64	70	31.19
80	27.15	80	27.52
90	24.59	90	25.85
100	24.59	100	25.85

Clearly the performance is not very different. The important point is that the earlier, more elaborate system certainly performs no better than the present, simple system.

(This test was done by Prof. C.J. van Rijsbergen.)

2. THE ALGORITHM

To present the suffix stripping algorithm in its entirety we will need a few definitions.

A *consonant* in a word is a letter other than A, E, I, O and U, and other than Y preceded by a consonant. (The fact that the term 'consonant' is defined to some extent in terms of itself does not make it ambiguous.) So in TOY the consonants are T and Y, in SYZYGY they are S, Z and G. If a letter is not a consonant it is a *vowel.*

A consonant will be denoted by c, a vowel by v. A list ccc . . . of length greater than 0 will be denoted by C, and a list vvv . . . of length greater than 0 will be denoted by V. Any word, or part of a word, therefore has one of the four forms:

CVCV . . . C
CVCV . . . V
VCVC . . . C
VCVC . . . V

These may all be represented by the single form

[C] VCVC . . . [V]

where the square brackets denote arbitrary presence of their contents. Using $(VC)^m$ to denote VC repeated m times, this may again be written as

$[C]\ (VC)^m\ [V]$.

m will be called the *measure* of any word or word part when represented in this form. The case m=0 covers the null word. Here are some examples:

m=0 TR, EE, TREE, Y, BY.
m=1 TROUBLE, OATS, TREES, IVY.
m=2 TROUBLES, PRIVATE, OATEN, ORRERY.

The *rules* for removing a suffix will be given in the form

(condition) S1 → S2

This means that if a word ends with the suffix S1, and the stem before S1 satisfies the given condition, S1 is replaced by S2. The condition is usually given in terms of m, e.g.

(m>1) EMENT →

Here S1 is 'EMENT' and S2 is null. This would map REPLACEMENT to REPLAC, since REPLAC is word part for which m=2.

The 'condition' part may also contain the following:

*S — the stem ends with S (and similarly for the other letters).
v — the stem contains a vowel.
*d — the stem ends with a double consonant (e.g. –TT, –SS).
*o — the stem ends cvc, where the second c is not W, X or Y (e.g. –WIL, –HOP).

And the condition part may also contain expressions with *and, or* and *not*, so that

(m>1 and (*S or *T))

tests for a stem with m>1 ending in S or T, while

(*d and not (*L or *S or *Z))

tests for a stem ending with a double consonant other than L, S or Z. Elaborate conditions like this are required only very rarely.

In a set of rules written beneath each other, only one is obeyed, and this will be the one with the longest matching S1 for the given word. For example, with

```
SSES → SS
IES  → I
SS   → SS
S    →
```

(here the conditions are all null) CARESSES maps to CARESS since SSES is the longest match for S1. Equally CARESS maps to CARESS (S1 = 'SS') and CARES to CARE (S1 = 'S').

In the rules below, examples of their application, successful or otherwise, are given on the right in lower case. The algorithm now follows:

Step 1a

```
    SSES → SS             caresses     → caress
    IES  → I              ponies       → poni
                          ties         → ti
    SS   → SS             caress       → caress
    S    →                cats         → cat
```

Step 1b

```
    (m>0) EED → EE        feed         → feed
                          agreed       → agree
    (*v*) ED  →           plastered    → plaster
                          bled         → bled
    (*v*) ING →           motoring     → motor
                          sing         → sing
```

If the second or third of the rules in Step 1b is successful, the following is done:

```
    AT → ATE                           conflat(ed)  → conflate
    BL → BLE                           troubl(ing)  → trouble
    IZ → IZE                           siz(ed)      → size
    (*d and not (*L or *S or *Z))
       → single letter                 hopp(ing)    → hop
                                       tann(ed)     → tan
                                       fall(ing)    → fall
                                       hiss(ing)    → hiss
                                       fizz(ed)     → fizz
    (m=1 and *o) → E                   fail(ing)    → fail
                                       fil(ing)     → file
```

The rule to map to a single letter causes the removal of one of the double letter pair. The –E is put back on –AT, –BL and –IZ, so that the suffixes –ATE, –BLE and –IZE can be recognised later. This E may be removed in step 4.

Step 1c

```
    (*v*) Y → I           happy        → happi
                          sky          → sky
```

Step 1 deals with plurals and past participles. The subsequent steps are much more straightforward.

Step 2

```
    (m>0) ATIONAL → ATE      relational      → relate
    (m>0) TIONAL  → TION     conditional     → condition
                             rational        → rational
    (m>0) ENCI    → ENCE     valenci         → valence
    (m>0) ANCI    → ANCE     hesitanci       → hesitance
    (m>0) IZER    → IZE      digitizer       → digitize
    (m>0) ABLI    → ABLE     conformabli     → conformable
    (m>0) ALLI    → AL       radicalli       → radical
    (m>0) ENTLI   → ENT      differentli     → different
    (m>0) ELI     → E        vileli          → vile
    (m>0) OUSLI   → OUS      analogousli     → analogous
    (m>0) IZATION → IZE      vietnamization  → vietnamize
    (m>0) ATION   → ATE      predication     → predicate
    (m>0) ATOR    → ATE      operator        → operate
    (m>0) ALISM   → AL       feudalism       → feudal
    (m>0) IVENESS → IVE      decisiveness    → decisive
    (m>0) FULNESS → FUL      hopefulness     → hopeful
    (m>0) OUSNESS → OUS      callousness     → callous
    (m>0) ALITI   → AL       formaliti       → formal
    (m>0) IVITI   → IVE      sensitiviti     → sensitive
    (m>0) BILITI  → BLE      sensibiliti     → sensible
```

The test for the string S1 can be made fast by doing a program switch on the penultimate letter of the word being tested. This gives a fairly even breakdown of the possible values of the string S1. It will be seen in fact that the S1-strings in step 2 are presented here in the alphabetical order of their penultimate letter. Similar techniques may be applied in the other steps.

Step 3

```
    (m>0) ICATE → IC         triplicate      → triplic
    (m>0) ATIVE →            formative       → form
    (m>0) ALIZE → AL         formalize       → formal
    (m>0) ICITI → IC         electriciti     → electric
    (m>0) ICAL  → IC         electrical      → electric
    (m>0) FUL   →            hopeful         → hope
    (m>0) NESS  →            goodness        → good
```

Step 4

```
    (m>1) AL    →            revival         → reviv
    (m>1) ANCE  →            allowance       → allow
    (m>1) ENCE  →            inference       → infer
    (m>1) ER    →            airliner        → airlin
    (m>1) IC    →            gyroscopic      → gyroscop
    (m>1) ABLE  →            adjustable      → adjust
    (m>1) IBLE  →            defensible      → defens
```

(m>1) ANT	→	irritant	→ irrit
(m>1) EMENT	→	replacement	→ replac
(m>1) MENT	→	adjustment	→ adjust
(m>1) ENT	→	dependent	→ depend
(m>1) and (*S or *T)) ION	→	adoption	→ adopt
(m>1) OU	→	homologou	→ homolog
(m>1) ISM	→	communism	→ commun
(m>1) ATE	→	activate	→ activ
(m>1) ITI	→	angulariti	→ angular
(m>1) OUS	→	homologous	→ homolog
(m>1) IVE	→	effective	→ effect
(m>1) IZE	→	bowdlerize	→ bowdler

The suffixes are now removed. All that remains is a little tidying up.

Step 5a

(m>1) E	→	probate	→ probat
		rate	→ rate
(m=1 and not *o) E	→	cease	→ ceas

Step 5b

(m>1 and *d and *L)	→	single letter	control
	→	controll	→
		roll	→ roll

The algorithm is careful not to remove a suffix when the stem is too short, the length of the stem being given by its measure, m. There is no linguistic basis for this approach. It was merely observed that m could be used quite effectively to help decide whether or not it was wise to take off a suffix. For example, in the following two lists:

list A	list B
RELATE	DERIVATE
PROBATE	ACTIVATE
CONFLATE	DEMONSTRATE
PIRATE	NECESSITATE
PRELATE	RENOVATE

–ATE is removed from the list B words, but not from the list A words. This means that the pairs DERIVATE/DERIVE, ACTIVATE/ACTIVE, DEMONSTRATE/DEMONSTRABLE, NECESSITATE/NECESSITOUS, will conflate together. The fact that no attempt is made to identify prefixes can make the results look rather inconsistent. Thus PRELATE does not lose the –ATE, but ARCHPRELATE becomes ARCHPREL. In practice this does not matter too much, because the presence of the prefix decreases the probability of an erroneous conflation.

Complex suffixes are removed bit by bit in the different steps. Thus GENERALIZATIONS is stripped to GENERALIZATION (Step 1), then to GENERALIZE (Step 2), then to GENERAL (Step 3), and then to GENER (Step 4). OSCILLATORS is stripped to OSCILLATOR (Step 1), then to OSCILLATE (Step 2), then to OSCILL (Step 4), and then to OSCIL (Step 5). In a vocabulary of 10,000 words, the reduction in size of the stem was distributed among the steps as follows:

Suffix stripping of a vocabulary of 10,000 words

Number of words reduced in step 1:	3597
" 2:	766
" 3:	327
" 4:	2424
" 5:	1373
Number of words not reduced:	3650

The resulting vocabulary of stems contained 6370 distinct entries. Thus the suffix stripping process reduced the size of the vocabulary by about one third.

ACKNOWLEDGEMENTS

The author is grateful to the British Library R & D Department for the funds which supported this work.

REFERENCES

1. LOVINS, J.B. Development of a Stemming Algorithm. *Mechanical Translation and Computational Linguistics.* 11 (1) March 1968 p. 22–31.
2. ANDREWS, K. The Development of a Fast Conflation Algorithm for English. *Dissertation for the Diploma in Computer Science*, Computer Laboratory, University of Cambridge, 1971.
3. PETRARCA, A.E. and LAY W.M. Use of an automatically generated authority list to eliminate scattering caused by some singular and plural main index terms. *Proceedings of the American Society for Information Science, 6* 1969 p. 277–282.
4. DATTOLA, Robert T. *FIRST: Flexible Information Retrieval System for Text.* Webster N.Y: Xerox Corporation, 12 Dec 1975.
5. COLOMBO, D.S. and NIEHOFF R.T. *Final report on improved access to scientific and technical information through automated vocabulary switching.* NSF Grant No. SIS75–12924 to the National Science Foundation.
6. DAWSON, J.L. Suffix Removal and Word Conflation. *ALLC Bulletin*, Michaelmas 1974 p. 33–46.
7. CLEVERDON, C.W., MILLS J. and KEEN M. *Factors Determining the Performance of Indexing Systems* 2 vols. College of Aeronautics, Cranfield 1966.

Robust Text Processing in Automated Information Retrieval

Tomek Strzalkowski
Courant Institute of Mathematical Sciences
New York University
715 Broadway, rm. 704
New York, NY 10003
tomek@cs.nyu.edu

Abstract

We report on the results of a series of experiments with a prototype text retrieval system which uses relatively advanced natural language processing techniques in order to enhance the effectiveness of statistical document retrieval. In this paper we show that large-scale natural language processing (hundreds of millions of words and more) is not only required for a better retrieval, but it is also doable, given appropriate resources. In particular, we demonstrate that the use of syntactic compounds in the representation of database documents as well as in the user queries, coupled with an appropriate term weighting strategy, can considerably improve the effectiveness of retrospective search. The experiments reported here were conducted on TIPSTER database in connection with the Text REtrieval Conference series (TREC).[1]

1 Introduction

The task of information retrieval is to extract *relevant* documents from a large collection of documents in response to user queries. When the documents contain primarily unrestricted text (e.g., newspaper articles, legal documents, etc.) the relevance of a document is established through 'full-text' retrieval. This has been usually accomplished by identifying key terms in the documents (the process known as 'indexing') which could then be matched against terms in queries (Salton, 1989). The effectiveness of any such term-based approach is directly related to the accuracy with which a set of terms represents the content of a document, as well as how well it contrasts a given document with respect to other documents. In other words, we are looking for a representation R such that for any text items $D1$ and $D2$, $R(D1) = R(D2)$ iff $meaning(D1) = meaning(D2)$, at an appropriate level of abstraction (which may depend on the types and character of anticipated queries).

[1] See (Harman, 1993) for a detailed description of TREC.

The simplest word-based representations of content are usually inadequate since single words are rarely specific enough for accurate discrimination, and their grouping is often accidental. A better method is to identify groups of words that create meaningful *phrases*, especially if these phrases denote important concepts in the database domain. For example, *joint venture* is an important term in the Wall Street Journal (WSJ henceforth) database, while neither *joint* nor *venture* are important by themselves. In fact, in a 800+ MBytes database, both *joint* and *venture* would often be dropped from the list of terms by the system because their inverted document frequency (*idf*) weights were too low. In large databases comprising hundreds of thousands of documents the use of phrasal terms is not just desirable, it becomes necessary.

To illustrate this point let us consider TREC Topic 104, an information request from which a database search query is to be built. The reader may note various sections of this Topic, with <desc> corresponding to the user's original request, further elaborated in <narr>, and <con> consisting of expert-assigned phrases denoting key concepts to be considered.

<top>
<num> Number: 104
<dom> Domain: Law and Government
<title> Topic: Catastrophic Health Insurance
<desc> Description:
Document will enumerate provisions of the U.S. Catastrophic Health Insurance Act of 1988, or the political/legal fallout from that legislation.
<narr> Narrative:
A relevant document will detail the content of the U.S. medicare act of 1988 which extended catastrophic illness benefits to the elderly, with particular attention to the financing scheme which led to a firestorm of protest and a Congressional retreat, or a relevant document will detail the political/legal consequences of the catastrophic health insurance imbroglio and subsequent efforts by Congress to provide similar coverages through a less-controversial mechanism.
<con> Concept(s):
1. Catastrophic Coverage Act of 1988, Medicare Part B, Health Care Financing Administration

2. catastrophic-health program, catastrophic illness, catastrophic care, acute care, long-term nursing home care
3. American Association of Retired Persons, AARP, senior citizen, National Committee to Preserve Social Security and Medicare
</top>

If the phrases are ignored altogether,[2] this query will produce an output where the relevant documents are scattered as shown in the first table below which lists the ranks and scores of relevant documents within the top 100 retrieved documents. On the other hand, if we include even simple phrases, such as *catastrophic-health program*, *acute care*, *home care*, and *senior citizen*, we can considerably sharpen the outcome of the search as seen in the second table.[3]

QUERY:104; NO. RELEVANT:21

REL DOCUMENT	RANK (no phrases)	RANK (phrases)
WSJ890918-0173	2	5
WSJ891004-0119	7	1
WSJ870723-0064	8	8
WSJ870213-0053	10	12
WSJ880608-0121	14	7
WSJ891005-0005	15	4
WSJ891009-0009	35	18
WSJ890920-0115	39	26
WSJ890928-0184	40	61
WSJ880609-0061	53	50
WSJ891009-0188	73	46
WSJ880705-0194	97	95
WSJ870601-0075	-	52
WSJ891005-0001	-	72
WSJ871028-0059	-	93

A query obtained from the fields <title>, <desc> and <narr> will be, as may be expected, much weaker than the one using <con> field, especially without the phrasal terms, because the narrative contains far fewer specific terms while containing some that may prove distracting, e.g., *firestorm*. In fact, Broglio and Croft (1993), and Broglio (personal communication, 1993) showed that the exclusion of the <con> field makes the queries quite ineffective, while adding the <narr> field makes them even worse as they lose precision by as much as 30%. However, adding phrasal terms can improve things considerably. We return to this issue later in the paper.

An accurate syntactic analysis is an essential prerequisite for selection of phrasal terms. Various statistical methods, e.g., based on word co-occurrences and mutual information, as well as partial parsing techniques, are prone to high error rates (sometimes as high as 50%), turning out many unwanted associations. Therefore a good, fast parser is necessary, but it is by no means sufficient. While syntactic phrases are often better indicators of content than 'statistical phrases' — where words are grouped solely on the basis of physical proximity, e.g., "college junior" is not the same as "junior college" — the creation of compound terms makes the term matching process more complex since in addition to the usual problems of synonymy and subsumption, one must deal with their structure (e.g., "college junior" is the same as "junior in college").

For all kinds of terms that can be assigned to the representation of a document, e.g., words, syntactic phrases, fixed phrases, and proper names, various levels of "regularization" are needed to assure that syntactic or lexical variations of input do not obscure underlying semantic uniformity. Without actually doing semantic analysis, this kind of normalization can be achieved through the following processes:[4]

(1) morphological stemming: e.g., *retrieving* is reduced to *retriev*;

(2) lexicon-based word normalization: e.g., *retrieval* is reduced to *retrieve*;

(3) operator-argument representation of phrases: e.g., *information retrieval*, *retrieving of information*, and *retrieve relevant information* are all assigned the same representation, *retrieve+information*;

(4) context-based term clustering into synonymy classes and subsumption hierarchies: e.g., *takeover* is a kind of *acquisition* (in business), and *Fortran* is a *programming language*.

Introduction of compound terms complicates the task of discovery of various semantic relationships among them. For example, the term *natural language* can often be considered to subsume any term denoting a specific human language, such as *English*. Therefore, a query containing the former may be expected to retrieve documents containing the latter. The same can be said about *language* and *English*, unless *language* is in fact a part of the compound term *programming language* in which case the association *language* – *Fortran* is appropriate. This is a problem because (a) it is a standard practice to include both simple and compound terms in document representation, and (b) term associations have thus far been computed primarily at word level (including fixed phrases) and therefore care

[2] All single words (except the stopwords such as articles or prepositions) are included in the query, including those making up the phrases.

[3] Including extra terms in documents changes the way other terms are weighted. This issue is discussed later in this paper.

[4] An alternative, but less efficient method is to generate all variants (lexical, syntactic, etc.) of words/phrases in the queries (Sparck-Jones & Tait, 1984).

must be taken when such associations are used in term matching. This may prove particularly troublesome for systems that attempt term clustering in order to create "meta-terms" to be used in document representation.

2 Overall Design

We have established the general architecture of a NLP-IR system, depicted schematically below, in which an advanced NLP module is inserted between the textual input (new documents, user queries) and the database search engine (in our case, NIST's PRISE system). This design has already shown some promise in producing a better performance than the base statistical system (Strzalkowski, 1993b). We would like to point out at the outset that this system is completely automated, including the statistical core, and the natural language processing components, and no human intervention or manual encoding is required.

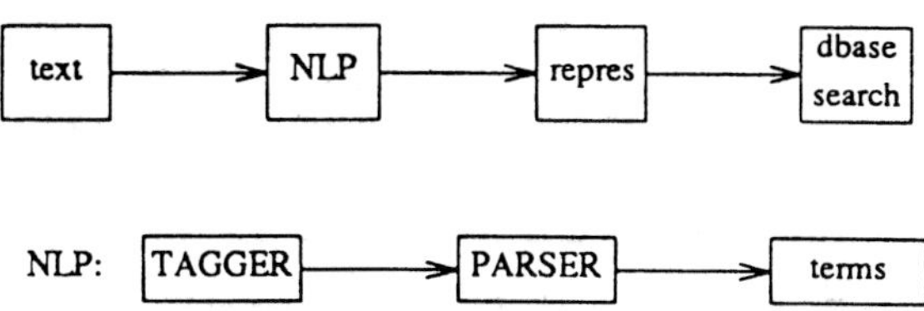

In our system the database text is first processed with a sequence of programs that include a part-of-speech tagger, a lexicon-based morphological stemmer and a fast syntactic parser. Subsequently certain types of phrases are extracted from the parse trees and used as compound indexing terms in addition to single-word terms. The extracted phrases are statistically analyzed as syntactic contexts in order to discover a variety of similarity links between smaller subphrases and words occurring in them. A further filtering process maps these similarity links onto semantic relations (generalization, specialization, synonymy, etc.) after which they are used to transform a user's request into a search query.

The user's natural language request is also parsed, and all indexing terms occurring in it are identified. Certain highly ambiguous, usually single-word terms may be dropped, provided that they also occur as elements in some compound terms. For example, "natural" may be deleted from a query already containing "natural language" because "natural" occurs in many unrelated contexts: "natural number", "natural logarithm", "natural approach", etc. At the same time, other terms may be added, namely those which are linked to some query term through admissible similarity relations. For example, "unlawful activity" is added to a query (TREC topic 055) containing the compound term "illegal activity" via a synonymy link between "illegal" and "unlawful".

One of the observations made during the course of TREC-2 was to note that removing low-quality terms from the queries is at least as important (and often more so) as adding synonyms and specializations. In some instances (e.g., routing runs) low-quality terms had to be removed (or inhibited) *before* similar terms could be added to the query or else the effect of query expansion was all but drowned out by the increased noise.

After the final query is constructed, the database search follows, and a ranked list of documents is returned. It should be noted that all the processing steps, those performed by the backbone system, and those performed by the natural language processing components, are fully automated, and no human intervention or manual encoding is required.

3 Fast Parsing with TTP Parser

TTP (Tagged Text Parser) is a full-grammar parser based on the Linguistic String Grammar developed by Sager (1981). It currently encompasses most of the grammar productions and many of the restrictions, but it is by no means complete. Unlike a conventional parser, TTP's output is a regularized representation of each sentence which reflects its logical predicate-argument structure, e.g., logical subject and logical objects are identified depending upon the main verb subcategorization frame. For example, the verb *abide* has, among others, a subcategorization frame in which the object is a prepositional phrase with *by*, as in *he'll abide by the court's decision*, i.e.,

ABIDE: *subject* NP *object* PREP by NP

Subcategorization information is read from the on-line Oxford Advanced Learner's Dictionary (OALD) which TTP uses.

Also unlike a conventional parser, TTP is equipped with a powerful skip-and-fit recovery mechanism that allows it to operate effectively in the face of ill-formed input or under severe time pressure. A built-in timer regulates the amount of time allowed for parsing any one sentence: if a parse is not returned before the allotted time elapses, TTP enters the skipping mode in which it will try to "fit" the parse. While in the skip-and-fit mode, the parser attempts to forcibly reduce incomplete constituents, possibly skimming over portions of input in order to restart processing at a next unattempted constituent; in other words, it will favor reduction over backtracking. The result of this strategy is an approximate parse, partially fitted using top-down predictions. In runs with approximately 130 million words of TREC's Wall Street Journal and San Jose Mercury texts, the parser's speed averaged 30 minutes per Megabyte or about 80 words per second, on a Sun SparcStation10. In addition, TTP has been shown to produce parse structures which are no worse than those generated by full-scale linguistic parsers when compared to hand-coded parse trees.[5]

Full details of TTP parser have been described in the TREC-1 report (Strzalkowski, 1993a), as well as in other works (Strzalkowski, 1992; Strzalkowski & Scheyen, 1993).

As may be expected, the skip-and-fit strategy will only be effective if the input skipping can be performed with a degree of determinism. This means that most of the lexical level ambiguity must be removed from the input text, prior to parsing. We achieve this using a stochastic parts of speech tagger to preprocess the text prior to parsing. In order to streamline the processing, we also perform morphological normalization of words on the tagged text, before parsing. This is possible because the part-of-speech tags retain the information about each word's original form. Thus the sentence *The Soviets have been notified* is transformed into *the/dt soviet/nps have/vbp be/vbn notify/vbn* before parsing commences.[6]

4 Head-Modifier Structures

Syntactic phrases extracted from TTP parse structures are represented as head-modifier pairs. The head in such a pair is a central element of a phrase (main verb, main noun, etc.), while the modifier is one of the adjuncts or arguments of the head. In the TREC experiments reported here we extracted head-modifier word pairs only, i.e., nested pairs were not used even though this was warranted by the size of the database.

Figure 1 shows all stages of the initial linguistic analysis of a sample sentence from the WSJ database. The reader may note that the parser's output is a predicate-argument structure centered around the main elements of various phrases. For example, BE is the main predicate (modified by HAVE) with 2 arguments (*subject, object*) and 2 adjuncts (*adv, sub_ord*). INVADE is the predicate in the subordinate clause with 2 arguments (*subject, object*). The subject of BE is a noun phrase with PRESIDENT as the head element, two modifiers (FORMER, SOVIET) and a determiner (THE). From this structure, we extract head-modifier pairs that become candidates for compound terms. In general, the following types of pairs are considered: (1) a head noun of a noun phrase and its left adjective or noun adjunct, (2) a head noun and the head of its right adjunct, (3) the main verb of a clause and the head of its object phrase, and (4) the head of the subject phrase and the main verb. These types of pairs account for most of the syntactic variants for relating two words (or simple phrases) into pairs carrying compatible semantic content. For example, the pair *retrieve+information* will be extracted from any of the following fragments: *information retrieval system; retrieval of information from databases*; and *information that can be retrieved by a user-controlled interactive search process.* We also attempted to identify and remove any terms which were explicitly negated in order to prevent matches against their positive counterparts, either in the database or in the queries.

One difficulty in obtaining head-modifier pairs of highest accuracy is the notorious ambiguity of nominal compounds. The pair extractor looks at the distribution statistics of the compound terms to decide whether the association between any two words (nouns and adjectives) in a noun phrase is both syntactically valid and semantically significant. For example, we may accept *language+natural* and *processing+language* from

INPUT SENTENCE
The former Soviet president has been a local hero ever since a Russian tank invaded Wisconsin.

TAGGED SENTENCE
The/*dt* former/*jj* Soviet/*jj* president/*nn* has/*vbz* been/*vbn* a/*dt* local/*jj* hero/*nn* ever/*rb* since/*in* a/*dt* Russian/*jj* tank/*nn* invaded/*vbd* Wisconsin/*np* ./*per*

TAGGED & STEMMED SENTENCE
the/*dt* former/*jj* soviet/*jj* president/*nn* have/*vbz* be/*vbn* a/*dt* local/*jj* hero/*nn* ever/*rb* since/*in* a/*dt* russian/*jj* tank/*nn* invade/*vbd* wisconsin/*np* ./*per*

PARSED SENTENCE
```
[assert
  [[perf [HAVE]] [[verb [BE]]
      [subject [np [n PRESIDENT] [t_pos THE]
              [adj [FORMER]] [adj [SOVIET]]]]
      [object [np [n HERO] [t_pos A] [adj [LOCAL]]]]
      [adv EVER]
      [sub_ord [SINCE
             [[verb [INVADE]]
                [subject [np [n TANK] [t_pos A]
                      [adj [RUSSIAN]]]]
                [object [np [name [WISCONSIN]]]]]]]]]
```

EXTRACTED TERMS & WEIGHTS

president	2.623519	soviet	5.416102
president+soviet	11.556747	president+former	14.594883
hero	7.896426	hero+local	14.314775
invade	8.435012	tank	6.848128
tank+invade	17.402237	tank+russian	16.030809
russian	7.383342	wisconsin	7.785689

Figure 1. Stages of sentence processing.

[5] Hand-coded parse trees were obtained from the University of Pennsylvania Treebank Project database.

[6] The tags are read as follows: *dt* is determiner, *nps* is a proper name, *vbp* is a tensed plural verb, *vbn* is a past participle.

natural language processing as correct, however, *case+trading* would make a mediocre term when extracted from *insider trading case*. On the other hand, it is important to extract *trading+insider* to be able to match documents containing phrases *insider trading sanctions act* or *insider trading activity*.

5 Term Weighting Issues

Finding a proper term weighting scheme is critical in term-based retrieval since the rank of a document is determined by the weights of the terms it shares with the query. One popular term weighting scheme, known as tf.idf, weights terms proportionately to their inverted document frequency scores and to their in-document frequencies (tf). The in-document frequency factor is usually normalized by the document length, that is, it is more significant for a term to occur in a short 100-word abstract, than in a 5000-word article.[7]

A standard tf.idf weighting scheme (see Buckley, 1993 for details) may be inappropriate for mixed term sets, consisting of ordinary concepts, proper names, and phrases, because:

(1) It favors terms that occur fairly frequently in a document, which supports only general-type queries (e.g., "all you know about X"). Such queries were not typical in TREC.

(2) It attaches low weights to infrequent, highly specific terms, such as names and phrases, whose only occurrences in a document are often decisive for relevance. Note that such terms cannot be reliably distinguished using their distribution in the database as the sole factor, and therefore syntactic and lexical information is required.

(3) It does not address the problem of inter-term dependencies arising when phrasal terms and their component single-word terms are all included in a document representation, i.e., *launch+satellite* and *satellite* are not independent, and it is unclear whether they should be counted as two terms.

In our post-TREC-2 experiments we considered (1) and (2) only. We changed the weighting scheme so that the phrases (but not the names, which we did not distinguish in TREC-2) were more heavily weighted by their idf scores while the in-document frequency scores were replaced by logarithms multiplied by sufficiently large constants. In addition, the top N highest-idf matching terms (simple or compound) were counted more toward the document score than the remaining terms.

[7] This is not always true, for example when all occurrences of a term are concentrated in a single section or a paragraph rather than spread around the article.

Schematically, these new weights for phrasal and highly specific terms are obtained using the following formula, while weights for most of the single-word terms remain unchanged:

$$weight(T_i)=(C_1*log(tf)+C_2*\alpha(N,i))*idf$$

In the above, $\alpha(N,i)$ is 1 for $i<N$ and is 0 otherwise. The selection of a weighting formula was partly constrained by the fact that document-length-normalized tf weights were precomputed at the indexing stage and could not be altered without re-indexing of the entire database. The intuitive interpretation of the $\alpha(N,i)$ factor is as follows. We restrict the maximum number of terms on which a query is permitted to match a document to N highest weight terms, where N can be the same for all queries or may vary from one query to another. Note that this is not the same as simply taking the N top terms from each query. Rather, for each document for which there are M matching terms with the query, only min(M,N) of them, namely those which have highest weights, will be considered when computing the document score. Moreover, only the global importance weights for terms are considered (such as idf), while local in-document frequency (eg., tf) is suppressed by either taking a log or replacing it with a constant.

Changing the weighting scheme for compound terms, along with other minor improvements (such as expanding the stopword list for topics, or correcting a few parsing bugs) has lead to an overall increase of precision of more than 20% over our official TREC-2 ad-hoc results. Table 1 includes statistics of these new runs for 50 queries (numbered 101-150) against the WSJ database. The gap between the precision levels in columns *txt2* and *con* reflects the difference in the quality of the queries obtained from the narrative parts of the topics (*txt2* = *title* + *desc* + *narr*), and those obtained primarily from expert's formulation (*title* + *desc* + *con*). The column *txt2+nlp* represents the improvement of *txt2* queries thanks to NLP, with as much as 70% of the gap closed. Similar improvements have been obtained for other sets of queries.

6 Conclusions

We presented in some detail our natural language information retrieval system consisting of an advanced NLP module and a 'pure' statistical core engine. While many problems remain to be resolved, including the question of adequacy of term-based representation of document content, we attempted to demonstrate that the architecture described here is nonetheless viable. In particular, we demonstrated that natural language

Run	txt1	txt2	txt2+nlp	con	con+nlp
Tot number of docs over all queries					
Rel	3929	3929	3929	3929	3929
RelRet	2736	3025	3108	3332	3401
%chg		+9.0	+14.7	+21.8	+24.3
Recall	(interp) Precision Averages				
0.00	0.6874	0.7318	0.7201	0.7469	0.8063
0.10	0.4677	0.5293	0.5239	0.5726	0.6198
0.20	0.3785	0.4532	0.4751	0.4970	0.5566
0.30	0.3060	0.3707	0.4122	0.4193	0.4786
0.40	0.2675	0.3276	0.3541	0.3747	0.4257
0.50	0.2211	0.2815	0.3126	0.3271	0.3828
0.60	0.1765	0.2406	0.2752	0.2783	0.3380
0.70	0.1313	0.1783	0.2142	0.2267	0.2817
0.80	0.0828	0.1337	0.1605	0.1670	0.2164
0.90	0.0451	0.0818	0.1014	0.0959	0.1471
1.00	0.0094	0.0159	0.0194	0.0168	0.0474
Average precision over all rel docs					
Avg	0.2309	0.2835	0.3070	0.3210	0.3759
%chg		+22.8	+33.0	+39.0	+62.8
Precision at N documents					
5	0.5000	0.5240	0.5200	0.5600	0.6040
10	0.4080	0.4600	0.4900	0.5020	0.5580
100	0.2380	0.2790	0.2914	0.3084	0.3346
R-Precision (after Rel)					
Exact	0.2671	0.3053	0.3332	0.3455	0.3950
%chg		+14.3	+24.7	+29.3	+47.9

Table 1. Run statistics for 50 ad-hoc queries against WSJ database with 1000 docs retrieved per query: (1) *txt1* - single terms of <narr> and <desc> fields — this is the base run; (2) *txt2* - <narr> and <desc> fields with low weight terms removed; (3) *txt2+nlp* - <narr> and <desc> fields including syntactic phrase terms using the new weighting scheme; (4) *con* - <desc> and <con> fields with low weight terms removed but with no NLP; and (5) *con+nlp* - <desc> and <con> fields including phrases with the new weighting scheme.

processing can now be done on a fairly large scale and that its speed and robustness can match those of traditional statistical programs such as key-word indexing or statistical phrase extraction. We suggest, with some caution until more experiments are run, that natural language processing can be very effective in creating appropriate search queries out of a user's initial specifications, which can be frequently imprecise or vague.

Acknowledgements

The author would like to thank Donna Harman of NIST for making her PRISE system available for this research. We would also like to thank Ralph Weischedel and Constantine Papageorgiou of BBN for providing and assisting in the use of the part of speech tagger. This paper is based upon work supported by the Advanced Research Projects Agency under Contract N00014-90-J-1851 from the Office of Naval Research, under Contract N00600-88-D-3717 from PRC Inc., under ARPA's Tipster Phase-2 Contract 94-FI57900-000, and the National Science Foundation under Grant IRI-93-02615.

References

Broglio, John and W. Bruce Croft. 1993. "Query Processing for Retrieval from Large Text Bases." Human Language Technology, Proceedings of the workshop, Princeton, NJ. Morgan-Kaufmann, pp. 353-357.

Buckley, Chris. 1993. "The Importance of Proper Weighting Methods." Human Language Technology, Proceedings of the workshop, Princeton, NJ. Morgan-Kaufmann, pp. 349-352.

Harman, Donna (ed.). 1993. *First Text REtrieval Conference*. NIST special publication 500-207.

Sager, Naomi. 1981. *Natural Language Information Processing*. Addison-Wesley.

Sparck Jones, K. and J. I. Tait. 1984. "Automatic search term variant generation." *Journal of Documentation*, 40(1), pp. 50-66.

Strzalkowski, Tomek. 1992. "TTP: A Fast and Robust Parser for Natural Language." Proceedings of the 14th International Conference on Computational Linguistics (COLING), Nantes, France, July 1992. pp. 198-204.

Strzalkowski, Tomek. 1993a. "Natural Language Processing in Large-Scale Text Retrieval Tasks." Proceedings of the First Text REtrieval Conference (TREC-1), NIST Special Publication 500-207, pp. 173-187.

Strzalkowski, Tomek. 1993b. "Robust Text Processing in Automated Information Retrieval." Proc. of ACL-sponsored workshop on Very Large Corpora. Ohio State Univ. Columbus, June 22.

Strzalkowski, Tomek, and Peter Scheyen. 1993. "Evaluation of TTP Parser: a preliminary report." Proceedings of International Workshop on Parsing Technologies (IWPT-93), Tilburg, Netherlands and Durbuy, Belgium, pp. 293-308.

TERM-WEIGHTING APPROACHES IN AUTOMATIC TEXT RETRIEVAL

GERARD SALTON and CHRISTOPHER BUCKLEY
Department of Computer Science, Cornell University, Ithaca, NY 14853, USA

(*Received* 19 *November* 1987; *accepted in final form* 26 *January* 1988)

Abstract—The experimental evidence accumulated over the past 20 years indicates that text indexing systems based on the assignment of appropriately weighted single terms produce retrieval results that are superior to those obtainable with other more elaborate text representations. These results depend crucially on the choice of effective term-weighting systems. This article summarizes the insights gained in automatic term weighting, and provides baseline single-term-indexing models with which other more elaborate content analysis procedures can be compared.

1. AUTOMATIC TEXT ANALYSIS

In the late 1950s, Luhn [1] first suggested that automatic text retrieval systems could be designed based on a comparison of content identifiers attached both to the stored texts and to the users' information queries. Typically, certain words extracted from the texts of documents and queries would be used for content identification; alternatively, the content representations could be chosen manually by trained indexers familiar with the subject areas under consideration and with the contents of the document collections. In either case, the documents would be represented by *term vectors* of the form

$$D = (t_i, t_j, \ldots, t_p) \quad (1)$$

where each t_k identifies a content term assigned to some sample document D. Analogously, the information requests, or queries, would be represented either in vector form, or in the form of Boolean statements. Thus, a typical query Q might be formulated as

$$Q = (q_a, q_b, \ldots, q_r) \quad (2)$$

or

$$Q = (q_a \text{ and } q_b) \text{ or } (q_c \text{ and } q_d \text{ and } \ldots) \text{ or } \ldots \quad (3)$$

where q_k once again represents a term assigned to query Q.

A more formal representation of the term vectors of eqns (1) and (2) is obtained by including in each vector all possible content terms allowed in the system and adding term weight assignments to provide distinctions among the terms. Thus, if w_{dk} (or w_{qk}) represents the weight of term t_k in document D (or query Q), and t terms in all are available for content representation, the term vectors for document D and query Q can be written as

$$D = (t_0, w_{d_0}; t_1, w_{d_1}; \ldots,; t_t, w_{dt})$$

and

$$Q = (q_0, w_{q_0}; q_1, w_{q_1}; \ldots; q_t, w_{qt}). \quad (4)$$

This study was supported in part by the National Science Foundation under grants IST 83-16166 and IRI 87-02735.

In the foregoing formulation, the assumption is that w_{dk} (or w_{qk}) is equal to 0 when term k is not assigned to document D (or query Q), and that w_{dk} (or w_{qk}) equals 1 for the assigned terms.

Given the vector representations of eqn (4), a *query-document similarity* value may be obtained by comparing the corresponding vectors, using for example the conventional vector product formula

$$\text{similarity}(Q,D) = \sum_{k=1}^{t} w_{qk} \cdot w_{dk}. \quad (5)$$

When the term weights are restricted to 0 and 1 as previously suggested, the vector product of eqn (5) measures the number of terms that are jointly assigned to query Q and document D.

In practice, it has proven useful to provide a greater degree of discrimination among terms assigned for content representation than is possible with weights of 0 and 1 alone. In particular, term weights in decreasing term importance order could be assigned, in which case the weights w_{dk} (or w_{qk}) could be allowed to vary continuously between 0 and 1, the higher weight assignments near 1 being used for the most important terms, whereas lower weights near 0 would characterize the less important terms. In some circumstances, it may also be useful to use normalized weight assignments, where the individual term weights depend to some extent on the weights of other terms in the same vector. A typical term weight using a vector length normalization factor is $\frac{w_{dk}}{\sqrt{\sum_{vector} (w_{di})^2}}$ for documents $\left(\text{or } \frac{w_{qk}}{\sqrt{\sum_{vector} (w_{qi})^2}} \text{ for queries} \right)$. When a length normalized term-weighting system is used with the vector similarity function of eqn (5), one obtains the well-known cosine vector similarity formula that has been used extensively with the experimental Smart retrieval system [2,3]:

$$\text{similarity}(Q,D) = \frac{\sum_{k=1}^{t} w_{qk} \cdot w_{dk}}{\sqrt{\sum_{k=1}^{t} (w_{qk})^2 \cdot \sum_{k=1}^{t} (w_{dk})^2}}. \quad (6)$$

A vector matching system performing global comparisons between query and document vectors provides ranked retrieval output in decreasing order of the computed similarities between Q and D. Such a ranked output is useful because controls are now available over the size of the retrieved document set, and iterative retrieval strategies based on successive query reformulations are simplified. A system that first retrieves those items thought to be of main interest to the users will necessarily prove helpful in interactive information retrieval.

In designing automatic text retrieval systems, two main questions must be faced. First, what appropriate content units are to be included in the document and query representations? Second, is the determination of the term weights capable of distinguishing the important terms from those less crucial for content identification?

Concerning first the choice of content terms, various possibilities must be considered. In most of the early experiments, *single terms* alone were used for content representation, often consisting of words extracted from the texts of documents and from natural language query formulations. [3–7] In many cases, quite effective retrieval output has been obtained using single-term content representations. Ultimately, however, sets of single terms cannot provide complete identifications of document content. For this reason, many enhancements in content analysis and text indexing procedures have been proposed over the years in an effort to generate complex text representations. The following possibilities have been considered in this connection:

1. The generation of sets of *related terms* based on the statistical cooccurrence characteristics of the words in certain contexts within the document collection. The assumption normally made is that words that cooccur with sufficient frequency in the documents of a collection are in fact related to each other [8–11].
2. The formation of *term phrases* consisting of one or more governing terms (the phrase heads) together with corresponding dependent terms (the phrase components). Phrases are often chosen by using word frequency counts and other statistical methods, possibly supplemented by syntactic procedures designed to detect syntactic relationships between governing and dependent phrase components [12–17].
3. The use of word grouping methods of the kind provided by *thesauruses*, where classes of related words are grouped under common headings; these class headings can then be assigned for content identification instead of the individual terms contained in the classes [18–20]. Alternatively, term relationships useful for content identification may also be obtainable by using existing machine-readable dictionaries and lexicons [21–24].
4. The construction of *knowledge bases* and related artificial intelligence structures designed to represent the content of the subject area under consideration; entries from the knowledge base are then used to represent the content of documents and queries [25–30].

From the beginning, it was evident that the construction and identification of complex text representations was inordinately difficult. In particular, it became clear that most automatically derived term dependencies were valid only locally in the documents from which the dependent term groups were originally extracted; this implies that dependent term groups could not be counted upon to produce useful content identifiers in new document contexts different from those originally used [11]. The experiences gained with the use of automatically generated term phrases proved similarly discouraging: for some collections, improvements in retrieval effectiveness of up to 20% (in search recall and precision) were obtainable by using phrase identifiers instead of single terms; but for other collections these same phrase procedures did not furnish any improvements at all. Moreover, even sophisticated syntactic analysis programs could not be relied upon to produce useful complex content identifiers [16].

As for the use of preconstructed vocabulary schedules and term classifications, the problem is that viable procedures for the construction of effective vocabulary tools covering subject areas of reasonable scope appear to be completely lacking. The same goes for the construction of knowledge bases designed to reflect the structure of disclosure areas. Until more becomes known about the desired form and content of dictionaries and thesauruses, little gain should be expected from these tools in text analysis and document indexing.

In reviewing the extensive literature accumulated during the past 25 years in the area of retrieval system evaluation, the overwhelming evidence is that the judicious use of single-term identifiers is preferable to the incorporation of more complex entities extracted from the texts themselves or obtained from available vocabulary schedules [31–37]. Two main problems appear in producing complex text identifiers:

1. When stringent conditions are used for the construction of complex identifiers, typified by the use of restrictive frequency criteria and limited cooccurrence contexts for the recognition of term phrases, then few new identifiers are likely to become available, and the performance of the retrieval system with complex identifiers will differ only marginally from the results obtainable with single term indexing.
2. On the other hand, when the construction criteria for the complex entities are relaxed, then some good identifiers are obtained, but also many marginal ones that do not prove useful. Overall, the single-term indexing will generally be preferred.

When single terms are used for content identification, distinctions must be introduced between individual terms, based on their presumed value as document descriptors. This leads to the use of term weights attached to the item identifiers. The considerations controlling the generation of effective weighting factors are outlined briefly in the next section.

2. TERM-WEIGHT SPECIFICATION

The main function of a term-weighting system is the enhancement of retrieval effectiveness. Effective retrieval depends on two main factors: one, items likely to be relevant to the user's needs must be retrieved; two, items likely to be extraneous must be rejected. Two measures are normally used to assess the ability of a system to retrieve the relevant and reject the nonrelevant items of a collection, known as *recall* and *precision*, respectively. Recall is the proportion of relevant items retrieved, measured by the ratio of the number of relevant retrieved items to the total number of relevant items in the collection; precision, on the other hand, is the proportion of retrieved items that are relevant, measured by the ratio of the number of relevant retrieved items to the total number of retrieved items.

In principle, a system is preferred that produces both high recall by retrieving everything that is relevant, and also high precision by rejecting all items that are extraneous. The recall function of retrieval appears to be best served by using broad, high-frequency terms that occur in many documents of the collection. Such terms may be expected to pull out many documents, including many of the relevant documents. The precision factor, however, may be best served by using narrow, highly specific terms that are capable of isolating the few relevant items from the mass of nonrelevant ones. In practice, compromises are normally made by using terms that are broad enough to achieve a reasonable recall level without at the same time producing unreasonably low precision.

The differing recall and precision requirements favor the use of composite term weighting factors that contain both recall- and precision-enhancing components. Three main considerations appear important in this connection. First, terms that are frequently mentioned in individual documents, or document excerpts, appear to be useful as recall-enhancing devices. This suggests that a *term frequency* (tf) factor be used as part of the term-weighting system measuring the frequency of occurrence of the terms in the document or query texts. Term-frequency weights have been used for many years in automatic indexing environments [1–4].

Second, term frequency factors alone cannot ensure acceptable retrieval performance. Specifically, when the high frequency terms are not concentrated in a few particular documents, but instead are prevalent in the whole collection, all documents tend to be retrieved, and this affects the search precision. Hence a new collection-dependent factor must be introduced that favors terms concentrated in a few documents of a collection. The well-known *inverse document frequency* (idf) (or inverse collection frequency) factor performs this function. The idf factor varies inversely with the number of documents n to which a term is assigned in a collection of N documents. A typical idf factor may be computed as $\log N/n$ [38].

Term discrimination considerations suggest that the best terms for document content identification are those able to distinguish certain individual documents from the remainder of the collection. This implies that the best terms should have high term frequencies but low overall collection frequencies. A reasonable measure of term importance may then be obtained by using the product of the term frequency and the inverse document frequency ($tf \times idf$) [39–41].

The term discrimination model has been criticized because it does not exhibit well substantiated theoretical properties. This is in contrast with the probabilistic model of information retrieval where the relevance properties of the documents are taken into account, and a theoretically valid *term relevance* weight is derived [42–44]. The term relevance weight—defined as the proportion of relevant documents in which a term occurs divided by the proportion of nonrelevant items in which the term occurs—is, however, not immediately computable without knowledge of the occurrence properties of the terms in the relevant and nonrelevant parts of the document collection. A number of methods have been proposed for estimating the term relevance factor in the absence of complete relevance information, and these have shown that under well-defined conditions the term relevance can be reduced to an inverse document frequency factor of the form $\log((N-n)/n)$ [45–46]. The composite (tf × idf) term-weighting system is thus directly relatable to other theoretically attractive retrieval models.

A third term-weighting factor, in addition to the term frequency and the inverse document frequency, appears useful in systems with widely varying vector lengths. In many situations, short documents tend to be represented by short-term vectors, whereas much larger-term sets are assigned to the longer documents. When a large number of terms are used for document representation, the chance of term matches between queries and documents is high, and hence the larger documents have a better chance of being retrieved than the short ones. Normally, all relevant documents should be treated as equally important for retrieval purposes. This suggests that a *normalization factor* be incorporated into the term-weighting formula to equalize the length of the document vectors. Assuming that w represents the weight of term t, the final term weight might then be defined as $w\Big/\sum_{\text{vector } i} w_i$, or $w\Big/\sqrt{\sum_{\text{vector } i}(w_i)^2}$.

In the preceding discussion of term-weighting systems, both documents and queries were assumed to be represented by sets, or vectors, of weighted terms. Term-weighting systems have also been applied to Boolean query statements, and extended Boolean systems have been devised in which Boolean query statements are effectively reduced to vector form [47–54]. The previous considerations regarding term weighting thus apply to some extent also to Boolean query processing.

3. TERM-WEIGHTING EXPERIMENTS

A number of term-weighting experiments are described in the remainder of this note in which combinations of term frequency, collection frequency, and length normalization components are used with six document collections of varying size, covering different subject areas. In each case, collections of user queries are used for retrieval purposes and the performance is averaged over the number of available user queries. For each experiment, the average search precision is computed for three different recall points, including a low recall of 0.25, an average recall of 0.50, and a high recall of 0.75. This average search precision is then further averaged for all available user queries. In addition, to the precision measure, the rank of the weighting methods in decreasing performance order is used as an evaluation criterion. A total of 1800 different combinations of term-weight assignments were used experimentally, of which 287 were found to be distinct. A rank of 1 thus designates the best performance, and 287 the worst.

In the present experiments, each term-weight combination is described by using two triples, representing, respectively, the term frequency, collection frequency, and vector normalization factors for document terms (first triple), and query terms (second triple). The principal weighting components are defined in Table 1. Three different term-frequency components are used, including a binary weight (b), the normal term frequency (t), and a normalized term frequency (n) that lies between 0.5 and 1.0. The three collection frequency components represent multipliers of 1(x) that disregards the collection frequency, a conventional inverse collection frequency factor (f), and a probabilistic inverse collection frequency (p). Finally, the length normalization factor may be absent (x as the third component) or present (c). (In the previously mentioned full set of 1800 different term-weight assignments, additional weighting components not included in Table 1 were also tried. These additional components did not supply any fundamentally new insights or advantages.)

Table 2 shows actual formulas for some well-known term-weighting systems. The

Table 1. Term-weighting components

Term Frequency Component		
b	1.0	binary weight equal to 1 for terms present in a vector (term frequency is ignored)
t	tf	raw term frequency (number of times a term occurs in a document or query text)
n	$0.5 + 0.5\dfrac{\text{tf}}{\max \text{tf}}$	augmented normalized term frequency (tf factor normalized by maximum tf in the vector, and further normalized to lie between 0.5 and 1.0)
Collection Frequency Component		
x	1.0	no change in weight; use original term frequency component (b, t, or n)
f	$\log\dfrac{N}{n}$	multiply original tf factor by an inverse collection frequency factor (N is total number of documents in collection, and n is number of documents to which a term is assigned)
p	$\log\dfrac{N-n}{n}$	multiply tf factor by a probabilistic inverse collection frequency factor
Normalization Component		
x	1.0	no change; use factors derived from term frequency and collection frequency only (no normalization)
c	$1\Big/\sqrt{\sum_{\text{vector}} w_i^2}$	use cosine normalization where each term weight w is divided by a factor representing Euclidian vector length

Table 2. Typical term-weighting formulas

Weighting System	Document term weight	Query Term weight
Best fully weighted system *tfc·nfx*	$\dfrac{\text{tf}\cdot\log\frac{N}{n}}{\sqrt{\sum_{\text{vector}}\left(\text{tf}_i\cdot\log\frac{N}{n_i}\right)^2}}$	$\left(0.5+\dfrac{0.5\ \text{tf}}{\max \text{tf}}\right)\cdot\log\dfrac{N}{n}$
Best weighted probabilistic weight *nxx·bpx*	$0.5+\dfrac{0.5\ \text{tf}}{\max \text{tf}}$	$\log\dfrac{N-n}{n}$
Classical idf weight *bfx·bfx*	$\log\dfrac{N}{n}$	$\log\dfrac{N}{n}$
Binary term independence *bxx·bpx*	1	$\log\dfrac{N-n}{n}$
Standard tf weight: *txc·txx*	$\dfrac{\text{tf}}{\sqrt{\sum_{\text{vector}}(\text{tf}_i)^2}}$	tf
Coordination level *bxx·bxx*	1	1

coordination-level match, which simply reflects the number of matching terms present in documents and queries, respectively, is described by the sextuple *bxx·bxx*. Similarly, the probabilistic binary term independence system that uses binary document terms, but a probabilistic inverse collection frequency weight for the query terms, is represented as *bxx·bpx*. A typical complex term-weighting scheme, described as *tfc·nfx*, uses a normalized tf × idf weight for document terms, and an enhanced, but unnormalized tf × idf factor for the queries. (Since the query vectors remain constant for all documents of a collection, a query normalization simply adds a constant factor to all query-document similarity measurements, which leaves the final document ranking unaffected.)

The six collections used experimentally are characterized by the statistics of Table 3. The smallest collection is a biomedical (MED) collection, consisting of 1033 documents and

Table 3. Collection statistics (including average vector length and standard deviation of vector lengths)

Collection	Number of vectors (documents or queries)	Average vector length (number of terms)	Standard deviation of vector length	Average frequency of terms in vectors	Percentage of terms in vectors with frequency 1
CACM					
documents	3,204	24.52	21.21	1.35	80.93
queries	64	10.80	6.43	1.15	88.68
CISI					
documents	1,460	46.55	19.38	1.37	80.27
queries	112	28.29	19.49	1.38	78.36
CRAN					
documents	1,398	53.13	22.53	1.58	69.50
queries	225	9.17	3.19	1.04	95.69
INSPEC					
documents	12,684	32.50	14.27	1.78	61.06
queries	84	15.63	8.66	1.24	83.78
MED					
documents	1,033	51.60	22.78	1.54	72.70
queries	30	10.10	6.03	1.12	90.76
NPL					
documents	11,429	19.96	10.84	1.21	84.03
queries	100	7.16	2.36	1.00	100.00

30 queries, whereas the largest collection (INSPEC) comprises 12684 documents and 84 queries, covering the computer engineering areas. In all cases, the query vectors are much shorter than the corresponding document vectors.

The NPL (National Physical Laboratory) collection of 11429 documents and 100 queries was available in indexed form only (i.e., in the form of document and query vectors) and not in original natural language form. This may explain its somewhat peculiar makeup. Both the document and the query vector are much shorter in the NPL collection than in the other collections, and the variation in query length (2.36 for a mean number of 7.16 query terms) is very small. Furthermore, the term frequencies are especially low for the NPL collection: each query term appears precisely once in a query, and the average frequency of the terms in the documents is only 1.21. In these circumstances, the term frequency weighting and length normalization operations cannot perform their intended function. One may conjecture that the NPL index terms are carefully chosen, and may in fact represent specially controlled terms rather than freely chosen natural language entries.

Typical evaluation output is shown in Tables 4 and 5. With a few minor exceptions, the results for the five collections of Table 4 are homogeneous, in the sense that the best results are produced by the same term-weighting systems for all collections, and the same holds also for the poorest results. The results of Table 4 do however differ substantially from those obtained for the NPL collection in Table 5. Considering first the results of Table 4, the following conclusions are evident:

1. Methods 1 and 2 produce comparable performances for all collections, the length normalization is important for the documents, and the enhanced query weighting is effective for the queries. These methods are recommended for conventional natural language texts and text abstracts.
2. Method 3 does not include the normalization operation for vector length, nor the enhanced query weights. This unnormalized (tf × idf) weighting method is poor for collections such as CRAN and MED where very short query vectors are used with little deviation in the query length. In such cases, enhanced query weights (n factor) prove important.
3. Method 4 represents the best of the probabilistic weighting systems. This method is less effective than the enhanced weighting schemes of methods 1 and 2. It fails especially for collections such as CISI and INSPEC where long query vectors are used and the term discrimination afforded by query term weighting is essential.
4. Methods 5 to 7 represent, respectively, the classical inverse document frequency weighting, the probabilistic binary term independence system, and the classical term frequency weighting. As can be seen, these methods are generally inferior for all collections.
5. The coordination level matching of binary vectors represents one of the worst possible retrieval strategies.

Table 4. Performance results for eight term-weighting methods averaged over 5 collections

Term-weighting methods	Rank of method and ave. precision	CACM 3204 docs 54 queries	CISI 1460 docs 112 queries	CRAN 1397 docs 225 queries	INSPEC 12,684 docs 84 queries	MED 1033 docs 30 queries	Averages for 5 collections
1. Best fully weighted (*tfc·nfx*)	Rank	1	14	19	3	19	11.2
	P	0.3630	0.2189	0.3841	0.2626	0.5628	
2. Weighted with inverse frequency *f* not used for docs (*txc·nfx*)	Rank	25	14	7	4	32	16.4
	P	0.3252	0.2189	0.3950	0.2626	0.5542	
3. Classical tf × idf No normalization (*tfx·tfx*)	Rank	29	22	219	45	132	84.4
	P	0.3248	0.2166	0.2991	0.2365	0.5177	
4. Best weighted probabilistic (*nxx·bpx*)	Rank	55	208	11	97	60	86.2
	P	0.3090	0.1441	0.3899	0.2093	0.5449	
5. Classical idf without normalization (*bfx·bfx*)	Rank	143	247	183	160	178	182
	P	0.2535	0.1410	0.3184	0.1781	0.5062	
6. Binary independence probabilistic (*bxx·bpx*)	Rank	166	262	154	195	147	159
	P	0.2376	0.1233	0.3266	0.1563	0.5116	
7. Standard weights cosine normalization (original Smart) (*txc·txx*)	Rank	178	173	137	187	246	184
	P	0.2102	0.1539	0.3408	0.1620	0.4641	
8. Coordination level binary vectors (*bxx·bxx*)	Rank	196	284	280	258	281	260
	P	0.1848	0.1033	0.2414	0.0944	0.4132	

Table 5. Performance results for NPL collection (11429 docs, 100 queries)

Evaluation	Best fully weighted *tfc·nfx*	Weighted restricted *f* *txc·nfx*	Classical tf × idf *tfx·tfx*	Best probabilistic *nxx·bpx*	Classical idf system *bfx·bfx*	Binary independence *bxx·bpx*	Standard weight *txc·txx*	Coordination level *bxx·bxx*
Rank	116	62	149	2	23	8	172	83
Average precision	0.1933	0.2170	0.1846	0.2752	0.2406	0.2596	0.1750	

The results of Table 5 for the NPL collection differs markedly from those of Table 4. Here the probabilistic schemes using binary query weights and unnormalized document vectors are preferred. This is a direct result of the special nature of the queries and documents for that collection: the very short queries with little length deviation require fully weighted query terms ($b = 1$), and the normally effective term frequency weights should be avoided because many important terms will then be downgraded in the short document vectors. An enhanced term frequency weight (n factor), or a full weight ($b = 1$) is therefore preferred. Retrieval results obtained for NPL were used earlier to claim superiority for the probabilistic term weighting system [55]. The results of Tables 4 and 5 do not support this contention for conventional natural language documents and queries.

4. RECOMMENDATIONS

The following conclusions may be drawn from the experimental evidence reported in this study:

4.1 *Query vectors*

1. Term-frequency component
   - For short query vectors, each term is important; enhanced query term weights are thus preferred: first component *n*.
   - Long query vectors require a greater discrimination among query terms based on term occurrence frequencies: first component *t*.
   - The term-frequency factor can be disregarded when all query terms have occurrence frequencies equal to 1.
2. Collection-frequency component
   - Inverse collection frequency factor *f* is very similar to the probabilistic term independence factor *p*: best methods use *f*.
3. Normalization component
   - Query normalization does not affect query-document ranking or overall performance; use *x*.

4.2 *Document vectors*

1. Term-frequency component
   - For technical vocabulary and meaningful terms (CRAN, MED collections), use enhanced frequency weights: first component *n*.
   - For more varied vocabulary, distinguish terms by conventional frequency weights: first component *t*.
   - For short document vectors possibly based on controlled vocabulary, use fully weighted terms: first component $b = 1$.
2. Collection-frequency component
   - Inverse document-frequency factor *f* is similar to probabilistic term independence weight *p*: normally use *f*.
   - For dynamic collections with many changes in the document collection makeup, the *f* factor requires updating; in that case disregard second component: use *x*.
3. Length-normalization component
   - When the deviation in vector lengths is large, as it normally is in text indexing systems, use length normalization factor *c*.
   - For short document vectors of homogeneous length, the normalization factor may be disregarded; in that case use *x*.

The following single-term weighting systems should be used as a standard for comparison with enhanced text analysis systems using thesauruses and other knowledge tools to produce complex multiterm content identifications:

Best document weighting *tfc*, *nfc* (or *tpc*, *npc*)

Best query weighting *nfx*, *tfx*, *bfx* (or *npx*, *tpx*, *bpx*)

REFERENCES

1. Luhn, H.P. A statistical approach to the mechanized encoding and searching of literary information. IBM Journal of Research and Development 1:4; 309–317; October 1957.
2. Salton, G., ed. The Smart Retrieval System – Experiments in Automatic Document Retrieval. Englewood Cliffs, NJ: Prentice Hall Inc.; 1971.
3. Salton, G., McGill, M.J. Introduction to Modern Information Retrieval. New York: McGraw-Hill Book Co.; 1983.
4. van Rijsbergen, C.J. Information Retrieval, 2nd ed. London: Butterworths; 1979.
5. Luhn, H.P. A new method of recording and searching information. American Documentation 4:1; 14–16; 1955.
6. Taube, M.; Wachtel, I.S. The logical structure of coordinate indexing. American Documentation 3:4; 213–218; 1952.
7. Perry, J.W. Information analysis for machine searching. American Documentation 1:3; 133–139; 1950.
8. van Rijsbergen, C.J. A theoretical basis for the use of cooccurrence data in information retrieval. Journal of Documentation 33:2; 106–119; June 1977.
9. Salton, G.; Buckley, C.; Yu, C.T. An evaluation of term dependence models in information retrieval. Lecture Notes in Computer Science, In: Salton, G.; Schneider, H.J., eds. 146, Berlin: Springer-Verlag, 151–173; 1983.
10. Yu, C.T.; Buckley, C.; Lam, K.; Salton, G. A generalized term dependence model in information retrieval. Information Technology: Research and Development 2:4; 129–154; October 1983.
11. Lesk, M.E. Word-word associations in document retrieval systems. American Documentation 20:1; 27–38; January 1969.
12. Klingbiel, P.H. Machine aided indexing of technical literature. Information Storage and Retrieval 9:2; 79–84; February 1973.
13. Klingbiel, P.H. A technique for machine aided indexing. Information Storage and Retrieval 9:9; 477–494; September 1973.
14. Dillon, M.; Gray, A. Fully automatic syntax-based indexing. Journal of the ASIS 34:2; 99–108; March 1983.
15. Sparck Jones, K.; Tait, J.I. Automatic search term variant generation. Journal of Documentation 40:1; 50–66; March 1984.
16. Fagan, J.L. Experiments in automatic phrase indexing for document retrieval: A comparison of syntactic and non-syntactic methods. Doctoral thesis, Report 87-868, Department of Computer Science, Cornell University, Ithaca, NY; September 1987.
17. Smeaton, A.F. Incorporating syntactic information into a document retrieval strategy: An investigation. Proc. 1986 ACM-SIGIR Conference on Research and Development in Information Retrieval, Pisa, Italy, Association for Computing Machinery, New York; 103–113; 1986.
18. Sparck Jones, K. Automatic Keyword Classification for Information Retrieval. London: Butterworths; 1971.
19. Salton, G. Experiments in automatic thesaurus construction for information retrieval. Information Processing 71, North Holland Publishing Co., Amsterdam; 115–123; 1972.
20. Dattola, R.T. Experiments with fast algorithms for automatic classification. In: Salton, G., ed. The Smart Retrieval System-Experiments in Automatic Document Processing. Chapter 12, pp. 265–297. Englewood Cliffs, NJ: Prentice Hall Inc.; 1971.
21. Walker, D.E. Knowledge resource tools for analyzing large text files. In: Nirenburg, Sergei, ed. Machine Translation: Theoretical and Methodological Issues, pp. 247–261. Cambridge, England: Cambridge University Press; 1987.
22. Kucera, H. Uses of on-line lexicons. Proc. First Conference of the U.W. Centre for the New Oxford English Dictionary: Information in Data, pp. 7–10. University of Waterloo; 1985.
23. Amsler, R.A. Machine-readable dictionaries. In: Williams, M.E., ed. Annual Review of Information Science and Technology, Vol. 19, pp. 161–209. White Plains, NY: Knowledge Industry Publication Inc.; 1984.
24. Fox, E.A. Lexical relations: Enhancing effectiveness of information retrieval systems. ACM SIGIR Forum, 15:3; 5–36; 1980.
25. Croft, W.B. User-specified domain knowledge for document retrieval. Proc. 1986 ACM Conference on Research and Development in Information Retrieval, pp. 201–206; Pisa, Italy. New York: Association for Computing Machinery; 1986.
26. Thompson, R.H.; Croft, W.B. An expert system for document retrieval. Proc. Expert Systems in Government Symposium, pp. 448–456. Washington, DC: IEEE Computer Society Press; 1985.
27. Croft, W.B. Approaches to intelligent information retrieval. Information Processing & Management 23:4; 249–254; 1987.
28. Sparck Jones, K. Intelligent retrieval. In: Intelligent Information Retrieval: Proc. Informatics, Vol. 7; 136–142; Aslib; London: 1983.
29. Fox, E.A. Development of the coder system: A testbed for artificial intelligence methods in information retrieval. Information Processing & Management 23:4; 341–366; 1987.
30. Salton, G. On the use of knowledge based processing in automatic text retrieval. Proc. 49th Annual Meeting of the ASIS, Learned Information, Medford, NJ: 277–287; 1986.
31. Swanson, D.R. Searching natural language text by computer. Science 132:3434; 1099–1104; October 1960.
32. Cleverdon, C.W.; Keen, E.M. Aslib–Cranfield research project, Vol. 2, Test Results. Cranfield Institute of Technology, Cranfield, England; 1966.
33. Cleverdon, C.W. A computer evaluation of searching by controlled languages and natural language in an experimental NASA database, Report ESA 1/432. European Space Agency, Frascati, Italy; July 1977.
34. Lancaster, F.W. Evaluation of the Medlars demand search service, National Library of Medicine, Bethesda, MD; January 1968.
35. Blair, D.C.; Maron, M.E. An evaluation of retrieval effectiveness for a full-text document retrieval system. Communications of the ACM 28:3; 289–299; March 1985.
36. Salton, G. Another look at automatic text retrieval systems. Communications of the ACM, 29:7; 648–656; July 1986.
37. Salton, G. Recent studies in automatic text analysis and document retrieval. Journal of the ACM 20:2; 258–278; April 1973.
38. Sparck Jones, K. A statistical interpretation of term specificity and its application in retrieval. Journal of Documentation 28:1; 11–21; March 1972.
39. Salton, G.; Yang, C.S. On the specification of term values in automatic indexing. Journal of Documentation 29:4; 351–372; December 1973.
40. Salton, G. A theory of indexing. Regional Conference Series in Applied Mathematics, No. 18, Society for Industrial and Applied Mathematics, Philadelphia, PA; 1975.

41. Salton, G.; Yang, C.S.; Yu, C.T. A theory of term importance in automatic text analysis. Journal of the ASIS 26:1; 33–44; January–February 1975.
42. Bookstein, A.; Swanson, D.R. A decision theoretic foundation for indexing. Journal of the ASIS 26:1; 45–50; January–February 1975.
43. Cooper, W.S.; Maron, M.E. Foundation of probabilistic and utility theoretic indexing. Journal of the ACM 67–80; 25:1; 1978.
44. Robertson, S.E.; Sparck Jones, K. Relevance weighting of search terms. Journal of the ASIS 27:3; 129–146; 1976.
45. Croft, W.B.; Harper, D.J. Using probabilistic models of information retrieval without relevance information. Journal of Documentation 35:4; 285–295; December 1975.
46. Wu, H.; Salton, G. A comparison of search term weighting: Term relevance versus inverse document frequency. ACM SIGIR Forum 16:1; 30–39; Summer 1981.
47. Noreault, T.; Koll, M.; McGill, M.J. Automatic ranked output from Boolean searches in SIRE. Journal of the ASIS 27:6; 333–339; November 1977.
48. Radecki, T. Incorporation of relevance feedback into Boolean retrieval systems. Lecture Notes in Computer Science, 146, G. Salton and H.J. Schneider, eds., pp. 133–150. Berlin: Springer-Verlag; 1982.
49. Paice, C.D. Soft evaluation of Boolean search queries in information retrieval systems. Information Technology: Research and Development 3:1; 33–41; 1983.
50. Cater, S.C.; Kraft, D.H. A topological information retrieval system (TIRS) satisfying the requirements of the Waller-Kraft wish list. Proc. Tenth Annual ACM–SIGIR Conference on Research and Development in Information Retrieval, C.T. Yu and C.J. van Rijsbergen, eds. pp. 171–180. Association for Computing Machinery, New York: 1987.
51. Wong, S.K.M.; Ziarko, W.; Raghavan, V.V.; Wong, P.C.N. Extended Boolean query processing in the generalized vector space model, Report, Department of Computer Science, University of Regina, Regina, Canada; 1986.
52. Wong, S.K.M.; Ziarko, W.; Wong, P.C.N. Generalized vector space model in information retrieval. Proc. Eighth Annual ACM–SIGIR Conference on Research and Development in Information Retrieval, Association for Computing Machinery, New York; 18–25; 1985.
53. Wu, H. On query formulation in information retrieval. Doctoral dissertation, Cornell University, Ithaca, NY; January 1981.
54. Salton, G.; Fox, E.A.; Wu, H. Extended Boolean information retrieval. Communications of the ACM 26:11; 1022–1036; November 1983.
55. Croft, W.B. A comparison of the cosine correlation and the modified probabilistic model. Information Technology: Research and Development 3:2; 113–114; April 1984.

SEARCH TERM RELEVANCE WEIGHTING GIVEN LITTLE RELEVANCE INFORMATION

KAREN SPARCK JONES
Computer Laboratory, University of Cambridge

Previous experiments demonstrated the value of relevance weighting for search terms, but relied on substantial relevance information for the terms. The present experiments were designed to study the effects of weights based on very limited relevance information, for example supplied by one or two relevant documents. The tests simulated iterative searching, as in an on-line system, and show that even very little relevance information can be of considerable value.

INTRODUCTION

Relevance weighting of search terms

CURRENTLY several research projects are investigating the use of relevance-based term weighting, i.e. the use of weights for search terms based on information about their occurrences in known relevant documents.[1–6] These weights are statistical in character, and relate term relevance occurrence to total occurrence in a specific way. The manner in which the weights are used varies, but appropriate applications would be to SDI or iterative on-line searching, where judgements on documents obtained in one search cycle may be exploited in the next. Search output is ordered by document scores derived from matching term weights. An attractive feature of the approach is that not merely the general value of relevance information, but specific choices of relevance weighting function can be given theoretical justification. That is, the output ordering obtained using relevance weights according to particular formulae should be superior to that given by simple co-ordinate term matching.

Robertson and Sparck Jones[7] considered a range of weighting functions and reported retrieval experiments with them. These applied the same set of requests to two very similar sets of documents represented by the pseudo-random division of a larger set into moieties by even and odd serial number. Weights derived from searches and assessments on the first, even, set were used in searching the second, odd, one. Performance for the latter represented by conventional recall/precision graphs showed large improvements over simple term matching, and also over matching using only term collection frequency information for weighting, without additional relevance information. The test results were further satisfactory in showing that a specific weighting formula recommended on theoretical grounds was superior to others in the set studied. Experiments by other projects also show the value of relevance weighting.

The tests carried out by Robertson and Sparck Jones used a relatively small set of 225 requests and 1,400 documents. A subsequent series of experiments was designed to investigate the value of relevance weights in a geater range of environments reflecting some characteristic properties of real information retrieval systems.[8] They would also provide further evidence relating to the theoretical arguments for a specific approach to weighting. Thus four tests were conducted referring to four environmental conditions, with performance comparisons in each case between unweighted term matching, weighting by collection frequency, and relevance weighting by the recommended formula and by another, simpler formula. First, to see whether relevance weighting would continue to perform well for much larger document sets than that originally used, the comparisons were made for a set of 27,361 documents, divided as before into even and odd subsets, with seventy-five requests. Second, to check whether weighting would be useful in poor matching conditions, i.e. with few documents and request terms, the 27,361 documents (given as titles) were searched with a version of the requests having far fewer terms than the originals. Third, to study the value of the weights when they are computed for one set of documents and applied to another rather different in character, the 27,361 documents were divided into two groups by subject rather than pseudo-randomly by even and odd serial number. Fourth, to discover how weights are affected by the amount of relevance information available for computing them, progressively smaller sets of documents, down to a sixteenth of the whole collection, were used to generate them. In all four experiments the relevance weights continued to perform well, compared with unweighted and frequency weighted terms: very substantial performance improvements were obtained, specifically with the recommended weighting formula, which was much superior to its simpler competitor.

The most obvious application of relevance weighting is in iterative on-line searching. But this is also a challenging application since the number of documents the user is willing to inspect to provide relevance judgements as a basis for further searching is probably small. From this point of view the results of the fourth experiment just described were particularly encouraging, since weighting performance was as good, except at highest recall, for weights derived from an average of 3·1 relevant documents per request as for weights derived from 24·9 relevant documents. However, if the initial search is done using simple term matching, or even frequency weights, obtaining two or three relevant documents seems, for the test data available, to require twenty to thirty assessments, which might be deemed unacceptable.

EXPERIMENTS

Weighting with little relevance information

The present set of experiments was therefore designed to investigate more fully the question of how little relevance information is required to achieve conspicuous performance improvements over none at all. (A comparison between statistical and human request modification using relevance information is also desirable, but appropriate test data is lacking and is not at all easily obtained.)

The general pattern of the tests was therefore an initial search using simple term matching to retrieve a specified small number of relevant documents, computation of weights, and a further search exploiting the weights. Performance for the latter was compared, as before, with that for terms without weights and with frequency weights. The iteration was confined to the two search cycles in this way, in the interest of experimental control. Further tests with several cycles allowing further weight modification are desirable, particularly since it is not clear how useful extensive iteration on the same set of request terms would be: Ide's experiments suggest, for example, that it may not be.[9] As a further control,

Journal of Documentation, Vol. 35, No. 1, March 1979, pp. 30–48.

and also to simplify the actual machine runs, the experiments were actually a simulation of iterative searching on the same document set. The complete set of documents was divided into even- and odd-numbered subsets, as in the previous experiments. The even set was searched and the output inspected to identify the required number of best matching relevant documents. Weights were then computed for the request terms using this relevance information and that for the term frequencies in the even set as a whole. The modified requests were then searched on the odd-numbered set, for performance comparison with the other search methods applied to the same set.

The justification for this procedure is that it ensures a strict comparison between the various methods as alternative techniques for extracting relevant documents from a document set, since the set for which performance is evaluated is identical for all methods, while the amount of relevance information considered for each request is the same. If a strictly iterative procedure is adopted, one or the other of two difficulties arises. Either the first cycle output is inspected until the required number of relevant documents is retrieved, leaving a variable collection for the different requests for the next search and performance evaluation: or the first cycle output has a fixed cutoff, which will give variable numbers of relevant documents per request as a base for weighting. The simulation is nevertheless acceptable since the two document sets used are produced by pseudo-random division of the complete set and hence are statistically very similar.

The experiments are also simulations in using test data with known relevant documents rather than on-the-spot user assessments. But there is no reason to suppose that real users judging first cycle output on the spot for a small number of relevant documents would produce overall evaluations different from those used.

Ideally, experiments with relevance weights should investigate their value in a systematic way with a series of collections differing by only one factor at a time, to see how these factors affect weight performance. But sequences of test collections of this kind are simply not available. The experiments were therefore based on the alternative strategy of using collections differing in virtually every way: if each shows relevance weights of value, this suggests that they are generally likely to be of value, though particular collection properties affecting their value are not identified.

The tests were therefore conducted with the small collection of 225 requests and 1,400 documents in aeronautics used in the original experiments of Robertson and Sparck Jones, and with the set of seventy-five requests and 27,361 chemical documents used in the subsequent tests. The first collection comes from the Cranfield project, with requests and documents manually indexed using extracted keyword stems, and with the documents indexed to a high level of exhaustivity.[10] The second collection, kindly made available by UKCIS, consists of document titles and request term lists taken from carefully constructed Boolean SDI profiles; the lists are long, and embody individual word truncation and also word strings.[11] It should be noted that while the relevance information available for the Cranfield data is exhaustive, that for the UKCIS data is limited to assessments of the pooled output of a variety of Boolean searches carried out by UKCIS: and as the use of the profile terms without their Boolean structure retrieves far more documents than were assessed, performance determined by the given relevant documents only is probably lower than the true level. For the data as supplied, both the average number of relevant documents per request and collection generality differ for the two collections, providing useful tests of relevance weight value.

Collection details are given in Table 1.

TABLE 1. *Data details*

Cranfield Data	
No. requests	225
Av. terms per request	7·9
No. documents	1,400
No. word stems in documents	2,683
Av. stems per document	29·9
No. different documents relevant to some request	831
No. relevant postings	1,614
Av. relevant per request	7·2
No. documents, even set	700
odd set	700
No. relevant postings, even set	834
odd set	780
Av. relevant per request, even set	3·8
odd set	3·7
UKCIS Data	
No. profiles	75
Av. terms per profile	18·3
No. documents	27,361
No. word stems in titles	17,537
Av. stems per document	6·6
No. different documents relevant to some profile	3,380
No. relevant postings	3,739
Av. relevant per profile	49·9
Av. documents assessed per profile by UKCIS	195·6
No. documents, even set	13,680
odd set	13,681
No. relevant postings, even set	1,837
odd set	1,902
Av. relevant per profile, even set	24·5
odd set	25·4

In the tests, relevance weights were derived from the one best matching relevant document obtained in the first cycle search, and from the two best (lower numbered documents were selected in cases of ties). The weights were calculated according to the formula

$$w = \log \frac{\left(\frac{r+0{\cdot}5}{R-r+0{\cdot}5}\right)}{\left(\frac{n-r+0{\cdot}5}{N-n-R+r+0{\cdot}5}\right)}$$

where r = the number of relevant documents containing the request term
R = the number of relevant documents
n = the number of documents containing the term
N = the number of documents.

Thus if one relevant document only is considered, $R = 1$, N = the collection size, $r = 0$ or 1, according to whether a specific request term is in the known relevant document, and n ranges from 0 to N; 0·5 is added to the formula components, following standard statistical practice, to allow for uncertainty. The rationale for this formula is given in Robertson and Sparck Jones; it is one way, and arguably the best way, of exploiting the information in the contingency table for a term, which is as follows:

		document relevant +	document relevant −	
document indexed	+	r	$n-r$	n
	−	$R-r$	$N-n-R+r$	$N-n$
		R	$N-R$	N

The matching score for a document is the sum of its matching term weights; and as terms may have negative weights, a document may be labelled not retrieved if its score is either zero or negative. Output for positively scoring documents is ordered by score, i.e. notional co-ordination level; recall and precision are used as performance measures and recall and precision averages over the request set are simply obtained by average of numbers, i.e. using the totals of documents retrieved for all requests at each level. For convenience the results are processed to give average precision at ten standard recall levels. Simple term matching gives document scores representing the numbers of terms shared by request and document, providing real co-ordination level output. Collection frequency weights are calculated according to the formula

$$w = -\log \frac{n}{N}, \text{ implemented as } w = -\log \frac{n}{\max n},$$

giving scores on notional levels.

Test results

The experimental results are listed in Table 2. This shows, for the two test collections, performance for searching the odd-numbered documents using terms, T, collection frequency weights, C, and relevance weights, R, respectively. The table also includes the case where relevance data is supplied not by the best matching relevant document but by a 'random' one, actually that in the known relevance set with the first serial number, or by two 'random' documents, the first two. Thus performance for relevance weights in the Table is given for B1, B2, F1 and F2, representing the use of the one or two best relevant documents and the one or two first. The use of the first documents allows an interesting comparison with that of the best. As the number of relevant documents is much larger for the UKCIS data, results are also given for B3 and F3 for this collection.

TABLE 2. *Experimental results*

	T	C	R									
Cranfield Recall			B1	B2	B3	F1	F2	F3	All	Y	F3a	F3b
100												
90	1	1								7		
80	1	2					3		4	12		
70	2	3	4	5		5	6		7	20		
60	3	5	7	8		8	9		10	29		
50	4	7	11	11		11	13		15	35		
40	6	8	15	17		17	18		20	43		
30	7	11	20	22		20	25		24	50		
20	9	15	24	27		25	28		28	57		
10	13	23	32	35		30	36		38	78		
UKCIS Recall												
100												
90												
80												
70	2	2							13	14	6	
60	2	3							28	31	10	7
50	2	8						7	29	42	10	18
40	3	10		18	24	8	18	25	39	54	16	23
30	4	11	18	25	25	26	24	22	44	69	19	23
20	7	12	16	26	34	23	26	30	45	81	19	35
10	8	13	48	47	49	41	42	40	53	97	18	38

A further view of the level of performance given by the selected best matching relevant documents as predictors of request term value in searching is supplied by the comparison with performance for weights derived from all the relevant documents in the weight generating document set, labelled All. The earlier experiments with relevance weights exploited all the available relevant documents in this way; it provides as good predictive information as may be got, but is unrealistic since it assumes far more extensive assessment than could actually be obtained, and is for comparative purposes only.

The final comparison is with 'optimal' weighting performance. This is obtained when the weights are derived from the same set of documents as they are used to search, in this case the odd-numbered ones. These retrospective weights provide the best weights for the request terms as relevant document selectors, given their actual patterns of occurrences. The resulting performance, labelled Y, defines a yardstick for the regular predictive weights. (As the information used is complete, 0·5 is omitted from the weighting formula in this case.)

Graphs comparing the selected performance for term matching, collection frequency weights, relevance weights using the first two relevant documents, and using all the relevant documents, along with the yardstick, are given for the two sets of data in Figs. 1 and 2.

As Table 2 shows, the results for the two collections are rather different. For the Cranfield data it is evident that, for the relevance weighting itself, there is little overall difference between B1 and B2 and between F1 and F2, and between B and F. The best results, F2, is superior to B1, the least good, and is, interestingly, the same as All; however, B1 is not much inferior, and all the relevance weighting results are much superior to collection frequency weighting (though they are also very far from the yardstick).

The most conspicuous feature of the UKCIS results is the loss of recall. At low recall precision is good for all the relevance weighting, and much superior to that for collection frequency weighting, though it is still inferior or much inferior to that for All. Some raising of the recall ceiling is associated with the progression from

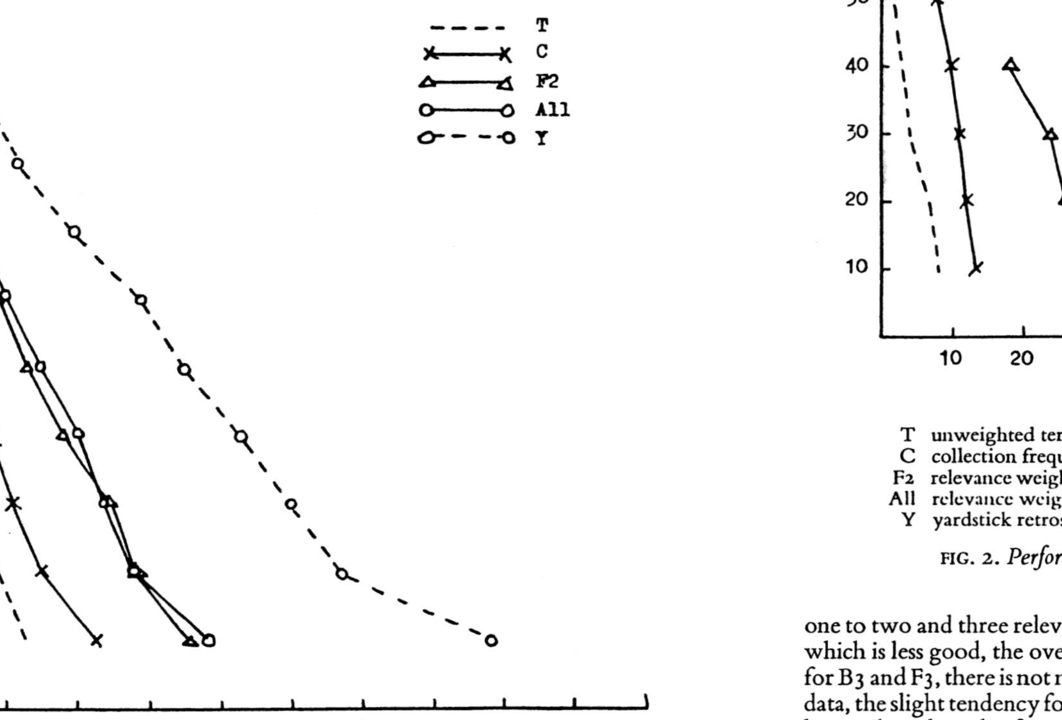

T unweighted terms
C collection frequency weighted terms
F2 relevance weighted terms, weights derived from two relevant documents
All relevance weighted terms, weights derived from all relevant documents
Y yardstick retrospective relevance weighted terms

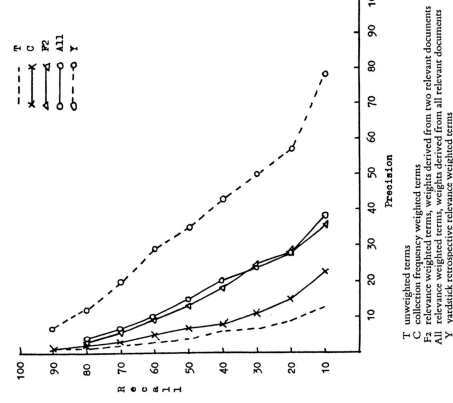

FIG. 1. *Performance comparison for the Cranfield collection*

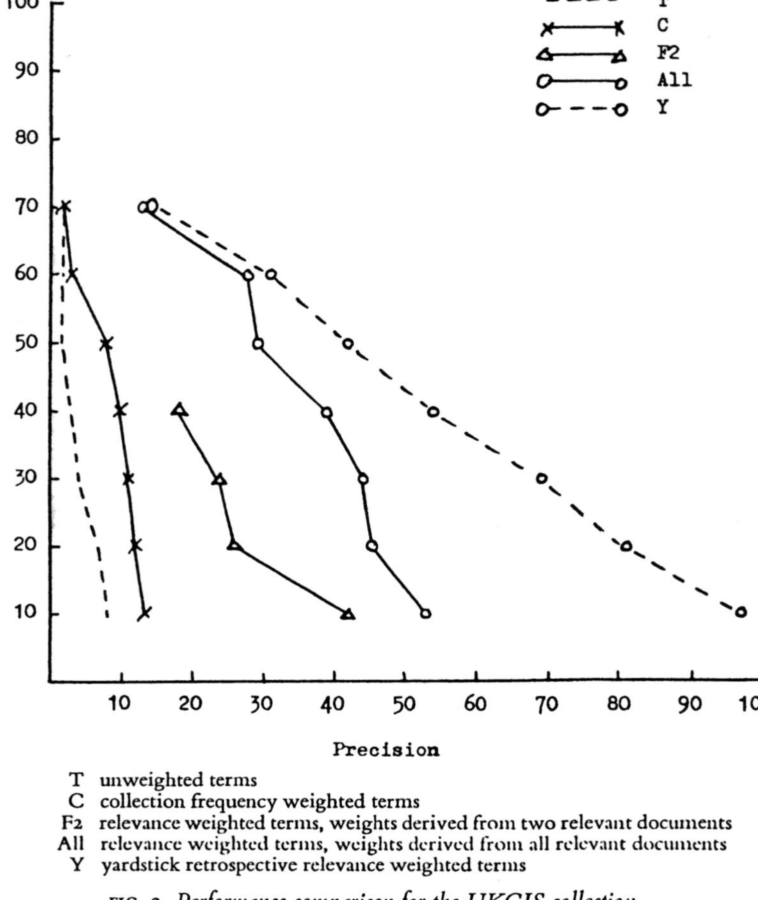

T unweighted terms
C collection frequency weighted terms
F2 relevance weighted terms, weights derived from two relevant documents
All relevance weighted terms, weights derived from all relevant documents
Y yardstick retrospective relevance weighted terms

FIG. 2. *Performance comparison for the UKCIS collection*

one to two and three relevant documents used for weighting. But apart from B1, which is less good, the overall difference is not large. Equally, for B2 and F2, and for B3 and F3, there is not much difference between B and F. As with the Cranfield data, the slight tendency for the F results to be superior to the B results can perhaps be attributed to the fact that the choice of relevant documents for weighting introduces less bias into the sample for F than for B.

DISCUSSION

The UKCIS results, especially the loss of recall, appear rather depressing. Possible reasons for this loss are best considered in the context of a more refined account of relevance weighting than that given above.

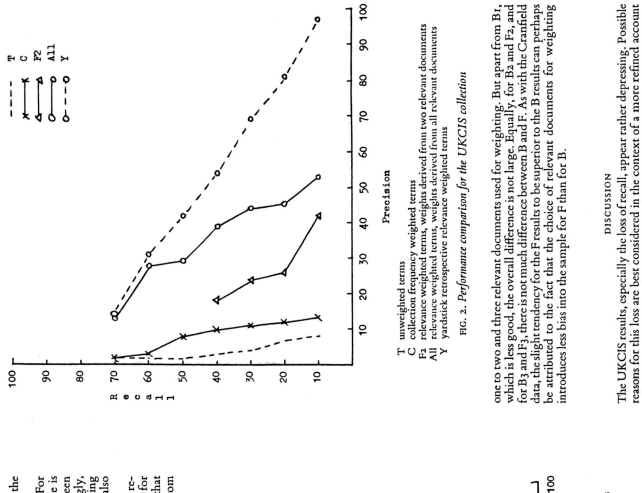

The structure of relevance weights

The relevance weighting function w as presented above orders the search output for a particular request, but, as described in Robertson and Sparck Jones, the actual matching values obtained for individual documents do not give a complete picture of their status. To obtain complete, fully significant matching values, i.e. document scores directly reflecting relevance probabilities, scaling is required. This is also necessary for averaging across requests by matching values rather than output rank position.

The approach to weighting underlying the function is based on the idea that both the presence and absence of search terms in a document is important: we want to accept documents with good terms, i.e. ones correlated with relevance, and reject ones with bad terms, correspondingly rejecting ones without good terms and accepting ones without bad terms. Of course for a request and document with several terms, the final result is the net balance for good and bad terms.

As theoretically developed in Robertson and Sparck Jones, the approach leads to term weights with explicit presence and absence components, contributing respectively to document scores according to whether each term is or is not present in the document. The presence component is

$$v = \log \frac{\left(\frac{r}{R}\right)}{\left(\frac{n-r}{N-R}\right)}$$

and the absence component is

$$u = \log \frac{\left(\frac{R-r}{R}\right)}{\left(\frac{N-n-R+r}{N-R}\right)}$$

The score for a document is thus the sum of the v's for all the request terms present in the document plus the sum of the u's for the request terms absent from the document.

This presence/absence form of weighting is reinterpreted, as described in Robertson and Sparck Jones, by the formula given earlier (in its yardstick form, without addition of 0·5), as a presence only weight which achieves the correct output ordering through the positive or negative weights it assigns to the search terms; good terms have positive weight and bad ones negative, and a document score is simply the sum of the weights for the matching terms. The effect of scoring for absence is achieved indirectly through the non-contribution of term weights to scores, but to obtain numerically significant scores, i.e. exactly those given by the explicit presence/absence form of weight, the simple sum of weights scores must be modified. This is achieved by calculating a scaling constant for each request which is applied to every document. The constant is the sum of u's for *all* the search terms. The net effect is, therefore, to modify the contribution to a document score for any matching term, and to make a contribution for any non-matching term. The relationship between the two techniques for arriving at the correct score is indicated by the fact that for a single term $w = v - u$.

Significant scores are also required to determine cutoff in searching. In simple term matching with output ordered by co-ordination level, the levels have a clear interpretation, and a natural cutoff is provided by level 0, representing no match, and also the minimum score. Note that this is the logical cutoff: it has no particular correlation with human cutoff, the point at which the average user declines to go to the effort of inspecting more documents. Simple weighting schemes like those using term collection frequency suggests a similar natural cutoff when level 0 is reached. In practice, in a large real collection, the bulk of the documents will be found at level 0.

The natural cutoff for the relevance weighting scheme is rather different. Specifically a document's score reflects the document's probability of relevance. Relevance probability is not systematically exploited in simple term searching, whatever *de facto* correlation of relevance with term matching observed. In relevance weighting as described a document score of 0 directly defines the point where the probability of retrieving a relevant document is that of retrieving one at random from the whole collection. The important point is that a score of 0 is not given simply by a document having no terms in common with a request, and is not the minimum possible score for a given query or query set. However, given the definition of zero score, we will expect, as for simple term searching, that in practice the bulk of the documents will fall below this cutoff. It is important to recognize that a particular score may be achieved by a variety of means, and that a class of scores, e.g. the positive ones, or the negative ones, do not reflect request/document matching in a simple way. Thus positive scores represent the finally positive outcome of combined v's and u's, where any v or u may be positive or negative; i.e. these scores may in fact reflect term presence only, or term absence, or a mixture of both. Negative scores represent a finally negative outcome for the same range of possibilities, though the negatively scoring documents will in practice typically include a large number of documents having no terms in common with the request, and hence no good ones. It is evident that the number of documents with exactly zero score will typically be small.

The results obtained for the UKCIS collection have a low recall ceiling, reflecting a high cutoff point in the output ordering. As described, the cutoff is determined by document scores equivalent to searching at random; and as document scores are based on estimates of the relative values of search terms present or absent as predictors of relevant or non-relevant documents, the low recall ceiling observed suggests that there is something wrong with the estimation. (A rather different view is that cutoff should not be determined absolutely, for the collection as a whole, but relatively, for the part not yet searched. But this implies continual recalculation and there is no available theoretical base or practical method for doing this.)

Approaches to estimation

Properly speaking, when relevance weighting is expressed through the term contingency table, we are estimating relevance probability. However, given this mode of expression, we may speak of estimation in a narrower sense when we attempt to use contingency table data for one document set to compute weights designed to retrieve relevant documents from another. In what follows estimation will be used in this sense. Thus, as described in Robertson and Sparck Jones, when relevance weights are applied retrospectively, to establish optimal performance, no estimation is needed and the contingency table is exploited unadorned. When relevance weights are applied predictively, using one document set as a sample for computing weights to be exploited in searching another, some allowance must be made for the inadequacy of the sample. This is clearly particularly necessary when a small document set is being used to generate weights for application to a large one. In the original experiments, following Cox,[12] allowance was made by adding 0·5 to the central elements of the table, and one or two, as required for consistency, to the marginal totals, and the same approach was adopted in the experiments reported here. However, we are dealing in these with a very small sample (specifically of relevant documents, supplying R and r*) and the results for the UKCIS data suggest that the method of estimation, while apparently adequate for small samples, is not adequate for very small ones, i.e. it becomes progressively less satisfactory.

Further study of Cox's argument suggested that a correct treatment of the table would be to add 0·5 to the marginal totals as to the central elements. A test of this, using F3 on the UKCIS collection, showed a rise in the recall ceiling, but a loss of precision. The method was not, therefore, more satisfactory than the first one. (The result is given as F3a in Table 2.)

A detailed study of the UKCIS data as a sample for estimation suggested that the particular feature of it described below probably accounted for the original result, though it is not obvious how this is to be dealt with in estimation. In both methods of estimation the central elements of the contingency table, which are used to calculate w, are the same; the change from one method to the other affects u, i.e. deals with the absence rather than presence of request terms. The Cranfield and UKCIS collections have requests with very different characteristics. The Cranfield collection has short requests consisting entirely of terms occurring in the document set as a whole, and as relatively frequent terms, typically occurring in the weight generation subset. The UKCIS collection has long requests containing many terms not occurring in the documents at all. Naturally, in calculating w and u for such a term, we are given $r = 0$, in fact because $n = 0$. The first estimation method used for the experiments described earlier, gives large positive w and small negative u for such a term, allowing any future documents containing the term to score positively and future documents not containing the term to score negatively. Unfortunately, if there are many such terms the net result will be that many documents are heavily penalised, with negative scores meaning that they are not retrieved. Some relevant documents are clearly lost in this way. The fact that the UKCIS document descriptions are very short probably contributes to this result, since counterbalancing matches on several good terms are not obtained. Overall, the position seems to be that given the various components of a document score, having or not having a term, and whether the term is good or bad, the overriding influence on the final score is not having any query terms, and specifically not having any of many query terms. Certainly the fact that the Cranfield collection achieves good performance with relatively small loss of recall, even for a relevance sample of 1, suggests that it is not the small sample in itself which is the sole problem with the UKCIS results. Equally, it is not only the estimation method, which works well enough for Cranfield, or for the larger sample represented by All for UKCIS. The problem is the conjunction of the two.

* Note that the document sample, supplying N and n, is the whole of the initially searched set, and not merely the assessed subset; but the different sources of R and N do not invalidate the estimation, and provide more information.

The second estimation method in fact corrects for the specific consequence of the first just described, since w is positive and u zero when r and n are zero. Indeed the recall ceiling is higher. But the fact that for a given recall level achieved by both methods, precision is lower for the second, suggests that this method is not right either. As noted, the difference between the two methods is confined to the treatment of u. The difference in precision performance must therefore be due to the overall effect of the u's on the document scores for each query, and their consequences when requests are averaged at each scoring level.

Further evidence that the treatment of u rather than w is presenting problems, and that these are shown up by the UKCIS data, is supplied by a test simply setting $u = 0$ when $n = 0$ but otherwise computing u by the first method. The results for F3, labelled F3b in Table 2, show that this raises the recall ceiling substantially, without lowering precision. Of course this is not a sufficiently proper procedure for general use, but it seems to be a clue to the main problem in estimating from very small samples. It is quite likely that good estimates for very small samples could still lead to some loss of recall, but this would be unlikely to matter if precision was very good.

Advantages of relevance weights

It is clear that better methods of estimation are required, but as van Rijsbergen points out,[6] it is far from obvious how these are to be derived. However, the experiments reported do show that very considerable improvements in performance can be obtained with relevance weights, even when these depend on very few relevant documents, as with the Cranfield collection, though with 'sparse' material like the UKCIS data the weighting formula as used may give large gains in precision only for a non-negligible loss of recall.

Further, even in these cases, the situation may not be what it appears to be. A rather different view of performance is obtained from an analysis of performance not in terms of recall and precision alone, but in terms of numbers of documents retrieved and hence requiring scanning by the user.

Table 3 shows the average number of relevant and non-relevant documents retrieved per request:

(a) at the lowest matching score, 1, for relevance weights, compared with the lowest and next lowest for simple term searching. (At the lowest score above cutoff performance for the different methods is properly comparable; the higher levels for terms are given for information only.)

(b) at specific (lower) recall levels. (The document numbers involved are derived from the interpolation data, and are therefore notional rather than actual.)

These figures show, in a strikingly clear way, how the average number of non-relevant documents retrieved is reduced with relevance weights. In real terms, the loss of some relevant documents is perhaps more than balanced by the huge reduction in non-relevant, given that for equal scores the user is scanning randomly to extract relevant documents from the total set retrieved. For example, for UKCIS F2 compared with terms, the user trades 18·9 relevant amidst 724·2 non-relevant for 12·0 relevant with 146·5 non-relevant. At recall 30%, he retrieves the same number of relevant documents, 7·7, as terms (7·6), but with only 23·9 non-relevant rather than 173·3. Thus, for each relevant document retrieved, he is scanning 12·2 rather than 38·3 at score 1, or 3·1 rather than 22·7 at recall 30%. As the final columns in each section of Table 3 show, there are substantial reductions, with relevance weighting, in the number of non-relevant documents scanned per relevant retrieved. If the emphasis is on precision, and more explicitly on reducing scanning effort, then the 'unfortunate' UKCIS results do not turn out so badly.

TABLE 3. *Numbers of retrieved documents*

	Av. rel. retr.	*Av. nrel. retr.*	*Av. nrel. per rel.*		*Av. rel. retr.*	*Av. nrel. retr.*	*Av. nrel. per rel.*
Cranfield							
Terms							
score 1	3·3	375·4	113·7	recall 40	1·4	21·0	
2	2·9	164·1		30	1·1	13·5	12·8
3	2·2	64·9		20	0·7	6·8	
B1				recall 40	1·4	7·9	
score 1	2·5	48·8	19·8	30	1·1	4·3	4·0
				20	0·7	2·2	
B2				recall 40	1·4	6·5	
score 1	2·6	52·8	20·6	30	1·1	3·6	3·4
				20	0·7	1·9	
F1				recall 40	1·4	6·5	
score 1	2·8	64·0	23·2	30	1·0	4·0	3·9
				20	0·7	2·1	
F2				recall 40	1·4	6·0	
score 1	2·8	67·4	24·1	30	1·1	3·2	3·0
				20	0·7	1·8	
All				recall 40	1·4	5·3	
score 1	2·8	64·1	22·7	30	1·1	3·3	3·1
				20	0·7	1·8	
Y				recall 40	1·4	1·8	
score 1	3·1	39·9	12·7	30	1·1	1·0	1·0
				20	0·7	0·5	
UKCIS							
Terms							
score 1	18·9	724·2	38·3	recall 40	10·2	298·5	
2	5·6	73·2		30	7·6	173·3	22·7
3	1·2	9·0		20	5·1	66·0	
B1				recall 40	—	—	
score 1	9·6	93·5	9·7	30	7·8	35·0	4·5
				20	5·3	26·0	
B2				recall 40	10·2	46·1	
score 1	11·7	116·9	10·0	30	7·7	22·6	2·9
				20	5·3	14·6	
B3				recall 40	10·4	32·5	
score 1	12·4	131·4	10·6	30	7·8	22·4	2·9
				20	5·2	9·7	
F1				recall 40	10·4	105·4	
score 1	10·5	114·5	11·0	30	7·6	20·9	2·7
				20	5·1	17·2	
F2				recall 40	10·4	44·4	
score 1	12·0	146·5	12·2	30	7·7	23·9	3·1
				20	5·3	14·7	
F3				recall 40	10·4	30·7	
score 1	14·4	183·7	12·8	30	7·6	25·9	3·4
				20	5·1	11·6	
All				recall 40	10·4	15·9	
score 1	18·7	335·5	18·0	30	7·8	9·6	1·2
				20	5·2	6·4	
Y				recall 40	10·2	8·6	
score 1	18·8	336·6	17·9	30	7·8	3·5	0·4
				20	5·1	1·2	
F3a				recall 40	10·2	51·1	
score 1	18·8	583·4	31·0	30	7·7	32·6	4·2
				20	5·1	21·3	
F3b				recall 40	10·3	33·6	
score 1	16·8	222·9	13·2	30	7·9	25·6	3·3
				20	5·2	9·6	

Maximum recall ceiling

	Terms	B1	B2	B3	F1	F2	F3	All	Y	F3a	F3b
Cranfield	95·3	71·0	74·1	—	79·5	80·5	—	81·4	90·6	—	—
UKCIS	74·6	37·9	46·3	48·8	41·2	47·5	56·7	73·6	74·1	74·1	66·4

The effectiveness of relevance weighting from this point of view is clearly shown by a detailed analysis of performance for individual requests.

Illustrative requests

Performance is determined by the collection frequency properties of the request terms. For discussion purposes in the present context we can distinguish six types of term of a marked character, according to whether their collection frequency, n, is high, low or medium relative to their high or low relevance frequency, r. The types are listed in Table 4a. Collection frequency clearly depends on overall collection size: here we may define $n > 70$ as high for Cranfield, $n = 20$–70 as medium and $n < 20$ as low, with $n > 100$, $n = 30$–100 and $n < 30$ as high, medium and low respectively for UKCIS. The examples to be discussed refer to relevance sets for weight generation of size 2, and specifically F2, so $r = 2$ is high and $r = 0$ is low. Most requests do not include all these types of term, and indeed typically contain terms of less definite character, but the two Cranfield examples and one UKCIS request illustrated cover the range of marked types and together exhibit the mechanism of relevance weighting very well.

Cranfield request 3 shows relevance weighting at its most effective. As Table 4b shows, unweighted term matching altogether retrieves five relevant documents and 278 non-relevant; but weighted searching retrieves the five relevant documents with only fifteen non-relevant ones. How is this achieved? Table 4c gives the value of n and r for the six request terms for the even-numbered weight generating document set, and the resulting weights in the explicit presence/absence form defined earlier. The presence component, v, of a term's weight is here referred to as its P-weight, and its absence component, u, as its A-weight. The table very clearly illustrates the different ways in which presence and absence components together define term value. The table also gives n and r for the odd-numbered document search set, and finally the types of those terms with a clear-cut character. Thus request 3 has two terms of type c, the best type, with low n and high r, and one of type b, the worst, with high n and low r.

In studying performance for request 3, we consider non-relevant documents first, as their elimination is the most striking feature of the weighted term results. Of the six terms, only two, 410 and 2,159, of type c, give positive scores on single-term document matches, that is have P-weights sufficiently large to counterbalance the combined A-weights for the remaining terms. The more frequently occurring terms in particular lead to negative scores on single term matches: and as the majority of documents sharing terms with the request share only one, which is typically a frequent term, it is easy to see how the number of documents retrieved when terms are not weighted is reduced when weighting is introduced. Further, as the number of relevant documents per query is small in relation to collection size, eliminating frequent term matches means that it is non-relevant documents which are not retrieved. One term in this request, 2,187, of the worst

TABLE 4. *Illustrative requests*

(a) Types of term

	n	r
type *a*	high	high
b	high	low
c	low	high
d	low	low
e	medium	high
f	medium	low

(b) Numbers of documents retrieved

		Unweighted term matching			*Weighted term matching*		
		Rel.	*Nonrel.*	*Total*	*Rel.*	*Nonrel.*	*Total*
Cranfield	request 1	12	300	312	4	30	34
	request 3	5	278	283	5	15	20
UKCIS	request 1	6	1,219	1,225	5	87	92

(c) Term properties and weights

		Even document set		*Weight*		*Odd document set*		
		n	r (F2)	P	A	n	r	*Type*
Cranfield								
request 1								
term	36	5	1	189	−29	4	1	
	54	36	2	123	−75	32	4	*e*
	985	151	1	37	−19	160	9	
	1,004	82	1	63	−24	72	2	
	1,256	18	0	80	−6	21	3	
	1,421	70	1	70	−25	64	6	
	2,134	24	0	68	−5	23	2	*f*
	2,211	84	2	85	−71	80	4	*a*
request 3								
term	410	9	2	189	−76	11	4	*c*
	422	36	1	99	−27	48	4	
	985	151	1	37	−19	160	4	
	1,829	24	0	68	−5	22	0	
	2,159	8	2	195	−76	12	4	*c*
	2,187	136	0	−6	2	140	0	*b*
UKCIS								
request 1	26 terms altogether							
term	1	70	2	222	−77	57	4	*e*
	2	20	0	205	−7	14	1	
	4	2	0	296	−7	2	0	*d*
	5	305	0	87	−6	335	2	*b*
	7	574	0	62	−5	567	4	*b*
	13	41	1	223	−29	31	0	

The selected terms for this request include all those in relevant documents in the even F2 or odd document sets.

The sum of the A-weights for the nine remaining terms occurring in some documents $= -62$.

The sum of the A-weights for the eleven terms not occurring in any documents $= -77$. So the total of A-weights for the terms not itemised above $= -139$.

(d) Matching terms, relevant documents UKCIS request 1

Document	*Terms*	*Score*	*Document*	*Terms*	*Score*
4,075	1 7	96	21,865	2 7	9
16,755	1 5	122	23,579	7	−202
17,301	1 7	96	27,171	—	(−270)
21,515	—	(−270)	27,221	1 5	122

type, *b*, indeed has a negative *P*-weight, so documents with it alone are easily lost; but such cases are not common. The specific way in which documents matching only on a common term with low *P*-weight are usually rejected is by their failure to match on other more valuable terms. Table 4c clearly shows that large *A*-weights are associated with good terms of type *c*, penalizing documents not possessing them. So, for example, any document matching on term 985, and not on 410, would be eliminated for this reason alone, irrespective of the negative absence contributions of other non-matching terms. Documents matching on 422, on the other hand, a medium frequency term with one relevance occurrence, start with a higher *P*-weight, but this is still outfaced by a combination of other term *A*-weights.

Matches on more than one common term are also rejected in this case, because one of the two has a negative *P*-weight, and combinations of a common term and a medium frequency term, like 985 and 1,829, are similarly eliminated. Those non-relevant documents which are retrieved are all but one indexed by the two good terms, and as these are rare terms, they do not pick up many non-relevant documents. The remaining one is jointly indexed by three terms with moderate *P*-weights.

The relevant documents for this query are all in fact indexed by several terms, though it is interesting to note that they all contain at least one of the two good terms, and so would have been retrieved by these alone.

Cranfield request 1 illustrates a less strikingly successful outcome for relevance weights, with a reduction in non-relevant documents retrieved from 300 to thirty, but also a reduction in relevant retrieved from twelve to four. Here again many non-relevant documents are eliminated because they only match on one or two frequent terms with low *P*-weight; but in this case there are also relevant documents indexed by few query terms, and especially by common terms, and such combinations are ineffective. There are also relevant document matching combinations involving terms with high *P*-weights, like 54, but there are not enough terms involved to counterbalance the high *A*-weights of other terms plus, since this is a rather longer request, the aggregated smaller *A*-weights of the remaining non-matching terms. The request, nevertheless, shows how the ratio of non-relevant to relevant documents retrieved is materially improved through weighting, though there is a loss of recall.

The effects observed for Cranfield request 1 are very clearly displayed by UKCIS request 1, where 1,219 non-relevant documents retrieved by unweighted term matching are reduced to eighty-seven by weighted matching, but also six relevant to five. This is, however, a manifestly better result than that for Cranfield request 1. The UKCIS request has twenty-six terms altogether, but eleven of these do not occur in either document set. Details of some representatives of the remaining fifteen are given in Table 4c. Of these fifteen, only five, for documents matching on one term alone, give positive scores. The more frequently occurring terms in particular lead to negative scores for single term matches, and as for this data more than 90% of the documents sharing terms with the request share only one, it is easy to see how the 1,225 documents retrieved by unweighted matching become ninety-two. Here again the specific part of the weighting mechanism accounting for the reduction, and especially that in non-relevant documents retrieved, is the contribution to document scores made by the absence of terms.

This is clearly illustrated by the terms shown in Table 4c. Term 7, for example, is of the worst type, *b*, and has such a low *P*-weight that any document containing only it would be eliminated by the higher *A*-weight of term 1 alone, let alone the combined *A*-weights of all the other terms. Term 5, also frequent and with a low *P*-weight, would be counterbalanced by terms 1 and 13. In contrast, term 4, of type *d*, has a sufficiently high *P*-weight to retrieve unaided, but it is rare, and is only responsible for one non-relevant document. Term 1, of the useful type *e*, also retrieves some non-relevant documents, but not very many. Some non-relevant documents are retrieved by term combinations, but a good many, like those jointly indexed by the bad terms 5 and 7, are lost.

The query term membership for relevant documents is shown in Table 4d. There are none containing only one of the more helpful terms, like 4 or 1, but any such would have been retrieved. One document does match on only one term, but as this is a bad one of type *b*, namely 7, the document is unfortunately lost. This is the penalty for the elimination of the many non-relevant documents indexed by 7 alone. The remaining relevant documents are indexed by one or other of the bad terms 5 and 7, but as all but one are also indexed by term 1, their small *P*-weights simply increase the already adequate score given by the *P*-weight for term 1. Document 21,865 is of interest in being just retrieved by terms 2 and 7 together, though neither would achieve this individually.

For this query the sum of absence weights for the eleven terms not occurring in any documents is not gross, but it is easy to see how such terms could affect recall.

These examples together show how effective relevance weighting can be in reducing the numbers of non-relevant documents retrieved. It should be emphasized that the discussion has been entirely concerned with the numbers of documents retrieved. Weighting produces ordered search output, and the performance graphs of Figs. 1 and 2 very clearly show the superiority of weighted searching at the high precision end of the performance curve, i.e. at higher output ranks: the different scores derived from the weights serve to promote relevant documents at the expense of non-relevant ones.

Problems of relevance weights

The illustrations exhibit the good side of relevance weighting in the elimination of relevant documents. But the penalty to be paid is in some cases very severe, in that there are requests which fail to retrieve any relevant documents at all. The number and per cent of requests failing (of those requests which in fact have any relevant documents to retrieve, as there are some without for the odd-numbered document subsets) is shown in Table 5. As the table also shows, the attempts to improve the estimation basis do not necessarily deal with this problem.

This may or may not be an inevitable consequence of the general conditions of relevance weighting as studied here: that is, of the amount of information available, of the difficulty of estimation, and most importantly, of the fact that in all these tests, and similar ones conducted by other projects, the weights are being applied to a given set of terms which is not altered; clearly there must be costs associated with the continued use of a query term which is a bad one. Modification of request composition in relation to weighting is clearly the next topic, as was proposed, for example, by van Rijsbergen,[6] and some very promising results in this area have recently been obtained by Harper and van Rijsbergen.[13] In the meantime, it should be noted that the problem of output cutoff has not been studied by other workers in this area, and that in the method of evaluation used, for example, by the SMART workers, where the entire collection is ranked, any natural cutoff is disregarded.

TABLE 5. *Retrieval failures*

	Total requests	*Requests with relevant documents to retrieve in odd set*	*No. requests failing to retrieve any of their relevant documents; hence per cent of requests with relevant failing to retrieve*										
			Terms	*B1*	*B2*	*B3*	*F1*	*F2*	*F3*	*All*	*Y*	*F3a*	*F3b*
Cranfield	225	210	0	12 (5·7)	9 (4·3)	—	8 (3·8)	7 (3·3)	—	8 (3·8)	0	—	—
UKCIS	75	72	1 (1·4)	7 (9·7)	5 (6·9)	5 (6·9)	6 (8·3)	5 (6·9)	5 (6·9)	5 (6·9)	1 (1·4)	1 (1·4)	5 (6·9)

ACKNOWLEDGEMENT

I am very grateful to Dr S. E. Robertson for suggestions on estimation and to Dr C. J. van Rijsbergen and a referee for comments on the paper.

REFERENCES

1. ROBSON, A. *and* LONGMAN, J. S. *Automatic aids to profile construction.* 2 vols. UKCIS, Nottingham, 1975. (OSTI Report 5230.)
2. ROBSON, A. *and* LONGMAN, J. S. Automatic aids to profile construction. *Journal of the ASIS, 27,* 1976, 213–23.
3. SALTON, G., WONG, A. *and* YU, C. T. Automatic indexing using term discrimination and term precision measurements. *Information Processing and Management, 12,* 1976, 43–51.
4. YU, C. T. *and* SALTON, G. Precision weighting—an effective automatic indexing method. *Journal of the ACM, 23,* 1976, 76–88.
5. YU, C. T. *and* SALTON, G. Effective information retrieval using term accuracy. *Communications of the ACM, 20,* 1977, 135–42.
6. VAN RIJSBERGEN, C. J. A theoretical basis for the use of co-occurrence data in information retrieval. *Journal of Documentation, 33,* 1977, 106–19.
7. ROBERTSON, S. E. *and* SPARCK JONES, K. Relevance weighting of search terms. *Journal of the ASIS, 27,* 1976, 129–46.
8. SPARCK JONES, K. Experiments in relevance weighting of search terms. *Information Processing and Management,* 1979 (in press).
9. IDE, E. Relevance feedback in an automatic document retrieval system. *Information storage and retrieval, Scientific Report No. ISR-15,* Department of Computer Science, Cornell University, 1969.
10. CLEVERDON, C. W., MILLS, J. *and* KEEN, M. *Factors determining the performance of indexing systems.* 2 vols. Cranfield Institute of Technology, Bedford, 1966.
11. BARKER, F. H., VEAL, D. C. *and* WYATT, B. K. *Retrieval experiments based on Chemical Abstracts Condensates,* Research Report No. 2, UKCIS, Nottingham, 1974.
12. COX, D. R. *The analysis of binary data.* London: Methuen, 1970.
13. HARPER, D. J. *and* VAN RIJSBERGEN, C. J. An evaluation of feedback in document retrieval using co-occurrence data. *Journal of Documentation, 34,* 1978, 189–216.

(Revised version received 14 January 1979)

USING PROBABILISTIC MODELS OF DOCUMENT RETRIEVAL WITHOUT RELEVANCE INFORMATION

W. B. CROFT

Department of Computer and Information Science, University of Massachusetts, Amherst

and

D. J. HARPER

Computer Laboratory, University of Cambridge

Most probabilistic retrieval models incorporate information about the occurrence of index terms in relevant and non-relevant documents. In this paper we consider the situation where no relevance information is available, that is, at the start of the search. Based on a probabilistic model, strategies are proposed for the initial search and an intermediate search. Retrieval experiments with the Cranfield collection of 1,400 documents show that this initial search strategy is better than conventional search strategies both in terms of retrieval effectiveness and in terms of the number of queries that retrieve relevant documents. The intermediate search is shown to be a useful substitute for a relevance feedback search. Experiments with queries that do not retrieve relevant documents at high rank positions indicate that a cluster search would be an effective alternative strategy.

INTRODUCTION

THE PROBABILISTIC models of document retrieval which have recently been proposed in the literature[1–5] have been successful both in improving the retrieval performance of experimental systems and in providing a theoretical basis for methods which have previously relied on heuristics. A major assumption made in these models is that *relevance information* is available. That is, some or all of the relevant and non-relevant documents have been identified. Partial relevance information can be obtained by retrieving documents on the basis of the query and presenting them to the user for judgement as relevant or non-relevant. This process of obtaining relevance information and using it in a further search is called *relevance feedback*. In general it is the information about the relevant documents that is the most important since the characteristics of the non-relevant documents can be approximated by those of the entire collection.[4] For relevance feedback to be effective, the initial search using the query should present relevant documents to the user in as many cases as possible. This paper investigates the application of probabilistic models to the initial search with the aim of improving the retrieval effectiveness of this search.

The design of methods for improving the initial search has been one of the major research topics in information retrieval. The simplest approach to this search is to rank the documents according to the number of index terms in common with the query (sometimes called a co-ordination level search). Some of the modifications which have been proposed are

(*a*) Using a normalized query–document similarity measure, such as the Cosine Correlation.[6]
(*b*) Weighting the terms using inverse document frequencies.[7]
(*c*) Searching clusters of documents rather than the documents themselves.[8]

These methods differ from the approach taken in this paper in that we use the same probabilistic model for the initial search as is used for the relevance feedback search. The retrieval process can be viewed as a two-stage application of a probabilistic model where the main difference between the stages is the increase in the amount of relevance information available.

The second stage of the retrieval process depends heavily on the relevance information obtained in the first stage by presenting documents to the user. Since the user will only want to judge a relatively small number of documents, the evaluation of the retrieval experiments reported here will emphasize the ability of the initial search to retrieve relevant documents at the top end of the ranked list of documents. This leads to the associated problem of methods for dealing with queries which do not retrieve relevant documents at the top of the ranked list.

THE PROBABILISTIC MODEL

Each document is assumed to be described by a binary vector $\mathbf{x} = (x_1, x_2, \ldots x_v)$ where $x_i = 0$ or 1 indicates the absence or presence of the ith index term. A decision rule can be formulated by which any document can be assigned to either the relevant or the non-relevant set of documents for a particular query. The obvious rule is to assign a document to the relevant set if the probability of the document being relevant given the document description is greater than the probability of the document being non-relevant, that is if

$$P(\text{Relevant}|\mathbf{x}) > P(\text{Non-Relevant}|\mathbf{x})$$

A more convenient form of the decision rule can be found by using Bayes' theorem. This new rule, when expressed as a weighting function is,

$$g(\mathbf{x}) = \log P(\mathbf{x}|\text{Relevant}) - \log P(\mathbf{x}|\text{Non-Relevant})$$

This means that instead of making a strict decision on the relevance of a document, the documents are ranked by their $g(.)$ value such that the more highly ranked a document is, the more likely it is to be relevant.

The probabilities $P(\mathbf{x}|\text{Relevant})$ and $P(\mathbf{x}|\text{Non-Relevant})$ are difficult to calculate directly. However, they can be approximated in a number of different ways. If the assumption is made that the index terms occur *independently* in the relevant and non-relevant documents then

$$P(\mathbf{x})|\text{Relevant}) = P(x_1|\text{Relevant})\, P(x_2|\text{Relevant}) \ldots P(x_v|\text{Relevant})$$

and similarly for $P(\mathbf{x}|\text{Non-Relevant})$.

Let $\quad p_i = P(x_i = 1|\text{Relevant})$ and $q_i = P(x_i = 1|\text{Non-Relevant})$

where these are the probabilities that an index term occurs in the relevant and non-relevant sets respectively.

Then

$$P(\mathbf{x}|\text{Relevant}) = \prod_{i=1}^{v} p_i^{x_i}(1 - p_i)^{1-x_i}$$

$$P(\mathbf{x}|\text{nNon-Relevant}) = \prod_{i=1}^{v} q_i^{x_i}(1 - q_i)^{1-x_i}$$

and

$$g(\mathbf{x}) = \sum_{i=1}^{v} x_i \log \frac{p_i(1 - q_i)}{(1 - p_i)\, q_i} + \sum_{i=1}^{v} \log \frac{1 - p_i}{1 - q_i}$$

The second term of this function will be constant for a given query and will not affect the ranking of the documents. The first term involves a summation over all the terms in the document collection but for reasons explained by van Rijsbergen,[8] this summation is usually restricted to just the query terms. This function is then equivalent to a simple matching function between the query and the documents where query term i has the weight $\log p_i(1 - q_i)/(1 - p_i)q_i$. This model was first used by Robertson and Sparck Jones.[1] If the terms are assumed to be *not* independently distributed, then more accurate approximations for $P(\mathbf{x}|\text{Relevant})$ and $P(\mathbf{x}|\text{Non-Relevant})$ are possible.[3] In this paper we shall (mainly) use the simpler model based on the independence assumption.

When the model is applied to a retrieval system, the binomial parameter p_i is estimated from the sample of relevant documents obtained by user judgements and q_i is usually estimated from the total collection of documents. In the initial search, that is, prior to relevance feedback, we have no information about the relevant documents and we could therefore assume that all the query terms had equal probabilities of occurring in the relevant documents. The effect of this assumption can be seen by splitting the first term of $g(\mathbf{x})$ into two parts.

$$\sum_i x_i \log \frac{p_i}{1 - p_i} + \sum_i x_i \log \frac{1 - q_i}{q_i}$$

where the summation is over all query terms. If we assume that all p_i are the same, then the first part of the above expression is simply a constant $(\log p_i/1 - p_i)$ times the number of common terms between the query and the document. If we estimate q_i by n_i/N where n_i is the number of documents in which the term i occurs and N is the size of the collection, then the second part of the expression is

$$\sum x_i \log \frac{N - n_i}{n_i}$$

For large N this query term weight is very similar to the inverse document frequency weight used by Sparck Jones and Bates,[7] $\log N/n_i$.* Therefore this probabilistic model indicates that in the case where no relevance information is available, the best function for ranking the documents is a combination of a simple match and a match using inverse document frequency weights. Previous experiments have of course used either one or the other of these methods but not both together. This function shall be referred to as the *combination match.*

As an example of the difference between the initial searches mentioned, consider the binary query description $\mathbf{r} = (r_1, r_2, \ldots r_v)$ and a document description $\mathbf{x}$. The simple match for this pair is

$$\sum x_i r_i$$

The summation is now over all terms because the query appears explicitly. The match with inverse document frequency weights is

$$\sum x_i r_i \log N/n_i \text{ implemented as } \sum x_i r_i \log (\max n_i)/n_i$$

The match with the Cosine Correlation is

$$\sum x_i r_i / (\sum x_i \sum r_i)^{\frac{1}{2}}$$

and the combination match is

$$C \sum x_i r_i + \sum x_i r_i \log (N - n_i)/n_i$$

where C is a constant. An interesting special case of the combination match is obtained by allowing p_i to approach 1·0, in which case the constant C becomes very large. The combination match then specializes to ranking the documents by inverse document frequency weighting (approximately) within co-ordination level, which will be referred to as the co-ordination/IDF match.

Another possible application of the model is to introduce an intermediate search between the initial search and the relevance feedback search. The documents at the top of the ranking produced by the initial search have a high probability of being relevant. The assumption underlying the intermediate search is that these documents *are* relevant, whether in actual fact they are or not. Therefore before asking the user to give relevance judgements, a search would be performed in which the top few documents are used to provide estimates for p_i. The effect of this search will vary widely from query to query. For a query which retrieved a high proportion of relevant documents at the top of the ranking, this search would probably retrieve additional relevant documents. For a query which retrieved a low proportion of relevant documents, this search may actually downgrade the retrieval effectiveness. The intermediate search would therefore be most useful if the process of interacting with the user to obtain relevance judgements is considered very expensive or even impractical by either the user or the system designer.

A different application arises when the query does not retrieve any relevant documents at a particular cutoff. In this case the user has judged all the retrieved documents as being non-relevant, whereas the intermediate search is performed before the user looks at any documents. The technique of using the characteristics of the judged non-relevant documents to perform another search for relevant documents (negative feedback) has been shown to have some merit by Ide.[9] The application of the probabilistic model to negative feedback could be done by performing an initial search with either of the following changes,

* They implement this weight as $\log (\max n_i)/n_i$, where $(\max n_i)$ is the maximum value of n_i observed for the particular document collection. The same implementation is adopted in the experiment reported in this paper.

(*a*) The terms in the judged non-relevant set of documents could provide estimates for q_i, in which case all p_i values remain equal.

(*b*) The terms in the non-relevant documents could be used to vary the estimates for p_i. If a query term occurs frequently in the judged non-relevant set, the p_i values for the term would be reduced. Experimental evidence suggests that the latter method is to be preferred.

In summary then, the combination match, the intermediate search and the negative feedback search are all based on the same probabilistic model and in each case no relevant documents are known. The difference in the searches is in the method of estimating the p_i values. The three searches are tested with retrieval experiments in the following section.

THE EXPERIMENTS

The experiments reported here were done with the Cranfield C1400I collection of 1,400 documents and 225 queries with binary indexing. A full description of this collection can be found in Sparck Jones and Bates.[7] Three evaluation methods are used. The first is a precision–recall table which gives average precision values at standard recall levels. The exact method of calculation of these values is described by Harper and van Rijsbergen.[4] To emphasize the performance of the searches at the top end of the rankings, the E measure[8] is used as the second evaluation method. The E measure is a weighted combination of precision and recall such that *the lower the* E *value, the better the effectiveness*. The parameter β is used to reflect the emphasis on precision or recall. $\beta = 1$ corresponds to attaching equal importance to precision and recall. $\beta = 0{\cdot}5$ and 2 corresponds to attaching half and twice as much importance to recall as to precision respectively. The E measure evaluates a set of retrieved documents so a ranked document list must be evaluated at cutoff points. However this has the advantage that the ranks within the retrieved set do not affect the evaluation whereas precision–recall figures can be very sensitive to the exact rankings. For example, at a cutoff of say ten documents the E measure considers simply the number of relevant documents in this set rather than their positions. Since the user must examine the ten documents anyway for the relevance feedback process, the E measure does seem appropriate.

Another advantage of the E measure is that significance tests are easy to apply because there is a single E value (for a given value of β) for each query rather than a set of recall-precision values. The significance test used here is the Wilcoxon signed-ranks test with a significance level of 5%. The E evaluation in the experiments is presented as average E values (over 225 queries) for $\beta = 0{\cdot}5,1,2$ at two arbitrary cutoffs of ten and twenty documents from the top of the document ranking.

The third evaluation method is simply to list the number of queries that do not retrieve relevant documents and the total number of relevant documents retrieved over all queries at a particular cutoff in the ranking. This gives a direct indication of the amount of relevance information that can be obtained from the user after the initial or intermediate search. The first figure is the most important because relevance feedback can be effective even with a single relevant document.[5]

The first experiment was to compare the usual methods for the initial search—the simple match (COORD), the match with inverse document frequency weights (INVWT) and the match using the Cosine Correlation (COS). Table 1 gives the results for these searches on the C1400I collection. The cutoff values used in the evaluation were ten and twenty documents. Values any higher than this would probably require too much effort for the user to judge documents for relevance.

These retrieval results indicate that there is little difference between the three initial searches. However, it does seem that the COS search does slightly better in terms of precision whereas the INVWT search does slightly better in terms of recall. In fact the only significant difference in the E values according to the Wilcoxon test is that the INVWT value for $\beta = 2$ (recall-oriented), cutoff $= 20$ is better than the other searches. In terms of the relevance information provided, the COS search is the best at cutoff $= 10$ whereas the INVWT search is the best at cutoff $= 20$.

TABLE 1. *Comparison of the COORD, INVWT and COS initial searches*

Recall	Precision COORD	Precision INVWT	Precision COS
10	47·5	45·8	49·1
20	41·2	39·7	43·2
30	34·4	33·5	34·9
40	30·0	30·3	29·9
50	27·6	27·7	27·5
60	20·5	22·1	21·0
70	16·5	18·2	16·1
80	12·9	15·1	13·7
90	10·1	11·5	10·0
100	9·5	11·0	9·2

Average E *values*

Search	Cutoff = 10, $\beta = 0{\cdot}5$	Cutoff = 10, 1·0	Cutoff = 10, 2·0	Cutoff = 20, 0·5	Cutoff = 20, 1·0	Cutoff = 20, 2·0
COORD	0·79	0·77	0·73	0·84	0·80	0·73
INVWT	0·80	0·78	0·73	0·84	0·79	0·71
COS	0·79	0·77	0·73	0·84	0·80	0·72

Relevance Information

Search	Cutoff = 10, # queries that fail	Cutoff = 10, Total rels retrvd	Cutoff = 20, # queries that fail	Cutoff = 20, Total rels retrvd
COORD	49	447	32	621
INVWT	50	432	28	648
COS	46	454	32	633

The next experiment tested the combination match. A number of searches were performed with the constant value of p_i set to values between 0·3 and 0·9. As p_i was increased from 0·3 to 0·6, material improvements in the search results were obtained. Increasing p_i above 0·6 improved the searches, but only marginally. As expected the results for $p_i = 0{\cdot}5 (C = 0)$ were almost identical to the INVWT results. The best* search results (COMB) for p_i set to 0·9 are given in Table 2. Search results (COOINV) are also given for the co-ordination/IDF match. This table shows that these match functions produce very similar results, and more importantly that they are the best overall initial searches. At a cutoff of ten documents, the COMB search is not significantly different to the other three searches but it provides approximately the same relevance information as the COS search. At a cutoff level of twenty the E values from the COMB search are significantly better (according to the Wilcoxon test) than the values for the other searches at each β value. The relevance information provided at this cutoff is much better than any other search.

TABLE 2. *The COMB and COOINV initial searches*

Recall	*Precision* COMB	*Precision* COOINV
10	48·1	48·2
20	41·6	41·6
30	35·3	35·2
40	31·8	31·7
50	28·5	28·5
60	22·7	22·2
70	18·6	18·0
80	15·5	14·8
90	11·4	11·1
100	10·9	10·6

Average E *values*

Search	*Cutoff = 10* $\beta = 0{\cdot}5$	*Cutoff = 10* 1·0	*Cutoff = 10* 2·0	*Cutoff = 20* 0·5	*Cutoff = 20* 1·0	*Cutoff = 20* 2·0
COMB	0·79	0·77	0·72	0·83	0·79	0·70
COOINV	0·79	0·77	0·72	0·83	0·79	0·70

Relevance Information

Search	*Cutoff = 10* # queries that fail	*Cutoff = 10* Total rels retrvd	*Cutoff = 20* # queries that fail	*Cutoff = 20* Total rels retrvd
COMB	44	449	23	670
COOINV	45	447	24	663

That the best results for the combination match were obtained for p_i almost equal to 1·0, is a consequence of the collection used for the experiment. The queries of the C1400I collection were manually indexed, with the indexers instructed to select 'significant' words from the query texts.[7] It is reasonable to suppose that significant words are those with potentially high probabilities of occurring in relevant documents. Therefore the combination match with a high constant value for p_i would be expected to produce the best results. It is conjectured that for automatically indexed queries the best value for p_i will be much less than 1·0, and that the resulting combination match will be more like inverse document frequency weighting than co-ordination/IDF weighting. The advantage of the combination match over the other match functions is that it can be tailored to a particular document collection. Note that for some collections it may be that the best constant value for p_i will be less than 0·5.

The next experiment was to perform an intermediate search by assuming that the top few documents from the ranking of the initial search are relevant. Two main variations of this search were used. The first used just the query terms in the intermediate search but with p_i estimates based on a specified number of the top documents. For this collection, the best performance was obtained by using the top five documents (and the search will be referred to as TOP5). The second variation of the intermediate search was to expand the query with terms from a maximum spanning tree of all terms in the collection. This maximum spanning tree is the tree of maximum edge weight connecting the index terms where the edge weight between two terms is a measure of the dependence of those terms. This form of query expansion, which comes from assuming that terms do not occur independently, is described in Harper and van Rijsbergen.[4] The p_i estimates for the expanded set of terms are found from the top few documents of the initial search, as for TOP5. The effect of this expansion is to provide extra terms which are not in the query but which may be in relevant documents. This search performed best when the top three documents of the initial search were used and it shall be referred to as EXTOP3. The initial search used for this experiment is the simple match (COORD) and the results for the intermediate searches given in Table 3 should be compared to the results for this search.

The significance tests on the E values showed that EXTOP3 is more effective than COORD at both cutoff levels and for all values of β. Even the simple TOP5 strategy was significantly better at a cutoff of ten documents, but not at twenty. However, the relevance information shows that while the total number of relevant documents retrieved has increased compared to the COORD search, the number of queries which do not retrieve any relevant documents at these cutoff levels also increases. Therefore there would not seem to be any advantage in having an intermediate search before a relevance feedback search. Any extra relevant documents retrieved by the intermediate search would almost certainly be retrieved by a relevance feedback search directly after an initial search. The intermediate search could however be used as a substitute for the relevance feedback search in systems where the interaction with the user was considered impractical.

The final experiment investigates methods of dealing with queries that retrieve no relevant documents at high cutoff levels. Even for the best initial search (COMB) there were still twenty-three of these queries at a cutoff of twenty documents. The best strategy used for the probabilistic model was to estimate p_i for the query terms by

$$p_i = 0{\cdot}5 + 0{\cdot}4 \times (1 - f_i)$$

where f_i is the ratio of the number of occurrences of term i in the judged non-relevant set to the size of that set. Therefore the p_i values range from 0·5 for a

* The idea of trying the combination match with various values for p_i, and then regarding the best of the searches as the result of the model is a little suspect. It would be better to optimize p_i on one set of queries, and then test the combination match with the best value on another set. However, given the similar search results observed over a wide range of p_i values (0·6–0·9), it would seem that such sophistication is unnecessary.

TABLE 3. *The TOP5 and EXTOP3 intermediate searches*

Recall	Precision	
	TOP5	EXTOP3
10	49·4	47·3
20	43·9	41·6
30	36·7	35·1
40	32·1	31·2
50	29·1	29·0
60	23·1	24·0
70	18·6	20·3
80	15·1	17·2
90	11·4	13·1
100	10·7	12·5

Average E values

Search	Cutoff = 10			Cutoff = 20		
	$\beta = 0·5$	1·0	2·0	0·5	1·0	2·0
TOP5	0·78	0·76	0·72	0·84	0·80	0·72
EXTOP3	0·78	0·76	0·71	0·83	0·79	0·70

Relevance Information

Search	Cutoff = 10		Cutoff = 20	
	# queries that fail	Total rels retrvd	# queries that fail	Total rels retrvd
TOP5	53	470	36	644
EXTOP3	54	469	39	673

query term which occurred in all the judged non-relevant documents to 0·9 for a term which occurred in none. This strategy is evaluated by giving the number of queries (out of twenty-three) that retrieved relevant documents in the top ten and twenty positions of the new ranking, excluding documents already seen by the user. The results for this search (NEGFD) and two other searches appear in Table 4. The search called EXTRA is simply looking at the next ten and twenty documents (after the first twenty) of the original COMB search. The other search, CLUSTER, uses the twenty-three queries for a bottom-up search of a cluster hierarchy.[10] It has been shown that this type of cluster search which retrieves one cluster of documents can achieve very high precision results but in many cases may not retrieve any relevant documents at all. Therefore the cluster search is not suitable for the initial search prior to relevance feedback in general but because it uses a different approach it may be a useful alternative strategy.

Table 4 shows that for this collection there is no advantage in using a negative feedback strategy because similar results can be obtained by simply looking at more documents from the initial search. The CLUSTER search seems to be particularly useful both in terms of the number of queries that retrieved relevant documents and the small number of documents that would have to be examined. The disadvantage of the cluster search is the overhead involved in setting up and maintaining the cluster hierarchy. This is discussed in detail by Croft.[10] The CLUSTER search and the EXTRA search together retrieved relevant documents for fourteen out of the twenty-three queries. Therefore it would seem advantageous to both retrieve a cluster and examine a few more documents from the initial search.

TABLE 4. *The NEGFD, EXTRA and CLUSTER searches with twenty-three queries that retrieved no relevant documents at cutoff twenty in the initial search*

Search	#queries that retrieved relevant docs in	
	next 10 docs	next 20 docs
NEGFD	5	4
EXTRA	5	4
CLUSTER	11*	–

* The average size of the retrieved clusters was three documents.

CONCLUSION

A probabilistic model of document retrieval was applied to two searches which can occur before relevance feedback—the initial search and the intermediate search. For the initial search there is no relevance information available whereas for the intermediate search the relevance information is derived from the top-ranking documents of the initial search. The experiments using the C1400I collection showed that the initial search based on this model and called the combination match performed better than the simple match, the match using inverse document frequency weights and the match using the Cosine Correlation. The improvements in retrieval effectiveness obtained were small but significant and this search also provided the most relevance information. However, this result should be taken as just an indication that the combination match is the most effective initial search because the experiments have only been done with one medium-size collection. The intermediate search, because it increases the number of queries that do not retrieve relevant documents at high ranks, would only be useful when a relevance feedback search was not possible or was too expensive.

A strategy based on the probabilistic model was also devised for queries which did not retrieve any relevant documents at high cutoff levels. This negative feedback strategy was shown to be ineffective for this collection since the same results could be achieved by examining more documents from the initial search. Finally, the results indicated that a cluster search would be a good alternative initial search strategy.

ACKNOWLEDGEMENTS

The work was carried out while D. J. Harper was in receipt of a CSIRO Postgraduate Studentship. Facilities were kindly provided by the Cambridge University Computer Laboratory. The authors thank Keith van Rijsbergen and Karen Sparck Jones for many helpful discussions. The document collection was generously made available by Karen Sparck Jones. The authors would like to thank the referees for their helpful suggestions.

REFERENCES

1. ROBERTSON, S. E. *and* SPARCK JONES, K. Relevance weighting of search terms. *Journal of the ASIS, 27*, 1976, 129–46.
2. YU, C. T. *and* SALTON, G. Precision weighting—an effective automatic indexing method. *Journal of the ACM, 23*, 1975, 76–88.
3. VAN RIJSBERGEN, C. J. A theoretical basis for the use of co-occurrence data in information retrieval. *Journal of Documentation, 33*, 1977, 106–19.
4. HARPER, D. J. *and* VAN RIJSBERGEN, C. J. An evaluation of feedback in document retrieval using co-occurrence data. *Journal of Documentation, 34*, 1978, 189–216.
5. SPARCK JONES, K. Search term relevance weighting given little relevance information. *Journal of Documentation, 35*, 1979, 30–48.
6. SALTON, G. *Automatic information organization and retrieval*. New York: McGraw-Hill, 1968.
7. SPARCK JONES, K. *and* BATES, R. G. Research on automatic indexing 1974–6. 2 vols. Computer Laboratory, University of Cambridge, 1977.
8. VAN RIJSBERGEN, C. J. *Information retrieval*, 2nd edition, London: Butterworths, 1979.
9. IDE, E. Relevance feedback in an automatic document retrieval system. M.Sc. thesis, Report ISR-15 to the National Science Foundation, Department of Computer Science, Cornell University, Ithaca, N.Y., 1969.
10. CROFT, W. B. Organizing and searching large files of document descriptions. Ph.D. thesis, Computer Laboratory, University of Cambridge, 1979.

(Revised version received 19 October 1979)

Some Simple Effective Approximations to the 2–Poisson Model for Probabilistic Weighted Retrieval

S.E. Robertson
ser@is.city.ac.uk

S. Walker
sw@is.city.ac.uk

Centre for Interactive Systems Research, Department of Information Science, City University
Northampton Square, London EC1V 0HB, UK

Abstract

The 2–Poisson model for term frequencies is used to suggest ways of incorporating certain variables in probabilistic models for information retrieval. The variables concerned are within-document term frequency, document length, and within-query term frequency. Simple weighting functions are developed, and tested on the TREC test collection. Considerable performance improvements (over simple inverse collection frequency weighting) are demonstrated.

1 Introduction

This paper discusses an approach to the incorporation of new variables into traditional probabilistic models for information retrieval, and some experimental results relating thereto. Some of the discussion has appeared in the proceedings of the second TREC conference [1], albeit in less detail.

Statistical approaches to information retrieval have traditionally (to over-simplify grossly) taken two forms: firstly approaches based on formal models, where the model specifies an exact formula; and secondly ad-hoc approaches, where formulae are tried because they seem to be plausible. Both categories have had some notable successes. A more recent variant is the regression approach of Fuhr and Cooper (see, for example, Cooper [3]), which incorporates ad-hoc choice of independent variables and functions of them with a formal model for assessing their value in retrieval, selecting from among them and assigning weights to them.

One problem with the formal model approach is that it is often very difficult to take into account the wide variety of variables that are thought or known to influence retrieval. The difficulty arises either because there is no known basis for a model containing such variables, or because any such model may simply be too complex to give a usable exact formula.

One problem with the ad-hoc approach is that there is little guidance as to how to deal with specific variables—one has to guess at a formula and try it out. This problem is also apparent in the regression approach—although "trying it out" has a somewhat different sense here (the formula is tried in a regression model, rather than in a retrieval test).

The approach in the present paper is to take a model which provides an exact but intractable formula, and use it to suggest a much simpler formula. The simpler formula can then be tried in an ad-hoc fashion, or used in turn in a regression model. Although we have not yet taken this latter step of using regression, we believe that the present suggestion lends itself to such methods.

The variables we have included in this paper are: within-document term frequency, document length, and within-query term frequency (it is worth observing that collection frequency of terms appears naturally in traditional probabilistic models, particularly in the form of the approximation to inverse collection frequency weighting demonstrated by Croft and Harper [4]). The formal model which is used to investigate the effects of these variables is the 2–Poisson model (Harter [5], Robertson, van Rijsbergen and Porter [6]).

2 Basic Probabilistic Weighting Model

The basic weighting function used is that developed in [6], and may be expressed as follows:

$$w(\underline{x}) = \log \frac{P(\underline{x}|R)\ P(\underline{0}|\overline{R})}{P(\underline{x}|\overline{R})\ P(\underline{0}|R)}, \tag{1}$$

where $\underline{x}$ is a vector of information about the document, $\underline{0}$ is a reference vector representing a zero-weighted document, and R and $\overline{R}$ are relevance and non-relevance respectively.

For example, each component of $\underline{x}$ may represent the presence/absence of a query term in the document or its document frequency; $\underline{0}$ would then be the "natural" zero vector representing all query terms absent.

In this formulation, independence assumptions (or, indeed, Cooper's assumption of "linked dependence" [7]), lead to the decomposition of w into *additive* components such as individual term weights. In the presence/absence case, the resulting weighting function is the Robertson/Sparck Jones formula [8] for a term-presence-only weight, as follows:

$$w = \log \frac{p(1-q)}{q(1-p)}, \tag{2}$$

where $p = P(\text{term present}|R)$ and $q = P(\text{term present}|\overline{R})$.

With a suitable estimation method, this becomes:

$$w = \log \frac{(r+0.5)/(R-r+0.5)}{(n-r+0.5)/(N-n-R+r+0.5)}, \tag{3}$$

where N is the number of indexed documents, n the number containing the term, R the number of known relevant documents, and r the number of these containing the term. This approximates to inverse collection frequency (ICF) when there is no relevance information. It will be referred to below (with or without relevance information) as $w^{(1)}$.

If we deal with within-document term frequencies rather than merely presence and absence of terms, then the formula corresponding to 2 would be as follows:

$$w = \log \frac{p_{tf}\, q_0}{q_{tf}\, p_0}, \tag{4}$$

where $p_{tf} = P(\text{term present with frequency } tf|R)$, q_{tf} is the corresponding probability for $\overline{R}$, and p_0 and q_0 are those for term absence.

2.1 Eliteness

The approach taken in reference [6] is to model within-document term frequencies by means of a mixture of two Poisson distributions. However, before discussing the 2–Poisson model, it is worth extracting one idea which is necessary for the model, but can perhaps stand on its own. (This idea was in fact taken from the original 2–Poisson work by Harter [5], but was extended somewhat to allow for multi-concept queries.)

We hypothesize that occurrences of a term in a document have a random or stochastic element, which nevertheless reflects a real but hidden distinction between those documents which are "about" the concept represented by the term and those which are not. Those documents which are "about" this concept are described as "elite" for the term. We may draw an inference about eliteness from the term frequency, but this inference will of course be probabilistic. Furthermore, relevance (to a query which may of course contain many concepts) is related to eliteness rather than directly to term frequency, which is assumed to depend *only* on eliteness. The usual term-independence assumptions are replaced by assumptions that the eliteness properties for different terms are independent of each other; although the details are not provided here, it is clear that the independence assumptions can be replaced by "linked dependence" assumptions in the style of Cooper [7].

As usual, the various assumptions of the model are very clearly over-simplifications of reality. It seems nevertheless to be useful to introduce this hidden variable of eliteness in order to gain some understanding of the relation between multiple term occurrence and relevance.

3 The 2–Poisson Model

The 2–Poisson model is a specific distributional assumption based on the eliteness hypothesis discussed above. The assumption is that the distribution of within-document frequencies is Poisson for the elite documents, and also (but with a different mean) for the non-elite documents.

It would be possible to derive this model from a more basic one, under which a document was a random stream of term occurrences, each one having a fixed, small probability of being the term in question, this probability being constant over all elite documents, and also constant (but smaller) over all non-elite documents. Such a model would require that all documents were the same length. Thus the 2–Poisson model is usually said to assume that document length is constant: although technically it does not require that assumption, it makes little sense without it. Document length is discussed further below (section 5).

The approach taken in [6] was to estimate the parameters of the two Poisson distributions for each term directly from the distribution of within-document frequencies. These parameters were then used in various weighting functions. However, little performance benefit was gained. This was seen essentially as a result of estimation problems: partly that the estimation method for the Poisson parameters was probably not very good, and partly because the model is complex in the sense of requiring a large number of different parameters to be estimated. Subsequent work on mixed-Poisson models has suggested that alternative estimation methods may be preferable [9].

Combining the 2–Poisson model with formula 4, under the various assumptions given about dependencies, we obtain [6] the following weight for a term t:

$$w = \log \frac{(p'\lambda^{tf} e^{-\lambda} + (1-p')\mu^{tf} e^{-\mu})\ (q' e^{-\lambda} + (1-q')e^{-\mu})}{(q'\lambda^{tf} e^{-\lambda} + (1-q')\mu^{tf} e^{-\mu})\ (p' e^{-\lambda} + (1-p')e^{-\mu})}, \tag{5}$$

where λ and μ are the Poisson means for tf in the elite and non-elite sets for t respectively, $p' = P(\text{document elite for } t|R)$, and q' is the corresponding probability for $\overline{R}$.

The estimation problem is very apparent from equation 5, in that there are four parameters for each term, for *none* of which are we likely to have direct evidence (because of eliteness being a hidden variable). It is precisely this estimation problem which makes the weighting function intractable. This consideration leads directly to the approach taken in the next section.

4 A Rough Model for Term Frequency

4.1 The Shape of the *tf* Effect

Many different functions have been used to allow within-document term frequency tf to influence the weight given to the particular document on account of the term in question. In some cases a linear function has been used; in others, the effect has been dampened by using a suitable transformation such as $\log tf$.

Even if we do not use the full equation 5, we may allow it to suggest the shape of an appropriate, but simpler, function. In fact, equation 5 has the following characteristics: (a) It is zero for $tf = 0$; (b) it increases monotonically with tf; (c) but to an asymptotic maximum; (d) which approximates to the Robertson/Sparck Jones weight that would be given to a direct indicator of eliteness.

Only in an extreme case, where eliteness is identical to relevance, is the function linear in tf. These points can be seen from the following re-arrangement of equation 5:

$$w = \log \frac{(p' + (1-p')(\mu/\lambda)^{tf} e^{\lambda-\mu})\ (q' e^{\mu-\lambda} + (1-q'))}{(q' + (1-q')(\mu/\lambda)^{tf} e^{\lambda-\mu})\ (p' e^{\mu-\lambda} + (1-p'))}. \tag{6}$$

μ is smaller than λ. As $tf \to \infty$ (to give us the asymptotic maximum), $(\mu/\lambda)^{tf}$ goes to zero, so those components drop out. $e^{\mu-\lambda}$ will be small, so the approximation is:

$$w = \log \frac{p'(1-q')}{q'(1-p')}. \tag{7}$$

(The last approximation may not be a good one: for a poor and/or infrequent term, $e^{\mu-\lambda}$ will not be very small. Although this should not affect the component in the numerator, because q' is likely to be small, it will affect the component in the denominator.)

4.2 A Simple Formulation

What is required, therefore, is a simple tf-related weight that has something like the characteristics (a)-(d) listed in the previous section. Such a function can be constructed as follows. The function $tf/(\text{constant} + tf)$ increases from zero to an asymptotic maximum in approximately the right fashion. The constant determines the rate at which the increase drops off: with a large constant, the function is approximately linear for small tf, whereas with a small constant, the effect of increasing tf rapidly diminishes.

This function has an asymptotic maximum of one, so it needs to be multiplied by an appropriate weight similar to equation 7. Since we cannot estimate 7 directly, the obvious simple alternative is the ordinary Robertson/Sparck Jones weight, equation 2, based on presence/absence of the term. Using the usual estimate of 2, namely $w^{(1)}$ (equation 3), we obtain the following weighting function:

$$w = \frac{tf}{(k_1 + tf)}\, w^{(1)}, \tag{8}$$

where k_1 is an unknown constant.

The model tells us nothing about what kind of value to expect for k_1. Our approach has been to try out various values of k_1 (values around 1–2 seem to be about right for the TREC data—see the results section 7 below). However, in the longer term we hope to use regression methods to determine the constant. It is not, unfortunately, in a form directly susceptible to the methods of Fuhr or Cooper, but we hope to develop suitable methods.

The shape of formula 8 differs from that of formula 5 in one important respect: 8 is convex towards the upper left, whereas 5 can under some circumstances (that is, with some combinations of parameters) be S-shaped, increasing slowly at first, then more rapidly, then slowly again. Averaging over a number of terms with different values of the parameters is likely to reduce any such effect; however, it may be useful to try a function with this characteristic. One such, a simple combination of 8 with a logistic function, is as follows:

$$w = \frac{tf^c}{(k_1^c + tf^c)} w^{(1)}, \tag{9}$$

where $c > 1$ is another unknown constant. This function has not been tried in the present experiments.

5 Document Length

As indicated in section 3, the 2–Poisson model in effect assumes that documents (i.e. records) are all of equal length. Document length is a variable which figures in a number of weighting formulae.

5.1 Hypotheses Concerning Document Length

We may postulate at least two reasons why documents might vary in length. Some documents may simply cover more material than others; an extreme version of this hypothesis would have a long document consisting of a number of unrelated short documents concatenated together (the "Scope hypothesis"). An opposite view would have long documents like short documents, but longer: in other words, a long document covers a similar scope to a short document, but simply uses more words (the "Verbosity hypothesis").

It seems likely that real document collections contain a mixture of these effects; individual long documents may be at either extreme or of some hybrid type. (It is worth observing that some of the long TREC news items read exactly as if they are made up of short items concatenated together.) However, with the exception of a short discussion in section 5.7, the work on document length reported in this paper assumes the Verbosity hypothesis; little progress has yet been made with models based on the Scope hypothesis.

The Verbosity hypothesis would imply that document properties such as relevance and eliteness can be regarded as independent of document length; given eliteness for a term, however, the number of occurrences of that term would depend on document length.

5.2 A Very Rough Model

The simplest way to incorporate this hypothesis is to take formula 8 above, but normalise tf for document length (d). If we assume that the value of k_1 is appropriate to documents of average length (Δ), then this model can be expressed as

$$w = \frac{tf}{(\frac{k_1 \times d}{\Delta} + tf)} w^{(1)}. \tag{10}$$

This function is used in the experiments described below (section 7). However, a more detailed analysis of the effect of the Verbosity hypothesis on the 2–Poisson model may reveal a more complex pattern.

5.3 Document Length in the Basic Model

Referring back to the basic weighting function 1, we may include document length as one component of the vector $\underline{\mathbf{x}}$. However, document length does not so obviously have a "natural" zero (an actual document of zero length is a pathological case). Instead, we may use the average length of a document for the corresponding component of the reference vector $\underline{0}$; thus we would expect to get a formula in which the document length component disappears for a document of average length, but not for other lengths. The weighting formula then becomes:

$$w(\underline{\mathbf{x}}, d) = \log \frac{P(\underline{\mathbf{x}}, d|R)\ P(\underline{0}, \Delta|\overline{R})}{P(\underline{\mathbf{x}}, d|\overline{R})\ P(\underline{0}, \Delta|R)},$$

where d is document length, and $\underline{\mathbf{x}}$ represents all other information about the document. This may be decomposed into the sum of two components, $w(\underline{\mathbf{x}}, d)_1 + w(\underline{0}, d)_2$, where

$$w(\underline{\mathbf{x}}, d)_1 = \log \frac{P(\underline{\mathbf{x}}, d|R)\ P(\underline{0}, d|\overline{R})}{P(\underline{\mathbf{x}}, d|\overline{R})\ P(\underline{0}, d|R)} \quad \text{and} \quad w(\underline{0}, d)_2 = \log \frac{P(\underline{0}, d|R)\ P(\underline{0}, \Delta|\overline{R})}{P(\underline{0}, d|\overline{R})\ P(\underline{0}, \Delta|R)}. \tag{11}$$

These two components are discussed separately.

5.4 Consequences of the Verbosity Hypothesis

We assume without loss of generality that the two Poisson parameters for a given term, λ and μ, are appropriate for documents of average length. Then the Verbosity hypothesis would imply that while a longer (say) document has more words, each individual word has the same probability of being the term in question. Thus the distribution of term frequencies in documents of length d will be 2–Poisson with means $\lambda d/\Delta$ and $\mu d/\Delta$.

We may also make various independence assumptions, such as between document length and relevance.

5.5 Second Component

The second component of equation 11 is

$$w(\underline{0}, d)_2 = \log \frac{P(\underline{0}|R, d)\ P(\underline{0}|\overline{R}, \Delta)}{P(\underline{0}|\overline{R}, d)\ P(\underline{0}|R, \Delta)} + \log \frac{P(d|R)\ P(\Delta|\overline{R})}{P(d|\overline{R})\ P(\Delta|R)}.$$

Under the Verbosity hypothesis, the second part of this formula is zero. Making the usual term-independence or linked-dependence assumptions, the first part may be decomposed into a sum of components for each query term, thus:

$$w(t, d)_2 = \log \frac{(p'e^{-\lambda d/\Delta} + (1-p')e^{-\mu d/\Delta})\ (q'e^{-\lambda} + (1-q')e^{-\mu})}{(q'e^{-\lambda d/\Delta} + (1-q')e^{-\mu d/\Delta})\ (p'e^{-\lambda} + (1-p')e^{-\mu})}. \tag{12}$$

Note that because we are using the zero-vector $\underline{0}$, there is a component for each query term, whether or not the term is in the document.

For almost all normal query terms (i.e. for any terms that are not actually detrimental to the query), we can assume that $p' > q'$ and $\lambda > \mu$. In this case, formula 12 can be shown to be monotonic decreasing with d, from a maximum as $d \rightarrow 0$, through zero when $d = \Delta$, and to a minimum as $d \rightarrow \infty$. As indicated, there is one such factor for each of the nq query terms.

Once again, we can devise a very much simpler function which approximates to this behaviour, as follows:

$$correction\ factor = k_2 \times nq \frac{(\Delta - d)}{(\Delta + d)}, \tag{13}$$

where k_2 is another unknown constant.

Again, k_2 is not specified by the model, and must (at present, at least) be discovered by trial and error (values in the range 0–2 appear about right for the TREC databases, although performance is not sensitive to this correction[1])—see the results section 7.

5.6 First Component

The first component of equation 11 is:

$$w(\underline{x}, d)_1 = \log \frac{P(\underline{x}|R, d)\ P(\underline{0}|\overline{R}, d)}{P(\underline{x}|\overline{R}, d)\ P(\underline{0}|R, d)}.$$

Expanding this on the basis of term independence assumptions, and also making the assumption that eliteness is independent of document length (on the basis of the Verbosity hypothesis), we can obtain a formula for the weight of a term t which occurs tf times, as follows:

$$\begin{aligned} w(t, d)_1 &= \log \frac{(p'(\lambda d/\Delta)^{tf} e^{-\lambda d/\Delta} + (1-p')(\mu d/\Delta)^{tf} e^{-\mu d/\Delta})\ (q'e^{-\lambda d/\Delta} + (1-q')e^{-\mu d/\Delta})}{(q'(\lambda d/\Delta)^{tf} e^{-\lambda d/\Delta} + (1-q')(\mu d/\Delta)^{tf} e^{-\mu d/\Delta})\ (p'e^{-\lambda d/\Delta} + (1-p')e^{-\mu d/\Delta})} \\ &= \log \frac{(p'\lambda^{tf} e^{-\lambda d/\Delta} + (1-p')\mu^{tf} e^{-\mu d/\Delta})\ (q'e^{-\lambda d/\Delta} + (1-q')e^{-\mu d/\Delta})}{(q'\lambda^{tf} e^{-\lambda d/\Delta} + (1-q')\mu^{tf} e^{-\mu d/\Delta})\ (p'e^{-\lambda d/\Delta} + (1-p')e^{-\mu d/\Delta})}. \end{aligned} \tag{14}$$

Analysis of the behaviour of this function with varying tf and d is a little complex. The simple function used for the experiments (formula 10) exhibits some of the correct properties, but not all. In particular, 14 shows that increasing d exaggerates the S-shape mentioned in section 4.2; formula 10 does not have this property. It seems that there may be further scope for development of a rough model based on the behaviour of formula 14.

---

[1] Values of this constant depend on the base of the logarithms used in the term-weighting functions

5.7 The Scope Hypothesis

As indicated above (section 5.1), an alternative hypothesis concerning document length would regard a long document as a set of unrelated, concatenated short documents. The obvious response to this hypothesis is to attempt to find appropriate boundaries in the documents, and to treat short passages rather than full documents as the retrievable units. There have been a number of experiments on these lines reported in the literature [10].

This approach appears difficult to combine with the ideas discussed above, in a way which would accommodate an explanation of document length in terms of a mixture of the two hypotheses. One possible solution is that used by Salton [11], of allowing passages to compete with full documents for retrieval. But there seems to be room for more theoretical analysis.

5.8 Document Length and Term Frequency—Summary

We have, then, a term weighting function which includes a within-document term frequency component, without (equation 8) or with (equation 10) a document-length component. We also have a document-length correction factor (equation 13) which can be applied to either 8 or 10.

6 Query Term Frequency

The natural symmetry of the retrieval situation as between documents and queries suggests that we could treat within-query term frequency (qtf) in a similar fashion to within-document term frequency. This would suggest, by analogy with equation 8, a weighting function thus:

$$w = \frac{qtf}{(k_3 + qtf)}\, w^{(1)}, \tag{15}$$

where k_3 is another unknown constant.

In this case, experiments (section 7) suggest a large value of k_3 to be effective—indeed the limiting case, which is equivalent to

$$w = qtf \times w^{(1)}, \tag{16}$$

appears to be the most effective. This may perhaps suggest that an S-shaped function like equation 9 could be better still, though again none has been tried in the present experiments.

The experiments are based on combining one of these qtf multipliers with the within-document term frequency and document length functions defined above. However, it should be pointed out that (a) the "natural symmetry" as between documents and queries, to which we appealed above, is open to question, and (b) that even if we accept each model separately, it is not at all obvious that they can be combined (a properly constructed combined model would have fairly complex relations between query and document terms, query and document eliteness, and relevance). Both these matters are discussed further by Robertson [12]. In the meantime, the combination of either qtf multiplier with the earlier functions must be regarded as not having a strong theoretical motivation.

7 Experiments

7.1 TREC

The TREC (Text REtrieval Conference) conferences, of which there have been two, with the third due to start early 1994, are concerned with controlled comparisons of different methods of retrieving documents from large collections of assorted textual material. They are funded by the US Advanced Projects Research Agency (ARPA) and organised by Donna Harman of NIST (National Institute for Standards and Technology). There were about 31 participants, academic and commercial, in the TREC-2 conference which took place at Gaithersburg, MD in September 1993 [2]. Information needs are presented in the form of highly structured "topics" from which queries are to be derived automatically and/or manually by participants. Documents include newspaper articles, entries from the Federal Register, patents and technical abstracts, varying in length from a line or two to several hundred thousand words.

A large number of relevance judgments have been made at NIST by a panel of experts assessing the top-ranked documents retrieved by some of the participants in TREC–1 and TREC–2. The number of known relevant documents for the 150 topics varies between 1 and more than 1000, with a mean of 281.

7.2 Experiments Conducted

Some of the experiments reported here were also reported at TREC–2 [1].

Database and Queries

The experiments reported here involved searches of one of the TREC collections, described as disks 1 & 2 (TREC raw data has been distributed on three CD-ROMs). It contains about 743,000 documents. It was indexed by keyword stems, using a modified Porter stemming procedure [13], spelling normalisation designed to conflate British and American spellings, a moderate stoplist of about 250 words and a small cross-reference table and "go" list. Topics 101–150 of the 150 TREC–1 and –2 topic statements were used. The mean length (number of unstopped tokens) of the queries derived from title and concepts fields only was 30.3; for those using additionally the narrative and description fields the mean length was 81.

Search Procedure

Searches were carried out automatically by means of City University's Okapi text retrieval software. The weighting functions described in Sections 4–6 were implemented as BM15[2] (the model using equation 8 for the document term frequency component) and BM11 (using equation 10). Both functions incorporated the document length correction factor of equation 13. These were compared with BM1 ($w^{(1)}$ weights, approximately ICF, since no relevance information was used in these experiments) and with a simple coordination-level model BM0 in which terms are given equal weights. Note that BM11 and BM15 both reduce to BM1 when k_1 and k_2 are zero. The within-query term frequency component (equation 15) could be used with any of these functions.

To summarize, the following functions were used:

(BM0) $$w = 1$$

(BM1) $$w = \log \frac{N - n + 0.5}{n + 0.5} \times \frac{qtf}{(k_3 + qtf)}$$

(BM15) $$w = \frac{tf}{(k_1 + tf)} \times \log \frac{N - n + 0.5}{n + 0.5} \times \frac{qtf}{(k_3 + qtf)} + k_2 \times nq \frac{(\Delta - d)}{(\Delta + d)}$$

(BM11) $$w = \frac{tf}{(\frac{k_1 \times d}{\Delta} + tf)} \times \log \frac{N - n + 0.5}{n + 0.5} \times \frac{qtf}{(k_3 + qtf)} + k_2 \times nq \frac{(\Delta - d)}{(\Delta + d)}.$$

In the experiments reported below where k_3 is given as ∞, the factor $qtf/(k_3 + qtf)$ is implemented as qtf on its own (equation 16).

Evaluation

In all cases the 1000 top-ranking documents for each topic were run against the supplied relevance assessments using a standard evaluation program from the SMART projects at Cornell University. (This was the official evaluation method used in TREC–2.) The evaluation program outputs a number of standard performance measures for each query, and finally a set of measures averaged over all the queries in the run. The measures used in the tables below are average precision (AveP), precision at 5, 30 and 100 documents (P5 etc.), R-precision (RP) (precision after the number of known relevant documents for a query have been retrieved) and recall (Rcl) (final recall after 1000 documents have been retrieved).

In TREC, a distinction is made between ad-hoc (retrospective) experiments and routing (SDI or filtering). All the results reported here have been obtained using the topics and documents (and methods) used for ad-hoc experiments in TREC–2.

7.3 Results

In these experiments the weighting functions involve three parameters (k_1, k_2 and k_3 above). It was to be expected that their values would interact, so there was a large number of preliminary runs to try to determine the extent of interaction, and to give clues as to the most fruitful ranges of values for further investigation. In should also be noted that k_1 and k_3 are parameters in expressions which are coefficients of a logarithmic value, whereas the document length correction involving k_2 is not a logarithm; hence the value of k_2 depends on the base of the logarithms used.[3]

Table 1 compares two of the new models with baseline $w^{(1)}$ weighting (BM1 with $k_3 = 0$), and with coordination level (BM0). For the shorter queries (title + concepts) BM15 appears somewhat better than BM1 (the difference is greater when a document length correction is added—Table 3). But its performance on the long queries is very poor. BM11 gives a very marked improvement over the baseline, particularly for the long queries.

---

[2] BM = Best Match

[3] To obtain weights within a range suitable for storage as 16-bit integers, the Okapi system uses logarithms to base $2^{0.1}$

Table 1. Comparison of term weighting functions

Function	k_1	k_2	k_3	AveP	P5	P30	P100	RP	Rcl
Query term source: titles + concepts									
BM11	1.0	0.0	0.0	0.300	0.624	0.536	0.440	0.349	0.683
BM15	1.0	0.0	0.0	0.214	0.504	0.435	0.347	0.278	0.568
BM1	0.0	0.0	0.0	0.199	0.468	0.416	0.326	0.261	0.542
BM0	—	—	—	0.142	0.412	0.336	0.270	0.209	0.411
Query term source: titles + concepts + narrative + description									
BM11	1.0	0.0	0.0	0.263	0.612	0.485	0.394	0.306	0.605
BM15	1.0	0.0	0.0	0.074	0.284	0.216	0.154	0.110	0.258
BM1	0.0	0.0	0.0	0.085	0.312	0.235	0.179	0.127	0.297
BM0	—	—	—	0.035	0.220	0.139	0.099	0.066	0.153
Database : TREC disks 1 and 2. Topics: 101–150									

Document Term Frequency

In Table 2 k_1 is varied for BM11 with the other parameters held at zero. As the value of k_1 increases from zero to about 2 performance improves sharply, then deteriorates gradually. Even very small values of k_1 have a marked effect, because the wide variation in document length implies that the term $\frac{k_1 \times d}{\Delta}$ in equation 10 can be quite large even when k_1 is as low as 0.05.

Table 2. Effect of varying the document term frequency parameter k_1

Function	k_1	k_2	k_3	AveP	P5	P30	P100	RP	Rcl
Query term source: titles + concepts									
BM11	0.0	0.0	0.0	0.199	0.468	0.416	0.326	0.261	0.542
BM11	0.2	0.0	0.0	0.263	0.616	0.499	0.404	0.311	0.633
BM11	0.5	0.0	0.0	0.287	0.628	0.525	0.432	0.338	0.664
BM11	1.0	0.0	0.0	0.300	0.624	0.536	0.440	0.349	0.683
BM11	2.0	0.0	0.0	0.303	0.640	0.524	0.443	0.359	0.689
BM11	5.0	0.0	0.0	0.285	0.612	0.506	0.431	0.342	0.666
BM11	10.0	0.0	0.0	0.259	0.540	0.485	0.404	0.324	0.635
BM11	50.0	0.0	0.0	0.179	0.412	0.400	0.317	0.254	0.537
Database : TREC disks 1 and 2. Topics: 101–150									

Document Length Correction

Values greater than 1 had a small detrimental effect in the BM11 model, but small positive values improved the performance of BM15, in which the document term frequency component is not normalised with respect to document length (Table 3).

Table 3. Effect of varying the document length correction parameter k_2

Function	k_1	k_2	k_3	AveP	P5	P30	P100	RP	Rcl
Query term source: titles + concepts									
BM11	1.0	0.0	0.0	0.300	0.624	0.536	0.440	0.349	0.683
BM11	1.0	1.0	0.0	0.300	0.632	0.532	0.438	0.349	0.678
BM11	1.0	2.0	0.0	0.296	0.632	0.523	0.437	0.347	0.671
BM11	1.0	5.0	0.0	0.275	0.624	0.506	0.424	0.335	0.631
BM15	1.0	0.0	0.0	0.214	0.504	0.435	0.347	0.278	0.568
BM15	1.0	1.0	0.0	0.229	0.512	0.453	0.364	0.292	0.598
Database : TREC disks 1 and 2. Topics: 101–150									

Query Term Frequency

Table 4 illustrates the effect of increasing k_3 from zero to infinity. For all functions and for both long and short queries performance improves fairly smoothly with k_3. For BM11 the increase in average precision is 37% on the long queries and 12% on the short. It is to be expected that k_3 would have a greater effect with the long queries, in which there are many "noisy" terms and in which most of the more apposite terms are likely to occur more than once. However, high values of k_3 increase the performance of BM15 by 24% even on the short queries.

Table 4. Effect of varying the query term frequency parameter k_3

Function	k_1	k_2	k_3	AveP	P5	P30	P100	RP	Rcl
Query term source: titles + concepts + narrative + description									
BM11	1.0	0.0	0.0	0.263	0.612	0.485	0.394	0.306	0.605
BM11	1.0	0.0	1.0	0.299	0.648	0.510	0.428	0.341	0.659
BM11	1.0	0.0	3.0	0.331	0.640	0.540	0.456	0.378	0.712
BM11	1.0	0.0	8.0	0.346	0.656	0.549	0.466	0.390	0.737
BM11	1.0	0.0	20.0	0.351	0.644	0.560	0.471	0.395	0.744
BM11	1.0	0.0	100.0	0.353	0.648	0.565	0.473	0.396	0.745
BM11	1.0	0.0	∞	0.360	0.652	0.569	0.479	0.401	0.754
Query term source: titles + concepts									
BM11	1.0	0.0	0.0	0.300	0.624	0.536	0.440	0.349	0.683
BM11	1.0	0.0	∞	0.335	0.636	0.560	0.468	0.375	0.723
BM15	1.0	1.0	0.0	0.229	0.512	0.453	0.364	0.292	0.598
BM15	1.0	1.0	∞	0.284	0.560	0.485	0.416	0.336	0.685
BM1	0.0	0.0	0.0	0.199	0.468	0.416	0.326	0.261	0.542
BM1	0.0	0.0	∞	0.232	0.504	0.435	0.361	0.289	0.601
Database : TREC disks 1 and 2. Topics: 101–150									

7.4 Discussion

On the short queries, and without a query term frequency component, the best version of BM11 gives an increase of about 50% in average precision, with somewhat smaller improvements in the other statistics, over the baseline Robertson/Sparck Jones weighting BM1. On the long queries the proportionate improvement is very much greater still. To put this in perspective, the best results reported here (Table 4, row 8), are similar to the best reported by any of the TREC–2 participants at the time of the conference in September 1993.

Many experimental runs were also carried out on two other sets of 50 topics and on two other databases: TREC disk 3 and a subdatabase of disks 1 and 2 consisting entirely of Wall Street Journal articles. The absolute values of the statistics varied quite widely, but the rank order of treatments was very similar to those shown in the tables here.

Applicability to Other Types of Database

If documents are all the same length, BM15 is the same as BM11. The fact that BM11 was so much better than BM15 must reflect the very large variation in document length in the test collection. BM15 without a document length correction is not very much better than BM1 (Table 1, rows 2 and 3). For this reason, experiments are currently under way searching relatively short, uniform documents. Clearly, statistical characteristics of different databases (e.g. abstracts, controlled and/or free indexing) will vary widely in ways which may substantially affect the performance of the weighting functions discussed here.

Relevance Feedback

No experiments have yet been conducted with any form of relevance feedback. However, all the functions used contain the Robertson/Sparck Jones weight $w^{(1)}$, which includes relevance information if it is available. Therefore in principle all the functions could be used in a relevance feedback situation (with or without query expansion). Clearly there may be interaction between the values of the ks and the use of relevance information, which would have to be investigated.

Effect of the Verbose Topic Statements

The best results reported here (e.g. row 8 of Table 4) rely on the use of BM11 with a query term frequency component from the "long" queries. Without a *qtf* component results from the long queries are not good (Table 1, bottom half). Even the "short" TREC-derived queries are very long compared with the searches entered by end-users of interactive retrieval systems. However, they are not long in comparison with user need statements elicited by human intermediaries. This suggests that it might be possible to make good use, even in an interactive system, of quite long and even rambling query statements, if users can be persuaded to enter them. We might even suggest a voice-recognition system!

Individual Queries

The statistics hide the variation over individual topics. In general, different topics did best with different functions and parameters. In many cases, though, varying a parameter brings about an improvement or deterioration which is almost uniform over the set of topics. Surprisingly, we found no very large difference between the variances of the statistics obtained from different treatments.

8 Conclusions

The approach of this paper has been that a theoretical analysis of the possible effects of a variable, within the framework of the probabilistic theory of information retrieval, can give us useful insights, which can then be embodied in very much simpler formulae. This approach has shown very considerable benefits, enabling the development of effective weighting functions based on the three variables considered (term frequency within documents and queries and document length). These functions are simple extensions of the Robertson/Sparck Jones relevance weight, and therefore fit well with some other work on the development of probabilistic models.

The approach complements a number of other current approaches. In particular, it fits somewhere in between formal modelling and pure empiricism, alongside regression-based methods, to which it seems to offer some ideas.

Acknowledgements

We are very grateful to Michael Keen, Karen Sparck Jones and Peter Willett for acting as advisors to the Okapi at TREC projects. Part of this work was undertaken with the help of grants from the British Library and ARPA.

References

1. Robertson S.E. *et al.* Okapi at TREC-2. In: [2].
2. Harman D.K. (Ed.) *The Second Text REtrieval Conference (TREC-2)*. NIST Gaithersburg MD, to appear.
3. Cooper W.S. *et al.* Probabilistic retrieval in the TIPSTER collection: an application of staged logistic regression. In: Harman D.K. (Ed.) *The First Text REtrieval Conference (TREC-1)*. NIST Gaithersburg MD, 1993. (pp 73–88).
4. Croft W. and Harper D. Using probabilistic models of information retrieval without relevance information. *Journal of Documentation* 1979; 35:285–295.
5. Harter S.P. A probabilistic approach to automatic keyword indexing. *Journal of the American Society for Information Science* 1975; 26:197–206 and 280–289.
6. Robertson S.E., Van Rijsbergen C.J. & Porter M.F. Probabilistic models of indexing and searching. In Oddy R.N. *et al.* (Eds.) *Information Retrieval Research* (pp.35–56). Butterworths London, 1981.
7. Cooper W.S. Inconsistencies and misnomers in probabilistic IR. In: *Proceedings of the 14th Annual International ACM SIGIR Conference on Research and Development in Information Retrieval* (pp.57-62). Chicago, 1991.
8. Robertson S.E. and Sparck Jones K. Relevance weighting of search terms. *Journal of the American Society for Information Science* 1976; 27:129–146.
9. Margulis E.L. Modelling documents with multiple Poisson distributions. *Information Processing and Management* 1993; 29:215–227.
10. Moffat A., Sacks-Davis R., Wilkinson R. & Zobel J. Retrieval of partial documents. In: Harman D.K. (Ed.) *The First Text REtrieval Conference (TREC-1)*. NIST Gaithersburg MD, 1993. (pp 59–72).
11. Buckley C., Salton G. & Allan J. Automatic retrieval with locality information using SMART. In: [2].
12. Robertson S.E. Query-document symmetry and dual models. (Unpublished.)
13. Porter M.F. An algorithm for suffix stripping. *Program* 1980; 14:130–137.

Improving Retrieval Performance by Relevance Feedback

Gerard Salton and Chris Buckley
Department of Computer Science, Cornell University, Ithaca, NY 14853-7501

Relevance feedback is an automatic process, introduced over 20 years ago, designed to produce improved query formulations following an initial retrieval operation. The principal relevance feedback methods described over the years are examined briefly, and evaluation data are included to demonstrate the effectiveness of the various methods. Prescriptions are given for conducting text retrieval operations iteratively using relevance feedback.

Introduction to Relevance Feedback

It is well known that the original query formulation process is not transparent to most information system users. In particular, without detailed knowledge of the collection make-up, and of the retrieval environment, most users find it difficult to formulate information queries that are well designed for retrieval purposes. This suggests that the first retrieval operation should be conducted with a tentative, initial query formulation, and should be treated as a trial run only, designed to retrieve a few useful items from a given collection. These initially retrieved items could then be examined for relevance, and new improved query formulations could be constructed in the hope of retrieving additional useful items during subsequent search operations.

Conventionally, the query formulation, or reformulation process is a manual, or rather an intellectual task. The *relevance feedback* process, introduced in the mid-1960s is a controlled, automatic process for query reformulation, that is easy to use and can prove unusually effective. The main idea consists in choosing important terms, or expressions, attached to certain previously retrieved documents that have been identified as relevant by the users, and of enhancing the importance of these terms in a new query formulation. Analogously, terms included in previously retrieved nonrelevant documents could be deemphasized in any future query formulation. The effect of such a query alteration process is to "move" the query in the direction of the relevant items and away from the nonrelevant ones, in the expectation of retrieving more wanted and fewer nonwanted items in a later search.

The relevance feedback procedure exhibits the following main advantages:

- It shields the user from the details of the query formulation process, and permits the construction of useful search statements without intimate knowledge of collection make-up and search environment.
- It breaks down the search operation into a sequence of small search steps, designed to approach the wanted subject area gradually.
- It provides a controlled query alteration process designed to emphasize some terms and to deemphasize others, as required in particular search environments.

The original relevance feedback process was designed to be used with *vector queries,* that is, query statements consisting of sets of possibly weighted search terms used without Boolean operators (Rocchio, 1966; 1971; Ide, 1971; Ide & Salton, 1971; Salton, 1971). A particular search expression might then be written as

$$Q_o = (q_1, q_2, \ldots, q_t) \quad (1)$$

where q_i represents the weight of term i in query Q_o. The term weights are often restricted to the range from 0 to 1, where 0 represents a term that is absent from the vector, and 1 represents a fully weighted term. A term might be a concept chosen from a controlled vocabulary, or a word or phrase included in a natural language statement of user needs, or a thesaurus entry representing a set of synonymous terms.

Given a query vector of the type shown in (1), the relevance feedback process generates a new vector

$$Q' = (q'_1, q'_2, \ldots, q'_t) \quad (2)$$

where q'_i represents altered term weight assignments for the t index terms. New terms are introduced by assigning a positive weight to terms with an initial weight of 0, and old terms are deleted by reducing to 0 the weight of terms that were initially positive. The feedback process can be represented graphically as a migration of the query vector from one area to another in the t-dimensional space defined by the t terms that are assignable to the information items.

This study was supported in part by the National Science Foundation under grant IST 83-16166 and IRI 87-02735.

Received February 12, 1988; revised April 28, 1988; accepted April 29, 1988.

Initially, the relevance feedback implementations were designed for queries and documents in vector form. More recently, relevance feedback methods have been applied also to Boolean query formulations. In that case, the process generates term conjuncts such as (Term *i and* Term *j*) or (Term *i and* Term *j and* Term *k*) that are derived from previously retrieved relevant documents. These conjuncts are then incorporated in the revised query formulations (Dillon & Desper, 1980; Salton, Voorhees, & Fox, 1984; Fox, 1983; Salton, Fox, & Voorhees, 1985). The application of relevance feedback methods in Boolean query environments is not further discussed in this note.

Many descriptions of the relevance feedback process are found in the literature. With the exception of some special-purpose applications (Vernimb, 1977), the method has, however, never been applied on a large scale in actual operational retrieval environments. Some recent proposals, originating in the computer science community, do suggest that a relevance feedback system should form the basis for the implementation of modern text retrieval operations in parallel processing environments (Stanfill & Kahle, 1986; Waltz, 1987). It is possible that the time for a practical utilization of relevance feedback operations is now finally at hand.

A study of the previously mentioned parallel processing application reveals that the relevance feedback process is easily implemented by using windowing and information display techniques to establish communications between system and users. In particular, ranked lists of retrieved documents can be graphically displayed for the user, and screen pointers can be used to designate certain listed items as relevant to the user's needs. These relevance indications are then further used by the system to construct modified feedback queries. Previous evaluations of feedback procedures have made it clear that some feedback methods are much more effective than others. Indeed, a poorly conceived arbitrary query reformulation can easily produce a deterioration in retrieval effectiveness rather than an improvement (Salton & Buckley, 1988).

The current note is thus designed to specify useful relevance feedback procedures, and to determine the amount of improvement obtainable with one feedback iteration in particular cases.

Basic Feedback Procedures

Vector Processing Methods

In a vector processing environment both the stored information items D and the requests for information Q can be represented as t-dimensional vectors of the form $D = (d_1, d_2, \ldots, d_t)$ and $Q = (q_1, q_2, \ldots, q_t)$. In each case, d_i and q_i represent the weight of term i in D and Q, respectively. A typical query-document similarity measure can then be computed as the inner product between corresponding vectors, that is

$$\mathrm{Sim}(D, Q) = \sum_{i=1}^{t} d_i \cdot q_i \tag{3}$$

It is known that in a retrieval environment that uses inner product computations to assess the similarity between query and document vectors, the best query leading to the retrieval of many relevant items from a collection of documents is of the form (Rocchio, 1966; 1971)

$$Q_{\mathrm{opt}} = \frac{1}{n} \sum_{\substack{\text{relevant}\\ \text{items}}} \frac{D_i}{|D_i|} - \frac{1}{N-n} \sum_{\substack{\text{nonrelevant}\\ \text{items}}} \frac{D_i}{|D_i|} \tag{4}$$

The D_i used in (4) represent document vectors, and $|D_i|$ is the corresponding Euclidian vector length. Further N is the assumed collection size and n the number of relevant documents in the collection.

The formula of expression (4) cannot be used in practice as an initial query formulation, because the set of n relevant documents is of course not known in advance of the search operation. Expression (4) can however help in generating a feedback query after relevance assessments are available for certain items previously retrieved in answer to a search request. In that case, the sum of *all* normalized relevant or nonrelevant documents used in (4) is replaced by the sum of the *known* relevant or nonrelevant items. In addition, experience shows that the original query terms should be preserved in a new feedback formulation. An effective feedback query following the retrieval of n_1 relevant and n_2 nonrelevant items can then be formulated as

$$Q_1 = Q_0 + \frac{1}{n_1} \sum_{\substack{\text{known}\\ \text{relevant}}} \frac{D_i}{|D_i|} - \frac{1}{n_2} \sum_{\substack{\text{known}\\ \text{nonrelevant}}} \frac{D_i}{|D_i|}, \tag{5}$$

where Q_0 and Q_1 represent the initial and first iteration queries, and the summation is now taken over the known relevant and nonrelevant documents. More generally, the following query formulation can be used for suitable values of the multipliers α, β, and γ.

$$Q_{i+1} = \alpha Q_i + \beta \sum_{\text{rel}} \frac{D_i}{|Di|} - \gamma \sum_{\text{nonrel}} \frac{D_i}{|D_i|} \tag{6}$$

In expressions (4) to (6), normalized term weights are used whose values are restricted to the range from 0 to 1. When larger weights greater than 1 can be accommodated, unnormalized weights are also usable.

The relevance feedback operation is illustrated in Figure 1 for the two-dimensional case where vectors carry only two components. The items used in the example are identified by the weighted terms "information" and "retrieval." Assuming that document D_1 is specified as relevant to the initial query Q_0, the feedback formula shown in Figure 1 produces a new query Q' that lies much closer to document D_1 than the original query. An analogous situation exists when document D_2 is identified as relevant and the new query Q'' replaces the original Q_0. Such new queries may be expected to retrieve more useful items similar to the previously identified documents D_1 and D_2, respectively.

The vector modification method outlined earlier is conceptually simple, because the modified term weights are directly obtained from the weights of the corresponding

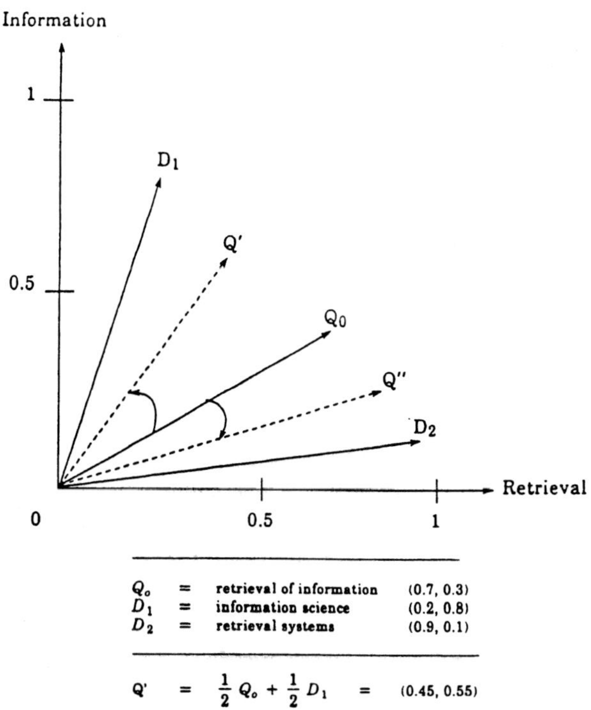

FIG. 1. Relevance feedback illustration.

terms in documents known to be relevant or nonrelevant to the respective queries. When the weight assignments available for initial queries and stored documents accurately reflect the values of the terms for content identification, the standard vector modification process provides a powerful query construction method.

Probabilistic Feedback Methods

An alternative relevance feedback methodology is based on the probabilistic retrieval model (van Rijsbergen, 1979; Harper, 1980; Robertson & Sparck Jones, 1976; Robertson, van Rijsbergen, & Porter, 1981; Yu, Buckley, Lam, & Salton, 1983). In that case an optimal retrieval rule is used to rank the documents in decreasing order according to expression

$$\log \frac{Pr(x \mid \text{rel})}{Pr(x \mid \text{nonrel})} \qquad (7)$$

where $Pr(x \mid \text{rel})$ and $Pr(x \mid \text{nonrel})$ represent the probabilities that a relevant or nonrelevant item, respectively, has vector representation x.

Assuming that the terms are independently assigned to the relevant and to the nonrelevant documents of a collection, and that binary term weights restricted to 0 and 1 are assigned to the documents, a query document similarity value can be derived from (7) between the query and each document $D = (d_1, d_2, \ldots, d_t)$, using two parameters p_i and u_i that represent the probabilities that the ith term has a value 1 in a relevant and nonrelevant document, respectively:

$$\text{sim}(D, Q) = \sum_{i=1}^{t} d_i \log \frac{p_i(1 - u_i)}{u_i(1 - p_i)} + \text{constants}$$

$$p_i = Pr(x_i = 1 \mid \text{relevant})$$

$$u_i = Pr(x_i = 1 \mid \text{nonrelevant}) \qquad (8)$$

The similarity formula of expression (8) cannot be used in practice without knowing the values of p_i and u_i for all document terms. A number of different methods have been suggested to estimate these quantities. For the initial search, when document relevance information is not available, the assumption is often made that the values of p_i are constant for all terms (typically 0.5), and that the term distribution in the nonrelevant items is closely approximated by the distribution in the whole collection (Croft & Harper, 1979). Referring to the term occurrence data of Table 1 specifying the occurrences of a typical term i in the relevant and nonrelevant document subsets, u_i can then be set equal to n_i/N, the proportion of documents in the collection that carry term i. For the initial run, expression (8) is then reduced to

$$\text{initial sim}(D, Q) = \sum_{i=1}^{t} d_i \log \frac{N - n_i}{n_i}. \qquad (9)$$

For the feedback searches, the accumulated statistics relating to the relevance or nonrelevance of previously retrieved items are used to evaluate expression (8). This is done by assuming that the term distribution in the relevant items previously retrieved is the same as the distribution for the complete set of relevant items, and that all nonretrieved items can be treated as nonrelevant. Applying the statistics of Table 1 to the retrieved portion of the collection, one finds that

$$p_i = \frac{r_i}{R} \quad \text{and} \quad u_i = \frac{n_i - r_i}{N - R}.$$

When these expressions are substituted in (8), one obtains the new form

feedback $\text{sim}(D, Q) =$

$$\sum_{i=1}^{t} d_i \log\left(\frac{r_i}{R - r_i} \div \frac{n_i - r_i}{N - R - n_i + r_i}\right) \qquad (10)$$

where R now represents the total number of relevant retrieved items, r_i is the total number of relevant retrieved

TABLE 1. Occurrences of term i in a collection of N documents.

	Relevant Items	Nonrelevant Items	All Items
$d_i = 1$	r_i	$n_i - r_i$	n_i
$d_i = 0$	$R - r_i$	$N - R - n_i + r_i$	$N - n_i$
All items	R	$N - R$	N

that include terms i, and n_i is the total number of retrieved items with term i.

Formula (10) poses problems for certain small values of R and r_i that frequently arise in practice—for example, $R = 1$, $r_i = 0$—because the logarithmic expression is then reduced to 0. For this reason, a 0.5 adjustment factor is often added in defining p_i and u_i, and the following formulas are used in the conventional probabilistic system to obtain p_i and u_i.

$$p_i = \frac{r_i + 0.5}{R + 1} \quad \text{and} \quad u_i = \frac{n_i - r_i + 0.5}{N - R + 1}. \tag{11}$$

The conventional probabilistic system has been criticized for a variety of reasons. For example, the 0.5 adjustment factor may provide unsatisfactory estimates in some cases, and alternative adjustments have been proposed to compute p_i and u_i, such that n_i/N or $(n_i - r_i)/(N - R)$ (Yu, Buckley, Lam, & Salton, 1983; Robertson, 1986; Wu & Salton, 1981). When no relevant items are initially retrieved (that is, $R = 0$), the best estimate for p_i, the probability that a term occurs in a relevant document, is simply its probability of occurrence in the complete collection. In that case, $p_i = n_i/N$. The test results for the adjusted probabilistic derivation presented later in this study correspond to the following estimates for p_i and u_i:

$$p_i' = Pr(x_i = 1 \mid \text{rel}) = \frac{r_i + n_i/N}{R + 1}$$

$$u_i' = Pr(x_i = 1 \mid \text{nonrel}) = \frac{n_i - r_i + n_i/N}{N - R + 1} \tag{12}$$

In expression (12), the adjustment factor is n_i/N instead of 0.5 as before. An alternative adjustment factor of $(n_i - r_i)/(N - R)$ is valid when the number of relevant documents not yet retrieved is assumed to be small. In practice, the output obtained with that factor differs only marginally from that obtainable with expression (12).

An additional ad hoc adjustment, similar to the one previously used to transform expression (4) into (5), may be made in (12) by enhancing the importance of document terms that also occur in the queries. This is achieved by assuming that a term occurrence in a query is equivalent to a term occurrence in 3 relevant documents (that is, for query terms $r_i' = r_i + 3$, $R' = R + 3$).

The advantage of all probabilistic feedback models compared with the conventional vector modification methods, is that the feedback process is directly related to the derivation of a weight for query terms. Indeed, the document similarity function of expression (8) increases by a weighting factor of $\log[p_i(1 - u_i)/u_i(1 - p_i)]$ for each query term i that matches a document, and this term weight is optimal under the assumed conditions of term independence and binary document indexing.

On the other hand, a good deal of apparently useful information is disregarded in the probabilistic environment in determining the form of the feedback query, including, for example, the weight of the terms assigned to the documents, and the weight of terms in the original query formulation. Furthermore, the set of relevant retrieved items is not used directly for query adjustment in the probabilistic environment, as it is in the vector model. Instead the term distribution in the relevant retrieved items is used indirectly to determine a probabilistic term weight. These indirections may account for the fact that the probabilistic relevance feedback methods do not in general operate as effectively as the conventional vector modification methods.

Relevance Feedback Evaluation

The relevance feedback methods are evaluated by using six document collections in various subject areas for experimental purposes. The collections ranging from a small biomedical collection (MED) consisting of 1033 documents and 30 queries to a large computer engineering collection (INSPEC) of 12684 documents and 84 queries are characterized in Table 2. In all cases the query vectors carry fewer terms than the corresponding document vectors.

A high-quality *initial* search was used for experimental purposes in all cases, consisting of the vector match of query and document vectors (expression (3)) using weighted query and document vectors. The term weights used for both documents and queries in the initial search were computed as the product of the term frequency multiplied by an inverse collection frequency factor, defined as

$$w_i = \frac{\left(0.5 + 0.5\dfrac{tf_i}{\max tf}\right) \cdot \log \dfrac{N}{n_i}}{\sqrt{\left(0.5 + 0.5\dfrac{tf_i}{\max tf}\right)^2 \left(\log \dfrac{N}{n_i}\right)^2}} \tag{14}$$

where tf_i is the occurrence frequency of term i in the document (or in the query), and N and n_i are defined in Table 1. The foregoing weight assignment produces term weights varying between 0 and 1. It is known that a high order of performance is obtained with the weight assignment of expression (14) (Salton & Buckley, 1988).

For the experiments, the assumption is made that the top 15 items retrieved in the initial search are judged for relevance, and the information contained in these relevant and nonrelevant retrieved items is then used to construct the feedback query.

To evaluate the effectiveness of the relevance feedback process, it is necessary to compare the performance of the first iteration feedback search with the results of the initial search performed with the original query statements. Normally, recall (R) and precision (P) measures are used to reflect retrieval effectiveness, where recall is defined as the proportion of relevant items that are retrieved from the collection, and precision is the proportion of retrieved items that are relevant. In evaluating a relevance feedback process, the evaluation is complicated by the fact that an artificial ranking effect must be distinguished from the true feedback effect. Indeed, any originally retrieved relevant item that is used for feedback purposes will necessarily be retrieved again in the first iteration feedback search, normally with a much improved retrieval rank. This occurs because the feedback query has been constructed so as to

TABLE 2. Collection statistics (including average vector length and standard deviation of vector lengths).

Collection	Number of Vectors (Documents or Queries)	Average Vector Length (Number of Terms)	Standard Deviation of Vector Length	Average Frequency of Terms in Vectors	Percentage of Terms in Vectors with frequency 1
CACM					
documents	3204	24.52	21.21	1.35	80.93
queries	64	10.80	6.43	1.15	88.68
CISI					
documents	1460	46.55	19.38	1.37	80.27
queries	112	28.29	9.49	1.38	78.36
CRAN					
documents	1398	53.13	22.53	1.58	69.50
queries	225	9.17	3.19	1.04	95.69
INSPEC					
documents	12684	32.50	14.27	1.78	61.06
queries	84	15.63	8.66	1.24	83.78
MED					
documents	1033	51.60	22.78	1.54	72.70
queries	30	10.10	6.03	1.12	90.76
NPL					
documents	11429	19.96	10.84	1.21	84.03
queries	100	7.16	2.36	1.00	100.00

resemble the previously obtained relevant items. When an item originally retrieved with a retrieval rank of 7 or 8 is again obtained with a rank of 1 or 2 in the feedback search, the resulting improvement in recall and precision is not a true reflection of user satisfaction, because a relevant item brought to the user's attention for a second time is of no interest to the user. Instead, the relevance feedback operation must be judged by the ability to retrieve *new* relevant items, not originally seen by the user.

Various solutions offer themselves for measuring the true advantage provided by the relevance feedback process (Chang, Cirillo, & Razon, 1971). One possibility is the so-called *residual collection* system where all items previously seen by the user (whether relevant or not) are simply removed from the collection, and both the initial and any subsequent searches are evaluated using the reduced collection only. This depresses the absolute performance level in terms of recall and precision, but maintains a correct relative difference between initial and feedback runs. The residual collection evaluation is used to evaluate the relevance feedback searches examined in this study.

Twelve different relevance feedback methods are used for evaluation purposes with the six sample collections, including six typical vector modification methods, and six probabilistic feedback runs. Six of these feedback methods are characterized in Table 3. In the first two vector modification methods, termed "Ide dec-hi" and "Ide regular" in Table 3, the terms found in previously retrieved relevant (or nonrelevant) documents are added to (or subtracted from) the original query vectors without normalization to obtain the new query statements (Ide, 1971; Ide & Salton, 1971). In the "dec-hi" system, all identified relevant items but only one retrieved nonrelevant item (the one retrieved earliest in a search) are used for query modification. The single nonrelevant item provides a definite point in the vector space from which the new feedback query is removed. The "ide regular" method is identical except that additional previously retrieved nonrelevant documents are also used in the feedback process.

The vector adjustment methods termed "Rocchio" in Table 3 uses reduced document weights to modify the queries as shown earlier in expression (6) (Rocchio, 1966; 1971). Several different values are used experimentally for the β and γ parameters of equation (6) to assign greater or lesser values to the relevant items compared with the nonrelevant, including $\beta = 1, \gamma = 0, \beta = 0.75, \gamma = 0.25$; and $\beta = \gamma = 0.5$. Other possible parameter values are suggested in Yu, Luk, and Cheung (1976).

Three probabilistic feedback systems are also included in Table 3, including the conventional probabilistic approach with the 0.5 adjustment factor, the adjusted probabilistic derivation with adjustments of n_i/N, and finally the adjusted derivation with enhanced query term weights.

A total of 72 different relevance feedback runs were made using the 12 chosen feedback methods. All the feedback methods produce weighted query terms. However, the weights of the terms attached to the documents are not specified by the feedback process. The document vectors may thus be weighted, using a weighting system such as that of expression (14); alternatively, the document vectors used

TABLE 3. Description of some relevance feedback methods.

Method	Description
Vector adjustment (Ide dec-hi)	Add document term weights directly to query terms; use all relevant retrieved for feedback purposes, but only the top-most nonrelevant items $$Q_{new} = Q_{old} + \sum_{\text{all relevant}} D_i - \sum_{\text{one nonrelevant}} D_i$$
Vector adjustment (Ide regular)	Add actual document term weights to query terms; use all previously retrieved relevant and nonrelevant for feedback: $$Q_{new} = Q_{old} + \sum_{\text{all relevant}} D_i - \sum_{\text{all nonrelevant}} D_i$$
Vector adjustment (Standard Rocchio)	Add reduced term weights to query following division of term weights by number of documents used for retrieval; choose values of β, γ in range 0 to 1 so that $\beta + \gamma = 1.0$ $$Q_{new} = Q_{old} + \beta \sum_{n_1 \text{ rel docs}} \frac{D_i}{n_1} - \gamma \sum_{n_2 \text{ nonrelevant docs}} \frac{D_i}{n_2}$$
Probabilistic conventional	$$Q_{new} = \log[p_i(1 - u_i)/u_i(1 - p_i)]$$ $$p_i = P(x_i \mid \text{rel}) = \frac{r_i + 0.5}{R + 1.0}$$ $$u_i = P(x_i \mid \text{nonrel}) = \frac{n_i - r_i + 0.5}{N - R + 1.0}$$
Probabilistic adjusted derivation	$$Q_{new} = \log[p_i'(1 - u_i')/u_i'(1 - p_i')]$$ $$p_i' = P(x_i \mid \text{rel}) = \frac{r_i + n_i/N}{R + 1}$$ $$u_i' = P(x_i \mid \text{nonrel}) = \frac{n_i - r_i + n_i/N}{N - R + 1}$$
Probabilistic adjusted derivation revised	Same as adjusted derivation, but for query terms use r_i' and R' instead of r_i and R, where $r_i' = r_i + 3$, $R' = R + 3$

in the feedback searches may carry binary weights, where terms that are present receive a weight of 1 and terms that are absent from a vector are assigned a weight of 0.

In addition to using weighted as well as binary document terms in the experiments, a number of *query expansion* methods can be applied in the feedback operations. The first possibility consists in not using any query expansion at all, and preserving only the original query terms appropriately reweighted for feedback purposes. Alternatively, a full query expansion can be used where all terms contained in the relevant previously retrieved items are added to formulate the new feedback query, as suggested in the previously given feedback equations. Finally, several partial query expansion methods can be used, where only some of the terms present in the previously identified relevant items are incorporated into the query. The partial query expansions are designed to produce superior query formulations at much reduced storage cost by restricting the query length to the average length of the relevant retrieved documents. In the expansion system presented in this study, the *most common* terms chosen for addition to the original query are those with the highest occurrence frequencies in the previously retrieved relevant items. Alternatively, the *highest weighted* terms—those with the highest feedback weight—have been used for query expansion.

Three measures are computed for evaluation purposes, including the *rank order* of each particular feedback method out of the 72 different feedback procedures tried experimentally. A rank order of 1 designates the best method exhibiting the highest recall-precision value, and a rank of 72 designates the worst process. In addition, a search precision figure is computed representing the average precision at three particular recall points of 0.75, 0.50, and 0.25 (representing high recall, medium recall, and low recall points, respectively). Finally the percentage improvement in the three-point precision feedback and original searches is also shown. Typical evaluation output for five of the six collections is shown in Table 4 for the runs using weighted document and query terms, and in Table 5 for runs with binary document terms.

With some minor exceptions, the results of Tables 4 and 5 are homogeneous for the five collections, in the sense that the best results are produced by the same relevance feedback systems for all collections, and the same holds also for the poorest results. These results differ, however, from those described later for the sixth collection (the NPL collection). The following main performance results are evident:

- A comparison of the results of Tables 4 and 5 for weighted and unweighted document vectors, respectively, shows that the weighted terms produce much better results in a feedback environment. This confirms results produced by earlier term weighting studies (Salton & Buckley, 1988).
- The paired comparisons included in Table 4 between full query expansion (where all terms from the previously retrieved relevant documents are incorporated in the feedback query) and restricted expansion by the most common terms from the relevant items, shows that full expansion is often preferable. However, the performance difference is modest, so that the expansion by most common terms should be used when storage requirements and processing times needed for fully expanded queries appear excessive. Other possible expansion systems (no expansion, or expansion by highest weighted terms) are inferior.
- The best overall relevance feedback method is the "Ide dec hi" method, where terms are directly added to the queries and only one nonrelevant item is used in the process. Because the vector processing model furnishes ranked retrieval output in decreasing order of the query-document similarity, it is convenient to choose the first (topmost) nonrelevant item that is retrieved for feedback purposes. The "dec hi" method is computationally very efficient.
- Other effective vector modification methods are the regular Ide process where additional nonrelevant items are used, and the Rocchio modification using normal-

TABLE 4. Evaluation of typical relevance feedback methods for five collections (weighted documents, weighted queries).

Relevance Feedback Method	Rank of Method and Avg Precision	CACM 3204 docs 64 queries	CISI 1460 docs 112 docs	CRAN 1397 docs 225 queries	INSPEC 12684 docs 84 queries	MED 1033 docs 30 queries	Average
Initial Run (reduced collection)		.1459	.1184	.1156	.1368	.3346	
Ide (dec hi)							
expand by	Rank	1	2	6	1	1	2.2
all terms	Precision	.2704	.1742	.3011	.2140	.6305	
	Improvement	+86%	+47%	160%	+56%	+88%	+87%
expand by	Rank	4	1	13	2	3	4.6
most common	Precision	.2479	.1924	.2498	.1976	.6218	
terms	Improvement	+70%	+63%	+116%	+44%	+86%	+76%
Ide (regular)							
expand by	Rank	7	18	15	4	2	9.2
all terms	Precision	.2241	.1550	.2508	.1936	.6228	
	Improvement	+66%	+31%	+117%	+42%	+86%	+68%
expand by	Rank	17	5	17	17	4	12
most common	Precision	.2179	.1704	.2217	.1808	.5980	
terms	Improvement	+49%	+44%	+92%	+32%	+79%	+59%
Rocchio (standard $\beta = .75$, $\alpha = .25$							
expand by	Rank	2	39	8	14	17	16
all terms	Precision	.2552	.1404	.2955	.1821	.5630	
	Improvement	+75%	+19%	+156%	+33%	+68%	+70%
expand by	Rank	3	12	12	10	24	12.2
most common	Precision	.2491	.1623	.2534	.1861	.5279	
terms	Improvement	+71%	+37%	+119%	+36%	+55%	+64%
Probabilistic (adjusted revised derivation)							
expand by	Rank	11	36	3	32	5	17.4
all terms	Precision	.2289	.1436	.3108	.1621	.5972	
	Improvement	+57%	+21%	+169%	+19%	+78%	+69%
expand by	Rank	14	10	18	9	14	13
most common	Precision	.2224	.1634	.2120	.1876	.5643	
terms	Improvement	+52%	+38%	+83%	+37%	+69%	+56%
Conventional Probabilistic							
expand by	Rank	18	56	1	55	13	28.6
all terms	Precision	.2165	.1272	.3117	.1343	.5681	
	Improvement	+48%	+7%	+170%	−2%	+70%	+59%
expand by	Rank	12	4	11	19	8	10.8
most common	Precision	.2232	.1715	.2538	.1782	.5863	
terms	Improvement	+53%	+45%	+120%	+30%	+75%	+65%

ized term weight adjustments. Relatively more weight should be given to terms obtained from the relevant items than to those extracted from the nonrelevant ($\beta = 0.75$, $\gamma = 0.25$). Other choices of the parameters, e.g., $\beta = \gamma = 0.5$, and $\beta = 1$, $\gamma = 0$) produce less desirable results.

The probabilistic feedback system is in general not as effective as the vector modification method. It should be noted that the probabilistic feedback processes tested here are directly comparable to the vector feedback methods. For the tests of Table 4, the same weighted document collections were used in both cases. Justification was previously offered by Croft and Harper (1979) for using probabilistic retrieval methods with weighted document collections. Of the probabilistic methods implemented here, the adjusted derivation with extra weight assignments for query terms was only somewhat less effective than the better vector processing methods. However, the probabilistic methods are, in any case, computationally more demanding than the vector processing methods.

The results of Tables 4 and 5 demonstrate that relevance feedback represents a powerful process for improving the output of retrieval system operations. The average improvement in the three-point precision obtained for a single search iteration is nearly 90% for the five test collections. Furthermore additional improvements of up to 100% may

TABLE 5. Relevance feedback evaluation for five collections (binary documents).

Relevance Feedback Method	Rank of Method and Avg Precision	CACM 3204 docs 64 queries	CISI 1460 docs 112 docs	CRAN 1397 docs 225 queries	INSPEC 12684 docs 84 queries	MED 1033 docs 30 queries	Average Five Collections
Initial Run (reduced collection)		.1459	.1184	.1156	.1368	.3346	
Ide (dec hi)							
expand by	Rank	24	8	28	5	23	17.6
most common	Precision	.1901	.1653	.1878	.1905	.5317	
terms	Improvement	+30%	+40%	+62%	+39%	+59%	+46%
Ide (regular)							
expand by	Rank	32	30	36	22	28	29.6
most common	Precision	.1812	.1445	.1751	.1734	.5061	
terms	Improvement	+25%	+22%	+51%	+27%	+51%	+35%
Rocchio (standard $\beta = .75$, $\gamma = .25$)							
expand by	Rank	31	49	35	45	56	43.2
most common	Precision	.1843	.1311	.1752	.1526	.4033	
terms	Improvement	+26%	+11%	+52%	+12%	+21%	+24%
Probabilistic (adjusted revised derivation)							
expand by	Rank	43	52	33	35	38	40.2
most common	Precision	.1669	.1305	.1777	.1616	.4766	
terms	Improvement	+14%	+10%	+54%	+18%	+42%	+28%
Conventional Probabilistic							
expand by	Rank	33	28	24	23	29	27.4
most common	Precision	.1800	.1484	.2042	.1732	.4962	
terms	Improvement	+23%	+25%	+77%	+27%	+48%	+40%

be obtainable when additional feedback searches are carried out (Salton et al., 1985).

The actual amount of improvement produced by one iteration of the feedback process varies widely, ranging from 47% for the CISI collection to 160 percent for the CRAN collection for the "Ide dec hi" system. The following factors may be of principal importance in determining the improvement obtained from the feedback process in particular collection environments:

- The average length of the original queries is of main interest. Because the feedback process involves the addition to the queries of new terms extracted from previously retrieved relevant documents, collections with short (often incomplete) queries tend to gain more from the feedback procedure than collections using longer, more varied initial query statements. The statistics of Table 2 show that the query length is directly correlated with relevance feedback performance (for the CRAN collection with an average query length of 9.2 an improvememt of over 150% is obtainable, but the gain is limited to about 50% for CISI with an average query length of 28.3 terms).
- Collections that perform relatively poorly in an initial retrieval operation can be improved more significantly in a feedback search than collections that produce satisfactory output in the initial search. For example, the MED collection with an initial average precision performance of 0.3346 has less potential for improvement than collections with an initial performance of 0.15 or less.
- Technical collections used with precisely formulated queries may be better adapted to the feedback process, than more general collections used with more discursive queries. In the former case, the set of relevant documents for any query may be concentrated in a small area of the document space, making it easier to construct high-performance queries in a feedback operation.

The relevance feedback results for the NPL collection shown in Table 6 do not follow the complete pattern established for the other collections. While the relative performance order for the feedback methodologies and the query expansion systems remains generally unchanged, the NPL results obtained for binary document vectors are in each case superior to those for the corresponding weighted term assignments. It was noted in earlier studies that the characteristics of the NPL collection differ substantially from those of the other collections (Salton & Buckley, 1988). The data of Table 2 show that both the document and the query vectors are much shorter for NPL than for the other collections, and the variation in query length (standard deviation of 2.36 for a mean number of 7.16 query terms) is very small. Furthermore, the term frequencies are especially low for the NPL collection: each query term appears precisely once in a query, and the average frequency of

TABLE 6. Relevance feedback evaluation for NPL collection (11429 documents, 100 queries),

Processing Method	Binary Documents Weighted Queries			Weighted Documents Weighted Queries		
	Rank	Precision	Improvement	Rank	Precision	Improvement
Initial run (reduced collection)					.1056	
Ide (dec hi)						
expanded by all terms	1	.2193	+108%	35	.1540	+46%
expanded by most common terms	3	.2126	+101%	40	.1334	+26%
Rocchio method						
$\beta = 0.75, \gamma = 0.25$ expansion by all terms	8	.1985	+88%	30	.1618	+53%
$\beta = 0.75, \gamma = 0.25$ expansion by most common terms	6	.2037	+93%	42	.1287	+22%
Probabilistic adjusted revised derivation						
expanded by all terms	21	.1879	+78%	33	.1547	+46%
expanded by most common terms	10	.1984	+84%	53	.1174	+11%
Probabilistic conventional derivation						
expanded by all terms	37	.1417	+34%	49	.1259	+19%
expanded by most common terms	18	.1916	+81%	43	.1285	+22%

the terms in the documents is only 1.21. In these circumstances, the term frequency weighting and length normalization operations cannot perform their intended function and binary term assignments are preferred. One may conjecture that the NPL index terms are carefully chosen, and may in fact represent specially controlled terms rather than freely chosen natural language entries. Because of the short queries, a substantial performance improvement of over 100% is, however, noted for the NPL collection, confirming the earlier results obtained for other collections with short query formulations.

In conclusion, the relevance feedback process provides an inexpensive method for reformulating queries based on previously retrieved relevant and nonrelevant documents. A simple vector modification process that adds new query terms and modifies the weight of existing terms appears most useful in this connection. Weighted document vectors should be used except when the occurrence characteristics of all terms are uniform as in NPL. The probabilistic feedback methods that disregard the original query term weights are not completely competitive with the simpler vector modification methods. Improvements from 50 to 150% in the three-point precision are attainable in the first feedback iteration. In view of the simplicity of the query modification operation, the relevance feedback process should be incorporated into operational text retrieval environments.

References

Chang, Y. K., Cirillo, C., & Razon, J. (1971). Evaluation of feedback retrieval using modified freezing, residual collection, and test and control groups. In G. Salton, ed., *The smart retrieval system—experiments in automatic document processing*, (355–370) Englewood Cliffs, NJ: Prentice Hall Inc.

Croft, W. B., & Harper, D. J. (1979). Using probabilistic models of document retrieval without relevance. *Journal of Documentation, 35*, 285–295.

Dillon, M., & Desper, J. (1980). Automatic relevance feedback in Boolean retrieval systems. *Journal of Documentation, 36*, 197–208.

Fox, E. A. (1983). Extending the Boolean and vector space models of information retrieval with *P*-norm queries and multiple concept types, Doctoral Dissertation, Cornell University, Department of Computer Science.

Harper, D. J. (1980). Relevance feedback in document retrieval systems, Doctoral Dissertation, University of Cambridge, England, 1980.

Ide, E. (1971). New experiments in relevance feedback. In *The Smart system—experiments in automatic document processing*, 337–354. Englewood Cliffs, NJ: Prentice Hall Inc.

Ide, E., & Salton, G. (1971). Interactive search strategies and dynamic file organization in information retrieval. In *The Smart system—experiments in automatic document processing*, 373–393. Englewood Cliffs, NJ: Prentice Hall, Inc.

Robertson, S. E. (1986). On relevance weight estimation and query expansion. *Journal of Documentation, 42*, 182–188.

Robertson, S. E., & Sparck Jones, K. (1976). Relevance weighting of search terms. *Journal of the American Society for Information Science, 27*, 129–146.

Robertson, S. E., van Rijsbergen, C. J., & Porter, M. F. (1981). Probabilistic models of indexing and searching. In R. N. Oddy, S. E. Robertson, C. J. van Rijsbergen, and P. W. Williams, (Eds.), *Information retrieval research*, (35–56) London: Butterworths.

Rocchio, J. J. Jr. (1966). Document retrieval systems—optimization and evaluation, Doctoral Dissertation, Harvard University. In *Report ISR-10, to the National Science Foundation*, Harvard Computational Laboratory, Cambridge, MA.

Rocchio, J. J. Jr. (1971). Relevance feedback in information retrieval. In *The Smart system—experiments in automatic document processing*, 313–323. Englewood Cliffs, NJ: Prentice Hall Inc.

Salton, G. (1971). Relevance feedback and the optimization of retrieval effectiveness. In *The Smart system—experiments in automatic document processing*, 324–336. Englewood Cliffs, NJ: Prentice-Hall Inc.

Salton, G., & Buckley, C. (1988). Parallel text search methods. *Communications of the ACM, 31*, 202–215; also Technical Report 87-828, Department of Computer Science, Cornell University, Ithaca, NY, April 1987.

Salton, G. & Buckley, C. (1988). Term weighting approaches in automatic text retrieval, *Information Processing and Management, 24,* 513–523; also Technical Report 87–881, Department of Computer Science, Cornell University.

Salton, G., Fox, E. A., & Voorhees, E. (1985). Advanced feedback methods in information retrieval. *Journal of the American Society for Information Science, 36,* 200–210.

Salton, G., Voorhees, & Fox, E. A. (1984). A comparison of two methods for Boolean query relevance feedback, *Information Processing and Management, 20,* 637–651.

Stanfill, C., & Kahle, B. (1986). Parallel free-text search on the connection machine. *Communications of the ACM, 29,* 1229–1239.

van Rijsbergen, C. J. (1979). *Information retrieval* (2nd ed.). London: Butterworths.

Vernimb, C. (1977). Automatic query adjustment in document retrieval. *Information Processing and Management, 13,* 339–353.

Waltz, D. L. (1987). Applications of the connection machine, *Computer, 20,* 85–97.

Wu, H., & Salton, G. (1981). The estimation of term relevance weights using relevance feedback, *Journal of Documentation, 37,* 194–214.

Yu, C. T., Buckley, C., Lam, K., & Salton, G. (1983). A generalized term dependence model in information retrieval. *Information Technology: Research and Development, 2,* 129–154.

Yu, C. T., Luk, W. S., & Cheung, T. Y. (1976). A statistical model for relevance feedback in information retrieval. *Journal of the ACM, 23,* 273–286.

Using Interdocument Similarity Information in Document Retrieval Systems

Alan Griffiths, H. Claire Luckhurst, and Peter Willett*
Department of Information Studies, University of Sheffield, Western Bank, Sheffield S10 2TN, United Kingdom

The first part of this paper reports a comparative study of the document classifications produced by the use of the single linkage, complete linkage, group average, and Ward clustering methods. Studies of cluster membership and of the effectiveness of cluster searches support previous findings that suggest that the single linkage classifications are rather different from those produced by the other three methods. These latter methods all produce large numbers of small clusters containing just pairs of documents. This finding motivates the work reported in the second part of the paper, which considers the use of clusters consisting of a document together with that document with which it is most similar. A comparison of the use of such clusters with conventional best match searches using seven document test collections suggests that the two types of search are of comparable effectiveness, but they retrieve noticeably different sets of relevant documents.

Introduction

A central problem in document retrieval is the identification of a few relevant documents that can form the basis for a relevance feedback search using probabilistic retrieval methods [1,2]. The simplest means of identifying such documents is to carry out a full search in which some matching function is used to determine the degree of similarity between each of the documents and the query. The calculated match values may then be used to identify the most similar documents, and thus those that are most likely to be relevant to the query [3]. A rather more sophisticated approach attempts to use approximate probabilistic models that do not involve the use of exact relevance information [4]. A third approach, and the one discussed in this paper, involves the use of clusters, or groups, of documents in which a query is matched against the clusters, rather than against individual documents [5–9]. Such a retrieval strategy may be more effective than a conventional search since the relationships between documents are taken into account when deciding which documents are to be retrieved, as well as the relationship between the query and the individual documents.

A wide range of clustering methods has been suggested for the grouping of documents in bibliographic retrieval systems [10]. Of these, the most effective would seem to be methods that are based on a similarity matrix that contains the similarities between all pairs of documents in a collection. Typical of such procedures are the hierarchic clustering methods that operate by means of a series of agglomerations in which the most similar pair of documents or clusters is fused together to form a new cluster. For a collection of N documents, $N - 1$ fusions take place to result in a hierarchic classification in which small clusters of closely related documents are nested within larger and larger clusters of less related documents. A recent study has investigated four such hierarchic agglomerative clustering methods for automatic document classification [8,9]. Experiments were carried out to study the structures of the hierarchies produced by the different methods, the extent to which the methods distort the input similarity matrix during the generation of the classifications, and the retrieval effectiveness obtainable from searches of the clusters. The results suggested that the single linkage method, which has been used extensively in previous work on document clustering [5–7] and which has a well-developed theoretical basis, was not necessarily the most effective procedure of those tested.

This paper starts by continuing the comparison of these four hierarchic clustering methods. The results of the experiments suggest a simple but effective approach to non-hierarchic document clustering that is described in the second part of the report.

*To whom correspondence should be addressed.

Received May 28, 1985; revised June 17, 1985; accepted July 10, 1985

Data Sets and Evaluation Measures

Document Test Collections

The experiments used seven collections of documents, queries, and relevance judgements to ensure that the results were not unduly influenced by the characteristics of a particular data set. The collections were as follows.

(1) Keen. A set of 800 document titles, augmented by manually assigned indexing terms, and 63 queries on the subject of librarianship and information science.

(2) Cranfield. A set of 1400 documents and 225 queries on the subject of aerodynamics. These are characterized by lists of manually assigned index terms, whereas all of the following sets of documents and queries have been automatically indexed from natural language query statements and abstracts and/or titles.

(3) Evans. A set of 2542 document titles and 39 queries from the INSPEC data base that was used in an evaluation of search strategy variations in SDI profiles [11].

(4) Harding. A set of 2472 documents and 65 queries from the INSPEC data base that was used in an evaluation of automatic indexing techniques [12]. The documents used are a subset of those in the Evans collection, but with the titles augmented by abstracts to provide more exhaustive document characterizations and with a larger set of queries.

(5) LISA. A set of 6004 document titles and abstracts, the 1982 input to the Library and Information Science Abstracts data base, together with 35 queries. These were obtained from students and staff in this department, and the relevance judgements were obtained from manual searches of the printed version of the data base, supplemented in some cases by online or exhaustive manual searches [13].

(6) INSPEC. A set of 12,684 document titles and abstracts from the INSPEC data base, together with 77 queries collected at Cornell and Syracuse universities.

(7) UKCIS. A set of 27,361 document titles from the Chemical Abstracts Service data base, together with 182 queries collected by the United Kingdom Chemical Information Service in the early 1970s. This data set has been used extensively in previous document retrieval research but suffers from a lack of exhaustive relevance judgements.

In each case, the words in the document and query representatives were stemmed using a suffix-stripping algorithm after the elimination of common words on a stopword list. Duplicate stems were then eliminated, and the documents and queries were represented for search by lists of binary stem numbers.

The frequency characteristics of these collections are detailed in Table 1 where it will be seen that they span a wide range of types and data. Thus, there are long document descriptions with long (Harding) and short (Cranfield) queries as well as short documents with long (Evans) and short (UKCIS) queries. Moreover there are both broad queries (INSPEC and UKCIS) and sets of very specific queries with few relevant documents (Cranfield and LISA).

As well as detailing the frequency characteristics of each of the collections, Table 1 also contains *overlap* figures. These are derived from the cluster hypothesis test of van Rijsbergen and Sparck Jones [14], which states that similar documents tend to be relevant to the same requests. This hypothesis is both intuitively reasonable and easily tested for a document test collection by calculating all of the relevant-relevant (RR) and relevant-nonrelevant (RNR) interdocument similarity coefficients for some query: if the hypothesis is correct, it is to be expected that the RR coefficients will tend to be larger than the RNR coefficients. The results may be illustrated graphically by calculating the sets of RR and RNR coefficients for all of the queries in a collection and then plotting them as a pair of frequency distributions. The figures in Table 1 are the fractions of the two distributions that overlap each other; an example of such a plot, for the Cranfield data, is shown in Fig. 1, with the overlap area shaded. A collection with a low overlap value, such as Cranfield, will be one in which the relevant documents for the set of queries cluster strongly together and are well separated from the great bulk of nonrelevant material. Such collections are likely to be well suited to search strategies that are based upon the retrieval of clusters of documents, whereas collections with high overlap values, such as UKCIS or Evans, would seem to be inherently less well suited to such strategies.

Evaluation of Retrieval Effectiveness

The cosine coefficient [3] was used to determine the degree of similarity between a query and each of the clus-

TABLE 1. Characteristics of the document test collections.

	Keen	Cranfield	Evans	Harding	LISA	INSPEC	UKCIS
Number of documents	800	1400	2542	2472	6004	12684	27361
Number of queries	63	225	39	65	35	77	182
Number of terms per document	9.8	28.7	6.6	36.3	39.7	36.0	6.7
Number of terms per query	10.3	8.0	27.5	32.4	16.5	17.9	7.4
Number of relevant per query	14.9	7.2	23.1	22.6	10.8	33.0	58.9
Overlap	0.63	0.43	0.80	0.66	0.58	0.56	0.83

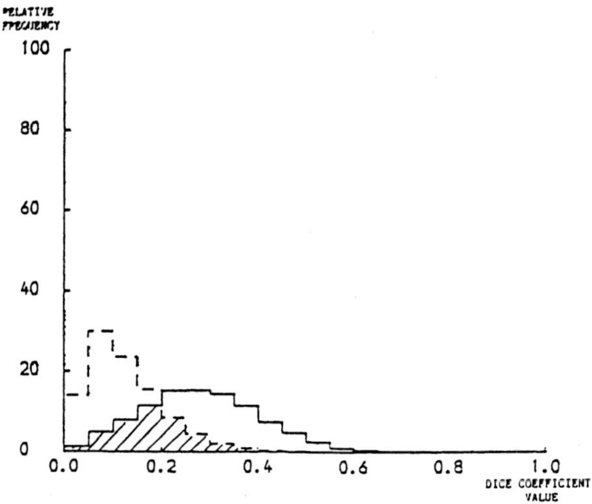

FIG. 1. Separation of RR and RNR distributions for the Cranfield test collection. The overlap area is shaded.

ters in a clustered search. For a cluster containing n_i occurrences of the ith term, the coefficient is defined as

$$\frac{\Sigma w_i n_i}{(\Sigma w_i^2 \Sigma n_i^2)^{1/2}}$$

where each of the query terms with a collection frequency of f_i in a collection of size N was assigned a weight, w_i, of

$$\log_e \frac{N}{f_i + 1},$$

and where the summation is over all of the terms in the indexing vocabulary. The clusters were ranked in descending order of similarity with each query for evaluation purposes.

The primary evaluation measure for the searches was the effectiveness measure, E [10]. For a search that retrieves a set of documents that give rise to recall and precision figures of R and P respectively, E is defined to be

$$1 - \frac{(1+\beta^2)PR}{\beta^2 P + R}$$

where β is a user-defined parameter reflecting the relative importance attached to recall and to precision. A value for β of 0.5 (or 2.0) corresponds to attaching twice (or half) as much importance to precision as to recall, while a value of 1.0 corresponds to attaching equal importance to the two factors.

The success of the searches in providing relevance information was evaluated using two further measures. The first of these was the total number of relevant documents that were retrieved by the entire set of queries in some test collection, while the second of these was the number of queries in a collection for which the set of retrieved documents contained no relevant documents at all. These two measures will be denoted subsequently by T and Q, respectively. Thus, if R_i is the number of relevant documents retrieved in response to the ith query, T is the sum of all of the individual R_i values, while Q is the number of occasions for which R_i is zero. The reader should note that effective retrieval corresponds to low E or Q and high T values.

Two different searches of the same data set may be compared for significant differences by means of the sign test [10]. It is assumed that a large number of queries is available, so that the binomial distribution may be approximated by the normal distribution, and that the E values are available for the sets of documents retrieved by the two search strategies in response to each of these queries. Then, if C is the number of cases for which the two searches retrieve different numbers of relevant documents, and if c is the number of cases for which the first search strategy retrieves more relevant material than does the second strategy, then the test statistic that is evaluated is

$$\frac{c \pm 0.5 - 0.5C}{0.5\sqrt{C}},$$

where c is increased by 0.5 if it is less than $0.5C$ and decreased by the same amount if it is greater. The statistic follows the z distribution, and thus a calculated value greater than the critical value for z in a one-tailed test at some chosen level of significance, .05 in the work reported here, may be taken to imply that one search strategy gives significantly better retrieval than does the other.

Comparative Studies of Hierarchic Document Clustering Methods

The four hierarchic agglomerative clustering methods used here are all based upon the following simple algorithm:

(1) Calculate all of the interdocument similarity coefficients.
(2) Assign each document to its own cluster.
(3) Fuse the most similar pair of current clusters.
(4) Update the similarity matrix by deleting the rows and columns corresponding to the clusters that have been fused and calculating the entries in the row and column corresponding to the newly formed cluster.
(5) Return to step 3 if there is still more than one cluster.

This paper considers four such methods: single linkage, complete linkage, group average, and Ward's method. The methods differ in the updating mechanism used in step 4 above; a discussion of this is given by Lance and Williams [15], while Griffiths et al. [8] provide a summary of previous comparative studies of these methods.

Experiments were carried out using the small Keen, Cranfield, and Evans test collections with the classifications being generated by the CLUSTAN package [16]. Although widely available and flexible in operation [17], this package is restricted in the size of the data set that can be processed. In practice, it was found that collections containing more than 800 documents could not be clustered, even when precomputed similarity matrices were used rather than the inefficient and time-consuming matrix generation routines in the package. Accordingly, only the Keen collection could be processed in toto; the Cranfield collection was hence split into two subsets, one of which contained the even-numbered documents and the other the odd; while a 1-in-4 systematic sample of the Evans documents was used for testing. The interdocument similarity measure that was used in the creation of the similarity matrices was the Dice coefficient.

Cluster Searches

The comparative studies in our previous paper [8] suggested that the single linkage classifications performed badly in optimal cluster searches for which full relevance data was available; however, the four methods gave more comparable levels of retrieval effectiveness in searches that retrieved a single cluster. These latter results are typified by the experimental runs reported in Table 2, which were obtained from searches of the bottom level clusters produced by the four methods. A *bottom level cluster* is the smallest cluster containing one of the documents in a collection, and thus corresponds to the cluster which that document joins when it first becomes connected into the cluster hierarchy [7]. Since it has been suggested that it is the small clusters that are important for good retrieval, a threshold cluster size of 40 documents was set so that only clusters smaller than this threshold size were included in the searches. The results are very similar to those reported previously [8] using a probabilistic model of cluster searching [7]; in particular, the group average method seems to perform consistently better than the other three methods in the $\beta = 2.0$ recall-oriented searches. This is confirmed by the sign test, since group average performs significantly better than all of the other methods with the two Cranfield subsets and better than single linkage when the Keen data are used.

Most experimental tests of cluster-based retrieval methods, such as those discussed above, have considered the retrieval of just a single cluster. However, this reflects a rather artificial retrieval environment since it would correspond to the retrieval of only two or three documents if a small bottom level cluster is identified as the best match for some query. In such cases, more than one cluster should be retrieved, and two sets of experiments were carried out to test the effect of retrieving additional documents. As before, the bottom level clusters were matched against each of the queries and ranked in descending order of the cosine coefficient. However, instead of retrieving

TABLE 2. Retrieval effectiveness of bottom level cluster searches.

	1 Cluster					5 Clusters					10 Documents				
	E Values					*E* Values					*E* Values				
Method	0.5	1.0	2.0	*T*	*Q*	0.5	1.0	2.0	*T*	*Q*	0.5	1.0	2.0	*T*	*Q*
Keen															
Single linkage	0.77	0.83	0.85	77	26	0.79	0.81	0.81	142	17	0.81	0.83	0.82	138	19
Complete linkage	0.76	0.82	0.84	80	20	0.75	0.78	0.78	144	11	0.75	0.76	0.74	182	8
Group average	0.74	0.79	0.81	99	21	0.74	0.76	0.75	169	13	0.74	0.76	0.75	186	8
Ward's method	0.72	0.79	0.82	83	19	0.70	0.74	0.74	150	9	0.72	0.73	0.71	197	5
Cranfield odd															
Single linkage	0.82	0.83	0.82	134	132	0.85	0.82	0.77	257	89	0.88	0.87	0.89	235	92
Complete linkage	0.79	0.80	0.80	129	118	0.80	0.77	0.71	255	77	0.84	0.80	0.72	297	63
Group average	0.78	0.78	0.76	186	109	0.81	0.77	0.70	302	72	0.84	0.80	0.72	302	69
Ward's method	0.79	0.81	0.81	120	122	0.80	0.77	0.72	236	78	0.85	0.81	0.73	288	66
Cranfield even															
Single linkage	0.78	0.79	0.79	165	121	0.86	0.83	0.78	251	92	0.88	0.84	0.78	255	92
Complete linkage	0.78	0.80	0.80	140	120	0.81	0.78	0.73	257	83	0.84	0.80	0.72	323	65
Group average	0.75	0.76	0.75	211	107	0.82	0.78	0.72	318	73	0.83	0.79	0.71	334	71
Ward's method	0.77	0.79	0.79	145	119	0.81	0.78	0.73	259	85	0.84	0.80	0.72	325	65
Evans															
Single linkage	0.83	0.87	0.88	30	22	0.85	0.84	0.82	54	12	0.85	0.84	0.81	55	12
Complete linkage	0.81	0.85	0.88	24	19	0.83	0.83	0.82	44	15	0.85	0.83	0.80	56	12
Group average	0.80	0.84	0.85	32	18	0.83	0.82	0.80	53	14	0.85	0.83	0.81	55	14
Ward's method	0.82	0.87	0.89	22	20	0.83	0.84	0.83	43	14	0.85	0.84	0.81	53	12

just the top-ranked cluster, either the 5 top-ranked clusters were retrieved or a sufficient number of clusters were retrieved to give a total of 10 distinct documents. If a greater number was obtained in the latter case, sufficient documents were randomly selected from the last of the retrieved clusters to ensure that all of the searches resulted in exactly the same fixed number of documents. It is felt that such searches provide a more realistic comparison of the merits of the different clustering methods than do experiments that involve the retrieval of just a single cluster. The results of the experiments using the top 5 clusters and top 10 documents are included in the right-hand portions of Table 2.

Few statistically significant differences in performance are evident in the case of the Evans collection; this may be due to the high overlap figure since, if there is little separation between the relevant and nonrelevant documents, there is unlikely to be large differences in retrieval effectiveness when the file is clustered for search in different ways. Both halves of the Cranfield collection show single linkage to be significantly worse than the other three methods for the retrieval of either 5 clusters or 10 documents. This is also the case for the retrieval of 10 documents from the Keen data; and for this test set, Ward's method gives significantly better results than does complete linkage when 5 clusters are retrieved. Griffiths and Willett [9] report experiments in which the use of the cosine coefficient was replaced by the use of a probabilistic cluster search. The results were very similar to those reported here, the only noticeable difference was that Ward's method was often significantly better than all of the other three methods and not just single linkage.

In summary, the cluster searches carried out here and previously would suggest that the single linkage method results in searches that are sometimes inferior to those obtained from the use of the other three methods; of these, Ward's method may give the best results if more than a single cluster is to be retrieved. However, it should be emphasized that the experiments have involved only a single basic search mechanism, and that different results might be obtained if, for example, top-down or bottom-up searches [6] of the full cluster hierarchies were to be undertaken.

Cluster Membership

A second set of experiments involved an investigation of the size and constitution of the bottom level clusters produced by the four methods.

The distribution of sizes in the bottom level clusters is shown in Table 3. Complete linkage, group average, and Ward's method show a similar distribution, with about three-quarters of the clusters containing just a pair of documents and with very few clusters containing more than 10 documents. Single linkage shows a quite different pattern of behavior, with a much less skewed distribution of cluster sizes and with very many large clusters. Thus, over 37% of the bottom level Keen clusters contain more than 400 documents, and over 10% contain more than 700; similar behavior is observed with the other test sets. Such a distribution of cluster sizes is a natural reflection of the highly unstructured character of single linkage hierarchies that has been noted in previous work [8,18].

TABLE 3. Distribution of sizes of bottom level clusters.

	Cluster Size					
Method	2	3	4	5–20	21–40	>40
			Keen			
Single linkage	234	74	30	59	8	395
Complete linkage	598	141	34	25	0	2
Group average	556	125	48	67	2	2
Ward's method	634	130	30	6	0	0
			Cranfield odd			
Single linkage	230	56	26	35	18	335
Complete linkage	520	126	30	23	0	1
Group average	468	125	43	60	2	2
Ward's method	546	126	18	10	0	0
			Cranfield even			
Single linkage	252	50	21	48	10	319
Complete linkage	540	115	26	17	0	2
Group average	478	121	41	55	3	2
Ward's method	550	121	21	8	0	0
			Evans			
Single linkage	184	58	25	51	3	314
Complete linkage	448	94	35	47	0	11
Group average	416	101	42	68	4	4
Ward's method	494	106	21	14	0	0

The figures in Table 3 raise some questions about the retrieval results in Table 2 since it may appear that the experiments had been biased against the single linkage method and toward clustering methods that tend to produce large numbers of small clusters. This is because the use of a threshold cluster size of 40 documents excludes considerable portions of the single linkage classifications from consideration during a search, whereas the great bulk of the bottom level clusters for the other three methods are smaller than this threshold size. To test whether the single linkage results were being affected, searches were carried out on the Keen data in which the threshold bottom level cluster size was progressively increased so that a greater and greater fraction of the file was available for search. The $\beta = 0.5$ and $\beta = 1.0$ searches showed a marked and progressive decrease in effectiveness as the threshold size was increased, although the $\beta = 2.0$, recall-oriented searches were less affected by the increase in the mean cluster size. The T and Q figures revealed an increasing amount of relevance information, but this was obtained only at the expense of a quite drastic increase in the numbers of documents retrieved as the mean cluster size grew. It would thus seem that the chosen methodology does not seriously disadvantage the single linkage method.

Two further points are of importance. First, it is intuitively reasonable that the larger a cluster becomes, the less accurately the representative describes the documents that are contained within that cluster, and it is thus to be expected that small clusters will give better search performance than do larger ones. This would certainly appear to be the case in the experiments reported here, while Croft [7] has reported results which confirm this expectation in an extended series of cluster based retrieval experiments using a single linkage classification of the full Cranfield test collection. The second point that needs to be made is a consideration of how an operational retrieval system based on document clusters might function. As noted in the first section of this paper, cluster searching has been advocated as a means of obtaining a few relevant documents that may then be used as the basis for a relevance feedback search. The feedback is based on user judgements of the relevance of the few documents retrieved in an initial search; thus, a cluster search that retrieved a very large cluster will require either very many relevance judgements from the user, which he or she may well not wish to provide, or a means for the selection of some small number of documents from the cluster. This latter approach may be accomplished by a variety of means—such as the matching of the individual documents in a cluster against the query, or the selection of those documents most similar to the representative—but this is at variance with the aim of retrieving document clusters in their entirety. Taking these two points together, it would seem that clustering methods that result in small numbers of large clusters are inherently less suitable for cluster based retrieval than are methods that result in large numbers of small clusters.

Luckhurst [19] describes additional experiments in which she measured the degree to which the same bottom level clusters were identified using different clustering criteria. A large degree of overlap was found among the complete linkage, group average, and Ward clusters that share many small clusters in common; for each of the test collections studied, about 75% of the bottom level clusters identified by these three methods were the same, whereas only about 40% of the single linkage clusters were identical with those produced by any one of the other three methods. This finding is again in line with other findings that single linkage gives classifications that yield rather different search results from the other three types of cluster.

Use of Nearest Neighbor Clusters

It must be emphasized that the results presented in the previous section have been obtained using very small sets of documents, and it is clear that the experiments should be repeated using significantly larger data sets. Until such tests have been completed, it may be noted that the results to date suggest that the best searches are obtained from the use of clusters containing only small numbers of documents. The smallest such clusters will contain just a document and its nearest neighbor, i.e., that document with which a specified document has its greatest similarity, and this section investigates the use of such *nearest neighbor clusters* (hereafter NNCs) for document retrieval. As before, the Dice coefficient was used for the determination of all of the interdocument similarity coefficients.

The organization of a file of documents on the basis of the NNCs represents an overlapping classification, since a given document may occur in more than one cluster. It should be noted that if a pair of documents are reciprocal nearest neighbors, i.e., if document j is the nearest neighbor of document i, and i is the nearest neighbor of j, the NNCs for i and j will be identical and only one cluster need be stored for search. Such occurrences will mean that, in general, less than N clusters need to be inspected in an NNC search of a file containing N documents.

The use of nearest neighbors has figured prominently in the general clustering literature [20–22] as well as in the specific context of document classification. Thus Goffman [23] and Mansur [24] have discussed retrieval methods based on chains of nearest neighbors, Willett [25] has considered using sets of nearest neighbors for generating single linkage clusters, while Croft [26] and Croft et al. [27] have described a network organization for information retrieval in which both documents and terms are linked to their nearest neighbors. However, these reports have not involved detailed retrieval experiments using document collections of realistic size; such tests are described below.

Effectiveness of Retrieval

A limitation of the work described in the previous section is that it considers only the comparison of one cluster search with another, without considering the retrieval effectiveness obtainable from conventional best match searching. Accordingly, the NNC searches are compared with *full searches* in which the queries are matched against each of the documents in the file. The full search is based on the collection frequency weights detailed above, with the similarity between a document and a query being calculated by the sum of the weights for the matching terms. The documents were ranked in descending order of similarity with each of the queries, and a threshold of 10 or 20 documents applied to the ranking to obtain a set of documents for the measurement of retrieval effectiveness. An entirely comparable procedure was used with the NNCs, these being ranked in descending order of the cosine match used in the previous section; sufficient clusters were then retrieved to obtain either 10 or 20 documents as required.

The effectiveness of the two types of search are detailed in Table 4. With one or two exceptions, the overwhelming impression is one of little or no difference between the two types of search strategy, with both giving similar levels of

TABLE 4. Retrieval effectiveness of full and NNC searches using a cutoff of 10 or 20 documents.

	Full Search					NNC Search				
	E Values					*E* Values				
	0.5	1.0	2.0	*T*	*Q*	0.5	1.0	2.0	*T*	*Q*
	10 documents									
Keen	0.73	0.74	0.72	186	4	0.72	0.73	0.71	202	6
Cranfield	0.80	0.78	0.73	433	52	0.75	0.73	0.68	533	35
Evans	0.78	0.83	0.85	113	3	0.80	0.84	0.85	103	4
Harding	0.83	0.86	0.88	155	19	0.83	0.87	0.89	149	24
LISA	0.80	0.80	0.78	74	9	0.79	0.80	0.77	78	7
INSPEC	0.80	0.85	0.87	233	10	0.83	0.87	0.89	203	11
UKCIS	0.89	0.91	0.92	340	75	0.90	0.93	0.94	316	77
	20 documents									
Keen	0.77	0.75	0.69	280	2	0.77	0.75	0.69	289	3
Cranfield	0.84	0.80	0.72	630	29	0.82	0.77	0.67	732	21
Evans	0.80	0.81	0.81	170	1	0.80	0.81	0.81	164	2
Harding	0.84	0.85	0.85	236	15	0.84	0.86	0.86	227	20
LISA	0.83	0.81	0.76	112	5	0.83	0.81	0.75	113	5
INSPEC	0.80	0.82	0.83	370	3	0.83	0.85	0.86	325	5
UKCIS	0.88	0.90	0.90	564	60	0.90	0.91	0.91	513	54

performance. This impression is confirmed, in general by the use of the sign test, since differences at the .05 level of statistical significance are observed only for the Cranfield and threshold-20 INSPEC searches. The Cranfield NNC results are significantly better than the full searches, even at the .0001 level of significance, and it is clear that the low overlap value for this collection is reflected in quite excellent cluster searches. It may be noted in passing that the difference between the two types of search is even more marked if a threshold of 5 documents is used, with the NNC search here retrieving some 35% more relevant documents than the full search and giving a $\beta = .05$ *E* value as low as 0.71. In the case of the INSPEC data, the threshold-20 NNC searches are significantly inferior to the full search at the .005 level of significance.

Early work on document clustering [28] found that cluster searches were markedly less effective than full searches. While more recent studies [3,29] have suggested that the two types of search may be rather less disparate in performance, the results obtained here do provide some form of justification for the use of clusters for organizing a document collection. Moreover, the results are acceptable even with the Evans and UKCIS collections where the overlap figures suggest that the data may not be amenable to a clustered organization. The most interesting results are those for the Cranfield collection since the NNC searches are far superior not only to the full search here but also to all of the strategies used by Croft and Harper in their studies of probabilistic searching in the absence of relevance information [3]. The NNC results are also noticeably better than those reported for bottom level cluster searches of a single linkage classification of this data set [7].

Combining the Two Types of Search

It has become increasingly clear that different search mechanisms result in the retrieval of quite different sets of documents [30], and it has accordingly been suggested that future document retrieval systems should incorporate a range of search strategies that can be selected, either by the system or by a user, as appropriate to the needs of a particular query [26]. That such a strategy can indeed increase the effectiveness of retrieval is shown by the "optimal" results listed in Table 5 where the full and NNC searches have been compared and the evaluation measures calculated using that type of search that gives the better result for each of the queries. The results are, of course, very much better than those listed in Table 4, not only in terms of the total numbers of relevant documents but also in terms of the queries retrieving relevant material since there are many cases where the full search retrieves at least one relevant document whereas the NNC search does not, and vice versa. Only in the case of the Cranfield data is there little improvement when the optimal results are compared with the individual types of search, this exceptional behavior arising from the fact that the NNC searches for this collection are so good that little benefit accrues from providing the full search as an alternative retrieval mechanism.

An analysis of the output from the two types of search shows that, although the total numbers of relevant document retrieved by the two types of search are very similar, the two sets of output often have relatively few relevant documents in common. For example, the full and NNC threshold-10 searches of the INSPEC data retrieved 233 and 203 documents, respectively, but only 90 of these were

TABLE 5. Retrieval effectiveness of combined and optimal full and NNC searches using a cutoff of 10 or 20 documents.

	Optimal Search					Combined Searth				
	E Values					*E* Values				
	0.5	1.0	2.0	*T*	*Q*	0.5	1.0	2.0	*T*	*Q*
	10 documents									
Keen	0.69	0.70	0.67	224	3	0.72	0.73	0.71	198	4
Cranfield	0.74	0.71	0.65	568	25	0.76	0.74	0.69	515	35
Evans	0.75	0.80	0.82	128	1	0.78	0.82	0.84	110	4
Harding	0.80	0.85	0.87	179	17	0.82	0.86	0.88	161	20
LISA	0.77	0.77	0.73	87	5	0.79	0.79	0.76	81	7
INSPEC	0.77	0.83	0.86	269	3	0.80	0.85	0.88	235	8
UKCIS	0.87	0.90	0.91	421	55	0.89	0.92	0.92	349	67
	20 documents									
Keen	0.74	0.72	0.65	324	2	0.77	0.75	0.69	291	2
Cranfield	0.81	0.76	0.65	774	13	0.82	0.78	0.68	709	21
Evans	0.77	0.78	0.78	195	1	0.79	0.80	0.80	174	1
Harding	0.82	0.83	0.83	264	14	0.83	0.84	0.85	246	17
LISA	0.81	0.79	0.72	126	3	0.83	0.81	0.75	114	5
INSPEC	0.78	0.80	0.81	413	1	0.80	0.83	0.83	370	3
UKCIS	0.86	0.88	0.88	672	38	0.89	0.90	0.90	556	49

common to both types of search. This suggests that an improved level of performance might be achieved from a retrieval strategy that encompassed both types of search so that some of the documents presented to a user had come from the full search and some of them from the NNC search. In the absence of any obvious rule as to what proportion of the documents should come from each type of search, and as to how this proportion should vary from one query to another, sets of 10 (or 20) documents were obtained for performance evaluation by merging the top 5 (or 10) documents from the full search ranking with the top 5 (or 10) documents from the NNC ranking (after the elimination of any duplicates). The results of these "combined" searches are listed in Table 5 and may be compared with the corresponding figures from Table 4. No large differences in performance can be seen with the exception of the UKCIS collection, where noticeably fewer queries retrieved no relevant material in the combined searches, and of the Cranfield data, where the NNC results are so good that the inclusion of material from a full search proves to be deleterious.

An alternative, and more sophisticated, means of combining two, or more, types of search is suggested in a recent paper by Croft and Thompson [31], who describe an adaptive mechanism that tries to learn which retrieval strategy is most appropriate for a given query. Unfortunately, the tests showed that, although the approach had some merit, it was not possible to obtain results that were superior to those obtainable from the consistent use of just a single strategy.

Implementation Details

The problem of identifying the document(s) most similar to some query, the nearest neighbor problem, has been intensively studied over the last few years, and several inverted file algorithms have been described that may be used for this purpose. The algorithm used here was that described by Noreault et al. [32]. This involves the addition of the inverted file lists corresponding to the terms in the query to yield a vector, the ith element of which contains the sum of the weights of the terms common to the query and to the ith document. The largest such element then specifies the nearest neighbor for that query. An example of an operational retrieval sysem based on this algorithm is given by Brzozowski [33], and it may be also used for the generation, search, and updating of a file of NNCs.

The clusters may be generated by using the algorithm to identify the nearest neighbor of each of the documents in a collection [34]. In such a case, the algorithm will have a running time of order $O(N^2)$, but the constant of proportionality is sufficiently small to make the algorithm practicable for files of nontrivial size. Our experiments used an elderly ICL 1906S computer with the programming in Algol 68, not a particularly efficient language. The identification of the 20 nearest neighbors, rather than just the single nearest neighbor as used here, for each of the documents in the SMART and UKCIS collections required about 5-½ and 3 hours of CPU time, respectively. This would suggest that the NNCs for files of up to 100,000 documents should be obtainable using a modern mainframe and assembly-level coding of the algorithm.

A further advantage of using an inverted file to support the searching of the NNCs is that, unlike most document clustering schemes that have been suggested, there are no overheads associated with the storage of cluster centroids, or representatives, since the requisite information is available from the inverted file. The only storage requirements additional to those of a conventional full search is an N-component array, the kth component of which contains the identifier for the nearest neighbor of the kth document, and the Σn_i^2 term in the denominator of the cosine coefficient for the kth NNC.

With one or two slight modifications, the algorithm may also be used to search the file of NNCs. This search may be carried out at the same time as a full search so that, once the set of NNCs has been generated, NNC searching involves little more processing than does a conventional full search of a document collection. Updating the lists of nearest neighbors as a new document, k, is added to the collection involves using the algorithm to calculate the similarity between k and each of the current members of the collection: the largest similarity corresponds to the nearest neighbor for k, while k becomes the nearest neighbor for some document l if the similarity between l and k is greater than that between l and its current nearest neighbor.

Very similar conclusions have been reached by Croft et al. [27] in a detailed study of the generation, search, and updating requirements of a network file structure that contains both documents and terms, rather than just documents as in the work reported here. These authors also report a simulation study of the numbers of disk accesses that are required for the searching of the network, and their results would be applicable, in large part, to a retrieval system that was based upon NNCs.

Conclusions

The first part of this article describes a comparison of four different hierarchic agglomerative clustering methods. These experiments show that the best results, in terms of the effectiveness of retrieval, are given by clustering methods that result in large numbers of small clusters. Since many of these clusters will contain just a document and its nearest neighbor, the findings would suggest the use of a file organization based upon clusters that contain a document and its nearest neighbor, an NNC. Such files may be generated, searched, and updated at a relatively low computational cost.

Searches of the sets of NNCs for seven document test collections were shown to give a level of retrieval effectiveness little different from that obtainable in conventional full searches. However, an analysis of the actual documents that were retrieved by the two types of search shows that they identify rather different sets of relevant documents. This would suggest that a retrieval system should contain both sorts of retrieval mechanism if it is to provide an effective response to as wide a range of queries as possible. Such a system would use one of the search types as the basic strategy, but could then switch to the other if the initial set of documents proved to be unsatisfactory.

Attempts were made in the experiments to combine the outputs from the two types of search into a single set of documents, but this was found to be less successful than a strategy that carried out both types of search and then selected the more effective one to provide the output. Such a retrospective approach can, of course, be used only in an experimental environment where full relevance information is available, and an operational retrieval system would need to have some selection mechanism that would allow it to select which strategy should be applied to a particular query. Studies are now in progress to identify appropriate selection methods for this purpose.

Acknowledgments

Thanks are due to Dr. K. Sparck Jones (Cambridge University), Prof. G. Salton (Cornell University), Mr. L. Evans, Mr. P. Harding, and Mr. J. Pache (INSPEC), and Mr. N. Moore (Library Association) for providing the document test collections used in this study. Funding was provided by the British Library Research and Development Department under grant number SI/G/564 and by the award of a Department of Education and Science Advanced Course Studentship to H. C. L.

References

1. Robertson, S. E.; Sparck Jones, K. "Relevance weighting of search terms." *Journal of the American Society for Information Science*. 27:129-146; 1976.
2. Harper, D. J.; van Rijsbergen, C. J. "An evaluation of feedback in document retrieval using co-occurrence data." *Journal of Documentation*. 34:189-216; 1978.
3. Salton, G.; McGill, M. J. *Introduction to Modern Information Retrieval*. New York, NY: McGraw-Hill; 1983.
4. Croft, W. B.; Harper, D. J. "Using probabilistic models of document retrieval without relevance information." *Journal of Documentation*. 35:285-295; 1979.
5. Jardine, N.; van Rijsbergen, C. J. "The use of hierarchical clustering in information retrieval." *Information Storage and Retrieval*. 7:217-240; 1971.
6. van Rijsbergen, C. J.; Croft, W. B. "Document clustering: an evaluation of some experiments with the Cranfield 1400 collection." *Information Processing and Management*. 11:171-182; 1975.
7. Croft, W. B. "A model of cluster searching using classification." *Information Systems*. 5:189-195; 1980.
8. Griffiths, A.; Robinson, L. A.; Willett, P. "Hierarchic agglomerative clustering methods for automatic document classification." *Journal of Documentation*. 40:175-205; 1984.
9. Griffiths, A.; Willett, P. *Evaluation of Clustering Methods for Automatic Document Classification*. London, UK: British Library Research and Development Department; 1984.
10. van Rijsbergen, C. J. *Information Retrieval*. London, UK: Butterworth; 1979.
11. Evans, L. *Search Strategy Variations in SDI Profiles*. London, UK: INSPEC; 1975.
12. Harding, P. *Automatic Indexing and Classification for Mechanised Information Retrieval*. London, UK: INSPEC; 1982.
13. Davies, A. *A Document Test Collection for Use in Information Retrieval Research*. M.S. dissertation, University of Sheffield, UK; 1983.
14. van Rijsbergen, C. J.; Sparck Jones, K. "A test for the separation of relevant and non-relevant documents in experimental retrieval collections." *Journal of Documentation*. 29:251-257; 1973.
15. Lance, G. N.; Williams, W. T. "A general theory of classificatory sorting strategies. I. Hierarchical systems." *Computer Journal*. 9:373-380; 1967.
16. Wishart, D. *CLUSTAN IC User Manual*. Edinburgh, UK: Edinburgh University Program Library Unit; 1978.
17. Aldenderfer, M. S. *A Consumer Report on Cluster Analysis Software*. University Park, PA: Pennsylvania State University; 1977.
18. Murtagh, F. "Structure of hierarchic clusterings: implications for information retrieval and multivariate data analysis." *Information Processing and Management*. 20:611-617; 1984.
19. Luckhurst, H. C. *A Comparison of Four Hierarchical Clustering Methods for Document Retrieval*. M.S. dissertation, University of Sheffield, UK; 1984.
20. Jarvis, R. A.; Patrick, E. A. "Clustering using a similarity measure based on shared nearest neighbours." *IEEE Transactions on Computers*. C-22:1025-1034; 1973.
21. Gowda, K. C.; Krishna, G. "Agglomerative clustering using the concept of mutual nearest neighbourhood." *Pattern Recognition*. 10:105-112; 1978.
22. Mizoguchi, R.; Shimura, M. "A nonparametric algorithm for detecting clusters using hierarchical structure." *IEEE Transactions on Pattern Analysis and Machine Intelligence*. PAMI-2:292-300; 1980.
23. Goffman, W. "An indirect method of information retrieval." *Information Storage and Retrieval*. 4:363-373; 1969.
24. Mansur, O. "An associative search strategy for information retrieval." *Information Processing and Management*. 16:129-137; 1980.
25. Willett, P. "A note on the use of nearest neighbours for implementing single linkage document classifications." *Journal of the American Society for Information Science*. 35:149-152; 1984.
26. Croft, W. B. "Incorporating different search models into one document retrieval system." *ACM SIGIR Forum*. 16:40-45; 1981.
27. Croft, W. B.; Wolf, R.; Thompson, R. "A network organization used for document retrieval." *ACM SIGIR Forum*. 17:178-188; 1983.
28. Salton, G. *The SMART Retrieval System*. Englewood Cliffs, NJ: Prentice-Hall; 1971.
29. Willett, P. "Document clustering using an inverted file approach." *Journal of Information Science*. 2:223-231; 1980.
30. Katzer, J.; McGill, M. J.; Tessier, J. A.; Frakes, W.; DasGupta, P. "A study of the overlap among document representatives." *Information Technology: Research and Development*. 1:261-274; 1982.
31. Croft, W. B.; Thompson; R. H. "The use of adaptive mechanisms for selection of search strategies in document retrieval systems." In: van Rijsbergen, C. J. (Ed.) *Research and Development in Information Retrieval*. Cambridge, UK: Cambridge University Press; 1984.
32. Noreault, T.; Koll, M.; McGill, M. J. "Automatic ranked output from Boolean searches in SIRE." *Journal of the American Society for Information Science*. 28:333-339; 1977.
33. Brzozowski, J. P. "MASQUERADE: searching the full texts of abstracts using automatic indexing." *Journal of Information Science*. 6:67-73; 1983.
34. Willett, P. "A fast procedure for the calculation of similarity coefficients in automatic classification." *Information Processing and Management*. 17:53-60; 1981.

Chapter 7

Systems

The SMART and SIRE Experimental Retrieval Systems 381
G. Salton and M.J. McGill

Architecture of an Expert System for Composite Document Analysis, Representation, and Retrieval 400
E.A. Fox and R.K. France

User-Friendly Systems Instead of User-Friendly Front-Ends 413
D.K. Harman

The Okapi Online Catalogue Research Projects 424
S. Walker

TREC and TIPSTER Experiments with INQUERY 436
J.P. Callan, W.B. Croft, and J.S. Broglio

RUBRIC: A System for Rule-Based Information Retrieval 440
B.P. McCune, R.M. Tong, and J. Dean

TARGET and FREESTYLE: DIALOG and Mead Join the Relevance Ranks 446
C. Tenopir and P. Cahn

INTRODUCTION

As an IR system seeks to provide users with items that in some way satisfy a user's information need, however expressed, it seemed entirely natural to the early workers in IR to carry out research by building a system and then ascertaining how well it worked in practice. While this approach had the obvious benefit that the implementers received rapid feedback from users, it also meant that it was often not possible to ascertain which particular feature(s) of one system resulted in it being judged as superior to another when two, or more, systems were compared with each other. The detailed studies carried out in Cranfield-2 focused the attention of the research community on the need for laboratory-based experiments, in which individual aspects of the overall retrieval process are carefully developed and optimised; these have formed the principal focus of IR research for many years. However, as the basic strategies necessary for effective retrieval have been established (as described in previous chapters), the research community has again started to address the implementation of systems based on these strategies.

There are several reasons for this renewed interest in system building. From a research viewpoint, the conclusions resulting from experiments that involve a single variable may need modification when other variables are allowed to interact in a less controlled manner; moreover, there are many important research questions (such as those relating to *user behaviour* and to *interface design*) that cannot be addressed, or are very difficult to address, in the absence of an actual implementation. Finally, the demonstration of basic system *efficiency, scalability,* and *robustness* is a necessary prerequisite for operational and, subsequently, commercial implementations of research ideas.

We have noted in Chapter 1 that IR involves two major tasks—indexing and searching—and we can clearly differentiate between systems on the basis of the particular approaches to these two tasks that they have adopted, even if we restrict ourselves, as we do in this chapter, to the retrieval of textual information. When dealing with working computer systems, rather than models or algorithms, it is also necessary to consider how the chosen indexing and searching strategies are to be implemented, since these will affect the system's efficiency in terms of the amounts of computer and human effort that are required; this forms the main substance of the papers we have chosen to include here. However, in structuring the chapter, we have also taken account of the sorts of *user* for which the system is intended, since this affects the way in which the underlying retrieval facilities are made available.

USERS AND INTERFACES

At the lowest level, a *level-1* system might consist of an assemblage of routines, typically developed within a single research group and bundled together primarily to facilitate additional research and development. The users here are likely to be members of the original research group, all of whom can be expected to have a fair degree of expertise, both in IR in general and in the use of the particular routines concerned. Such users will be tolerant of system limitations (both software and hardware), have little or no requirement for support and documentation, will accept the most minimal user interface, and view a core dump, for example, as a challenge rather than as a cause for complaint. For such a user community, the actual databases that can be searched are likely to be dictated by availability to the originating group rather than to any real user information needs.

A much greater level of sophistication is required if an academic research group wishes to make their system available to external users, i.e., individuals with a need to access text databases containing information that may be able to answer real information needs. The decision to extend a level-1 to a *level-2* system is not taken lightly since it will require the construction of a large body of supporting software that is only tangentially related to the research questions that motivated the development of the system in the first place; for example, the basic level-1 functionality will need to be augmented by modules that overcome the limitations noted in the previous paragraph, and sufficient attention must be paid to efficiency to enable an interactive response to be provided to queries that are matched against databases of nontrivial size. There may, however, still be inherent limitations, which mean, e.g., that such level-2 software is tied to the databases and software/hardware environment of a particular institutional setting.

Finally, commercial, *level-3* software must be hospitable to a wide range of users from all sorts of background, accessing all sorts of databases mounted on all sorts of platforms without recourse to the original system developers. Such software may have resulted from initial level-1 and then level-2 systems, or may have been developed from scratch by a commercial supplier, albeit one that (hopefully) has taken at least some account of the work of the research community.

The focus on users in this three-part categorisation means that the interface to the system will play a central role in determining the overall effectiveness of a search: not only does the interface provide the means by which the user activates the various retrieval facilities that are available but it may also provide a range of methods to support users in their search. Indeed, in a wide-ranging review of searching online database hosts, Vickery and Vickery (1993) identify no less than 14 such supportive roles that an interface might provide, ranging from assistance in the selection of appropriate databases and hosts, via the normal minutiae of transmitting search statements and output to and from the database host, to the provision of multilingual facilities. In practice, of course, the functionality of the interfaces to most IR systems is far more constrained than this ideal.

Such considerations matter little in a level-1 system, but they become of increasing importance as the user population becomes more heterogeneous, with less and less knowledge of the underlying indexing and searching routines embodied in the system that is being used. One way of handling such a user population is to adopt an explicitly minimalist approach, as is most obviously demonstrated by many of the current generation of Web search engines. Here, the user is restricted to typing in a natural language query statement and then scrolling through the search output, with the only other facilities being those that are provided by the Web browser that is being used, rather than by the IR system. As people become more familiar with the idea of content-based searching, it is likely that a much wider range of facilities will be provided, with the plummeting costs of computer hardware leading to sophisticated, graphics-based interfaces such as those currently being investigated in the context of digital libraries (Lesk, 1997; Rao et al., 1995). Such work will become of increasing importance with the development of the multimedia IR systems discussed in Chapter 8, which will provide content-based access not only to text but also to sound, images, and video, etc. At the same time, we can expect that the initial haphazard response, by builders of the new wave of Web systems, to previous IR research and practice will be succeeded by a more considered one.

Historically, the interfaces to conventional (i.e., Boolean) level-3 systems were entirely character based and provided little or nothing in the way of user support, e.g., by explicitly asking for lists of synonyms that could then be automatically linked with an OR operator. The systems thus generally required the user to have a considerable degree of knowledge of the system's functions if a successful search was to be achieved, this being one of the reasons why Boolean systems have traditionally been used by *intermediaries*, rather than the *end users* for which they were originally intended. Windowing systems of various sorts are now widely available, as is, increasingly, Web-based access, but these often represent a simple repackaging, rather than an enhancement, of the available retrieval facilities: an exception to this general rule is the library metaphor adopted by Pejtersen (1989) for designing the icons in a system for the retrieval of fiction. A more radical change in the facilities available from an IR interface may arise from work on *visualisation*, i.e., the process of forming a mental image of a domain. Much effort has gone into the development of visualisation systems for scientific and, increasingly, business computing to enable end users to achieve insights about the information contained in large numeric datasets, and there is now interest in the use of analogous techniques to allow users to interact with files of textual (more generally, multimedia) data. The concepts of "nearness" and "similarity" in the vector processing model make it particularly well suited to visualisation in geometric terms, as noted by Olsen et al. (1993), but spatial metaphors can also be developed for systems based on other IR models. For example, Hemmje et al. (1994) describe LyberWorld, a system for visualising and interacting with full texts that invokes the functionality of the INQUERY system (described below) by means of direct manipulation of a range of visualised information structures.

CURRENT IR SYSTEMS

To put the following system descriptions in context, it is appropriate to consider how a conventional Boolean retrieval system operates, such as one of the online database hosts (Hartley et al., 1990).

A user or an intermediary skilled in the use of the system, such as a librarian or information specialist, draws up an initial query formulation. This will typically consist of both natural language keywords or phrases and terms drawn from the controlled vocabulary if, as is often the case, there is such a vocabulary associated with the database that is to be searched. The various components of the query, each of which may have an associated word-type descriptor such as "Thesaural Term" or "Word in Title", are then linked by the Boolean logical operators AND, OR, and NOT. These three operators are normally supplemented by a range of pattern matching facilities to allow the specification and searching of text substrings; examples of these facilities include embedded strings, fixed-length and variable-length don't-care characters, right-hand and (much less commonly) left-hand truncation, and adjacency and proximity searching. When a query contains several different components, such as two lists of synonyms that are to be ANDed together, bracketing may be required to define the precise nature of the logical constraints that are to be applied to each document during the search.

Searching is normally effected by means of an *inverted file,* which contains two main components: the *dictionary file* and the *postings file.* The dictionary file contains a list of all of the keywords, classification terms, journal titles, etc., occurring in the database that can be used as retrieval keys. Associated with each entry in the dictionary file is a count, specifying how frequently that key occurs. The postings file contains a series of lists, one for each of the entries in the dictionary file. Each such list contains the identifiers of all documents that contain a given term, so that the postings file enables a search to be restricted to just those documents that contain the term combinations that have been specified in the query. It is also common to store not just the presence of a term in a document but also its location, so as to permit the efficient implementation of proximity searching and adjacency-based phrase identification.

Both of these components of an inverted file are used in a database search. (The reader should note that the following is a highly simplified description of the processing that takes place, and modifications are needed to encompass, e.g., proximity or truncated term searches.) Once the initial query terms have been submitted, they are looked up in the dictionary file to determine whether they have been used to index any of the documents in the database. If they have, their frequencies of occurrence in the database may be displayed. Associated with each entry in the dictionary file is a pointer to the corresponding list in the postings file. It is these lists that form the basis for most of the processing, with pairs of the lists being combined in accordance with the logical operators that are specified. Thus, in a search for two ANDed terms, the lists corresponding to these terms would be intersected to obtain a new postings list that contained the identifiers of those documents indexed by both of these terms; the size of the resulting list, i.e., the number of hits, may be reported to the searcher, and the list can then be used in subsequent operations. Once all of the specified logical operations have been carried out on the postings lists, the end result is a new list that contains the identifiers of all of those documents that satisfy the logical constraints in the query. The dictionary file and postings file operations may need to be repeated several times until an appropriate output size has been obtained. At this point, the system will access the original source texts, which are normally arranged as a simple serial file, for the documents that match the query. These documents are displayed to the user, who may then need to reformulate the query and thus start the whole procedure over again.

It should be noted that, while inverted file systems provide extremely rapid access to even the largest online databases, they can have substantial storage overheads and are not well suited to the provision of access to dynamic files that require frequent updating. There has, accordingly, been much interest in the use of an alternative file structure, the *text signature,* for IR: examples of systems based on this file structure have been described, using both conventional (Calderbank, 1990) and nonconventional (Stanfill and Kahle, 1986) computer hardware.

SELECTED READINGS

The classic example of a level-1 research system is the SMART system, which was developed by Salton at Harvard in the early sixties and which, after his move to Cornell, has played a significant role in the development of IR, as discussed in detail in previous chapters. The paper we have chosen for inclusion here is taken from the book by Salton and McGill (1983). This paper provides not only an overview of the vector processing model on which SMART is based but also a description of how SIRE, a similar system to SMART, uses an inverted file for the implementation of best-match searching (rather than for the Boolean searching with which this file structure is normally associated). The paper also describes the historical development of SMART up to the time of writing, in the early eighties. This last point is important since this, like all of the papers chosen for inclusion in this chapter, provides a description of a particular system at a *particular point in time,* whereas any successful system will evolve during its lifetime, in terms of the facilities that are available and/or the computational techniques that are used to implement these facilities. SMART, indeed, provides an excellent example of this, since one of the early descriptions of the system (Salton, 1968) goes as far as giving detailed accounts of the punched card and magnetic tape operations needed to invoke the functionality available at that time but says nothing about the term discrimination routines that later became central to SMART's procedures for the automatic generation of noun phrases and thesaural classes (and that are discussed in the paper included here). In just the same way, the selected paper in this chapter says nothing about the work carried out subsequently on retrieval and browsing in full texts (Salton et al., 1994). In its later life, SMART became a level-2 system, since it was provided to many groups for their own IR research projects, while SIRE subsequently evolved into a commercial IR system, PLS.

The second level-1 system discussed here is CODER (Fox and France, 1987). CODER (Composite Document Expert Retrieval) was an attempt to apply AI methods to document retrieval. The basic model is that of a distributed expert system in which individual problem-solving modules communicate with each other via blackboards that serve as holding areas for knowledge pertinent to the current retrieval problem. This model attracted much attention in the eighties (Belkin et al., 1983; Croft and Thompson, 1987), as did other attempts to integrate AI and IR (Vickery et al., 1987; Pollitt, 1987). In retrospect, this work was premature in that it had not then been realised how difficult it would prove to extend the domain-specific character of expert systems to encompass the very broad subject domains that characterise most IR systems. Moreover, the very general blackboard models that were used proved to be insufficiently well defined to converge on the desired outcome, i.e., sets of relevant documents.

Both of the level-2 systems included here are based on one of the retrieval models described in Chapter 5. Harman (1992) describes the PRISE system, which was developed at the National Institute of Standards and Technology during the mid-eighties and which sought to demonstrate that the vector processing model embodied in SMART could be implemented to allow rapid end user searching of large text databases. The implementation of the inverted-file, nearest-neighbour searching algorithm used in PRISE is detailed in Harman and Candela (1990), while the paper included here describes the interface that was developed to permit testing of the system in a real-world environment and the reactions of end users (many of whom had never, or only seldom, used an online IR system) to searches with PRISE. With subsequent development, PRISE is now available for use by the academic research community. Harman also includes brief descriptions of the interfaces for four other best-match retrieval systems of the period and thus provides a snapshot of the state of the art in best-match retrieval systems in the late eighties and early nineties; an analogous snapshot from a few years earlier is provided by Willett (1988).

The OKAPI system has been developed in the UK, initially at the Polytechnic of Central London (now the University of Westminster) and more recently at the City University. The origins of OKAPI date back to the early eighties, when a project was started to implement an OPAC on networked microcomputers, rather than the minicomputers and mainframes that then formed the basis for library automation systems. The project resulted in an operational OPAC that ran at the Polytechnic of Central London for several years, and it is this version of the system that is described here in the paper by Walker (1989). Since 1989, the focus has changed from OPACs to IR, and OKAPI now provides a robust test bed for the implementation of probabilistic models of retrieval, such as the relevance weighting and term frequency weighting schemes described in Chapter 6. A special issue of the *Journal of Documentation* (1997) contains ID articles on various aspects of OKAPI and of the experiments that have been carried out with it.

INQUERY and RUBRIC can be regarded as level-3 systems since both of them have led to full-scale commercial implementations, these being WIN (for Westlaw Is Natural) from West Publishing Company and TOPIC from Verity Inc. Detailed technical descriptions of these implementations are, hardly surprisingly, not available in the literature, and we have hence selected papers describing the original research that subsequently led to these systems. INQUERY (Callan et al., 1995) is based on the inference network model discussed in Chapter 5, in which documents are ranked in order of decreasing probability that they satisfy the user's information need. Searching involves calculating the belief in a document due to the occurrence in it of a single query term and then the combination of these individual beliefs by means of several different types of logical operator that include both Boolean and natural language searching. INQUERY, like SMART and OKAPI, is being used by both its developers and others in the ongoing series of TREC conferences.

Searching in RUBRIC (which stands for RUle-Based Retrieval of Information by Computer) is based on a weighted thesaurus in which concepts are arranged in trees, called *topics*, the leaves of which are strings that may occur in document texts, so the identification of such strings is taken as weighted proof of the relevance of concepts higher up the tree. Query terms are searched for in the various topics that are available to the system, and the weights for matching strings are propagated up to the root of a topic by means of a range of combination operators (such as minimum or maximum); the resulting weights then provide the basis for ranking the documents in the database. RUBRIC thus differs from the other systems considered here in its provision of what is, in effect, a modern implementation of the manual thesaural approaches that have been described in Chapters 2 and 3.

Finally, Tenopir and Cahn (1994) discuss two commercial online database hosts (DIALOG and Mead Data Central) that have recently introduced best-match searching facilities to complement their long-established Boolean search services. The technical details of the resulting systems, called TARGET and FREESTYLE, are not generally available (Keen, 1994), and we have thus here selected a paper that focuses upon system use rather than system implementation. Specifically, the paper reports a series of searches that have been carried out on the two systems, illustrating the use of both best-match and Boolean searching. The experiments are less detailed than those that can be carried out if a document test collection is available—as in the comparison of Boolean and best-match searching on the Westlaw system reported by Turtle (1994)—but they suffice to demonstrate the considerable benefits that accrue from the use of searching techniques that are very new to the great majority of current online searchers. Detailed discussions of searching using a conventional, purely Boolean system are presented by Blair and Maron (1985) in their discussion of the STAIRS evaluation.

Even these brief summaries will suffice to demonstrate the wide range of searching facilities that are available in the various systems, and the indexing facilities are equally varied. The lowest level of document indexing is exemplified by PRISE, which uses keyword stems extracted from the natural language texts of the database being searched, and a similar strategy is followed by the TREC version of OKAPI. Subject searching in the OPAC version of OKAPI involves the title, subject heading, corporate name, and classification number components of a catalogue record, with the addition of automatic stemming and cross-referencing and semiautomatic spelling correction of user input. SMART is like PRISE in that it is based on individual keyword stems extracted from document and query texts. It does, however, also include routines for the automatic generation of keyword clusters, these groupings typically being generated only for the less frequently occurring words in a database, and (more recently) of noun phrases, these being generated by either syntactic (Salton et al., 1990) or nonsyntactic (Fagan, 1989) means: the latter have become the main additional term formation device in SMART in the present decade. RUBRIC does little at the document indexing stage but then uses the topics at search time to facilitate the matching of document and query texts.

The two operational systems, TARGET and FREESTYLE, are analogous to their parent Boolean systems, while CODER and INQUERY both involve extensive processing of input texts. Thus, CODER augments the natural language of document and query texts by means of a lexicon generated from several machine-readable dictionaries, these providing access to a number of linguistic relationships that can be used to facilitate the matching of query terms at search time. In addition to conventional keyword-stem extraction, INQUERY includes a feature recognition routine that identifies the names of companies, cities, and countries occurring in document texts. INQUERY also provides an interactive approach to query expansion that identifies sets of noun sequences that occur in documents near to a concept that has been specified in the query.

These long-standing systems, and others like CLARIT (Evans and Lefferts, 1995), collectively show that a wide range of specific approaches may be successfully used within a broad natural language framework. The current TREC Programme shows how these systems are being further developed, how a wide range of other possibilities is being explored, and both how very different systems can give similar results and how quite simple but well-founded systems continue to give competitive performance.

In conclusion, the systems selected for inclusion in this chapter provide an overview of the many different indexing and searching facilities that can be implemented, using present-day technology, in operational IR systems that search textual databases of nontrivial size. We thus hope that the research ideas presented here will rapidly be taken up by the implementers of operational IR systems. In this respect, it is encouraging to note the emergence of Web search engines such as MUSCAT, which are firmly based on the lessons learnt by IR researchers over the years (Porter, 1982; Porter and Galpin, 1988), and others, such as AltaVista or Lycos, which make at least some use of these ideas. However, even if there is a rapid take-up of research findings, there are many outstanding developmental problems that need to be addressed, most obviously evidenced by the fact that most Web search engines (like OPACs that provide subject searching) have to process far shorter queries, containing just two or three words, than are common with IR systems: the sophisticated techniques that have been developed thus far for query weighting and expansion will need much further work if they are to be applied to their best effect in this new retrieval environment.

REFERENCES

*Note: *** after a reference indicates a selected reading.*

Belkin, N.J., Seeger, T., and Wersig, G. (1983) Distributed expert treatment as a model of information system analysis and design. *Journal of Information Science*, **5**, 153–167.

Blair, D.C., and Maron. M.E. (1985) An evaluation of retrieval effectiveness for a full-text document retrieval system. *Communications of the ACM*, **28**, 289–299.

Brajnik, G., Guida, G., and Tasso, C. (1990) User modelling in expert man-machine interfaces: A case study in intelligent information retrieval. *IEEE Transactions on Systems, Man, and Cybernetics*, **20**, 166–185.

Calderbank, V.J. (1990) TITAN: An information management system for faster retrieval from massive databases using text signatures. *Program*, **24**, 253–268.

Callan, J., Croft, W.B., and Broglio, J. (1995) TREC and TIPSTER experiments with INQUERY. *Information Processing and Management*, **31**, 327–332, 343.***

Callan, J., Croft, W.B., and Harding, S.M. (1992) The INQUERY retrieval system. In A. Min Tjoa and I. Tamos (Eds.), *Proceedings of the 3rd International Conference on Database and Expert Systems Applications*, pp. 78–83. Berlin: Springer-Verlag.

Croft, W.B., and Thompson, R.H. (1987) I^{3}R: A new approach to the design of document retrieval systems. *Journal of the American Society for Information Science*, **38**, 389–404.

Evans, D.A., and Lefferts, R.G. (1995) CLARIT—TREC experiments. *Information Processing and Management*, **31**, 385–395.

Fagan, J.L. (1989) The effectiveness of a non-syntactic approach to automatic phrase indexing for document retrieval. *Journal of the American Society for Information Science*, **40**, 115–132.

Fox, E.A., and France, R.K. (1987) Architecture of an expert system for composite document analysis, representation, and retrieval. *Journal of Approximate Reasoning*, **1**, 151–175.***

Fox, E.A., and Koll, M.B. (1988) Practical enhanced Boolean retrieval: Experiences with the SMART and SIRE systems. *Information Processing and Management*, **24**, 257–267.

Harman, D.K. (1992) User-friendly systems instead of user-friendly front-ends. *Journal of the American Society for Information Science*, **43**, 164–174.***

Harman, D.K., and Candela, G. (1990) Retrieving records from a gigabyte of text on a minicomputer using statistical ranking. *Journal of the American Society for Information Science*, **41**, 581–589.

Hartley, R.J., Keen, E.M., Large, J.A., and Tedd, L.A. (1990) *Online Searching: Principles and Practice*. London: Bowker Saur.

Hemmje, M., Kunkel, C., and Willett, A. (1994) LyberWorld—a visualization user interface supporting full text retrieval. In W.B. Croft and C.J. van Rijsbergen (Eds.), *Proceedings of the 17th Annual International Conference on Research and Development in Information Retrieval*, pp. 249–259. London: Springer-Verlag.

Journal of Documentation (1997) Special issue: Okapi Projects. *Journal of Documentation*, **53**, 3–87.

Kahle, B., Morris, H., Goldman, J., Erickson, T., and Curran, J. (1993) Interfaces for distributed systems of information servers. *Journal of the American Society for Information Science*, **44**, 453–467.

Keen, E.M. (1994) How does Dialog's TARGET work? *Online and CD-ROM Review*, **18**, 285–288.

Lesk, M.E. (1997) *Practical Digital Libraries: Books, Bytes and Bucks.* San Francisco: Morgan Kaufmann.

McCune, B.P., Tong, R., and Dean, J. (1985) RUBRIC, a system for rule-based information retrieval. *IEEE Transactions on Software Engineering*, **SE-11**, 939–944.***

Noreault, T., Koll, M., and McGill, M.J. (1977) Automatic ranked output from Boolean searches in SIRE. *Journal of the American Society for Information Science*, **28**, 333–339.

Oddy, R.N. (1977) Information retrieval through man-machine dialogue. *Journal of Documentation*, **33**, 1–14.

Olsen, K.A., Korfhage, R.R., Sochats, K.M., Spring, M.B., and Williams, J.G. (1993) Visualisation of a document collection: The VIBE system. *Information Processing and Management*, **29**, 69–81.

Paijmans, H. (1993) Comparing the document representations of two IR-systems: CLARIT and TOPIC. *Journal of the American Society for Information Science*, **44**, 383–392.

Pejtersen, A.M. (1989) A library system for information retrieval based on a cognitive task analysis and supported by an icon-based interface. In N.J. Belkin and C.J. van Rijsbergen (Eds.), *Proceedings of the 12th Annual International Conference on Research and Development in Information Retrieval*, pp. 40–47. New York: Association for Computing Machinery.

Pollitt, A.S. (1987) CANSEARCH: An expert systems approach to document retrieval. *Information Processing and Management*, **23**, 119–138.

Porter, M.F. (1982) Implementing a probabilistic information retrieval system. *Information Technology: Research and Development*, **1**, 131–156.

Porter, M.F., and Galpin, V. (1988) Relevance feedback in a public access catalogue for a research library: MUSCAT at the Scott Polar Research Institute. *Program*, **22**, 1–20.

Pritchard-Schoch, T. (1993) Natural language comes of age. *Online*, **17**(3), 33–43.

Rao, R., Pedersen, J.O., Hearst, M.A., Mackinlay, J.D., Card, S.K., Masinter, L., Halvorsen, P.-K., and Robertson, G.G. (1995) Rich interaction in the digital library. *Communications of the ACM*, **38**(4), 29–39.

Robertson, S.E., Walker, S., Hancock-Beaulieu, M.M., Gull, A., and Lau, M. (1993) Okapi at TREC. In D.K. Harman (Ed.), *The First Text REtrieval Conference (TREC-1)*. NIST Special Publication 500–207, pp. 21–30. Gaithersburg, MD: National Institute of Standards and Technology.

Salton, G. (1968) *Automatic Information Organisation and Retrieval.* New York: McGraw-Hill.

Salton, G., Allan, J., Buckley, C., and Singhal, A. (1994) Automatic analysis, theme generation, and summarisation of machine-readable texts. *Science*, **264**, 1421–1426.

Salton, G., Buckley, C., and Smith, M. (1990) The application of syntactic methodologies in automatic text analysis. *Information Processing and Management*, **26**, 73–92.

Salton, G., and McGill, M.J. (1983). *The SMART and SIRE Experimental Retrieval Systems*, pp. 118–155. New York: McGraw-Hill.***

Stanfill, C., and Kahle, B. (1986) Parallel free-text search on the Connection Machine system. *Communications of the ACM*, **29**, 1229–1239.

Tenopir, C., and Cahn, P. (1994) TARGET and FREESTYLE: DIALOG and Mead join the relevance ranks. *Online*, **18**(3), 31–47.***

Turtle, H. (1994) Natural language vs Boolean query evaluation: A comparison of retrieval performance. In W.B. Croft and C.J. van Rijsbergen (Eds.), *Proceedings of the 17th Annual International Conference on Research and Development in Information Retrieval*, pp. 213–220. London: Springer-Verlag.

Vickery, A., Brooks, H., Robinson, B., and Vickery, B. (1987) A reference and referral system using expert system techniques. *Journal of Documentation*, **43**, 1–23.

Vickery, B., and Vickery, A. (1993) Online search interface design. *Journal of Documentation*, **49**, 103–187.

Walker, S. (1989) The Okapi online catalogue research projects. In C. Hildreth (Ed.), *The Online Catalogue. Developments and Directions*, pp. 84–106. London: Library Association.***

Walker, S., and Hancock-Beaulieu, M.M. (1991) *Okapi at City: An Evaluation Facility for Interactive IR.* British Library Research and Development Department, report no. 6056. London: British Library.

Willett, P. (Ed.) (1988) *Document Retrieval Systems.* London: Taylor Graham.

The SMART and SIRE Experimental Retrieval Systems

G. Salton and M.J. McGill

0 PREVIEW

This chapter deals with analysis, file organization, search, and retrieval methodologies that may be used with the advanced information retrieval systems of the future. The SMART system is perhaps the best known of the experimental systems that are not based on a standard inverted file technology. The SMART system design is described in detail in this chapter, including the automatic indexing methods, the clustered file organization, which collects related records into common classes; and the interactive search process which is used to construct improved query formulations based on relevance information supplied by the users to the system.

Various other experimental retrieval systems, including SIRE, also utilize novel features that are not common in conventional retrieval. Some of these extensions are examined at the end of this chapter. The use of local clustering methods and the incorporation of weighted terms in Boolean retrieval are considered in this connection together with additional user feedback and query reformulation methods.

1 INTRODUCTION

Conventional retrieval systems are based for the most part on a common set of principles and methodologies. The documents are normally indexed manually by subject experts or professional indexers using a prespecified, controlled vocabulary; alternatively, some systems use the words included in document texts or text excerpts as index terms. Users or search intermediaries formulate search statements using terms from the accepted vocabulary together with appropriate Boolean operators between terms. The main file search device is an auxiliary, so-called inverted directory which contains for each accepted content identifier and for some of the objective terms a list of the document references, or markers, to which that term has been assigned. In a free text search system, the inverted directory contains the text words from the documents and the references to all documents containing each given word. The documents to be retrieved in response to a given search request are then identified by obtaining from the inverted directory the document reference lists corresponding to each query term, and performing appropriate list comparison and merging operations in accordance with the logical search term associations contained in the query statements. An *exact match* retrieval strategy is used which consists of retrieving all items whose content description contains the term combination specified in the search requests. Furthermore, all retrieved items are considered by the system to be equally relevant to the user's needs, and normally no special methods are provided for ranking the output items in presumed order of goodness for the user.

The existing methodology has certain obvious advantages. In some cases, the indexers and search intermediaries may become expert in assigning useful content indicators to the stored documents and incoming user queries. The retrieval system will then exhibit a high level of effectiveness. The inverted file design also produces rapid response times, because the inverted file manipulations will identify all matching documents before the main document file is ever used. The document file must then be accessed only for those documents which will be shown to the user in response to the query.

The benefits of the conventional retrieval designs are available only under special circumstances, however. In particular, when the indexing and search operations are not carried out consistently by the several intermediaries, the effectiveness of the retrieval operations will suffer. If, for example, one indexer uses "search" when another would use "retrieval," some documents may not be retrieved when wanted. The use of controlled vocabulary lists can minimize this problem, but cannot eliminate it. In practice, the required degree of indexing consistency cannot be guaranteed when similar information items are treated by different indexers and searchers. In such circumstances, the various documents pertaining to a common subject area may be identified very differently, and many of these items may not be retrievable when wanted.

The inverted directory of index terms is most useful in situations where the search vocabulary remains static over long periods of time and is limited to a relatively small number of terms. In such cases, the directory size will remain manageable and relatively little updating may be needed. In practice, the indexing vocabulary is often large, consisting of several tens of thousands of terms for each subject area, and the vocabulary is not stable. The inverted directories to be stored may then become very large, and these directories must be kept up to date when new documents are added to the file or new vocabulary terms are introduced.

The customary library file organization which places in related or adjacent file positions all items that exhibit similar subject content is not followed by the existing inverted file systems. Instead, the main document file is often kept in arbitrary order, and it becomes difficult, given the location of a particular useful document, to determine the location of other related documents. This complicates the file search process, which ideally consists in locating certain useful items, and then proceeding from there to identify additional items resembling the ones found earlier. For the same reason, the inverted file strategy is not well suited to the processing of approximate queries designed to approach a given subject area in small steps, and to the kind of browsing which proves so useful in conventional libraries. Instead, it becomes necessary to formulate complete and specific queries, in the hope of retrieving the entire set of relevant items from the start.

The standard inverted file technology is difficult to change because of the large investments already made in the existing commercial systems. Nevertheless, substantial improvements are possible in the operations of the conventional systems. Thus, in some partly experimental systems, term weighting facilities have been superimposed on the standard Boolean query formulations and inverted file search procedures, leading to the ranking of retrieved documents in accordance with the weights of the matching query and document terms. This makes it possible to present the retrieved documents to the user in decreasing order of the sum of certain term weights. Presumably the user will find it easier to prepare improved query formulations when the items judged by the system to be most relevant are retrieved ahead of other more marginal items.

Systems have also been developed that are based on totally new conceptions of the retrieval task. One of the best known of these, the SMART system, is described in the remainder of this chapter together with certain other nonstandard retrieval system designs.

2 THE SMART SYSTEM ENVIRONMENT

*A Vector Representation and Similarity Computation

The SMART system distinguishes itself from more conventional retrieval systems in the following important respects: (1) it uses fully automatic indexing methods to assign content identifiers to documents and search requests; (2) it collects related documents into common subject classes, making it possible to start with specific items in a particular subject area and to find related items in neighboring subject fields; (3) it identifies the documents to be retrieved by performing similarity computations between stored items and incoming queries, and by ranking the retrieved items in decreasing order of their similarity with the query; and finally, (4) it includes automatic procedures for producing improved search statements based on information obtained as a result of earlier retrieval operations [1,2,3,4].

	$TERM_1$	$TERM_2$	...	$TERM_t$
DOC_1	$TERM_{11}$	$TERM_{12}$	...	$TERM_{1t}$
DOC_2	$TERM_{21}$	$TERM_{22}$	...	$TERM_{2t}$
⋮	⋮			
DOC_n	$TERM_{n1}$	$TERM_{n2}$	...	$TERM_{nt}$

Figure 4-1 Term assignment array (n documents, t terms).

In the SMART system each record, or document, is represented by a *vector* of terms. That is, a particular document, DOC_i, is identified by a collection of terms $TERM_{i1}, TERM_{i2}, \ldots, TERM_{it}$, where $TERM_{ij}$ is assumed to represent the weight, or importance, of term j assigned to document i. By "term" is meant some form of content identifier, such as a word extracted from a document text, a word phrase, or an entry from a term thesaurus. A given document collection may then be represented as an array, or matrix, of terms where each row of the matrix represents a document and each column represents the assignment of a specific term to the documents of the collection. A sample term assignment array is shown in Fig. 4-1. In the SMART system, positive term weights are chosen for terms actually assigned to the documents (that is, $TERM_{ij}$ is a positive number when term j actually occurs in document i); and $TERM_{ij}$ is set equal to zero when term j is not present as an identifier of document i.

A particular query, say $QUERY_j$, can be similarly identified as a vector $QTERM_{j1}, QTERM_{j2}, \ldots, QTERM_{jt}$, where $QTERM_{jk}$ represents the weight, or importance, of term k assigned to query j. Instead of insisting on a complete match between all nonzero query and document terms before a document is retrieved by the system, the retrieval of a stored item can be made to depend on the magnitude of a similarity computation measuring the similarity between a particular document vector and a particular query vector as a function of the magnitudes of the matching terms in the respective vectors. A similarity measure often used with the SMART system is the cosine measure, defined as

$$\text{COSINE}(DOC_i, QUERY_j) = \frac{\sum_{k=1}^{t} (TERM_{ik} \cdot QTERM_{jk})}{\sqrt{\sum_{k=1}^{t} (TERM_{ik})^2 \cdot \sum_{k=1}^{t} (QTERM_{jk})^2}} \qquad (1)$$

The cosine correlation measures the cosine of the angle between documents, or between queries and documents, when these are viewed as vectors in the multidimensional term space of dimension t. In three dimensions, when only three terms identify the documents, the situation may be represented by the configuration of Fig. 4-2. Each axis corresponds to a different term, and the position of each document vector in the space is determined by the magnitude

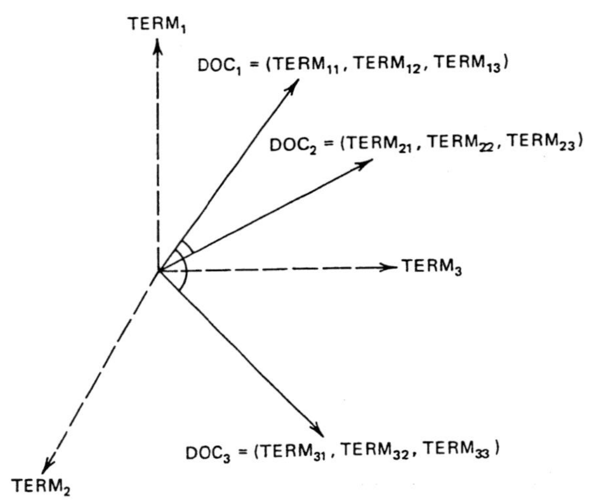

Figure 4-2 Vector representation of document space.

(weight) of the terms in that vector. The similarity between any two vectors is then represented as a function inversely related to the angle between them. That is, when two document vectors are exactly the same, the corresponding vectors are superimposed and the angle between them is zero.

The numerator of the cosine coefficient gives the sum of the matching terms between DOC_i and $QUERY_j$ when the indexing is binary, that is, when $TERM_{jk}$ is assumed equal to 1 whenever term k actually occurs in document i. When the indexing is not binary, the numerator represents the sum of the products of the term weights for the matching query and document terms. The denominator acts as a normalizing factor (by dividing the expression by the product of the lengths of the query and document vectors). This implies that each item is represented by a vector of equal length. If the angle between vectors is small and the normalized vectors are used, the cosine of the angle between the vectors may also be approximated by the distance between the tips of the corresponding vectors.

When a numeric measure of similarity is used for documents and queries, it is no longer necessary to retrieve all documents that exactly contain all the query terms. Instead the retrieval of a document can be made to depend on a particular threshold in the similarity measure or on a specific number of items to be retrieved. Assuming, for example, that a threshold of 0.50 is used, all items are retrieved for which the value of expression (1) is greater than or equal to 0.50; alternatively the top n items may be retrieved, where n is the number of items originally wanted. The retrieved documents may be conveniently presented to the user in decreasing order of their similarity values with the respective search requests. This is of special importance in an interactive retrieval situation where users are directly tied into the retrieval system, because new improved query formulations can then be constructed by utilizing information extracted from previously retrieved documents. Since the first few documents retrieved in response to a search request are those exhibiting the greatest query-document similarity, they are also the ones most likely to be relevant to the users' information needs. Hence they may be most important for query reformulation purposes.

*B Vector Manipulation

The query reformulation process incorporated into the SMART retrieval system is known as "relevance feedback" because relevance assessments supplied by the users for previously retrieved documents are returned to the system and used to construct new query vectors. The reformulated queries can then be compared with the stored documents in a new search operation. The aim is to construct new queries exhibiting a greater degree of similarity with the documents previously identified as relevant by the user than the original queries; at the same time, the new queries are expected to be less similar to the documents identified as nonrelevant by the user than the originals. The assumption is that the reformulated queries will retrieve more items resembling the relevant ones previously retrieved, and fewer items resembling the nonrelevant ones.

The query reformulation process is then based on the following complementary operations:

1 Terms that occur in documents previously identified as relevant by the user population are added to the original query vectors, or alternatively the weight of such terms is increased by an appropriate factor in constructing the new query statements.

2 At the same time, terms occurring in documents previously identified as nonrelevant by the users are deleted from the original query statements, or the weight of such terms is appropriately reduced.

Obviously, the query reformulation process can be carried out automatically by the retrieval system, given only an indication of relevance or nonrelevance of certain previously retrieved items obtained from the user population.

The effect of the relevance feedback operation is represented in the illustration of Fig. 4-3. In Fig. 4-3 and the related diagrams that follow, each document is identified by a point representing the tip of the corresponding vector, and the distance between two points is assumed to be inversely related to the respective cosine similarities between the vectors. Thus when two points appear close together in the space of Fig. 4-3, a substantial similarity exists between the vectors; the reverse is true for two points that appear far apart in the space. In Fig. 4-3, an original query vector (represented by an open triangle) appears with three retrieved documents of which one was identified as nonrelevant and two as relevant. Following the previously mentioned changes in the original query, a new query (the closed triangle) is constructed which appears shifted in the space: the distance to the relevant items is now smaller than be-

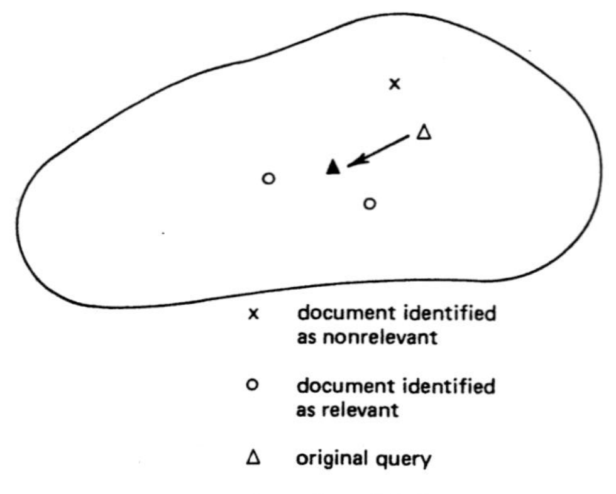

Figure 4-3 Relevance feedback illustration.

fore, and the distance to the nonrelevant one has increased. The relevance feedback process can be repeated several times in the hope of eventually obtaining adequate search output.

The cosine coefficient was introduced earlier to obtain a measure of similarity between a query vector and the various documents in a collection. The same measure also lends itself to the determination of similarities between pairs of documents. Thus, given the term vectors for two documents, DOC_i and DOC_j, the similarity between them may be defined as

$$\text{COSINE}(\text{DOC}_i,\text{DOC}_j) = \frac{\sum_{k=1}^{t} (\text{TERM}_{ik} \cdot \text{TERM}_{jk})}{\sqrt{\sum_{k=1}^{t} (\text{TERM}_{ik})^2 \cdot \sum_{k=1}^{t} (\text{TERM}_{jk})^2}} \tag{2}$$

By determining the similarity between various pairs of documents, it now becomes possible to construct a *clustered document file*, consisting of classes or clusters of documents such that the documents within a given class exhibit substantial similarities with each other. A clustered file resembles in concept the normal classified document arrangement used in conventional library situations, where items dealing with related subject areas are placed together in a common subject class. The clusters are, however, derived automatically and the construction method may be adapted to the particular collection environment under consideration. Thus, it is possible automatically to construct clustered files incorporating a large number of small clusters or a small number of large clusters; the classes may also overlap in the sense that certain documents may appear in more than one class. This last feature represents a substantial advantage over conventional library classification systems.

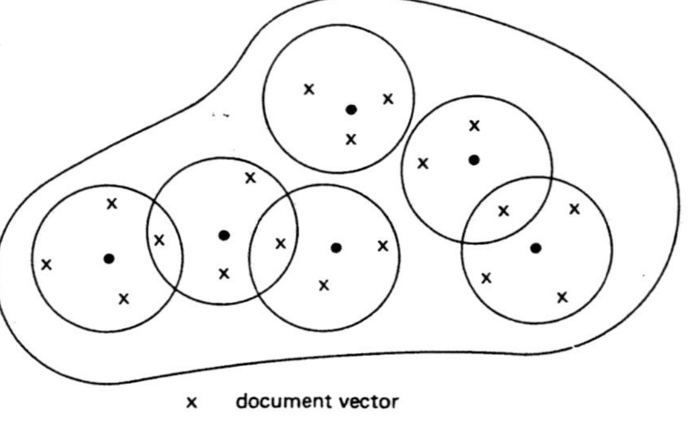

Figure 4-4 Sample clustered document collection.

A clustered document file is represented schematically in Fig. 4-4, where each x represents a document vector, and the distance between two particular x's is again assumed inversely proportional to their similarity. The large circular groupings in the figure identify the document clusters. It may be seen that some overlap exists between the clusters: certain documents located near the periphery of some classes actually appear in several classes. In order to render possible the manipulation of a clustered collection, it is convenient to use a special class vector, or *centroid*, to represent a given cluster. The centroids are similar to the centers of gravity of a set of points, and are represented by heavy dots in the illustration of Fig. 4-4. Given a set of m documents constituting a certain document class p, a given centroid vector $\text{CENTROID}_p = \text{CTERM}_{p1}, \text{CTERM}_{p2}, \ldots, \text{CTERM}_{pt}$ may be computed as the mathematical average of the document vectors included in the pth class. Thus, following the model used in the previous chapter for the construction of term classes, the weight of term k in the centroid for class p can be computed as the average of the weight of term k in all m document vectors incorporated into class p. That is,

$$\text{CTERM}_{pk} = \frac{1}{m} \sum_{i=1}^{m} \text{TERM}_{ik} \tag{3}$$

where the summation covers the m documents of class p.

Given a clustered collection of the type shown in Fig. 4-4, a document search is now carried out in two main steps. Each query is first compared with the various centroid vectors by computing the corresponding centroid-query similarity coefficients. For classes whose centroids exhibit a sufficiently high similarity with the query, the individual documents are next compared with the query, using the formula of expression (1), and documents showing sufficiently high similarities with the query are retrieved for the user's attention. Assuming that n documents exist in a collection which is divided into x clusters each containing approximately n/x documents, the number of vector comparisons needed to compare a query with the best cluster is x + n/x (instead of the n comparisons needed in an unclustered file). The number of needed vector comparisons is minimized when the number of clusters x equals $\sqrt{n}$.

For large collections involving many heterogeneous documents, a great many clusters may need to be defined. In that case, the number of required query-centroid comparisons may become excessively large. The search efficiency may then be increased by taking the set of centroids and applying the clustering methodology previously used for the document vectors to compare pairs of centroid vectors. Centroids that are sufficiently similar are then grouped into superclasses identified by supercentroids, as shown in Fig. 4-5, where two superclasses are represented. The file search now requires three steps: first a comparison of the query with the supercentroid vectors; then for some supercentroids, a comparison with the individual centroids included in the corresponding superclusters; finally, for certain centroids, a comparison with the individual document vectors located in the respective document clusters.

The clustered file organization is adaptable to a growing collection environment, because new incoming documents can be treated just like incoming queries. The new items are compared with the existing supercentroids and centroids, and eventually they are included in those clusters for which the document-cluster similarity is sufficiently large. As in the standard inverted file organization, two distinct files are needed for the file search process:

1 The main document file, arranged in order by clusters such that all items included in a common cluster are retrievable in a single access to the main file

2 The auxiliary file of cluster centroids, and supercentroids arranged in a hierarchical tree format where each supercentroid contains pointers specifying the locations of the individual centroids for that superclass, and each centroid in turn points to the locations of the individual document vectors for that class

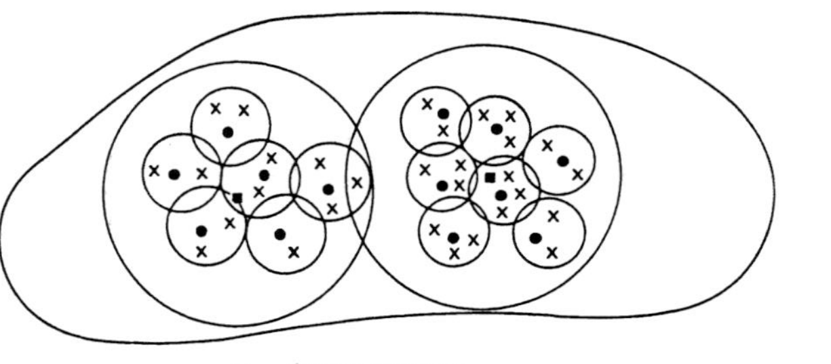

Figure 4-5 Introduction of superclusters.

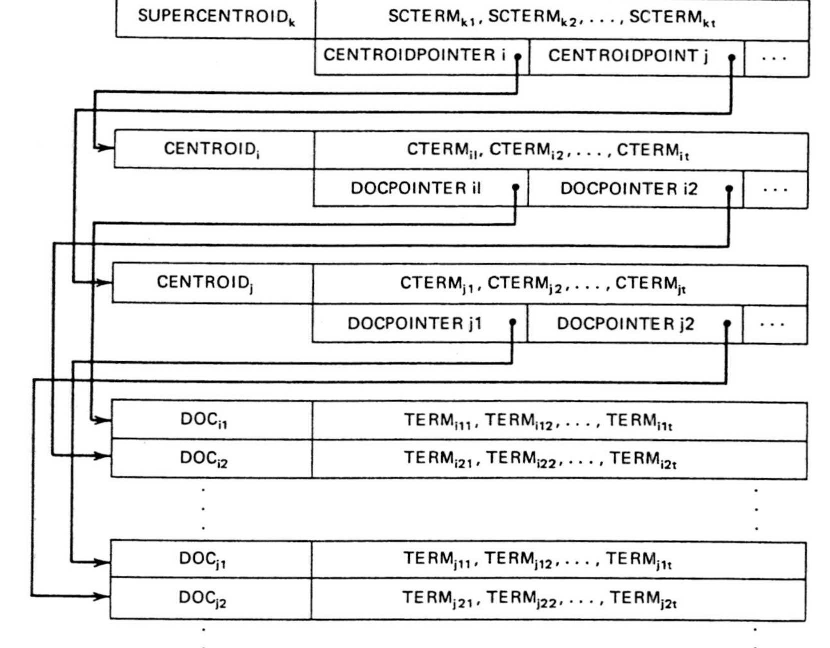

Figure 4-6 Hierarchical vector arrangement for clustered file.

The file arrangement is illustrated in simplified form in Fig. 4-6.

C Vector Generation

Consider now the document indexing process, that is, the method used to construct the document vectors. The basic function of an indexing system is the segregation of the subset of documents relevant to some query from the remainder of the collection. Preferably, all the relevant items might then occur in one or more document clusters, whereas the nonrelevant items would be placed in separate clusters. A situation of this type is shown in Fig. 4-7. Such an ideal document space might be constructed by assigning to the relevant document set the terms utilized by the user population to formulate the corresponding search requests. Unfortunately, it is difficult to know in advance what terms will be considered useful for query formulation purposes, and even in interactive systems where information can be generated about the usefulness of certain terms with respect to certain topic areas, it is still necessary to make the somewhat hazardous assumption that all users interested in specified subject areas would choose the same query terms to express their information needs. Similarly, one would have to assume that all such users would accept the same set of documents as relevant to their queries.

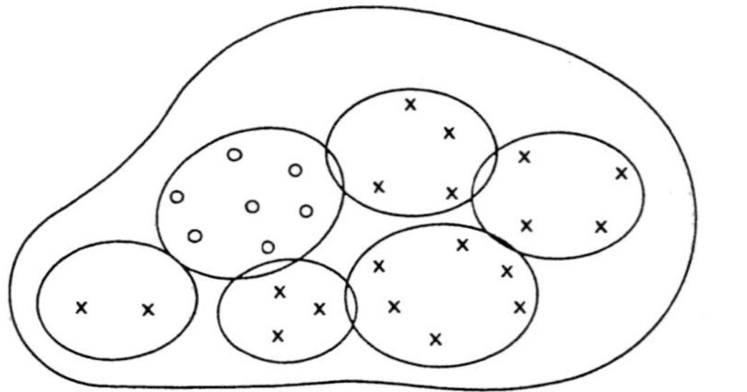

Figure 4-7 Ideal document space.

In practice, it is not possible to find a single clustering which is ideal for all subject areas and all users, even given full relevance information in advance. Furthermore, new documents that are added to the collection must necessarily be processed without the use of document relevance information. The best policy may then lead to the use of index terms capable of distinguishing each particular document from the remainder of the collection. This can be achieved by using as a controlling criterion the document frequency of each term in the collection, that is, the number of documents to which a term is assigned. The term discrimination theory examined in the previous chapter indicates that the terms to be preferred are medium-frequency terms that are assigned to a few documents but not to the rest of the collection.

In the SMART system, the text of the document abstracts (or the text of the query statements obtained from the user population) is analyzed automatically. Terms whose document frequency is neither too large nor too small are incorporated directly into the document or query vectors for indexing purposes. Terms whose document frequency exceeds a given threshold are considered too broad and unspecific; they are rendered more specific by being combined with other terms into *term phrases* before assignment to the document and query vectors. On the other hand, terms with a very low document frequency that are assigned to one or two documents only are considered too specific; they can be broadened by grouping them into term classes of the kind found in a *thesaurus* of terms. The thesaurus class identifiers are then incorporated into the term and document vectors instead of the individual rare terms. These operations are described in more detail in the next section, where the SMART procedures are treated more thoroughly.

A simplified flowchart of the SMART processing chain is shown in Fig. 4-8. The processes represented on the left side of the chart consisting of the

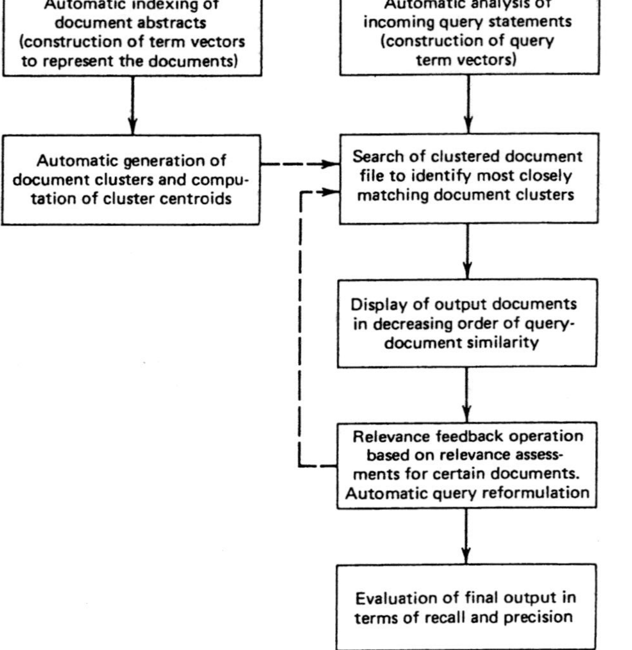

Figure 4-8 Simplified SMART system flowchart.

initial construction of term vectors for the documents and the generation of clustered files are carried out only once, or in any case at infrequent time intervals. The query-processing operations, on the other hand, including the generation of query vectors, the clustered file search, and the relevance feedback operations are performed for each query. Only the query-handling operations need to be done in real time while the user is present.

The SMART system is designed to make available a large variety of experimental methods, including many different automatic indexing procedures, query-document similarity functions, cluster file generation methods, and query-reformulation processes. The system can then serve as a test vehicle to validate the various experimental procedures. For this reason evaluation methods have been incorporated into the system which produce recall and precision information following the retrieval operations.

The following assumptions are implicit in the model used by the SMART environment for the representation of document and query operations:

1 Each document is represented by a particular vector, that is, a particular position in a t-dimensional vector space, where t is the number of permissible terms available for indexing purposes.

2 Each term included in a given document or query vector is assumed to be unrelated (orthogonal) to the other terms, and all terms are considered equally important (except for distinctions inherent in the assignment of weights to the individual terms).

The assumptions are in fact only first-order approximations to the true situation because documents exhibit not only subject content but also extent, or scope. A survey or tutorial text normally has greater scope than a research article. This suggests that the subject matter of a document be represented by a point in a certain location of the subject space as suggested by Figs. 4-3 to 4-5, and that an area of space surrounding the subject points be used to denote scope and extent. The document scope might be determined by using the frequencies with which individual documents are cited in the literature. Thus documents attracting many citations could be assumed to have wide scope.

The second area of simplification in the SMART model is the orthogonality assumption for the various index terms. In the SMART system, each term represents a separate coordinate in the vector space, and no term relationships are assumed to exist. In actual fact, words do not, however, occur independently of each other in the document texts, and neither do the index terms assigned to a collection of items. In recent years, a great deal of work has been devoted to the study of retrieval models which take into account certain term dependencies. These models tend to be complex and difficult to use. The available experimental evidence suggests that the greatest deviations from independence arise for the very rare terms that occur in a few documents only. The discrimination value theory indicates that these terms are not very important for retrieval purposes. For the vast majority of the medium- and high-frequency terms, the independence assumption is not in fact unreasonable.

Perhaps in a few years, some experimental retrieval systems will make provision for the representation of document scope and impact and for the use of term dependencies. At the present time efforts in this direction are in a very preliminary state.

3 SMART SYSTEM PROCEDURES

*A Automatic Indexing

When the SMART system was originally designed in the middle 1960s the experts generally felt that sophisticated language analysis procedures would be required in a machine indexing system to replace the intellect normally applied by the human indexer. Accordingly, the original SMART indexing system was based on the following language analysis tools:

1 Synonym dictionaries, or *thesauruses*, would be used to group the individual terms into classes of synonymous or related terms. When a thesaurus is available, each original term can be replaced by a complete class of related terms, thereby broadening the content description.

2 *Hierarchical term arrangements* could be constructed to relate the content terms in a given subject area. With such preconstructed term hierarchies, the standard content descriptions can be "expanded" by adding to a given content description hierarchically superior (more general) terms as well as hierarchically inferior (more specific) terms.

3 *Syntactic analysis* systems would serve for the specification of the syntactic roles of the terms, and for the formation of complex content descriptions consisting of term phrases and larger syntactic units. A syntactic analysis system can be used to supply specific content identifications, and it prevents confusion between compound terms such as "blind Venetian" and "Venetian blind."

4 *Semantic analysis* systems might supplement the syntactic units by using semantic roles attached to the entities making up a given content description. Semantic analysis systems utilize various kinds of knowledge extraneous to the documents, often specified by preconstructed "semantic graphs" and other related constructs.

The early test results obtained with the SMART system showed that some complicated linguistic methodologies that were believed essential to attain reasonable retrieval effectiveness were in fact not useful in raising performance [5,6]. In particular, the use of syntactic analysis procedures to construct syntactic content phrases and the utilization of concept hierarchies could not be proved effective under any circumstances. It may be that these failures were attributable not to the actual processes themselves but rather to the particular implementations used in the test situations. The fact is that linguistic theories were not sufficiently well understood 15 years ago to permit the construction of effective semantic maps and hierarchical term arrangements, or to design accurate and complete syntactic analysis systems. Some progress has been made in this area in the last few years. However, versatile linguistic methodologies that would be applicable to a wide variety of subject areas are still not easily incorporated into an unrestricted language processing environment at the present time. For this reason the standard SMART indexing procedures are based on simpler language process considerations that are by now well understood. These simple automatic methods can be shown to be superior to conventional indexing methodologies in laboratory test situations [6,7]:

1 The individual words that make up a document excerpt (abstract) or a query text are first recognized.

2 A stop list, comprising a few hundred high-frequency function words, such as "and," "of," "or," and "but," is used to eliminate such words from consideration in the subsequent processing.

3 The scope of the remaining word occurrences is broadened by reducing each word to word stem form; this can be done by using relatively simple suffix removal methods together with special rules to take care of exceptions, as previously explained [8,9].

4 Following suffix removal, multiple occurrences of a given word stem are combined into a single term for incorporation into the document or query vectors.

At this point, the standard query-document vector matching methods introduced in the previous section could be used to identify all documents whose word stem vectors are sufficiently similar to the query vectors. The SMART system retains a much larger number of content indicators than is customary in conventional systems, and the larger number and greater diversity of the terms compensate to some extent for the lack of precision in the term selection. Nevertheless, the foregoing process would provide inferior search results in many cases, because some word stems are obviously more important for the representation of document content than others. Two main operations are needed to transform the word stem vectors into useful term vectors: first a term weight can be assigned to each term reflecting the usefulness of the term in the collection environment under consideration; and second, terms whose usefulness is inadequate as reflected by a low term weight can be transformed into better terms [10–13].

As explained earlier, it is convenient to separate the term weighting task into two parts: first, one must take into account the term characteristics within a given document or document excerpt; second, it is important to consider also the function of the term in the remainder of the collection. The considerations detailed in Chapter 3 favor terms that exhibit high importance in the documents to which they are assigned, as measured, for example, by their occurrence frequencies in the individual documents. At the same time, the best terms must be able to distinguish the documents to which they are assigned from the remainder of the collection; hence their importance factor in the document collection as a whole ought to be low. The importance of a given term k in an individual document i is conveniently measured by the frequency of occurrence in the document $FREQ_{ik}$. The usefulness of the term in the collection as a whole may be reflected by the term discrimination value $DISCVALUE_k$, or alternatively by an inverse function of the document frequency $DOCFREQ_k$ (that is, the number of documents to which the term is assigned). Two possible term weighting functions reflecting the usefulness of term k in document i are

$$WEIGHT_{ik} = \frac{FREQ_{ik}}{DOCFREQ_k} \tag{4}$$

$$\text{and } WEIGHT_{ik} = FREQ_{ik} \cdot DISCVALUE_k$$

Terms with a low weight according to expression (4) could in principle be deleted from the indexing vocabulary. In practice, the deletion of broad, high-frequency terms is likely to cause losses in recall, and the elimination of specific, low-frequency terms may impair the precision. It is then preferable to alter such terms completely. The most obvious methods available for this purpose consist in creating specific *term phrases* incorporating the high-frequency terms that are originally considered too broad, and forming *thesaurus classes* of the low-frequency terms that may be too specific to be used by themselves.

Consider first the phrase-formation process. Ideally, a phrase is a language construct with specific syntactic and semantic properties. Because a full syntactic and/or semantic analysis of document and query texts is not currently possible for normal information retrieval purposes, a simple phrase-formation process must be used. The following phrase-formation criteria are of greatest importance:

1 The phrase components should occur in a common context within the document or query to which the phrase is assigned as a content identifier.

2 The phrase components should represent broad concepts, and their frequency of assignment to the documents of a collection should be sufficiently high.

In the SMART system a phrase is defined as a pair of two distinct word stems not contained on the stop list, such that the components occur in the same sentence within a document or query text, and at least one component has a document frequency in the collection exceeding a given threshold. A more stringent phrase-construction process is obtained by also taking into account the distance in the text between potential phrase components, that is, the number of intervening words between them. The following phrase-construction process can be used in practice:

1 Start with the query and document texts; use a stop list to eliminate common function words; generate word stems by using a suffix deletion process to reduce the original words.

2 Take pairs of the remaining word stems, and let each pair define a phrase provided that the distance in the text between components does not exceed n words (at most n − 1 intervening words), and that at least one of the components of each phrase is a high-frequency term; this frequency cutoff is manipulated to reduce the number of generated phrases to manageable size.

3 Phrases for which both components are identical are eliminated, as are duplicate phrases where all components match an already existing phrase.

4 Phrase weights are assigned as a function of the weights of the individual phrase components; if the term weights are restricted to values between 0 and 1, the phrase weight can be defined as the product of the individual component weights.

The phrase-generation process is illustrated for a sample sentence in Table 4-1. Some of the original words, such as "in," "need," "of," and "require," are deleted following a comparison with the entries contained in a stop list. The remaining words are transformed into word stems: this generates INFORM from "information" and RETRIEV from "retrieval." A maximum distance of four is assumed between phrase components in the text, leading to the generation of the seven phrases listed in Table 4-1c.

The phrase-formation process increases the specificity of the content identifiers attached to queries and documents. The converse operation consists in using thesaurus classes for content identification. A thesaurus contains groupings of similar or related terms into term classes. The use of thesauruses is

"People in need of information require effective retrieval services"

(a)

"PEOPLE INFORM EFFECT RETRIEV SERVICE"

(b)

PEOPLE	INFORM	EFFECT	RETRIEV
INFORM	EFFECT	EFFECT	SERVICE
INFORM	RETRIEV	RETRIEV	SERVICE
INFORM	SERVICE		

(c)

Table 4-1 Phrase-generation process. (a) Original sentence. (b) Word stems generated from original sentence. (c) Word pairs (phrases) generated assuming maximum component distance of four.

often advocated for purposes of synonym recognition: when the query specifies "manufacture" and the document contains "production," a term match is obtainable by including both terms in a common thesaurus class. Because the frequency of assignment of a thesaurus class is approximately equal to the sum of the frequencies of the individual terms in the class, thesauruses are most useful for the classification of the low-frequency terms that need to be broadened. Since the automatic term classification (thesaurus) construction methods are all based in one way or another on the computation of similarities between terms, thesauruses are not easily generated automatically. Normally, the term similarities would be obtained by computing similarity coefficients between the term vectors (columns) of the term assignment array (see Fig. 4-1). In effect the similarity between two terms will then depend on co-occurrences of the terms in the documents of a collection. Unfortunately, the terms of most interest for thesaurus construction purposes are those whose overall occurrence frequency in a collection is low. These terms do not co-occur very often in the same documents, and their computed similarity measure must be expected to be very low and may not then furnish an accurate indication of term relationship.

In practice, it becomes necessary either to use a manually constructed thesaurus that obeys the thesaurus construction principles described in the previous chapter, or else to use an automatic thesaurus construction method in which the grouping criteria are relatively weak [14,15]. The well-known *single-link* classification method appears to be most useful in this connection [16]. The single-link process is based on a computation of the term-term similarities for all term pairs. The process then proceeds iteratively as follows:

1 For each term pair ($TERM_i$, $TERM_j$) whose similarity exceeds a given threshold, an attempt is made to add a third term, $TERM_k$, to the group by computing the similarity between $TERM_k$ and each of the original terms; the new term is added whenever its similarity with *at least one* of the original terms exceeds a stated threshold.

2 The process is then repeated for term triples, quadruples, etc., by adding a new term whenever its similarity with one of the original terms exceeds the stated threshold.

An example of this process is shown in Fig. 4-9. The significant term-pair similarities are shown in Fig. 4-9a in tabular form. Figure 4-9b presents the same information in graph form, where the nodes of the graph designate terms, and the branches between nodes represent the corresponding term similarities. The final term clusters are given in Fig. 4-9c. The initial cluster is obtained by first forming the class $\{T_1, T_2\}$. To this are added terms T_3 and T_7 because of the similar term pairs (T_2, T_3) and (T_2, T_7). This produces a new class $\{T_1, T_2, T_3, T_7\}$. This group can be increased to its full size by adding T_8 because of the connection between T_3 and T_8. A second class is formed of terms T_4, T_5, and T_6 in view

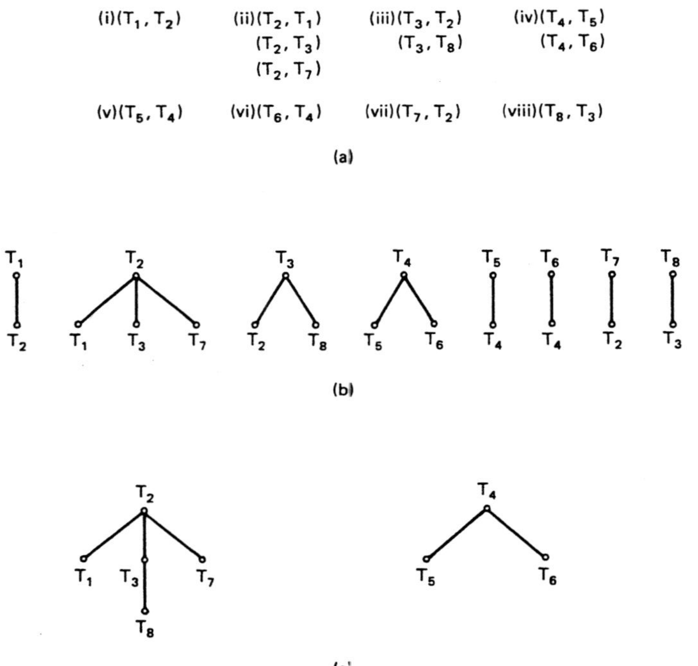

Figure 4-9 Single-link cluster example. (a) Initially available term pairs. (b) Corresponding graphical representation. (c) Corresponding single-link clustering.

of the existence of the similar pairs (T_4, T_5) and (T_4, T_6). For the example under consideration the thesaurus classes produced are as follows: $\{T_1, T_2, T_3, T_7, T_8\}$ and $\{T_4, T_5, T_6\}$.

The single-link cluster process requires of the order of n^2 term comparisons to classify n terms, since each term is associated with at most $(n - 1)$ other terms. This method has been used to cluster large collections of items [17], and it may be applicable to the general term classification problem because the number of terms does not normally exceed several tens of thousands.

For document clustering, where the file size may comprise hundreds of thousands or even millions of items, less expensive methods may turn out to be more appropriate. A summary of the SMART automatic indexing system is presented in the flowchart of Fig. 4-10.

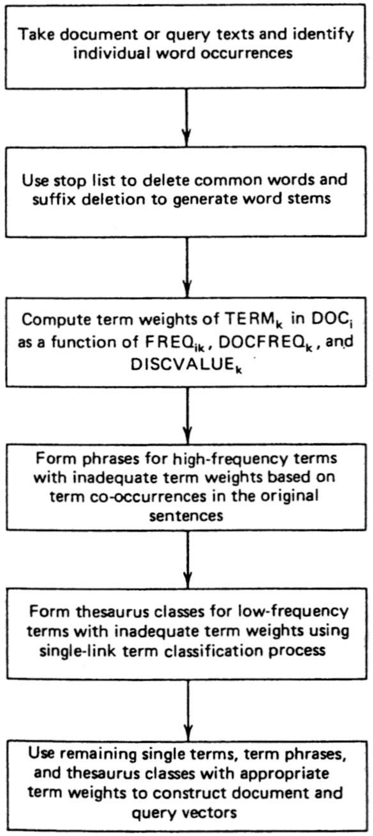

Take document or query texts and identify individual word occurrences

↓

Use stop list to delete common words and suffix deletion to generate word stems

↓

Compute term weights of $TERM_k$ in DOC_i as a function of $FREQ_{ik}$, $DOCFREQ_k$, and $DISCVALUE_k$

↓

Form phrases for high-frequency terms with inadequate term weights based on term co-occurrences in the original sentences

↓

Form thesaurus classes for low-frequency terms with inadequate term weights using single-link term classification process

↓

Use remaining single terms, term phrases, and thesaurus classes with appropriate term weights to construct document and query vectors

Figure 4-10 Typical SMART automatic indexing process.

*B Automatic Document Classification

It was seen earlier that the preferred file organization in the SMART environment is a clustered collection where the incoming queries are compared first with the centroids of certain document classes and then with the individual documents for those classes whose centroid similarity with the queries is sufficiently large. The clustered file organization lends itself to rapid collection searches and to fast and possibly effective retrieval strategies because all the related documents in a given class are in principle retrievable in a single file access. Furthermore, a clustered file is updated easily, because new documents can be treated like incoming queries in that comparisons with the existing centroids lead to the incorporation of new items into the most closely fitting classes.

The available clustering methods fall into two main types according to whether an initial set of classes already exists or on the contrary new classes must be constructed for a given collection of items. When document sets are to be clustered, a prior classification is not generally available; it is then necessary to construct a new classification for the given set of items. A second clustering criterion distinguishes the *hierarchical grouping* methods which utilize a full document-document similarity matrix specifying the similarity for all document pairs, from the *iterative partitioning* procedures where a rough classification is first generated which is then refined in several steps.

The hierarchical grouping methods which include the previously mentioned clique and single-link procedures are theoretically more satisfying than the alternative partitioning methods because in these methods each item is effectively considered as a possible "seed point" around which a new class is to be built, whereas the classes formed with the iterative partitioning process depend on the strategy used for the initial cluster generation. A form of iterative partitioning is nevertheless used with the SMART system because the number of required document comparisons to cluster n items is of the order of n log n, whereas n^2 comparisons may be needed to obtain the document pair similarities needed by the hierarchical grouping strategies. When the collections are large, a relatively inexpensive clustering method seems essential.

The SMART "single-pass" clustering proceeds in a bottom-up fashion by considering the records one at a time in arbitrary order, while attempting to group them into clusters [18,19]. The first item is initially identified with cluster one. The next item is compared with cluster one and merged with it if found to be sufficiently similar. If the new item is not similar to any already existing cluster, a new cluster is generated. Subsequent items are compared with all existing cluster centroids and entered into classes whenever the centroid similarity is sufficiently large. When a new item is entered into a cluster, the corresponding cluster centroid must be redefined by incorporating terms from the new term vector into the original cluster centroid.

In principle, the single-pass clustering process should serve to assign each item to at least one cluster, and the classification should be complete after one pass through the file. In practice, the resulting classes may not be usable for search purposes without additional refinements. Several problems may arise:

1 The number of clusters produced by the initial pass may become excessively large, implying that a query submitted to the system may have to be compared with a very large number of centroids before access to the individual records is actually obtained.

2 The size of certain clusters may become too large, particularly if a great many records in a collection cover fairly homogeneous subject areas.

3 Alternatively, the cluster size may be very small, and could indeed be limited to a single record in cases where so-called loose records exist that do not match any other records in the collection.

4 The overlap among clusters, that is, the number of items jointly contained in more than one cluster may be too large or too small.

To respond to these eventualities, controls must be introduced to regulate cluster size, cluster overlap, and number of clusters generated, and to handle any "loose" items remaining at the end of the first pass. The loose items actually present no severe problem, since they can naturally be merged with the closest existing clusters. To control the size and the number of clusters, a *cluster splitting* operation is carried out whenever a given cluster size exceeds some preestablished threshold. This is done by generating a term-term similarity matrix for all terms located in the excessively large clusters, and using a new *local* clustering operation to produce two or more new centroids replacing each centroid originally attached to a cluster that had grown too large.

The cluster splitting operation is illustrated in the example of Fig. 4-11 where the assumption is that no class may contain more than four elements. The initial state consists of four clusters, each containing between two and four records. These four centroids are themselves grouped into a supercluster with supercentroid S as shown in Fig. 4-11a. If a new record is added to cluster A, an illegal situation arises, since the cluster size is assumed limited to four elements. The A centroid must then be split thereby creating two new centroids A′ and A″ as shown in Fig. 4-11c. At this point the supercluster S is no longer viable since it now contains five elements. This is remedied by splitting S into S′ and S″, thereby creating a new hypercluster H included in Fig. 4-11d. The cluster splitting process thus propagates upward in the "cluster tree," starting with the lowest level clusters and moving upward as shown in the example.

A simplified flowchart of the single-pass cluster generation and search process is shown in Fig. 4-12. Generation and search differ in substance only for the lowest-level centroids: during cluster generation a new record must be added to the lowest level of the cluster tree and the cluster splitting routine may need to be invoked; during normal searching, on the other hand, the low-level clusters simply lead to the individual records on the lowest level. The program of Fig. 4-12 maintains a list of centroids to be split. When that list is not empty, the splitting routine is invoked following the placement of each incoming item.

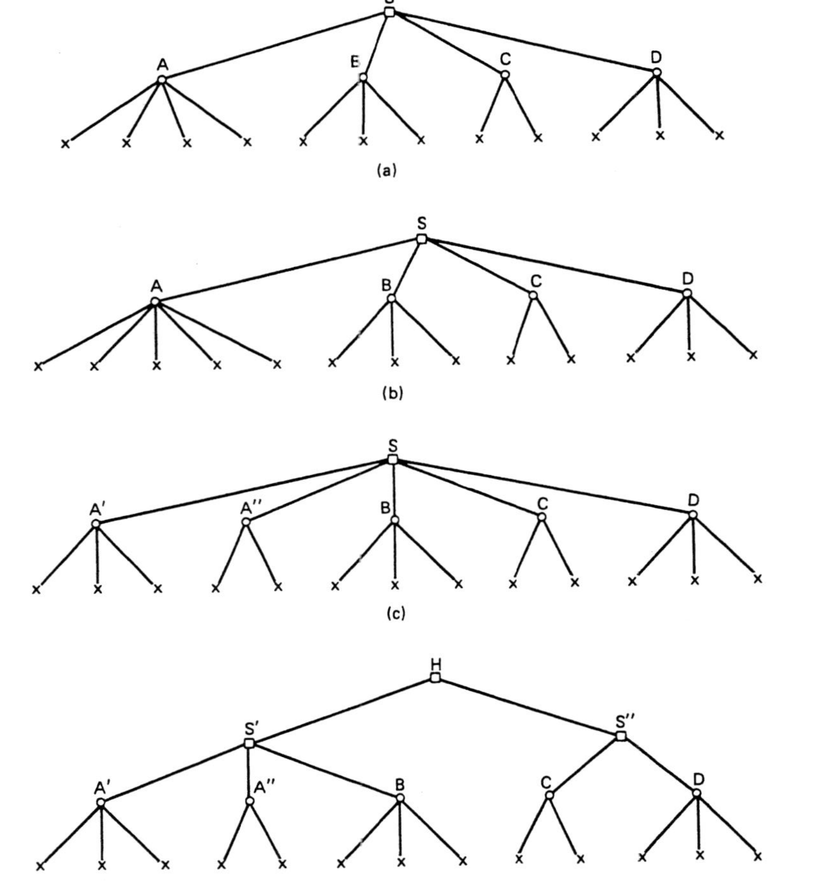

Figure 4-11 Example of cluster splitting process. (a) Initial state of cluster structure. (b) Addition of one more item to cluster A. (c) Splitting cluster A into two pieces A′ and A″. (d) Splitting supercluster S into two pieces S′ and S″.

The cluster generation method may be adapted to special retrieval requirements: when a premium is placed on search precision and the retrieval of nonrelevant items must be avoided, the cluster structure should consist of a large number of small, disjoint clusters on the lowest level of the search tree. When the recall proves more important a smaller number of larger, partly overlapping clusters should prove more effective. Suitable adjustments in the thresholds that control the clustering process can be used to satisfy varying retrieval requirements.

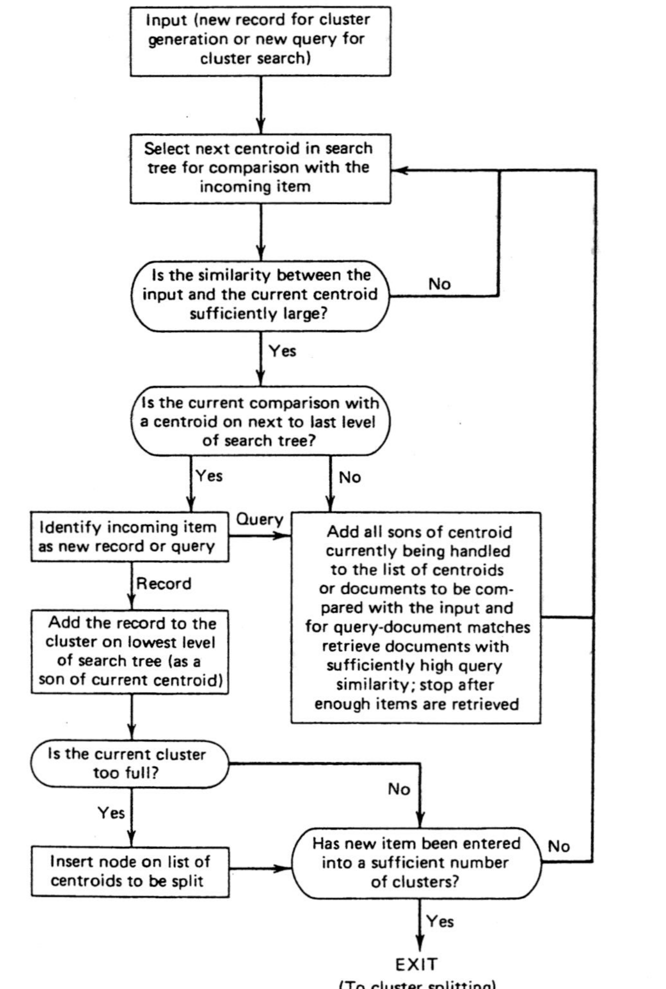

Figure 4-12 Cluster generation and search. (*Adapted from reference 18.*)

*C Relevance Feedback Operations

Most modern on-line search and retrieval environments make provisions for the utilization of flexible search procedures that can generate satisfactory query statements and useful retrieval output in several small steps. An iterative search system is typically implemented by initially submitting a tentative query, and then using system facilities to improve these query statements and the resulting set of retrieved items.

The methods used to construct improved query formulations fall into two broad classes: those which are applied before a file search is actually carried out, and those which depend on the prior retrieval of some retrieved items. In the former case, it is possible to use displayed vocabulary excerpts, term frequency information, and citations to so-called source documents previously identified as relevant by the user to construct improved queries. More specifically, a stored thesaurus of terms can be used to obtain synonym lists for the terms originally included in a search formulation. In addition, frequency data about the number of documents to which a term is assigned can also be stored in the thesaurus to provide an indication of the potential effect of the term for search purposes. When relevant source documents are known in advance, a query might simply be replaced by the terms assigned to such documents in the hope of retrieving additional documents similar to those originally identified as relevant.

An alternative query alteration process is based on the execution of an initial search operation and an initial retrieval of certain stored documents. The display of information relating to these items such as the titles or abstracts of the previously retrieved documents is then used to modify the query statements, normally by adding terms from documents that appear relevant to the user and by deleting terms included in the items that appear useless. This produces new queries whose resemblance to the relevant documents is greater than before while their resemblance to the nonrelevant items is smaller, as suggested in the example of Fig. 4-3. In the SMART system, this process has been called "relevance feedback." It has been shown experimentally that the relevance feedback process can account for improvements in retrieval effectiveness of up to 50 percent in precision for high-recall (broad) searches, and of approximately 20 percent in precision for low-recall searches [20].

Consider first the unrealistic situation where the complete set of relevant documents D_R is known in advance, and hence also the complete set of nonrelevant documents $D_{N-R} = N - D_R$. (In such a case, there is no point in submitting a search request because the known relevant documents can then simply be retrieved from the file without performing a file search.) It can be shown that in such a situation the optimal query which is best able to distinguish the relevant from the nonrelevant documents is a vector obtained by taking the difference between the set of relevant and the set of nonrelevant documents, respectively. More formally, if $TERM_{ik}$ represents the value, or weight, of term k in document i as before, then the average value of term k in the set of R relevant documents is $\left(\frac{1}{R}\right)\left(\sum_{i \in D_R} TERM_{ik}\right)$. Similarly, the average value of term k in the set of N − R nonrelevant documents is $\left(\frac{1}{N-R}\right)\left(\sum_{i \in D_{N-R}} TERM_{ik}\right)$. The value of term k in the optimal query Q_{opt} is then defined as

$$(Q_{opt})_k = C\left(\frac{1}{R}\sum_{i\epsilon D_R} TERM_{ik} - \frac{1}{N-R}\sum_{i\epsilon D_{N-R}} TERM_{ik}\right) \tag{5}$$

where C is a constant [21]

In practice the sets of relevant documents D_R and of nonrelevant items D_{N-R} are not known in advance. However, the relevance judgments obtained from the user population for previously retrieved relevant documents furnish approximations to the sets D_R and D_{N-R}. The assumption is then made that a near-optimal query can be obtained by taking the difference between the subsets of relevant and of nonrelevant items known at any particular time. By repeating the relevance feedback operation several times, and retrieving at each point a new set of documents with an improved query formulation, one may eventually obtain a reasonable approximation to the actual set of relevant and nonrelevant items.

Several formulations are now possible for a new improved query vector Q', starting with an initial query formulation Q and a set $D_{R'}$ of R' documents identified as relevant as well as a set $D_{N'}$ of N' nonrelevant documents, where $D_{N'}$ and $D_{R'}$ are initial representations of the actual set of nonrelevant and relevant documents, respectively. First it is possible by analogy to the optimal formula of expression (5) to define the new query as simply the difference between the known sets of relevant and nonrelevant items, respectively:

$$Q' = C\left(\frac{1}{R'}\sum_{i\epsilon D_{R'}} DOC_i - \frac{1}{N'}\sum_{i\epsilon D_{N'}} DOC_i\right) \tag{6}$$

DOC_i again represents the vector for the ith document. In formula (6) the information contained in the original query Q is not used. In practice the original query formulation may contain important information; hence an improved feedback strategy may be produced by using the original query and adding terms from the relevant documents, and/or deleting terms from the nonrelevant ones:

$$Q' = \alpha Q + \beta\left(\frac{1}{R'}\sum_{i\epsilon D_{R'}} DOC_i\right) - \gamma\left(\frac{1}{N'}\sum_{i\epsilon D_{N'}} DOC_i\right) \tag{7}$$

where α, β, and γ are suitable constants. Expression (7) specifies a new query as the vector sum of the old query plus the weighted difference between the average of the known relevant and the average of the known nonrelevant items.

The operations specified by expression (7) are illustrated in the example of Fig. 4-13, where a query Q comprising five terms is shown together with a relevant document D_1 and a nonrelevant document D_2. The constants α, β, γ are assumed to take on values of 1, 1/2, 1/4, respectively. The new query derived in Fig. 4-13c exhibits increased weights for terms 1 and 3, a decreased weight for term 5, and a new term (term 2) not present in the original query. Correspondingly, the query-document similarity obtained with the new query Q' is larger than before for document D_1 and smaller than before for D_2.

	Term 1	Term 2	Term 3	Term 4	Term 5
Q = (	5 ,	0 ,	3 ,	0 ,	1)
D_1 = (	2 ,	1 ,	2 ,	0 ,	0)
D_2 = (	1 ,	0 ,	0 ,	0 ,	2)

(a)

$$Q' = Q + \frac{1}{2}\left(\sum_{D_{R'}} D_i\right) - \frac{1}{4}\left(\sum_{D_{N'}} D_i\right)$$

$$Q' = (5,0,3,0,1) + \frac{1}{2}(2,1,2,0,0) - \frac{1}{4}(1,0,0,0,2)$$

$$= 5\tfrac{3}{4}, \tfrac{1}{2}, 4, 0, \tfrac{1}{2}$$

(b)

Assume $S(Q, D_i) = \sum_{j=1}^{t} (Q_j, D_{ij})$

$S(Q,D_1) = (5\cdot 2) + (0\cdot 1) + (3\cdot 2) + (0\cdot 0) + (1\cdot 0) = 16$

$S(Q',D_1) = (5\tfrac{3}{4}\cdot 2) + (\tfrac{1}{2}\cdot 1) + (4\cdot 2) + (0\cdot 0) + (\tfrac{1}{2}\cdot 0) = 20$

$S(Q,D_2) = (5\cdot 1) + (0\cdot 0) + (3\cdot 0) + (0\cdot 0) + (1\cdot 2) = 7$

$S(Q',D_2) = (5\tfrac{3}{4}\cdot 1) + (\tfrac{1}{2}\cdot 0) + (4\cdot 0) + (0\cdot 0) + (\tfrac{1}{2}\cdot 2) = 6\tfrac{3}{4}$

(c)

Figure 4-13 Relevance feedback operation. (a) Originally available query Q, relevant document D_1, nonrelevant document D_2. (b) Query alteration. (c) Query-document similarities.

In practice one finds that the information contained in the relevant documents is more valuable for query reformulation purposes than the terms which originate in the nonrelevant items. The reason is that the set of relevant documents with respect to a given query may be expected to be located in a reasonably homogeneous area of the document space, as in the example of Fig. 4-7. The addition to the query of terms from these relevant items will then produce a definite movement of the query in the direction of these relevant items (see Fig. 4-3). The set of nonrelevant items, on the other hand, is normally much more heterogeneous. The average nonrelevant item may therefore be located almost anywhere in the document space, and subtraction of the corresponding terms

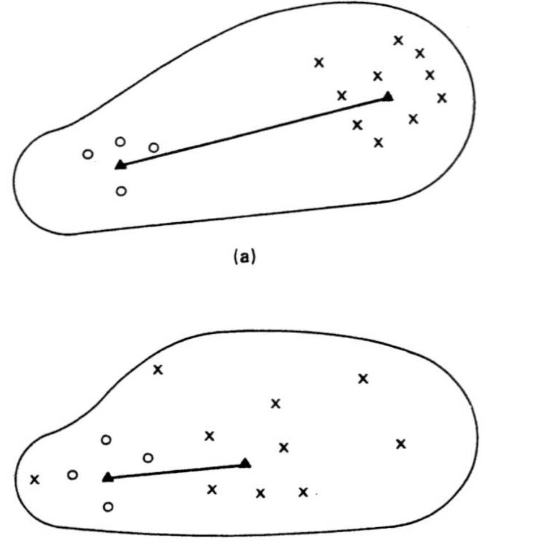

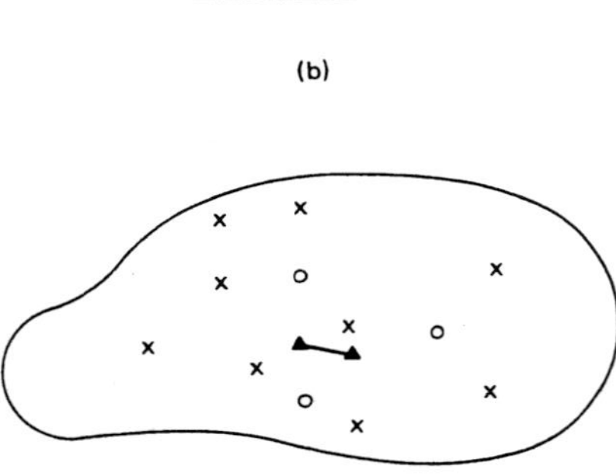

Figure 4-14 Relevance feedback environment. (a) Ideal relevance feedback situation. (b) Tight relevant document set, but loose nonrelevant set. (c) Intermingled relevant and nonrelevant documents.

removes the query from that area of the space without specifying a definite alternative direction. The feedback equation [expression (7)] should then be used with a smaller weight for γ than for β. Alternatively γ might be specified as 0, thereby creating a *positive feedback* strategy. A third alternative consists in using only a small set of nonrelevant documents by including in the feedback equation only one or two documents—for example, the nonrelevant documents retrieved earliest in a given search (those exhibiting the lowest ranks when the documents are arranged in decreasing order of the query-document similarity).

Since the difference between the average relevant and the average nonrelevant documents is equivalent to the distance between the corresponding vectors in the vector space, it is not surprising that the formal as well as experimental test results show that the retrieval operation is most effective when the relevant documents as well as the nonrelevant documents are tightly clustered, and the difference between the two groups is as large as possible. Such a situation is represented in Fig. 4-14a.

The relevance feedback operation is less favorable in the more realistic case where the set of nonrelevant documents covers a wider area of the space. The corresponding distance between the average relevant and nonrelevant items is much smaller in Fig. 4-14b than in Fig. 4-14a. Finally, the situation is distinctly unfavorable when relevant and nonrelevant are intermixed as shown in Fig. 4-14c. That situation represents a failure of the basic assumption of the SMART document analysis, namely that document content can be represented for retrieval purposes by the term occurrence vectors. Additional information must then be added to the document vectors to distinguish those which are useful from the others. Some approaches to this problem are mentioned in the next section.

The experimental evidence available for relevance feedback indicates that one or two feedback operations are quite effective in raising retrieval performance. Following the second query reformulation a state of diminishing returns sets in and not much further improvement can be expected.

*D Dynamic Document Space

The query alteration process described in the previous subsection was based on information obtained from the user population in the course of the normal retrieval process. In a system where customer intelligence is available, an attempt can also be made to improve the document vector representation (instead of only the query vectors) by incorporating into the document representations new information obtained from the users during the search operations. One possibility consists in adding to the originally available document terms new information derived from relevance assessments furnished by the users in the course of a retrieval operation.

Specifically, when a number of documents retrieved in response to a given query are labeled by the user as relevant, it is possible to render these documents more easily retrievable in the future by making each item somewhat more similar to the query used to retrieve them. Analogously, retrieved documents labeled as nonrelevant are rendered less easily retrievable by being shifted away from the query. Following a large number of such interactions, documents which are wanted by the users will have been moved slowly into the active portion of the document space—that part in which a large number of user queries are concentrated, while items which are normally rejected will be located on the periphery of the space. Eventually, such items could be discarded.

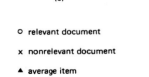

By analogy to the relevance feedback operations, the dynamic document vector alteration can be carried out by constructing a new document representation DOC_i' from the old document representations DOC_i and the terms contained in query Q. The query terms are added to the original document vector using the positive weighting factors α, β, γ, δ, and ϵ:

1 For documents designated as relevant, which must be rendered more similar to query Q:
   a A query term *not* present in the document is added to the document with a weighting factor of α.
   b A query term also present in the document receives increased importance by incrementing its weight by a factor β.
   c A document term not present in the query is decreased in weight by a factor $-\gamma$.
2 For documents designated as nonrelevant which must be rendered less similar to the query:
   a Document terms also present in the query are rendered less important by decreasing their weight by a factor of $-\delta$.
   b Document terms absent from the query are increased in weight by a factor ϵ [22,23].

Several laboratory tests were carried out to test the foregoing dynamic document space alteration methods. In each case, a collection of user queries was first used to generate a modified document space. A new query set, distinct from the original one, could then be processed against both the originally available document space and the modified space. Improvement in recall and precision of from 5 to 10 percent could be detected for the modified space compared with the original space. One would expect that the document vector modification process carried out for a given time period with a particular user population would eventually produce an equilibrium position where documents important to the users could become easily retrievable whereas extraneous documents would be easily rejected. Such a conjecture remains to be verified in practice.

4 AUTOMATIC ENHANCEMENTS OF CONVENTIONAL RETRIEVAL

*A Document Ranking and Term Weighting

Various retrieval systems and procedures have been implemented over the last few years that are based in one way or another on the SMART model [24,25]. Possibly the most useful of these from a practical viewpoint are systems that preserve as much as possible the conventional processing methodology while adding enhancements to simplify the retrieval operations and to improve system effectiveness. The main characteristics of currently existing retrieval technologies are the inverted file organizations and the use of Boolean query formulations. This suggests that improved retrieval services could be obtained by combining the basic inverted file systems with SMART-like "back-end" procedures, designed to overcome some of the disadvantages of conventional systems.

Among the methods usable for improving the output produced by conventional file systems are the incorporation of weighted instead of binary terms and the presentation of the retrieved output in decreasing order of the query-document similarity. The generation of *ranked* document output increases user satisfaction and retrieval precision. Furthermore, the ranked retrieval can substantially enhance the chances of success of the relevance feedback process by bringing the relevant items to the user's attention early in the search; this in turn leads to the construction of useful feedback queries.

Ranked retrieval and relevance feedback can in principle be implemented in binary indexing systems where the index terms are either present or absent from the document and query vectors. However, the documents are easier to rank when *weighted terms* are assigned to the queries, and possibly also to the documents, because a composite query-document similarity coefficient can then be computed for each query-document pair based on the weights of matching query-document terms.

In a system such as SMART where each document is represented by a vector of terms and each vector is stored as a complete entity, the use of term weights presents no conceptual problem, because a term weight can simply be listed with each term identification in the corresponding term vector. Thus a particular document i dealing with "fruit" might be listed as

$$DOC_i = (APPLE,4; PEAR,3; \; . \; . \; . \; ; PLUM,1)$$

to indicate that the document deals rather more with pears than with plums, and even more with apples. In inverted file systems, the term weighting information must be included in the various inverted lists. Thus the term list for a given term k must now be expanded to include not only the document references for documents to which term k is assigned but also the particular weights for that term in the various documents. A sample inverted file of that kind is shown in Table 4-2.

Given some particular query Q_j, a file organization such as that of Table 4-2 now makes it possible to compute a similarity measure between the query and the document terms. For each term k included in query j, the corresponding term list is extracted from the inverted file, and the weights of terms that occur in both query j and document i are appropriately combined to produce a similarity measure between the given query j and each document that shares

Table 4-2 Typical Inverted Term Lists with Weights

$TERM_1$	DOC_i,WT_{i1}; DOC_j,WT_{j1}; . . . ; DOC_m,WT_{m1}
$TERM_2$	DOC_i,WT_{i2}; DOC_k,WT_{k2}; . . . ; DOC_n,WT_{n2}
⋮	
$TERM_s$	DOC_j,WT_{js}; DOC_m,WT_{ms}; . . . ; DOC_p,WT_{ps}

terms with the query. Consider a query consisting of three terms r, s, and t, and let the similarity measure between the query j and document i be defined as the sum of the products of the matching terms [that is, the numerator of the cosine formula of expression (1)]. To compute the similarity measure between the given query and document, it suffices to enter first the inverted list for term r and pick out $TERM_{ir}$ representing the weight of term r in document i. This leads to the computation of the product $QTERM_{jr} \cdot TERM_{ir}$. A subsequent access to the inverted lists for terms s and t makes it possible to add to the earlier product the terms $QTERM_{js} \cdot TERM_{is}$ and $QTERM_{jt} \cdot TERM_{it}$.

To compute the cosine measure of expression (1) an additional normalization factor consisting of the sum of the squares of all term weights included in each document and each query is needed. This makes it necessary to provide for each document i the factor $\sum_{k=1}^{t} (TERM_{ik})^2$. These factors can be computed in advance for each document and stored in a special "document length" file which is accessed for all documents that have a nonzero similarity with the query. The expanded inverted document reference lists together with the document length file permit the computation of the full cosine similarity measure for all documents sharing one or more terms with the query, followed by the ranking of documents in decreasing order of the query-document similarity.

The SIRE (Syracuse information retrieval experiment) system includes the normal inverted file processing facilities used for the Boolean query operations, as well as the expanded term weighting operations that provide ranked document output [26–28]. The SIRE file organization is shown in Fig. 4-15, and the corresponding processing chain is presented in simplified form in Fig. 4-16. In essence, the SIRE processing chain consists of two main sections. Initially, a Boolean query formulation is processed in the conventional manner. This step identifies all documents whose term assignment precisely matches the query formulation. This subset of documents is then further processed by computing a cosine similarity measure between each document and a "flattened" query consisting of all the original query terms connected by Boolean OR operators. Thus an original query formulated as (A AND B) OR (C AND D) becomes A OR B OR C OR D, or simply the query vector (A,B,C,D).

In the SIRE system the users are not expected to assign weights to the terms. Instead the weight of term k in document i is defined as $FREQ_{ik}$, that is, as the frequency of occurrence of the term in the document. Correspondingly, the document length needed in the denominator of the cosine computation is obtained as the sum of the squares of the individual term frequencies in the document. It is easy to see how the file organization of Fig. 4-15 leads to the proper computation of the cosine measure. A directory to the inverted lists is used to gain access to the document reference numbers and the weights (term frequencies) for all query terms. This produces the numerator of the cosine for each relevant document (each document retrieved by the Boolean query) and the corresponding query. The document length is next obtained for each document from the document length list (Fig. 4-15c). Following the computation of the

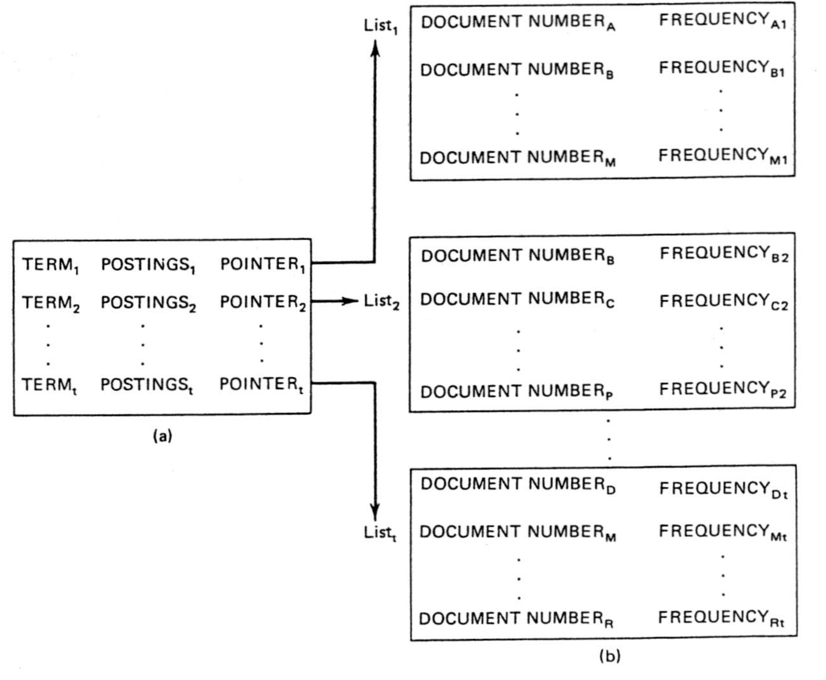
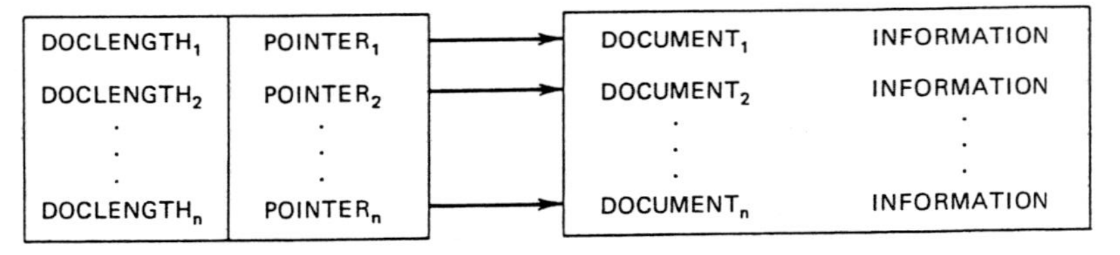

Figure 4-15 SIRE file organization. (a) Directory to inverted lists. (b) Inverted document reference lists. (c) Document length list. (d) Main document file.

query-document similarities, the output information may be extracted from the main document file in decreasing order of the cosine measure by using the file pointers provided for that purpose.

In the SIRE system, the cosine computations and the ranking algorithms are completely divorced from the Boolean retrieval operations. Alternatively, it is possible to give up the Boolean operations completely and process query formulations expressed simply as sets of weighted query terms. In the BROWSER system, a file organization substantially equivalent to that shown in Fig. 4-15 is used together with term weights based on an inverse document

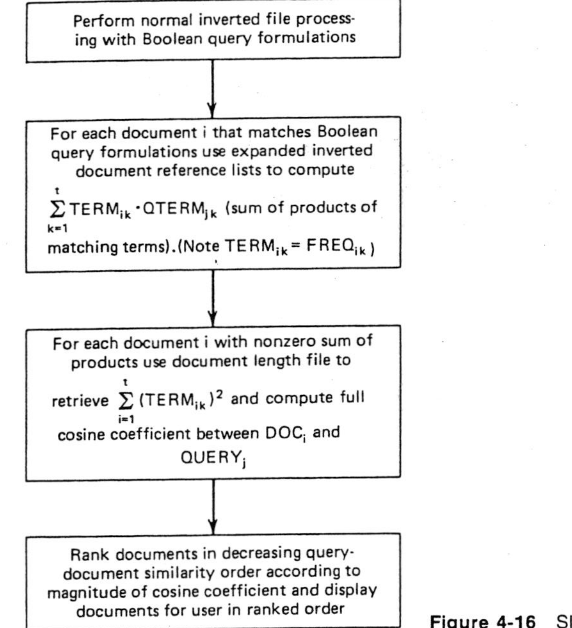

Figure 4-16 SIRE processing chain.

frequency factor [29]. CITE is another system that uses the conventional inverted file technology with term weights, document ranking, and relevance feedback based on the methods described earlier [30].

Another possibility for combining Boolean query processing with term weighting systems is to allow weighted terms directly as part of the normal Boolean formulations. Unfortunately, this approach raises a number of difficult problems, because the normal two-valued logic used to process Boolean queries assumes that a term is either present in or absent from a document or query identification. When the Boolean system is extended to include term weight or importance factors, it becomes necessary to interpret the meaning of compound expressions consisting of weighted terms and Boolean operators such as A_a AND B_b, where a,b represent the weights for terms A and B, respectively. In so doing one would like to define matching functions that resemble the normal Boolean operations and produce equal output for distinct query formulations that are logically equivalent [31,32].

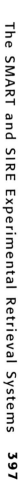

It is possible to design retrieval models that furnish unambiguous retrieval output for weighted Boolean queries. The theory of fuzzy sets provides a model in which the weight of term k in document i represents the degree to which the document is a member of the set of documents indexed by the term k [33]. A weight of 1 then indicates that DOC_i is a full member of the document set indexed by $TERM_k$, a weight of 0 says that the document does not belong to the set, and an intermediate weight designates a partial degree of membership. The effect of compound Boolean expressions can also be defined in the fuzzy set model. Whether weighted Boolean queries will ever become popular in retrieval remains to be seen.

*B Retrieval through Man-Machine Dialogue and Local Clustering

The previously described relevance feedback process is based on a somewhat rudimentary type of user-system interaction, because the system generates query formulations based on relevance assessments returned by the user for previously retrieved documents. There exist interactive systems where the user is expected to take a much more active role in the retrieval operations. Thus users may be asked to carry out the query reformulations by individually choosing good terms for incorporation into the queries; the corresponding terms may then be chosen from among a set of potentially useful terms displayed by the system. Users may also be asked to assign positive and/or negative weights to the terms considered for incorporation into the query. Finally the users may be asked to assign weights (positive or negative) to displayed documents that may or may not have been retrieved in earlier searches [34].

Relevance judgments can be used as a basis for query reformulation also in conventional retrieval environments where Boolean query statements are used to retrieve documents manually indexed by keywords. The user feedback process devised for the European Community retrieval service consists of the following main steps [35]:

1 Relevance assessments are obtained for some of the documents retrieved in response to an initial search request.

2 The set of terms used to index some of the items known as relevant is examined [for example, (A AND B AND C AND D) and also (E AND F AND G)].

3 Some terms from the query statements chosen under step 2 are removed so as to broaden the resulting search statements [for example, statements (A AND B AND D) and also (E AND F) are constructed].

4 These shortened queries are used as new search statements to retrieve additional documents; the relevance of some of these newly retrieved documents is then assessed.

5 For each of the new query statements a "query quality factor" is computed as the ratio between the new relevant items retrieved divided by the new nonrelevant items retrieved.

6 Those partial queries with sufficiently high query quality factors are chosen and a final feedback query is constructed by inserting OR connectives between the corresponding partial query formulations [for example, the new statement used could be (A AND B AND D) OR (E AND F)].

7 The newly constructed query is used for search purposes, and the process is repeated if desired.

Additional feedback techniques incorporating slight variations of such a process can easily be devised.

One of the virtues of the relevance feedback and related query reformulation methods is the *local* nature of the operations involved; normally only the previously retrieved documents are used, rather than the whole document set. Such considerations lie at the root of a number of *local clustering* systems designed to improve the final search output. A standard inverted file search is used as a fast preliminary step, and the automatic classification procedures previously described then serve to cluster the (local) set of documents retrieved in response to particular search efforts in the hope of improving the final search output. The corresponding document classes can be used to determine a specific ranking order in which the output items can be brought to the user's attention. By displaying together whole groups of related documents and bringing them to the user's attention simultaneously, the choice of new terms to be incorporated into a feedback query may also be simplified [36].

Local clustering operations can be applied to terms as well as to documents. This produces a *local thesaurus* specifically applicable to each query which is obtained by grouping terms extracted from previously retrieved documents. A typical query reformulation process based on local term clustering might be carried out as follows [37,38]:

1 Relevance assessments are obtained for certain documents retrieved in earlier search operations.

2 Terms from the documents identified as relevant are ranked in decreasing order of relative frequency (frequency of occurrence in the relevant retrieved documents divided by total frequency in the collection), and terms with large relative frequency are used for query reformulation purposes.

3 Alternatively, or in addition, term similarity coefficients may be obtained for pairs of terms occurring in the relevant documents, the size of the coefficients being dependent on common occurrence patterns in the respective documents or document sentences.

4 Terms with large enough similarity coefficients are then clustered, and each original query term is considered as the kernel of a cluster of related terms to be used for query reformulation purposes.

It is not hard to generate extensions and refinements of the local clustering operations previously described. Thus local term association procedures can in principle also incorporate syntactic considerations where syntactic relationships between terms lead to the generation of term groups [39,40]. Document grouping methods, on the other hand, might utilize the similarities not only between the assigned terms but also between bibliographic citations shared jointly by a number of documents [41]. As the use of computers for document processing becomes more widespread, one may expect that the query refinement procedures based on user-system cooperation and on local clustering operations will also become more widespread.

REFERENCES

[1] G. Salton, Automatic Information Organization and Retrieval, McGraw-Hill Book Company, New York, 1968.

[2] G. Salton, editor, The SMART Retrieval System—Experiments in Automatic Document Processing, Prentice-Hall, Inc., Englewood Cliffs, New Jersey, 1971.

[3] G. Salton and M.E. Lesk, The SMART Automatic Document Retrieval System—An Illustration, Communications of the ACM, Vol. 8, No. 6, June 1965, pp. 391–398.

[4] G. Salton, A. Wong, and C.S. Yang, A Vector Space Model for Automatic Indexing, Communications of the ACM, Vol. 18, No. 11, November 1975, pp. 613–620.

[5] G. Salton and M.E. Lesk, Computer Evaluation of Indexing and Text Processing, Journal of the ACM, Vol. 15, No. 1, January 1968, pp. 8–36.

[6] G. Salton, Recent Studies in Automatic Text Analysis and Document Retrieval, Journal of the ACM, Vol. 20, No. 2, April 1973, pp. 258–278.

[7] G. Salton, A New Comparison between Conventional Indexing (MEDLARS) and Automatic Text Processing (SMART), Journal of the ASIS, Vol. 23, No. 2, March–April 1972, pp. 75–84.

[8] J.B. Lovins, Development of a Stemming Algorithm, Mechanical Translation and Computational Linguistics, Vol. 11, No. 1–2, March and June 1968, pp. 11–31.

[9] A. Tars, Stemming as a System Design Consideration, ACM SIGIR Forum, Vol. 11, No. 1, Summer 1976, pp. 9–16.

[10] G. Salton, C.S. Yang, and C.T. Yu, A Theory of Term Importance in Automatic Text Analysis, Journal of the ASIS, Vol. 26, No. 1, January–February 1975, pp. 33–44.

[11] K. Sparck Jones, A Statistical Interpretation of Term Specificity and Its Application in Retrieval, Journal of Documentation, Vol. 28, No. 1, 1972, pp. 11–21.

[12] G. Salton and C.S. Yang, On the Specifications of Term Values in Automatic Indexing, Journal of Documentation, Vol. 29, No. 4, December 1973, pp. 351–372.

[13] G. Salton and A. Wong, On the Role of Words and Phrases in Automatic Text Analysis, Computers and the Humanities, Vol. 10, 1976, pp. 69–87.

[14] G. Salton, Experiments in Automatic Thesaurus Construction for Information Retrieval, Information Processing 71, North Holland Publishing Company, Amsterdam, 1972, pp. 115–123.

[15] K. Sparck Jones, Automatic Keyword Classification for Information Retrieval, Butterworths, London, 1971.

[16] G. Salton, Dynamic Information and Library Processing, Prentice-Hall Inc., Englewood Cliffs, New Jersey, 1975.

[17] W.B. Croft, Clustering Large Files of Documents Using the Single Link Method, Journal of the ASIS, Vol. 28, No. 6, November 1977, pp. 341–344.

[18] R.E. Williamson, Real Time Document Retrieval, Doctoral Thesis, Cornell University, Ithaca, New York, June 1974.

[19] G. Salton and A. Wong, Generation and Search of Clustered Files, ACM Transactions on Data Base Systems, Vol. 3, No. 4, December 1978, pp. 321–346.

[20] E. Ide and G. Salton, Interactive Search Strategies and Dynamic File Organization, in The SMART Retrieval System—Experiments in Automatic Document Processing, G. Salton, editor, Prentice-Hall, Inc., Englewood Cliffs, New Jersey, 1971, Chapter 16.

[21] J.J. Rocchio, Jr., Relevance Feedback in Information Retrieval, in The SMART Re-

trieval System—Experiments in Automatic Document Processing, G. Salton, editor, Prentice-Hall, Inc., Englewood Cliffs, New Jersey, 1971, Chapter 14.
[22] G. Salton, Dynamic Document Processing, Communications of the ACM, Vol. 15, No. 7, July 1972, pp. 658–668.
[23] T. Brauen, Document Vector Modification, in The SMART Retrieval System—Experiments in Automatic Document Processing, G. Salton, editor, Prentice-Hall, Inc., Englewood Cliffs, New Jersey, 1975, Chapter 24.
[24] N.S. Malthouse, Indexgen—Index Term Generation Heuristics, Oak Ridge National Laboratory, Report ORNL-EIS-104, Oak Ridge, Tennessee, June 1978.
[25] Informatics Inc., RADC Automatic Classification On-Line (RADCOL)—User's Manual, Final Technical Report, Rome Air Development Center, Rome, New York, May 1975.
[26] T. Noreault, M. Koll, and M.J. McGill, Automatic Ranked Output from Boolean Searches in SIRE, Journal of the ASIS, Vol. 28, No. 6, November 1977, pp. 333–339.
[27] M.J. McGill, L. Smith, S. Davidson, and T. Noreault, Syracuse Information Retrieval Experiment (SIRE): Design of an On-Line Bibliographic Retrieval System, SIGIR Forum, Vol. 10, No. 4, Spring 1976, pp. 37–44.
[28] M.J. McGill and T. Noreault, Syracuse Information Retrieval Experiment (SIRE): Rationale and Basic System Design, Report, School of Information Studies, Syracuse University, Syracuse, New York, May 1977.
[29] J.H. Williams, BROWSER, An Automatic Indexing On-Line Text Retrieval System, IBM Federal Systems Division Report, Gaithersburg, Maryland, 1969.
[30] T.E. Doszkocs and B.A. Rapp, Searching MEDLINE in English: A Prototype User Interface with Natural Language Query, Ranked Output and Relevance Feedback, Proceedings of the ASIS Annual Meeting, Minneapolis, Minnesota, October 1979, R.D. Tally, editor, Knowledge Industry Publications, White Plains, New York, 1979, pp. 131–139.
[31] A. Bookstein, On the Perils of Merging Boolean and Weighted Retrieval Systems, Journal of the ASIS, Vol. 29, No. 3, May 1978, pp. 156–158.
[32] W.G. Waller and D.H. Kraft, A Mathematical Model of a Weighted Boolean Retrieval System, Information Processing and Management, Vol. 15, No. 5, 1979, pp. 235–245.
[33] A. Bookstein, Fuzzy Requests: An Approach to Weighted Boolean Searches, Journal of the American Society for Information Science, Vol. 31, No. 4, July 1980, pp. 240–247.
[34] R.N. Oddy, Information Retrieval through Man-Machine Dialogue, Journal of Documentation, Vol. 33, No. 1, March 1977, pp. 1–14.
[35] V. Vernimb, Automatic Query Adjustment in Document Retrieval, Information Processing and Management, Vol. 13, No. 6, 1977, pp. 339–353.
[36] D.S. Becker and S.R. Pyrce, Enhancing the Retrieval Effectiveness of Large Information Systems, IIT Research Institute, Report PB 266 008, Chicago, Illinois, 1977.
[37] R. Attar and A.S. Fraenkel, Local Feedback in Full-Text Retrieval Systems, Journal of the ACM, Vol. 24, No. 3, July 1977, pp. 397–417.
[38] T.E. Doszkocs, AID—An Associative Interactive Dictionary for On-Line Searching, On-Line Review, Vol. 2, No. 2, 1978, pp. 163–173.
[39] D.J. Hillman, Customized User Services via Interactions with LEADERMART, Information Storage and Retrieval, Vol. 9, No. 11, 1973, pp. 587–596.
[40] D. Taeuber, CONDOR—Ein Integriertes Datenbank und Informationssystem, Nachrichten für Dokumentation, Vol. 29, No. 3, 1978, pp. 127–130.
[41] H. Small, Cocitation in the Scientific Literature: A New Measure of the Relationship between Two Documents, Journal of the ASIS, Vol. 24, No. 4, July–August 1973, pp. 265–269.

BIBLIOGRAPHIC REMARKS

Many materials dealing with modern information retrieval appear as user manuals and reports issued by the sponsoring organizations. A summary of many existing, advanced systems is included in:

F.W. Lancaster and E.G. Fayen, Information Retrieval On-Line, Melville Publishing Company, Los Angeles, California, 1973.

Additional information about the SMART system can be obtained from:

G. Salton, editor, The SMART Retrieval System—Experiments in Automatic Document Processing, Prentice-Hall, Inc., Englewood Cliffs, New Jersey, 1971.

Advanced bibliographic retrieval services are also examined in various survey papers. The following references may serve as a convenient introduction:

D.B. McCarn and J. Leiter, On Line Services in Medicine and Beyond, Science, Vol. 181, July 27, 1973, pp. 318–324.

T.E. Doszkocs, B.A. Rapp, and H.M. Schoolman, Automated Information Retrieval in Science and Technology, Science, Vol. 208, April 4, 1980, pp. 25–30.

G. Salton, Progress in Automatic Information Retrieval, Computer, Vol. 13, No. 9, September 1980, pp. 41–57.

Architecture of an Expert System for Composite Document Analysis, Representation, and Retrieval

Edward A. Fox and Robert K. France
Department of Computer Science, Virginia Tech

ABSTRACT

The CODER (COmposite Document Expert/extended/effective Retrieval) project is a multi-year effort to investigate how best to apply artificial intelligence methods to increase the effectiveness of information retrieval systems handling collections of composite documents. To ensure system adaptability and to allow controlled experimentation, CODER has been designed as a distributed expert system. The use of individually tailored specialist experts, coupled with standardized blackboard modules for communication and control and external knowledge bases for maintenance of factual world knowledge, allows for quick prototyping, incremental development, and flexibility under change. The system as a whole is being implemented under UNIX as a set of MU-Prolog and C modules communicating through pipes and TCP/IP sockets.

KEYWORDS: ***information retrieval, artificial intelligence, distributed expert system, knowledge bases, blackboard architecture, lexicon construction***

INTRODUCTION

As the world's pool of information, particularly of machine-readable text, rapidly expands, it becomes increasingly necessary to engage the help of computers to control and manipulate it. Initial attempts at computer-aided information storage and retrieval (ISR) made centralized databases accessible to a large community of users [1] but focused principally on performance and have achieved only moderate levels of effectiveness [2]. Today, end users often prefer to search for themselves [3], using gateways, front ends, intermediaries, and interfaces [4], or aided by powerful microcomputers attached to optical disk stores. These end users need more effective and adaptable tools such as have been investigated by the research community [5]. CODER (*CO*mposite *D*ocument *E*xpert/extended/effective *R*etrieval) is a research system intended to address these needs through the mechanisms of knowledge-based and goal-directed artificial intelligence (AI) techniques.

Problem Description

The CODER system is aimed at investigating issues of meaning representation and the effective matching of user needs with relevant (passages of) documents. Although the SMART system has been evolving for more than 25 years with similar objectives [6], recent experience with reimplementing a modern version [7] and with using its latest form [8] suggests than an AI-based architecture would make further development and experimentation much easier. Questions in key subject areas that could then be studied (along with references to related work) include:

COMPOSITE DOCUMENTS

1. Can composite documents that include text, factual information, and references to other documents [9] be effectively analyzed [10] so that entire documents or appropriately sized passages [11] can be retrieved?
2. Can document analysis and modeling improve with findings about abstract document structure [12], message composition [13], office modeling of documents and other objects [14, 15], document formatting [16], and related standards [17]?

EFFECTIVE RETRIEVAL

3. Can effective retrieval methods suitable for the growing number of full text databases [18] be developed [2] using automatic techniques [19]?
4. Because the overlap between results of different retrieval methods is small [20], can overall effectiveness increase by use of several? Can retrieval systems be tailored to different users' understandings of relevance?
5. Can rule-based processing allow more effective combination of bibliographic information about documents [21] with other factual and content components than has been achieved with statistically based approaches [22]?

Project funded in part by grants from the National Science Foundation (IST-8418877), the Virginia Center for Innovative Technology (INF-85-016), and by an AT&T equipment contribution. An earlier version of this paper was presented at the Third Annual USC Computer Science Symposium; Knowledge-Based Systems: Theory and Applications, Columbia, South Carolina, March 31–April 1, 1986.

Address correspondence to Edward A. Fox, Department of Computer Science, Virginia Tech, Blacksburg, Virginia 24061.

6. Can a heuristic approach allow selection for each query of the most appropriate search strategy (e.g., choice between clustered versus inverted file searching, according to findings in [23]), the best retrieval approach (e.g., extended Boolean [24] versus vector space [25] versus probabilistic [26, 27]), and the fastest method for identifying good documents [28]?

AI METHODS

7. Is the logic programming paradigm in general [29, 30] and the Prolog language in particular [31] mature enough to use for natural language analysis [32], the rule-based processing commonly used in expert system development [33], and general AI programming [34] in a large, complex system?
8. Is the blackboard model [35] of a distributed expert information-providing mechanism [36] suitable for an ISR system?

KNOWLEDGE REPRESENTATION

9. In light of the many knowledge representation schemes suggested for information retrieval [37], can computationally tractable ones [38] be developed [39]?
10. In particular, are frames [40] useful in representation and reasoning [41] about document content in a way that can aid information retrieval [42]?
11. Can temporal data be suitably represented and used [43] in retrieval?

COMPUTATIONAL LINGUISTICS

12. Can linguistic analysis aid information retrieval [44], not only through improved analysis of queries [45] but also in document analysis [46] through skimming [47, 48] or far more robust and detailed analysis [49, 50] of more than a constrained sublanguage [51]?
13. Can machine-readable dictionaries [52] support expansion of the small lexicons used to date in text analysis systems [53]?

HUMAN-COMPUTER INTERFACE

14. Does current knowledge about human-computer interaction [54] and information retrieval [55] allow development of interfaces that can adapt to individual needs and preferences?
15. Can information retrieval systems satisfy some of the needs for tutoring systems by making books [56], encyclopedias [57], and other reference works more accessible?
16. Does a graphics-based interface [58] where problem formulation, query construction, term expansion, feedback, browsing, and profile-based filtering are all interwoven in a highly interactive human-computer dialogue [59] lead to more effective and pleasant retrieval?

Related Work

Several research investigations are related to the CODER project. The earliest use of expert system methods in the retrieval area was probably in the CONIT system [60]. The closest contemporary effort is development of I^3R by Thompson and Croft [61]. I^3R differs by being coded as a monolithic system in Lisp, interfaced with a database system, aimed to explore retrieval methods that access a statistically analyzed document collection, and implemented using fewer but more complex experts. Yet like CODER, I^3R is built around a blackboard that coordinates retrieval processing. The RUBRIC system, which uses a rule-based approach whereby queries become small knowledge bases [62], incorporates a variety of techniques for combining evidence [63] that have been included in CODER. TOPIC is also of interest, as it attempts to parse documents to condense their content and identify important concepts [46]. The more ambitious Project Minstrel, applying retrieval and AI methods of office modeling, is based on a comprehensive knowledge representation facility [15].

Although CODER incorporates many ideas from other research efforts, it is unique in its aim and scope. CODER provides a unified paradigm for the entire process of information storage, representation, and retrieval based on a tailor-made encoding of knowledge (see [64] and the section on knowledge administration below) and a flexible architecture designed to support the storage and manipulation of that knowledge. This article concentrates on the architectural issue; the interested reader is referred to France and Fox [64] for more details on how knowledge is used.

ARCHITECTURE

CODER is organized as an integrated system for document entry, analysis, storage, retrieval, and display. It should be adaptable as a standalone system, as a server for interactive or batch entry of documents or queries, or as an intelligent intermediary to another database system. The following discussion relates to the most comprehensive case: standalone implementation.

In keeping with design principles of modularity and object-oriented programming, CODER is made up of four different types of objects differentiated by their use of knowledge (see Figure 1). *Experts* are specialists in particular restricted domains pertinent to the tasks at hand. They communicate with each other only through *blackboards*, which serve as holding areas for session-specific knowledge. Each blackboard is the external knowledge source for a *strategist* that also has a local knowledge base of planning rules to coordinate the activities of experts in the community. *External knowledge bases* store information of common interest to several experts. Because they deal only with factual world knowledge, they require only limited inference abilities. Finally, there are

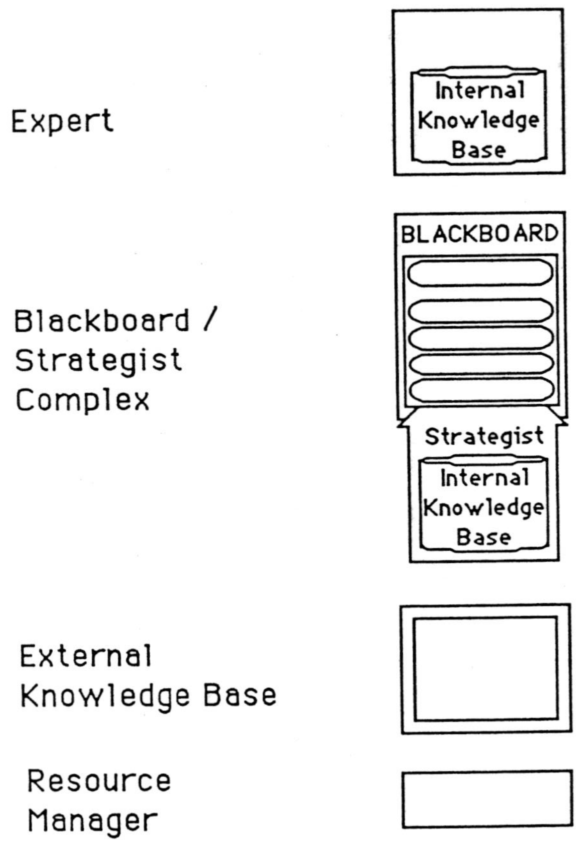

Expert — Internal Knowledge Base

Blackboard / Strategist Complex — BLACKBOARD, Strategist, Internal Knowledge Base

External Knowledge Base

Resource Manager

Figure 1. CODER Object Classes

resource managers mediating between low-level machine structures and the abstract representations used by the rest of the system. These may be implemented in a procedural language, as they do not require special knowledge or inference capabilities..

The internal structure of CODER is shown in Figure 2. The central region or ''spine'' includes external databases for documents and terms, along with the knowledge administration complex. The resources of the spine are shared by two expert communities, one for document analysis and one for retrieval. From an external perspective the system wraps so that users (shown at either end of the figure) are inside the system; they can both enter documents and retrieve them, possibly in an integrated fashion. Each user communicates with a resource manager specialized to his or her preferred interface, which in turn communicates with a group of translation specialists to effect a two-way dialogue between the user and the rest of the system. The interaction of these specialists with each other and with other experts is mediated by a blackboard. Each expert community may also reference additional external knowledge bases, such as the user model base. Attached to each blackboard and coordinating all the activities of the subsystem is a strategist.

The overall operation of CODER is shown in Figure 3. Because one or more parts of CODER can be assigned to separate processors, it is logical to view the system as made up of groupings of modules needed for common functions. For example, one user might be entering new documents so the system can analyze and store them, while other users are searching and retrieving documents. In both these cases, state information about the progress of the system's services for a user is maintained entirely on the blackboard involved. Finally, at the

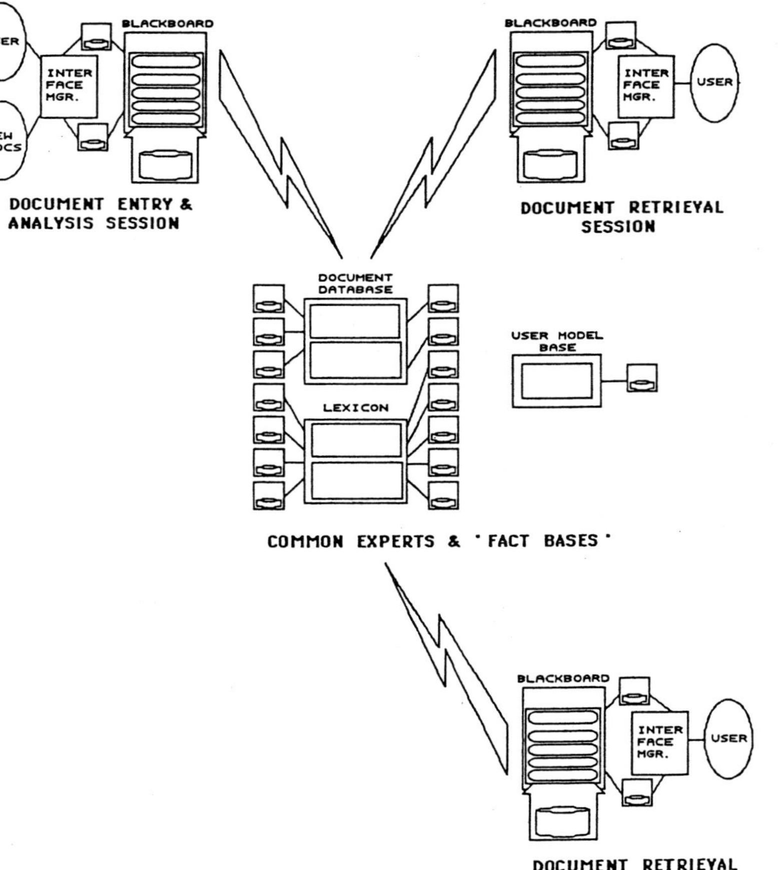

Figure 3. Overview of System Operation in a Distributed Environment

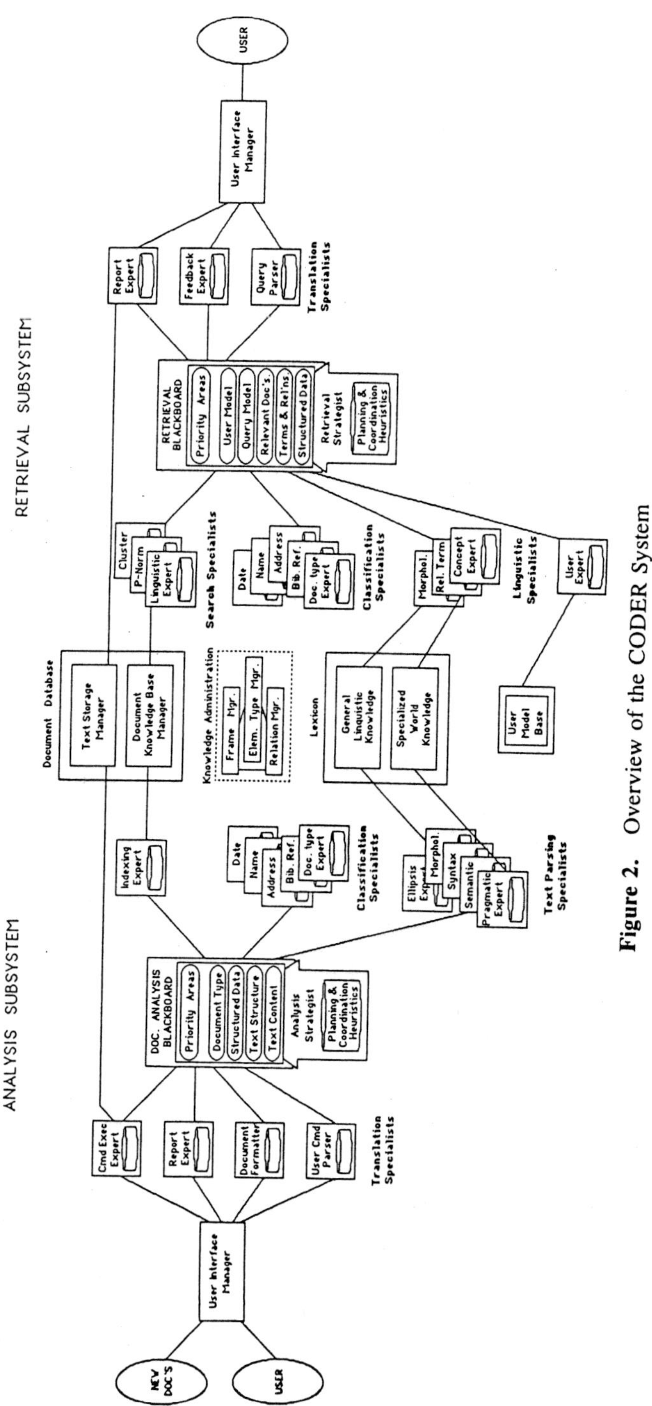

Figure 2. Overview of the CODER System

center of the figure are the shared experts and external knowledge bases involved in supporting these tasks.

The sections that follow provide more detailed information about the various CODER components.

Knowledge Administration

Knowledge in CODER is partitioned both *horizontally* between the two subsystems and among the modules of each subsystem, and *vertically* along what Sterling [65] refers to as the "logical levels of problem solving." The top level of this second division is the goal-oriented planning knowledge that guides the session strategists. In the current CODER implementation this *strategic knowledge* is encoded in rules for recognizing and reacting to stages in the problem tasks. Actual steps in the problem solution are carried out by the experts in each community using *tactical knowledge* of how to accomplish their designated tasks. Finally, the characteristics of the problem universe are represented as *world knowledge* in the external knowledge bases.

Strategic and tactical knowledge are stored locally in the modules that use them. The same is not true for world knowledge. Facts about the world provide the premises from which the experts reason about their tasks, and facts and hypotheses about the world make up the problem-state descriptions that inform the strategists' decisions. Thus, the factual representation language used in CODER to encode world knowledge also serves as a *lingua franca* for communication among the modules that make up each subsystem community. This language, defined in Figure 4, is itself made up of three levels. Elementary data types include distinct sets of names for entities of different sorts, as well as such familiar primitives as character, integer, and atom. Frames provide a facility for building definite descriptions of entities according to prototypical descriptions drawn from a tangled hierarchy of classes. And relations are predications on those entities, either ascribing accidental properties to them or describing relations among them.

Relations are familiar to AI programmers by analogy to Prolog predicates. CODER relations differ from Prolog predicates in having specified type signatures (arity and types on arguments) and algebraic attributes (whether they are transitive, symmetric, and so forth). Elementary data types are also familiar; restricted data types are defined through a type of restriction polymorphism [66]. The semantics of frames, however, may require some explanation. The subsumption relation given in Figure 5*a* defines the inheritance hierarchy that can be specified for frame types. The frame with no slots subsumes all other frames, and two frames are equivalent if they subsume one another.

Figure 5*b* defines the matching of frame objects, in terms of the types of the various slots and their values. Frame object A matches frame object B if every filled slot of A matches a filled slot of B, where elementary objects match

```
relation  ::= relation_name {argument} +

  argument ::= relation
             | frame
             | elementary_object
             | quantifier argument

frame     ::= frame_name  { slot_name slot_filler } *

  slot_filler ::= frame
                | elementary_object
                | quantifier slot_filler

elementary_object ::= {quantifier} {primitive_object  restriction}

  quantifier ::= list_of  |  non_empty_list_of
               | set_of   |  non_empty_set_of
               | integer
```

Figure 4. Definition of Factual Knowledge Representation Formalism

```
subsumes(ancestor_frame, descendent_frame) ≡
   slot_list(ancestor_frame, anc_list),
   slot_list(descendent_frame, desc_list),
   ∀x (x ∈ anc_list ⊃ ∃y (y ∈ desc_list ∧ name(x)=name(y) ∧
        subsumes(type(x), type(y)) )).
```

Figure 5a. Semantics of Frames: Frame Subsumption

```
match(frame1, frame2) ≡
   slot_list(type(frame1), list1) ∧
   slot_list(type(frame2), list2) ∧
   ∀x (x ∈ list1 ∧ has_value(frame1, x, v) ⊃ ∃y (y ∈ list2 ∧
      name(x)=name(y) ∧ has_value(frame2, y, r) ∧ match(v, r) )).

match(elt1, elt2) ≡
   elt1 = elt2.
```

Figure 5b. Semantics of Frames: Frame Matching

if and only if they are equal. This asymmetric matching is based only on filled slots, so objects of differing types can still match. Matching of frames is computationally inexpensive and mirrors whether the two objects, or two descriptions of the same object, are indeed similar. By defining suitable frame types, the knowledge administrator can describe the various entities to be handled in a particular CODER system. Experts can then instantiate objects of these types and store them on the blackboard or in external knowledge bases.

Consistent use of this formalism is maintained system-wide by the modules of the knowledge administration complex (see Figure 6), which include type managers for each component of the language. For example, the frame type manager keeps track of the classes suitable for describing entities and the attributes appropriate to each class; the relation type manager keeps track of the relations existing among entities and the characteristics of each relation. New types are added only by an external system administrator rather than by the modules of the system: deciding what sorts of types should be recognized by the system is part of the knowledge engineering involved in constructing CODER. Knowledge objects, by contrast—concrete expressions in the representation language—are created, modified, and destroyed dynamically during the operation of the system.

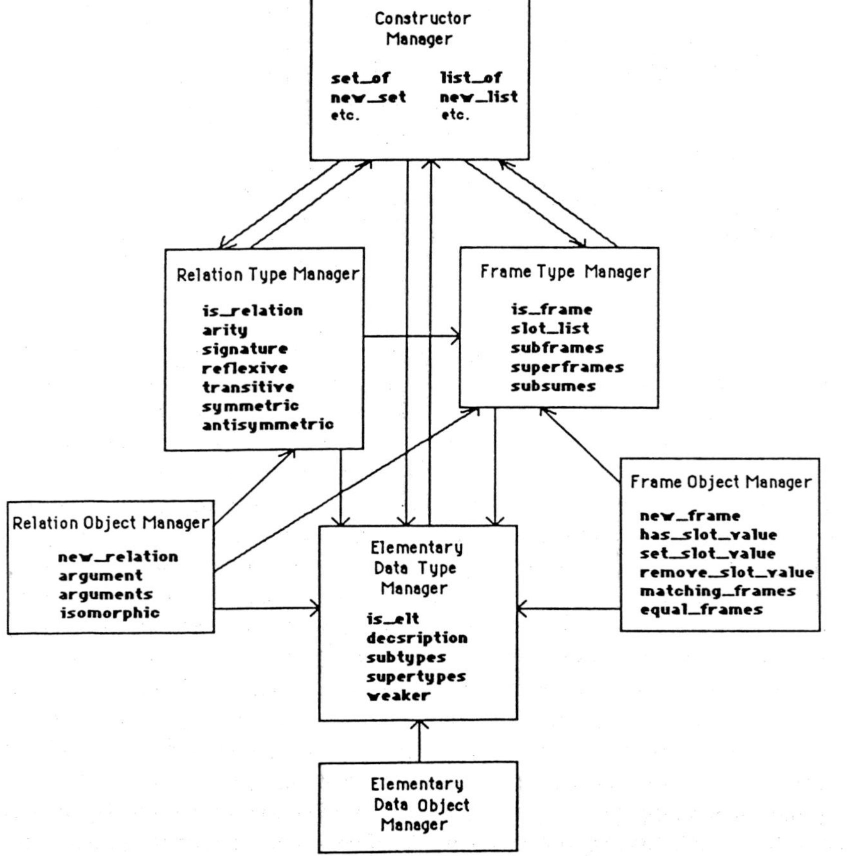

Figure 6. Internal Structure of the CODER Knowledge Administration Complex (arrows indicate dependencies)

External Knowledge Bases

Whereas the knowledge administration complex aids with control of the types of knowledge representations employed in a particular system, the external knowledge bases (EKBs) provide storage and access to large numbers of facts. The document knowledge base, the lexicon, and the user model base are all EKBs that each maintain knowledge about a particular class of objects as specific statements of fact.

The functionality of external knowledge bases is specified by the operations shown in Figure 7. Formally, propositions entered into a fact base are required to be *ground instances* of logical relations known to the system; that is, to involve neither unbound variables nor meta-terms. These propositions are added to an external knowledge base as single statements but may be retrieved in either of two ways. The knowledge base may be queried with a skeletal fact, that is, a fact containing one or more variables, and will return the set of all facts in the knowledge base that match the skeleton. Alternately, the knowledge base may be queried with an object (an elementary datum, a frame, or a relation) and will return the set of all facts involving that object. In addition, a knowledge base may be queried about the *number* of facts that match an object or a skeletal fact:

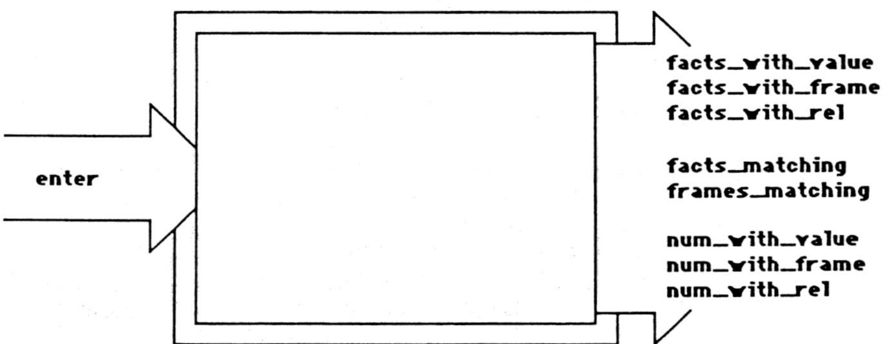

Figure 7. The Functionality of an External Knowledge Base. An EKB has no implementation independent internal structure.

this information can be used by the querying entity for statistical purposes or simply to avoid receiving excessively large sets of facts.

The lexicon maintains knowledge about terms in the language. It can be conceptually divided into two parts, one of general linguistic knowledge and the other of specialized world knowledge particular to the collection of documents employed. Although knowledge from both conceptual halves may be recalled for a given request, tagging the knowledge in this way promotes portability by allowing knowledge of general use to be decoupled from the pragmatics of a given document collection and reused in other applications. Construction of the current CODER lexicon following these principles is highlighted in Figure 8. The initial loading of facts portrayed at the top of the figure is from one large machine-readable dictionary [67]. Table 1 describes the various relations initially derived from the more than 80,000 headwords present. Further analysis such as of the definitions (see c_DEF) should lead to additional relations that would be more directly usable for parsing.

The document knowledge base maintains facts about the documents as assertions relating a document (passage) and a knowledge structure. A simple attached resource manager provides storage and retrieval for raw document text. Together these modules constitute the document database. Finally, there is a user model base of facts about individual users. These include reports of occurrences during a single session and general statements about the user, such as the type of information that has proven relevant in the past, background knowledge particular to or supplied by the user, and common characteristics of relevant documents. This body of knowledge about users, and the bodies of knowledge discussed above, inform the system's response in intelligently analyzing and retrieving documents for a particular individual.

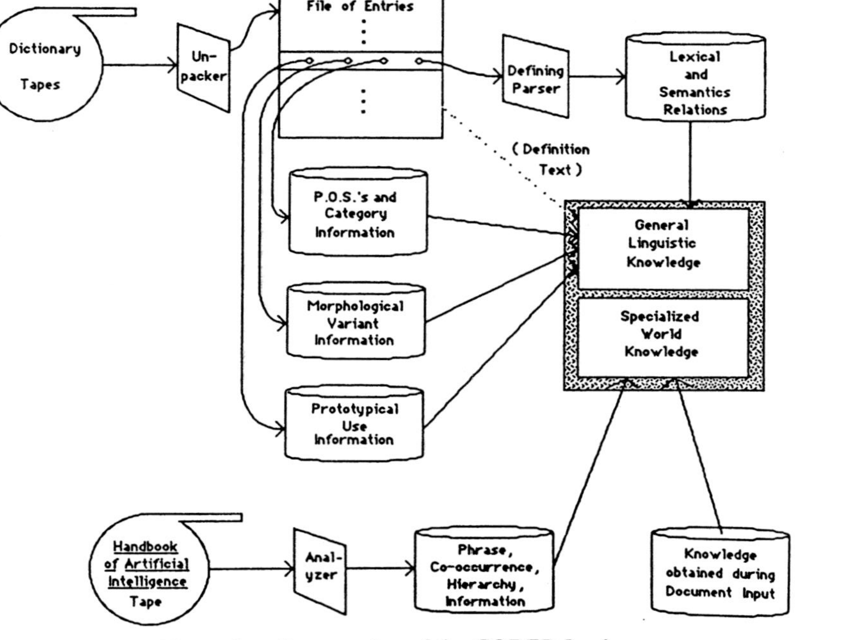

Figure 8. Construction of the CODER Lexicon

Table 1. Relations abstracted from the *Collins Dictionary of the English Language* [70] tapes

c_ABBREV	Abbreviation of headword
c_ALSO_CALLED	Headword also commonly called this
c_CATEGORY	Category (semantic label) of headword
c_COMPARE	Compare to another headword and sense(s)
c_DEF	Definition of headword
c_DEF_NUM	Number of (up to) 80-character blocks of definition
c_HEADWORD	Headword entry
c_MORPH	Morphological variant of headword (including part of speech)
c_NLAST	Rest (e.g., first/middle name) of proper noun headword
c_PAST	Past form of headword
c_PLURAL	Plural of headword (sometimes just the ending)
c_POS	Part of speech
c_RELADJ	Related adjective to headword
c_SAMP	Example of headword in context
c_SINGULAR	Singular form of headword (sometimes just the ending)
c_SYLL	Syllabification of headword
c_USAGE	Usage notes providing guidance on usage of headword
c_USAGE_NUM	Number of (up to) 80-character blocks in usage note
c_VAR_SPELL	Variant spelling(s) (if any)
c_VAR_SYLL	Syllabification of variant spelling(s)

Experts

Conceptually, an expert is a specialist in a certain restricted domain pertinent to the task at hand. Experts are designed to be implemented in relative isolation from one another: no expert has knowledge of the internal behavior of the other experts in the community, and all experts communicate with the community strictly through the given blackboard. Part of the specification of an individual expert is the set of predicates that it may view in a given blackboard area and the (possibly overlapping) set of predicates that it may post back. Obviously, there must be agreement among the expert implementors on the structure and bounds of those predicates if the experts are to work together. What each expert does with those predicates, however, and what internal knowledge and processes it uses to produce new hypotheses are left to the implementor of the individual expert. Each expert can therefore be built in the way that best takes advantage of the characteristics of its particular domain of expertise.

An expert has only two requirements for its operation: it should be knowledge driven, and it must recognize the appropriate commands from the strategist scheduler. The first is philosophical in nature: it is part of the CODER design that the complexities of the system tasks be realized in the knowledge required for their execution rather than the process of execution itself. For experts this implies that expertise be represented as explicit knowledge, separate from whatever engine manipulates it. The knowledge in the expert, moreover, is constrained by system design to be on a higher level than factual knowledge: either rules for finding and manipulating factual knowledge in an external knowledge base or facts that relate to classes of objects in the problem universe. The second requirement is pragmatic: for the strategist to schedule their activity properly, experts must go through a canonical cycle of operations.

The typical CODER expert consists of a communications interface, a local knowledge base, and an inference engine (see Figure 9). The interface provides for communication with the blackboard and optionally with external knowledge sources such as resource managers or EKBs. The local knowledge base contains the particular expertise necessary for the proper execution of the expert's tasks; the inference engine is chosen to best execute those tasks. Possible engines include both forward-chaining and backward-chaining rule interpreters, frame-based classification engines, and pattern-matching engines. These engines could then be associated with different rule bases, classification trees, and similarity measures, respectively, to produce specialized experts in a variety of disciplines.

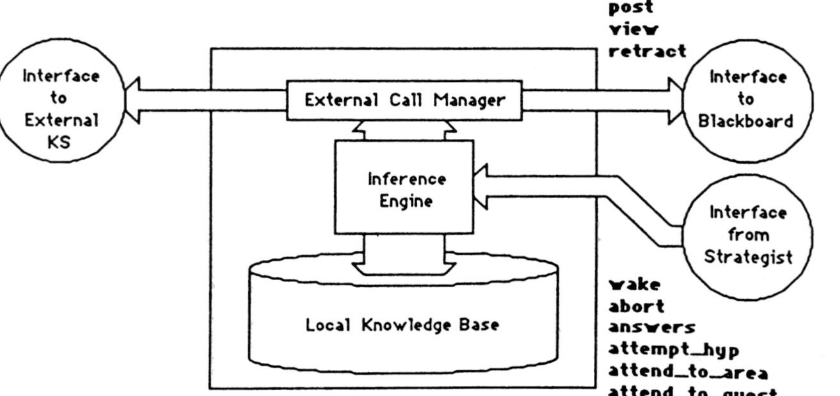

Figure 9. Canonical CODER Expert Showing Internal Structure and Functionality of Interface with Blackboard/Strategist Complex

Some examples of expert knowledge bases and inference techniques are given in Table 2. Recent research supports the view that it is possible to build engines that cover a broad range of problems without falling into the computational trap of general inference (see [38] for a formal analysis of this effect).

This method of problem decomposition is particularly well suited to the tasks of document analysis and retrieval, where the relevance of a given document to a given information need is influenced by many factors. Assigning an expert to a

Table 2. Knowledge bases and inference types for some sample experts

Expert Name	Local Knowledge Base	Inference Engine
Date	Mappings from different natural representations for dates into a canonical internal representation	Forward chaining (rule based)
Bibio. Ref.	Different types of biblographic entities and clues to recognize them; lexical conventions for representations of biblio. entities in text and in bibliographies	Classificational
Doc. Type	Different types of documents (both hard and soft types) and clues to recognize them and their component fields	Classificational
Morphology	Declension, conjugation and case-changing rules for English; irregular morphological variants (or how to find them in the lexicon)	Hard coded
Related Term	Methods and metrics for navigating relation networks in the lexicon	Relational
Cluster	Heuristics for finding document passages in the database that are similar to those identified by the user as close to current needs	Special purpose
P-Norm	Methods to transform a fact-based representation of a search request to a p-norm representation and conduct a search	Hard coded
Linguistic	Methods and metrics for identifying documents in the database that share linguistic substructures with the retrieval request	Relational

small area of specialization and decoupling it from the remainder of the system, however, has additional advantages. First, the development of the expert is separated from that of the surrounding system. Interaction problems, normally a plague of AI systems, are thereby kept to a minimum. In addition, the experts are kept small, so problems of rule interaction *within* the expert are minimized. Furthermore, tasks that are found to require too much complexity can be further subdivided according to the areas of expertise required to solve them, until they are reduced to manageable size.

Blackboard/Strategist Complex

A blackboard is an area for communication among experts [35]. This communication takes place through posting and reading hypotheses in specialized subject areas. In CODER blackboards (see Figure 10), a specialization of this process provides a means for asking and answering questions, which are

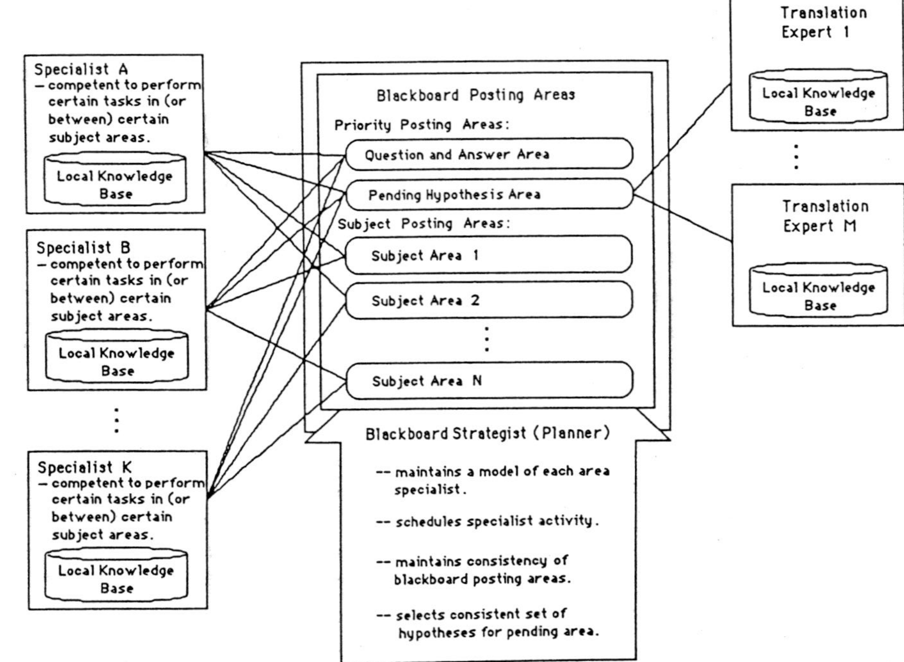

Figure 10. Blackboard/Strategist Complex Showing Mapping of Experts in the Immediate Community to Blackboard Areas

contained in a separate area of the blackboard. The importance of this type of communication was noted convincingly by Belkin and colleagues [36]. In addition, the CODER blackboards provide a special area, maintained by the blackboard strategist, containing a small set of consistent hypotheses of high certainty. This pending hypothesis area is available for read access by all experts and thus, indirectly, by the outside world. It provides an instantaneous picture of the ''consensus'' of the blackboard: what the system as a whole hypothesizes about the problem under consideration at any moment.

A hypothesis is a higher-order knowledge structure built on the factual knowledge forms supported by the knowledge administration complex. It consists of five parts:

1. The fact hypothesized.
2. The identifier of the expert hypothesizing it.
3. The confidence that the expert has in it (which can be assigned by different methods for different types of hypotheses, according to whatever knowledge aggregation scheme is appropriate for the set of constraints and knowledge sources at hand).
4. The hypothesis identifier.
5. The dependencies on other hypotheses.

This latter information, apart from aiding selection of the set of pending hypotheses, allows truth maintenance functions to be performed within the blackboard subject areas. If an expert withdraws a hypothesis, for instance, or radically changes the associated confidence level, this information makes it possible to schedule tasks to reconsider the dependent hypotheses.

Monitoring the blackboard for this class of event is one function of the blackboard strategist, shown in the lower part of Figure 11. Because the logic task scheduler's rules governing truth maintenance are independent of the particular predicates involved in the facts hypothesized, this function is independent of the application domain of the blackboard community. The strategist also monitors the blackboard for domain-specific events and conditions that trigger new processing. These categories of function are kept separate in the strategist, so the truth maintenance function can be transported to other tasks. Both task schedulers in the strategist have been designed as rule interpreters, as neither the strategies involved in truth maintenance nor those involved in information analysis or retrieval are yet well understood.

The final component of the strategist is a dispatcher of the tasks identified by the other components. On the basis of the mix of tasks scheduled by the truth maintenance and task oriented components, it attempts to make optimal use of all available machine resources by issuing appropriately timed commands to the experts in the blackboard community. This allows different groups of experts to be active at different phases in the community task, but also allows experts outside the currently active group to be called up to answer a question or to reconsider a hypothesis. In an ideal environment with one processor per expert,

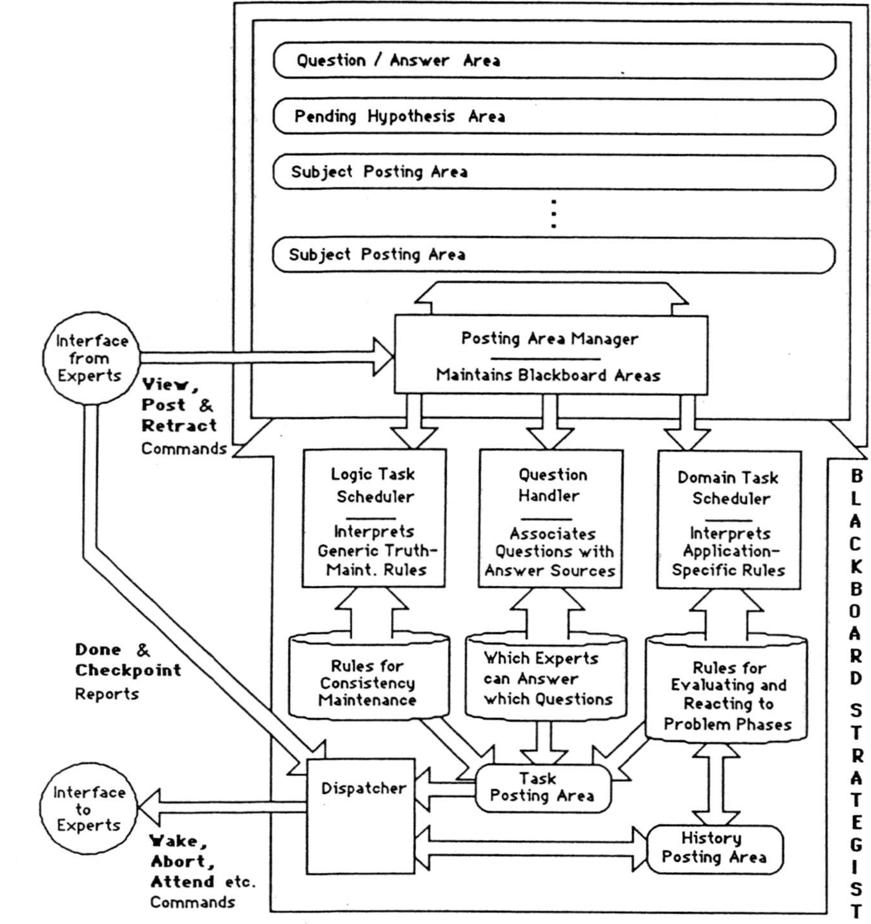

Figure 11. Internal Structure of Blackboard/Strategist Complex

such dispatching duties would be kept at a minimum, and the normal cycle of activities of each expert would ensure highly parallel processing.

IMPLEMENTATION STATUS AND FUTURE WORK

Early work on the CODER system concentrated on design and on preparation of the knowledge to be loaded into the external knowledge bases. A test collection was needed that would allow investigation of the many questions of interest, so the decision was made to collect all issues of *AIList Digest*, an electronic mail publication distributed from the DARPA Internet to many networks, beginning with the first one edited by Kenneth Laws in 1984. As of May 1987, roughly 13 megabytes of data, including over 6500 messages by many different authors in widely differing formats, have been collected. To provide domain knowledge relevant to this collection as a supplement to the general English lexicon, *The Handbook of Artificial Intelligence* has also been obtained in machine-readable form. Queries and relevance judgments on this test collection have been captured using the SMART system.

Experimentation in natural language processing is best supported by a large, comprehensive lexicon. The most efficient construction approach was to reformat machine-readable dictionaries and to parse entries into suitable structures. Because the G.&C. Merriam Company and the Longman Group Limited both refused to provide their dictionaries, it was decided to use four separate dictionaries obtained from the Oxford Text Archive [68–71] so that the resulting lexicon could be made freely available to other researchers. Initial efforts focused on the largest of these, the *Collins Dictionary of the English Language*.

Development of CODER is taking place in the UNIX[1] environment. Pipes and TCP/IP sockets [72] allow intermodule and intermachine communication. Thus, procedural modules like interface managers can be coded in C or C++, a dialect supporting the class-object paradigm [73]. MU-Prolog was selected as the AI implementation language, as it includes a clause indexing facility for medium-size collections of facts or rules, and two types of database support [74]. The first scheme uses hashing, and the second employs a two-level superimposed coding scheme [75] that performs well for partial matches [76] and can easily support large Prolog databases [77]. MU-Prolog also has tools for information hiding, interfacing with the UNIX operating system, and reducing dependence on rule ordering and extra-logical operations.

Implementation of the modules of the CODER system began early in 1986. At the end of the summer of 1986, the knowledge administration and blackboard/strategist complexes were nearly complete, the communication routines were well underway, interface managers using CURSES and SUN-Windows packages had been prototyped (see Figure 12), a p-norm search routine had been tested, and a first version of the document-type specialist developed. Further coding according to the detailed specifications given in France [78] should lead to a working prototype in 1987.

Subsequent efforts will aim first at demonstrating the feasibility of using CODER for document analysis and retrieval and at comparing different approaches to see if CODER will indeed simplify experimentation regarding the application of AI methods to ISR problems. Much of this work, however, will require development of a more refined lexicon, specification of heuristics regarding appropriate retrieval methods for particular types of queries, and

[1] Trademark of AT&T Bell Laboratories.

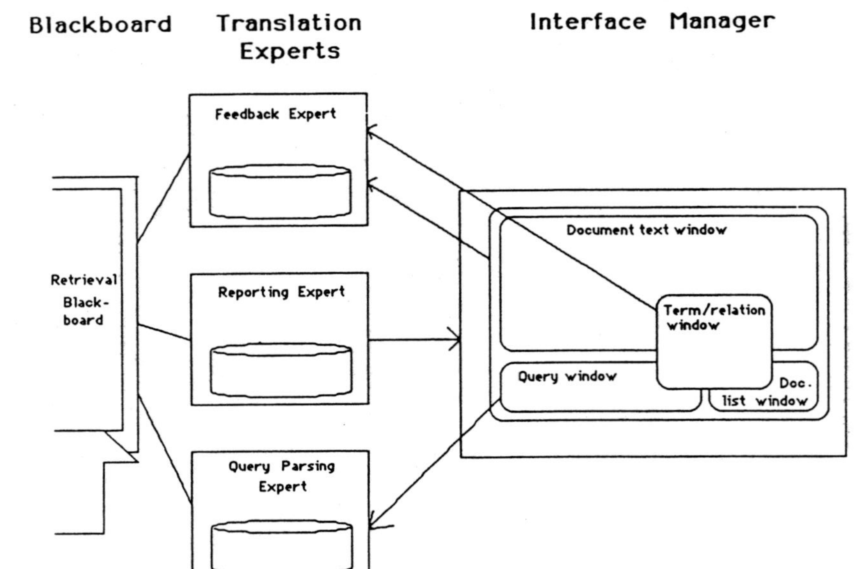

Figure 12. Retrieval Subsystem User Interface

thorough integration of user models into a truly interactive system for satisfying information needs. It is hoped that initial success with CODER will be followed by a long period of productive research and experimentation that will contribute to the human knowledge base about ISR.

ACKNOWLEDGMENTS

Numerous students enrolled during the last two years in Virginia Tech's two-quarter graduate sequence on information storage and retrieval have played a role in the development of CODER. For an MS project, Robert Wohlwend made an initial version of the Prolog lexicon from the typesetting tapes of one major dictionary. Research assistants Mary Beth Weaver and Qi Fan Chen are currently involved in system implementation. Pat Cooper and Joy Weiss have provided secretarial support.

The Oxford Text Archive and the Melbourne University Department of Computer Science have supplied tapes with dictionaries and Prolog interpreters, respectively. The staff of the SUMEX Computer Project at the Stanford University Medical Center, with permission of the authors and William Kaufman, provided the machine-readable version of the *Handbook of Artificial Intelligence*. Kenneth Laws has helped assure the project of a complete backfile of *AIList Digest* issues.

References

1. Neufeld, M. L., and Cornog, M., Database history: From dinosaurs to compact discs, *J. Am. Soc. Inf. Sci.* 37(4), 183–190, 1986.
2. Blair, D. C., and Maron, M. E., An evaluation of retrieval effectiveness for a full-text document-retrieval system, *Commun. ACM* 28(3), 289–299, 1985.
3. Ojala, M., Views on end-user searching, *J. Am. Soc. Inf. Sci.* 37(4), 197–203, 1986.
4. Williams, M. E., Transparent information systems through gateways, front ends, intermediaries, and interfaces, *J. Am. Soc. Inf. Sci.* 37(4), 204–214, 1986.
5. Fox, E. A., Information retrieval: Research into new capabilities, in *CD-ROM: The New Papyrus* (S. Lambert and S. Ropiequet, Eds.), Microsoft Press, Redmond, WA, 143–174, 1986.
6. Salton, G., The SMART system 1961-1976: Experiments in dynamic document processing, *Encyclopedia of Library and Information Science* 28, 1–36, 1980.
7. Fox, E. A., Some considerations for implementing the SMART Information Retrieval System under UNIX, TR 83-560, Dept. of Computer Science, Cornell Univ., 1983.
8. Buckley, C., Implementation of the SMART Information Retrieval System. TR 85-686, Dept. of Computer Science, Cornell Univ., 1985.
9. Fox, E. A., Composite document extended retrieval: An overview, *Research and Development in Information Retrieval, Eighth Annual Int. ACM SIGIR Conference.,* Montreal, 42–53, 1985.
10. Fox, E. A., Analysis and retrieval of composite documents, *ASIS '85, Proceedings of the 48th ASIS Annual Meeting,* 54–58, 1985.
11. O'Connor, J., Answer-passage retrieval by text searching, *J. Am. Soc. Inf. Sci.* 31(4), 227–239, 1980.
12. Kimura, G. D., A Structure Editor and Model for Abstract Document Objects, Dissertation, Tech. Report No. 84-07-04, Univ. of Washington, Dept. of Computer Science, 1984.
13. Babatz, R., and Bogen, M., Semantic relations in message handling systems: Referable documents, Paper presented at IFIP Working Group 6.5 Symposium, 1985.
14. Horak W., and Kronert, G., An object-oriented office document architecture model for processing and interchange of documents, *Proceedings of the Second ACM-SIGOA Conference on Office Information Systems,* 152–160, 1984.
15. Harper, D. J., Dunnion, J., Sherwood-Smith, M., and van Rijsbergen, C. J., Minstrel-ODM: A basic office data model, *Inf. Proc. & Mgmt.* 22(2), 83–107, 1986.

16. Peels, A., Janssen, N., and Nawijn, W., Document architecture and text formatting, *ACM Trans. Office Inf. Sys.* 3(4), 347–369, 1985.

17. Rauch-Hindin, W., Upper level OSI protocols near completion, *Mini-Micro Systems* (18)9, 53–66, 1986.

18. Tenopir, C., Full-text databases, *ARIST* 19, 215–246, 1984.

19. Salton, G., Another look at automatic text-retrieval systems, *Commun. ACM* 29(7), 648–656, 1986.

20. Katzer, J., et al., A study of the overlap among document representations, *Inf. Tech.: Res. & Dev.* 1(4), 261–274, 1982.

21. Bichteler J., and Eaton III, E. A., The combined use of bibliographic coupling and cocitation for document retrieval, *J. Am. Soc. Inf. Sci.,* 31(4), 278–282, 1980.

22. Fox, E. A., Extending the Boolean and Vector Space Models of Information Retrieval and P-Norm Queries and Multiple Concept Types, Dissertation, Cornell Univ., University Microfilms Int., Ann Arbor, Mich., 1983.

23. Voorhees, E. M., The Effectiveness and Efficiency of Agglomerative Hierarchic Clustering in Document Retrieval, Dissertation, TR 85-705, Dept. of Computer Science, Cornell Univ., 1985.

24. Salton, G., Fox, E. A., and Wu, H., Extended boolean information retrieval, *Commun. ACM* 26(11), 1022–1036, 1983.

25. Salton, G., Wong, A., and Yang, C. S., A vector space model for automatic indexing, *Commun. ACM* 18(11), 613–620, 1975.

26. Robertson, S. E., and Sparck Jones, K., Relevance weighting of search terms, *J. Am. Soc. Inf. Sci.* 27(3), 129–146, 1976.

27. Van Rijsbergen, C. J., *Information Retrieval,* 2nd ed., Butterworths, London, 1979.

28. Buckley, C., and Lewit, A. F., Optimization of inverted vector searches, *Research and Development in Information Retrieval, Eighth Annual International ACM SIGIR Conference,* Montreal, 97–110, 1985.

29. Kowalski, R. A., *Logic for Problem Solving,* Elsevier North-Holland, New York, 1979.

30. Genesereth, M. R., and Ginsberg, M. L., Logic programming, *Commun. ACM* 28(9), 933–941, 1985.

31. Clocksin, W. F., and Mellish, C. S., *Programming in Prolog,* 2nd ed., Springer-Verlag, New York, 1984.

32. Pereira, F., Logic for Natural Language Analysis, Tech. Note 275, SRI International, 1983.

33. Helm, A. R., Marriott, K., and Lassez, C., Prolog for expert systems: An evaluation, *Proceedings of the Expert Systems in Government Symposium,* 284–293, 1985.

34. Bobrow, D. G., If Prolog is the answer, what is the question? Or what it takes to support AI programming paradigms, *IEEE Trans. Software Eng.* 11(11), 1401–1408, 1985.

35. Nii, H. P., Blackboard systems: The blackboard model of problem solving and the evolution of blackboard architectures, *AI Mag.* 7(2), 38–53, 1986.

36. Belkin, N. J., Hennings, R. D., and Seeger, T., Simulation of a distributed expert-based information provision mechanism, *Inf. Tech.: Res. Dev. Applications* 3(3), 122–141, 1984.

37. Smith, L. C., and Warner, A. J., A taxonomy of representations in information retrieval system design, in *Representation and Exchange of Knowledge as a Basis of Information Processes* (H. J. Dietschmann, Ed.), North-Holland, New York, 31–49, 1984.

38. Levesque, H. J., A fundamental tradeoff in knowledge representation and reasoning, *Proceedings of the Fifth CSCSI National Conference,* London, Ontario, 141–152, 1984.

39. Patel-Schneider, P. F., Brachman, R. J., and Levesque, H. J., ARGON: Knowledge Representation Meets Information Retrieval, Proceedings of the First Conference on Artificial Intelligence Applications, December 1984, Denver, CO. Washington, D.C.: IEEE Computer Society Press; 280–286, 1984.

40. Minsky, M., A framework for representing knowledge, *The Psychology of Computer Vision,* (P. Winston, Ed.), McGraw-Hill, New York, 1975.

41. Fikes, R., and Kehler, T., The role of frame-based representation in reasoning, *Commun. ACM* 28(9), 904–920, 1985.

42. Patel-Schneider, P. F., Small can be Beautiful in Knowledge Representation, Proceedings of the IEEE workshop on Principles of Knowledge-Based Systems. Denver, CO, 11–16, 1984.

43. Zarri, G. P., An outline of the representation and use of temporal data in the RESEDA system, *Inf. Tech.: Res. Dev. Applications* 2(2/3), 89–108, 1983.

44. Sparck Jones, K., and Kay, M., *Linguistics and Information Science,* Academic Press, New York, 1973.

45. Sparck Jones, K., and Tait, J. I., Automatic search term variant generation, *J. Doc.* 40(1), 50-66, 1984.

46. Hahn, U., and Reimer, U., Heuristic text parsing in "Topic": Methodological issues in a knowledge-based text condensation system, in *Representation and Exchange of Knowledge as a Basis of Information Processes* (H. J. Dietschmann, Ed.), North-Holland, New York, 143–163, 1984.

47. DeJong, G., An overview of the FRUMP system, in *Strategies for Natural*

Language Processing, (W. G. Lehnert and M. H. Ringle, Eds.), Lawrence Erlbaum, Hillsdale, N.J., 149–176, 1982.

48. Mauldin, M. L., Thesis proposal: Information retrieval by text skimming, unpublished manuscript, Dept. of Computer Science, Carnegie-Mellon Univ., Pittsburgh, Penn., 1986.

49. Riesbeck, C. K., Realistic language comprehension, in *Strategies for Natural Language Processing,* (W. G. Lehnert and M. H. Ringle, Eds.), Lawrence Erlbaum, Hillsdale, N.J., 435–454, 1982.

50. Selfridge, M., Integrated processing produces robust understanding, *Comp. Ling.* 12(2), 89–106, 1986.

51. Sager, N., Sublanguage grammars in science information processing, *J. Am. Soc. Inf. Sci.* 26(1), 10–16, 1975.

52. Amsler, R. A., Machine-readable dictionaries, *ARIST* 19, 161–209, 1984.

53. White, C., The linguistic string project dictionary for automatic text analysis, *Proceedings of the Workshop on Machine-Readable Dictionaries,* SRI, Menlo Park, Calif., 1983.

54. Borgman, C. L., Psychological research in human-computer interaction, *ARIST* 19, 33–64, 1984.

55. Sewell, W., and Teitelbaum, S., Observations of end-user online searching behavior over eleven years, *J. Am. Soc. Inf. Sci.* 37(4), 234–245, 1986.

56. Weyer, S. A., The design of a dynamic book for information search, *Int. J. Man-Machine Stud.* 17(1), 87–107, 1982.

57. Weyer, S. A., and Borning, A. H., A prototype electronic encyclopedia, *ACM Trans. on Office Info. Syst.* 3(1), 63–68, 1984.

58. Frei, H. P., and Jauslin, J. F., Graphical presentation of information and services: A user oriented interface, *Inf. Tech.: Res. Dev.* 2(1), 23–42, 1983.

59. Oddy, R. N., Information retrieval through man-machine dialogue, *J. Doc.* 33(1), 1–14, 1977.

60. Yip, M.-K., An Expert System for Document Retrieval, MS Thesis, M.I.T., 1979.

61. Thompson, R. H., and Croft, W. B., An expert system for document retrieval, *Proceedings of the Expert Systems in Government Symposium,* IEEE, 448–456, 1985.

62. McCune, B. P., et al., RUBRIC: A system for rule-based information retrieval, *IEEE Trans. Software Eng.* SE-11(9), 939–945, 1985.

63. Tong, R. M., et al., A rule-based approach to information retrieval: Some results and comments, AAAI-83: Proceedings of the National Conference on Artificial Intelligence. Washington, DC, 411–415, 1983.

64. France, R. K., and Fox, E. A., Knowledge structures for information retrieval: Representation in the CODER project, *Proceedings of the Second IEEE Expert Systems in Government Conference,* McLean, Va., 135–141, 1986.

65. Sterling, L., Logical levels of problem solving, *Proceedings of the Second International Logic Programming Conference,* Uppsala Univ., Uppsala, Sweden, 231–242, 1984.

66. Cardelli, L., and Wegner, P., On understanding types, data abstraction, and polymorphism, *ACM Computing Surveys* 17(4), 471–522, 1985.

67. Wohlwend, R. C., Creation of a Prolog Fact Base from the Collins English Dictionary, MS Report, Dept. of Computer Science, Virginia Tech, Blacksburg, Va., 1986.

68. Cowie, A. P., and Mackin, R., *Oxford Dictionary of Current Idiomatic English. Volume 1: Verbs with Prepositions & Particles,* Oxford UP, Oxford, England, 1975.

69. Cowie, A. P., Mackin, R., and McCaig, I. R., *Oxford Dictionary of Current Idiomatic English. Volume 2: Phrase, Clause & Sentence Idioms.* Oxford U.P., Oxford, England, 1983.

70. Hanks, P. (Ed.), *Collins Dictionary of the English Language,* William Collins, London, 1979.

71. Hornby, A. S., (Ed.), *Oxford Advanced Dictionary of Current English,* Oxford, U.P., Oxford, England, 1974.

72. Leffler, S. J., Fabry, R. S., and Joy, W. N., A 4.2BSD interprocess communication primer, in *ULTRIX-32, Supplementary Documents,* vol. III, 3-5-3-28, 1984.

73. Stroustrup, B., *The C++ Programming Language*, Addison-Wesley, Reading, Mass., 1985.

74. Naish, L., *MU-Prolog 3.2db Reference Manual,* Dept. of Computer Science, Univ. of Melbourne, Melbourne, Australia, 1985.

75. Sacks-Davis, R., and Ramamohanarao, K., A two level superimposed coding scheme for partial match retrieval, *Info. Syst.* 8(4), 273–280, 1983.

76. Sacks-Davis, R., Performance of a multi-key access method based on descriptors and superimposed coding techniques, *Info. Syst.* 10(4), 391–403, 1985.

77. Ramamohanaro, K., and Shepherd, J., A Superimposed Codeword Indexing Scheme for Very Large Prolog Databases, Tech. Report 85/17, Dept. of Computer Science, Univ. of Melbourne, Melbourne, Australia, 1985.

78. France, R. K., An Artificial Intelligence Environment for Information Retrieval Research, MS Thesis, Dept. of Computer Science, Virginia Tech, Blacksburg, Va., 1986.

User-Friendly Systems Instead of User-Friendly Front-Ends

Donna Harman
National Institute of Standards and Technology, Gaithersburg, MD 20899

Most commercial online retrieval systems are not designed to service end users and, therefore, have often built "front-ends" to their systems specifically to serve the end-user market. These front-ends have not been well accepted, mostly because the underlying systems are still difficult for end users to use successfully in searching. New techniques, based on statistical methods, that allow natural language input and return lists of records in order of likely relevance, have long been available from research laboratories. This article presents four prototype implementations of these statistical retrieval systems that demonstrate their potential as powerful and easily used retrieval systems able to service all users.

In an article entitled "In search of the elusive end user" (Summit, 1989), Roger Summit, founder, and president of Dialog Information Services, Inc., estimated that the current usage of DIALOG by end users was about 12% of overall usage, and that that number was growing only at about 20% a year. He mentioned many problems encountered by end users, and described some of the necessary features of user-friendly front-ends. In a subsequent letter to the editor (Cleverdon, 1990), Cyril Cleverdon, however, commented:

> I do not argue with the points he raises, but I find it astonishing that he makes no mention of the problem which far outweighs all others. I refer to the insistence on Boolean searching.

A look at most user-friendly front-ends shows many important features, such as easy dialup and logins, easy file management, and help in selecting databases. All these are clearly necessary and useful, but at the heart of these retrieval systems is a Boolean search engine requiring users to supply AND's and OR's (either directly or indirectly using graphic interfaces), and, more critically, returning an unranked list of document or record titles. At least one study (Miller, Kirby, & Templeton, 1988) found that 45% of search statements issued using a front-end to MEDLINE retrieved no documents. Equally problematic are searches that are so broad that a very large number of documents are returned; with no ranking, the perusal of this list is intimidating to many users. In addition to the problem of submitting adequate initial queries, there is the problem of improving these queries. Boolean systems seldom have any mechanism for aiding the user in producing a better query, and never have any mechanism for automatically improving that query.

A viable alternative to these Boolean retrieval engines are the statistical retrieval engines that take a natural language query and return a list of titles ranked in order of likely relevance to that query.

These systems have been developed over the past 30 years in various information retrieval research laboratories, but have had very little influence on commercial online systems. Several operational prototypes (or small operational systems) have been built, particularly recently, to demonstrate the strengths of these statistical retrieval engines, and several small companies are beginning to market systems based on this technology. These new retrieval methods will be seen, it is hoped, in more and more major commercial systems. This article describes several of the operational prototypes in order to show the power of these retrieval methodologies and to encourage developers to consider this alternative—and users to request these enhanced retrieval services.

The first prototype described, the PRISE system, was designed to test these laboratory technologies using a textual data set of nearly a gigabyte, with testing being done by a group of real users with real information needs. This system is presented in full detail to show how these systems work in general, and to show the results of user testing. The second prototype, the CITE system, was a system designed to access the MEDLINE and CATLINE databases at the National Library of Medicine, but using a ranking technology instead of Boolean methods. The third prototype, the MUSCAT system, was an outgrowth of research done at Cambridge University, and runs at the Scott Polar Research Institute as a bibliographic retrieval system. The fourth and final prototype is the News Retrieval Tool, a prototype retrieval system being built by the University of Glasgow for the Financial Times (a major international newspaper). Whereas all these prototypes have statistical retrieval engines, and return ranked lists of documents, the exact features and interfaces of the systems are very different.

Statistical Ranking

The mechanism behind all these prototypes is called *statistical ranking* or *probabilistic ranking*. Various theoretical models have been used to describe this concept (Bookstein, 1985; Robertson & Sparck Jones, 1976; Salton & McGill, 1983), but the methodology is basically one of statistically comparing each record in an information file with the user's query and estimating the likelihood that the record is pertinent or relevant to the query. This approach has proven useful in many laboratory experiments such as those at Cornell University (Salton, 1971; Salton & Buckley, 1988), Cambridge University (Harper, 1980; Sparck Jones, 1979), University of Massachusetts at Amherst (Croft, 1983), and others. An excellent survey of both the underlying models and the retrieval experiments run using them was written by Belkin & Croft (1987).

At the simplest level, the statistical comparison of a query and a document could be a count of the number of matching terms between them. Documents would then be ranked on this count. This was one of the first methods tried and is referred to as quorum or coordination matching. Several commercial retrieval systems offer this option (within a Boolean environment), but find that users do not select it very often because of poor performance. These are several reasons for this poor performance:

(1) There is no technique for resolving ties. If there are three words in a query, maybe only a few documents match all three words, but many will match two terms, and these documents are essentially unranked.

(2) There is no allowance for word importance within a data set. A query such as "human factors in menu design" could return a single document containing all four noncommon words, and then an unranked list of documents containing the two words "human" and "factors" or "menu" and "design," all in random order. This could mean that the possibly ten documents containing "menu" and "design" are buried in 500 documents containing "human" and "factors."

(3) There is no allowance for word importance within a document. Looking again at the query "human factors in menu design," the correct order of the documents containing "menu" and "design" would be by frequency of "menu" within a document, so that the highest ranked document contains multiple instances of "menus," not just a single instance.

(4) There is no allowance for document length. Whereas this factor is not as important as the first three factors, it can be important to normalize ranking for length, because otherwise long documents often rank higher than short documents, even though the query terms may be more concentrated in the short documents.

These problems can be largely avoided by using more complex statistical ranking routines involving proper term weighting or accurate similarity measures.

Various experiments in laboratories have been concerned with developing optimal methods of weighting the terms and optimal methods of measuring the similarity of a document and the query. One of the term weighting measures that has proven very successful is the inverted document frequency weight or IDF (Sparck Jones, 1972), which is basically a measure of the scarcity of a term in the data set. A second measure used is some function of a term's frequency within a record. These measures are often combined, with appropriate normalization factors for length, to form a single term weight. Statistically ranked retrieval using this type of term weighting has a retrieval performance that is significantly better in the laboratory than using simple quorum or coordination matching (Croft, 1983; Harman, 1986; Salton & McGill, 1983).

The PRISE System

The PRISE system, developed at the National Institute of Standards and Technology, is an implementation based on laboratory experiments done in 1985 (Harman, 1986). Results from these experiments suggested an optimal weighting formula (see Appendix), and the similarity of a document and a query is calculated by summing the weights of all matching terms. Results on standard test collections using this weighting method are not superior to other methods such as Salton & McGill (1983) and Croft (1983); however, the goal of this prototype was to show that this type of retrieval technique is capable of being efficiently implemented. Experiments were run to test various efficiency algorithms, with the results always being tested using the standard test collection to ensure that improvements in response time had not sacrificed effective performance. A detailed description of the prototype data structures, the algorithms selected, and the experiments themselves is given in an earlier paper (Harman & Candela, 1990).

A user interface was added to the system to enable testing in real-world environments. Figure 1 shows the first screen seen by a user, prompting for selection of a data set for searching. Only one data set is shown for illustration; the actual user testing had five data sets to select from, with the option of selecting multiple data sets for simultaneous searching. The screen shown in Figure 1 shows the selected data set highlighted. (The

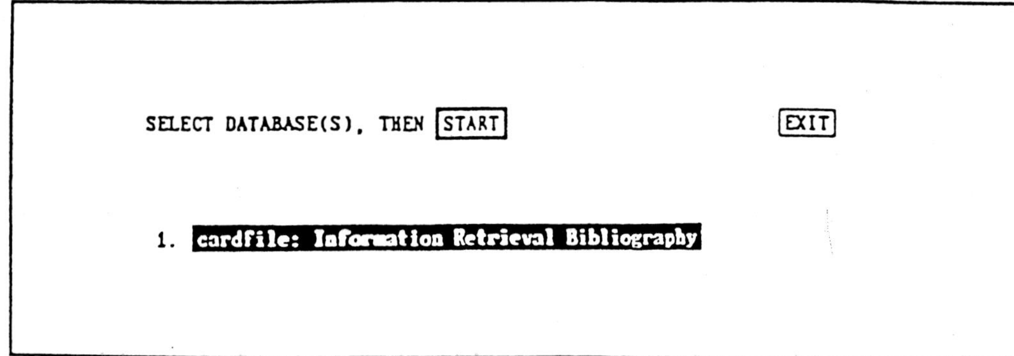

FIG. 1. User screen for data set selection.

actual screens are in color, so the highlighting is much more effective.)

Figure 2 shows the title selection screen. The user has typed in a natural language query "human factors in information retrieval systems" (by simply typing into the query window) and the system has searched the data set, selected appropriate bibliographic records, ranked those records based on their similarity to the query, and returned the titles of those records along with a list of all the query words that are contained in each selected bibliographic record. The query issued by the user is in natural language, with no need for Boolean connectors, proximity operators, or other such devices needed in traditional online systems. The first four titles show some of the effects of ranking; record 4 is probably not relevant to the query, but the top three records are all likely candidates. If more titles were to be examined, the next screen holding titles 5–8 contains only one record of interest. Whereas the system does not do a perfect job of ranking, clearly a user can easily scan down the titles and do a rough selection. This is contrasted to a Boolean system, where the same query (without connectors or other limiting devices) would pull in many records, all in random order.

Figure 3 shows a display of a selected record. The portion of the record shown is from a personal bibliographic file of about 1400 such records, each with a summary to indicate the items of interest in that reference. All query terms are highlighted, and the banners at the top help to orient the user. The seven mouse-selectable buttons allow the user to scroll through the record by page, by line, or to the next query word. The user could alternatively exit, select a new data set, input a new query, or go back to the title screen to select another title.

User Testing

Five different data sets were involved in the testing: a 1.6-megabyte manual, a 50-megabyte legal code book, and almost one gigabyte of the text of 40,000 court cases. The users who tested the system consisted of more than 40 people, all proficient in doing research (usually manual research) in the various test data sets as part of their regular job. About two-thirds of these users had never or seldom used an online retrieval system. Nine of the testers used Boolean retrieval systems regularly, and five others had used Boolean retrieval systems, but not regularly enough to develop expertise. All users brought trial queries with them—often questions they were currently manually researching or had researched in the past. These queries covered a wide range of the subject areas contained in the data sets.

The system (running on a 3-mip processor) was very fast, easily providing real-time response to the users. Initial response time for most queries on the largest data set usually tested (268 megabytes) was on the order of 1 second. Table 1 gives the average response time using a test group of user queries for each data set.

The response time for the 806-megabyte data set assumes parallel processing of the three parts of the data set, and would be longer if the data set could not be processed in parallel.

The system was also very effective. A test set of queries was assembled from all those queries tried during user testing. The records providing the correct answers (relevant records) were noted for each test query. Looking only at the test queries, 53 of 68 queries retrieved at least one relevant record in the top ten, with 25 of these retrieving relevant records as the first record. Other user queries not recorded as test queries worked equally well, and users were very pleased with the results.

User Reactions

The main reason the natural language/ranking approach is more effective for casual users is that all the terms in the query are used for retrieval, but the results are ranked based on co-occurrance of query terms, as modified by the term weighting, based on term and term-within-record attributes. This method not only eliminates the often-wrong Boolean syntax used by casual users, but provides some results even if a query term is incorrect, that is, it is not the term used in the data, it is mispelled, etc. The longer the query the bet-

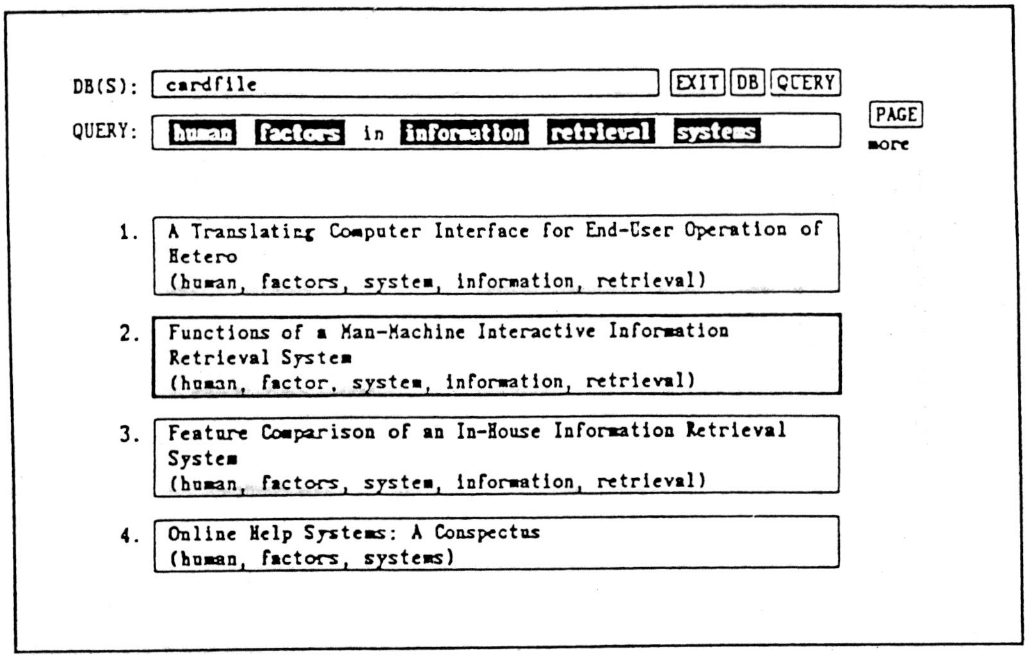

FIG. 2. User screen for title selection.

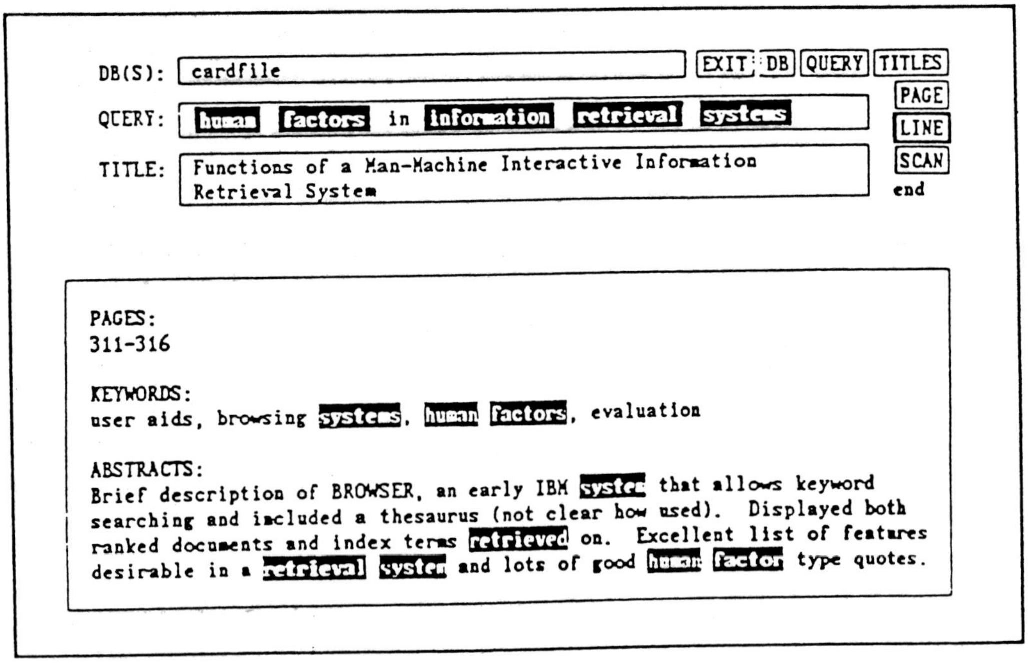

FIG. 3. User screen for record display

TABLE 1. Response time.

Size of data set	1.6 Mb	50 Mb	268 Mb	806 Mb
Number of queries	13	38	17	17
Average number of terms per query	4.1	3.5	3.5	3.5
Average response time per query (in seconds)	0.28	0.58	1.1	1.6

ter the system tends to work, although the average query in the tests was only 3.5 words. The ranking methodology works well for the complex queries that may be difficult to express in Boolean, especially for casual users. For example, "human factors and/or system performance in medical databases" is difficult in Boolean because it contains many high or medium frequency words without any clear necessary Boolean syntax. The ranking methodology would do well with this query.

All users were able to get satisfactory results within a short time of seeing a demonstration, and those that had never used an online retrieval system did as well as those with experience. Five of the nine users who regularly used Boolean systems, and the five people in the test group who used Boolean systems only occasionally, all preferred the ranking system because it consistently gave good results—results equivalent to those normally achieved by experts using the Boolean systems. Allowing the system to supply some of this expertise actually resulted in better test results. In one testing session, users brought in ten queries that previously had been run against a Boolean system. The system retrieved the single relevant record within the top five records for all ten queries, whereas the Boolean system had missed the relevant record completely in three of the queries. These are clearly not exhaustive tests, but they do suggest that the ranking methodology is very effective.

The user testing also pointed out several other critical design features. One of these was the importance of the information shown in the title selection screen (Fig. 2). The users had to have enough information to allow a rough judgment of record usefulness based only on this screen. The title itself needs to be not only descriptive but to carry additional information. For court cases, this information would be dates, case numbers, and court locations. For reference manuals, the particular chapter and section numbers and page numbers are important. Good titles are especially important in a retrieval system outputting the titles in a ranked order rather than random order, because the user is likely to scan further looking for information rather than automatically accepting or rejecting the results of the search. Once the user has selected a record for display, the ability to highlight query words (and other user-selected words) allows quick scanning of the records (See Fig. 3).

Several features were added to the query input to facilitate searching. All query terms automatically had their singular/plural variations added, along with other simple semantic variations (a user override was provided). Upper and lower case were ignored. Note that these features tend to add more retrieved records, but because the output is ranked, the search can be more extensive without overwhelming the user. Users were able to use phrases instead of single terms. This was particularly useful when those phrases were the kind normally used in place of sets of individual terms, such as the phrase "human factors." All these features improved searching.

Future work on the PRISE prototype will add the ability to access the data in several distinct manners besides keyword access, such as by using the table of contents or the back-of-the-book index, and will add the ability to use simple hypertext to access cross-references (possibly in other data sets) or to link to accompanying tables and figures. Query modification techniques, such as relevance feedback to improve the initial query are currently being added, and the prototype will be further tested with different users in other retrieval environments.

The CITE System

The CITE system was a statistically based prototype retrieval system developed as a sophisticated front-end to MEDLINE, the National Library of Medicine's largest and most heavily used data base. It was built during the 1970s, making it the first large-scale prototype to be built using the statistical ranking methodology (Doszkocs & Rapp, 1979).

Many of the features of the system were designed to take advantage of (or make up for) the characteristics of the MEDLINE database. This database had approximately 500,000 online records in 1979, and was traditionally accessed by a Boolean search system using controlled vocabulary and "free-text" words from the title and abstract of each record. However, at the time the CITE system was developed, less than 50% of the records contained abstracts, thus requiring heavy use of the controlled vocabulary, Medical Subject Headings (MeSH). This provided problems in matching the controlled vocabulary against the natural language queries normally input to statistical retrieval systems. An additional limitation was the enormous size of the database relative to computer capabilities in the late 1970s.

The first problem—and also opportunity—was the existence of the controlled vocabulary. Whereas this posed a problem in that the natural language was being matched only against titles in over half the database, it presented an opportunity in that manually indexed terms were available. It has been shown (Katzer, McGill, Tessier, Frakes, & Das Gupta, 1982) that retrieval using manually indexed terms brings in a different (and complementary) set of articles than does retrieval using "free-text" terms. Therefore, the existence of the manually indexed terms could help performance; however, there needed to be a way of mapping between natural language and the MeSH-controlled vocabulary. Although there are many ways of doing this, the initial CITE system used relevance feedback. The initial user query was run as if all documents contained suitable "free-text" for matching. The matched documents were ranked in a manner similar to the PRISE system, but without any document frequency or length information, since these were not available in MEDLINE (i.e., documents were ranked by sums of matching IDF weights only; see Appendix for definition of the IDF measure). The users were shown the ranked list, asked to mark relevant records, and the MeSH headings assigned to each relevant record were added to the query. In this manner, an indirect mapping was made from the natural language terms to the MeSH-controlled vocabulary.

The enormous size of the MEDLINE database was handled by partitioning the data into 48,000 record segments for searching, starting with the most current records (Doszkocs, 1982). Segment size was dependent on the desired speed and available memory, and more modern machines would likely be able to work with larger segments. Note that this technique of dividing the data into partitions for separate searching can be applied today in a distributed manner; that is, with different server machines processing segments of a database and the results being combined on one client workstation, allowing very fast processing of very large databases (Harman, McCoy, Toense, & Candela, 1991).

The CITE system was also used as an online catalog access method (Doszkocs, 1983). In 1980, the National Library of Medicine closed its physical card catalog, substituting an interim online system. This proved unsatisfactory and, in 1982, a plan was developed (Siegel, Kameen, Sinn, & Weise, 1984) to user test two different in-house systems, the first a sophisticated but traditional library system specifically designed to maintain card catalogs and provide Boolean access (the ILS system), and the CITE system. The use of the CITE system was particularly aimed at solving the problem of subject searching, although the usual author, title, and call number capabilities were available on both systems. The data in this case was the CATLINE database containing more than 500,000 references, each with a title and one or two subject headings from MeSH.

Several modifications were made to CITE to better handle this new environment. Because of the extremely short records, stemming was added that reflected the special characteristics of medical English (Ulmschneider & Doszkocs, 1983). These stems were used both in matching query terms against the "free-text" titles and in attempting to match the query terms against MeSH (either the headings themselves or text in the cross-references, scope notes, or annotation files of the medical subject heading records). Additionally a manual mapping of keywords was made to the 82 topical MeSH subheadings in CATLINE.

The modified CITE (the CITE/CATLINE system) first accepted a user query in natural language, and then prompted the user to select and rank order from a list of suggested keywords, medical subject headings, and topical subheadings. This revised list was used for retrieval, with a ranked set of titles being returned. Relevance feedback was used to suggest new medical subject headings for user selection and to permit CITE/CATLINE to add automatically the classification numbers of the relevant records. CITE/CATLINE also provided an "electronic shelflist" displaying keywords from related classification numbers or similar medical subject headings as possible additional terms.

The results of the comparison showed that the CITE/CATLINE system was rated very favorably by 84% of its users, as compared with only 65% of the users liking the more traditional ILS system (Siegel, Kameen, Sinn, & Weise, 1984). In particular, users found the largest proportion of relevant information with the CITE/CATLINE system, and four of five felt that their search was easier using this system. Of 40 sample subject searches, over one-half failed using the more traditional Boolean system, with only one failing using CITE/CATLINE.

The CITE (and CITE/CATLINE) system is no longer used at the National Library of Medicine.

The Muscat System at the Scott Polar Research Institute

The Muscat system (Porter & Galpin, 1988) currently in use at the Scott Polar Research Institute in Cambridge, England, is based on the probabilistic retrieval model originally proposed by Robertson and Sparck Jones (1976), but uses essentially the same statistical methods of ranking documents as the previously described systems—but with different weighting techniques. The Muscat system is designed not only to do information retrieval, but also to handle all aspects of the catalog records normally maintained in libraries. The Scott Polar Research Institute is a research department of the University of Cambridge and serves as a specialized library for information about polar regions for the entire world. Users may be University researchers or members of polar expeditions, or other persons particularly interested in Arctic and Antarctic regions. This means that the retrieval system must serve librarians, experienced end users, and casual end users. The data being retrieved is basic card catalog data, involving more than 43,000 records currently.

The interface consists of function keys or direct commands (for more experienced users). Users can issue a natural language query consisting of sentences or strings of terms, titles, or the Universal Decimal Classification numbers for use in polar libraries (an officially recognized subset of the full UDC schedule). Figure 4 shows some sample queries.

title search: "reproduction and mortality of wandering albatrosses on Macquarie Island"
free-text search: "penguin breeding habits"
UDC search: "595.78(*49)"
words plus UDC: "moth Alaska 595.78 (*49)"

FIG. 4. Sample queries (from Porter & Galpin, 1988).

The system returns a ranked list of records from the catalog, ranked using a probabilistic retrieval system in a manner very similar to the other systems (see Porter & Galpin (1988) for the exact ranking formula). The major differences are the additional features added to the Muscat system to better serve a library environment and the inclusion of relevance feedback.

In addition to the ability to input UDC numbers, searchers have the ability to request author searches and to input standard Boolean queries. As input, the author search takes an author surname and outputs a list of authors with that surname. Users select from that list, and then catalog entries by that author are presented to the user. The Boolean query option requires that a user preface the query with the tag "boolean" which allows standard Boolean syntax to be used (see Fig. 5). The Boolean query returns the number of hits found and will return an unranked list of records. It is possible to combine a Boolean query with a probabilistic query, with the results being a ranked list of records, but with that list restricted to those documents that satisfy the Boolean query.

"query Alaskan moths"
"boolean 'alaska' and 'moth'"

FIG. 5. Probabilistic queries and Boolean queries (from Porter & Galpin, 1988).

One of the most useful features of the Muscat system is relevance feedback. After a user sees the ranked list of documents, he/she has the option of modifying the query using relevance feedback. In this case, the user marks the relevant or useful documents in the list, and the system processes this document list to produce statistics about the terms contained in the relevant documents. Original query terms contained in the relevant documents are given higher weights, and terms not in the original query but appearing often in the relevant documents are suggested to the user as possible additional query terms. The terms shown to the user are ranked in order of likely importance (see Porter & Galpin (1988) for the exact formulas). Figure 6 shows a list of the terms that would be generated from 11 relevant documents retrieved in response to the query "Falklands Wars."

(*72)	[Falkland Islands region]
(*7)	[Antarctic region]
355.489	[Aviation warfare, history]
occup	
stamp	
truth	
argentin	
656.835	[Postage stamps]
disturb	
britain	
(*721)	[Falkland Islands]
355.48	[Military history]
341.223	[Territorial claims]

FIG. 6. Feedback terms (from Porter & Galpin, 1988).

The square brackets giving the interpretation of the UDC codes are provided only for clarification (Fig. 6), and do not appear on the screen. The user selects some or all of these terms for addition to the query and the search is rerun. In this manner, the query can grow to include many terms not in the original query but highly useful in retrieving more relevant documents. This is particularly important in research libraries where users often require high recall and are willing to work with a retrieval system to obtain it.

In general, users have liked the flexibility of the system and found the probabilistic retrieval beneficial. A basic inquiry routine had to be set up, however, for some users to enable them to use the system in an elementary way with minimal assistance from the staff. Muscat has also been installed in other innovative applications, with new features developed to cope with these environments.

The News Retrieval Tool

The News Retrieval Tool (NRT) currently being built at the University of Glasgow is another outgrowth of the probabilistic retrieval model from the University of Cambridge (Robertson & Sparck Jones, 1976; van Rijsbergen, 1979). The data and prototype retrieval engine are located at the *Financial Times* Profile Office in London. Users connect via telephone from Macintosh personal computers. This prototype runs a set of 1988 and 1989 articles from the *Financial Times* (approximately 130,000 articles), and is designed to test retrieval improvements for users of the existing profile retrieval service.

The interface is a basic Macintosh interface, with multiple windows for different functions. The following five screen figures were taken from the *News Retrieval Tool User's Guide* (Sanderson, 1991), with additional information taken from a technical note on the project (Campbell, Sanderson & van Rijsbergen, 1990). Figure 7 shows a query search screen.

The user has typed in the query, "the Brazilian rain forests." In addition to the probabilistic weighting that is similar to the previously described prototypes, the NRT system allows users to add weight to terms by moving the knobs attached to the slider bars shown in the lower right-hand corner. After users are satisfied with the query, they request a search by "clicking on" the search button. The results of that search are shown in Figure 8.

Users can view a document by "clicking on" a title, which is then highlighted, and a third window is brought up (overlaid) to display the document (Fig. 9).

Using the scroll bars users can then browse that document. The documents are presented in a manner that allows easy browsing, with the headline in bold, enlarged type, the first (summary) paragraph in enlarged type, and noncritical identifications in reduced type. This style is particularly useful for the newspaper environment, and allows a much greater ease of scanning large volumes of text.

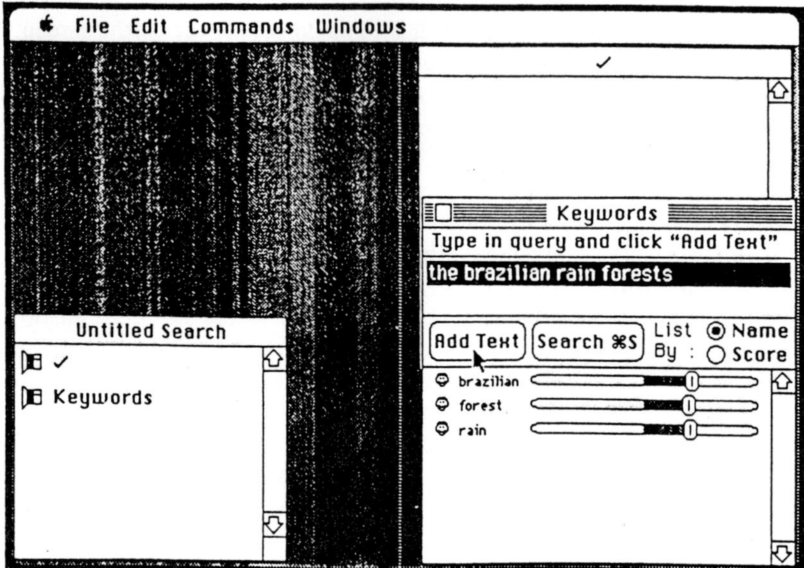

FIG. 7. User screen for query search.

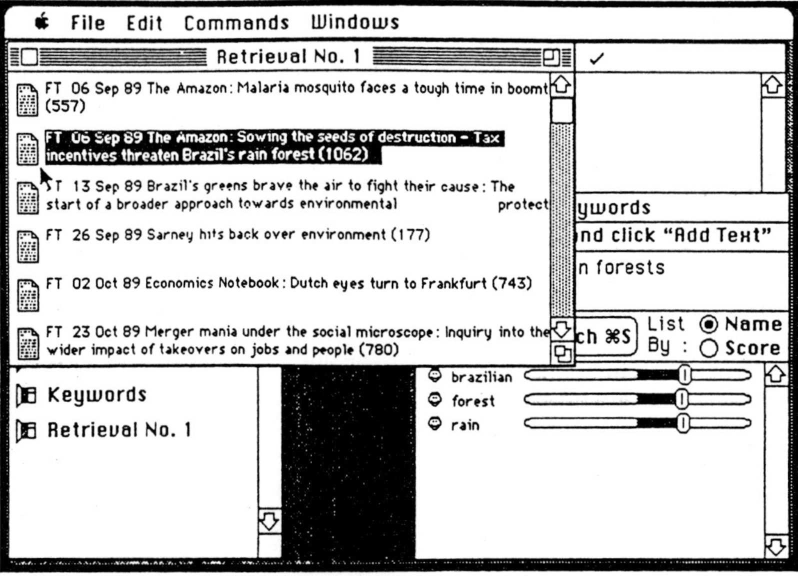

FIG. 8. Search results.

The NRT system makes heavy use of relevance feedback for query modification. It is assumed that end users in this environment want a high recall, and are willing to work with the system to obtain more documents. To start relevance feedback, users select relevant documents from the title screen and "drag" those documents into a "tick box" (history list) of relevant documents (shown in the top right-hand section of Fig. 10).

They then ask for a second search by "clicking on" the search button again. The system uses statistics from the occurrence of the terms in relevant documents to both reweigh initial query terms and to automatically add new terms to the query. Figure 11 shows the results of the second search.

Note that new terms have been added in the term box (lower right-hand corner), with document icons next to the terms to indicate that they are coming from relevance feedback rather than from user input terms. The results of the second search are a new set of titles, showing the two previously found relevant documents (marked with a check), plus four new titles, including one previously seen nonrelevant document (marked as a blank icon). Feedback can continue for multiple iterations, with the query words always being taken from the original query plus a selection of words from the documents currently in the "tick box."

The NRT system has several other highly interesting features. Users can select words directly from a docu-

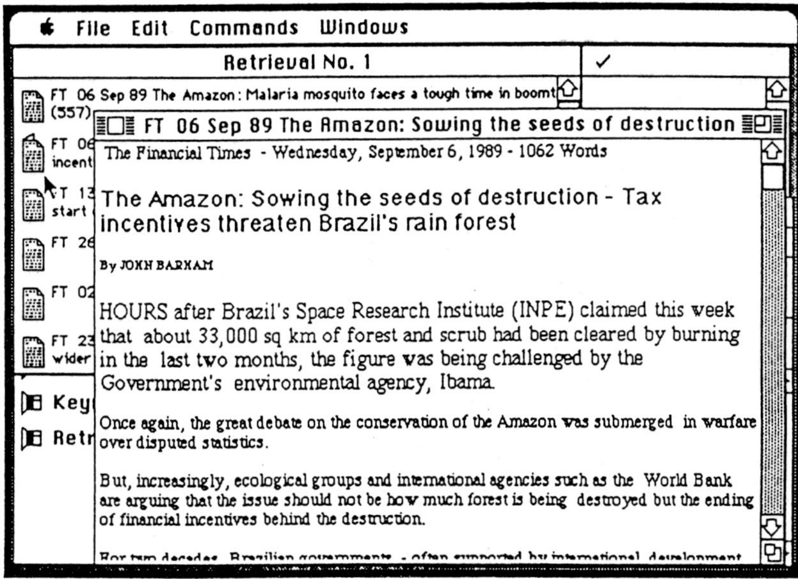

FIG. 9. Document display.

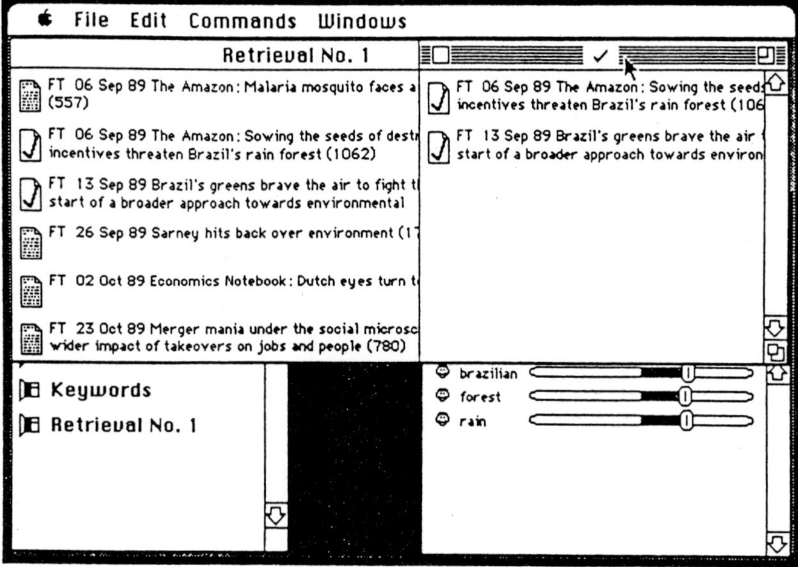

FIG. 10. Relevance feedback.

ment for adding to the query. Users can also edit lists, such as the "tick box" of relevant documents, as their perceived needs change. To help users better understand the term weighting, keywords can be ordered by "score" (term weight) rather than alphabetically ("name"). Standard Macintosh commands are also available for those users desiring more complex operations.

User testing is just starting on the NRT system. One of the initial observations has been that:

> after the first retrieval, users simply pick articles based upon the headline, mark them as relevant, and then use the relevance feedback mechanism to perform another retrieval. After this second (usually more effective) retrieval users begin to look more closely at the documents themselves. Having scanned the first paragraph, they discard non relevant articles from the "tick" window and add some new (relevant) articles found in the second retrieved set. This larger, and more precise set of relevant articles are then used (by relevance feedback) to perform another search. (Campbell et al., 1990)

Conclusion

The prototype retrieval systems using statistically based ranked retrieval of records not only perform at speeds suitable for real-time retrieval, but provide high-quality retrieval results. User testing for these prototypes showed the effectiveness of these systems for text retrieval (the PRISE system and the NRT system) and for bibliographic records (the CITE/CATLINE system

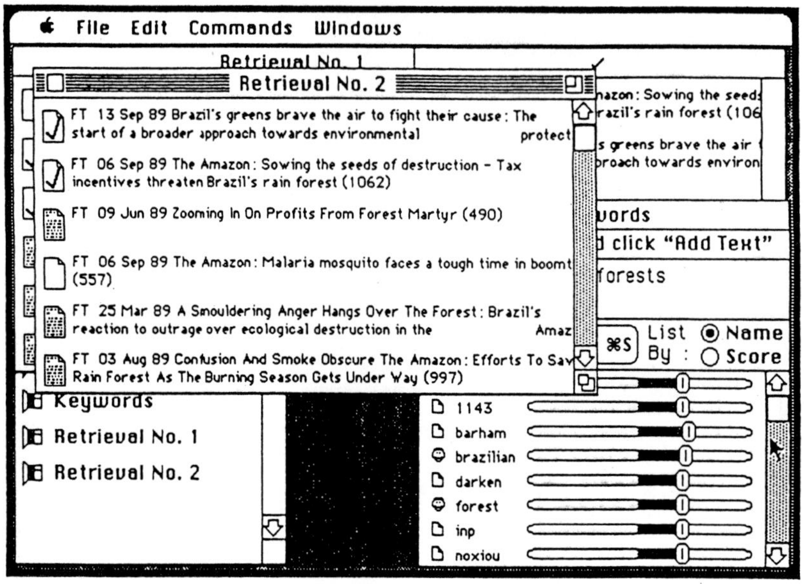

FIG. 11. Results from relevance feedback.

and the Muscat system). The ranking schema allowed novice users the opportunity to be successful searchers with minimal training, and, as importantly, with no learning curve for searchers using the system only occasionally. This is in sharp contrast to Boolean-based retrieval systems, where continual use is necessary to obtain consistently good results. In each of the prototypes it was important to provide an appropriate interface and appropriate tools tailored to the retrieval environment. Clearly, these systems also need a proper "front-end" to handle logins, file management, etc. However, by adding an effective retrieval engine that caters to end users, these prototypes are truly user-friendly systems and not just user-friendly front-ends.

Appendix

Ranking Using the IDF Weighting Measure

$$\text{rank}_j = \sum_{k=1}^{Q} \frac{(\log_2(\text{Freq}_{jk} + 1) \times \text{IDF}_k)}{\log_2 M_j}$$

where: Q = the number of terms in the query,
Freq_{jk} = the frequency of query term k in record j,
IDF_k = the inverse document frequency weight of term k for a given database, and
M_j = the total number of significant terms (including duplicates) in the record (length factor) j.

$$\text{IDF}_k = \log_2 \frac{N}{\text{Num}D_k} + 1$$

where: N = the number of records in the database, and
$\text{Num}D_k$ = number of records in the collection that contain one or more instance of term k.

References

Belkin, N. J. & Croft, W. B. (1987). Retrieval techniques. In M. Williams (Ed.), *Annual review of information science and technology* (pp. 109–145). New York: Elsevier.

Bookstein, A. (1985). Probability and fuzzy-set applications to information retrieval. In M. Williams (Ed.), *Annual review of information science and technology* (pp. 117–151). New York: Knowledge Industry Publications, Inc.

Campbell, I., Sanderson, M., & van Rijsbergen, K. (1990). *News Retrieval Tool technical notes,* Glasgow University: Computing Science Department.

Cleverdon, C. (1990). Letter to the editor. *Online Review, 14,* 35.

Croft, W. B. (1983). Experiments with representation in a document retrieval system. *Information Technology: Research and Development, 2,* 1–21.

Doszkocs, T. E. (1982). From research to application: The CITE natural language information retrieval system. In G. Salton and H. J. Schneider (Ed.), *Research and development in information retrieval* (pp. 251–262). Berlin: Springer-Verlag.

Doszkocs, T. E. (1983). CITE NLM: Natural language searching in an online catalog. *Information Technology and Libraries, 2,* 364–380.

Doszkocs, T. E. & Rapp, B. A. (1979). Searching MEDLINE in English: a prototype user interface with natural language query, ranked output, and relevance feedback. In *Proceedings of the 42nd Annual Meeting of the American Society for Information Science,* Minneapolis, MN.

Harman, D. (1986, September). An experimental study of factors important in document ranking. In F. Rabitti (Ed.). *Proceedings of the 1986 ACM conference on research and development in information retrieval,* Pisa, Italy.

Harman, D. & Candela, G. (1990). Retrieving records from a gigabyte of text on a minicomputer using statistical ranking, *Journal of the American Society for Information Science, 41*(8), 581–589.

Harman, D., McCoy, W., Toense, R., & Candela, G. Prototyping a distributed information retrieval system that uses statistical ranking. *Information Processing and Management, 27*(5), 449–460.

Harper, D. J. (1980). *Relevance feedback in document retrieval systems: an evaluation of probabilistic strategies.* Doctoral dissertation, Jesus College, Cambridge, UK.

Katzer, J., McGill, M. J., Tessier, J. A., Frakes, W., & Das Gupta, P. (1982). A study of the overlap among document representations. *Information Technology: Research and Development, 2,* 261–274.

Miller, N., Kirby, M., & Templeton, E. (1988). End user searching in a medical school library. *Medical Reference Service Quarterly, 7,* 1–13.

Porter, M. & Galpin, V. (1988). Relevance feedback in a public access catalogue for a research library: Muscat at the Scott Polar Research Institute. *Program, 22,* 1–20.

Robertson, S. E. & Sparck Jones, K. (1976). Relevance weighting of search terms, *Journal of the American Society for Information Science, 27,* 129–146.

Salton, G. (1971). *The SMART retrieval system — experiments in automatic document processing,* Englewood Cliffs, NJ: Prentice-Hall.

Salton, G. & Buckley, C. (1988). Term-weighting approaches in automatic text retrieval. *Information Processing and Management, 24,* 513–523.

Salton, G. & McGill, M. (1983). *Introduction to modern information retrieval.* New York: McGraw-Hill.

Sanderson, M. (1991). *NRT (News Retrieval Tool): A user's guide.* Glasgow University: Computing Science Department.

Siegel, E. R., Kameen, K., Sinn, S. K., & Weise, F. O. (1984). A comparative evaluation of the technical performance and user acceptance of two prototype online catalog systems. *Information Technology and Libraries, 3,* 35–46.

Sparck Jones, K. (1972). A statistical interpretation of term specificity and its application in retrieval. *Journal of Documentation, 28,* 11–20.

Sparck Jones, K. (1979). Search term relevance weighting given little relevance information. *Journal of Documentation, 35,* 30–48.

Summit, R. K. (1989). In search of the elusive end user. *Online Review, 13,* 485–491.

Ulmschneider, J. E. & Doszkocs, T. (1983). A practical stemming algorithm for online search assistance. *Online Review, 7,* 301–318.

van Rijsbergen, C. J. (1979). *Information Retrieval (2nd ed.).* London: Butterworths.

The Okapi online catalogue research projects

Stephen Walker

Introduction

Online catalogue research at the Polytechnic of Central London (PCL) has now been going on, mainly funded by the British Library Research and Development Department, for about five years. This article contains a historical survey of the projects from 1982 up to December 1987, a summary of the results of some of the more recent work and a brief discussion of some specific aspects of online catalogue research and design.

The research has given rise to a series of more or less operational online catalogues, three fairly lengthy reports and a number of articles and published and unpublished talks.[1-8] (The name 'Okapi' is not, strictly, an acronym, but see Mitev, 'Designing an online public access catalogue', p.5. The okapi, according to Gill Venner, is shy and elusive and has a long gestation period.)

All the research has consisted of work towards the design and production of catalogue systems which satisfy the following criteria: they must be usable at sight without any appreciable need for learning or relearning, and this must be achieved without sacrificing effectiveness and without making them tedious for experienced users. Much online catalogue research has been carried out on outdated, first-generation systems, or on specially developed 'toy' systems which do not access real files and are in no way suitable for live use in a library. While such research can be of value, there is much work which can only be done on 'live' systems. All the Okapi work has been done on systems which have been developed at least to a point where they are reliable and complete enough to be installed in a library unattended. Hence, as with CITE at the National Library of Medicine,[9, 10] or the catalogues produced during the Dewey Decimal Classification (DDC) online project,[11] a large proportion of the Okapi work consists of design and programming.

The purpose of the Okapi research is to test the applicability, in the online catalogue context, of findings from research in interactive computer systems, cognitive psychology and information retrieval (IR). In a sense, our results are the systems which we produce. Formal system evaluation and comparison is done by observation and interviewing, and by study and repetition by experimenters of searches performed under natural conditions by (mainly undergraduate) PCL library users. Two of the catalogue systems have undergone extended live use in one of PCL's site libraries, and a considerable amount of transaction log data have been collected.

The Okapi projects arose from a research proposal entitled 'Microcomputer networking in libraries'. The proposers, Neil McLean and Mel Collier, head and deputy head of library services at PCL, wanted to see what could usefully be done in the way of library automation using networked microcomputers rather than the conventional multi-user access to a mainframe or large mini. They suggested that a public access catalogue would be a suitably demanding trial application. Because of the interests of the researchers who were appointed, the 'networking' aspect soon became subsidiary to the main aim of working towards effective IR systems for untrained, non-dedicated users.

Okapi '84

Okapi '84 was the prototype system developed during the original project in 1983 and 1984. This system was demonstrated at the conference and exhibition 'Public access to library files' at the Centre for Catalogue Research, Bath University, in September 1984. It is described by Mitev.[12]

Features of Okapi '84 included the following:

- There were only two types of search – 'Books about something' or 'Specific books' (Figure 5.1).

```
                P.C.L. ON-LINE CATALOGUE                  ** OKAPI
Do you want to look for :
            1.   SPECIFIC BOOK(S)
                 (if you know the author and/or title)
            2.   BOOK(S) ABOUT SOMETHING
                 (any topic(s) you have in mind)
Indicate your choice by typing 1 or 2 : █
IF YOU HAVE A PROBLEM DURING YOUR SEARCH, PRESS THE
     YELLOW KEY FOR EXPLANATIONS, OR ASK A MEMBER
                    OF THE STAFF
```

Figure 5.1 Search type choice screen – Okapi '84

- For a subject search, the words of the user's search were looked up in an index containing words from title-like fields and subject headings, and from corporate names. The system would first perform an implicit AND on the search words. If this failed, words were assigned weights on an inverse term frequency basis (uncommon words are worth more than common words), and the system would look for records containing just some of the words of the search. For example, a search for 'women and their fight in society' would lead to a message to the effect that there is no book described by all the words of the search, but the system would nevertheless retrieve four items (in the PCL catalogue), the first of which is titled *Hidden from history: 300 years of women's oppression and the fight against it*. Records were given a score equal to the sum of the weights of the words by which they were indexed, and would be output in decreasing score order.
- For specific item searches, Okapi '84 presented the user with a form-filling type of screen on which could be entered a title and/or an author's name. The system would follow different paths (search trees) according to the data elements which the user had entered and the results of initial searches. (Figure 5.2 gives a view of one possible configuration of this screen.) In a title search, for example, a search for an incomplete or garbled title would lead to the choice of a title index display or a search for 'titles containing the words of the search, and thenceforth behave rather as if it were doing a subject search. There is no title 'Banking and industrialization', but such a search could lead to 'Banking and industrialization in Europe' or 'Banking in the early stages of industrialization' and a number of other titles.
- All commands, or menu selections (there is no clear distinction between *command* and *selection*) were performed by a single keystroke. There were six coloured 'function' keys. Single digits and occasionally letters were also used for selection.
- Record displays were either single line, six to a screen, with column headings AUTHOR, TITLE, etc., or 'full'. Full records contained up to five elements: AUTHOR (which includes any added names, personal or corporate), TITLE (including any subtitle, series title, part title), PUBLICATION (publisher(s), edition, date), SUBJECT (Library of Congress and/or PREserved Context Indexing System headings) and location information (including classmark). Full records were selected by line number from a brief display screen. When only a few records were retrieved the default display would be full. (Okapi '84 record displays were similar to the screens shown in Figures 5.6 and 5.7. The red key took the user back from a brief display to the input screen, and there was no 'See books classified near this one' option.)

SPECIFIC BOOK SEARCH ** OKAPI

To find a book the computer needs the TITLE (one or two words are often enough), or the AUTHOR (you need not know the entire name) or BOTH.

TITLE (if known) : banking and in█........................

AUTHOR :

GREEN KEY	When you have finished entering the title, or if you don't know the title.
WHITE KEY	If you want to correct what you have typed.
BLUE KEY	To enter again and delete your word(s).
YELLOW KEY	If you need explanations.
RED KEY	To choose a SUBJECT search instead.

Figure 5.2 Specific book search input screen – Okapi '84

It is difficult to know how well Okapi '84 succeeded in meeting the goal of combining effectiveness with ease of learning and use. A certain amount of fairly informal evaluation was carried out late in 1984, and is described by Mitev.[13] Okapi was certainly easy to use and most people found that it needed minimal learning and relearning. Later, Richard Jones did a study of samples of specific item and subject searches from Okapi '84 transaction logs.[14] He estimated that 25% of subject searches and 18% of author/title searches failed at the first attempt. The session failure rate would have been considerably lower, but it is very difficult to estimate this from log data alone. Note that failure does not include collection failure – the absence of the sought item or topic from the collection; one of the functions of a good catalogue is to inform users as quickly as possible that the library does not hold what they are looking for.

The subject search, which is extremely simple, was probably relatively successful given the intrinsic difficulty of subject searching in files of records with inadequate subject description. For various reasons the specific item search, into which the designers had put a good deal of effort, was less successful. It was somewhat over-elaborate, or, rather, the complications were in the wrong places. In particular, the designers did not realize that in a relatively small collection (PCL's catalogue contained about 90,000 titles) by far the most frequent cause of a specific item search 'failure' is collection failure. The catalogue of a small library should not encourage its users to be too persistent without warning them that the library may hold nothing relevant. (The effects of collection size have been little mentioned by writers on online catalogues, perhaps because many of the writers are from North America and are used to university libraries which are larger than many national collections.)

Okapi '84 was used for almost two years at one of PCL's site libraries. Most user and system activity was captured and stored in machine-readable log files. Because of storage limitations these transaction logs do not directly identify the records which were displayed. These can only be identified with certainty by 'replaying' the search with the same programs and files. Unfortunately this will not be possible for much longer, because the original hardware is no longer being maintained. However, it is hoped that the logs themselves, which contain a wealth of information about user activity, will continue to be available in hard copy or in unix *tar* format on ¼in. cartridge tape.

Improving subject retrieval: Okapi '86

Despite the fact that Okapi '84's specific item search was probably relatively less effective than its subject search, recent work has concentrated on subject retrieval. Subject searching is generally, and probably correctly, seen as a richer and more important research area than investigation of author and other known-item search activity. Some interesting and useful things can be done in the way of improving specific item search systems, but only if the catalogue has considerable 'knowledge' of bibliographic items (for example, one can envisage a catalogue which could say, 'We haven't got Joseph Matthews on online catalogue screen displays, but there is an article in *Library trends* which might be of some interest.'). Such a catalogue would 'know' a large number of titles and names even if the library being searched did not possess them. It would be prepared to 'flip' name-words and it would have access to useful cross-reference files derived from the forms of names and titles which people actually search for.[15]

Okapi '86 is a subject-only system, using the same hardware as Okapi '84. The file structures, much of the code and the general appearance of the screens are similar to Okapi '84.

All searches are processed on a combinatorial, best-match basis. This means that a search may retrieve items which are indexed under only some of the terms in the search, although any records containing all the terms are output first and described as 'matching your search closely'. Each term in the search is given a 'weight' which is determined by its relative frequency in the file being searched. This results in a common word like 'history' being assigned a weight which is very low compared with that assigned to a rare word such as 'swords'. A search for 'history of swords' will output anything under both words first, followed by everything under 'swords' only. Items indexed under 'history' but not 'swords' will not be retrieved. The cut-off rules which determine which records will be retrieved, and what weight a record has to achieve for it to be counted as a possible match, are fairly complex and purely pragmatic, being based on experience from repetition of real searches. The aim is to achieve a reasonable balance between exhaustiveness and accuracy, between 'recall' and 'precision'. Since there are few books indexed under 'swords', the 'history of swords' searcher may well be prepared to look through them all; there are thousands of books under 'history', and only a minute proportion will contain anything of relevance to this searcher.

Okapi '86 underwent live evaluation in PCL's Riding House Street site library late in 1986. It incorporated three devices aimed at automatically or semi-automatically improving retrieval. These are:

- automatic stemming of search terms,
- automatic cross-referencing,
- semi-automatic spelling correction.

Okapi '86 is described in some detail in the report by Walker and Jones.[16] The first few stages of a typical search are shown in Figures 5.3, 5.4 and 5.5.

```
SUBJECT SEARCH                                  ** OKAPI
The computer will look for books which include all (or most) of
your words in their titles or subject descriptions:
Type a word or a phrase which describes the books you want:
emploument of women during the 1st world war█.............
Press the GREEN KEY when you have finished
WHITE KEY to change what you have typed
BLUE KEY to get rid of what you have typed
```

Figure 5.3 Subject search input screen – Okapi '86

```
Your search: "employment of women during the first world war"

Looking up these words

CAN'T FIND "emploument" – closest match found is employment"

GREEN KEY to use "employment" instead █

BLUE KEY to type a different word


(RED KEY to abandon this search)
```

Figure 5.4 Okapi '86 offering a replacement word during look-up

```
Your search: "employment of women during the first world war"

Looking up these words

 713 books under "employment"
 822 books under "women"
  81 books under "1st world war"

Looking for books described by your search – please wait..

One book matches your search closely
(95 books found altogether)

GREEN KEY to look at the book(s) found █
(the most similar books should appear first)


BLUE KEY to correct or change your search

RED KEY to do a different search
```

Figure 5.5 Look-up and search results screen – Okapi '86

Stemming

Neither Okapi '84 nor any commercially available online catalogue will find any books in PCL libraries in response to the reasonable subject searches 'accounts dictionary' or 'terminal illness', although there are at least half a dozen books on each subject. Library of Congress uses 'accounting–dictionaries' and 'terminal care'. There are PREserved Context Indexing System (PRECIS) headings 'accountancy' and 'patients with terminal illnesses'. A persistent searcher might find some records by browsing subject headings, but one would think that any subject catalogue worthy of the name could go straight to the records described by the above headings.

Stemming procedures have been in use for many years, mainly as a relatively cheap way of conflating terms which are morphologically similar in the hope that they are also semantically similar. Most of them use small sets of rules about what constitutes an affix which can safely be removed, and any stem 'normalization' which may thereafter be needed to achieve conflation (e.g., 'absorption' → 'absorb', 'travelling' → 'travel'). There has been research which suggests that moderately strong automatic stemming can be applied in specialized online reference retrieval searching.[17] The National Library of Medicine's CITE catalogue uses a stemming procedure designed for medical terminology (it knows about '. . . itis' and '. . . ectomy').[18]

It seems almost self-evident that a subject catalogue should at least conflate singular and plural noun forms, and remove possessive endings and the English 'ing' suffix. We refer to this as 'weak' stemming. Weak stemming is defined to be any stemming which can be done almost unconditionally without making an appreciable difference to the meaning of the stemmed words (within the language of subject searches). On the other hand, it is fairly obvious that 'strong' stemming – the removal of longer and more 'meaningful' suffixes such as 'ization', 'ism' and 'ability' – often cannot be done without drastically altering the sense of a search (consider 'organ', 'organic', 'organism' and 'organization'). The converse also holds. At least outside the hard sciences, words which are closely related in meaning in the context of a subject search are often morphologically and etymologically unrelated ('alcoholism' and 'drunkenness', 'communism' and 'marxism'). If strong stemming does not seem to introduce too much noise in reference retrieval searching this is probably because typical searches include, explicitly or implicitly, at least three words and often more. In online catalogue searching, the mean number of significant words is usually a little over two, and few searches contain more than three words.

We decided to use both weak and strong stemming. Records retrieved only under strong stems would not be given high weight. A search for 'industrialization' must retrieve the 98 books indexed under 'industrialisation' or 'industrialization' before offering to show the 2,000 books under 'industry'. The stemming procedure used is substantially that of Martin Porter,[19] split into weak and strong phases and with the addition of a certain amount of spelling standardization at the weak level. Weak stemming removes regular English plurals and possessives, and the 'ing' and 'ed' suffixes. The associated spelling standardization is mainly an attempt to cope with the differences between British and American spelling: there are 13 rules, including 'iz' → 'is', non-terminal 'ae' → 'e' and terminal 'tre' → 'ter'. The spelling rules are given in full by Walker and Jones.[20] Strong stemming removes the endings given in steps 2 to 5 of Porter's algorithm.[21]

At first we considered the design of a search system in which strong stems would not be introduced at all unless weak-stem searching found little or nothing. This has several drawbacks, including the fact that even when all the weak stems of the words in a search co-occur, they may do so in only a very few records, and there may be other relevant records retrievable by adding one or more strong stems. It would often be necessary to go back to the user and ask for guidance on whether to broaden the search. One could use rules of thumb about thresholds below which the search would be automatically repeated using strong stems. There is a danger of falling into over-elaboration of the search sequencing, as in Okapi '84's specific item search.

The method we used leads to an increase in the computational load but a gain in simplicity. The search and merge procedure always uses both strong and weak stems, but ensures that records retrieved under weak stems usually come out nearer the top of the list than those retrieved under strong stems. It is simply necessary to ensure (a) that no strong stem contributes to the score of a record which is indexed under the corresponding weak stem, and (b) that a strong stem, if distinct from the corresponding weak stem, has lower weight than the weak stem. The algorithm is described by Walker.[22]

Automatic cross-referencing

After studying some thousands of searches made by users of PCL's business studies, social sciences and communications library, we constructed a list of several hundred classes of terms which are treated as synonymous. This was primarily an attempt to deal with synonyms which cannot be conflated by a rule-based stemming procedure. It is intended to cope with irregular plurals ('child' = 'children'), other morphological variation which is too context dependent to be handled algorithmically ('Hebrides' = 'Hebridean'), abbreviations ('BBC' = 'British Broadcasting Corporation'), words with alternative spellings ('gaol' = 'jail') and near synonyms ('Great Britain' = 'United Kingdom' = 'Britain' = 'UK' = 'British Isles'). The list also contains a very few phrases which apparently have no equivalents ('soap opera', 'Z cars', 'facts of life'), but are included on the grounds that their constituent words have no relation to the meaning of the phrase. These are phrases which behave, and are treated, exactly like words.

The index also contains both strong and weak stems of the individual words of phrases in the cross-reference list, because a search for 'broadcasting' may well be satisfied by books about the BBC.

Dealing with words which the system cannot find

Nearly all those keyword-type online catalogues which use an implicit Boolean AND will simply report a failed search (it might display 'No entries' or 'Nothing found') if the search contains a word which they cannot find. Users often do not notice that they have miskeyed a word, and many systems do not make it clear why they have failed to find anything. This can lead to the mistaken assumption that the catalogue contains nothing relevant. Miskeyings (like 'Amwerica') and misspellings ('rascism' or its companion 'Facism') – the former are more common among Okapi users – are frequent. About 10% of searches of Okapi contain at least one dubious spelling. In searching a small file it is also likely that users will enter a good many words which are correct but which the system does not know.

The only satisfactory way to deal with a word which cannot be found is to negotiate it with the user; such a word can be ignored (i.e., removed from the search) or replaced, or the search can be abandoned on the ground that the word is correct and essential to the success of the search. The decision must rest with the user. However, it may be helpful if the system can sometimes suggest a correction for a miskeyed word. Okapi '86 automatically invokes a procedure which tries to find a likely correction before asking the user for a decision. This procedure can suggest a replacement for about half the genuine miskeyings it receives, and the replacement is usually right (although it does suggest 'teacher' for 'Thacher'). Some of the dialogue is shown in Figures 5.4 and 5.5 and the matching procedure is described by Walker and Jones.[23]

Evaluation of Okapi '86

Method

Two terminals were installed in PCL's Riding House Street site library, one running Okapi '86, as described above, and the other running a system which appeared to be almost identical, but used weak stemming only, no cross-reference table and no semi-automatic spelling correction. The two systems are referred to as *EXP* and *CTL* respectively. They were alternated daily between the two terminals. By each terminal was a prominent notice displaying 'OKAPI '86 is an experimental computer catalogue for subject searches . . . Please use one of the other catalogues if you have to look up the title or author of a book . . .' The 'other catalogues' were terminals to the LIBERTAS system of SWALCAP Library Services Ltd. There were also one or two microfiche readers. Some thousands of searches were logged automatically, and about a thousand were studied in some detail. About 120 users were briefly interviewed as they left one of the terminals. These users were asked whether they had used the catalogue before, whether they found what they were looking for, and whether they had any particular problems or would like to make any suggestions for improving the catalogue. The times were recorded so that session boundaries could be marked in the machine logs and the log data correlated with the interview results.

A set of 255 of the logged searches – those which were almost certainly the first search in a session or which bore no apparent relationship to the previous search – were repeated by the experimenters on *EXP*, *CTL* and a third system (*OSTEM*) which did no stemming at all.

Interview results

There was no significant correlation between perceived success and system (*EXP* or *CTL*). The overall perceived session success rate was very high (86%). More than half the users interviewed felt unable to make any comments or suggestions. There were about 30 comments of the type, 'Very easy to use', 'No problems' and 'Straightforward'. In addition there were about 20 interesting and enlightening comments ranging from, 'You can search on what you want with this if you just type in some buzz-words' to 'It only looks for keywords – doesn't analyse the search'. The comments are given in full by Walker and Jones.[24]

As will be seen below in the section on search repetition results, the objective difference between the two systems was not great, and it is not at all surprising that users did not seem to find any difference. (It is most unlikely that any user noticed that there were two systems – the terminals were labelled identically and the screen layouts were the same. For a discussion of a controlled comparison of two explicitly different catalogue systems, see below under 'Comparative evaluation of two catalogues'.) In the section 'Relevance feedback, query expansion and adaptive systems' there is further discussion of users' catalogue needs and expectations.

Search repetition results

A hundred of the 255 searches did quite well (or too well), even on the system which did no stemming at all (*OSTEM*), finding more than 20 records. Of the remaining 155, 74 (48%) found more records on the weak-stemming (*CTL*) system than on *OSTEM*. Precision was not markedly decreased: in four of the searches the extra records were all false drops (e.g., 'skiing' and 'sky' become conflated), and in another six there were some false drops. There were very few searches of the 'accounts dictionary' type in which stemming makes the difference between success and total failure.

The difference between *EXP* (the system with both strong and weak stemming and automatic cross-referencing) and *CTL* was less marked. Fifty-three (34%) of the 155 searches found more records. Of these 53, 37 were affected by the strong stemming and 23 by cross-referencing. In 15 of the 37 cases, strong stemming decreased precision, but the cross-referencing was never detrimental.

We concluded that weak stemming is almost entirely beneficial in a subject search system. The Okapi '86 procedure would be improved by the use of an exception list containing words which cannot safely be made singular or have an 'ing' ending removed ('rights', 'housing', 'painting'). 'Ed' endings are rare in catalogue searching and there is no point in removing them at the 'weak' level.

Strong stemming is more contentious. Words for strong stemming might be filtered through a table of exceptions which are not to be stemmed ('organism', 'organist', etc.) Strong stemming is an economical but crude way of automatically bringing in some of the halo of *see also* terms which surround many search words. For words which occur frequently in searches, this may be better done by using a thesaurus-like structure, prepared using a ranked list of words actually used in searches, with their contexts. This would be an extension of the automatic cross-reference list of classes of words to be treated as synonymous with each other which we have used in Okapi '86.

More generally, it is quite difficult to find sensible ways of combining phrase searching with word searching. Users who have commented that, 'It should look for phrases' or 'Why does it do it word by word?', can only be answered by saying that phrase searching often does not work very well because many books are not described in the catalogue by the phrases which searchers use. It is likely that a procedure in which search statements were split into portions which match subject heading subfields as well as into (weak-stemmed) words would be something of an improvement. However, informal repetition experiments suggest that no more than about 30% of searches contain a close match with any subject heading more than one word long.

Spelling correction

Using the machine logs of searches on *EXP* and *CTL*, we classified responses to the situation where the system cannot find a word into 'good' or 'bad'.

A 'good' response is one where the user enters an appropriate replacement (corrects a misspelling or enters a synonym), accepts a correct suggestion (*EXP* system), or aborts the search when the word is correct and essential to the meaning of the search. Any other case is 'bad'.

On the *CTL* system 23 of 36 (64%) of responses were good and on *EXP* 41 of 57 (78%). These results may be due to chance, but the figures suggest that it is worth trying to do semi-automatic correction. The Okapi '86 word-matching procedures do not require much storage and the look-up is quick and efficient, and they could readily be implemented in commercial library systems.

There are signs that users may come to expect a reasonable tolerance of miskeyings from any interactive computer system. Many catalogue users will by now have had experience of word-processing systems with instant spelling verification. One user interviewed by Richard Jones said (of spelling correction) that he 'thought computers did that anyway'.

Cross-referencing

About 25% of the searches studied contained a member of the cross-reference list. This is not surprising, since it was derived from a study of past searches by users of the same library. In almost all cases this led to an increase in recall (the ratio of the number of relevant records retrieved to the total number of relevant records in the catalogue) without decrease in precision (the proportion of relevant records in the retrieved set). Again, we found no search where this made the difference between success and total failure, nor is there any evidence that users were better satisfied.

Since the Okapi '86 experiments, the simple database of classes of approximate synonyms ('child' = 'children'), go phrases ('french chalk') and stop words has been extended somewhat. A 'universal thesaurus' is indeed an impossibility,[25] but it is not particularly difficult to construct a fairly substantial network of simple facts about relationships between words and phrases. Relationships include those of the *see also* type ('butterflies'↔'entomology') and that of homography ('IT', 'aids', 'china'). Some kind of context must often be known ('china'↔'ceramics' or 'china'↔'Beijing').

There is a rather easy way of making use of a generalized *see also* relationship between terms. Conventional thesauri are often arranged hierarchically, so that of two terms one may be 'broader' or 'narrower' than the other. Users do not need to be informed that 'rat' is (in one sense) more specific than 'rodent'. This is part of their knowledge of the language. In a search system like Okapi, which ranks records by weighting terms, the system also does not need to know anything about the nature of the relationship. It can treat classes of related terms in the same way as it treats strong and weak stems: include them all, but ensure that co-occurrences of related terms in a record do not contribute multiply to the weight of the record. If the user is searching for 'rats', records indexed under 'rat(s)' should come out first. A title 'Rodent control : rats and mice' must not be assigned a higher weight than 'Rats in the European Economic Community', although the first contains two additional terms linked to the sought term in a *see also* relationship. Nevertheless, this searcher may well be interested in titles like 'The ecology of the smaller rodents', but these should be ranked lower than the first two. Conversely, the searcher for 'rodents' retrieves the same set of books, but the 'rodent' records appear first. This is achieved by assigning a higher weight to the actual terms in the search than to any *see also* terms, regardless of the direction of the relation.

In practice, a notion of the 'distance' between related terms is helpful: the system should not expect the person who searches for 'cryogenics' to be particularly satisfied with general works on 'physics'.

A ranked output IR system such as Okapi can also use several other kinds of knowledge about words to modify the way in which weights are assigned to them in an individual search. Conjunctions like 'and' and 'or', and prepositions, can sometimes be used with reasonable accuracy to separate a search query into 'concepts'. 'And' is by no means always used in its Boolean sense (consider 'yachting and boating'), but 'or' usually is so intended (people use 'or' rather than 'and' when they do not see the concepts which it separates as being particularly closely related). It is generally used in an exclusive rather than an inclusive sense. The preposition 'of' is common in online catalogue subject searches. There is some evidence that in searches containing a single 'of' (like 'objectives of common agricultural policy') the portion to the left of the preposition should be weighted somewhat lower than the portion to the right. Finally, there are expressions of scope, form or time, as in 'the Russian contribution to international economy since the revolution' or 'principles of contestable markets'. A search system should treat these as dangerous and relatively unimportant. They are not difficult to recognize. They cannot be ignored, but should always be given low weight compared with other terms in the search.

Comparative evaluation of two catalogues

During the spring of 1987, Richard Jones carried out a comparison experiment in the Riding House Street site library of PCL.[26] The catalogues were a version of Okapi '86 and the SWALCAP LIBERTAS system. The Okapi system had a subject search which was almost identical with that of the *EXP* catalogue described above. It had one important additional feature: the ability to move from a full record display into a sequence of brief records in Dewey number order (Figures 5.6 and 5.7). To make the comparison more realistic, this version of Okapi (known as Okapi '87) also had a rather rudimentary specific item search, along the lines of that of Okapi '84 but simplified.

```
                     FULL DISPLAY                 Book 2 of 95
 "employment of women during the 1st world war"
---------------------------------------------------------------
    AUTHOR(S):  BRAYBON G
     TITLE(S):  Women workers in the First World War : the
                British experience.
  PUBLICATION:  Croom Helm, 1981.
   SUBJECT(S):  European War, 1914-1918 - Women's work.
                Women - Employment - Great Britain -
                History - 20th century. Labor and laboring
                classes - Great Britain - History - 20th
                century. Working class women. Social aspects.

 Not in this branch
 No. of copies in other PCL libraries : RHS (2)
                         Shelved at : 331.40941 BRA
---------------------------------------------------------------
 RED KEY to search again or to finish
 BLUE KEY to see the previous book again
 GREEN KEY to see the next book
 Or press the YELLOW KEY to see books classified near this one
```

Figure 5.6 Full-record display – Okapi '87

```
                        SHORT DISPLAY
 "employment of women during the 1st world war"
 No. Class.      Title                           Author
---------------------------------------------------------------
 1   331.40941   Sex discrimination in the       CHIPLIN B
                 labour market.
 2   331.40941   Women at work.                  MACKIE L
 3   331.40941   Women workers in the First      BRAYBON G
                 World War : the . .
 4   331.40941   Women workers in the Second SUMMERFIELD P
                 World War : pro..
 5   331.40941   Schooling for women's work.     (DEEM R)
 6   331.40941   Work, women and the labour      (WEST J)
                 market.
---------------------------------------------------------------
 RED KEY to go back to where you were
 BLUE KEY to see previous books
 GREEN KEY to see next books

 Or type a NUMBER for fuller details of one book : █
```

Figure 5.7 Brief-record display after pressing yellow key from the screen of Figure 5.6 – Okapi '87

The experiment was based on the Siegel and Markey comparison experiments.[27,28] Users were intercepted as they approached a terminal to either catalogue and asked to undertake their searches under controlled conditions. A considerable inducement was offered, but the refusal rate was high. Subjects were taken, singly, to a room containing a terminal to each system and asked to carry out their search first on one system, then on the other. The searches were observed and followed by a fairly loosely structured interview. There was no use of log data, because LIBERTAS produced none.

The experiment obtained data on user preferences and general assessments of the performance of the two catalogues on ease of use and learning, display formats, selection menu design and the ease and speed of navigation and browsing. Since the sample size was small (about 50 subjects) and the whole experiment was intentionally rather open ended the results are fairly soft. However, they should prove of considerable interest to researchers and designers. This may be the first time there has been a broad comparison of two fairly 'complete' catalogue systems which are also internally quite similar (the present writer had a hand in the design of both of them) with the same users in the same library. There follows a taste of the results.

Ease of use and learning
Most of the subjects were more familiar with LIBERTAS than with any version of Okapi. Almost all of them were familiar with some online catalogue. There was a measure of agreement that Okapi was easier to learn, particularly by users with little previous experience of computers. People who were familiar with computers (terminals to the Polytechnic network for example) or with LIBERTAS generally found LIBERTAS easier to use; they often found Okapi's coloured keys more difficult than LIBERTAS's mnemonic commands (LIBERTAS is not what most people would understand by a command-driven system, but most of the choices and options are single letters or words like BACK, and these have to be followed by pressing the RETURN key). Some of those familiar with LIBERTAS also found the use of coloured keys and the wording of some of Okapi's prompts ' . . . condescending and a bit babyish'. On the whole, then, users who were mainly familiar with LIBERTAS preferred its general tone and did not perceive it as slower or more tedious to give commands to. Objectively, it is quicker to give commands to Okapi, but there is a stage in the search procedure (the merge) which is sometimes faster on LIBERTAS.

Performance
Most users thought that Okapi retrieved more useful material in subject searching than LIBERTAS did. Two factors may have contributed to this: the stemming and cross-reference table, and the fact that in subject searching Okapi always showed 'full' records which often contain subject headings and are more easily classifiable into relevant and non-relevant than LIBERTAS's brief (one- or two-line) records or its card-like full record. Objectively, it is true that Okapi nearly always retrieves as much as or more than LIBERTAS, but LIBERTAS sometimes outputs records in a more sensible order, keeping editions of the same work together and taking word adjacency into account in the weighting procedure (so that records containing the actual search statement come out first).

In specific item searching, LIBERTAS was both subjectively and objectively more successful. It should be mentioned that the specific item search in Okapi '87 was knocked up rather hastily for this experiment; the Okapi projects have not been concerned with specific item searching since 1985.

Display formats
There was a clear preference for the Okapi full-record displays. It does not appear that subjects were specifically asked to compare the brief display formats.

Selection menu design
The LIBERTAS catalogue menu offered a choice of six search modes (author and title, title, subject, etc.). These are chosen by a single digit (followed by RETURN). This was uniformly preferred to the Okapi '87 mode selection screen (similar to Figure 5.1). Some users thought it gave greater 'precision' or 'tied down their ideas'. Some thought it meant there were a greater number of search modes. Objectively, the two catalogues provide almost exactly the same search functions.

Browsing
Some users preferred LIBERTAS's default brief-record display in subject searching because it is quicker to scan than Okapi's full records. At the same time they wanted 'everything on one screen', meaning location information (in LIBERTAS neither brief nor full records include location or a class number). This poses something of a quandary for the designer. In Okapi one can browse backwards or forwards at either brief- or full-record level. If the default display (in a subject search) is brief, there is a real danger of a user missing relevant items with non-indicative titles. Perhaps the default display should be full with an initially prominent option to move to brief.

Subjects were asked to evaluate the effectiveness of Okapi's 'See books classified near this one' option. Most of them found additional useful material, but found it difficult to understand 'their location in relation to the original search' (Figure 5.7). This again poses a serious problem for the designer of a system which allows users to range widely through a catalogue (see the section below). However, this feature was new to all the subjects, and it may be that after one or two sessions most people would find it easy to use.

Relevance feedback, query expansion and adaptive systems
It is probably true that in most online catalogue searching both recall and precision are much lower than that which a good intermediary would obtain in reference retrieval searching. There are three reasons for this. First, the subject descriptive content of most bibliographic records is slight and of poor quality, using non-current language,

descriptors which are too general and not enough of them. Second, many online catalogues do not provide search functions which are powerful or flexible enough to permit exhaustive or precise searching. Finally, even if the subject content of the records were to be greatly enhanced and adequate functionality provided in the search systems, a large proportion of end-users would not be able to make use of the functions. Unless some approach to a standard emerges – something which is extremely unlikely; neither online nor offline training even begins to tackle the problem – most people will use many different catalogues, and even with instruction a substantial proportion will never be able to grasp the principles of Boolean logic and the combination of sets.

At the same time, we are finding very high perceived success rates with simple, transparent catalogues such as the Okapi series. Many users are not at present very demanding of a catalogue. Perhaps 80% of subject search sessions are short and successful, the searcher being satisfied by one or two apparently relevant items in the first dozen or so. If these 'successful' sessions are the important ones, and if users' expectations do not increase, it is probably not worth trying to do much more in the way of improving online catalogues. Most people are satisfied: why bother about the others? However, if we look at the remaining 20% of sessions we find that they fall into two classes. There are short sessions which are total failures – there is a total mismatch between the user and the system. Then there are long sessions, lasting up to an hour and involving the display of hundreds, occasionally thousands, of records. These users are very strongly motivated and persistent. More than half the machine time is spent handling sessions of this type.

With the advance of communication and storage technology, and the proven inadequacy of passive, unhelpful search programs – both of the keyword Boolean type and the browsing, phrase-matching type – it seems likely that in the not-far-distant future the old reference retrieval software will fall into disuse, intermediaries will be redeployed and we shall be able to throw away our front-ends to DIALOG. The same system will be used to access the catalogue of our local library and to search ERIC or MEDLINE (not to mention services which retrieve facts rather than references). These search systems must still be suitable for casual use by inept or inexperienced users. But they must also provide powerful facilities to reduce the proportion of total failures and to aid demanding and persistent users.

The guiding principle of the Okapi research is that the system must adapt itself to the user rather than the converse. The original Okapi team, Mitev, Venner and Walker, were inspired by, among others, Charles Hildreth[29] and Ward Shaw.[30] Tentative proposals for research towards highly interactive systems which adapt themselves to individual users and uses were put forward in 1984. The resulting systems would try to incorporate some of the ideas of Hayes and others,[31] adapting to users' needs, aptitude and experience.

In 1986 the then current team started work towards a system which would do automatic or semi-automatic query expansion by using terms extracted from records which the user had seen and judged relevant. There is, of course, a long history of research into uses of relevance information in IR systems, going back to the 1960s,[32-4] but it only appears to have been used in one online catalogue: CITE, at the National Library of Medicine.[35,36]

We wrote procedures for extracting words, subject headings and classification numbers from displayed records, and for recombining these in new searches. Repeating searches from Okapi logs, we found, not surprisingly, that it is often possible to obtain additional relevant records which would not otherwise have been found. However, interaction problems seemed to be almost insuperable if the system were to remain suitable for casual use. Richard Jones's comparison experiment, briefly reported above, showed that users felt lost if they moved just one step from their original searches by choosing to 'look at books classified near this one', although the dialogue would appear to be a reasonable compromise between clarity and verbosity (Figures 5.6 and 5.7). It is probably too intrusive even to unconditionally ask the subject searcher to provide relevance information, and we believe that relevance judgements should only be requested if the system can detect that the user is either in trouble or being fairly persistent. Having obtained relevance information and performed one or more subsequent searches, the navigation problems multiply. There will often be a considerable number of courses of action which the system itself will not be able to choose between. The user is going to be faced with a substantial processing load. Options might include the following:

Look for other books like this one.
Look for more books like the ones you chose.
See books with subject descriptions similar to this one.
See books classified near this one.
Add this book to the list you told the computer to remember.
Go back to what you were doing before . . .
Review what you have done.

In addition, there will be the usual semi-constant options, like seeing next or previous book or starting another search.

Currently we are experimenting with the use of windows to

provide context-sensitive advice, search history information and act as 'dialogue windows'. The greatest part of most searches is spent in looking at record displays, so information and dialogue windows would usually overlay a portion of a bibliographic display.

Whatever display and interaction techniques are used, it seems clear that a system which aims to satisfy the widely differing needs of widely differing types of user must already incorporate some degree of adaptivity. The system must be able to form some picture ('model' is the currently fashionable word) of the user's needs, competence and experience. In most cases 'advanced' options would not even appear. It seems that work on the use of relevance feedback cannot help but include an element of research in the design of adaptive systems.

Availability of the Okapi software

All versions of Okapi up to Okapi '87 were written in Z80 assembly language and operated on a network of Apple IIe microcomputers connected to a Nestar PLAN/4000 file server. This is a historical accident owing to the nature of the original research proposal. Writing the software was somewhat tedious, but having to work at this level did help the designers to get away from preconceptions about interaction which they might have had if they had been working within the input/output facilities provided by a conventional mini or mainframe operating system (for example, that it needs a RETURN to terminate user input or that the operating system can properly handle the echoing of characters to the terminal). With Okapi '86 we were already up against hardware constraints, as much due to disk access times as to CPU speed. It was decided to produce future versions in a form suitable for 32-bit processors and relatively fast disk access.

Currently, the Okapi software is being rewritten in C to run under Unix, and possibly also under VMS on DEC equipment. The next implementation will operate on ANSI-type terminals (VT100 compatible) connected to Sun workstations or other 32-bit byte-addressable machines running BSD Unix. The source code and minimal documentation will be available to researchers and libraries. No charging policy has yet been decided, but it is hoped that it would not be priced above the means of researchers and educational establishments.

This public software will not take the form of a turnkey system which can simply be loaded and run. Apart from anything else, Okapi systems do not use machine readable cataloguing (MARC) files, and it is unlikely that a MARC tape conversion program will be supplied. The file specifications will be documented, and users wishing to load their own files must convert them into the Okapi format. Nor is there any way of inputting or editing individual records. To do anything interesting with the software a good programmer and designer will be needed. The distribution will consist of indexing and searching utilities, including functions to make use of the database of rather simple knowledge about words and phrases referred to above. At the time of writing the only categories are *see*, *go*, *stop* and *syntax* (syntax words are words like 'in', 'of' and 'and', which would not be indexed or searched for in a subject search system, but which can possibly be used to modify the weighting of other words in a search request). There is also a library of functions for record display and for implementing the necessary highly interactive user–system dialogue.

References

1 Mitev, N. N., Venner, G. M. and Walker, S., *Designing an online public access catalogue: Okapi, a catalogue on a local area network*, London, British Library, 1985 (Library and Information Research Report 39).

2 Walker, S. and Jones, R. M., *Improving subject retrieval in online catalogues: 1. Stemming, automatic spelling correction and cross-reference tables*, London, British Library, 1987 (British Library Research Paper 24).

3 Jones, R. M., *A comparative evaluation of two online public access catalogues: user opinions about the design of online catalogues*, London, British Library (in press, to be published 1988).

4 Walker, S., 'The free language approach to online catalogues', in Bryant, P. (ed.), *Keyword catalogues and the free language approach*, Bath, University of Bath Library, 1985.

5 Mitev, N. N. and Walker, S., 'Intelligent retrieval aids in an online public access catalogue: automatic intelligent search sequencing', in *Informatics 8: advances in intelligent retrieval*, Proceedings of an Aslib/BCS Conference, Oxford, 16–17 April 1985; London, Aslib, 1985.

6 Jones, R. M., 'Improving Okapi: transaction log analysis of failed searches in an online catalogue', *VINE*, **62**, May 1986, 3–13.

7 Walker, S., 'Ease of use in online catalogues: a plea for the user', in Kinsella, J. (ed.), *Online public access to library files*, 2nd National Conference Proceedings, University of Bath, April 1986; Oxford, Elsevier, 1986.

8 Walker, S., 'Improving subject access painlessly: recent work on the Okapi projects', *Program*, **22**, (1), 1988.

9 Doszkocs, T. E., 'CITE NLM: natural language searching in an online catalog', *Information technology and libraries*, **2**, (4), 1983, 364–80.

10 Doszkocs, T. E., 'Natural language processing in information retrieval', *Journal of the American Society for Information Science*, **37**, (4), 1986, 191–6.

11 Markey, K. and Demeyer, A. N., *Dewey Decimal Classification online project: evaluation of a library schedule and index integrated into the subject searching capabilities of an online catalog*, Dublin, Ohio, Online Computer Library Center, 1986.

12 Mitev, N. N., op. cit.
13 Ibid.
14 Jones, R. M., 'Improving Okapi', op. cit.
15 Taylor, A. G., 'Authority files in online catalogs: an investigation of their value', *Cataloging and classification quarterly*, **4**, (3), 1984, 1–17.
16 Walker, S. and Jones, R. M., op. cit.
17 Frakes, W. B., 'Term conflation in information retrieval', in van Rijsbergen, C. J. (ed.), *Research and development in information retrieval*, Proceedings of the Third Joint BCS and ACM Symposium, King's College, Cambridge, 2–6 July 1984, Cambridge, Cambridge University Press, on behalf of the British Computer Society.
18 Ulmschneider, J. E. and Doszkocs, T. E., 'A practical stemming algorithm for online search assistance', *Online review*, **7**, (4), 1983, 301–15.
19 Porter, M. F., 'An algorithm for suffix stripping', *Program*, **14**, (3), 1980, 130–7.
20 Walker, S. and Jones, R. M., op. cit., 65.
21 Porter, M. F., op. cit.
22 Walker, S., 'Improving subject access painlessly', op. cit.
23 Walker, S. and Jones, R. M., op. cit., Appendices 1 and 2.
24 Walker, S. and Jones, R. M., op. cit., Chapter 8.
25 Walker, S., 'The free language approach', op. cit.
26 Jones, R. M., *A comparative evaluation of two online public access catalogues*, op. cit.
27 Siegel, E. R. *et al.*, 'A comparative evaluation of the technical performance and user acceptance of two prototype online catalog systems', *Information technology and libraries*, **3**, (1), 1984, 35–46.
28 Markey, K. and Demeyer, A. N., op. cit.
29 Hildreth, C. R., *Online public access catalogs: the user interface*, Dublin, Ohio, Online Computer Library Center, 1982.
30 Shaw, W., 'Design principles for public access', in Divilbiss, J. L. (ed.), *Public access to library automation, 17th clinic on library applications of data processing*, Urbana, Illinois, University of Illinois at Urbana-Champaign, Graduate School of Library and Information Science, 1981.
31 Hayes, P. J. and Reddy, D. R., 'Steps towards graceful interaction in spoken and written man–machine communication', *International journal of man–machine studies*, **19**, (3), 1983, 231–84.
32 Maron, M. E. and Kuhns, J. L., 'On relevance, probabilistic indexing and information retrieval', *Journal of the Association of Computing Machinery*, **7**, 1960, 216–44.
33 Robertson, S. E., Maron, M. E. and Cooper, W. S., 'Probability of relevance: a unification of two competing models for information retrieval', *Information technology: research and development*, **1**, (1), 1982, 1–21.
34 Robertson, S. E. and Sparck Jones, K., 'Relevance weighting of search terms', *Journal of the American Society for Information Science*, **27**, 1976, 129–46.
35 Doszkocs, T. E., 'CITE NLM', op. cit.
36 Doszkocs, T. E., 'Natural language processing', op. cit.

TREC AND TIPSTER EXPERIMENTS WITH INQUERY

JAMES P. CALLAN, W. BRUCE CROFT, and JOHN BROGLIO
Computer Science Department, University of Massachusetts, Amherst, MA 01003-4610, U.S.A.
E-mail: {callan, croft, broglio}@cs.umass.edu

Abstract — INQUERY is a probabilistic information retrieval system based upon a Bayesian inference network model. This paper describes recent improvements to the system as a result of participation in the TIPSTER project and the TREC-2 conference. Improvements include transforming forms-based specifications of information needs into complex structured queries, automatic query expansion, automatic recognition of features in documents, relevance feedback, and simulated document routing. Experiments with one- and two-gigabyte document collections are also described.

1. INTRODUCTION

The effectiveness of an information retrieval (IR) system depends upon representation and matching. The system must *represent* the information need, it must *represent* the documents, and it must determine how well the information need *matches* each document. Our approach has been to use improved representations of document text and queries in the framework of the inference network model of retrieval. This model uses Bayesian networks to describe how text and queries should be used to identify relevant documents (Turtle & Croft, 1991a; Croft & Turtle, 1992; Turtle & Croft, 1992). Document retrieval and routing are viewed as probabilistic inference processes that compare text representations based on different forms of linguistic and statistical evidence to representations of information needs based on similar evidence from natural language queries and user interaction. Learning techniques are used to modify the initial queries both for short-term and long-term information needs (relevance feedback and routing, respectively).

This approach, generally known as the inference net model and implemented in the INQUERY system (Callan *et al.*, 1992), emphasizes retrieval based on combination of evidence. Different text representations (such as words, phrases, paragraphs, or manually assigned keywords) and different versions of the query (such as natural language and Boolean) can be combined in a consistent probabilistic framework. This type of "data fusion" has been known to be effective in the information retrieval context for a number of years, and was one of the primary motivations for developing the inference net approach.

Another characteristic of the inference net approach is the ability to capture complex structure in the network representing the information need (i.e., the query). A practical consequence of this is that complex Boolean queries can be evaluated as easily as natural language queries to produce ranked output. It is also possible to represent "rule-based" or "concept-based" queries in the same probabilistic framework. This has led to our concentrating on automatic analysis of queries and techniques for enhancing queries, rather than on in-depth analysis of the documents in the database. In general, it is more effective (as well as efficient) to analyze short query texts rather than millions of document texts. The results of the query analysis are represented in the INQUERY query language, which contains a number of operators, such as #SUM, #AND, #OR, #NOT, #PHRASE, and #SYN (Turtle & Croft, 1991a; Callan *et al.*, 1992). These operators implement different methods of combining evidence.

Some of the specific research issues we are addressing are morphological analysis, the use of phrases and other syntactic structure, the use of feature recognizers (for example, company and country name recognizers) in representing documents and queries, analyzing natural language queries to build structured representations of information needs, learning techniques appropriate for routing and structured queries, techniques for acquiring domain knowledge by corpus analysis, and probability estimation techniques for indexing.

The TIPSTER and TREC evaluations have made it clear that much remains to be learned about retrieval and routing in large, full-text databases based on complex information needs. On the other hand, we have made considerable progress in developing effective techniques for this environment, and the evaluations have shown that good levels of performance can be achieved.

2. THE INQUERY SYSTEM

The INQUERY document retrieval and routing system is based on the inference network model (Turtle & Croft, 1991a; Callan *et al.*, 1992). The main processes in INQUERY are document indexing, query processing, query expansion, query evaluation, and relevance feedback. Each is described below.

2.1 *Document indexing*

The *document parser* is a set of text processing modules, organized into four phases: (1) layout analysis, (2) lexical analysis, (3) syntactic analysis, and (4) feature recognition. *Layout analysis* is the only phase in which the document can be modified. It transforms the raw document into a canonical format, saving structural information as necessary, and identifies which portions to index. *Syntactic analysis* verifies that the document conforms to an expected format. The other two phases, *lexical analysis* and *feature recognition*, record the locations of terms (words or numbers) and features (company names, countries, etc.) in the document text.

The *lexical analysis* module identifies and records word boundaries, recognizes *stopwords*, *stems* the words, and indexes the words for retrieval. In theory, every word in the document collection will be indexed. In practice, it is helpful to identify very common words, such as *operators* or *closed-class* words, which do not carry any meaningful information for retrieval purposes, although they may offer significant information for text extraction (Sundheim, 1991). These *stopwords* are usually not indexed, although they are retained in the text so that subsequent textual analysis (syntactic analysis, feature recognition) may make use of them. Stopwords can be indexed, however, if they are capitalized (but not at the start of sentences) or joined with other words (e.g., "the The-1 system"). Stemming is performed to conflate words that have the same root form or stem, in spite of different endings.

Feature recognition is an important step in representing text at different levels of abstraction. Feature recognizers search text for words that correspond to simple semantic components, for example, company names or country names. The document is indexed by both the words (e.g., "Lotus Development Corp") and the feature (e.g., #company). The set of feature recognizers delivered with INQUERY is shown below.

> Company name recognizer: For each mention of a company in the text, it generates a transaction for the special term #COMPANY.
>
> U.S. city recognizer: For each mention of a U.S. city in the text, it generates a transaction for #CITY.
>
> Country recognizer: For each mention of a country in the text, it generates a transaction for either #USA or #FOREIGNCOUNTRY.

These *features* extend the range of queries that can be specified. Figures 1 and 2 illustrate the role that these features play in document indexing. This completes the usual processing for document text.

The INQUERY text processing behavior is customized easily. We have discussed the default behavior, but these modules can be replaced easily if some other behavior is desired.

The document indexing process also involves building the compressed inverted files necessary for efficient performance with very large databases. Since positional informa-

John Davenport, 52 years old, was appointed chief executive officer of this international telecommunications concern's U.S. subsidiary, Cable & Wireless North America Inc. Mr. Davenport, who succeeds John Zrno, is currently general manager of the group's operations in Bermuda.

Fig. 1. Indexing example: original document text.

tion is stored, the indices are typically about 40% of the size of the original document collection, after compression.

2.2 *Query processing*

Queries can be made to INQUERY by using either natural language, or a structured query language, or a mixture of the two. Natural language queries are transformed incrementally into complex structured queries in the INQUERY query language by a series of query text processing modules (Callan & Croft, 1993). Query text processing must minimally mirror the indexing text processing. But because query texts are much shorter than document collections, it is practical to experiment with more thorough textual analysis at the research and development stage. This reduces the need to repeatedly index large document collections in order to make small experimental adjustments. All query text processing is experimental, and the sequence of operations is adjusted frequently as more is learned about the effects of this processing.

Currently, INQUERY has a small number of internal query text processors (Callan & Croft, 1993). These include stop-phrase removal (e.g., "A document must discuss"), conversion of hyphenation and sequences of capitalized words (proper names) into proximity constraints, insertion of features, case conversion, stopword removal, and stemming (Figs. 3 and 4).

Orthographic clues such as hyphenation and capitalization, when reliable, are very good clues to phrasal grouping. Hyphens are generally discarded during indexing so that expressions such as *Iran-Contra* or *voice-activated* are indexed as terms *Iran* and *Contra* or *voice* and *activated*, respectively. In query processing, the corresponding procedure is to remove the hyphen and to place a proximity constraint on the words, as shown below.

```
voice-activated ⇒ #1 (voice activated)
```

Groups of capitalized words are similarly constrained, as shown.

```
House of Representatives ⇒ #1 (House of Representatives)
```

2.3 *Query expansion*

Our approach to query expansion (called *PhraseFinder**) is based on the assumption that concepts found in similar lexical contexts may also be related semantically. For example, the words "connectionist" and "neural networks" might occur in similar lexical contexts, but rarely in the same documents. The semantic relationship captured is not necessarily synonymy, because PhraseFinder also might relate "connectionist" and "back propagation," which co-occur but have different meanings.

*PhraseFinder was called WordFinder until we discovered that WordFinder is the trademark name of a commercial software product.

john davenport 52 year old appoint chief execut offic intern telecommun concern u.s. #USA subsidiar cabl wireless north america inc #COMPANY davenport succee john zrno current gener manag group oper bermuda #FOREIGNCOUNTRY

Fig. 2. Indexing example: document text indexed.

Document will describe marketing strategies carried out by U.S. companies for their agricultural chemicals, report predictions for market share of such chemicals, or report market statistics for the chemicals. pesticide, herbicide, fungicide, insecticide, fertiliser, predicted sales, market share, stimulate demand, price cut, volume of sales

Fig. 3. Natural language query text.

A PhraseFinder database is an INQUERY database of *pseudo-documents*. Each pseudo-document represents a *concept*, in this case a noun sequence, that occurs in the document collection. The "text" of the pseudo-document consists of words that occur near the concept in the document collection. For example, a PhraseFinder document for a *Wall Street Journal* collection contains an *amnesty program* pseudo-document indexed by *1986, act, control, immigrant, law* (Fig. 5),. . . . Although very different in implementation, the approach is similar in spirit to the distributed representations employed by the MatchPlus and Bellcore systems (Caid *et al.*, 1995).

The usual document retrieval algorithms (discussed in Section 2.4) are used to retrieve the pseudo-documents that represent concepts. Thus, INQUERY can use any structured query to retrieve a ranked list of concepts. The most highly ranked concepts are those that are most highly associated (*in that collection*) with the query. Figure 6 shows the top 20 concepts returned by INQUERY for two TIPSTER topics, filtered to remove concepts that already appeared in the query.

A query is expanded by evaluating it against a PhraseFinder database, selecting the top ranked concepts, weighting them, and adding them to the query. Our current approach is to select the top *n* concepts and weight them at one half the weight of the initial query terms.

PhraseFinder is sensitive to several parameters, including the size of the collocation window, decisions about what syntactic classes to include in the window, and whether low- and/or high-frequency noun groups are removed from the database. The current implementation of PhraseFinder shows promise on the TIPSTER data, but more work is necessary to build a PhraseFinder that would be effective on a variety of document collections (Jing & Croft, 1994).

2.4 *Query evaluation*

The query evaluation process uses the inverted files and the query represented as an inference net to produce a document ranking. Documents are ranked according to the belief that they are relevant to the query.

Query evaluation involves probabilistic inference based on the operators defined in the INQUERY query language. These operators define new concepts and how to calculate the belief in those concepts using linguistic and statistical evidence. The belief in a document due to the occurrence of a single term t is:

$$bel_{term}(t) = d_b + (1 - d_b) \cdot \left(d_t + (1 - d_t) \cdot \frac{\log(tf + 0.5)}{\log(max\_tf + 1.0)} \right) \cdot \frac{\log\left(\frac{C + 0.5}{df}\right)}{\log(C + 1.0)}, \quad (1)$$

market strateg carr #usa compan #company agricultur chemic report predict market share chemic report market statist market agrochem #usa pesticid herbicid fungicid insecticid fertil predict sale stimul demand price cut volum sale

Fig. 4. Query text, after stopword and stop-phrase removal.

<DOC>
<TITLE> amnesty program </TITLE>
<TEXT>
... 1986(3), act(3), control(2), immigrant/immigration(16), law(8), reform(4), 1982(2), 1987(3), agency(3), aliens(13), duarte(2), el-salvador(2), employers(8), documentation(2), guatemala(2), file(3), government(6), fear(2), entered(3), illegal(14), naturalization(2), mandates(2), legalization(3), nelson(5), nicaragua(2), new-york(2), permanent(4) ...
</TEXT>
</DOC>

Fig. 5. A PhraseFinder pseudo-document for the concept *amnesty program*. Numbers in parentheses indicate the number of repetitions of the word preceding.

where

tf = the frequency of term t in the document,
max_tf = the frequency of the most frequent term in the document,
df = the number of documents in which term t occurs,
C = the number of documents in the collection,
d_t = minimum term frequency component when a term occurs in a document,
d_b = minimum belief component when a term occurs in a document.

This equation is a variation of the well known *tf.idf* approach, with values normalized to remain between 0 and 1, and further modified by default term frequency (d_t) and default belief (d_b) values that the user may define at program invocation. d_t and d_b default to 0.4.

The belief in a document due to a given query language operator depends on the type of operator and the belief in its arguments. The query language operators have been discussed in detail elsewhere (Turtle & Croft, 1991; Callan *et al.*, 1992), so we merely provide several examples to illustrate their general operation. #WSUM is a weighted sum operator, #UW*n* is an unordered window proximity operator, and #PROX*n* is an ordered interword proximity operator.

Query 115: Impact of the 1986 Immigration Law - will report specific consequence consequences of the U.S.'s Immigration Reform and Control Act of 1986.	Query 132: "Stealth" Aircraft - will provide cost, technical, and/or performance data on U.S. "stealth" aircraft projects.
illegal immigration	northrop corp.
illegals	tactical fighter
undocumented aliens	aerospace companies
amnesty program	flying wing design
immigration reform law	enemy radar
editorial-page article	stealth bomber
naturalization service	development program
civil fines	radar-evading aircraft
new immigration law	bat-winged aircraft
legal immigration	cost overruns
employer sanctions	expensive plane
simpson-mazzoli immigration reform	stealth fighter
statutes	radar-evasion standards
applicability	full-scale production
seeking amnesty	palmdale
legal status	radar-evading
immigration act	pentagon official
undocumented workers	flying wing
guest worker	air force officials
sweeping immigration law	development costs

Fig. 6. Query expansion example: concepts discovered automatically for TIPSTER topics 115 and 132.

$$bel_{wsum}(w_1 \cdot Q_1, \ldots, w_m \cdot Q_m) = \frac{(w_1 \cdot bel(Q_1) + \ldots + w_m \cdot bel(Q_m)) \cdot w_q}{w_1 + \ldots + w_m} \tag{2}$$

$$bel_{proxn}(Q_1, Q_2, \ldots Q_m) = bel_{term}(Q') \tag{3}$$

$$bel_{UW_n}(Q_1, Q_2, \ldots Q_m) = bel_{term}(Q'') \tag{4}$$

where

m = the number of arguments to an operator,
n = a positive integer argument to the proximity operator,
Q_i = a term or a nested query net operator,
w_i = a positive real number, used as a query term weight,
w_q = the maximum value that the #wsum operator can yield (normally 1.0),
Q' = a compound term created temporarily during query evaluation to represent the locations where $Q_i, \ldots, Q_n$ occur in order with an interword separation $<n$, and
Q'' = a compound term created temporarily during query evaluation to represent the locations where $Q_1, \ldots, Q_n$ occur in any order within a text window of size $\leq n$.

The efficiency of retrieval is comparable to commercial information retrieval systems.

2.5 *Relevance feedback*

The INQUERY system is able to refine queries automatically based upon relevance feedback by a user. The general approach is for the system to select terms from relevant documents, add them to the query, and then reweight all of the query terms.

Early experiments (Haines & Croft, 1993) showed that ranking terms by the product of their frequency in relevant documents (*rdf*) and their inverse document frequency (*idf*) was best on small and medium-sized collections with relatively small numbers of relevance judgments. The number of terms added was set empirically to 5. Term weights were determined by their frequency in relevant documents (*rtf*). The INQUERY system still uses this model for interactive relevance feedback, where the number of relevance judgments per query is generally low (e.g., <15).

REFERENCES

Caid, W.R., Dumais, S.T., & Gallant, S.I. (1995). Learned vector-space models for document retrieval. *Information Processing & Management, 31*, 419–429.

Callan, J.P. (1994). Passage-level evidence in document retrieval. In *Proceedings of the Seventeenth Annual International ACM SIGIR Conference on Research and Development in Information Retrieval*, pp. 302–310, Dublin, Ireland. Association for Computing Machinery.

Callan, J.P. & Croft, W.B. (1993). An evaluation of query processing strategies using the TIPSTER collection. In R. Korfhage, E. Rasmussen, & P. Willett (Eds.), *Proceedings of the Sixteenth Annual International ACM SIGIR Conference on Research and Development in Information Retrieval*, pp. 347–356, Pittsburgh, PA. Association for Computing Machinery.

Callan, J.P., Croft, W.B., & Harding, S.M. (1992). The INQUERY retrieval system. In *Proceedings of the Third International Conference on Database and Expert Systems Applications*, pp. 78–83, Valencia, Spain. Berlin: Springer-Verlag.

Church, K. (1988). A stochastic parts program and noun phrase parser for unrestricted text. In *Proceedings of the 2nd Conference on Applied Natural Language Processing*, pp. 136–143.

Croft, W.B. & Turtle, H.R. (1992). Text retrieval and inference. In P. Jacobs (Ed.), *Text-Based Intelligent Systems*, pp. 127–156. Lawrence Erlbaum.

Haines, D. & Croft, W.B. (1993). Relevance feedback and inference networks. In R. Korfhage, E. Rasmussen, and P. Willett (Eds.), *Proceedings of the Sixteenth Annual International ACM SIGIR Conference on Research and Development in Information Retrieval*, pp. 2–11, Pittsburgh, PA. Association for Computing Machinery.

Harman, D. (Ed.) (1994). *The Second Text REtrieval Conference (TREC2)*. National Institute of Standards and Technology Special Publication 500-215, Gaithersburg, MD.

Jing, Y. & Croft, W.B. (1994). An association thesaurus for information retrieval. In *RIAO 94 Conference Proceedings*, pp. 146–160. New York.

Sundheim, B. (Ed.) (1991). *Proceedings of the Third Message Understanding Evaluation and Conference*. Los Altos, CA: Morgan Kaufmann.

Turtle, H.R. & Croft, W.B. (1991a). Evaluation of an inference network-based retrieval model. *ACM Transactions on Information System, 9*(3), 187–222.

Turtle, H.R. & Croft, W.B. (1991b). Efficient probabilistic inference for text retrieval. In *RIAO 3 Conference Proceedings*, pp. 644–661. Barcelona, Spain.

Turtle, H.R. & Croft, W.B. (1992). A comparison of text retrieval models. *Computer Journal*.

RUBRIC: A System for Rule-Based Information Retrieval

BRIAN P. MC CUNE, MEMBER, IEEE, RICHARD M. TONG, MEMBER, IEEE, JEFFREY S. DEAN, MEMBER, IEEE, AND DANIEL G. SHAPIRO

Abstract—A research prototype software system for conceptual information retrieval has been developed. The goal of the system, called RUBRIC, is to provide more automated and relevant access to unformatted textual databases. The approach is to use production rules from artificial intelligence to define a hierarchy of retrieval subtopics, with fuzzy context expressions and specific word phrases at the bottom. RUBRIC allows the definition of detailed queries starting at a conceptual level, partial matching of a query and a document, selection of only the highest ranked documents for presentation to the user, and detailed explanation of how and why a particular document was selected. Initial experiments indicate that a RUBRIC rule set better matches human retrieval judgment than a standard Boolean keyword expression, given equal amounts of effort in defining each. The techniques presented may be useful in stand-alone retrieval systems, front-ends to existing information retrieval systems, or real-time document filtering and routing.

Index Terms—Artificial intelligence, evidential reasoning, expert systems, information retrieval.

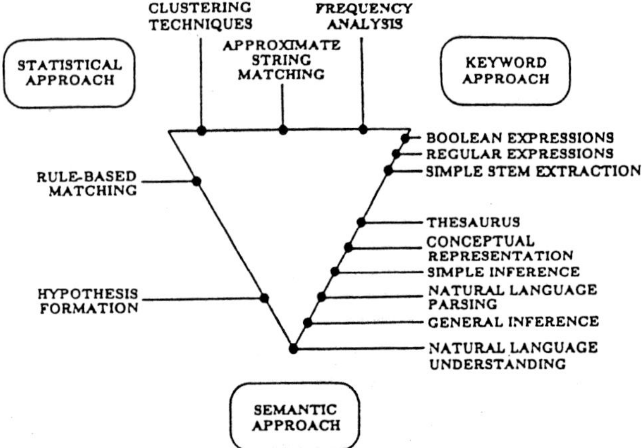

Fig. 1. The information retrieval triangle.

I. The Information Retrieval Problem

THE three most common approaches to the textual information retrieval (see the vertices of the triangle in Fig. 1), when used in isolation, suffer from problems of precision and recall, understandability, and scope of applicability. For example, Boolean keyword retrieval systems such as the commercial DIALOG system operate at a lexical level, and hence ignore much of the available information that is syntactic, semantic, pragmatic (subject-matter specific), or contextual. The underlying reasoning behind the responses of statistical retrieval systems [2] is difficult to explain to a user in an understandable and intuitive way. Systems that rely on a semantic understanding of the natural language that is present in documents [3] must severely restrict the vocabulary and document styles allowed (e.g., to partially formatted, stereotypic messages).

In addition to being used by specialists, in the near future large on-line document repositories will be made available via computer networks to relatively naive computer users. For both classes of users, it is important that future retrieval systems possess the following attributes.

- Detailed queries should be posed at the user's own conceptual level, using his or her vocabulary of concepts and without requiring complex programming.
- Partial matching of queries and documents should be provided, in order to mirror the imprecision of human interests.
- The number of documents retrieved should be dependent upon the needs of the user (e.g., uses for the documents, time constraints on reading them).
- A logical, understandable, and intuitive explanation of why each document was retrieved should be available.
- The user should be able to easily experiment with and revise the conceptual queries, in order to handle changing interests or disagreement with previous system performance.
- Conceptual queries should be easily stored for periodic use by their author and for sharing with other users.

II. A Knowledge-Based Approach

In order to address the issues raised above, we have created a prototype knowledge-based full-text information retrieval system called RUBRIC (for RUle-Based Retrieval of Information by Computer). RUBRIC integrates some of the best characteristics of all three basic approaches to information retrieval (Fig. 1) within the framework of a standard artificial intelligence technique. Queries are represented as a set of logical production rules that enable the user to define retrieval criteria using much better semantic and heuristic controls than can be found in current retrieval systems.

The rules define a hierarchy of retrieval topics (or concepts) and subtopics. By naming a single topic, the user automatically invokes a goal-oriented search of the tree defined by all of the subtopics that are used to define that topic. The lowest level subtopics are defined in terms of pattern expressions in a *text reference language*, which allows keywords, positional contexts, and simple syntactic and semantic notions. Each rule may have a user-provided heuristic weight. This weight defines how strongly the user believes that the rule's pattern indicates the presence of the rule's subtopic. Technical issues that arise when information retrieval is viewed as a problem in evidentiary reasoning are discussed in [6].

To perform a retrieval RUBRIC uses the set of rules for a topic to create a heuristic AND/OR goal tree that defines at its leaves what patterns of words should be present in documents, and in what combinations.

Document recall by RUBRIC is enhanced by the use of higher level notions than simple Boolean combinations of keywords. Retrieval precision is improved by the use of variable weights on each rule to define the certainty of match. These weights make it possible to present to the user only partial matches above some threshold. By tracing through rule invocation chains, an explanation facility allows the user to see exactly why a document was retrieved and why it was assigned its overall certainty or importance weight. This promotes experimentation and appropriate modification of the rule base. The retrieval vocabulary to be used is unrestricted, being left up to whoever creates the rules. Rule sets may be stored in public or private rule "libraries," so that useful subtopics may be shared among users, thus simplifying the task of defining new topics.

A rule-based query can be more complex than the keyword expression that might be used with a Boolean retrieval system. Therefore, we expect rule-based retrieval to be used initially for applications in which the same query is made repetitively over some period of time. In such situations people who are trained RUBRIC users but not programmers should be willing to expend more effort to develop a detailed rule-based definition of the query topic.

Although RUBRIC is a knowledge-based system, it really is not an expert system in the usual sense. In an expert system the system's knowledge base is an attempt to define what is known about some field of inquiry (e.g., infectious diseases, geology) in a useful form analogous to that used by human experts. Although the knowledge is never complete and perhaps not agreed upon by all experts, there exists some underlying theory or physical model that all concerned believe. In the case of information retrieval, as in other areas of preference such as politics or matters of style, there is no "right" answer. Hence, RUBRIC is really a system for capturing and evaluating human preferences. Preference systems are likely to play a much larger role in the future, as artificial intelligence tackles the problem of supporting complex, multiattribute decision making.

III. Expressing Query Topics as Production Rules

RUBRIC gains its power from the knowledge base of retrieval rules at its disposal. An example set of rules that defines the topic of the 1982 World Series of Baseball is given in Fig. 2. These 15 rules define a main topic, called World_Series, and a number of subtopics. The subtopics are used to define the main topic, but may also be used as query topics on their own or as subtopics of other main topics. This rule set is by no means complete; however, extensions in the form of additional rules are easy to make.

Each rule defines a logical implication; that is, the existence of the pattern on the left-hand side of the arrow ("=>") implies the existence of the topic named on the righthand side. Thus, a rule defines the topic or concept named in its right-hand side. There may be multiple rules about the same topic, and RUBRIC

```
team | event => World_Series

St._Louis_Cardinals | Milwaukee_Brewers => team

"Cardinals" => St._Louis_Cardinals (0.7)
Cardinals_full_name => St._Louis_Cardinals (0.9)

saint & "Louis" & "Cardinals"
   => Cardinals_full_name

"St." => saint (0.9)
"Saint" => saint

"Brewers" => Milwaukee_Brewers (0.5)
"Milwaukee Brewers" => Milwaukee_Brewers (0.9)

"World Series" => event
baseball_championship => event (0.9)

baseball & championship => baseball_championship

"ball" => baseball (0.5)
"baseball" => baseball

"championship" => championship (0.7)
```

Fig. 2. Rule base for topic of world_series.

will use each as an equally valid alternate definition (i.e., there is an implicit OR). The left-hand side of a rule is its body, which defines a pattern to be matched. This can be the topic named in the right-hand side of another rule, a text reference expression (defined below), or a compound expression that defines the logical AND (denoted by "&") or OR ("|") of two or more other rule topics of text reference expressions. Explicit text to be matched without further interpretation is surrounded by quotation marks; names of topics and text reference language constructs are not. The last element in a rule is its weight, which is a real number in the interval [0, 1]. It represents the rule definer's confidence that the existence in a document of the pattern defined by the rule's left-hand side implies that the document is about the topic named in the rule's right-hand side. If a weight is omitted, it is assumed to be 1.0 (i.e., absolute confidence). Note that a weight is a number made up by a human user, based upon his or her experience and insight; a weight is *not* a statistical quantity.

A text reference expression may be a single keyword or phrase, or a lexical context within which two keywords or phrases must be found (e.g., word adjacency, same sentence, same paragraph). So, for example, one can specify that two patterns are of interest only if they occur in the same sentence. Fuzzy (partial) matching versions of these contexts are also allowed. RUBRIC's fuzzy pattern matcher returns a value in [0, 1] that is proportional to the degree that the phrases are in the desired context, i.e., inversely proportional to the logical distance between the two objects in the document. For example, when matching a fuzzy same-sentence context, two phrases in the same sentence might receive a weight of 1.0, within adjacent sentences 0.8, etc.

Rules often define alternate terms, phrases, and spellings for the same concept. Thus, rules can also provide a simple hierarchical thesaurus, with variable weights defining the degree of certainty with which a particular variant is to match. For example, in English "St." is used as the abbreviation for both "Saint" and "Street," and thus "St." is weighted less that the keyword "Saint" in Fig. 2. Rules can also aid multilingual information retrieval. For example, if the database contains text in multiple languages, then the lowest level(s) of rules

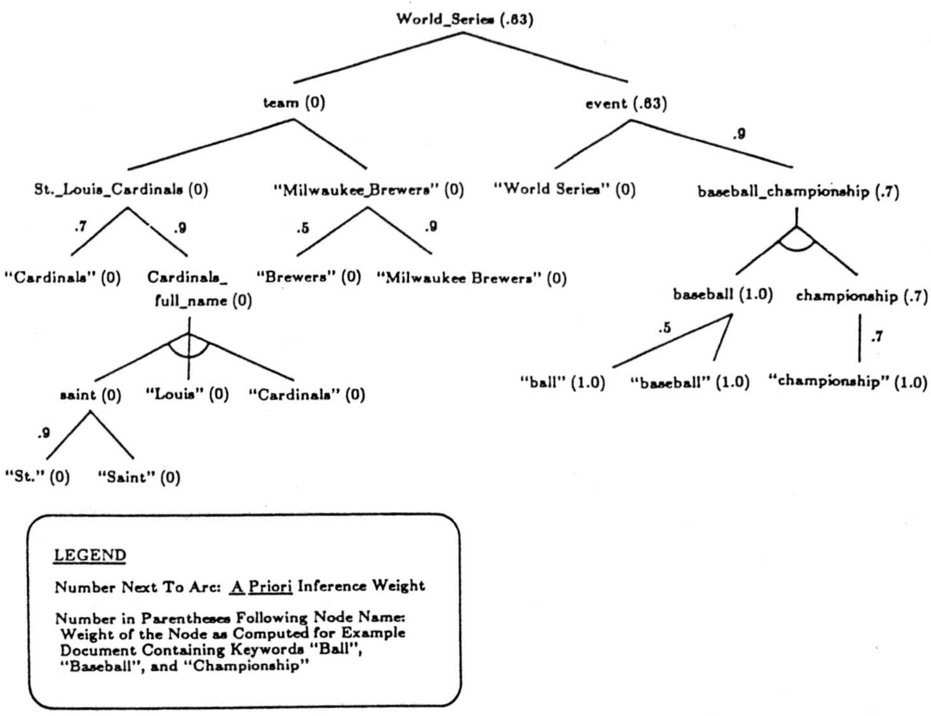

Fig. 3. Rule evaluation tree for world_series topic.

might define synonyms in each language of interest. The more conceptual language-independent rules higher in the hierarchy would remain unchanged.

It has been found useful to provide a new type of rule in RUBRIC, called a *modifier rule*, which enables the user to incorporate auxiliary (or contextual) evidence into the query. Auxiliary evidence is evidence that by itself neither confirms nor disconfirms a hypothesis, but which may increase (or decrease) our belief if seen in conjunction with some primary evidence. The form of such a rule is

if A, **then** C to degree w_1;
  but if also B, **then** C to degree w_2

where if w_1 is greater than w_2 then B is disconfirming auxiliary evidence, and if w_1 is less than w_2 then B is confirming auxiliary evidence. This has the effect of interpolating between w_1 and w_2, depending upon the certainty computed for the auxiliary clause B. Thus we might have a rule of the kind:

if (the story contains the literal string "bomb"),
  then (it is about an *explosive device*)
    to degree 0.6;
  but if also (it mentions a *boxing match*),
  then (reduce the strength of the conclusion)
    to degree 0.3

Here we see the concept of disconfirming evidence in operation; notice that by itself being about the concept *boxing match* is not evidence that can be used to support or deny the conclusion we are trying to establish.

Knowledge bases of rules are expected to evolve over time. Initially the set of rules provided in a knowledge base will capture a small portion of the kinds of knowledge required. New rules are easily added to RUBRIC, currently by means of a standard display-oriented text editor. Existing rules may be modified for experimentation to provide feedback for honing their logical structure, keywords, and weights.

IV. Query Processing

A set of rules defines a logical hierarchy of retrieval topics and subtopics (Fig. 3). A specific retrieval request is carried out by a goal-oriented inference process similar to that used in the MYCIN medical diagnosis system [4]. This process creates and evaluates an AND/OR tree of logical retrieval patterns. The root node of this tree represents a semantic topic or concept that the user wants retrieved; nodes farther down in the tree represent intermediate topics with which the root topic is defined; and nodes at the leaves of the tree represent patterns of words that are to be searched for in the database. Each arc in the tree is weighted such that the intermediate topics and keyword expressions contribute, according to their weight, to the overall confidence that the root topic has also been found. (Unlabeled arcs in Fig. 3 have an implicit weight of 1.0.) Arcs representing the conjuncts of an AND expression are linked together near their common base in Fig. 3.

RUBRIC supports a number of calculi for interpreting the rule weights. Weights are treated as certainty or partial truth values, not as probabilities. Each calculus defines how to combine the uncertainties during such logical deductions as AND, OR, and implication. The default method is to use the functions minimum, maximum, and product to propagate the weights across AND and OR arcs and implication nodes, respectively [4].

Referring to Figs. 2 and 3, we now describe how RUBRIC processes a query. (Annotated traces of the system's operation are found in [1].) When the user types in the conceptual query World_Series, RUBRIC searches its rule base for all rules that

Phrases Present in Document	Support for World_Series Topic
"World Series"	1.00
"Saint", "Louis", "Cardinals"	0.90
"Milwaukee Brewers"	0.90
"St.", "Louis", Cardinals"	0.81
"Cardinals"	0.70
"baseball", "championship"	0.63
"Brewers"	0.50
"ball", "championship"	0.45
none of the above	0.00

Fig. 4. Possible weights for world_series topic.

provide definitions for this topic (i.e., that have World_Series on their right-hand sides). There is only one such rule in Fig. 2, so RUBRIC expands that rule according to its lefthand side. The result is that the World_Series, team, and event nodes of Fig. 3 are created, as well as the two arcs between them. Since team and event are themselves the names of topics, rather than textual patterns, RUBRIC searches its rule base for their definitions. This process continues recursively until all leaf nodes of the tree contain textual patterns.

At this point each document in the database is matched against all of the phrases in the leaves of the tree. For a given document, if a phrase is found somewhere in the document, the corresponding node in the tree is assigned a value of 1.0, otherwise 0. Then the weights at the leaves are combined and propagated up through the tree to determine the overall weight to be assigned to this document.

For example, if a document contained the words "ball," "baseball," and "championship," and no other words referred to in the example rule base, then the nodes of the tree would be assigned the weights shown in parentheses in Fig. 3. The "ball," "baseball," and "championship" leaf nodes all receive a weight of 1.0, and all other leaves receive a weight of 0. The baseball node would then be assigned the value 1.0 because that is the maximum of (1.0 multipled by 0.5) and (1.0 times 1.0). Similarly, the championship node receives the value 0.7. Then, because it is an AND node, the baseball_championship node gets the value 0.7, which is 1.0 times the minimum of 1.0 and 0.7. The event node then gets the value 0.63, which is the maximum of (0 times 1.0) and (0.7 times 0.9). Since there are no keywords in the document that support the team subtopic, the overall weight of the match of the World_Series topic on this document is 0.63 (1.0 times the maximum of 0 and 0.63).

Other combinations of keywords and phrases in a document can satisfy the concept of World_Series to varying degrees. Fig. 4 shows the other weights possible for the World_Series topic, depending upon the dominant phrases that occur in the document.

V. User Interface

A user need only see the highest weighted documents. After the database has been searched, each document that was considered has an associated weight that represents the system's confidence that the document is relevant to the topic requested by the user. RUBRIC sorts these documents into descending order based upon their weights, and groups the documents by applying statistical clustering techniques to the weights. The user is then presented with those documents that lie in a cluster containing at least one document with a weight above a threshold provided by the user (e.g., 0.8 or above). Clustering prevents an arbitrary threshold from splitting closely ranked documents. The threshold may be varied depending upon how much time the user has available to read documents, how important it is not to miss any potentially relevant ones, etc.

RUBRIC is able to explain why a particular document was retrieved. This capability is very important for instilling confidence in users and helping them get a good enough feel for the operations of the system that they can successfully write and use their own retrieval rules. RUBRIC can display each rule that results in a nonzero weight being propagated, as well as the value of that weight. RUBRIC can also show each attempt to match a word or phrase to the document, along with whether or not it matched.

VI. Experimental Results

We have done preliminary experiments with RUBRIC to examine the improvements that can be achieved over a conventional Boolean keyword approach. As an experimental database for testing the retrieval properties of RUBRIC, we have used a selection of thirty stories taken from the Reuters News Service. Our basic experimental procedure is to rate the stories in the database by inspection (i.e., define a subjective ground truth), construct a rule-based representation of a typical query, apply the query to the database, and then compare the rating produced by RUBRIC with the *a priori* rating.

We concentrate on two basic measures of performance. Both of these are based on the idea of using a selection threshold to partition the ordered stories so that those above it are "relevant" (either fully or marginally) and those below it are "not relevant." In the first we lower the threshold until we include all those deemed *a priori* relevant, and then count the number of unwanted stories that are also selected (denoted N_F). In the second we raise the threshold until we exclude all irrelevant stories, and then count the number of relevant ones that are not selected (denoted N_M). The first definition therefore gives us an insight into the system's ability to reject unwanted stories (precision), whereas second gives us insight into the system's ability to select relevant stories (recall).

We selected as a retrieval concept "violent acts of terrorism," and then constructed an appropriate rule-based query. This is summarized in Fig. 5, where we make extensive use of modifier rules. An auxiliary clause is shown linked to its conclusion by a directed arc labeled "Modifier". Application of this query to the story database results in the story profile shown in Fig. 6. (Notice that for presentation purposes the stories are ordered such that those determined to be *a priori* relevant are to the left in Figure 6.) The performance scores for this experiment are

Precision: $N_F = 1$ when we ensure that $N_M = 0$, and

Recall: $N_M = 5$ when we ensure that $N_F = 0$.

This is almost perfect performance, being marred only by the selection of story 25, which, although it contains many of the

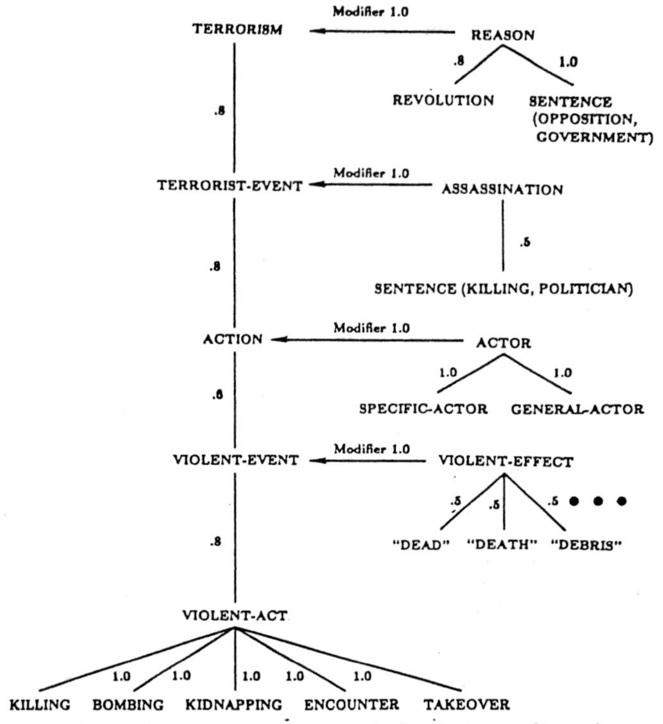

Fig. 5. Rule base structure for concept of violent acts of terrorism.

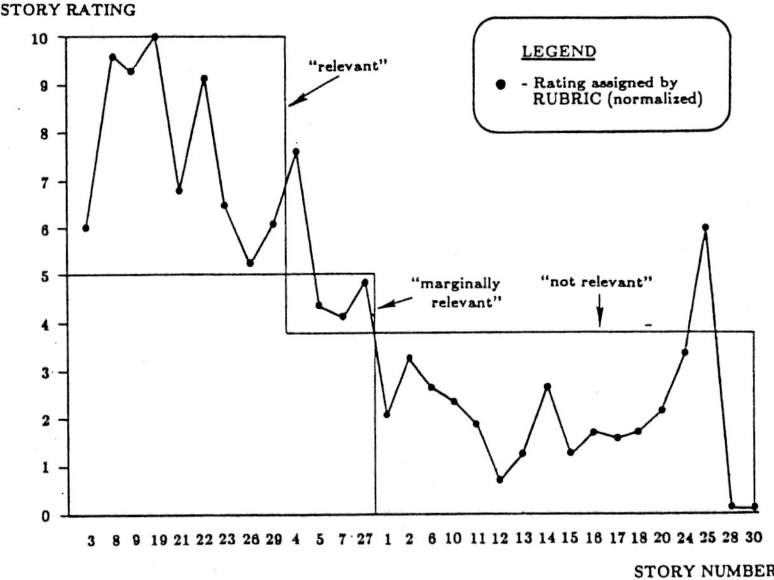

Fig. 6. Story profile from RUBRIC experiment.

elements of a terrorist article, is actually a description of an unsuccessful bomb disposal attempt.

To compare RUBRIC against a more conventional approach, we constructed two Boolean queries by using the rule-based paradigm and setting all rule weights to 1.0 (thus incidentally showing that our method subsumes Boolean retrieval as a special case). One of these queries is shown in Fig. 7 as an AND/OR tree of subconcepts. The only difference between the two Boolean queries is that in the first we insist on the conjunction of ACTOR and TERRORIST-EVENT (as shown), whereas in the second we require the disjunction of these concepts. The conjunctive form of the Boolean query misses five relevant stories and selects one unimportant story, whereas the disjunctive form selects all the relevant stories, but at the cost of also selecting seven of the irrelevant ones.

While these results represent only a preliminary test, we believe that they indicate that the RUBRIC approach allows the user to be more flexible in the specification of his or her query, thereby increasing both precision and recall. A traditional Boolean query tends either to over- or under-constrain the search procedure, giving poor recall or poor precision. We feel that, given equal amounts of effort, RUBRIC allows better

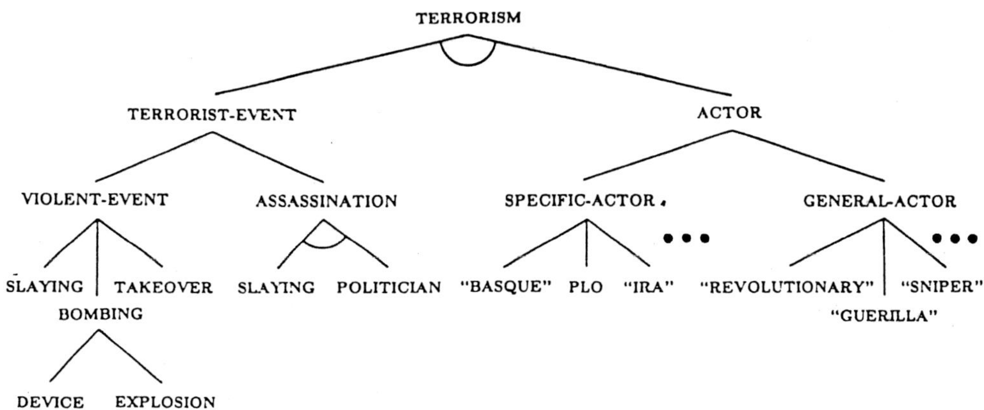

Fig. 7. AND/OR concept tree for Boolean query.

models of human retrieval judgment than can be achieved with traditional Boolean mechanisms.

We have also explored the effects of using different calculi for propagating the uncertainty values within the system [5]. Among these calculi are well-known classes such as those that use "max" and "min" as disjunct and conjunct operators, and those (so-called "Bayesian-like") that use "sum" and "product". Our initial conclusion is that the calculus used is not the major determinant of performance, but that it does interact with how rules are defined.

VII. Future Work

Much additional research and system development are needed to make RUBRIC usable. We are currently providing a better user interface and conducting more complete experiments. The interface for end users will include more focused interactive explanation, analysis of results for sensitivity to specific rules and weights, display of graphs such as Fig. 6, and rule editing. Experimentation will consist of defining, in conjunction with users, larger rule sets for a realistic retrieval domain and then using these rules to retrieve documents from a realistic database.

Other areas of possible future work include making rule evaluation and textual pattern matching more efficient, possibly through the use of heuristics to limit rule evaluation; exploring additional ways of representing and propagating uncertainty in both numeric and symbolic representations; ablative testing to measure how useful each system feature is; extending the text reference language to allow specification of the syntactic role that a word plays in a sentence (e.g., "ship" used as a noun versus as a verb); constructing a more general thesaurus that has a network structure rather than a hierarchical one like rules; and allowing retrieval from multiple remote databases.

VIII. Potential Applications

Application systems based on RUBRIC may be useful for information routing and change detection, in addition to information retrieval. For information retrieval RUBRIC could be extended to work on formatted documents such as messages or bibliographic entries, to work as a front end to existing databases and information retrieval systems, and to segment larger documents by subtopics. RUBRIC could be used to process messages in real-time, filtering the important ones and routing them to the appropriate recipient (human or another program). With RUBRIC, analyses of documents over time could detect statistical changes at a conceptual level rather than just in the use of individual keywords.

References

[1] B. P. McCune, J. S. Dean, R. M. Tong, and D. G. Shapiro, "RUBRIC: A system for rule-based information retrieval," Advanced Information & Decision Systems, Mountain View, CA, Tech. Rep. 1018-1, Feb. 1983.

[2] G. Salton and M. J. McGill, *Introduction to Modern Information Retrieval*. New York: McGraw-Hill, 1983.

[3] R. C. Schank and G. DeJong, "Purposive understanding," in *Machine Intelligence*, vol. 9, J. E. Hayes, D. Michie, and L. I. Mikulich, Eds. 1979, ch.24, pp. 459–478.

[4] E. Hance Shortliffe, *Computer-Based Medical Consultations: MYCIN*. New York: Elsevier, 1976.

[5] R. M. Tong, D. G. Shapiro, J. S. Dean, and B. P. McCune, "A comparison of uncertainty calculi in an expert system for information retrieval," in *Proc. Eighth Int. Joint Conf. Artificial Intell.*, A. Bundy, Ed. Los Altos, CA: William Kaufman, Aug. 1983, vol. 1, pp. 194–197.

[6] R. M. Tong, D. G. Shapiro, B. P. McCune, and J. S. Dean, "A rule-based approach to information retrieval: Some results and comments," in *Proc. Nat. Conf. Artificial Intel.* Los Altos, CA: William Kaufman, Aug. 1983, pp. 411–415.

TARGET & FREESTYLE:

DIALOG and Mead Join the Relevance Ranks

by Carol Tenopir and Pamela Cahn
University of Hawaii

Everyone undoubtedly has seen announcements of the new, non-Boolean, natural language search techniques from West, DIALOG, and Mead Data Central. Some of you may already be experimenting with or using Westlaw's WIN, DIALOG's TARGET, or Mead's FREESTYLE. All are based on the assumption that our standard command-driven online systems coupled with Boolean logic searching are not only difficult to learn, but may sometimes miss relevant documents. This assumption is based not only on searchers' experiences, but on years of controlled tests in the information retrieval laboratories.

There is no doubt that this new way to search old systems is gaining a lot of attention. Westlaw Is Natural (WIN) was introduced in the fall of 1992 and on its first anniversary won the *ONLINE* Product of the Year award at ONLINE/CD-ROM '93. It continues to garner favorable reviews and is now the search method that Westlaw trainers teach first to new searchers. DIALOG's TARGET and Mead's FREESTYLE were announced at ONLINE/CD-ROM '93 to great fanfare, and became publicly available in late 1993 and early 1994.

Searchers are definitely interested. It was standing-room only at ONLINE/CD-ROM '93s session on natural language systems. Teresa Pritchard-Schoch's article, "Natural Language Comes of Age" [1], won the IAC Best Article award for 1993.

COMMAND BOOLEAN ... RELEVANCE RANKING

THE NATURAL ALTERNATIVE

Although each product works somewhat differently, all three offer an alternative to searching with command interfaces and Boolean/proximity operators. (Proximity operators such as specifying within a paragraph or within a specified number of words are an extension of the Boolean AND.) They offer (somewhat) natural language input, with no need for commands or logical operators. This input method is coupled with so-called "associative," "probabilistic" or "statistical" retrieval techniques that provide relevance ranking of search results.

Unlike exact-match Boolean logic systems, where all concepts or terms linked with AND or a proximity operator must be present, relevance retrieval techniques are partial-match systems. They retrieve all documents that contain any words used to represent a concept (as if all words were ORd together). These documents are then run against a mathematical algorithm that weights and ranks the documents.

Statistical methods compare, for example, how many times the search words appear in each record with how many times they appear in the database as a whole. Documents that contain many of the search words are given higher weights. If those terms appear relatively less frequently in the database as a whole, the documents that contain them are weighted even more heavily. Relative lengths of each document are taken into account as well. The documents are then sorted by the assigned weights to display first those documents that best match the query. Pritchard-Schoch provides a clear explanation of the history and methods of these techniques, which have been tested for decades. They have been available on smaller online or CD-ROM systems and in software for in-house databases for several years [2].

> TARGET...is best suited for full-text databases...

The most important question for experienced searchers is what will relevance search systems retrieve compared to the tried-and-true Boolean search engines? Should experienced searchers use the new methods? Will your search results be better with one technique or the other? Which method should we teach our end-users? Do all of the new systems achieve the same results?

WESTLAW IS NATURAL

Since WIN has been around the longest of these three, it is setting the standard for the other relevance retrieval search systems [3]. WIN goes beyond just statistical relevance ranking by offering a powerful combination of natural language input, automatic word-stemming, automatic recognition of legal phrases, and a thesaurus.

We did not study WIN for this article, because others are doing so and because Westlaw's subject domain is limited to law. Legal searchers should carefully compare WIN with Mead's new FREESTYLE in the LEXIS service, since both include many of the same legal reference sources.

We chose to look more closely at the relevance retrieval systems on DIALOG and Mead's NEXIS as they might be used for searching full-text newspapers. Full-text searching of newspapers poses unique challenges since the topics and lengths of documents vary so widely, and thus is an apt test of relevance retrieval techniques.

TARGET

DIALOG officially announced TARGET in October 1993 and made it available for all users in December 1993. Although it was under development off and on for several years, it wasn't until WIN's success that DIALOG decided to get TARGET ready for release. The DIALOG development staff looked at many different relevance methods and tested a variety of algorithms before programming what we see now.

TARGET works on all DIALOG databases, but it is best suited for full-text databases or those with lengthy abstracts. These are the databases that rely on free-text searching and often retrieve excessive false drops with conventional searching. Since relevance retrieval compares how many times words occur in a document in relation to the length of each document, entire documents about a topic can be differentiated from those with only a single paragraph or a mention in passing of the desired subject. The *most* relevant documents should be placed at the top of the set for display first in relevance-ranked retrieval.

TARGET FOR SUBJECT SEARCHING

TARGET works best for text searching. Just as with DIALOG's Boolean system, TARGET defaults to the basic index. Those of you who are regular DIALOG searchers are aware of this distinction in its indexes. Unlike NEXIS and many other online systems, DIALOG maintains separate indexes for subject and non-subject searching. The "basic index" typically includes only words from titles, words from abstracts, words from full text, and words or phrases from descriptors or identifiers—fields which are all considered to represent the subjects of documents. The basic index is searched by default if a searcher doesn't specify any particular field.

To search for an author, journal name, corporate source, or other non-subject field in Boolean DIALOG, the searcher must explicitly name that field. (e.g., SELECT AU=Asimov, Isaac or SELECT JN=Library Journal). This separation helps avoid false drops in the regular Boolean system, because you will not, for example, retrieve articles authored by Mr. Carpenter when searching for the subject carpenter.

TARGET provides two ways of searching these non-subject fields:

1) By putting the prefix search in single quotes (e.g., target 'au=asimov, isaac')

2) An author set created in a Boolean search can be added to a TARGET search (e.g., s au=asimov, isaac; target *s1 'life science' biology zoology).

HOW TO SEARCH WITH TARGET

TARGET can be used in a single database or in multiple databases. Searchers can use a predefined OneSearch grouping or BEGIN in whichever databases they desire. Databases are searched with the CURRENT option by default (current calendar year plus one year) in databases that support the CURRENT feature, but searches can be modified to include other date ranges. If the database does not support CURRENT, TARGET will search the entire database.

After beginning in a database or database group, a searcher inputs the word TARGET to get into the TARGET menu search mode. TARGET menu mode provides helps, prompts, and some menu choices to guide the novice user through the search process. Figure 1 shows the beginning of a TARGET menu mode search session.

Alternatively, experienced searchers can use the word TARGET as a command, if they follow it with search terms. Inputting: target radiation

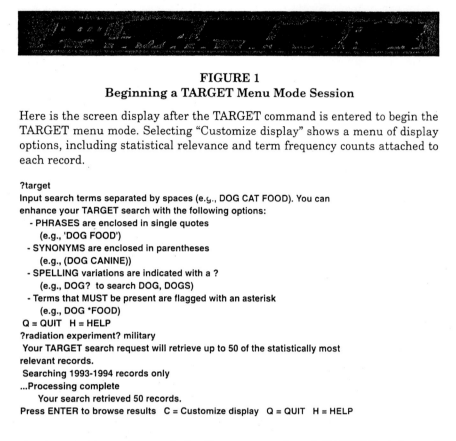

FIGURE 1
Beginning a TARGET Menu Mode Session

Here is the screen display after the TARGET command is entered to begin the TARGET menu mode. Selecting "Customize display" shows a menu of display options, including statistical relevance and term frequency counts attached to each record.

```
?target
Input search terms separated by spaces (e.g., DOG CAT FOOD). You can
enhance your TARGET search with the following options:
  - PHRASES are enclosed in single quotes
     (e.g., 'DOG FOOD')
  - SYNONYMS are enclosed in parentheses
     (e.g., (DOG CANINE))
  - SPELLING variations are indicated with a ?
     (e.g., DOG?  to search DOG, DOGS)
  - Terms that MUST be present are flagged with an asterisk
     (e.g., DOG *FOOD)
Q = QUIT   H = HELP
?radiation experiment? military
 Your TARGET search request will retrieve up to 50 of the statistically most
relevant records.
 Searching 1993-1994 records only
...Processing complete
     Your search retrieved 50 records.
Press ENTER to browse results   C = Customize display   Q = QUIT   H = HELP
```

experiment? military will search for the three terms using the relevance retrieval engine, but without bringing up any of the TARGET system prompts or menus. It will not allow special TARGET display features, unless TARGET menu mode is turned on for that search session with the SET TARGET command.

NOT NATURAL LANGUAGE

Even in the novice TARGET mode, TARGET does not claim to support natural language. It does replace the need for Boolean or proximity connectors, but only the actual words or phrases to be searched should be entered. This differs from Westlaw's WIN, since WIN allows a user to enter a natural language statement directly. WIN's natural language interface supports a search statement such as **what is the government's obligation to warn military personnel about their exposure to radiation?** The system then strips out common phrases (e.g., "what is the"), identifies legal phrases matched from a phrase thesaurus, and eliminates stopwords.

TARGET requires formalized input of major terms, phrases, and synonyms and does little automatic processing. A TARGET statement might look like this: **government? obligation warn? ('military personnel' soldier? sailor?) expos? *radiation.** Just as with DIALOG Boolean searching, understanding the required syntax is necessary.

The question mark indicates truncation, just as it does in the regular DIALOG system. Unlike full Boolean, however, TARGET does not support single or specified character truncation. The single ? retrieves any number of characters after the input stem; DIALOG's ? ?, ??, ???, etc. (used to specify maximum number of characters following a stem) are not supported in TARGET, because TARGET is intended to be easier to use than the Boolean system.

Unlimited truncation of course works best for relatively long character strings such as government. TARGET help screens use the search examples of **dog cat food** and recommends truncating dog as **dog?** to retrieve dog or dogs. Most experienced searchers would hesitate to input a three-character stem such as **dog?** with unlimited truncation, for fear of retrieving such words as dogfish, doggerel, dogma, dogwood, etc. TARGET does no automatic stemming, so even singulars/plurals must be indicated by the user. In the dog example it is safer to explicitly search for **dog dogs.**

Synonyms can be, but don't have to be, grouped with parentheses by the searcher (but without placing a Boolean OR between them). In the earlier example, 'military personnel,' soldier, and sailor are all synonyms. Grouping synonyms cuts down the weighting for each individual term.

TARGET does not have a thesaurus, so the burden of identifying and inputting synonyms is completely on the user, just as it is in DIALOG's Boolean system. Creating a thesaurus that would serve all of the databases on a supermarket system such as DIALOG would be a daunting task. Westlaw has an easier time of it, building a thesaurus of legal terms and phrases. FREESTYLE has a general synonym-type thesaurus. To make natural language search techniques truly useful for novices, databases and systems will have to spend the time and effort to develop and maintain complete multitopic thesauri.

TARGET searchers can indicate bound phrases with quotation marks (e.g., **'military personnel'**). The phrases will then be searched as adjacent, bound phrases only, rather than as separately weighted search terms. No phrases are automatically identified, again the searcher must explicitly mark all phrases for the system. The relevance algorithm does, however, weight individual search words more heavily if they occur within several words of another search word.

The asterisk (used in this example in front of ***radiation**) can be used by the TARGET searcher to indicate a term that *must* be present in a search. Records that do not have this term will not be retrieved, just as if a Boolean AND were used. Individual terms can be marked as mandatory, or a concept can be marked as mandatory by putting the asterisk outside the parentheses. For example, if the military personnel concept is considered mandatory, the searcher would input ***('military personnel' soldier? sailor)** to indicate any one of these terms *must* be present in retrieved records.

TARGET MODIFICATIONS AND DISPLAY

Search statements in the TARGET menu mode can be modified by choosing the Modify option (but only after a search is run and after the first three items are displayed). Modifications can be made to add or delete terms, to change the designation of a term as a required term, or to change the dates being searched. TARGET statements build a set which can then be used in a Boolean search.

TARGET examines all of the records that contain any of the input words and calculates likely relevance of each. The formula goes beyond just counting word frequency by comparing how many of the search terms appear in each record with how many times each word appears in the database as a whole. Uncommon words that appear frequently in a document are given more weight. Unequal document lengths are taken into account as well as are proximity of search words.

The resulting document ranking is used as the basis for order of display. Unlike Boolean's reverse chronological display or a user-specified sorting order such as alphabetically by author, relevance ranking displays first documents that are most likely to answer the user's query. This is good output for browsing until an information need is satisfied, and for those questions where the user doesn't need a comprehensive search. "Relevance" is always ultimately subjective of course, so there is no guarantee that the fiftieth item displayed will be of less interest in a particular case than the fortieth, or even the first, item.

TARGET displays up to 50 items. Most searches retrieve at least the full 50 items because with multiple words or concepts in a search, documents with even only one of the words will be retrieved. It may be more intuitive to end-users that inputting a fuller description (more terms) of their information needs will retrieve more documents.

The default brief display format includes title, publication, and date. Customizing the display in any way desired can be done as a modify function after a search is run. In addition to specifying the fields desired in a custom display, TARGET can attach to each record in the display term, frequency counts for each term in the search statement and an overall statistical relevance percentage that is used by the system to determine the order of display.

FREESTYLE... will automatically strip stop-words from an input query.

FREESTYLE

Mead's FREESTYLE is available for both the LEXIS legal service and NEXIS news service. FREESTYLE's performance in LEXIS is best compared to WIN, since LEXIS and Westlaw share many of the same legal databases and compete head-to-head in the legal research market. We chose instead to examine FREESTYLE only in NEXIS, specifically in full-text newspapers.

FREESTYLE works on all NEXIS files, either selected individually, selected as NEXIS pre-specified group files, or mixed together in *ad hoc* groupings by the searcher. After selecting a filename, searchers enter the command .FR to get to FREESTYLE mode. To return to Boolean mode, enter .BOOL.

PLAIN ENGLISH

FREESTYLE is closer to plain English than is TARGET, because it will automatically strip stopwords from an input query. Singulars and plurals are automatically searched (but other word form variations such as past tense and gerunds are not). As with the full NEXIS system, common abbreviations, British/American spelling, and equivalencies (e.g., 4 and four) are also automatic.

As with WIN, a FREESTYLE search could be directly entered as what is the government's obligation to warn military personnel of exposure to radiation? or using a shorter, more formalized statement as in TARGET. If entered in the former way, "what, is, the, to, of" and "to" will all be discarded as stop (noise) words. (In plain English searches we tested, effect, services, and information were not discarded as

FIGURE 2
FREESTYLE Thesaurus Screen

The thesaurus can be reached from the Search Options screen.

SYNONYM SELECTION

Synonyms for: EXPERIMENT
Enter synonym numbers to include in search and press ENTER (e.g. 1,2,3-4)

<=1> Return to Search Options <=2> Return to Term Selection

Term Variations

1	experimented	2	experimenter	3	experimenting
4	experimentor				

5	assay	6	attempt	7	dry run
8	endeavor	9	examination	10	first attempt
11	investigation	12	periculum	13	research
14	search	15	test	16	testing program
17	trial	18	tryout		

For further explanation, press the H key (for HELP) and then the TRANSMIT key.

stopwords.) Government's will be searched as government, governments, or government's. The other words will be searched as singulars or plurals, but obligation will not be truncated to oblige, warn to warning, exposure to expose or exposed, etc.

In the first version of FREESTYLE (February 15-May 30, 1994), these variations need to be explicitly input by the searcher (oblige obliged obligation) because truncation, other than automatic plurals, is not supported by FREESTYLE. The NEXIS symbols for user-specified truncation (! and *) did not work in the version of the software we tested.

FREESTYLE THESAURUS

Unlike TARGET, FREESTYLE does have an accompanying thesaurus where searchers can look for synonyms or variant word forms to add to their search. The thesaurus is not invoked automatically; searchers must select the thesaurus option from a Search Options screen and specify which of their search terms they want to check for synonyms [4]. Figure 2 (see page 34) shows a sample FREESTYLE thesaurus screen.

FREESTYLE does not invoke the thesaurus automatically, according to Mead, because of the variety of word meanings in the English language. Searches would retrieve too many false drops from homographs (e.g., strike, plant, etc.), or from variant endings that change the meaning of the stem word (e.g., injury, injurious). A Mead spokesperson said, "Until we can parse for parts of speech, we will not invoke the thesaurus automatically, and that's a long way off."

Searchers may specify bound phrases by putting them in quotation marks (e.g., "military personnel"). These phrases will then be treated as adjacent words and counted together in the relevance ranking algorithm. Unlike TARGET, some terms not explicitly bound by the searcher will be recognized as phrases by FREESTYLE. Mead has a dictionary of over 300,000 phrases that are checked each time a search is entered. These include general phrases (e.g., red carpet); legal phrases (e.g., personal injury); pharmaceutical phrases (e.g., names of

FIGURE 3
Questions Searched And Strategies Used*

Category 1: Single Concepts:

Question #1. What can you find out about EMFs?
DIALOG Boolean: (electromagnetic or electro(w)magnetic)(w)field? or emf?
DIALOG TARGET: 'electromagnetic field?' emf? 'electro magnetic field?'
NEXIS Boolean: electromagnetic field! or emf! or electro magnetic field!
NEXIS FREESTYLE: What can you find out about emfs (electromagnetic fields)

Question #2. Find any mention of Hopis.
DIALOG Boolean: hopi? ?
DIALOG TARGET: (hopi hopis)
NEXIS Boolean: hopi
NEXIS FREESTYLE: hopi

Category 2: Two Concepts

Question #3. What is the effect of PCBs on fish?
DIALOG Boolean: (pcb? ? or polychlorinated()biphenyl?)(s)fish?
DIALOG TARGET: pcb? polychlorinated biphenyl? fish?
NEXIS Boolean: pcb or polychlorinated biphenyl w/50 fish!
NEXIS FREESTYLE: What is the effect of PCB on fish "polychlorinated biphenyl"

Question #4. Is there abusive behavior and battering in lesbian relationships?
DIALOG Boolean: (abus? or batter?)(20n)lesbian? ?
DIALOG TARGET: (abus? batter?) *lesbian?
NEXIS Boolean: abus! or batter! w/20 lesbian
NEXIS FREESTYLE: Is there abusive abuse behavior and battering in <u>lesbian</u> relationships

Category 3: Three Concepts Or More

Question #5. Should the state provide emergency medical services for illegal immigrants?
DIALOG Boolean: (state? ? or government?)(s)emergency(5n)(health or medical)(s)(legal? or illegal?)(s)(immigrant? ? or alien? ?)
DIALOG TARGET: (state states government?) *emergency (health medical) (legal? illegal?)(immigrant immigrants alien aliens)
NEXIS Boolean: state or government! w/50 emergency w/5 health or medical w/50 legal! or illegal! w/50 immigrant or alien
NEXIS FREESTYLE: Should the state government provide <u>emergency</u> medical health services to illegal legal immigrants aliens

Question #6. Find information about employment discrimination against gays.
DIALOG Boolean: (employment or job or work or workplace)(4n)discriminat?(s)(gay? ? or lesbian? or homosexual?)
DIALOG TARGET: employment job work workplace *discriminat? gay? lesbian? homosexual?
NEXIS Boolean: employment or job or work or workplace w/4 discriminat! w/50 gay or lesbian or homosexual
NEXIS FREESTYLE: find information about employment <u>discrimination</u> against gays job work workplace lesbians homosexuals

** All DIALOG searches were done using CURRENT. NEXIS searches were modified to date after 1992. An asterisk (*) in DIALOG TARGET searches indicates terms marked mandatory. Underlined terms in NEXIS FREESTYLE are terms marked mandatory.*

FIGURE 4
DIALOG Test Search Results

DIALOG		Set Size	# Relevant	# Not Relevant	PRECISION
Question 1	Boolean	86	26	60	30%
	TARGET	50	20	30	40%
	Boolean Uniques	36	5	31	14%
	TARGET Uniques	0			
Question 2	Boolean	80	51	29	64%
	TARGET	50	40	10	80%
	Boolean Uniques	30	9	21	30%
	TARGET Uniques	0			
Question 3	Boolean	30	4	26	13%
	TARGET	50	6	44	12%
	Boolean Uniques	7	0	7	0%
	TARGET Uniques	27	2	25	7%
Question 4	Boolean	8	7	1	88%
	TARGET	50	12	38	24%
	Boolean Uniques	0			
	TARGET Uniques	42	5	37	12%
Question 5	Boolean	29	27	2	93%
	TARGET	50	46	4	92%
	Boolean Uniques	9	8	1	89%
	TARGET Uniques	30	27	3	90%
Question 6	Boolean	45	36	9	80%
	TARGET	50	45	5	90%
	Boolean Uniques	26	20	6	77%
	TARGET Uniques	31	26	5	84%
TOTAL AVERAGES	Boolean	46	25	21	61%
	TARGET	50	28	22	56%
	Boolean Uniques	18	7	11	42%
	TARGET Uniques	22	15	18	48%

specific drugs); and medical phrases (e.g., names of diseases).

SEARCH OPTIONS/RESULTS

After inputting a search statement but before FREESTYLE runs the search, a Search Options screen is displayed. Search Options include viewing the thesaurus, editing the search statement, or running the search as is.

Edit choices include adding or deleting search terms or phrases, designating terms as mandatory, or adding restrictions such as date, byline, etc. (If date restrictions are not selected, FREESTYLE defaults to searching the full file. Date edits allow users to specify a specific date or date range.) If more than one edit is desired the process can take a while. The Search Options screen must be entered for each modification and each must be done individually. Command stacking provides a shortcut through the restrictions and allows users to enter more than one option at a time.

Like the asterisk (*) in TARGET, designating a term as mandatory means that the term *must* be present

FIGURE 5
Differences Between TARGET and FREESTYLE

	TARGET	FREESTYLE
Maximum retrieval set size	50	1,000
Unlimited truncation	YES	NO
Autoplurals (enter singular or plural form)	NO	YES
Autoequivalencies	NO	YES
Field limiting	YES	YES, for DATE, HLEAD, HEADLINE, BYLINE, TERMS only
Date limiting	CURRENT automatic. Can also limit by Current Year + 0-6 or all, in whole year increments *only*, after query is run and first 3 items browsed.	YES
Modify query (Add/delete/edit terms)	YES (in menu mode, only after query is run and first 3 items browsed).	YES, before and/or after query is run.
Thesaurus for synonyms lookup	NO	YES
Display records forwards and backwards	NO, forwards only. Must leave Target and display set in Dialog boolean mode to browse already displayed items (exception: full text of record)	YES

FIGURE 6
NEXIS Test Search Results

NEXIS		Set Size	# Relevant	# Not Relevant	PRECISION
Question 1	Boolean	75	23	52	31%
	FREESTYLE	50	18	32	36%
	Boolean Uniques	25	5	20	20%
	FREESTYLE Uniques	0			
Question 2	Boolean	61	40	21	66%
	FREESTYLE	49	36	13	73%
	Boolean Uniques	21	6	15	29%
	FREESTYLE Uniques	9	1	8	11%
Question 3	Boolean	36	5	31	14%
	FREESTYLE	50	5	45	10%
	Boolean Uniques	27	1	26	4%
	FREESTYLE Uniques	41	1	40	2%
Question 4	Boolean	10	8	2	80%
	FREESTYLE	50	8	42	16%
	Boolean Uniques	2	2	0	100%
	FREESTYLE Uniques	42	2	40	5%
Question 5	Boolean	46	43	3	93%
	FREESTYLE	50	45	5	90%
	Boolean Uniques	20	17	3	85%
	FREESTYLE Uniques	24	19	5	79%
Question 6	Boolean	59	57	2	97%
	FREESTYLE	50	46	4	92%
	Boolean Uniques	45	43	2	96%
	FREESTYLE Uniques	36	32	4	89%
TOTAL AVERAGES	Boolean	48	29	19	64%
	FREESTYLE	50	26	24	53%
	Boolean Uniques	23	12	11	56%
	FREESTYLE Uniques	25	11	19	37%

in any documents retrieved and ranked by FREESTYLE. It adds more precision to the search by combining a Boolean-like search technique with relevance ranking. However, in FREESTYLE the mandatory designation must be made *after* an initial search statement is entered, and the desired term must be retyped after the mandatory option is selected.

Since NEXIS has one large inverted index, rather than a subject-related basic index and non-subject field additional indexes like DIALOG, authors (bylines) and publication years will be searched if they are entered as part of the initial search statement. Searching for **isaac asimov** as a byline in FREESTYLE can be done just by entering his name, but documents that include mentions of Isaac Asimov in the text or as a subject will be retrieved in addition to articles written by him. To gain more precision by searching for him only as a byline, use the Restrictions choice on the Search Options screen, followed by selecting **byline**. This can only be done if you have already entered a basic search query, however. You cannot select an author alone.

When the search is run, a Search Results screen is displayed. The screen reports any stopwords that were input in the search statement and any phrases found in the phrase dictionary. It summarizes which terms were designated mandatory and any restrictions applied.

FREESTYLE DISPLAY

After a FREESTYLE search is run and the system calculates relevance, up to 25 documents will be displayed in ranked order. (This number can be changed at the Search Options screen to anywhere between one and 1,000.) All NEXIS display options are supported, including CITE, KWIC, and FULL. SuperKWIC is a new display format that displays only the portion of each document that is most heavily weighted and therefore most likely to be most relevant. FREESTYLE records can be sorted in reverse chronological order for current event searching.

WHERE AND WHY

While DIALOG has included information about the occurrences of words and relevance ranking score as a display option with each record, Mead has chosen to make this diagnostic information part of two separate commands. The WHERE and WHY commands are unique to Mead.

WHERE shows which documents contain each of the search terms, and WHY shows the level of importance assigned to each term by the system. If you have changed the display to more than 25 documents, WHERE will only display information about the first 25 documents retrieved in any FREESTYLE search. This will be changed in the new release expected in June 1994.

WHERE and WHY have been favorably received, especially by experienced searchers [5]. WHERE helps searchers determine which documents to browse according to their own idiosyncratic view of relevance. WHY helps an experienced searcher determine if a new strategy should be used, if a Boolean search might get better results, or even if they are in the wrong database.

COMPARING TARGET AND FREESTYLE

The main purpose of this article is to compare DIALOG Boolean searching with DIALOG TARGET and NEXIS Boolean with NEXIS FREESTYLE. We did not set out to compare TARGET and FREESTYLE head-to-head, although some comparison is obvious. Most of the differences in the approaches taken by the two systems reflect their differing basic philosophies.

TARGET puts the searcher more in control and does very little automatically. FREESTYLE, on the other hand, does some things automatically and attempts to lead the searcher by the hand a bit more. This is consistent with the different focuses of these systems—experienced searchers for DIALOG and novice end-users for NEXIS. Figure 5 summarizes the main features of TARGET and of FREESTYLE and shows where they differ.

COMPARING RELEVANCE AND BOOLEAN

An in-depth comparison of these Boolean search engines with relevance search techniques requires testing real questions and searches. This should be done over time by many searchers—we have just scratched the surface.

We gathered questions from reference librarians in four libraries and selected six questions to test. Each question was translated into four search queries:

1) TARGET
2) DIALOG Boolean
3) FREESTYLE
4) NEXIS Boolean

We did all of the searches in the same newspapers, in an *ad hoc* grouping of the Los Angeles Times, Boston Globe, and Washington Post papers for 1993-1994.

Search results were downloaded and judged for relevance on a four-point scale, from not at all relevant (1) to very relevant (4). We compared the order in which documents were displayed, as well as the total number of documents retrieved, the number of relevant documents retrieved, and unique documents retrieved by each search method.

Figure 3 (on page 36) is a list of questions searched and the corresponding search statements in both DIALOG and NEXIS. The questions represent three levels of search complexity:

1) single-concept searches
2) two-concept searches
3) three- or more concept searches

Known item searches (such as retrieving a known article from a specified journal issue) were not tested, since both systems recommend Boolean techniques for these.

TEST SEARCH RESULTS

Figures 4 and 6 show how many items were retrieved by each search method for each question, and how many relevant documents were retrieved. The maximum display was set to 50 in both TARGET and FREESTYLE. Presumably many more documents that contained at least one of the search terms are in the databases, but the displayed items should be the 50 most relevant items. As expected, because of the restricting properties of adding concepts in a Boolean search, simple Boolean searches (one or two concepts) usually retrieved more items than relevance searching, but more complex searches (three or more concepts) retrieved fewer.

On DIALOG, an average precision ratio (relevant retrieved/all retrieved) of 56% was achieved by TARGET, compared to 61% by Boolean. NEXIS results were similar, with 53% for FREESTYLE and 64% by Boolean (Figures 4 and 6). (For the precision calculations, documents judged definitely relevant (a rating of 4) and probably relevant (a rating of 3) were both counted as relevant.)

The better overall precision with Boolean should be contrasted with the greater number of total documents retrieved and, at times, greater *number* of relevant documents, obtained by relevance searching.

DISPLAY ORDER

Since relevance searching presumably ranks items in decreasing order of relevance, display order and degrees of relevance were examined as well. Figures 7 and 8 present a relevance judgment map of each search question.

As you can see, the display order of TARGET and FREESTYLE generally puts more relevant items first, but not always. The pattern is inconsistent and difficult to anticipate. Searchers should not assume that because they have viewed some non-relevant items, that the next items will also be false drops.

In the electromagnetic fields question, for example, many highly relevant documents were displayed after

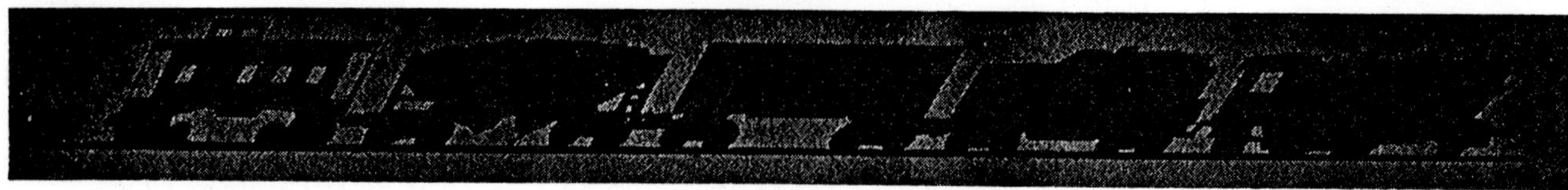

FIGURE 7
Relevancy Rankings (TARGET)

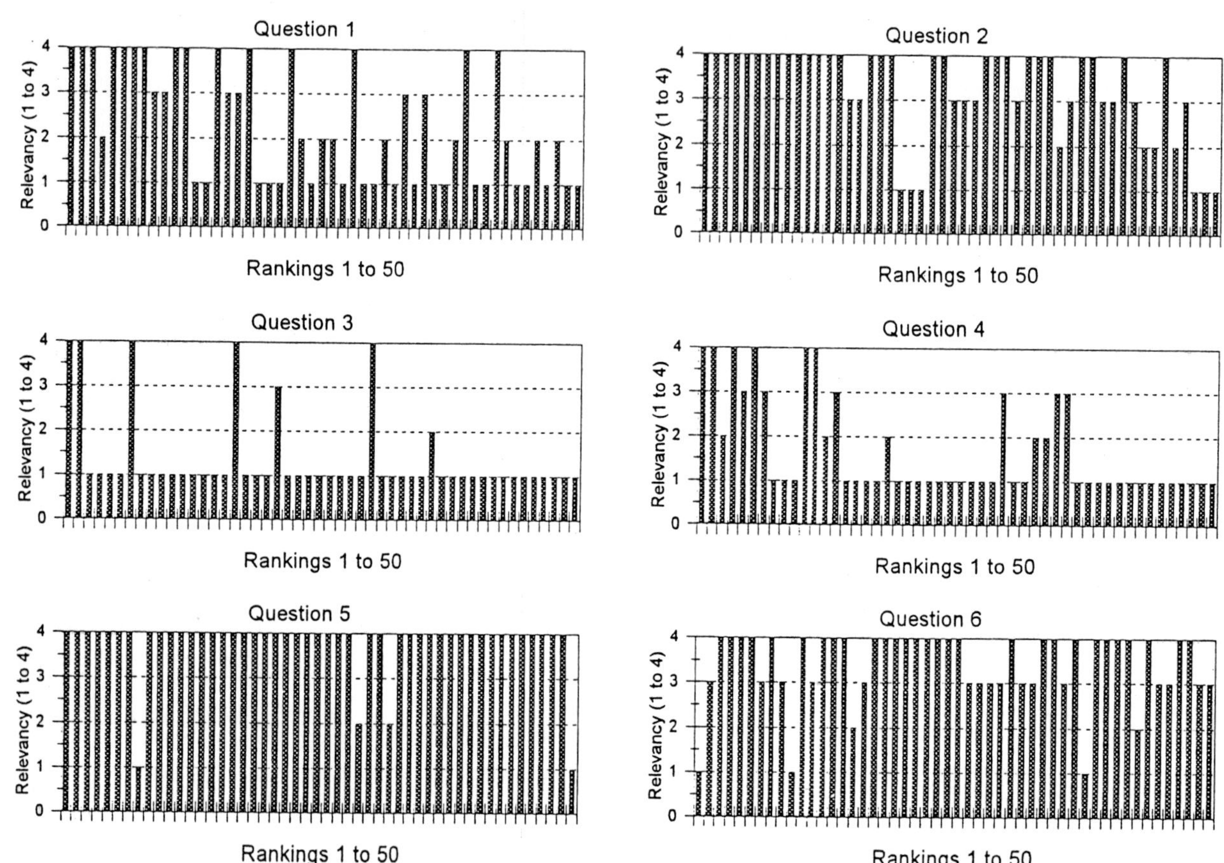

NOTE: Relevance was judged on a 4-point scale. 1 = Definitely not relevant 2 = Probably not relevant 3 = Probably relevant 4 = Definitely relevant

three obvious false drops on the British Rock Group EMF. Several false drops were scattered among highly relevant and probably relevant documents in discrimination against homosexuals in the workplace and other topics.

UNIQUE RETRIEVALS

Finally, we examined unique retrievals for each search method. In most questions, both Boolean methods and relevance methods retrieved unique documents. In fact, in only one question on DIALOG and none on NEXIS, were all the documents retrieved in the Boolean search also retrieved in the relevance search. In two questions on DIALOG and one on NEXIS, all of the items retrieved in the relevance search were retrieved by the Boolean. The other questions had documents that were uniquely retrieved by relevance searching or Boolean searching. Uniquely retrieved documents, both false drops and relevant items, were examined in more detail.

Relevance search methods often retrieved false drops that contained only one or two, but not all of the search terms. In the question on the effect of PCBs on fish, for example, many articles that mentioned only PCBs and many others only about fishing were retrieved by both TARGET and FREESTYLE. (Unfortunately, sometimes these were displayed before relevant items that included both terms.) This could have been avoided by designating both terms as mandatory, much as a Boolean AND (or a proximity operator) would do. The only advantage to using TARGET or FREESTYLE in that case would be to rank the PCB and fish articles in order by how often in each document the terms occur.

Boolean methods, on the other hand, retrieved full articles that only contained words in passing, such as mentioning job discrimination as one type of discrimination faced by gays. False drops also sometimes resulted from figurative speech or one-time misspellings. (Relevance searching

FIGURE 8
Relevancy Rankings (FREESTYLE)

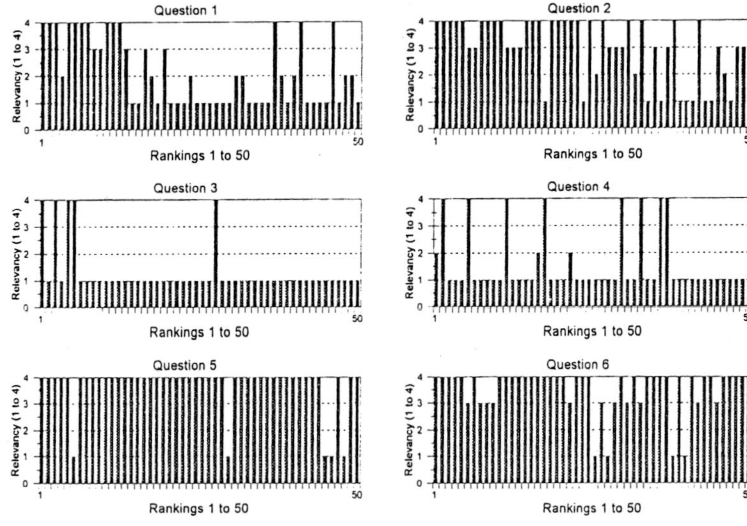

NOTE: Relevance was judged on a 4-point scale. 1 = Definitely not relevant 2 = Probably not relevant 3 = Probably relevant 4 = Definitely relevant

might retrieve these as well, but would put them at the end of a display, sometimes beyond the fifty documents displayed.) For example, one Boolean false drop in the EMF question contained one misspelling "*Emf*rem Zimbalest" in the text. Another described the situation in Bosnia as "two electromagnetic fields in conflict."

Unique relevant documents also were retrieved by Boolean searching when the search words used by the searcher did not occur frequently, but alternative terms did. For example, one highly relevant EMF document included that term only once, so it fell out of the TARGET and FREESTYLE searches, but was retrieved in the larger Boolean set. Throughout the body of the article, terms such as "high voltage power lines" were used instead. Others referred more often to "cellular phones" or "cellular antennas." A system thesaurus can sometimes help with this problem.

Finally, every searcher approaches search strategies differently. We chose to link DIALOG Boolean concepts with the "within the same paragraph" operator (S) instead of the Boolean AND or the proximity operator NEAR (N). We used the w/50 connector (within 50 words) in NEXIS Boolean. Some of the relevant documents uniquely retrieved by TARGET and FREESTYLE contained words further apart than this. Although a Boolean AND would have retrieved these, there would have been so many additional false drops that the value would be obscured. TARGET and FREESTYLE were clearly better for those searches where (S) or w/50 were not enough, but AND would be too much.

WHEN DOES RELEVANCE WORK BEST?

What does all of this tell us about the important question of when should you use TARGET or FREESTYLE and when should you use Boolean searching? Unfortunately, there are no absolute answers, but some general advice is emerging. Based on our tests, recommendations from DIALOG, Mead, and West, and comments from other searchers, we can make some recommendations.

Use relevance searching:

- Only when you are doing primarily a subject search.
- Especially when you are searching full-text databases or databases with lengthy abstracts.
- When you want just a few, highly relevant items on a subject.
- When you will be satisfied with no more than the system maximum number of items, even if there are more than that in the database.
- When concepts are of unequal weight and some peripherally relevant items may not contain all of the concepts.
- When you want to browse through a subject to be brought up-to-date on a topic.
- When a Boolean search is too broad and retrieves too many items.
- When search terms are common words that retrieve too much in a Boolean search.
- When a Boolean search is too precisely specified and retrieves too few items.
- If you don't know the database or the information you are searching well.
- You are training novice users who don't want to have to memorize commands and learning operators.

WHEN DOES BOOLEAN WORK BEST?

Continue to use Boolean and proximity operators when:

- You are looking for a known item or known citation.
- You want everything by a particular author.
- Non-subject fields are an important part of your search.
- Your search has concepts that are of equal weight and you want everything on the topic.
- You are an experienced Boolean searcher and it works for you.

Both methods are powerful search techniques. Boolean has the advantage of over twenty years of testing in the real world of searching. Relevance searching is the newcomer in commercial applications, with many enhancements yet to come. Perhaps in another twenty years, with comprehensive thesauri; natural language input, including parsing for parts of speech; and further testing of the best statistical weighting algorithms in large multitopic full-text databases, relevance retrieval will be all we need. For now it is another weapon in the good searcher's arsenal.

REFERENCES

[1] Pritchard-Schoch, Teresa. "Natural Language Comes of Age." *ONLINE* 17, No. 3 (May 1993): pp. 33-43.

[2] Tenopir, Carol. "The New Generation of Online Search Software." *Library Journal* 117 (October 1, 1993): pp. 67-68.

[3] WIN is not the first commercially available online system to go beyond Boolean. That honor probably belongs to Congressional Quarterly's Washington Alert, which has used the Personal Librarian search engine since 1989.

[4] The FREESTYLE thesaurus is a synonym list thesaurus such as *Roget's*, not the kind of thesaurus defined in the ANSI (American National Standards Institute) or ISO (International Standards Organization) standards for use with indexing. It lists only synonyms and word form variants, and does not specify term hierarchies, such as broader terms, narrower terms, etc.

[5] Bjørner, Susanne N. "Output Options: The .WHERE and .WHY of FREESTYLE" *ONLINE* 18, No. 2 (March 1994): pp. 88-91.

Chapter 8
Extensions

A Hypertext Environment for Interacting with Large Databases 469
M. Agosti, G. Gradenigo, and P.G. Marchetti

Automatic Analysis, Theme Generation, and Summarization of Machine-Readable Texts 478
G. Salton, J. Allan, C. Buckley, and A. Singhal

Querying Across Languages: A Dictionary-Based Approach to Multilingual Information Retrieval 484
D.A. Hull and G. Grefenstette

Experiments in Spoken Document Retrieval 493
K. Sparck Jones, G.J.F. Jones, J.T. Foote, and S.J. Young

Video Parsing, Retrieval and Browsing: An Integrated and Content-Based Solution 503
H.J. Zhang, C.Y. Low, S.W. Smoliar, and J.H. Wu

The Automatic Indexing System AIR/PHYS—From Research to Application 513
P. Biebricher, N. Fuhr, G. Lustig, M. Schwantner, and G. Knorz

A News Story Categorization System 518
P.J. Hayes, L.E. Knecht, and M.J. Cellio

Conceptual Information Extraction and Retrieval from Natural Language Input 527
L.F. Rau

A Production Rule System for Message Summarization 534
E. Marsh, H. Hamburger, and R. Grishman

The Application of Linguistic Processing to Automatic Abstract Generation 538
F.C. Johnson, C.D. Paice, W.J. Black, and A.P. Neal

INTRODUCTION

We have so far treated document retrieval as defined or, at any rate, bounded in critical ways. We have restricted ourselves, from the functional point of view, to retrieval as a means of providing access to end documents, offered for the user's consideration as (hopefully) about the topic for which he has an information need. We have also focused, from the data point of view, on documents consisting of continuous natural language text and of familiar or orthodox kinds, like scientific papers or news stories. Finally, we have also limited ourselves, implicitly, from the "spatiotemporal" point of view, to material covering relatively short time spans and in a single language.

But, as the reference in Chapter 2 to searching only titles or assigned subject headings rather than full text, and in Chapter 7 to OKAPI's use for conventional library catalogues, both imply, the notion of retrieval system is far richer and more hospitable than the de facto restrictions listed above might suggest. This is illustrated even by conventional library catalogues. These are intended to provide the user with access to end documents (notably books), but while the file being searched is very limited in the descriptive information it contains about the end documents, it may exploit restricted or artificial description languages or cover a range of natural languages; it may cover end documents from a long period of time; and it may lead to many types of documents, including ones not in continuous text, like dictionaries, or not even in natural language at all, like recorded music or picture books. It is evident, moreover, that retrieval naturally extends both to long-familiar related cases like museum catalogues and, more importantly, to the new cases represented by the wide variety of document and file types in electronic form.

Thus it is not only that the key system concepts we have considered are very general and, hence, widely pertinent ones. It is more importantly the case that the basic models and retrieval techniques we have illustrated are very general ones with a wide range of potential applications. The statistical techniques, in particular, have been claimed as of very broad utility simply because sign systems of many kinds exhibit the same fundamental distributional behaviour (unless they have been knowingly designed, as for some special-purpose codes, to avoid this). The argument is that the kind of statistical apparatus illustrated earlier may be adopted for other neighbouring uses over a range of information access functions—for example, for data extraction or document condensation; to files containing documents of very unconventional kinds, like advertising directories or archives of chemical compounds; to other language modalities, notably speech; and even to other media, like images. However, while statistical facts about information-conveying entities may be useful for many forms of information access, it does not follow that the best specific techniques will be the same or of the same type, or that they do not have to be combined with other, nonstatistical processes. This is well shown by summarising, where, even if lexical statistics about the source text may help to identify key content, simply concatenating important source sentences does not necessarily deliver output summaries that are coherent discourses. Thus for cases involving language, the question is what the relative emphasis on statistical and nonstatistical NLP should be, and how they may complement one another.

It is evident that, in looking outward from core retrieval, there are many distinctive kinds of application, and a family of related tasks, all sharing the common requirement for *content-based* information access. In this chapter, we give illustrative examples, to draw attention especially to the potential uses of existing techniques, to the importance of information access broadly conceived, and to the need to develop and combine methods for a range of access functions in different situations. Technology developments, especially in networking, are offering new opportunities for rapid, end user access to large resources, but, as these are often extremely heterogeneous, they also impose new requirements not only to provide individual functions effectively but to integrate these for the user within a single working environment.

The topics covered in this chapter, and papers chosen, are thus seen as representing the untilled frontier as far as effective automated systems are concerned, not the orderly fields of established information farming. However, because the frontier is an exciting one and because the tasks we consider both spread out in different directions from the core and individually present very difficult challenges, we cannot do more in this section than indicate the main features of the various applications and tasks and the current state of the art. The specific papers we have chosen and cite are thus offered only as leads into the research areas in question, of use now but not necessarily with long-term standing. As further leads, we have also included some collections and surveys in the secondary references.

We have grouped the material under two broad headings: *document and data types* and *information-processing tasks.* Under the first, we consider "nonstandard" types of document, involving special kinds of language or text, like formulae, documents with complex structures and, especially, hypertext as constituting a special type of retrieval file; multilingual or cross-language retrieval as a special case for automated methods; and multimedia retrieval, particularly for speech and image, where automatic content-based indexing and searching is in its infancy. Under the second heading, we examine categorisation, filtering and routing, information extraction, and summarising. Categorisation and filtering are both document allocation tasks, of different kinds, while extraction and summarisation are different versions of the content characterisation task. The terminology used for this whole family of tasks is far from consistent, and the relationships between the tasks are complicated not only because of some intrinsic similarities but because of the fact that some individual pioneer systems subsume several subtasks or can be viewed under several lights (for instance, as addressing extraction or routing), and because of the cross-application of the same processing techniques.

Thus, while statistical techniques may extend quite far toward the more demanding content identification and representation tasks but eventually meet their limit in the areas of extraction and summarisation, there is a complementary extension of NLP techniques across tasks, primarily summarisation and extraction, where some such processing is mandatory but may range from more comprehensive to partial and from "deep" to "shallow", according to the individual application. We do not attempt here to cover or even comment on the current state of NLP but simply include some papers in which, because of the task, it necessarily plays a role, only observing here that the same kind of robust parsing as is described in Strzalkowski's paper in Chapter 6 figures in these other tasks. In the same way, while noting that categorisation and filtering, like relevance feedback in mainstream retrieval, are all cases of machine learning, we do not attempt any comment on learning in general.

DOCUMENT AND DATA TYPES

Specialised Text Forms

Considering first document and data types, some technical application areas are long established as fields for automated retrieval, using both older, conventional controlled-language approaches and newer, natural language–based ones. This is well illustrated by the medical case, with the MEDLINE service offering both MeSH (a thesaurus) and plain natural language searching; by the legal area, where full text was early of interest and where particular types of query, e.g., for case citations, and user need, e.g., for high recall, may occur; and by the chemical world, where searching extends over technical nomenclatures (including subwords like *vinyl* with front and back truncation) and formulae. Patent searching is another specialised retrieval context.

But apart from the sublanguage or even artificial code aspects of, say, chemical formulae, these applications usually fall within the general scope of retrieval as we have hitherto considered it and, further, appear to be essentially amenable to the straightforward, statistically based techniques that have proven themselves for "ordinary" material: this is certainly the case with legal material. However, as the development of full-text searching of news wires illustrates, it may be practically useful, within the context of a routine retrieval system, to offer supplementary resources like the specialised parsers developed by the NLP community and gazetteers to deal with proper names: these may figure in bewilderingly many variants and can present considerable problems of identification (in both senses), especially if they are multiword items or have internal punctuation.

At the same time, as the medical case early showed and as is nowadays common with records and databases of all kinds, it is possible on the one hand to treat controlled language data not only by the same techniques as "ordinary" natural language but also, whenever its terms are named using words drawn from the natural vocabulary, to take them along with any natural text for searching. This is because controlled terms, even if their uses are specialised, have some sense relationships to their usual meanings. Similarly, regardless of whether constraints are placed on attribute values in a conventional (e.g., relational) database, fields may be searched as if their entries were ordinary words or text. Equally, where there are different fields but natural language appears in all of them, the same search technique can sometimes be usefully applied across the fields, disregarding category boundaries, as in conventional library and museum catalogues.

These points are well known, but nevertheless emphasise the flexibility and wide reach of the retrieval notions and technology that we have considered. Thus they can be extended on the one hand to treat *metalevel* documents as *object-level* ones (e.g., the table of contents of a book as just the same as its chapter texts), i.e., to "flatten" multilevel data, but also to treat file items at any level as autonomous documents including, for example, whole organisational directory structures. This is natural in the familiar form of "grepping" as well as in World Wide Web operation, though this does not always also involve the kind of statistical indexing techniques we have presented. The implication, as new Web-browsing services are assuming, is that complex, multilevel, and variegated bodies of information can be treated, as far as retrieval techniques go, as homogeneous both across or at different grain levels, allowing on the one hand rapid skimming over broad areas and on the other more considered analysis in narrow ones. There is, however, a new challenge, for both statistical and nonstatistical techniques, in managing all this data scale and variety effectively. For example, while something useful can nearly always be retrieved even with crude searches, extremes of document length can have drastic effects on document ranking, with very short or very long documents far too highly rated. Again, unexpected term frequency effects may occur because of the very large document and file sizes now available.

It should also be noted that, in complementary fashion, where it is necessary to preserve record structure and explicitly different fields, the statistical techniques developed for simple text data can be extended to combine matching information appropriate to different types of *index key* within the framework of weighted searches delivering a ranked output. This is illustrated by Croft et al. (1990), exploiting inference networks.

Hypertext

Hypertext was often seen, in the eighties, as a panacea for information access problems (see, e.g., Frisse, 1988). But, like expert systems, it has not altogether lived up to that early promise, even while benefiting from the technology development that has made displays and interfaces for the user much more powerful. From the conventional librarian's point of view, some of the claims for hypertext novelty and value as supplying a superstructure for convenient information access, and especially browsing, read much like rediscoveries of familiar notions of indexing and classification.

From one point of view hypertext, and now hypermedia, has been a wild success. The World Wide Web's URLs are hypertext in rampant form, and the direct manipulation interface with its click-and-point modus operandi has made nonsequential "reading" of an information resource easy and productive. But from the point of view of automatic indexing and searching, the reality is more primitive, so hypertext systems have deficiencies that the glossy user tools do not wholly overcome. Thus, as far as the creation of hypertext structure is concerned, links reflecting deeper conceptual relations are normally man-made, while automatic links are limited to syntactically defined or primitive lexical ones. The man-made links have the same advantages and disadvantages in sometimes capturing, and sometimes missing, relationships as human indexing elsewhere. At the same time, recognising, automatically, that two sources are "really" about the same thing and should thus be directly linked has made no more advance within the hypertext world than in the retrieval one, though in some cases hypertext structure can be leveraged from the rich and explicit formats that characterise many machine sources.

From the searching point of view, making navigation easy for the user has its well-known downside, the user lost far from home. But while in individual applications helpful search mechanisms can be implemented, the challenge of providing effective general strategies that combine techniques developed for document retrieval with the use of other, independently provided link structures, and with direct manipulation, has still to be met. There is further interest here in the need to support searching across both object and metalevels of information (i.e., over the end sources and the hypertext structure), and also over the yet higher level of the user's own temporal session.

The facility with which hypertext links can now be created and manipulated, and the value that is added to hypertext structures by the multiple presentation resources now available with any windows interface, nevertheless make hypertext a significant new file and search environment; and the development of text-based methods in document retrieval has suggested similar approaches to the creation and use of hypertext. These are primarily extensions of the very old idea of association nets (see Chapter 2) but applied to connect smaller text segments rather than large documents as wholes. The essential point is that, while automatically created links based on single words are far too weak, the perception of content relations that justifies manual linking can be automatically replicated through the computation of similarities between text passages based on many shared (and weighted) words. The work reported in Salton and Allan (1993) illustrates these ideas, showing in particular how the same basic comparison notions apply both to form and search hypertext. This paper and the one by Salton et al. included here further show how the approach naturally leads to the creation of simple, excerpt-based summaries. Relevance feedback techniques common for retrieval can also be applied within this framework, for adaptive hypertext. Such work needs, however, validation on a much larger scale.

An alternative point of view on the relationship between hypertext and retrieval is that the notion of hypertext should be the conceptual base for information systems, so retrieval is simply embedded in a hypertext environment. The paper by Agosti et al. selected for this chapter adopts this position. The approach thus emphasises the role of system architectures and also, given that human decision making plays an important part, however much hypertext construction and use is automated, the provision of tools for hypertext management, as shown in Agosti et al. (1996).

The many issues to be addressed, and possibilities offered, by hypertext and more generally hypermedia are explored in the *Information Processing and Management* (1993) special issue, and in Agosti and Smeaton (1996). The problems that hypermedia indexing and searching present are also considered later in connection with speech and image retrieval.

Multilingual Files

Much of the mainstream IR work covered in this volume has been done for English language material. In general, statistically based techniques can be applied to other languages (as the TREC work on Spanish, for instance, shows), though much more work is needed on Asian languages, and any processes relying on explicitly linguistic knowledge, whether stemming or phrasal parsing, cannot be generic in the same way. Indeed stemming in particular is a problem for word compounding languages. But in all these cases, as in our discussion as a whole, the tacit assumption has been that systems are confined to a single language and thus that query formation, albeit by general methods, is geared to one specific language or another. It is only if explicitly *interlingual* indexing languages, like the Universal Decimal Classification (UDC), are used that a single query can be applied regardless of the language or number of languages in the file. For ordinary natural language searching, the user's request has to be reformulated in as many languages as are represented in the file. With the growth of full-text files and easier access to multiple files in different languages, there is increasing interest in appropriate strategies for *cross-language* retrieval by automatic query translation or for multilingual query formation without undue user effort.

In conventional retrieval contexts, as exemplified by the many international bibliographic services providing access to databases in different languages, a number of intermediate strategies are applied. In some cases, where document and request indexing make use of thesaurus or subject headings, translation equivalents for the index terms are provided by specially constructed multilingual thesauri. In others, reference resources are provided to assist the human request translator, notably in the area of technical terminology. The increasing use of corpora to gather specific data about word uses and contexts, typically as a support for machine translation, and the spread of automatic and semiautomatic translation methods along with the increasing provision of large translation lexicons, may all facilitate the request translation process for the human searcher and help to automate it. However, the key problem is that with the short contexts typical of requests, there is little leverage for word sense selection. On the other hand, the fact that index descriptions can be simple means that when a little more text is available, current language analysis techniques may be able to deliver enough information for contextual disambiguation and may also be applied to files to gather pertinent collocational information to filter alternative translations.

Salton (1970) is an early study of multilingual retrieval within an IR framework of a modern type, but it crucially relied on a manually constructed translation thesaurus. Fully automatic cross-language and multilingual retrieval exploiting only general text-processing methods or conventional, existing *word* dictionaries is an area where very little has been done so far, primarily because of the difficulty of obtaining suitable test data. But we have included one recent paper, by Hull and Grefenstette (1996), to signal the growing importance of this theme.

Multimedia

So far, also, we have considered only written language(s). The most exciting current developments are in content-based retrieval for other media and from multimedia files, in particular from speech, graphics, and image files. The individual characteristics of the different media mean that they each present distinctive indexing and searching problems. However, there are also important issues where documents are intrinsically combinations of media, as with television and video but also with more conventional data like museum catalogues (cf. Lees 1993). Thus, in some cases, the information provided by any one medium is only partial and perhaps even completely incomprehensible out of context (e.g., an enlarged detail photograph of a painting). But more generally, full information is recovered only from the integrated combination of the several media. This is clear from many news reports, for example. Multimedia sources like video may also present difficult segmentation problems to recover natural units since these are not necessarily externally marked and have to be recovered from the various internal features of the file item. This is exemplified by the separation of stories in a newscast, which is not simply correlated with visual scene changes.

Automatic retrieval for spoken documents, especially when these are autonomous items without accompanying images, would appear the least challenging case, if only because speech is language and spoken documents have the same general language properties as written ones; but word recognition is much more difficult, especially for more informal material like spontaneous dialogue.

From a logical point of view, speech recognition can be treated as *transcription* to text, even if this is not explicitly, or cannot be fully, done in practice. Speech recognition performance can thus be characterised in terms of transcription errors. The continuing advance of speech recognition technology, especially over the last decade, has achieved very high performance for good quality (i.e., clearly spoken, quietly surrounded) speech, but for natural speech in ordinary surroundings, the transcription success rate may be no more than 25%, and in general with speech all kinds of transcription error can be expected. Nevertheless, as recorded speech is everywhere, there is a natural interest in spoken document retrieval and in whether established retrieval methods can be successfully adapted to this new context.

In principle, the way these techniques exploit redundancy should be highly appropriate to the speech case, since language redundancy should overcome both deficiencies in the correct recognition of any individual word in all its occurrences (including the incorrect recognition in its stead of some other word) and deficiencies in the overall indexing coverage of whole documents. Thus it could be expected that search term combination will be important as a noise filter in a manner analogous to, and enhancing, its content filtering function. (Though we are not covering optical character recognition [OCR] directly in these readings, we should note that such retrieval strategies should be effective for OCR for similar reasons [Taghva et al., 1996].)

Earlier work with speech data focused on so-called "topic spotting" for known information categories, rather than regular retrieval (see, e.g., Rose, 1991; Rose et al., 1992). Spoken document retrieval in the more usual sense of retrieval is represented by the paper by Sparck Jones et al. selected here, with its follow-up in Jones et al. (1996), and by Wechsler and Schäuble (1996). These show that speech retrieval using state-of-the-art speech recognition and retrieval technology works respectably, though more robustness and significant scaling up are required for practical applications.

The type of technique applied is also used to deal with the speech element of combined multimedia retrieval, as in Hauptmann and Witbrock (1997), where the combination of different media can act as another reinforcement device to overcome the noise in individual media. At the same time, media combinations may make it easier to deal with one of the major problems of retrieval in the speech, as opposed to text, case, namely that it takes time to scan output documents. Other media may help to focus on specific segments of a speech stream, for instance, corresponding discontinuities in a picture stream: failing this help, techniques analogous to those applied in passage retrieval are needed to locate the best "stretches" of speech for the user to sample.

Technological advances have brought not only speech but, more strikingly, image processing to the fore, particularly in the attractive form of direct image display at the user interface. However, retrieval from graphics and image files present far more, and far more varied, problems for indexing and searching than any of the other media considered, especially for the development of general as opposed to application-specific techniques. Conventional picture files are ordinarily indexed by explicitly assigned text keys or perhaps via naturally accompanying text. The challenge is to provide automatic content identification, building up from primitive, content-relevant features to higher-level combination keys and descriptions that are both generally applicable and powerful enough for retrieval queries couched in such terms as "Find pictures of plants" when submitted to a broad coverage file.

The underlying problem is of course a hard AI one, so the current question is what modest but useful approaches can be provided. The present situation is that some general-purpose features can be recognised (e.g., lines), though this is of little value unless they are understood to have some specific semantic interpretation (as in military applications), as can higher-level shapes (e.g., a yellow blob) and overall colour characterisation (as by a histogram). These higher-level characterisations may be of use for matching an input query in picture form. But even with such rudimentary forms of image description, search is tricky because of such factors as change of orientation and zooming. Particular forms of higher-level feature configuration can also be useful for specialised applications like face recognition.

The difficulties of handling images alone, especially without images as queries or a reasonably easy way of expressing queries in terms of picture-relevant features, have therefore encouraged combination strategies using a variety of search keys, including nonimage ones. These are illustrated on the one hand by Ogle and Stonebraker's extension of conventional database technology (1995), and on the other by the multimedia projects reported in Wactlar et al. (1996) and Hauptmann and Witbrock (1997), and in Faloutsos et al. (1994) and Flickner et al. (1995), the latter showing basic image retrieval techniques that are already in the marketplace. The paper we have included here, by Zhang et al. (1995), illustrates the range of problems to be addressed and techniques under investigation for video retrieval. Video is an interesting case since some methods, for individual images, may be applicable elsewhere, while others are connected with the existence of extended image sequences.

The overview papers by Enser (1993) and Cawkell (1993), the *IEEE Computer* (1995) special issue, and the two collections in Ruthven (1996) and Maybury (1997) cover the state of the multimedia retrieval art as a whole.

RELATED TASKS

The other dimension to be examined here is related information access tasks. We have excluded, for these readings, database query in the conventional sense, where the information in the base has already been "codified". However, there are other important tasks that are related to document retrieval in critical respects: because they are concerned with what is important, from a content point of view, in documents; and because they do, or may, exploit similar techniques to identify this. It is indeed proper to assume a family of information access needs and tasks with no hard-and-fast divisions between them and to seek automated information management systems that offer a corresponding range of functions.

Categorisation

IR is essentially a *classification* problem, concerned with separating wanted (or preferred) from unwanted. It subsumes the classification achieved by indexing and the classification imposed by searching. From another point of view, IR is primarily concerned with *assignment,* as in assignment of documents to subject pigeonholes or to search queries. Under this perspective, some forms of classification (as in the initial construction of document or term groups) are not concerned with assignment but when established become vehicles for future assignment. For automated assignment, suitable assignment key sets or rules are needed (as with entry words with a thesaurus), and there is an obvious advantage if these keys can themselves be automatically identified by the analysis of already classified training data. This is a *learning* process and, as category membership changes with new assignments so the key sets or rules are themselves modified, it may become a *dynamic* learning process.

The term *categorisation,* while sometimes used broadly as a synonym for classification, is more often restricted to the assignment case, and we use it thus here. Categorisation may still take various forms within retrieval. One is text assignment to index headings not themselves just extracted from the text as simple index terms are. An obvious example is assignment to independently defined subject headings or thesaurus labels so the learning stage is designed to identify distinguishing text terms or term combinations that will justify future assignment to one such index category rather than another. Maron (1961) was an early study in this area, while the paper by Biebricher et al. (1988) in this chapter illustrates this application of classification in an operational setting.

The underlying presumption in this case is, of course, that such indexing categories will be useful for future retrieval, not necessarily only individually but in combination as specified by requests. At the same time, as mentioned earlier, ad hoc retrieval can be viewed as direct document assignment to some single, and perhaps very specific, user-defined category (with embedded learning in the relevance feedback case). There are clearly intermediate states. One common one is where there are broad topic categories, designed perhaps for classes of users (often information analysts), to which documents are assigned. This is illustrated for the speech case by Rose (1991) already mentioned, and for text in the paper by Hayes et al. (1988) reproduced here, as well as by Apte et al. (1994), Lewis (1992, 1995), and Lewis and Gale (1994); see also the *ACM Transactions on Information Systems* (1994) special issue.

Hayes et al.'s paper does not apply statistical techniques but, rather, illustrates both the use of some explicit (though rather crude) NLP and of a rule-based approach, with manually constructed patterns; and it has been applied operationally (Hayes and Weinstein, 1991). Riloff and Lehnert (1994) describe a more elaborate use of information extraction by NLP techniques for a more refined text categorisation case. This work, and other categorisation effort figuring in Jacobs (1993), falls in the overlap area for several tasks, including information extraction in its own right, and summarising, where common techniques for robust language processing like those also used by Strzalkowski (as discussed in Chapter 6) are particularly useful or indeed essential. The disadvantage of Hayes et al.'s approach is that the patterns have to be built manually: in the statistical approaches, like Apte et al.'s, rule induction is automatic.

Filtering

Categorisation, especially when applied to an incoming stream of documents and followed by transmission to selected users, leads to retrieval in another guise.

Thus we have in principle so far assumed that retrieval is for the one-off request. However, persistent or standing interest *profiles* also represent a familiar form of user need, and automated services, following traditional library practice, early offered "selective dissemination of information". Here individual users or user groups were circulated with potentially relevant documents from incoming material (see Barker et al. [1972] and Sprague and Freudenreich [1978]). Modern manifestations of this process are usually labelled *routing* or *filtering.*

The particular version of the document categorisation task it requires, while having much in common with conventional searching, has some distinctive features. The situation is essentially the inverse of the usual one (see Belkin and Croft, 1992): in the usual case, all the documents in the file are considered in relation to a query, and hence ranked for it. In the filtering case, a new document is considered in relation to all the queries and either assigned to each or not, so each user's output is either just one document or none. However, when taken over time, filtering system performance can be evaluated using recall and precision, as in the one-off case.

But the main, significant distinctive feature of the filtering task is that it is much more open to performance improvement through learning than is retrieval for ad hoc requests. Information about the user's preferences can be accumulated over time, and hence over substantial data samples, making techniques like statistically based relevance feedback very effective. The TREC Programme clearly shows this (see the Harman paper in Chapter 4 and other TREC references there). In addition, the user may be more committed to query formulation or output assessment, since the cost-benefit payoff is likely to be better.

Document filtering is thus, as Belkin and Croft (1992) argue, a task where modern statistically based methods drawn from retrieval appear particularly appropriate; and the task itself is becoming increasingly important as a way of dealing with, e.g., high-volume news feeds or incoming material flooding the networks. The well-tried methods we have introduced in earlier sections may have much more to offer as a base for World Wide Web "crawlers" than some existing, very naive, implementations of putatively intelligent agents. We have not, however, been able to include a modern paper reporting actual tests on this fine-grained routing, as opposed to the broader categorisation examples, largely because there has been no serious experiment with it outside the TREC context, where it has been somewhat artificially interpreted.

Information Extraction

Two other key tasks in the present broad family are information extraction, or mining (with consequent knowledge-base construction), and summarising. The distinction between these two is essentially between selection from, and condensation of, source document content, though there is also a secondary distinction in that a summary is normally a new text, while extracted information may not be reformulated as text but rather entered into an information base. These two tasks are nevertheless clearly related to one another and to retrieval in that extracting a key fact and expressing it linguistically is providing one form of abstract, just as an index description even consisting only of a list of words constitutes another, very weak, form of summary. A phrasal subject description of a document is more obviously a summary, albeit a minimal one, through having the textual character that summaries also have. Extracted facts, on the other hand, may also have a complex individual or linked structure, e.g., indicating the properties and relations of entities, which may be represented in a sub- or controlled language like an indexing language.

The range of possibilities in this area as a whole is considerable. It covers, for example, whether the definition of what is important is determined by the source document itself or is externally supplied to guide the selection of information; whether the selected information, especially if it is at all complicated, is viewed more as a means to the end of reaching the source document or as constituting a new autonomous document in its own right; and so forth.

Fact extraction, or *information extraction* as it is now usually called, has been of interest, especially for restricted types of text or subject domain, since the sixties, as illustrated by Sager's early work on (so-called) formatted databases (1978). It is currently an active research area under the US Message Understanding Conferences (MUC) Programme, where there is less concern with obtaining a regularised representation of the content of a source and more with identifying specific types of information within it (Chinchor et al., 1993; MUC-6, 1996; Sundheim and Chinchor, 1993). The main feature of this work is thus on the one hand the specification of the kind of domain information to be identified in and extracted from a source, and on the other the development of methods for recognising this information under all the variant forms in which it may figure in a text. Fact extraction thus requires explicit NLP, ranging from the more or the less shallow, according to the needed coverage of the source and nature of the required information. Work in this area has called for robust as well as flexible processing to allow at least some of the required information to be recovered, even if not all can be captured. This task is typically distinguished from indexing by the need to determine true discourse entities, to recognise abstract entities like events, and to establish patterns of entity relationship. However, corpus statistics can support robust processing by indicating syntactic or semantic preferences for interpretation.

Some work in this area has been demonstrably successful and is the outcome of well-developed experience of NLP. The work includes some focusing on both the extraction of units of information and their integration into an integrated knowledge base supporting retrieval. This is represented by Rau's paper reproduced in this section and also by Jacobs and Rau (1988, 1990). Anderson et al. (1992) report on extraction and subsequent report generation. The work being done in this area, both within and apart from MUC, is by now substantial and cannot be considered in detail here, beyond noting a general convergence on robust parsing designed to pick up key text elements and the continuing dependence on application-specific content requirements and representation frames. The MUC work involves extensive evaluation for correctness of extraction and frame filling, but, in general in this area, there has been little serious evaluation on the use of the knowledge bases for retrieval (though McKeown and Radev [1995] describe the formation of summaries from such inputs). The types of approach adopted for extraction are further illustrated in Jacobs and Rau (1993) and MUC-6 (1996).

Summarising

Progress in summarising has been much less visible. Extraction-type strategies have been applied to summarising, as in DeJong's notable early work (1982), but their dependence on prior specification of the kind of source content that is important (and hence is meat for the summary) is a serious limitation, and there are real problems about providing guiding hands for open and unrestricted documents. Some research work, applying various text understanding strategies, including the use of discourse structure but confined to particular application areas, is illustrated by Hahn (1990) and Ciravegna (1995). The paper by Marsh et al. (1984), which has been selected for inclusion in this chapter, shows how largely-general NLP techniques, when supplemented by application-specific semantic categories and patterns, can be successfully applied to the derivation of very simple summaries.

At the same time, for summarising—unlike fact extraction—there has also been a serious attempt, initiated by Luhn in the fifties (see several papers in Schultz, 1968), to apply the statistical approach so successfully used for indexing and retrieval to the identification not of key words, but of key sentences, which could then be run together to form an abstract text. Source document content was not directly, but only indirectly, condensed. This statistical approach has never been very successful. This is in part because of the difficulty of bringing methods well suited to the coarser needs of indexing as the means of indicating important concepts to bear on the much finer needs of summarising; and in part because of the difficulty of producing coherent summary text by concatenating independent extracted sentences. Attempts have been made to "soup up" purely statistical extraction by exploiting other importance cues and to smooth the output text, especially to deal with dangling anaphors. We illustrate some of this work, in a fairly sophisticated form, in the paper by Johnson et al. (1993).

Paice (1990) chronicles the early stages of this persistent line of research, following Luhn through such work as that reported by Pollock and Zamora (1975) and by Paice (1981) and Paice and Husk (1987), further seen recently in Brandow et al. (1995). The conclusion to be drawn from it is that there appear to be clear limits to the scope of statistical techniques when applied to surface text to seek information entities more complex than simple or compound "unit concepts", so the challenge is whether statistics can be effectively combined with limited NLP, given that full NLP, other than for specific applications, is off the horizon.

We conclude with summarising, as this task both extends over a range from modest to full blown and is one that needs, urgently, to be addressed to help users trying to cope with the masses of material they are nowadays offered. Sparck Jones (1993) presents a framework for thinking about summarising, while the range of issues and ideas in this area of growing interest appear in Endres-Niggemeyer et al. (1995) and in the *Information Processing and Management* (1995) special issue.

Finally, as general references for this whole section, we note Jacobs (1993) and Cole et al. (1997).

SELECTED READINGS

Agosti et al. (1992) propose a conceptual architecture as a basis for hypertext systems, in fairly formal terms, and illustrate the functionality this basic model supports, including semantic association, navigation, and sequential and associative reading. The model is illustrated by a prototype system showing its retrieval mode. The authors' concern is to provide a systematic underpinning for hypertext in general, avoiding ad hoc aggregations of facilities lacking real power.

The work reported here by Salton et al. (1994) describes a range of studies relating to hypertext and covering automatic text decomposition and linking at different levels, text theme identification, travel over associated sets of texts, and the selection of text excerpts from related nodes to form summaries. The whole is a systematic application of the statistical approaches originally developed for mainstream retrieval, illustrated by examples taken from tests with a large encyclopedia. The main issue left open is scaling up to much larger and more varied files.

Hull and Grefenstette (1996) present an experiment in multilingual document retrieval via query translation. The approach used for the test was to take French versions of English requests, carefully prepared by human translators, and then translate these automatically back into English for retrieval from an English file. This allowed comparison between native and foreign language retrieval. The automatic translation was done with a conventional bilingual dictionary. The tests showed that query translation was feasible, though, when done simplistically without regard to multiword expressions, with considerable loss of performance.

Sparck Jones et al. (1996) address spoken document retrieval, combining state-of-the-art speech recognition methods with established retrieval techniques hitherto used for text, in experiments with a small database of spoken messages. The paper reviews issues in speech retrieval, reports on the data preparation, and describes the speech processing used in the tests, along with retrieval performance comparisons for different term weighting schemes as well as against a text retrieval benchmark. This last shows that the loss of performance with speech was not large, but this was for a favourable data case.

Video data requires considerable manipulation for retrieval, not least because it is extremely bulky. Zhang et al. (1995) describe the parsing techniques they use to segment video data and extract representative key frames from the larger source to form the retrieval file. The images in this file are then indexed by simple, general content representation features like colour, texture, and shape, as well as temporal features like camera motion. The paper illustrates retrieval methods using these image descriptions, which are applied within an interactive facility supporting browsing.

AIR/PHYS is an established automatic indexing system supported by a large descriptor dictionary and applied to a substantial document database. Biebricher et al.'s paper (1988) describes the very sophisticated assignment system used to determine the appropriate index terms for incoming documents, applying statistical methods in an iterative way intended to allow for dependencies between the descriptors. The work shows how ideas stemming from retrieval research are used in a large operational system.

The categorisation work presented here by Hayes et al. (1988) relies on sets of manually constructed pattern-action rules to correlate text features with class labels. The patterns include linguistic features like syntactic word classes, as well as pseudolinguistic criteria like proximity. Unlike the previous system, that described here does not use statistics as a basis for categorisation. The paper reports a test on news material, with evaluation measured by recall and precision and complemented by failure analysis.

Rau (1988) describes the SCISOR system, developed to process news stories. This applies robust parsing, combining top-down expectation methods with bottom-up ones to extract information about entities, their properties, and relationships, which can then be incorporated in an integrated network representation of the real-world situations or events reported in the stories. For retrieval, this network can be searched using marker-passing techniques. It can also be exploited to produce summaries instantiating generic semantic frames.

A rather different approach to text interpretation and representation is used by Marsh et al. (1984). In this case, processing is used to build a regularised version of the text in a format in which text information constituents are assigned to application-specific headings. Summarisation is designed to extract format lines, guided by general criteria as to the type of information that is most important for the application domain. It is driven by rules drawing inferences to connect the initial text information items and to score the different lines in a representation. The paper reports a test and evaluation.

Finally, Johnson et al. (1993) describe strategies for improving abstracts based on sentence selection. Abstracts consisting of extracted source sentences normally suffer from lack of coherence, attributable largely to the presence of unresolved anaphoric expressions. In this work, sentence selection is guided by rules exploiting both indicator words and phrases and information about sentence structure obtained from parsing. The rules are designed to identify important, free-standing sentences that could form an appropriate and readable abstract.

REFERENCES

*Note: *** after a reference indicates a selected reading.*

ACM Transactions on Information Systems (1994) Special issue: Text categorisation. *ACM Transactions on Information Systems*, **12**, 231–333.

Agosti, M., Crestani, F., and Melucci, M. (1996) Design and implementation of a tool for the automatic construction of hypertexts for information retrieval. *Information Processing and Management*, **32**, 459–476.

Agosti, M., Gradenigo, G., and Marchetti, P.G. (1992) A hypertext environment for interacting with large databases. *Information Processing and Management*, **28**, 371–387.***

Agosti, M., and Smeaton, A.F. (Eds.) (1996) *Information Retrieval and Hypertext*. Boston: Kluwer Academic Publishers.

Anderson, P.M., Hayes, P.J., Huettner, A.K., Schmandt, L.M., Nirenburg, I.B., and Weinstein, S.P. (1992) Automatic extraction of facts from press releases to generate news stories. In *Proceedings of the Third Conference on Applied Natural Language Processing, Association for Computational Linguistics*, pp. 170–177. San Francisco: Morgan Kaufmann.

Apte, C., Damerau, F., and Weiss, S.M. (1994) Towards language-independent automated learning of text categorisation methods. In W.B. Croft and C.J. van Rijsbergen (Eds.), *Proceedings of the 17th Annual International Conference on Research and Development in Information Retrieval*, pp. 23–30. London: Springer-Verlag.

Barker, F.H., Veal, D.C., and Wyatt, B.K. (1972) Towards automatic profile construction. *Journal of Documentation*, **28**, 44–55.

Belkin, N.J., and Croft, W.B. (1992) Information filtering and information retrieval: Two sides of the same coin? *Communications of the ACM*, **35**(12), 29–38.

Biebricher, B., Fuhr, N., Lustig, G., Schwanter, M., and Knorz, G. (1988) The automatic indexing system AIR/PHYS—from research to application. In Y. Chiaramella (Ed.), *Proceedings of the 11th Annual International Conference on Research and Development in Information Retrieval*, pp. 333–342. New York: Association for Computing Machinery.***

Brandow, R., Mitze, K., and Rau, L.F. (1995) Automatic condensation of electronic publications by sentence selection. *Information Processing and Management*, **31**, 675–686.

Cawkell, A.E. (1993) *Indexing Collections of Electronic Images: A Review*. British Library Research Review 15. London: British Library.

Chinchor, N., Hirschman, L., and Lewis, D.D. (1993) Evaluating message understanding systems: An analysis of the Third Message Understanding Conference (MUC-3). *Computational Linguistics*, **19**, 409–449.

Ciravegna, F. (1995) Understanding messages in a diagnostic domain. *Information Processing and Management*, **31**, 687–702.

Cole, R.A., Mariani, J., Uszkoreit, H., Zaenen, A., and Zue, V. (Eds.) (1997) *Survey of the State of the Art of Human Language Technology*. Cambridge: Cambridge University Press. (Available via http://www.cse.ogi.edu/CSLU/HLTsurvey/.)

Croft, W.B., Krovetz, R., and Turtle, H. (1990) Interactive retrieval of complex documents. *Information Processing and Management*, **26**, 593–613.

DeJong, G.F. (1982) An overview of the FRUMP system. In W.H. Lehnert and M.D. Ringle (Eds.), *Strategies for Natural Language Processing*, pp. 149–176. Hillsdale, NJ: Lawrence Erlbaum.

Endres-Niggemeyer, B., Hobbs, J., and Sparck Jones, K. (Eds.) (1995) *Summarising Text for Intelligent Communication*. Dagstuhl Seminar Report 79, 13.12–19.12.93 (9350), IBFI, Schloss Dagstuhl, Wadern, Germany. (Available via http://www.bid.fh-hannover.de/SimSum/Abstract/.)

Enser, P.G.B. (1993) Query analysis in a visual information retrieval context. *Journal of Document and Text Management*, **1**, 25–52.

Faloutsos, C., Barber, R., Flickner, M., Hafner, J., Niblack, W., Petkovic, D., and Equitz, W. (1994) Efficient and effective querying by image content. *Journal of Intelligent Information Systems*, **3**, 231–262.

Flickner, M., Sawhney, H., Niblack, W., Ashley, J., Huang, Q., Dom, B., Gorkani, M., Hafner, J., Lee, D., Petkovic, D., Steek, D., and Yankee, P. (1995) Query by image and video content: The QBIC system. *IEEE Computer*, **28**(9), 23–32.

Frisse, M.E. (1988) Searching for information in a hypertext medical handbook. *Communications of the ACM*, **31**, 880–887.

Hahn, U. (1990) Topic parsing: Accounting for text macro structures in full-text analysis. *Information Processing and Management*, **26**, 135–170.

Hauptmann, A.G., and Witbrock, M.J. (1997) Informedia: News on demand; multimedia information acquisition and retrieval. In M. Maybury (Ed.), *Intelligent Multimedia Information Retrieval*. Cambridge, MA: AAAI Press/MIT Press. In the press.

Hayes, P.J., Knecht, L., and Cellio, M. (1988) A news story categorisation system. In *Proceedings of the Second Conference on Applied Natural Language Processing, Association for Computational Linguistics*, pp. 9–17. San Francisco: Morgan Kaufmann.***

Hayes, P.J., and Weinstein, S.P. (1991) CONSTRUE/TIS: A system for content-based indexing of a database of news stories. In *Proceedings of the Second Annual Conference on Innovative Applications of Artificial Intelligence*, pp. 49–64. Cambridge, MA: AAAI Press/MIT Press.

Hull, D.A., and Grefenstette, G. (1996) Querying across languages: A dictionary-based approach to multilingual information retrieval. In H.-P. Frei, D.K. Harman, P. Schäuble, and R. Wilkinson (Eds.), *Proceedings of the 19th Annual International Conference on Research and Development in Information Retrieval*, pp. 49–57. New York: Association for Computing Machinery.***

IEEE Computer (1995) Special issue: Content-based image retrieval systems. *IEEE Computer*, **28**(9), 18–62.

Information Processing and Management (1993) Special issue: Hypertext and information retrieval. *Information Processing and Management*, **29**, 383–396.

Information Processing and Management (1995) Special issue: Summarising text. *Information Processing and Management*, **31**, 625–751.

Jacobs, P.S. (Ed.) (1993) *Text-Based Intelligent Systems.* Hillsdale, NJ: Lawrence Erlbaum.

Jacobs, P.S., and Rau, L.F. (1988) Natural language techniques for intelligent information retrieval. In Y. Chiaramella (Ed.), *Proceedings of the 11th Annual International Conference on Research and Development in Information Retrieval,* pp. 85–99. New York: Association for Computing Machinery.

Jacobs, P.S., and Rau, L.F. (1990) SCISOR: Extracting information from on-line news. *Communications of the ACM,* **33**(11), 88–97.

Jacobs, P.S., and Rau, L.F. (1993) Innovations in text interpretation. *Artificial Intelligence,* **63**, 143–191.

Johnson, F.C., Paice, C.D., Black, W.J., and Neal, A.P. (1993) The application of linguistic processing to automatic abstract generation. *Journal of Document and Text Management,* **1**, 215–241.***

Jones, G.J.F., Foote, J.T., Sparck Jones, K., and Young, S.J. (1996) Retrieving spoken documents by combining multiple index sources. In H.-P. Frei, D.K. Harman, P. Schäuble, and R. Wilkinson (Eds.), *Proceedings of the 19th Annual International Conference on Research and Development in Information Retrieval,* pp. 30–38. New York: Association for Computing Machinery.

Lees, D. (Ed.) (1993) *Museums and Interactive Multimedia: Proceedings of an International Conference held in Cambridge, England, 20–24 September 1993.* Cambridge, England: Museum Documentation Association; Pittsburgh, PA: Archives and Museum Informatics.

Lewis, D.D. (1992) An evaluation of phrasal and clustered representations on a text categorization task. In N.J. Belkin, P. Ingwersen, and A.M. Pejtersen (Eds.), *Proceedings of the 15th Annual International Conference on Research and Development in Information Retrieval,* pp. 37–50. New York: Association for Computing Machinery.

Lewis, D.D. (1995) Evaluating and optimising autonomous text classification systems. In E.A. Fox, P. Ingwersen, and R. Fidel (Eds.), *Proceedings of the 18th Annual International Conference on Research and Development in Information Retrieval,* pp. 246–254. New York: Association for Computing Machinery.

Lewis, D.D., and Gale, W.A. (1994) A sequential algorithm for training text classifiers. In W.B. Croft and C.J. van Rijsbergen (Eds.), *Proceedings of the 17th Annual International Conference on Research and Development in Information Retrieval,* pp. 3–12. London: Springer-Verlag.

McKeown, K., and Radev, D.R. (1995) Generating summaries of multiple news articles. In E.A. Fox, P. Ingwersen, and R. Fidel (Eds.), *Proceedings of the 18th Annual International Conference on Research and Development in Information Retrieval,* pp. 74-82. New York: Association for Computing Machinery.

Maron, M.E. (1961) Automatic indexing: An experimental inquiry. *Journal of the Association for Computing Machinery,* **8**, 404–417.

Marsh, E., Hamburger, H., and Grishman, R. (1984) A production rule system for message summarisation. In *AAAI-84, Proceedings of the American Association for Artificial Intelligence,* pp. 243–246. Cambridge, MA: AAAI Press/MIT Press.***

Maybury, M. (Ed.) (1997) *Intelligent Multimedia Information Retrieval.* Cambridge, MA: AAAI Press/MIT Press.

MUC-6 (1996) *Proceedings of the Sixth Message Understanding Conference (MUC-6).* San Francisco: Morgan Kaufmann.

Ogle, V.E., and Stonebraker, M. (1995) Chabot: Retrieval from a relational database of images. *IEEE Computer,* **28**(9), 40–48.

Paice, C.D. (1981) The automatic generation of literature abstracts: An approach based on the identification of self-identifying phrases. In R.N. Oddy, S.E. Robertson, C.J. van Rijsbergen, and P. W. Williams (Eds.), *Information Retrieval Research,* pp. 172–191. London: Butterworths.

Paice, C.D. (1990) Constructing literature abstracts by computer: Techniques and prospects. *Information Processing and Management,* **26**, 171–186.

Paice, C.D., and Husk, G.D. (1987) Towards the automatic recognition of anaphoric features in English text: The impersonal pronouns. *Computer Speech and Language,* **2**, 109–132.

Pollock, J.J., and Zamora, A. (1975) Automatic abstracting research at the Chemical Abstracts Service. *Journal of Chemical Information and Computing Science,* **15**, 226–232.

Rau, L.F. (1988) Conceptual information extraction and retrieval from natural language input. In *RIAO 88,* pp. 424–437. Paris: Centre des Hautes Etudes Internationales d'Informatique Documentaire.***

Riloff, E., and Lehnert, W. (1994) Information extraction as a basis for high-precision text classification. *ACM Transactions on Information Systems,* **12**, 296–333.

Rose, R.C. (1991) Techniques for information retrieval from speech messages. *Lincoln Laboratory Journal,* **4**, 45–59.

Rose, R.C., Chang, E.I., and Lippman, R.P. (1992) Techniques for information retrieval from voice messages. In *ICASSP-92, Proceedings of the International Conference on Acoustics, Speech and Signal Processing, S5-17,* pp. 317–320. New York: Institute of Electrical and Electronics Engineers.

Ruthven, I. (1996) (Ed.) *Multimedia Information Retrieval, Glasgow 1995.* London: Springer-Verlag.

Sager, N. (1978) Natural language information formatting: The automatic conversion of texts to a structured database. *Advances in Computers,* **17**, 89–162.

Salton, G. (1970) Automatic processing of foreign language documents. *Journal of the American Society for Information Science,* **21**, 187–194.

Salton, G., and Allan, J. (1993) Selective text utilisation and text traversal. In *Proceedings of Hypertext-93,* pp. 131–144. Washington, DC: Association for Computing Machinery.

Salton, G., Allan, J., Buckley, C., and Singhal, A. (1994) Automatic analysis, theme generation, and summarization of machine-readable texts. *Science,* **264**, 1421–1426.***

Schultz, C.K. (Ed.) (1968) *H.P. Luhn: Pioneer of Information Science.* New York: Spartan Books.

Sparck Jones, K. (1993) What might be in a summary? In G. Knorz, J. Krause, and C. Womsa-Hacker (Eds.), pp. 9–26. *Information Retrieval 93: Von der Modellierung zur Anwendung,* Konstanz, Germany: Universitaetsverlag Konstanz.

Sparck Jones, K., Jones, G.J.F., Foote, J.T., and Young, S.J. (1996) Experiments in spoken document retrieval. *Information Processing and Management,* **32**, 399–419.***

Sprague, R.J., and Freudenreich, L.B. (1978) Building better SDI profiles for users of large, multidisciplinary data bases. *Journal of the American Society for Information Science,* **29**, 278–282.

Sundheim, B.M., and Chinchor, N.A. (1993) Survey of the Message Understanding Conferences. In *Proceedings of the Human Language Technology Workshop,* pp. 56–60. San Francisco: Morgan Kaufmann.

Taghva, K., Borsack, J., and Condit, A. (1996) Evaluation of model-based retrieval effectiveness with OCR. *ACM Transactions on Information Systems,* **14**, 64–93.

Wactlar, H.D., Kanade, T., Smith, M.A., and Stevens, S.M. (1996) Intelligent access to digital video. *IEEE Computer,* **29**(5), 46–53.

Wechsler, M., and Schäuble, P. (1996) Indexing methods for a speech retrieval system. In I. Ruthven (Ed.), *Multimedia Information Retrieval, Glasgow 1995.* London: Springer-Verlag.

Zhang, H.J., Low, C.Y., Smoliar, S.W., and Wu, J.H. (1995) Video parsing, retrieval and browsing: An integrated and content-based solution. In *Proceedings of ACM Multimedia '95,* pp. 15–24. New York: ACM Press.***

A HYPERTEXT ENVIRONMENT FOR INTERACTING WITH LARGE TEXTUAL DATABASES

M. AGOSTI,[1] G. GRADENIGO[1] and P.G. MARCHETTI[2]
[1]Dipartimento di Elettronica e Informatica, Universitá di Padova, Via Gradenigo 6/a, 35131 Padova, Italy
[2]European Space Agency—IRS, Via Galileo Galilei, 00044 Frascati, Italy

Abstract—This paper presents a design and implementation project based on a two-level conceptual architecture for the construction of a hypertext environment for interacting with large textual databases. The conceptual architecture has been proposed to be used for a semantic representation of the informative content of a collection of documents and for the organisation of the document collection itself. The hypertext environment is based on a set of functions that permits one to exploit the potential capabilities of the two-level architecture. Those functions are presented in detail. The paper reports some results of a more general project whose final goal is the definition of a new model for information retrieval: a model with information retrieval capabilities embedded within a hypertext environment. Finally, an outline is presented of the characteristics of a prototype, named HYPERLINE, of the hypertext environment. This prototype has been developed by the Information Retrieval Service of the European Space Agency (ESA-IRS)

INTRODUCTION

In Agosti *et al.* (1989, 1990) a conceptual architecture has been proposed that can be used for a conceptual representation of the informative content of a collection of documents and for the organisation of the document collection itself. The main scope of this architecture is to support the user with a reference model that makes explicit the semantic representations of the documents that are managed and used by the system to solve the user's query. Work is under way to make use of that conceptual architecture for two different requirements:

1. to experimentally verify the soundness of the architecture as a basis for the construction of a hypertext environment to be used as a conceptual reference and interface tool for the final user; and
2. to act as a basis for the definition of a new information retrieval model and the related approach in defining and retrieving information on documents (structural and dynamic aspects).

This paper presents the results of the application of the architecture for purpose 1; thus the paper introduces the guidelines of the design and implementation project that uses the architecture as a basis for the construction of a hypertext environment interacting with large textual databases; in Agosti *et al.* (1991) an initial report of the work was given.

The paper is structured as follows: The first section gives the motivations of the work. Then the main characteristics of the reference architecture are presented together with the description of the basic model of the interface and the different functions that have been designed and implemented. Finally, the highlights of the usable prototype are given.

MOTIVATIONS

Information retrieval systems (IRS) are designed for efficient storage and retrieval of large numbers of bibliographic references or short textual documents. The architecture of these systems does not foresee a formal and explicit representation of the information items stored in the database and relationships among them. This representation (called "schema" in the database management area) is actively used by a database management system and its final user. The lack of such a formal representation of the database content managed by an IRS deprives the user of an *explicit reference* for formulating the query and the IRS of the possibility to capture the semantic of the query. This is not, however, a serious drawback when the query involves information of a deterministic type (e.g., "find all documents with date of publication = 1990"), but it becomes very limiting when the information sought concerns the informative content of documents (e.g., "find documents about database modelling and documents about related concepts").

On currently available information retrieval systems, the user is able to see a single indexing term or a list of indexing terms used in a representation of the informative content of the documents. Browsing, during a query, through the indexing terms related to a term of interest for the user and through the structure of the indexing terms would be helpful for a proper understanding of the semantic context in which the *meaning* of each term is defined by its relationships with other terms.

Few information retrieval services support the user, providing the possibility to see the structure of indexing terms used in representing the semantic content of documents, for example, to see the connection of an indexing term with other related indexing terms. A facility like this is very useful, but it is not sufficient to really inform the user on the structure of the indexing terms. In fact:

- the facility is available only on a stand-alone basis; that is, if users browse the semantic structure of the indexing terms they are unable to see related documents, because browsing through the thesaurus or some other semantic structure is not entirely integrated with the bibliographic database search function; and
- the user is required to know at least an indexing term in order to begin searching for the semantic structure. Otherwise access tot he structure would be impossible.

Some interesting research efforts (see, for example, Croft & Thompson, 1987, and McMath *et al.*, 1989), have been addressed towards making the structure of the indexing terms more explicit to the user. The research work based on a two-level architecture (Agosti *et al.* 1989, 1990) here reported, presents a conceptual tool that makes the structure of the indexing terms explicit and directly available to the final user; together with the research results, a prototype implementation, which is available for public access and use through public networks is also presented.

The issue of defining an architecture is discussed here. This architecture is able to support the explicit conceptual modelling of information retrieval data in order to produce a schema of concepts that describes the informative content of a document collection. This schema is defined as a network of concepts for a specific information retrieval application domain. This schema can be used in an active manner by the user, because this network has to provide the user with a frame of reference in the query formulation process.

Furthermore, the interface provides some elements of information transfer and interaction mechanisms that can be considered complementary to the usual search strategy development process (Belkin & Marchetti, 1990). The present implementation of the HYPERLINE hypertext environment has been urged by the functional elements made available by the two-level model. These hypertext functional elements will have to melt with the traditional information retrieval ones in a future interface implementation. A cognitive task analysis (CTA) approach will be used to cast the large resulting interactivity (Marchetti & Belkin, 1991).

THE REFERENCE CONCEPTUAL ARCHITECTURE

The part of an informative service that is automated by means of an information retrieval (IR) system presents highly complex characteristics due to the complex nature of the

A shorter version of this paper was presented at RIAO91—Conference on Intelligent Text and Image Handling, Autonomous University of Barcelona; Barcelona, Spain, 2-5 April 1991.

data such a service handles. The database managed by an operational IR system is usually made up of:

1. a collection of documents, and
2. a structured collection of auxiliary data.

The *collection of documents* usually consists of a large collection of textual documents. It is possible to characterise the stored documents by means of structured data such as the author's name and the date of publication. The structured data is therefore a deterministic representation of the documents of the collection.

The *structured collection of auxiliary data* is associated to each document in order to represent its semantic content, and is also used to select and retrieve the documents from the database in response to the user's queries. The auxiliary data by which the content of a document is represented is associated to the document itself by means of an indexing process. Each auxiliary data item is assumed to describe the document content only to a certain extent, neither completely nor uniquely, and different auxiliary data items may be assigned to each document. In fact, the description of the content of a document derives from a subjective process, because either the content can be visualized and described in different ways by different persons or different descriptions simply reflect different users' requirements for information.

All specific information retrieval models differ from each other basically because of the kind and structure of the auxiliary data used in the system operations. The auxiliary data represents the vocabulary to be consulted by the IR system; thus such data exists even if the documents have not yet been inserted into the database. It is important to note that the auxiliary data items have very different semantic values; therefore this type of vocabulary takes on a rather complex structure, having to represent the complex semantic relationships that exist between auxiliary data items. Furthermore, some IR systems make use of different auxiliary data structures to permit multiple descriptions of the informative content of documents; these descriptions highlight different aspects and make use of several vocabularies for heterogeneous categories of users. Previous considerations make it clear that the complexity of data modelling in IR depends more on the auxiliary data modelling than on the modelling of the document collection.

The proposed architecture

The auxiliary data describes the document information contents, but the meaning of an auxiliary data item becomes fully defined only by means of the semantic relationship that exists between this auxiliary data item and others. As previously shown, a database managed by an IR system usually consist of two main parts: a collection of documents and a structured collection of auxiliary data. Because of the different roles these two parts play in the architecture of an IR system, it is necessary to make it explicit and to consider an architecture that permits working on at least two different levels of classification abstractions (see Fig. 1):

First level. This is the lowest level that contains the elementary objects of interest; it is therefore the level where the collection of documents D that is managed by an IR system can be placed.

Second level. This level arises from the application of the classification abstraction mechanism to the elementary objects of the first level; this level can be identified as the level of concepts—that is, the locus on which the semantically related concepts are placed; this is the plane of abstraction where the set T of auxiliary data items used by an IR system can be placed; each item represents a concept that is pertinent to a certain set of documents on the basis of their semantic content.

The classification mechanism can be further applied to produce a third level or plane of meta-classes, where by meta-class we mean a class of classes—that is, a class whose members are classes of elementary objects. A meta-class can be, for example, the class of thesauri. This level of classification arises from the repeated application of the classification abstraction process. This third level has been described in Agosti *et al.* (1990); it is mentioned here because it completes the reference architecture, but its role is out of the scope of this paper. The abstraction mechanisms (classification, generalisation-specialisation, and aggregation) included in the paradigm that underlines the proposed architecture are sufficient for the organisation of the representations of the information contained within the documents of the collection.

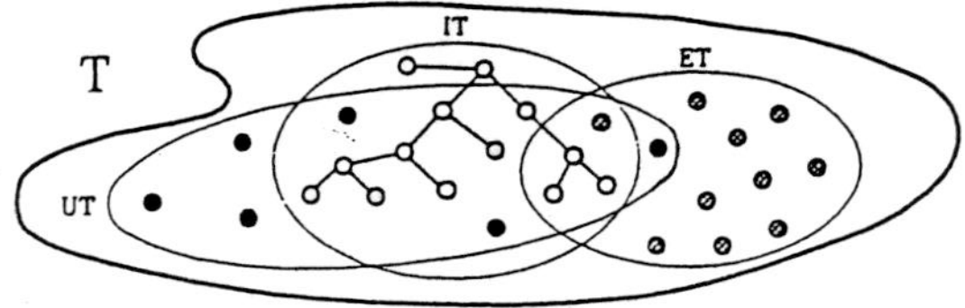

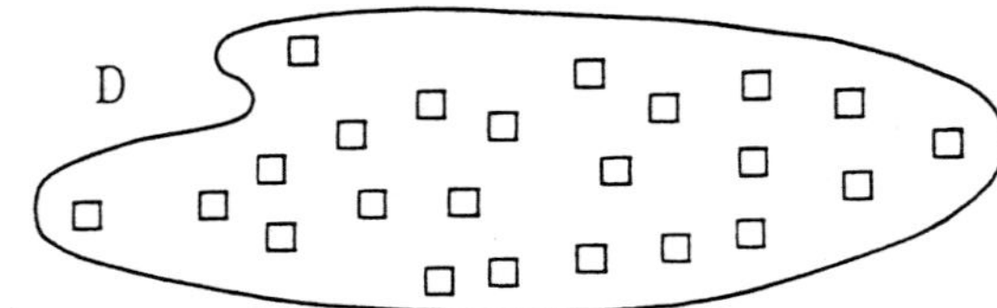

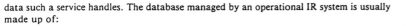

Fig. 1. Two-level architecture and basic model.

The collection of documents

The collection of documents is represented at the first level of the architecture. Each document has its own identity and status; the identity of the document is independent of the way it is represented or structured and the values it may assume.

The structured collection of auxiliary data

The structured collection of auxiliary data is represented at the second level of the architecture. An object-oriented approach is adopted for the design and management of the structured collection of auxiliary data because with this approach it is possible to use the multiple inheritance mechanism, which permits the implementation of this natural property of IR: An IR object can be related to many different terms and hence the object can belong to several different classes. The conceptual tool necessary for designing and managing the auxiliary data must be able to support polythetical classification of the IR objects. In this approach each auxiliary data item is viewed as a class of objects; instances of each of these classes are the documents pertinent to the specific concept expressed by the class term. Hence one of these classes is a set of documents, and from a higher abstraction level may be seen as a single conceptual object of a structure representing the semantic relationships between different concepts. Each *class* can be considered on two different abstraction levels: as a set of instances and as a whole entity.

The *properties of the class* can be subdivided into:

- the properties of the class as an object—that is, the properties of the auxiliary data as such, and
- the properties of the objects of the class—properties of the documents belonging to the class identified by the auxiliary data.

FUNCTIONS FOR A HYPERTEXT ENVIRONMENT FOR INTERACTION WITH LARGE TEXTUAL DATABASES

The introduced architecture has been used as a basis for the construction of a hypertext environment to be used as a conceptual reference and intermediary tool by the final user of an available IR system. Since the available IR system is one of Boolean nature, as is almost any IR system presently used in large applications, the functional model can be generalised for all the applications using a Boolean IR system. The first level of the architecture, the plane of the collection of documents, is implemented and managed by the available IR system; the second level of the architecture has been designed and implemented as a conceptual interface between the user and the collection, which operates as an environment with hypertext capabilities. The interface implements the interactive use of the auxiliary data conceptual structure and the relationships between the level of documents and that of concepts and vice versa; the interface makes transparent to the user the way the IR system makes use of Boolean logic. The next section describes the functions of the tool that has been designed to make a hypertext environment for browsing large textual databases available to the user. A prototype based on these general functions has been developed by the IR Service of the European Space Agency (ESA-IRS). In the following section the prototype's highlights together with examples of the prototype implementation of the environment are presented.

As has been underlined in the introduction of this paper, the complete project, of which this paper presents a part, has as its final target the definition of a new model of information retrieval, which is going to use a hypertext environment as a browsing mechanism embedded within an IR system. Many hypertext functionalities have been shown to be very useful for the retrieval of information from informative resources (Frisse, 1988; Frisse *et al.*, 1990; Nielsen, 1990; Ritchie, 1989). The problem of retrieving information from large informative resources is still an open one. This work gives some positive results in the direction of solving the problem.

Functional capabilities of the environment: The basic model

The basic model is based on the two-level architecture (see Fig. 1). At the first level is placed the collection of documents of interest; in the following the collection of documents is identified and represented by the set D. The second level can be considered as the level of concepts, that is, the conceptual plane on which the semantically related concepts are placed. This is the plane of abstraction where indexing terms used by an IR system can be placed; each term identifies a concept.

Since different structures of auxiliary data (or different indexing techniques) can provide different conceptual representations of the same collection of documents to satisfy different users' requirements, a basic model has been designed that foresees this possibility. Thus, this model permits users to choose at "runtime" in a transparent way the indexing and retrieval techniques most familiar to them or that most suit their informative requirements.

At the second level there is the set T, which represents the universe of possible usable terms. The set ST (System Terms), a subset of T, is the set of terms used and managed by the system. This is the set resulting from the union of all terms used by the different structures of auxiliary data managed by the interface. Two different auxiliary data structures used concurrently by the system have been taken into consideration in this work: the set ET and the set IT, where:

1. ET (Extracted Terms) is the set of terms produced by the application of an automatic parsing algorithm to the textual parts of the managed documents; the terms of the set are all the terms extracted by the algorithm not included in a list of stop-words or non-significant words; and

2. IT (Indexing Terms) is the set of indexing terms of an auxiliary data structure adopted by the system; for the first prototype of the interface, a thesaurus has been used as an example of a complex auxiliary data structure. A thesaurus consists of a complex semantic structure of indexing terms associated with the documents by experienced indexers. In this context the thesaurus is seen as a repository of human knowledge and ability in concept classification. The fundamental types of semantic relationships expressed in a thesaurus are: scope, equivalence, and hierarchical and associative relationships; see Aitchison & Gilchrist (1987) for further details on a thesaurus structure.

The set of possible usable terms T could contain other auxiliary data structures, but it always contains also another set of terms: the set of User Terms (UT). The elements of the set UT are the free terms that the user of the system can insert into a query. That is the set of terms that are not necessarily present in the set of terms extracted from the documents of the collection or in the set IT of indexing terms. It is important to note that the ET, IT, and UT sets are not necessarily disjoined. The architecture of the basic model is depicted in Fig. 1, where

$$T = ET \cup IT \cup UT.$$

The proposed architecture can be used as a frame of reference by the user in the process of query formulation. Through the architecture the structure of the auxiliary data is made available to users, so they can see and navigate through the semantic structure of the indexing terms describing the informative content of the documents.

The functions made available in the environment have been designed taking into account some hypertext functionalities that have been shown to be useful and relevant for the user; see, for example, Nielsen (1990) and Shneiderman & Kearsley (1989). Furthermore, as a first step towards the integration of hypertext and information retrieval environments, it has been provided the possibility of using the result of the concept navigation process to construct a search strategy for the user. The hypertext environment makes the functions described in the following sections available to the user:

1. semantic association;
2. navigation;
3. sequential reading;
4. associative reading from a single document or from many documents;
5. backtracking;
6. history; and
7. support of search strategy development.

Semantic association. The semantic association function operates in the following way: When the user expresses interest in a subject using a specific term, a list of conceptually related indexing terms that are concepts of the auxiliary data structure are suggested to the user. The aim of the semantic association function is to make more transparent and to communicate to the user the meaning the system gives to the term used by the user in the expression of his or her information needs. In the formulation of a query, the user can use natural language; each word given by the user is mapped by the system in a set $IT(i)$ of semantically close concepts which is a part of the auxiliary data structure managed by the system. Moreover, the set $IT(i)$ given to the user by the semantic association function operates for the user as an entry point to the auxiliary data structure; the user can via this entry point start interacting with the system. The aim of this interaction is the acquisition of information via concept navigation and document browsing. In this way we do expect to help the various IR searcher groups by means of an extensive support of their conceptual knowledge (Ingwersen, 1986). The semantic association function moves from the classical term analysis potentially useful for probabilistic relevance feedback (Robertson *et al.*, 1986) and in other semi-automatic feedback modes (McAlpine & Ingwersen, 1989). The semantic association function performs a concept analysis (Belkin & Marchetti, 1990) and knowledge extraction as described in the following.

Suppose the term ut that the user initially enters is itself an indexing term, in this case: $ut = it$. Thereby the connections that the term has with the other indexing terms (e.g., the thesaurus relations) are presented to the user and made available to the other environment functions (e.g., navigate, show, . . .). If the term *ut* that the user initially enters is not a term of *IT*, but a term of *ET*, then the list of conceptually related indexing terms is constructed making use of the documents and through an inference mechanism on the indexing terms. The procedure is based on the fact that each term of the set *ET* has been extracted during the indexing procedure (parser) from a set of documents and its relationship with them is maintained. These functional relationships are acknowledged and made usable in an active way. Thus, a term *et* is related to a set of documents $D(i)$. When the set $D(i)$ has been constructed by the interface, the interface can construct and make use also of the set of indexing terms with which the documents of the set $D(i)$ have been associated during the indexing procedure. Since the resulting set of terms of the set *IT* could have too high cardinality, an inference mechanism is applied to reduce the cardinality of the set and to present the user only the set $IT(i)$ of the most pertinent indexing terms. The way this function operates is shown in Fig. 2.

If the term *ut* that the user initially enters is not a term of the set *IT* nor of the set *ET*, a stemming algorithm is used for suggesting an alphabetical list of terms morphologically close to the term *ut*. After the users' choice of a term from those suggested, the interaction continues in one of the two previously presented ways. In the present implementation a list of conceptually related indexing terms (elements of *IT*) is suggested only if the used term *ut* is also an element of the set *ET*, that is:

$$UT - ET = \varnothing, \quad \text{where the symbol } \varnothing \text{ denotes the empty set.}$$

When the semantic association function has completed its operations, the set $IT(i)$ is available to the user as input to one of the other functions.

Navigation. Before presenting the navigation function, it is important to recall that the user of an IR system is usually looking for documents only to find information stored in the collection of documents. The navigation function gives the user the possibility to browse the structure of the semantic concepts representing the information content of the collection of documents, that is, the conceptual structure of auxiliary data items and of the complex relationship that exists between them. This function enhances the user-system communication, because the user has the possibility to navigate within the semantic structure of concepts (the auxiliary data structure), and a more powerful interaction with the information stored in the collection of documents managed by the IR system is made possible.

The navigation can start from any term of the set *IT*. If the user has had in response to a previously entered term a set $IT(i)$ of indexing terms, or has directly entered a term *it*, the user can navigate the semantic structure of the auxiliary data in order to find out the way in which the terms have been connected and chosen by the indexers. Figure 3 shows the functional relationships in the navigation procedure.

Sequential reading. The sequential reading function allows browsing of the documents associated with any specific term of the set *IT*; in fact, each term of the auxiliary data structure is connected to a set of documents that are semantically related to the term itself. Sequential reading allows the user to move from the second level of the architecture (level of the auxiliary data structure) to the first level (where the documents are managed). In Fig. 4 the sequential reading function is graphically represented. Reading or browsing of the set of the related documents can be done in a sequential manner, one after the other; this function is usually defined as a "documents browsing facility" by the operative information re-

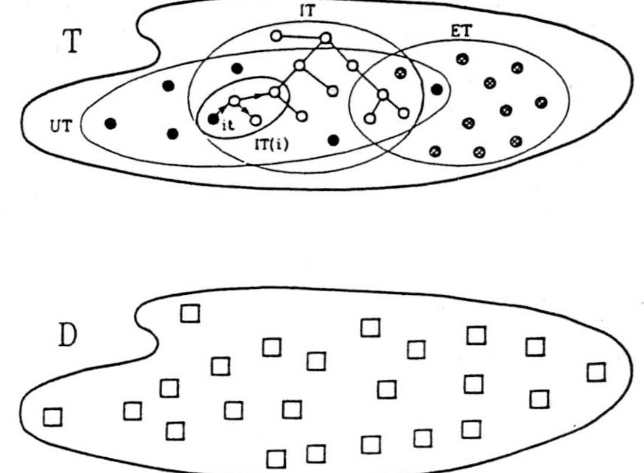

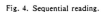

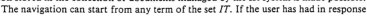

Fig. 2. Semantic association.

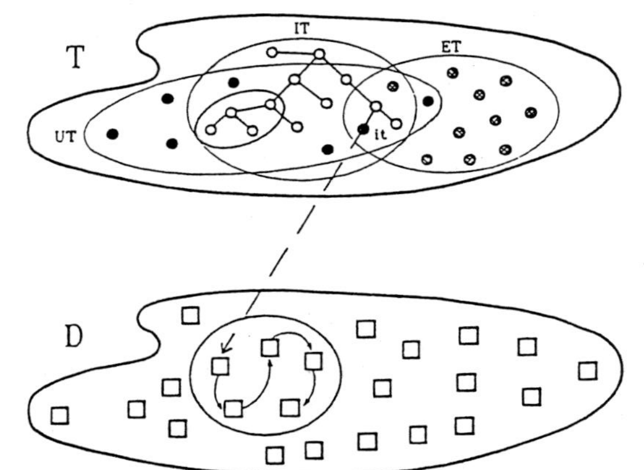

Fig. 3. Navigation.

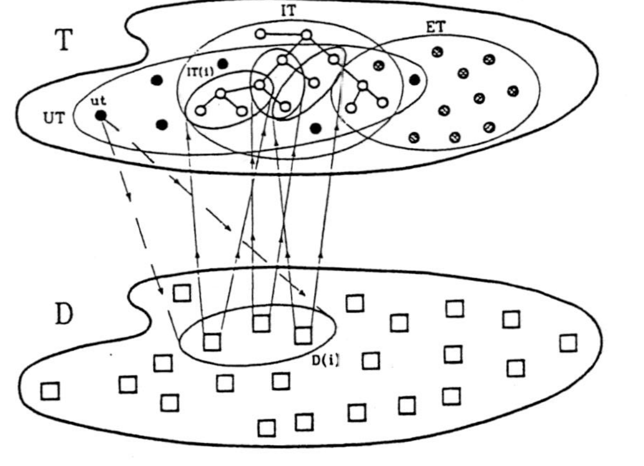

Fig. 4. Sequential reading.

trieval services. It is important to note that this facility is available from operative information retrieval services when the user has formulated a query that has retrieved a set of documents; the user can "browse" (sequentially read) the documents of the set identified as a result of the query. The sequential reading function, instead, permits reading of the documents of the set related to every indexing term of the auxiliary data structure without any query formulation.

Associative reading from a single document or from many documents. The user can invoke the function of associative reading from documents to return from the level of documents to the level of auxiliary data and navigate along the auxiliary data structure. This facility permits navigation between the two levels of the architecture; depending on the level where the user is (first or second), he or she can navigate on that level using the suitable functions. The associative reading function has been designed to be made available from a single document or from many documents.

Two different modes of associative reading can be triggered by the user when using the sequential reading function:

1. First mode of associative reading from a single document: During sequential reading of a set of documents, the user can ask to see the set of indexing terms $IT(k)$ associated with the document *Dk* being read at that precise moment. In Fig. 5 this mode of associative reading is graphically represented by the arrows connecting a document of the first level to a set of terms of the second level.

2. Second mode of associative reading from a single document: During sequential reading of a set of documents the user can leave the reading of that precise set of documents and express interest in knowing the indexing terms associated to the term *it* which indexes the document *Dk* the user is reading in that moment. The user can obtain this list of terms associated to *it* and continue reading through the documents indexed by them. The interface prepares the list of associated terms passing from the level of documents to the level of terms and back to the level of documents, thus obtaining again a semantic association from the index term *it* to other associated index terms. This semantic association is not constrained by the auxiliary data structure hierarchy, but it is driven by the choices made by the knowledge engineers who indexed the documents. In Fig. 6 this mode of associative reading is graphically represented as for the previous mode of reading, with the arrows connecting a specific term of the set of terms to a set of documents belonging to the first level.

Backtracking. The user could be interested in the possibility to come back to a previous situation generated during the user's interaction with the environment. Depending on

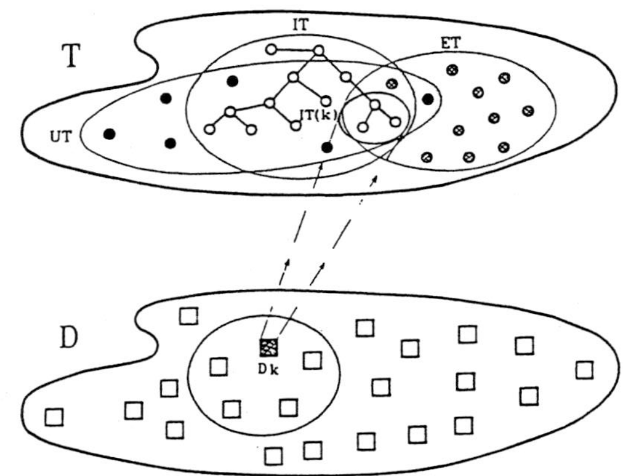

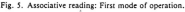

Fig. 5. Associative reading: First mode of operation.

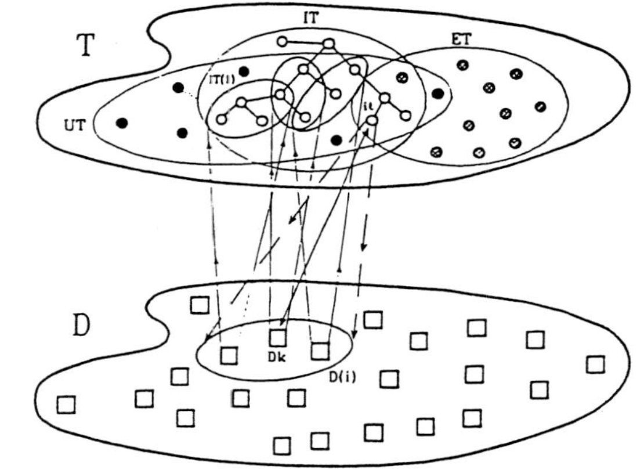

Fig. 6. Associative reading: Second mode of operation.

the level and on the specific function the user has just used, the backtracking function implements different ways of returning to the previous situation or possibility to navigate through the previously selected set of terms or documents.

History. The history function keeps details on the history of the user-system interaction during an interactive session. Since one of the major usability problems connected with tools that permit navigation in an information space (e.g., hypertext and hypermedia) is the user's risk of disorientation (Nielsen, 1990), the history function has been designed to be used in case the user loses the sense of context. Another useful aspect of this function is to keep details of all steps of the interaction, so the user can read through the interaction history to review the different interaction steps and to formulate new interaction strategies for future usage of the tool.

Support to search strategy development. At any time during the auxiliary data structure navigation or during the associative reading the user can identify some terms (indexing terms) as good candidates for a subsequent search strategy formulation. A function has been implemented in order to save these terms in a term pool. The experienced users or professional searchers can then re-use the terms in the term pool for search strategy development. In this way the classical query formulation techniques benefit also from the browsing mechanisms of the hypertext interface.

PROTOTYPE HIGHLIGHTS

A prototype based on the general functions of a hypertext environment described in this paper has been designed and developed. The prototype is available as one of the facilities of ESA-QUEST, the information retrieval system of ESA-IRS. The purpose of the project has been the integration under a unique user framework of two basic information retrieval elements: reference browsing and the concept-to-concept navigation. The project has been developed in the framework of the unifying model previously presented and with the specification of a functional environment capable of making the model and the functionality effectively available to the ESA-IRS users. The operative online environment in which the prototype is running entailed several constraints, as well as a variety of practical drawbacks. In the ESA-IRS service there is an availability of large, good bibliographic collections specifically designed for professional usage. The collection size can span up to about 3.5 million references, and the auxiliary data structure that we use is identified with a network of indexing terms reaching the size of 15 thousands terms. The user population

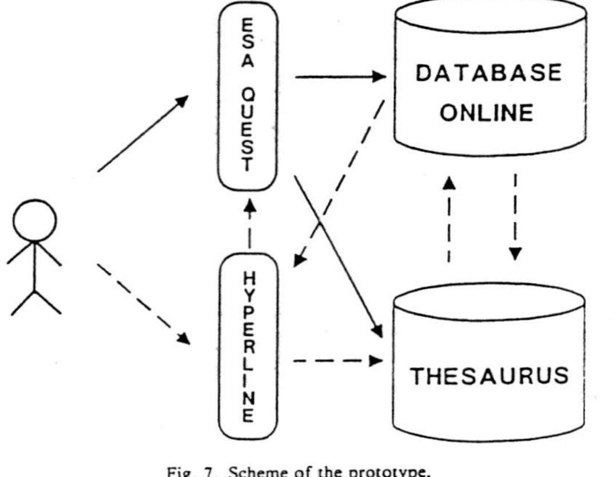

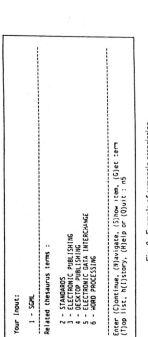

Fig. 7. Scheme of the prototype.

is rather heterogeneous in interests, level of knowledge of the IR system, and of the query language. This kind of environment, with the richness and variety of online data and the presence of a large user population, has made the steps of formative design and usability testing easier. On the other hand, the distribution of the user population over several countries, as well as the difference in equipment used for the online searches (it ranges from teletypes to personal computers and mainframes), has imposed strong constraints in the design. In order to make the prototype available to all ESA-IRS users, it has been decided to implement the prototype for accessing the ESA-IRS service from "dumb" terminals.

The prototype has been named HYPERLINE and has been officially and publicly presented in December 1990 in London during the 14th International Online Information Meeting. The scheme of the prototype and its relationships with the ESA-QUEST system are presented in Fig. 7. At present the prototype can be used with 10 different large textual databases. It is important to note that HYPERLINE is domain-independent, and it works on topics ranging from Aerospace to Metallurgy. Some tests have been performed on other multilingual collections; first results on these tests are encouraging, but further research needs to be carried out. It seems important to show here some examples of the most interesting features of how the prototype implements the semantic association, document reading, and navigation functions.

Significative examples of prototype functions

Semantic association. As stated above, the hypertext environment is designed to allow concept navigation through the auxiliary data structure. If the concept the user is interested in is not an index term, the hypertext environment performs a semantic association from the user term to the index terms conceptually associated to it. In the example shown in Fig. 8 the user is interested in the meaning and getting information concerning the acronym "SGML." SGML is not an index term for the bibliographic file (INSPEC) used in this example. This means that the user would not be able to know which concepts are associated to it without having an in-depth knowledge of the query language. What HYPERLINE does is provide the user with a list of suggested index terms conceptually related to the term expressed by the user. As previously introduced, the semantic association is performed using the knowledge stored in the auxiliary data of the bibliographic file. The ranking of conceptually related index terms is performed according to their occurrence in the most recent references. So, for the term SGML, the suggested concepts are those depicted in Fig. 8.

```
Your Input:

  1 - SGML
--------------------------------------------------------------------------
Related thesaurus terms :

  2 - STANDARDS
  3 - ELECTRONIC PUBLISHING
  4 - DESKTOP PUBLISHING
  5 - ELECTRONIC DATA INTERCHANGE
  6 - WORD PROCESSING

--------------------------------------------------------------------------
Enter (C)ontinue, (N)avigate, (S)how item, (G)et term
(T)op list, h(I)story, (H)elp or (Q)uit : n5
```

Fig. 8. Example of semantic association.

Navigation. If users wish to navigate the auxiliary data structure, they can choose, for example, the term "ELECTRONIC DATA INTERCHANGE." In this case the user obtains the answer reported in Fig. 9.

Document reading. At any time during auxiliary data structure navigation the user can choose the option of showing document references. This option allows reading of the reference items indexed by the actual indexing term (Fig. 10).

The first results of the feedback coming from formative evaluation of HYPERLINE are extremely encouraging: Users understand quickly the meaning of the messages in the menus and are amazed at being free to browse multi-million reference databases without knowing a single search command. The navigation aids that are usually in a hypertext context and implemented also in HYPERLINE (backtracking and history functions) seem to be sufficient to avoid the common feeling of "being lost." In this regard we feel that a strong support to the user is given by the explicit presence of the network of indexing terms built up with the thesaurus whose visibility has been maximised in this environment.

User session example

In the following an example from a user session interaction is given. The user is interested in "INFORMATION RETRIEVAL USER INTERFACE." In Fig. 11 the concepts HYPERLINE found semantically associated to it are shown. The user is interested in reading the bibliographic references sought (Fig. 12). The first reference read (Fig. 12) is cen-

```
----- thesaurus term ELECTRONIC DATA INTERCHANGE ---------------------------
Ref  Items term                                      Relationship
  1   1026 ELECTRONIC DATA INTERCHANGE
  2   5100 DATA HANDLING                             Previous
  3   1047 EFTS                                      Narrower term
  4   6481 CAD/CAM                                   Related term
  5    823 INTEGRATED SOFTWARE                       Related term
  6  41817 STANDARDS                                 Related term
  7   5100 DATA HANDLING                             Broader term
  8   5100 DATA HANDLING                             Top term
  9        DATA CONVERSION (SOFTWARE)                Used for
 10    396 DATA EXCHANGE                             Used for
 11     97 DATA INTERCHANGE                          Used for
 12     31 DATA INTERFACES                           Used for
 13     11 DATA PORTABILITY                          Used for
 14      6 DATA TRANSFER FORMATS                     Used for
 15    115 EDIF                                      Used for
 16        PORTABILITY, DATA                         Used for
 17        TRANSFER FORMATS FOR DATA                 Used for
----------------------------------------------------------------------------
Enter (N)avigate, (B)ack navigate, (S)how item, (G)et term,
(T)op list, h(I)story, (H)elp or (Q)uit : sl
```

Fig. 9. Example of navigation.

```
Show item 1 of 1026
Quest Accession Number: 91180726
  891052097, C91053012  INSPEC  Issue 9117
  Communications support for EDI
  Author(s): Debenham, M.J.
  IEE Colloquium on 'Standards and Practices in Electronic Data Interchange'
(Digest No.106), p. 8/1-3
  Published: 1991, IEE, London, UK
  Pages: 34
  Country of Publication: UK
  Meeting: 21 May 1991, London, UK
  Sponsor(s): IEE
  Document Type: CA (Conference Article)
  Treatment: P (Practical)

  There are many parallels between passing structured commercial messages
between computer systems (which is the objective of EDI communications) and
passing unstructured text between users' terminals (which is the objective of
                                                                        -More-
------------------------------------------------------------------------------
Enter n(E)xt item, (V)iew thesaurus,
(A)ssociated terms in this item,
Associate(D) terms to <ELECTRONIC DATA INTERCHANGE>
or (Q)uit :
```

Fig. 10. Example of document reading for the index term: "ELECTRONIC DATA INTERCHANGE."

tered around the hypermedia concept, and the user tries to understand which are the possible associated concepts (Fig. 13). At this moment the user is therefore performing an associative reading, jumping to the concept "HYPERMEDIA" showing a bibliographic reference related to it (Fig. 14). Reading of the reference opens a new scenario, since the title is now talking about hypertext standardization. The user feels a bit too far away from the original starting point and asks for the list of concepts associated to "HYPERMEDIA." There (Fig. 15) the user receives proof that "HYPERMEDIA" and "USER INTERFACE" are associated concepts and this stimulates the user to return to the original list proposed by HYPERLINE (Fig. 11). A list of concepts is there to elicit associations. The user this time chooses to see the "DATABASE MANAGEMENT SYSTEMS" (DBMS) associated terms. Figure 16 gives the list of concepts associated to "DATABASE MANAGEMENT SYSTEMS." The user reads a few references related to "OBJECT-ORIENTED DATABASES" and then decides to browse the semantic structure again (Fig. 16). Then, getting the idea that "OBJECT-ORIENTED DATABASES" could be an interesting issue to look at, the user selects to navigate the thesaurus structure, choosing the path 6 in Fig. 16: "OBJECT-ORIENTED DATABASES." Figure 17 shows the associated concepts. Among the related concepts there is something that is again worth exploring, like "OBJECT-

```
EsaQuest is looking for related candidate terms

Your Input:

   1 - INFORMATION RETRIEVAL USER INTERFACE
------------------------------------------------------------------------------
Related thesaurus terms :

   2 - INFORMATION RETRIEVAL
   3 - USER INTERFACES
   4 - INFORMATION RETRIEVAL SYSTEMS
   5 - EXPERT SYSTEMS
   6 - DATABASE MANAGEMENT SYSTEMS

------------------------------------------------------------------------------
Enter (C)ontinue, (N)avigate, (S)how item, (G)et term
(T)op list, h(I)story, (H)elp or (Q)uit : sl
```

Fig. 11. Terms semantically related to "INFORMATION RETRIEVAL USER INTERFACE."

```
Show item 1 of 46
Quest Accession Number : 91075354
  C91023775  INSPEC  Journal Paper  Issue 9107
  The rhetoric of hypertext
  Carlson, P.A.
  Human Resources Lab., Intelligent Systs. Branch, Brooks AFB, TX, USA
  Hypermedia (UK)
  Hypermedia  vol.2, no.2, 1990, p.109-31, 8 Refs, ISSN: 0955-
8543, Country of Publ.: UK
  Treatment: P (PRACTICAL)

  As a fundamental orientation, the author adopts the view that
hypertext may eventually bring about a paradigm shift in
text delivery and in human information processing. However,
paradigm shifts do not occur overnight; they are evolutionary
rather than revolutionary. Because of the considerable
commitment of western knowledge and culture to the written word
and to linear text, it seems likely that successful hypertext
systems will electronically emulate many of the strategies a
sophisticated reader uses in dealing with hard
                                                        -More-
------------------------------------------------------------------------------
Enter n(E)xt item,(V)iew thesaurus,
(A)ssociated terms in this item,
 Associate(D) terms to <INFORMATION RETRIEVAL USER INTERFACE>
or (Q)uit : a
```

Fig. 12. Display of the first bibliographic reference indexed by "INFORMATION RETRIEVAL USER INTERFACE."

```
Associated terms :
------------------------------------------------------------------------------
   1 - APPLE COMPUTERS
   2 - HYPERMEDIA
   3 - INFORMATION RETRIEVAL SYSTEMS
   4 - WORD PROCESSING
------------------------------------------------------------------------------
(S)how item, (V)iew thesaurus, or (Q)uit : s2
```

Fig. 13. Terms associated to the bibliographic reference shown in Fig. 12.

```
Show item 2 of 789
Quest Accession Number : 91079387
  C91023811  INSPEC  Conference Paper  Issue 9107
  An interchange format for hypertext systems: the Intermedia model
  Riley, V.A.
  Inst. for Res. in Inf. & Scholarship, Brown Univ., Providence, RI, USA
  Proceedings of the Hypertext Standardization Workshop (NIST SP 500-178)
  Gaithersburg, MD, USA  16-18 Jan. 1990
  1990, p.213-22, 10 Refs, Country of Publ.: USA
  Publisher: NIST. Gaithersburg, MD, USA
  Pages: vi+269
  Moline, J.; Benigni, D.; Baronas, J. (Editors)
  Sponsor: NIST
  Treatment: P (PRACTICAL)

  Realization of the potential for information sharing that
is inherent in hypertext systems depends on the ability to
readily exchange data between those systems.  A format for
exchanging link-related data between first-order
                                                        -More-
------------------------------------------------------------------------------
Enter n(E)xt item, p(R)evious-one,(V)iew thesaurus,
(A)ssociated terms in this item,  Associate(D) terms to <HYPERMEDIA>
or (Q)uit : d
```

Fig. 14. Bibliographic reference indexed by the "HYPERMEDIA" term.

```
Associated terms :
--------------------------------------------------------------------------------
   1 - INFORMATION RETRIEVAL
   2 - USER INTERFACES
   3 - INFORMATION RETRIEVAL SYSTEMS
   4 - EXPERT SYSTEMS
   5 - DATABASE MANAGEMENT SYSTEMS
   6 - MICROCOMPUTER APPLICATIONS

--------------------------------------------------------------------------------
(S)how item, (V)iew thesaurus, or (Q)uit : v
```

Fig. 15. List of terms associated to "HYPERMEDIA."

```
----- thesaurus term DATABASE MANAGEMENT SYSTEMS -----------------------------
Ref   Items term                                    Relationship
 1    15009 DATABASE MANAGEMENT SYSTEMS
 2     4755 FILE ORGANISATION                       Previous
 3     9503 MANAGEMENT INFORMATION SYSTEMS          Previous
 4      228 DEDUCTIVE DATABASES                     Narrower term
 5     1444 DISTRIBUTED DATABASES                   Narrower term
 6      153 OBJECT-ORIENTED DATABASES               Narrower term
 7     4208 RELATIONAL DATABASES                    Narrower term
 8      515 APPLICATION GENERATORS                  Related term
 9      677 CONCURRENCY CONTROL                     Related term
10      706 DATA INTEGRITY                          Related term
11     2055 DATABASE THEORY                         Related term
12     4021 DECISION SUPPORT SYSTEMS                Related term
13      935 GEOGRAPHIC INFORMATION SYSTEMS          Related term
14      789 HYPERMEDIA                              Related term
15      782 INTEGRATED SOFTWARE                     Related term
16      110 MULTIMEDIA SYSTEMS                      Related term
17     1399 QUERY LANGUAGES                         Related term
18      612 TRANSACTION PROCESSING                  Related term
                                                   -More 0.10-
--------------------------------------------------------------------------------
Enter (N)avigate, (B)ack navigate, (S)how item, (G)et term,
(T)op list, h(I)story, (H)elp or (Q)uit : s6
```

Fig. 16. The thesaurus structure for the term "DATABASE MANAGEMENT SYSTEMS."

ORIENTED PROGRAMMING" (OO), so the user performs some sequential reading on references related to (OO).

The user has grasped a certain number of ideas and therefore decides that it is time to go back again to the concept network (Fig. 17) and to view the history of his or her navigation (Fig. 18). The user, starting from the concept "INFORMATION RETRIEVAL USER INTERFACE," has explored areas like hypermedia, DBMS, and OO databases and programming. A final look at the concept network around the DBMS concept (Fig. 16)

```
----- thesaurus term OBJECT-ORIENTED DATABASES -------------------------------
Ref   Items term                                    Relationship
 1      153 OBJECT-ORIENTED DATABASES               Narrower term
 2    15009 DATABASE MANAGEMENT SYSTEMS             Previous
 3     2233 OBJECT-ORIENTED PROGRAMMING             Related term
 4    15009 DATABASE MANAGEMENT SYSTEMS             Broader term
 5     6447 COMPUTER APPLICATIONS                   Top term
 6     4755 FILE ORGANISATION                       Top term
--------------------------------------------------------------------------------
Enter (N)avigate, (B)ack navigate, (S)how item, (G)et term,
(T)op list, h(I)story, (H)elp or (Q)uit : s3
```

Fig. 17. Terms associated to "OBJECT-ORIENTED DATABASES" in the thesaurus.

```
----- Navigation History -----------------------------------------------------
0 Your input  - INFORMATION RETRIEVAL USER INTERFACE
1 Show        - INFORMATION RETRIEVAL USER INTERFACE
2 Show        - HYPERMEDIA
3 -Top List - - ---------------
4 Navigate    - DATABASE MANAGEMENT SYSTEMS
5 Show        - OBJECT-ORIENTED DATABASES
6 Navigate    - OBJECT-ORIENTED DATABASES
7 Show        - OBJECT-ORIENTED PROGRAMMING
8 B-Navigate  - DATABASE MANAGEMENT SYSTEMS
(V)iew list again or (Q)uit : v
```

Fig. 18. History of the navigation conducted by the user.

shows that since the original interest was centered around the user interface, it is worth looking at references dealing with "MULTIMEDIA SYSTEMS." With this last browsing operation the user decides to quit the session.

This session example shows some of the peculiar characteristics of the hypertext environment when embedded in an information retrieval system. It is very easy to jump from concept to concept and perform sequential and associative reading. The concepts proposed are related to the one entered by the user, but the retrieved documents do not necessarily overlap the original topic. Therefore the hypertext tool can lead the user far away from his original aim. The richness of concepts and references available in a large operative information retrieval system can then require a considerable intellectual effort on behalf of the user and challenge one's ability to perceive and classify concept associations. On the other hand, it seems that concept association is a straightforward task for human beings, and it is the most basic unit of thinking and learning (Iran-Nejad, 1989). We do expect, therefore, that users will appreciate the large wealth of associations elicited by the HYPERLINE hypertext environment for large bibliographic collections.

CONCLUSIONS

This paper has described the conceptual design and functions of an operational prototype, named HYPERLINE, of a hypertext environment for interaction with large textual databases. The functions that are made available by the environment have been introduced and specified. Scope of the prototype is to make explicitly available to the final user the auxiliary data structure, which in this environment is a thesaurus structure. The prototype is based on a two-level architecture that permits the conceptual separation between auxiliary data structure and document collection. The prototype permits the direct use of the auxiliary data structure by the user together with the possibility of navigating the document collection, and the relationships between these two conceptual levels. This is made available through a set of functions that have been described. HYPERLINE is already in experimental usage by ESA-IRS users. From the beginning of the experimental usage of HYPERLINE, log data of the user-system interaction are collected. From an initial statistical analysis of the log data, it emerges that the effectiveness of the retrieval is improved by the possibility of moving between the two conceptual levels and a navigation in each of them.

Acknowledgements – The work of Maristella Agosti and Girolamo Gradenigo has been partly supported by the Italian National Research Council (CNR) under the project, "Sistemi informatici e calcolo parallelo–P5: Linea di Ricerca Coordinata MULTIDATA."

REFERENCES

Agosti, M., Gradenigo, G., & Mattiello, P. (1989). The hypertext as an effective information retrieval tool for the final user. A.A. Martino (Ed.), *Preproceedings of the III International Conference on Logics, Informatics and Law*, Vol. I, Firenze, 1-19.

Agosti, M., Crestani, F., Gradenigo, G., & Mattiello, P. (1990). An approach for the conceptual modelling of IR auxiliary data. *Ninth Annual IEEE International Phoenix Conference on Computers and Communications*, March 21–23, 1990, Scottsdale, Arizona, 500–505.

Agosti, M., Gradenigo, G., & Marchetti, P.G. (1991). Architecture and functions for conceptual interface to very large online bibliographic collections. *Intelligent Text and Image Handling, RIAO 91*, Barcelona, Spain, April 1991, Vol. 1, 2-24.

Aitchison, J., & Gilchrist, A. (1987). *Thesaurus construction – A practical manual* (2nd Ed). London: Aslib.

Belkin, N.J., & Marchetti, P.G. (1990). Determining the functionality and features of an intelligent interface to an information retrieval system. In J.-L. Vidick (Ed.), *Proc. 13th ACM-SIGIR Int. Conf. on Research and Development in Information Retrieval*, Brussels, Belgium, 151–177.

Croft, W.B., & Thompson, R.H. (1987). I^{3}R: A new approach to the design of document retrieval systems. *Journal of the American Society for Information Science, 38*(6), 389–404.

Frisse, M.E. (1988). Searching for information in a hypertext medical handbook. *Communications of the ACM, 31*(7), 880–886.

Frisse, M.E. (Chairman), Agosti, M., Bruandet, M.F., Hahn, U., & Weiss, S. (1990). Panel Session: Hypertext: "Growing Up?" In J.-L. Vidick (Ed.), *Proc. 13th ACM-SIGIR Int. Conf. on Research and Development in Information Retrieval*, Brussels, Belgium, 343–347.

Ingwersen, P. (1986). Cognitive analysis and the role of the intermediary in information retrieval. In R. Davies, (Ed.), *Intelligent Information Systems: progress and prospects*, (pp. 206–237) New York: Wiley.

Iran-Nejad, A. (1989). Associative and nonassociative schema theories of learning. *Bulletin of the PSYCHONomic Society* (US), *27*(1), 1-4.

Marchetti, P.G., & Belkin, N.J. (1991). Interactive online search formulation support. *Proc. Online Meeting N.Y.*, May 1991.

McAlpine, G., & Ingwersen, P. (1989). Integrated information retrieval in a knowledge worker support system. In N.J. Belkin & C.J. van Rijsbergen (Eds.), *Proc. of ACM-SIGIR 1989 Conf.*, Cambridge, MA (pp. 48–57).

McMath, C.F., Tamaru, R.S., & Rada, R. (1989). A graphical thesaurus-based information retrieval. *Int. J. Man-Machine Studies, 31*, 121–147.

Nielsen, J. (1990). The art of navigating through hypertext. *Communications of the ACM, 33*(3), 296–310.

Ritchie, I. (1989). HYPERTEXT – Moving towards large volumes. *The Computer Journal, 32*(6), 516–523.

Robertson, S.E., Thompson, C.L., Macaskill, M.J., & Bovey, J.D. (1986). Weighting, ranking and relevance feedback in a front-end system (information retreival). *Journal of Information Science, 12*(1–2), 71–75.

Shneiderman, B., & Kearsley, G. (1989). *Hypertext hands on! An introduction to a new way of organizing and accessing information*. Reading, MA: Addison-Wesley.

Automatic Analysis, Theme Generation, and Summarization of Machine-Readable Texts

Gerard Salton, James Allan, Chris Buckley, Amit Singhal

Vast amounts of text material are now available in machine-readable form for automatic processing. Here, approaches are outlined for manipulating and accessing texts in arbitrary subject areas in accordance with user needs. In particular, methods are given for determining text themes, traversing texts selectively, and extracting summary statements that reflect text content.

Many kinds of texts are currently available in machine-readable form and are amenable to automatic processing. Because the available databases are large and cover many different subject areas, automatic aids must be provided to users interested in accessing the data. It has been suggested that links be placed between related pieces of text, connecting, for example, particular text paragraphs to other paragraphs covering related subject matter. Such a linked text structure, often called hypertext, makes it possible for the reader to start with particular text passages and use the linked structure to find related text elements (*1*). Unfortunately, until now, viable methods for automatically building large hypertext structures and for using such structures in a sophisticated way have not been available. Here we give methods for constructing text relation maps and for using text relations to access and use text databases. In particular, we outline procedures for determining text themes, traversing texts selectively, and extracting summary statements that reflect text content.

Text Analysis and Retrieval: The Smart System

The Smart system is a sophisticated text retrieval tool, developed over the past 30 years, that is based on the vector space model of retrieval (*2*). In the vector space model, all information items—stored texts as well as information queries—are represented by sets, or vectors, of terms. A term is typically a word, a word stem, or a phrase associated with the text under consideration. In principle, the terms might be chosen from a controlled vocabulary list or a thesaurus, but because of the difficulties of constructing such controlled vocabularies for unrestricted topic areas, it is convenient to derive the terms directly from the texts under consideration. Collectively, the terms assigned to a particular text represent text content.

The authors are in the Department of Computer Science, Cornell University, Ithaca, NY 14853–7501, USA.

Because the terms are not equally useful for content representation, it is important to introduce a term-weighting system that assigns high weights to terms deemed important and lower weights to the less important terms. A powerful term-weighting system of this kind is the well-known equation $f_t \times 1/f_c$ (term frequency times inverse collection frequency), which favors terms with a high frequency (f_t) in particular documents but with a low frequency overall in the collection (f_c). Such terms distinguish the documents in which they occur from the remaining items.

When all texts or text queries are represented by weighted term vectors of the form $D_i = (d_{i1}, d_{i2}, \ldots, d_{it})$, where d_{ik} is the weight assigned to term k in document D_i, a similarity measure can be computed between pairs of vectors that reflects text similarity. Thus, given document D_i and query Q_j (or sample document D_j), a similarity computation of the form $sim(D_i, Q_j) = \sum_{k=1}^{t} d_{ik}d_{jk}$ can produce a ranked list of documents in decreasing order of similarity with a query (or with a sample document). When ranked retrieval output is provided for the user, it is easy to use relevance feedback procedures to build improved queries on the basis of the relevance of previously retrieved materials.

In the Smart system, the terms used to identify the text items are entities extracted from the document texts after elimination of common words and removal of word suffixes. When the document vocabulary itself forms the basis for text content representation, distinct documents with large overlapping vocabularies may be difficult to distinguish. For example, the vectors covering biographies of John Fitzgerald Kennedy and Anthony M. Kennedy, the current Supreme Court justice, will show many similarities because both Kennedys attended Harvard University, were high officials of the government, and had close relationships with U.S. presidents. The global vector similarity function described earlier cannot cope with ambiguities of this kind by itself. An additional step designed to verify that the matching vocabulary occurs locally in similar contexts must therefore be introduced as part of the retrieval algorithm. This is accomplished by insisting on certain locally matching substructures, such as text sentences or text paragraphs, in addition to the global vector match, before accepting two texts as legitimately similar (*3*).

Consider, as an example, a typical search conducted in the 29-volume Funk and Wagnalls encyclopedia, using as a query the text of article 9667, entitled "William Lloyd Garrison" (Garrison was the best known of the American abolitionists, who opposed slavery in the early part of the 19th century) (*4*). The upper portion of Table 1 shows the top 10 items retrieved in response to a global vector comparison. The top retrieved item is article 9667 itself, with a perfect query similarity of 1.00, followed by additional articles dealing with abolitionism and the slavery issue, retrieved with lower similarity values.

The upper portion of Table 1 consists of relevant items only, with the exception of article 9628, entitled "Gar," retrieved in position eight on the ranked list. Gar is a type of fish, obviously unrelated to the slavery issue but erroneously retrieved because truncated terms were used in the text vectors, and the truncated form of "Garrison" matches "Gar." (Removal of "-ison" as part of the stemming process first reduced "Garrison" to "Garr," as in "comparison" and "compar"; removal of the duplicated consonant then reduced "Garr" to the final

"Gar.") The lower portion of Table 1 shows the results obtained with an additional local text comparison that required at least one matching text sentence between the query article and each retrieved document. There are no matching sentences in documents 9667 ("Garrison") and 9628 ("Gar"), because gar, meaning fish, and "Gar" derived from the name Garrison are obviously not used in similar contexts. Hence the offending document 9628 was removed from the retrieved list. Most linguistic ambiguities are similarly resolvable by this global-local vector-matching process. The lower portion of Table 1 also differs from the upper in that certain text passages are retrieved (labeled "c" for section and "p" for paragraph) in addition to certain full document texts. The passage retrieval issue is examined in more detail in the next section.

Text Decomposition and Structure

Practical retrieval searches deal with text items that are heterogeneous in both subject matter and text length. Thus, in the same text environment it may be necessary to cope with short e-mail messages as well as long book-sized texts. In an encyclopedia, three-word articles representing cross-references from one subject to another occur routinely, in addition to many long

Table 1. Text retrieval strategies. Query: article 9667, "William Lloyd Garrison." Section indicated by "c"; paragraph indicated by "p."

Document number	Query similarity	Title of retrieved item
	Global text comparison only	
9667	1.00	Garrison, William Lloyd
18173	0.53	Phillips, Wendell
76	0.48	Abolitionists
21325	0.40	Slavery
827	0.36	American Anti-Slavery Society
21326	0.35	Slave Trade
8097	0.35	Emancipation Proclamation
9628	0.30	Gar
2883	0.27	Birney, James Gillespie
5584	0.27	Clay, Cassius Marcellus
	Global-local text comparison and retrieval of text passages	
9667	1.00	Garrison, William Lloyd
18173	0.53	Phillips, Wendell
2974.c33*	0.50	Blacks in Americas
76	0.48	Abolitionists
21325.c8	0.42	Slavery
827	0.36	American Anti-Slavery Society
8097	0.35	Emancipation Proclamation
23173.c97*	0.31	United States of America
23545.p5*	0.29	Villard, Henry
5539.c28*	0.28	Civil War, American

*New article retrieved in restricted search.

treatments such as the 175-page article entitled "United States of America." In a vector-processing environment, long articles that deal with diverse subject matter are difficult to retrieve in response to short, more specific queries, because the overall vector similarity is likely to be small for such items. Thus, the full article "United States of America" is not retrieved in the top 10 items in response to the query about William Lloyd Garrison, even though certain sections in the article specifically deal with abolitionism.

The rejection of long articles can reduce retrieval performance in some cases. More generally, long articles are difficult for users to handle even when retrieval is possible, because long texts cannot easily be absorbed and processed. This suggests that long texts be broken down into smaller text passages and that access be provided to shorter text excerpts in addition to full texts. Various attempts have been made in the past to implement passage retrieval capabilities, but flexible systems capable of handling text excerpts do not currently exist (5).

The Smart system can deal with text segments of varying length, including text sections, paragraphs, groups of adjacent sentences, and individual sentences. The lower portion of Table 1 thus shows the results of a mixed search in which text sections and paragraphs are retrieved instead of full texts whenever the query similarity for a shorter text passage exceeds the similarity for the full article. A number of new items are promoted into the top 10 list when text passages are retrievable, including section 33 of document 2974, "Blacks in the Americas," and section 97 of "United States of America." The text of document 2974.c33 (section 33 of document 2974) covers the founding of the American Anti-Slavery Society by William Lloyd Garrison in 1833. The relevance of this text to abolitionism and William Lloyd Garrison explains its good retrieval rank and high similarity coefficient of 0.50.

The available evidence indicates that when searching an encyclopedia, the use of the combined global and local similarity computations improves retrieval effectiveness by about 10% over the use of global vector similarity measurements alone. An additional 10% improvement is obtainable by use of the passage retrieval capability that identifies document excerpts in addition to full texts (6). The results obtained by extensive testing in the TREC (Text Retrieval Evaluation Conference) environment indicate that the Smart system produces consistently superior retrieval performance (7). Furthermore, response times are comparable to those obtainable in commercial retrieval environments. A Smart search of the TREC collections (700,000 full-text documents, or 2.4 gigabytes of text) has typical response times of 3 s for a 10-term query or 6 s for a 20-term query.

When text passages are available for processing and similarity measurements are easily computed between texts and text excerpts, text relation maps can be generated that show text similarities that exceed a particular threshold value. Figure 1 shows a relation map for four encyclopedia articles related to William Lloyd Garrison ("Slavery," "U.S. Civil War," "Abolitionists,"

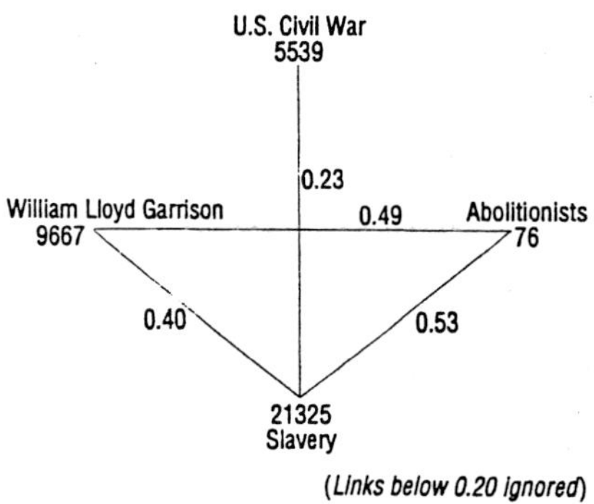

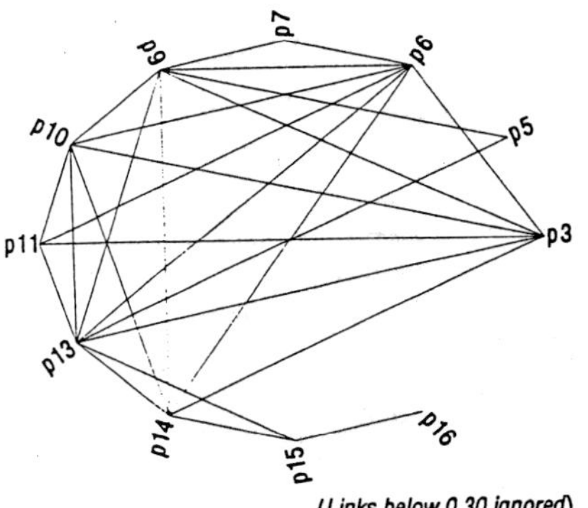

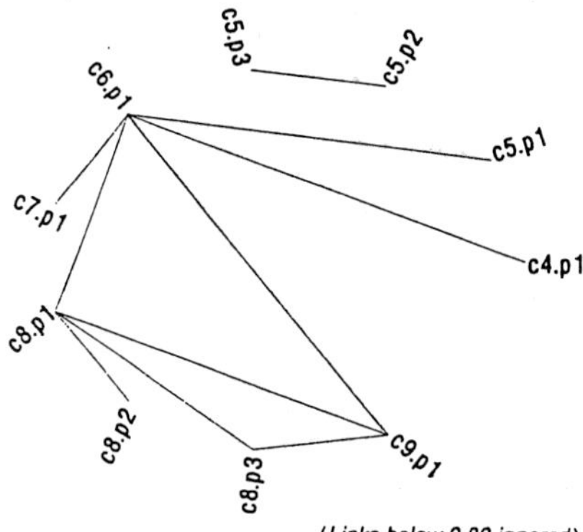

Fig. 1 (top). Basic text relation map. Vertices (nodes) represent texts; lines (links between nodes) represent text relations above a similarity threshold of 0.20. In all figures, "c" indicates section, "p" indicates paragraph. **Fig. 2 (middle).** Well-connected text relation map for paragraphs of article 21385, "Smoking." **Fig. 3 (bottom).** Poorly connected text relation map for paragraphs of article 21933, "Symphony."

and "Garrison"). The texts themselves are represented by nodes (vertices) of the map, and the pairwise text similarities are indicated by links (branches) between the corresponding node pairs. Figure 1 shows all similarities between full articles exceeding a similarity threshold of 0.20 (8). Text linking has been used in the past to build hypertext structures, but the links between related text pieces are normally assumed to be placed subjectively by individual text authors—a procedure manifestly impractical in environments where large masses of heterogeneous texts are stored for processing (9).

A study of various kinds of text relations between texts and text excerpts can reveal a good deal of information about the internal structure of individual texts, as well as the relations between different texts. Consider, as an example, the paragraph map for article 21385, "Smoking," shown in Fig. 2, which includes all pairwise paragraph similarities exceeding 0.30. In the corresponding graph, there are no disconnected components, and many similarities exist between adjacent paragraphs. The convex graph structure reflects a homogeneous treatment of the topic; in this case, the "Smoking" article emphasizes the health problems connected with smoking and the difficulties that arise when people attempt to quit smoking. For a homogeneous map such as this, it should be easy to determine the basic text content by looking at only a few carefully chosen paragraphs.

In contrast, consider the paragraph relation map in Fig. 3, which shows paragraph similarities for article 21933, "Symphony," and uses the same similarity threshold of 0.30. This map is much less dense; there are many outliers consisting of a single node only, and there is a disconnected component that includes paragraphs 2 and 3 of section 5. Clearly, the "Symphony" topic does not receive the same homogeneous treatment in the encyclopedia as "Smoking," and a determination of text content by selectively looking at particular text excerpts is much more problematic in this case. Attempts have been made in the past to relate certain manually linked hypertext structures to the corresponding text characteristics, but a detailed structural text analysis based on automatically linked structures at various levels of detail has not so far been undertaken (*10*).

In Figs. 1 to 3, the text nodes are equally spaced around the circumference of a circular structure. This makes it easy to recognize the links between individual text excerpts, but the actual link location in the running text is obscured. In particular, it is difficult to tell whether a link is placed at the beginning, in the middle, or at the end of a text. An alternative display format is shown in Fig. 4, in which the space assigned to each text along the circumference is proportional to the text length, and each text link is placed in its proper position within the texts. Figure 4 shows a paragraph map for four related articles ("Mohandas Gandhi," "Indira Gandhi," "Nehru," and "India") with the use of a similarity threshold of 0.30. It is obvious that the text of article 12017 ("India") is much longer than that of the other articles and that the coverage of Mohandas Gandhi (the Mahatma) is in turn more detailed than that of Indira Gandhi and Nehru.

Various kinds of topic relationships can be distinguished in Fig. 4, depending on the particular linking pattern between text elements. For example, when multiple links relate a particular (shorter) document such as "Indira Gandhi" (9619) and a subsection of a longer document such as "India" (12017), a narrower-broader text relation normally exists. Similarly, when a particular section of one document has multiple links to a particular section of another document, the two text items usually share a common subtopic. One can thus conclude that "Nehru" (16579) and the two "Gandhis" (9619 and 9620) represent subtopics of "India" (12017). Similarly, "Mohandas Gandhi" and "Nehru," and "Indira Gandhi" and "Nehru," are pairs of related documents that share common subtopics. Finally, the lives of the two Gandhis appear to be largely unrelated—a single linked paragraph pair exists that refers to unrest in India, a condition that plagued both politicians. The relation between Mohandas and Indira Gandhi is entirely through Nehru, who was a disciple of the Mahatma and also the father of Indira.

This type of analysis gives an objective view of the topic coverage in individual texts and of the information shared among sets of related texts. In the rest of this article, we examine three kinds of text analysis systems in more detail, which leads to the identification of text themes, the selective traversal of texts, and the summarization of text content by extraction of important text excerpts.

Text Theme Identification

A text theme can be defined as a specific subject that is discussed in some depth in a particular text or in a number of related texts. Themes represent centers of attention and cover subjects of principal interest to text authors and presumably also to text readers. The identification of text themes is useful for many purposes—for example, to obtain a snapshot of text content and as an aid in deciding whether actually to read a text.

Various approaches based on linguistic text analysis methods suggest themselves for the identification of text themes (*11*). In the present context, the text relation maps are used as inputs to a clustering process that is designed to identify groups of text excerpts that are closely related to each other but also relatively disconnected from the rest of the text (*12*). The following simple process leads to text theme identification: First, the triangles in the relation map are recognized (a triangle is a group of three text excerpts, each of which is related to the other two to a degree that is above the stated similarity threshold). A centroid vector is then constructed for each triangle, as the average vector for the group of three related items. Finally, triangles are merged into a common group (theme) whenever the corresponding centroids are sufficiently similar (that is, when the pairwise centroid similarity exceeds a stated threshold). Each theme may be represented by a global centroid vector that is constructed as the average vector of all text excerpts included in the theme.

Figure 5 shows the four themes derived by this method for the Gandhi-India subject area shown in Fig. 4. The following themes are apparent: (i) the single solid triangle consisting of paragraphs 9619.p5, 16579.p4, and 16579.p5 on the right-hand edge of Fig. 5 (main subject: Nehru); (ii) the single hashed triangle consisting of paragraphs 9619.p3, 12017.p219, and 12017.p220 (main subject: Sikhs, Punjab); (iii) the group of dark triangles consisting of paragraphs 9619.p7, 12017.p211, 12017.p216, 12017.p218, and 12017.p222 (main subject: Indira Gandhi); (iv) the group of light triangles consisting of paragraphs 9620.p3, 9620.p6, 9620.p8, 9620.p11, 9620.p14, 9620.p15, 9620.p18, 12017.p148, and 16579.p4 (main subject: Mohandas Gandhi). The clear separation between the two Gandhis already noted in the map of Fig. 4 is present also in the theme map of Fig. 5, in which no overlap exists between the dark and light triangle groupings.

An alternative, less onerous but also less refined theme generation method is to build a text relation map with the use of a high similarity threshold (where the number of linked text excerpts is small). Each disconnected component of the map, consisting of groups of highly related text excerpts, is then identified with a particular theme. The graph obtained by use of a text similarity threshold of 0.50 for the Gandhi-India subject area is shown in Fig. 6. The high similarity threshold reduces the similarity map to three areas, identified as Mohandas Gandhi (top theme), Indira Gandhi (middle), and Nehru (bottom). These themes duplicate those of Fig. 5, but the second theme in Fig. 5, which covers Indira Gandhi's problems with the Sikhs in Punjab, is no longer recognized as a separate subject.

When text relation maps are used as the main input, themes can be generated at various levels of detail. The larger the text excerpts used for text grouping purposes, the wider in general is the scope of the corresponding themes. Contrariwise, when sentences and other short excerpts are used in the grouping process, the theme coverage is normally narrow. Thus, when themes are derived from the texts of documents 9667 and 76 ("William Lloyd Garrison" and "Abolitionists," respectively), a theme derived from paragraph relations might cover the "beginnings of U.S. abolitionism"; a more detailed theme derived from sentence relations might cover the "founding of the newspaper *Liberator*," which was a milestone in the early years of the abolitionist movement. By suitable variation of the scope of the theme generation process, it is thus possible to derive a smaller number of broader themes or a larger number of narrower themes.

Selective Text Traversal

When large text collections are in use, flexible methods should be available that will skim the texts while concentrating on text passages that may be of immediate interest. Such a skimming operation can then be used both for selective text traversal, in which only text passages deemed of special importance are actually retrieved or read, and for text summarization, in which summaries are constructed by extraction of selected text excerpts.

In selective text traversal (*13*), starting with a text relation map and a particular text excerpt of special interest, a user may follow three different traversal strategies: (i) The path may cover many of the central nodes, which are defined as nodes with a large number of links to other nodes of the map. (ii) The path may use text excerpts located in strategic positions within the corresponding documents—for example, the first paragraphs in each text section or the first sentences in each paragraph. (iii) The path may use the link weight as the main path generation criterion by starting with the desired initial node and choosing as the next node the one with maximum similarity to the current node. This last strategy is known as a depth-first search.

When individual text excerpts are selected for path formation or summarization, a number of factors must receive special attention; among these are the coherence of the resulting text, that is, the ease with which the text can be read and understood; the exhaustivity of coverage of the final text, that is, the degree to which all the main subject areas are covered; the text chronology, that is, the accuracy with which timing factors are recognized; and finally, the amount of repetition in the selected text excerpts. Some of these factors are handled relatively easily; for example, text chronology is often maintained by the use of only forward-pointing paths and backtracking is not allowed (if a particular paragraph is included in a path, no other text excerpt appearing earlier in the same document can appear in the same path).

In the present context, text coherence is used as the main criterion, and forward depth-first paths are used in which each chosen text excerpt is linked to the most similar text excerpt not yet seen at this point. In a depth-first path, each chosen excerpt is closely related to the next one, and the chance of poor transitions between selected paragraphs is minimized. Consider, as an example, the paragraph map in Fig. 7, which is based on six documents related to the Greek god Zeus (article 24674). The assumption is that the path starts with the initial text paragraph of "Zeus" (24674.p3). A short depth-first path may be defined as a single-link path that includes only the initial text excerpt plus the next most similar excerpt. In Fig. 7, this defines path 24674.p3 to 17232.p4 (paragraph 4 of the

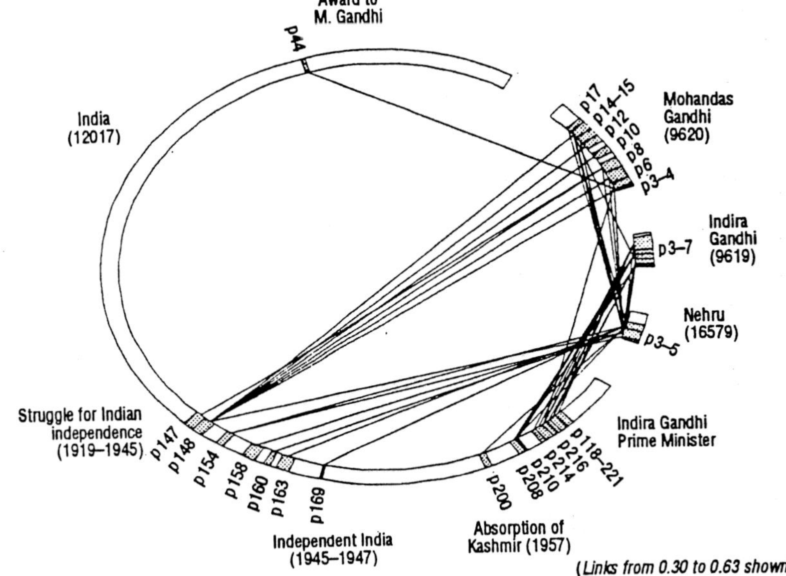

Fig. 4. Paragraph similarity map for articles related to "India" (12017). Length of curved segments is proportional to text length; links are placed in correct relative position within each text.

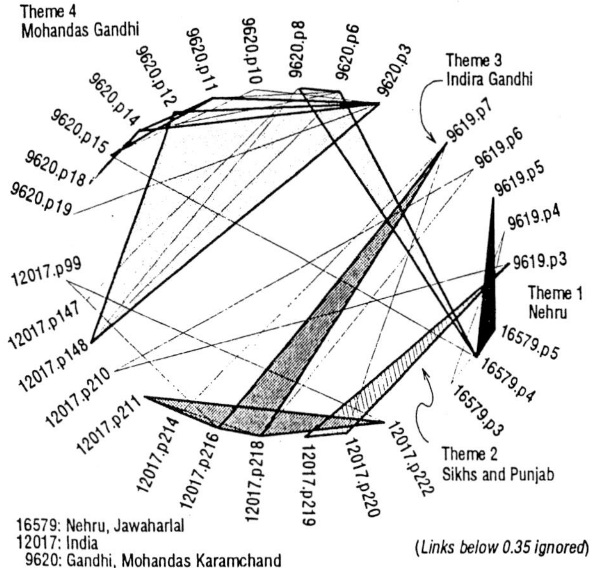

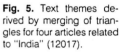

Fig. 5. Text themes derived by merging of triangles for four articles related to "India" (12017).

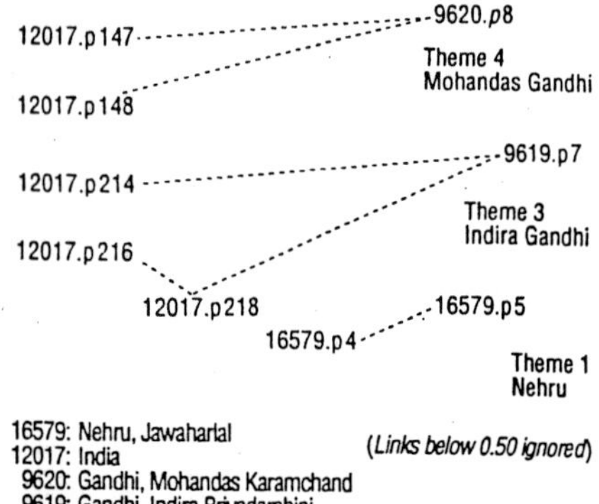

Fig. 6. Simplified text themes derived from high-threshold (disconnected) text relation map for articles related to "India" (12017).

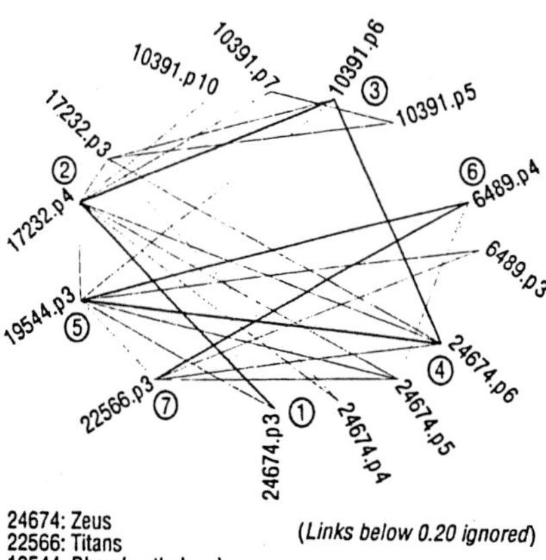

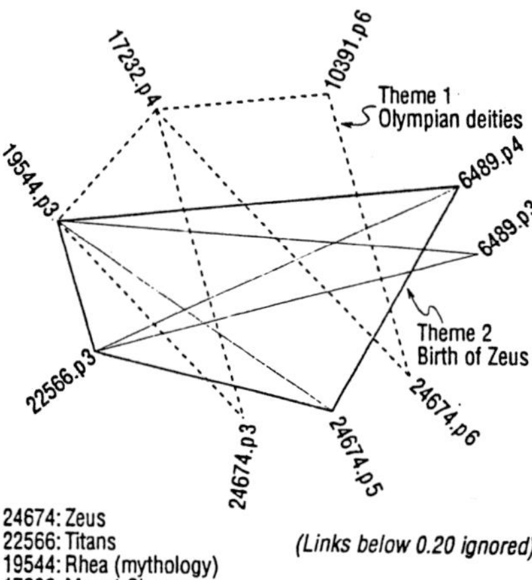

Fig. 7 (top). Depth-first paragraph-traversal order for six articles related to "Zeus" (24674). Path starts with initial paragraph of "Zeus" (24674.p3) and covers, in order, 17232.p4 ("Mount Olympus"), 10391.p6 ("Greek Religion and Mythology"), 24674.p6 ("Zeus"), 19544.p3 ("Rhea"), 6489.p4 ("Cronus"), and 22566.p3 ("Titans"). **Fig. 8 (bottom).** Two themes, "Olympian deities" (dashed triangles) and "birth of Zeus" (heavy lines), for articles related to "Zeus" (24674).

article "Mount Olympus"). The corresponding paragraphs introduce Zeus as the god of the sky and the ruler of the Olympian gods and then proceed by identifying the 12 major Olympian deities, including Zeus, his wife Hera, and his siblings and children.

A more complete forward depth-first path proceeds from item 17232.p4 to include 10391.p6 (paragraph 6 of 10391, "Greek Religion and Mythology") and four additional paragraphs presented in detail in Fig. 7. The complete forward depth-first path includes information about Rhea, Zeus' mother; Cronus, Zeus' father; and the Titans, a race of giants that included Rhea and Cronus, among other gods.

Instead of initiating the text traversal at the beginning of a text, it is also possible for a searcher to use context-dependent text-traversal strategies that start with a special text excerpt of immediate interest. For example, someone interested in the foreign policy of President Nixon might locate paragraph 622 of article 23173 ("United States of America") by using a standard text search. A depth-first path starting at 23173.p622 can then be used to obtain further information. Such a path also includes paragraphs 9086.p13 (paragraph 13 of article 9086, "Gerald R. Ford") and 16855.p11 (paragraph 11 of 16855, "Richard M. Nixon"). The corresponding texts deal with the exchange of visits between President Nixon and Leonid Brezhnev; the continuation of detente between the United States and the Soviet Union that was pursued by President Ford and Secretary of State Kissinger; and finally, Nixon's approach to the People's Republic of China. A completely different topic will be covered by a depth-first path starting with paragraph 23173.p624, describing the Watergate break-in. The corresponding coverage includes Nixon's presumed implication in the Watergate burglary (23173.p624), Vice President Ford's staunch defense of Nixon during his term as vice president (9086.p8), and finally, Nixon's resignation on 9 August 1974 and Ford's pardon (23848.p19).

Current experience indicates that a depth-first path provides a reasonably coherent body of information in practically every subject environment. The resulting paths may, however, be flawed in some ways. For example, there may be repetition of subject coverage in two or more excerpts in a given path; in the previous example, Nixon's resignation is mentioned in paragraphs 9086.p8 and 23848.p19. Repeated text passages may be eliminated by a sentence-sentence comparison, followed by the removal of duplicate occurrences of sufficiently similar sentences. Alternatively, a larger text excerpt in a path can sometimes be replaced by a shorter excerpt whose similarity to the previous text element is large. In the depth-first path of Fig. 7, the long paragraph 10391.p6 that deals with the divine hierarchy on Mount Olympus (node 3 in the figure) may be replaced by a group of three adjacent sentences (10391.g17) consisting of the first three sentences of the paragraph. Similarly, paragraph 22566.p13 is replaceable by sentence group 22566.g7, which includes only the last three sentences of the paragraph.

An alternative way of reducing the path size is to use theme generation methods to obtain text excerpts covering the desired subject area. Figure 8 shows a theme generation map obtained by triangle merging for the Zeus subject area used in Fig. 7. Two themes are distinguished, "Olympian deities" and "birth of Zeus." The two text excerpts that are most similar to the respective theme centroids are 17232.p4 ("The 12 major Olympian deities were Zeus and his wife Hera. . .") and 24674.p5 ("Zeus was the youngest son of the Titans Cronus and Rhea. . ."). An appropriate short path covering Zeus can then be obtained as 24674.p3 (the initial paragraph of the Zeus article), followed by 17232.p4 and 24674.p5, representing the most important paragraphs in the two themes, respectively.

Text Summarization

In the absence of deep linguistic analysis methods that are applicable to unrestricted subject areas, it is not possible to build intellectually satisfactory text summaries (*14*). However, by judicious text extraction methods, collections of text passages can be identified that provide adequate coverage of the subject areas of interest. For example, when homogeneous text relation maps are available, a good summary is normally obtainable by use of one of the longer text-traversal paths in chronological (forward) text order.

Consider, as an example, the paragraph map for document 16585 ("Horatio, Viscount Nelson") (Fig. 9). Two paths are shown that start with the initial text paragraph 16585.p3. The dashed path traverses all "bushy" nodes—that is, nodes in which the number of incident links is large (≥6). The path marked by a heavy line is a complex depth-first path—that is, a depth-first path obtained by starting at each of the bushy nodes, proceeding in depth-first order, and assembling the resulting excerpts into a single path in forward text order. The shorter, dashed path covers the highlights of Nelson's life in paragraphs 16585.p3, p6, p9, and p11, which deal, respectively, with a summary of Nelson's achievements as a British naval commander, his role in the battle of Copenhagen in 1801 after he had

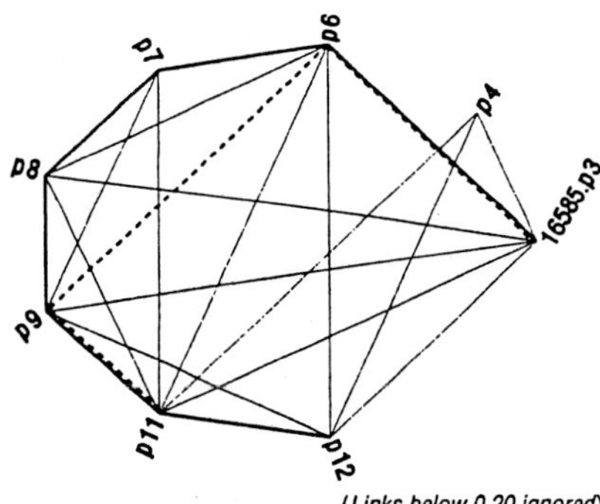

Fig. 9. Complex paths used for text summarization. Dashed path 16585.p3-p6-p9-p11 includes all bushy nodes; solid path 16585.p3-p6-p7-p8-p9-p11-p12 is a depth-first path.

become a vice admiral, and the crucial defeat of Napoleon during the battle of Trafalgar in 1805. The longer, solid path adds paragraphs p7, p8, and p12 of document 16585 to the paragraphs already present in the dashed path. This adds information about the battle of the Nile in 1798, plus a wrap-up paragraph covering Nelson's burial in St. Paul's Cathedral.

When the text relation map is substantially disconnected, the text-traversal process will not produce comprehensive summaries. In that case, adequate subject coverage is generally obtained by taking the initial paragraph of the main document under consideration, followed by the best paragraph for each text theme, as explained earlier. For the Zeus subject matter in Figs. 7 and 8, the resulting summary consists of paragraphs 24674.p3, 6489.p4, and 17232.p4. The corresponding summary introduces Zeus, the ruler of the Olympian Gods (24674.p3), mentions the story of the birth of Zeus as the sixth child of Cronus and Rhea (6489.p4), and terminates with an introduction to the 12 major Olympian deities (17232.p4).

When paths and themes are used for text summarization, longer summaries will be obtained when the text relation map is generated with low similarity thresholds. This produces denser maps with large numbers of text links. The themes may then partly overlap, and the summaries obtained by text extraction will be discursive. Contrariwise, when high similarity thresholds are used, the maps and themes tend to be disconnected and the summaries become sparser.

Conclusion

Formal evaluation data on the effectiveness of the methods introduced here are difficult to produce in the absence of detailed relevance information relating the content of many kinds of text excerpts to large numbers of subject queries. The experience accumulated with the wide-ranging subject matter in the Funk and Wagnalls encyclopedia indicates that useful output products are obtained in most cases. Because the approaches described here are robust and generally applicable to a wide variety of texts in many different environments, one may anticipate that such text-processing and knowledge-extraction capabilities will soon be widely used.

REFERENCES AND NOTES

1. M. Bernstein, J. D. Bolter, M. Joyce, E. Mylonas, in *Proceedings of Hypertext-91*, Association for Computing Machinery, San Antonio, TX, 15 to 18 December 1991 (ACM Press, Baltimore, MD), pp. 246–260; G. P. Landow, *Comput. Humanities* **23**, 173 (1989); J. D. Bolter, *Writing Space—The Computer, Hypertext, and the History of Writing* (Erlbaum, Hillsdale, NJ, 1991); P. Delaney and G. P. Landow, Eds., *Hypermedia and Literary Studies* (MIT Press, Cambridge, MA, 1991).
2. G. Salton, Ed., *The Smart Retrieval System—Experiments in Automatic Document Processing* (Prentice-Hall, Englewood Cliffs, NJ, 1971); ———, C. S. Yang, A. Wong, *Commun. ACM* **18**, 613 (1975); G. Salton, *Automatic Text Processing—The Transformation, Analysis, and Retrieval of Information by Computer* (Addison-Wesley, Reading, MA, 1989); *Science* **253**, 974 (1991).
3. G. Salton and C. Buckley, *Science* **253**, 1012 (1991); ———, in *Proceedings of SIGIR-91—Fourteenth International ACM-SIGIR Conference on Research and Development in Information Retrieval*, Chicago, IL, 13 to 16 October 1991, A. Bookstein, V. Chiaramella, G. Salton, V. V. Raghavan, Eds. (Association for Computing Machinery, New York, 1991), pp. 21–30.
4. An electronic version of the Funk and Wagnalls encyclopedia containing approximately 26,000 articles of text was used as a sample database in this study.
5. J. O'Connor, *Inf. Process. Manage.* **11**, 155 (1975); *J. Am. Soc. Inf. Sci.* **32**, 227 (1980); S. Al-Hawamdeh and P. Willett, *Electron. Publ.* **2**, 179 (1989).
6. G. Salton, C. Buckley, J. Allan, *Electron. Publ.* **5**, 1 (1992); G. Salton, J. Allan, C. Buckley, in *Proceedings of SIGIR-93—Sixteenth International ACM-SIGIR Conference on Research and Development in Information Retrieval*, Pittsburgh, PA, 27 June to 1 July 1993, R. Karfhage, E. Rasmussen, P. Willet, Eds. (Association for Computing Machinery, New York,1993), pp. 49–58.
7. C. Buckley, G. Salton, J. Allan, in *The First Text Retrieval Conference*, D. K. Harman, Ed. (NIST Special Publication 500-207, Government Printing Office, Washington, DC, 1993), pp. 59–72; C. Buckley, J. Allan, G. Salton, in *The Second Text Retrieval Conference*, D. K. Harman, Ed. (NIST Special Publication, Government Printing Office, Washington, DC, in press).
8. All text relation maps in this study are based on global text similarity as well as local context check restrictions. The similarity thresholds used to construct the text relation maps can be chosen so that the number of links does not greatly exceed the number of nodes appearing in the maps.
9. M. H. Anderson, J. Nielsen, H. Rasmussen, *Hypermedia* **1**, 255 (1989); M. Bernstein, in *Proceedings of the European Conference on Hypertext*, Versailles, France, November 1990, A. Rizk, N. Streitz, J. Andre, Eds. (Cambridge Univ. Press, New York, 1990), pp. 212–223; M. H. Chignell, B. Nordhausen, J. F. Valdez, J. A. Waterworth, *Hypermedia* **3**, 187 (1991); R. Furuta, C. Pleasant, B. Shneiderman, *ibid.* **1**, 179 (1989); P. Gloor, in *Proceedings of Hypertext-91—Third ACM Conference on Hypertext*, San Antonio, TX, 15 to 18 December 1991 (ACM Press, Baltimore, MD, 1991), pp. 107–121; T. C. Rearick, in *Hypertext/Hypermedia Handbook*, J. Devlin and E. Berk, Eds. (McGraw-Hill, New York, 1991), pp. 113–140.
10. R. A. Botafogo, E. Rivlin, B. Shneiderman, *ACM Trans. Inf. Sys.* **10**, 142 (1992); R. S. Gilyarevskii and M. M. Subbotin, *J. Am. Soc. Inf. Sci.* **44**, 185 (1993); C. Guinan and A. F. Smeaton, in *Proceedings of ECHT-92—ACM-ECHT Conference*, Milan, Italy, 30 November to 4 December 1992 (ACM Press, Baltimore, MD, 1992), pp. 122–130.
11. M. A. Hearst and C. Plaunt, in *Proceedings of SIGIR-93—Sixteenth International ACM-SIGIR Conference on Research and Development in Information Retrieval*, Pittsburgh, PA, 27 June to 1 July 1993, R. Korfhage, E. Rasmussen, P. Willet, Eds. (Association for Computing Machinery, New York, 1993), pp. 55–68.
12. F. Murtagh, *Comput. J.* **26**, 354 (1982); W. B. Croft, *J. Am. Soc. Inf. Sci.* **28**, 341 (1977); G. Salton and A. Wong, *ACM Trans. Database Syst.* **3**, 321 (1978).
13. G. de Jong, in *Strategies for Natural Language Processing*, W. G. Lehnert and M. H. Ringle, Eds. (Erlbaum, Hillsdale, NJ, 1982), pp. 149–176.
14. H. P. Luhn, *IBM J. Res. Dev.* **2**, 159 (1958); H. P. Edmundson and R. E. Wyllys, *Commun. ACM* **4**, 226 (1961); C. D. Paice, *Inf. Process. Manage.* **26**, 171 (1990); J. E. Rush, R. Salvador, A. Zamora, *J. Am. Soc. Inf. Sci.* **22**, 260 (1964).
15. The authors are grateful to the Microsoft Corporation for making the Funk and Wagnalls encyclopedia available in machine-readable form. Supported in part by NSF grant IRI 93-00124.

Querying Across Languages: A Dictionary-Based Approach to Multilingual Information Retrieval

David A. Hull **Gregory Grefenstette**

Rank Xerox Research Centre
6 chemin de Maupertuis, 38240 Meylan France
{hull,grefen}@grenoble.rxrc.xerox.com

Abstract

The multilingual information retrieval system of the future will need to be able to retrieve documents across language boundaries. This extension of the classical IR problem is particularly challenging, as significant resources are required to perform query translation. At Xerox, we are working to build a multilingual IR system and conducting a series of experiments to understand what factors are most important in making the system work. Using translated queries and a bilingual transfer dictionary, we have learned that cross-language multilingual IR is feasible, although performance lags considerably behind the monolingual standard. The experiments suggest that correct identification and translation of multi-word terminology is the single most important source of error in the system, although ambiguity in translation also contributes to poor performance.

1 Introduction

As Internet resources such as the World Wide Web become accessible to more and more countries, and technological advances overcome the network, interface, and computer system differences which have impeded information access, it will become more common for searchers to wish to explore collections of documents that are not written in their native language. Beyond merely accepting extended character sets and performing language identification, the text retrieval systems of the future will have to provide help in searching for information across language boundaries. At Xerox, we have begun a series of experiments to explore what factors are most important in making multilingual information retrieval systems work.

After presenting our definition of multilingual information retrieval, we introduce several basic approaches to the problem and discuss the previous research work in this area. We then describe our first round of experiments using French queries and an English document collection (TIPSTER). We demonstrate that multilingual information retrieval is feasible using a general language bilingual dictionary and some basic linguistic analysis tools, but that there is a significant gap between monolingual and multilingual performance. From a failure analysis of the results, we learn that translation ambiguity and missing terminology are the two primary sources of error, and we conclude by suggesting some methods for resolving these problems.

Our goal in these experiments is not to build the ideal fully-functional multilingual IR system, as the time and resources required for this task are considerable. Rather, we restrict our attention to a single language pair and try to understand the basic requirements for effective multilingual IR and the problems that arise from a simple implementation of such a system. From this research, we can begin to understand which components of the system are most important and find some directions for our future research. Therefore, the examples of when and the reasons why the system failed are more important than the numerical results of the experiments.

2 Defining Multilingual Information Retrieval

There is no common currently accepted definition for multilingual information retrieval (MLIR). The term has been used in the past to cover a broad range of different approaches to information retrieval (IR) using one or more languages. In this section, we will present a number of different descriptions of the multilingual IR task that have been used by previous authors and outline our own approach to the problem. Five different definitions for MLIR are outlined below.

(1) IR in any language other than English.

(2) IR on a parallel document collection or on a multilingual document collection where the search space is restricted to the query language.

(3) IR on a monolingual document collection which can be queried in multiple languages.

(4) IR on a multilingual document collection, where queries can retrieve documents in multiple languages.

(5) IR on multilingual documents, i.e. more than one language can be present in the individual documents

Definition (1) comes from the recent TREC conferences [Harman, 1995], where the IR experiments in Spanish are referred to as the multilingual track. A number of modern IR systems claim that they are performing multilingual information retrieval because they are capable of handling extended character sets and can be modified to perform text retrieval in other languages. An expanded version of this definition is (2), where it is assumed that the system is working with a multilingual document collection but the documents in each language are viewed as separate and independent parts of the collection. Once the query is entered, the language of interest is fixed, and only documents in that language are searched. This definition also covers parallel document collections[1], which can be searched in any of their component languages.

Definition (3) assumes that the document collection is monolingual, but the retrieval system is capable of processing queries in a number of different languages and retrieving documents across language boundaries. With (4), a simple extension of the previous definition, we can move to a multilingual document collection which can be searched in any of its component languages and where documents can be retrieved in multiple languages in response to a single search. Finally, we can generalize this definition still further to multilingual documents (5). The MLIR problem descriptions above are listed in order of their complexity. Recent work on Spanish IR [Broglio et al., 1995, Buckley et al., 1995] suggests that modern IR systems and techniques can be applied effectively to other languages. However, researchers are only beginning to address the problem of cross-language document access using full-text retrieval systems.

The MLIR problem as we would like to define it (3-5) requires some form of query translation. This adds an entirely new order of complexity to the traditional IR problem and requires that an extensive knowledge base be incorporated into the system to support document access across language barriers. However, MLIR is a far more tractable problem than machine translation, as the translated representations of documents or queries are for automatic machine use only and need never be read by a human being. Therefore the entire issue of syntactic generation and the problems associated with incorrect resolution of ambiguity [Oard et al., 1994] can be avoided. Information retrieval is such an inexact science that it is not clear whether direct query translation is necessary or even optimal for identifying relevant documents. It may be possible to achieve a reasonable level of performance by relying primarily on statistical similarity information. However, recent research by Davis and Dunning suggests that such information alone is not sufficient [Davis & Dunning, 1996]. This is one of the important issues which needs to be explored in this expanding field of research.

Our research concentrates on problem (3) above for several reasons. First, in order to obtain experimental results that are both reliable and quantifiable, it is necessary to have test document collection with large numbers of relevance judgements. For the moment, such resources are scarce to non-existent in the multilingual domain. Therefore, we are able to leverage off the extensive previous work in traditional IR if we rely upon a monolingual test collection. Second, following a long tradition of experimental research, we attack the simplest problem first, and worry later about generalizing our results to multilingual document collections.

Definition (4) adds an additional layer of complexity to the IR problem because of the language-dependent nature of the translation process. There is no guarantee that document similarity scores obtained by translation of the query into several different languages will be comparable, so creating a single ranked list of documents requires research into merging strategies that is only beginning to happen for monolingual merging problems [Voorhees et al., 1995]. Definition (5) requires that scores be combined on the level of the individual documents. We also restrict ourselves to a single language pair (English/French) in order to minimize the resource requirements of our experiments.

3 Basic Approaches to MLIR

Information Retrieval systems rank documents according to statistical similarity measures based on the cooccurrence of terms in queries and documents. For our approach to MLIR, which tries to capture relevant documents across language boundaries, some mechanism for query or document translation is required. Our MLIR system has been designed to use query translation. There is no reason in principle why the problem could not be approached using document translation instead. Queries tend to be very short (often only one or two words), which does not provide much context for the translation process, so it is quite possible that document translation could lead to better performance. However, when faced with the choice between translating the query once or translating every document in the collection, the former seems much more realistic in terms of efficiency. The query translation module can easily be built on top of an already existing IR software package without having to redesign the entire system. Furthermore, for document translation, the storage costs increase linearly with the number of supported languages (unless document translation is performed dynamically, which is not currently a realistic option).

Oard [Oard et al., 1994] defines three major approaches to the problem of interlingual term correspondence, which they call text translation, term vector translation, and Latent Semantic Coindexing[2]. Text translation describes the process of mapping the query from the source language directly into one or more target languages using a machine translation (MT) system. This represents the high-end approach to MLIR, since machine translation generally involves the sophisticated use of natural language processing and text generation techniques. It is characterized by the direct resolution of ambiguity in translation using structural information from the source language text. This strategy for MLIR might allow the researcher to take advantage of the extensive body of research on machine translation and the availability of commercial products. However, the performance of current MT systems in the setting of general language translation is dismal enough to make this option less than entirely satisfactory. Experiments by Radwan [Radwan, 1994] confirm these suspicions.

As a more robust alternative, we can consider using term vector translation[3], a process by which each word in the source language is mapped to all of its possible definitions in the target language. Retrieval strategies based on the vector space model can seamlessly evaluate this extended representation of the translated query. However, this approach raises a number of important issues with respect to term weighting strategies. Should each term be weighted according to the number of translations? For example, a term with four translations may have its importance artificially inflated with respect to a term with a single translation unless this

[1] A parallel document collection is defined as one where the same documents are presented in two or more languages.

[2] Latent Semantic Indexing [Landauer & Littman, 1990] applied to a parallel document collection.

[3] Oard [Oard et al., 1994] expected that the term vectors would be extracted from a parallel aligned corpus, but we find this concept useful for describing our dictionary-based approach also.

one to many mapping is accounted for in the term weights. Perhaps an extended or weighted Boolean model where all translations of each term are linked by disjunction would be more appropriate. Furthermore, some translations of a term will be much more common than others. Should more common translations be weighted proportionally higher? What resources do we use to obtain this information? These questions suggest that corpus-driven methods for MLIR should be considered.

While direct translation of the query seems like the most viable approach to MLIR, one can also consider methods that derive query translations indirectly using a training corpus. Landauer and Littman [Landauer & Littman, 1990] and Evans et al. [Evans et al., 1991] present very compelling techniques based on Latent Semantic Indexing, which uses the singular value decomposition of a parallel document collection to obtain term vector representations which are comparable across all the languages of the collection. Unfortunately, this technique has not yet been seriously tested for the MLIR problem. Davis and Dunning [Davis & Dunning, 1996] examine several interesting alternative approaches which also use a parallel document collection. For example, one can match the query against sentences in the same language and find terms in matching sentences in other languages that are strongly associated with the query topic. Indirect query translation using training corpora may be able to capture domain and context dependent relationships that would be missed by other techniques. We consider exploiting parallel corpora for direct or indirect translation to be a promising line of research.

4 Resource requirements for MLIR

Extending information retrieval to the multilingual domain requires that researchers obtain a significant number of additional resources, even for the simplest approaches, where the query and the documents returned are both in the same language. The MLIR system must be able to handle the character sets of each language that is supported and multilingual document collections may benefit from some facilities for automatic language recognition [Sibun & Spitz, 1994, Grefenstette, 1995]. Support for accented character sets may seem simple on the surface, but there are some important issues that must be addressed. In many text collections, accenting is inconsistent, and capitalized letters sometimes lose their accents. Our approach is to handle these problems during the stemming process.

Efficient stemming algorithms for English have been developed over the past twenty-five years, but most of this work will not generalize to other languages. It is not known what investment would be required to create high-performance stemmers for languages other than English. Stemmers are being developed for other languages but most have not been extensively tested. Fortunately, Xerox linguists have developed an alternative solution based on the use of inflectional analysis. This approach is particularly valuable for term translation, as it only conflates word forms which have the same inflectional root, so no additional ambiguity is introduced before translation. In terms of IR performance, it works as well as traditional stemming algorithms in English [Hull, 1996] and provides similar improvements for Spanish [Hearst et al., 1996].

Xerox has developed a methodology [Chanod, 1994] which can be used to construct a morphological analyzer for a new language in 8-10 person/months, and tools have already been built for most Western European languages. These analyzers recognize the possible parts of speech of each token in a text and provide a normalized form for a variety of surface forms. For example, the French word *joignaient* (joined) is morphologically analyzed as the 3rd person plural preterite form of *joindre*. The German word *Weingärtnergenossenschaften* is analyzed as the feminine plural noun *Wein#Gärtner#Genosse(n)#schaft* composed of the agglutination of the words *Wein*, *Gärtner*, *Genosse*, and *schaft*. In addition to providing principled stemming, morphological analysis is a necessary step in any subsequent natural language processing, such as noun phrase recognition. It is also crucial for finding term entries in bilingual dictionaries.

Query translation requires extensive resources for each language pair under consideration. Depending on the approach, this may include (1) a machine translation system, (2) bilingual thesauri or transfer dictionaries, (3) information derived from parallel texts and/or monolingual domain-specific corpora. Machine translation systems are useful for direct query translation. Bilingual dictionaries are one source of definitions for term vector mapping. Parallel corpora can be used to extract relationships between terms for term vector translation or as a reference for the indirect query translation strategies described in the previous section. Domain-specific monolingual corpora can be an important source for terminology and can be used as a surrogate when parallel corpora are not available in the field of interest, although the process of extracting translations is much more difficult and manual effort may be required.

Bilingual general language dictionaries in machine readable form are more and more available, although they tend to be expensive to obtain. Unfortunately, they are designed with human readers in mind and thus need to be adapted for use by automatic retrieval systems. For term vector translation, the system needs only the direct translations of each entry, which we will define as a bilingual transfer dictionary (also sometimes called a bilingual thesaurus). Bilingual general language dictionaries contain more verbose definitions and examples including large amounts of vocabulary that would not be suitable for IR. Converting a bilingual dictionary to a transfer dictionary is a non-trivial effort.

Parallel text collections can also be used for term vector translation, but doing so accurately requires immense quantities of training text and statistical models of great sophistication. The work of Brown et al. [Brown et al., 1993] from IBM epitomizes this strategy. They generate not only term translation vectors but corresponding translation probabilities for each link which accurately model the distribution of the training corpus. This approach is extremely compelling but the translation probabilities must be applied with caution, as they may not generalize to other domains and they are generated independent of context. The IBM work is designed for machine translation and has not been tested on the MLIR problem. Much simpler approaches, such as the matching of associated terms from aligned sentences suggested by Davis and Dunning have not yet been proven to be effective.

Of these two resources, bilingual general language dictionaries are more prevalent than parallel texts of sufficient size to have similar coverage. While creating a transfer dictionary is not a simple process, the effort required to implement the IBM approach makes the former task seem simple in comparison. Therefore, our experiments use a bilingual transfer dictionary. In a sense, one can consider these two approaches as complementary. The transfer dictionary provides broad but shallow coverage of the language. All major words in the language are defined but most technical terminology is missing and translation probabilities are not available. On the other hand, parallel corpora provide narrow but deep coverage, particularly when they concentrate on a single domain. The ideal MLIR system of the future will want to take advantage of both of these resources.

5 Previous Experiments in MLIR

There is a long history of multilingual text retrieval in the context of controlled vocabulary systems. Salton [Salton, 1970] and Pevzner [Pevzner, 1972] demonstrated in the early 70's that cross-language text retrieval systems perform as well as their single-language counterparts given a carefully constructed bilingual thesaurus. A large number of governmental and commercial applications have been developed based on this approach. However, controlled vocabulary systems are less than ideal for modern text retrieval for a number of reasons [Oard & Dorr, 1996]. First and foremost, these systems require considerable human effort in thesaurus contruction and document indexing (which is often not fully automated), something that is just not feasible for large modern text collections which use language in a much more dynamic fashion. As retrieval is generally based on a simple boolean model, these systems also require considerable skill to be utilized effectively and tend to be less robust and less effective than systems which can rank documents using full-text statistical matching techniques. For more information on multilingual text retrieval research and applications, readers are encouraged to consult Oard's comprehensive review [Oard & Dorr, 1996].

Experimental work on the application of MLIR to full text retrieval systems is sparse indeed, with two notable exceptions. Christian Fluhr and colleagues at INSTN have developed a ranked boolean system which uses bilingual term, compound, and idiom dictionaries to work on English-French and French-German cross-language retrieval[4]. Radwan and Fluhr [Radwan, 1994] conducted experiments using the Cranfield collection and translated French queries and obtained the following results [p. 244]: monolingual system - 0.345, MLIR using term vector translation and transfer dictionaries - 0.270, MLIR using machine translation (SYSTRAN) - 0.215, as measured by average precision at 10-90% recall. These experiments provide strong evidence that term vector translation is more effective than machine translation. Mark Davis and Ted Dunning from NMSU have tried a variety of corpus learning methods on English queries and a Spanish document collection (the Mexican newspaper El Norte) and have found that all of their translated query sets performed far worse than the monolingual baseline [Davis & Dunning, 1996]. Their research suggests that corpus learning strategies alone will not be sufficient to provide acceptable performance for MLIR. In contrast to Fluhr's system, it appears that Davis and Dunning generated their query translations entirely automatically. No one has yet been able to build an automatic system that performs effectively without considerable human intervention in the dictionary contruction process.

6 The Xerox Experimental Approach

Multilingual IR systems can be evaluated automatically in much the same fashion as monolingual IR systems, using queries with known relevance judgements. However, in the multilingual context, there is a strong desire to compare the results against the optimal performance of the system if the query were perfectly translated. This gives rise to the following approach to evaluation in MLIR. Start with queries, documents, and relevance judgements in a single language. Have the queries translated into another language by human translators. These translated queries are retranslated by the MLIR system, and the results can then be compared to the original queries to get a good sense of the relative performance of the MLIR system. All the experiments described in the previous section use some variant of this strategy.

Following this well-motivated and well-tested methodology, we worked with translated French queries and English documents. Our experiments used the TIPSTER text collection and queries 51-100 from the recent TREC experiments [Harman, 1995]. We chose to use only the news component of the collection, which consists of articles from the Wall Street Journal, AP newswire, and the San Jose Mercury News, and amounted to roughly half a million documents or about 1.6 GB of text. The 50 selected queries were translated into French externally by a professional translator. We used the term vector translation model, with query translations generated by a bilingual transfer dictionary.

A careful examination of the queries and some preliminary experiments made it clear that the original queries were not suitable for multilingual information retrieval due to their length and content. In particular, the *Concept* fields of the queries contain large amounts of specific terminology, much of which has no good translation and was therefore left in English by the human translator. For example, most acronyms (GATT, LBO, OSHA, SALT II, OPEC, FDIC, NRA, LAN) and proper names (Reagan, Bush, Iran-Contra, Toshiba, M-1 Abrams, AH-64 Apache) are not translated and most technical terminology has one unique translation. Using this information, the MLIR system was able to attain unrealistically high levels of performance. While this may be reasonable for a technical domain, we wish to obtain a more general picture of the problems associated with query translation. Researchers have recognized that most real queries are only a few words long, and this is even more likely to be the case when users are not working in their native language. To address this issue, we decided to work with short versions of the queries (average length of seven words) that had been created for previous TREC experiments and translated them into French. While some acronyms and terminology remain, the overwhelming majority of the language independent evidence has been removed.

We also converted an on-line bilingual French $\Longrightarrow$ English dictionary (Oxford Hachette, 1994) to a word-based transfer dictionary suitable for text retrieval, which involved the removal of large amounts of excess information. Unfortunately, this was neither a simple nor a fully automatic process. Although the dictionary was formatted in SGML, which allowed for automated filtering of sections such as pronunciation, etymology, and examples, these markings were not always coherent or correct, creating one source of errors in our translation assignments. In some cases it was possible to detect these marking errors. For example, we would label for manual treatment any translation containing personal pronouns such as *I* or *we*. 462 of the 34000 definitions were manually treated based on this filter. Sometimes, especially for common words, the dictionary entry was so long and complex that the automatic filtering would fail, either due to bugs in the filter or misplaced SGML markers. For example, automatic extraction of translations of the com-

[4] Much of this work is from the EMIR European Project: http://www.newcastle.research.ec.org/esp-syn/text/5312.html.

English: politically motivated civil disturbances
French: troubles civils à caractère politique
Term vector retranslation:
trouble – turmoil discord trouble unrest disturbance disorder
civil – civil civilian courteous
caractère – character nature
politique – political diplomatic politician policy

Table 1: An example of the query translation process for short query Q67

mon French word *prendre* (to take) gave 23 words including *success, break, catch, set, sink, stiffen, take, thicken, find, oneself, lay, idea, bring, charge, handle, pick, client, put, accent, one's, arm, waist, customer.* We left such noisy definitions as they were produced, but a serious manual cleaning of the dicionary would be beneficial. 521 of the transfer dictionary entries (mostly common words) had ten or more translations. Duplicate terms were removed from each definition.

A further and more pernicious error for our system was the use of encyclopedic definitions which elaborate on the translation of the word, introducing contextual words that are not proper translations of the dictionary head word, but rather clues to a human user about how and where the word is used. These clues are often embedded in the heart of the definition and thus reappear after automatic filtering. For example, the French word *radiation* was filtered to: *radiation, expulsion, striking off from the register, loss of the license to practice medicine, disbarring.* Filtering out stopwords still left *disbarring, expulsion, radiation, striking, register, loss, license, practice, medicine* as translation equivalents. Ideally, one would only retain *radiation, expulsion,* and perhaps *disbarring.* In an IR setting, it is evident that the terms *register, license,* and *medicine* add considerable noise to the results. Our automatic filtering created an object that more resembles a thesaurus than a dictionary.

The MLIR process consists of three basic steps. First, the query is morphologically analyzed and each term is replaced by its inflectional root. Second, the system looks up each root in the bilingual transfer dictionary and builds a translated query by taking the concatenation of all term translations. Terms which are missing from the transfer dictionary are passed unchanged to the final query. The translated query is then sent to a traditional monolingual IR system. Documents are also normalized to their inflectional roots. This is the simplest possible approach to MLIR, since all issues relating to specialized term weighting and resolving ambiguity in translation are ignored. It is designed to serve as a baseline, and future efforts will improve upon this model. Table 1 shows a sample query.

These experiments use a modified version the SMART information retrieval system [Buckley, 1985], which measures the strength of the link between the query and each document using the vector space model. We apply the square-root function to term and document frequencies. Query term weights are multiplied by the traditional IDF factor while documents are normalized to have unit length. Documents are ranked in descending order of their inner product score with respect to the query and performance is evaluated by comparing the ranked list to known relevance judgments.

The unique characteristics of MLIR suggest specific strategies for evaluation. One would expect in general that translated queries (particularly short ones) will tend to perform worse than the original queries due to errors and ambiguity introduced by the translation process. Success in information retrieval depends on the ability of the user (with help from the system) to find vocabulary which appears in the documents of interest. This task becomes much more difficult when the terminology must cross language boundaries. This suggests that relevance feedback techniques, which improve the query by incorporating information from previously discovered relevant documents will be a particularly important tool in the multilingual setting.

In addition, the user cannot be expected to quickly read and evaluate (or have translated) lots of documents in a foreign language. Therefore, high precision should be an important goal for an MLIR system. Once a few relevant documents have been collected, the system can resort to monolingual relevance feedback to find more relevant documents if high recall is the final goal. Note that for these experiments, we are assuming that the user is working with a monolingual collection. For a multilingual document collection, good relevance feedback would probably necessitate obtaining at least one relevant document in each language of interest. For these reasons, we choose to use precision averaged at 5, 10, 15, and 20 documents retrieved as the evaluation measure.

7 Experimental Results

Our experiment compares the original English queries to three retranslations generated by different versions of the transfer dictionary. The first version uses the dictionary constructed automatically by the process described in the previous section. Given that many dictionary entries have extraneous terms and sometimes the correct definition is missed completely, we decided to also build a clean version of the transfer dictionary manually for the query terms used in the experiment. Since the queries are short with some duplication, there are only about 300 unique terms to look up. We used the 3rd edition Robert and Collins French-English dictionary (not online) for this work. In hindsight, we realized that using different dictionaries for automatic vs. manual translation[5] may cause some inconsistency in the results, largely because one dictionary may be more comprehensive than another, resulting in more definitions for some terms. The second query representation is generated from this manually constructed transfer dictionary.

Q53: rachat financé par emprunt ⟹ leveraged buyout
Q55: délit d'initié ⟹ insider trading
Q56: taux d'emprunt préférentiels ⟹ prime lending rate
Q58: chemin de fer ⟹ railroad
Q62: coup d'état ⟹ coup d'etat
Q64: prise d'otage ⟹ hostage-taking
Q65: système de recherche documentaire ⟹ information retrieval system
Q66: langage naturel ⟹ natural language
Q70: mère porteuse ⟹ surrogate mother
Q82: génie génétique ⟹ genetic engineering
Q88: pétrole brut ⟹ crude oil
Q90: gaz naturel ⟹ natural gas
Q96: programme informatique ⟹ computer program

Table 2: A list of the important multi-word expressions in the query sample

[5] We remind the reader that in this context *translation* means replacing a source language term with all entries from the transfer dictionary. No lexical ambiguity is resolved.

During the manual construction process, we realized that the translation of multi-word noun phrases as an individual unit is particularly important. The automatically created transfer dictionary provided word-based translation only. Therefore, whenever we found a multi-word expression (MWE) in the bilingual dictionary which was also matched in the query, we added it to the transfer dictionary. See Table 2 for a list of these expressions. This multi-word transfer dictionary serves as the basis for the third query representation. In summary, we generated four different experimental runs: (a) the original English queries and translated queries constructed from (b) the automatically generated word-based transfer dictionary, (c) the manually built word-based transfer dictionary, and (d) the manually built multi-word transfer dictionary. Experiments (c) and (d) are artificial, in the sense that this level of performance could not be obtained for a different set of queries without additional manual effort. They are included to help us understand the inherent limitations of this methodology by factoring out problems with the current implementation. The evaluation results averaged over the 50-query sample are presented in Table 3.

Original English	Automatic word-based transfer dict.	Manual word-based transfer dict.	Manual multi-word transfer dict.
0.393	0.235	0.269	0.357

Table 3: Average Precision at 5, 10, 15, and 20 documents retrieved for the original English queries and translation via three different versions of the transfer dictionary.

When we analyze the average performance figures using the Friedman Test [Hull, 1993], we find that queries (b) and (c) perform significantly worse than queries (a) and (d), but that the difference between translation by the multi-word transfer dictionary (d) and the original English queries (a) is not statistically significant. While there is probably a real difference present which we were unable to detect due to the small size of the query sample, these results indicate that an IR system can perform almost as well across languages as it can in a monolingual setting, provided that a sufficiently accurate and comprehensive transfer dictionary is available. Correct translation of multi-word expressions makes the biggest difference in average performance.

There are several caveats which should be applied to these results. We had to manually construct the multi-word transfer dictionary in order to obtain the best results. Building a similar dictionary with full coverage of the language would be an immense task, therefore the final column of Table 3 should be interpreted as an optimal performance benchmark for transfer dictionary-based translation and represents a level of performance which is not currently attainable. Second, most modern IR systems have many additional features, such as automatic query expansion or phrase matching which improve performance. Our original English performance baseline has none of these features (i.e. MWE's are scored by individual term matching only). Were such techniques applied, the gap in performance between the original and translated queries could well increase. There are other ways in which we might be able to improve the English baseline, such as adopting term-weighting strategies that are better suited for short queries.

7.1 Detailed Query Analysis

The average performance analysis shows only part of the picture. In order to get a different view of the results, we break down the performance by query in Table 4. We begin by removing the 8 queries whose original English version have an average precision of 0.0 from the sample (corresponding to no relevant documents ranked in the top 20). The goal of the MLIR system is to obtain performance equivalent to its monolingual counterpart. However, there is an important difference between systems that perform equally well at a high level and equally poorly (i.e. score zero according the evaluation measure). In the top half of the table, we arbitrarily define an absolute difference of average precision of more than 0.10 as important and partition the remaining queries according to whether their translated versions fall above or below this threshold. In the bottom half the table, we divide the queries that perform worse in translation according to whether they have an average precision greater than zero.

Performance	Automatic word-based trans dict	Manual word-based trans dict	Manual multi-word trans dict
Tr > Orig	1	3	4
Tr ≈ Orig	19	22	26
Tr < Orig	22	17	12
0.0 < Tr < Orig	10	9	9
Tr = 0.0	12	8	3

Table 4: Comparison of the performance of the translated (Tr) and original (Orig) English queries. Values given are the number of queries in each category.

We notice a steady improvement in performance as more manual effort is applied to the dictionary constuction process. This difference is reflected primarily in queries moving from having no relevant documents ranked in the top 20 to at least some relevant documents scoring well, which is important. Recovering at least one relevant document is substantially better than finding none, because monolingual relevance feedback becomes a viable option. There are even some queries which perform much better in their translated versions.

In order to gain a better understanding of the problems associated with query translation, we selected the 17 queries which did worse when translated using the manual word-based transfer dictionary and performed a detailed failure analysis. We found that 9 lost information as a result of the failure to translate multi-word expressions correctly, 8 had problems due to ambiguity in translation (i.e. extraneous definitions added to query), and 4 suffered from a loss in retranslation. Note that the total is greater than 17 because some queries suffered from more than one problem.

Our experimental results demonstrate that recognizing and translating multi-word expressions is crucial to success in MLIR. This is in distinct contrast to monolingual IR, where identifying noun phrases or word pairs generally helps but does not produce dramatic gains in average performance. The key difference is that the individual components of phrases often have very different meanings in translation, so the entire sense of the phrase is often lost. This is not always the case, but it happens often enough to make correct phrase translation the single most important factor in our multilingual experiments. About half of the expressions given in Table 2 lose vital semantic content when translated on a word by word basis.

Ambiguity in translation can also cause serious problems by adding noise to the query in the form of irrelevant translations. Here are some examples which illustrate the problem:

- machine ⟹ machine ⟹ machine engine
- amendment ⟹ amendement ⟹ amendment enrichment enriching agent
- measure ⟹ mesure ⟹ measure measurement moderation tempo
- failure ⟹ faillite ⟹ fail bankruptcy collapse failure
- military ⟹ militaire ⟹ military army serviceman
- affair ⟹ affaire ⟹ matter business affair case deal bargain transaction

In those case where rare and inappropriate definitions are added to the query (machine, amendment, measure), the ambiguity seriously hurts performance. In other cases (failure, military), the expanded terms all have similar meaning, and the results remain unchanged (since the query using failure is on bank failures). In the last example (affair - taken from *Iran-Contra affair*), the additional terms are valuable for query expansion, and cause a dramatic improvement in performance. Thesauri are legitimate tools for query expansion and this benefit can sometimes extend to the multilingual domain.

As mentioned previously, the simple concatenation of dictionary entries (giving all terms in the query equal weight) is a particularly naive approach to the problem of term weighting in query translation. However, it performs quite well given its simplicity. An alternative approach might be to adopt a probabilistic scheme that adjusts the weights according to the number of translations. For example, the three English translations of a French term would each get 1/3 of their normal term weight, corresponding to the uncertainty of the system regarding the correct definition. We tried this experiment, and found that the average precision dropped from 0.357 to 0.297 as a result of this measure. However, we should note that the 11-pt average precision remained constant and average precision of the reweighted queries was actually higher for 50% and greater recall.

How can we explain this result? A scan through the list of translations reveals that the occurrence of many translations is not necessarily a sign of uncertainty, as definitions are often close synonyms of one another. Full weighting of the dictionary expansion of *affair* above sharply improved performance. While words with only a single translation appear in general to be more valuable, we have not found an effective way to verify or exploit this observation. Most modern IR systems weight each term fully in query expansion, so our naive approach to term weighting (in the absence of more valuable information) seems reasonable.

Translation is not a isomorphic mapping. There are many humorous examples of how quickly meaning decays with repeated translation. In our experiments, there is only one intermediate language, but this alone can lead to confusion. We describe problems of this kind as loss in retranslation. It is important to remember that there is an additional source of error in our experiments that comes from the fact that we translate the queries into French before they are translated back into English. A French user working directly with the MLIR system would not have this additional layer of indirection. Here are some examples of this process (braces link multiple translations of the same term).

- financial crunch ⟹ pertes financières ⟹ [loss ruin waste] financial
- proven ⟹ confirmé ⟹ confirmed
- demographic shifts ⟹ déplacements de population ⟹ population [movement displacement transfer travel trip]
- valued ⟹ représentant ⟹ represent stand portray depict representative

Many of these examples could be correctly resolved with a perfect transfer dictionary, but the variety and richness of language is such that a complete reference of this kind cannot be created.

7.2 Sample Query Profile

In order to give a concrete picture of the general problems discussed in the previous section, we present a detailed profile of a single query. Table 5 shows the original text and the results of retranslation using the manually-generated version of the transfer dictionary for query Q76. This query is definitely not a triumph for our system, as the average precision score of 0.54 for the English text decays to 0.05 after retranslation. The course of this decay is measured in Table 6.

English: original intent or interpretation of amendments to the U.S. Constitution
French: l'intention première ou une interprétation d'un amendement de la constitution des USA
Term vector retranslation:
intention – intention benefit
première – first initial bottom early front top leading basic primary original
interprétation – interpretation
amendement – amendment enrichment enriching agent
constitution – formation settlement constitution
USA – USA

Table 5: An example of the query translation process for short query Q76

version	prec.	reasons for decay
orig Eng	0.54	
LR	0.34	intent ⟹ intention, U.S. ⟹ USA
TA 1	0.19	constitution, amendment
TA 2	0.10	original, intention
trans Eng	0.05	

Table 6: The decay in performance of query 76 from the original English (orig Eng) to the translated English (trans Eng) due to translation ambiguity (TA) and loss in retranslation (LR)

The first drop is caused by loss in retranslation. These differences are very subtle, but surprisingly important for IR performance, and demonstrate that search success is highly dependent on seemingly random choices in word selection. Intent and intention are close synonyms, and even native speakers of English might not distinguish between them in this context. These particular errors are partly due to the experimental methodology[6], but they are representative of the kinds of problems that a non-native speaker might have in finding the best vocabulary to describe a query topic. The two subsequent drops are the results of translation ambiguity, due to the fact that each word is replaced by all

[6] Many traditional stemming algorithms (such as Porter) would normalize these words to the same root, but inflectional morphology maintains the distinction as each word has a separate dictionary definition.

of its translations. Clearly, words like enrichment, settlement, and formation are unrelated to the primary topic of the query. If this ambiguity could somehow be resolved, we could expect some real improvements in performance.

Fr: amendement	Fr: constitution	χ^2 score
amendment	formation	4
	settlement	71
	constitution	11961
enrichment	formation	8
	settlement	7
	constitution	9

Table 7: Chi-square scores generated from a likelihood ratio test applied to contingency tables of document cooccurrences

One possible approach to resolving ambiguity would be to use the target language text to determine which translations tend to occur together. If translations of different query terms are used in the same context then this is evidence in favor of these particular translations. For example, it would not be too difficult to identify *amendement de la constitution* as a noun phrase and look at the document cooccurrence patterns among the translations of the component terms. The statistical significance of the cooccurrence pattern for the contingency table generated by each pair of translations is measured using the likelihood ratio test [Dunning, 1993] and presented in Table 7. The higher the score, the less likely that these words would occur together by chance. From these results, the correct translation can easily be recognized. However, when we repeated the same experiment for *intention première* we found no such evident pattern. It would also be difficult to determine which pairs of words to compare on a general basis. A serious effort to resolve ambiguity would require a much more comprehensive approach, but this example suggests that the development of such a strategy might be feasible. We plan to attack this problem in our future research.

8 Future Extensions

There are two primary sources of error in our current implementation of a multilingual information retrieval system, missing translations of multi-word expressions and unresolved ambiguity in word-based translation. In addition, there will be some loss in retranslation due to the experimental design which cannot be avoided (i.e. the ambiguity introduced by the human translator). We find a substantial gap in performance between the original English queries and the translated queries which are generated from our noisy automatic word-based transfer dictionary. However, the dramatic improvements that result from manual corrections and additions to this dictionary indicate that with work, one can expect the MLIR system of the future to approach the performance level of its monolingual counterpart. We hope to move in that direction with our future efforts.

To obtain multi-word expressions, one could simply attempt to gather together terminology lists from various specialized domains. However, such resources are precious and tend to be carefully guarded by their owners, making them expensive and not easily available. A natural alternative to the direct approach is to perform terminology extraction from corpora. There has been extensive research on the automatic recognition of terminology translations in parallel corpora [van der Eijk, 1993, Dagan & Church, 1994] and even some work on using non-parallel domain-specific corpora [Peters & Picchi, 1991]. Information extracted by these techniques could be used to supplement the transfer dictionary in an MLIR system.

The error due to ambiguity could probably be reduced with proper term weighting strategies, although this is a difficult problem. The term alignment work of IBM [Brown et al., 1993] directly generates vectors of translation probabilities which could be incorporated into an MLIR system. This might help to reduce the importance of rare translations. However, these translation probabilities are likely to be highly domain-dependent so it is unclear how much they would help performance unless the training corpus is closely related to the collection used for retrieval. A multilingual collection, a fraction of which was available in parallel form, would be ideal for this kind of experiment. The vector space model is based on a term independence assumption, which is a questionable approximation of the true nature of language. This becomes a particularly cogent problem when one considers that the translation probabilities generated by IBM's word alignment follow this assumption. A very rare translation may always be correct in a particular context. Given the amount of data required to reliably estimate a word alignment model, the additional goal of estimating context based translation rules is probably still out of reach, as this step goes a long way towards solving the machine translation problem.

The term vector translation model tends to assume that retrieval strategies rely solely on the vector space model. In many ways, a weighted Boolean model might be more appropriate for MLIR. Linking term translations by disjunction would represent an elegant solution to the term weighting questions discussed in previous section. User derived conjunctions between query terms could serve as a natural filter for extraneous translations. Weighted boolean models deserve serious consideration in the context of multilingual information retrieval.

Direct translation filtering strategies applied to the target language text collection represent a promising direction of research. One very simple method was presented in Table 7. More complex strategies could be devised that filter using context from the document collection. This approach has the nice advantage that the same collection is being used for both disambiguation and retrieval, so domain relevance of the filtering process is guaranteed. In this light, the translation disambiguation problem bears a strong resemblence to term disambiguation in a monolingual setting. In fact, a number of researchers [Dagan et al., 1991, Brown et al., 1991] have used cross-language relationships to help with disambiguation. Given the limited success of term disambiguation as a tool for IR [Sanderson, 1994], there is some question about whether we can hope to gain any benefits out of translation filtering. Translation disambiguation may well work better as an interactive tool. If the user has some familiarity with the target language, he or she could be given a list of items and asked to select the intended definition, or perhaps eliminate the few that are clearly not relevant. This would be a lot cheaper and probably a lot more effective than automatic disambiguation.

Our experiments examine a very basic approach to multilingual information retrieval, simply replacing each term by the concatenation of its translations, as found in a transfer dictionary. This approach can work quite well if the dictionary is robust and comprehensive and translations for multiword expressions are available. The current challenge in MLIR is to find ways to automatically extract the terminology lists and translation probabilities that are not available in the current generation of bilingual dictionaries. There is also a need to explore more structured query models of the translation process and determine whether or how much automatic disambiguation is desirable. Work has only begun on this broad class of problems, so there are plenty of challenges ahead.

Acknowledgments We are grateful to Doug Oard for his many helpful comments on this paper and for his comprehensive survey of the MLIR literature [Oard & Dorr, 1996].

References

[Broglio et al., 1995] Broglio, J., Callan, J., Croft, W., & Nachbar, D. (1995). Document retrieval and routing using the INQUERY system. In *Overview of the 3rd Text Retrieval Conference (TREC-3), NIST SP 500-225*, pp. 29–38.

[Brown et al., 1991] Brown, P., Pietra, S. D., Pietra, V. D., & Mercer, R. (1991). Word-sense disambiguation using statistical methods. In *Proc. of the Association for Computational Linguistics (ACL)*, pp. 169–176.

[Brown et al., 1993] Brown, P., Pietra, S. D., Pietra, V. D., & Mercer, R. (1993). The mathematics of statistical machine translation: Parameter estimation. *Computational Linguistics*, 19(2),263–311.

[Buckley, 1985] Buckley, C. (1985). Implementation of the smart information retrieval system. Technical Report 85-686, Cornell University. SMART is available for research use via anonymous FTP to ftp.cs.cornell.edu in the directory /pub/smart.

[Buckley et al., 1995] Buckley, C., Salton, G., Allen, J., & Singhal, A. (1995). Automatic query expansion using SMART: TREC-3. In *Overview of the 3rd Text Retrieval Conference (TREC-3), NIST SP 500-225*, pp. 69–80.

[Chanod, 1994] Chanod, J.-P. (1994). Finite-state composition of french verb morphology. Technical Report MLTT-005, Rank Xerox Research Centre - Grenoble Laboratory.

[Dagan et al., 1991] Dagan, I., A.Itai, & Schwall, U. (1991). Two languages are more informative than one. In *Proc. of the Association for Computational Linguistics (ACL)*, pp. 130–137.

[Dagan & Church, 1994] Dagan, I., & Church, K. (1994). Termight: Identifying and translating technical terminology. In *Proceedings of the ANLP*, pp. 34–40.

[Davis & Dunning, 1996] Davis, M., & Dunning, T. (1996). A TREC evaluation of query translation methods for multi-lingual text retrieval. In *The 4th Text Retrieval Conference (TREC-4)*. To appear.

[Dunning, 1993] Dunning, T. (1993). Accurate methods for the statistics of surprise and coincidence. *Computational Linguistics*, 19(1),61–74.

[Evans et al., 1991] Evans, D., Handerson, S., Monarch, I., Pereiro, J., & Hersh, W. (1991). Mapping vocabularies using latent semantics. Technical Report CMU-LCL-91-1, Laboratory for Computational Linguistics, Carnegie Mellon University.

[Grefenstette, 1995] Grefenstette, G. (1995). Comparing two language identification schemes. In *Proc. of Analisi Statistica dei Dati Testuali (JADT)*, pp. 263–268.

[Harman, 1995] Harman, D. (1995). Overview of the 3rd text retrieval conference (TREC-3). In *Overview of the 3rd Text Retrieval Conference (TREC-3), NIST SP 500-225*, pp. 1–19.

[Hearst et al., 1996] Hearst, M., Pedersen, J., Pirolli, P., Schütze, H., Grefenstette, G., & Hull, D. (1996). Xerox site report: Four TREC-4 tracks. In *The 4th Text Retrieval Conference (TREC-4)*. To appear.

[Hull, 1993] Hull, D. (1993). Using statistical testing in the evaluation of retrieval performance. In *Proc. of the 16th ACM/SIGIR Conference*, pp. 329–338.

[Hull, 1996] Hull, D. (1996). Stemming algorithms - a case study for detailed evaluation. *Journal of the American Society for Information Science*, 47(1),70–84.

[Landauer & Littman, 1990] Landauer, T. K., & Littman, M. L. (1990). Fully automatic cross-language document retrieval using latent semantic indexing. In *Proc. of the 6th Conference of UW Centre for the New OED and Text Research*, pp. 31–38.

[Oard et al., 1994] Oard, D., DeClaris, N., Dorr, B., & Faloutsos, C. (1994). On automatic filtering of multilingual texts. In *Proc. of the 1994 IEEE Conference on Systems, Man, and Cybernetics*.

[Oard & Dorr, 1996] Oard, D. W., & Dorr, B. J. (1996). A survey of multilingual text retrieval. Technical Report UMIACS-TR-9619, University of Maryland. http://www.ee.umd.edu/medlab/mlir/mlir.html.

[Peters & Picchi, 1991] Peters, C., & Picchi, E. (1991). Capturing the comparable: a system for querying comparable text corpora. In *Proc. of Analisi Statistica dei Dati Testuali (JADT)*, pp. 247–254.

[Pevzner, 1972] Pevzner, B. (1972). Comparative evaluation of the operation of the Russian and English variants of the Pusto-Nepusto-2 system. *Automatic Documentation and Mathematical Linguistics*, 6(2),71–74.

[Radwan, 1994] Radwan, K. (1994). *Vers l'Accès Multilingue en Langage Naturel aux Bases de Données Textuelles*. PhD thesis, Université de Paris-Sud, Centre d'Orsay.

[Salton, 1970] Salton, G. (1970). Automatic processing of foreign language documents. *Journal of the American Society for Information Science*, 21,187–194.

[Sanderson, 1994] Sanderson, M. (1994). Word sense disambiguation and information retrieval. In *Proc. of the 17th ACM/SIGIR Conference*, pp. 142–150.

[Sibun & Spitz, 1994] Sibun, P., & Spitz, A. L. (1994). Language determination: Natural language processing from scanned document images. In *Proceedings of the ANLP*, pp. 15–21.

[van der Eijk, 1993] van der Eijk, P. (1993). Automating the acquisition of bilingual terminology. In *Proceedings of the EACL*, pp. 113–119.

[Voorhees et al., 1995] Voorhees, E., Gupta, N., & Johnson-Laird, B. (1995). Learning collection fusion strategies. In *Proc. of the 18th ACM/SIGIR Conference*, pp. 172–179.

EXPERIMENTS IN SPOKEN DOCUMENT RETRIEVAL*

K. SPARCK JONES[1], G. J. F. JONES[1,2], J. T. FOOTE[2] and S. J. YOUNG[2]

[1] Computer Laboratory, University of Cambridge, New Museums Site, Pembroke Street, Cambridge CB2 3QG, and [2] Engineering Department, University of Cambridge, Trumpington Street, Cambridge CB2 1PZ, U.K.

(Received 15 June 1995; accepted in final form 7 December 1995)

Abstract—This paper describes experiments in the retrieval of spoken documents in multimedia systems. Speech documents pose a particular problem for retrieval since their words as well as contents are unknown. The work reported addresses this problem, for a video mail application, by combining state of the art speech recognition with established document retrieval technologies so as to provide an effective and efficient retrieval tool. Tests with a small spoken message collection show that retrieval precision for the spoken file can reach 90% of that obtained when the same file is used, as a benchmark, in text transcription form.

1. INTRODUCTION

This paper presents a set of experiments constituting initial work on a novel multimedia retrieval application. This research combines state of the art speech recognition and document retrieval technologies for spoken message retrieval, envisaged as one function among many provided on a workstation equipped with multimedia video facilities.

The paper discusses the problems involved, the strategies being deployed to overcome these, an initial system implementation, and the design and results of a first set of retrieval tests. Our claims are on the one hand, that the straightforward probabilistic methods that have been established for text retrieval can be naturally extended to the speech case; and on the other, that current speech recognition technology can support adequate message retrieval performance, even if this is not as accurate as that obtained with written text. Our further claim is that spoken message retrieval can be conveniently implemented to enhance the capabilities of an office computer system with video facilities. Although the message corpus used for the work described here has been necessarily limited in scale, the results reported provide data to support these claims, though as this is research in progress we have much more development and testing to do. Specifically, our experiments constitute the first serious tests of spoken document retrieval combining modern recognition and retrieval technologies.

Section 2 discusses the distinctive problems to be overcome in speech retrieval, taking the particular application with which we are concerned, the retrieval of video messages in their audio form, as a motivating context: this research is being carried out under the joint Cambridge University/Olivetti Research Limited Video Mail Retrieval (VMR) Project. Section 3 summarizes the specific technical problems to be tackled in spoken document retrieval. The overall strategy we have adopted for the work is outlined in Section 4, which is followed by Sections 5 to 7 describing our work so far in detail, covering data provision in 5, speech processing in 6 and retrieval testing in 7, concluding with an assessment of what we have done to date. The final section, 8, considers the tests in their broader context and comments on current and planned future research. The paper includes some previously published material, reproduced here for comparative purposes or completeness.

* Address for reprint requests: Karen Sparck Jones, Computer Laboratory, University of Cambridge, New Museums Site, Pembroke Street, Cambridge CB2 3QG, U.K. (Tel: +44 1223 334631; Fax: +44 1223 334678; email: sparckjones@cl.cam.ac.uk).

2. BACKGROUND

2.1. *The Pandora/Medusa systems*

The research under the VMR Project described here was stimulated by the wish to retrieve messages from the kind of archive that can naturally accumulate when voice or video mail facilities are routinely available in an office environment, as with the Pandora multimedia system developed jointly by Olivetti Research Limited (ORL), Cambridge, and the Computer Laboratory. For this, content-based searching on message bodies is needed, not just access via administrative *header* data.

The Pandora and its successor Medusa systems offer interactive video as well as video mail, but dialogue retrieval is currently well beyond the speech processing state of the art, as is general-purpose image retrieval: we have therefore been concerned only with audio message retrieval, allowing for images in accompanying displays. The research reported here thus takes the VMR application, aimed at retrieving naturally but relatively clearly spoken messages, which are also normally more concentrated and definite in content than dialogue, as illustrative of a potentially large class of practical speech retrieval cases. At the same time, experience of this comparatively less intractable type of application should provide a base for conversation (or meeting record) retrieval, which is often taken as a desideratum for the future wired workplace.

2.2. *Related retrieval applications*

The project naturally applies retrieval techniques suited to full text; however, some specific text retrieval applications, most obviously to email, are more germane than others.

2.2.1. Email. Video messages, especially where the speaker naturally adopts a dictation-like style, may resemble conventional abstracts in length, content density and presentational coherence. However they may be much more informal and incomplete, like email messages, especially where they are elements of an extended exchange of messages. Operational systems are already available for searching large email files [e.g. Usenet (Burrows, 1991)], and search facilities for data sources including email are proliferating on the Internet, though the retrieval techniques used are often rudimentary and performance has not been properly assessed. The email case may nevertheless suggest effective ways of combining search keys referring to message headers with ones referring to message bodies. But while email often embeds previous message material in new messages, this does not presently apply to video mail and might not become common even if technologically feasible, because of increasing the time taken to 'read' messages.

2.3. *Retrieval involving speech*

Spoken access to text files is a developing area (Kupiec *et al.*, 1994), but in general transcribing spoken queries for text file searching is much less challenging than speech file searching. For instance, it is more reasonable to expect the searching user to speak clearly and accept verification of search terms, and to participate in query development. Spoken query work is pertinent to VMR, but the much more important challenge in the VMR case is clearly that of dealing with the spoken document files.

2.3.1. Access to speech files. The current dominant applications for speech recognition, illustrated by the (D)ARPA initiatives on Continuous Speech Recognition (CSR) and Spoken Language Systems (SLS), have helped to raise speech processing standards. They are not directly relevant, in terms of the system purposes involved, to VMR, though they supply generic performance data for word identification in continuous speech and have acted as a testbed for the specific speech recognition system (Young *et al.*, 1993) being used for VMR. The kind of performance measure for recognition exemplified by the ARPA Word Error Rate (Woodland *et al.*, 1995) is not, however, especially suited to the retrieval context, since it treats *all* words equally. Much of this work has also been based on read speech: spontaneous speech recognition is much harder and Word Error Rates are typically much higher (Young *et al.*, 1994).

2.3.2. Word spotting. An alternative recognition requirement is for *word spotting*, i.e. approaching word identification for the retrieval task by focusing only on the recognition of important content-bearing words. Since video mail messages are often informally structured (from a linguistic point of view) and there is much greater variation in utterance style over time, recognition is harder than for read speech and is thus most usefully treated as a word spotting enterprise. This does however involve more than a method of identifying just required words: since a speech recognizer must hypothesize the occurrence of some speech event at all times, word spotters usually incorporate additional models to cover periods of silence along with a "filler" model for recognizing all non-keyword acoustic events.

Word spotting has long been an intelligence agency concern, but it is not made easy to know what has been achieved here, and how specifically pertinent it is to VMR. Some work on word spotting has been reported, for example by Rose (1991), Wilcox and Bush (1992) and McDonough *et al.*, (1994), though for varied application tasks. In some cases there are similarities to retrieval, e.g. in message categorization (Rose, 1991; McDonough, 1994), where selective word identification serves topic spotting for category assignment; in other cases word spotting has been for quite different purposes (Wilcox & Bush, 1992). However even with good speech performance, the categorization work described used classes that were much coarser than those normally defined by message retrieval requests, so this work has little direct bearing on our own.

The forms of performance measure used in this work on word spotting are however far more appropriate than the Word Error Rate. They exploit notions, with respect to matching for sought words, of *hit*, *miss* and *false alarm* which have obvious analogues in document matching. However a measure like the False Alarm (FA) Rate, used in conjunction with the percentage of this to provide a Figure of Merit (FOM) characterizing performance, is still somewhat remote and needs to be related to the realities of search term occurrence in documents.

2.3.3. Conventional retrieval. Little work has been done in this area, and what had been done has been limited in scope or evaluation. Schäuble and others (Glavitsch & Schäuble, 1992, Schäuble & Glavitsch, 1994; Glavitsch *et al.*, 1994) have proposed a system for speech retrieval based on predefined acoustic units, and have considered the effect of term occurrence errors of semantic and acoustic origin, but only by simulation. In particular, while Glavitsch and Schäuble and their colleagues show that retrieval performance can hold up reasonably well under some noise (as is required for actual spoken document retrieval), their 'consonant/vowel' index key model drawn from text does not carry over in an unproblematic way to speech: the indexing keys are so brief they may be very unreliable (cf. James, 1995); and their error simulation is not acoustically motivated, so no account is taken of the important matter of substitution errors, and insertion and deletion errors are assumed to be simply distributed over all documents. Further, their tests with some classical IR test collections have used written documents which do not necessarily have the same linguistic and discourse properties as spoken ones.

Genuine spoken document retrieval experiments have, however, been recently carried out by James (1995), using short news stories and semi-realistic prompted request. James applied conventional term weighting in a straightforward way in conjunction with indexing by phones, and explored a range of alternative strategies for term recognition. He obtained best performance for a combination of word recognition for a standing vocabulary, using triphones and a bigram language model, with matching via a biphone lattice for out-of-vocabulary words. This gave average precision performance, for forty requests and over three hundred documents, reaching 90% of that obtainable with the same methods for text versions of the data.

James's experiments are valuable in suggesting that speech processing and information retrieval technologies can be effectively combined. However the data used, professionally spoken and consisting of short items with a high information content, cannot be taken as typical of many applications. The tests described below were motivated by the need to develop methods suited to more demanding conditions, especially in relation to the discourse properties of file documents; and they also exploited consistent methods of term weighting.

3. PROBLEMS IN SPOKEN DOCUMENT RETRIEVAL

Our research applies well-understood probabilistic retrieval techniques (Robertson & Sparck Jones, 1994) and equally well-established speech recognition techniques (Rabiner, 1989). Thus the retrieval methods use simple natural language units (stems, words, phrases) in coordination with statistically-based weighting to produce a ranked search output. The speech techniques rely on hidden Markov models (HMMs), where the identification of any particular speech unit (phone, word, word string) is computed using a sequence of transition probabilities for items given their predecessors, based on data from a prior training sample. For any given unit, identification takes the form of an acoustic score, or *a-score*. However, in combining these retrieval and speech techniques for spoken document retrieval there are a number of key problems.

These problems are primarily those arising from the use of speech as such, and secondarily those associated with the particular kind of documents involved, but both have implications for any attempt to apply the retrieval methods hitherto successfully suited for written text. Thus the project focuses on the interaction effects of speech and retrieval factors, seeking retrieval offsets to speech challenges. But this is made difficult by the current lack of experience of speech retrieval and by the difficulties of getting performance reference data for large speech files. The problems we have are as follows.

3.1. Term constraints

For individual terms, the project has to tackle all the usual problems of word recognition in continuous speech: compared with the text case there is always, in the most fundamental way, some uncertainty, reflected in a-score values, about whether a putative word is actually present in the speech at that time. Lexical category and sense ambiguity are familiar in text retrieval. But while such ambiguities may be resolved in the speech case by different pronunciation, new ambiguities appear through homophones and, especially, alternative word boundary allocations (e.g. 'Hello Kate' vs 'locate'). There is a further problem with stemming, since in the spoken case the same stem may be differently pronounced depending on its full form context. A more fundamental problem is that word spotting on shorter words is inherently more unreliable and hence generalizing search terms by suffix stripping may actually degrade word spotting reliability.

The natural strategies for dealing with the uncertainty and ambiguity problems are the query formulation ones already applied to reduce ambiguity in the text case, namely increasing the number of search terms, exploiting redundancy to secure multiterm matches. Thus these techniques can be readily combined with the use of thresholds on acoustic scores, which are useful as a means of avoiding false alarms in word matching. However because thresholds also mean that true hits that happen to have low a-scores are lost, it is necessary to study the effects of threshold setting on trade-offs between hits, misses and false alarms and, more importantly, to see how the potentially valuable data provided by actual a-scores could be exploited. This is a complicated matter both because the occurrences of a word naturally have different a-scores and because ways have to be found of combining numerical term values given by the distinct procedures used for acoustic processing and term weighting. Thus, while the speech recognition and document retrieval approaches we are using are both probabilistic, it is still necessary to find proper ways of combining speech recognition a-scores with the usual types of term weights in order to derive single, meaningful index term values and consequent query–document matching scores.

3.1.1. Term data limitations. A file of spoken documents consists of digitised acoustic records, i.e. contains sound streams, not explicit word sequences; and because speech recognition will be far from perfect in the kinds of context with which we are concerned, while document retrieval is essentially a bulk task, we cannot rely on being able to gather any very reliable, detailed or exhaustive data about the occurrences of words in the document file from direct operations on the file. This affects design and testing and can be expected to affect retrieval strategies too, since it implies that applying the statistical techniques successfully used for text is not completely straightforward.

Thus even if there is a good reference lexicon supplying word pronunciations, which can be used to find what words may occur in the speech file, this cannot be guaranteed to deliver a correct or complete list of all the words in the file with accompanying correct or complete incidence data; and there are further obvious difficulties about phrase extraction. Data management has therefore to be leveraged from search term vocabularies, though they need not be exclusive and speech processing techniques are available for out-of-vocabulary request words (see James, 1995); and retrieval procedures may have to allow for filtering and multiple processing cycles to gather and apply occurrence data for weighting, even when working just with search terms from input requests.

3.2. *Message constraints*

The specific ways in which term uncertainty and ambiguity are managed naturally depend on the properties of queries and documents, e.g. their length, content density etc, as this affects the chances of matching on single occurrences of search terms. The VMR messages also present particular challenges to normal document retrieval protocols through their informality and/or brevity. Past retrieval experience for short documents (e.g. abstracts, news) is not narrowly applicable, and there is not yet (as noted earlier) any pertinent data about file behaviour and search performance under established retrieval methods for the more similar email case. Moreover with speechmail, individual documents may be more casual, dilute or cryptic than written ones, and while less likely to involve extensive repetitive quoting, perhaps be repetitive in other ways.

Thus the lack of reliable information about words implies a lack of information about important properties of documents. Information about the gross properties of a file, e.g. about average message length and variation in length can be obtained and also, from listening to audio samples or inspecting illustrative transcriptions, information about the flavour and style of the documents. Inferences can also be made from any dictionary-driven vocabulary identification. But the lack of correct or complete information about words affects dependent information about internal message characteristics like content word density and about external message relationships, as well as information about the content properties of the message set as a whole, with implications for system design and operation. There are also potential difficulties with some specific techniques found helpful in the text case, notably query expansion in relevance feedback. It may not be possible to fully identify other retrieved message words to offer the user as candidate additions to the query or to add to it automatically. The user may have to process the retrieved output more minutely than in the written case, and explicit file processing may be needed to gather frequency data to assign relevance weights to new terms for further searching, again implying more complex operations than with text systems.

3.3. *User interface constraints*

Speech retrieval also presents extra challenges for interface design to promote effective user searching. The most obvious point is that listening to speech takes far more time than scanning text, so where for example, 20 abstracts might take 30 seconds to read, 20 messages of similar word length could take 15 minutes to listen to. It may be possible to supply (playback) short extracts, e.g. parts of messages where search terms are concentrated, but these may not be very informative if there are few or common search terms, or the extract is short. (It cannot however be assumed that written transcription, even if feasible, would be helpful since it cannot be expected to deliver anything like normal, properly punctuated, text.) It is at the same time desirable to display other document information, notably message headers, and in principle in the VMR context displaying the accompanying sender image may be helpful. The retrieval interface has therefore to be developed to allow the user to exploit the various types of information associated with messages in a convenient way, especially by combining these for searching, in *hybrid* searches.

4. RESEARCH STRATEGY

The difficulties of speech retrieval, together with the form of previous work on word spotting, naturally suggest a staged strategy for tackling the spoken message retrieval task. This progresses from the most favourable, but least realistic, situation with a known speaker set and known search word set, to an open speaker set and open search vocabulary. State of the art retrieval strategies may in principle be applied throughout though, as noted, it is not obvious how query expansion may be implemented, and equally it may be necessary to develop strategies that are especially adapted to compensate for defects in speech recognition proper.

The tests described here were for the first case, with a known message speaker community and a known search vocabulary. Though on a very small scale compared with current text retrieval test, they represent a material step forward as a feasibility study on spoken document retrieval, and are now being followed up, on a larger scale, for the more realistic open speaker and open vocabulary situation.

5. DATA PROVISION

Our first message set, VMR1,* was designed to meet various criteria arising from the requirements of both the document retrieval component of the system and the speech recognition element (since there was no existing public, properly recorded video or audio message file we could use). From the document retrieval perspective the database had to consist of messages with the same general properties as could be expected in Pandora/Medusa-type installations. But in order to meet the specification for Stage 1 of our project, it also had to consist of messages making natural use of a set of fixed search keywords, while at the same time forming a corpus with the kinds of message similarities and differences, that pose challenges for recall and precision, as could be deemed typical of expected VMR situations. Messages should also have similar acoustic properties to those found in an operational system and be of comparable length. At the same time, we could not rely on having many people to generate messages specifically for us, independent of any operational video system with a natural user community. We also wished to transcribe the message set to provide a reference base for testing, but could not carry out large-scale transcription since this is a comparatively expensive process. VMR1 is therefore a very small document collection from the retrieval point of view, serving primarily as a tool for development of our speech processing technology and general approach, but not allowing serious retrieval experiments in terms of the file sizes customary in text retrieval tests.

Apart from messages, VMR1 had also to contain spoken material for use as training data for the speaker-dependent acoustic models in the word spotter. The appropriate training of acoustic model parameters is an important feature in the building of speech recognition systems and it is vital to have suitable and sufficient data to construct a high performance system.

VMR1 is fully described in Jones *et al.* (1994); the main points about it are as follows.

5.1 *Message definition*

While the structure of the message set is important if a small database is to be viable for retrieval research, it is also necessary to have messages that are natural in both content and speaking style. To meet the first requirement we sought messages on *topics* within a set of topic *categories*: each category has an associated set of *keywords* drawn from a fixed keyword *vocabulary* from which search *terms* in Stage 1 must be taken. To meet the second requirement, since the messages were collected specially and not drawn from a natural mail community, we utilized prompting *scenarios*. These stumulated the speaker to talk on a topic within a category

* Also previously called Database 1 and sometimes referred to as a corpus.

without constraining them to produce messages strictly tied to pre-specified topics. The scenarios also encouraged the speakers to use the keywords for the category, though keywords were not exclusive to categories and could well occur in messages in other categories. However as the scenarios were only prompts, messages for the same scenario could be on quite different individual topics within the same general content area. Overall, our approach led to messages that varied in their individual topics but that clustered round the prompting categories, while maintaining links, through broader relations between categories marked by shared keywords, with messages in other categories.

In addition, since the keyword vocabulary is not very large, we provided a set of *otherwords* as a further prompting and potential search vocabulary.

It should be noted that while our general notion of topic also applies to requests, the message database was not constructed with any test requests already in mind. The provision of test requests and relevance assessments is described in Section 7.

5.2. *VMR1 database formation*

We used a total keyword vocabulary of 35 words (e.g. badge, date, rank, workstation), along with 31 related otherwords, and 10 broad subject categories (e.g. Document, Windows, Schedule). We collected 300 messages, taken as the maximum practicable for transcription and as the minimum sufficient for initital testing of our speech retrieval processes in conditions that share critical properties with real ones, though we of course do not regard a set of 300 documents as a proper IR test collection. Thus all the choices of keywords, topics and categories were motivated by the need for a ''representatively' naturalistic message set and the same considerations, applying both to the characteristics of their messages and to their speech, determined the number of speakers used and number of messages per speaker.

Thus we sought 20 messages each from a subset of 4 categories from the 10 available, with 15 speakers overall, so that for any one category there were messages from 6 speakers. The assignment of speakers to categories was randomized, and the actual data collection protocol was designed to encourage an even distribution of messages across the scenarios within a category for each speaker, although this could not be enforced.

The *prompt* for each spontaneous message consisted of the scenario and the keywords and otherwords for the category. Speakers were asked to favour the use of the listed keywords and otherwords, but not at the expense of construction of realistic messages. They were also not restricted to the keywords precisely as shown to them but could use them in variant *word forms*: for example, the keyword mail might be used in the forms mailed, mails or mailing. (The word spotter should pick up the common stem as long as there is not too much pronounciational variation, and so get correct hits on the keyword). The speakers were not shown a complete list of the keywords available, but only those relevant to the current category.

Speakers were assigned to categories about which they were deemed knowledgeable, to encourage plausible messages; but to avoid sequencing effects for categories and scenarios both category and scenario orders were distributed per speaker on a Latin square basis (Tague, 1981).

Training data, in the form of material read by each speaker in our set, was collected for all the keywords; the phonetically varied training data needed for the filler models for words outside the predefined keyword vocabulary was obtained by collecting 50 read sentences from the standard TIMIT corpus (Lamel *et al.*, 1986) for each speaker.

5.3. *Recording and transcription*

The acoustic quality of the target recognition system for VMR is defined by the ORL Medusa system, which incorporates a specified desk mounted microphone and custom-designed audio preamplifier stage. However experimental speech recognition systems frequently rely on very high-quality and low-noise acoustic channels. To study the effects of channel quality, VMR1 was recorded using both head and desk microphones in parallel. All data was recorded in a partially soundproofed room, so that the basic recorded signals would be as noiseless as possible. The effect of various noise conditions likely to be encountered in the real Medusa environment will be investigated later by mixing separately recorded noise with the recorded speech signal.

The prompted messages were fully transcribed by hand, including not only non-speech events, for example loud breaths and tongue clicks, but also disfluencies such as partially spoken words, pauses and hesitations such as "um" and "ah". Non-speech events were transcribed in accordance with the Wall Street Journal data collection procedures (Garafolo *et al.*, 1993). Basic punctuation was also added for ease of reading. This full transcription was required both for word spotter evaluation purposes and also for retrieval performance testing and bench marking.

5.4. *VMR1 database details*

In total therefore, VMR1 consisted, for each speaker, of:

(1) 77 read sentences ("r" data): sentences containing keywords, constructed such that each keyword occurred a minimum of five times.
(2) 170 isolated keywords ("i" data): 5 occurrences of each of the 35 keywords spoken in isolation.
(3) 150 read sentences ("z" data): phonetically-rich sentences from the TIMIT corpus.
(4) 20 natural speech messages ("p" data): the response to 20 unique prompts from 4 categories.
(5) 20 "tags" ("t" data): natural speech responses to a prompt requesting a summary for each of their "p" messages.

The "r", "i", and "z" sets are for use as training data; the "p" and "t" material, along with their transcriptions, serves as a test corpus for both keyword spotting and preliminary IR experiments (though the tag data was not used for the work reported here). The messages, the prime material for actual retrieval, average about 137 words each, with an average of 7 keywords (tokens) each; they vary somewhat in length, but a 2-min upper limit was imposed in recording. The amount of training and test data we have (5 hours each) is typical of other speech recognition development databases, though very small in terms of retrieval testing.

6. WORD SEARCHING

In acoustic processing, natural language words may be treated as integral wholes or as composed from constituent units like syllables or phones; and as noted, hidden Markov modelling can in principle be used for any kind of unit in context. However while integral words may be appropriate for some applications, a compositional approach using underlying phones is more flexible and refined, and has therefore been used in all our experiments. Whole words are thus characterized as strings of phones drawn from the set of about 50 phones representative of spoken English; and words are identified, and distinguished from preceding or following other words, noise, or silence, by Markov modelling. A word occurrence's acoustic score is the likelihood that this file word is the required one; so a threshold may be applied to remove false alarms.

For experimental purposes the message file has been preprocessed to obtain an inverted keyword file. This preprocessing is in fact done by the word spotting techniques described below, and there are therefore in our experimental system several inverted files, each representing a different a-score threshold. Word spotting thus plays a critical role in forming the retrieval search files, as well as being the test area for spoken word recognition techniques. With large message files it would probably be necessary to invert explicitly on variant forms of words, but we judged that the full-word models for our keywords would subsume the variants actually occurring in the files. This judgement was shown to be sound since examination of the acoustic stems of keywords occurring in VMR1 revealed the vast majority to be identical to the fixed keyword form used by the word spotter. A preprocessing strategy like that used for our Stage 1 tests is however only viable with a fixed keyword vocabulary: we return to the need to allow open search terms in Section 8.

6.1. *Word spotting experiments*

Our initial experiments were designed to study keyword spotting solely from the acoustic point of view, identifying individual keyword occurrences in the message set. For this we used the HMM toolkit, HTK, developed in Cambridge (Young *et al.*, 1993), which applies standard algorithms both in training HMM parameters and in finding the most likely word model sequence given unknown speech (for full details see Jones *et al.*, 1995a).

After processing the raw acoustic data to obtain a spectral representation, we constructed compositional keyword models* and monophone filler models for each speaker; we used the "i" and "r" data for the former, and the TIMIT sentence "z" data along with the non-keyword parts of the "r" data for the latter. Hence each phone within each individual keyword was trained uniquely within its acoustic context from the 10 read examples of the keyword. We have separate model sets for the two microphones.

Keyword spotting is done with a two-pass recognition procedure using Viterbi decoding, in a manner similar to Rose and Paul's (Rose, 1991). The first step analyses the stored speech just for filler monophones, using a filler network. The second identifies keywords in parallel against a background of noise and silence using a network combining individual keyword nets, the filler net and silence, as illustrated in Fig. 1. The recognition output in the former case is a sequence of filler phones and silence, and in the latter case a sequence of putative keywords, filler phones and silence. The acoustic score for each putative keyword occurrence found in the latter pass is computed by calculating the ratio between the Viterbi score for the keyword and the Viterbi score for the same section of speech data in the first pass. This procedure is described in more detail in Knill and Young (1994). In practice we found it necessary to compensate for limited training data by using phone triple filler models to discourage the word spotted from fitting the filler model to actual speech occurrences in the recognition pass that includes the keyword models.

The accepted figure-of-merit (FOM) for word spotting is defined as the average percentage of correctly detected keywords as the a-score threshold is varied from 1 to 10 false alarms per

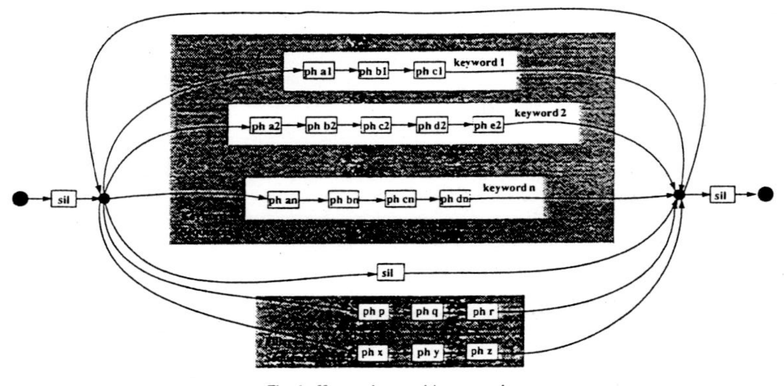

Fig. 1. Keyword recognition network.

* Via a pronouncing dictionary.

keyword per hour. The keyword spotting results were evaluated against time-aligned text transcriptions containing the keywords. The FOMs for the two microphones, averaged across both the 15 talkers and 35 keywords, are 81.2% for head and 76.4% for desk. The receiver operating characteristic (ROC) curve for the two microphones, plotting percent correct against thresholds set to range from 1 to 10 false alarms, is given in Fig. 2. This shows that the desk microphone (the realistic office case) is not much inferior to the head one, and also that a high performance level can be obtained for only a few false alarms. These results were exploited for our message retrieval experiments.

7. MESSAGE RETRIEVAL EXPERIMENTS

Our tests so far have used VMR1 with two different request sets defining two retrieval test collections, VMR Collection 1a and VMR Collection 1b. The primary purpose of these tests has been to establish that spoken document retrieval is feasible and viable. For this purpose we have calibrated against text matching performance. However the tests have also, equally importantly, been used to experiment with different term weighting schemes (Robertson & Sparck Jones, 1994; Robertson *et al.*, 1995), to see whether using spoken as opposed to written documents affects these schemes and in particular their comparative performance. We have naturally also used these tests to check the relative performance for head and desk microphones implied by the word-spotting experiments, and we have used them to study the impact of training data differences on recognizer performance: this is important in relation to speaker-independent systems.

From the point of view even of past retrieval testing, let alone present-day TREC, a file of 300 documents is extremely small. But the constraints imposed by the need to calibrate speech retrieval performance by reference to transcribed data are quite severe, and we thought it important to make some initial trials to see whether actual rather than simulated retrieval for naturally-spoken material was practicable. Speech data is also significantly more bulky than

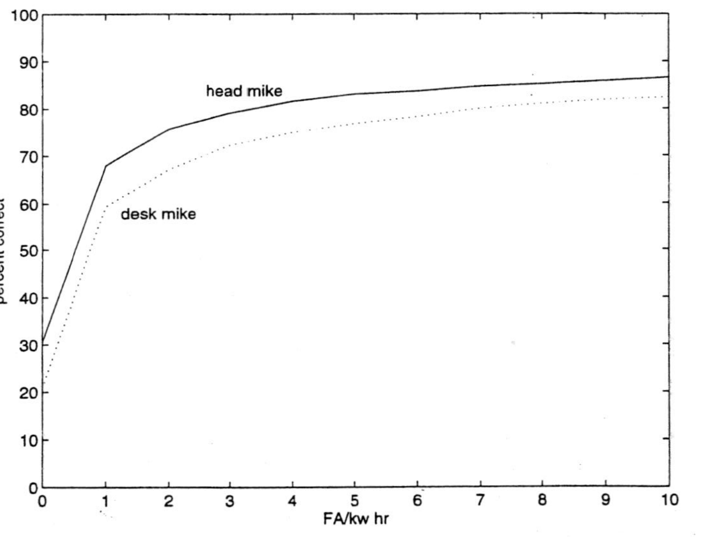

Fig. 2. VMR task keyword spotting ROC.

text, so processing is not trivial. Of course one consequence of such small data sets, quite apart from other factors mentioned below, is that absolute performance levels have no real meaning and performance differences have to be treated with caution. We return to the question of larger data sets later.

It must however be emphasized that though we were using a limited search vocabulary and test data generated via a set of subject categories, this does not imply we were in fact engaged in message categorization as opposed to retrieval or that retrieval itself was trivial. The test search requests were never designed to map onto the categories, and though both search vocabulary and message set were small we still had a good range of requests and messages on specific distinct topics. At the same time, from the retrieval point of view, while there was a considerable topic spread across the category set as a whole, discrimination within categories was required.

We nevertheless expect, because the keyword queries did not fully cover their source requests, to get better performance through more flexibility when we allow open search terms in more realistic, albeit larger-scale, retrieval.

7.1. *Methodology*

7.1.1. Collection 1a. In order to obtain some test requests quickly, given a lack of users, we decided simply to exploit the prompts used to obtain messages in the database recording. To reduce variations in word form, query words were suffix stripped to stems using the standard Porter algorithm (Porter, 1980). Queries were formed from the prompts by selecting those stems also found in a stemmed list of the keywords. For example, given the prompt:

> Your current project is lagging behind schedule. Send a message pointing this out to the other project management staff. Suggest some days and times over the next week when you would be willing to hold a meeting to discuss the situation.

the following query was obtained:

> project messag [project] manag staff time meet.

With this expedient we obtained a total set of 50 requests with corresponding simple term list queries, averaging 4.6 distinct terms (average 5.68 occurrences).

To obtain relevance assessments, the 6 recorded messages generated in response to each prompt were assumed relevant to the query constructed from that prompt. The 24 other messages in the same category, which are quite likely to contain similar keywords, are assumed to be not relevant. This whole procedure was somewhat crude, but we believe it gave us adequate material, from a term distribution point of view, for fair experiments.

As mentioned earlier, we are only working with written queries in this project. Moreover, as the messages have been preprocessed, identifying search term stem occurrences in the files is a purely mechanical operation via the written forms of the keywords that act as access points to the inverted file.

7.1.2. Collection 1b. We subsequently obtained a second set of more realistic requests and relevance assessments, from the user community that supplied the database messages. A total of 50 requests was collected, 5 for each of the 10 categories defined previously. These were gathered from 10 users who each generated 5 requests and corresponding relevance assessments. This was achieved by forming 10 unique sets of 5 categories and assigning each to a user knowledgeable about the subject matter of the categories in the set. As for the data collection, the category subsets were ordered using a Latin square to prevent sequencing effects. For each category requests and relevance assessments were generated as follows.

Requests

Subjects were asked to form a natural language request based on the information given in a text prompt. One such prompt was framed for each of the message categories, described earlier, by combining the information given in the 5 message scenario prompts asociated with the category. Hence there were 10 prompts in total. Subjects were asked that their request include at least one of the fixed keywords associated with the category, as defined for the message collection phase. Subjects were also shown the list of otherwords associated with the category.

Relevance Assessment

Each request was converted to a query consisting only of the suffix stripped fixed keywords present in the request. For example, given the request

> In what ways can the windows interface of a workstation be personalized.

the following query was obtained:

> window interfac workstat

The query was used to score each document transcription in the message archive; keyword terms in the messages were collection frequency weighted (Robertson & Sparck Jones, 1994). The messages were then ranked in order to decreasing score.

Ideally users should assess the relevance of all messages in the archive to their request; however, even with the 300 document archive this was considered impractical. Thus a suitable message subset for assessment must be generated. For Collection 1b the list of messages for assessment was formed by combining the 30 messages generated for the category to which the original message prompt belonged together with the highest scoring 5 messages which were not associated with the category. Thus there were 35 messages to assess for each request. The order of these messages was randomised using a random number generator seeded with a unique request number.

The subjects were presented with the transcription of each potentially relevant message and asked to mark it as "relevant", "partially relevant", or "not relevant".

A full description of the formation of the Collection 1b naturalistic request set is contained (in Jones *et al.* 1995b).

Apart from the greater realism, the main differences between Collection 1a and Collection 1b were that there were far fewer terms per query for the latter, an average of 2.58 distinct terms (average 2.64 occurrences, but one case 0), while there was naturally variation in the number of relevant documents per query as well as, in fact, a larger average number, 10.8 highly relevant and 17.22 highly or partially relevant.

7.2. *Calibration via text retrieval*

Retrieval performance for speech documents can be expected to suffer degradation relative to that for text documents due to either misses or false alarms. The extent of the degradation can be measured, when transcribed texts are available, by comparing performance for spoken word spotting results with that for the transcriptions. We used our transcribed corpus to provide us with this performance standard.

However as indicated earlier with the 'Hello Kate' example, there is a further problem with word spotting in that unrelated acoustic events will often resemble valid keywords: even the most accurate acoustic models cannot discriminate in these cases. The output of an ideal word spotter that reports all keyword phone sequences thus provides a more legitimate standard of comparison than text. We simulated this ideal 'phonetic text' performance by scanning phonetic transcriptions of the messages for phone sequences that match those of a keyword. In the tables which follow the two forms of reference are labelled *text* and *phonetic*, respectively.

7.3. *Spoken message retrieval performance*

Our tests have compared unweighted term (*uw*) matching performance with two forms of weighting. As mentioned, the aim was primarily to check that the same sort of comparative performance was obtained as for text (insofar as this could be done with a small collection). We thus used the conventional collection frequency weight (*cfw*) (alias inverse document frequency weights), and the 'combined weight' (*cw*), incorporating within-document term frequencies, normalised for document length, defined in (Robertson & Sparck Jones, 1994) and derived in (Robertson & Walker, 1994): the *cw* scheme reflects the City University work for TREC (Robertson *et al.*, 1995). The *cw* weight for each term in each document is calculated as follows,

$$cw(i, j) = \frac{cfw(i)*tf(i, j)*(K+1)}{K*ndl(j)+tf(i, j)}$$

where $cw(i, j)$ represents the *cw* weight of term i in document j, $tf(i, j)$ is the document term frequency and $ndl(j)$ the normalized document length. The combined weight constant K has to be tuned empirically: after testing we set $K = 1$.

To measure performance we used only precision metrics, namely precision at selected document cutoff levels in the ranked search output, and average precision as defined in the TREC evaluation (Harman, 1994). We believe that document cutoff is highly appropriate where it is very likely that the user will not be willing to consider many output documents in this case because listening to them takes time. The implementation for average precision requires a ranking of the entire collection.

The word spotter outputs a list of putative keyword hits and associated acoustic scores. As these are probabilistic, it would naturally appear sensible to combine information they provide with that given by the term weighting schemes. However it is not completely clear how this should be done (though we are currently investigating the question), and as the basic retrieval schemes require only the presence/absence of a keyword in a message, we have applied a threshold to the a-scores. This has in any case the advantage that, because acoustic false alarms typically score worse than true hits, thresholding removes a greater proportion of the false alarms. Clearly, it is desirable in practice to choose an operating threshold that optimizes retrieval performance in trading false alarms against 'pseudo'-misses, i.e. hits with scores below the threshold. This question is discussed in more detail in Jones *et al.*, (1995a): for the Stage 1 studies the optimal threshold values were chosen *a posteriori* for both head and desk microphone systems, though an *a priori* fixed threshold value would have to be used in an operational system.

We present our retrieval results first for collection 1a (Tables 1, 2, 3), and then for Collection 1b (Tables 4, 5, 6, 7, 8, 9). As we have tried the same weighting schemes for both collections the consequences of collection differences are easily seen in the parallel tables; however for Collection 1b there are additional figures for the full as opposed to highly relevant assessments. We comment on the results for each collection individually, and then discuss the complete set of tests.

7.3.1. Collection 1a results. Table 1 shows retrieval performance for the standard transcribed messages (*text*) and for the ideal phonetic text (*phonetic*), using different cutoff matching scores. The behaviour is as expected: first, the text transcription performs better than the phonetic reference; second, when weighting is introduced, *cfw* weighting gives a substantial improvement

Table 1. Collection 1a: Retrieval precision values for text transcription and ideal phonetic word spotter

		Text			Phonetic		
Weight Scheme		*uw*	*cfw*	*cw*	*uw*	*cfw*	*cw*
Precision	5 docs	0.264	0.296	0.300	0.248	0.292	0.308
	10 docs	0.222	0.250	0.270	0.216	0.240	0.268
	15 docs	0.192	0.213	0.236	0.189	0.211	0.233
	20 docs	0.170	0.193	0.208	0.169	0.183	0.203
Av Precision		0.293	0.332	0.358	0.279	0.317	0.349

in performance over the unweighted case, and *cw* in turn does better than *cfw*. It must however again be emphasized that with these artificial queries and assessments, absolute performance values are not indicative of expected real performance levels; and equally that while our claim is that the relative orderings should hold for the weighting schemes, the small collection means that the observed differences must be treated with caution.

Retrieval performance results for head and desk microphones, at document cutoffs, are shown in Table 2. The acoustic threshold th_{mco} gives best performance at the 5 document cutoff, and threshold th_{map} best average position. Again application of *cfw* and, further, of *cw* weighting is highly advantageous.

Finally, Table 3 shows average precision performance acoustic matching using head and desk microphones compared with both transcribed and ideal phonetic text standards. These results show that ideal phonetic retrieval performance is degraded by about 5% relative to that of the standard text transcriptions, because of homophones, so retrieval using even a perfect word spotter will not perform as well as retrieval from text. However, even for an imperfect word spotting system, and considering both head and desk microphones, retrieval performance is encouragingly around 90% of the ideal phonetic figure. As anticipated from the lower FOM reported earlier, retrieval performance for the desk microphone is slightly lower, though it appears it will still be good enough for the eventual Medusa system.

One reason for the good performance of the retrieval system is the inherent robustness of term weighting with respect to false alarms. *Cfw* weighting penalizes both frequently occurring, and hence undiscriminating, keywords (as in the text case), and also keywords having high numbers of acoustic false alarms across the document set. *Cw* moreover, as well as being generally preferable on independent grounds, is yet more robust in relation to speech. Figure 3 shows

Table 2. Collection 1a: Retrieval performance for head and desk microphone data, thresholds chosen to maximize precision cutoff values (th_{mco}) and average precision (th_{map})

		Head					
Weight Scheme		*uw*		*cfw*		*cw*	
		th_{mco}	th_{map}	th_{mco}	th_{map}	th_{mco}	th_{map}
Precision	5 docs	0.248	0.232	0.288	0.256	0.272	0.260
	10 docs	0.212	0.192	0.218	0.222	0.244	0.234
	15 docs	0.164	0.169	0.185	0.195	0.211	0.213
	20 docs	0.143	0.156	0.160	0.171	0.192	0.187
Av Precision		0.256	0.259	0.293	0.295	0.311	0.316
		Desk					
Weight Scheme		*uw*		*cfw*		*cw*	
		th_{mco}	th_{map}	th_{mco}	th_{map}	th_{mco}	th_{map}
Precision	5 docs	0.252	0.244	0.264	0.260	0.272	0.272
	10 docs	0.176	0.182	0.224	0.214	0.238	0.238
	15 docs	0.164	0.167	0.192	0.191	0.210	0.210
	20 docs	0.141	0.142	0.173	0.166	0.177	0.177
Av Precision		0.232	0.241	0.279	0.283	0.299	0.299

Table 3. Collection 1a: Relative average precision retrieval performance

		Text	Phonetic	Head	Desk
cfw	Relative to Text	100%	95.5%	88.8%	85.2%
	Relative to Phonetic	—	100%	93.2%	89.4%
cw	Relative to Text	100%	97.5%	88.3%	83.5%
	Relative to Phonetic	—	100%	90.5%	85.7%

Table 4. Collection 1b: Retrieval precision values for text transcription and ideal phonetic word spotter with highly relevant message set

Weight Scheme		Text			Phonetic		
		uw	*cfw*	*cw*	*uw*	*cfw*	*cw*
Precision	5 docs	0.342	0.350	0.342	0.338	0.346	0.354
	10 docs	0.281	0.308	0.294	0.288	0.321	0.310
	15 docs	0.260	0.297	0.299	0.263	0.301	0.299
	20 docs	0.242	0.281	0.280	0.251	0.283	0.282
Av Precision		0.296	0.332	0.346	0.302	0.339	0.355

spoken message retrieval performance for Collection 1a using head microphone data at different acoustic score thresholds for *uw*, *cfw* and *cw* schemes. It can be seen from this figure that the performance trends observed for *a posteriori* best performance thresholds are consistent across the different threshold levels; and also, significantly, that as well as achieving the best retrieval performance in absolute terms, the *cw* scheme is also less sensitive to the choice of threshold than the other schemes.

7.3.2. Collection 1b results. As Collection 1b is rather more realistic than Collection 1a (or at least is less artificial), we replicated all the tests done with Collection 1a on Collection 1b. Tables 4, 5, and 6 thus show comparative performance for the three retrieval strategies for the

Table 5. Collection 1b: Retrieval performance for head and desk microphone data for highly relevant message set, thresholds chosen to maximize precision cutoff values (th_{mco}) and average precision (th_{map})

Weight Scheme		Head					
		uw		*cfw*		*cw*	
		th_{mco}	th_{map}	th_{mco}	th_{map}	th_{mco}	th_{map}
Precision	5 docs	0.333	0.333	0.358	0.350	0.346	0.333
	10 docs	0.265	0.265	0.306	0.321	0.308	0.296
	15 docs	0.238	0.238	0.283	0.285	0.283	0.289
	20 docs	0.207	0.207	0.253	0.260	0.270	0.266
Av Precision		0.265	0.265	0.310	0.312	0.320	0.330

Weight Scheme		Desk					
		uw		*cfw*		*cw*	
		th_{mco}	th_{map}	th_{mco}	th_{map}	th_{mco}	th_{map}
Precision	5 docs	0.296	0.296	0.308	0.308	0.338	0.338
	10 docs	0.273	0.273	0.300	0.300	0.302	0.302
	15 docs	0.246	0.246	0.274	0.274	0.282	0.282
	20 docs	0.215	0.215	0.245	0.245	0.254	0.254
Av Precision		0.254	0.254	0.296	0.296	0.307	0.315

Table 6. Collection 1b: Relative average precision retrieval performance for highly relevant message set

		Text	Phonetic	Head	Desk
cfw	Relative to Text	100%	102.4%	94.00%	89.4%
	Relative to Phonetic	—	100%	91.8%	87.3%
cw	Relative to Text	100%	102.7%	95.3%	91.2%
	Relative to Phonetic	—	100%	92.9%	88.9%

Table 7. Collection 1b: Retrieval precision values for text transcription and ideal phonetic word spotter with full relevant message set

Weight Scheme		Text			Phonetic		
		uw	*cfw*	*cw*	*uw*	*cfw*	*cw*
Precision	5 docs	0.472	0.488	0.508	0.472	0.484	0.508
	10 docs	0.430	0.466	0.462	0.434	0.474	0.464
	15 docs	0.391	0.436	0.448	0.396	0.444	0.443
	20 docs	0.371	0.418	0.425	0.375	0.419	0.427
Av Precision		0.403	0.450	0.460	0.409	0.455	0.464

two reference standards, for spoken document retrieval for the head and desk microphones, and speech performance relative to the two standards. These tables give the figures for the highly relevant documents only: performance for the highly and partially relevant documents taken together is given in Tables 7, 8, and 9.

The results again show the three strategies in the same rank order, with *cw* better than *cfw* better than *uw*, and results for the head microphone better than the desk one. (These comparisons are subject to the same caveats as those for Collection 1a.) The difference between Collections 1a and 1b is that for the latter performance is better against the phonetic than against the text standard. This is somewhat surprising, but seems to be attributable to the fact that the queries have so few terms. Where there are only one or two query terms, the retrieval of text

Table 8. Collection 1b: Retrieval performance for head and desk microphone data full relevant message set, thresholds chosen to maximize precision cutoff values (th_{mco}) and average precision (th_{map})

Weight Scheme		Head					
		uw		*cfw*		*cw*	
		th_{mco}	th_{map}	th_{mco}	th_{map}	th_{mco}	th_{map}
Precision	5 docs	0.492	0.492	0.516	0.516	0.492	0.476
	10 docs	0.400	0.400	0.434	0.434	0.456	0.452
	15 docs	0.363	0.363	0.413	0.413	0.429	0.431
	20 docs	0.330	0.329	0.381	0.381	0.408	0.401
Av Precision		0.364	0.364	0.410	0.410	0.418	0.423

Weight Scheme		Desk					
		uw		*cfw*		*cw*	
		th_{mco}	th_{map}	th_{mco}	th_{map}	th_{mco}	th_{map}
Precision	5 docs	0.412	0.412	0.444	0.444	0.496	0.496
	10 docs	0.384	0.384	0.430	0.430	0.436	0.436
	15 docs	0.368	0.368	0.399	0.399	0.416	0.416
	20 docs	0.324	0.324	0.370	0.370	0.384	0.384
Av Precision		0.333	0.333	0.385	0.385	0.409	0.409

Table 9. Collection 1b: Relative average precision retrieval performance, full relevant message set

		Text	Phonetic	Head	Desk
cfw	Relative to Text	100%	101.3%	91.1%	85.7%
	Relative to Phonetic	—	100%	90.0%	84.6%
cw	Relative to Text	100%	101.0%	92.1%	88.9%
	Relative to Phonetic	—	100%	91.2%	88.0%

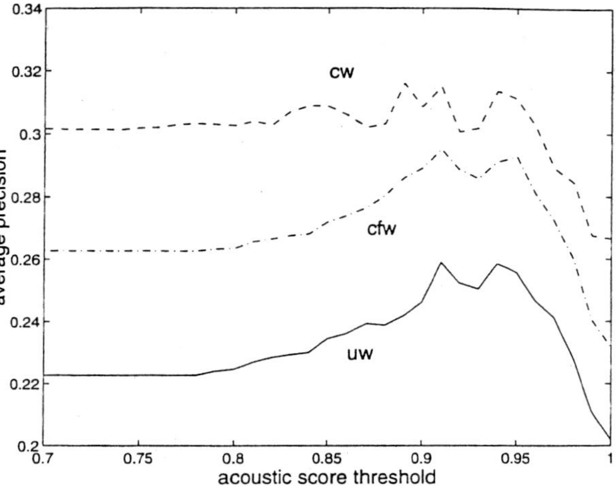

Fig. 3. Collection 1a: average retrieval precision for head microphone data versus threshold.

transcriptions is particularly susceptible to failures arising from occasional inconsistent suffix stripping of different word forms. This problem is less likely in the phonetic case where the matching is based on comparison of the document contents to the acoustic composition of the standard keyword form.

Figure 4 shows the effect of differing thresholds on retrieval performance for Collection 1b for the highly relevant message set.

7.3.3. Discussion of test results. Apart from the differences for the two standards, the picture for the two collections, with their rather different requests and assessments, is similar. This

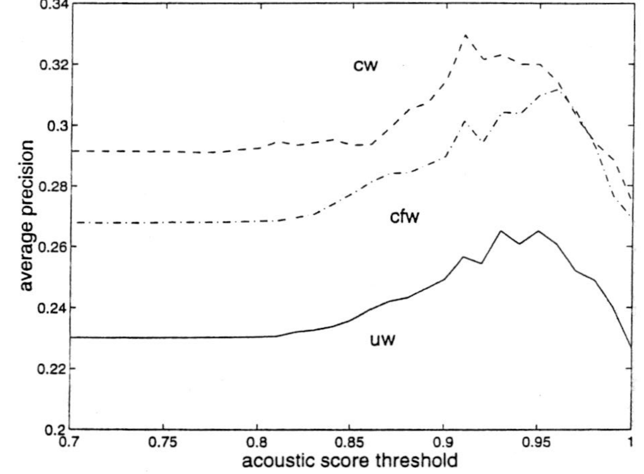

Fig. 4. Collection 1b: average retrieval precision for head microphone data versus threshold for the highly relevant message set.

includes good levels of performance for spoken document retrieval relative to the standards, suggesting that reasonable speech retrieval performance can be envisaged in real situations like the intended VMR office context, even if the circumstances in which our Collection 1 materials were created and recorded were favourable ones.

By comparison with James's tests (James, 1995), our absolute levels of performance were lower. But this is not surprising since James's data, consisting of brief and well-defined, summary-type documents, provided unnaturally favourable conditions. The categories covered in our message set are closely related and much less orthogonal than the individual news stories used as documents in his database. However we anticipate that use of an open search term vocabulary, as in James's experiments, would lead to an improvement in absolute performance levels in our system. The general trend towards better performance as more factors are taken into account in weighting is the same in both cases. while we also achieve performance of around 90% in comparison with text transcriptions.

Both sets of experiments relied on known speakers, a limitation that has to be removed before operational deployment is possible. The major advances in the experiments described above, compared with James's, relate mainly to the composition and acoustic quality of the spoken documents. The messages in VMR1 are entirely unscripted and spoken by people not trained for or used to recording. As noted earlier, recognition on this type of spontaneous spoken material is much more difficult than on read speech. Further, our comparative tests between head and desk micophone data show that retrieval performance is only slightly degraded by reduced acoustic channel quality.

8. CONCLUSION: CURRENT AND FUTURE WORK

Referring back to our retrieval strategy summary, these experiments constitute a fair, if not very large, set of spoken document retrieval tests assuming a known speaker community and search vocabulary. (They also assume typed requests, but this is not a material limitation). The results in relation to speech recognition performance and to the behaviour of retrieval strategies in the speech case confirm the first tests reported by James (1995). We have begun work on speaker independent and open vocabulary searching, initially with the two test collections used here: thus speaker-independence is achieved simply by removal of the explicit training data associated with Database 1 (Foote *et al.*, 1995). At the same time, we must again emphasise that, compared with text retrieval, it is much harder to get test data, while processing, for the same number of file items, is much more onerous.

We have also already taken some first steps towards the provision of a convenient user interface (Brown *et al.*, 1994), in particular addressing the issue of user scanning and browsing when listening to any significant amount of speech is slow. Thus we have experimented with a visual display of file contents as a horizontal bar showing putative positions of search terms, which enables the user to manually select potentially interesting sections for playback. But we have not been able, with our existing data, to include hybrid searching and we have also not made any serious attempt to incorporate image presentation. The obvious purely technical questions we have to consider are the possible use of the actual acoustic scores delivered by the speech processing, in conjunction with other incidence data for terms, and means of providing for query expansion in relevance feedback and not just relevance reweighting.

Acknowledgement—This project is supported by the UK DTI Grant IED4/1/5804 and SERC (now EPSRC) Grant GR/H87629. Olivetti Research Limited is an industrial partner of the VMR project. The VMR corpus used for this work will be available for public distribution in the near future.

REFERENCES

Brown, M. G., Foote, J. T., Jones, G. J. F., Sparck Jones. K., & Young, S. J. (1994). Video mail retrieval using voice: An overview of the Cambridge/Olivetti retrieval system. In *Proceedings of the ACM Multimedia '94 Conference*

Workshop on Multimedia Database Management Systems, (pp. 47–55). San Francisco, Calif.

Burrows, M. (1991). DEC Systems Research Centre, Palo Alto, pers. commun.

Foote, J. T., Jones, G. J. F., Sparck Jones, K., & Young, S. J. (1995). Talker-independent keyword spotting for information retrieval. In *Proceedings of Eurospeech 95* (Vol. 3, pp. 2145–2148). ESCA.

Garafolo, J., Paul, D. & Phillips, M. (1993). CSR WSJ0 Detailed orthographic transcription (.dot) specification (ftp: jaguar.ncsl.nist.gov /csr/csr-dot-spec.doc).

Glavitsch, U., & Schäuble, P. (1992). A system for retrieving speech documents. In *Proceedings of SIGIR '92* (pp. 168–176). ACM.

Glavitsch, U., Schäuble, P, & Wechsler, M. (1994). Metadata for integrating speech documents in a text retrieval system. *SIGMOD Record 23*(4), 57–63.

Harman, D. K. (Ed.) (1994). *The Second Text REtrieval Conference (TREC-2)*, Special Publication 500–215, National Institute of Standards and Technology, Gaithersburg, Md.

James, D. A. (1995). *The Application of Classical Information Retrieval Techniques to Spoken Documents*. Dissertation, Engineering Department, University of Cambridge.

Jones, G. J. F., Foote, J. T., Sparck Jones, K., & Young, S. J. (1994). *Video Mail Retrieval Using Voice: Report on Keyword Definition and Data Collection*. Technical Report 335, Computer Laboratory, University of Cambridge.

Jones, G. J. F., Foote, J. T., Sparck Jones, K., & Young, S. J. (1995a), Video mail retrieval: the effect of word spotting accuracy on precision. In *Proceedings of ICASSP 95* (Vol. 1, pp. 309–312). IEEE.

Jones, G. J. F., Foote, J. T., & Sparck Jones, K. (1995b). Video mail retrieval using voice: Report on collection of naturalistic requests and relevance assessments. VMR Project Working Document.

Knill, K. M., & Young, S. J. (1994). *Speaker Dependent Keyword Spotting for Hand-Held Devices*. Technical Report 193, Cambridge University Engineering Department, July 1994.

Kupiec, J., Kimber, D., & Balasubramanian, V. (1994). Speech-based retrieval using semantic co-occurrence filtering. In *Proceedings of HLT 94 (ARPA)* (pp. 350–354). San Francisco: Morgan Kaufmann.

Lamel, L. F., Kassel, H. K., & Seneff, S. (1986). Speech database development: Design and analysis of the acoustic-phonetic corpus. In *Proceedings of the DARPA Speech Recognition Workshop* (pp. 26–32).

McDonough, J., Ng, K., Jeanrenaud, P., Gish, H., & Rohlicek, J. R. (1994). Approaches to topic identification on the switchboard corpus. In *Proceedings of ICASSP 94* (Vol. 1, pp. 385–388). IEEE.

Porter, M. F. (1980). An algorithm for suffix stripping. *Program 14*(3), 130–137.

Rabiner, L. R. (1989). A tutorial on hidden Markov models and selected applications in speech recognition. *Proceedings of the IEEE 77*(2), 257–286.

Robertson, S. E., & Sparck Jones, K. (1994). *Simple, Proven Approaches to Text Retrieval*. Technical Report 356, Computer Laboratory, University of Cambridge.

Robertson, S. E., & Walker, S. (1994). Some simple effective approximations to the 2-Poisson model for probabilistic weighted retrieval. In *Proceedings SIGIR '94* (pp. 232–241). ACM.

Robertson, S. E., Walker, S., Jones, S., Hancock-Beaulieu, M. M., & Gatford, M. (1995). Okapi at TREC-3. In D. K. Harman (ed.), *The Third Text REtrieval Conference (TREC-3)* (pp. 109–126). Special Publication 500–225, National Institute of Standards and Technology, Gaithersburg, Md.

Rose, R. C. (1991). Techniques for information retrieval from speech messages. *Lincoln Laboratory Journal 4*(1), 45–60.

Schäuble, P., & Glavitsch, U. (1994). Assessing the retrieval effectiveness of a speech retrieval system by simulating recognition errors. In *Proceedings HLT 94 (ARPA)* (pp. 347–349). San Francisco, Morgan-Kaufmann.

Tague, J. M. (1981). The pragmatics of information retrieval experimentation. In K. Sparck Jones (Ed.), *Information Retrieval Experiment*. (Chap 5, pp. 59–102). London: Butterworths.

Wilcox, L. D., & Bush, M. A. (1992). Training and search algorithms for an interactive wordspotting system. In *Proceedings of ICASSP 92* (Vol. II, pp. 97–100). IEEE.

Woodland, P. C., Leggetter, C. J., Odell, J. J., Valchev, V., & Young, S. J. (1995). The 1994 HTK large vocabulary speech recognition system. In *Proceedings of ICASSP 95* (Vol. 1, pp. 73–76). IEEE.

Young, S. J., Woodland, P. C., & Byrne, W. J. (1993). *HTK: Hidden Markov Model Toolkit V1.5*, Entropic Research Laboratories, Inc., 600 Pennsylvania Ave. SE, Suite 202, Washington, DC 20003 USA.

Young, S. J., Woodland, P. C., & Byrne, W. J. (1994). Spontaneous speech recognition for the Credit Card corpus using the HTK Toolkit. *IEEE Transactions on Speech and Audio Processing*, 2(4), 615–621.

Video Parsing, Retrieval and Browsing: An Integrated and Content-Based Solution

H. J. Zhang, C. Y. Low, S. W. Smoliar and J. H. Wu
Institute of Systems Science, National University of Singapore
Heng Mui Keng Terrace, Kent Ridge, Singapore 0511
Republic of Singapore
+65 772-6725
zhj@iss.nus.sg

ABSTRACT

This paper presents an integrated solution for computer assisted video parsing and content-based video retrieval and browsing. The uniqueness and effectiveness of this solution lies in its use of video content information provided by a parsing process driven by visual feature analysis. More specifically, parsing will temporally segment and abstract a video source, based on low-level image analyses; then retrieval and browsing of video will be based on key-frames selected during abstraction and spatial-temporal variations of visual features, as well as some shot-level semantics derived from camera operation and motion analysis. These processes, as well as video retrieval and browsing tools, are presented in detail as functions of an integrated system. Also, experimental results on automatic key-frame detection are given .

KEYWORDS

Video parsing, video indexing, video retrieval, video browsing, multimedia, database.

1. INTRODUCTION

Interfaces to multimedia information systems, such as video on demand (VOD), are in general very weak in interactive functionality (even if some are very visually appealing). Selection rarely involves anything better than key words; and any manipulation of the video itself is limited to the lowest level of VCR control. The problem is that, from the point of view of content, the resources managed by such systems are *unstructured*. The source material is not subject to any structural analysis (parsing) and therefore can be neither indexed nor accessed on the basis of structural properties. Fundamentally, such a system is a database which must support extended capabilities for retrieval (for the user) and insertion (for the system manager). Parsing is the primary extension which serves insertion, while retrieval must exploit parsing results. In addition, because of the subjective nature of the source material, retrieval must be supplemented by capabilities for browsing.

Our use of the term "parsing" differs slightly from linguistic conventions. We see it as encompassing two tasks: *temporal segmentation* of a video program into elemental units, and *content extraction* from those units, based on both video and audio semantic primitives [29]. Many effective algorithms are now available for temporal segmentation [17; 28]. However, fully automated content extraction is a much more difficult task, requiring both signal analysis and knowledge representation techniques; so human assistance is still needed. We thus feel the most fruitful research approach is to concentrate on *facilitating tools*, using low-level visual features . Such tools are clearly feasible and research in this direction should ultimately lead to an intelligent video parsing system [23, 30, 31].

Retrieval and browsing require that the source material first be effectively *indexed*. While most previous research in indexing has been text-based [6, 20], content based indexing of video with visual features is still an research problem. Visual features can be divided into two levels: low-level image features, and semantic features based on objects and events. To date automation of low-level feature indexing[8, 19, 10] has been far more successful than that of semantic indexing[6]. Perhaps the biggest problem with indexing video using the low-level image features of every frame is its enormous volume, but a viable solution seems to be to index representative key-frames [18] extracted from the video sources.

While we tend to think of indexing supporting retrieval, *browsing* is equally significant for video source material. By "browsing" we mean an informal perusal of content which may lack any specific goal or focus. The task of browsing is actually very intimately related to retrieval. On the one hand, if a query is too general, browsing is the best way to *examine the results*. This should provide some indication of *why* the query was poorly expressed; so browsing also serves as an aid to *formulating queries*, making it easier for the user to "just ask around" in the process of figuring out the most appropriate query to pose [32].

Unfortunately, the only major technological precedent for video browsing is the VCR (even available in "soft" form for computer viewing), with its support for sequential fast forward and reverse play. Browsing a video this way is a matter of skipping frames: the faster the play speed, the larger the skip factor. The "content-based" browser of [3] takes this approach, but a uniform skip factor really does not account for video content. Furthermore, there is always the danger that some skipped frames may contain the content of greatest interest. A *truly* content-based approach to video browsing should be based on some level of analysis of the actual image content, rather than simply providing a more sophisticated view of temporal context. However, only few research efforts published [31] that have discussed how parsing results may be applied to support more powerful browsing tools.

This paper presents our work on developing an integrated system to parsing, retrieval, and browsing based on three levels of automated content analysis. What makes our solution effective is its use of the content information represented by the visual feature extracted video parsing processes. There are three processes in our solution which capture different levels of content information: The first is temporal segmentation. At the second level each segment is abstracted into key-frames, based on a simple analysis of content variation which yields results far more useful than sub-sampling at a fixed rate. Finally, visual features, such as color and texture, are used to represent the content of key-frames. In addition, variations among key-frames from the same shot are calculated and integrated with information about camera operation and object motion to provide event-based cues. Indexing is then supported by a clustering process which classifies key-frames into different visual categories; this categorization may also support manual user annotation. These results facilitate retrieval and browsing in a variety of ways. Retrieval may be based on not only the annotated index but also low-level image features of key-frames and temporal variation, object motion and camera operation features of segments. The key-frames enable browsing with a fast forward/backward player, a hierarchical time-space viewer, and cluster-based clip windows.

This paper is organized as follows: Section 2 presents our approaches to video parsing, including a brief summary of temporal segmentation and a detailed discussion of key-frame extraction. Section 3 reviews the visual features of key-frames used in content representation. The resulting approach to retrieval and browsing is then presented in detail in Section 4. Finally, Section 5 offers concluding remarks and a brief view of our current and future work.

2. VIDEO PARSING: SEGMENTATION AND ABSTRACTION

2.1 Temporal Segmentation and Camera Operation Detection

The basic unit of video to be represented or indexed is usually assumed to be a single camera shot, consisting of one or more frames generated and recorded contiguously and representing a continuous action in time and space. Thus, temporal segmentation is the problem of detecting boundaries between consecutive camera shots. The general approach to the solution has been the definition of a suitable *quantitative* difference metric which represents significant *qualitative* differences between frames. Our own system detects not only simple camera breaks but also gradual transitions implemented by special effects such as fades, wipes, and dissolves [28].

For compressed video data, it would be advantageous to segment it directly, saving on the computational cost of decompression and lowering the overall magnitude of the data to be processed. Also, elements of a compressed representation, such as DCT coefficients and motion vectors in JPEG and MPEG data streams, are useful features for effective content comparison [30, 27]. Our experiments have shown that proper use of both DCT coefficients and motion vectors can achieve both fast processing speed and very high segmentation accuracy [30].

To obtain motion features of video, our system also identifies frames involving camera operations, such as panning, tilting, and zooming, as false positives, and dominant object motions. The simple and effective approach in our system analyzes the characteristic patterns of motion vectors [28]. An alternative approach, implemented in our system, is to examine spatio-temporal slices of video sequences [1]. These images also provide characteristic patterns for camera operation, and they may be used for abstraction and representation of shot content [33].

2.2 Automated Video Abstraction: Key-Frame Extraction

Even when videos are compressed, it is rarely feasible or desirable to index and/or store all frames for retrieval purposes. Instead, an abstraction process is necessary, which may be effectively applied at the individual segment level. We view abstraction as a problem of mapping an entire segment to some small number of representative images, usually called *key-frames*. An index may be constructed from key-frames, and retrieval queries may be directed at key-frames, which can subsequently be displayed for browsing purposes. Also, if storage space is limited, only these key-frames need to be maintained on-line. Furthermore, aThese techniques will be discussed at greater length in the sequel.

Key-frames are still images which best represent the content of the video sequence in an abstracted manner, and may be either extracted or reconstructed from original video data. Key-frames are frequently used to supplement the text of a video log [18], but there has been little progress in identifying them automatically. The challenge is that the extraction of key-frames needs to be automatic and content based so that they maintain the important content of the video while remove all redundancy. In theory semantic primitives of video, such as interesting objects, actions and events should be used. However, because such general semantic analysis is not currently feasible, we have to rely on low-level image features and other readily available information instead. Based on these constraints, we have developed a robust key-frame extraction technique which utilizes information computed by the parsing processes:[1]

[1] US Patent pending.

- *Color features:* The basic representation of the color of a video frame is a histogram of the distribution of color components. Also, average brightness, color moments (including mean), dominant color are used. Our specific mathematical definitions will be presented in Section 3. If compressed data are used, these features may be calculated from DCT coefficients of video frames[27].
- *Motion*: Dominant motion components resulting from camera operations and large moving objects are the most important source of information, since motion is the major indicator or content change. For instance, a zoom shot is usually best abstracted by three frames—the first, the last, and one in the middle. When MPEG video is used, motion vectors from B and P frames can be directly extracted for motion analysis.

In our implementation, the key-frame extraction process is integrated with the processes of segmentation. Each time a new shot is identified, the key-frame extraction process is invoked, using parameters already computed during segmentation. Certain heuristics are also applied, such as the decision to use the first frame of every shot as a key-frame. In addition users can adjust several parameters to control the density of key-frames in each shot. The default is that at least two key-frames will be selected for each shot; and, in the simplest case, they could be the first and last frames of the shot. The process is faster with compressed video data, and real time extraction can be achieved.

2.3 Experimental Results

The performance of various temporal segmentation systems has been discussed elsewhere [17, 28, 3, 29, 27] and will not be repeated here. **Table 1** summarizes key-frame extraction results obtained from four test sets, which represent the effectiveness of the techniques described in Section 2.2 in abstracting different types of video material. The first test was based on two "stock footage" videos consisting of unedited raw shots of various lengths, covering a wide range of scenes and objects. "Singapore," the second test set, is travelogue material from an elaborately produced documentary which draws upon a variety of sophisticated editing effects. Finally, the "Dance" video is the entirety of *Changing Steps*, a "dance for television" containing shots with fast moving objects (dancers), complex and fast changing lighting and camera operations, and highly imaginative editing effects, many of which are far less conventional than those in "Singapore." We feel that these four source videos are representative of both the content material and style of presentation that one will generally find in professionally produced television and film.

Because key-frame extraction takes place at the segment level, segmentation results are also listed in **Table 1**. Furthermore, because it is hard to quantitatively measure the accuracy of key-frame extraction (even human selection can be subjective), only the number of key-frames extracted for each test is given. **Table 1** shows that segmentation performs with an accuracy of over 95% (counting both missing and false detection as errors) in the first three tests. The dance video yields the lowest accuracy, due to the elaborate production technique, and can be considered the lowest achievable accuracy of the segmentation techniques. For all segments which were correctly detected, key-frames were correctly extracted, yielding an average of between two and three key-frames per shot, which tends to be a suitable abstraction ratio. In addition the test results demonstrate that camera operations (both panning and zooming) have been properly abstracted by the key-frames detected.

It is also worth observing that, particularly in the "Dance" example, key-frame extraction actually compensated for segmentation errors. That is, in many of the cases where a shot boundary was missed, one or more additional key-frames were detected to represent the material in the missed shot. In other words key-frame detection is more robust than shot boundary detection.

Video	Length (sec.)	N_d	N_m	N_f	N_k
Stock footage 1	451.8	35	1	1	116
Stock footage 2	1210.7	78	1	5	271
Singapore	173.8	31	1	0	71
Dance	2109.1	90	17	4	205

Table 1: Video segmentation and key-frame extraction results: N_d: number of shots correctly detected; N_m: number of shots missed by the detection algorithm; N_f: false detection of shot boundaries; N_k: number of key-frames extracted.

To systematically evaluate the effectiveness and accuracy of our key-frame extraction system, we conducted a user trial comparing automatic extraction with human identification of key-frames from the two stock footage videos listed in **Table 1**, which were provided by the Singapore Broadcasting Corporation (SBC).[2] Members of the SBC Film/Videotape Library staff were instructed to identify key-frames from these source tapes, on the basis of which they then evaluated the results of our system. Our system did not miss any of the key-frames selected by the librarians. The only difficulty was that our results were more "generous," extracting more key-frames than were selected manually; but this discrepancy has been remedied by providing user control of the density of frames selected. On the other hand the librarians agreed that our automatic extraction was more objective (our system always tried to identify at least one key-frame per shot), while they sometimes tended to ignore certain shots which they felt were not important.

3. SHOT CONTENT REPRESENTATION AND SIMILARITY MEASURES

After partitioning and abstraction the next step is to identify and compute *representation primitives*, based on which the content shot can be indexed, compared, and

[2] Now the Television Corporation of Singapore.

classified. Ideally these should be semantic primitives that a user can employ to define "interesting" or "significant" events. However, such an ideal solution is not feasible; so that our representation primitives are based on information accessible through the techniques described in Section 2. The resulting representation is divided into two parts: primitives based on key-frames and those based on temporal variation and motion information. These parts complement each other and can be used either separately or together.

3.1. Representation of Shot Content Based on Key-frame Features

Following the techniques used in image database systems[8, 19, 10], key-frames are represented by properties of color, texture, shape, and edge features, each of which will now be reviewed.

3.1.1 Color features

Color has excellent discrimination power in image retrieval systems. It is very rare that two images of totally different objects will have similar colors [22]. Our representation primitives for color features include mean brightness, color histogram, dominant colors, and statistical moments.

Color histogram: A histogram of the distribution of color intensities is a quantitative representation which is especially useful for textured images which are not well served by segmentation techniques. Also, color histograms are invariant under translation and rotation about the view axis and change only slowly under change of angle of view, change in scale, and occlusion [22]. We have chosen the Munsell space to define color histograms because it is close to human perception of colors [16]. As in QBIC, we have quantized the color space into 64 "super-cells" using a standard minimum sum of squares clustering algorithm [8]. A 64-bin color histogram is then calculated for each key-frame where each bin is assigned the normalized count of the number of pixels that fall in its corresponding supercell.

The distance between two color histograms, I and Q, each consisting of N bins, is quantified by the following metric :

$$D^2_{his}(I,Q) = \sum_i^N \sum_j^N a_{ij}(I_i - Q_i)(I_j - Q_j) \tag{1}$$

where the matrix a_{ij} represents the similarity between the colors corresponding to bins i and j, respectively. This matrix needs to be determined from human visual perception studies, and we have derived it using the method of [11]. Notice that if a_{ij} is the identity matrix, then this measure becomes Euclidean distance.

Dominant colors: Because, in most images, a small number of color ranges capture the majority of pixels, these dominant colors can be used to construct an approximate representation of color distribution. These dominant colors can be easily identified from color histograms of key-frames. Experiments have shown that using only a few dominant colors will not degrade the performance of color image matching [22, 10]. In fact, performance may even be enhanced, since histogram bins which are too small are likely to be noise, thus distorting similarity computations. Our current implementation is based on twenty dominant colors, corresponding to the histogram bins contains the maximum numbers of pixels.

Color moments: Because a probability distribution is uniquely characterized by its moments, following [20] we represent a color distribution by its first three moments:

$$\mu_i = \frac{1}{N}\sum_{j=1}^{N} p_{ij} \tag{2}$$

$$\sigma_i = \left(\frac{1}{N}\sum_{j=1}^{N}(p_{ij} - \mu_i)^2\right)^{\frac{1}{2}} \tag{3}$$

$$s_i = \left(\frac{1}{N}\sum_{j=1}^{N}(p_{ij} - \mu_i)^3\right)^{\frac{1}{3}} \tag{4}$$

where p_{ij} is the value of the i-th color component of the j-th image pixel. The first order moment, μ_i, defines the average intensity of each color component; the second and third moments, σ_i and s_i, respectively, define the variance and skewness.

Using these three moments, distance may be computed as follows [21]:

$$D_{mom}(I,Q) = \sum_{i=1}^{r}(w_{i1}|\mu_i(I) - \mu_i(Q)| + w_{i2}|\sigma_i(I) - \sigma_i(Q)| + w_{i3}|s_i(I) - s_i(Q)|) \tag{5}$$

where r is the number of color components and the w_{ij} $(1 \le j \le 3)$ weight the contributions of the different moments for each color component. As we use only a small set of moments, it is possible for two qualitatively different color images to have a D_{mom} value of 0. Nevertheless, experimental evidence has shown that this measure is more robust in matching color images than color histograms [21].

Mean brightness: This number reflects the overall lighting conditions, and is defined similar to and can be derived from (2).

3.1.2 Texture features

Texture has long been recognized as being as important a property of images as is color, if not more so, since textural information can be conveyed as readily with gray-level images as it can in color. Nevertheless, there is an extremely wide variety of opinion concerned with just what texture is and how it may be quantitatively represented [26]. Among all these alternatives we have chosen two models which are both popular and effective in image retrieval: Tamura features [25] and the Simultaneous Autoregressive (SAR) model [14].

Tamura Features: The Tamura features are *contrast*, *directionality*, and *coarseness*, which were introduced as

As we pointed out earlier, another advantage to using key-frames in browsing is that we are able to browse the video content down to the key-frame level without necessarily storing the entire video. This is particularly advantageous if our storage space is limited. Such a feature is very useful not only in video databases and information systems but also to support previewing in VOD systems. What is particularly important is that the network load for transmitting small numbers of static images is far less than that required for transmitting video; and, because the images are static, quality of service is no longer such a critical constraint. Through the hierarchical browser, one may also identify a specific sequence of the video which is all that one may wish to "demand." Thus, the browser not only reduces network load during browsing but may also reduce the need for network services when the time comes to request the actual video.

The browsing tools presented above are basically *programs* or *clips* based. That is, video programs or clips are loaded into the browser either from a list of names specified by retrieval result, a database index or a user. As shown in Figure 3, the only criteria used to select the representative icons displayed at the top level of the hierarchy is time: they are the first key-frame of the first shot among all shots represented. In other words, the shots at the high levels are grouped only according to their sequential relations not their content. As a result, though random access is provided, a user has to browse down to the second or third level to get a sense of content of all shots in a group. This is less a problem if the browsing is launched from retrieval result such as shown in *Figure 1* and *Figure 2*, but it will not be very convenient when we use it to brows raw video data or parsing result.

To support *class-based* browsing, we have been working on clustering algorithms using the same content representation as used in retrieval. Two types of algorithms, ISODATA partitioning and hierarchical clustering[7], have been used for this task. With such clustering processes, when a list of video programs or clips are provided, the parsing system will use either key-frame and/or shot features to cluster shots into classes, each of which consists of shots of similar content. After such clustering, each class of shots can be represented by an icon, which can then be displayed at the high levels of hierarchical browser. As a result, user can know roughly the content of each calls of shots even without moving down to lower level of the hierarchy. Such clustering is also useful in index building and computer-assisted video content annotation. We are currently working on integrating this part into our system.

5. CONCLUDING REMARKS AND FUTURE WORK

In this paper we have presented an overview of our work in developing an integrated and content-based solution for computer-assisted video parsing, abstraction, retrieval and browsing. The most important feature of our approach is its use of low-level visual features as a representation of video content and its automatic abstraction process. Such a representation and extracted key-frames, together with spatio-temporal features and some semantic primitives derived at shot level, can then be used to facilitate indexing, retrieval and browsing. Experimental results and usibility studies have shown that such a solution is effective and feasible and will be useful in many multimedia applications, though tranditional text-based indexing and retrieval tools will still be part of the integrated system.

We are now working on more robust algorithms to extract event-based features. Case studies on parsing and indexing news broadcasts have already allowed us to support queries such as "find me all interview shots in a news program" [31]. An inportant extension of our work is to incorporate audio analysis and text parsing into both video parsing and content representation[4].

6. REFERENCES

1. E. H. Adelson and J. R. Bergen, Spatiotemporal Energy Models for the Perception of Motion, *Journal of the Optical Society of America A* 2 (2), pp. 284-299, 1985.
2. E. M. Arkin *et al.*, An Efficiently Computable Metric for Comparing Polygonal Shapes, *IEEE Transactions on Patt. Analy. and Mach. Intell.*, 13 (3), pp. 209-216, 1991.
3. F. Arman *et al.*, Content-based Browsing of Video Sequences, *Proc. ACM Multimedia 94*, San Francisco, CA, 1994.
4. W. Bender and P. Chesnais, Network Plus, Proc. SPIE Electronic Imaging Device and Systems Symposium. Vol. 900, p81-86, 1988.
5. D. Daneels *et al.*, Interactive Outlining: An Improved Approach Using Active Geometry Features, *Proc. IS&T/SPIE. Conf. on Storage and Retrieval for Image and Video Databases II*, San Jose, CA, 1993.
6. M. Davis, Media Streams: An Iconic Visual Language for Video Annotation, *Proc. Symposium on Visual Languages*, Bergen, NORWAY, 1993.
7. R. Duda and P. Hart, *Pattern recognition and scene analysis*, Wiley, New York, 1973.
8. C. Faloutsos *et al.*, Efficient and Effective Querying by Image Content, *Journal of Intelligent Information Systems* 3, pp. 231-262, 1994.
9. W. T. Freeman and E. H. Adelson, The Design and Use of Steerable Filters, *IEEE Trans. on Patt. Analy. and Mach. Intell.*, 13 (9), pp. 891-906, 1991.
10. Y. Gong *et al.*, An Image Database System with Content Capturing and Fast Image Indexing Abilities, *Proc. International Conference on Multimedia Computing and Systems*, Boston, MA, 1994, pp. 121-130.

11. M. Gorkani and R. Picard, Texture Orientation for Sorting Photos at a Glance, *Proc. 112h International Conference on Pattern Recognition*, Jerusalem, ISRAEL, 1994.

12. M. Ioka, A Method Of Defining the Similarity of Images on the Basis Of Color Information, *Technical Report RT-0030*, IBM Tokyo Research Laboratory, 1989.

13. T. Kato *et al.*, A Sketch Retrieval Method for Full Color Image Database: Query by Visual Example, *Proc. 11th International Conference on Pattern Recognition*, Amsterdam, HOLLAND, 1992, pp. 530-533.

14. J. Mao and A. K. Jain, Texture Classification and Segmentation Using Multiresolution Simultaneous Autoregressive Models, *Pattern Recognition*, 25 (2), pp.173-188, 1992.

15. M. Mills, J. Cohen, and Y. Y. Wong, A Magnifier Tool for Video Data, *Proc. CHI '92*, Monterey, CA, pp. 93-98, 1992.

16. M. Miyahara, and Y. Yoshida, Mathematical Transform of (R,G,B) Color Data to Munsell (H,V,C) Color Data, *Proc. of SPIE Visual Communication and Image Processing*, 1001, pp. 650-657, 1988.

17. A. Nagasaka and Y. Tanaka, Automatic Video Indexing and Full-Video Search for Object Appearances, *Visual Database Systems, II*, E. Knuth and L. M. Wegner, editors, North-Holland, pp. 119-133, 1991.

18. B. C. O'Connor, Selecting Key Frames of Moving Image Documents: A Digital Environment for Analysis and Navigation, *Microcomputers for Information Management*, 8(2), pp. 119-133, 1991.

19. A. Pentland, R. W. Picard, and S. Scarloff, Photobook: Tools for Content-Based Manipulation of Image Databases, *Proc. IS&T/SPIE. Conf. on Storage and Retrieval for Image and Video Databases II*, San Jose, CA, 1994, pp. 34-47.

20. L. A. Rowe, J. S. Boreczky, and C. A. Eads, Indexes for User Access to Large Video Databases, *Proc. IS&T/SPIE Conf. on Storage and Retrieval for Image and Video Databases II*, San Jose, CA, 1994, pp. 150-161.

21. M. Stricker and M. Orengo, Similarity of Color Images, *Proc. IS&T/SPIE. Conf. on Storage and Retrieval for Image and Video Databases III*, San Jose, CA, 1995.

22. M. J. Swain and D. H. Balllard, Color Indexing, International Journal of Computer Vision, Vol.7, pp.11-32, 1991.

23. D. Swanberg, C.-F. Shu, and R. Jain, Knowledge Guided Parsing in Video Databases, *Proc. IS&T/SPIE Conf. on Storage and Retrieval for Image and Video Databases*, San Jose, CA, 1993.

24. L. Teodosio and W. Bender, Salient Video Stills: Content and Context Preserved, *Proc. ACM Multimedia 93*, Anaheim, CA, 1993, pp. 39-46.

25. H. Tamura, S. Mori, and T. Yamawaki, Texture Features Corresponding to Visual Perception, *IEEE Trans. on Syst., Man, and Cybern.*, 6 (4), pp.460-473, 1979.

26. M. Tuceryan and A. K. Jain, Texture Analysis, *Handbook of Pattern Recognition and Computer Vision*, C. H. Chen, L. F. Pau, and P. S. P. Wang, editors, World Scientific, pp. 235-276, 1993.

27. B.-L. Yeo and B. Liu, Rapid Scene Analysis on Compressed Video, *IEEE Transactions on Circuits and Systems for Video Technology*, to appear.

28. H. J. Zhang, A. Kankanhalli, and S. W. Smoliar, Automatic Partitioning of Full-motion Video, *Multimedia Systems* 1 (1), pp. 10-28, 1993.

29. H. J. Zhang and S. W. Smoliar, Developing Power Tools for Video Indexing and Retrieval, *Proc. IS&T/SPIE Conf. on Storage and Retrieval for Image and Video Databases II*, San Jose, CA, 1994, pp. 140-149.

30. H. J. Zhang *et al.*, Video Parsing Using Compressed Data, *Proc. IS&T/SPIE Conf. on Image and Video Processing II*, San Jose, CA, 1994, pp. 142-149.

31. H. J. Zhang *et al.*, Automatic Parsing and Indexing of News Video, *Multimedia Systems*, 2 (6), pp. 256-266, 1995.

32. H. J. Zhang, S. W. Smoliar, and J. H. Wu, Content-Based Video Browsing Tools, *Proc. IS&T/SPIE Conf. on Multimedia Computing and Networking 1995*, San Jose, CA, 1995.

33. H. J. Zhang and W. C. Ho, "Video sequence parsing," *Technical Report*, Institute of Systems Science, National University of Singapore, 1995.

The Automatic Indexing System AIR/PHYS — From Research to Application

Peter Biebricher, Norbert Fuhr, Gerhard Lustig, Michael Schwantner
Technische Hochschule Darmstadt, Fachbereich Informatik
Karolinenplatz 5, D 6100 Darmstadt / West Germany

Gerhard Knorz
Fachhochschule Darmstadt, Fachbereich Information und Dokumentation
Schöfferstraße 8, D 6100 Darmstadt / West Germany

Abstract

Since October 1985, the automatic indexing system AIR/PHYS has been used in the input production of the physics data base of the Fachinformationszentrum Karlsruhe/West Germany. The texts to be indexed are abstracts written in English. The system of descriptors is prescribed. For the application of the AIR/PHYS system a large-scale dictionary containing more than 600 000 word-descriptor relations resp. phrase-descriptor relations has been developed. Most of these relations have been obtained by means of statistical and heuristical methods. In consequence, the relation system is rather imperfect. Therefore, the indexing system needs some fault- tolerating features. An appropriate indexing approach and the corresponding structure of the AIR/PHYS system are described. Finally, the conditions of the application as well as problems of further development are discussed.

1 Introduction

The automatic indexing system AIR/PHYS was developed at the Technische Hochschule Darmstadt/West Germany. In 1983, the system was evaluated by a retrieval test comprising about 300 queries and 15 000 documents. The results, though inferior to those obtained with manual indexing, turned out to be acceptable for application [Fuhr & Knorz 84]. Subsequently, the AIR/PHYS system was improved [Knorz 86], in particular by the development of the new dictionary PHYS/PILOT. Since October 1985, the system has been used in the input production of the physics data base PHYS of the Fachinformationszentrum Karlsruhe/West Germany (Fachinformationszentrum Energie Physik Mathematik GmbH). The data base PHYS comprises more than one million documents, and the annual increment amounts to about 125 000 documents. As there are only few large-scale applications of automatic indexing so far, it may be justifiable to describe in this paper the underlying theoretical approach, the main components, and the application environment of the AIR/PHYS system. (More detailed presentations are given in [Lustig 86] and [Biebricher et al. 88]. Finally, the possibilities of improving the system are discussed.

2 The indexing dictionary

The research on automatic indexing performed at the Technische Hochschule Darmstadt is restricted by the following preconditions:

(1) The texts to be indexed are abstracts (including titles) written in English.

(2) The system of descriptors is prescribed.

In consequence, an automatic indexing system needs a special dictionary containing term-descriptor relations for as many *terms* (i.e. single words, phrases and formulas) of the application field as possible. The lack of such dictionaries seems to have been the main obstacle for putting results of indexing experiments into practice. In order to overcome this difficulty, we have investigated different techniques of automatic dictionary construction. Association factors derived from texts alone did not produce satisfactory results. However, the association factor $z(t,s)$, introduced into automatic indexing with encouraging results twenty years ago [Fangmeyer & Lustig 69,Fangmeyer & Lustig 70], has proved to be extremely useful. Its generation requires a large set M of documents indexed manually with the prescribed descriptor system. The association factor $z(t,s)$ is defined for a term-descriptor pair (t,s) by

$$z(t,s) = \frac{h(t,s)}{f(t)}$$

where

$f(t)$ = number of documents of M containing the term t in the abstract text and

$h(t,s)$ = number of those among the $f(t)$ documents to which the descriptor s is manually assigned.

This leads to the definition of a weighted relation Z consisting of all term-descriptor pairs (t,s) for which $z(t,s)$ and $h(t,s)$ exceed certain cut-off values c_1 and c_2, respectively.

The association factor $z(t,s)$ is an estimate of the probability for the descriptor s to be assigned to a document if the abstract of this document contains the term t. Obviously, $z(t,s)$ is not a purely semantic measure but it depends also on the significance of the occurrence of term t in an abstract (cf. table 1). It is this property which makes the association factor $z(t,s)$ an important tool in automatic indexing.

For the construction of the PHYS/PILOT dictionary [Biebricher et al. 86] $|M| =$ 392 000 documents have been used to generate the relation Z. With the cut-off values $c_1 = 0.29$ and $c_2 = 2$, more than 800 000 pairs (t,s) have been obtained. Because of performance reasons only 350 000 of these pairs have been included in the PHYS/PILOT dictionary. They have been chosen according to their probable importance estimated by means of some heuristic criteria. The other term-descriptor relations of PHYS/PILOT are

Term t	Descriptor s	$h(t,s)$	$f(t)$	$z(t,s)$
stellar wind	STELLAR WINDS	359	479	0.74
molecular outflow		11	19	0.57
hot star wind		13	17	0.76
terminal stellar wind velocity		12	13	0.92
molecular cloud	MOLECULAR CLOUDS	254	731	0.34
dense molecular cloud		23	64	0.35
incline joint		18	36	0.50
small crack extension		35	70	0.50
Orion	ORION NEBULA	122	347	0.35
small crack extension		32	70	0.45
Orion	NEBULAE	108	347	0.31
bipolar outflow		10	17	0.58
cloud core		25	83	0.30
molecular outflow		11	19	0.57

Table 1: Examples of the association factor $z(t,s)$.

- the USE relation of the thesaurus of the data base PHYS,
- the identity relation connecting each of the 22 680 descriptors with itself,
- the Broader-Term relation of the thesaurus,
- a formal inclusion restricted to descriptor-descriptor pairs (s_1, s_2). This relation holds if and only if each word occurring in s_1 occurs also in s_2, e.g. (collision, atom collision), (beam injection, ion beam injection).
- a contrast relation between opposite descriptors, e.g. (elastic scattering, inelastic scattering).

The size of the dictionary is illustrated by table 2.

3 The indexing approach

Let D be a set of documents, S be the set of the descriptors prescribed, and G the set of the indexing weights admitted. Then indexing can be considered as a mapping g of the Cartesian product $D \times S$ into G. An automatic indexing process can be subdivided into two steps x and a (see fig.1).

Descriptors	22 683
Other terms	179 675
Single terms	85 017
Phrases	94 658
Pairs (t,s) in the relations:	
Relation Z	355 933
t = single term	159 930
t = phrase	170 697
t = term derived from formulas	25 306
Relation USE	50 138
Identity relation $t = s$	22 683
Broader-term relation	165 020
Formal inclusion	27 787
Contrast relation	100
Total of related pairs	621 661

Table 2: Survey of the PHYS/PILOT dictionary

We name $x(d,s)$ *the description function*. It defines for any element (d,s) of $D \times S$ a *relevance description* ("Relevanzbeschreibung") $x(d,s)$ consisting of all information needed for the decision about the weighted assignment of the descriptor s to the document d. This decision is described by the *indexing function* $a(x)$ which maps into G the set X of all relevance descriptions the indexing system under consideration is able to process. Thus the indexing weight $g(d,s)$ of descriptor s relative to document d is given by

$$g(d,s) = a(x(d,s)).$$

In general, relevance descriptions are rather complex, but they can be decomposed into local portions which we call *indications* ("Hinweise").
A term t is said to give an *indication of a descriptor s relative to a document d* if and only if

- t occurs in the abstract of d and
- the indexing system recognizes a relation between t and s.

We denote this indication by $y(t,s,d)$.
In order to find the indications, first the relevant terms occurring in the abstract must be identified by a dictionary look-up. We distinguish different *forms of occurrence* of a term which correspond to different degrees of exactness resp. reliability of its identification. For example, a single noun in the text after reduction to its standard form (e.g. computers → computer), and the corresponding dictionary-entry may completely coincide, or they may only have the same stem (e.g. the stem "comput" in "computer" and "computation"). The form of occurrence of a phrase is defined by means of the forms and the distances of its components [Beinke-Geiser et al. 86].

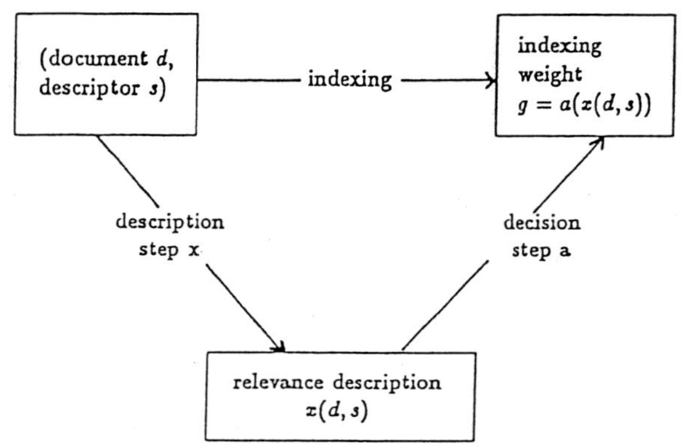

Figure 1: Subdivision of automatic indexing into two steps: Description and decision

The *description of the indication* $y(d,s,d)$ consists of all information used as a contribution from $y(d,s,t)$ to the corresponding relevance description $x(d,s)$. Typical examples of such information are

- the form and position in which the term t occurs in the text,
- the kind of relation between t and s,
- in the case of the relation Z the values of $z(t,s)$ and $h(t,s)$.

Let $Y(d,s)$ be the set of all indications $y(d,s,t)$ given by any term t. The most important information contained in the relevance description $x(d,s)$ is derived from the descriptions of the indications belonging to $Y(d,s)$, e.g.

- the greatest value of $z(t,s)$ and the corresponding value of $h(t,s)$ for which t is a phrase occurring in adjacent form in the abstract of d,
- the number of occurrences of s in the abstract,
- a binary variable is set $= 1$, if and only if at least one indication of $Y(d,s)$ is given by a term in the title of d,
- the number of indications of $Y(d,s)$ given by phrases.

Other information of a relevance description does not come from indications, e.g. the number of words in the abstract. However, such information is ignored, if the set $Y(d,s)$ is empty; for in this case $x(d,s)$ is defined as empty.
Many indexing experiments have been performed in order to find out

- which information is best suited for being inserted into the relevance descriptions and
- which indexing function produces the best results (cf. [Knorz 83a,Knorz 83b,Knorz 83c,Knorz 86]).

In these investigations the quality of automatic indexing usually has been judged according to the coincidence with manual indexing, measured by the consistency factor

$$q = \frac{|AUT \cap MAN|}{|AUT \cup MAN|}$$

where AUT and MAN denote for a given test set of documents the set of all automatic resp. manual descriptor assignments. The results of this evaluation were confirmed in the retrieval test mentioned above.

In the AIR/PHYS system a relevance description x has the form of a vector with 33 components, and the indexing function $a(x)$ is a linear polynom

$$a(x) = a_0 + \sum_{i=1}^{33} a_i \cdot x_i$$

where $x_1, ..., x_{33}$ denote the components of x. The coefficients a_i are determined by the condition

(3) $E((a(x) - P(s \text{ relevant to } d \mid x(d,s) = x))^2) = \text{minimum}$,

and therefore $a(x)$ is an approximation of the probability

(4) $P(s \text{ relevant to } d \mid x(d,s) = x)$.

In practice, the expected value E is approximated by the mean value calculated in a sample of pairs (d,s) and the event "s is relevant to d" is substituted by "s is manually assigned to d". The indexing weights produced by the function $a(x)$ are independent of any descriptor-descriptor relations. However, the indexing weights of related descriptors should generally increase each other. In order to take into account the relations between descriptors the AIR/PHYS system iterates some parts of the indexing process [Knorz 86]. In this iteration other relevance description vectors $x'(d,s)$ are formed. The components of $x'(d,s)$ are

- the indexing weight $a(x(d,s))$ obtained before,
- some data derived from the set of all weights $a(x(d,s_i))$ of descriptor assignments $s_i \rightarrow d$,
- some data derived from the weights $a(x(d,s_i))$ of those descriptors s_i which are related with s,
- some components of the vector $x(d,s)$.

The relevance descriptions $x'(d,s)$ are mapped into the set G of indexing weights by means of another indexing function $a'(x')$ which is a linear polynom, too. Its coefficients are determined by a condition analogous to (3). The indexing function $a'(x')$ is a somewhat better approximation of the probability (4) than $a(x)$, but the difference is not very important.

A more theoretical presentation of the "Darmstadt Indexing Approach" described in this section is given in [Fuhr 85].

4 Description of the AIR/PHYS system

We now describe the components of the AIR/PHYS system.

(1) *Text preparation.* This subsystem prepares the dictionary look-up of the words in the texts to be indexed [Beinke-Geiser et al. 86]. A text is broken down into sentences, the sentences are decomposed into words. Stop words are identified. A dictionary-independent algorithm reduces each word to its standard form, e.g. a verb form to the infinitive [Kuhlen 77].

(2) *Processing of formulas.* Numerical data as well as physical or chemical formulas in a text are identified and, after a bottom-up analysis, substituted by standardized terms according to the rules for manual indexing [Muhler & Repp 86]. In the following steps these terms are treated like original text terms.

(3) *Assembling of the indication descriptions.* All terms of a text for which a relation to a descriptor can be found in the dictionary are identified, i.e. all indications given by text terms are determined. For each such indication a description is formed [Beinke-Geiser et al. 86].

(4) *Calculation of the relevance description vectors.* The descriptions of all indications of a set $Y(d,s)$ (see Section 3) are used to calculate the 33 components of the corresponding relevance description vector $x(d,s)$ [Knorz 86].

(5) *Calculation of the indexing weights* $a(x(d,s))$.

(6) *Iteration of parts (4) and (5)* As explained in section 3, the parts (4) and (5) are iterated in order to correct the indexing weights $a(x(d,s))$. In this way the relevance description vectors $x'(d,s)$ and the improved indexing weights $a'(x'(d,s))$ are calculated.

(7) *Transformation into unweighted indexing.* In this final part an unweighted indexing is derived by means of the definition

$$a'(x'(d,s)) = \begin{cases} \geq g_o & \rightarrow \text{s is assigned to d} \\ < g_o & \rightarrow \text{s is not assigned to d} \end{cases}$$

with an appropriate cut-off value g_o. This reduction is necessary because of the compatibility with the manual indexing for the data base PHYS.

5 Fault toleration

The use of statistical and heuristical methods in the dictionary construction as well as in the text analysis leads to partly imperfect — i.e. incomplete, uncertain, vague, and even faulty — information to be processed by the indexing system. In spite of these deficiencies the indexing system has to produce results of acceptable quality. This problem is quite different from the usual problem of fault toleration in hardware or software systems. So, other forms of fault toleration have to be inserted into an indexing system.

In the AIR/PHYS system this has been done in several different ways, mainly by

- labelling or weighting of information according to its kind and degree of imperfection estimated by means of heuristic criteria,
- accumulating high redundancy in the relevance descriptions,
- probabilistic weighting of the descriptor assignments,
- optimizing the indexing function by means of a multiple regression analysis method,
- iterating parts of the indexing process in order to check and correct the results already obtained.

6 Application of AIR/PHYS

The physics data base PHYS contained at the end of 1987 about one million documents. In 1987, 125 000 new documents were incorporated into the system. All incoming documents have to be included into the abstract journal PHYSICS BRIEFS. For this reason they have to be classified into a classification system of 3 hierarchical levels with about 600 classes at the lowest level. Further, another indexing is needed in order to represent the documents in the subject index of the abstract journal.

After the Fachinformationszentrum Karlsruhe had decided to apply automatic indexing to the input of the data base PHYS we studied these further tasks of content analysis in order to accomplish them automatically, too. Experimental research has been done using modified versions of our approaches to dictionary construction and indexing. However, the results obtained until now are far below the quality level needed for a printed journal.

Thus, the application of the indexing system AIR/PHYS does not make superfluous the manual content analysis of the same documents. Simultaneously with the classification and the register indexing, the human indexers check and correct the automatic indexing output. This can be done on-line or off- line.

With an appropriate cut-off value g_o (cf. part (7) of section 4) an average indexing depth of 12 descriptors/document is realized. From this kind of a proposal the indexers cancel an average of 4 descriptors/document, and substitutes them by 4 other descriptors. In comparison with the previous average of 8.5 descriptors/document in the manual indexing for the data base PHYS, we have now an average of 12 manually checked resp. corrected descriptors/document. As a consequence higher recall ratios of retrieval results without substantial precision losses can be expected.

For each of the first 20 000 documents to which the AIR/PHYS system has been applied the indexers had to judge globally if this contribution to the indexing work was really useful [Lück 88]. The automatic indexing of 19 per cent of the documents was considered to be good. Furthermore, the indexers accepted the automatic indexing of 63 per cent of the documents as being useful in spite of some corrections needed. However, in 18 per cent of the documents there were too many faults so that the automatic indexing was of no help for the indexers' work. After this evaluation the Fachinformationszentrum Karlsruhe decided to continue the application of the AIR/PHYS system and even to extend it to other databases.

The above-mentioned figures vary significantly between the different subfields of physics. Special difficulties arise when many formulas of high complexity must be treated, e.g. in nuclear physics and in the subfield of elementary particles.

The main source of indexing faults is the incompleteness of the already very large dictionary. Though most of the lacking data are needed only rarely their absence cumulates to a considerable error ratio. For example, the most effective relation Z covers only 10 000 (44 per cent) of the descriptors. The other descriptors had not been assigned often enough in the manual indexing used for the generation of the relation Z (cf. section 2). In consequence, the continuous maintenance of the dictionary is not limited to the insertion of new descriptors and their relations, but also more relations covering the already known descriptors have to be generated [Schwantner 88]. For this purpose, the manual corrections of the automatic indexing are evaluated.

7 Problems of further development

Beside the dictionary also the indexing procedure could still be improved, mainly by the following:

- In the text analysis the significance of the occurrence of a term as well as the syntagmatic relations between terms should be considered more precisely.
- The formula processing subsystem is to be revised and extended.
- Some new elements should be inserted into the relevance description, and in the following the indexing function must be optimized again. The same is necessary for the relevance description and the indexing function of the iterated decision step (see part (6) in section 4) which should be made more important.

Another aspect of our future work derives from the fact that the automatic indexing produced by the AIR/PHYS system is manually checked and corrected. This kind of man-computer cooperation could be considerably improved by an appropriate assistance system. Above all, such a system must be able to explain to the indexer, why a descriptor is automatically assigned, i.e. the indications of the descriptor (cf. section 3) must be described. These explications should be offered in variable depth, comprehensiveness, and lay-out. Obviously, the system should also answer questions concerning statistical or dictionary information. Further, the indexer should have the possibility to modify the number of automatic descriptor assignments. Finally, more intelligent techniques could be applied in order to react immediately to the indexers' assignment corrections. For example, the conformity of the corrections with the indexing rules of the PHYS database could be checked, and new dictionary information could be inferred.

References

Beinke-Geiser, U.; Lustig, G.; Putze-Meier, G. (1986). Indexieren mit dem System DAISY. In: Lustig, G. (ed.): *Automatische Indexierung zwischen Forschung und Anwendung*, pp. 73–97. Olms, Hildesheim.

Biebricher, P.; Fuhr, N.; Knorz, G.; Schwantner, M. (1986). Indexierungswörterbücher für das Fachgebiet Physik. In: Lustig, G. (ed.): *Automatische Indexierung zwischen Forschung und Anwendung*, pp. 52–72. Olms, Hildesheim.

Biebricher, P.; Fuhr, N.; Knorz, G.; Lustig, G.; Schwantner, M. (1988). Entwicklung und Anwendung des automatischen Indexierungssystems AIR/PHYS. *Nachrichten für Dokumentation 39(3)*.

Fangmeyer, H.; Lustig, G. (1969). The EURATOM Automatic Indexing Project. In: International Federation for Information Processing (ed.): *IFIP Congress 68, Edinburgh*, pp. 1310–1314. North Holland Publishing Company, Amsterdam.

Fangmeyer, H.; Lustig, G. (1970). Experiments with the CETIS Automatic Indexing System. In: International Atomic Energy Agency (ed.): *Proceedings of the Symposium on the Handling of Nuclear Information*, pp. 557–567.

Fuhr, N.; Knorz, G. (1984). Retrieval Test Evaluation of a Rule Based Automatic Indexing (AIR/PHYS). In: Van Rijsbergen, C. (ed.): *Research and Development in Information Retrieval*, pp. 391–408. Cambridge University Press, Cambridge.

Fuhr, N. (1985). A probabilistic model of dictionary based automatic indexing. In: *Proceedings of the riao 85, Recherche d'Informations Assistée par Ordinateur*, pp. 207–216.

Knorz, G. (1983a). *Automatisches Indexieren als Erkennen abstrakter Objekte. Sprache und Information.* Vol. 8, Niemeyer, Tübingen.

Knorz, G. (1983b). A Decision Theory Approach to Optimal Automatic Indexing. In: Salton, G.; Schneider, H. (ed.): *Research and Development in Information Retrieval*, pp. 174–193. Springer, Berlin, Heidelberg, New York.

Knorz, G. (1983c). *Development of automatic indexing for the AIR retrieval test. Experiments by means of ALIBABA.* Report DVII 83-3, TH Darmstadt, FB Informatik, Datenverwaltungssysteme II.

Knorz, G. (1986). Die Anwendung von Polynomklassifikatoren für die automatische Indexierung. In: Lustig, G. (ed.): *Automatische Indexierung zwischen Forschung und Anwendung*, pp. 98–126. Olms, Hildesheim.

Kuhlen, R. (1977). *Experimentelle Morphologie in der Informationswissenschaft.* Verlag Dokumentation, München.

Lück, W. (1988). Erfahrungen mit dem automatischen Indexierungssystem AIR/PHYS. In: Deutsche Gesellschaft für Dokumentation (ed.): *Deutscher Dokumentartag 1987*, pp. 340–352. VCH Verlagsgesellschaft, Weinheim.

Lustig, G. (ed.) (1986). *Automatische Indexierung zwischen Forschung und Anwendung.* Olms, Hildesheim.

Muhler, I.; Repp, J. (1986). Die Verarbeitung von Formeln in physikalischen Texten. In: Lustig, G. (ed.): *Automatische Indexierung zwischen Forschung und Anwendung*, pp. 31–42. Olms, Hildesheim.

Schwantner, M. (1988). Entwicklung und Pflege des Indexierungswörterbuches PHYS/PILOT. In: Deutsche Gesellschaft für Dokumentation (ed.): *Deutscher Dokumentartag 1987*, pp. 329–339. VCH Verlagsgesellschaft, Weinheim.

A News Story Categorization System

Philip J. Hayes, Laura E. Knecht, and Monica J. Cellio

Carnegie Group Inc
650 Commerce Court at Station Square
Pittsburgh, PA 15219

Abstract

This paper describes a pilot version of a commercial application of natural language processing techniques to the problem of categorizing news stories into broad topic categories. The system does not perform a complete semantic or syntactic analyses of the input stories. Its categorizations are dependent on fragmentary recognition using pattern-matching techniques. The fragments it looks for are determined by a set of knowledge-based rules. The accuracy of the system is only slightly lower than that of human categorizers.

1. Introduction

The large economic potential of automatic text processing is leading to an increasing interest in its commercial applications. This paper describes a pilot version of a commercial application of natural language processing techniques to the problem of categorizing news stories into broad topic categories.

The conventional way to process natural language texts is to have people read them and perform some action based on what they have read. People, for instance, currently categorize news stories for routing purposes and extract information from banking payment telexes so that transactions can be executed.

Unfortunately, using people tends to be:

- **slow** - people read text slowly;
- **expensive** - if the volume of text is high, processing it requires the efforts of many people;
- **inconsistent** - it is very hard to get a group of people to make consistent decisions about text.

In many cases, the proper processing of text is central to a company's revenue stream, so that improvements in the processing can provide major leverage and justify major contract system expenditures.

Automatic text processing offers the possibility of such improvements in all three areas. A single text processing machine can potentially do the job of several people faster, cheaper, and more consistently.

This paper describes an implementation of a system to do text categorization. The texts it operates on are news stories, but similar techniques could be employed on electronic mail messages, telex traffic, technical abstracts, etc.. Once categorization has been accomplished, the results can be used to route the texts involved to interested parties or to facilitate later retrieval of the texts from an archival database.

The system described here uses the well-established natural language processing technique of pattern-matching [1, 5]. Since the input to the system is an arbitrary news story on any topic whatsoever, no attempt is made to perform a complete syntactic or semantic analysis. Instead, categorization is based on the presence of particular words and phrases in particular lexical contexts. As the more detailed description in Section 3 will make clear, however, the approach used goes well beyond the keyword approaches used in information retrieval (e.g. [6]). In particular, the words and phrases the system looks for and the context in which it looks for them are specified through a modified version of the powerful pattern matching language used in Carnegie Group's Language Craft^{TM} product[1] [3]. Moreover, the system determines which words and phrases to search for in a given story and how to interpret the presence of these words and phrases according to knowledge-based rules.

As simple as these techniques are by current natural language processing standards, the accuracy of the system is high. As described in more detail in Section 4, the system had an average accuracy of

[1]Language Craft also uses caseframe parsing techniques for complete linguistic analyses.

93%[2] on a sample of 500 random stories that had not been previously processed by the system or seen by its developers. Moreover, this accuracy was obtained without sacrificing computational efficiency. The average processing time was 15 seconds per story[3] on a Symbolics 3640, a figure which we believe could be considerably improved through a detailed performance optimization which we have not performed.

The remaining sections of the paper describe in more detail: the problem tackled by the system, the approach used, and the results obtained.

2. The Problem

The primary goal in developing the system described in this paper was to demonstrate the feasibility of categorizing news stories by computer in small amounts of time (a few seconds) using natural language processing techniques. The specific task chosen to do this was emulation of the performance of a group of human categorizers. Our raw material was a data base containing many thousands of news stories that had been hand-categorized[4] for any of 72 categories. Our system was required to assign 6 of the 72 categories: acquisitions/mergers, metals, shipping, bonds, war, and disorders. A story could be assigned one or more of these codes, or no code at all if none of the chosen six was appropriate. The restriction to six codes was imposed to keep the effort required to build the system within certain budgetary limits. As Section 3 will show, the approach taken is equally applicable to the larger set of categories.

Modelling the categorizations produced by human beings presented some difficulties. To summarize:

- The text processing techniques used in the system were oriented to identifying concepts explicitly mentioned in a story. They were not well suited to identifying the class of people that a story might be of interest to. The human categorizers of the stories in our data base used both these kinds of considerations when they assigned topic codes to stories.
- Some topic codes had relatively vague, subjective definitions.
- The human categorizers were not always consistent in the way they made their topic assignments.

The news stories themselves posed another challenge. Though the set of topics to be assigned by the system was narrowed from 72 to 6, there was no parallel narrowing of the stream of stories that would serve as input to the system. The full range of story types found in a newspaper occurred in the data base of news stories. As a consequence, our task was not the relatively simple one of, for instance, distinguishing a story about war from one about bonds. War stories also had to be distinguished from military, disaster, crime, diplomacy, politics, and sports stories, to name just a few.

It was often the case that we could characterize the kind of stories that might mislead the system. We were prepared for sports stories that looked like metals stories (*"...captured the gold medal at the summer Olympics..."*) or like war/disorders stories (*"...the battle on center court at Wimbledon..."*). A more difficult challenge was posed by words and phrases that were good predictors of a particular topic but occurred randomly across all story types, sometimes with the same meaning, sometimes not. For instance, the noun *note*, in the sense of financial instrument, was useful for finding stories about bonds; however, numerous, random stories used that word in a different sense. Metaphorical language was also a problem -- not use of fixed phrases (we had no trouble failing to assign the category **metals** to a story that contained the phrase *like a lead balloon*) -- but rather creative metaphorical language. So, a story about a series of battles in the continuing disposable diaper war between Proctor and Gamble and its competitors was assigned to the disorders category.

[2]More precisely, its average recall was 93% (i.e. it made 93% of the topic assignments it should have made) and its average precision was also 93% (i.e. 93% of the topics it did assign were correct).

[3]The average story length was 250 words; stories varied from about a 100 to about 3000 words.

[4]The hand-categorizations were done by a group of people who had no involvement with or knowledge of the system we developed.

3. Approach

3.1. Overview

The system tackles story categorization in two distinct phases:

- **hypothesization**: an attempt to pick out all categories into which the story might fall on the basis of the words and phrases it contains; if particular words and phrases suggest more than one category, they will contribute to the hypothesization of each of these categories;
- **confirmation**: an attempt to find additional evidence in support of a hypothesized topic or to determine whether or not the language that led to the topic's being hypothesized was used in a way that misled the system; it is this phase, for instance, that would detect that conflict vocabulary was being used in the context of a sports story and disconfirm the **war** and **disorders** categories for that story. This phase thus has an expert system flavor to it.

Both phases use the same basic kind of processing: a contextually limited search for words and phrases using pattern-matching techniques. They are also both organized (conceptually) as a collection of knowledge-based rules. The phases differ only in the directedness with which the search is conducted. Hypothesization always looks for the same words and phrases. Confirmation looks for different words and phrases using specific knowledge-based rules associated with each of the topics that have been hypothesized.

The search for words and phrases in both phases is organized around *patternsets*. A patternset represents a collection of words and phrases that are associated with a given concept, such as *conflict*. The concepts associated with patternsets sometimes correspond to the topics we are trying to categorize stories into, but they may also be more specific or may span several topics.

The basic operation on a patternset is to determine how many of the words and phrases it represents appear in a story. System actions are taken when the number of matches crosses a threshold, at which point we say that the patternset has matched. The thresholds are empirically determined and differ from patternset to patternset and even from use to use of the patternset.

Hypothesization is typically performed on the basis of matches of single patternsets. Confirmation rules typically involve branching conditions depending on the results of multiple patternset matches. Individual patternsets may be involved in both hypothesization and confirmation phases.

The remainder of this section describes the operation of the system in greater technical detail.

3.2. Patterns and Patternsets

Patternsets are collections of *patterns*. A pattern is an expression in a pattern-matching language that corresponds to one or more words and phrases that might appear in a story. A pattern is said to match the story if any of the words or phrases that it specifies appear in the story. Each pattern has a weight, either *probable* or *possible*, with matches of *probables* counting more than matches of *possibles*, according to a scheme explained below. Patterns also have names.

The following pattern, called "titanium", will match the word *titanium* and assign the match a weight of "probable".

```
(titanium) -> probable
= titanium
```

Eight operators are available to allow individual patterns to specify several words and phrases. They are:

- ?: specifies an optional subpattern;
- ! and !!: specify alternatives (i.e. they both mean "or");[5]
- ~ and ¬: specify a subpattern that should not be matched;[6]
- &skip: specifies the maximum number of words to skip over;
- +N: specifies that a word is a noun and can therefore be pluralized;
- +V: specifies that a word is a verb and can therefore occur with the full range of verbal inflections.

The following examples illustrate how these operators are used.

---

[5]The operator !! is more efficient than !, but there are some situations where it cannot be used.

[6]The operator ¬ filters out a subpattern to the left of the subpattern to be matched; ~ filters out a subpattern to the right.

- (par (pricing !! ?issue price))
  -> probable
  = parprice
  [This rule matches the phrases *par pricing, par issue price*, and *par price*.]

- ((¬ ratings) war +N) -> possible
  = war
  [This rule matches *war* or *wars* preceded by anything except the word *ratings*.]

- (sell +V (&skip 6 (company !! business !! unit))) -> possible
  = sell-co
  [This rule matches any form of the verb *sell* followed by *company, business*, or *unit*, with as many as 6 words intervening.]

The pattern operator **&skip** deserves special comment. It allows us to find key expressions even when it is impossible to predict exactly what extraneous words they will contain. Consider, for example, the phrases *sell the business* and *sell the unit*; these phrases must be matched if the system is to detect stories about acquisitions. The problem is that expressions like *sell the business* are rare. Examples of the sorts of phrases that we actually find in acquisitions stories are given below:

sell the Seven-Up business
sell the ailing Seven-Up unit
sell its Seven-Up soft drink business
sell 51 pct of the common stock of its unit
sell the worldwide franchise beverage business
sell about 5 mln dlrs worth of shares in the company

With **&skip**, we can look for the verb *sell* followed by *company, unit*, or *business* without having to specify what the intervening words might be.

In addition to pattern operators, a set of **wildcards** is also available to rule-writers for matching words that cannot be specified in advance. $ is the general wildcard: it matches any single word or other symbol. **$d** matches any determiner (*a, the, this*, etc.); **$n** matches any number; **$q** matches any quantifier (*much, many, some*, etc.); and **$p** matches any punctuation mark.

3.3. Hypothesization and Confirmation

After a story has been read in, the system begins the process of topic determination by applying its hypothesization rules. A hypothesization rule tells the system to hypothesize one or more specified topics if a given patternset matches the story with a strength greater than a given threshold.

For example, one of the system's hypothesization rules specifies that the topics **war** and **disorders** should be hypothesized if the score for matches in the "conflict" patternset is 4 or greater; another rule specifies that the **metals** topic be hypothesized if the "metals" patternset matches with a score greater than 2. The thresholds for each rule are determined empirically based on the rule developer's observation of the performance of the system when different thresholds are used. Note also that there is not necessarily a direct correlation between topics and patternsets; some patternsets could provide evidence for more than one topic, and some topics could make use of more than one patternset.

The scores for patternset matches are calculated according to the formula:

```
(2 x probables) + possibles
```

i.e. a match with a "probable" pattern has a weight of 2 while a match with a "possible" pattern has a weight of 1. In the course of establishing this weighting system, we experimented with several more complex and finely-grained schemes, but found that they provided no significant advantage in practice.

After the hypothesization phase comes confirmation. This involves more detailed topic-specific processing to determine whether or not the vocabulary used in hypothesizing the topic was used in a misleading way. The confirmation phase uses topic-specific knowledge-based rules which may try to match additional patterns or patternsets.

The most complex confirmation rules in the system are those for the **war** and **disorders** topics. These topics were difficult to tell apart, so considerable additional processing was involved. The rules use additional specialized patternsets: one patternset looked specifically for words (including proper names) that occur in war but not disorders stories and another looked for vocabulary that occurs in stories that are both war and disorders stories. There are also patternsets for sports, crime, and disaster vocabulary. The confirmation rules associated with **war** and **disorders** attempt to match these rules according to a branching set of conditions.

Consider the following story, for example. The

words and phrases in boldface match patterns in the "conflict" patternset; the total value of matches is great enough to get the story hypothesized as **war** and **disorders.** In the confirmation phase, additional patternsets are run against the story. As soon as *Iran* and *Iraq* are matched, the topic **war** is confirmed and the topic **disorders** is disconfirmed.

> IRAN ANNOUNCES END OF MAJOR **OFFENSIVE** IN GULF **WAR**
>
> LONDON, Feb 26 - Iran announced tonight that its major **offensive against** Iraq in the Gulf **war** had ended after dealing savage blows against the Baghdad government.
>
> [...]
>
> The statement by the Iranian High Command appeared to herald the close of an **assault** on the port city of Basra in southern Iraq.
>
> [...]
>
> It said 81 Iraqi **brigades** and **battalions** were totally destroyed, along with 700 **tanks** and 1,500 other vehicles. The victory list also included 80 **warplanes downed,** 250 **anti-aircraft guns** and 400 pieces of military hardware destroyed and the seizure of 220 **tanks** and **armored personnel carriers.**

For the story that follows, the topics **war** and **disorders** are also originally hypothesized. In the confirmation phase, two things are discovered: the story mentions no wars by name nor contains any references to countries or organizations involved in conflicts that are classified as wars; and there is nothing in the story that suggests that the topic **disorders** should be disconfirmed. Hence **war** is disconfirmed and **disorders** is confirmed.

> **RIOT** REPORTED IN SOUTH KOREAN PRISON
>
> Seoul, July 5 - Twelve South Korean women **detainees** refused food for the fifth consecutive day today after a **riot** against their maltreatment in a Seoul prison was put down, dissident sources said.
>
> The 12, **detained** for **anti-government protests** and awaiting trial, pushed away prison officials, smashed windows and occupied a prison building on Tuesday as a **protest** against what they called "suppression of prisoners' human rights".
>
> After two hours, about 40 **riot** police, **firing tear** gas, stormed the building and overpowered the **protesters,** the sources said. Some **protesters** were injured, they added.

For the story below, both **war** and **disorders** are hypothesized and then disconfirmed because *tennis* is matched during the disconfirmation phase.

> LENDL **DEMONSTRATES** GRASS COURT MATURITY
>
> LONDON, July 2 - Czechoslovak top seed Ivan Lendl served warning that he may finally have come of age on grass when he emerged victorious from a pitched **battle** with one of the finest exponents of the fast court game at Wimbledon today.
>
> The U.S. and French Open tennis champion has never won a title on grass but he outlasted American 10th seed Tim Mayotte 6-4 4-6 6-4 3-6 9-7 over three and a half hours to join Boris Becker, Henri Leconte and Slobodan Zivojinovic in Friday's semifinals.
>
> The titanic **struggle** on court one upstaged the centre court **clash** between seventh seed Leconte and the remarkable Australian Pat Cash, which had been billed as the day's main attraction [...]

The story below is the rare sports story which is also a disorders story. Even though the name of a sporting event, *Asian Games*, occurs in the text, the topic **disorders** is not disconfirmed. The reason is that the confirmation patternsets match words and phrases in the story (e.g. *radicals* and *violent protests*) that very strongly suggest that real disorders are being described.

> POLICE SEEK 160 SOUTH KOREAN **RADICALS**
>
> SEOUL, July 2 - Police said today they wanted to **detain** 160 South Koreans to stop **sabotage** attempts during September's Asian Games in Seoul.
>
> The 160, mostly students and workers, masterminded various **violent protests** against the government and the United States in the past months but managed to escape arrest, police said.
>
> They had been tipped that the **radicals** were trying to organise big **demonstrations** against the government during the Asiad, which is to run from September 20 to October 5.
>
> "It is highly probable that they will form **radical** underground groups to step up their **anti-government** and anti-U.S. **protests** and may disrupt the Asian Games in an attempt to defame the government," a senior police officer told reporters.
>
> [...]

3.4. Flow of Control

Rather than being expressed in a formal rule language, topic hypothesization and confirmation rules are specified through a lisp program. Having a program allows for fine-grained control by the rule developer. Rather than having a set of hypothesization and confirmation rules which are processed in a fixed order, we allow the rule developer to specify the order and manner of processing in a topic-dependent manner. The major kinds of activities available to rule developers for incorporation into the control code are the following: running one or more patternsets, applying evaluation functions to the resulting matches, and confirming or disconfirming topics.

In developing the system, we observed many regularities in the lisp code which controls the flow of processing and we believe it would be possible and profitable to provide rule developers with a more restricted control language which embodies many of these regularities in its primitives.

3.5. Rulebase Development

The process of formulating the *rulebase* of the system, i.e. the collection of patterns, patternsets, and hypothesization and confirmation rules it uses, is an empirical one. It requires human rule developers to examine many stories, create rulebase components according to their intuitions, run stories through the system, observe the results, and modify the system to avoid any miscategorizations that have occurred without introducing new miscategorizations. This task is time-consuming and sometimes tedious. Nevertheless, our experience with the system suggests that it does tend to converge without undue oscillation at an accuracy level that while far from perfect is adequate for many tasks of practical importance (see Section 4). The rule development effort on this system took approximately six person months.

An important factor in the success of the rulebase development effort was the separation of the vocabulary the system looks for into a collection of abstract concepts represented by patternsets. The patternsets provide rule developers with a way of thinking about the themes they are looking for in a story when they write the hypothesization and confirmation rules without becoming mired in questions about which specific words and phrases indicate those themes.

In designing the system, we also considered a different approach in which the selection of words and phrases to look for would be determined automatically by a statistical method. Since we did not adopt this approach, we have no direct evidence that it would not have worked as well as the labor-intensive method chosen. However, our choice was influenced by a belief that a statistical method would not provide us with a choice of words and phrases that could be used to make distinctions as precisely as the patterns of the kind described above that were chosen by humans.

As shown in [2], accuracy is particularly problematic with a traditional keyword approach regardless of whether the keywords are selected by humans or statistically. And if we had adopted a statistical approach, it would have been computationally expensive to vary the length of the phrases chosen as much as human rule developers do. It would also have been difficult to establish the contextual restrictions that human rule developers establish (e.g. this word, so long as it is not followed by one of these four others). Rules of the complexity of the confirmation rule for **war** and **disorders** described in Section 3.3 are of course essentially impossible to establish by statistical means.

Some interesting possibilities for a statistical approach to defining keywords have appeared recently in conjunction with semantic information about potential keywords [7] and in conjunction with very powerful parallel hardware devices [4]. However, given the current state of the art, we continue to believe that our decision to use rules formulated and refined by human developers was a sound one from the point of view of the accuracy of the resulting system.

4. Performance

4.1. Measuring Performance

The accuracy of the system for topic assignments was measured through two percentages for each of the six topics:

- **recall**: the percentage of stories assigned the topic code by human categorizers that were also assigned that code by the system;
- **precision**: the percentage of stories assigned the topic code by the system that actually carried the topic code assigned by the human categorizers.

The recall rate serves as a measure of the number of stories for which the system misses an appropriate topic code; a high recall percentage will therefore mean few such false negatives. The precision rate, on the other hand, measures the number of stories for which the system chooses an incorrect topic. A high precision percentage means few such false positives. We emphasized high recall over high precision.

4.2. Results

The results obtained from the system were very promising. After certain necessary adjustments (described below) to the raw results, the system had an average recall rate of 93% (i.e. it made 93% of the topic assignments it should have made and missed only 7%) and an average precision rate also of 93% (i.e. 93% of the topics it did assign were correct). Another way of expressing this is that it had on average only 7% false negatives and 7% false positives in its topic assignments. This level of accuracy was achieved in an average of around 15 seconds per story on a Symbolics 3640 in Common Lisp. Little effort was spent to optimize the execution time and we believe that a substantial improvement in speed is possible.

Adjustments to the raw recall and precision figures produced by the system were necessary because, as described in Section 2, we discovered three problematic features of the hand-categorizations against which the system was being evaluated: they were not always content-based; they were not always consistent; and some topic definitions were vague. Given this, it was clear that raw performance scores would not give a meaningful picture of how well the system worked, so we devised a score-adjustment procedure to provide results that would reflect system performance more accurately. The remainder of this section describes that procedure and presents the raw and adjusted results we obtained.

We used an adjustment procedure that was based on the assumption that there are three explanations for disagreements between the system and the human categorizers about the assignment of a topic to a story:

- The human categorizer is clearly wrong.
- The system is clearly wrong.
- The topic assignment is debatable. This case can typically be attributed to one of the three sources of difficulty described above.

A set of 500 stories was run through the system. These stories had never before been processed, and no hypothesization or confirmation rules had ever been based on them. A Carnegie Group employee who was not involved with the system produced score adjustments for each topic disagreement between the system and the human categorizers. The employee was presented with a story and told that there was a disgreement on a specific named topic; she was not told which choice the system or the human categorizers had made. The employee was asked to decide whether the topic was appropriate for the story, inappropriate, or debatable. Debatable cases counted in favor of the system.

The results of this experiment before and after adjustment of the system's scores were as follows (where **acq** is acquisitions/mergers, **mtl** is metals, **shp** is shipping, **bnd** is bonds, and **dis** is disorders).

	Raw Rec.	Raw Prec.	Adj. Rec.	Adj. Prec.
acq	85%	82%	92%	92%
bnd	91%	89%	97%	100%
dis	90%	58%	93%	84%
mtl	80%	70%	95%	90%
shp	72%	49%	88%	92%
war	88%	82%	92%	100%

Recall is 92% or higher, except in the case of the **shipping** code. This is not surprising because it turned out that **shipping** was a strongly interest-based category, as far as the human categorizers were concerned. So, stories about rough weather in the St. Lawrence seaway (but not the Rhine) and the devaluation of the rupee (but not the Turkish lira) were classified as shipping stories because human categorizers possessed the expert knowledge that shippers are interested in that particular waterway and that particular currency.

The precision scores are actually higher than the corresponding recall scores in the case of **war** and **bonds**. Since we have found that precision can be traded off against recall by appropriate manipulation of thresholds associated with our rulebase, this suggests that the recall rate for those two topics could be further improved while still maintaining an acceptable precision rate.

The adjustment procedure also allowed us to

measure the performance of the hand-categorizers. While adjusted precision scores were perfect for all six topics, adjusted recall scores ranged from 81% to 100%, with an average of 94%.

	Adj. Rec.	Adj. Prec.
acq	100%	100%
bnd	97%	100%
dis	81%	100%
mtl	95%	100%
shp	100%	100%
war	90%	100%

While human performance on precision is clearly superior to that of the system, the average recall rates of human categorizers and of the system are very similar (94% v. 93%). Closer examination of the results, however, shows that the kind of errors made are quite different. Human errors stem mainly from inconsistent application of categories, especially the categories with the vaguest definitions, and from failing to specify all the categories when several should have been assigned to a story. System errors on the other hand stem largely from misinterpretation of the way in which language is being used. This sometimes results in ridiculous categorizations of a kind that humans never produce.

Out of 500 stories, the system produced a total of 28 "lemons" (stories that were clearly assigned the wrong categories). We analyzed these stories and discovered six sources of errors:

- The system did not match useful words or phrases, or the disconfirmation rules were too powerful.
- The topic vocabulary was not much used in the story.
- The system used the story background to derive the topic.
- The topic vocabulary came too late in the story.
- The topic vocabulary was used with different meanings.
- The topic vocabulary was used with the same meaning, but different focus.

Examples and further discussion follow.

4.2.1. Topic Vocabulary Not Much Used In Story

Some stories did not use the topic vocabulary more than one or two times. Setting thresholds very low would catch these stories, but generate many false positives as well. Most stories that had this problem were also very short, so we added length-dependent thresholds to address the problem. This technique worked for **metals** stories, where the vocabulary is somewhat distinctive, but would not work for **acquisitions** stories, where the vocabulary consists of very common words like *buy* and *sell*.

4.2.2. Story Background Used To Derive Topic

News stories sometimes have background information included which does not have much to do with the main point of the story. For example, the following story, about the Pope's visit to Colombia, was miscategorized as a **metals** story because of the background information about the country. Solving this problem requires a deep understanding of the structure of the story.

> SECURITY FOR POPE TIGHTENS
> Chiquinquira, Colombia, July 3 - Security precautions for Pope John Paul II were tightened today, with hundreds of troops making thorough body searches of visitors to this colonial town high in the Andes mountains.
> [...]
> Chiquinquira has been spared the guerilla warfare which has torn much of Colombia over the past three decades. But the nearby Muzo emerald **mines**, the country's biggest, have attracted adventurers who often feud violently in the town.
> Some Muzo **miners** have moved on to the more lucrative drug traffic [...].

4.2.3. Topic Vocabulary Used With Different Meaning

Sometimes stories are miscategorized because of the metaphorical language they use. For example, in one story the word *revolution* appeared numerous times: the British government was calling for a revolution in broadcasting. Another contained the phrases *ready to go to war*, *make peace*, *make war*, *target*, and *heavy losses*; the subject of the story was labor negotiations in the automobile industry. Since the system does not really understand the texts it processes, it is inevitable that it will be fooled from time to time by such usage.

4.2.4. Topic Vocabulary Used with Same Meaning But Different Focus

The following story illustrates another problem for which there is no obvious solution. The word *army* occurs four times (not all shown), and the sense of the word in this **military** story is exactly the sense it might have in an actual **war** or **disorders** story.

> CHINESE **ARMY** TO HAVE NCOS FOR FIRST TIME
>
> Peking, July 4 - The Chinese **army** will allow non-commissioned officer ranks for the first time as part of its reform program, the New China News Agency said today.
>
> It said soldiers who have been in the **army** for one year and had a good record would, after training at two special schools, serve as NCOS.
>
> [...]

5. Conclusion

This paper has shown that high accuracy automatic text categorization is feasible for texts covering a diverse set of topics, using the well-established natural language processing technique of pattern matching applied according to knowledge-based rules, but without requiring a complete syntactic or semantic analysis of the texts. Automatic text processing of this kind has many potential applications with high economic paybacks in the routing and archiving of news stories, electronic messages, or other forms of on-line text. We expect that many such systems will be in commercial use within the next few years.

Acknowledgements

Peter Neuss and Scott Safier contributed substantially to the design and implementation of the system described in this paper.

References

1. Carbonell, J. G., Boggs, W. M., Mauldin, M. L., and Anick, P. G. The XCALIBUR Project: A Natural Language Interface to Expert Systems. Proc. Eighth Int. Jt. Conf. on Artificial Intelligence, Karlsruhe, August, 1983.

2. Furnas, G. W., Landauer, T. K., Dumais, S. T., and Gomez, L. M. "Statistical semantics: Analysis of the potential performance of keyword information systems". *Bell System Technical Journal 62*, 6 (1983), 1753-1806.

3. Hayes, P. J., Andersen, P., Safier, S. Semantic Case Frame Parsing and Syntactic Generality. Proc. of 23rd Annual Meeting of the Assoc. for Comput. Ling., Chicago, June, 1985.

4. Hillis, W. D.. *The Connection Machine.* MIT Press, Cambridge, Mass., 1985.

5. Parkison, R. C., Colby, K. M., and Faught, W. S. "Conversational Language Comprehension Using Integrated Pattern-Matching and Parsing". *Artificial Intelligence 9* (1977), 111-134.

6. Salton, G. and McGill, M. J.. *Introduction to Modern Information Retrieval.* McGraw-Hill, New York, 1983.

7. Walker, D. E. and Amsler, R. A. The Use of Machine-Readable Dictionaries in Sublanguage Analysis. In *Analyzing Language in Restricted Domains: Sublanguage Description and Processing*, R. Grishman and R. Kittredge, Ed., Lawrence Erlbaum Associates, Hillsdale, New Jersey, 1986, pp. 69-83.

CONCEPTUAL INFORMATION EXTRACTION AND RETRIEVAL FROM NATURAL LANGUAGE INPUT

Lisa F. Rau
Artificial Intelligence Program
GE Research and Development Center
Schenectady, NY 12301

Abstract

Recent progress in understanding texts in constrained domains has increased the potential for storing texts in conceptual format. Storing texts in conceptual format has a number of advantages. A conceptual format facilitates and encourages natural language interrogation. It can support imprecise and inexact queries, conceptual information summarization, and ultimately, document translation.

In this paper, a method for extracting information from texts in constrained domains is described. Information extracted is stored in a conceptual format, and can be retrieved with natural language queries. Due to the conceptual format of both the queries and the information, partial or inexact matches of desired information is supported through the representation of concepts in the domain. Information may also be summarized using heuristics for expository text summarization.

These capabilities have been implemented in a prototype intelligent information retrieval system called SCISOR (System for Conceptual Information Summarization, Organization and Retrieval).

1 Introduction

Typically, information obtained from natural language texts, in the end, is extracted by human beings. Although relevant texts may be found through a process of document retrieval, after those relevant documents are retrieved, a person isolates and digests the portions of particular interest. This paradigm is appropriate when obtaining the "source" document is important. However when conceptual information is desired *from* the source document, Artificial Intelligence techniques can aid in automating the information extraction process.

Within the last decade, there have been some limited successes in the development of AI systems that partially parse and understand short texts in constrained domains [1,2,3,4]. Based on these successes, a prototype intelligent information system, SCISOR, is currently under development at GE's Research and Development Center. SCISOR is designed to read short articles from an on-line source of information and extract information from the articles. This information is stored in a conceptual form, and users may then ask questions in natural language. Answers to questions are formulated and passed to a natural language generator for response.

SCISOR currently operates in the domain of stories about corporate mergers and acquisitions, although it is built with domain-independence in mind. Below is an example of the kind of interaction SCISOR is designed for:

1. User: Did ACE hardware take over the ACME food company?

System: *Yes it did. The ACE hardware company completed the takeover last Friday.*

2. User: What were the events in the ACE-ACME takeover deal?

System: *Rumors that ACME was to be taken over started May 13, 1985. The stock rose $5 a share to $65. On May 16, the ACE company announced that it had made an offer to ACME valued at $66 a share. The offer was a cash offer to purchase all 2 million outstanding shares of ACME. After a month of deliberation involving some potential conflict of interest matters, the ACE-ACME deal was completed last Friday.*

3. User: What happened yesterday in the HAL Corporation bid for BIG?

System: *HAL Corporation increased its bid for the BIG company yesterday, up $4 to $70 a share. BIG has not commented on the new offer.*

Figure 1 illustrates the architecture of the SCISOR system. Each of the boxes in Figure 1 represents a major component of SCISOR. First, newspaper stories, or questions about the stories that deal with corporate takeovers are interpreted using two parsing systems, one labeled "TRUMP" and the other labeled "partial parser". Input questions are parsed with the same understanding mechanism as is used for

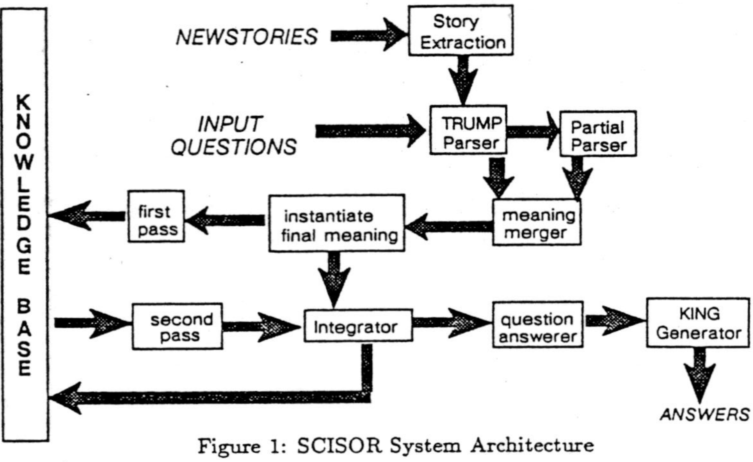

Figure 1: SCISOR System Architecture

the input stories, but without the partial parser. The questions are stored along with the stories, for future user modeling, and to enable the system to answer a user's question when the answer becomes known, if it is not known to the system at the time the question is posed. The integration mechanism "fills in" new information in stories with the story summary obtained thus far. It also unifies references to past events with the previously stored representation of those events, if necessary. Answers to input questions are retrieved with a two-pass retrieval mechanism. After answers have been retrieved, they are passed to the KING (Knowledge INtensive Generator) [5] natural language generator for expression.

Input stories and questions are represented in the KODIAK [6] knowledge representation language. KODIAK has been augmented with some scriptal knowledge [7] of typical sequences of events in the domain. These domain-dependent scripts must be encoded by hand for each application area. The following is a typical input to the SCISOR system:

Group Offers to Sweeten Warnaco Bid

```
April 8 - An investor group said yesterday that it is
prepared to raise its cash bid for Warnaco, Inc. from
$40 a share to at least $42.50, or $433.5 million, if
it can reach a merger agreement with the apparel maker.

The California-based group, called W Acquisition Corp.,
already had sweetened its hostile tender offer to $40
a share from the $36 a share offered when the group
launched its bid in mid-March.
```

SCISOR is a complex system with many components. In the sections that follow, three capabilities of the SCISOR system in particular will be focussed on in more detail. These capabilities are the text processing mechanisms, the two-pass retrieval mechanism and the summarization mechanism.

2 Text Processing

Natural language analysis of free text is an extremely difficult and challenging problem. However, in constrained domains with sufficient knowledge about the domain, various techniques have been successfully applied to the problem. Two such techniques are to perform a "top-down", expectation-driven conceptual analysis as in [1,8], or to analyze the domain in terms of a sublanguage [3,9], and use that sublanguage to guide understanding. The approach to the problem of text processing taken in SCISOR is to use multiple techniques and sources of information *together* to increase both the quantity of information extracted from texts, as well as the quality.

The two primary techniques integrated in SCISOR are top-down conceptual analysis and bottom-up linguistic analysis. The combination of top-down (full parsing) and bottom-up (partial parsing) processing allows a text processing system to make use of all sources of information it may have in the understanding of texts in a domain. It can perform in-depth analysis when more complete grammatical and lexical knowledge is present, or perform more superficial analysis when faced with unknown words and constructs. This flexibility in processing is necessary to achieve robust text processing. Bottom-up methods tend to produce more accurate parses and semantic interpretations, account for subtleties in linguistic expression, and detect inconsistencies and lexical gaps. Top-down methods are more tolerant of unknown words or grammatical lapses, but are also more apt to derive erroneous interpretations, fail to detect inconsistencies between what is said and how it is interpreted, and often cannot produce any results when the text presents unusual or unexpected information. Integration of these two approaches can improve the depth and accuracy of the understanding process.

The bottom-up processing is performed by TRUMP. TRUMP (TRansportable Understanding Mechanism Package) is a suite of natural language processing tools. The system currently includes a parser, a semantic interpreter, and a set of lexical acquisition tools, although its theoretical foundation lies in work done on knowledge representation for natural language generation [5]. Some of the background of TRUMP is described in [10].

The TRUMP parser combines words into phrases and sentences, checks syntactic constraints, and instantiates linguistic relations. The system's acquisition strategy is to facilitate the addition of domain-specific vocabulary while preserving a core of linguistic knowledge across domains. Consider a phrase such as "the investor group seeking control of Warnaco". TRUMP may be capable of parsing the phrase without much knowledge about corporate takeovers, but with such knowledge it will produce both a more precise interpretation and a better choice in the case of ambiguity. "The investor group" describes a group of investors, not a group that also invests; "seeking control" refers to the takeover objective, not really a "search"; "of Warnaco" means that Warnaco is to be controlled, and not that Warnaco is currently in control of something else. These decisions are obvious, yet they all actually require a great deal of knowledge on the part of the system. This knowledge is sometimes used to help parsing, but mostly it is used to produce more specific interpretations from general concepts.

TRUMP is designed to allow a variety of knowledge sources to contribute to the interpretation of the input. TRUMP does not really care where additional information is coming from, but tries to fit any more specific interpretations with what it has already produced. Thus the specific interpretation of "investor group" may be derived from a lexical entry for that compound nominal, while the interpretation of "seeking control" depends on domain knowledge about corporate takeovers.

Top-down processing in SCISOR is performed by a partial parser called TRUMPET (TRUMP Expectation Tool). TRUMPET incorporates a more "top-down" or expectation-driven mode of operation. In this mode, various sources of information are combined to aid in the extraction of expected pieces of information from text. These pieces of information are integrated to derive as complete an interpretation as possible.

TRUMPET uses the following sources of information to perform its top-down interpretation of the input.

1. **Role-filler Expectations:** Constraints on what can fill a conceptual role add to the confidence of assignments. These are implemented as declarative properties of the roles.

2. **Event Expectations:** Event expectations created from previous stories are used to predict values in new events. These are implemented as dæmons that are activated upon the instantiation of a typically continuing event.

3. **World knowledge Expectations:** World knowledge expectations can disambiguate multiple interpretations through domain-specific heuristics. These heuristics are implemented as special-purpose procedures.

The program can operate with any combination of these information sources. When one or more sources are lacking, the information extracted from the texts is more superficial, or has a smaller degree of reliability. This flexibility in depth of processing is an interesting feature in its own right, in addition to having the practical advantage of allowing the system to "skim" efficiently when a text overlaps with material already processed or not pertaining to the topic at hand.

As an example, consider the following sample text:

```
Warnaco received another merger offer,
valued at $36 a share, or $360 million.
```

Role-filler expectations allow SCISOR to make reliable interpretations of the dollar figures in spite of incomplete lexical knowledge. Event expectations lead to the deeper interpretation that this offer is an increase over a previous offer. World knowledge allows the system to predict whether the offer was an increase or a competing offer, depending on what other information is available. A unique feature of SCISOR is that partial linguistic knowledge contributes to all of these interpretations, and to the understanding of "received" in this context. This is noteworthy because general knowledge about "receive" in this case interacts with domain knowledge in understanding the role of Warnaco in the offer.

This top-down, or expectation-driven, approach, offers the benefit of being able to "skim" texts for particular pieces of information, passing gracefully over unknown words or constructs and ignoring some of the complexities of the language. A typical, although early, effort at skimming news stories was implemented in FRUMP [1], which accurately extracted certain conceptual information from texts in preselected topic areas. FRUMP proved that the expectation-driven strategy was useful for scanning texts in constrained domains. This strategy includes the banking telex readers TESS [4] and ATRANS [11].

Clearly, a robust parser and semantic interpreter could obtain predefined features from the texts without the use of expectations. This would make predefining items of interest unnecessary. Robust in-depth analysis of texts, however, is beyond the near-term capabilities of natural language technology; thus SCISOR is designed with the understanding that there will always be gaps in the system's knowledge base that must be dealt with gracefully. SCISOR's text processing techniques are more fully described in [12].

After information has been extracted using the text processing system just described, it is instantiated and stored in processes not described here. This is the manner in which graphs such as in Figures 2 and 3 are constructed. In the next sections, the mechanism to perform retrieval and summarization of conceptual information will be described.

3 Information Retrieval

SCISOR provides capabilities for improving the usefulness of an information retrieval system by exploiting the conceptual nature of the information. In particular, SCISOR's method of retrieval allows for close matching between the items of interest to a user and items actually present in the source documents. The implementation of this capability will now be described in more detail.

SCISOR can answer questions when the questions provide information that may be *partial*, *similar*, or *wrong*. The following examples illustrate these three "anomalous states of knowledge".

ANSWER: GE took over RCA.

1. **Partial:** *What did GE do?*

2. **Similar:** *Did GE buy up RCA's stock?*

3. **Wrong:** *Did RCA take over GE?*

Question 1 provides partial information in that although the user asks about a particular company, they do not further specify what kind of action they were interested in. Question 2 is similar in that the user asked if GE bought RCA's stock whereas in fact GE has taken over RCA. Buying up a company's stock is similar in some sense to taking over a company. Finally, in question 3, the user is incorrect in their assumption that RCA was trying to take over GE. Finding answers to questions that contain partial, similar or incorrect information is a difficult problem in general.

SCISOR performs retrieval with a form of constrained marker-passing [13] and intersection search. In this technique, features in user requests are relaxed by passing markers heuristically up and down the abstraction (or "isa") hierarchy. Answers

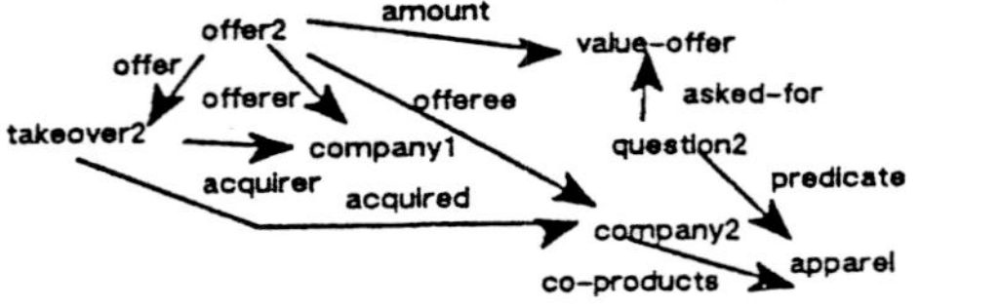

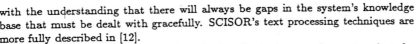

Figure 2: How much are offers for apparel companies in takeovers?

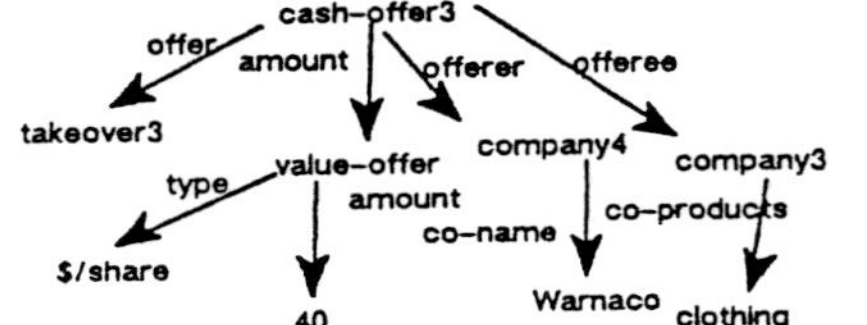

Figure 3: Part of Story Episode .

are located when enough markers intersect in a conceptual representation of a portion of a document.

For example, consider the conceptual representation of the question "How much has a company offered to take over an apparel company?" given in Figure 2. Previously stored in the system is part of a story episode that should be retrieved to give an answer to the question, shown in Figure 3.

The instantiation of the concepts in the question (OFFER2, COMPANY1, COMPANY2, QUESTION2, TAKEOVER2, APPAREL) causes related concepts to be activated That is, COMPANY1 causes COMPANY3 and COMPANY4 to be marked. TAKEOVER2 causes CASH-OFFER1 to be marked. Note how the instantiation of an OFFER causes a more specific kind of offer; a CASH-OFFER, to get marked. Similarly, CLOTHING is marked even though the input question specified an APPAREL company. This marker-passing to related concepts allows SCISOR to find answers to questions even when the questions ask for information at a different level of conceptual generality than is present in the story.

This process of marker-passing serves to find an initial set of likely candidates for retrieval. This initial set is then examined in more detail to further narrow down the possibilities. The additional examination is a kind of filtering process to determine the exact nature of the match between input question and the answer in a story. This process examines the nature of the *relationships* between the features

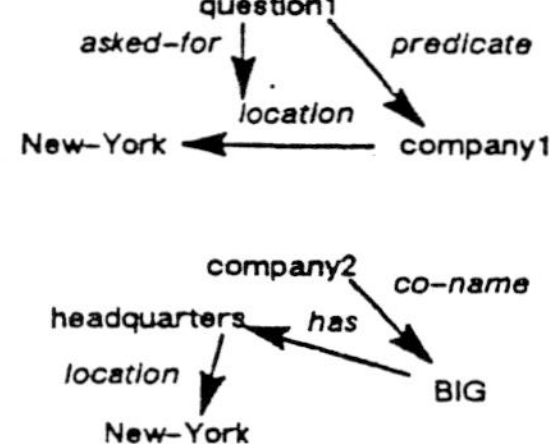

Figure 4: Inexact Matching

matched in the first pass. For example, the first pass determines that COMPANY1 matches COMPANY4, and OFFER2 matches CASH-OFFER3. The second pass looks at whether COMPANY1 is the OFFERER of OFFER2, and whether COMPANY4 is the OFFERER of CASH-OFFER3.

Figure 4 illustrates another simple example of the kind of matching that SCISOR can perform efficiently. In this example, the question asks what companies are located in New York. The representation of the story contains the information that the BIG company has its headquarters in New York. These two conceptual graphs can still be matched to each other even though they do not match exactly, due to the partial node-to-node matching information obtained from the first pass of the retrieval mechanism. This type of flexible, partial, relaxed matching greatly increases the system's ability to find information related to what the user *means*, as opposed to what they may *say*.

This two-step retrieval process is very efficient, in that only likely candidates are examined closely. Also, it is very tolerant of erroneous, incomplete or partial input information. This is important in many domains where events take place over time. For example, in the corporate takeover domain, it is necessary to ensure retrieval of previous events even when a new state of affairs may contradict the previous events. For example, SCISOR must find that Warnaco was trying to take over W Acquisition if today W Acquisition announced that it was trying to take over Warnaco.

This method of information retrieval and some of its advantages are more fully described in [14]. In the next section, SCISOR's summarization capabilities will be described.

4 Text Summarization

In application areas dealing with events that take place over time, the ability to summarize information is especially important. For a user interested in a concise summary, a large set of documents, each describing one event in an ongoing story plus a rehash of all events up to that point, might constitute acute information overload.

For the purposes of summarization, the distinction between narrative texts and expository texts is an important one. In narrative texts where a story is being told, there is a plot. Events central to the plot are described in the same way as superfluous events. Thus the task of summarization becomes one of determining what the plot is, and gathering together descriptions of events central to that plot. Some examples of approaches to narrative text summarization may be found in [15,16,17].

Expository texts do not have "plots" *per se*. As a result of this, the events described in an expository text may all be relevant. For example it can be assumed that the facts present in a newspaper story are all somehow relevant to that story. The task in expository text summarization then becomes one of determining the appropriate *level of detail* for the summary.

With expository texts the conciseness of a summary can be roughly approximated to a linear function of the distance of the concepts to be expressed from the containing category that represents what is to be summarized. In narrative texts, a program must have a more complicated method of determining the relative importance of the events described in the story. Although the "linear function of the distance" heuristic does not always produce an optimal summary, it is a starting point for more complex heuristics.

In the SCISOR system, summaries are to be produced by generating (in natural language) the contents of a particular category, such as CORPORATE-TAKEOVER-SCENARIO1. The "contents" of this category are the events that have taken place in this particular corporate takeover "script". To limit the depth of description, a limit is placed on the number of nodes that will be passed to the language generator for expression. If the number of nodes at any given level of description is too large, other heuristics may be used to capture generalities that can be expressed to the user. The simplest heuristic is to check if there are two or more concepts that are members of the same category. If this is the case, this generalization can be expressed more succinctly to the user.

For example, in Figure 5, three components of the representation of the corporate takeover scenario are members of the LEGAL-COMPLICATION category. This would cause the sentence "..involving some potential conflict of interest matters..." to be generated in place of the details of those legal complications.

Figure 5 also illustrates a portion of a corporate takeover scenario. The encircled concepts are the concepts that are to be expressed in the summary. This figure corresponds to one summary that might be given below.

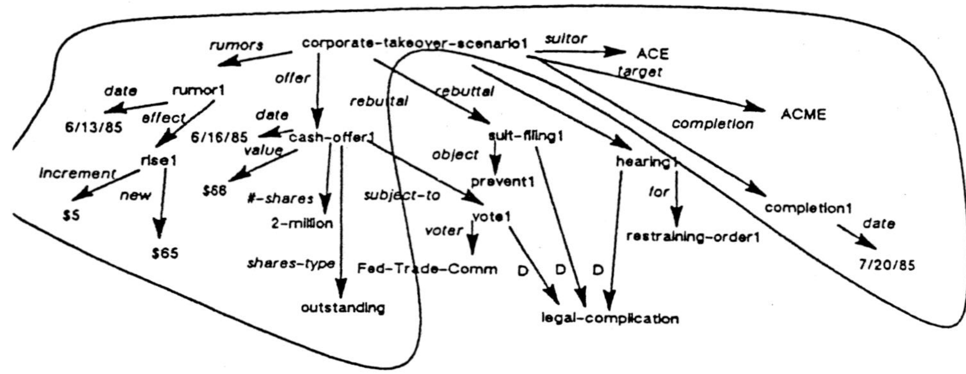

Figure 5: Story to be Summarized

Summary: *Rumors that ACME was to be taken over started May 13, 1985. The stock rose $5 a share to $65. On May 16, the ACE company announced that it had made an offer to ACME valued at $66 a share. The offer was a cash offer to purchase all 2 million outstanding shares of ACME. After a month of deliberation involving some potential conflict of interest matters, the ACE-ACME deal was completed last Friday.*

The natural language generator of SCISOR has not yet been connected so that output such as this is currently "canned".

SCISOR also uses the "linear function of distance" heuristic to produce appropriate summaries. For example, a very long article about a takeover may have many extraneous, historical details and surrounding context that might not be appropriate for a summary of that takeover. Although these details are included in the representation of the article, they are not used in summarization because of their conceptual distance from the corporate takeover script.

In order to guide the summary of an event, the user must refer to the event at an appropriate conceptual level. For example, to elicit the summary above, the user might request "Please give me a summary of the events in the ACE - ACME takeover". The program outputs the contents of any conceptual category that is inquired about by the user. If that category is a high level one, a summary will be produced. If it is very specific, something very specific such as an answer to a specific question will be produced. If the user asks for a "short" summary or an "extended" summary, SCISOR uses heuristics to compute a relative measure of length, based on the longest paths existing in the particular representations.

5 Implementation and Status

SCISOR is an implemented system written in Common Lisp. It is capable of processing stories at the rate of a few seconds per sentence. It currently has available to it a core lexicon of over 5,000 words. An on-line news service is currently being connected to SCISOR, to enable extensive testing of the system with a continuous source of on-line stories.

Although the text processing mechanism is still being refined, SCISOR can currently extract a dozen or so features from articles in the domain, and answer questions about those features. Although the natural language generator has been implemented, it has not been converted yet to Commonlisp to run with SCISOR.

In the immediate future, we plan to connect SCISOR directly to a continuous source of on-line information to begin collecting large amounts of conceptually analyzed material, and extensively testing the system. In the longer term, we hope to continue to increase the size of the lexicon and system grammar, and to improve the capabilities of the bottom-up TRUMP parser. The most important extension, however, will be to test SCISOR in real-life information gathering tasks.

As the system has been engineered to be portable across domains, we will eventually choose another application and tailor the system for this new domain. This should provide valuable insight into issues of system extensibility and portability, and the prospects for potential "generic" text processing packages.

6 Summary

SCISOR represents a unique integration of knowledge sources to aid in its goal of robust and reliable extraction of information from naturally occurring texts in constrained domains. Its ability to use lexical and syntactic knowledge when available separates it from purely expectation-driven semantic analyzers. At the same time, its lack of reliance on any single source of information and multiple "fall-back" heuristics give the system the ability to focus attention and processing on those items of particular interest to be extracted.

Large conceptual knowledge bases pose their own special problems in conceptual information retrieval. SCISOR retrieves complex conceptual events using a two-pass retrieval mechanism. During the first marker-passing pass, concepts related to the concepts in an input query are activated. This initial pass finds events that have features that are not identical to features in the inputs. The second pass continues to determine a best match to an input query, and formulate an informative reply that is passed to a natural language generator.

SCISOR also supports expository text summarization through a simple technique of mapping the depth of description to the number of nodes away from the event being summarized. This simple process is augmented with some heuristics to provide summaries of complex events.

This paper has presented an overview of the SCISOR system and described the techniques it uses to perform conceptual information extraction, retrieval and summarization.

References

[1] G. DeJong, "Skimming stories in real time: an experiment in integrated understanding," Research Report 158, Department of Computer Science, Yale University, 1979.

[2] M. Lebowitz, "Generalization from natural language text," *Cognitive Science*, vol. 7, no. 1, pp. 1–40, 1983.

[3] R. Kittredge and J. Lehrberger, *Sublanguages: Studies of Language in Restricted Domains*. New York: Walter DeGruyter, 1982.

[4] S. Young and P. Hayes, "Automatic classification and summarization of banking telexes," in *The Second Conference on Artificial Intelligence Applications*, (), pp. 402–208, IEEE Press, 1985.

[5] P. S. Jacobs, "Knowledge-intensive natural language generation," *Artificial Intelligence*, vol. 33, pp. 325–378, November 1987.

[6] R. Wilensky, "Knowledge representation - a critique and a proposal," in *Experience, Memory, and Reasoning*, (J. Kolodner and C. Riesbeck, eds.), pp. 15–28, Hillsdale, New Jersey: Lawrence Erlbaum Associates, 1986.

[7] R. C. Schank and R. P. Abelson, *Scripts, Plans, Goals, and Understanding*. Halsted, NJ: Lawrence Erlbaum, 1977.

[8] R. E. Cullingford, *Natural Language Processing: A Knowledge-Engineering Approach*. Totowa, NJ: Rowman and Littlefield, 1986.

[9] R. Grishman and L. Hirschman, "PROTEUS and PUNDIT: research in text understanding," PROTEUS Project Memorandum 1, NYU, 1986.

[10] P. S. Jacobs, "Language analysis in not-so-limited domains," in *Proceedings of the Fall Joint Computer Conference*, (Dallas, Texas), 1986.

[11] S. Lytinen and A. Gershman, "ATRANS: automatic processing of money transfer messages," in *Proceedings of the Fifth National Conference on Artificial Intelligence*, (Philadelphia), 1986.

[12] L. F. Rau and P. S. Jacobs, "Integrating top-down and bottom-up strategies in a text processing system," in *Proceedings of Second Conference on Applied Natural Language Processing*, (), p. , Forthcoming, February 1988.

[13] E. Charniak, "Passing markers: a theory of contextual influence in language comprehension," *Cognitive Science*, vol. 7, no. 3, pp. 171–190, 1983.

[14] L. F. Rau, "Knowledge organization and access in a conceptual information system," *Information Processing and Management, Special Issue on Artificial Intelligence for Information Retrieval*, vol. 23, no. 4, pp. 269–283, 1987.

[15] W. G. Lehnert, "Plot Units: A Narrative Summarization Strategy," in *Strategies for Natural Language Processing*, (W. Lehnert and M. Ringle, eds.), pp. 375–412, Hillsdale, NJ: Lawrence Erlbaum Associates, 1982.

[16] S. Klein, "Meta-compiling text grammars as a model for human behavior," in *Proceedings of TINLAP-1*, (Cambridge, Massachusetts), 1975.

[17] M. G. Dyer, *In-Depth Understanding*. Cambridge, MA: MIT Press, 1983.

A PRODUCTION RULE SYSTEM FOR MESSAGE SUMMARIZATION

*Elaine Marsh and Henry Hamburger**

Navy Center for Applied Research
in Artificial Intelligence
Naval Research Laboratory - Code 7510
Washington, D.C. 20375
*Also at George Mason University

Ralph Grishman

Department of
Computer Science
New York University
New York, New York 10012

ABSTRACT

In summarizing a message, it is necessary to access knowledge about linguistic relations, subject matter knowledge about the domain of discourse, and knowledge about the user's goals for the summary. This paper investigates the feasibility of integrating these knowledge sources by using computational linguistic and expert system techniques to generate one-line summaries from the narrative content of a class of Navy messages. For deriving a knowledge representation of the narrative content, we have adapted an approach developed by Sager *et al.* at New York University. This approach, called *information formatting*, uses an explicit grammar of English and a classification of the semantic relationships within the domain to derive a tabular representation of the information in a message narrative. A production system, written in OPS5, then interprets the information in the table and automatically generates a summary line. The use of a production rule system provides insight into the mechanisms of summarization. A comparison of computer-generated summaries with those obtained manually showed good agreement, indicating that it is possible to automatically process message narrative and generate appropriate, and ultimately useful, summaries.

INTRODUCTION

Behavior modeled in expert systems has generally been held distinct from that modeled in natural language understanding systems. Attempts at practical expert systems have been directed toward design [McDermott 1980], diagnosis [Shortliffe 1976], and interpretation [Buchanan 1978], among others. Practical systems for natural language understanding have concentrated largely on database interfaces [Grosz 1983, Ginsparg 1983, Grishman 1983] and database creation [Sager 1978]. In this paper we investigate the feasibility of integrating techniques from computational linguistics and expert system technology to summarize a set of Navy equipment failure messages called CASREPs (casualty reports). A natural language analysis procedure automatically generates a tabular representation of the information contained in message narrative. A production rule system then interprets the tabular representation and identifies a clause that is appropriate as a message summary. We have chosen to use a production system for a natural language application because it facilitates understanding and modification of the system. More important for research purposes, a production system makes the operations involved in summarization explicit and, thus, can provide insight into the general problem of summarization.

Summarization can be approached at several different levels. Typically, strategies for summarization have taken a single-level approach. Summaries of stories have been derived at the high level of conceptual representation. Structural features of a graph reveal the central concepts of a story [Lehnert 1980]. Goal-directed summaries have also been investigated in some detail [Fum 1982]. We, on the other hand, have taken a multi-level approach, incorporating several sources of knowledge in the linguistic analysis and production rule system. This permits us to investigate not only the requirements of individual knowledge sources, but also their interactions.

NATURAL LANGUAGE PROCESSING

Each CASREP message contains a set of structured (i.e. *pro forma*) fields and a narrative describing the equipment failures. These narratives typically consist of two to twelve sentences and sentence fragments.

The central task of narrative analysis is the extraction and representation of information contained in narrative portions of a message. This task is difficult because the structure of the information, and often much of the information itself, is implicit in the narrative. Several formalisms, such as *scripts* and *frames*, have been developed to describe such information and have been used in text analysis [Schank 1977; Montgomery 1983]. We are using an approach called *information formatting* that was developed at New York University for the representation of the information in medical narratives [Sager 1978, Hirschman 1982]. In simple terms, an information format is a large table, with one column for each type of information that can occur in a class of texts and one row for each sentence or clause in the text. It is derived through a distributional analysis of sample texts. The narrative is automatically transformed into a series of entries in the information format table. This procedure involves three stages of processing: (1) parsing, (2) syntactic regularization, and (3) mapping into the information format.

First the text sentences are parsed using a top-down parser and the broad-coverage Linguistic String Project English grammar [Sager 1981] extended to handle the sentence fragments and special sublanguage constructions (e.g. date expressions, such as *NLT 292300 Z SEP 82*) that appear in these messages. The grammar consists of a set of context-free definitions augmented by grammatical restrictions. It also uses a Navy sublanguage lexicon that classifies words according to their major parts of speech (e.g. noun, verb, adjective), as well as their special subfield classes (e.g. PART, FUNCTION, SIGNAL), and certain English syntactic subclasses. The parsing procedure identifies the grammatical relations that hold among parts of the sentence, principally subject-verb-object relations and modifier-host relations.

The syntactic regularization component utilizes the same machinery as the parser, augmented by standard transformational operations. The principal function of the regularization component is to reduce the variety of syntactic structures and word forms to be processed, without altering the information content of the sentences, thereby simplifying the subsequent mapping into the information format. Regularization includes: (1) standardization into subject-verb-object word order, e.g. passive to active; (2) expansion of conjoined phrases into conjoined assertions; (3) reduction of words to "canonical form" plus information marker(s); (4) filling in of certain omitted or reduced forms of information.

The third stage of processing moves the phrases in the syntactically regularized parse trees into their appropriate format columns. It involves two steps: (1) identifying connectives and (2) mapping into the information format. A connective word indicates a causal, conjunctional, or time relation between the two clauses it connects. The connective is mapped into the CONNective column of the format table; arguments of the connective are mapped into separate format rows, and their words are mapped into the appropriate format columns. The mapping process is controlled in a large part by the sublanguage (semantic) word classes associated with each word in the lexicon. In general, the formatting procedure is straightforward because most word classes are in a one-to-one correspondence with a particular format column.

The production system for message summarization operates on the information format that is generated for each message.

PRODUCTION RULE SYSTEM FOR SUMMARIZATION

We have implemented prototype knowledge bases for two application areas: dissemination and summary generation [Marsh 1984]. While the dissemination application relies on information obtained from both *pro forma* and narrative data sets of a message, summary generation is based entirely on information contained in narrative portions of the messages. Such summaries, which up to now have been generated by hand, are used to detect patterns of failure for particular types of equipment. This failure information is crucial to decision-makers who procure equipment for new and existing ships. Typically, the manually derived summary consists of a single clause, extracted from the sentences of text. Only rarely is a summary generated from material not explicitly stated in the narrative. The single line summary results in a five- to ten-fold reduction of material. Clearly, the sharp reduction in reading material can ease the decision-making process, provided that the key information from the report regularly finds its way into the summary.

Our current system consists of a set of productions, implemented in a Lisp-based version of the OPS5 production system programming language. OPS5 permits the assignment of attributes and numerical values, or scores, to the working memory elements, and our system takes advantage of this. Productions operate on an initial database of working memory elements that includes data from the the information formats and identify the crucial clause that will be used for the summary. Criteria for production rules are based on the manual summarization that is currently performed.

Several types of knowledge are required for message summarization. Knowledge of the possible relationships is reflected in the initial choice of what fields are available in the format system devised for the domain. This is represented by the columns of each message's information format table. Additional domain knowledge and knowledge of the nature of the application are embodied in the production rules of the expert system.

Each production rule incorporates one of three different types of knowledge necessary for summarization. The first type reflects an understanding of the subject matter of the equipment failure reports. These production rules assign semantic attributes or categories to working memory elements by explicitly specifying these words in a list in the rule. For example, the working memory element containing the word *inhibit* is assigned a category IMPAIR. Elements indicating a bad status (e.g. broken, corroded, failure, malfunction, etc.) have the category BAD assigned and so on. Other category assignment rules are concerned with level of generality, flagging equipment failures at the assembly level, and not at the more detailed part or more general system level, since assemblies are most important to the summary.

Other production rules are based on general principles of summarization, and these rules are typically inferencing rules. These identify causal relationships among working memory elements and may add information to the data base in the form of new working elements. We will see an example of this type below.

Finally, the end use that will be made of the summaries is also a guiding factor in some of the productions. To guide future equipment specification and procurement, one must know not only what went wrong and how often, but also why. Format rows that contain such information are identified as being more important by having the score of the row boosted. For example, causality is important to the summaries. Once a causal relationship is identified, the row specifying the 'cause' has its score boosted. Taken together, the productions are attentive to such matters as malfunction, causality, investigative action, uncertainty, and level of generality. In addition, the system has rules excluding from summaries format rows containing very general statements. For instance, universal quantification and mention of the top level in a *part-of* tree betray a clause that is too general for a summary line.

Summarization proceeds in three stages: (i) inferencing, (ii) scoring the format rows for their importance, and (iii) selection of the appropriate format row as the summary. First, inferences are drawn by a set of production rules. For example, the presence of one of the words in the IMPAIR category triggers an inferencing rule. If part1 impairs part2, we can infer that part1 causes part2 to be bad, and we can also infer that part1 is bad. A set of production rules, summarized as rules (1) and (2) below, operate on the format lines to draw such inferences. The production rule in (1) infers that the second argument (part2) of CONN is bad.

(1) if both (a) CONN contains an 'impair' word
  and (b) the STATUS column of the 2nd argument of
    CONN [the connective] is empty
  then both (c) fill the STATUS column of the
    2nd argument with 'bad'
    and (d) assign the word in CONN
    the attribute 'cause'.

For example, in Table 1, the connective word ***inhibit*** has been mapped by the formatting procedure into the CONN column, connecting two format rows, its first argument, *APC-PPC circuit*, a PART, and its second, *PA driver*, also a PART. Both rows have the PART column of the format filled.

CONN	PART	STATUS
	APC-PPC circuit	
inhibit		
	PA driver	

Table 1: Simplified information format for the sentence: *APC-PPC is inhibiting PA driver*

By a previous production rule, the ***inhibit*** has been categorized in the class of impairment verbs. Rule (1) replaces impairment by a format version of "cause to be bad." Specifically, the verb *inhibit* in the CONN column gets assigned the attribute 'cause'. Since the STATUS column of the second argument is empty, ***bad*** is inserted into that STATUS column. Thus, it is inferred that the PA driver is bad because it has been impaired.

Another production rule, summarized as (2), infers that

the STATUS column of the first argument (part1) of CONN is also 'bad' and inserts *bad* into the STATUS column since it has caused something else to be bad.

(2) if both (a) CONN has the attribute 'cause'
and (b) the STATUS of the first argument of CONN is empty
and (c) the STATUS of the second argument of CONN is 'bad'
then (d) insert 'bad' into the empty STATUS column.

In our example Table 1, 'inhibit' in the CONNective column has been assigned the attribute 'cause', and the STATUS of *APC-PPC circuit* is empty. The STATUS of the *PA driver* contains 'bad', by rule (1). So 'bad' is inserted into the STATUS column of the first argument, yielding *APC-PPC circuit bad*.

The second stage of the summarization system rates the format rows for their importance to the summary. When it comes time to score the various formats to determines the most appropriate one for the summary, since "bad" is a member of the class of words signifying malfunction, it will cause both arguments of *inhibit* to be promoted in importance. An additional scoring increment will accrue to the first argument but not the second because it is a cause rather than an effect. Another rule increments a format row referring to an assembly (a mid-level component), since such a format is more revealing than a format containing a statement about about a whole unit or an individual part (such as a transistor). For example, *circuit*, the head of the PART phrase of the first argument is identified as belonging to a class of components at the assembly level. As a result, the score of the row containing *APC-PPC circuit bad* is incremented again.

The third and final stage of summarization is to select the format row or rows with the highest rating. As a result of the various production rule actions, the winning format row is "PART: *APC-PPC circuit*; STATUS: *bad*." While other format rows may also have positive scores, only the row with the highest score is selected. The system does not preclude selecting several format rows if they have equally high scores.

IMPLEMENTATION

The LSP parser is implemented in about 15,000 lines of Fortran 77 code. The parser runs on a DEC VAX 11/780 under the UNIX and VMS operating systems and requires 2 megabytes of virtual memory when executing, of which two-thirds is list space for holding the grammar, dictionary entries, etc. The English grammar, regularization component, and information formatting components are written in Restriction Language, a special language developed for writing natural language grammars [Sager 1975]. The dissemination and summary generation applications programs are written using the OPS5 production system. In total, there are 63 production rules in the applications programs.

EXPERIMENTAL RESULTS

The purpose of this experiment was to test the feasibility of automatically summarizing narrative text in Navy equipment failure messages using techniques of computational linguistics and artificial intelligence. Computer-generated results were compared to those obtained by manual summarization procedures to evaluate the performance of the system. The manual summaries were prepared independently of our experiment by experts who routinely summarize such messages.

Since both the natural language processing components and the applications programs were under development while this experiment was being carried out, 12 casualty reports were used for debugging the programs. Subsequently, 12 other reports were used for the computer-human comparison. For an appropriate summary line to be generated, it is necessary that 100% of the sentences in a text be processed correctly by the natural language procedures. The natural language analysis procedures processed 100% of the sentences contained in the documents; this percentage includes 9 sentences (25%) that were paraphrased and rerun because they were not correctly processed on their first run. Paraphrasing these sentences brought the total number of sentences from 36 to 38. The sentences were paraphrased to expedite processing since the major purpose of running the messages was to investigate methods of summarization and not the performance of the natural language processing system. 70 format lines were generated from 38 sentences in 12 messages.

The computer-generated results of the summarization program compare favorably to those obtained manually. Figure 1 shows a comparison of the two sets of results for the 12 test documents. The discrepancies between the computer-generated results and the manual results are summarized in Figure 2.

Doc.	Machine *# format rows*	Manual *# sentences*	Agreement *Machine/Manual*
1.	1	1	1/1
2.	1	1	1/1
3.	1	1	1/1
4.	1	1	0/1
5.	1	2	1/2
6.	2	1	1/1
7.	1	1	1/1
8.	2	1	1/1
9.	1	1	0/1
10.	1	2	1/2
11.	1	1	1/1
12.	1	2	1/2
	14	15	10/15

Fig. 1: Comparison of machine and manual summary results

#	Discrepancy	Doc.
1	word not included in category list	4
1	second manual summary not about bad-status	5
1	second manual summary not in narrative text	10
2	different summaries generated	9,12

Fig. 2: Analysis of machine and manual summary results

Agreement between machine and manual summaries is obtained when the text contained in the format row selected by the automatic procedure agrees with the text in the manually generated sentences. The discrepancies in the *Agreement* column of Figure 1, as specified in Figure 2, can be categorized as follows. One (message 4) is the result of a failure to enter a word on a category list in the production rule system. As a result, the word was not categorized as a BAD-STATUS, and the score of its format row was not correspondingly boosted. Two errors (messages 5 and 10) were due to the program selecting one format line, although manual generation produced two sentences. In the first case (message 5), the additional text in the manual summary did not concern a description of a bad status. Rather it was a description of a good function status (i.e. *Drive shaft was found to rotate freely.*). In message 10, the extra manual summary consisted entirely of text that was not contained in the message narrative. Our system does not automatically generate text, nor could it have made the inferences necessary to do so. In both these cases, however, the line that the program selected agreed with one of the manual summaries.

The most significant discrepancies (a total of 2) were caused by the system selecting more specific causal information than was indicated in the manual summary. In message 9, which contains the sentence *Loss of lube oil pressure when start air compressor engaged for operation is due to wiped bearing* the manual summary line generated was *Loss of LO pressure,* while the system selected the more specific information that indicated the cause of the casualty, i.e. *wiped bearing.* Similarly, in message 12, the system selected the line *low output air pressure* from the assertion *low output air pressure resulting in slow gas turbine starts* since it indicated a cause. The program did not identify the second part of the manual summary because its score was not as high as that of the cause *low output air pressure.* However, its score was the second highest for that message. This suggests that it may be more appropriate to select all the summary lines in some kind of score window rather than only those lines that have the highest score.

In two cases (messages 6 and 8), the system generated two summary texts, although the manual summary consisted of only one sentence. Two summary lines were selected because both had equally high scores. Nonetheless, one of the two summaries was also the manual summary.

In conclusion, the summarization system was able to identify the same summary line as the manual summary 10/15 times (66.6%). For 10 out of 12 messages, the summarization system selected at least one of the same summary lines as the manual generation produced. For two messages, the system was not able to match the manual summary, in one case, because the crucial status word was not in the appropriate list in the production rule system and, in a second case, because the automatic procedure identified the more specific causal agent.

CONCLUSION

The results of our work are quite promising and represent a successful first step towards demonstrating the feasibility of integrating computational linguistic and expert system techniques. We recognize that much remains to be done before we have an operational system. Our work up to now has pointed to several areas that require further development.

Refinement of the semantic representation. Our current information format was developed from a limited corpus of 38 messages, including those in the test set. Even within that corpus not all types of information have been captured - for example, modes of operation, relations between parts and signals, and relations and actions involving more than one part. Some of this information has been incorporated into the expert system. For example, part-assembly-system information has been encoded as a categorization rule. However it is clear that enrichment of our semantic representation is a high priority. We are considering the use of some external knowledge sources to obtain this information. One possibility is to access machine-readable listings of Navy equipment.

Intersentential processing. Our current implementation does almost no intersentential processing. This has proved marginally adequate for our current applications, but clearly needs to be remedied in the long run. One aspect of this processing is the capture of information that is implicit in the text. This includes missing arguments (subject and objects of verbs) and anaphors (e.g. pronouns) that can be reconstructed from prior discourse (earlier format lines); such processing is part of the information formatting procedure for medical records [Hirschman 1981]. It should also include reconstruction of some of the implicit causal connections The reconstruction of the connections will require substantial domain knowledge, of equipment-part and equipment-function relations, as well as "scriptal" knowledge of typical event sequences (e.g. failure - diagnosis - repair).

ACKNOWLEDGMENTS

This research was supported by the Office of Naval Research and the Office of Naval Technology PE-62721N. The authors gratefully acknowledge the efforts of Judith Froscher and Joan Bachenko in processing the first set of messages and providing the specifications for our dissemination system.

REFERENCES

[Buchanan 1978] Buchanan, B.G., Feigenbaum, E.A. DENDRAL and Meta-DENDRAL: their applications dimension, *Artificial Intelligence* **11**, 5-24.

[Fum 1982] Fum, D., Guida, G., Tasso, C. Forward and backward reasoning in automatic abstracting. *COLING 82* (J. Horecky (ed)). North Holland Publishing Company.

[Ginsparg 1983] Ginsparg, J.M. A robust portable natural language data base interface. *Proceedings of the Conference on Applied Natural Language Processing,* ACL.

[Grosz 1983] Grosz, B.J. TEAM, a transportable natural language interface system.*Proceedings of the Conference on Applied Natural Language Processing,* ACL.

[Grishman 1983] Grishman, R., Hirschman, L., Friedman, C. Isolating domain dependencies in natural language interfaces.*Proceedings of the Conference on Applied Natural Language Processing,* ACL.

[Hirschman 1982] Hirschman, L., Sager, N. Automatic information formatting of a medical sublanguage. In *Sublanguage: Studies of Language in Restricted Domains* (Kitttedge and Lehrberger, eds). Walter de Gruyter, Berlin.

[Hirschman 1981] Hirschman, L., Story, G., Marsh, E., Lyman, M., Sager, N. An experiment in automated health care evaluation from narrative medical records. *Computers and Biomedical Research* **14**, 447-463.

[Lehnert 1980] Lehnert, W. Narrative text summarization. *AAAI-80 Proceedings*: 337-339.

[Marsh 1984] Marsh, E., Froscher, J., Grishman, R., Hamburger, H., Bachenko, J. Automatic processing of Navy message narrative. NCARAI Internal Report.

[McDermott 1980] McDermott, J. R1: A rule-based configurer of computer systems. Carnegie-Mellon University, Department of Computer Science Report CMU-CS-80-119, April 1980.

[Montgomery 1983] Montgomery, C. Distinguishing fact from opinion and events from meta-events. *Proceedings of Conference on Applied Natural Language Processing,* 55-61, Assn. for Computational Linguistics.

[Sager 1975] Sager, N., Grishman, R. The Restriction Language for computer grammars of natural language. *Communications of the ACM,***18**, 390.

[Sager 1978] Sager, N. Natural language information formatting: The automatic conversion of texts to a structured data base. In *Advances in Computers***17** (M.C. Yovits, ed), Academic Press.

[Sager 1981] Sager, N. *Natural Language Information Processing.* Addison-Wesley.

[Schank 1977] Schank, R., Abelson, R. *Scripts, Plans, Goals, and Understanding.* Lawrence Erlbaum Associates.

[Shortliffe 1976] Shortliffe, E.H. *Computer-based medical consultations: MYCIN.* American Elsevier.

The application of linguistic processing to automatic abstract generation

F. C. Johnson, *Centre for Computational Linguistics, UMIST, PO Box 88, Manchester M60 1QD, UK. (currently at the Department of Library and Information Studies, The Manchester Metropolitan University, All Saints, Manchester M15 6BH, UK.)*

C. D Paice, *Department of Computing, University of Lancaster, Bailrigg, Lancaster LA1 4YR, UK.*

W. J. Black, *Centre for Computational Linguistics, UMIST, PO Box 88, Manchester M60 1QD, UK.*

A. P Neal, *Department of Computing, University of Lancaster, Bailrigg, Lancaster LA1 4YR, UK.*

One approach to the problem of generating abstracts by computer is to extract from a source text those sentences which give a strong indication of the central subject matter and findings of the paper. Not surprisingly, concatenations of extracted sentences show a lack of cohesion, due partly to the frequent occurrence of anaphoric references. This paper describes the text processing which was necessary to identify these anaphors so that they may be utilised in the enhancement of the sentence selection criteria. It is assumed that sentences which contain non-anaphoric nounphrases and introduce key concepts into the text are worthy of inclusion in an abstract. The results suggest that the key concepts are indeed identified but the abstracts are too long. Further recommendations are made to continue this work in abstracting which makes use of text structure.

1. INTRODUCTION

This paper describes a project which was funded by the British Library Research and Development Department to develop techniques for generating abstracts of technical papers by computer. The approach taken was to select from source text sentences which give a strong indication of the central subject matter and findings of the paper. In general, sentences may be selected on the basis of various statistical, grammatical, positional and presentational clues[1]. Not surprisingly, concatenations of extracted sentences show a lack of cohesion, due partly to the frequent occurrence of anaphoric references. This paper describes the text processing which was necessary to identify these anaphors so that they may be utilised or their effects neutralised in the sentence selection criteria.

This work brings together established automatic abstracting techniques with newly developed sentence selection and rejection rules. Not only are there traditional reasons for pursuing this work (i.e., to reduce human costs and to speed up information dissemination), but there are also new developments which could benefit. The use of networks for electronic journals and for knowledge dissemination is possibly the key issue for the future. The electronic medium offers sophisticated searching, with browsing and navigation at the full-text level, and with the ability to move within and between articles via hypertext links. The use of automatic abstracting techniques to identify key points and passages in a text may offer a way further to enhance these facilities.

2. BACKGROUND RESEARCH IN AUTOMATIC ABSTRACTING

Interest in the problem of how to identify *topic* sentences for abstracting dates from Luhn's[2] influential paper in 1958. Luhn's approach was to score each sentence in a text according to the weights, based on frequency of occurrence, of all the keywords in a sentence. The highest scoring sentences were extracted to produce an abstract. At about the same time, Baxendale[3] drew attention to the strong tendency of topic sentences to appear first, or sometimes last, in a paragraph. These ideas were subsequently taken up by other workers, in particular Edmundson,[4] who in 1969 published the results of an experiment to compare the effectiveness of four extracting methods: the keyword, the title, the location and the cue method. The last, which scores sentences according to the presence of bonus words and stigma words, was found to produce the best result.

Paice[5] later proposed the use of *indicator constructs* such as *In this paper we show that ...*, which introduce statements about the topic, aim or findings of an article. More recently an experiment was conducted to test the effectiveness of abstracts produced using the keyword and indicator phrase methods with respect to the function an abstract purports to serve [6]. The results highlighted the problem of cohesion in the abstracts. In particular, the presence of dangling anaphoric references resulted in a disjointed, and at worst unintelligible abstract. This is not surprising, seeing that these techniques take no account of the structure of text in the task of identifying sentences for abstracting.

The aim of our research was to obtain a fuller understanding of the problem of cohesion in automatic abstracts. Research at Lancaster during the late 1980s[1,7] focused on the recognition of anaphors (pronouns and demonstratives) using local, i.e., within sentence, contextual information to decide whether potentially anaphoric words were actually being used anaphorically and to resolve or neutralise them in constructing a passage for extraction. *Anaphora* is often used only to designate pronouns as they operate within the sentence.[8] Our project addressed the problem posed by discourse phenomena in text. Coherent texts comprise sequences of sentences or other linguistic units each with a discernable relation of meaning to its predecessors. In other words, successive sentences either discuss further properties of a real or abstract object, related objects, or events instigated or affected by the objects. Although texts can be quite long, they have a *cast* of relatively few objects and events. A consequence of this characteristic of text is the use of definite noun phrases (DNP). These are phrases like ***the motor*** which can refer over long distances. DNPs may involve reference to objects introduced into the discourse by quite different noun phrases (***a Ford car, the vehicle or the engine*** etc). DNPs can also refer back to events, "X bought the purchase".

The outcome of our work to address the problems caused by DNPs in automatic abstracting was the development of grammatical criteria used to identify points in the text where new concepts are introduced. Those sentences which introduce important concepts and do not refer to discourse entities previously mentioned in the text are surely candidates for extraction. Thus we had thrown light on a new criterion for selecting isolated sentences for abstracting.

The principles behind this approach are described in detail in Neal.[9] The motivation was to analyse texts to find chains of DNPs and to ascertain how far back in the text one should be expected to look to resolve each DNP. A sentence containing such referring expressions may refer to discourse entities in a previous sentence. Likewise a sentence containing connectives or comparatives may only be interpreted with reference to some previous sentence(s). If such sentences are selected for an abstract they presuppose something that was said in another sentence which may not have been selected. Neal, using the terminology of logic, states that these sentences fail to be propositions. That is, a translation to a classical logical form would include free variables. Using this perspective, it may be assumed that the anaphors must be resolved within the boundaries of a proposition: thus the aim was to identify the points in the text where new propositions begin.

For most referring expressions unsatisfied within the extract, the discourse entity referred to (which may itself be an anaphor) lies in the preceding sentence. With a DNP this entity may be a long way off, requiring a special strategy. Neal proposed that if all propositional sentences, which contain no unresolved connectives, anaphors or comparatives, were selected for inclusion in an abstract, then it may be assumed that any DNP in later selected sentences will be resolved. Taking this approach eliminates the need to search backwards for the entity referred to. The outcome was a set of heuristics to identify non-anaphoric noun phrases and to select sentences containing these key concepts for abstracting. A summary of those which form part of the sentence selection or rejection criteria are presented here. Following this, we describe in some detail the text processing which is necessary to exploit the grammatical clues and text structure in abstracting.

3. SENTENCE SELECTION RULES

The methodology of the project represents an extension of the ***extract and rearrange*** methods described above. The system is constructed out of two rule sets, the first of which is a selective tagger and parser derived from a similar approach.[10] The tagger assigns grammatical ***tags*** to each word in the text according its morphological structure using criteria on the kinds of ending (or suffixes) words will take. Since this does not result in an unique interpretation for each word, the parser is used to disambiguate the tags and in the process structures the sequence of these word categories according to a grammar. The second rule set identifies two classes of sentence in the source text for inclusion in the abstract. The sentence selection/rejection rules are devised to make use of and develop techniques which deserve further attention in abstracting: the use of indicator phrases[5] and clue words.[4] Some of the rules specify rhetorical constructs indicating the relative salience of sections of text (conclusions have high salience, references to previous work have low salience and so on). These are mostly concerned with sentence rejection. Other rules rely on logical and linguistic hypotheses about text structure, and exploit more narrowly grammatical criteria to identify points in the text where new concepts are introduced. From an analysis of ten papers from the journal ***Nature*** Vol 340 consisting of approximately 30,000 words, the authors found that sentences lacking anaphors and not introduced by rhetorical connectives frequently introduce key information into a discourse. The development of the rules to identify indicator phrases is outlined in Paice.[5] These two rule sets, to identify non-anaphoric sentences and to identify sentences containing an indicator phrase, are the only sentence *selection* rules used in the system. Further rules, as stated above, are concerned with the ***elimination*** or ***rejection*** of sentences.

The sequence of the sentence selection rules is shown below with corresponding lists.

CASE 1. Select a sentence if it contains an indicator phrase. List 1 presents a sample of phrases recognised by the system. These are defined by structural patterns rather than enumerated as a list of cases. The representation and implementation, based on an adaptation of Definite Clause Grammar (Pereira and Warren[11]) rules are described in Black and Johnson.[6]

List 1. Indicator phrases

The | _ | objective | of | this | study | is ...
The | primary | aim | of | the present | investigation | was ...
The | main | hypothesis | of | the | research | was ...

The | procedures | introduced | in | the following | study ...
The | problem | considered | by | our | research ...
The | subject field | examined | in | this | project ...
The | ideas | presented | here ...
The | model | outlined | below ...

The | results | of | this | analysis | confirm ...
The | findings | from | our | research | show ...

We | have | proved | that ...
We | may | conclude | that ...
We | have tried to | demonstrate | that ...

CASE 2. Reject a sentence if it is introduced by a connective or by an anaphoric prepositional phrase (List 2). These sentences are dependent on others in the text and should not be included. This also applies to a connective which occurs before or just after the main verb. For example, the following sentence would be rejected because the connective "however" appears just after the verb indicating that the statement relies on some previous sentence for its full interpretation:

Enhanced activities are, however, most apparent at very low ionic strengths.

List 2. Connectives

also, then, therefore, firstly, secondly, thirdly, even, although, while, first, second, third, finally, consequently, similarly, since, hence, perhaps, even if, however, for example, in all, in contrast, as a result, in conclusion.

CASE 3. Reject a sentence if the subject is an anaphoric pronoun (List 3). The following sentence would be rejected because "they" refers to some group of people or a set of results discussed in a previous sentence(s).

They appear to support our hypothesis.

List 3. Anaphoric subject pronouns

he, she, it, they, that, this, those, all, his, her, their.

CASE 4. Reject a sentence if the first conjunct contains an incomplete comparative construction (i.e., missing the comparand which follows *than*) (List 4). The first sentence given below is rejected because the comparative "greater" suggests a comparand in some earlier sentence; but the second is not rejected since the comparand of generated enzymes, "wild types", is given following "than" :

The yield loss was considerably greater in 1986
Enzymes generated were far more active than wild types under certain conditions

List 4. Comparatives

larger, smaller, shorter, higher, greater, other, another, more, less, further, since.

CASE 5. If a sentence begins with any of the following phrases (List 5), then the remainder of the sentence following the phrase must be tested against all the rules for rejection or selection. These phrases cannot be used to resolve anaphors in later sentences and so they are in a sense ignored in the rules. For example, the following sentence starts with an "it ... that" phrase. The remainder of the sentence, "the incremental change of adoption ..." would eventually be selected as non-anaphoric using rule no 9 given below:

It may be remarked that the incremental change of adoption rates were more pronounced in other provinces than in the punjab in the case of almost all the new technologies.

List 5. Non-antecedents

I, we, the author, my, our, it...that, it...to

CASE 6. Reject a sentence if the subject noun phrase begins with an anaphoric quantifier (List 6). The following sentence would be rejected because "each modal peak" refers to some previously introduced entity for its full description:

Each modal peak corresponds to a larval instar.

List 6. Anaphoric quantifiers

each, all, no, total

CASE 7. Reject a sentence if it contains the demonstratives *this* or *these* and others (List 7) anywhere in the sentence. For example, the following sentence would be rejected because "this" refers to some previously observed event:

This could be due to inadequate sampling methods.

List 7. Demonstratives etc.

this, these, the same, the above, the following, the former, the latter

CASE 8. Reject a sentence if the subject noun phrase before the main verb is anaphoric. These generally begin with a quantifier or determiner (*some, every, the*) and are anaphoric (e.g.,The pupae gave rise to adults at the end of the 6 month period) *unless* every occurrence of the determiners or demonstratives (*the, that, those*) is justified by a following preposition, *of* (e.g., the rotation of crops).

CASE 9. Otherwise accept sentence. These sentences are those which are non-anaphoric and should introduce key concepts into the text. Thus the idea of chains of anaphoric reference, whereby subsequent sentences rejected by the above rules, refer to these concepts. The following sentence would be considered to be non-anaphoric since the subject nounphrase cannot be rejected by any of the above rules. Subsequent sentences in the text will be expected to refer to these soil samples:

Soil samples were taken at approximately monthly intervals during November 1985 to June 1987 in an established lucerne field at the Upington Agricultural Research station.

The preliminary analysis of the sentences selected using these definitive rules has begun to suggest how they might be augmented. Tentative statements ***perhaps*** or ***might*** may indicate deselection of a sentence. Likewise, verb tense may also indicate deselection. Furthermore, contextual rules, such as those used in GARP[1,7], to reduce the number of false identifications may be introduced. It is expected that future work to extend and improve the rule set will require the use of a success rate analysis to measure the performance of each rule and the expected enhancement to the system from the addition of further rules.

4. THE ARCHITECTURE OF THE ABSTRACTING SYSTEM

This approach to sentence selection depends on the ability to recognise anaphoric noun-phrases in a sentence and also any rhetorical structures. Most of the rules can be implemented without recourse to real parsing (The GARP rules[7] to recognise anaphors and connectives clearly show this). However, parsing is necessary for the implementation of rule 8 which requires that DNPs can be recognised. As such, it requires that text is unambiguously tagged to permit noun-phrase parsing.

The architecture defines an implementation of the sentence selection and rejection rules as a series of text filters, using the tagger and parser developed for this purpose. The first filter subjects a text to morphological and lexical analysis, assigning grammatical tags to words. This is referred to as initial tagging. Multiple tag assignments are then disambiguated by partial parsing to identify the noun-phrases required by the abstracting rules. This filter works selectively, only assigning tags where they are required by the sentence selection rules. The important feature of the system is that it is designed to be reasonably fast in operation. The use of a parser to disambiguate tags means that a corpus for statistical analysis is not necessary, as in the stochastic methods.[12-14] Also, the parser segments the sentence into phrasal units (in line with O'Shaughnessy[10]) rather than relying on a full linguistic analysis with an extensive grammar. This ensures that there is no restriction on the type of sentence structure which the system will attempt to parse, thus for example it will not *fail* when faced with a *garden path* sentence, e.g., *The largest rocks during the experiment,* where local ambiguity forces a parser to backtrack to arrive at a single correct interpretation.

The only manual intervention required is the initial pre-editing of the texts to separate out headings, captions, figures and formulae, and to mark up the start of each new paragraph. This is, in principle, automatable, particularly assuming access to marked up (e.g., SGML) versions of the text. The information is used at a later automated stage to record structural information which may be used in abstracting.

4.1 Initial word tagging

4.1.1 The dictionary

The construction of a dictionary plays an important part in tagging, especially since the closed class words in the dictionary carry a great deal of information about the syntactic structure of a sentence. The initial tag assignment is performed on the basis of a limited dictionary (ca. 300 words) consisting of most function words and some content words (such as all adverbs not ending in *-ly* and common verbs ***do, be*** and ***have***). Exceptions to the morphology rules are included, e.g., the irregular forms of the nouns ***women, men***. This allows for the assumption that all plural nouns and s-forms of verbs can be identified. The dictionary lists all the possible parts-of-speech for each word. For instance, the word *after* has the possible tags preposition, adverb, or adjective.

An extract of the dictionary with its information in the format **word &tag(features,** is shown in Fig. 1. The features associated with determiners (ana,non) state whether they form anaphoric noun-phrases and the second feature (s,p) state whether the determiner when combined with a noun will form a singular or plural noun-phrase. The features of verbs and auxiliaries (pres,past,ing) state the tense.

Comparison of text words against the dictionary is performed, a sentence at a time, by a sequential merging process coded in the C language. The words of the sentence are first sorted alphabetically in order to facilitate the look-up process. Afterwards, any word found in the dictionary will have received one or more tags.

```
a &det(non,s
about &adv(_,_
about &prep(_,_
again &adv(_,_
against &prep(_,_
alive &adv(_,_
all &predet(_,_
almost &adv(_,_
did &aux(pres,_
did &v(past,_
do &aux(pres,_
do &v(pres,_
doing &v(ing,_
done &v(past,_
during &prep(_,_
each &det(ana,s
```

FIG. 1. *A dictionary extract.*

4.1.2 The morphology analyser

The majority of content words not listed in the dictionary can be tagged using morphological information about suffixes (usually, *-ment, -ity, -ness* indicate nouns, *-ous, -cal* indicate adjectives and *-ly* adverbs). These, with the associated part-of-speech, are listed in Fig. 2. Various checks are used to avoid incorrect assignments. In general, the stem must contain at least three letters. For example, only words with more than three letters ending in *-s* are assigned the associated tag of plural noun or s-form verb. This excludes *bus* and *gas*. A check to ensure that the penultimate letter is not *s, u* or *i* rules out s-form tagging of *discuss, surplus* and *analysis*. In addition to these rules, a word containing a capital letter is tagged as a likely proper noun. The program for the recognition of word endings was written in C using the UNIX LEX utility for pattern matching.

The default categories of single noun or baseform verb are assigned to any word which does not comply with the morphology rules. Research into lexicon construction has shown that the majority of new words will be nouns, abbreviations or proper names (Amsler[15]). An unknown word may also be an adjective, but since adjectives and nouns occur interchangeably in similar positions in our grammar the information lost by treating adjectives as nouns is not considered to be important in this application.

NOUN(-ness, -ics, -ster, -eer, -izer, -grapher, - loger, -er*, -al*, -ty, -ory*, -ry, -cy, -ectomy,. -fy, -y*, -on, -ment, -ance, -art, -ic*, -ick*, -igue*, -ism, -hood, -et, -ship, -age, -encence, -ful*, -ive*, -ard, -or, -ar*, -tude, -um, -ice, -eme, -ean*, -arian*, -ician, -gram, -ete, -ia, -ock, -ode, -ome, -ile*, -ot, -ote, -cule, -cle, -ist, -ade, -ad, -il*, -ese*, -form*, -ine*, -id*, -nd*, -oid*, -gen, -cide, -th, -ule, -ure, -stat, -phil*, -phile*, -phobe*, som*, -some*)

ADJECTIVE(-cal, -ble, -lytic, -logic, -genic, -like, -ward, -lent, -ior, -ular, -an, -ose, -ac, -ant, -esque, -excent, -ern)

ADVERB(-wards, -ively, -ibly, -fully, -ily, -ically, -edly, -itive, -ativc, -fuge, -wise)

ADJECTIVE & ADVERB(-less, -ways, -way, -ly, -st, -fold)

POSS(-'s)

NOUN(plural) & VERB(sform) (-s)

VERB(edform) (-ed)

VERB(ingform) & NOUN (-ing)

ADJECTIVE & VERB (-ish)

VERB(-ize, -esce)

*may also indicate an adjective

FIG. 2. *Morphology information.*

The output from this stage is a set of Prolog clauses describing the text in the following form, **con(SN,SP,EP,Word,Category,Feature1,Feature2)** where,

[SN] is the Sentence Number in which the word occurs.
[SP] is the Start Position of the word in the sentence.
[EP] is the End Position of the word in the sentence.
[Word] is the word in question.
[Category] is the assigned category as indicated by the recognised ending of the word, or by the dictionary.
[Feature1] is the tense of a verb or the anaphoric indicator of a determiner.
[Feature2] is the number feature of singular or plural.

Example predicates for a sentence are shown below in **Figure 3.**

```
con(8,0,1,developing,v,ing,_).con(8,0,1,developing,n,_s).
con(8,1,2,countries,n,_p).con(8,1,2,countries,v,pres,_).
con(8,2,3,today,n,_s).
con(8,3,4,do,aux,pres,_).con(8,3,4,do,v,pres,_).
con(8,4,5,not,adv,_,_).
con(8,5,6,have,aux,past,_).con(8,5,6,have,v,pres,s).
con(8,6,7,a,det,non,s).
con(8,7,8,world,n,_s).con(8,7,8,world,v,pres,s).
con(8,8,9,of,prep,_,_).
con(8,9,10,resources,n,_p).con(8,9,10,resources,v,pres,_).
con(8,10,11,to,adv,_,_).con(8,10,11,to,aux,_,_).con(8,10,11,to,prep,_,_)
con(8,11,12,freely,adj,_,_).con(8,11,12,freely,adv,_,_).
con(8,12,13,exploit,n,_s).con(8,12,13,exploit,v,pres,s).
con(8,13,14,and,coord,_,_).
con(8,14,15,a,det,non,s).
con(8,15,16,few,det,non,p).
con(8,16,17,are,aux,ing,_).con(8,16,17,are,v,pres,_).
con(8,17,18,now,adv,_,_).con(8,17,18,now,subord,_,_).
con(8,18,19,beginning,v,ing,_).con(8,18,19,beginning,n,_s).
con(8,19,20,',',punct,_,_).
con(8,20,21,out,adv,_,_).con(8,20,21,out,prep,_,_).
con(8,21,22,of,prep,_,_).
con(8,22,23,necessity,n,_s).
con(8,23,24,',',punct,_,_).
con(8,24,25,to,adv,_,_).con(8,24,25,to,aux,_,_).con(8,24,25,to,prep,_,_)
con(8,25,26,look,n,_s).con(8,25,26,look,v,pres,s).
con(8,26,27,towards,prep,_,_).
con(8,27,28,a,det,non,s).
con(8,28,29,more,adj,_,_).con(8,28,29,more,adv,_,_).con(8,28,29,more,n,_s)
con(8,29,30,self,n,_s).con(8,29,30,self,v,pres,s).
con(8,30,31,reliant,adj,_,_).
con(8,31,32,road,n,_s).
con(8,32,33,to,adv,_,_).con(8,32,33,to,aux,_,_).con(8,32,33,to,prep,_,_)
con(8,33,34,development,n,_s).
```

FIG. 3. *Prolog predicates containing tag information.*

4.2 Disambiguation by local syntactic context
Clearly this process of initial tagging creates a number of tags which are extremely unlikely in the immediate context. We experimented with the possibility of using a set of heuristic constraint rules to eliminate some of these. These rules comprise a trigger and a consequence. The trigger is the presence of a certain assigned tag and the consequence is the selection from a choice of tags following the trigger by the removal of the unlikely tags. These rules are presented in Table 1 with an example of the original set of predicates resulting from the morphology and lexicon analysis. These rules state: if a noun-or-verb follows a determiner, retract the verb; if an auxiliary follows an auxiliary-or-verb, retract the verb; if an adjective-or-adverb follows a verb, retract the adjective; if a noun-or-present verb follows a verb-or-nonpresent auxiliary, retract verb and the auxiliary; and finally, if a modal-or-noun follows a determiner, retract the modal. The italics in the examples indicate the removal of a predicate from the database as a result of the rule.

RULE	EXAMPLE
con(_n,_p1,_p2,_det,_,_), con(_n,_p2,_p3,_n,_,_), con(_n,_p2,_p3,_v,_,_), retract(con(_n,_p2,_p3,_v,_,_)	con(4,0,1,the,det,ana,_) con(4,1,2,detectors,n,_p) *con(4,1,2,detectors,v,pres,_)*
con(_n,_p1,_p2,_aux,_,_) con(_n,_p1,_p2,_v,_,_) con(_n,_p2,_,_aux,_,_) retract(con(_n,_p1,_p2,_v,_,_)	con(1,0,1,it,pron,_s) con(1,1,2,has,aux,past,_) *con(1,1,2,has,v,pres,s)* con(1,2,3,been,aux,_,_)
con(_n,_p1,_p2,_v,_,_) con(_n,_p2,_,_adj,_,_) con(_n,_p2,_,_adv,_,_) retract(con(_n,_p2,_,_adj,_,_)	con(1,3,4,suggested,v,past,_) *con(1,4,5,recently,adj,_,_)* con(1,4,5,recently,adv,_,_)
con(_n,_p1,_p2,_aux,_t,_), not(_t=pres), con(_n,_p1,_p2,_v,pres,_), con(_n,_p2,_,_n,_,_), con(_n,_p2,_,_v,pres,_), retract(con(_n,_p1,_p2,_aux,_,_)), retract(con(_n,_p2,_,_v,pres,_))	*con(5,6,7,are,aux,ing,_)* con(5,6,7,are,v,pres,_) con(5,7,8,20cm,n,_p) *con(5,7,8,20cm,v,pres,s)* con(5,8,9,apart,adv,_,_)
con(_n,_p1,_p2,_det,_,_) con(_n,_p2,_,_modal,_,_) con(_n,_p2,_,_n,_,_) retract(con(_n,_p2,_,_modal,_,_)	con(2,0,1,the,det,ana,_) *con(2,1,2,will,modal,_,_)* con(2,1,2,will,n,_s)

Table 1 : *Heuristic Constraint Rules*

These rules were applied to a text of 470 words: 236 of these words were correctly and unambiguously tagged by the morphology and lexicon. A further 70 words had their tags correctly selected by these constraint rules. This gives a total success rate of 65% and leaves 164 words to be resolved. It is possible to continue developing the rules to deal with more cases. Hindle[16] developed a set of about 350 rules of this type using a corpus of texts and statistical analysis to determine the frequency with which certain categories are likely to occur together in a sentence. However, he reported a success rate of 81%, which meant that nearly 1 out 5 of the ambiguous words are incorrectly disambiguated in any given sentence. SIMPR, a knowledge-based text storage and retrieval system,[17] pre-processes text for automatic indexing using morphological analysis to identify the word tokens, or tags, in text. Using a lexicon considerably larger than ours, of approximately 57000 entries, and approximately 400 rules for context-dependent disambiguation according to the particular location in which each word occurs, it was able to resolve about 95% of the morphological ambiguities. In addition, the rules expressed as a constraint grammar eliminate around 90% of syntactic ambiguities and produces a syntactic representation giving a structure name (such as noun-phrase) for each major groupings of words.

The use of existing tagging and parsing software, such as CLAWS[18] was considered. However, the output of CLAWS, an unstructured sequence of tags, did not appear to suit our requirements for later processing. We only became aware of the constraint grammar parser used in SIMPR,[19-21] once the work reported here had got under way. Our approach was, then, to adapt in-house components using the fragments of grammar rules to capture much of what is stated in the heuristic constraint rules described above. In this way, further ambiguity following initial tagging will be resolved during the parsing process. Since the aim was to parse the sentences to identify noun-phrases it was decided to continue the tag disambiguation process using grammar rules, the *local parser*, with an added mechanism to deal with the problems of partial parsing, the *global parser*. The five heuristic constraint rules are retained since they will make subsequent parsing significantly faster.

4.2.1 The tag disambiguator

Locally, a bottom-up chart parser is used with a grammar to group words together that are likely to form noun groups or verb groups by exploiting the word order in these groups. Thus boundaries may be identified; for example, a quantifier generally starts a noun group and an auxiliary initiates a verb group. In this way, unrestricted text can be partially analysed using the fixed lower level structure of some constituents to disambiguate tags. At a global level, the parser attempts to link a phrasal unit found to earlier units so that clauses can be identified.

A major problem in locating phrase boundaries is encountered when they are not marked by function words. For example, consider the sentence: ***The blue book defines file transfer,*** where all the words apart from ***the*** are possible verbs or nouns. Faced with this sequence of unidentified words, number agreement may be used to decide that ***defines*** is the verb following a singular nounphrase (NP). However, there are always some difficult cases, consider: ***The boy adores fish*** **and** ***The boy scouts fish.*** Based on number agreement alone, it is not possible to state when the verb is in the s-form. Likewise ed-forms of verbs may also present problems. Consider: ***The machines scattered papers*** and ***The machine disentangles scattered papers.*** In such cases, it is hoped that the remaining words in the sentence will force the decision. Thus, at present, these undecided cases are dealt with in the global parser.

4.2.2 The parser

Definite Clause Grammar rules are adapted for use with a bottom-up parser by storing the results on the arcs of a chart. The basic principle of bottom-up parsing is to reduce the words whose categories match the right hand side of a grammar rule to a phrase of the type on the left hand side of the rule. There are several rule invocation strategies for chart parsing. A left corner parsing strategy[22] was used which is based on an interaction of data-driven analysis and prediction based on grammar rules. Some state-of-the-art heuristics[23] were used to cut the parser's search space roughly by a third. Details of the implementation are recorded in Johnson, Black, Neal and Paice.[24]

4.2.3 The grammar

The left corner chart parsing strategy is used with a predominantly noun-phrase grammar to return a partial analysis of the text. The NP grammar can correctly identify NPs especially when they are separated by an auxiliary verb, a common verb (shown in Sentence 1 below) or a determiner which signals the end of a verbphrase (VP, as shown in Sentence 2 below). The NPs selected for these sentences are given from their start to end position.

Sentence 1.

0 another 1 important 2 feature 3 of 4 expert 5
systems 6 is 7 their 8 mode 9 of 10 operation 11.

```
0 6    np(nom(nom(prmod(adj(another,adj(important))),n(feature)),
         pmod(pp(of,np(n(expert,n(systems)))))))
7 11   np(poss(poss(ppron(their))),nom(n(mode),
         pmod(pp(of,np(n(operation))))))
```

Sentence 2.

0 this 1 paper 2 considers 3 the 4 need 5 to 6
provide 7 some 8 form 9 of 10 local 11 area 12 network
13 management 14 .

```
0 2np   (det(this),n(paper))
3 5np   (art(the),n(need))
7 14np  (quant(some),nom(n(form),pmod(pp(of,np(nom(prmod(
          adj(local)),n(area,n(network,n(management)))))))))
```

4.2.4 The global parser

The determining of higher-level syntactic structures that link these groups together is difficult, especially when dealing with unrestricted text. The approach taken is to recover the units that occur in-between the NPs initially selected. In sentence 2 above from positions 2 to 3 there is a verb and from positions 5 to 7 NPs. In the global parser these are acceptable units to occur between NPs and so the NPs are accepted as correct. Further illustration of the global parsing is shown below to indicate the categories which may appear between two NPs. Square brackets are used to indicate the optional presence of a category, e.g., [,]. Notice that the parser is fairly rudimentary. For example, it is not necessary to identify whether a preposition occurs in or between NPs. The parser only does what is necessary in this application and in doing so reduces the search space and thus the time taken.

{np} [,] prep {np}	{a primary factor} in {public health}
{np} [,] conj {np}	{large numbers of people in the rural areas} and {old quarters of cities}
{np} conj prep {np}	{the areas in the rural quarter of the city} and in {the poorer quarters}
{np} relative clause	{technologies} which are efficient in the use of local materials
prep {np} [,] {np}	By {cosmic ray events}, {the distribution}
{np} vp {np}	{the west's technological development} was founded on {the cheap raw materials}

In addition to the global parsing rules, a set of recovery procedures are needed when the group appearing between two NPs is not accepted. These are given below and are all performed on the arcs built up during the chart parsing.

{np1} relative {np2} **& np1** ends with a past particle →	{the results suggested} that {the larvae}
reduce np1 to **recover vp "suggested"**	{the results} suggested that {the larvae}
{np1} aux {np2} →	{each packet} may {travel by the same route}
reduce np2 to recover vp "may travel"	may travel by {the same route}
{np1} vp conj {np2} →	{we} must research and {develop}
recover np2 as vp	{we} must research and develop
{np1} adverb prep {np2} →	{the rate of n release depends} essentially on {the soil temperature}
reduce np1 to recover vp	{the rate of n release} depends essentially on {the soil temperature}
{np1} {np2} →	{industries depend on selling}{their wares}
reduce np1 to recover vp	{industries} depend on selling {their wares}
pron {np2} →	it {depends on the rules}
reduce np2 to recover vp	it depends on {the rules}

5. EVALUATION OF THE PARSER

The results in Table 2 were obtained for 310 sentences parsed from test texts, Test A, which were not used in the development of the parser. Similar results were obtained during earlier experiments, Test B, over a total of 1200 sentences.

TYPE	NO.OF SENTENCES Test A	Test B	PERCENTAGE Test A	Test B
ALL CORRECT	135	516	43.3%	43%
CORRECT 1ST NP&VP	124	504	40.2%	42%
INCORRECT	51	180	16.5%	15%

Table 2: *Evaluation of the parser*

The types of analysis used to obtain these statistics are described below.

The following sentence is an example which was considered to be correctly parsed: ***Seeds of both species were germinated on moist filter papers which were soaked in de-ionized water in a constant temperature box.*** The parse results are as follows:

```
np(0,4,np(ana,p):(np(n(seeds)),pp(of),np(art(both),n(species))))
vp(4,7,vp(_,_) : vp(aux(were),vp(vp(v(germinated)),on))).
np(7,21,np(non,s):((np(nom(prmod(adj(moist,np(n(filter)))),
n(papers))),relnp(rel(which,seq(vp(aux(were),vp(vp(v(soaked)),in)),
np(nom(prmod(part(de-ionized)),n(water))))))),pp(in),
np(art(a),n(constant,n(temperature,n(box)))))).
```

The following sentence has only its first NP and VP correctly parsed (this being adequate for our purposes): ***Sprinkler irrigation was provided with the rows configured in such a way that runoff was prevented from contaminating adjacent treatment areas.*** Although all the NPs and VPs were found, the word ***such*** was tagged as an adjective and not as a predeterminer. The expression ***such a way*** could not be recognised. This meant that it was unable to find a permissible construction between the NPs: ***the rows configured*** and ***a way***. As a consequence, the relative clause starting ***that runoff*** could not be joined to the NP.

```
np(0,2,np(_,s):np(n(sprinkler,n(irrigation)))).
vp(2,5,vp(_,_):(vp(aux(was),vp(v(provided))),pp(with))).
np(5,8,np(ana,_):np(art(the),n(rows,pmod(part(configured))))).
vp(15,17,vp(past,_):vp(aux(was),vp(v(prevented)))).
np(18,21,np(_,p):np(n(adjacent,n(treatment,n(areas)))))).

unselected(10,12,np(non,s):np(art(a),n(way))).
unselected(13,14,np(_,s):np(n(runoff))).
```

However, this does demonstrate an advantage of this approach. There are many expressions which may occur in sentences but which may cause difficulties when trying to write a grammar for unrestricted text. For example, along with the example ***in such a way*** we might also find the expressions, ***is some what surprising*** or ***greater than that of***. The partial parser is able to ignore these expressions, which means that the delimitation of NPs would rely on other clues such as a noun-phrase begins with a determiner.

Finally, in some sentences the first noun-phrase or verb-phrase is not correctly identified owing to restrictions in coverage of the grammar. More compendious grammars exist but the project lacked the resources to assimilate them with its software environment.

Although there is much scope for improvement it was decided that the tag disambiguation method by partial parsing was adequate for this application. Such improvements may be obtained by simply extending the grammar rules. For example, the errors outlined above may be dealt with by including idiomatic phrases in the dictionary (e.g., ***more than ever***), and by assigning more tags in the dictionary (***such*** tagged as a predeterminer). However, at present the tagger and noun-phrase parser has allowed us to produce abstracts using the sentence selection rules outlined at the start of this paper.

6. EVALUATION OF THE EXTRACTS

This system should, according to the principle, produce abstracts which are cohesive pieces of English and reproduce the sense of the original text. An example abstract produced is given in Appendix 1, abstract 1. Alongside this are abstracts produced using a technique which relies on keywords, using Earl's[25] algorithm, (abstract 2) and one which relies on the identification of indicator constructs outlined in Paice,[5] (abstract 3), for comparison. The methods for producing these additional abstracts are outlined in Black and Johnson.[6]

At a glance, it may be said that our objectives have been met. None of the selected sentences in any of the three abstracts is obviously inappropriate. However, whilst both abstracts 1 and 2 are more informative than abstract 3, abstract 1 is more cohesive than 2. However, it could be argued that abstract 1 is too long, which raises the question, is there a *correct* length for an abstract? Clearly, there are limits: the abstract should convey more information than the title alone, and it should be shorter than the full text. As a rule of thumb, the length of an abstract of 250-500 words is often stated.[26] Biological Abstracts, on the other hand, advised its abstractors to aim at 3-5% of the length of the original text.[27] Thus, although we can give the actual length of the abstracts in the appendix in terms of a percentage of the full text, it is generally accepted amongst abstractors that an abstract does not need to be a specified length but should be long enough to convey the information to allow the abstract to fulfill its function.

There are a number of problems to address when seeking an objective framework for the evaluation of these abstracts. In particular, it is not realistic to base the evaluation on a target set of extracted key sentences from the source text: a given idea might be expressed in two or three different alternative sentences[4] and the whole abstract by many valid alternative subsets of the sentences in the text. We instead propose evaluation in terms of the information conveyed in the selected sentences. A template is created, before looking at the abstracts obtained, which sets out the information found in the text under certain headings: for an example, see Fig. 4. The scores in Fig. 4 are arbitrary values, assigned by the authors, intended to indicate the relative importance of the various ideas. A score of 5 is used for a concept which is assumed to be central to the paper, and which must be mentioned in the abstract. A score of 0 is used for a concept which, although is not necessary, would not appear out of place in the abstract. The assignment of intermediate weights is a rather subjective activity. However, what is important is not the actual scores but the ranking they imply. The plausibility of this scheme used to score the abstracts was tested by composing an abstract by hand, based on the tabulation. This is shown in Fig. 5 with the automatic abstract and an abstract produced by CAB for comparison.

It is important to note that evaluation is not only a matter of information selection. We also need to find some means of evaluating the abstracts in terms of their cohesiveness. In addition, we also found that we had to evaluate the success of the tagger and parser in its use in the sentence selection rules. As stated above, with limited resources this system is obviously rather rudimentary.

Despite these problems, a preliminary analysis of one abstract is demonstrated below. To indicate the success of our prime objective of producing a coherent piece of text, anaphoric references are categorised in the abstract as follows. If apparently anaphoric expressions occur which are considered to be acceptable, they are marked by italics. If the anaphoric expression is resolved by other sentences included in the abstract, they are marked by bold type and a subscript marks the sentence number in which the reference is found. Finally, as in sentence 35, any unresolved anaphor would be marked in capitals. Sentence 35 was selected for its indicator phrase: but the expression referred to, ***the results***, is provided in the previous sentence:*Since recovery of first-instar larvae in field collected samples was unsatisfactory, the head-capsules of 20 first-instar larvae, hatched in the laboratory, were measured.* Unfortunately this sentence was rejected. Our rules include *since* as a connective, although it is used here as an *intra* sentence connective. This highlights our need to develop and refine our rules based on the results.

Text: "Some aspects of the biology of the white-fringed beetle, in the Lower Orange River irrigation area of South Africa."

NO	Topic:-		score	extract	CAB
1.	Subject sp. is:	White-fringed Beetle	5	5 [1]	5
		(or 'beetle' 1)	-	-	-
2.	Origin of sp. is:	S.America	0	0 [1]	-
3.	Incidence of sp. is:	E.US, SE.Australia etc	0	0 [1]	-
4.	Role of sp. is:	pest of Lucerne	4	-	4
		(or 'pest'or 'lucerne' 2)	-	2 [1]	-
5.	Parts damaged are:	roots	1	-	1
		underground stems	0	-	-
6.	Stage of 1. causing 5:	larva	1	-	1
	Aim:-				
7.	Purpose of study is:	biology of 1.	1	1 [20]	1
8.	Stage of focus is:	larva	0	-	0
	Setting:-				
9.	Locality of study:	LOR irrign. area of S.Africa	3	[3]title	3
		(or Lower Orange River 1)			
		(or 'S.Africa 1)			
	Methods:-				
10.	General method is:	survey	0	-	0
11.	number of localities:	several	0	-	0
12.	specific methods:	soil sampling in lucerne fields	2	2 [25]	-
		(or just 'soil sampling' 1)			
		count & sort larvae	0	0 [26]	-
13.	Measurements:	head capsule widths of larvae	2	2 [41]	1
14.	Analysis method:	probit analysis	0	0 [41]	-
Findings:-					
15.	Geographical distribn.	recent eastward spread	0	-	-
16.	Infestation rates	highest in central & east			
		parts of region	0	-	-
17.	No. of larval instars:	7	3	-	3
18.	Life cycle period	12-15 months	2	-	2
19.	Larval period	9-12 months	2	-	2
20.	Maturation of larvae:	faster at higher temperature	2		
		(or affected by temp. 1)	-	1[53]	-
21.	Peak populations:	February	0		
22.	Distribn. in soil:	mostly in top 300 mm.	0		
		depths down to 750 mm.	1	-	-
		disagrees with earlier report	1	-	-
	TOTALS		30	16	23

FIG. 4. *Evaluation of the abstracts*

The abstract is then scored against the template, as shown in the column headed *extract* in Fig. 4. The square brackets show the sentence numbers from the abstract given below. This abstract only gets a score of 16, including the title which covers idea 9. This low score could be shown in a better light if it is considered that an abstract for this text from CAB Abstracts, shown in Figure 5, scores 23 out of a possible 30. Due to the arbitrary nature of the scores, the exact numerical totals are not intended to be taken too seriously. For example, idea 4, *pest of Lucerne*, is not explicitly stated in the abstract, only implied and therefore is assigned a score of 2 instead of 4. The main point is that where the highly scored ideas are not included then the abstract is penalised accordingly. In this example abstract, findings are almost unrepresented. In the template, it was considered that idea 17 referring to the findings was especially worth reporting. This does not appear in the abstract, but is included in the CAB abstract which again scores higher.

MODEL Abstract.
This paper concerns the White-fringed Beetle, G.leucoloma, a pest whose larvae cause damage to the roots of lucerne. A study of the biology of this insect was carried out in the Lower Orange River irrigation area of South Africa. Soil samples were taken, and head-capsule widths of larvae were measured. Seven larval instars were found to occur. The total life cycle took 12-15 months. The larvae matured in 9-12 months: the period was shorter at warmer seasons of the year. Larvae occurred down to 750mm below the soil surface, in disagreement with an earlier report.
(**11%** of the full text)

CAB Abstract.
The biology of Graphognathus leucoloma was studied in the Lower Orange River irrigation area of South Africa in 1985. Information is presented on its geographic distribution within the region, number and size of larval instars, and phenology. Larvae caused severe damage to the roots of lucerne throughout the region. During its life cycle of 12 to 15 months, 7 larval instars were present over a period of 9-12 months.
(**6.3%** of the full text)

AUTOMATIC Abstract
Note/ Sentences marked with '?' could be excluded using further criteria which have been considered for the development of the system. These are sentences which begin with a verbal noun (e.g., *readings*) or a relational noun (e.g., *yields, measurements*) which assume a relation with some previously mentioned entity (e.g., *measurements of larvae size*). Sentences marked with *i* are selected on the basis that they contain an indicator construct. The only occurrence of unresolved anaphora is in sentence 35. In the text the results refers to the measurement of the head-capsule width of first-instar larvae hatched in the laboratory.

1 the white fringed beetle, graphognathus leucoloma, a south american insect, is an established pest of pastures and crops in *the* eastern united states, south eastern australia, new zealand and south africa.
10? reproduction is parthenogenetic and only females are known.
15? pupation takes place in **the**$_{1:crops}$ upper soil layers from where **the**$_{15:pupation}$ adults make their way to the soil surface.
20i in *this* paper results of *our* investigations on *the* biology of **this**$_{1:beetle}$ insect are reported.
24 a single survey was conducted during september 1985 in established lucerne at seven localities in *the* lower orange river irrigation area.
25 five soil samples were taken at random in lucerne fields at **each**$_{24}$ locality.
26? larvae were sorted from **the**$_{25}$ soil samples by hand and stored in 70 percent ethyl alcohol.
28 soil samples were taken at approximately monthly intervals during November 1985 to June 1987 in an established lucerne field at *the* Upington Agricultural Research Station.
30? larvae and pupae were removed from **the**$_{28}$ soil samples by hand and stored in 70 % ethyl alcohol.
31? adults were sampled in 50 **pit traps** in **the**$_{28}$ soil which were placed at random in **this**$_{28}$ lucerne field.
35i **THE** results were subjected to probit analysis.
39 the highest percentage rate of infestation occurred in the central parts **of the region.**
41 as instar sizes frequently overlap, probit analysis was used to calculate instar head capsule size using the method of frampton.
53 temperature appears to play an important role in the duration of especially **the**$_{20:biology}$ pupal and adult stages.
(**22%** of the full text)

FIG. 5. *Abstracts*

7. CONCLUSION

This paper has described an enhanced sentence selection method for automatic abstracting. These rules rely on grammatical criteria to identify desirable isolated sentences to include in an abstract. A simple system, based on the limited resources of a dictionary, morphological analyser and noun-phrase parser, is used to satisfy this requirement. The advantage of using a partial grammar and a chart parser for simple recovery procedures means that no restrictions are placed on the text handled.

The results suggest that this work may be a step in the right direction for automatic abstracting. However, much remains to be done. The output from our program is far from perfect and our sentence selection rules need to be refined to produce shorter, more acceptable abstracts. We have identified the need to extend the dictionary, particularly to recognise idiomatic phrases, and the need to refine the parsing rules. At present, the system is rather rudimentary, designed to be fast in its operation while allowing us to explore various automatic abstracting techniques. We have been encouraged by the results of the sentence selection rules outlined in this paper. The main drawback is that the abstracts produced are too long, although this could be helped by use of alternative sentence selection criteria. Positional criteria may be employed to eliminate sentences which occur in the middle of the text or paragraphs.[3,4]

It is not generally sufficient to concatenate a set of isolated key sentences from a text. An understanding of the structure of texts and how they are organised beyond the level of the sentence must be utilised in the process. After all, the author of the text will have endeavoured to use the structure to help convey meaning and to ensure that key concepts are introduced at appropriate places.

8. FUTURE WORK

Further understanding of rhetorical structure theory and text grammars (e.g. [28,29]) may provide a way of analysing text according to the way in which the meaning is organised to convey some kind of message. Ideally, it may provide a means to allow us to keep track of the relationships between a text's propositions *and* to determine the relative importance of the sentences concerned (ideas along these lines have been expressed by Paice [30]). Integrating this work into that of automatic abstracting may enable us to further our ultimate goal of producing coherent and useful abstracts.

REFERENCES

1. PAICE, C.D. Constructing literature abstracts by computer: techniques and prospects. *Information Processing and Management*, 26(1) 1990, 171-186.
2. LUHN, H.P. The automatic creation of literature abstracts. *I.B.M. Journal of Research and Development*, 2(2) 1958, 159-165.
3. BAXENDALE, P.B. Man-made index for technical literature - an experiment. *I.B.M. Journal of Research and Development*, 2(4) 1958, 354-361.
4. EDMUNDSON, H.P. New methods in automatic abstracting. *Journal of the Association of Computing Machinery*, 16(2) 1969, 264-285.
5. PAICE, C.D. The automatic generation of literature abstracts: an approach based on the identification of self-indicating phrases. *In*: R.N.Oddy, S.E Robertson, C,J van Rijsbergen and P.W Williams, *(eds). Information Retrieval Research.* Butterworths, 1981, 172-191.
6. BLACK, W.J AND F.C JOHNSON. A practical evaluation of two rule-based automatic abstracting techniques. *Expert Systems for Information Management*, 1(3) 1992, 159-177.
7. PAICE, C.D AND G.D HUSK. Towards the automatic recognition of anaphoric features in English text: the impersonal pronoun it. *Computer Speech and Language*, 1(3) 1987, 109-132.
8. ALLEN, J. *Natural language understanding.* Menlo Park: Benjamin/Cummings Publishing, 1987.
9. NEAL, A.P. A tool for the syntactic resolution of anaphora. *In*: K. Jones *(ed). The Structuring of Information.* Proceedings of Informatics 11. London: Aslib, 1991, 27-36.
10. O'SHAUGHNESSY, D.O. Parsing with a small dictionary for applications such as text to speech. *Computational Linguistics*, 15(2) 1989, 97-109.
11. PEREIRA, F.C.N AND D.H.D WARREN. Definite clause grammars for language analysis - a survey of the formalism and a comparison with augmented transition networks. *Artificial Intelligence*, 13 1980, 231-278.
12. CHURCH, K. A stochastic parts program and NP parser for unrestricted text *Proceedings of the second Association of Computational Linguistics conference on Applied Natural Language Processing.* 1988, 136-144.
13. DEROSE, S.J. Grammatical category disambiguation by statistical optimization. *Computational Linguistics*, 14(1) 1988, 31-39.
14. MARKEN, C.G. Parsing the LOB corpus. *Association of Computational Linguistics Annual Meeting*, 1990, 243-251.
15. AMSLER, R.A. Research toward the development of a lexical knowledge base for natural language processing. *In*: N.J. Belkin and C.J. Van Rijsbergen, *(eds). Proceedings of the 12th Annual International ACM SIGIR Conference on Research and Development in Information Retrieval.* Cambridge MA, New York: ACM, 1989, 242-249.
16. HINDLE, D. Acquiring disambiguation rules from text. *Association of Computational Linguistics Annual Meeting*, 1989, 118-125.
17. GIBB, F. Knowledge-based indexing in SIMPR: Integration of natural language processing and principles of subject analysis in an automated indexing system. *Journal of Document and Text Management* 1(2), 1993, 131-154.
18. GARSIDE, R. The CLAWS word tagging system. *In*: R. Garside, G. Leech and G. Sampson *(eds). A computational analysis of English: A corpus-based approach.* London: Longman, 1987.
19. KARLSSON, F. Constraint Grammar as a Framework for Parsing Running Text. *In*: Hans Karlgren *(ed). Proceedings of the XIIIth International Conference on Computational Linguistics*, Vol 3, Helsinki 1990, 168-173.
20. KARLSSON, F., VOUTILAINEN, A., HEIKILLA, J. and ANTTIL, A. *Natural Language Processing for Information Retrieval Purposes.* Helsinki: Research Unit for Computational Linguistics, 1990, (SIMPR-RUCL-1990-13.4e).
21. KARLSSON, F., VOUTILAINEN, A., ANTTILA, A. and HEIKILLA, J. Constraint Grammar: a Language-Independent System for Parsing Unrestricted Text, with an Application to English. *In*: *Workshop Notes from the Ninth National Conference on Artificial Intelligence (AAAI-91)*, California: American Association for Artificial Intelligence, July 15, 1991.
22. GAZDAR, G. AND C. MELLISH. *Natural language processing in Prolog: An introduction to computational linguistics.* Wokingham: Addison-Wesley, 1989.
23. WIREN, M. A comparison of rule-invocation strategies in context-free chart parsing. *Association of Computational Linguistics Proceedings, Third European Conference, 1987*, 226-235.
24. JOHNSON, F.C., BLACK, W.J., NEAL, A.P. AND C.D. PAICE. Development and

evaluation of a parser for use in an automatic abstracting system. *British Library Abstracting Report*, no. 3, May 1992.
25. EARL, L.L. Experiments in automatic abstracting and indexing. *Information Storage and Retrieval*, 6(4) 1970, 313-334
26. ROWLEY, J. *Abstracting and indexing*. London:Clive Bingley, 1992, p.14.
27. BATTEN, W.E (ed). *Handbook of special libraries and information work*. London:ASLIB, 1975, p.131.
28. MANN, W.C AND S.A THOMPSON. Rhetorical structure theory: A theory of text organisation. *ISI Reprint Series ISI/RS-87-190*, Information Science Institute, 1987.
29. SILLINCE, J.A.A. Argumentation-based indexing for information retrieval from learned articles. *Journal of Documentation*, 48(4) 1992, 387-406.
30. PAICE, C.D. The rhetorical structure of expository texts. *In:* K. Jones *ed. The Structuring of Information*. Proceedings of Informatics 11. London: Aslib, 1991, 1-25.

APPENDIX 1

These abstracts are taken from the same paper to illustrate the results of using three different techniques for sentence selection. The first is produced using the sentence selection rules described in this paper; the second is produced using Earl's[20] keyword technique; and the third is produced using the identification of Paice's[5] indicator constructs. The original article contained 107 sentences and each abstract is expressed as a percentage of this length.

1. British Library project for Abstracting technique.

Developing countries today do not have a world of resources to freely exploit and a few are now beginning, out of necessity, to look towards a more self reliant road to development. This article deals particularly with the indigenous technologies of cooling, using largely natural sources of energy and techniques which have been developed by people locally. The supply of safe drinking water is a primary factor in the maintenance of public health in developing countries. Consideration must be given not only to the water source and its quality but also to the distribution and storage systems. Nile water and water from irrigation channels is unfit for drinking and often carries dangerous pathogens such as bilharzia larvae. Drinking water is usually scooped out of the pot with a dipper, though it was discovered that water collected at the base after it had been filtered through the pot is much cleaner. An experiment was set up using portable meteorological testing equipment in order to evaluate the cooling action of the maziara. Water samples were taken at various stages in the system, to be measured later in the laboratory for purity. Over a 16 hour test period a single jar produced 1700 k cal of cooling. Samples were taken from the river source and from the effluent runoff after water had been allowed to filter through the maziara system. Samples were tested in the government laboratories in the luxor hospital and it was found that the filtered outflow water was pure to the government's drinking water standards, even though the original nile water that was put into the jar was contaminated. The result of the purification tests illustrates that chances of drinking water contamination can be reduced if the maziara's filtering action is used. Technological sophistication is usually measured in terms of the number of transistors or moving parts. If we evaluate sophistication in terms of efficiency we find the opposite. The hazards of modern air conditioning systems are rarely advertised in the glossy brochures distributed by companies dealers in the third world. Mild shocks sometimes occurs at the entry of an excessively cooled building, if the temperature differences between the inside and outside are too great. Comparative experiments are currently being planned by the authors in Iran, in the use of water jars for air cooling within buildings as against mechanical cooling. In Iran, wind shafts often lead to basement water cisterns. A domestic cooler was developed using a porous compartment to hold the food. This article has dealt with some of the technological innovations that have grown out of an indigenous scientific approach to a basic problem cooling in many third world countries. **(18.7%)**

2. Keyword Method

The maziara is a traditional water cooling and purification system used in rural areas of upper Egypt. As the air becomes drier more water evaporates from the water jar's surface and the cooling rate increases. The hazards of modern air conditioning systems are rarely advertised in the glossy brochures distributed by companies' dealers in the third world. Comparative experiments are currently being planned by the authors in Iran, in the use of water jars for air cooling within buildings as against mechanical cooling. This article has dealt with some of the technological innovations that have grown out of an indigenous scientific approach to a basic problem cooling in many third world countries. **(4.7%)**

3. Indicator Method

This article deals particularly with the indigenous technologies of cooling, using largely natural sources of energy and techniques which have been developed by people locally. The result of the purification tests illustrates that chances of drinking water contamination can be reduced if the maziara's filtering action is used. This article has dealt with some of the technological innovations that have grown out of an indigenous scientific approach to a basic problem cooling in many third world countries. **(2.8%)**

Chapter 9
Envoi

Historical Note: Information Retrieval and the Future of an Illusion 555
D.R. Swanson

As previous chapters have shown, IR has developed slowly but consistently since the initial studies some four decades ago. The wide range of models and techniques that have been developed since that time provide a firm basis for the current generation of IR systems, which provide interactive, end user access to textual information resources on a scale that would have been unthinkable, even just a few years ago.

It is inevitable, indeed appropriate, that the Reader should focus on successes such as these. However, the sheer scale and technological sophistication of present-day systems must not blind people to the substantial, inherent problems that lie at the heart of IR. These are problems that relate to concepts such as use of language and the perception of relevance, and that cannot be eliminated simply by the application of massive machine power and glitzy user interfaces. We hence close with a paper written by Swanson (1988), based on his more than three decades of research in IR. Swanson refers to these inherent problems in terms of "postulates of impotence", which are statements about the nature of the IR world and the necessary limits it imposes on retrieval systems. They thus show why an IR system can never be expected to provide the "perfect" performance that characterises many other types of information processing system.

At first sight, the reader may be dismayed by Swanson's downbeat assessment of the limits of the feasible; we, conversely, prefer to regard it as demonstrating why IR is such an inherently fascinating subject for study and why there will always be scope for novel approaches to content based retrieval. Swanson, indeed, sees positive opportunities in three "postulates of fertility" that he also discusses in this paper. The current intense interest in IR engendered by the World Wide Web and the rich technological resources that computing offers, mean that IR is becoming of importance to a much wider range of researchers and practitioners than has been the case in the past. We believe that constructive responses to the state of affairs that Swanson describes can lead to better systems than we have now.

REFERENCES

*Note: *** after a reference indicates a selected reading.*

Swanson, D.R. (1988) Historical note: information retrieval and the future of an illusion. *Journal of the American Society for Information Science*, **39**, 92–98***

Historical Note: Information Retrieval and the Future of an Illusion

Don R. Swanson
Graduate Library School, University of Chicago, 1100 East 57th Street, Chicago, IL 60637

More than thirty years ago there was good evidence to suggest that information retrieval involved conceptual problems of greater subtlety than is generally recognized. The dramatic development and growth of online services since then seems not to have been accompanied by much interest in these conceptual problems, the limits they appear to impose, or the potential for transcending such limits through more creative use of the new services.

In this article, I offer a personal perspective on automatic indexing and information retrieval, focusing not necessarily on the mainstream of research but on those events and ideas over a 34-year period that have led to the view stated above, and that have influenced my perception of important directions for future research.

Some experimental tests of information systems have yielded good retrieval results and some very poor results. I shall explain why I think that occurred, why I believe that the poor results merit special attention, and why we should reconsider a suggestion that Robert Fairthorne put forward in 1963 to develop postulates of impotence — statements of what cannot be done. By understanding such limits we are led to new goals, metaphors, problems, postulates, and perspectives.

The Limits of Information Retrieval

In the beginning was Calvin Mooers, who in 1950 introduced the term "information retrieval" (IR) into the literature of documentation [1]. For better or worse the name stuck, notwithstanding the question it raises of what an information retriever might be, or the image it invites of a bird-dog fetching the New York Times. Bar Hillel's warning a few years later that Mooers had confused IR with literature searching led to Mooers' rebuttal that Bar Hillel had confused IR with question-answering, both failing to notice that the bird-dog was neither searching literature nor answering questions [2,3]. In any event, the problem context in which the dispute arose was that of subject access to information, and how to index scientific articles and reports. Apropos of indexing and access, the first use of "information retrieval" in Volume 1 of this journal did not become an entry point in the index to that volume [4]. Automatic keyword-in-context indexing was not yet born, though its conceptual origin dates back at least to the year 1247 when Hugo de St. Caro employed 500 monks to compile the first concordance of the bible [5]. Hugo's monk-powered ecclesiastical data processing system (allegedly called the MP/EDP-1, or possibly System 1 — history is obscure on this point) must have been worth seeing.

The decade of the 1950s was marked by endless disputes among proponents of various breeds of indexing schemes, classification systems, and bird-dogs. In 1953, the first large scale experiment intended to test retrieval effectiveness only inflamed the controversy. In effect, the test was a contest between the uniterm system of Documentation, Inc. (aka DocInc, a company founded by Mortimer Taube in 1951) and the Armed Services Technical Information Agency (ASTIA) subject heading system, using 98 questions applied to a test collection of 15,000 technical documents. Before the results could be evaluated, it was necessary for the contestants to decide jointly which among the retrieved documents were or were not relevant to the questions. As reported by Dake Gull, both teams agreed that 1390 documents were relevant to one or more of the 98 questions, but there were another 1577 documents that one team or the other, but not both, considered to be relevant — a colossal disagreement that was never resolved [6]. Both sides claimed victory, but the performance of the uniterm system attracted more notice, for it was novel and challenged the more conventional system. In any event, the partisan spirit seemed to overshadow what for me was the more compelling question of why the two teams disagreed on the matter of relevance, on so massive a scale. That hiatus was the first clue that the idea of a "relevant" document might be more problematic than it appeared.

That an IR system should be judged by two measures — how well it captures relevant documents, and how well it rejects the irrelevant — was implicit in the experiment. However, the idea was not formalized until 1955 when Kent, Berry, Luehrs, and Perry defined the two measures as "recall" (proportion of relevant documents that are retrieved) and "pertinency factor" (proportion of retrieved documents that are relevant) [7]. The latter measure was later to be called "relevance ratio" and then, about 1965, "precision ratio" became more or less standard. These authors, and hundreds of IR researchers since, seemed to accept uncritically the idea that relevance is additive. The possibility, for example, that two irrelevant documents might become relevant if put together has never been adequately considered, so far as I know.

At about the same time as the DocInc/ASTIA contest, Oliver Lilley at the Columbia library school was investigating the extent to which subject headings assigned to books was predictable by prospective users of the catalog. The results were amazing. 340 graduate students in the library school, asked to chose subject headings appropriate to six books, came up with an average of 62 headings per book, of which 61 were different from the headings actually used on the catalog card. Whether that says more about subject headings or Columbia students isn't clear; nonetheless here was the second clue that subject-oriented indexing and retrieval might be either far more or far less than it seemed [8].

Interest in the problems and process of indexing was stimulated during the latter part of the fifties by the work of Hans Peter Luhn at IBM who devised a method of automatic abstracting (more accurately, extracting) with obvious implications for indexing and searching [9,10]. His method was based on the selection of words according to frequency, avoiding those that were either too rare or too common. Phyllis Baxendale at IBM San Jose tested a similar method for indexing by comparing human with machine procedures for word extraction [11].

Bar Hillel seemed to enjoy intellectual skeet shooting; he would often toss out good ideas and then blast them to bits. Others would pick up the pieces and find them interesting. In November, 1958, at the Teddington conference, in criticizing the Luhn approach to automatic extracting, he proposed an alternative approach that he thought superior to any other that he knew of, but about which he nonetheless had the gravest doubts—namely to base index words, or, even better, word-pairs, on the ratio of relative frequency within the document to relative frequency within the language [12]. Substantially the same idea was developed at about the same time, and carried much further, by Harold Edmundson, Vic Oswald, and Ron Wyllys at the Planning Research Corporation [13]. Soon after its birth this neat new theory collided with a few untidy facts. John O'Connor at the University of Pennsylvania, who, around 1960, was studying the relationship between word frequency and indexing in the drug literature, noted among other things that 11 out of 23 documents properly indexed with the term "toxicity" did not contain any word at all with the stem "toxi" [14]. Thus O'Connor provided a third category of clues that nothing was going to be simple about automatic indexing and retrieval.

The Edmundson-Wyllys ideas, together with early work on associative indexing by Lauren Doyle at System Development Corporation (SDC) and by Ed Stiles at an unmentionable government agency, as well as work on automatic classification by Harold Borko at SDC, and especially the seminal work on probabilistic indexing and ranked-output retrieval by Bill Maron and Lary Kuhns, at Thompson Ramo Wooldridge, had by 1960 set the stage for subsequent research based on statistical approaches to IR [15–18]. I have mentioned only a few of the people and projects that I knew at the time and that influenced my work. Mary Stevens wrote a definitive review of the early work on automatic indexing, citing 662 references [19]. (Regrettably, she neglected to mention Hugo).

My own approach to investigating the mysteries of indexing and retrieval, during the late 1950s, was to dump a small collection of physics articles into a computer word by word, along with a thesaurus or synonym dictionary, and then try to retrieve articles relevant to a set of test questions. For small enough a collection, I thought I could settle in advance the matter of which articles were and which were not relevant to each question. Automatic indexing, information retrieval, text searching, and literature searching in effect could then be studied as one and the same problem. Judgments of relevance were made with some care by subject experts, with a three-person consensus to resolve disagreements prior to any retrieval tests. The point of using a computer was mainly to force a mode of description that was rigorous, and that would separate purely mechanical problems—what a computer can do—from conceptual problems, or problems of meaning. As Christine Montgomery then put it, we were trying to distinguish the temporal from the eternal.

Early in 1959, my colleagues and I at Thompson Ramo Wooldridge put these ideas before Verner Clapp, then President of the Council on Library Resources. Not only was financial support quickly forthcoming, but the project was sustained as well by Verner's enthusiasm and encouragement—for he did not take lightly the bets he placed. In August 1959 we were awarded a nine-month contract that was completed more or less on schedule, with the help of a team that included Paul Garvin, Lary Kuhns, Donald Black, and twelve physicists who participated in relevance assessments and in formulating searches.

Two publications, in 1960 and 1962, reported the outcome of this work [20,21]. I was impressed with how poor our retrieval results were and the kind of difficulties that we encountered. To anticipate the words that would be used in a document to express the idea in a search question was as difficult in practice as it was in principle.

Nearly a year before these experiments were initiated, Vic Yngve, at the International Conference on Scientific Information (ICSI) held in Washington, D.C. in 1958, presented a paper on the feasibility of text searching. His insights on the ubiquity of ambiguity and on the need to find "formal connections between widely divergent ways of saying essentially the same thing" must be considered prophetic [22, p. 977–978]. Bar Hillel a few years later similarly stated:

> Though scientific and technological writers may not make full use of the theoretically unlimited number of ways of expressing their thoughts, put at their disposal by natural languages, they do make use of a large enough number to defeat any system based upon simple matching of expressions [23].

A recent experiment in text searching reported by Blair and Maron corroborates these basic difficulties and offers an illuminating discussion of their nature and causes for specific types of search questions [24]. Comparison of the measured effectiveness of retrieval in my 1960 Science paper with this 1985 work by Blair and Maron is also of interest. First, I should correct a misunderstanding. Blair and Maron indicated that their results were at variance with more favorable results that I had reported in 1960. In fact, in both cases the average proportion of relevant documents retrieved—that is, "recall"—was very low, about 20%, at comparably high levels of "precision" (about 70%). The following statement by Blair and Maron is similar to my explanation of why the results were so poor.

> Stated succinctly, it is impossibly difficult for users to predict the exact words, word combinations, and phrases that are used by all (or most) relevant documents and only (or primarily) by those documents, as can be seen in the following examples [24, p. 295].

In my own experiments, I did obtain substantially higher recall, but lower precision, with thesaurus-aided methods; my point is not that the reported 20% is a magic limit, but that retrieval even at best is seriously problematic, and it is worth trying to understand why that is so.

My experiment shares with the Blair-Maron experiment two design features that might explain the similarly low values of recall. First, each test dealt with fairly homogeneous material—mine with nuclear physics scattering problems, and Blair & Maron with litigation support material relevant to a particular case. Second, in both cases a high level of expertise was applied to the judgment of relevance. Thus relevance judgments tended in many instances to reflect subtle distinctions that could not be discerned by anticipating word usage. The Blair-Maron experiment, based on a collection of some 400,000 documents, offers valuable insight into the nature and the subtlety of what I call the "conceptual" problems of IR—the problems of meaning. To expect that machines can be instructed to solve such problems may be an illusion without a future.

The Crucial Role of Relevance Judgments

Among the many retrieval tests conducted between 1960 and 1985, I have reviewed four of the more notable ones [25–27]. Although there have been many reports of high values of recall and precision, I know of no solutions that have been offered to the problems of meaning—problems that account for the low values reported by me and by Blair and Maron. Consistently high values of recall and precision seem to be attributable to the conditions under which questions are created and relevance is judged. For example, some experiments used relevance judgments based only on inspection of titles, or titles and abstracts. Others involved circular reasoning based on "source" documents, and still others the delegation of pre-screening, hence irrelevance judgment, to nonexperts. Under these and similar circumstances the possibility for taking into account subtle relevance relationships based on expert judgment appears to be precluded at the outset.

Thus I suspect that the outcome of retrieval tests depends more strongly on the nature of the questions and the circumstances of the relevance judgments than on the characteristics of the systems under test. The best retrieval results are obtained when relevance judgments are hasty or simplistic—that is, based on obvious words or phrases, particularly in titles. The poorest results are obtained when relevance judgment depends on any subtle process of extracting meaning from text by persons with expert knowledge of the subject.

For the foregoing reasons, I believe we stand to learn more from the poor retrieval results reported by Blair and Maron than from the reportedly successful tests. I have not, however, attempted an exhaustive review of the literature on retrieval experiments, and so will quote the opinion of Karen Sparck Jones who did conduct such a review, covering the period 1958–1978. "Overall, the impression must be of how comparatively little the nonnegligible amount of work done has told us about the real nature of retrieval systems" [28, p. 245]. In the same book, Bill Cooper, commenting on the state of theorizing in document retrieval, says pretty much the same thing: "Deep down . . . it's shallow" [29, p. 201].

Postulates of Impotence

In 1963, Robert Fairthorne, arguing that information science was a branch of science, not of mathematics, pointed out the necessity of formulating principles valid in the outside world, and suggested that such principles might be statements of what cannot be done—of what Whittaker called "postulates of impotence" (PI) [30,31, p. 58–60].

The fundamental laws of physics and cosmology can take the form of PI, statements about what it is impossible to achieve. Whittaker noted that any well-developed branch of physics can be exhibited as a set of logical deductions from PI. Numerous examples can be cited, including the impossibility of "perpetual motion". Some progress has been made in other fields as well; the theory of economics follows from the nonexistence of a free lunch, and political theory from the impossibility of fooling all of the people all of the time.

So far as I know, no one has explicitly accepted Fairthorne's challenge to come up with such postulates for information science, but a number of perceptive writers—Bar Hillel [12,23], Lauren Doyle [32], Robert Taylor [33], and no doubt others — laid at least some of the groundwork even before Fairthorne's paper. Whether useful and rigorous PI for "information science" can be invented is difficult to say, for that really depends on just what we are trying to explain, but it seems worthwhile at least to stimulate argument on the matter. In that spirit I propose the following postulates. They apply only to the problem of subject-oriented information retrieval — that is, the problem of meeting information needs with items the exact nature and even existence of which are unknown to the requester.

PI 1: An information need cannot be fully expressed as a search request that is independent of innumerable presuppositions of context — context that itself is impossible to describe fully, for it includes among other things the requester's own background of knowledge. Indeed, because the search is for something that is unknown at the outset, the question cannot be precisely formed until the answer is found.

PI 2: It is not possible to instruct a machine to translate a stated request into an adequate set of search terms. Search terms are hypotheses, inventions, or conjectures; there are no rules.

PI 3: A document cannot be considered relevant to an information need independently of all other documents that the requester may take into account. Relevance is not fixed, it is judged within a shifting framework. With each document examined, a requester is faced with a continually branching web of associations. Two documents that are thought similar in one context, or in the light of one hypothesis, may be quite different in another. The phenomenon of "changing salience as a function of the object set considered" is well known in the behavioral sciences. For example, two objects, such as Pepsi and Coke, are judged more similar if a third object, 7up, is introduced into the situation [34]. Two separate pieces of a puzzle might be irrelevant, but, when fit together, reveal a relevant pattern.

PI 4: It is never possible to verify whether all documents relevant to any request have been found, for relevance can be ascertained only by examining the relevant document and one can never in practice or even in principle examine all documents. Any claim or conjecture that all relevant documents have been found is, however, open to potential refutation by someone who might exhibit a relevant document that was not found [35]. This postulate is parallel to the principle that the universal laws of empirical science can in principle be refuted but never verified.

PI 5: Machines cannot recognize meaning and so cannot duplicate what human judgment in principle can bring to the process of indexing and classifying documents. Corollary: Some indexers all of the time, and all indexers some of the time, also cannot duplicate what human judgment in principle can bring to the process of indexing.

PI 6: Word-occurrence statistics can neither represent meaning nor substitute for it. Such data, however, can be used, with occasional success, to signal or point out potentially fruitful areas of text where a human being might then seek meaning or relevance.

PI 7: The ability of an IR system to support an iterative process cannot be evaluated in terms of single-iteration human relevance judgment. For repeated iterations, new criteria emerge, such as the ability of the system to stimulate creative revision of the question.

PI 8: You can have either subtle relevance judgments or highly effective mechanized procedures, but not both.

PI 9: In sum, the first eight postulates imply that consistently effective fully automatic indexing and retrieval is not possible. The conceptual problems of IR — the problems of meaning — are no less profound than thinking or any other form of intelligent behavior. There is no evidence yet that thinking can be reduced to rule-ordered manipulation of a database of facts. Our relevance judgments and our thinking entail, among other things, artful leaps of the imagination unconstrained by logic, reasoning, or the clammy hand of consistency; more important, they entail knowing who we are, what we are, the kind of world we live in, and why we want what we seek. It is hardly imaginable that a mechanism other than a human could acquire such self-knowledge, be given it, or do the job without it.

All of that is not to deny that machines are unsurpassed as an aid to information retrieval, and that continued research to improve such capability is warranted. That we can retrieve more information faster, however, does not by itself mean that we have learned how to do it better. My postulates of impotence are not precise or rigorous but perhaps they can serve as reminders of the enormity of our presuppositions. I hope they will start arguments.

Transcending the Limits

Beginning about 1955, I participated for eight years in various studies of problems related to military intelligence analysis. These studies were focused not on collection of data but on the process by which massive amounts of raw or low-level fragmentary data are transformed into much smaller quantities of finished, high-level intelligence. That focus creates a new perspective within which information retrieval can be seen as part of a broader process of information exploration, correlation and synthesis. Our purpose was to develop machine techniques for aiding and stimulating these and other creative activities associated with intelligence analysis.

An illuminating comparison can be drawn between the intelligence analyst and the scientist, with respect to their use of recorded information. The scientist typically sees new knowledge as originating in measurements on the physical world; such knowledge is then recorded, stored in libraries and retrieved as needed — usually keeping the chore of literature searching to the absolute minimum insofar as possible and then delegating to an assistant whatever cannot be avoided. Such a generalization is of course hazardous, but I suspect that my impression is at least more right than it is wrong. The Weinberg report of 1963 similarly notes: "To the working scientist or engineer, time spent gathering information or writing reports is often regarded as a wasteful encroachment on time that would otherwise be spent producing results that he believes to be new" [36, p. 9]. More recently, Weissberg, Caponio, and Lunin state: "Despite the enormous growth of information, there remains for many scientists the belief that they can maintain awareness of developments in their field by very conventional means; that is, attendance at scientific meetings, direct communication with other scientists, and the review of the literature in their own specialization" [37, p. 52].

The intelligence analyst, by contrast, is much more intimate with the available base of recorded information. New knowledge, or finished intelligence, is seen as emerging from large numbers of individually unimportant but carefully hoarded fragments that were not necessarily recognized as related to one another at the time they were acquired. Use of stored data is intensively interactive; "information retrieval" is an inadequate and even misleading metaphor. The analyst is continually interacting with units of stored data as though they were pieces selected from a thousand scrambled jigsaw puzzles. Relevant patterns, not relevant documents, are sought.

Imagine for a moment that the scientific community adopted the culture, attitudes, and metaphors of the intelligence community with respect to recorded information. Scientists might then take seriously the idea that new knowledge is to be gained from the library as well as from the laboratory, through processes of correlation, synthesis, and exploration of the literature.

A number of national committees on which I served during the 1960s, particularly the National Science Foundation's Science Information Council (SIC), stressed the importance of securing more involvement of scientists in the process of scientific communication. Burt Adkinson, chairman of the SIC and peerless facilitator of productive discussions, saw to it that council members were provided with abundant background documentation pertinent to the agenda for each meeting. The Weinberg report mentioned earlier was required reading for more than one of our meetings. Most of its conclusions strike with even more force today than they did 24 years ago. It called upon scientists to become more deeply involved in creating new science by synthesizing the literature of science, and to develop attitudes toward information indistinguishable from attitudes toward research itself [36].

The Weinberg report also stressed the dangers of specialization, arguing that science can flourish only if every branch of science interacts with other branches of science. Moreover: "The ideas and data that are the substance of science and technology are embodied in the literature; only if the literature remains a unity can science itself be unified and viable" [36, p. 7].

An important unintended consequence of specialization is the failure of the various branches of science to fertilize one another. This theme continued to be of interest to Weinberg, writing four years later: "I suppose the most obvious danger lurking in the fragmentation of science can be seen by reflecting on the historical fact that the various branches of science have always fertilized each other" [38, p. 42]. Fertilization was also of interest much earlier to J. D. Bernal at the 1958 ICSI conference: "Here what science loses by such enforced specialisation is the cross fertilisation of ideas from different fields such as lead to all great discoveries" [39, p. 80].

Perhaps these two authors are implying that we need postulates of fertility. Because that idea would seem to merit at least as much attention as impotence, I offer three postulates just for a start.

Postulates of Fertility (PF)

PF 1: The literatures of different scientific specialities tend to develop independently of one another, but the connectedness inherent in the physical world suggests that there are many fertile, unintended logical connections between these distinct literatures.

PF 2: Owing to inadequate communication between scientific specialities, these literatures tend to be mutally isolated bibliographically; that is, they do not adequately cite one another, and are not co-cited — they are noninteractive. There is reason to think therefore that the logical connections between them may be not only unintended, but unnoticed, unexplored, and unfertilized.

PF 3: Sufficiently creative use of online systems can lead to detection of both the logical connections and the bibliographic isolation of the connected literatures, and so eventually to the impregnation of these virginal connections.

These postulates add up to this; the fragmentation of science into specialities, and therefore the relative isolation of specialized literatures from one another, suggests that there may exist numerous unintended and unnoticed relationships among these isolated literatures. If that is so, then a systematic search for such connections ought to be a worthwhile pursuit — a pursuit that goes beyond information retrieval, and may resemble the correlation and synthesis functions of intelligence analysis.

Implications for Future Research

In a series of recently published studies [35,40–42], I have tried to confirm my three postulates of fertility by analyzing two separate, noninteractive or bibliographically isolated, chunks of literature — sets of journal articles — that together contain implications that cannot be seen within the two sets considered separately. That is, the two literatures taken together contain a chain of reasoning, with some of the links being in one literature and other links in the other literature. Only by retrieving the two literatures and bringing them together can any one person become aware of the complete argument, and so be led to the implied conclusion. (And so it is, incidentally, that articles which taken alone are irrelevant become relevant when put together.) Moreover, because the two literatures were noninteractive it was plausible to suppose that they had not before been brought together, and so one can assume that their logical relationship had not been noticed, an assumption supported by the fact that apparently the conclusion had not before been published.

I have described then how new discoveries might in principle be extracted or constructed from existing literature through retrieving, assembling, and understanding the individual parts that make up the whole, parts that had not previously been assembled.

The metaphor of the jigsaw puzzle should not go unnoticed in connection with the postulates of fertility; fitting the pieces together results in fertilization. Any pattern thus revealed we may assume was not designed by anyone. The pieces fit together neither intentionally nor by chance, but because of the inherent connections within the physical world. In principle, new patterns can emerge that have never before been seen.

Perhaps the discovery of new knowledge within the scientific literature is commonplace, and I am doing no more than describing some obvious ways that it might happen. Indeed, I have found instances of such discoveries by others, but I am not yet sure how common it is. One characteristic feature of the kind of discovery to which I refer is the bibliographic pattern that supports it. The author making the discovery would have to bring together literatures that have not before been seen as related.

In any event, the main problem is to systematize and describe a process by which new connections can with some regularity and consistency be discovered in the scientific literature. I have taken an initial step toward a solution, in the form of a structured trial and error-elimination process that appears to hold promise; it is, in effect, a paradoxical quest for the absence of retrieval clues. The trial part consists of browsing among article titles that are selected in such a way as to enhance their suggestiveness of logical connections. Connections that are well known are considered "errors" and eliminated at one level by simple online search for certain co-occurrences, and more deeply by analyzing co-citation patterns [42].

Co-citation, or rather the absence of co-citation, plays a central role in this process. As a matter of historical interest, here is probably the first suggestion (1957) that co-citations might have significance—another good idea put forward, and dismissed, by Bar Hillel:

> And one can think of many other easily establishable relationships between documents that stand a better chance [than co-requests] of being a useful approximation, e.g., co-occurrence of their references in reference lists printed at the end of many documents, co-quotation, and so on [2, p. 111].

This offhand remark does not of course diminish the importance of Henry Small's independent development of the co-citation idea in 1973 [43]. Incidentally, this Bar Hillel paper has not before now been co-cited with any paper by Henry Small according to Scisearch® and Social Scisearch®, on Dialog® (June, 1986), suggesting therefore that the passage quoted has gone unnoticed.

Although the goal of much advanced IR research is to make computers do humanlike things, the possibility that people can be humanlike should not be overlooked. The dazzling capability that the online services already offer opens new horizons for human creativity in exploring the world of recorded knowledge, and new opportunities for research into humanized information retrieval. The potential for improving human interaction with recorded knowledge is immediate, but there seem to be few signs of interest in so practical a goal. Waiting for Godot, we fail to grasp what is now in reach.

References

1. Mooers, C. N. "The Theory of Digital Handling of Non-Numerical Information and Its Implications to Machine Economics." Technical Bulletin No. 48. Cambridge, MA: Zator Co., 1950 (Paper presented at the Association for Computing Machinery, Rutgers Univ., New Brunswick, NJ, 1950 March 29.)
2. Bar-Hillel, Y. "A Logician's Reaction to Recent Theorizing on Information Search Systems." *American Documentation.* 8(2):103–113; 1957.
3. Mooers, C. N. "Comments on the Paper by Bar-Hillel." *American Documentation.* 8(2):114–116; 1957.
4. Mooers, C. N. "Coding, Information Retrieval, and the Rapid Selector." *American Documentation.* 1(4):225–229; 1950.
5. Wheatley, H. B. What is an Index? A Few Notes on Indexes and Indexers. London, UK: Longmans, Green & Co.; 1879, p. 28.
6. Gull, C. D. "Seven Years of Work on the Organization of Materials in the Special Library." *American Documentation.* 7(4):320–329; 1956.
7. Kent, A.; et al. "Operational Criteria for Designing Information Retrieval Systems." *American Documentation.* 6(2):93–101; 1955.
8. Lilley, O. L. "Evaluation of the Subject Catalog." *American Documentation.* 5(2):41–60; 1954.
9. Luhn, H. P. "A Statistical Approach to Mechanized Encoding and Searching of Literary Information." *IBM Journal of Research and Development.* 1:309–317; 1957.
10. Luhn, H. P. "The Automatic Creation of Literature Abstracts." *IBM Journal of Research and Development.* 2:159–165; 1958.
11. Baxendale, P. B. "Machine-Made Index for Technical Literature—An Experiment." *IBM Journal of Research and Development.* 2:354–361; 1958.
12. Bar-Hillel, Y. "The Mechanization of Literature Searching." In: *Mechanization of Thought Processes.* Proceedings of a Symposium held at the National Physical Laboratory, 10th; 1958 November 24–27; London: HM Stationery Office; 1959: 791–807.
13. Edmundson, H. P.; Oswald, V. A., Jr.; Wyllys, R. E. "Automatic Indexing and Abstracting of the Contents of Documents." Los Angeles, CA: Planning Research Corp. Document PRC R-126, ASTIA AD No. 231606; 1959. Cited by Doyle [15].
14. O'Connor, J. "Some Remarks on Mechanized Indexing and Some Small-Scale Empirical Results." In: *Machine Indexing: Progress and Problems.* Papers presented at the Third Institute on Information Storage and Retrieval. The American University; 1961 February 13–17.
15. Doyle, L. B. "Semantic Road Maps for Literature Searchers." *Journal of the Association for Computing Machinery.* 8:553–578; 1961.
16. Stiles, H. E. "The Association Factor in Information Retrieval." *Journal of the Association for Computing Machinery.* 8:271–279; 1961.
17. Borko, H. "Automatic Document Classification Using a Mathematically Derived Classification System." Santa Monica, CA: Sys-

tem Development Corp. FN-6164; 1961 December 28. Cited by Stevens [19].
18. Maron, M. E.; Kuhns, J. L. "Relevance, Probabilistic Indexing and Information Retrieval." *Journal of the Association for Computing Machinery*. 7:216–244; 1960.
19. Stevens, M. E. *Automatic Indexing: A State of the Art Report*. Washington D.C.: National Bureau of Standards Monograph 91; 1965 March 30.
20. Swanson, D. R. "Searching Natural Language Text by Computer." *Science*. 132(3434):1099–1104; 1960.
21. Swanson, D. R. "Interrogating a Computer in Natural Language." In: Popplewell, Cicely M. Information Processing 1962. Proceedings of IFIP Congress 62. Amsterdam: North Holland Publ. Co.; 1963: 288–293.
22. Yngve, V. H. "The Feasibility of Machine Searching of English Texts." In: *Proceedings of the International Conference on Scientific Information*. Washington, D.C.: National Academy of Sciences-National Research Council; 1959: vol. 2: 975–995.
23. Bar-Hillel, Y. "Theoretical Aspects of the Mechanization of Literature Searching." In: Hoffmann, Walter, ed. *Digital Information Processors*. New York: Wiley Interscience Publ.; 1962: 406–443.
24. Blair, D. C.; Maron, M. E. "An Evaluation of Retrieval Effectiveness for a Full-Text Document-Retrieval System." *Communications of the Association for Computing Machinery*. 28(3):289–299; 1985.
25. Swanson, D. R. "The Evidence Underlying the Cranfield Results." *Library Quarterly*. 35(1):1–20; 1965.
26. Swanson, D. R. "Some Unexplained Aspects of the Cranfield Tests of Indexing Performance Factors." *Library Quarterly*. 41(3):223–228; 1971.
27. Swanson, D. R. "Information Retrieval as a Trial-and-Error Process." *Library Quarterly*. 47(2):128–148; 1977.
28. Sparck Jones, K. "Retrieval System Tests 1958–1978." In: Sparck Jones, K., ed. *Information Retrieval Experiment*. London: Butterworths; 1981:213–255.
29. Cooper, W. S. "Gedanken Experimentation: An Alternative to Traditional System Testing?" In: Sparck Jones, K., ed. *Information Retrieval Experiment*. London: Butterworths; 1981: 199–209.
30. Fairthorne, R. "Mathematics, Mechanics, and Statistics for the Information Science Curriculum or, What Mathematics Does an Information Scientist Need?" In: Luhn, H. P., ed. *Automation and Scientific Communication*. Washington, D.C.: American Documentation Institute. Annual Meeting, 26th; 1963 October 6–11: Part 1: 39–40.
31. Whittaker, E. Taylor. *From Euclid to Eddington. A Study of Conceptions of the External World*. Cambridge: Univ. Press; 1949; AMS reprint ed. 1979.
32. Doyle, L. B. "Is Relevance an Adequate Criterion in Retrieval System Evaluation?" In Luhn, H. P., ed. *Automation and Scientific Communication*. Washington, D.C.: American Documentation Institute. Annual Meeting, 26th; 1963 October 6–11: Part 2: 199–200.
33. Taylor, R. "The Process of Asking Questions." *American Documentation* 13(4):391–396; 1962.
34. Einhorn, H.; Hogarth, Robin M. "Behavioral Decision Theory; Processes of Judgment and Choice." *Annual Review of Psychology*. 32: 53–88; 1981.
35. Swanson, D. R. "Undiscovered Public Knowledge." *Library Quarterly*. 56(2):103–118; 1986.
36. U.S. President's Science Advisory Committee. Science, Government, and Information. Washington, D.C.: The White House; 1963 January 10.
37. Weissberg, A.; Caponio, J. F.; Lunin, L. F. "The Neurological Information Network" *Journal of the American Society for Information Science*. 38(1):52–59; 1987.
38. Weinberg, A. M. *Reflections on Big Science*. Cambridge, MA: MIT Press; 1967.
39. Bernal, J. D. "The Transmission of Scientific Information: A User's Analysis." In: *Proceedings of the International Conference on Scientific Information*. Washington, D.C.: National Academy of Sciences-National Research Council; 1959: vol. 1; 77–95.
40. Swanson, D. R. "Fish Oil, Raynaud's Syndrome, and Undiscovered Public Knowledge." *Perspectives in Biology and Medicine*. 30(1):7–18; 1986.
41. Swanson, D. R. "Two Medical Literatures that are Logically but not Bibliographically Connected." *Journal of the American Society for Information Science*. 38(4):228–233; 1987.
42. Swanson, D. R. "Online Search for Logically-Related Noninteractive Medical Literatures: A Systematic Trial-and-Error Strategy." *Journal of the American Society for Information Science*. (In Press).
43. Small, H. "Co-citation in the Scientific Literature: A New Measure of the Relationship Between Two Documents." *Journal of the American Society for Information Science*. 24(4):265–269; 1973.

Author Index

Agosti, M., 471
Allan, J., 480
Belkin, N.J., 135, 300
Biebricher, P., 515
Black, W.J., 540
Broglio, J.S., 438
Brooks, H.M., 135, 300
Buckley, C., 325, 357, 480
Cahn, P., 448
Callan, J.P., 438
Cellio, M.J., 520
Chamis, A.Y., 175
Cleverdon, C.W., 47, 98
Cooper, W.S., 191, 265
Croft, W.B., 288, 341, 438
Daniels, P.J., 135
Dean, J., 442
Doyle, L.B., 25
Foote, J.T., 495
Foskett, D.J., 111
Fox, E.A., 402
France, R.K., 402
Fuhr, N., 515
Gradenigo, G., 471
Grefenstette, G., 486
Griffiths, A., 367
Grishman, R., 536
Hamburger, H., 536
Harman, D.K., 247, 415
Harper, D.J., 341
Hayes, P.J., 520
Hull, D.A., 486
Hutchins, W.J., 93
Johnson, F.C., 540
Jones, G.J.F., 495
Joyce, T., 15
Kantor, P., 175
Keen, E.M., 217
Knecht, L.E., 520
Knorz, G., 515
Kuhns, J.L., 39
Lancaster, F.W., 223
Lesk, M.E., 60
Low, C.Y., 505
Luckhurst, H.C., 367
Luhn, H.P., 21
Lustig, G., 515
Marchetti, P.G., 471
Maron, M.E., 39
Marsh, E., 536
McCune, B.P., 442
McGill, M.J., 383
Mills, J., 98
Neal, A.P., 540
Needham, R.M., 15
Oddy, R.N., 300
Paice, C.D., 540
Porter, M.F., 315
Rau, L.F., 529
Robertson, S.E., 282, 347
Salton, G., 60, 274, 325, 357, 383, 480
Saracevic, T., 143, 175
Schwantner, M., 515
Singhal, A., 480
Smoliar, S.W., 505
Sparck Jones, K., 331, 495
Strzalkowski, T., 319
Swanson, D.R., 557
Tague-Sutcliffe, J., 205
Tenopir, C., 448
Tong, R.M., 442
Trivison, D., 175
Turtle, H., 288
van Rijsbergen, C.J., 269
Walker, S., 347, 426
Willett, P., 367
Wong, A., 274
Wu, J.H., 505
Yang, C.S., 274
Young, S.J., 495
Zhang, H.J., 505

Index

A

aboutness
  definition, 85
  and eliteness, 346
  indexing, 91, 93–97
  and meaning, 85–86
  and relevance, 144, 156, 269
  retrieval effectiveness, 196
  topic discrimination, 35
  see also pertinence; relevance

abstract
  automatic derivation, 22, 30, 34–36, 538–551, 556
  generic and discriminating, 35–37
  information retrieval function, 1, 87, 97
  keyword in context index, 24
  keyword representation, 49, 87
  Luhn-type, 36
  relation to relevance, 146
  retrieval effectiveness, 201
  sentence selection procedure, 465
  term abstract creation, 18

abstraction
  by association, 25–37
  automatic, 538–551, 556
  hypertext environment, 470
  video parsing, 504–505

acceptability, evaluation, 169

accuracy
  automated retrieval, 317
  automatic text processing, 518, 523
  evaluation, 206
  head-modifier pair, 320–321
  see also precision

adaptation, OKAPI system, 432–434

aggregate probability
  SMART system evaluation, 63
  see also probability

AI. *see* artificial intelligence

AIR/PHYS, 464
  automatic indexing, 513–517

alphabetical list
  thesaurus, 112, 113, 124
  see also dictionary

alphabetical subject catalogue, operational performance investigation, 47

ambiguity
  multilingual document translation, 490–491
  semantic, 40
  spoken document retrieval, 494

American Psychological Association (APA), thesaurus, 114

anaphoric word
  identification for abstraction, 539
  text structure, 94

anomalous state of knowledge (ASK), 136
  ASK hypothesis, 299–304
  discussion, 299–301
  question formulation, 179
  structure, 301–304
  see also knowledge

architecture, definition procedure, 469

artificial intelligence (AI), 10
  CODER system, 377–378
  expert system, 401
  in natural language processing, 177, 180

artificial language, common, 21–22

ASK. *see* anomalous state of knowledge

assignment. *see* categorization

association
  indexing and abstraction, 25–37
  text-derived, 26–30
  see also term association

association factor
AIR/PHYS, 513–514
co-occurrence of word, 27
Association Hypothesis, 308
see also Cluster Hypothesis
association map
co-occurrence of word, 28–30
retrieval system component, 30–37
term linkage display, 12
association net, 459
associative reading, hypertext environment, 473
associative relationship, thesaurus, 120, 121–122
associative retrieval, best-match principle, 300
author name, keyword, 87, 88
automated retrieval, 10–12, 15
conventional approach, 40–41
cost-effectiveness, 11
file time vs. search time, 306
hypertext, 459
information retrieval encodements, 20–24
multilingual document, 487–488
OKAPI system, 378
procedures, 93
robust text processing, 317–322
setup, 168, 172
term weighting approaches, 323–328
see also information retrieval; retrieval
automatic abstraction, 556
linguistic processing application, 538–551
see also abstract; abstraction
automatic document classification
SMART system, 390–392
see also classification; clustering
automatic indexing
AIR/PHYS, 513–517
compared to manual indexing, 81, 83, 86–87, 89, 93, 305–306
SMART system, 387–390
vector space model, 273–280
see also indexing
automatic text processing
categorization system, 518–526
see also text processing
auxiliary data
hypertext environment, 470, 471–473
structured collection, 470

B

backtracking, hypertext environment, 473
batch retrieval system, 3, 310
Bayes' theorem, 282, 292
Bayesian inference network, 260
definition and function, 287–288
see also inference network
behavioural retrieval model, 260
benchmark, 89
best match principle, 3
ASK hypothesis, 300–301
see also matching
best match search
techniques, 305, 307
see also matching
bibliographic distribution, models, 258
bibliographic classification, 122–123
bibliographic coupling, index language, 100
bibliographic search, 1
bibliometrics
models, 258
relation to relevance, 151–153
binary independence model, inference network, 292
blackboard
CODER system, 401, 408–409
document retrieval, 378
Boolean logical operators, 3, 271, 377, 413, 419
confusion about, 265
link matrix form, 291
logical models, 258
OKAPI system, 425
probabilistic interpretation, 295
Boolean search model, 3, 12, 148, 269, 376, 487
alternatives to, 265–267, 378
conventional, 376–377
in hypertext environment, 471–473
index term variables, 42
limitations, 258
PRISE system, 415
SIRE system, 396–397
terms, 10
vs. FREESTYLE system, 446–456
vs. ranked-output, 9, 217, 220–221, 417
vs. RUBRIC system, 440–441
vs. TARGET system, 446–456

broader/narrower terms (BT/NT)
thesaurus relationship, 120–124
see also term

browsing
exploitation, 12, 459
hypertext environment, 87, 472–473
information retrieval, 1, 90
OKAPI system, 432
precision and recall failure, 241–242
and video parsing, 503–510
see also World Wide Web

BT/NT. *see* broader/narrower terms

C

Cambridge Language Research Unit, thesaurus approach, 17

catalogue system
library, 457
OKAPI, 424–434

categorization
facet, 123
information retrieval, 2, 462, 464
news story, 518–526

category
automatic derivation, 22
automatic generation and assignment, 26
index language, 99

CATLINE system, 413, 418

centroid. *see* class centroid

change, relevance affecting, 146–147

character set, multilingual document, 486

citation analysis, 258

CITE system, 413, 424, 427
searching procedure, 417–418

CLARIT system, automated retrieval, 379

clarity, classification of questions, 180

class
definition function, 104, 107
document, 42

class centroid
document space, 274–275
SMART system, 384–385

class formation
index language term, 49–50
performance improvement, 58
recall device, 47

class label, categorization, 464

classification
automatic, 308
bibliographic, 122–123
document, 390–392
facet, 47, 122–123, 265–266
hierarchical, 18
hypertext environment, 470
information retrieval, 2, 15, 462
library, 25, 86
question, 177
relevance, 159
thesaurus, 111–112, 122, 129
weaknesses, 15
see also hierarchical classification

closeness
conversion to distance, 45–46
measurement in index space, 44–45
probabilistic search determination, 42–43
see also distance; nearness

clue
automatic derivation, 22
document exclusion probability, 42
machine-readable text interpretation, 22

CLUSTAN package, 367

cluster
analysis, 308
association map, 30, 31, 33
designation, 33, 34
membership, 369–370
nearest-neighbor, 370–372
see also document clustering

Cluster Hypothesis
document relevance, 308
interdocument similarity, 366
probability ranking, 285
vector processing model, 259
see also Association Hypothesis

clustering
associated term, 12
document space, 274–275
interdocument similarity information, 365
retrieval effectiveness, 214
SMART system, 390–391, 398
techniques, 308–309
see also classification; document clustering; term clustering

CODER system
  artificial intelligence retrieval, 377–379
  expert system architecture, 400–412
cognitive model, 257, 260–261, 301
cognitive task analysis (CTA), hypertext environment, 469
collection
  evaluation data, 167
  see also document collection
collection frequency. *see* inverse document frequency
color histogram, video parsing and retrieval, 506
combination match
  probabilistic model, 340–341
  see also matching
command
  classification and evaluation, 207
  OKAPI system, 425
communication ecology, 145–146
communication effectiveness, relevance review, 143–165
communication theory
  concepts, 41
  relevance, 146–147
  scientific, 145–146
complex expression, description, 306
complexity
  classification of questions, 181
  suffix stripping, 313–315
composite document analysis, expert system architecture, 400–412
compound term, 119, 306
  index language evaluation, 88–89
  see also index term; term
concept
  location in thesaurus, 112–113
  ranking in INQUERY system, 437
concept association method, natural language, 75
concept indexing
  definition, 98
  performance measure, 101–103, 108–110
  procedure, 99
  see also indexing
concept number, word stem replacement, 61
conceptual information extraction, natural language input, 527–533
confirmation, automatic text processing, 520, 521–523
conflation algorithm, 306
  multilingual document, 486–487
  see also n-gram coding, stemming
confounding of word form
  index language, 99, 104
  index language device, 49–50, 58
  recall device, 47
  see also n-gram coding, stemming
CONIT system, 401
consonant
  definition, 314
  spoken document retrieval, 494
content
  document, 86, 93
  identification concerns, 39–41, 318
  representation terms, 323–324
  retrieval in information retrieval system, 1
  specification in index, 40
content indicator, direct and indirect, 87
content-based retrieval, 458
  video, 508–511
context
  index language, 104–105
  information seeking, 176, 178–179
  meaning determination, 39–40
continuous speech recognition (CSR), 493
controlled term index language, 56, 58
controlled vocabulary. *see* vocabulary control
conventional system, 9
co-occurrence, consensus of, 27
co-occurrence pattern
  compound term, 119
  phrase recognition, 75–78
  statistical association, 61
  term, 308
co-occurrence of word pairs
  association map, 30, 32–33
  error rate, 318
  generic and discriminating, 35–37
  sentence, 26–28, 36
  use for term clustering, 308
coordinate indexing
  operational performance investigation, 47
  search constraint, 113

see also pre-coordinate, post-coordinate entries; Uniterm system

coordination, precision device, 47

coordination level, 3
- ranking in non-Boolean search, 266
- search exhaustivity, 236

coordination level match, 269–270
- term-weighting, 325–326
- *see also* matching

correlation coefficient, SMART system evaluation, 72

correlation of term, index language, 100

cosine correlation
- SMART system, 382–383, 384
- SMART system evaluation, 72

cost-effectiveness
- automated retrieval system, 11
- evaluation, 61, 209, 284
- relevance, 157
- retrieval measure, 193–197

Cranfield tests, 3, 13, 91, 217, 305, 375
- evaluation, 171, 377
- index language, 99, 100–101, 104–105
- index language devices, 47–59
- relevance, 149–150

cross-reference
- automatic, 426, 428, 429, 430
- closeness of terms, 39, 43
- hierarchical expansion, 81
- thesaurus, 112, 117, 123

CSR. *see* continuous speech recognition

CTA. *see* cognitive task analysis

current awareness, 3

cut-off value
- AIR/PHYS, 516
- document cutoff, 217–218, 221–222
- SMART system relevance judgement, 62–63

D

DAG. *see* directed acylic dependency graph

DARPA/NIST
- speech recognition, 493–494
- TRECs, 4, 11, 411

data fusion
- cognitive model, 261
- inference net approach, 436
- techniques, 310

data retrieval
- analysis and evaluation, 212–214, 215
- compared to fact retrieval, 1
- distinction from document retrieval, 85, 104
- *see also* information retrieval; retrieval

database
- Boolean partition, 258
- computer implementation, 1
- hypertext environment interaction, 469–477
- online search, 175
- retrieval evaluation, 209, 215, 353
- searching, 377
- variable operationalization, 206

database management systems (DBMS), compared to information retrieval systems, 1, 2, 3

DBASE, retrieval evaluation, 210

DBMS. *see* database management systems

decision theory, Bayesian, 283

decomposition
- description, 89
- factor, 11
- inference network, 292
- IR systems, 91
- text, 479–480

definite article, text structure, 94

definite noun phrase, 539
- *see also* phrase

definition
- good definition, 150, 156
- notion standardization, 21

demand search function, MEDLARS, 223–224

Dempster-Shafer evidence theory, 287–288

dependency, inference network, 297

DEPT. *see* Distributed Expert Problem Treatment

description
- complex expression, 306
- decomposition, 89
- document, 12, 87
- final, 87
- index description, 89
- initial, 87
- retrieval evaluation, 213
- *see also* indexing

descriptor
- indexing vocabulary, 10
- thesaurus, 115–116, 118, 123–124

vector processing model, 259
Zatocoding, 16

destination, information exchange, 147

destination view, relevance, 150–151, 155, 157, 160

device. *see* index language device; precision device; recall device

DIALOG
automated retrieval, 11
information seeking investigation, 182, 185
interactivity, 3
usage estimation, 415
see also TARGET system

dictionary
abstraction system, 541–543
AIR/PHYS, 513–515
bilingual general language, 486–487
indexing, 513–515
statistical phrase, 75
see also synonym dictionary; thesaurus

dictionary file, searching, 377

digital libraries, 376

directed acylic dependency graph (DAG), Bayesian inference network, 287–288, 289

directory, search and retrieval, 2

discrimination
abstracting procedure, 35–37
relation to representation, 89–90
term, 324
vector processing model, 259

discrimination value model, 259, 277–280, 324

distance
closeness conversion, 45–46
expectations for, 430
see also closeness; nearness; similarity

Distributed Expert Problem Treatment (DEPT), 136

distributed expert systems model, 258
see also expert system

document
coefficient of similarity determination, 22–24
definition, 85–86
division, 87
relation to indexing, 7
relation to information need, 436
relation to request, 269, 282
relationship among, 281–282
relevance determination, 47–49
representation, 312, 318
retrieval status value, 88
as sentence, 268–269
structure, 87–88
term abstract creation, 18
term association evaluation, 16
see also text

document association, automatic search, 12–13

document class
effect on precision measure, 231
generation, 42

document classification
automatic, 390–392
see also classification

document clustering, 11, 305, 308
comparative study, 367–372
inspection probability, 88
model, 296
SMART system, 384–385, 390
see also cluster; term clustering

document collection
hypertext environment, 470
multilingual, 485
TREC, 249
variable operationalization, 206

document description
keyword, 12
modern retrieval system, 87
see also description

document length
SMART system evaluation, 68
TARGET system, 449
2-Poisson model, 348–350, 352

document network, model, 289

document parser
INQUERY system, 436
see also parsing

document partitioning, 100

document ranking, 88, 305
SMART system, 395
see also ranking

document reading, hypertext environment, 474

document representation, 312, 318
relevance in information science, 161–162
see also representation

document retrieval
- compared to information retrieval, 1
- goals, 136–137
- inference network, 287–297
- *see also* information retrieval

document set
- definition, 99
- statistical characteristics, 90

document space
- configuration for vector space, 273–275
- heuristics, 45–46
- SMART system, 394–395

document surrogate
- variable operationalization, 206
- *see also* abstract; title

document vector, term weighting retrieval, 327

domain, classification of questions, 180

E

E measure, probabilistic model, 341–342

e-mail
- search and retrieval, 2, 87, 493–494
- *see also* spoken document retrieval; video document

effectiveness
- communication, 143
- evaluation, 2, 169, 183
- OKAPI system, 425
- probabilistic model, 341–343
- relevance, 146–147, 156
- SMART/SIRE retrieval, 381
- traditional measure, 282–283
- *see also* retrieval effectiveness

efficiency
- economic, 99
- evaluation, 169, 375
- index language, 103–104
- information retrieval experimentation, 205
- IR system, 5
- MEDLARS, 224–225
- operating, 99, 100–103

element
- index language evaluation, 88–89
- in thematic structure, 93–94, 96

eliteness, probabilistic weighted retrieval, 346

encyclopedia
- multilingual text retrieval, 489
- text decomposition and retrieval, 479

environment. *see* system environment

environment variable, 168

ERIC Thesaurus, "Descriptor Groups", 123–124

estimation
- inference network, 292–293
- relevance number, 42
- relevance weighting, 333–334

ethics, retrieval evaluation, 212

evaluation
- experimental design, 210–212
- information retrieval testing, 169–170
- interactive system, 171
- investigation, 169
- methodology, 168–169
- relevance judgements, 167–168
- remit, 168
- retrieval effectiveness, 191–204
- system evaluation, 168
- test collections, 170
- TREC, 251–252

exact match strategy, SMART/SIRE retrieval, 381

exhaustivity
- and aboutness, 96–97
- concept indexing, 98
- definition, 107
- description, 89
- evaluation, 206
- indexing and searching, 107–108
- MEDLARS evaluation, 227–232
- performance factor, 11
- performance measure, 58, 101–104
- recall failure, 232–235
- *see also* specificity

existence search, retrieval effectiveness, 200

expansion. *see* query expansion

expert, CODER system, 406–408

expert assistant, 272

expert system
- CODER architecture, 400–412
- compared to hypertext, 459
- distributed model, 258
- information seeking investigation, 177, 178
- production rule system, 534
- RUBRIC system, 441

extension heuristics, 45
- *see also* heuristics

extension of request language, 46
extract, automatic derivation, 22
extraction. *see* information extraction

F

facet
  bibliographic classification, 123
  thesaurus, 113, 124
facet classification
  Boolean search, 265–266
  operational performance investigation, 47
  see also classification
fact extraction. *see* summarizing
fact retrieval, as information retrieval, 1
factor. *see* performance factor
factor analysis, association map, 29–30, 31
factor decomposition, test design, 11
fallout, performance measure, 207–208, 282, 284
fallout ratio, index language evaluation, 51
false drop
  document structure, 19
  free-text search, 447
  relevance malpractice, 149
  TARGET/FREESTYLE system, 454
  term allocation, 16
fault tolerance, AIR/PHYS, 516
feature recognition, INQUERY system, 436
feedback
  information exchange, 147
  probabilistic model, 340, 357–358, 361
  retrieval evaluation, 212
  vector processing method, 356–357
  see also relevance feedback
file, weighting, 307
file structure, text signature, 377
file time, vs. search time, 87, 306–307
file time indexing, 87, 306
filtering
  abstraction system, 541
  information retrieval, 2, 462–463, 530–531
  multilingual text retrieval, 488, 491
  performance increase, 309–310
  spoken document retrieval, 495
  see also routing
foreign language literature
  search evaluation, 225, 244
  see also multilingual document
format, MEDLARS, 224
frame
  CODER system, 404–405
  key-frame extraction, 504–506
  production rule system, 534
FREESTYLE system
  automated retrieval, 378–379
  discussion, 446–456
frequency ranking
  text reduction, 22
  see also ranking
frequency vector, normalization, 19
frequency of word
  abstracting, 35
  definition, 27
  relevance, 36–37, 152
  see also term frequency
frozen ranks, 221
fuzzy set model, 258
  SIRE system, 397

G

generality, performance measure, 282
goal
  human-computer dialogue, 139–141
  information seeking, 178
good term, 150, 156, 278
  relevance weighting, 335–337
  see also term; word
goodness of fit, best match search, 305
graphic display, thesaurus, 126–129
Greco-Latin square design, retrieval evaluation, 211

H

head-modifier pair, syntactic phrase, 320–321
heading, syntactic indexing, 98
heuristics
  automatic abstracting program, 36, 543
  document space, 45–46
  extension heuristics, 45
  index space, 43–45
  non-anaphoric noun phrase identification, 539

hierarchical classification
  index language, 99–100, 104–105, 107
  MEDLARS, 223
  SMART system, 60, 61
  thesaurus, 112
  word ordering, 18
  see also classification

hierarchical expansion, SMART system, 78–81

hierarchical link
  indexing language, 86
  see also linkage

hierarchical relationship
  document clustering, 367–372
  thesaurus, 112, 120, 121, 123, 127

hierarchical term arrangement, SMART system, 387

HYPERLINE system, hypertext environment, 474

hypertext
  automatic analysis, 478–492
  compared to expert systems, 459–460
  interaction with database, 469–477
  model, 258

hypertext environment, auxiliary data, 470

hypothesis, definition, 408, 558

hypothesization, automatic text processing, 520, 521–523

I

ideoglossary, to remove semantic ambiguity, 40

IDF. *see* inverse document frequency

image retrieval, 2
  multi-media system, 85, 460–461
  see also video document

index
  accuracy evaluation, 206
  associative organization, 28
  conventional approach, 40
  keyword in context, 22–24
  relation to relevance, 146

index key, 87, 459

index language
  controlled term, 56, 58
  crude, 106–107
  function, 86
  multilingual, 460
  pre-coordinate or post-coordinate, 98
  recall and precision failure, 237–241
  revision, 129–131
  simple concept, 49, 56, 58
  single term, 49, 56
  specificity control, 230
  thesaurus, 10, 112
  vocabulary control, 10, 99–100

index language device
  confounding of word form, 49–50
  Cranfield tests, 47–59, 104–105
  natural language terms, 49
  properties and features, 87, 91
  synonym groups, 49–50
  system context, 90
  testing and evaluation, 98–110

index preparation, procedures, 99

index space
  closeness measures, 44–45
  movement within, 43–44
  probabilistic search determination, 43

index term
  class definition, 104
  closeness relationship determination, 43
  definition, 98
  document and request as, 269–270
  error and omission, 231
  good, 278
  hypertext environment, 469
  index language evaluation, 88–89
  relation to document natural language term, 56–58, 86
  relation to specificity, 58
  see also term

indexing
  associative, 25–37, 556
  co-ordinate, 47
  computer evaluation, 60–84
  concept, 98–99, 101–103, 108–110
  defined, 1
  file time, 87, 306
  in document retrieval, 1
  manual, 81
  objectives, 96–97
  policy, 89
  probabilistic, 39–46, 293–295
  and reader needs, 96
  retrieval system, 86
  search time, 87, 306
  semantic, 253–254
  sources, 87

statistical, 305–306
techniques, 305–307
term selection, 15
video material, 503–504
weighted, 98, 266
see also automatic indexing

indexing dictionary, AIR/PHYS, 513–515

inference network, 258
Bayesian, 260, 287
data fusion, 436
for document retrieval, 287–297
probabilistic model, 260

infometrics. *see* bibliometrics

information
communication of, 146–148
definition, 85
expectations for, 95–96
and probability, 285
quantitative measure, 41–42
and relevant information, 146
see also knowledge

information extraction
requirements, 2, 463
see also summarizing

information formatting, production rule system, 534

information need, 1, 3, 558
document exclusion probability, 42
and documents, 85–86, 95–96
inference network, 296
model and concept, 177
natural language description, 287
origination, 299–300
relevance, 154
system representation, 436

information provision mechanism (IPM), design concerns, 135–136

information retrieval (IR)
compared to document retrieval, 1
compared to machine translation, 17–18
definition and function, 5, 269, 317
essay procedure, 17
expert system architecture, 400–412
holistic view, 257
limits of, 555–557
multilingual, 484–485
non-classical logic, 268–272
origins of, 2–3
probabilistic, 12
thesaurus approach, 15–20
see also automated retrieval; data retrieval; probabilistic retrieval; retrieval

information retrieval (IR) encodement, automatic derivation, 20–24

information retrieval (IR) model. *see* model

information retrieval (IR) research, practice-based vs. theory-based, 257

information retrieval (IR) strategy, berrypicking, 90

information retrieval (IR) system
compared to database management systems, 1, 2, 3
conventional compared to modern, 9
definition, 98, 301–303, 469
interdocument similarity information use, 365–373
model, 178
pseudo-interactive, 310
relevance concerns, 146
traditional compared to automated, 9
see also AIR/PHYS; CATLINE; CITE; CLARIT; CODER; CONIT; DIALOG; FREESTYLE; HYPERLINE; INQUERY; MEDLARS; MEDLINE; MUSCAT; NEXIS; NRT; OKAPI; PRISE; RUBRIC; SCISOR; SIRE; SMART; STATUS/IQ; TARGET; THOMAS; WIN

information retrieval (IR) task, 2

information retrieval (IR) theory, concepts, 41

Information Retrieval System Subject Authority List (API), 117

information science
definition, 145
relation to relevance, 143–148, 161–164

information seeking behavior, 260

information seeking, investigation, 175–189

information space, multidimensional, 258–259

information system
evaluation, 168
relevance notion, 148

initial weight
inverse document frequency, 307, 310
see also term weighting; weighting

INMAGIC, retrieval evaluation, 210

INQUERY system
automated retrieval, 378–379
probabilistic model, 260
TREC and TIPSTER experiments, 436–439

inspection, search operation, 88

intent, information seeking, 178

interaction, relation to relevance, 145

interactive system, evaluation, 171

interactivity
- information retrieval systems, 3, 178
- pseudo-interactive retrieval system, 310
- retrieval system design, 301
- *see also* multi-media system

interdocument similarity information
- use in retrieval system, 365–373
- *see also* document classification; document clustering; similarity

interest, assumptions for, 95

interface
- expert system, 401
- human-computer, 135–142, 401
- RUBRIC system, 443, 445
- spoken document retrieval, 501
- user-friendly, 375–376, 413–421

interfixing
- effect on relevance, 56
- index language, 100

intermediary, 376

Internet. *see* World Wide Web

interpretive relevance, definition, 144

inverse document frequency (IDF)
- automated retrieval, 317
- initial weight, 307
- term weighting, 321, 324, 422
- theory, 219

inverted directory, SMART/SIRE retrieval, 381–382

inverted file
- IR system implementation, 5
- retrieval evaluation, 209
- search time indexing, 87
- searching, 372, 377
- SIRE system, 396
- spoken document retrieval, 496–497

IPM. *see* information provision mechanism

IR. *see* information retrieval

iterative process
- associative index, 33
- precision and recall failure, 241–242
- retrieval system design, 301, 558
- search term weighting, 329
- SMART system, 61
- *see also* relevance feedback

K

key
- index, 459
- non-language, 87

key-frame, video retrieval, 504–505, 506, 508–509, 511

keyword
- aboutness definition, 93
- association map, 28–29, 30, 32
- automatic indexing, 12
- automatic text processing, 523
- index language, 86–87, 377
- index language representation, 49
- RUBRIC system, 440–441, 443
- spoken document retrieval, 495–497
- stemmed, 305
- thesaurus, 115–116
- *see also* term

keyword in context
- index generation, 22–24
- performance measure, 101–102

keyword-matching
- SMART system evaluation, 72
- *see also* matching

knowledge
- assumptions for, 95, 96
- communication of, 147–148
- relevance affecting, 146–147
- *see also* anomalous state of knowledge; public knowledge

knowledge base
- CODER system, 401, 404–406, 407
- construction, 324
- multilingual document retrieval, 485
- RUBRIC system, 440–441

knowledge representation
- expert system, 401
- indexing by association, 25–26
- *see also* representation

knowledge retrieval, as information retrieval, 1

L

language
- common language practicality, 21–22
- *see also* natural language

language normalization, suffix process, 72–75
Latent Semantic Coindexing, multilingual document, 485
Latin square design, retrieval evaluation, 211
lattice
  algebraic properties, 18
  bibliographic classification, 123
  thesaurus organization, 12
learning style inventory (LSI), information seeking process, 181–182
legal phrase, search procedure, 450–451, 458
lexical analysis, INQUERY system, 436
lexicon, CODER system, 406
library
  circulation data, analysis of, 258
  definition, 98
  indexing system specialization, 40
  organization, 25–26
library problem, 39
"light gun", 34
linguistic processing, automatic abstraction, 538–551
Linguistic String Grammar, Tagged Text Parser, 319
linguistics
  expert system, 401
  relation to relevance, 145
link matrix form, inference network, 290–291
linkage
  evaluation, 206
  hierarchial, 86
  index language, 86, 100, 105
  interdocument similarity information, 365
  paradigmatic, 89
  precision device, 47
  thesaurus, 126
logic
  conditional, 270–271
  non-classical, 268–272
  relation to relevance, 144, 145, 154, 159–160
  logical model, 258
  Logical Uncertainty Principle, 271–272
  loss function, decision theory, 283
  LSI. *see* learning style inventory

M

machine search, compared to association method, 30
machine translation, compared to information retrieval, 17–18
machine-readable text
  analysis and summarization, 478–492
  automatic retrieval of encodement, 20–24
Macrothesaurus, 132–133
Manual for Building a Technical Thesaurus (ONR-55), format, 113
manual indexing
  compared to automatic indexing, 81, 83, 86–87, 89, 93, 305–306
  see also indexing
manual indexing vocabulary, 9, 13
  cost-effectiveness, 11
marker-passing
  information retrieval, 530–531
  news story search, 464
matching
  combination match, 340–341
  coordination level, 269–270, 325–326
  information structure, 19
  keyword, 72
  MEDLARS demand search, 223
  modulation operation, 89
  relation, 86
  request-document, 61
  retrieval operation, 88
  search term weighting, 329–333
  SMART system evaluation, 68–72
  terms, 133
  see also best match
mathematical model, 258
Maximum Entropy Formalism, 267
meaning
  and aboutness, 85–86
  automated retrieval, 317
  determination of, 39–40, 268
  multilingual document translation, 490–491
  and relevance, 144
  verbal tag affecting, 26
  word in context, 17
measure. *see* performance measure
Medical Subject Headings (MeSH)
  evaluation, 173, 418
  index language, 86
  text form, 458
  thesaurus, 117, 458

MEDLARS
automated retrieval, 11
background, 223–224
evaluation, 171, 173, 223–246
thesaurus, 113

MEDLINE system
interactivity, 3
partitioning, 418
search statement, 413, 418
text form, 458

"Memex" machine, 15

memory, structure affecting, 122

MeSH. *see* Medical Subject Headings

Message Understanding Conferences (MUC) Programme, 463

meta-data. *see* auxiliary data

Minicard system, 40

miskeying, OKAPI system, 428

MLIR. *see* multilingual information retrieval

model
characteristics, 257–258
cognitive, 260–261
discrimination value, 277–280
fuzzy set, 258
inference network, 288–291
logical, 258
probabilistic, 259–260
retrieval testing, 169
term frequency, 347–349
underlying assumptions, 257, 261
vector processing, 258–259
see also specific models

modern system, 9

modifier, keyword in context, 22

modifier rule, RUBRIC system, 442

MONSTRAT model, 140, 142

motivational relevance, definition, 144

MUC. *see* Message Understanding Conferences

multi-media system
document definition, 85
interface, 376
retrieval procedures, 460–461
video parsing and retrieval, 503–510
see also interactivity

multilingual document
dictionary approach query, 484–492
foreign language literature, 225, 244
retrieval procedure, 460, 464

multilingual information retrieval (MLIR), dictionary-based approach, 484–492

multiple aspect indexing, false drop production, 16

multivariate technique
clustering, 308
retrieval effectiveness, 214

MUSCAT system, 413
automated retrieval, 379
evaluation, 418–419

N

n-gram coding, stemming, 306

name, search procedure, 458

natural language
automatic text processing, 519
compared to thesaurus, 111
conceptual information extraction, 527–533
data collection, 212–213
indexing and searching, 10, 11, 39
information need, 287
performance improvement, 58–59
probabilistic model, 259
redundancy, 10
retrieval system, 85–86, 171, 252

natural language processing (NLP), 9–10
artificial intelligence, 177, 180
automated retrieval system, 319
database routines, 309
information extraction, 462
large-scale, 317
production rule system, 534–535
see also text processing

natural language terms, index language devices, 49

navigation, hypertext environment, 472, 474

nearest neighbor cluster (NNC), 370–372
see also cluster

nearest neighbor searching, 5

nearness
best match search, 305
vector processing model, 376
see also closeness; distance

network representation
  information retrieval, 287, 458
  see also representation
News Retrieval Tool (NRT), evaluation, 419–421
news story
  categorization system, 518–526
  retrieval procedure, 464
newspaper, free-text searching, 447
NEXIS system, 447, 449, 450, 452, 453
NLP. *see* natural language processing
NNC. *see* nearest neighbor cluster
node
  document network, 289
  inference network, 295–296
noise
  automatic derivation system, 22
  affecting spoken document retrieval, 496
  relevance malpractice, 149
  semantic, 40–41
  terms, 353
non-relevance, rejection in associative search, 33–34
nonreplicability, evaluation, 171
notion, standardization, 21
notional element, document encoding, 17
notional family, word groupings, 17
novelty, information retrieval experimentation, 205
NRT. *see* News Retrieval Tool
null output, Boolean search, 265–266

O

off-line mode, association map retrieval, 30–34
OKAPI system
  automated retrieval, 378–379
  probabilistic model, 260
  research project evaluation, 424–434
  2-Poisson model, 351
on-line mode, association map retrieval, 30–34
on-line public-access catalogue (OPAC)
  OKAPI system, 378
  retrieval effectiveness, 215
  user operated, 3
on-line search, 177, 212
  search term weighting, 329
on-line system, 4, 559
  see also World Wide Web
OPAC. *see* on-line public-access catalogue
operating efficiency
  definition, 99
  performance measure, 100–103
  see also efficiency
operator, identification in INQUERY system, 436
  see also Boolean logical operators
output
  logical model, 258
  search operation, 88
output overload, Boolean search, 265–266

P

PA. *see Psychological Abstracts*
paired comparison, SMART system evaluation, 63
paradigmatic relations, 86, 89
parsing
  automatic abstraction, 544–546
  document parser, 436
  natural language index terms, 11
  natural language text processing, 528–529
  Tagged Text Parser (TTP), 319–320
  video, 503–510
partial-match algorithm, 3
  see also matching
partitioning
  Boolean retrieval, 258
  document, 100
  effect on relevance, 56
  theme, 107
passage, document division, 87
patent search, retrieval effectiveness, 200
pattern expression, RUBRIC system rules, 440–441
pattern-action, categorization, 464
pattern-matching
  automatic text processing, 518–526
  see also matching
Pearson correlation coefficient, co-occurrence of word, 27–28
"peekaboo" card
  index, 98
  search procedure, 12, 19
people, relation to relevance, 163–164
performance factor, 11, 168

performance measure, 13
  automatic text processing, 523–524
  closeness, 44–45
  description, 2, 11, 47
  economic efficiency, 99
  index language, 100–104, 237–241
  OKAPI system, 432
  relevance, 106, 150, 167–168
  relevance weighting, 335–337
  retrieval effectiveness, 191–204
  retrieval evaluation, 169, 170, 207–209
  RUBRIC system, 443–445
  space density, 275–277
  spoken document retrieval, 499–500
  suffix stripping, 313–314
pertinence
  retrieval effectiveness, 196
  vs. relevance, 106, 153–154, 155, 160, 208–209
  see also aboutness; meaning
philosophy
  relation to relevance, 144, 145, 155
  retrieval effectiveness, 191–192
phrase
  automated retrieval, 317–319
  bound, 448, 450
  conceptual unit, 306
  definite noun, 539
  head-modifier pairs, 320–321
  term phrase, 386, 388
  translation, 489
  see also sentence; term
phrase extraction, document network, 289
phrase recognition
  co-occurrence pattern, 75–78
  SMART system, 75–78
  statistical, 61, 75, 309
  syntactic, 309
  syntactic analysis, 61, 309, 319
PhraseFinder, INQUERY system, 437
Poisson
  2-Poisson model, 351
  see also 2-Poisson model probabilistic weighted retrieval
Porter algorithm, 309
post-coordinate retrieval, compared to pre-coordination, 10
post-coordination, index language, 56, 87, 98
postings file, searching, 377
postulates of impotence, 557–558
pragmatic view, relevance, 155–158
pragmatics
  information retrieval experimentation, 205–216
  relation to relevance, 145
pre-coordination
  compared to post-coordination, 10
  index language, 98, 99, 239–240
  MEDLARS, 223
pre-coordination of term, evaluation, 206
PRECIS, aboutness in indexing, 93
precision
  automatic routing, 255
  automatic text processing, 523–525
  definition, 324, 556
  document class affecting, 231
  evaluation, 169
  extension of request language, 46
  FREESTYLE system, 452
  index language evaluation, 47, 51
  MEDLARS, 226–227
  MEDLARS evaluation, 224, 226, 234, 244–245
  normalized, 62
  performance measure, 2, 11, 61, 183, 208–209, 275–276, 282, 321
  relation to recall, 51, 56, 61, 172, 219
  relation to relevance, 149–150
  retrieval evaluation, 218, 556
  see also accuracy
precision device
  effect on relevance, 56
  function, 47
  SMART system, 83
precision failure
  exhaustivity, 228, 230, 236–237
  false coordination, 240
  inappropriate term, 236
  index language, 237–241
  specificity, 237
  user-system interaction, 241–244
precision ratio. *see* precision
predicate, coefficient of association, 44
presupposition
  classification of questions, 181
  given and hidden, 95–97
prevalence of word, definition, 27

PRISE system, 309, 413–417
  automated retrieval, 378–379
  user interface, 414–417
probabilistic indexing, 39–46, 260
  relevance number determination, 41–42
  retrieval, 293–295
  see also indexing
probabilistic model, 259–260
  feedback, 340, 357–359, 361
  inference network, 287–288, 289, 292–293
  use without relevance, 339–344
probabilistic ranking, 259, 260, 283
  retrieval systems, 414
  see also probability ranking principle; ranking
probabilistic retrieval, 12
  MUSCAT system, 418–419
  non-Boolean, 266–267
  OKAPI system, 378–379, 424–435
  relevance estimation, 270, 271
  spoken document, 494
  TARGET/FREESTYLE system, 446
  see also information retrieval; probability ranking principle; retrieval
probabilistic weighted retrieval, 2-Poisson model, 345–354
probability
  generic association search, 25
  and information, 285
probability measure, SMART system evaluation, 63–64
probability ranking principle (PRP), 3, 259, 266
  discussion, 281–286
  inference network, 290
  see also probabilistic model; ranking
problem
  definition, 178
  force in information retrieval, 301
problem structure, in human-computer dialogue, 135–142
profile, 462
pronoun, anaphoric, 94
PRP. *see* probability ranking principle
pseudo-interactive retrieval system, 310
Psychological Abstracts (PA), thesaurus, 114
public knowledge, 145–146, 147, 154
  and information seeking, 178–179
  see also knowledge

Q

quasi-synonym (QS) list
  SMART system, 75
  see also synonym
query
  constitution change, 307–308
  definition, 207
  evaluation, 207, 215
  for multilingual document, 484–492
  relation to request, 86
  relation to search, 1
  relevance in information science, 162
  retrieval evaluation, 209–210
  rule-based/concept-based, 436
  as sentence, 268
  see also request; search
query concept, inference network, 289–290
query development
  automatic, 248, 252–255
  Boolean, 413
  effect on recall, 89
  hypertext environment, 471–472
  News Retrieval Tool, 420
  TREC, 247–248
query expansion
  INQUERY system, 437
  OKAPI system, 432–434
  relevance feedback, 308, 360
query network, model, 288, 289–290
query node, inference network, 296
query processing
  INQUERY system, 437
  RUBRIC system, 442–443
query term frequency, 2-Poisson model, 350, 352
query topic, expression as production rule, 441–442
query translation, multilingual document, 485–486, 489–490
query vector, term weighting retrieval, 327
query-term weight, initial weight/relevance weight, 307
question
  model and concept, 176–177, 178–179
  structure and characteristics, 180–181
quorum search, 3

R

Radar Research Establishment, 17

Ramsey test, 271, 272

ranked-output model, compared to Boolean search model, 9

ranking
- frequency ranking of words, 22
- index key, 459
- INQUERY system, 437
- News Retrieval Tool, 420
- OKAPI system, 430–431
- probabilistic, 259, 260, 283, 414
- relevance number, 12, 39, 41–42
- statistical testing, 220, 222
- *see also* probability ranking principle

Rapid Selector, 40

RAT. *see* remote associates test

reader
- assumptions and expectations, 95–96
- indexing needs, 96
- *see also* user

recall
- automatic text processing, 523–525
- definition, 99, 324, 556
- index language evaluation, 47, 51–56
- MEDLARS, 224, 226–227, 232, 244–245
- normalized, 51, 56, 58, 62
- performance measure, 2, 11, 61, 100, 183, 207–208, 275–276, 282, 284
- relation to exhaustivity, 228, 230
- relation to precision, 51, 56, 61, 172, 219
- relation to relevance, 102–103, 105, 107, 149–150
- relation to specificity, 230
- relevance weighting effect, 332–333
- RUBRIC, 441
- vocabulary control, 287

recall device
- function, 47
- SMART system, 83

recall failure
- error and omission, 231–232
- exhaustivity, 232–234, 236–237
- index language, 237–241
- specificity, 234–235, 237
- user-system interaction, 241–244

recall ratio. *see* recall

recall target, retrieval evaluation, 218

recall-precision graph
- retrieval evaluation, 218
- SMART system, 62–64, 72
- TREC, 251–252

record, information retrieval of, 1–2

redundancy
- retrieval function, 10, 88
- speech recognition, 461

reference retrieval system, priorities, 281

references
- explicit, 469
- information retrieval of, 1

related term (RT), thesaurus, 120–124, 128
- *see also* synonym; thesaurus

relatedness, library organization, 25

relationship
- generic, 25
- generic vs. discriminating, 36
- library organization, 25
- retrieval effectiveness, 214
- semantical vs. statistical, 43–44
- thesaurus, 120–124

relative clause, text structure, 94

relevance, 1, 3, 91
- and aboutness, 144, 156, 269
- definition, 183, 281–282, 558
- destination view, 150–151, 155, 157, 160
- document content, 86
- and eliteness, 346
- evaluation, 183, 317
- knowledge view, 154
- logical view, 144, 145, 154, 159–160
- multiple representation, 287
- performance measure, 106
- pragmatic view, 155–158, 160, 161
- probabilistic indexing, 39–46
- relation to recall, 102–103, 105, 107
- retrieval effectiveness, 195–196, 199–200
- review and framework, 143–165
- situational, 157
- subject knowledge view, 153–155, 160, 161
- subject literature view, 151–153
- system view, 148–150
- systems of, 144–145
- term relevance weight, 324–325
- vs. pertinence, 106, 153–154, 155, 160, 208–209

relevance description, AIR/PHYS, 514–515
relevance evaluation
  index language devices, 47–49
  information quantity, 41
  scale, 18–19
  spoken document retrieval, 498
relevance feedback
  automatic query modification, 307–309
  best-match principle, 300, 305
  definition, 339
  evaluation, 171, 358–363
  hypertext, 460
  INQUERY system, 438
  multilingual retrieval, 488
  MUSCAT system, 419
  OKAPI system, 432–434
  probabilistic model, 343
  and retrieval performance, 355–363
  retrieval system design, 301
  SMART system, 383, 392–394, 397–398
  spoken document retrieval, 495
  2-Poisson model, 353
  user feedback, 10–11
  vector processing model, 259
  vs. non-iterative approach, 221–222
  see also feedback
relevance information, probabilistic model use, 339–344
relevance judgement
  evaluation, 167–168
  in information science, 162–163, 164
  retrieval effectiveness, 195, 200, 557, 558
  SMART system, 397–398
  TREC, 250–251, 253
relevance number
  definition procedure, 45–46
  derivation procedure, 41–42
  document ranking, 39, 158–159
relevance probability
  best match search, 305
  term searching, 333
relevance ratio
  performance measure, 100, 101–102, 556
  retrieval effectiveness, 200
  see also precision
relevance weight
  advantages, 334–335
  comparison with initial weights, 307
  structure, 333
  see also term weighting; weighting
relevant document, 86
  see also relevance
reliability, information retrieval experimentation, 205
remit, evaluation, 168–169
remote associates test (RAT), information seeking process, 181
representation
  document, 86, 161–162, 312, 318
  expert system architecture, 400–412
  index language matching, 86
  knowledge, 25–26, 401
  network, 287, 458
  relation to discrimination, 89–90
  request, 86
  state of knowledge, 301
request
  improvement, 242–244
  natural language, 86
  relation to document, 269, 282
  relation to indexing, 1
  search failure, 235
  spoken document retrieval, 498
  see also query; search
request language, extension, 46
request set, averaging, 169
request-document matching
  SMART system, 61
  see also matching
residual collection, relevance feedback, 359
resource manager, CODER system, 402
response time
  MEDLARS, 224, 244
  SMART/SIRE retrieval, 381
retrieval effectiveness, 191–204
  comparison, 217–222
  expert system, 400–401
  interdocument similarity, 366–367
  RUBRIC, 441
  vector processing model, 259
  see also effectiveness
retrieval performance
  evaluation, 207–209

and relevance feedback, 355–363
space configuration, 277
spoken message, 498–500
see also performance measure

retreival status value, 88

retreival system. *see* information retreival system

retrieval with probabilistic indexing (RPI) model
inference network comparison, 293–295
see also probabilistic indexing

rheme, sentence structure, 94

robustness, systems, 375

role, precision device, 47

role indicator, index language, 100, 104

routing
information need, 436
information retrieval task, 2, 462
TREC, 253–254, 255
see also filtering

RUBRIC system, 401
automated retrieval, 378–379
discussion, 440–445
inference network, 290

rulebase development, automatic text processing, 523

rules
association map, 32
index language evaluation, 51
suffix stripping, 313, 314

S

scalability, systems, 375

SCISOR system, 464
information retrieval, 530–532
natural language input, 527–529

scope hypothesis, document length, 350

scope note (SN), thesaurus, 116

scoring, retrieval operation, 88
see also matching

search
cluster, 368–369
demand search function, 223–224
generic, 25
hybrid, 2, 495
indexing during, 87
information seeking process, 181–184, 185–186
inverse conditional, 44
online, 177, 212
probabilistic strategy, 42–43
see also query; request

search engines, World Wide Web, 4, 376, 379

search failure
MEDLARS evaluation, 235–237
OKAPI system, 426

search process, definition, 207

search program
definition, 99
specificity/exhaustivity affecting, 102–103

search statement
definition, 207
evaluation, 207

search term relevance weighting, discussion, 329–338

search time, vs. file time, 87, 306–307

search time indexing, 87, 306

searching
defined, 1
delegated vs. end-user, 207
in document retrieval, 1
exhaustivity and specificity, 230–231
lower-level operations, 88
nearest-neighbor, 5
spoken document retrieval, 496–497
strategy, 89
TARGET/FREESTYLE system, 447–449
techniques, 307–308
text, 556–557

segmentation, video parsing, 504–505

semantic analysis, SMART system, 387

semantic association, hypertext environment, 471–472, 474

semantic noise, 40–41
see also noise

semantic progression, sentence structure, 95

semantics
and logic, 268, 271
possible-world, 271
relation to relevance, 145

sentence extraction, text reduction, 3

sentence
document as, 268–269
identification, 538
meaning determination, 39

- parsing, 319–320
- thematic structure, 93–94
- word co-occurrence, 26–28, 308
- *see also* phrase; term

sequential reading
- hypertext environment, 472–473
- *see also* browsing

sign test, SMART system, 64–66, 72

significance
- aboutness determination, 93, 96
- retrieval evaluation, 220
- *see also* aboutness; meaning

significance test SMART system, 63–67

similarity
- best match search, 305, 307
- interdocument, 365–373
- query/document, 323
- SMART system, 382–383
- vector processing model, 376
- video parsing and retrieval, 505–508

similarity coefficient, 307

simple concept index language, 49, 56, 58

single term index language, 49, 56

single-link classification
- SMART system, 389
- *see also* linkage

SIRE system
- best match search, 377
- experimental retrieval, 381–397
- inverted file processing, 396

skimming, text traversal, 481–482

SLS. *see* Spoken Language Systems

SMART system, 13, 169, 378–379, 400
- basic organization, 60–67
- environment, 382–387
- experimental retrieval, 381–397
- index language evaluation, 51–56
- multilingual retrieval, 488
- phrase vocabulary creation, 306
- probabilistic model, 259–260
- research system, 377
- text analysis and retrieval, 478–479
- weighting, 309

software, retrieval system, 3, 210, 215

source, information exchange, 147

specificability assumption, information retrieval characteristic, 300

specificity
- classification of questions, 180–181
- concept indexing, 98
- definition, 107
- description, 89
- evaluation, 206
- index term, 58
- indexing and searching, 107–108
- MEDLARS evaluation, 227–231, 236
- performance measure, 102, 104
- precision failure, 237
- recall failure, 234–235
- relation to recall, 102
- *see also* exhaustivity

speech recognition, 460–461, 464

spelling correction, automatic, 426, 428, 430

spoken document retrieval
- experiments, 493–502
- procedures, 460–461

Spoken Language Systems (SLS), 493

SRT. *see* symbolic reasoning test

STAIRS system, evaluation, 171, 378

statistical analysis
- approaches, 11, 12
- automatic text processing, 523
- closeness of meaning, 39–40
- cluster, 33
- co-occurrence of word, 27
- document set, 90
- information seeking, 186–189
- key word, 32
- phrasal representation, 309
- retrieval effectiveness, 202, 213–214, 217, 219
- text reduction, 22
- weighting, 10

statistical association, co-occurrence pattern, 61

statistical independence, of terms, 260

statistical phrase dictionary, language normalization, 75

statistical ranking, retrieval systems, 414

STATUS/IQ system, 3–4

stem
- keyword, 305
- language normalization, 10, 72–75, 78

text reduction, 60
weighted/nonweighted comparison, 72
see also suffix

stemming
algorithm, 306
automatic, 426, 427–428, 429
INQUERY system, 436
measure, 309
multilingual document, 486
n-gram coding, 306
SMART system, 387
string similarity, 306

Stiles formula, co-occurrence of word, 27

stop word list, 306
INQUERY system, 436
SMART system, 387

string similarity, stemming, 306

subheading, search evaluation, 240–241, 245–246

subject, information need, 85

subject heading system, ASTIA, 555

subject index
library, 98
performance measure, 104
see also index

suffix
effect on performance, 58–59
language normalization, 72–75
specificity reduction, 58
see also stem

suffix "s" dictionary, language normalization, 72–75, 81

suffix stripping
algorithm, 313–316
right-hand truncation, 306
SMART system, 387–388
spoken document retrieval, 494

summarizing
information retrieval task, 2, 96–97, 458, 463–465
requirements, 463
see also aboutness

summarization
machine-readable text, 478–492
production rule system, 534–537
text, 531–532

surrogate, 87

symbolic reasoning test (SRT), information seeking process, 181

synonym
effect on retrieval, 16–18, 319
index language requirement, 99
inference network, 297
quasi-synonym list, 75
recall device, 47
specificity reduction, 58

synonym dictionary
language normalization, 72–75
quasi-synonym (QS) list, 75
SMART system, 60, 61, 68, 75, 387
see also dictionary; thesaurus

synonym group
index language devices, 49–50, 56, 58–59
TARGET system, 448

synonym/near-synonym relationship, 120

synonymity, effect on retrieval, 16–18

synonymy, definition, 111

syntactic analysis
INQUERY system, 436
phrase, 61, 309, 318
SMART system, 387

syntactic control, evaluation, 206

syntactic indexing, definition, 98

syntactic phrase, 306
see also phrase; term

syntagmatic relations, index language, 86, 88

system
information need representation, 436
users and interface levels, 375–376

system design, search time indexing, 87

system environment, 90

system parameter, 168

system view, relevance, 148–150

T

t test, SMART system, 64

tag
abstraction system, 539–541, 543–544
closeness measurement, 44
machine-readable, 28, 30, 40–41
meaning determination, 40–41
use in document, 26

Tagged Text Parser (TTP), 319–320

Tamura features, video parsing and retrieval, 506–507

TARGET system
  automated retrieval, 378–379
  discussion, 446–456

term
  association, 10, 12, 318–319
  broader/narrower (BT/NT), 120–124
  clustering, 308
  combination in search, 10, 19, 40
  compound, 88–89, 119, 306, 321
  correlation of, 100
  cross-referencing, 39
  differentiation in systems, 15–16
  document representation, 312
  pluralization, 118
  proper name, 118
  related (RT), 120–124, 128, 324
  relations, 88
  representation, 100
  synonymous, 18, 319
  thesaurus, 115–119
  see also index term; word

term abstract, creation, 18

term allocation, false drop frequency, 16

term association, 10
  automatic search, 12–13
  evaluation concerns, 16
  in relevance feedback, 11
  in thesaurus, 17, 18
  see also association

term clustering, 308

term dependency, probabilistic retrieval, 267

term discrimination. *see* discrimination value model

term frequency (TF)
  document size affecting, 459
  and eliteness, 346
  model, 347–348
  searching, 307
  term weighting system, 324
  see also frequency of word

term grouping, function, 103

term phrase
  SMART system, 386, 388
  see also phrase

term relevance weight, definition, 324–325

term vector, automatic text analysis, 323

term vector translation, multilingual document, 485–486, 491

term weighting
  automated retrieval, 321, 323–328
  automatic, 275
  Boolean search, 258, 266
  concept indexing, 110
  content characterization, 41
  differentiation, 306, 421
  document set, 90
  experiments, 325–326
  index language, 100
  indexing, 306, 307
  initial weight, 307
  link matrix form, 291
  multilingual document, 486, 490, 491
  OKAPI system, 426
  print term as, 232
  probabilistic model, 253–254, 259–260
  relevance feedback, 11
  relevance number ranking, 12
  relevance weights, 307
  similarity measure, 307
  SMART system, 68–72, 78, 388, 395, 397
  spoken document retrieval, 499–500
  text analysis and retrieval, 478
  see also relevance weight; weighting

TEST. *see Thesaurus of Engineering and Scientific Terms*

test. *see* evaluation

test collection. *see* document collection

text
  machine-readable, 21–22
  reduction into stem form, 60
  summarization, 531–532
  thematic structure, 93–96

text analysis, machine-readable text, 478–492

text compression, 5

text decomposition and structure
  machine-readable text, 479–480
  see also decomposition

text identifier, generation, 324

text node, 295–296
  text decomposition, 480

text processing
  automatic, 518–526
  computer evaluation, 60–84

natural language, 528–530

text reference language, RUBRIC system, 440–441

text relation map, 480–481, 483

text retrieval, compared to information retrieval, 1

Text REtrieval Conferences. *see* TREC

text searching, 556–557
- *see also* searching

text signature, file structure, 377

text theme
- identification, 480–481
- *see also* theme

text windows, 308

TF. *see* term frequency

thematic progression, sentence structure, 94

thematic structure, text, 93–96

theme
- indexing partition, 107
- interfixing within, 100
- sentence structure, 94
- text, 480–481

theme generation, machine-readable text, 478–492

Thesaurofacet, 114, 117, 119, 131, 133

thesaurus
- definition, 111
- format, 113–115
- FREESTYLE system, 450–451
- graphic display, 126–129
- index language, 10, 13, 86, 91
- language normalization, 72–75
- lattice organization, 12
- layout, 124–126
- machine compilation, 131
- multilingual, 487
- purpose, 112–113
- relations between, 131–133
- relationships, 120–124
- revision, 129–131
- SMART system, 61, 81, 386–389, 399
- structure, 124
- term, 115–118, 324
- term forms, 118–119
- *see also* dictionary; synonym dictionary; vocabulary control

thesaurus approach, information retrieval, 15–20

Thesaurus of Engineering and Scientific Terms (TEST), format, 113–114, 133

THOMAS system, 299–301

TIPSTER database, 10
- automated retrieval, 317–322
- INQUERY experiments, 436–439
- multilingual document retrieval, 487–488

title
- associative index, 33
- information retrieval, 1, 87
- keyword in context index, 24
- keyword representation, 49, 87
- request enhancement, 243
- retrieval effectiveness, 201
- searching by, 415, 417, 419

topic
- identification, 538
- indexing requirements, 235
- and information need, 85–86
- relatedness between, 25
- relation in abstract, 35
- spoken document retrieval, 495
- TREC, 247–248, 249–250, 254

topic relationship, text decomposition, 480

topic spotting, speech recognition, 461

TOPIC system, 401
- automated retrieval, 378

topical relevance
- definition, 144
- *see also* relevance

traditional system, 9

translation
- automatic, 464
- index language, 99
- interlingual term correspondence, 485
- machine, 17–18
- machine-readable texts, 21–22
- multilingual document, 484–492

TREC, 4, 89
- automated retrieval, 379
- discussion, 247–256
- INQUERY experiments, 436–439
- retrieval evaluation, 169, 170–171, 173–174, 378
- text decomposition and retrieval, 479
- 2-Poisson model, 350–351, 353
- weighting, 307, 309

tree structure, demand search, 223–224
TRUMPET, parsing, 529
truncation, 306
  TARGET system, 448
  see also stem; suffix
TTP. *see* Tagged Text Parser
2-Poisson model, probabilistic weighted retrieval, 345–354

U

UNISIST, thesaurus, 111, 113, 115, 118, 119, 121, 127–128
Uniterm system, 15–16, 18, 30
  index language, 99, 100
  operational performance investigation, 47
Universal Decimal Classification System
  index term, 98
  operational performance investigation, 47
  performance measure, 105
URL
  interactive system evaluation, 171
  see also hypertext; World Wide Web
US Digital Libraries Initiative, 5
user
  and information seeking, 175–177, 178–179, 184
  and interfaces, 375–376
  MEDLARS, 224
  model derivation, 140
  retrieval evaluation, 209
  typical needs, 90, 91
  see also reader
user friendliness, retrieval system, 208
user satisfaction, definition, 283–284
user-friendly system, 413–421
user-system interaction, precision and recall failure, 241–244
utility
  information system, 168, 183–184
  and ranking, 281, 284–285
  retrieval effectiveness, 194–196, 199, 201–202, 208–209
utterance
  definition, 137
  goals, 139
  see also sentence

V

validity, information retrieval experimentation, 205
variable
  effect on index language evaluation, 51
  evaluation methodology, 168–169, 170, 215
  index language, 99
  information retrieval experimentation, 205–206
  operationalization, 206–209
variance analysis, retrieval effectiveness, 214
vector distance relation, matching operation as, 19
vector generation, SMART system, 385–387
vector manipulation, SMART system, 383–385
vector processing model, 258–259
  feedback, 356–357
  nearness, 376
  PRISE system, 378
  text decomposition, 479
vector query, use with relevance feedback, 355–356
vector representation, SMART system, 382–383
vector space model
  automatic indexing, 273–280
  text analysis and retrieval, 478
Verbosity hypothesis, document length, 348–349
video document
  retrieval procedures, 460–461, 464, 493–495
  see also image
Video Mail Retrieval (VMR), experiments, 493, 495
video parsing
  retrieval and browsing, 503–510
  segmentation and abstraction, 504–505
  see also parsing
visualization, interface, 376
VMR. *see* Video Mail Retrieval
vocabulary
  automatic text processing, 525–526
  controlled term, 56, 58
  descriptors, 10
  index language, 98
  normalization, 10
  similarity determination, 22
vocabulary control
  evaluation, 206, 417
  index language, 86, 103, 377
  MEDLARS, 223, 231, 245
  multilingual text retrieval, 487
  performance measure, 238–239
  professional, 26

recall, 287
SMART/SIRE retrieval, 381–382
spoken document retrieval, 495–496
suffix stripping, 316
thesaurus, 112–113
traditional, 10

vowel
definition, 314
spoken document retrieval, 494

W

weighted indexing, definition, 98

weighting
concept and term, 110
index key, 459
index term, 41, 47, 89
initial, 307
inverse document frequency, 317
PRISE system, 414
retrieval operation, 88
RUBRIC system, 440–441
search term, 329–338
statistical, 10
TARGET/FREESTYLE system, 447, 449
see also term weight

West Publishing Company, 4

Western Reserve University, evaluation, 102

WIN system, automated retrieval, 378, 446, 447

windows
effect on interaction, 171, 459
use with relevance feedback, 357

word
anaphoric, 94, 539
document representation, 312
factor analysis, 26
generic and discriminating, 35
meaning and context, 17
meaning determination, 39–40
statistical evaluation, 22
stopword list, 306
in thesauri, 10
thesaurus format, 118
see also sentence; term

word list, automatic derivation system, 22

word pairs co-occurrence
association map, 30, 32–33
relative frequency, 558
sentence, 26–28, 36

word spotting, spoken document, 494, 495, 497, 499

word stem. *see* stem

World Wide Web
"grepping", 459
interactive system evaluation, 171
retrieval requirements, 1, 484
search engines, 4, 376, 379
services, 11, 553
Web crawler, 462

Z

Zatocoding system, 15–16